We Japanese

This delightful work – the best ever popular encyclopaedia of Japanese culture, history and society – contains answers to all the questions that anyone curious about Japan might ask. First written in 1934 and subsequently expanded into three volumes, all of which are contained in this work, it is a treasury of exotic facts and useful information, profusely illustrated with charming line drawings and period photographs. Written with great style, this work brings traditional Japan to life in a way that no contemporary guide book can, explaining all the curious features of daily life that visitors to Japan still see, such as the luck cat figures, the blinds over tea house doors, the symbolism of guardian figures at the gates of temples and significance of Japan's many picturesque festivals as well as practices such as acupuncture, incense burning, fortune- telling and many, many more. *We Japanese* is a passport to the timeless essence of Japan.

FREDERIC DE GARIS, scholar and writer, lived in Japan for over twenty years. **ATSUHARU SAKAI** was a noted translator, editor and compiler.

www.keganpaul.com

THE KEGAN PAUL JAPAN LIBRARY

The National Faith of Japan • *D.C. Holtom*
The Japanese Enthronement Ceremonies • *D.C. Holtom*
History of Japanese Religion • *Masaharu Anesaki*
Ainu Creed and Cult • *Neil Gordon Munro*
Japan: Its Architecture, Art and Art Manufactures • *Christopher Dresser*
An Artist's Letters from Japan • *John La Farge*
Japanese Girls and Women • *Alice M. Bacon*
The Kwaidan of the Lady of Tamiya • *James S. de Benneville*
The Haunted House • *James S. de Benneville*
We Japanese • *Frederic de Garis and Atsuharu Sakai*
Shogi: Japanese Chess • *Cho-Yo*
The Nightless City of the Geisha • *J. E. de Becker*
Landscape Gardening in Japan • *Josiah Conder*
Things Japanese • *Basil Hall Chamberlain*
The Gardens of Japan • *Jiro Haneda*
Ancient Japanese Rituals and the Revival of Pure Shinto • *Sir Ernest Satow with Karl Florenz*
History of Japanese Thought • *Hajime Nakamura*
The Mikado's Empire • *W. E. Griffis*
Quaint Customs and Manners of Japan • *Mock Joya*

We Japanese

THE CUSTOMS,

MANNERS, CEREMONIES, FESTIVALS,

ARTS AND CRAFTS

OF JAPAN

BESIDES NUMEROUS OTHER SUBJECTS

KEGAN PAUL
London • New York • Bahrain

First published in 2002 by
Kegan Paul Limited
UK: P.O. Box 256, London WC1B 3SW, England
Tel: 020 7580 5511 Fax: 020 7436 0899
E-Mail: books@keganpaul.com
Internet: http://www.keganpaul.com
USA: 61 West 62nd Street, New York, NY 10023
Tel: (212) 459 0600 Fax: (212) 459 3678
Internet: http://www.columbia.edu/cu/cup
BAHRAIN: bahrain@keganpaul.com

Distributed by:
Turpin Distribution
Blackhorse Road
Letchworth, Herts. SG6 1HN
England
Tel: (01462) 672555 Fax: (01462) 480947
Email: books@turpinltd.com

Columbia University Press
61 West 62nd Street, New York, NY 10023
Tel: (212) 459 0600 Fax: (212) 459 3678
Internet: http://www.columbia.edu/cu/cup

Printed in the USA by IBT/Biddles

ISBN: 0-7103-0719-5

British Library Cataloguing in Publication Data
Garis, Frederic de
We Japanese : the customs, manners, ceremonies, festivals,
Arts and crafts of Japan. – (The Kegan Paul Japan library)
1.Japan – Civilization 2.Japan – History
I.Title II.Sakai, Atsuharu
306'.0952

ISBN 0710307195

Library of Congress Cataloging-in-Publication Data
Applied for.

PREFACE FOR COMBINED EDITION

The popular practices of a nation mirror its spirits and psychology. Hence we conceived an idea that we would present the true aspects of the Japanese nation to the guests of the Fujiya Hotel by describing the festivals, ceremonies, and other customs, including history, art, religion and tradition, on the menu-cards of the Hotel.

Our information met with the demands not only of the Hotel guests, but of the foreign tourists and residents of Japan in general, and we published it in book-form, entitled "We Japanese". Edition after edition appeared and it was followed by "We Japanese", Vol. II, with equal success. This was some time before the war.

We printed the third volume of "We Japanese" during the war, but bombing came to destroy it all while it was being bound. We were rather lucky, however, to have it destroyed by bombing, because unawares we were influenced more or less by the current ideas of nationalism during the prewar and war periods. We have re-written "We Japanese", Vol. III, since the close of the war.

"We Japanese" narrates Japan in her natural and unattired garb, and its perusal may lead the foreign reader to think that, after all, the Japanese are a superstitious nation. True, the Japanese are over-religious, superstitious or not, depending upon the definition of religion and superstition that one may make. But the Japanese believe in Kami (lit. unseen) and most of their life, daily and national, is influenced by their fear of the Unseen.

There is not a single village or hamlet throughout the country but has a shrine dedicated to the Unseen, and most Japanese venerate the Unseen in their family-altars. Practically all the mountains in Japan are named and dedicated to the Unseen, each with a shrine built on the top. Even a pedestrian-traveller in the country is committed to the care of the roadside Unseen. Birth is considered to be due to the power of the Unseen, and a baby is taken to a tutelary shrine to be committed to the care of the Unseen. Even marriage is attributed in this country to an arrangement made by the Unseen, and this is one chief reason why Japan has a negligibly low rate of divorce. All our houses are dedicated to the Unseen, and the Japanese clean their houses for fear that the Unseen will not dwell in an unclean house. The Japanese are known the world over for their industrial and industrious activities and honest hospitality, attributable to their sense of devotion and piety. Their classical art-objects of exquisite beauty are produced through their piety and sincerity for devotional purposes, not at all lucrative. Dishonesty is inconsistent with the fear of the Unseen.

When a foreigner is served with a kind of food that is typically Japanese, its taste unpalatable to him will appeal to his tongue sooner than does its nice taste for which the Japanese like the food. The same can be said about the observation of a nation. Its strange customs and other popular practices attract the attention of a casual observer sooner than do the true characteristics of the nation. He is often blindfolded too much by the common practices to see the essential aspects of the nation.

Now that we have completed a set of three volumes, we have decided to present a handy edition of "We Japanese" in one book to the public. It is our sincere desire and hope that the foreign reader of the book will go deeper than casual observations to see the true spirits of the Japanese, who are at heart as honest and peaceful as any other nations of the world because they also are a race which God has created.

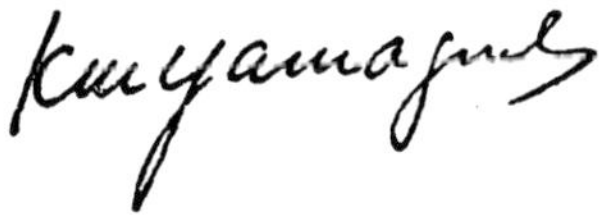

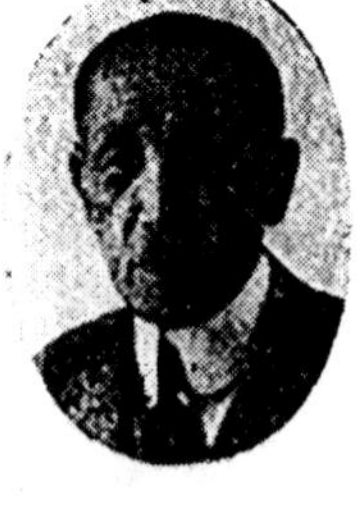

President, Fujiya Hotel

PREFACE

BOOK I

In offering this second edition of "*We Japanese*" to a gracious public which welcomed so heartily the first edition, I can only explain its popularity by the fact that it does answer a real purpose and provide for a genuine need.

This, I suppose on second thoughts, is hardly surprising, as those who visit any country are sure to ask more questions of their hotel host than they do even of their professional guides. However, this is natural, since they are in contact with him most. Moreover, in the course of many years as a hotel manager a man is certain to learn in the best school of all just what are those questions which visitors tend to ask most, and therefore what are the subjects in which visitors tend to ask most, and therefore what are the subjects in which they are most interested. These are naturally questions concerning those things which are different in Japan from the countries from which the visitors come. Just as it is true to say that human nature is the same the world over, so also it is true that human nature is more interested in differences than in resemblances when travelling in various countries. This natural curiosity is healthy, though like all things that are good can became vicious if carried to excess, as it often is. Just therefore as any large hotel is a natural clearing-house for such questions, this book merely claims to answer a large number of the oft-repeated questions put to me in that clearing-house, with which so long an association, and with the most charming people from all over the world, has taught me most people really wish to know about Japan.

I need hardly say that I owe a debt of gratitude to many sources of information on Japan, of which there is happily an increasing number. First among these must come Professor Chamberlain's "Things Japanese," that extraordinarily compact and reliable authority providing the well from which all writers on Japan must at some time or another draw. It is while preparing this second edition that I learn of Professor Chamberlain's death, and I feel it a duty here to pay homage to that illustrious scholar who has done more than anyone else to introduce Japan to a world-wide public. Japan deplores his passing, but will for all times venerate his memory.

Among other sources of information I am greatly obliged to such excellent current tourist magazines as the "Travel Bulletin" published monthly by the N. Y. K. and the "Tourist" published also monthly by the Japan Tourist Bureau. There is also the magazine "Japan" to which I owe a lot, as well as to a number of people who from time to time have provided me with much that appears in these pages. I ask them all to accept my sincere gratitude.

MY HONORABLE BOW

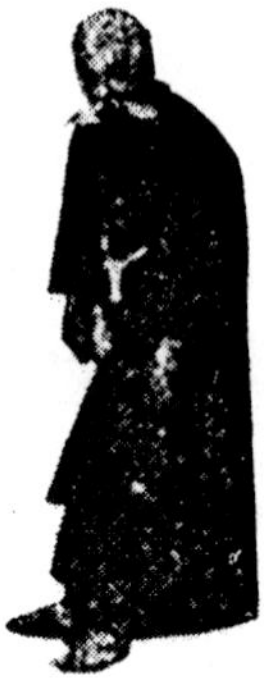

It is now 28 years ago that I began to manage the Fujiya Hotel at Miyanoshita. During these years the many thousands of guests from overseas who have done me the honor of staying at the Fujiya Hotel must have asked me so many questions concerning the various Japanese customs, festivals and the daily life of our people. In order to satisfy their natural curiosity, I conceived the idea some years ago of giving a brief printed answer to these questions on the back of the hotel menu cards so that all our guests might profit from the information.

I am happy to say that the idea proved immediately successful, to such an extent in fact that many of our guests have asked me to supply them with a complete set of the menu cards for their reference, intellectual as well as gastronomic. In the course of time, however, this complete set of menu cards became too bulky so that I was constrained to seek some other solution. This I found in the happy idea of publishing the description in question in book form, so that the guests might keep them for handy and convenient reference in their libraries, for themselves and their families. Such a book, said many of my guests, would also provide an ideal sourvenir of their stay in Japan. This book has therefore no pretentions to nobility of birth other than that, and no claim to prosperity other than that it has proved to supply a real need. In this I feel that its publication is justified. If it can supply, moreover, an added inducement to old guests to visit Japan again, and to introduce her charms to new guests, the book will have served just that purpose that I am optimistic enough to believe it may.

May I here be pardoned for explaining the occasional mention of the Fujiya Hotel in the book. This is not in any way to advertize the hotel, which frankly has, like good wine, no need of any bush, but it so happens that as the original descriptions appeared on the back of our menu cards the name of the Hotel was given. At that time of course there was not the least intention of publishing the descriptions. As, however, those original descriptions were published in our own hotel printing-shop and the type is what we have used to print them in book form, it is evident that it would be an expensive matter to eliminate the reference to the Fujiya Hotel from the electro plates. We therefore beg our readers' clemency in this, as well as for any errors which may have crept into the book.

In an endeavour to satisfy the growing public demand for this book we therefore have pleasure in publishing this second edition. It now behoves me to acknowledge the help received from Mr. F. de Garis, who was responsible for the literary side of the work. I am also deeply indebted to Mr. Senji Isono of the Fujiya Hotel Staff who helped so much in the translation of the description of things Japanese, and as compiler of the volume.

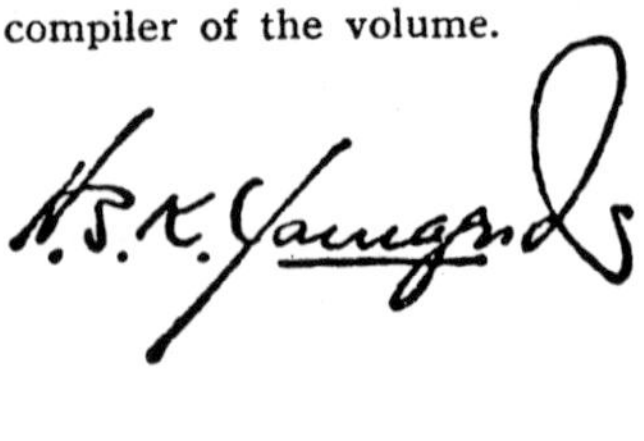

PREFACE

BOOK II

The first volume of "We Japanese" met with such success that many friends persuaded me to continue to publish these miniature sketchei of Japan and Japanese life. It is indeed most gratifying to me to see that there is such a growing interest in my country, her life, customs and manners. Feeling therefore that such a series of books as this may in some ways help my friends to appreciate Japan the better, I consented to publish this second volume. In fact, my friends have been so insistent that I have prepared a third volume, now in the press, and to continue to do my best to satisfy them so long as my readers do me the honour of showing that they are interested in Japan.

In preparing this second volume, I have thought it best to omit the quainter things of Japan, and to offer my friends some phases of Japanese life which appeal to the deeper thinkers. In other words, since the first volume catered for the general public for the most part, I now purpose to offer profounder material on Japan for those readers who are not content merely to know that there are certain quaint customs in Japan which are not practised in their own country. Happily, there is a growing public for this more substantial diet on Japanese culture. This most encouraging, and for this reason I am convinced that this volume will meet with the wishes of many. Subsequent volumes will be of the same graduated style, so that by the time the series is complete, I hope to have offered to my friends what I believe will be a valuable compendium to the study of Japan and her ways, and in an appealling manner artistically produced in a volume such as this, bound in a style which is genuinely Japanese.

I therefore dedicate this second volume to my many friends in the four corners of the earth. In doing so I pray that it may provide them with entertainment, and instruction, and fire them with a genuine desire to continue learning of Japan, and in knowing her more to love her.

I am deeply indebted to Professor A. F. Thomas for his assistance in compiling and revising the book. Also to Mr. Atsuharu Sakai and Mr. Senji Isono for the very valuable aid they have given in helping me to publish this volume, which I believe is a worthy successor to volume one.

N.B.—Since volume One of "We Japanese" was published there has appeared on the market a book entitled "Their Japan." I should like to point out that the book "Their Japan" has no connection whatever with the series "We Japanese." This I feel it neces sary to point out since from the correspondence and personal inquiries I have received it appears that confusion is likely to arise.

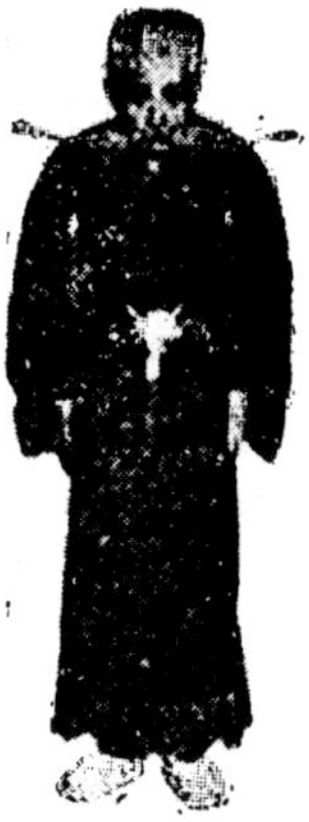

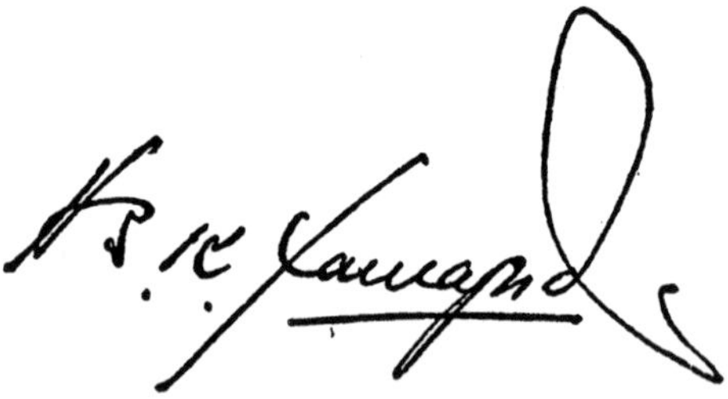

Managing Director
FUJIYA HOTEL

PREFACE

BOOK III

"We Japanese", Vols, I and II, was so well received by foreign tourists who visited Japan in the prewar days because it was one of the best books on Japan, giving extensive information concerning the Japanese and their customs and popular practices. When the war ended in 1945, the book was out of print, and we could not meet the demands of the Occupation Personnel, which demanded the book in order to study Japan.

H.S.K. Yamaguchi, author of "We Japanese", prepared its third volume, but it was totally destroyed by bombing during the war while it was in the press. And Yamaguchi died a sudden death in 1944, without realizing the preparation of the third volume. So we asked Mr. Atsuharu Sakai, writer of "We Japanese" Vol. II, to prepare another volume for the present author, and he has just completed its writing.

Japan, as a defeated nation, has the great mission of rising up again on her war-devasted debris. She must stand up again on her own feet and reconstruct a peaceful country by entirely forgetting the hostilities of the war. All the Japanese must work in perfect cooperation in the reconstruction of the country as a truly democratic nation.

Our national reconstruction requires foreign cooperation and guidance, which we cannot get unless the foreign countries have good knowledge of Japan. We must first show our true aspects to the foreign countries and also that we are a peaceful nation, not at all jingoistic and warlike.

"We Japanese", Vol. I & II, describes the customs and manners of the Japanese which are the real aspects of the nation. As successor to the late author of the book, the present author was resolved to send a new edition of the book to the public.

Many printing-presses were bombed out during the war, and the printing materials were difficult to secure. Nor were skilled labourers more available But we were lucky enough to overcome all these difficulties and succeeded in sending to the public new editions of "We Japanese", Vols. I & II, twice in 1948. But demands were so great for the book that they were all sold out in a few months. In this volume we presented Japan from another vewpoint. While "We Japanese", Vols. I & II, gives popular practices, this third volume is given more to the spiritual and mental phases of the Japanese. The new volume gives more historical aspects of the nation than the first and second volumes do.

The present author of "We Japanese", Vol. III, has been associated with the late H.S.K. Yamaguchi for over thirty long years in the same business of the hotel industry. We have the same common ambition; namely, we want to make Japan and the Japanese known as much to the outside world as possible. No misunderstanding is possible where there is true knowledge. We send this volume to the world hoping that it will be found worthy of a third volume of "We Japanese", Vols. I & II, which is received so well by its readers.

We express our indebtedness to Mr. Atsuharu Sakai, who has prepared "We Japanese", Vol. III, for the present author.

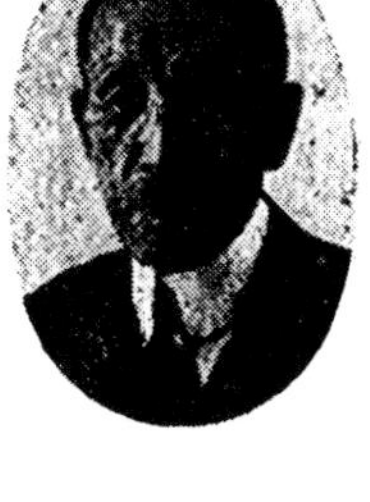

June, 1949

President, Fujiya Hotel,
Miyanoshita, Japan

CONTENTS

BOOK I

CONTENTS

Drama, Dance, Shakespeare:

Sports and Games:

Flowers:

Names of the Years:

Fine Arts, Porcelains, Products, Industries:

Sundry:

CONTENTS

CONTENTS

BOOK II

National:

Historical:

Japanese Characteristics:

Arts and Inventions:

CONTENTS

CONTENTS

CONTENTS

BOOK III

CONTENTS

We Japanese

BOOK I

Written by

FREDERIC DE GARIS

for

H. S. K. YAMAGUCHI,

Managing Director

THE NATIONAL FLAG OF JAPAN

HINOMARU ("THE ROUND OF THE SUN")

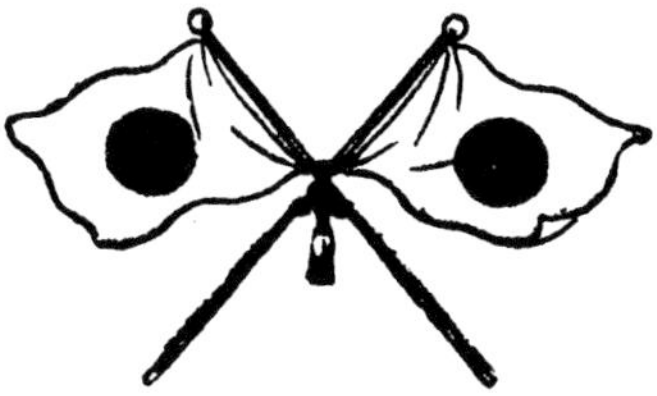

Flags showing the rising sun were used by some of the noted clan heads in ancient days. A record of these flags appears in annals written about 600 years ago. When the ban against building large vessels was lifted—after the advent of Commodore Perry's squadron in 1853-54—the necessity arose to distinguish Japanese ships in foreign commerce, and the flag, about as it now appears, was suggested as a national ensign by Lord Nariakira Shimazu, head to the Satsuma clan.

By official proclamation issued in January, 1870, the standard form and size of the flag were fixed in a rectangular proportion of 3 for the length and 2 for the width, with the diameter of the sun three-fifths of the width, placed in the center of the flag. The material, whether silk, cotton or muslin, was not stipulated. This ordinance was made to clarify the confusion then existing relative to the flag. The flag-staff universally used is of bamboo, painted black every few inches. It is capped with a golden ball.

The first display of the sun flag as the symbol of the nation was on the occasion of the trip to the United States, in 1860, of the first embassy ever sent abroad by the government. It numbered 70 in all. The Powhattan, a steamship of the U. S. navy, was placed at the disposal of the Shogunate for this purpose. The ship flew the American flag at the stern, the Japanese flag at the bow. In a national rite the flag was first used in Yokohama on the occasion of the opening of the first railway in Japan, by Emperor Meiji, on September 17, 1872. The people of Yokohama and those who lived along the rail line hit upon the happy idea of displaying sun flags in front of every house in honor of the Emperor, and in celebration of the occasion.

KIMIGAYO

("Sovereign Reign")

THE NATIONAL ANTHEM OF JAPAN

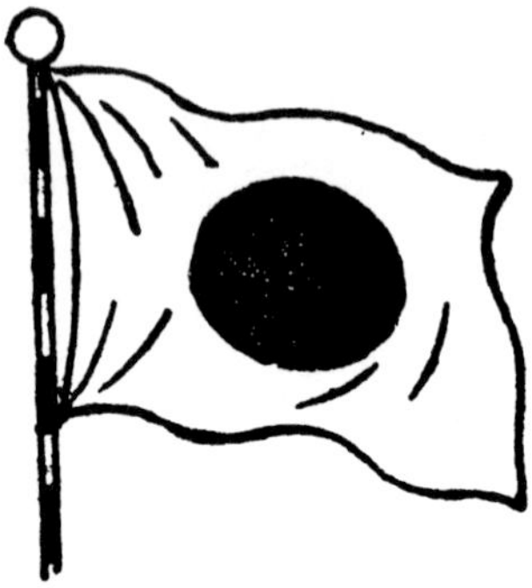

The Kimigayo is recognized as one of the most dignified and most beautiful national anthems in the world. This noble and sonorous melody was harmonized by a German bandmaster, Franz Eckert, director of the Marine Band of Japan from 1879-98. He also founded the military band of Toyama Gakko, Tokyo, and established the military band of the Imperial Guards. In his selection and harmonization of the Kimigayo, Herr Eckert's own modest statement is recorded in the Asiatic Society Transactions:

"Some time ago I was asked by the Ministry of Marine to compose a national anthem, as one did not exist at that time. Having asked for them, I received several Japanese melodies from which I selected the following. I harmonized it and arranged it for European instruments. As I think it unnecessary to write down the instrumentation, I give the original melody only. The poem is from the famous Kokinshu and is about a thousand years old."

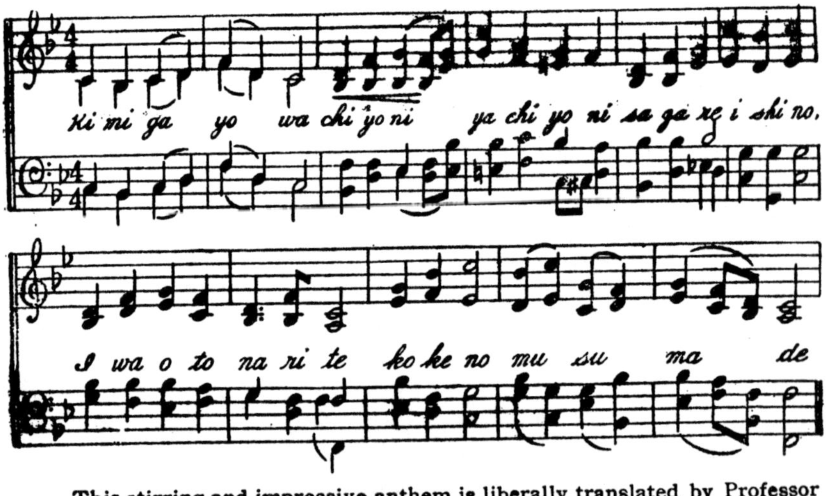

This stirring and impressive anthem is liberally translated by Professor B. H. Chamberlain, author of "Things Japanese", as follows:

Kimi ga yo wa	Ten thousand years of happy reign be thine;
Chiyo ni yachiyo ni	Rule on, my lord, till what are pebbles now
Sazare ishi no	By ages united to mighty rocks shall grow
Iwao to nari te	Whose venerable sides the moss doth line.
Koke no musu made.	

The Kimigayo was played for the first time at Court on the birthday of Emperor Meiji in 1880.

ERAS—YEAR NAMES ("NENGO")

Time, in Japanese chronology, is not reckoned as in Christian countries. It is divided into eras with variable numbers of years, which now correspond with the reigns of the respective Emperors, each era being designated by a particular name called a "year name." For instance, 1933 was the 8th year of *Showa*—the 1st year of the present *Showa* being 1926—and this *Showa* is the 230th era. Also, Japanese chronology is dated from the ascension to the throne of the first Emperor, *Jimmu Tenno*, in 660 B.C.—by which reckoning 1933 becomes 2593—a system employed in Government offices, including post offices, by some historiographers, and in school textbooks. The word *Tenno* is the equivaent of the English word, Emperor.

The meanings of recent eras are: *Meiji* ("Enlightened Era")—1868–1912, *Taisho* ("Way of Heaven" or "Era of Great Equity")—1912–26, *Showa* ("Radiant Peace")—1926–

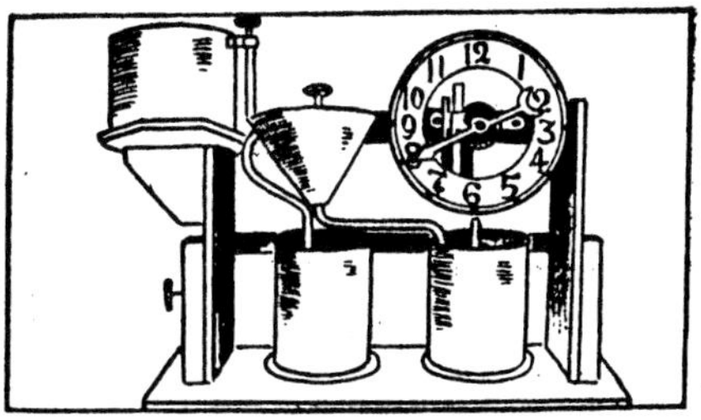

An ancient Japanese clock and Sun dial.

There are advocates who desire that this system be reformed, as with it Japanese history and other records are perplexing even to Japanese. For instance, it is recorded that major earthquakes in Japan occurred in the 13th year of the Hakuho Era, the 7th year of the Meio Era, the 1st year of the Keicho Era, the 6th year of the Genroku Era, the 1st year of the Bunka Era, the 4th year of the Koka Era, the 1st year of the Ansei Era, and so on, but offhand it is difficult to determine how long the intervals were between these occurrences. Reference tables are required by the average person to obtain such information. The difficulties of this system are further illustrated in relation to the present Showa Era, which began, automatically, at 1.25 a.m., December 25, 1926, upon the death of *Emperor Taisho*—which, up to the moment of the Empreror's death, was the 15th year of the Taisho Era. At the Emperor's death the era year became Showa 1, and at 1 a.m. of January 1, 1927, it was Showa 2, which began one hour before, at midnight, in accordance with the Japanese custom. Thus there were three era years in one week. It is worth noting that as Showa 1 was less than a week in length, this fact will cause considerable confusion to future students of Japanese chronology. However, so long has this system been followed, it is not anticipated that it will be changed.

Officially, for communications and trasanctions with foreign Governments and peoples, the Christian (Gregorian) calendar went into effect in Japan on January 1, 1873, and unofficially this calendar is becoming widely used in poplular and technical literature.

VOLCANOES IN JAPAN

Situated as she is in a volcanic zone, Japan suffers from frequent earthquakes and consequently from many volcanic eruptions, which, according to the ancient idea of the Japanese, are a furnace for burning up all dust and garbage of the sea. This is so because our ancients believed that a crater leads to the bottom of the sea. According to tradition, Mt. Fuji made its sudden appearance simultaneously with Lake Biwa in one night in the 6th month (June) in the 5th year (286 B.C.) during the reign of the Emperor Korei (the 7th).

The first volcanic eruption recorded in Japanese history took place on the 14th day of the tenth month (October) in the 12th year (684 A.D.) of the reign of the Emperor Temmu (the 40th), when a new island appeared to the north-west of an Izu island. In the 3rd month (March) of the following year, because of ashes falling from heaven, "all plants in the province of Shinano were killed." During a period of 1246 years, 684 to 1931, 61 mountains erupted 761 times in Japan.

Active volcanoes: There are some active volcanoes in Japan and the following list gives the names of some of the chief ones and the date and number of their eruptions:

Mountain	*Date of First Eruption*	*No. of Violent Eruptions*
Mt. Asama	685 A.D.	266
Mt. Shirane	1882	9
Mt. Fuji	781	15
Miyake-jima Island	1085	12
Ao-ga-shima Island	1652	5
Mt. Iwo-ga-Take	1907	68
Mt. Hakusan	1177	6
Mt. Shirouma	1625	5
Mt. Nasu-dake	1397	5
Mt. Asama-san	1893	12
Mt. Za-o-san	1624	10
Mt. Chokai	578	17
Mt. Iwaki	1596	17
Mt. Kirishima	742	58
Mt. Sakura-jima	716	26
Suwanose-jima Island	1813	8
Mt. Tarumae	1667	26
Mt. Koma-ga-Take	1640	9
Alaid Island	1770	7

BANZAI-THE JAPANESE "HURRAH"

Banzai (Ban—"10,000"; zai, or sai—"years")
Ban-Banzai ("Ten Times Ten Thousand Years")
Wan-sui (Chinese), its characters being read "Banzai" in Japan.

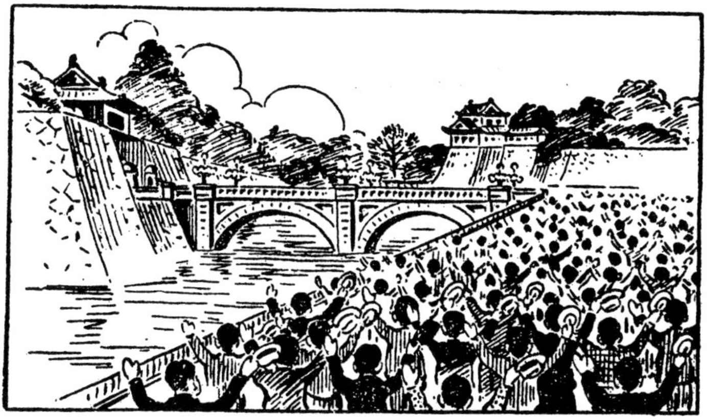

A Banzai at the Niju-bashi Bridge of the Imperial Palace, Tokyo.

What is generally considered to be the origin of Banzai occurred during the Chinese Chin Dynasty (255–207 B.C.) when the King-Emperor Chou of that dynasty, coveting a famous jewel, called Ho-Shih-Pi ("Gem of Ho-Shih," a man's name), owned by King Hui of the Chou Dynasty, offered a considerable territory in exchange for the jewel. Hui, fearing the powerful Chou, had to comply with what was practically a demand. He sent Lin-Hsiang-Ju as his messenger to present the jewel to Chou. When this was done all the courtiers of Chou joined in a mighty shout, "Wan-sui" (Banzai).

There are a number of joyous occasions recorded during the ancient days of both China and Japan when Wan-sui or Mansai (another pronunciation of the present Banzai) was shouted. In Japan, in 788, in the reign of Kammu, the 50th Emperor, there was a great drought. It lasted for five months. Irrigation of crops ceased, as there was no rain. The people were in desperate straits. Early one morning, the Emperor, after observing his ablution rites, went into the garden and there asked in prayer that the drought be broken. Soon banks of clouds appeared in the sky, and from them the rain fell in torrents. Every courtier, stamping his feet in joy, shouted "Mansai."

In 1889, when the Constitution of Japan was promulgated, "Banzai", as it is now shouted, was heard in many places. On February 11 of that same year, when Emperor Meiji held a military review in front of the Niju-bashi bridge of the Imperial Palace, the Tokyo Imperial University students joined in a loud "Banzai." It is now used whenever the occasion demands. At New Year, street singers, called Manzai (which here is not synonymous with Banzai), visit every house and sing songs that are supposed to exorcise the evil spirits from the premises and bring happiness to the family.

THE POPULATION OF JAPAN

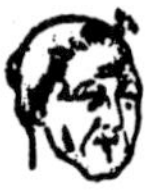
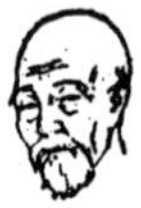

A national census is taken every five years. In 1930 (the last official census) the total population of the Empire was 90,396,045. Of this total 64,450,005 were registered in Japan proper—which is the Empire excluding Korea, Formosa, and Japanese Saghalien. This is an increase of 4,713,183, or 7.9% in the five years since the census of 1925—which showed a population for Japan proper of 59,736,822. The ratio of increase in the five years was 15.30 for each 1,000 as agianst 13.14 of the previous five years from 1920 to 1925—which registered an increase of 3,773,769. These figures, etc., evidence the steady growth of the population of Japan—which necessarily is in constant acceleration, in the same way that money increases at compound interest.

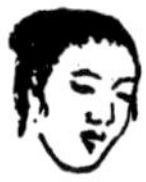
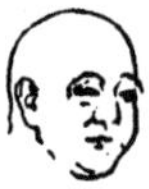

In 1932, the total population of Japan proper was estimated at 66,296,000—the average density being 173 per sq. kilometer, or 2,494.83 per sq. ri, or 430.14 per sq. mil. This density is exceeded by Java, certain parts of India, and by Belgium, the Netherlands, and England. In other words, in Japan proper, a country that is four-fifths mountainous or otherwise unfitted for farming, with a total area only slightly larger than that of Montana, one of the states of the U.S.A., dwell over sixty-six million people, or, putting the situation in another way, Japan proper maintains a population over half as large as that of the United States on an area of cultivated land less than half that of California.

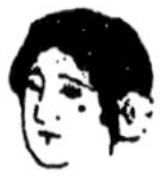
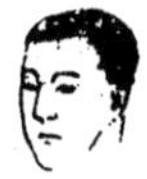

According to the 1933 report of the Statistical Bureau of the Cabinet, there were added in 1932, through excess of births over deaths, 115 babies every hour. This population increase presents a serious problem for the Government—which is searching for means for its solution, and ways for providing employment for its productive male population which matures yearly.

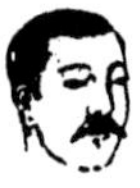
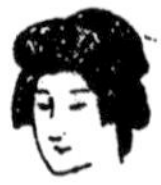

On Oct. 1, 1933, the population of Japan proper totaled 67,238,000, an increase of 942,000 over that of 1932—of which 33,796,000 were males, 33,442,000 were females.

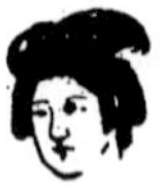
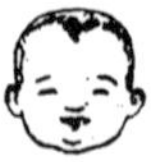

In 1920 the birth rate for Japan proper reached its highest figure of 36.19 per 1,000, but since then it has slightly decreased up to 1932.

Population experts calculate that the Japanese population will never reach the hundred million mark—that the population will become stabilized around eighty million in 1960, and from then on the increase will stop entirely, as was the case with European countries.

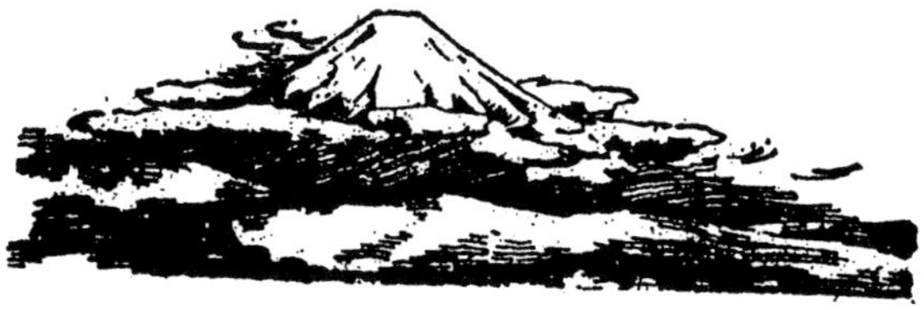

Mt. Fuji may be seen in whole or in part, more or less distinctly, from 22 prefectures, but nowhere in Japan are the views of this regal mountain so beautiful or varied as those of the Hakone District.

The perfect, majestic conical peak of Mt. Fuji, rising in sublime grandeur 12,395 feet (3,778 metres) above sea-level, is the highest, as well as the most famous mountain in all Japan. It is the "National Mountain," regarded as sacred by Japanese and it has been the Mecca for over 1,000 years for pilgrims and other folk who have climbed its slopes during July and August, the only time in the year when the mountain's robe of snow is laid aside. It extends into three provinces: Suruga, Kai, and Totomi. At its base it is about 100 miles in circumference.

Peerless Fuji-yama defies description. You may read about it, see scores of pictures of it, hear what other travelers say about it, but when you see it in its varied aspects, never twice alike, you will realize that the real Fuji is far beyond anything you have ever imagined. Sometimes it appears in faultless white and silver against a blue sky, sometimes its perfect crest seems to float phantom-like above the clouds, and sometimes at sunset it lifts its purple mystery into a rosy sky—and its charm graces all the arts of Japan and appears in countless Japanese and foreign writings, and poems.

Ascent: The ideal way to make the trip from Miyanoshita and to avoid staying overnight in an overcrowded hut is to take a motor car or a Gotemba bus in time to reach Nagao-toge (Long-tail Pass) for the superb sunset view of the ethereal mountain. At Gotemba transfer to a Subashiri bus, resting at an inn there until 7 p.m. before starting the climb. The night climb avoids the sun and the way seems shorter. The Subashiri is the shortest route (8 m.), but other routes are available. Each is divided into 10 stages, with a stone hut at nearly every stage where one may rest, or lodge for the night. Arrive at the summit in time for the impressive sunrise view—and the wonderful panorama of land, sea, mountains, and lakes. A circuit of the crater is usually made in order that all phases of the peak can be viewed. Horses are available to the 8th station. Descend by the Gotemba sand trail. The trails are opened about July 5–10; accommodations at the huts are available up to about September 10. The ascent requires about 9 hours, the descent about 4 hrs., which with a 2 hrs. rest and the walk around the crater totals 15 hours. Guides can be hired at Subashiri.

Mt. Fuji is reported to have been an active volcano up to about the 14th century. It has been quiescent since 1707, but small wisps of steam issue from fissures in its crater.

PRECEPTS AND MAXIMS OF THE SHOGUN IEYASU

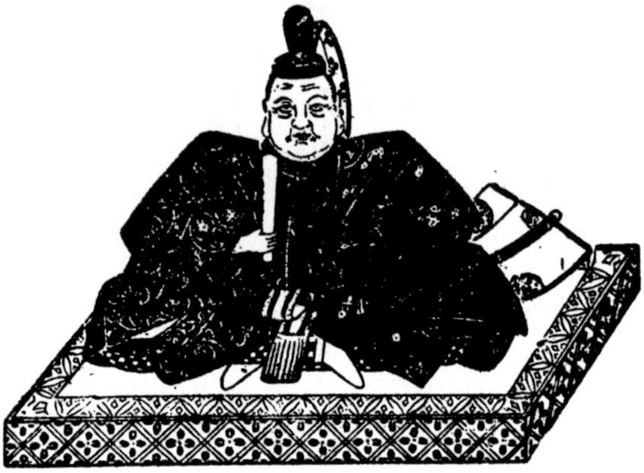

Life is like unto a long journey with a heavy load. Let thy steps be slow and steady that thou stumble not.

Persuade thyself that imperfection and inconvenience is the natural lot of mortals and there will be no room for discontent . . . neither for despair.

When ambitious desires arise in thine heart, recall the days of extremity thou hast passed through.

Forbearance is the root of quietness and assurance forever.

Look upon wrath as thine enemy.

If thou knowest only what it is to conquer, and knowest not what it is to be defeated, woe unto thee!—it will fare ill with thee.

Find fault with thyself rather than with others.

Better the less than the more.

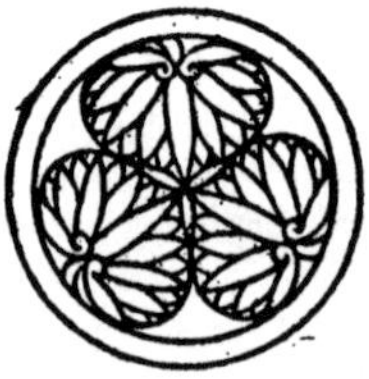

Tokugawa *mon*, or crest—three leaves of *aoi*, or hollyhock.

Ieyasu (E-yay-yasu)—b. 1542; d. 1616—Founder of the Tokugawa Shogunate, which existed during the period between 1603 and 1867, was one of the most illustrious men of Japan. His mausoleum is at Nikko, in the precincts of the Toshogu or Ieyasu Shrine. During the 264 years of Tokugawa rule the arts and crafts of Japan flourished as never before.

MOMOTARO or LITTLE PEACHLING

(*Momo*=peach; *taro*=a popular name for boys)

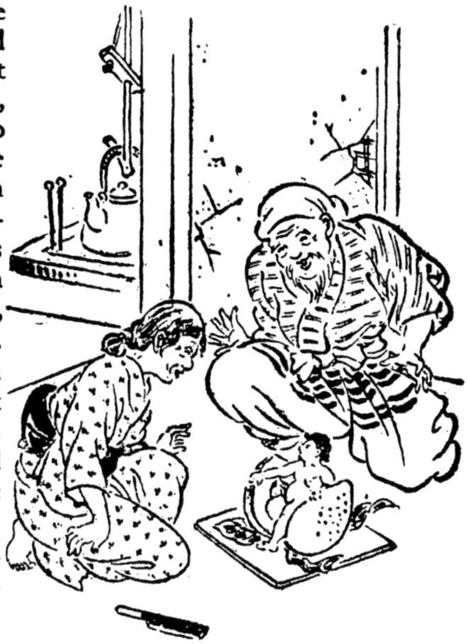

A long, long time ago there lived an honest old wood-cutter and his wife. One day the old man went off to the hills to gather faggots, while his wife went to the river to wash clothes. While doing this she noticed a large object floating down the stream. With a stick she managed to draw it to her, and was much surprised to find that it was a very large peach. She took it home, intending to give it to her husband. Upon his return, setting the peach before him, she was about to cut it when the fruit split apart and a little boy baby came forth. The old couple, rejoicing, named the babe Momotaro, or Little Peachling, because he came out of a peach, and brought him up as their own child.

In the course of time the boy grew up to be remarkably strong and brave, and at last one day he said to his foster-parents: "I am going over to the Ogres' Island to carry off the riches they have stored there; so please make me some millet dumplings for my journey." This they did—and Momotaro cheerfully started out with the dumplings in his pouch, and a complete equipment. As he journeyed a dog came to his side and said: "Momotaro! What is that hanging from your belt?" He replied: "I have some of the very best Japanese dumplings." "Give me one and I will go with you," said the dog. So Momotaro took a dumpling out of his pouch and gave it to the dog. Then a monkey came and got one the same way. A pheasant flew up and said: "Give me a dumpling too, and I will go along with you." So all three traveled with him.

When they arrived at the Ogres' Island, the pheasant flew over the castle gate and by signals reported the ogres' movements, the monkey clambered over the castle wall and tore off the gate chain, while Momotaro, leading the dog, forced the gate and got into the castle. There they battled with the ogres, pressing them back, and finally took their chief, Akandoji, prisoner. So all the ogres did homage to Momotaro and laid their treasures before him—a great pile of precious things. Momotaro went home laden with riches, and maintained his foster-parents in peace and plenty for the remainder of their lives. He became a man of influence, very rich and honorable.

A festival in Momotaro's honor is held yearly at Kurusu, on the Kiso River, the little village where the legendary Momotaro was brought up.

Stories of Momotaro's exploits are embedded in the heart of every Japanese boy, and his figure is always a conspicuous decoration in the annual Boy's Festival celebration.

WHICH IS YOUR CHOICE?

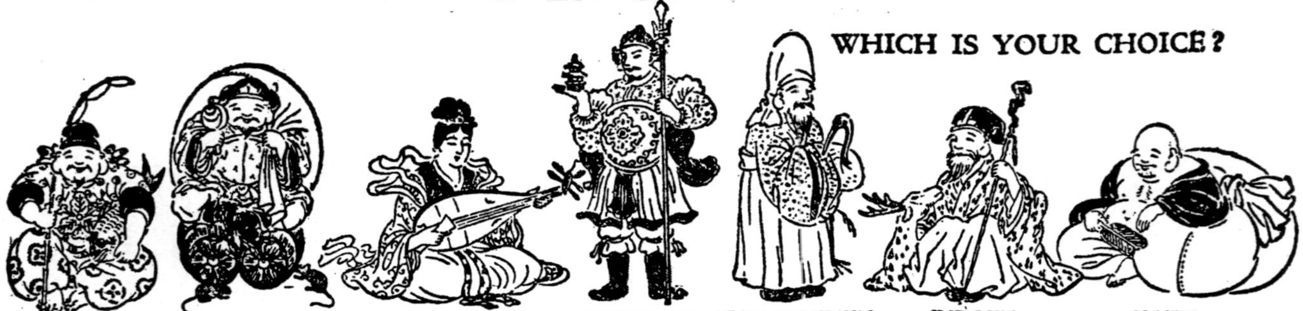

EBISU: The deity of fishermen and tradesmen. He carries a fishing rod and huge *tai* (sea-bream). He is not a dilettante angler but a hard worker who believes in earning his living by honest toil.

DAIKOKU: The happy god of wealth, patron saint of farmers—a disseminator of good humour and happiness. He stands or sits on two rice bales, holding the lucky hammer from which he can shake out anything that human heart desires. On his shoulder is a huge sack of treasures. So vast is his wealth he does not mind the rat nibbling at one of his rice bales.

BENTEN: The maiden deity, the only woman among the seven gods. She represents art, literature, music and eloquence. Maidens who wish to improve in female accomplishments are her devoted worshippers. She is pictured playing on the *biwa,* her favorite instrument, and is always shown with a sea serpent.

BISHAMON: Clad in armour from crown to toe and armed with a spear of formidable length, Bishamon is the god of militarism, but the toy pagoda he carries signifies his dual role of religious missionary and warrior, determined to conquer the world through the virtues of his spear and pagoda.

FUKU-ROKUJIN: A deity with a short trunk and shorter legs and preternaturally long head, even longer than his legs. He was a Chinese philosopher who was able to "live on the mists of heaven and the dews of earth". He could prophesy events and he performed miracles to the improvement of mankind

JUROJIN: The God of longevity, a copious drinker of *sake*, depicted as a venerable old man with a snow-white beard and carrying a *shaku* or holy staff, to which is tied a scroll containing all the wisdom of the world. He is always accompanied either by a crane, a stag or a tortoise.

HOTEI: Distinguished by his huge protuberant abdomen, which is thought to indicate a largeness of soul and an inward wealth of resources, characteristic of a man who has attained the wisdom of Buddhism.

These Seven Deities are worshipped at all times but at New Year they are particularly remembered and feted. Temples dedicated to each of them are found throughout Japan.

HAGOROMO (Feather Robe)

The Legend of the Angel Who Came to Earth

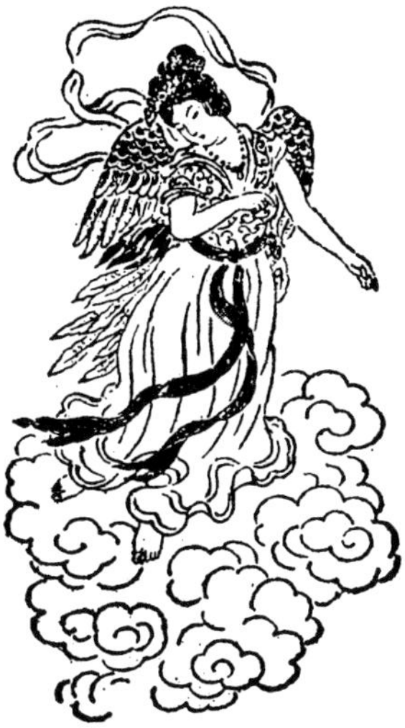

Hagoromo is one of the favorite "No" plays. The legend is as follows:

A fisherman, Hakuriu (White Dragon) by name, beached his boat at Miho-no-Matsubara, and while admiring the superb beauty of this bit of seashore and Mt. Fuji in the distance, he chanced to see a beautiful feather robe hanging on a pine-tree branch. At the same time perfumed flowers fluttered down from the sky to the accompaniment of majestic music, which swelled as the blue waters of the bay swirled. The man took down the robe and was amazed at its magnificence. An angel appearing, asked what he was doing with her robe. "I want to take it home, as it is so beautiful", replied the fisherman. "No, you may not do so. Please return it to me. Without it I cannot fly back to Heaven". The argument continued thus until at last her appeals were effective, and the robe was given back. Instantly, the angel ascended to Heaven, flying away over Mt. Fuji, fast disappearing toward the west. She was, however, good enough to perform a dance in mid-air in grateful recognition of the man's kindly act. This was the Hagoromo-no-Mai, a celestial dance.

Miho-no-Matsubara, famed in poetry and art, is a sandy pine-clad point about 7 m. from Shimizu, Shizuoka Prefecture. The Hagoromo-no-Matsu (The pine-tree of the heavenly robe of feathers) stands there. The present tree, planted about 50 years ago, replaces the original tree, which is said to have been 90 feet in height, with a girth of 11 feet.

According to the researches of Professor Shinji Nishimura of Waseda University, this legend is of world-wide knowledge and had its origin independent among various races. It is neither the exclusive invention of the Japanese people nor their sole property. It belongs to the class of the "Bird-maiden myth" or the "Swan-maiden myth" of the mythologies of the world. The legend, in various forms, is known in most of the European countries, in Asia, the South Pacific Islands, and was known among the tribes of North and South America.

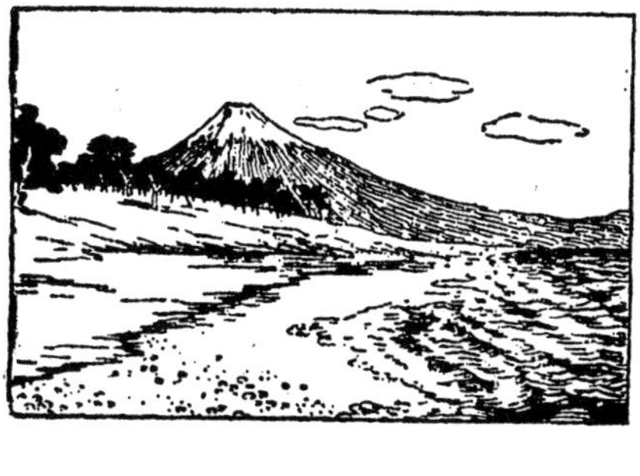

In Japan, there are several places which claim its origin: Omi, Tango, and others.

TENGU

Tengu, the most popular of all supernatural beings, are, according to legend, a class of goblins or gnomes that haunt high mountains and deep forests, and play many pranks.

Tengu have enormously long red human noses and human mouths, and they use a leaf of the Yatsude tree for a fan. They are guarded by Karasu tengu ("Crow tengu"), smaller beings with bodies like a person, but with two wings, which enable them to fly. Their nails are like a tiger's claws and their eyes are round, exuding light like a lightning bolt, and they have long beaks like a bird, instead of a mouth. They are armed with clubs.

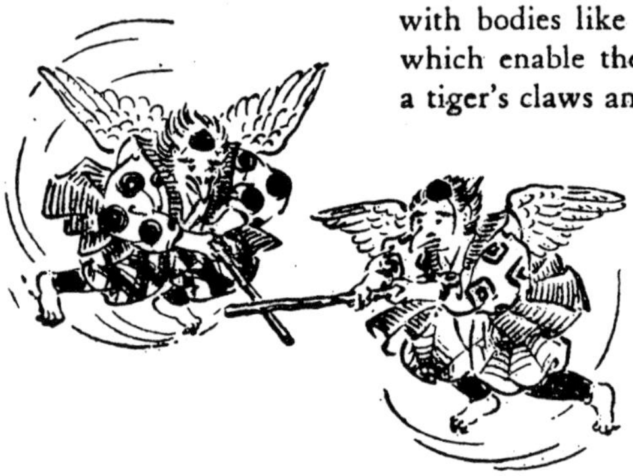

Legend has it that in the mystic past there drifted to Japan large, powerful Europeans with red, sunburned faces, and red hair, and with prominent noses which seemed enormous to people with small noses without much of a bridge—and which in course of time, by hearsay, became exaggerated into the long noses peculiar to tengu. These men wore capes, which are shown in tengu effigies. Some people think that these men were the origin of the tengu of popular tradition.

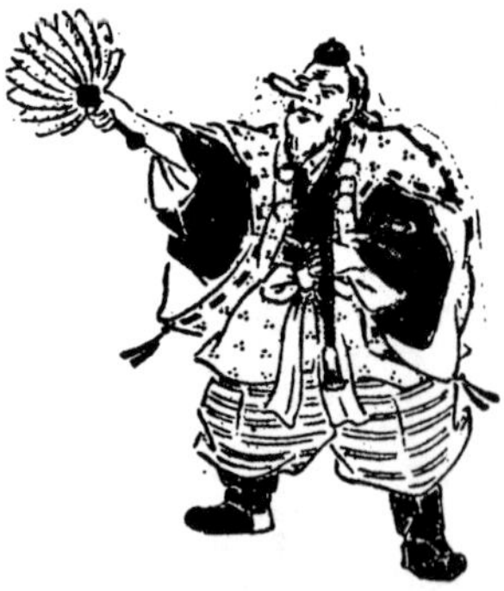

Many temples are dedicated to tengu, and some of them are very wealthy, due to the fact that for some reason tengu are included among the patron saints of farmers, who yearly give a portion of their crops to the temples. The nearest to Miyanoshita is the Doryo-san temple. A visit to this temple makes an interesting trip. The largest tengu temple in this neighborhood is at Oyama, near Hiratsuka, half-way between Miyanoshita and Yokohama. It is visited annually by thousands of pilgrims.

At Kamakura, back of the Kencho-ji temple-grounds, on the hillside, reached by stone steps, is a small temple dedicated to tengu. Two large guardian tengu with noses shaped like an eagle's beak, and eight smaller tengu on the rocks on the approach to the temple, are rather striking objects.

FANTASTIC KAPPA, or RIVER BOY, STORIES

Japanese dictionaries define *Kappa* as a fabulous amphibious animal, but many persons claim to have seen this aquatic biped, which walks like a man —and which is said to be about the size of a 13 or 14-year-old boy, and looks like one—and it is so widely known in Japan that many places have a local story about it. Every case of drowning in a river is attributed to a kappa, and as kappa are said to be fond of cucumbers, it is a custom for mothers, at the beginning of the bathing season, to propitiate them by throwing a cucumber into the river so that their children will not be seized and drowned by a kappa.

Quoting from *Netsukes*, a book by A. Brockhaus: "Kappa is of pure Japanese origin. It is a fantastic animal, mostly depicted with a body resembling a tortoise, frog legs, and a monkey-like head—on the top of which is a hollow which is filled with his watery elixer of life. This creation, nevertheless, is 'scientifically' described as a froggy creature, 4 ft. 9 in. in height, and in 1830 was still caught in swamps. He falls in love, he is dangerous to young ladies, has a fighting spirit, but is as ceremonious as a nobleman. Before engaging a duel with a kappa, man is advised to request that the kappa make a polite bow. The kappa is such a gentleman that he will comply with the request of his adversary, but this causes the life-giving water to flow out of the hollow on his head so that he is easily conquered!"

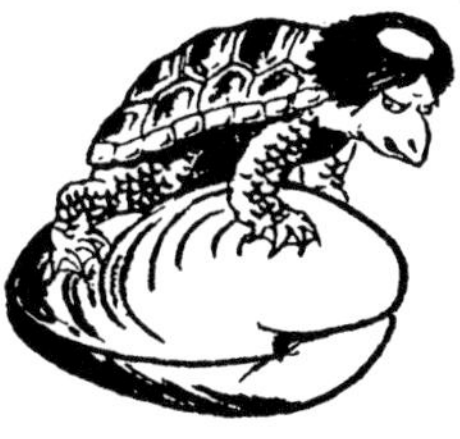

Wood-Netsuke.
Kappa with its toes caught by a clam.

In Japan, bobbed hair is called O-Kappa ("Honorable Kappa") and is so named after the style of hair which kappa favor.

Among the scores of Kappa stories, space permits only the following:

A kappa was caught in Idzumo province. About to be killed it begged for its life, stating that it would never more drown a child in the river—and gave a written promise to this effect. It is asserted in some parts of Idzumo that if a child says *Unshu-Nishikawatsu-Mura* (meaning the village of Nishikawatsu in Idzumo province) it will never be drowned.

Near Fukuoka, Kyushu, there is an Itsushima Shrine, built in the Horeki era (1751–64). Upon being repaired, just before the enthronement of the present Emperor (1928), three flat stones, each 3×13×13 ft. in dimensions, and each inscribed in Sanskrit, were found buried underground. It is said that three kappa were once caught in that neighborhood. The people were about to kill them in retaliation for the children drowned there. The three kappa pleaded for their lives, declaring that never again would they drown any children. In proof of their vow, each of them incised a stone in Sanskrit.

In Higo (Kumamoto) province a child was drowned—it was thought by a kappa. A *samurai*, Ishiwara Kanainosuke, angered by the child's death, plunged into the river and fought with a kappa. He cut off one of the kappa's arms. It looked like a dried stick. A few days later the kappa came and asked for his arm. It was given to him on condition that he would drown no more children. It is said that no child of Ishiwara village has since then been drowned.

THE BECKONING CAT

In china-shops throughout Japan there are on sale *Maneki-Neko* or Beckoning Cats, which are porcelain cats with their left paw raised in the Japanese beckoning manner, *i.e.*, summoning a person by waving the hand palm out instead of with the palm towards him, as do foreigners. Such cats are very popular as mascots among people depending upon the public's favor for their success.

About 150 years ago there were two tea-houses near the gate of the Ekoh-in Temple, Ryogoku, Tokyo. Both houses vied with each other in attracting guests by means of large porcelain cats with paw uplifted as if beckoning to passers by. The eastern house had a golden cat, the western, a silver cat. These particular cats seem to have been well known inasmuch as mention of them is made in various old books, and also in 17-syllable poems written on the Beckoning Cat.

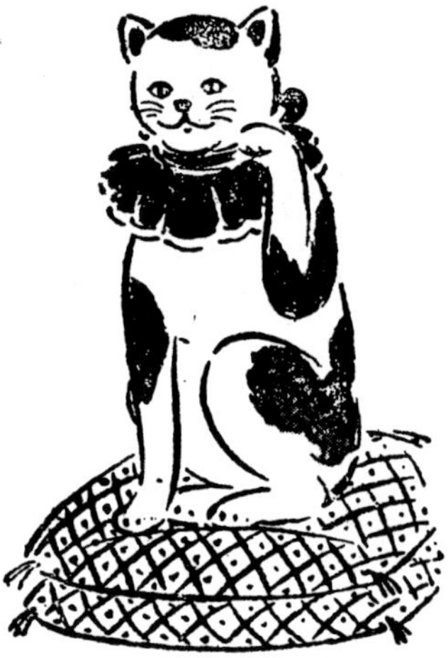

Yahei, the host of the eastern house, became dissolute, but his wife O-Tsuna, on the contrary, was a most amiable and charming woman, overflowing with smiles, and was popular with their guests—one of whom, named Hachirobei, an old-clothes dealer, was enamored by O-Tsuna's cheerful ways, until she cajoled him out of a large sum of money he had collected for another old-clothes dealer. Hachirobei, determining to atone with his life for his misconduct, went one evening to the Ryogoku-Bashi bridge over the Sumida intending to throw himself into the river. He was leaning against the bridge railing, ruminating over his fate, when along came O-Tsuna, his love.

"What are you doing here, Hachirobei, my dear?" she said. "No more of you, O-Tsuna!" replied Hachirobei, in a fury. "You have taken all my money and you have ruined me." He then told her about his situation, and O-Tsuna, repentant, proposed that she should join her lover on his journey to the world beyond. They committed suicide (*shinju*—"double suicide") in the Sumida River.

Their suicide made such a sensation in Yedo (old Tokyo) that their story was staged, and the Golden-cat Tea-house became so popular that the rival tea-house had to close.

Beckoning Cats are kept by merchants and tea-house and restaurant keepers as luck-bringers, and in the belief that they attract customers—and a Beckoning Cat usually has a place in the house-altar of the demimonde.

SHIBUI KONOMI

An elusive phase of Japanese Aestheticism

The Japanese have given the word *shibumi* to a quality which is literally a "rough or astringent taste," i.e., the reverse of "sweet taste." Its adjective, *shibui,* is derived from *shibu,* an astringent quality. Japanese-English dictionaries define *shibui* as simple, unaffected, tasty, or elegant. None of these words, however, gives more than the barest hint, if any hint at all, of what *shibui* really is.

Like all transcendent qualities, the word *shibumi* eludes definition. To the Japanese, those externals which soothe and satisfy the spirit are *shibumi.* These things are instinctive, not shaped by reason and not easily put into speech, but *shibumi* suggests art appreciation, culture, ultra-refinement, quiet tastes, and a great consideration for others. "Nothing too much" is in it, and the word is in itself a protest against ostentation. There is something in it which conforms to the traditional appreciation of serenity, introspection, modesty, formality, nobility and reserve, and conservatism, and, as the antithesis of bizarre, it is opposed to everything that is garish, gay, loud or noisy, or sensuous.

No single English word exactly describes *shibumi* as the Japanese understand it. By an artistic foreign visitor *shibumi* has been described as "the acme of elegance and refinement—the result of the use of restraint in the highest sense." Japanese speak of *shibui* in relation to customs, houses, rooms, decorations and ornaments, persons, dress, as well as to the tone of voice. It marks the character of the old order of things, and sometimes of the new. In short, the parts must be related to the whole, and the whole must be seemly to place and circumstance. *Shibumi* is found in all the arts of Japan—that esoteric quality introduced into Art by the Zen Sect of Buddhism. It is the art that conceals art.

A certain color scheme is essential in producing a *shibui* effect. A sculptured piece of white marble, for instance, cannot be *shibui* because it is devoid of color, but the prevalence of brilliant or bright color is antagonistic to *shibui.*. The color of bran, the outer coat of kernels of rice, wheat, etc., is commonly called *shibu-kawa* (meaning astringent skin), and this color, or that of various shades of chestnut or russet in an art object is usually essential in securing a *shibui* effect. The color of ashes, unpolished silver and gold, and other colors, constitute factors for producing a subdued and tranquil effect in an art object and it is the artistic employment of such colors or combinations of colors that imparts to Japanese art an indescribable *shibui* effect. A careful study of a guest-room in a Japanese house will reveal that the color scheme is obtained by the contrast of the colors of the walls, ceiling, pillars, and other parts of the room. In no part of it is there a color which departs from the traditional color that makes the room *shibui.*

A Japanese, in commenting upon a woman's kimono, might say: "Look at her *shibui konomi*"—meaning that the woman was dressed with discrimination in silk material of the traditional color, not showy, but rich in quality. In speaking of a voice as *shibui,* reference is made to its quality through the cultivation and training it has received.

Perhaps a liberal rendition of the meaning of *Shibui Konomi* would be: An inherent appreciation of the elements, properly arranged and balanced, that enters into art, and into one's life and personality.

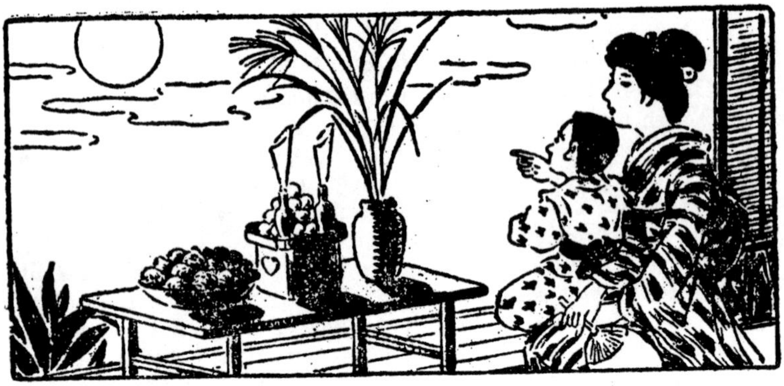

ARTISTIC, AESTHETIC, and POETIC TASTES OF THE JAPANESE

MOON-VIEWING

An inherent love of nature is a strong national characteristic of the Japanese, shared by all classes, from the humblest person to the most exalted —and the yearning to express and perpetuate the impressions made on refined tastes by nature in her varied moods has resulted in producing the paintings and exquisite fine arts in metal, wood, clay, and other materials for which Japan is famous the world over. Japanese genius touches perfection in small things, for which the Japanese flexible, artistic hands are peculiarly adapted. The graceful, tapering Japanese hand deserves a chapter in itself, and is so treated in Hamilton Wright Mabie's "Japan To-day and To-morrow," and reference is made to it on another Fujiya Hotel menu.

The aesthetic tastes of the Japanese are evidenced in the *Cha-no-yu* or Tea Ceremony, in their annual moon-viewing parties, in flower arrangement, in their *bonsai* and *bonkei* creations, their insect-hearing and incense-smelling parties and in many other ways—those mentioned being described on Fujiya Hotel menu cards.

Moon-viewing: There are two moon-viewings, determined by the lunar calendar, the "Jugoya" on Aug. 15, the "Jusanya" on Sept. 13, and it is a superstition that if the *Jugoya* is observed it is also necessary to observe the *Jusanya* in order to avoid bad luck. By the Gregorian calendar these moon-viewings are about a month later, varying somewhat every year.

When the moon is in the full and at its best, thousands of families on the prescribed nights place tiny altars on the veranda where the moonlight falls and make offerings of food, fruits, flowers and the autumn grasses to the brilliant satellite. Poems are composed for the occasion and appropriate stories are told in the light of the moon.

CHA-NO-YU ("TEA CEREMONY")

Cha-Tea (*no*-a particle)-*Yu*-hot water

Overseas visitors to Japan usually desire to witness at least one *Cha-no-yu*, an ancient observance which has come down through the ages and which is a development by certain priests of the Buddhist Zen sect of simple tea drinking into what is now an aethetic cult, its outstanding tea-master being Rikyu, once a close friend of the great *Taiko-Hideyoshi*. From its inception the *Cha-no-yu* ceremony has been regarded as a promotor of mental composure. In the mere handling of the utensils employed there must be the utmost exactness, and not a single error must occur in the performance of the function itself. It is declared by its devotees that the accurate and delicate performance of each act teaches precision, poise and tranquility, courtesy, sincerity, unselfishness and daintiness, and produces harmony in every sense.

Situated in every large garden and in some small gardens is a tea-ceremony house, constructed on prescribed lines, and in the homes of many wealthy families a room is set aside for the *Cha-no-yu*. These rooms are only 9 feet square, their floors being covered with 4½ mats (*tatami*), each mat being about 6×3 feet in size.

Space does not permit a description of the ceremony itself, or of the "Don'ts" in connection with it, or of the utensils employed—but it may be said that while to Occidental eyes some of these utensils may appear crude crockery ware, many of them are valued at thousands of yen. The tea itself

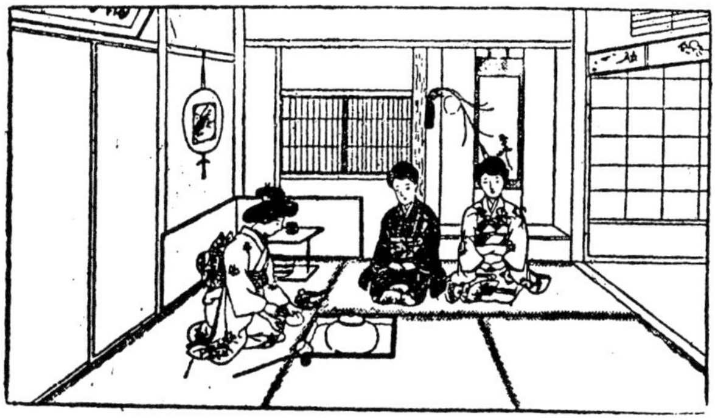

is made of powdered green tea-leaves and when made has the consistency of thick pea soup. This thick-tea ceremony is called *Koi-cha*. There is another style of tea ceremony, the *Usu-cha*, which differs from the *Koi-cha* in some respects. It is less ceremonious, and the tea, of good quality, is drunk like ordinary tea and is made with lukewarm water, and the bowl is filled afresh for each guest, being rinsed out with water each time. The tea used in both these ceremonies comes from Uji, near Kyoto, the most noted tea district of Japan. See "Japanese Green Tea" description. An authoritative work on *Cha-no-yn* is *The Book of Tea*, by Okakura Kakuzo (Duffield & Co., New York).

The tea ceremony with its long formalities cannot be fully appreciated by the casual Westerner, but when he witnesses it he cannot fail to be impressed by the sincere enjoyment evidenced by the Japanese participants in the function—which for them still carries a trace of its religious element.

IKE-BANA

The Aesthetic Art of Flower Arrangement in Japan

While there are different methods of arranging flowers according to various schools, the fundamental principles underlying the first steps are the same in that every arrangement must be made to symbolize "Heaven," "Man," and "Earth." If a single plant or tree branch is used, the main part that shoots upward represents "Heaven," a twig on the right, bent side ways, denotes "Man," and the lowest twig or branch on the left, the end slightly bent so that it points upward, signifies "Earth." This is the *Yo,* or male style. The female style is shown in the picture. Three separate plants or branches placed closely together, not necessarily of the same kind, are often used to represent these three elements; for instance, a bamboo may be used to symbolize "Heaven," with a pine and plum-blossom branch as "Man" and "Earth" respectively, and sometimes grasses are used to signify "Earth." Invariably, there is an odd number of stalks or branches in an *ike-bana* for the reason that odd numbers are considered lucky; even numbers are unlucky and are never used in flower arrangements. Flower arrangement is an important factor in the decoration of a Japanese room. The word "flower," in Japan, is used in a broad sense and covers not only the flowers of plants but also the blossoms of fruit and other trees, and even flowerless trees and shrubs: the pine, willow, bamboo, maple, etc.

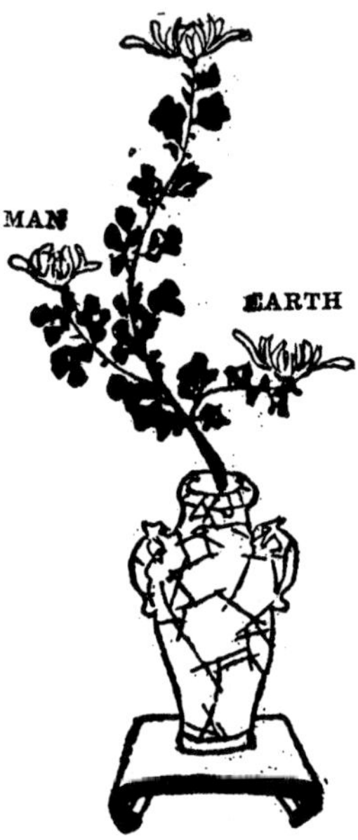

"*In*," or female style of arrangement.

The receptacles for *ike-bana,* and the relative height of the vases and flowers are important essentials in the art. Volumes have been written on *ike-bana.* The most instructive books in English are "The Flowers of Japan and the Art of Japanese Flower Arrangement," by Josiah Conder, and "Japanese Flower Arrangement Applied to Western Needs," by Mary Averill. The following quotation is a translation of a Japanese saying, taken from the latter book.

"Heaven and earth are flowers—
Gods as well as Buddha are flowers.
The heart of man is also the soul of flowers."

THE INSECT-HEARING FESTIVAL

The insect-hearing festival is a picturesque rite which has come down from feudal days. This poetic and sentimental pastime is usually held on late August and September evenings in temple and shrine precincts, public parks, and in many gardens, when the "seven grasses of autumn" are in full bloom. Singing insects are dear to the hearts of Japanese and their chirpings are believed to be clearer and more resonant at that time. Old and young foregather in chosen spots in gardens and other places where the festival is held, carrying their insects in tiny cages, some of which have been brought from the gardens of individual homes, others that have been bought, from one of the many vendors, especially for this ceremony of "Freeing the Insects." In cool glens and in softly lighted bowers the cages are opened and the tiny captives freed. Then, almost breathless, the liberator waits for the insects to get their new bearings, realize their freedom, and send forth their rejoicings in sibilant song.

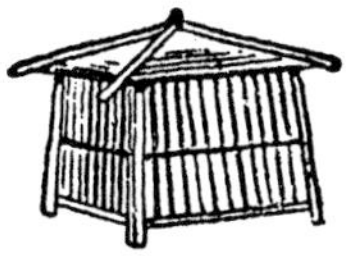

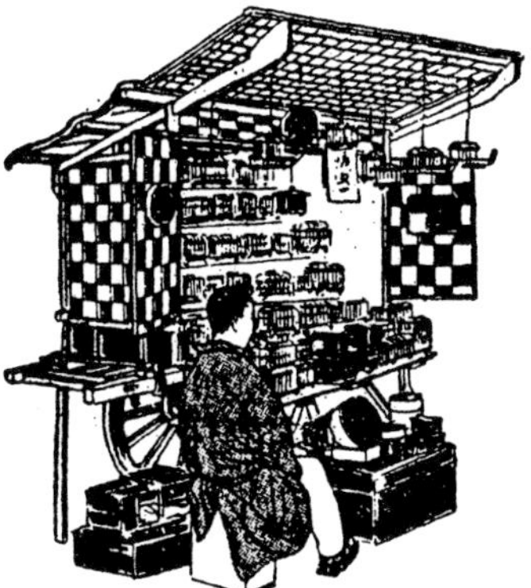

The insect season begins on May 28, at the time of the Fudō Temple festival.

The *Mushi-uri* ("Insect-seller") then appears with his wares. He need not advertise his stock in trade as the chirping insects in their small cages attract buyers—who hang the cages on trees or under the eaves of their houses, where, during the hot summer nights, the stillness is broken by the songs of the insects. The cages sell from a few sen to as high as ¥185 for artistic cages—of split bamboo, highly polished. There are more than a dozen different kinds of singing insects; their average life is from 40 to 60 days. They are sold at prices from 15 sen to 60 sen for the best singers. Many dealers specialize in breeding the insects. When they are hatched out six out of every ten are females. But as only the males sing, the females are sacrificed. Ordinarily they are fed with a slice of cucumber or eggplant, fresh daily.

Mr. Chosei Motoori, a musician, has succeeded in recording the notes of some of the most popular singing insects. The *Kusahibari* ("Grass-Lark"), the smallest of the insects, produces its song in the G key, one octave higher than the highest G key on the piano. It is very clear and has a metallic ring to it. The *Katan,* almost as small as the Kusahibari, produces the sweetest sound—a long continued, monotonous tremolo. *Matsumushi* ("Pine-insect"), so named because its wings look like pine-tree bark, sings in the E or F key in a series of different staccato notes. The *Suzumushi* ("Bell-insect") is the violinist of the insect world. Its tune is *sforzando piano,* a delicate "Liin-liin-liin," like soft tones from a bell. While most singing insects tune up only at night, the *Kirigirisu* ("Long-horned grasshopper") sings in the day time. The *Emma-Korogi,* a variety of cricket, sings with a trill in tremolo, and with a somewhat slower tempo than other insects. *Emma* means the ruler of hell.

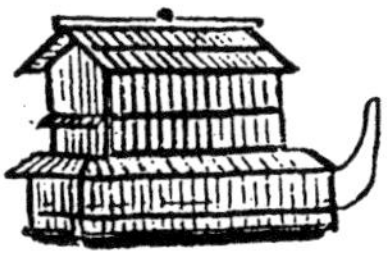

BONSAI

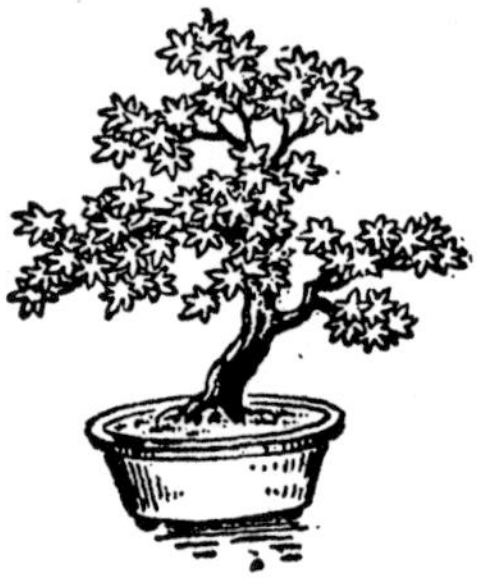

Bonsai, or potted plants, are dwarfed trees, trained to show the beauty of large normal trees, or of ancient trees. The favorite trees for *bonsai* are pines (matsu), principally of the needle-leaf family, and a species of broad-leaf Mongolian oak (keyaki), Some specimens of these trees, potted for 100 years or more, bring several thousand yen when sold. At one of the recent exhibitions of *bonsai* there were two pines each said to be over 500 years old. Trees also used in *bonsai* are cryptomeria (sugi), maple (momiji), ground cypress (hinoki), cherry (sakura), and others. Some trees have two trunks, some a single trunk; sometimes a different species is grafted into the main tree. Some of these dwarfed trees, from one foot up in height, have all the characteristics of normal trees.

The usual method of producing these dwarfed trees is as follows: the main roots of selected seedlings of small trees, not more than 3 to 5 in. in height, are cut away, only the small roots being allowed to develop—a procedure which is carried out periodically. Weights are hung on the branches in order to make them hang in downward curved shapes and the branches are tied with string or wire to form them into artistic shapes. The treatment differs with each tree. The trees are kept in a shaded location. Six to ten years are required to produce a desirable tree. *Bonsai* for decorative and exhibition purposes are common all over Japan.

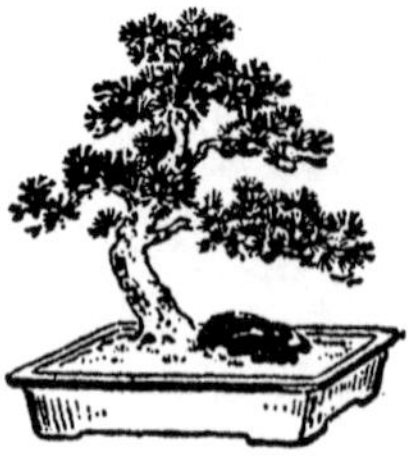

BON-KEI

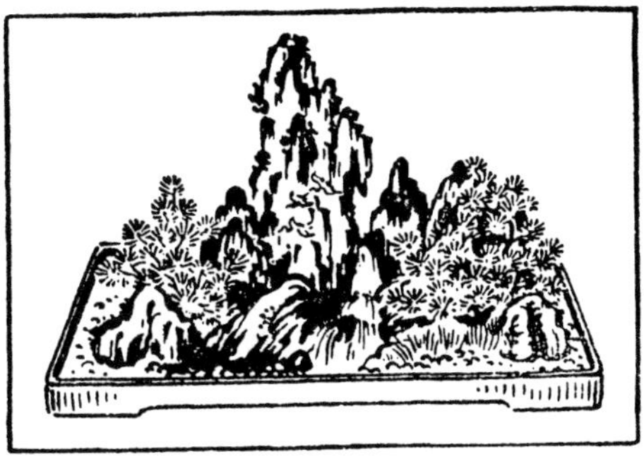

Bon-kei are tray landscapes representing in miniature natural scenery by means of stones and sand placed in a shallow porcelain dish or tray. Sometimes artificial trees and flowers, as well as tiny models of men, animals, houses and other objects

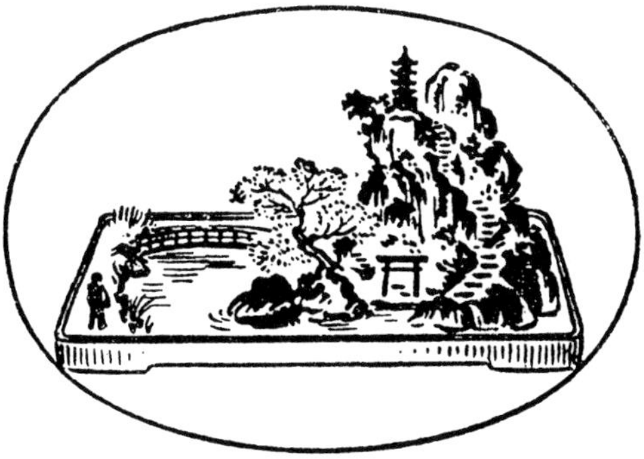

are used in the composition, which in this case is called *hako-niwa*.

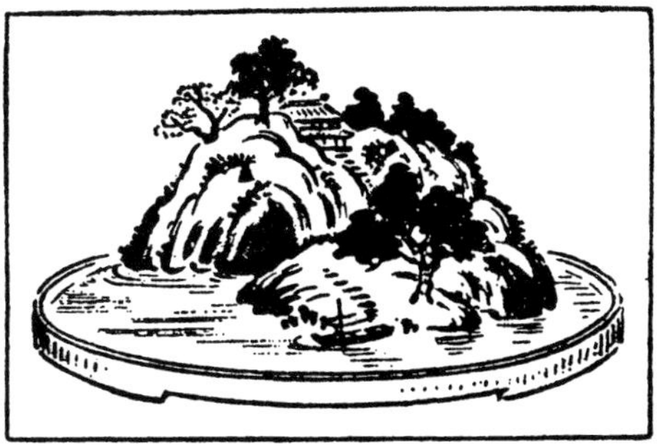

Sometimes *bon-kei* are designed to depict, in miniature, favorite mountain and seashore views.

Bon-kei are used as decorative features in many Japanese homes.

INCENSE BURNING (KŌDŌ)

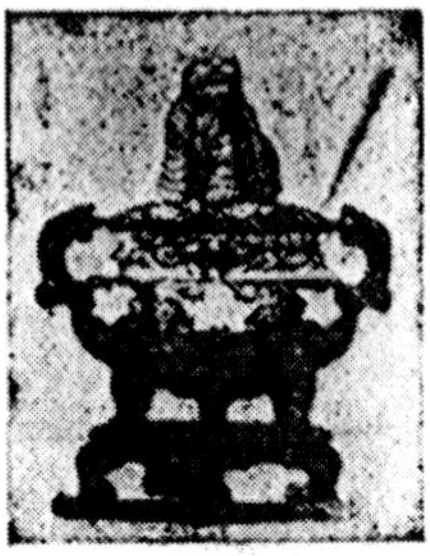

At this aesthetic pastime the guests, as rare incenses are burned, try to guess the name of the incense. Sometimes the participants form two groups, the group making the greatest number of correct guesses winning the prizes. In olden days, when nobles formed the parties, swords, armour, and many other treasures were given away as prizes.

The burning of incense has always been associated with Buddhism, but as a cult it was developed by the luxurious 8th Ashikaga *Shogun*, Yoshimasa (*shogun* from 1443–73), a patron of the fine arts, landscape gardening, tea ceremony, etc. A pastime of the aristocracy, it was later dropped to a large extent by them but it still has its votaries among the upper classes of Japan.

A description of a recent *Ko-kwai* ("Incense-party") held at the Gokokuji ("Protection-of-the-Country Temple"), Tokyo, by the Shoin-sha Society, will serve to explain the procedure at these parties. A master of ceremonies, one well versed in the incense ritual, was chosen to preside. In turn, each guest burned his favorite incense in an appropriate burner—which in itself was a work of art—and passed it around so that the other guests could enjoy the fragrance of the burning incense. After all had become acquainted with the various fragrances offered, the master of ceremonies chose one other incense from the many sampies brought to the party, and burned. This was passed around and each guest in turn tried to name the incense, and the effect it created on his senses, its "character," its "color," and its "taste"—for, according to the devotees, incense possesses these qualities. Twelve different kinds of incense were burned.

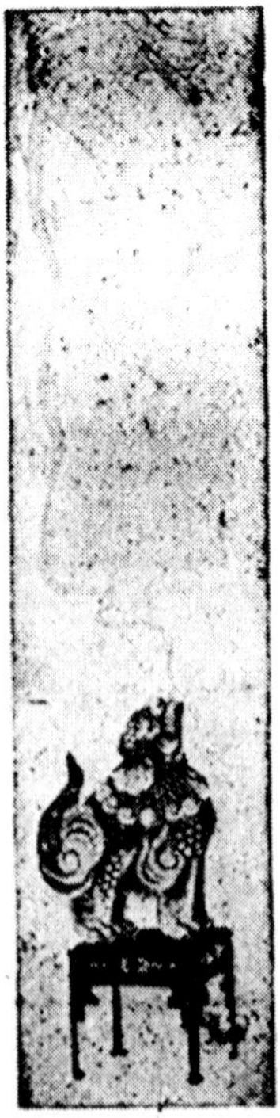

The refined sense of smell developed by incense burning is believed to cultivate mental composure in the same way that the tea-ceremony (*cha-no-yu*) and flower arrangement (*ike-bana*) cultivate mental and physical poise.

The basis of the incense of the present day is *awase-ko* ("combined incense"), introduced from China in the 10th century.

In the 15th century, as previously noted, besides the cult of burning incense practised by Japanese dilettanti, the use of incense was started for secular and recreation purposes—a use which has prevailed up to the present time. In the secular sense burning incense serves to scent the air of a room, and it is used as well to impart an agreeable perfume to clothing, toilet accessories, etc. In its recreation aspect, it tests the accuracy of the sense of smell. When the olfactory nerves become somewhat numbed by much smelling, their sensitivity is partially restored by rinsing the mouth at intervals with vinegar.

There are nearly a hundred distinct kinds of incense that are recognized and distinguished by names derived from literary allusions.

JAPANESE POETRY

Japanese poetry is almost entirely an impressionist rendering of nature. The poems suggest but do not elucidate. In outline they are intended to appeal to the reader, the details of which his own nature-love will enable him to fill in for completion. The most popular subjects are flowers, or birds, cherry and plum blossoms, the moon and the falling leaves of autumn; the winter snow and the mist upon the mountains; a pine tree on the sea-shore or the sun rising above the waves; nature in all her forms and under every aspect.

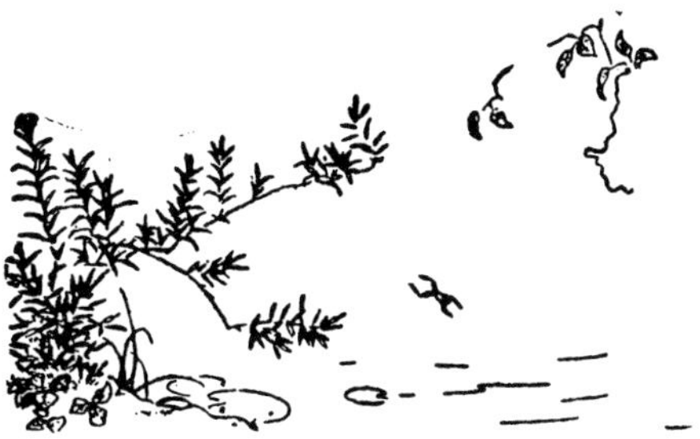

Yearly the whole nation is invited to compete in writing odes on a subject selected by Imperial direction, and in this competition the Emperor and Empress, and today the Dowager Empress, and Princes and Princesses of the Blood, all submit poems. The subjects are chosen and announced usually in November. The selected poems are read in January in the Phoenix Hall of the Imperial Palace. The 1929-30 subject was "Farm House at Dawn," that of 1930-31 was "Cock-crow at Dawn." The 1932-3 subject was "Morning Sea"

About 35,000 poems are received annually in this competition; the best five, after those of the Imperial Family, are selected by the Poetry Bureau as poems worthy to be read before the Emperor and Empress. The poems are written in the *tan-ka* style—a 31 syllable composition in which the idea is couched in choice language. The poem is divided into five sections of 5-7-5-7-7 syllables. Each contestant is allowed to submit one poem, which must be written on a specified piece of paper. There is no substantial reward for the fortunate composers, but they deem it the highest honor to have their poems read before Their Majesties. As soon as the contest is over every important newspaper in the land publishes the poems of the Imperial Family, together with the poems selected. Ancient records show that this contest was inaugurated in the 14th century.

The following, liberally translated, are poems of Basho, the famous 17th century pilgrim poet. Basho was a *samurai*, who, in his youth, renounced the life of nobleman and courtier to become a pilgrim priest, a poet and teacher of poetry. He lived from 1644 to 1694, blameless and almost saintly, yet a lover of life and adventure, a wanderer, a devotee of Nature in all her aspects.

Starting on a Summer outing he wrote:

"Butterfly, awake, awake
Come let us take
Our comrade way together!"

Of a Winter jaunt:

"Now off we go
Acrcss the snow
Until we tumble in it!"

One of the most famous of Basho's apparently simple nature poems is this:—

"A lonely pond in age-old stillness sleeps.
Apart, unstirred by sound or motion till
Suddenly into it a little frog leaps . . . !"

For an intelligent exposition of the Japanese poem the reader is referred to *Japanese Poetry*, by Dr. Curtis Hidden Page (Houghton Mifflin Co., Boston), from which the above translations are taken.

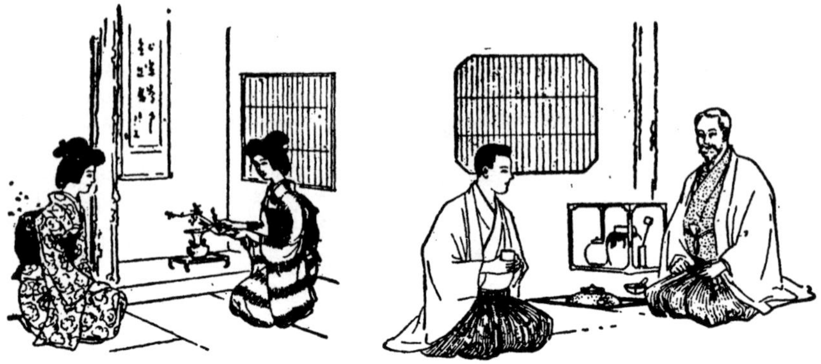

JAPANESE EMOTION—AND ITS SUPPRESSION

The Japanese are highly emotional but early acquire the habit of suppressing evidences of their deep-seated emotion, and encase themselves in an armor of inscrutability impossible of penetration by the Westerner. But occassionally emotion cannot be suppressed and it breaks out violently even in high places, as revealed in the scenes which sometimes occur during the sittings of the Diet. Only a few years ago at some of the great baseball games even the most exciting plays did not move the huge crowds to shout or yell in the approved manner; they sat, thousands of men and boys absolutely silent as if at a funeral. However, today a Japanese baseball crowd is not much different from the ardent American fans of the game. There is one place, however, where emotion cannot be wholly suppressed, and that is at a theater where, during pathetic scenes, men and women weep with little restraint but this does not alter the fact that suppression and not expression is a characteristic of the Japanese.

When telling about some misfortune or about the death of a parent, wife, child or near relative, a Japanese will smile in a way which a Westerner considers heartless, although the teller, because of grief, may be near the breaking-down point. One reason for this attitude is the characteristic consideration for the feelings of others in that one's personal grief should not be inflicted upon others. However, though a rigid repression of emotions is exercised, the emotion of grief is sometimes so strong that in spite of self-control tears will glisten in the eyes. The English language has many expletives—and they fill a useful function, but in Japanese swear words are practically non-existent, which would indicate that in that language no provision is made for the expression of emotions of anger.

This suppression leads to a poise seldom found among the people of other countries; and even the children have this poise. Tranquility and absence of haste are the outward manifestations of Japanese life except, of course, in the major activities in the great cities.

Japanese regard self-control as the highest of the virtues, and from time immemorial self-control has emanated from the Zen Sect of Buddhism down through the masses. Their ascetic practice of the tea ceremony, and of flower arrangement, are methods of training Japanese in self-control and poise which long have been practised.

THE JAPANESE PHYSIQUE

Stature. Recent observers have noted that Japanese boys and girls are stronger, better developed, and taller than their parents. A decade ago a person 5 ft. 6 in. tall, when in a crowd, could look over the heads of most of the people. This is not the case today. This increase of height is due to the use of benches and chairs in the schools and elsewhere taking the young folk off their knees on the matted floors, and to the practice of outdoor and indoor sports of every kind—which has developed them in many ways.

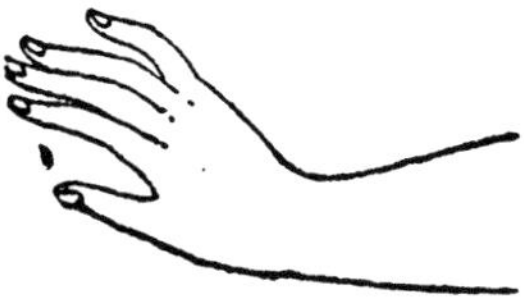

Hands. Quoting Hamilton Wright Mabie in *Japan To-day and To-morrow*, the author writes: "The Japanese hand is one of the most significant facts in Japan. Like the dyer's hand, which Shakespeare found significant, it shows what the Japanese have been doing for many centuries. It is as unlike the big, potential, unlined hand of the untrained races as the faces of rudimentary peoples are unlike the faces of highly cultivated peoples. The Japanese hand is sinewy, flexible, sensitive. It has been shaped by ancient industry, by the use of weapons, by the discipline of art, and by the use of the *fude* (brush) in the development of the art of calligraphy, which is more than a medium of communication, and examples of it are shown side by side with beautiful pictures." Foreign visitors frequently remark upon the beauty and neatness of the Japanese hand—the artistic hand, narrow, with long fingers, tapering symmetrically—the hand which enables a Japanese to fabricate the tiniest objects, as well as to demonstrate the dexterity of Japanese surgeons in their operations.

Feet. While the Japanese foot, generally, is shorter and more stocky than that of Westerners, it is more perfect in shape, for the reason that it has not been cramped by tight-fitting shoes. The *tabi* (ankle sock) and Japanese footgear have permitted freedom of foot movement, but the increasing use of shoes, especially among males, is bound, eventually, to have its effect, and in time the feet of Japanese shoe-wearers will be as unlovely to look at as those of the majority of Westerners. See "Footgear" description.

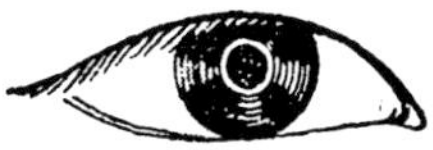

Eyes. In caricature, so long has the Oriental eye been drawn on a slant that many Occidentals believe that Orientals have slant-eyes. The principal difference between Occidental and the great majority of Oriental eyes is that the thick upper lid of the latter on its inner side, toward the nose, has a sharp curve somewhat like the end of a bow that has been drawn taut by its string in order to propel the arrow. In color, the Oriental eye is seal-brown with shades to darker coloring.

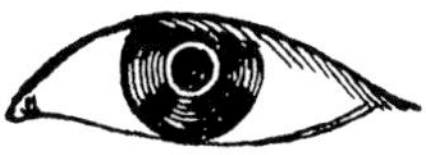

In quickness of movement there is no race on earth quicker than the Japanese. In any work in which the hands are employed such work is done with great speed, and this is equally true of work requiring movement of the feet, or in walking, with some specific object in view. In quick movements of the body when startled, or when danger is imminent, the quickness of movement of the Japanese has been likened to that of a cat under similar circumstances.

The people of every country in the world have their special hoodoos and superstitions, also their lucky charms and omens. What are yours?

Here are some of the outstanding Japanese superstitions, as recorded by *Amanojaku*, of the *Osaka Mainichi* and *Tokyo Nichi-Nichi* staff.

JAPANESE SUPERSTITIONS

There is a countless number of superstitions in Japan—those peculiar to certain localities, to certain professional groups, and those common to all classes throughout the country.

* * *

There are superstitions concerning direction (*Hogaku*), Physiognomy (*Ninso*), House Structure (*Kaso*), Omens (*Engi*), Dates (*Higara*), Fortune Telling (*Bokuzei*), Exorcism (*Majinai*), etc.

* * *

Let Amanojaku give an example or two of superstitions falling under each of these general divisions.

* * *

The Japanese divide the horizontal space into 12 directions, each bearing the name of an animal such as monkey, horse, rabbit, etc., and each day has its lucky and unlucky directions. See diagram, *Wood Carvings, Fujiya Hotel* description.

* * *

On the day when the Dragon-snake direction is declared unlucky, people postpone till another day their trips in that direction, or they go by a round about way, avoiding that particular course.

* * *

Just as each day has its own lucky and unlucky directions, so each person has his own good and bad *Hogaku*, which vary each day.

* * *

If, accordingly, any person meets, say, a railway accident while travelling, the mishap is explained by the evil *Hogaku* he was following rather than by the attendant physical conditions.

* * *

One direction which is always dreaded as unlucky is Northeast, which the Japanese call *Kimon* or the Devils' Gate.

The Japanese also believe their physiognomy has a great deal to do with determining their career. Many go to physiognomists with the pictures of the girls proposed for their brides and ask for their decision.

* * *

In choosing a career for their children, many parents attribute greater importance to the advice of the physiognomist than to the native aptitude of the children.

* * *

Some parents even take their babies to fortune tellers and have them fix their names.

* * *

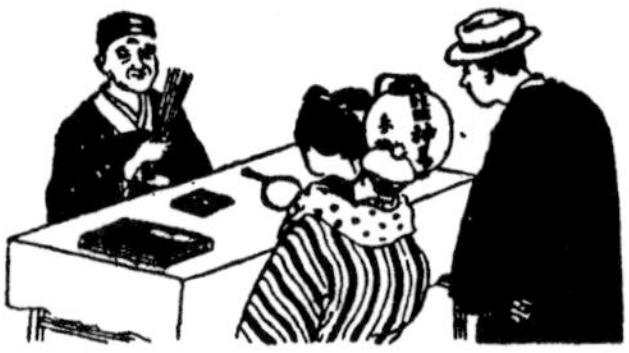

If each person has his physiognomy (*Ninso*), each house has its house fortune (*Kaso*). Some houses have good "Kaso" while others have bad "Kaso."

* * *

When the owner of a newly built house dies from accident or illness, people attribute the cause of his death to certain defects in the *Kaso*.

* * *

Many a house cannot be sold or rented because it is built in an unlucky *Hogaku* or has a protruding part in the direction of *Kimon*.

* * *

When a house is burnt, or burglars break into it, or the family living in it decline in fortune, the house is more often blamed than the carelessness or indolence of its occupants.

(*Continued*)

JAPANESE SUPERSTITIONS

Engi, which, broadly translated, means the ascribing of lucky or unlucky omens to things or happenings, includes perhaps the greatest number of popular superstitions in Japan.

* * *

For instance, Japanese believe the ages of 19, 33, 42, and 47 to be unlucky years (*yakudoshi*) when persons should expect some serious misfortunes to happen to them.

* * *

Some Westerners also believe in climacterical years, but they base their belief upon general experiences, such as the change in the life of a woman, etc.

* * *

The Japanese)*yakudoshi*, on the contrary, are based upon a childish play of words: 19 is a bad year because its Japanese pronunciation, *juku*, can be taken for "repeated sorrows."

* * *

Similarly, .33 is a bad year because its sound, *san-zan*, also means "hopeless miseries"; 42 is unlucky because its pronunciation, *shini*, signifies death.

* * *

Japanese always use specific objects for each ceremony, fixed by tradition, such as eating beaten rice-cake (*mochi*), dried eggs of herring (*kazunoko*), beans (*mame*), etc., and decorating their house with sprays of pine, bomboo, etc., for New Year's Day.

* * *

These objects are used either because their names can be twisted to mean some other object thought to be happy, or because they have qualities which people wish to have themselves.

The *mochi* also means, in Japanese, "to have"—to have wealth—*kazunoko* means "many children"—*mame* means "good health."

Pine is used because its other name is *chitose*, which means "a thousand years"; bamboo is employed because it is a symbol in Japan for 10,000 years (*yorozuyo*).

* * *

Japanese are particularly sensitive about *engi* in a wedding ceremony. In sending engagement presents to the girl's family the young man must not forget to include a handsome piece of sea-weed (*kobu*).

* * *

This is regarded as a lucky object because *kobu* is the suffix of *yorokobu*, which means "to be happy," or "to be glad."

* * *

But in making a list of the sundry objects included among the presents the would-be-bridegroom must spell the *kobu*, *kombu*, which means a woman who bears many children.

* * *

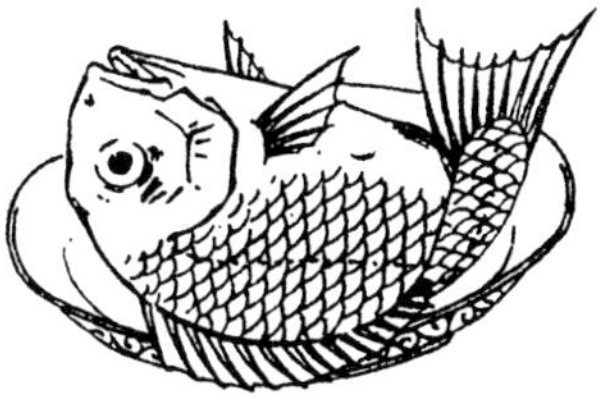

At the wedding dinner the red fish, *medetai* (sea-bream), called *tai*, must be served whole to each person because *medetai* means "happy"—to cut it is ominous of separation, incompleteness, etc.

* * *

The dinner must also include a soup of clams in the shells because these have two shells which when closed make a complete whole. The sea-ear is never used because it has only one shell.

(*Continued*)

JAPANESE SUPERSTITIONS

Another food indispensable not only at wedding and birthday dinners, but on all other happy occasions is lobster. The crustacean is served because its body is bent, which to Japanese means old age.

* * *

When invited to a dinner Japanese never eat one bowl of rice only; they eat at least two because one bowl of rice means an offering to the spirit of a dead person (*hotoke*).

* * *

Superstitions about dates (*Higara*), like those concerning directions, (*Hogaku*), exercise a vast influence upon the Japanese people.

* * *

Thus in fixing the date on which to start an enterprise, like opening a store, building a home, or departing on a long journey, Japanese choose one which they believe to be lucky (*kichinichi*).

* * *

They are specially particular in holding happy occasions like engagement dinners or wedding ceremonies only on a day which an expert chirosophist pronounces to be fitting for the event.

* * *

There is a day named *Tomobiki* which comes once in every six days and on which Japanese never hold a funeral.

* * *

It is believed that if on that particular day any family holds a funeral ceremony, six other members of it will subsequently pass away. The reason is that *Tomobiki* means "to pull friends."

* * *

If, therefore, for any reason a funeral is unavoidable on that day, Japanese put six earthen dolls in the coffin so that the God of Death will be satisfied by proxies.

The daily variation of personal fortune is largely fixed by the day, month, and year in which a person is born.

* * *

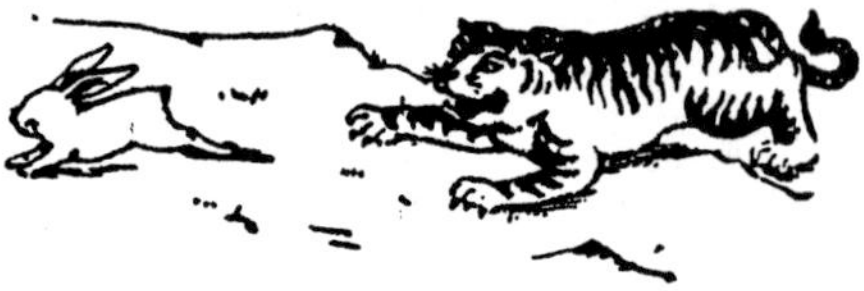

One born in the Rabbit year cannot expect good luck on a Tiger day, similarly one born in the Second Star (*Jikoku*) day because the two stars do not agree.

* * *

Persons born in a certain year, such as girls born in the year of Firehorse (*Hinoe-uma*) have little chance of marriage because they are believed to burn their husbands, that is, cause their death.

* * *

Bokuzei or fortune-telling by means of Chinese *Eki* is an expert practice widely sought by the Japanese in order to find out everything they wish to know, but have no means of learning.

* * *

In case a husband or wife disappears, by accident, by eloping, or due to other causes, Japanese go to the *Eki-sha* and ask him to tell where the missing person may be, whether that person will return or not, etc.

* * *

Many Japanese go to the *Eki-sha* to know when they will fall ill, when death will occur, what profession they should choose in order to succeed, whether they will have children or not, and the like.

(*Continued*)

JAPANESE SUPERSTITIONS

The classes of people who are most superstitious are those who are engaged in professions which involve a large element of chance, such as geisha, wrestlers, gamblers, variety show actors, etc.

* * *

These people, therefore, are exceedingly sensitive to uncleanliness or impurity which they believe will cause the wrath of the gods and bring about bad luck.

* * *

They accordingly "purify" themselves after having been in a filthy place, having met a person whom they hate, or, having met with an accident, by means of sprinkling a generous quantity of salt around them, or by producing sparks by striking flint with steel.

* * *

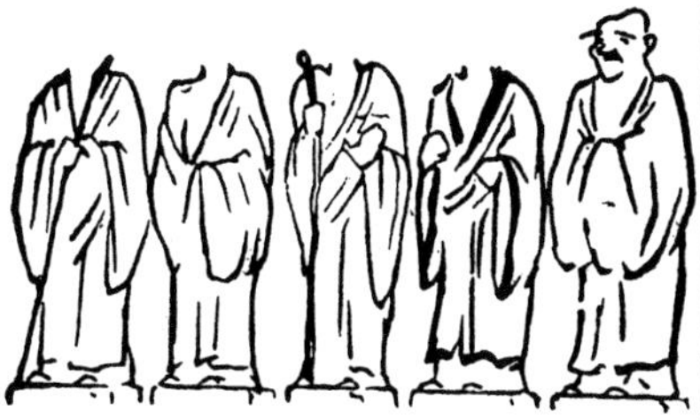

Wherever the idols of *Rakan* (Buddha's disciples) are found they are seen mostly with their heads missing. The reason is that among Japanese speculators the heads serve as talismans of good fortune and hence they are stolen.

* * *

There are many kinds of "holy" amulets in Japan; Shintō, Buddhistic, or zoolatrous in character, used as safeguards against all kinds of natural calamities, diseases, etc.

Some of them consist of a sheet of paper upon which the seal of a shrine or temple is affixed; others are made up of fragments of wood or metal that have been ' consecrated."

* * *

These objects are put up in such places in the house where their influence is desired—those against pestilence at the entrance, those against fire at the fireplace, those against thunder on the ceiling, and so forth.

* * *

Exorcism, or belief in the mystical power of certain things or practices to produce the desired effect, which Japanese call *Majinai*, is a form of superstition which very extensively prevails in Japan.

* * *

The sign "House to let" is never posted straight; it is always put up slantwise. Japanese believe that this is the *majinai* to rent the house promptly.

* * *

The practice is the remnant of the early custom when two signs were put on to form the shape of the character (入) which means "to enter."

* * *

Inside the buses running on the streets in a great metropolis like Osaka, people see a talisman placed above the driver's seat. This is the *majinai* against accident.

* * *

Likewise, when people encounter a snake, venomous or otherwise, they quickly pronounce *aburaunkensowaka.* The incantation will cause the reptile to recoil and disapper. No one knows what the charm means.

(Continued)

JAPANESE SUPERSTITIONS

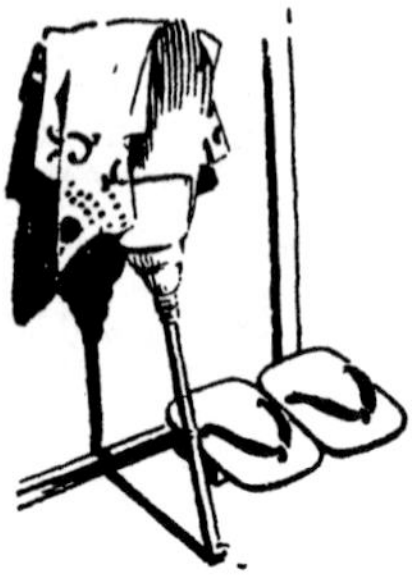

When Japanese are annoyed by visitors who outstay their welcome and wish to get rid of them, they usually set a broom upside down and tie around it a towel (*tenugui*) in the same way that a scarf or other wrap is sometimes tied around the face, and the caller's footgear or geta are warmed up and placed next the handle in order to speed the visitor's departure.

* * *

In case this charm fails to produce results, they cauterize the footgear of the visitors with the moxa, believing that the burning treatment will set the objects into action.

* * *

This practice is said to have originated through the idiosyncrasies of an old man who had a great aversion to dust. Upon the departure of a caller his invariable habit was to have the house thoroughly dusted. If the call ran into a late hour, as his maid servants had to stay awake to do their master's bidding, they devised this schem to speed the caller's departure.

* * *

When people suffer from *okori*, a kind of fever similar to malaria and very prevalent in Japan, they make effigies of themselves out of straw, rub their bodies with these, and after due ceremony throw them into a river.

* * *

When people suffer from some kind of a disease the effects of which appear on the skin, such as smallpox, the itch, etc., they wear large hats and dip themselves in water in a lake or the sea until the hat floats on the surface. The disease is left with the hat.

There are many interesting kinds of charms that are used in healing various illnesses, particularly epidemics, but here only one or two can be presented.

* * *

One of the best known charms extensively employed even today among lovers is secretly to cause the person whom one loves to eat the ashes of a burnt newt, a species of little salamander which Japanese call *imori*.

* * *

In some country districts, when children get some kind of a growth on their heads, their parents write upon it the Chinese character (馬)—horse. The growth is called, in Japanese, *kusa*, which also means "hay." The idea is that the horse will eat up "hay"—or the growth.

* * *

When any person dies the body is always laid with the head toward the north; hence people avoid sleeping in that position presumably for fear that they may pass away while asleep.

* * *

Whenever Japanese set out on a long journey, or leave for a battle ground, or attempt a dangerous undertaking like a flight in an airplane, they generally go armed with at least a dozen different talismans, or *ofuda*.

* * *

True to the Japanese saying, *Heta no naga dangi*, Amanojaku's description of Japanese superstitions has dragged on much too long without recounting anything of real interest. It is time he stopped it.

(Concluded)

JAPANESE CUSTOMS

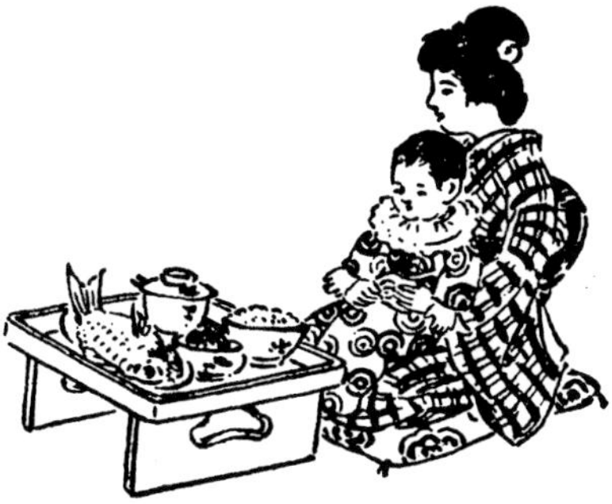

Birth: Seven days after the birth of a child it is named during a celebration at the home, attended by relatives, friends, and neighbors, and at that time the infant's head is shaved. If the child is a boy, his grandmother or nurse, on the thirty-second day, takes him, beautifully attired, to a shrine by way of thanksgiving, and to pray for his welfare—that he may grow up strong and healthy. If a girl, this ceremony is held on the thirty-third day. (See "Miyamairi" description.)

After 120 days, when one or two teeth have appeared, the ceremony of *Okui-zome*, or the "First Eating," takes place. On a tiny table are placed a rice-bowl, a tea-cup, chopsticks, etc., and the mother, holding the infant, sits down at the table and makes the baby go through the form of eating from the rice-bowl. The first anniversary of a child's birth is celebrated by a banquet. In the case of the eldest son and heir of the family, when he reaches the age of 17 years a ceremony called the *Gempuku* takes place. This indicates that the boy, now grown to man's estate, is proclaimed the heir. Ordinary birthdays are not celebrated like those abroad, except that a special rice with red beans is served for the occasion.

Ages: Should a child be born on December 31st, or on any day of the year prior to that date, the infant on January 1st of the year following is regarded as being two years old. Therefore, when a Japanese states his age it is always one year less reckoned in the Occidental way.

Auspicious and Calamitous Years: In the life of a man, the 25th and 42nd years are considered calamitous years; with women, the 19th and 33rd years. In these years, festivities are held to ward off misfortune. The 61st year (*Kanreki*) is regarded as an auspicious year inasmuch as one cycle of the Ten Calendar Signs and of the Twelve Zodiacal Signs is completed, and both men and women enter on a new lease of life—a second childhood, as it were—and, to celebrate the event, a man at that time dons a red cap. He visits a shrine to express his thanksgiving at attaining his age, and invites his relatives and friends to his home to help him celebrate. The 70th year is celebrated as *Koki*, the "rarely reached age." The 77th (*Ki-no-ji*), or year of "gladness," and the 88th (*Bei-ju*), or "rice" year, are also celebrated, the former by wearing a red *chanchan-ko* (a loose coat-like garment worn over the *kimono*), the latter by wearing red apparel throughout. Silver and golden weddings are often celebrated, similar to the Western customs.

CUSTOMS—VARIOUS

Adoption: The custom of adopting boys and girls, and even adults, into Japanese families is widespread, and has been practised for centuries, as the discontinuance of a family is regarded as a great disgrace.

A man without an heir to perpetuate the family name usually adopts a boy (a relative, if possible), who becomes a member of the family. Should there be a daughter in the family the boy will marry her, or, in case there is no daughter, the man may adopt a girl and a boy, who will marry, or he may even adopt a married couple, all these taking the family name. Also, like the Occidental custom, young children are adopted into a Japanese family.

This may seem a sad breaking of home ties, but as the custom is deeply rooted in Japanese family life it is generally accepted without question—and those adopted still remain loyal to their own families.

Mogusa (*Artemisia absinthium*—wormwood—*moxa*): A cotton-like fibre obtained from the small, dried leaves of this plant, common in Japan. It is a custom to burn *mogusa* on the human body in order to increase the circulation of the blood. It is used to reduce boils and skin eruptions, swellings, and to relieve pains, and is also used for kidney and stomach disorders, for rheumatism, swollen legs, etc. At many large temples there is a special building where *mogusa* treatments are given, but it is in common use in homes. The burning always leaves a white scar. Also, a parent sometimes burns *mogusa* on the clenched hand, or on the top junction of the little and its next toe, of a misbehaving boy as a reminder to behave.

Gifts of Soba (Buckwheat Macaroni): It is the Japanese custom that when a house is first occupied a gift of *soba* shall be presented to the new neighbors of the occupant, one on each side of the house, and to the three opposite, making five (a lucky number). *Soba* homonymously means "close-by," so friendly intercourse is sought with near neighbors by this gift of *soba* ("friendship"). Japanese families eat *soba* on New Year's Eve. It then is called *Toshikoshi Soba*, or "Year-going-over-soba," so that they may have long life. *Toshi*—year, *koshi*—going over.

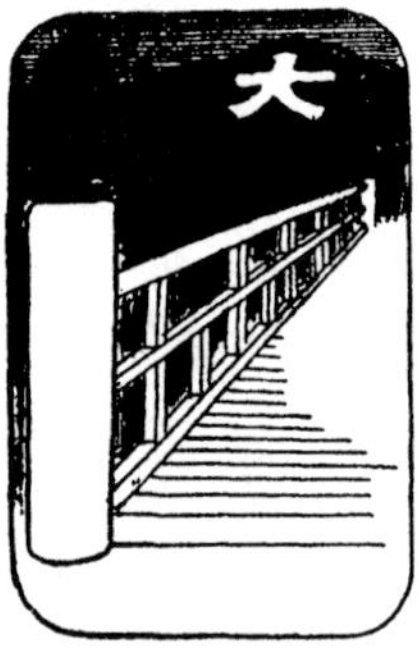

Daimonji (*Dai*—"Great," or "Big," *Monji*—"Character," or "Letter"): Spectacular bonfires in the shape of the character *Dai*, of large propotions, are burned on many mountain- and hill-sides in Japan on the last day of the *O-Bon* Festival (which see) by way of bidding farewell to the spirits of the dead who, on that day, are supposed to return to their respective homes. The *Daimonji* of Kyoto are especially noted—the picture showing one of the largest as seen from the Sanjo bridge. The horizontal stroke of this character is 228 ft. long, the left vertical one is 510 ft. long, and the right vertical stroke is 408 ft. long. Legend relates that when the Jodoji temple burned, the Buddha upon the altar fled to the mountain and emitted a great light there. In memory of this, the people make a fire every year at this place.

On the same night, on other hills around Kyoto, there are bonfires, some with different characters, some with figures. The best place to view all these illuminations at a glance is on Yoshidayama Hill, Kyoto.

CUSTOMS—VARIOUS

Citron Baths: On the day of *Toji* (winter solstice—December 21 or 22), when winter officially begins, according to the lunar calendar (which see), the fragrant odor of sliced citron rises from public bath-houses throughout Japan, and from the private baths of many citizens—slices of citron having been placed in the hot baths.

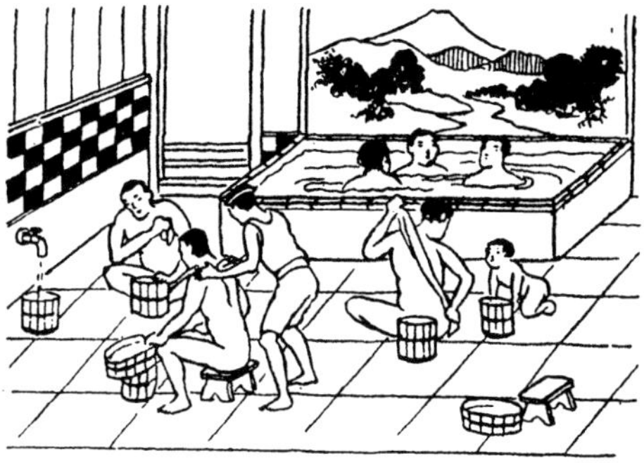

This custom, which has been observed from time immemorial, came from China and is yet widely celebrated in that country, and on *Toji* day many Chinese residents in Japan make it a holiday.

In former days, poets and artists held special meetings on "toji" spending the day in composing poems, writing ideographs, or practising such arts as flower arrangement ("Ike-bana") and the tea ceremony ("Cha-no-yu").

There are many interesting beliefs in connection with "toji." It is a superstition among farmers that their winter wheat crops will be bumper ones if fair weather prevails on the advent of winter. In the event of thunder being heard on that day, they believe that the ensuing year will have an abundance of rain. A southerly wind at *toji* is said to insure, generally, fine weather during the coming year.

Blacking the Teeth is a custom which, it is said, began in 920 A.D.; but the reason for it is unknown. It may be that it was to show the married state, inasmuch as every married woman in Japan blackened her teeth until the late Empress Shoken set the example of discontinuing the practice—and as the efficacy of the preparation used for the blackening wears out after a few days, the married women of the land experienced no difficulty in ridding their teeth of their blackness. Men also followed this practice until they were finally prohibited from doing so in the year 1870. Mitford, in his *Tales of Old Japan*, gives the following recipe for tooth-blacking, as having been supplied to him by a fashionable Yedo druggist:—"Take three pints of water, and, having warmed it, add half a tea-cupful of wine (*sake*). Put into this mixture a quantity of red-hot iron; allow it to stand for five or six days, when there will be a scum on the top of the mixture, which should then be poured into a small teacup and placed near a fire. When it is warm, powdered gall-nuts and iron-filings should be added to it, and the whole should be warmed again. The liquid is then painted on to the teeth by means of a soft feather brush, with more powdered gall-nuts and iron, and, after several applications, the desired color will be obtained." Today one must go to remote country districts to see women with blackened teeth.

Widows: Many women upon becoming widows have their hair cut short and eyebrows shaved as an indication that they have renounced the world. It is a custom to place the hair in their husband's coffin. Thus it appears that the fashion of hair bobbing originated in Japan.

CUSTOMS—VARIOUS

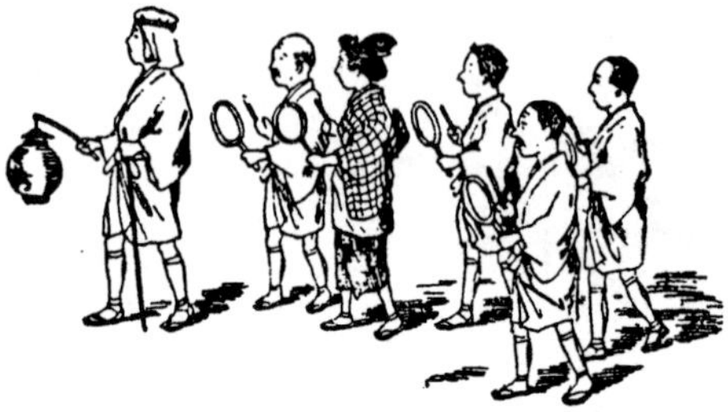
Nichiren-sect pilgrims.

Kan-Mairi or *Kan*-Worship. During the *Kan*, or Coldest Season, which generally lasts for 30 days —from early January to early February—many devout Buddhists make pilgrimages on each night to various temples. In former days, these devotees were naked, save for a loin cloth, and were barefoot, and at each temple visited they would often pour cold water over their naked bodies.

Similar ablutions are sometimes observed today, with the idea that their prayers will be accepted because of this devotion. Special prayers are offered during these pilgrimages: for more skill in their calling, for the cure of a sick relative, etc. Nowadays, as they are not permitted to go naked, they wear a thin, white outer garment, also a white cloth or a band around the head—white signifying purification. It is an arresting sight at night to see the various groups on their way to and from the temples, especially those of the Nichiren Sect with their flat fan-drums (*Uchiwa-Daiko*), which are beaten while they chant the solemn, mystic formula of the sect: *Namu-myoho-renge-kyo* ("Glory to the Sutra of the Lotus of Truth"), as they walk. Many of the groups carry lighted paper lanterns, which add much to the picturesque sight. Buddhists of other sects chant the formula: *Namu-Amida-Butsu*, which, popularly interpreted, is "Save me, Amida-Buddha," and often they carry bells.

CUSTOMS—VARIOUS

Relative to Gifts: When a neighbor makes a gift of fruit, mushrooms, or similar things, a maid servant usually brings it on a lacquered tray, covered with a *fukusa*, a silken cloth. Custom and courtesy stipulate that when the tray is handed back, a sheet of special writing paper, *hanshi*, or a box of matches, must be placed on the tray. If this were not done, its omission would indicate that the recipient did not care to receive further gifts from that particular giver. The Japanese say that only a beggar returns an empty tray. The box of matches is a survival of the custom of placing on the tray the old-time flat, broad carton of matches then in use—a gift of some value in the days when matches were not so cheap as they are today.

Taking off Overcoats: The Japanese overcoat is a cloak-like garment with long wing-sleeves, cape-like in effect, so made to allow the sleeves of the *kimono* and *haori* to be placed in them. It is regarded as an extra to ordinary garments, much as a raincoat is regarded—and so Japanese keeps his overcoat on, even when making a business call. It would not show respect were he to do so. Before entering temples, shrines, or homes, overcoats, hats, and in the majority of cases, shoes, are left on the outside porch or steps, and in the *genkan* (entrance way) of private houses.

Railway Tickets: In Japan, railway tickets are not taken up on trains. After the ticket is purchased, it is punched by an employee as the passenger steps through the wicket at his boarding station. Upon reaching his destination the ticket is handed to an employee at the "out" wicket of the station. Occasionally the train guards examine tickets en route to see that the passenger is not travelling in a class higher than his ticket allows, and to ascertain whether or not he is on the right train, many country folk unaccustomed to railway travel often being found on a wrong train.

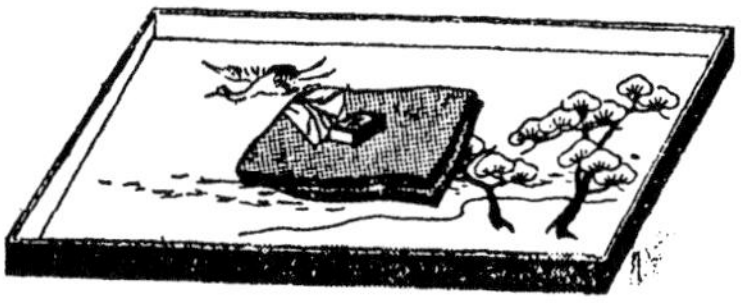

This system is in direct contrast to that of the United States, but is similar, in most respects, to the English system on short runs, though on long runs in Britain tickets are taken up on the trains.

Cartmen Lead Horses: In Japan, one seldom sees a horse being driven; horses are led by a short rope—and rarely does one see a cartman sitting on his cart, whether or not it is loaded. As it is estimated that there are 200,000 horse-drawn carts in Japan, some idea of the time wasted by these cartmen can be formed.

Extra-legal Punishment: In some old communities there is an ancient autumn festival custom which permits the villagers to punish the most hated person in the village—and sometimes this custom and privilege are observed in very strenuous ways. On October 18, 1932, in the village of Shiosaki, Wakayama Prefecture, this custom was carried out vigorously, but as the victim happened to be the lone policeman of the village, the action brought down the wrath of the authorities on the offenders.

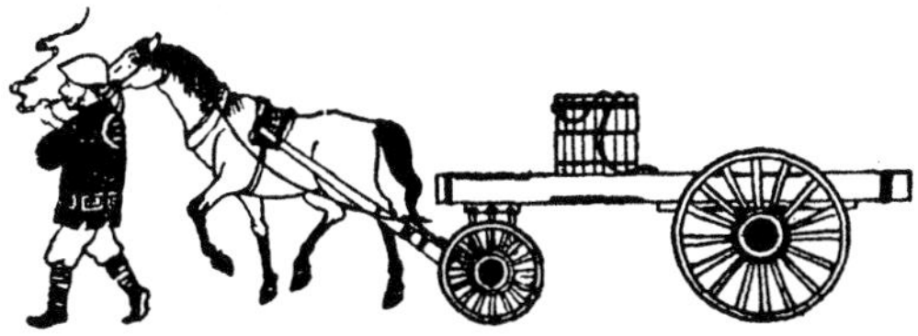

CUSTOMS—VARIOUS

One or Three Slices: No orthodox Japanese will serve one or three slices of any food, like pickled *daikon* or pineapple, because one, *hito-kire* (*hito*-one, *kire*-piece), means "kill someone," and three, called *mikire* (*mi*-three, *kire*-pieces), means homonymously, in the Japanese language, "kill me," *mi* in this case meaning "body," while *kire* is the imperative form of the verb "to kill"—"kill yourself." It is therefore considered an unlucky sign for a Japanese to be served with one or three slices of any food. Two or four slices may be served with impunity, though the number "four," homonymously suggesting death (*shi*), is generally regarded as an unlucky number and is avoided as much as possible among Japanese.

Red Rice: While plain boiled-rice is a common food in Japan, it is a general custom to serve *Sekihan* ("Red boiled-rice") on every happy occasion: a festival, wedding, child-birth, recovery from a protracted illness, graduation from school, return from a long journey, and so on. *Sekihan*, which consists of glutinous rice boiled with *azuki* ("red beans"), is generally offered to the deity of an orthodox Japanese family on the 1st and 15th of every month. On the day of *Tenchosetsu* (Emperor's birthday) the majority of Japanese families serve this rice.

Stale Tea: Japanese never drink tea which has been kept overnight. It is considered an insult if one is served with such tea. In feudal days, every criminal condemned to death was served with overnight tea before he was beheaded—which explains the Japanese aversion to stale tea.

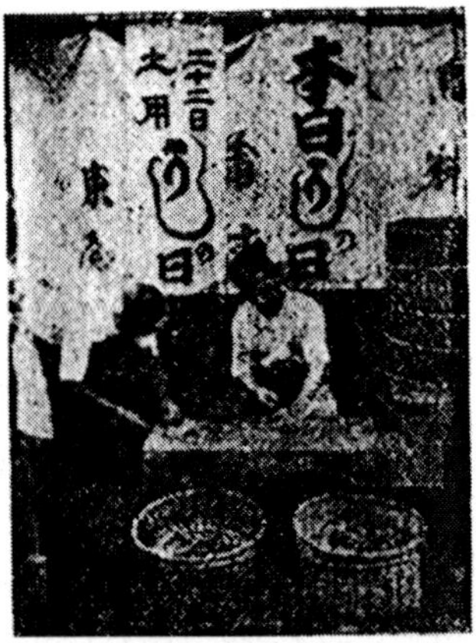

AN EEL-SHOP

Eating Eels: *Ushi-no-Hi*, or the first Day of the Ox in the *Doyo*—Dog-day (which varies yearly by the lunar calendar, but occurs in the dog-days of either late July or early August) is the particular day upon which broiled eels are eaten in Japan—a custom that has come down from olden days—in the belief that this practice will secure immunity from disease during the following 12 months and in fact, in the same belief, eels are eaten on any Day of the Ox that may occur during this *Doyo*. Medical men naturally ridicule the truth of this belief, but it is said to be a well-established fact that the eating of eels by the people of Tokyo was a factor in checking the alarming spread of the form of eye weakness known as *torime* (night blindness of nyctalopia) which developed immediately after the 1923 earthquake-fire—this alleged curative power of eels being attributed to their rich content of Vitamin A. While the present generation in Japan places little stock in this superstition, the custom persists and all eel restaurants in the cities and country are crowded on the prescribed day except the large Tokyo eel restaurants, which are closed, and which sacrifice profits in order to retain their regular customers who maintain their business the year round—the proprietors generally attending a Buddhist memorial service to console the spirits of the eels used in their business. On the Ox-days, it is estimated that the people of Tokyo alone consume 100,000 lbs. of eels, valued at about $50,000.

CHADAI ("TEA MONEY")

With few exceptions, in addition to the rates quoted at Japanese inns, the custom of giving a sum of money, known as *chadai* ("tea money"), upon the guest's departure, still prevails. It is a troublesome matter to foreigners and to many Japanese who would much prefer to pay a fixed rate as in foreign-style hotels, but coming down the ages from time immemorial the practice is well established, although associations of travelling and business men are trying to have the custom abolished, and in many cases have succeeded.

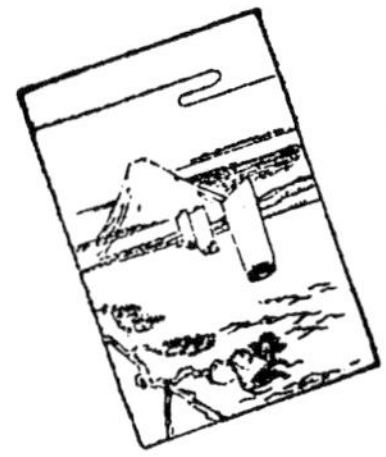

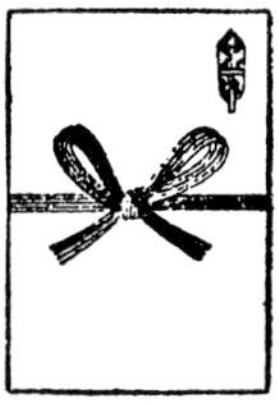

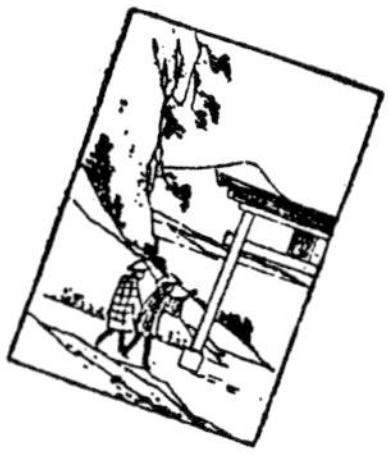

To foreign visitors tea money appears to be a gift to the innkeeper for his good will, general care of the guest, and possibly for sundry cups of tea of welcome upon arrival. In view of the fair rate made for lodging and meals, Japanese regard it as part of the regular charge, based largely upon the location, size and furnishings of the room occupied, bedding, food supplied, grade of inn, etc., but in any event it is highly speculative from the innkeeper's point of view, some guests giving nothing, others being lavish. If every one refrained from giving the custom would soon die out, but this, as with the question of tips in all countries, is a discouraging problem.

As this matter now stands, the ordinary guest commonly gives, as a minimum, from one-half up of the daily rate per person for tea money, according to service required or favors extended. But on special occasions from 100 to 1000 yen is given. No punishment, except perhaps a subtle suggestion of dissatisfaction on the part of the innkeeper, follows the omission of tea money.

This custom, it is said, originated long ago when inns were not so numerous as they are today. In those olden days, when devotees made their pilgrimages, the only accommodation available was in the temples visited—which is still the case today in many places. The temple authorities made no charge for lodging or meals, but it became the custom for guests to offer a sum of money, carefully wrapped up, a sum in accordance with the guest's circumstances, upon their departure. This custom spread to the inns.

Gifts: Upon the guest's departure it is customary for the innkeeper to present some small gift: a towel, a cup, or some article made or produced in the vicinity. The omission of a gift may sometimes be traced to the omission of "the money," or perhaps to the innkeeper's opinion that the sum given was too small.

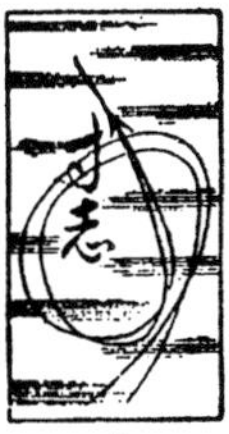

The illustrations show various styles of money envelopes in which *chadai* is placed before giving it to the innkeeper.

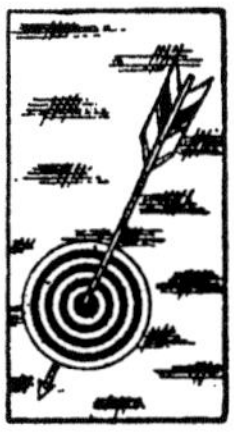

ENVELOPES FOR TIPS (“*Shugi-bukuro*”)

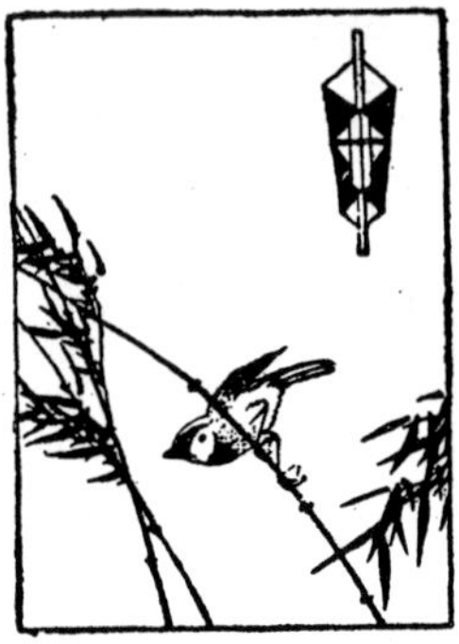

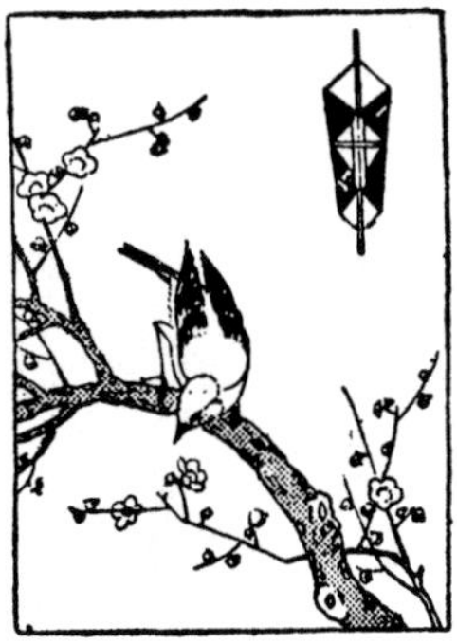

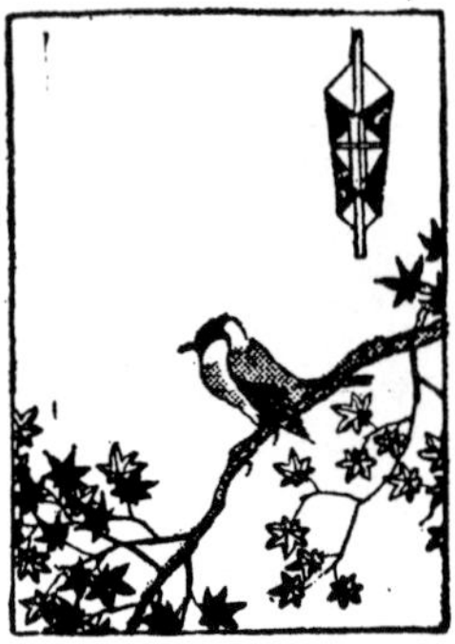

Japanese etiquette requires that in presenting a tip, the money shall be wrapped in white paper or placed in a *Shugi-bukuro,* a special envelope made for that purpose. In no case should the money be handed uncovered, although in these days modern people do not always conform to this old custom.

The practice probably originated through “Bushido,” the moving spirit of the country. In days gone by, money was rather despised, especially by the *samurai,* and its possession was looked down upon, and, consequently, the crude presentation of naked money offended the Japanese sense of politeness and consideration.

There are now hundreds of varieties of *Shugi-bukuro* on

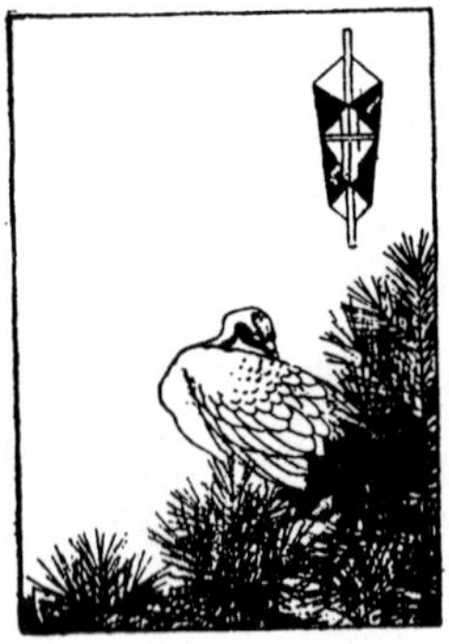

sale at stationers' shop—envelopes of all sizes and in many colors and designs.

Besides their use for tips, some folk collect them as a hobby.

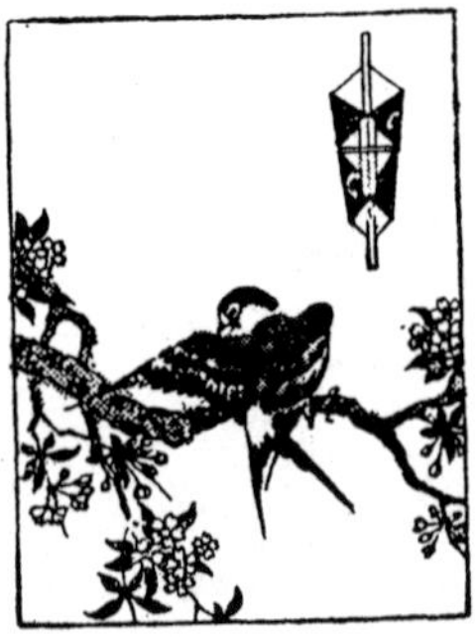

BONITO—AS A MASCOT OR A GIFT

Bonito (*Katsuo*) is a fish well-nigh indispensable in the Japanese cuisine, especialy in its dried form, called *katsuo-bushi*. Marketable *katsuo* are generally about a foot long, with fat, round bodies. The fish has small scales, back bluish-black, belly lead-white. On its sides are four to six blue lines.

The fish is cut into large pieces, from which the bones are taken out. These pieces, after being steamed, are dried in the sun until they become as hard as the hardest wood. This is called *katsuo-bushi*—and is used as a flavoring for countless Japanese dishes and soups. With a sharp knife, or a piece of broken glass, or a specially made plane, it is shaved into thin flakes—which are put into the pots where vegetables, fish, or other foods are being cooked. In shops that specialize in selling dried foodstuffs *katsuo-bushi* is displayed in quantity. The pieces look like mahogany or like the whetstones used by western farmers to sharpen scythes and sickles—and their use is always a puzzle to uninformed foreign visitors.

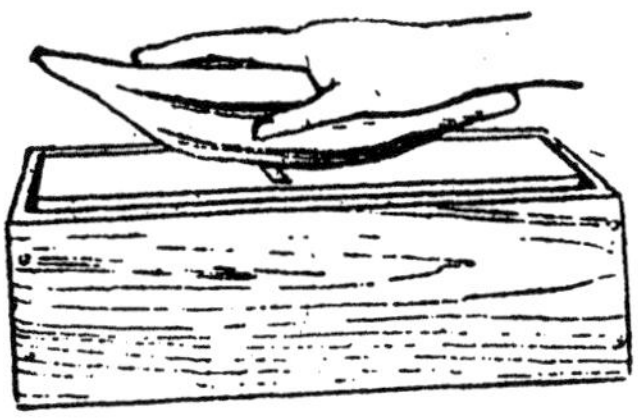

The ideographs of *katsuo-bushi* mean "Bonito-knot," which homonymously suggest a "victorious samurai" (*katsuo*-victory; *bushi*-samurai) and it is on account of this meaning, implying victory, that dried bonito is so much valued in Japan, and is the reason that it is presented as a token of congratulation, or more properly as a mascot, on every felicitous occasion, such as a birth of a child, a marriage, or success of any kind. Several *katsuo-bushi* are placed in a bamboo basket or on a laquered tray or in a large envelope especially made for that purpose, and are presented by friends on these happy occasions.

It is recorded that in 1537 Ujimasa Hojo went offshore to see bonito-fishing. While a banquet was being served him a large bonito jumped into his boat—and it was thought a "Victory-fish" must surely be a good omen. On the following day Hojo defeated his life-long enemy, Lord Uyesugi, in battle. Afterward it became an established custom of the Hojo to serve bonito every time a member of the family went to war.

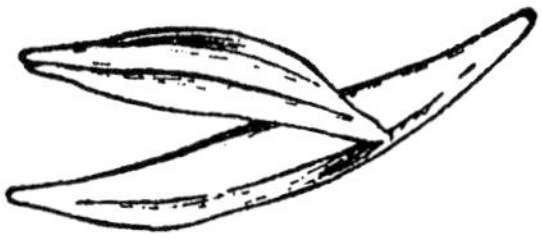

From ancient times sea products have been regarded as valuable gifts in Japan and the customs of former days still remain in the people's idea and habit of giving *katsuo-bushi*, *kombu* (a delectable seaweed), or *awabi* (see Awabi and Noshi descriptions)—which all mean joy and happiness.

AWABI AND NOSHI

Noshi, the Japanese gift emblem, is a narrow, semi-transparent strip of yellow substance, wrapped in red and white papers folded into the shape shown in the picture. This substance is the meat of Awabi (Sea-ear), dried, stretched, and sliced. In former days, a longer piece of this meat, almost two feet long, was used as the gift emblem. The modern noshi is merely an informal or abbreviated form of the old-time ***awabi-noshi.***

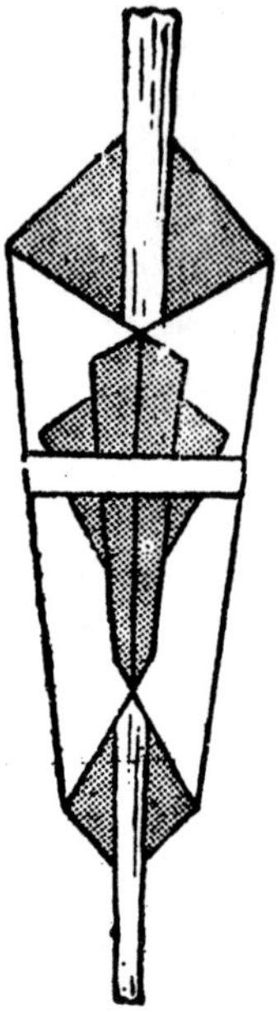

Awabi (the Western abalone): which grows on rocks under the sea, like a limpet, has only one shell, and consequently Japanese have the expression *Awabi no kata-omoi*, meaning "One-sided love."

This shell-fish is gathered mostly by women divers, and it requires skill and experience to be successful at the work as not only does one have to dive, but the shell becomes so firmly attached to the rock when the fish is disturbed that it has to be pried off.

The beautiful awabi shell is used in making various objects. Sometimes pearls are found in the shell, though of inferior quality to those found in pearl oysters.

Awabi meat is delicious and is used in many ways; in soups, and in the same way that ordinary fish is cooked. When dried it is often sliced in thin flakes and used as a substitute for *katsuobushi* (dried bonito). As its dried meat has been used from ancient times as gifts, it is probably from this custom that the idea of *noshi* originated.

Besides the *noshi* an essential part of a gift is the *mizuhiki* or red and white cords, or, sometimes gold or silver and white cords, which is tied outside the wrapping of the box or package, but red and white cord is never used with a present consisting of fish, meat, or any organic thing. In mourning gifts the *mizuhiki* is made of black and white cords, and the *noshi* is omitted.

TOPSY-TURVYDOM

It is often remarked that Japanese do things in ways directly opposite to those of "foreigner." To the Japanese, foreign ways appear equally unaccountable. They wonder why foreigners do so many things topsy-turvy instead of doing them naturally, in the Japanese way.

Here are a few instances of this contrariety:—

Japanese books begin at the back, or what foreigners call the end, the word finis being put where foreigners begin their books. Sometimes the type runs from top to bottom, in which case the page is read from right to left, as in a newspaper. Sometimes the type runs across the page and is read from right to left. The footnotes are printed at the top of the page. In newspaper paragraphs, a full stop is put at the beginning of each paragraph. A letter is written in perpendicular lines from top to bottom and is read from right to left; its salutation and complimentary phrases are written at the close of the letter. In addressing a letter the general detail is put first, the particulars afterward, thus: "Japan, Tokyo, Kojimachi (or whatever the ward may be), such-and-such street, the particular number, Smith John Mr." The writer's name and address is written or printed on the envelop back. For writing, a brush, not a pen, is used. Japanese ink is made as needed, from an inkstone rubbed on a slab. The seal is more important than the signature.

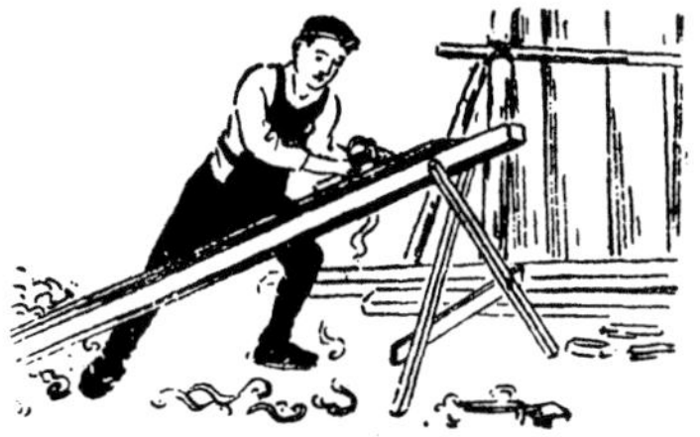

Japanese say "east-north," "west-south," not "north-east," "south-west," also "four or three" when Westerners say "three or four."

Boats are hauled up on the beach stern first. Oarsmen push, punt, or scull their oars; they do not pull them as do Westerners. Carpenters saw and plane towards, instead of away from, their bodies. The handles of saws are straight, like those of western hammers. In building a house the roof is constructed first on a nearby piece of ground, then the parts are numbered, separated, and stored away until the frame is up. The roof is then placed in position on it by firemen.

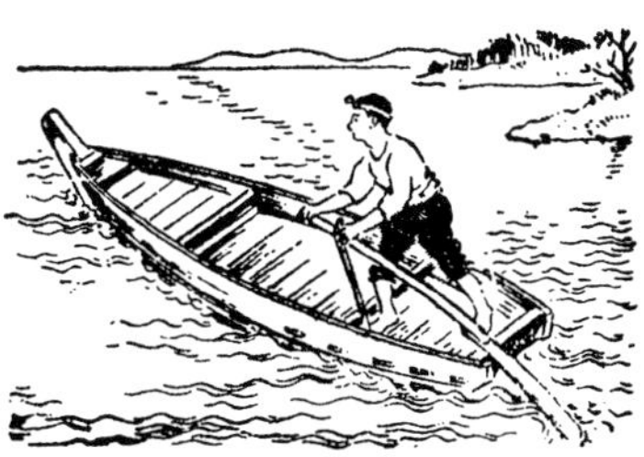

Cartmen lead their horses, whether the cart is loaded or empty.

The best rooms in a house are at the back, the garden also is at the back.

In making up accounts the figures are written first, the corresponding items next.

TOPSY-TURVYDOM

Japanese never use soap in the bath-tub. Soaping is done outside the tub and the body rinsed off before entering the bath. They dry the body with a wet towel wrung out of hot water. People indulge chiefly in hot baths (112°—120° F.) the year round. The water for Western style baths is heated before being run into the tub; Japanese bath-water is heated by means of a fire underneath or alongside the bath. Bath tubs are of wood, either oval or square, and are just large enough to accommodate a bather in a sitting position with knees drawn up close to the chin. They are so made to save the cost of the fuel needed for heating a large quantity of water.

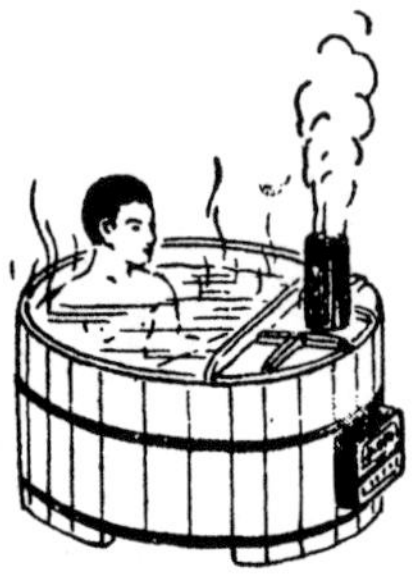

When the bath is ready the head of the house takes the first bath, then the wife, followed by the children according to age, the oldest first, and finally the servants, but there is a constant trickle of cold water into the bath to keep it clean, and because soap has not been used the water is not discolored. The fire keeps the water at an even temperature.

Men in Japan are most emphatically the superior sex. When a man and wife go off in rickshas it is my lord's ricksha that bowls off first.

Entering or leaving a room, or on the street, etc., the man precedes the woman. He is served first at meals. At movie theaters the best orchestra seats are reserved for men and boys; women and girls sit on the sides.

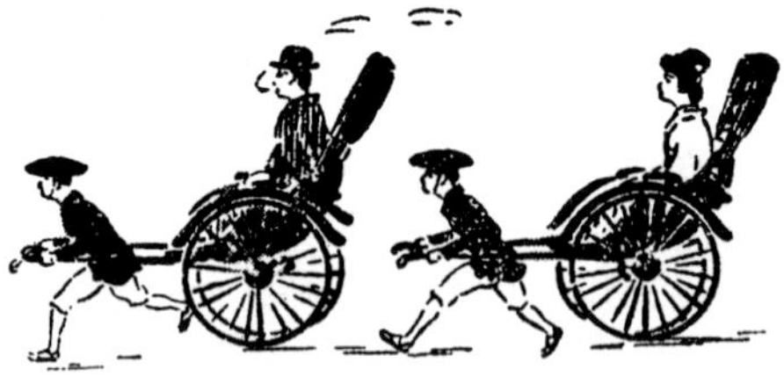

It is the lot of Japanese women to carry the baby and the bundles; the baby usually on the woman's back, the bundles on the upturned arm, not under the arm. Per contra, salesmen and other business men usually carry their brief cases under the arm, not in the hand by its strap handle.

TOPSY-TURVYDOM

The Japanese deny themselves the satisfaction of self-expression and delight in understatements: thus, when forced to speak about their possessions they always belittle them as being of no especial value. When speaking about his household, a husband refers to his wife as *kanai* or "inside the house," or as *gusai*, "my stupid wife." But when he inquires as to the health, etc., of his neighbour's wife he always designates her as *okusan* (*oku*—farthest inside, *san*—synonymous with Mr., Mrs., Master, or Miss), but never does he so designate his own wife—he would be thought mad if he did so. His son, though a bright lad, is described as "a good-for-nothing boy," or as a "sucking pig" (*tonji*).

When pedestrians, motor cars, etc., approach from opposite directions, the Rule of the Road in the United States is to pass on the right. In Japan, Great Britain, Canada, and elsewhere the rule is to pass on the left. Therefore, Japanese wonder at the contrariety of the United States.

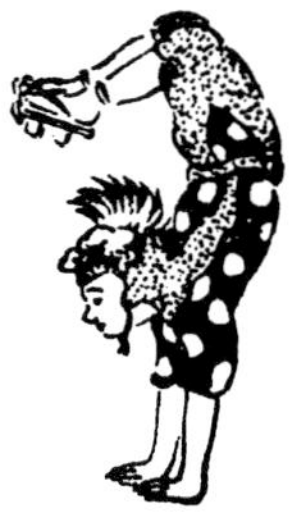

A gift is never presented ostentatiously, it is always "a mere trifle."

When a titbit is offered, a Japanese will say: "Although this does not taste good, please have it."

Comparatively few Japanese embroiderers are women. All the best peices are the work of men and boys.

Japanese usually wear their wrist watches with the watch turned to the inside of the wrist and on the left instead of the right wrist.

TOPSY-TURVYDOM

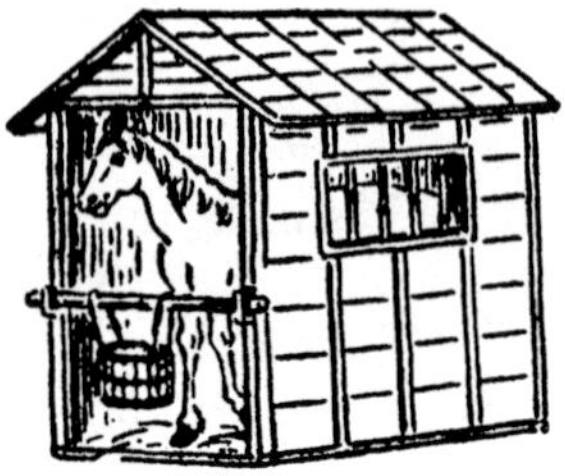

When a horse is stabled it is backed into the stall, its head being toward the entrance, and the animal is fed from a tub at the stable door. There is no manger as in the West.

The majority of Japanese cats are short-tailed, or have no tail. The bones are all there, but not normally developed, and usually the tail is crooked, as though broken. It often happens that should a litter be born with one long-tailed kitten, the tail will be chopped off to a respectable shortness. However, the objection to long-tailed cats prevails only in certain provinces. This objection has doubtless been augmented by the snaky aspect of a normal cat's tail when waved from side to side, and by the superstition that there exist cats furnished with one or several long tails, which possess the power of bewitching human beings after the manner of foxes and badgers.

Irreverent foreigners sometimes describe a malevolently gossipy woman as a cat. In Japan that appellation is colloquially applied to geisha, for the reason that geisha bewitch men with their artful, sham, coy ways, like the magic cats alluded to above.

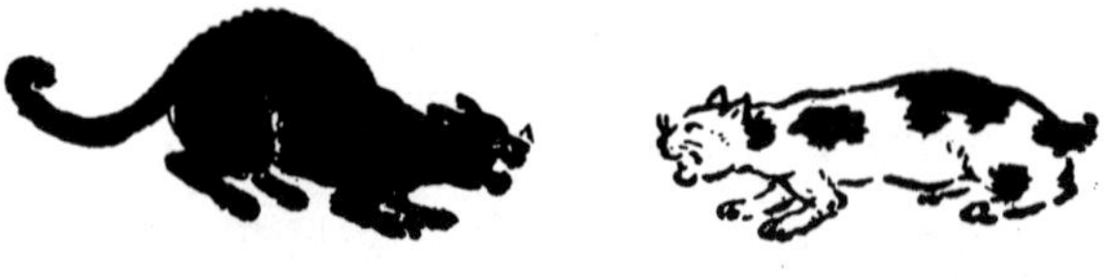

TOPSY-TURVYDOM

Should a child be born on December 31st, or any day of the year prior to that date, on January 1st of the year following the child is regarded as being two years old—hence, when a Japanese age is stated it is always one year less-reckoned in the Occidental way.

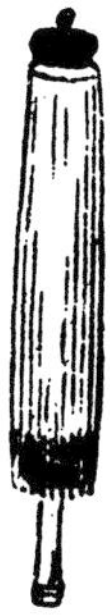

There are no swear words in the Japanese language. The alphabet has no "l," "r" is the nearest approach into which the Japanese tongue can be twisted when pronouncing an English word containing an "l."

The Japanese umbrella is made of oiled paper and when closed is carried handle down by means of a ring or loop at the top. The ribs and shaft are of bamboo.

Seven in Japan, and all numbers containing seven, as 17, 27, 37, etc., are considered more a less unlucky numbers.

Japanese count on their fingers, beginning with the thumb until all the fingers are down at 5, they turn up the little finger for 6 and so on, the counting being done quickly.

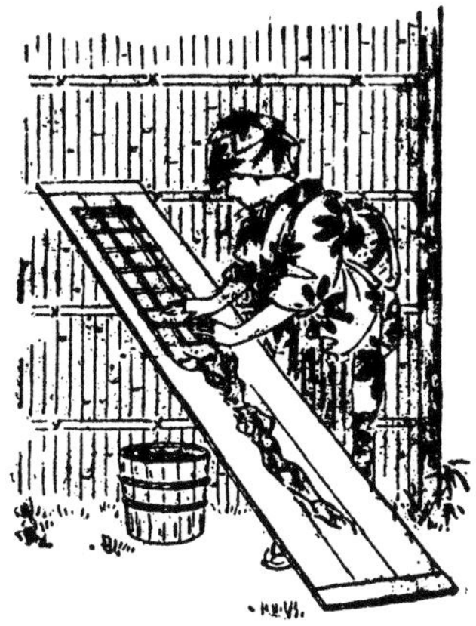

Japanese use the *soroban* (abacus) for all calculations, mental arithmetic being little practised.

A Japanese generally sharpens his pencil with outward cuts. Also he strikes a match away from him.

A lady in Japanese costume, owing to her dress, turns her feet inward. The kimono is crossed left over right, except for the dead. Western clothing is buttoned or hooked. The Japanese kimono has no fastening, and obi or sash holding it together. When ready for the wash, the kimono is taken to pieces, washed and when starch is required it is spread on boards to dry.

Japanese wear white for funerals and black for weddings.

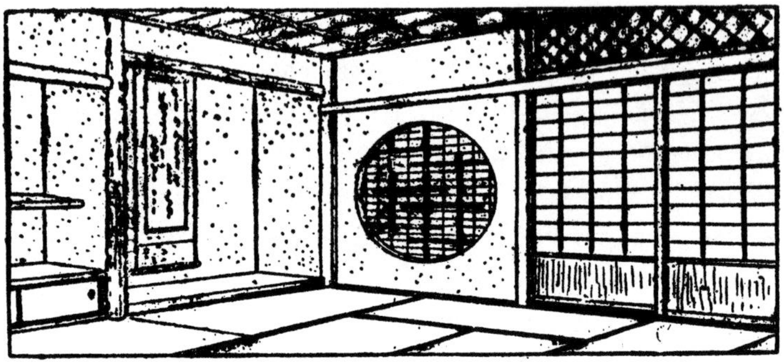

Babies' heads are shaved. Children are not weaned till they are 2, 3, or even 4 years old—which corresponds to the 1, 2, 3, years of the West. The second of a pair of twins is considered the elder.

A Japanese house has hardly any furniture to speak of. Stoves, fireplaces, and stair-rails are conspicuous by their absence. Doors do not open, they slide in grooves. Doors inside the house are never locked, the rooms being intercommunicating, more or less.

Japanese pack away their pictures, curios, and ornaments, and have as little as possible in their rooms, in contrast to the Western custom. Pictures are hung in a certain order. The principal, and usually the only one in a room, is the *kakemono* or scroll picture, hung in the *tokonoma,* or alcove (the holy of holies), in the best room. Ideographs hold the first rank, then black and white pictures, lastly colored pictures. These are changed according to the season and to conform with fixed aesthetic rules. This order is in contrast to the Western way of hanging pictures wherever they will go, often with little artistic consideration.

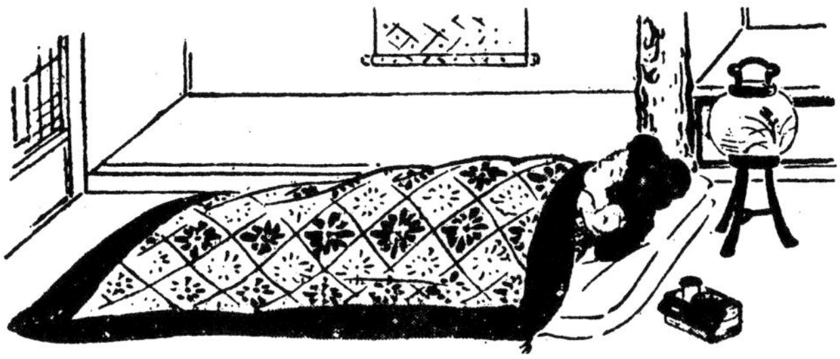

A Japanese woman's marriage is usually arranged by a gobetween. Wedding receptions are usually held at the bridegroom's home. Wedding banquets of wealthy families are generally given at hotels. There are few old bachelors or spinsters in Japan.

A Japanese set of cups, plates, etc., is 5 or 10, not 6 or 12.

Japanese mostly drink hot, not iced, tea. It is made with boiling water, but is drunk lukewarm.

On entering a house people slip off their footgear.

The housemaid dusts first, then sweeps.

Japanese have very hard pillows. They sleep on *futons* (wadded bed) on the floor, and avoid the North position in sleeping, for the reason that the dead are placed in that position. Their bedding is put away in closets. They sit on *zabuton* (cushions) on the floor.

In Japan, newcomers call first on residents who are immediate neighbours, and also send them bowls of *soba* (like macaroni).

TOPSY-TURVYDOM

Western people use trays to carry food to the table. Japanese meals are eaten from the *ozen*, a high tray, on the floor, each individual having his own tray. The constituents of a meal, each in a small bowl, are arranged on the tray so that the color effect will be pleasing to the eye. The meal is eaten with chopsticks, one-handed. Except among the cultivated class, noisy supping or intake of breath evinces appreciation—and as to this, a Japanese derives pleasure in having the meal appeal to his senses of taste and sight, of smell and hearing. Sake wine is heated. Sweets are eaten before the dinner.

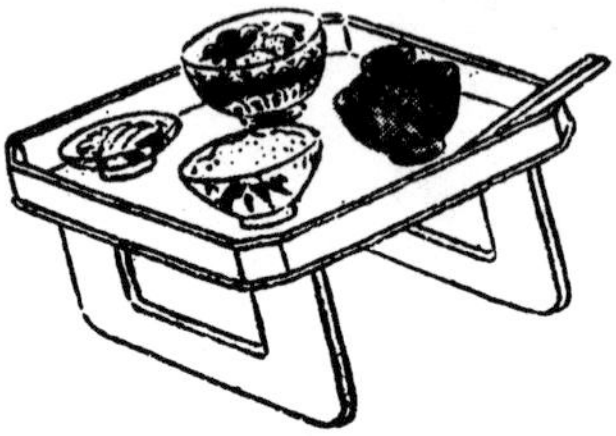

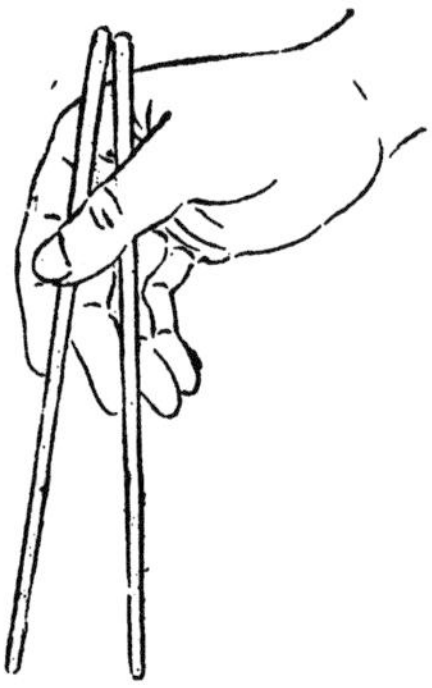

At banquets, an extra portion is provided for each guest to take away with him so that the homefolks can also enjoy the good food served at the banquet.

Many Japanese eating together do not make so much noise as the same number, or fewer, of foreigners, i.e., there is little conversation during a Japanese meal.

A Japanese tips before leaving, sometimes upon entering an inn, not the servants only but the innkeeper also—who is given what is known as *chadai* ("tea money"). Japanese inns present souvenirs to their guests, upon leaving.

TOPSY-TURVYDOM

Japanese say "yes" when Westerners would say "no," as: "You have no spinsters in Japan, have you?" The reply would be: "Yes, we have none." There are no words in the language which exactly express the same meaning as the terse English "yes" and "no."

Respect is shown by the drawing in of the breath.

There are no flowers in a Japanese landscape garden.

The names of streets are not of the throughfare, but of the section or piece of land through which the streets run.

Watchmen, in making their rounds at night, sound warnings by clapping two sticks together in a regular cadence at intervals of a few seconds. Instead of clappers they sometimes use a palmer's staff, a long iron staff surmounted by loose iron rings, carried by priests on their pilgrimages, the rings jingling when the end of the staff is struck on the ground.

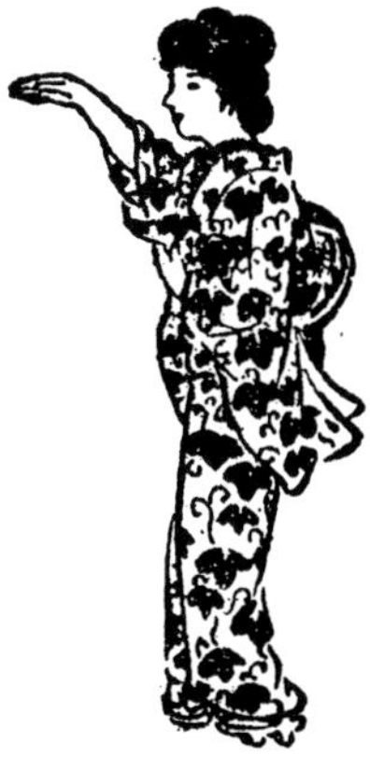

Japanese, when they wish to summon a person, beckon by waving the hand palm out, foreigners with palm towards them.

Japanese do not open gifts in the presence of the giver. Some Japanese allow little finger nails to grow long. It indicates that they do no manual labor—a custom derived from China.

Distant views are shut out from houses; miniature reproductions of natural scenery inside the fence take their place.

In shooting with bow and arrow Japanese archers place their arrows outside the bow. Westerners places them inside. The bows are made of several layers of bamboo, not of a single piece of wood.

TOPSY-TURVYDOM

Japanese bow their heads when they meet acquaintances. Westerners shake hands while looking at each other.

In a Japanese theater the performance lasts for six hours or more with long intermissions between the acts: some of them are 25 minutes long in order to permit the audience to partake of a meal in one of the restaurants in the theater building.

In a Japanese fencing bout the bamboo "sword" is held by both hands.

In Japanese footgear the whole foot is visible. The great toe is segregated in the *tabi* or short ankle sock so that the thong of the *geta* or shoe can pass between the great toe and the next toe and thus hold the *geta* in place.

Brokers on the exchanges accept bids and close contracts with hand raised, palm towards them—shutting the hand to clinch the offer, i.e., the reverse of the Western custom.

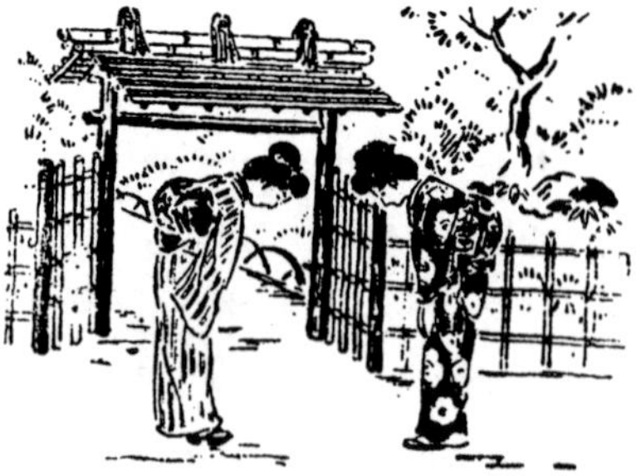

In summer, men as well as women carry fans—and use them.

Japanese say *achi-kochi* ("there-here"); Westerners say "here and there."

TOPSY-TURVYDOM

When telling about the death of a parent, wife, child, or some near relative a Japanese will often smile, his face in no way evidencing the grief he feels, which is in direct contrast to a Westerner's expression under similar circumstances. This custom comes through a desire to suppress all signs of deep emotion, and not to inflict a personal grief on another person.

Foreign scaffolding is made of milled lumber, spiked together. In Japan, scaffolds are made of poles which are tied together with straw ropes. The sight of Japanese workmen erecting a scaffold, with bunches of long straw ropes dangling, like tails, from their waists, is of amusing interest to most foreign visitors.

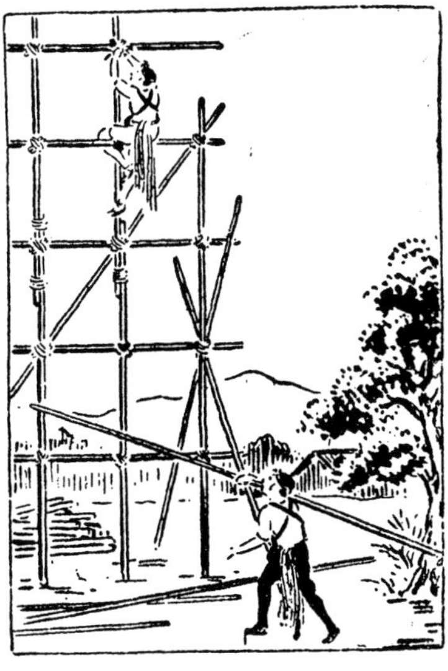

A Japanese woman, when in Japanese dress, never wears a hat. When putting on a foreign-style coat of any kind a Japanese man first thrusts his arm into the left sleeve, then, swinging the coat high on the back of his neck and shoulders, works his right arm into the sleeve.

A Westerner stirs his tea in the way the hands of a watch move, a Japanese does it in the reverse way. In Japan the wife holds the purse strings, and is economical in expenditures for the family. How is it in the West?

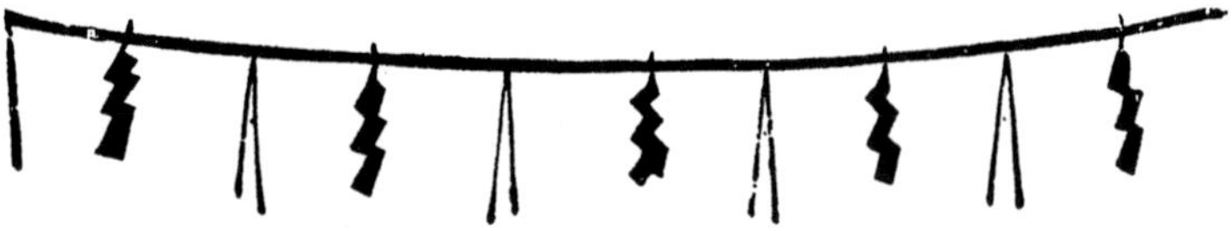

THE JAPANESE NEW YEAR

DECORATIONS

The greatest holiday of the nation is the New Year. In every household unusual preparations are made to celebrate the holiday in the most joyful manner, and business is suspended so far as possible during the period. Houses are cleaned throughly and formally on New Year's eve, the brooms bound with red and white strings as a seal against their use lest the Gods of Good Luck, which the New Year brings into the house, should be startled out of it by the bustle. New costumes are made—a new kimono for each child. Debts are paid—a moral, not a legal, obligation, but a custom so strongly rooted that people unable to meet their financial obligations at this time have been known to commit suicide.

At the front entrance to the house are decorations which though they may vary somewhat in different places consists usually of two pine trees, one with smooth bark (denoting the female), the other of rough bark (denoting the male), one on each side of the entrance. At the back of each pine tree are three stalks of bamboo. Across the top of the gate or the house entrance is the *Shimenawa*, a deep fringe of straw along which is strung *gohei*, little angular strips of white paper, an emblem supposed to represent offerings of cloth to the deities of a *Shinto* shrine, and somewhere in its decorations are fern leaves, an orange, and a small bent lobster—all of which symbolizes a host of good wishes for a long, strong, and prosperous life. The pine tree, because of its hardiness, denotes long life, the bamboo stalks, constancy and virtue, from a pun on its name; the fern, with its multiplicity of leaves, suggests an expanding good fortune throughout the years; the orange, daidai, has the same pronunciation as the Chinese word signifying "generation to generation," and, therefore, cannot be left out of the good wishes; the small lobster is also supposed to suggest old age because of its curved back. Since the lobster's back is also crooked when it is young this symbol expresses the special wish: though old age's back may be bent (the back of an old person in Japan often being bent)—that the spirit in the worn body may remain young.

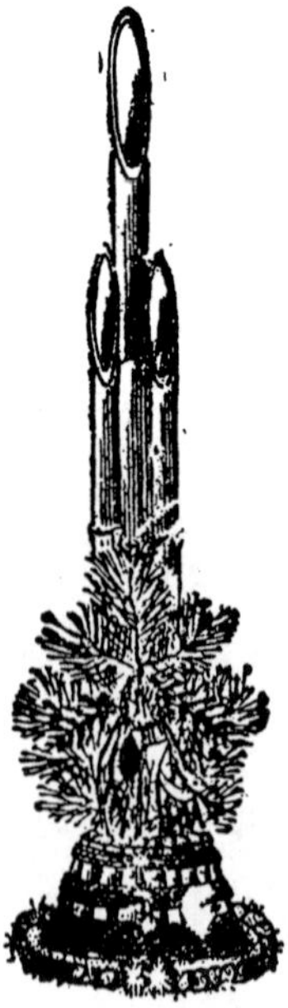

THE JAPANESE NEW YEAR

FOOD AND DRINK

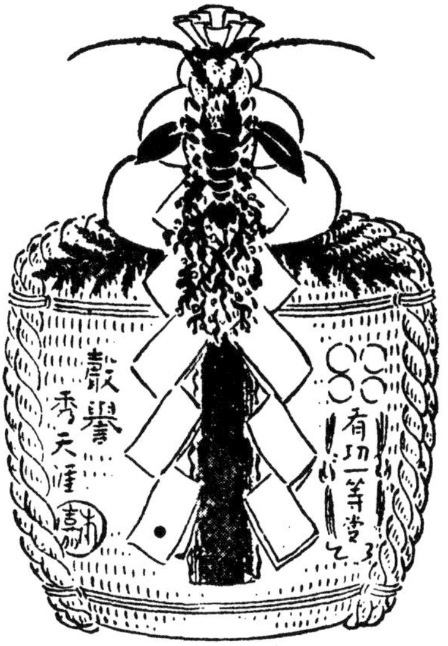

Special food is eaten at New Year and the first meal on New Year's day is a great event. For this meal fresh water is drawn at daybreak by the servants—if possible from a well or a neighboring stream. This water is known as "young water" and is believed to have the power of preserving health throughout the year. The special dish is *O-zoni*, a sort of broth containing *mochi* (rice-cake or paste) and vegetables. Many other foods are served, including carp, raw and cooked, because of the energy and determination of this fish to surmount obstacles, leap waterfalls, etc.; black peas, because the Japanese name for them is pronounced the same, though written differently, as another Japanese word meaning "robust"; chestnuts, deliciously cooked, in order that success may come to one inasmuch as part of the written character for chestnut means "mastery"; *daikon* (a variety of radish), and dried *kombu*, a seaweed, for happiness; also lotus root —the lotus being a sacred plant. A variety of yellow chrysanthemum petals (eaten as a salad), though believed to have little food value, is frequently used principally to enrich the color scheme on the table—the preparation of this meal and in fact all Japanese meals being made with an artistic eye as regards color.

Besides the food mentioned, a special drink, *O-toso*, is served and drunk at this time in the belief that it possesses a preventative power against sickness in general. *O-toso* is a sweet sake (*mirin*) flavored with Japanese pepper, Cassia bark, etc. *Mochi*, a kind of rice-paste, made into flat round cakes of many sizes is eaten throughout the holiday.

THE JAPANESE NEW YEAR

NEW YEAR CALLS

Everywhere there is evidence of leisure and joyousness. From the houses comes the sound of cheerful conversation and gaiety: the older folk chatting and the younger folk hilarious over a game of cards (*Hyaku-nin-isshu*—"Single Songs of 100 Poets") which is played only at this season. In the streets groups of small boys are flying their kites and here and there and everywhere young girls indescribably gorgeous of dress are playing battledore and shuttlecock. See the Fujiya Hotel menu card, "Battledore and Shuttlecock."

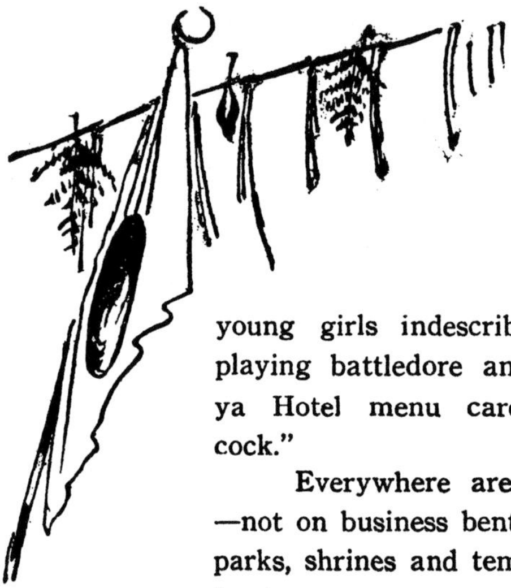

Everywhere are ricksha, motor cars, bicycles—not on business bent but on calls, to theaters, the parks, shrines and temples, to banquets, fetes and feasts.

There is no day in Japan quite like the New Year and the two days following, for these holidays cover three at least, and even five days. Friendliness is the keynote of this season. All enmity is forgotten for the nonce, if not forgiven forever, and foes of yesterday are friends at this time. Callers leave cards at the houses of their friends and acquaintances, wishing them a "Happy New Year." So universal is this custom that it is impossible to receive each and every visitor and return his compliments, so at the entrance to most houses is placed a receptacle for the callers' cards. Also, millions of personal and greeting cards are sent through the mails. Presents are given as at Christmas time in other countries, and gifts of orders for merchandise, and of merchandise itself, are made by tradesmen and business men to their customers and clients. Work, unless unavoidable, is taboo while this gala spirit prevails. Hot-spring resorts are crowded to capacity and there is relaxation everywhere.

THE JAPANESE NEW YEAR

2nd, 3rd, 4th, 5th, 6th, and 7th Days

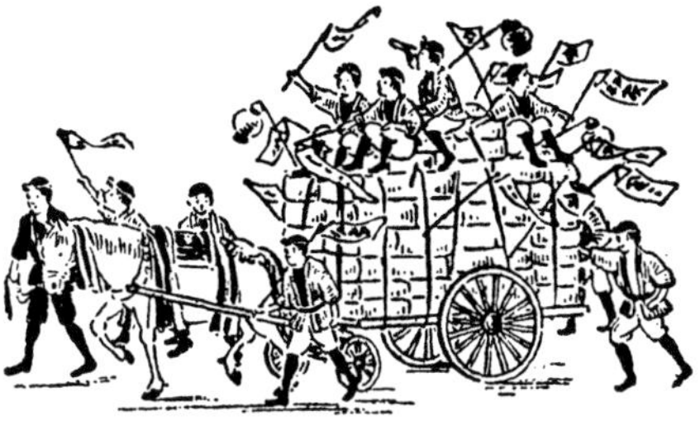

On the streets the day after New Year are seen carts piled high with merchandise and decorated like floats in a procession with flags and streamers in color. On top are lads in spickspan new apprentice suits—jolly fellows. The horse is decorated as if for a circus parade. These are the carts of wholesale dealers making the first deliveries of the year. This is called "Hatsuni."

On the third, fourth, fifth, and sixth days there is still much hilarity and the country hardly settles down to its wonted industry until the seventh day, called "Nanakusa," the day on which, in the early morning, all the New Year decorations within and outside the houses are taken down and either burned or tossed into a river or the sea as a token of purification. The day is also known as the "Early Herb Fete Day" *Wakana-no-Sekku* because of the special dish served on that day: a rice-gruel seasoned with *nanakusa* or the seven kinds of early herbs. On the sixth day, called *Dezome*, in many parts of the country firemen give their exhibitions in the streets, and that of the Tokyo firemen, given on the plaza of the Imperial Palace, is worth seeing.

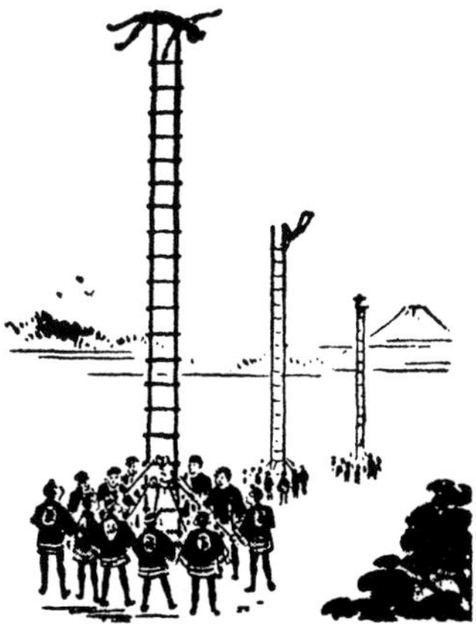

As part of the New Year ceremonies of the Court, the Emperor, on the Yoyogi parade ground, Tokyo, reviews the troops—usually at some time between the 5th and the 9th. And the spirit of the season still prevails on the 15th and 16th of January when employees who have been too busily occupied during the New Year to have much leisure are given a holiday at this time. This holiday is called *Yabu-iri.*

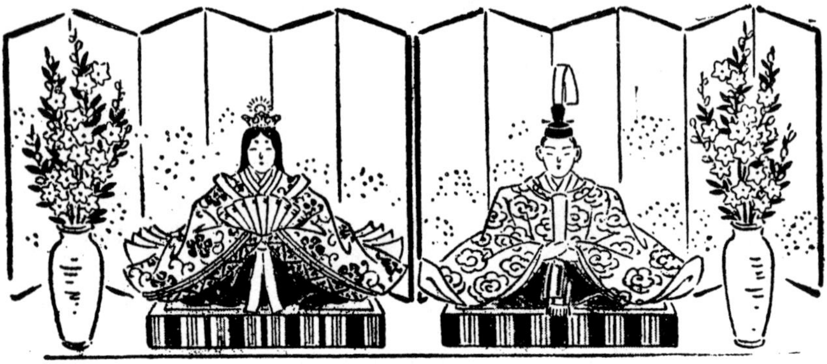

DAIRI-SAMA

THE DOLL FESTIVAL

The **Peach Fete,** more popularly known as the "Festival of the Dolls," a time-honored festival for girls, is held yearly on the 3rd day of the 3rd month—March 3rd. The dolls are not the everyday dolls usually played with but are ceremonial dolls, a heritage of the household, handed down, many of them, from generation to generation for a few days' display in the best room of the house at this festival time, after which they are carefully boxed and put away until the next year. Parents who are able to do so buy new sets of dolls for a girl baby born since the preceding festival, and relatives and friends make gifts of dolls.

Usually a set consists of at least 15 dolls, all in ncient costumes. The display also includes miniature household articles which often are exquisite artistic productions: a chest of drawers, *hibachi* (charcoal heater), a dinner table set, bowls, toilet stand, musical instruments, a palanquin in which the dolls are supposed to go out, and other tiny articles—laquered, if the purse permits. The dolls most highly valued are the **Dairi-sama,** which represent the Emperor and Empress in resplendent court costumes of silk. They are attended by their ministers, court ladies and musicians. All are displayed on a tier of steps, usually five, from 3 to 6 ft. long and covered with bright red cloth. The Imperial couple occupy the top step, the Emperor at the left of the Empress. Court ladies and banquet trays and dishes occupy the second tier; the other dolls are arranged on the lower tiers.

Peach blossoms, symbolizing happiness in marriage, are always among the decorations of the stand; also, being full and round, the peach blossoms signify the feminine characteristics of softness, mildness, peacefulness. Many marriages take place on the day of the Doll Festival.

The dolls are made to suit every purse, the best being highly finished objects of art. Regulation sets cost from $3.50 to $150 and up.

Many interpretations are given the festival. Families observe it to encourage filial piety, ancestor worship, loyalty, but above all else is the love of children by Japanese parents, their joy and pride in them, and their desire to please them—and this love often impels poor parents to sell some of their belongings to buy dolls and decorations for the festivals.

BUDDHA'S BIRTHDAY CELEBRATION

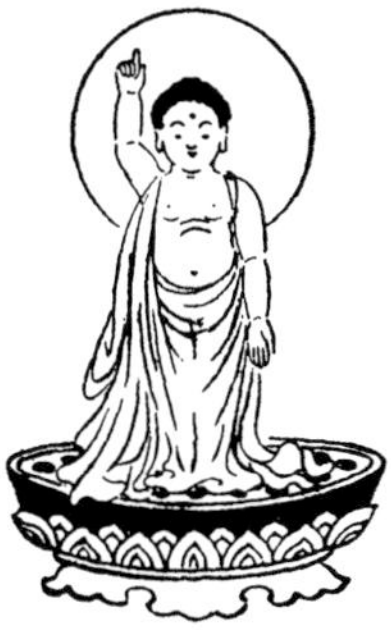

Annually, on April 8th, the birthday of ***Shakamuni*** the founder of Buddhism, is celebrated throughout Japan. Every temple of note observes the ceremony of ***Kan-butsu-e*** or "Baptising Ceremony of Buddha," which consists mainly of pouring "sweet tea" from tiny ladles over a small statue of the infant Buddha as an expression of devotion, and then drinking the beverage. Erected over the statue, which usually is from 12 to 16 inches high, is a temporary miniature temple beautifully decorated with flowers, called the *Hanamido* ("Flowery Temple") This day, also called the "Flower Day," generally marks the commencement of the cherry-blossom season. In the large cities the celebration is becoming increasingly popular: for instance, in Tokyo thousands of young children (Buddhist Sunday School pupils), in gala attire, each carrying flowers, assemble in Hibiya Park, where the *Hanamido* has been installed, and hold exercises and dances in honor of Buddha. This celebration has become one of the prettiest of the annual festivals of the capital.

BOYS' FESTIVAL

For centuries the Boys' Festival has been celebrated yearly on the 5th day of the 5th month, May 5th. It is called *Tango-no-Sekku*. One interpretation of *tango* is "the First Day of the Horse." The horses displayed in the Festival symbolically imply the attributes of manliness, bravery and strength desired in boys. The Festival is also known as *Shobu-no-Sekku* or "Iris Festival" and calls for many leaves of *shobu*, variety of iris, whose long, narrow leaf is somewhat like a sword-blade in shape. The boys bathe in the *Shobu-yu*, or Iris hot-bath, on this day to instil a warrior spirit in them. The wooden sword used on this day is called *Shobu-katana* ("Iris Sword").

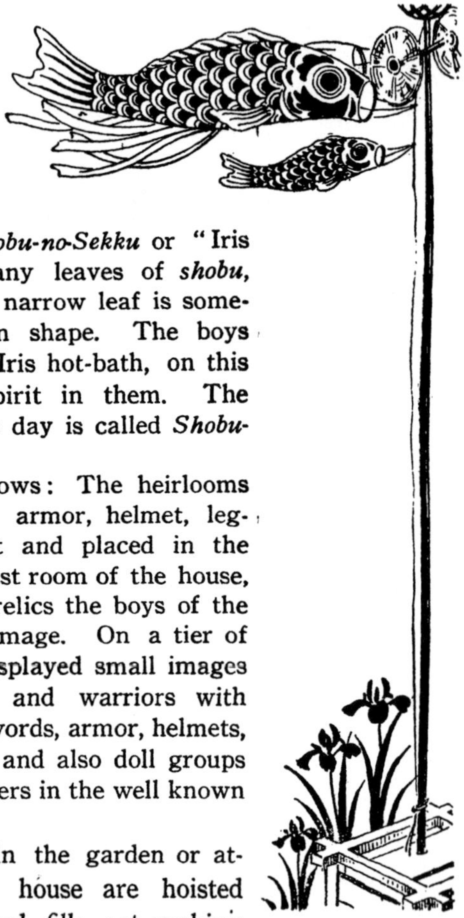

The Festival is as follows: The heirlooms of a warrior ancestor: the armor, helmet, leg-guards, etc., are brought out and placed in the *tokonoma* or alcove of the best room of the house, and before these precious relics the boys of the family bow in reverent homage. On a tier of shelves in this room are displayed small images of famous feudal generals and warriors with miniature paraphernalia of swords, armor, helmets, banners, drums, spears, etc., and also doll groups depicting scenes and characters in the well known hero stories of Japan.

On a long pole set in the garden or attached to the roof of the house are hoisted balloon carp which the wind fills out making them apparently swim in the air like real fish. Usually a carp is flown for each son: one (perhaps 15 ft. or more) for the eldest and the others grading down to a small one if there is a baby boy in the family. The carp has the power to fight its way up swift streams, and because of its determination to overcome obstacles is held to be a fitting example for growing boys, typifying, as it does, ambition, strength and the will to overcome difficulties.

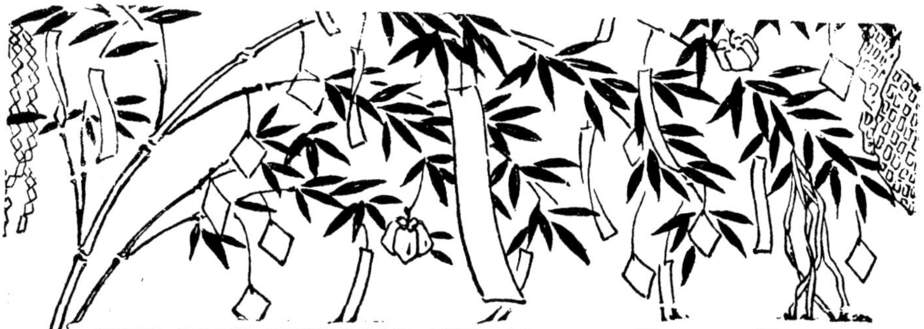

THE STAR FESTIVAL ("Hoshi-matsuri"), more Popularly TANABATA (" Weaving-loom ") MATSURI—celebrated on July 7th.

This is a festival in which children and young women find much enjoyment. Fairylike in its fantasy is its legend: That on the eve of July 7 *Shokujo*, or Weaver Princess Star, is supposed to meet *Kengyu*, or Herdboy Star, on the bank of the *Amanogawa* ("River of Heaven"), or Milky Way, for their annual tryst. Veda is the Princess Star, Altair, the Herdboy Star—the stars known as Lila Aquila. The legend back of this meeting is that the celestial princess, daughter of the celestial king, a most skilful weaver and the embodiment of industry, while engaged in weaving cloth for the king's garments, fell in love with a handsome lad, a cowherder, and as a reward for her diligent industry the king allowed them to marry. But so much in love were they that the princess gradually neglected her weaving and the herder allowed his cows to stray, which so exasperated the king that he finally separated the couple forcing them to remain on opposite sides of the Milky Way, and permitting them to approach each other only once a year. But there is no bridge over the Milky Way and the princess, on her first visit, wept so bitterly at the impossibility of meeting her husband that she roused the sympathy of a *kasasagi* (magpie) who assured her that a bridge would be contrived for her. This was done, the magpies with wings spread forming a bridge on which the princess crossed. But, further says the legend, if the eve of July 7 is rainy the magpies will not form the bridge and the celestial lovers must wait another year before meeting.

The princess, as an accomplished weaver, receives on this day the supplications of those who wish to improve their own weaving, sewing, and their knowledge of the gentle arts: music, poetry, handwriting, etc., of which the princess later became the patron, and farmers ask the herder for bounteous harvests. The festival is observed in a spirit of joy. Bamboo trees are set up in front of the houses or before garden shrines and to their branches are hung poems on the love theme of the festival, also papers cut in the shape of kimono (as a tribute to the weaver princess), and to represent cows (for the herder), also threads of five colors: green, red, yellow, white, and black (or purple). Melons, peaches, egg-plant and other fruit and vegetables, cakes and sweetmeats are likewise offered. The next morning the bamboos are taken to a stream and are floated away on the current.

O-BON or "FEAST OF THE DEAD", or "FESTIVAL OF LANTERNS", sometimes called the "FESTIVAL OF SOULS", is considered by some as similar to the Christian "ALL SOULS' DAY". Observed yearly in Japan on July 13-14-15.

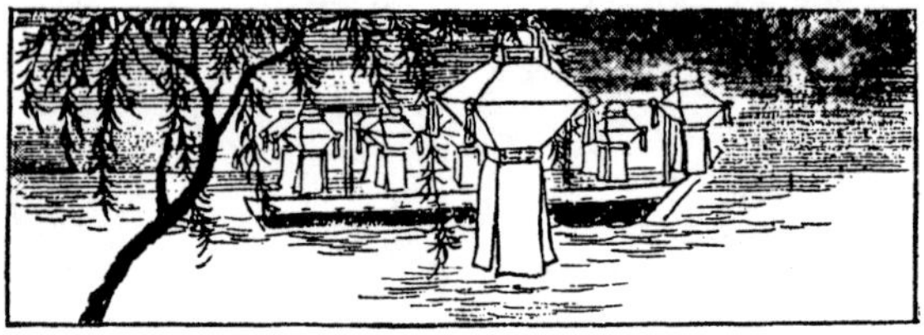

The *O-Bon* is a memorial festival which has been observed by Japanese Buddhist families ever since the introduction of Buddhism into Japan about 1300 years ago. It is a 3-day reunion of the living with the spirits of the dead. Its purpose is to perpetuate the memory of ancestors and to stimulate ancestor worship and filial piety.

On the 13th, at the graveyards, the living pay homage to their dead relatives, and much incense is burned. As darkness sets in they hung lighted white paper lanterns on the graves and invite the spirits to come forth and visit their old homes. With a lighted lantern they escort them there, pointing out the bad spots in the road and evincing the greatest concern for their comfort. In the homes the people talk to the spirits as if they were present in the flesh; to them the visit and imagined conversation of their spirit guests are as real as any actual affair of the moment.

In the best room, in front of the family altar, is spread a small mat: on it are placed the ancestral tablets, other articles and sweets, and around it is a leaf fence. On the table for the dead, is placed a meal in tiny portions which, besides the favorite dishes of the departed, includes a plate of Japanese potatoes, sesame, egg-plant, and gourd. The family usually call in a Buddhist priest to chant sutras for the dead.

On the 15th "farewell rice ball" lunches are offered the spirit guests to cheer their departure to the *Meido*, the Celestial World of Darkness, and "farewell fires" are lighted at the house front as beacons to show the return way.

At the conclusion of the *O-bon* the sacred articles used in the festival are placed at night by one of the family in a small straw-boat (a small lighted lanterns or candle at the bow; at the stern, burning incense) which is floated on a running stream or cost on the sea—both methods as a means of comforting those who have no grave but the river or the ocean bed.

BON-ODORI ("Bon Dance"). The Dance of Rejoicing for the Souls that have been liberated from their sufferings in the Buddhist Hells into a state of celestial bliss.

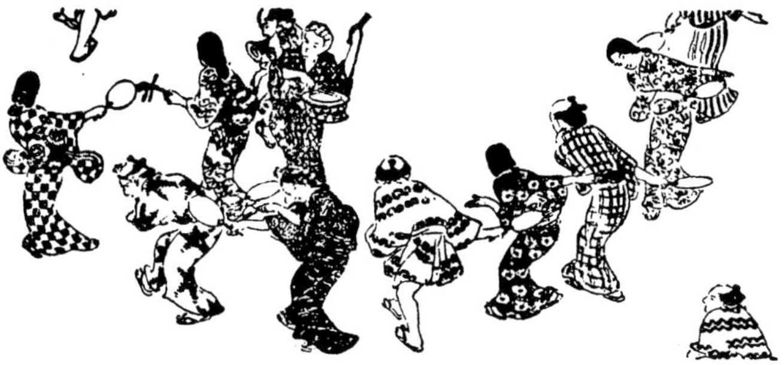

The *Bon-Odori* is a primitive community dance—a religious folk-dance—usually held on the last night of *O-Bon*, July 15th. It is best seen in country districts where it has become the most delightful event of the season for the young folk who, having been rehearsed many times, gather at their local shrine, temple grounds, or village common, and there dance far into the night—sometimes until dawn. It is a rhythmic dance in which the performers singly and in groups assume graceful postures, like living statues, and sing or chant folk and other songs. At other times they sway their bodies in unison and whirl faster and faster as the singing, clapping of hands, stamping of feet and beating of drums increase in measure. Some of the numbers last a half-hour, after which another folk-song with a different rhythm is given. The performers seem tireless.

A large outdoor night dance, sometimes with more than 1,000 performers, is held yearly at Nikko, in the precincts of the Iyeyasu, or Toshogu Shrine, usually in mid-August, at which time the shrine buildings are illuminated, the only time in the year that this is done. An *Odori* (the largest in Japan) is celebrated yearly on the nights of August 6th and 7th at Kiyotaki, 4 miles from Nikko, in commemoration of the visit in 1916 of the late Emperor Taisho and the Empress, the Emperor having visited the place on August 6th, the Empress on August 7th.

THE SHICHIGOSAN (Lit., "Seven-Five-Three") FESTIVAL

The *Shichi-go-san*, said to be over 400 years old, held yearly on November 15, is a pretty festival. At that time, parents with children 7, 5, and 3 years old go to a shrine to express their

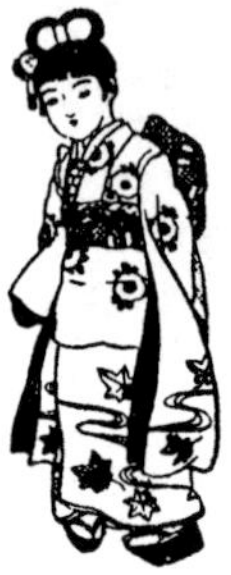

Seven years

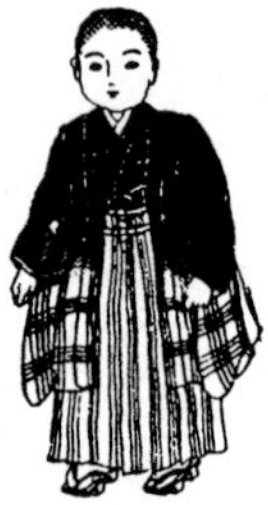

Five years

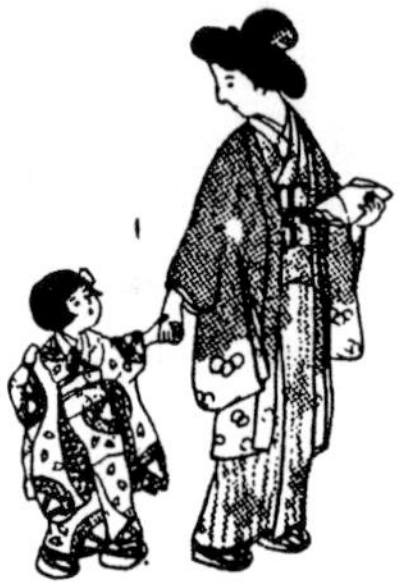

Three years

gratitude to the tutelary deity that the children have reached these critical ages and to invoke future blessings. These ages correspond to the 6, 4, 2 years of age in Western countries. In former days (not so much today) the festival was marked by ceremonies of putting up the hair of a 3-year old girl, of placing a *hakama* (pleated skirt) on a 5-year old boy, and of giving a 7-year old girl an *obi* (silk girdle), to be worn for the first time.

In Tokyo the most popular shrines frequented for this festival are the Myojin (Kanda), Hiei (Sanno Hill, Kojimachi), Hachiman (Fukagawa), Ushijima (Mukojima), and Hikawa (Akasaka). The first two named draw the largest numbers. At the Hiei, during the day, sometimes over 20,000 parents and children in their finest clothing visit the shrine. The children are given talismans and sweetmeats by the shrine authorities and receive presents from relatives and friends.

As to attire in Japan, the tinier the tot the more brilliantly is it dressed. After childhood, there is a gradual decline of color in costume all the way to old age, which is marked by severe simplicity and dark shades of clothing.

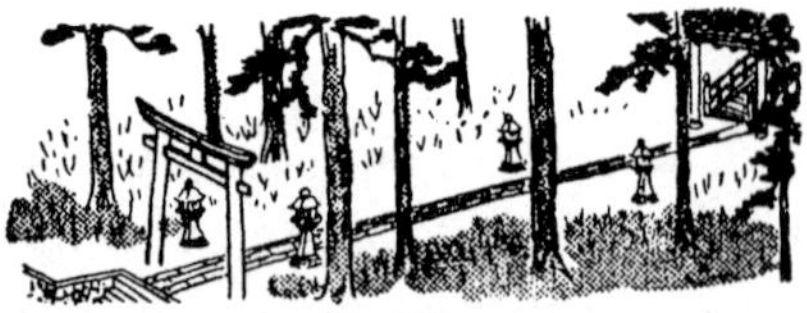

Leading to the Shrine.

Some of the talismans previously mentioned as being given to children by shrine authorities at the time of the *Shichi-go-san* Festival are shown in accompanying illustrations. They are printed in striking colors on the front and back of the long, narrow paper bags of sweetmeats presented to the children at the shrines. Those on the left represent some of the actual objects on sale at booths in the shrine precincts. The bottom figure depicts *Kintoki*, a strong boy who grew to manhood in the Hakone mountains. He became friendly with wild animals of the district, wrestled with bears and performed many other strenuous feats. He is shown riding a dog—a very popular toy. Some of the other pictures are of squat *Daruma*, whose eyes must be painted in when he brings Good Luck to his owner. *Daruma* is regarded as a lucky toy for the reason that no matter how much one tries to keep him down he is never beaten but always bobs up serenely. The dice is also for luck. Coral was a prized treasure in olden days. The striking hammer has the same significance as that of Aladdin's magic lamp. Each toy dangling from its bamboo stem has its particular meaning.

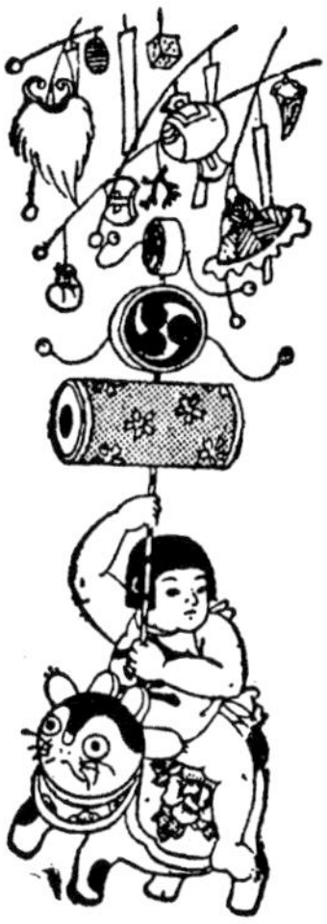

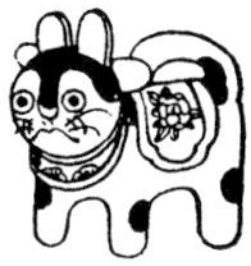

In the third picture the characters in the circle, top, read "Celebration." Those below it read "Longevity." Their background consists of two crossed *noshi*—one of which always accompanies a gift. In the picture under it are the sun and its rays, symbols of Japan, the crane, said to live for 1,000 years, and the tortoise, popularly believed to live for 10,000 years, both signifying long life. The pine and the bamboo, both ever-green, also signify long life and youthfulness. The plum is shown because it is the first blossom that appears in spring, often when snow lies on its branches. It signifies vigor. The old man with the rake is *Jo*, who with his wife, *Uba*, typify the spirit of the evergreen pine tree of Takasago beach. Takasago is one of the "*No*" plays. Symbolizing long life and happiness the old couple are generally a feature of the decorations at times of congratulation: weddings, the girls' festival, etc. Usually they are shown together standing on a *shimadai*, as in the picture. The ideographs between them give the name of the contents of the bag: *Chitose* ("1,000 years") *Ame*, a confection.

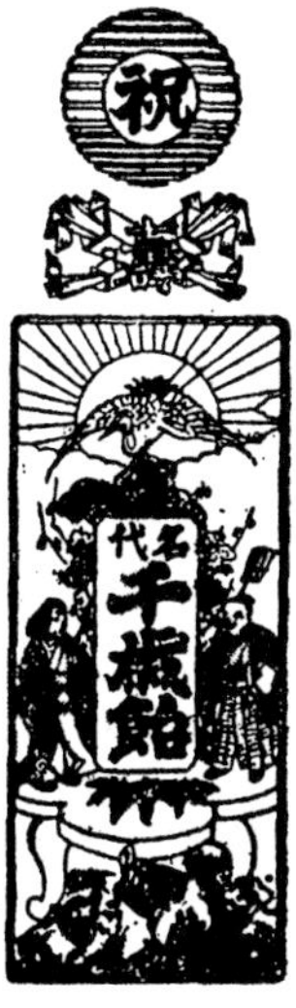

For more detailed descriptions see Kintoki, Daruma, Noshi, Cranes, Pines, Bamboo, Turtles, and Toys.

MIYAMAIRI ("Shrine Visit")

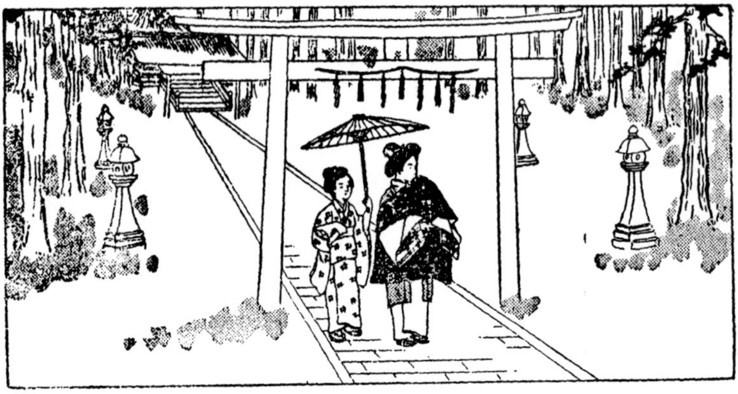

Miyamairi, the first real festival in a baby's life, has a deep religious significance. Upon its observance the baby is taken to the shrine of the local deity, *Ujigami,* the guardian and protector of the people of the district.

The day for this fete differs according to the sex of the baby For a boy it is usually held on his thirty-second day; for a girl, on her thirty-third day. The baby, in its best dress, is carried in the arms or on the back of its nurse or on its grandmother's back. In cities, motor cars or rickshas are now employed for this service, but modern conveyances detract greatly from the beauty and significance of the custom. The mother does not go because she is considered impure and cannot yet approach the presence of the *Kami,* or god. The party, consisting of relatives and friends, forms a procession to the shrine. On their back each one in it carries one of the baby's beautiful kimono—thus making the procession highly picturesque

Arriving at the shrine, the priest is requested to perform the ceremony of purifying and blessing the baby In his impressive formal robes the priest leads the way to the presence of the *Kami,* recites the sacred ritual, and waves the *gohei* or sacred cut paper over the baby's head in order to drive away evil and to bring upon the child the love and blessing of the *Kami.* In this way is the baby freed from all evil that it may have brought from the other world and the child then enters this life clean, pure, and noble.

When the ceremony is ended the baby is taken to visit relatives and friends. At this time bags of *ame* (wheat gluten) are given as presents from the baby In olden days when a mother lacked milk, the baby was fed on *ame* and thus *ame* became established as baby's food. To give *ame* as a present evidences the baby's willingness to share its food with its friends

In return for the *ame,* the recipients present the baby with *Inu-hariko* (papiermache dogs) symbolizing the hope that the child will grow as fast and be as healthy as a puppy. Hemp is also presented because it is strong. Then the procession proceeds homeward carrying the baby's clothes and long strings of *inu-hariko,* of all sizes. The mother joyously welcomes the baby and a banquet is then served to all.

EBISU-KO FESTIVAL

The festival of *Ebisu-ko*, held yearly on October 20, is so called after *Ebisu*, one of the Seven Gods of Luck, who is also the patron of fisherman the only one of the eight million deities of Japan who remains at large during October, which is called the "godless month" because all the other gods then leave their proper shrines and assemble at the great temple at Izumo, on the Japan Sea side of Western Japan, where they discuss momentous affairs, and arrange for the marriages of Japanese maidens. It is said the reason *Ebisu* does not accompany them is that, being deaf, he does not hear the summons. In times past tradesmen on this day sold off their surplus stock and gave entertainments to their customers, correspondents, etc., as an amend—so it was half-jocularly said—for cheating them during the rest of the twelve months, but today when many old-time customs are falling into desuetude, the 20th of October has come to be regarded as a day for social gatherings of the members of guilds, political and literary societies, and so forth.

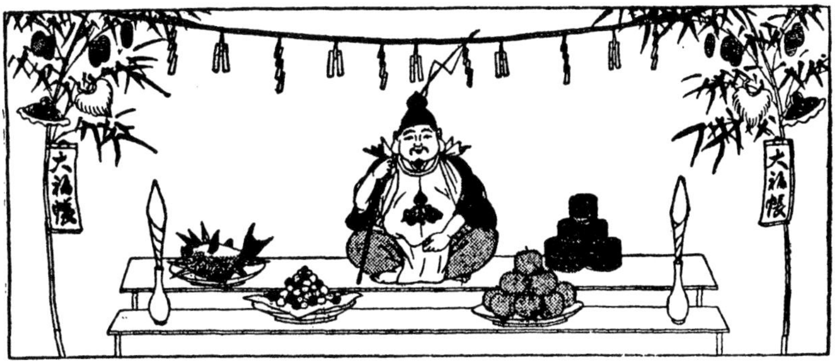

At New Year, *Ebisu* is a feature of the festivals at all shrines dedicated to this fat and jolly god of good luck, his devotees then going in merry crowds to the shrines to make their small offerings and to insure their share of good luck during the coming year. In particular, the grounds of the Osaka Imamiya shrine, the head shrine of this deity, are so packed and overflowing every year at this time that traffic in the vicinity of the shrine is tied up. Almost everyone carries a green branch of bamboo, to which they tie the gaily colored good-luck charms and talismans they buy at the booths: red cardboard *tai* fish, a picture of *Ebisu* himself, tokens symbolizing wealth—gilt paper shaped like the old oblong *koban* coins, treasure chests, purses, and modern cloth moneybags in miniature—small cardboard godowns filled to bursting with rice bags, dice suggesting luck, a target with an arrow in the center of the bullseye as an appeal for success in undertakings of all kinds, besides other trinkets. This observance is repeated again and again, in lesser degree, at all Ebisu shrines throughout the land.

JIZO

In the tenets of Buddhism, *Jizo* is the patron saint and guardian of the souls of dead children.

According to Buddhist belief the souls of all children must go after death to the *Sai-no-Kawara*—which to some extent corresponds to the Styx, the mythological river of the ancient Greeks. Here a merciless she-devil, the hag *Shozuka-no-Baba*, after she has stolen the children's clothing, sets them to the task of piling up stones on the bank of the river, telling the children that if they make towers high enough Holy Paradise will be reached. The task is everlasting because the hag and her company of devils scatter the heaps of stones as fast as the children can pile them.

Then comes benign *Jizo*. Impelled by his love and pity for the little ones, he drives the demons away, comforts the children, and hides them in his great sleeves. Thus comes the belief that every stone placed with a prayer in the lap of a statue of *Jizo* will lighten the labor and shorten the penance of some young soul; and that each bit of the pitiful little pieces of children's clothing that is hung about images of *Jizo* will clothe the soul of some child.

Jizo images are found everywhere in Japan, but principally along traveled roadways.

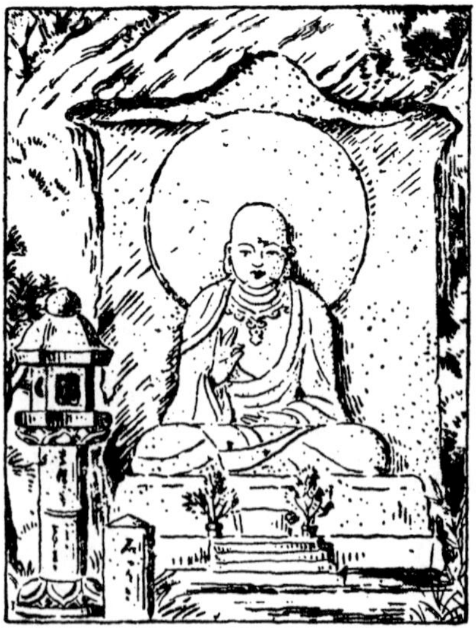

On the way to Lake Hakone, beyond Ashinoyu, left of the road, is a famous *Jizo* image, carved in high relief from the native andesite, the dull grey basaltic lava common to the vicinity. It is depicted in the picture on the left. It is said that the sculptured image is over 1,000 years old, and that it was carved in a single night by the great Buddhist saint, Kobo Daishi. A festival in its honor is held yearly on August 23.

KOBO DAISHI and the 1100 YEARS FLAME

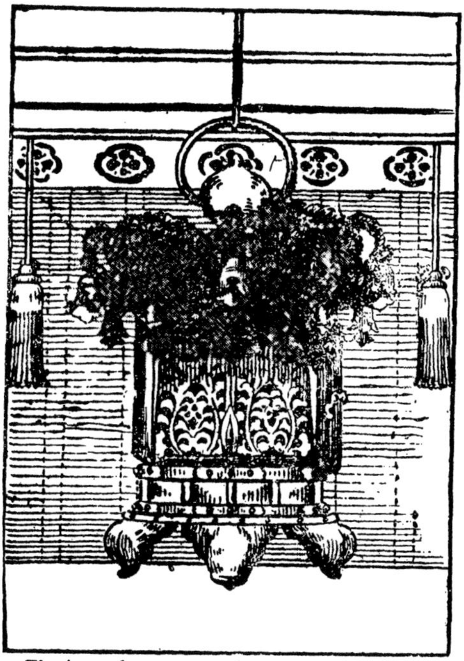

The irregular mass at the top of the lantern is the accumulated soot.

This flame has burned constantly for over 1100 years in front of the tomb of the great Buddhist saint, Kobo Daishi, on Koya-san ("Plateau Mountain"), near Nara, at the monastery he founded (A. D. 816) near the top of the mountain. The monastery consists of several temples. In the early days the flame was maintained by the use of heavy vegetable oils. Several lanterns are kept in reserve so that in case of repairs or anything happening to the flame lantern, the flame can be quickly transferred, priests from the various monasteries performing these religious duties, thus keeping the flame burning.

The real name of Kobo Daishi (A. D. 774-835) was Priest Kukai, Kobo Daishi being the posthumous name given him by Emperor Daigo in 921—it means "Law-spreading Great Teacher." "Daishi" means "great master," "apostle," or "saint." He was the great exponent of the Shingon doctrines of China, and the inventor of the Japanese syllabary known as *Hira-gana*. It is no exaggeration to say that he is to Japanese what the apostles, put together, are to Christians. He was equally noted as a preacher, traveler, painter, and sculptor. Throughout Japan, in temples and elsewhere, are sculptures and carved images and paintings accredited to him. So much so that it seems almost incredible that during his 60 years of life he could work so many miracles, do so many things, scale so many mountains, etc.

The immense Koya-San cemetery is the most unique in Japan. It extends through a large grove of noble cryptomarias to the Toro-do, a building containing over 3000 lanterns, gifts of devotees. Here are tombs, pagodas, sotobas and monuments of every description, erected in memory or over the remains, or a portion of them, of some of the most celebrated men of Japan. At the entrance, just beyond the Ichi-no-hashi ("First Bridge"), is a replica of the famous Nestorian Stone, at Si-an, China. Near the end of the cemetery is the Kotsu-do ("Hall of Bones") wherein are deposited bones of persons who desired some part of their anatomy to rest as near as possible to the remains of Kobo Daishi—and beyond is the Gobyo (the mausoleum) occupying a high point on the hill, the burial place of part of the ashes of the venerated priest—the most revered spot of the Shingon sect adherents in Japan. And since his interment, prayers have been offered daily before his tomb.

In the old days women were allowed to advance only to a certain gate where they worshiped the Buddha from a distance. Today the monastery is open to women. Visitors are put up at the temples. For food, only vegetables are served—no meat—which is one of the tenets of the sect.

SHINTŌ ("THE WAY OF THE GODS")

Shintōism is a cult which embraces nature—and ancestor—worship. The chief deity in its pantheon (of the so-called "8,000,000 gods") is *Amaterasu-O-Mikami*, the Sun Goddess and Great Ancestress of the Japanese Imperial House. Although this pantheon embraces gods and goddesses of the sea, river, wind, fire, and mountains, and celebrated warriors and loyal servants of the Imperial House, it is the worship of the first Imperial Ancestress and many of her relatives and descendants which constitutes the leading characteristic of Shintōism.

The underlying principle in Shintō services is that of purity and purification. It is almost compulsory to wash the mouth and hands before worshiping, and the frequent ablutions of the body practised by Shintō priests and devout believers all show the paramount importance attached by Shintōism to purification. The impurities from which believers are to be cleansed consist of contact with dead bodies and human blood, and of the evil imaginings of the mind. Divine protection is also prayed for against natural evils of all kinds: floods, pestilence, hurricanes, earthquakes, etc.

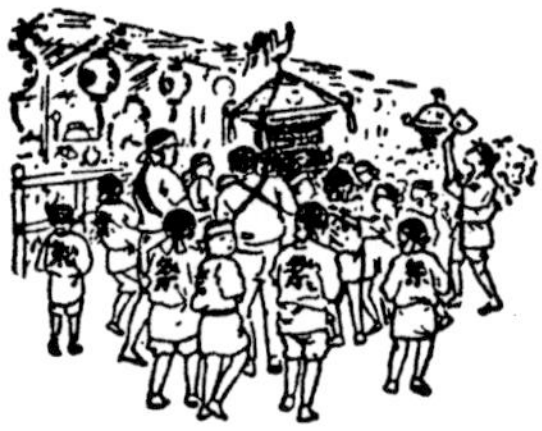

Young boys carrying a Mikoshi.

Shintōism has no system of theology or of ethics. It is not a religion in the strict sense—but regarded as a form of religion it comprises only thirteen sects. It teaches the innate goodness of the human heart. "Follow the genuine impulses of your heart" is the essence of its ethical teachings. Its teaching regarding future reckoning for the good and bad deeds of the present life is not quite clear, though it explicitly declares that the spirit lives after death. Shintōism knows no asceticism, no celibate clergy; its priests may marry or eat animal food, just as may the laity. Women serve in the shrines as priestesses or *kagura* dancers, but they never become nuns. The offerings to the gods consist of rice, fruit, vegetables, *sake*, and on stated occasions, the products of the looms.

BUDDHISM—IN JAPAN

Buddhism first entered Japan in 552 A.D. when the King of Kudara, Korea, troubled by civil war, solicited the aid of Japan—and at that time presented *sutra* (scriptures) and images to Emperor Kimmei. These presents were soon followed by priests and nuns, as well as by temple architects and image carvers. The Emperor instructed his minister to propagate the new religion, but it was only after a half century of much dispute and hard struggle that the Regent, Prince Shotoku, in the reign of Empress Suiko (592-628) established the Buddhist religion on a firm footing in the Court and the Empire. What King Asoka did for Buddhism in India, and what Constantine did for Christianity in the Roman Empire, was effected by Prince Shotoku for Buddhism in Japan—and sometimes he is designated as "the Constantine of Japan."

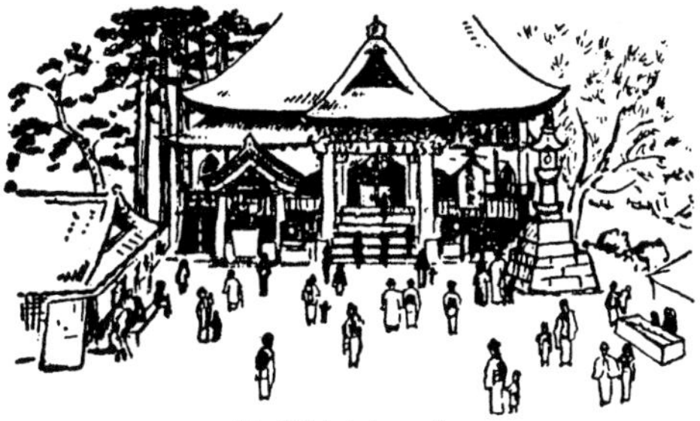

Buddhist temple.

The first Buddhist sect arose in 624. It propagated the teachings of the San-ron sect, *Mahoyamika*. Other sects arose, but for about 130 years Buddhism in Japan remained Chinese in its main features. Then through the efforts of two great priests, *Saicho* or *Dengyo-Daishi* (founder of the Tendai sect) and *Kukai* or *Kobo-Daishi* (founder of the Shingon sect), a strong national bent was given to the imported religion, chiefly by the application of the doctrine of the *Honji-suijaku*, according to which the Shinto deities were regarded as various manifestations of Buddhas and Bodhisattvas. This bold teaching was carried to its logical conclusion with the growth of two-fold Buddhism (or two-fold Shintoism, *Ryobu-Shinto*, speaking from the Shintoist standpoint). Buddhism then became all powerful, with its two great and rival centers: the monastery on Mt. Koya, near Nara, where was taught the Shingon sect's esoteric philosophy, with its complex symbolism, and that on Mt. Hiei, Kyoto, the seat of the Tendai sect, and these became the fountain heads of Buddhist learning.

In 1930 Buddhism had 41,179,740 adherents, who maintained 106,223 temples. The largest sect is the Shin Shu, with over thirteen million adherents, next the Zen Shu with over nine million (3 branches), followed by the Shingon Shu with over eight million, and the Jodo Shu and the Nichiren Shu, each with over three million adherents. Space does not permit statements of the tenets or principles of the various sects—but it may be said that the Shin Shu and Nichiren Shu are the most democratic sects in Japanese Buddhism. As to Buddhism in Japan, Indian religious men have remarked that devotion to Buddha was greater in Japan than in India, where the Sage was born.

* Shu means sect.

CHRISTIANITY—IN JAPAN

For nearly a century, or between 1549 and 1638, Roman Catholic missionaries in Japan were active in their efforts to make converts—the first named date marking the landing of Francis Xavier, one of the founders of the Society of Jesus, the last, that of the expulsion of the missionaries. During that time it is claimed that over 200,000 Japanese became Roman Catholics, the number including famous *daimyo*, generals, and cultivated ladies of high rank. At first favored by *Nobunaga*, missionaries were placed under a ban by *Hideyoshi*, their activities strinctly prohibited by *Iyeyasu*—and finally they were driven away. In 1637 Kyushu's 20,000 Catholics rose in desperate revolt against the relentless persecutions they suffered, in what is known as the Shimabara insurrection—a rising due, according to some accounts, to local misgovernment as much as to religious causes: the latter factor, changing the attitude of the ruling powers, was brought about by the over-zeal of the Jesuit, Dominican, and Franciscan missionaries, the quarrels which arose between these religious orders, and their intrigues with the feudal nobility—and with the Court at Kyoto. The insurrection ended in 1638 with the massacre of the Christians, the great majority of whom were affiliated with the Jesuits, in and about Hara Castle, at Arima (S. part of Shimabara Penin.), where they had taken refuge. This tragic event practically rooted out all outward traces of Christianity in Japan for over two centuries, because apart from the converts made to the Roman Catholic faith by the Portuguese and Spanish missionaries there was no other form of Christianity in Japan at that time. Before the final extirpation of the Church in 1639, native Christians continued to be ruthlessly persecuted—many of them being crucified, thousands burned. But despite all this, Christianity was never entirely eradicated in certain parts of Kyushu—as is proven by the remarkable fact that in about a month after the erection of a Roman Catholic Church in Nagasaki in 1865 there occurred a memorable scene known as "The Finding of Christians," when thousands of Christians in the Nagasaki neighborhood, who secretly had kept the faith transmitted by their forebears through successive generations for about 225 years, made open confession of their religion.

Protestant missions and Roman Catholic missionaries next began their work about 1859, and at first all missionaries met with the greatest obstacles—all Japanese being strictly forbidden to believe in the "Evil Christian Religion." With the Restoration (1868), the doors began to be thrown open to missionary teaching. The old edicts prohibiting Christianity were removed from the noticeboards in 1873. The Constitution, promulgated in 1889, granted full religious liberty. All the well-known larger churches are self-supporting.

In 1930 there were 254,038 adherents to Christianity, the largest denomination being the Roman Catholic, followed in their order by the Presbyterian, Methodist, Congregational, Episcopal, Baptist, and other denominations.

RELIGION IN JAPAN

FROM A FOREIGNER'S VIEWPOINT

Japan keeps her faith and her many shrines and temples; they are seen wherever one travels. Yet notwithstanding these evidences of faith many observers declare that the Japanese take their religion lightly. There is no set day of worship, and as a rule shops are open and business goes on every day in the week, except in the government departments and in some of the large stores in the cities, other shops being closed only twice a month, on specified days, to afford a holiday for their employees. There is nothing in the shrines and temples similar to a Christian service. Worshipers alone or in small groups continually visit these sacred edifices. If it is a Shinto shrine they stand in front of the main entrance, pull the bell rope and clap their hands three times to attract the attention of the enshrined deity, toss a coin into the offertory-box, bow their head and say a brief prayer; before a Buddhist temple a gong is struck with a small stick to announce their presence to the gods of that temple, and if they have a rosary it is rolled between their hands, making slight sounds, as they pray. This act of worship occupies less than a minute and appears to be perfunctory; apparently it does not matter whether they pray before a Shinto shrine dedicated to ancestor worship, or before a Buddhist temple which stands as an exponent of a highly developed philosophic creed, but whatever their faith they show the greatest respect for other faiths. A Buddhist will remove his hat and bow before a Shinto shrine with the same respect that he shows before his own temples—and vice versa.

They accept their religion cheerfully and are tolerant of other religions, but underneath it all the old faith lives, and few are the Japanese who at their death are not buried under Buddhist rites. In Spring and Autumn, bands of pilgrims, robed in white, go their way through the countryside from temple to temple—an arresting sight. A multitude of sincere and devout believers follow the Buddhist doctrines and contribute to keep their respective sects of many shades of thought—which today have more than 41 million adherents. The Shintoists have close to 18 million followers.

The hundreds of thousands of shrines and temples throughout Japan serve as a bulwark for the people, who, though they may be lax in their visits to them, nevertheless cherish them as a link between themselves and the myriad of deities to whom they are dedicated. They look forward with delight to the annual religious festivals and periodical religious ceremonies—which are times for foregathering, for sauntering along the rows of booths, buying trifles, and for amusing the children at the side shows.

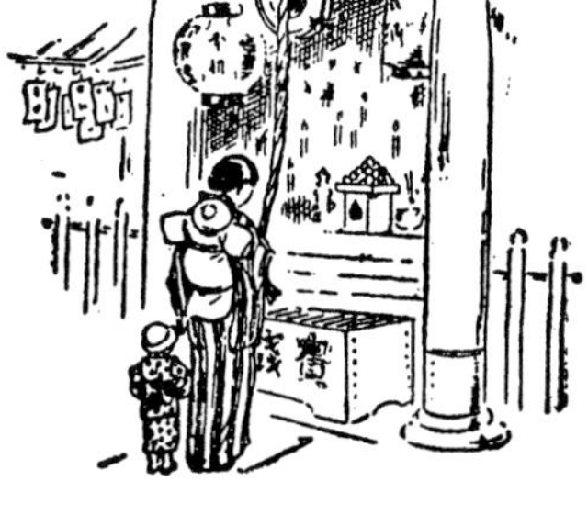

THE JAPANESE CLASSIC "NO" PLAYS

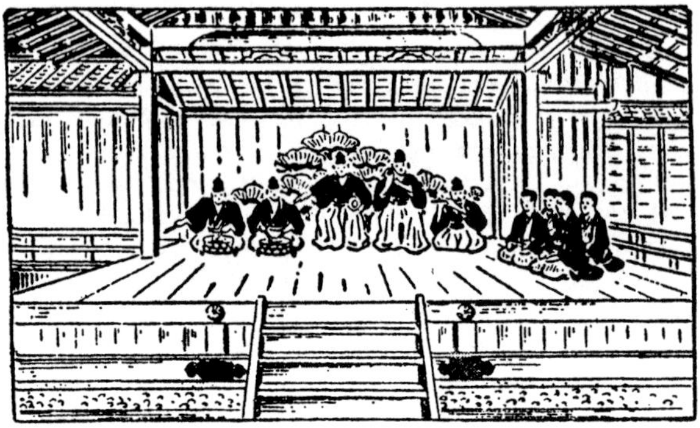

A "No" Stage.

The word *No*, used to designate a certain kind of theatrical performance, is obscure in its origin, and Japanese scholars and Buddhist priests have various theories. One of the most plausible is that *No* was a term in Buddhism and that it referred to the unity of mind between the audience and the actors, chorus and musicians. The *No* is not a dance, since it is a creative movement, a unity of the arts rather than a mere dance.

The *No* has a history of over 1,000 years. However, it was in 1368, under the patronage of Shogun Yoshimitsu, that it was elevated and became the aristocratic entertainment of the court and nobility which it continues to be today.

There are similarities in the *No* to the ancient Greek drama in its principle of unity and use of pure sound in the place of music. The *shite*, or leading actor, is the pivot upon which the whole performance turns. The chorus and the musicians are like his two arms—they aid and support him. The music is not music in the western sense; it is pure sound only. Three drums and a flute are the instruments employed, while the chorus, kneeling at the right of the stage, comments on the characters and describes the changing scenes. The principal actors speak, but present all the emotions of the play by their actions and the type of mask they wear for various interpretations—the masks succeeding in concentrating attention upon the theme of the play.

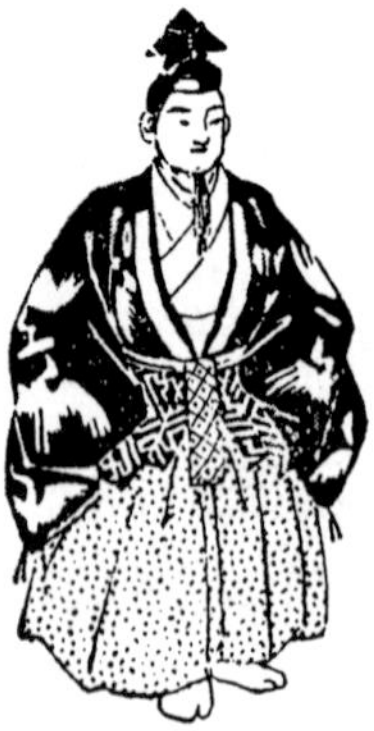

Among the most interesting things about the *No* are the imaginative, wonderfully suggestive properties, the houses, castles, shrines, boats, bell towers, etc., being made of pieces of bamboo.

There are six different types of plays: the divine *No* in which the gods appear; the fighting *No* where the character describes war, involving much acrobatic performance; the Katsura Hagoromo, featuring the life of women; the Dojoji, or the devils—which always are in the form of women, though acted by men; the *No* dealing with human affairs, presenting some of the cardinal virtues of fidelity, justice, charity, etc.; and the Congratulation pieces, which form a lively ending.

"NO" MASKS

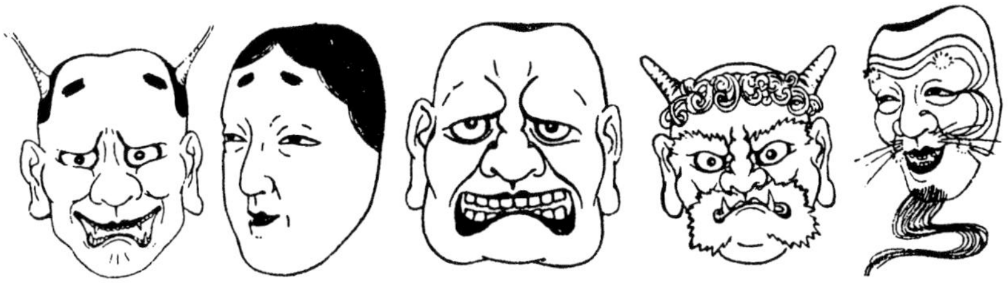

The chief performers of *No* plays wear masks indicating the characters portrayed. Mask carvers in olden days were master craftsmen. Such of their masks which have been handed down are highly prized and valued.

The masks are neutral and expressionless, as the essence of the art is to show emotions by gestures and poses, not by facial expressions, and marvellously well do these masks of painted wood differentiate the most delicate shades of human feeling. The plays themselves are brief, all having close connection with Buddhism. In fact, there is not a single play among the 300 *No* dramas in existence in which a priest does not appear—one whose divine power of meditation or prayer does not invariably lead the ghost of a warrior or lady, a flower or a tree into the blessing of Nirvana.

The aim of the *No* play is to express a desire or yearning, not for beauty, but for the beauty we dream of, therefore the worth of the play depends, not upon the truth or moral, but upon the total effect of the beauty produced—which is poetry.

The language of the *No* is classic, a mixture of the Chinese and old-Japanese styles, which cannot be readily comprehended by those who are not versed in these styles. At a play most of the audience closely follows the actors in the book of the play, the actors employing *utai*, or recitative chanting, in speaking their parts, which are composed, as a rule, of 7 and 5 syllabled phrases alternately. The actors' costumes are always similar to those worn in ancient days. Only a few actors are on the stage at the same time, and the stage itself has, except in rare cases, little setting.

ODORI ("DANCE")

The Japanese *Odori* is a dance very different from the Western dance; not the least difference is that women are not held in men's arms. In fact, apart from men who make it a profession, the *odori* is seldom danced by men.

The *Odori* is a posture dance, with slow movements of the body, feet, arms and hands. The dancers employ fans, sprays of blossoms, baskets of flowers, flags and other accessories according to the story the dancers endeavor to interpret. They are accompanied by one or more *samisen* players, and frequently by players on Japanese drums. At banquets and parties, geisha are often hired to perform for the entertainment of guests. They are well trained in the *Odori*. Neither expression nor emotion is shown on the faces of *Odori* dancers. In society, *Odori* dancing by young maidens is frequently engaged in as part of the entertainment of the evening.

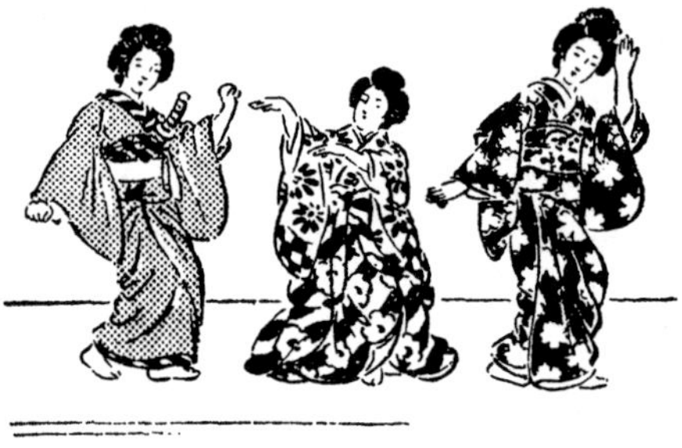

The *odori* of today is the same as that of the Tokugawa period. Many *odori* are adopted from the "No" plays, and the dancers strive to keep their faces as expressionless as the masks of the "No". No *odori* represents the present life of the Japanese. Each *odori* depicts a story, one of the *samisen* players singing the story—but the music is only supplemental to the dance itself, it is not paramount as in the Western dance.

The most elaborate and spectacular of the *odori* dances is the Miyako-*Odori*, which is performed at Kyoto five times daily during the month of April. It is one of the greatest stage spectacles in Japan. The 32 uniformly and richly-clad participants are all young and attractive geisha, from 15 to 18 years old, specially chosen and trained for this dance. They are assisted by a chorus of six singers, called *jikata*, and six *samisen* players on one side of the approach to the stage, and an orchestra of eleven girls on the opposite side who beat the *taiko* with drum-sticks, and *tsuzumi*, or "long snare drum beaten with the hand," both being drums of different shapes. Each season several different themes are portrayed: "The music of the Fifty Bells," "The Morning Sun on the Waves," etc., etc. The dance is always divided into nine scenes or acts, eight of them being shown with a graceful posture dance and one with music only. All are in beautiful settings and the costumes of the dancers are gorgeous creations.

In the spring-time in Tokyo, at the Shimbashi Embujo, geisha perform the Cherry and other dances.

See "Japanese Musical Instruments" descriptions.

(*Continued*)

ODORI ("DANCE")

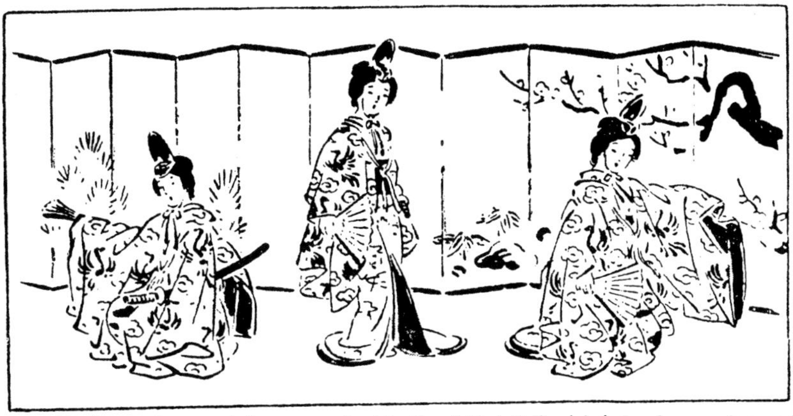

Perhaps the most famous *odori* is the "Dojoji," which is also performed in the "No". Its accessories are fans and *eboshi* ("priest hat"). Its legendary story is as follows :

Anchin, a young, handsome prince, brother of Emperor Sujaku, who, disguised as a priest, while on his travels with his sweetheart, Princess Onoutama, was entertained by a Wakayama *samurai* of high rank whose residence was near the river Hidaka-gawa. Kiyohime, the *samurai's* beautiful daughter, fell madly in love with Anchin, and ardently pressed her suit. Anchin declared it was impossible for him to marry her as he was betrothed to Princess Onoutama. Upon their departure, Kiyohime, wildly excited, tried to intercept Anchin, but, eluding her, the prince and princess fled, like deer, to the river,—jumped into a boat and were ferried across. Kiyohime, in hot pursuit, reached the river bank—but there was no boat or means of crossing the river. She ran hither and thither, bemoaning her fate, praying fervently for aid. So intense was her desire and emotions that she was transformed into a dragon, and easily made the crossing. In the meantime Anchin had taken refuge inside the bronze temple bell of Dojoji, not far from the river, but his weight caused the bell to crash to the ground—and he was entrapped. Kiyohime, following his train, wound her dragon-like form 7½ times around the bell, creating such an intensive heat that the bell, Anchin, and herself were dissolved into hot water.

The lengend does not say what became of Princess Onoutama, but as women were not allowed to enter the temple precincts, it is assumed that she remained outside the grounds.

Dojoji, a temple of the Tendai sect, is over 1000 years old. In its precincts memorial stones for Anchin and Kiyohime may still be seen. The moral of this legend, which the dance is supposed to inculcate, is that a woman's love for a man is more vivid and emotional than that of a man's love for a woman, and therefore a woman's love should not be lightly spurned.

Almost as famous as the "Dojoji" are the Odori : *Shiokumi*, *Urashima*, and *Matsushima*, among others. The last portrays sightseeing at Matsushima. It is regrettable that space does not permit descriptions of these dances.

Many places in Japan are noted for their Odori : Niigata, Akita, and other cities and towns, but these are local dances, not universal dance like those mentioned.

Concluded.

SHAKESPEARE IN JAPAN

The Shakespeare Association of Japan was organized on April 23, 1929, and, yearly, on April 23, a "Shakespeare Day" is celebrated by the Association—this day being generally regarded as the day of Shakespeare's birth, on the strength of a tradition that he died upon an anniversary of his birthday, his death occurring on April 23, 1616. The object of the Association is to collect works by and about Shakespeare, and material relationg thereto, and to encourage and promote the study of Shakespeare in Japan.

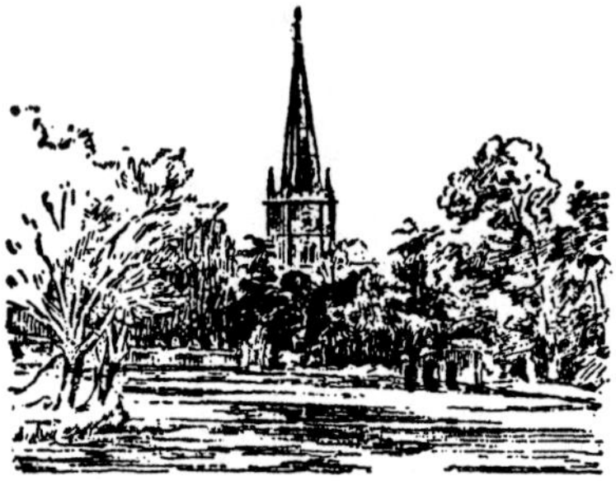

HOLY TRINITY CHURCH. The burial place of William Shakespeare. View from the garden of the Memorial Theatre on the River Avon.

"He was not of an age but for all time."

In 1877, W. A. Houghton, an American professor, was called by the Tokyo University (now the Tokyo Imperial University) to the newly-established chair of English Literature to lecture on Shakespeare. He is generally considered the first Shakespearian lecturer in Japan. Among others of his famous students were Yuzo Tsubouchi, now D. Lit., the Honorary President of the Association, Sanae Takata, D. Lit., former President of Waseda University, Tokyo—the latter being the first Japanese teacher of Shakespeare. In 1929, Dr. Tsubouchi finished his translation into Japanese of the complete works of Shakespeare, in 40 volumes—a monumental task in the face of unusual linguistic barriers. The Tsubouchi Memorial Theatre Museum was so named in honor of the Doctor, and to commemorate his great achievement.

Prior to the foundation of the Association, the study of Shakespeare's works had been carried on, though not systematically, for about sixty years, and occassionally some of Shakespeare's plays are staged in the theatres, at Waseda, and elsewhere.

* * *

In the villa garden of Prof. Sanki Ichikawa, D. Lit., President of the Association, there has been laid out a Shakespeare garden, the first of its kind in Japan, which contains about 100 species of flowers and plants mentioned in the poet's works.

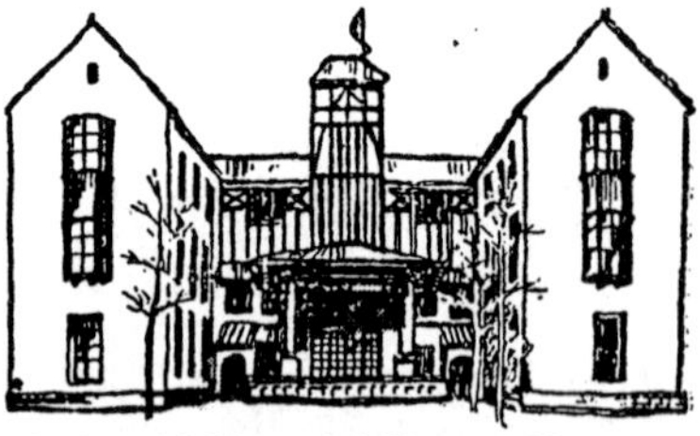

Tsubouchi Memorial Theatre Museum.

Tsubouchi Memorial Theatre Museum.

Modelled architecturally after the Fortune Theatre, London, formerly situated in Golden Lane,—when it was known as "Master Alley's Fortune Theatre." In its lobby there was a statue of the "God of Fortune." The theatre was located at Bankside, on the Thames.

KEN-JUTSU OR THE ART OF HANDLING A SWORD

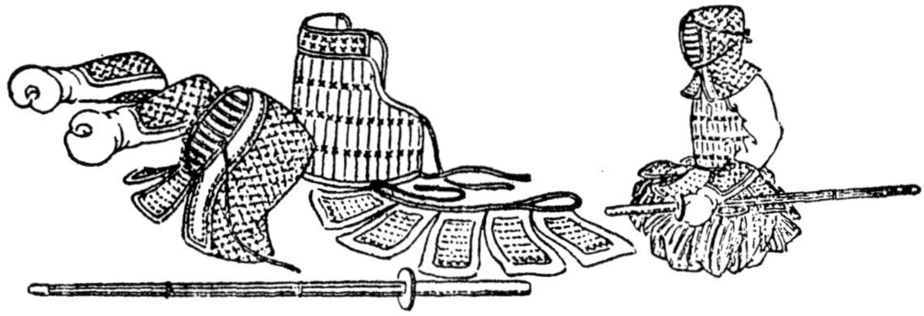

Fencing is an art as old as Japanese history. This art developed rapidly with the rise of the military class in the 12th century. Simultaneously the art of sword making was also developed. Every samurai looked upon his sword as the embodiment of his spirit. With the introduction of modern military methods, fencing was almost forgotten for a time, but was revived later as an interesting kind of gymnastic exercise and as an aid to mental discipline, particularly among students and military officers.

In fencing bouts each contestant wears a face-guard, a plastron to cover the trunk, and gauntlets to protect the arms and hands. Swords made of four bamboo strips 4 ft. 4 in. long, of which the leather-covered handles are 1 ft. 3 in. long, are used instead of real swords, and are held by both hands, 5 in. apart. In making a slash one aims at the face (front or side), the trunk, or the arms; in making a thrust, at the throat of one's opponent. When either contestant is hit in any one of these places, he is considered beaten. A match consists of three contests, the winner of two of them being the victor. Mere skill in hitting an antagonist is not prized so much as are exhibitions of coolness, presence of mind, and the few openings offered—which are characteristic of the attack and defence of an accomplished fencer.

In many of the large cities of Japan, halls for instruction in fencing are maintained. Visitors who desire to witness the contests are welcomed. In all Japanese boys' schools above the primary grade fencing is taught as a physical exercise.

KYU-JUTSU OR THE ART OF ARCHERY

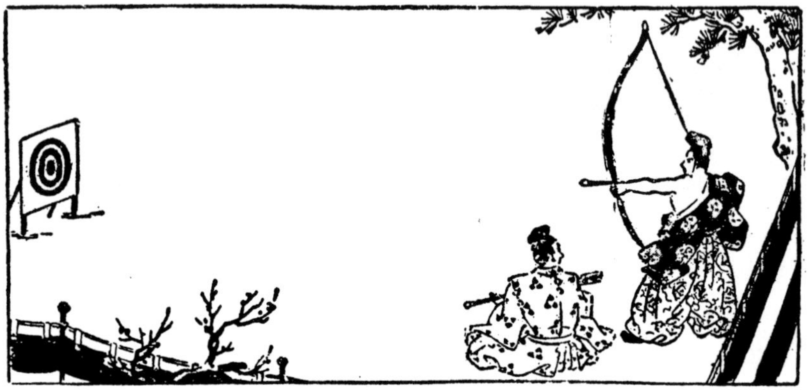

In olden days archery was an important branch of Japanese military art, but due to the widespread use of firearms in the later years of the Tokugawa period, bows and arrows lost their value as implements of actual warfare. However, today, archery practice is in vogue throughout Japan, and on suburban trains of large cities, and elsewhere, one frequently sees devotees of the art, old and young, recognizable by their long bows in cloth cases, on their way to or from archery grounds. Archery practice is now regarded as a graceful exercise which develops a coordination of eye and brain.

A famous archery court in olden days was the 396 ft. range back of the Sanju-sangen-do ("The Hall of 33 ken") temple, Kyoto. An archer's frame was proportionate to his success at this long range. Similar ranges were established in other places.

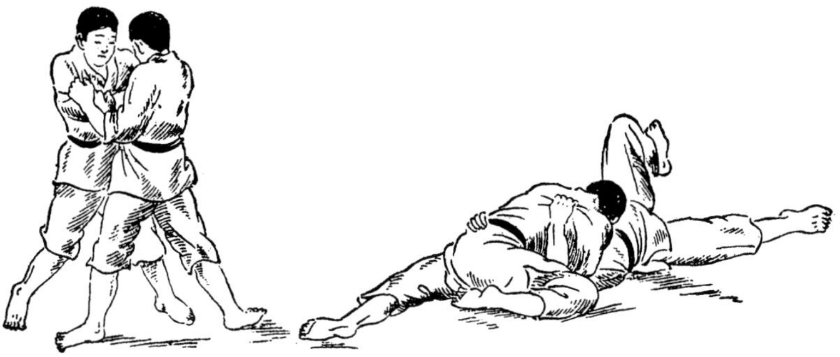

JU - JUTSU or JUDO

Ju-jutsu a kind of wrestling, once confined to Japan, is now known the world around. *Ju-jutsu* means the "Art of Suppleness." It is a mode of self-defence for women as well as men. Certain grades of the police are instructed in *ju-jutsu*, many colleges and schools have classes in it, and there are many private schools of instruction. Modern *ju-jutsu*, due to the effort of Mr. Jigoro Kano, M.P., is a combination of the best methods of the different schools of this art.

The secret of *ju-jutsu* consists in utilizing the strength of an antagonist to one's own advantage, not to match strength with strength, but to win by yielding to strength, in other words, by pliancy, and it often happens that a skilful weak man is victor over a stronger opponent. There are several methods: to hurl an antagonist down, to hold him down on the ground so that he cannot move, or to strike or push him with the fist, and to kick a vulnerable spot with the foot in order to bring him down. To attain skill in *ju-jutsu*, mental discipline constitutes an essential qualification. One must be self-composed, self-reliant, and above all alert to utilize either the strength or the mistakes of one's opponent. Contestants wear cotton jackets and trousers—no shoes. The jacket is reinforced in its upper part and in its short sleeves with a heavy layer of strong hand-knitted cotton, and is held in place by a belt of the same material. Included in the course of instruction are various ways of causing apparent death by pressure, and of recalling to life from such swoons, also methods of disjointing bones as well as principles connected with moral training.

Through the Japan Tourist Bureau, foreign visitors are permitted to witness the exhibitions at the Kodokwan, the famous training headquarters in Tokyo. Yearly on January 12, when the Kagami-biraki is celebrated there, the contests and programs are elaborate, but Kodokwan *ju-jutsu* is worth seeing at any time.

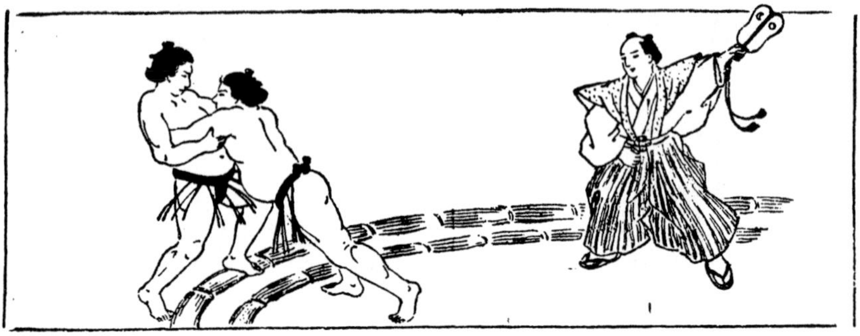

SUMO OR JAPANESE WRESTLING

Sumo (lit., "horn power") is a characteristic sport of Japan. Established over 1950 years ago it long has been regarded as the national game of Japan. Tokyo wrestlers, under the control of the Wrestlers' Association, constitute two camps, the "East" and the "West." Yearly, in January and May, these camps compete in championship tournaments, each of 10 days duration, at the Kokugi-kwan, in Tokyo, the great, roofed wresting amphitheatre which seats about 13,000 spectators. When champions wrestle, the place is packed. Victory or defeat means much to the contestants inasmuch as their rank is respectively raised or lowered according to the result, and incidentally the amount of their pay is affected. During the rest of the year these wreslers give exhibitions throughout the country.

The wrestlers are gigantic men of enormous girth. They often eat ten or more times as much as the average man and drink quantities of sake and beer, disregarding all the training rule so rigorously followed in the Western world. They appear to be overburdened with fat but underneath the fat constant practice gives their muscles great power and flexibility. Also, as many of the rules are based on principles of leverage, weight counts to advantage. They habitually wear their hair long, twisted into a knot on the crown of the head, in the samurai manner. In the ring they are naked, except for a black loin cloth.

The outer edge of the wrestling ring is square. The small elevated platform rests on a foundation of heavy straw rice-bales. The ring itself, 12 ft. in diameter, is sanded, its boundary line being marked by a double circle of thick straw ropes about 4 in. apart, half-buried in the sand, the inner circle constituting the stage of the contest. From each corner of the platform rise slanting pillars of wood that support a roof, the pillars draped in red, black, green, and white for the four directions of the compass, the roof draped in purple bunting. At each pillar sit retired wrestlers, the trainers, who act as judges in disputed cases. For centuries the families of Shiga and Yoshida, the latter represented to this day by a descendant, have acted as umpires. They wear the ancient style of costume and carry a lacquered fan (their badge of office) of the type once used by generals to signal in battle. By lifting or lowering the fan, the umpire emphasizes his orders. A contestant wins if he throws his opponent or if any part of his body, his knee or hand touches the ground or if even one foot is forced or placed outside the ring. There are 48 paramount rules governing the 12 throws, 12 twists, and 12 throws over the back.

Each contest is brief; the action rapid and exciting. It generally lasts less than a minute though the getting-ready process may take 15 minutes or more, for the reason that each contest waits for the psychological moment when their preparedness is perfectly balanced so that the two may begin their contest on an equal basis.

FOOTBALL IN JAPAN

Kemari—" Kicking Ball "

You may be surprised to learn that football has been played in Japan for a thousand years: but the Japanese game is not at all like the lively soccer game of the West, or like its strenuous rugger. On the contrary, the Japanese game is played by men dressed in ancient constumes, their gowns of gold and silk brocade, their hats of strange shape, and fans and paper handkerchiefs are included in their outfit At the present time this ancient sport is preserved and fostered at the Peers' Club, Kyoto, and the players are of the noblest blood of Japan although they have been forced to become everyday business men.

Lady Murasaki Shikibu, a lady-in-waiting to Empress Akiko, author of the famous classic romance *Genji-Monogatari* (probably written about 1001-15 A.D.—long before Chaucer, Dante, and Boccaccio flourished in European literature) mentions that her hero, Prince

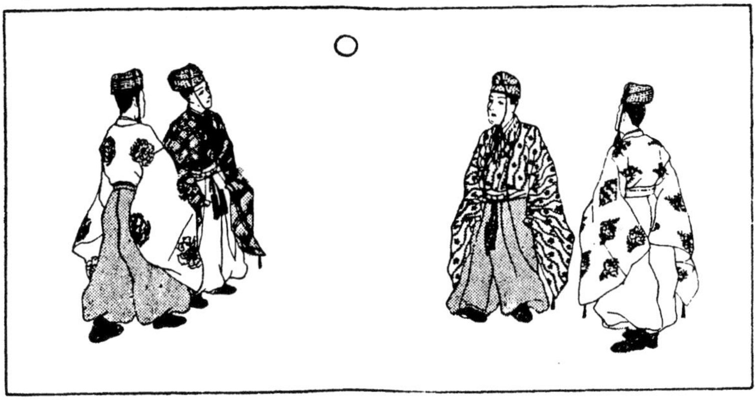

Genji, watched a game played by some of his courtiers. At that period, football was a more active game than that described below. The players formed opposing teams and there were goal-posts: a pine tree, a maple, a willow, and a cherry-tree, growing in tubs, two on each side of the grounds, between which the ball was kicked.

Kemari originally came from China, about 611 A.D. The sport was a diversion for emperors, princes, and lesser folk, but from about the middle of the last century there were no longer oppotunities for elegant diversions, and *Kemari* was one of the pastimes that fell into discue—except at the Kyoto Peers' Club, where it has never been allowed to die, and where on New Year's Day, on May 17, July 7, October 20, and on December 22, semi-public exhibitions are given. The playing ground is a space about 50 ft. square. The ball, somewhat smaller than a modern volley ball, is made of leather on a bamboo framework and is inflated to give it resiliency. It is not perfectly round, but is bound around the middle to produce a slight bulge on either side, and a small string, like a lace, can be used to pick it up. The players wear shoes of leather, their ankles being thickly bound with cloth, as the kicking is done with the instep.

Kemari now is an individual sport, not a contest. It requires a high degree of skill. The players stand in a cirle and the ball is kicked from one to another with the object of keeping it going as continuously as possible, and it is the desire of each individual player to perform the feat with graceful ease.

Before the play an ancient ceremonial ritual is observed, conducted by the oldest player. After that, formality ceases, faces break out into happy grins and the game becomes lively, but not rough, with shouting and by-play, like that of a lot of youngsters. The play covers several periods, each limited to the time required (about 20 minutes) for a stick of incense to burn out.

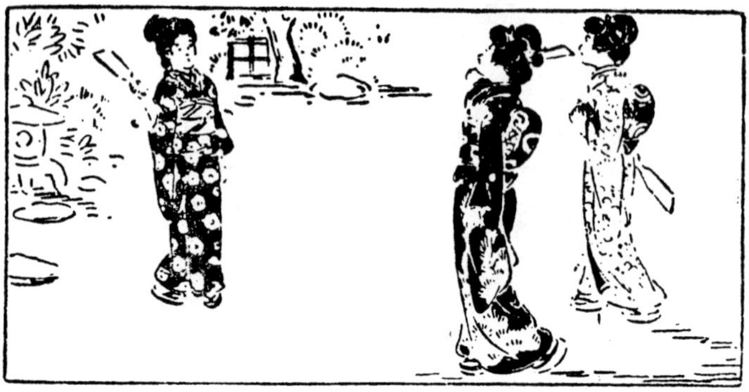

BATTLEDORE and SHUTTLECOCK

Oibane, or Battledore and Shuttlecock is, in Japan, a game played during the New Year holidays. In December magnificent displays of *hagoita,* or battledore, begin to appear at the large toy shops and department stores. They are priced five sen to several hundreds of yen. The more expensive ones are elaborately decorated on one side, often representing a popular actor in a play of the current year. Some of the *hagoita* are about 4 feet long and 1½ feet wide at the broader end. These larger ones are purchased by wealthy men for their favorite geisha but are never used in play. Many subjects are painted or worked out in padded silk on the back of both the large *hagoita* and the smaller ones: the Seven Gods of Luck, their Treasure Ship, dancers, beautiful women, pictures of the cranes, pine trees, bamboo, and plum trees. In olden days some *hagoita* were embellished with gold and silver decorations.

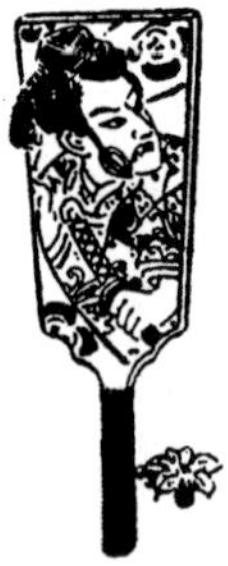

The game consists in batting the shuttlecock to and fro with the battledore. The one who misses the shuttlecock more times than the opponent often has her face marked with charcoal or white powder as a penalty, and it is a laughable sight to see a number of young girls in their beautiful holiday clothes with their faces so besmudged.

It is believed that the game originally came from China. One version of the origin of this New Year amusement is that it grew out of the belief that it was a charm against mosquitoes. In autumn dragon flies devour mosquitoes and the shuttlecock is said to resemble a dragon fly. The playing of battledore and shuttlecock is believed to have become a definitely established New Year pastime about the year 1800.

JAPANESE INDOOR GAMES

"GO"

Go is the national indoor game of Japan. To the Japanese this ancient pastime symbolizes the never-ending battles between the "black crow and the snowy heron." As a mere pastime *Go* is easily learned and a moderate amount of study enables one to become a fair player, but higher ranges of skill are attained only by persistent labour. Professional players often carry on one game for many hours, sometimes for days, and even without keeping a record they remember the exact order of their hands when replacing them upon resumption of the game.

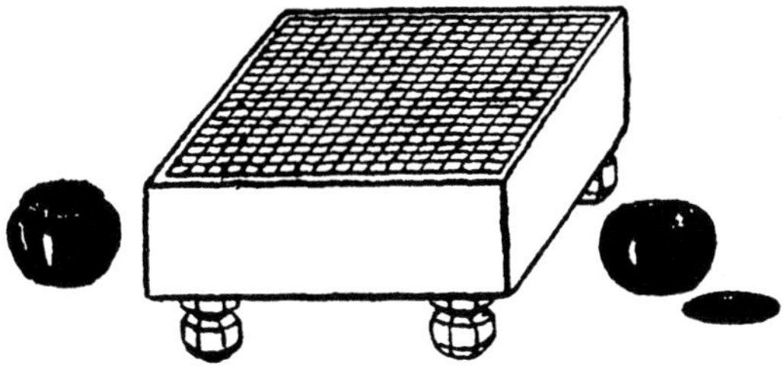

Casual foreign observers of *Go* inappropriately liken it to "checkers." With justice, *Go* is considered more difficult than chess, its wider field affording more numerous ramifications.

Go is played on a square wooden block, called *Goban*, its surface being lined so that the intersections of the lines make 361 *me*, or crosses. These crosses may be occupied by 180 white and 181 black stones (*ishi*). The white stones are made of shell, the black, of slate. Nine spots on the board, called ***seimoku***, are supposed to represent the chief celestial bodies; the white and black stones represent day and night, and the number of crosses, the 360 degrees of latitude, exclusive of the central cross, called *taikyoku*, that is, the Primordial Principle of the Universe. Once a stone is placed on the cross lines it cannot be lifted unless captured by the opponent.

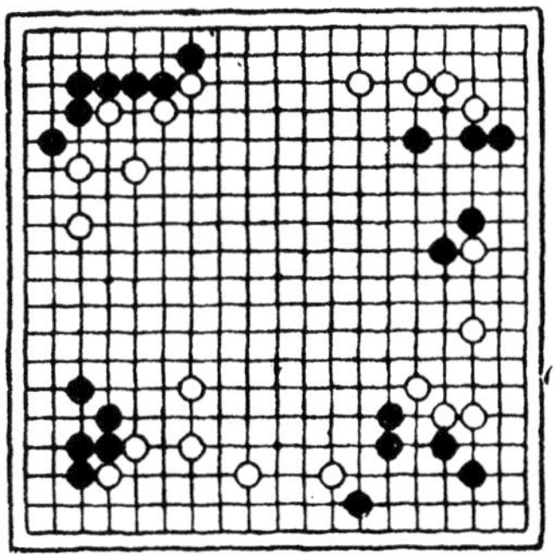

Notwithstanding that *Go* was introduced into Japan from China some time between 724-56 A.D., Chinese now come to Japan for instruction by experts in the higher intricacies of the game.

This description is continued.

JAPANESE INDOOR GAMES

"GO"

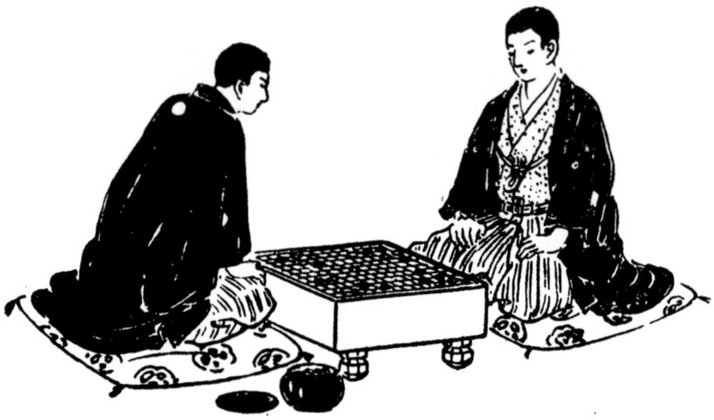

The object of the game of *Go* is to obtain possession of the larger portion of the board. This is done by so surrounding the mé of one's opponent that they are bottled up, so to speak.

The placing of the stones calls for so much skill, and the many plans of campaigns are so complicated that a teacher is indespensable. Guests may obtain a teacher upon request. Few foreigners have succeeded in getting beyond a rudimentary knowledge of this interesting game.

There are nine degrees, or classes, of proficiency in the game, the ninth being the highest point of excellence attainable.

Etiquette of *Go*. If the players are equally matched, they alternate in playing with the white stone; if unequal, the weaker always takes the black, and odds are given by allowing him to occupy several, or all, of the nine spots or advantage points on the board, i.e., to place stones upon them at the outset, and even with such handicap, the more skilful player often wins.

Gomoku, the simple pastime played here and abroad, is a very different game, although it is played on a *Go* board, with the regulation *go-ishi* (round black and white stones). The object of this game is to be the first in getting five stones in a row in any direction.

KITSUNE-KEN (*Kitsune*—Fox, *Ken*—game; "game" is derived from "fist"), or TONOSAMA (*Lord Daimyo*)-KEN. More popularly, TOHACHI-KEN.

Tohachi-Ken is a popular game at convivial parties, especially when geisha are present, among whom the game is known as *Kitsune-Ken*. Three symbols or signs are employed: a lord or daimyo is represented by placing a hand on each knee; a rifle by one arm, generally the right, thrust out with closed fist; a fox, by placing the hands open near the ears—representing the ears of a fox.

Their values in this game are as follows: the daimyo is superior to the rifle, because he commands it; the rifle is superior to the fox because with it the fox can be killed; and the fox is superior to the daimyo because it can bewitch him, but the daimyo cannot kill the fox without the rifle, nor the fox use the rifle against the daimyo. This leads to a number of combinations.

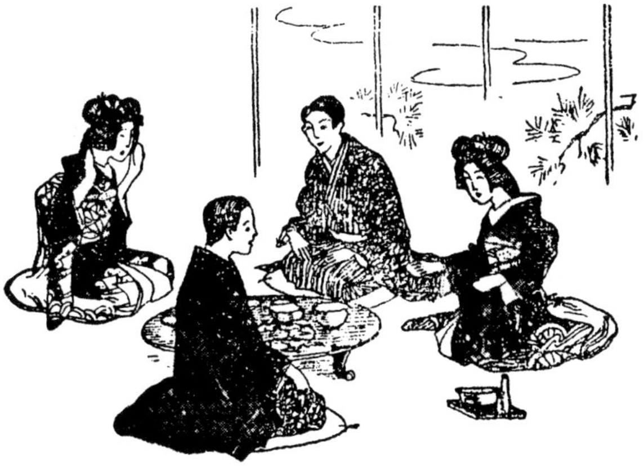

The players, always two, on beginning each game, first individually clap their hands, in unison one-two-three times, and then each quickly indicates one of the three signs. The game is continued until one player wins three times in succession. The losing player must drink a cup of *sake*, or give a forfeit. Monthly, contests are held in Tokyo.

The origin of the name, *Tohachi*, is said to be as follows: Tohachi Okumura, a patent-medicine pedlar, who lived during the last years of the Tokugawa Shogunate, imported from Holland what he called "mysterious medicine," which he hawked about the streets of Yedo, selling the compound for one-tenth of a sen a package, claiming it would cure all the ills the body is heir to. Stopping occasionally, he set up his stand and lauded the efficacy of his medicine. Gradually he collected his audiences, consisting principally of children—and, to entertain them, showed them how to play the game—which was named after him.

This *ken* was a favorite game with the *Hatamoto* ("Under the Flag"), the feudatory nobles who aided the *shogun* in wartime, furnishing men in proportion to the rice revenues granted them. They numbered 80,000. With the elimination of the *shogun*, the *Hatamoto* were dispersed—most of them ruined and driven either into trade, or poverty. During their existence they were perhaps the proudest and most over-bearing class in Japan, writes Lord Redesdale in his *Tales of Old Japan*.

JAN-KEN-PON

Jan-Ken-Pon, the most popular game in Japan, is played throughout the length and breadth of the land—principally by children—but also by adults of either sex, irrespective of class or social standing. It is played by two or more persons as a means of deciding priority of choice or preference in anything on occasions similar to those abroad when straws or lots are drawn, when persons are counted out with—" Ene, mene, mina, mo," etc., a coin tossed up, or matched—heads or tails—for a decision, etc.,

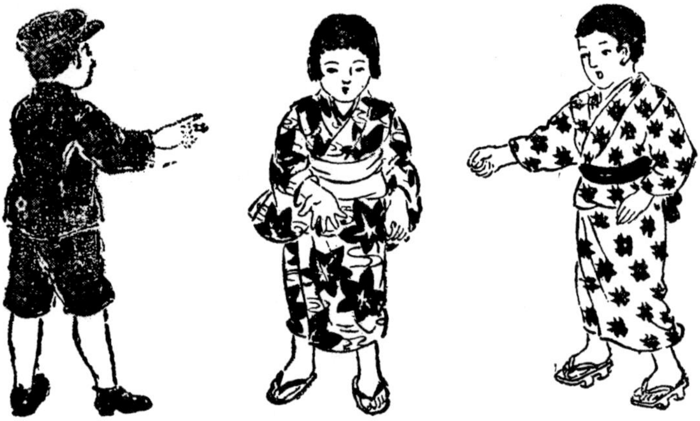

It is played with one hand held out respectively representing "paper," "scissors," "stone." " Paper is represented by the open hand, " stone " by the closed hand, and " scissors " by the closed hand with the index and middle fingers open. They have equal value, i.e., should three be playing and their hands happen to show the three forms there is no decision, and they try again. This also holds when two play. When one hand shows, " paper," the other " scissors," the latter wins as " scissors " will cut paper. If a " stone " and " scissors " are shown, the former wins because stone will dull scissors. If " paper " and " stone " are shown, " paper " wins because paper can cover or wrap up stone.

Beginning the game the players wave a closed hand in the air three times, generally calling out " Jan ! Ken ! Pon ! " as if to beat time, often stamping their feet in unison with each call. The form of the hand presented at the third stroke decides the winners. It is a fair game, no cheating can be done or dishonest practices employed. One is under the eyes of a rival all the time.

Jan-Ken-Pon, which according to some authorities literally means " Two, Fist and Open hand," seems to be of Chinese origin. It was first played at Nagasaki during the latter years of the Tokugawa regime.

JAPANESE INDOOR GAMES

HYAKU-NIN-ISSHU or "100-Persons-each one-Poem" Game

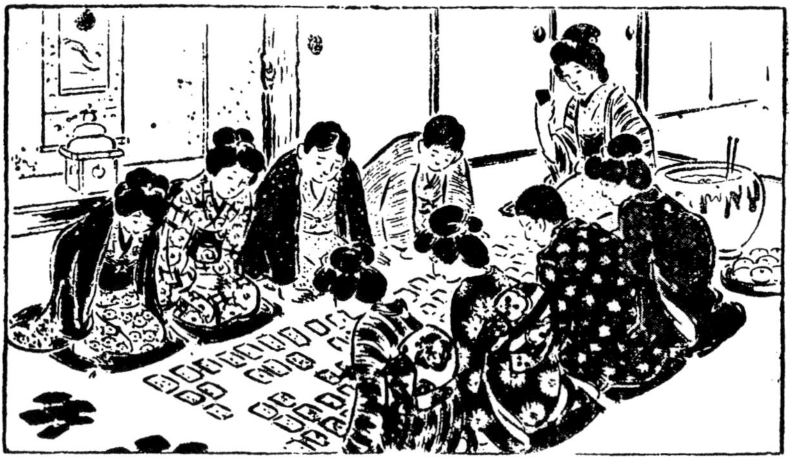

The ***Hyaku-nin-Isshu*** is a collection of 100 31-syllable poems, said to have been selected by Teika Fujiwara in the 12th century. They include poems written by 7 Emperors, 1 Empress, 20 Court Ladies, 57 Courtiers and 15 Priests. They consist of two sets of cards: one for the reader with the full poems; the other for the players with only the latter half of each poem. A Japanese 31-syllable poem consists of two parts—the upper made of 5-7-5 syllables and the lower of 7-7 syllables.

The game shown in the picture, which, as a rule, is played only at New Year, is called *Uta-garuta* (Uta: poem; garuta: card). In this game the players form two opposing groups and the cards, 50 to each group, are placed, face up, on the mat floor in full view of all. The first half of each poem is read out loudly by the reader and the corresponding card bearing the second half of the same poem is picked up. Cards may be picked up on either side. When a card of one group is picked up by an opponent that group is penalized by having a card added to their lot. The group that first gets rid of its cards wins the game. If an error is made in picking up a card from the opposing group, such card must be added to the side that made the error. When two play only 50 cards are used—25 for each player. There are different ways of playing this game although in all cases the skill in picking up quickly the second half of the poem upon hearing the first half, is the decisive factor.

The players must master all the 100 poems so thoroughly that one or two first words of the reader may suggest the whole poem instantly. Retentive memory as well as quickness of action is equally necessary for proficiency in *Hyaku-nin-Isshu.*

DUCK NETTING IN THE IMPERIAL PRESERVES

The netting of ducks, a pastime in olden days of the Tokugawa *shoguns*, is believed to be peculiar to Japan. In the grounds of the Hama Palace, Tokyo, are two lakes, from each of which leads a number of twisting, tortuous canals, 6 or 7 ft. wide, and rather shallow. At the end of each canal is an embankment. Tame ducks are kept on these lakes the year round to act as decoys for wild ducks. Both tame and wild ducks are fed daily at the ends of the canals, the low embankments concealing the feeders—and the ducks are not frightened. Gradually the wild ducks become accustomed to this trip from the lake down the canals to the feeding ground.

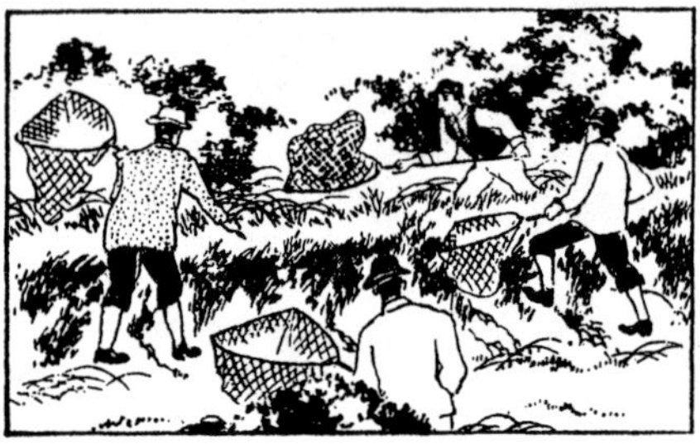

When a hunt is on, and while the ducks are feeding, a man creeps stealthily toward the lake and quietly lowers a steel screen into the water, cutting off the return passage of the ducks by water to the lake, thus confining them in restricted space. The netters, five on each side, then cautiously take their assigned places along the canal, keeping out of sight. The ducks, sensing trouble, rise into the air from the water. Then such of the netters who have the luck and the knack bag them in large long-handled nets in much the same way that a butterfly is netted. It is not considered especially difficult to catch ducks in this manner since they are slow in getting a start when rising from the water.

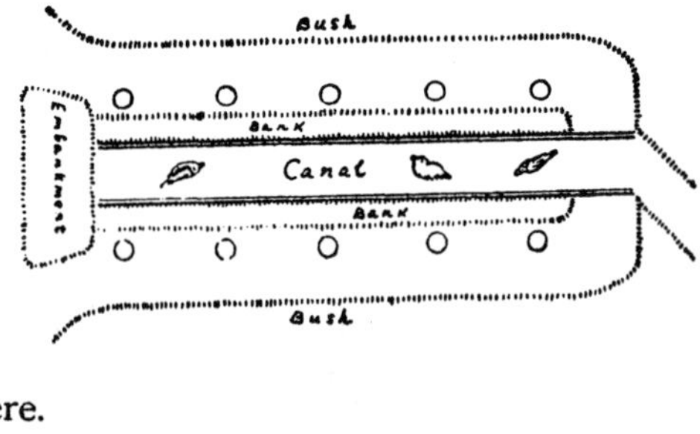

Other Imperial preserves are located elsewhere.

When the Imperial Family entertain visiting princes, distinguished persons, diplomats, or others, they usually invite such guests to a duck-netting party as one feature of their entertainment. Among the notables entertained in this way are the Prince of Wales, Marshal, Madam, and Mlle. Joffre, besides many others.

THE CHERRY (*Sakura*)

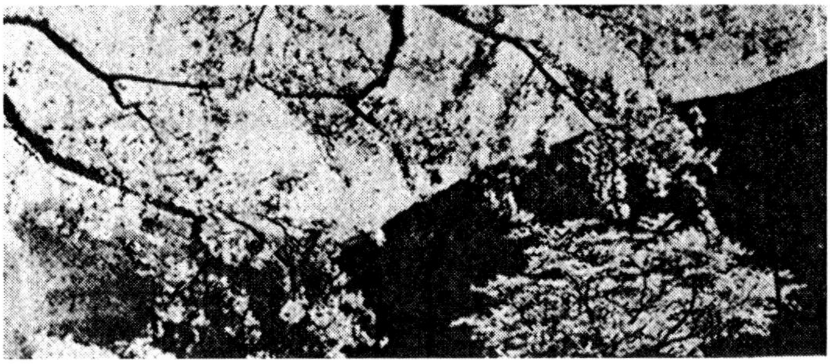

Cherry Blossoms at Kowakidani, near Miyanoshita.

The cherry, the pride of Japan, the coronation of spring, breaks out into pink clouds of blossoms that gradually spread over the Empire in early April. They transform the country into a fairyland of loveliness which has given Japan its floral name of "The Land of the Cherry-Blossoms." All through the month of April, the railway cars and all other conveyances are crowded with old and young, rich and poor, on their way to some noted place for cherry viewing (*hana-mi*).

Some of the young people are dressed in fantastic costumes as an incentive to merry-making—for it is a festive time, and for the brief life-time of the blossoms, a period usually not more than two weeks, the nation is practically on holiday and the cherry blossoms are the topic of the hour.

The *Sakura-no-hana*, the cherry blossom of Japan, is glorified and worshiped as no other flower in all the world. It symbolizes perfection to the Japanese and satisfies their aesthetic sense. It has been the inspiration and theme of thousands of poems by the rulers, by the "100 poets," and by the mass of the people.

Among many varieties of cherry trees there are sixteen principal species of blossoming trees. Almost all varieties bear their blossoms on leafless branches. The first trees to flower are the single white and pink varieties. After them arrive the double blossoms which last about two weeks. The trees do not bear fruit; only a few varieties bear tiny red pellets. The single mission of the tree is to be beautiful.

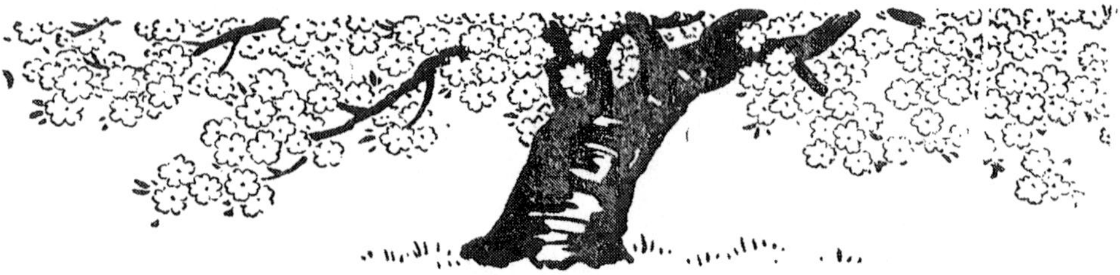

THE JAPANESE FLORAL CALENDAR

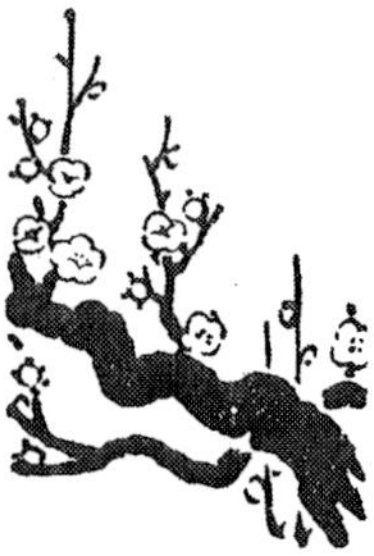

Each month of the year has its favorite flower or tree, their blooming seasons varying a little according to latitude and location in Japan's long stretch from north to south. January, the pine; February, plum; March, the peach and the pear; April, cherry; May, azalea, the peony, and wistaria; June, iris; July, morning-glory; August, lotus; September has the "seven grasses of Autumn"; October, the chrysanthemum; November, the maples; and December, the camellia. The "seven grasses" are the hagi (bush, or Japanese clover), susuki (pampas grass), kuzu (arrow-root), nadeshiko (wild carnation), ominaeshi (maiden flower), fujibakama (Chinese agrimony), and hirugao (convolvulus—wild morning-glory).

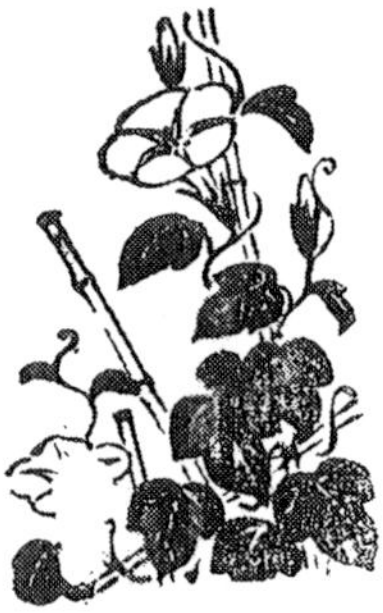
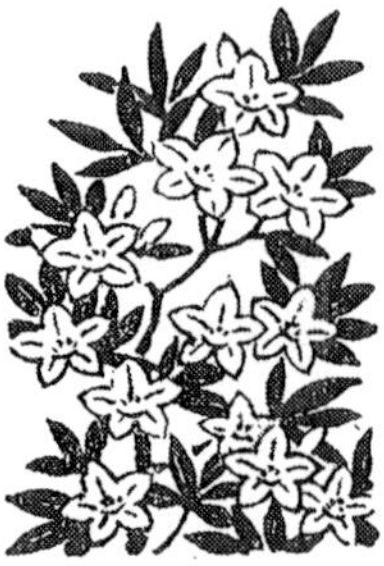

At Miyanoshita the seasonal blossoms appear as follows:
Plum (Ume), February and March. Peach (Momo) and Pear (Nashi), March and April. Cherry (Sakura) from April 10 to 30. Azalea (Tsutsuji), May and early June. Wistaria (Fuji), last half of May. Peony (Shakuyaku) and Tree-Peony (Botan), first half of May. Iris (Shobu), late May and early June. Morning-glory (Asagao), July to mid-September. Lotus (Hasu), late July to mid-August. Chrysanthemum (Kiku), October and November. Maples (Momiji), in full color from mid-October to the end of November.

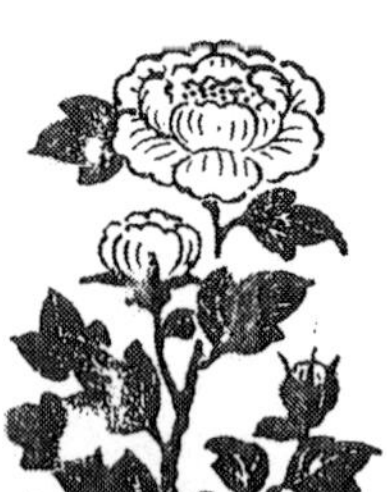
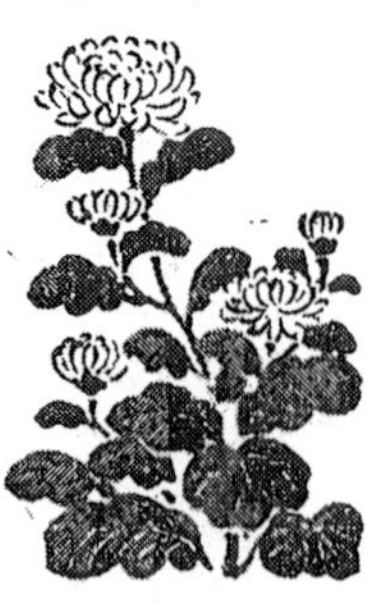

The orchids and other flowers in our greenhouses, heated by natural hot-spring water, are worth seeing.

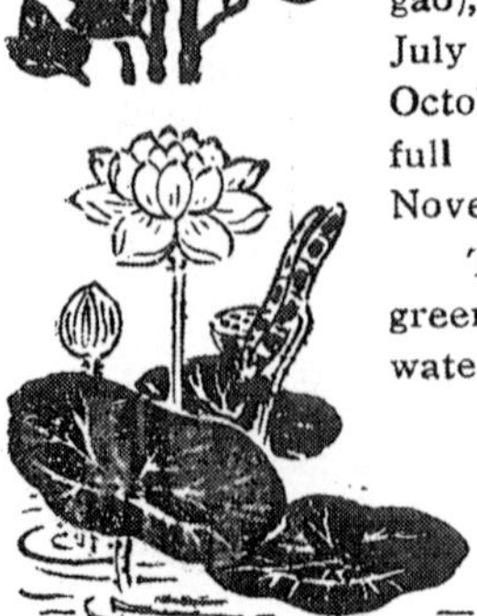
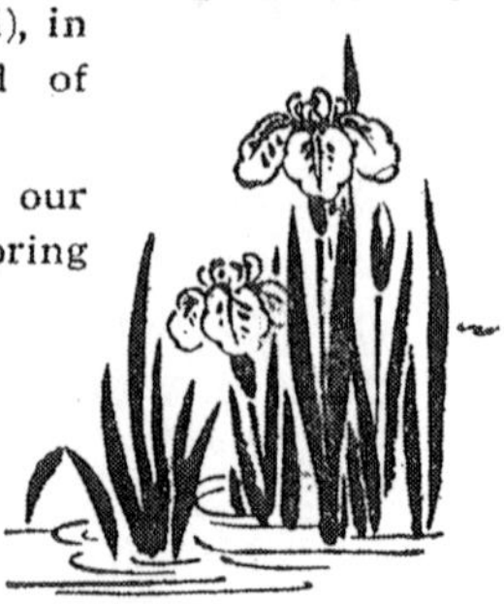

THE PINE TREE IN JAPAN

The real beauty of the pine tree can be seen only in Japan. In other countries, however large the trees may grow, shapely ones are very rare. Not a few pine trees in Japan are over 800 years old. During a long period of time the climate and other natural causes have combined to form the picturesque pine tree. Especially has this been the case with trees not growing in forests but standing alone, probably because their branches have been bent by the winter winds and thus formed into artistic shapes.

Pine trees are always to be found in Japanese garden. A very special art is required in the shaping of these trees. In late spring a gardener climbs the tree and trims the young sprouts by picking off the imperfect sprouts and allowing the tree to concentrate its nutriment on the perfect sprouts. From five to seven years are given these sprouts to grow into graceful shapes. While still very young the tree is formed into a desired shape by means of a system of strings or wires. The "Sailboat" at the Kinkakuji Temple, Kyoto, is a good example of the artificially shaped trees. It is made out of one pine tree and about a hundred years is supposed to have been spent in its making. When the tree was young a branch was bent into shape by means of strings and left for several years in that condition. The branch formed the hull of a boat. Then the central trunk was allowed to grow and was formed into the sail of the boat. Seventy or eighty years were needed for this operation. It is presumed that at present the tree is about four hundred years old. "Hair Dressing", or trimming, has been practised on the tree every spring during these four hundred years.

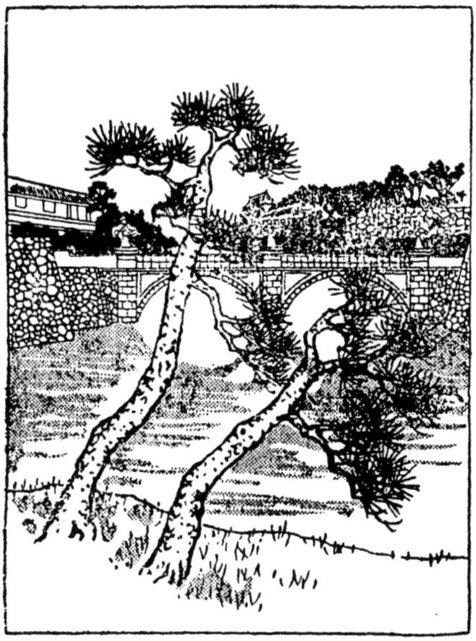

THE WOOD-CARVINGS IN THE FUJIYA HOTEL DINING-ROOM, MIYANOSHITA, HAKONE, JAPAN

Among the 44 large wood-carvings in the Fujiya Hotel dining-room are 12 representing the Year Names. In Japan each year in a cycle of 12 years bears the name of an animal, real or fabulous. The Year Names are as follows:

1. Rat............(*Ne*)
2. Ox ....(*Ushi*)
3. Tiger.........(*Tora*)
4. Rabbit ......(*U*)
5. Dragon......(*Tatsu*)
6. Snake.........(*Mi*)
7. Horse.........(*Uma*)
8. Sheep.........(*Hitsuji*)
9. Monkey......(*Saru*)
10. Cock ....(*Tori*)
11. Dog............(*Inu*)
12. Wild Boar...(*I*)

The same symbols are used in specifying certain hours:

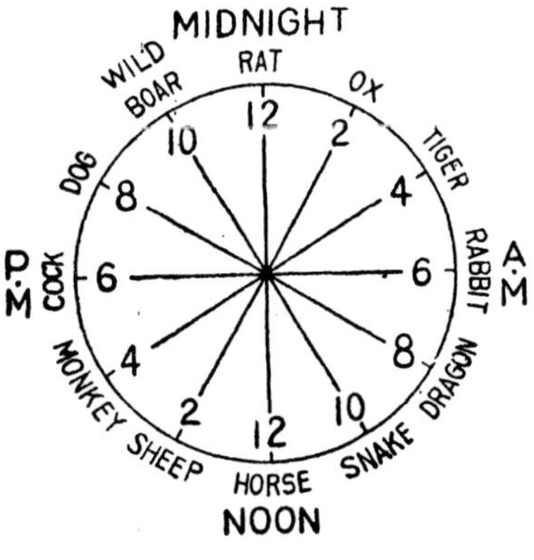

4 a.m. is the Tiger hour
4 p.m. is the Monkey hour

1932 was the Monkey Year; 1933, the Cock Year; 1934, the Dog Year; 1935, the Year of the Wild Boar—a new cycle beginning with that of the Rat of the following Year, i.e., 1936.

These symbols are used also to indicate points of the compass:

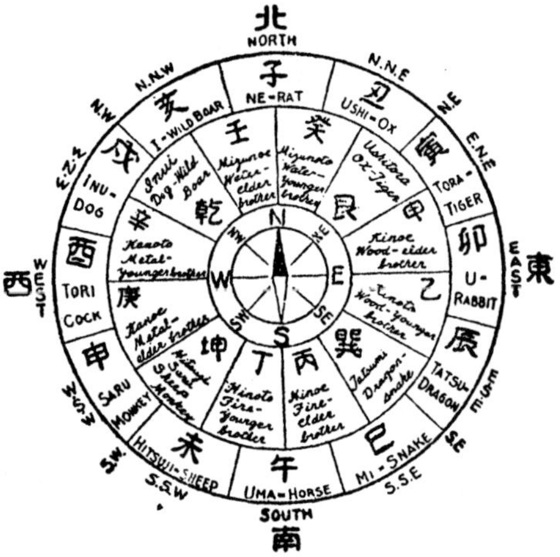

"Rat," N.; "Horse," S.; "Rabbit," E, and so on. The five "elements" are: Wood, Fire, Earth, Metal, Water. The each "element" is not used in compass diagrams. Each of the five elements is divided into two parts, termed respectively the "elder" and the "younger" brothers (*e* and *to*). They are known as the *juk-kan*, or "ten celestial stems."

DEPICTING SOME OF THE WOOD-CARVINGS IN THE FUJIYA HOTEL DINING ROOM—THESE SYMBOLIZE THE YEAR NAMES

By Edith de Garis

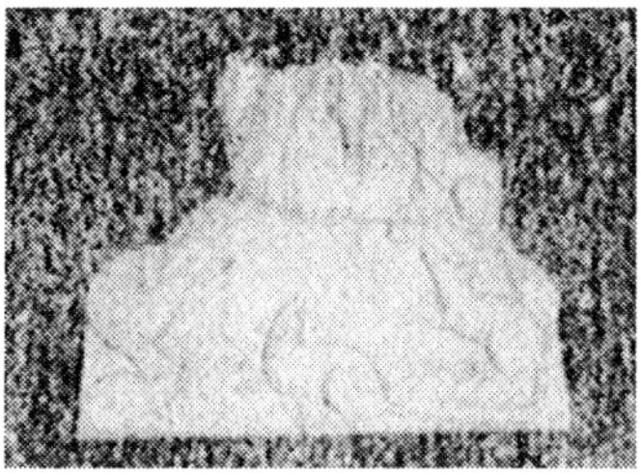

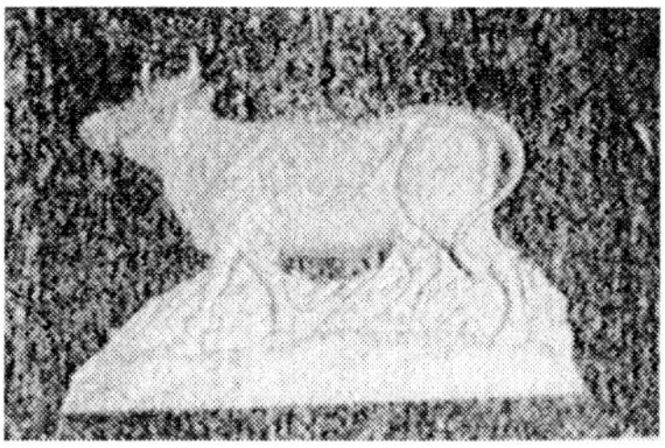

The rat of the first year is not an ordinary rat posed for a picture—It has seven rats joyously feasting on the New Year *mochi* (rice cake) with eyes ever alert for the terrible house cat.

The ox, sturdy and faithful, contemplates the cosmos as he chews his cud—while the tiger of the third year has caught a poor little animal, who, as can be seen, hopelessly pleads for mercy.

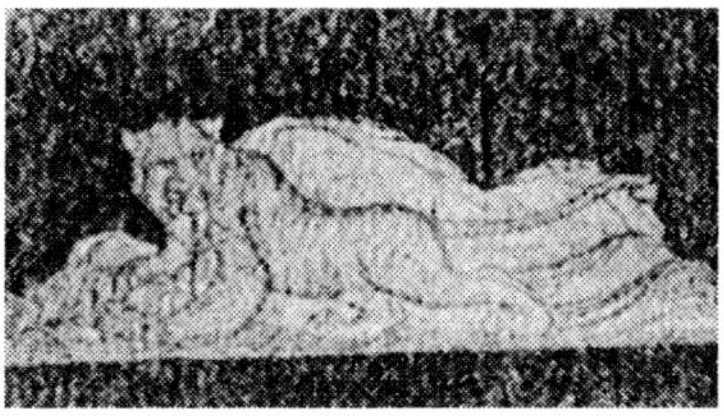

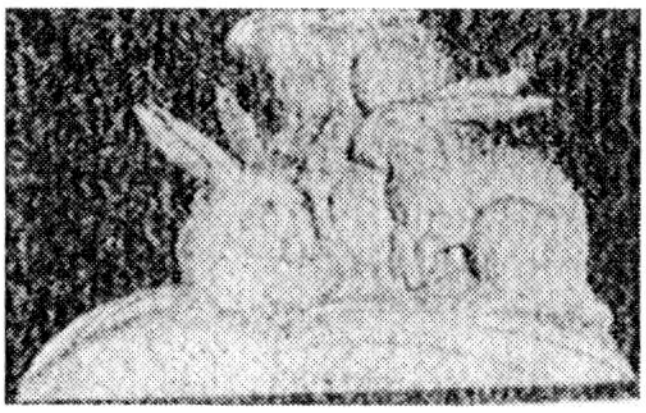

The three hares, or rabbits, of the fourth year wait expectantly for a titbit of lettuce-perhaps-and the dragon of the fifth year coils its spiked back around the base of Mt. Fuji, and in doing so figuratively embraces the three provinces which Mt. Fuji touches. While the dragon typifies benevolent constructive forces, the sign of the sixth year, the snake, or serpent, represents the destructive forces, and for this reason is depicted as struggling in the clutches of a ferocious tiger who will soon settle its malevolence.

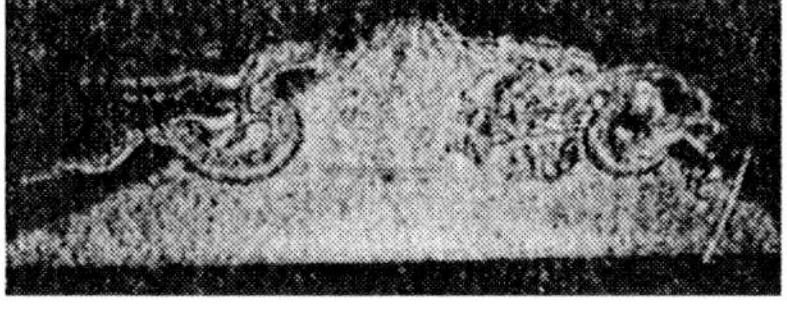

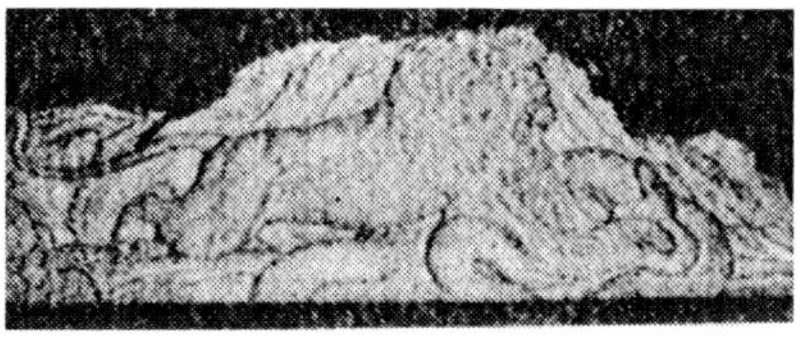

WOOD CARVINGS IN THE FUJIYA HOTEL DINING ROOM THAT SYMBOLIZE THE YEAR NAMES

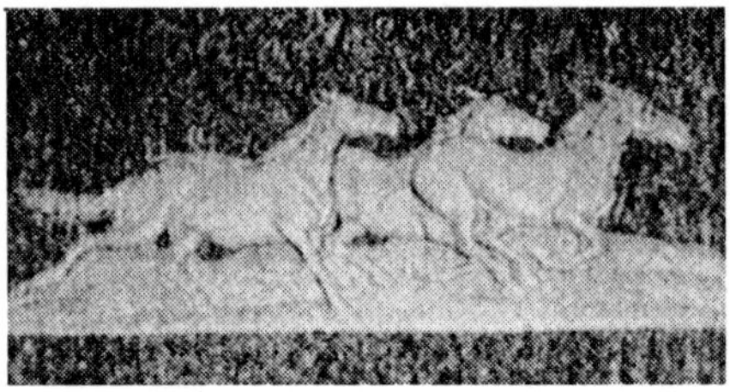
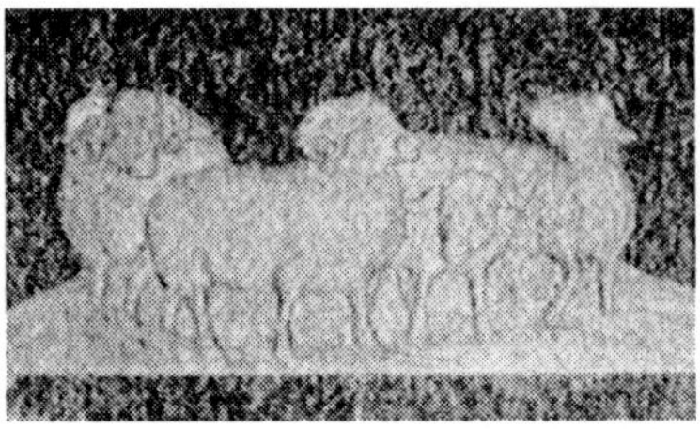

The horses of the seventh year gallop in a wild freedom across a plain, while the sheep of the eighth year huddle together for mutual protection, and the monkeys of the ninth year consider the meaning of life as applied to their own problems.

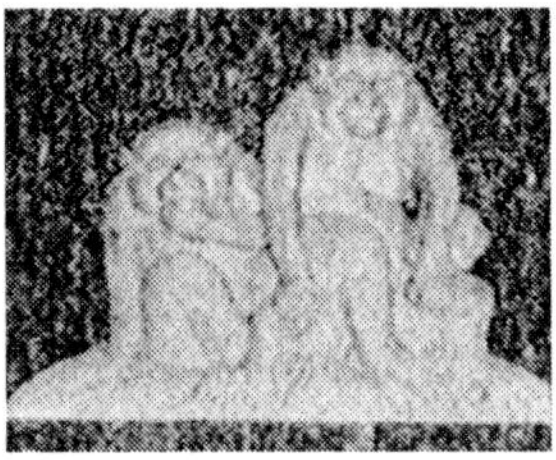
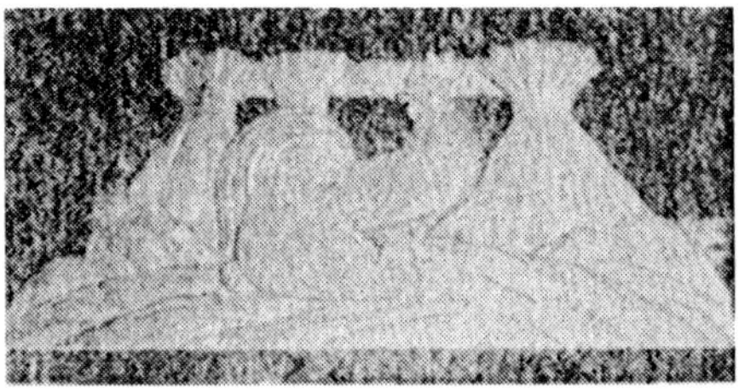

The cock, of all birds the most pugnacious and fearless, has become in Japanese symbolism the representative of valor: and this lord of the barnyard on the Fujiya Hotel wall is admonishing his family—is telling his wife that *her* children are all rascals.

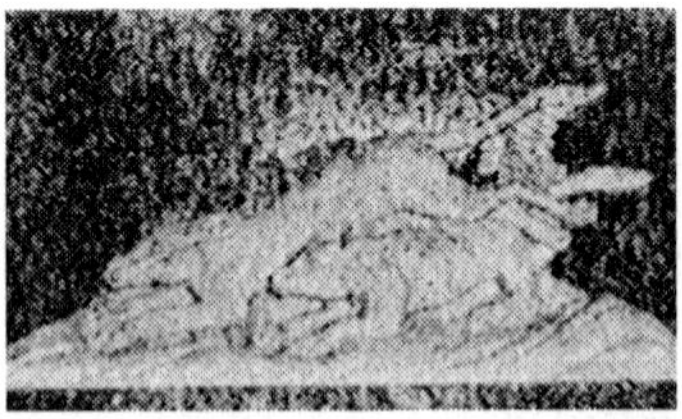
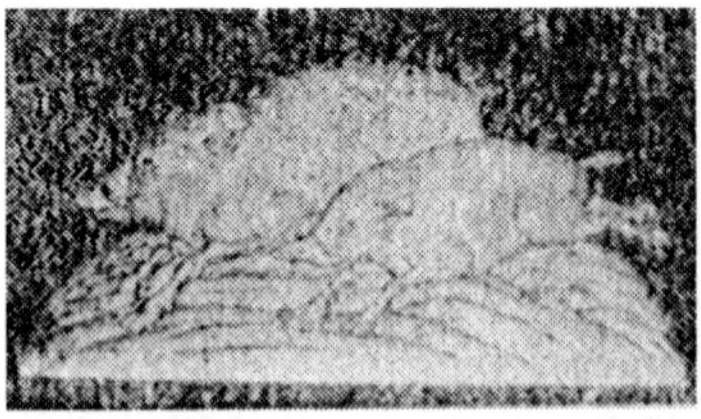

The two dogs of the eleventh year are making a spirited dash across the garden for the luscious bone they have somehow learned has just been thrown out, and the wild boars of the twelfth and last year of the cycle are in mad flight from a foe—one can almost hear the *cr-aa-ck* of the gun of the invisible hunter.

NAMES OF THE ORIENTAL ZODIAC

In Japan, the years, days, and hours each have their distinctive signs of the zodiac (*juni-shi*), whose order is as follows: rat, ox (or bull), tiger, hare (or rabbit), dragon, serpent (or snake), horse, sheep (or goat), monkey, cock (or bird), dog, and wild boar. The year 1933 was the year of the Cock (*Tori*) in the current 12-year cycle—which terminates in 1935, at the end of the Year of the Wild Boar (*I*)—the 12-year cycle beginning with the Year of the Rat (*Ne*) in 1936. These animals and the bird are often referred to in Japanese history, story, folklore, literature, art, and heraldry. The reader is referred to *The Wood Carvings in Our Dining Room* description.

The Japanese and Chinese also use what are called *juk-kan* ("10 celestial stems"), which are formed by dividing each of the five elements of wood, fire, earth, metal, and water, into two parts. These sub-divisions, called *e* and *to*, are said to signify natural and artificial, or elder and younger (brother), or upper and lower, or active and passive, or male and female. These ten stems, taken in conjunction with the twelve signs of the zodiac, form a sexagenary cycle, or cycle of sixty years, often called the "Cycle of Cathay." The current sexagenary cycle began on January 1, 1924; it will terminate at the end of 1983.

The 1st Year—The Year of the Rat ("Ne")

"Ne"—short for nezumi, the real word for rat

It is somewhat of a paradox that the rat should be so highly honored in Japan, inasmuch as that rodent is a real nuisance as well as a pest. It has the freedom of Japanese houses (also European houses) except as that freedom is interrupted by a weasel—which, when it chases a rat above the ceiling, causes sounds that are much like those of a clog dance going on above one's head. In Japan, as elsewhere, the rat is a disease carrier, and often a bounty of two or more *sen* is offered for every dead or live rat that is brought to a police-man at his box. Various are the rat-poisons, literally "rough on rats." One of them is named *neko-irazu* ("cat needed not"). Inouye, in his *Sketches of Tokyo Life*, says "a picture of a cat by Nitta Manjiro, a descendant of a famous loyalist general of the 14th century, will, if hung on a wall, keep rats at a distance." It is said that the famous carving of the "Sleeping Cat," by Hidari Jingoro, at the Tōshōgu Shrine, Nikko, serves to keep rats away from the premises.

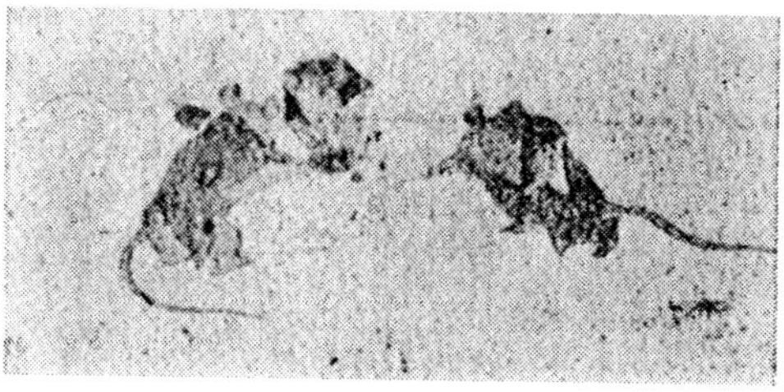

The rat is the symbol of the first year.

In Japanese art, the rat is often depicted upon metal-work, and in paintings. In literature, it figures only slightly. But the rat is most honored by its association with *Daikoku* ("God of Wealth"), one of the *Seven Gods of Luck*. While Daikoku is usually depicted standing, he is sometimes shown seated on two rice bales—indicative of the wealth of the country, and of individual wealth. Often rats are pictured gnawing at the bales, and so have become familiar attendants of this god. It is said that the rodents are introduced to suggest that all wealth must be well guarded, but it is more likely that the *nezumi* are associated with *Daikoku* because the festival of that happy deity is held on the "Day of the Rat."

The 2nd Year—The Year of the Ox or Bull ("Ushi")

The ox is the symbol of the 2nd year of the Oriental Zodiac.

There are many stories and tales in Japan in which the ox figures prominently, but the limitations of space prevent repetition here. In general, it may be said that the Ox year is considered a lucky year.

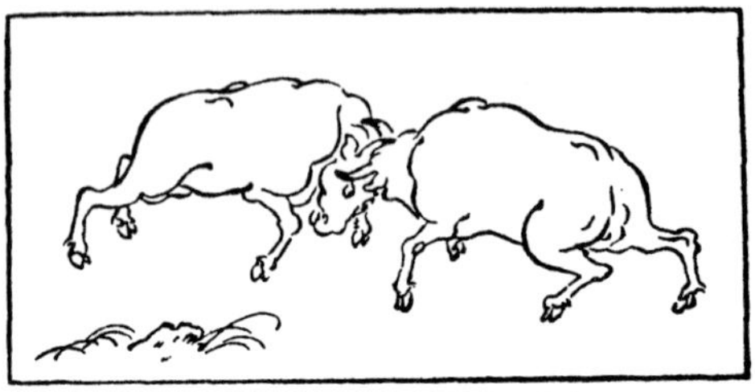

From a painting by Toba Soja.

The ox figures in a few Japanese proverbs. One to the effect that "a bee stings the horn of an ox" corresponds to the English proverb that "an elephant does not feel a fleabite," and "to kill the ox by straightening its horns" is the Japanese way of saying that "the remedy is worse than the disease"; and the Western proverb that "birds of a feather flock together," is expressed in Japanese by the saying, "oxen herd with oxen." Then the Japanese saying about "changing a cow for a horse" expresses the idea of "a change for the better." A "snail's pace" becomes in Japanese "as slow as an ox."

Ushi appears sometimes in the names of places and of persons. *Ushigome* in Tokyo seems to point back to the old ox-pasture stage in its early history—(*ushi*—ox, *gome*—come in). *Ushijima* is one sample of a family name with a bovine origin. Hearn, in his *Shadowings* (p. 117) includes *Ushi* in a list of given names of girl students. He calls it an "extraordinary name" and surmises that "Miss Ushi was born at the Hour of the Ox (1 to 3 a.m.), on the Day of the Ox, in the month of the Ox, and the Year of the Ox." The youthful name of Yoshitsune, one of Japan's great heroes, was *Ushiwaka*, or "Young Ox" which, as history records, was an appropriate name.

In art, the ox is often associated, in a recumbent attitude, with the revered minister, Sugawara Michizane, who used to ride it when he was driven into exile, and who is now deified as *Tenjin* ("Heavenly God"). There are many shrines known as *Ushi tenjin*, of which the most famous near Tokyo is at Kameido, noted for its wistaria blossoms. The ox is also associated with the peach-tree and is an emblem of the Zen sect.

The Hour of the Ox was "sacred to women crossed in love for taking vengeance upon a straw image of a recreant lover at the shrine of Fudo." This was called *ushi-toki-mairi* ("ox-hour-visit"). It is described by Dr. Griffis in his *The Mikado's Empire* (p. 474) · "Her feet are shod with high clogs, her limbs are lightly robed in a loose night-dress of white, her hair is dissheveled, and her eyes sparkle with the passion within her. Sometimes she wears a crown, made of an iron tripod reversed, on which burn three candles. In her left hand she carries the straw effigy; in her right she grasps a hammer. On her bosom is suspended a mirror. She carries nails in her girdle or in her mouth. Reaching the sacred tree, which is encircled with a garland of rice straw, before the shrine, and near the *torii*, she impales upon the tree with nails, after the manner of a Roman crucifier, the straw image of her recreant lover. The visit is repeated nightly, several times in succession, until the object of her incantation sickens and dies." And Griffis also tells of having seen such trees, "plentifully studded with nails," "wounded unto death by repeated stabs of the iron nails driven home by arms nerved to masculine strength," "all scarred and stained by rust."

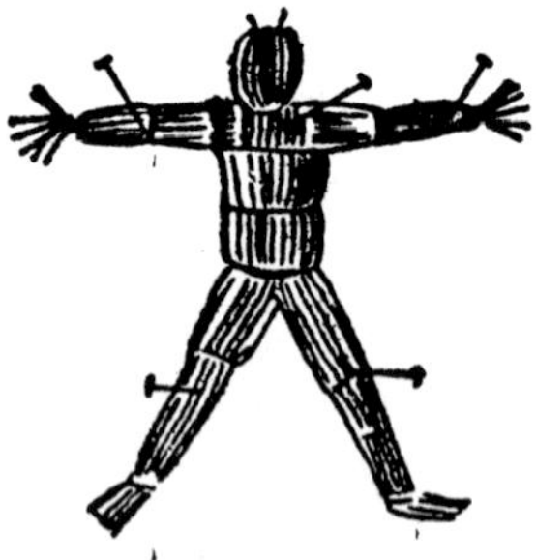

The 3rd Year—The Year of the Tiger ("Tora")

The Tiger is the symbol of the 3rd year of the Oriental Zodiac.

The statement that "there are no snakes in Ireland" may likewise be applied to tigers in Japan. Brinkley writes: "There is no evidence that the tiger (or lion) ever existed in Japan, and yet both of these animals play an important part in Japanese institutions." As another writer expresses it: "By the Japanese the tiger is considered more as a symbol than as a zoological reality, and is drawn in accordance with a type handed down by the old Chinese artist."

In Japanese art there is a conventional connection between the tiger and bamboo. Maude R. Allen, in her *Japanese Art Motives*, says that "the tiger is often drawn forcing its way through the luxurious and poisonous undergrowth of the jungle (which signifies sin), symbolizing Will overcoming Evil. Crouching besides a clump of bamboo during a storm, the tiger is symbolic of the power of faith." The tiger was often painted on the screens before the doors of magistrates, "to produce in all who approach a feeling of awe and terror"; on the gates of homes and of temples, "as a symbol of bravery"; and it is honored by gamblers, and "drawings of it, holding money in its front paws, are hung in gambling halls, and incense is burned before them.

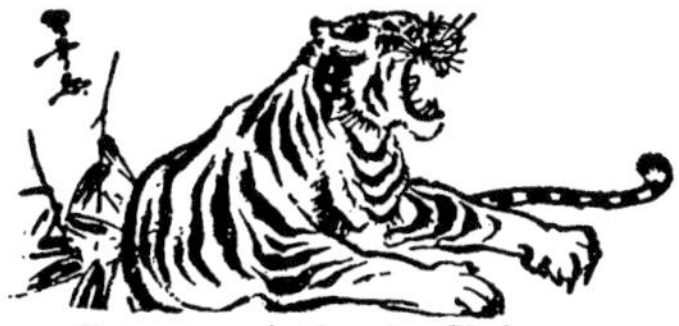
From a painting by Kakuen.

De Visser, in his discussion of "The Dog and Cat in Japanese Superstition," in the Transactions of the Asiatic Society of Japan, gives the natural connection between cats and tigers, as follows: "There was a cat kept by a Zen priest for a long time, till it was killed by a dog. He deplored its death and said: 'As you are an animal, you cannot become a Buddha; but because the tiger is the highest of all animals, you must be reborn a tiger'. Thirteen years later, on the same day of the same month, the cat appeared to him in a dream and told him that it had actually been reincarnated as a tiger." That special kind of cat is called *nekomata* ("monster cat"): and one Japanese writer says of them, that "they are animals of Darkness considered as being tigers; therefore, the cat is also called *tegai no tora*, or a tiger fed by the hand." In reckoning time, the tiger gives nature to one day in every 12, and it exerts an influence upon those days. Should it be learned that an observance or a ceremony has been scheduled to take place on a Tiger Day that was not auspicious for the event, the function is postponed. The Tiger "Hour" of every 24 hours is from 3 to 5 a.m.

In nomenclature, the tiger (*tora*) appears often in boys' names. It is often used as a prefix: *torage no koma* is a colt with hair striped like a tiger: *torafu-ishi* is a stone striped like a tiger, used in making inkstones; *torahige* is a nickname for a bristling beard or mustache; *tora-ko-watashi* is a phrase meaning "makeshift"; *tora-no-maki* is an "open sesame," or a "key" or "crib," especially for students taking an examination!

The tiger also gives point to several proverbs. Besides others—The fox that borrows the tiger's power; or, in Western parlance, the ass in the lion's skin. To cherish like the tiger's cub, i.e., to keep as the apple of the eye. Feeding a tiger, trouble afterwards, i.e., to warm a viper in one's bosom. If you do not enter the tiger's den, you cannot get her cub, seems to be the equivalent of "nothing ventured, nothing gained." If you keep the tiger out of the front gate, there is a wolf at the back gate—one Japanese version of "out of the frying pan into the fire."

The 4th Year—The Year of the Rabbit ("U") or Hare ("Usagi")

The rabbit, or hare, is the symbol of the 4th year of the Oriental Zodiac

The Japanese word for hare, *usagi*, abbreviated to *u*, appears in some names. For instance, a boy named *Uhachi* (*hachi*=8) was probably born in the eighth month of a hare year. *Usagi* is also used in composition with other words: *usagi-komori* (the long eared bat), *usagi-mimi* (quick-eared), *usagi-tobi* (a rabbit-jump), *usagi-uma* (donkey, jackass), *usagi-saru* (the woolly monkey), and others.

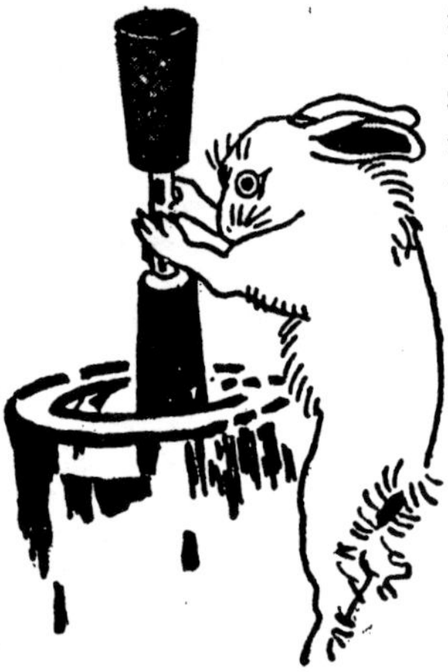

The hare appears early in Japanese tradition, or folklore, as is shown in the tale *The White Hare of Inaba* in the *Kojiki* ("Record of Ancient Matters"), the earliest work in Japanese literature, dating from the year 712—which contains the mythology and the earliest history of the nation.

In Japan, the hare is especially connected with the moon. The Sanskrit word for "moon" means, literally, "one who carries the hare"—which accounts for its association with the full moon for ages past in every quarter of the globe, except where the hare becomes "the man in the moon." Commonly, the hare with his mortar and pestle, is pictured as pounding the *mochi*, of which rice cakes are made.

Gyokuto ("Jeweled hare") is a poetical expression for the "moon," just as *Kin-u* ("Golden crow"), said to be three legged, is used for the "sun."

"Hare Day" also figures in folklore and customs. Thus the *mayu-dama*, a sort of Christmas tree decorated with cakes in honor of the silkworm, makes its appearance on whatever date in January may happen to be the "First Day of the Hare" (*Hatsu U*), at which time a celebration is held at the Kameido Temple, Tokyo. And, on the first "Hare Day" of the 10th month, there is a singular celebration at Wasa, Kishu province, called the "Laughing Festival of Wasa." The 10th month (October) is often called the "godless month" because all the deities are supposed to repair to the great shrine in Izumo. It is said that, when this conclave was first convened, one deity mistook the date and did not appear until the conference was over, and, naturally, he was laughed at by the other deities. The Wasa festival commemorating that mistake, is a time of "merriment from morning till evening."

A number of heraldic designs utilize the hare, one or more, in various poses. Only a few proverbs center around the hare. "There's not even the hair of a rabbit" means that there is not even a small particle of a thing. "He who runs after two hares will not catch either" has its counterpart in an Italian and an English proverb. The "Hare Hour" is the time between 5 and 7 a.m.

The 5th Year—The Year of the Dragon ("Tatsu")

The dragon (tatsu or ryo or ryu) is the symbol of the 5th year of the Oriental Zodiac

Of all mythical beasts the most important, by far, is the dragon. The fabulous creature reached Japan through China and is supposed to have had its origin in the Indian serpent, or some prehistoric monster. It is not always possible to establish a clear line of demarcation between the serpent and the dragon.

For instance, one description characterizes it as a " composite monster with scowling head, long straight horns, a scaly serpentine body, a bristling row of dorsal spines, four limbs armed with claws, and curious flame-like appendages on its shoulders and hips. The claws are usually three on each foot, but are sometimes four and even five." Another description calls it essentially a serpent, " with the horns of a deer, the head of a horse, eyes like a devil, neck like a snake, belly like that of a red worm, scales like those of a carp, ears like a cow, paws like a tiger, and claws like an eagle." Can anything be more composite ? Furthermore, it is said to be "all powerful, for it is possessed of the strongest characteristics of each of the creatures from which it is formed."

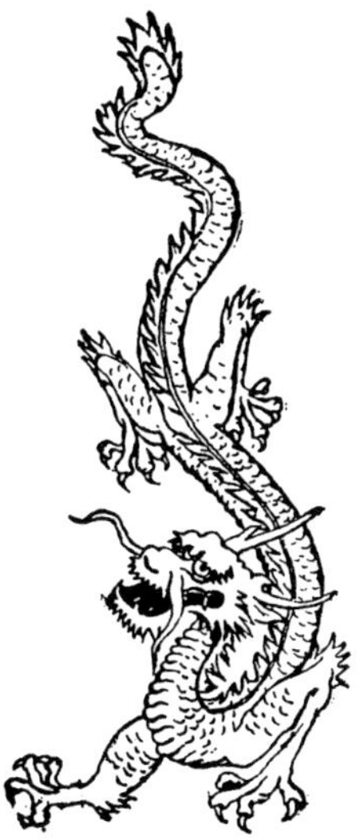

Dragons are represented as of various colors: black, green, red, white, or yellow. "When the white dragon breathes, its breath turns to gold; the spittle of the violet dragon turns to crystal balls"—and in Japanese art the dragon is generally accompanied "by a ball of varied form, but usually spherical," which is " the gem of omnipotence." Huish, in his *Japan and its Art*, states that "the Japanese artist uses the dragon in every possible way for the purposes of adornment." He cites the following examples, " as the holder for a fan, the gem forming the knob or rivet, as the handle to a spoon, as a pouch ornament, upon sword guards, as a handle to bells." He suggests that this is due to " the wonderful adaptability of its lissome body to all manner of ornament."

The dragon figures extensively in figures of speech: Bowes, in his *Japanese Pottery*, among others, lists the following; *riu-me* (a fine horse), *riu-o* (Dragon King, who governs the rain), *riu-dzu* (dragon's head from which temple bells are suspended). Maude Rex Allen, in her *Japanese Art Motives*, cites other cases: the Emperor's garments are spoken of as " dragon robes "; his seat is known as the " dragon throne." Professor Ernest W. Clement adds *ryu-ga* (Imperial Carriage); *ryo-tai* (Imperial person); *ryu-to* (dragon's lantern, a phosphorescent light at sea); *ryo-hangyo* (water lizard); *ryu-ketsu-ju* (dragon's-blood tree); *tatsumaki* (water-spout); *tatsu-no-kuchi* (dragon's mouth, for a tap or siphon), besides others.

The dragon appears early in Japanese mythology, and figures in many of the so-called Japanese fairy-tales. Moreover, the dragon is not confined to the Orient. The European dragon of the middle ages, a winged serpent with a crocodile's tail, was the symbol of sin in general and of paganism in particular. Its name, in English, is Greek, and is derived from a verb meaning to see or look at, or, more remotely, to flash.

The 6th Year—The Year of the Snake ("Mi") or Serpent

The snake is the symbol of the 6th year of the Oriental Zodiac

In its use as a year name the snake is a fabulous creature often undistinguishable from the serpent, or the dragon, and is treated here in that sense. In Japan there are several harmless varieties of snakes and one poisonous snake called *mamushi*. For the use of snakes as medicine, see that description.

The serpent is especially associated with *Benten*, the Japanese Venus, sea goddess and goddess of love and beauty, one of the seven Gods of Good Luck. She is often represented with a serpent coiled around the rock on which she is seated. On account of this association, snakes are held sacred in some parts of Japan, especially on Enoshima island, near Kamakura.

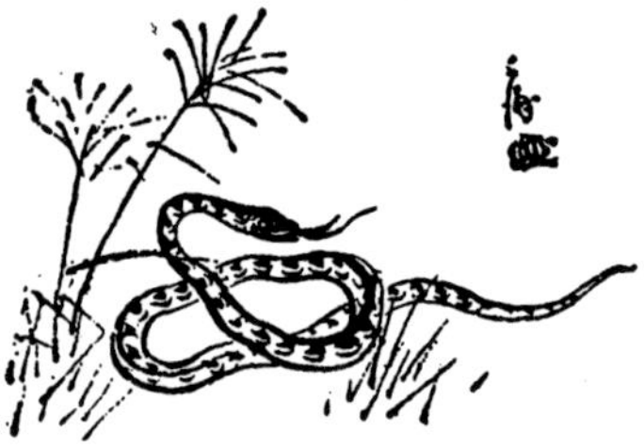

From a painting by Chiura.

Huish, in his *Japan and Its Art*, says that "snakes are favorites with the artists in metal-work, who excel to a greater extent in portraying them than in anything else." Allen, in her *Japanese Art Motives*, emphasizes the fact that "the snake is of symbolic importance in Japan. For instance, it is a symbol of woman's jealousy, as in the story of *Kiyohime*, who revenged herself by becoming transformed into a dragon and destroying her lover." This story is given in the "Odori" description.

There is an old superstition that, "if you cut a bamboo on a moonlight night, you will find a snake in the hollow of it between the third and fourth joints." The time of the hour of the snake is from 9 to 11 a.m.

Ja, another word for snake, appears in many combinations. For some reason, a "mouthpiece" is *ja-guchi;* for an obvious reason, a coiled pipe is *jakan;* a long bamboo basket filled with stones is called *jakago; jabara* is literally "snake's belly," and *jakotsu*, "snake's bones"; *jabisen* or *jamisen*, is a kind of musical instrument made of snake's skin, and *janome* is literally "serpent's eye." *Jasoku*, "serpent's feet," is used in rhetoric for anything redundant.

The Japanese equivalent of "a thief to catch a thief" may be freely translated "a snake to find a snake": *ja* (*hebi*) *no michi wa hebi.* Another proverb is *yabu wo tsutsuite hebi wo dasu*, which is often abbreviated into *yabu-hebi*, and means "poke a canebrake and drive out a snake" and is apparently the equivalent of the western expression about "letting sleeping dogs lie" and "stirring up a hornet's nest." *Mekura hebi ni ojizu*, "a blind man is not afraid of a snake," seems to be one version of the western proverb, "Where ignorance is bliss, it is folly to be wise." Another proverb warns—"avoid three things: a snake, a smooth-tongued man, and a wanton woman." "The man who has once been bitten by a snake fears every piece of rope" is more suggestive than "the burnt child dreads the fire." These are only a few of the proverbs in which snakes figure.

The 7th Year—The Year of the Horse ("Uma")

The horse is the symbol of the 7th year of the Oriental Zodiac

Chronologically, the horse is an ancicnt animal in Japan. Murdoch says that "perhaps the most suggestive among the archeological spoils of the dolmens is the abundant horse furniture and trappings which are recovered."

The horse is specially mentioned in connection with the death of Emperor Suinin (29 B.C.—A.D. 70), when, for the first time, instead of living beings buried alive, terra-cotta images of men, horses, and various other things were set up around the grave. But really good horses seem to have been rare till more modern days. In recent times the horses of north-eastern Japan and of Hokkaido have been held in high repute. The favorite horse of Emperor Meiji was Hokkaido bred, and referring to Emperor Meiji's love for horses, Dr. Griffis, in his *The Mikado*, writes: "He was passionately fond of high bred horses and of riding them. He frequently attended the races, in both Tokyo and Yokohama. He had been well trained by the best teachers of horsemanship when a lad in Kyoto."

The horse figures prominently in Japanese art, but is usually not depicted with great skill. In the Japanese language and literature the horse plays a not insignificant part. *Baka*, "fool," is written with the ideographs for "horse" and "deer"; a Chinese emperor is said to have declared that a stag could be called a horse, and a horse a stag—a declaration which was considered the height of folly. From I1 a.m. to 1 p.m. is the hour of the horse; on the compass, the horse stands at the south.

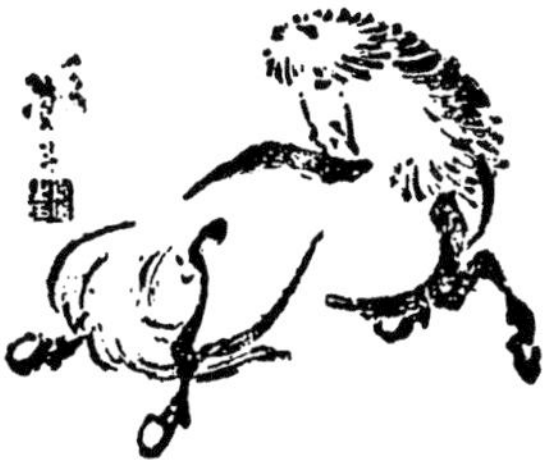

From a wood-cut by Keisai.

Harukoma is the title of a popular song that was sung at the beginning of spring by singers who went from door to door and usually carried a miniature horse's head above their own heads. The same word is also the name of a children's toy which was used in the early spring season. To a long bamboo pole was attached the head of a horse made of paper or cloth, and at the other end was attached a small wooden wheel. Children straddled the pole and rode on this "horse." Now, *takeuma* (bamboo-horse) is used instead; it is really a pair of bamboo stilts.

There are a few Japanese proverbs about horses, among them: "Preaching to deaf ears" of the west becomes 'like prayers to a horse's ear"; while the western "water off a duck's back" is "like wind to a horse's ear." In English, "when one sheep is over the dam the rest follow"; the Japanese say practically the same thing about "one horse" and a "thousand horses."

About "the day of the horse," Brinkley, in Vol. V of his encyclopedic work, in one of his paragraphs on this subject, writes: "The innumerable shrines of Inari throughout the country are thronged with worshippers on the first 'day of the horse,' *hatsu-uma*, generally about the 2nd of the 2nd month (February); lights are placed in the pillar lamps; flags are hoisted and, after praying for agricultural prosperity, the people feast on red-rice, *seki-han*.

As cures, a horse's tooth, if rubbed upon pimples on the face is thought to remove them; and a piece of red paper with three of the characters for "horse" may be used to ward off an attack of small pox. The superstition which persists relative to the misfortune of a girl born in a certain year of the horse, *Hinoe-uma* ("Fire-Horse"), is given in "Japanese Superstitions."

The 8th Year—The Year of the Sheep ("Hitsuji") or Goat

The sheep is the symbol of the 8th year of the Oriental Zodiac

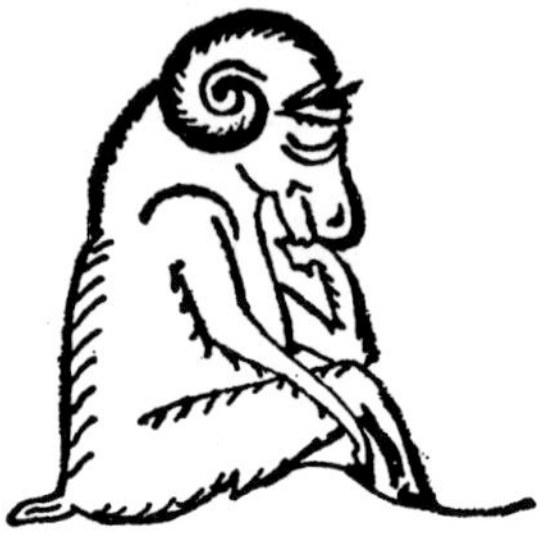

Drawing by Rocky.

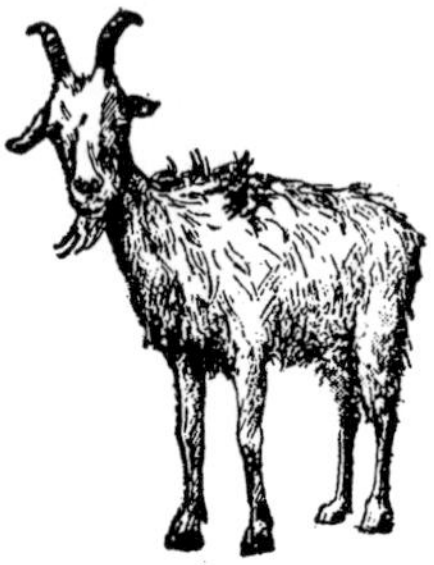

In China, the goat, in all probability, was the original zodiacal animal, but in Japan the sign of zodiac is called *hitsuji* ("sheep"), although the pictures usually show goats. Moreover, in the Japanese language, the goat is called by a word (*yagi*) that means "mountain sheep," i.e., "wild sheep"—which seems to indicate that there is no such sharp distinction as the Biblical one between the sheep and the goats—of the Far East.

In Japan, goats and sheep are not very numerous—and in art they are rare—and this sign of the zodiac does not figure so prominently as the other signs. There has been much discussion concerning the reason for the scarcity of goats and sheep in Japan. Some authorities attribute this scarcity to the damp atmosphere and frequent summer rains. Miss Harteshorn, in *Japan and Her People*, puts the cause as "dampness of the climate, which causes foot-rot."

The annual production of wool in Japan is negligible in comparison with the amount used. The greater part of this important textile material is imported. The war and the practical cessation of importations from Australia and elsewhere warned the government that suitable measures should be adopted for supplying wool at home. Accordingly, beginning with the 1918-19 Diet session, funds have been provided for encouraging sheep farming by importing blooded stock from sheep breeding countries, and distributing this stock among government and private pastures, and a small subsidy is granted to farmers for each head of sheep kept. In 1930, the latest available, there were in the Japanese Empire approximately 24,000 sheep, 88,000 goats—figures which show a steady increase over prior years.

The Japanese words for "sheep" (*hitsuji, menyo, rashamen*) and for "goat" (*yagi*) are not very common in composition with other words. In Inouye's *Japanese English Dictionary* six examples are cited of the former and one of the latter (*yagi-so*), "far-flower." There is a Japanese word for "goatee," which seems to be merely a translation (*hitsuji-hige*). The animal known to the West as "alpaca" becomes a "sheep-camel" (*hitsuji-rakuda*) in Japanese. Brinkley's Dictionary gives *hitsuji-ine* as a name for "the second crop of rice." *Hitsuji no ayumi* ("sheep's walk") means "walking slowly, like a sheep to the slaughter."

The 9th Year—The Year of the Monkey ("Saru")

The monkey is the symbol of the 9th year of the Oriental Zodiac

The monkey affords much of interest in both fact and fiction, and is an animal of general good standing in Japan. Monkey year is fortunate as a birth year because Hideyoshi, the "monkey-faced adventurer," was born in a monkey year and succeeded in raising himself from a low-born station to that of administrator of the Empire, with the title of *Taiko* ("Great Prince"). On the other hand, monkey year is unlucky for marriage, because the word for monkey (*saru*) has the same pronunciation as the Japanese verb, "to leave," and suggests divorce. For that reason, among the superstitious, there are few weddings in a monkey year, but there are an unusually large number in either the year before or the year after.

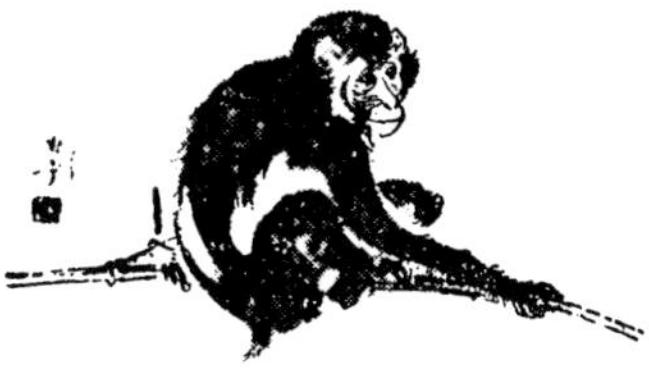

From a painting by Kakunen.

The monkey figures in many Japanese proverbs. "To teach a monkey to climb a tree" would be as foolish as "To teach your grandmother to suck eggs"; but "even a monkey sometimes falls from a tree"—just as "Even Homer nods," or "a good marksman may miss." A conceited man who makes a display of wisdom is only "a monkey with a hat on." While the West uses "a cat and a dog" as typical of unfriendly relations, the Japanese use "a dog and a monkey." "The monkey seizes the moon" is the Japanese variant of Aesop's fable about the dog that tried to catch the shadow of his bone in the brook, and is founded on the following story. Some long-armed monkeys, seeing the reflection of the moon in a well under a tree, resolved to catch it. They made a long chain of apes from the tree to the water, when suddenly the branch to which they clung broke, and the apes were drowned. This is a Buddhist parable.

The monkey is also prominent in the so-called Japanese fairy tales: *Momotaro*, or Little Peachling (see that description). *The Battle of the Monkey and the Crab*, and *The Silly Jellyfish*. Space does not permit listing some of the words of which *saru* forms a part. Sosen, "the Japanese Landseer," made a specialty of monkeys after a most careful study of the creatures in the woods; and his productions are masterpieces in Japanese art.

The carving of the three monkeys at Nikko is famous. The group is called "the monkeys of the three countries" and are said to represent India, China, and Japan. One covers his eyes with his hands; another, his ears; and the third, his mouth. They present a good example of punning in the Japanese language: *saru* is monkey and *zaru* is a negative ending for a verb—*mi-zaru, kika-zaru, iwa-zaru*, or "seeing-not," "hearing-not," "speaking-not." These three monkeys are commonly found by the roadside, as they are connected with Koshin, god of the roads. By another pun, they are also associated with the Shinto god Saruta, often, confused with Koshin. These monkeys are used to teach the moral lesson of "seeing no evil, hearing no evil, speaking no evil."

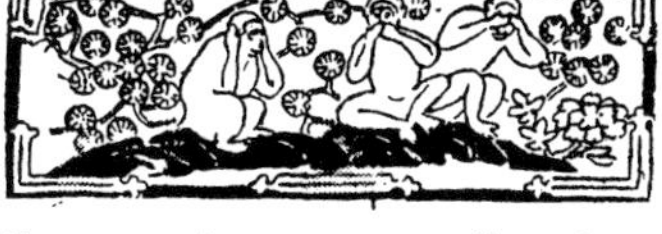

The 10th Year—The Year of the Cock ("Tori")

The cock is the symbol of the 10th year of the Oriental Zodiac

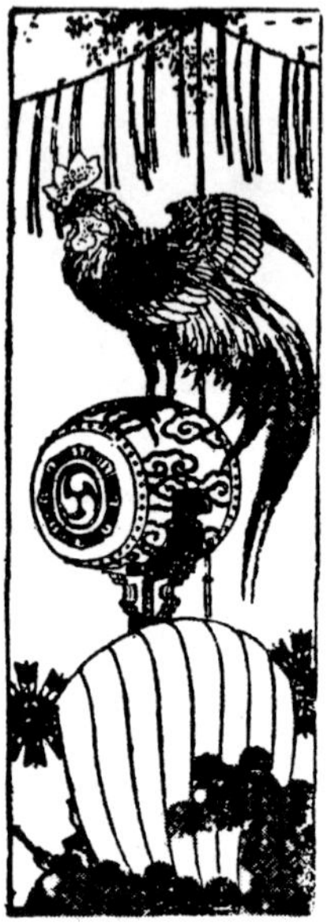

From Hokusai's "Ehon Teikin Orai"

Fortune tellers say that persons born in the year of the cock are generally intelligent and kind by nature. As the years of the zodiac recur in 12-year cycles, persons born in prior years of the cock were, in 1933 (the last cock year), 12, 24, 36, 48, 60, 72, 84, and 96 years old, respectively. In each case, one year older if age is reckoned in the Japanese way. Cock year is considered to be a lucky year, for the following reasons: "It is believed by Japanese that the cock has five virtues. Its comb represents civilization, and its strong feet denote military strength. With an enemy it fights well—demonstrating courage. Having found food, it calls friends for the sake of humanity. Watching for the dawn it is faithful." *Tori-no-ato* ("Bird's footprints"), is applied to Chinese ideographs, which are said "to have been invented by a Chinese from observing the footprints of birds"—a somewhat more honorable appellation than the Westerner's "hen tracks"!

In Western countries, the cock is also a symbol of watchfulness, and therefore of protection. In that sense it is often placed on weather vanes. In Japan there are many interesting traditions and beliefs about the cock; its crow at day break is believed to drive away the evil spirits of darkness that have roamed abroad throughout the night. Due to this belief the cock has become a talisman against evil spirits.

The cock appears early in Japanese rscords; for it is an "important element in the Shinto sun-myth," "When the Sun Goddess retired to a cave in anger at the violence of her brother, Susano-o, and left the world in darkness, the cock's crow outside the cave made the angry goddess think that the day had dawned even without her august presence"—and this was one of the lures by which she was induced to come forth from her retirement. At the Grand Shrine of Ise, the cock is regarded as a messenger of the Sun Goddess, and always some of these beautifully plumaged birds may be seen in the shrine's precincts.

Perhaps, because the cock is a common domestic fowl, he does not figure so extensively in Japanese art and folklore as other animals. There is, however, one very striking design of a cock, with or without a hen, on a drum. This is known as *Kanko* or Drum of Remonstrance, which in China it was customary to set up before the Imperial Palace, "to be struck by an official in charge whenever a letter of remonstrance was offered to the Sovereign." The expression *Kanko Koke wo shozu,* or "The Drum of Remonstrance is covered with moss," was used concerning a Chinese Emperor, "whose administration was so popular that not a letter of remonstrance was presented during his whole life"—suggesting that when the drum was not beaten because there were no complaints against the ruler, the fowls became accustomed to it, and, as the years passed, moss grew on the unused drum. And in Japan, the cock on a drum, *Kanko-dori,* is symbolical of peace and prosperity, with no cause for complaint.

The crowing of a cock does not sound like "cock-a-doodle-doo" to the Japanese, who hear "Kok-ke—kok-ko"—which may mean "Happiness to our land."

The common Japanese word for egg is *tama-go* (lit., "jewel-child")—which seems to indicate that the Japanese have decided the famous question, "which was first, the chicken or the egg?" in favor of the chicken! In fact, *tori-no-ko* ("chicken's child") is another term for "egg"—which suggests a favorite dish known as *oyako-domburi* ("parent-child-bowl"), which consists of a bowl of rice with chicken and egg.

The 11th Year—The Year of the Dog ("Inu")

The dog is the symbol of the 11th year of the Oriental Zodiac

The dog is a friendly character in Japanese stories, folklore, and literature—a beneficent and protective character—only rarely, as in China, demonical character. In the so-called Japanese fairy tale, *Momotaro* or *Little Peachling*, a dog is one of Momotaro's faithful companions and aids in the successful campaign against the ogres. In another tale, *The Old Man Who Made Dead Trees Blossom*, this miracle was accomplished through the instructions of the "Old Man's" pet dog, which in anger had been killed by a spiteful neighbor, and which appeared to the old man in his dreams. In many cases and places the dog is really a sacred animal. The dog, for instance, is the only animal admitted on Koya-San, south of Nara, where is situated the head temple of the Shingon sect of Buddhism. In the Harima mountains there is a Buddhist temple called *Inu-dera* ("Dog Temple"), and there are other shrines to dogs in various places, and the dog, *Koma-Inu*, together with the lion, guard the entrance to many temples and shrines in Japan.

In Japanese literature, Bakin has immortalized the dog in his famous novel, *Hakkenden* ("Story of Eight Dogs"); and Lady Sei Shonagon, in her *Makura-no-Soshi* ("Pillow Sketches"—A.D. 991-1000) relates an incident of a dog which was exiled because it barked at a cat which had been honored with court rank!

One of the most common toys in Japan is a papier-mache dog, which is considered the perpetual protector of little children, and, when hanging above their heads, is said to make them stop crying—and the words, *inu-no-ko, inu-no-ko* ("puppy, puppy") are believed to make a Japanese baby quiet when it cries in its dreams. Moreover, the placing of the ideograph for dog (犬) upon a child's forehead is done to drive away the demons of disease.

The word *inu* is not uncommon in proper names. In Bizen province is an island *Inushima* (*Shima*=island), to which dogs are said to have been exiled. *Inubushi* ("Dog warrior," i.e., an unfit warrior), *Inuyama* ("Dog mountain"), *Inugawa* ("Dog river"), *Inukai* ("Dog rearer"), *Inumaru* ("Dog circle") are other names compounded with the Japanese word for "dog."

In Japanese proverbs, *Inujini* means "dog's death" and signifies, as in the West, a base or useless death. "To have the hand bitten by the dog you feed" means "to be betrayed by one's own dependent." "When a dog barks, a hundred follow" expresses a pretty general truth all the world over. The word *inu*, appearing in the composition of about forty common names of plants, generally means "wild."

In Japanese history the dog appears in connection with *Shogun Tsunayoshi* (1860-1709) who was so fond of dogs that he was given the nickname of *Inu-Kubo* ("Dog Prince").

The 12th Year—The Year of the Wild Boar ("I")

The wild boar is the symbol of the 12th year of the Oriental Zodiac

The wild boar is known in Japan as ***i-no-shishi***, often contracted to ***i***, and also as *yama-kujira* ("mountain whale"). The boar years are called ***i-no-toshi***, or the year (*toshi*) of the wild boar. This animal stands to the Japanese as a type of reckless courage. Huish in his *Japan and Its Art* says: the boar is "a great favorite with *netsuke* makers." A common *netsuke* design is a representation of Nitan killing a wild boar. This incident is shown in a carving on the long office counter of the Fujiya Hotel—which depicts the story of "The Hunting Party of the Shogun Yoritomo at the base of Mt. Fuji." An army of beaters had driven the wild game of the district to an appointed rendezvous—a wounded, maddened boar among them. It was as big as an ox. Showing its tusks, raising a cloud of dust as it ran, the desperate animal came rushing toward the hunters at lightning speed. It was too swift and fierce to be shot down with bows and arrows. In an instant, a warrior named Nitan-no-Shiro Tadatsune sprang out from Yoritomo's bodyguard and, throwing away his bow and arrows, mounted his horse and made straight for the boar, which at once turned and attacked him. Quick as a flash, Nitan leaped on the back of the beast with his own back turned toward the animal's head. Grasping its tail, Nitan clung to the back of the boar, which now redoubled its speed. As he got the chance, Nitan drew his dagger and stabbed the beast until it fell dead. The ovation Nitan received from Yoritomo and his party is said "to have been so great as to shake the surrounding hills"!

The wild boar figures rather extensively in Japanese history, folklore, literature and art. Mention is made of it in the *Kojiki*, the earliest work in Japanese (dating from A.D. 712). Likewise, it figures in Japanese poetry, first in a poem by Akahito, the famous 8th century poet, and in many subsequent long and short poems by various poets. In art, there are many examples in which the *i-no-shishi* appears. *Usa Hachiman* ("God of War") is sometimes represented as riding on the back of a boar. Years ago there were ¥10 bills with the picture of a wild boar on the back. This represented one of the 30,000 boars sent by *Hachiman* to protect and encourage Wakeno Kiyomaro, a great loyalist, who was dragging his weary feet to the place of his exile. A picture of this loyalist was on the face of these bills. In some back country districts the people still use the word *i-no-shishi* as a nickname for a ¥10 bill.

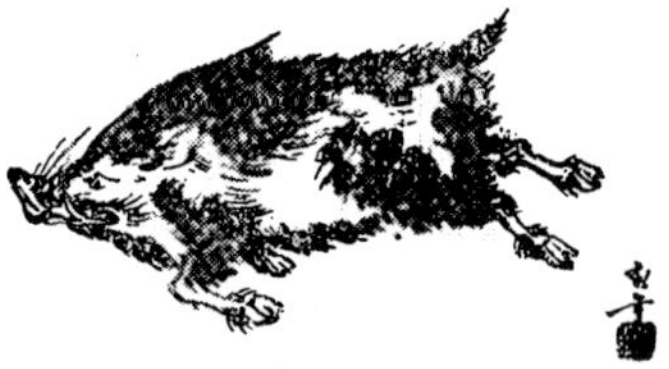

From a painting by Kakunen.

It was one of the rites and ceremonies of the year, in October, to celebrate the young of the wild boar by making special *mochi* (rice cake) and offering them at the family altar. It was believed that if one ate *mochi* pounded at the hour of the boar (9–11 p.m.) on the day of the boar, he would be free from all disease. Women especially celebrated the day by offering *mochi* to their patron saints and praying that they might be favored, as is the wild boar, with many children who would possess the reckless courage of the wild boar.

NETSUKE (Pron., Net-ske: the U almost silent)

Ne=root as of a plant; *tsuke*=to fasten. Perhaps derived from the old tale that peasants used twisted wistaria-roots as a device to prevent their water gourds slipping from their girdles (*obi*).

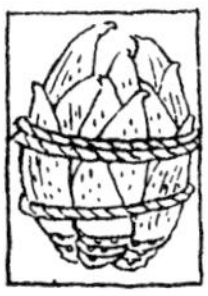

Bamboo-shoots. (*Wood*).

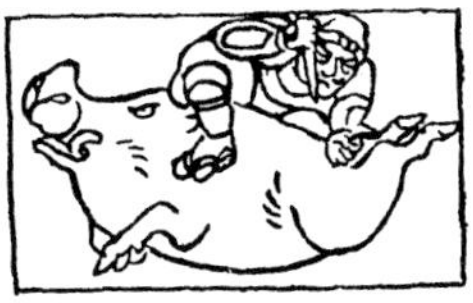

Nitan-no-Shiro killing wild-boar, single-handed. (*Ivory*).

The *netsuke* is a toggle affixed by a cord to a purse, tobacco-pouch, pipe-case, *inro*, or to anything which a man may desire to suspend from his girdle, its purpose being to prevent the suspended article from falling. It is particularly adapted to the Japanese form of dress which requires a waistband, but is not so much in use now as in olden days. It is distinctly Japanese—useful yet ornamental—often it is a marvel of minuteness, alive with humor and the grotesque.

Netsuke are made of wood (some colored), lacquered wood, bamboo, elephant or walrus ivory, boars' tusks, deer horns, walnut or other shells, sea-pine, jade, metal, porcelain, amber, onyx, coral, crystal, and other material. *Netsuke* always have two holes, usually in the back, or some means by which a cord may be attached. If in the form of a figure, an arm or a leg perhaps answers the purpose.

Even a partial list of the most renowned names amongst *netsuke*-carvers of old and modern Japan would occupy more space than is available here—and as to the designs, it may be said that they embrace the whole range of Japanese subjects, told with the utmost lucidity. Religion, history, folk-lore, incidents of daily life, all provide subjects for the carver—most of them treated in a comic or even flippant vein. All the gods and goddesses, demons, and fabulous animals of Japan and China have been done again and many times again, but they are all different. Each carver, according to his skill, will achieve an entirely different result with the same subject.

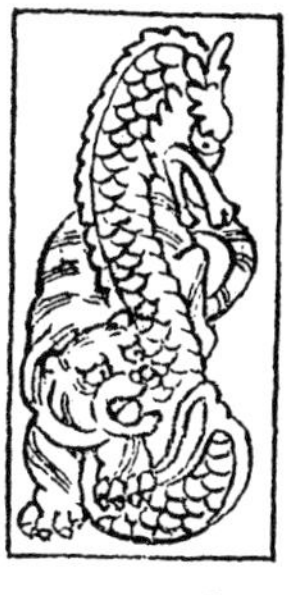

Dragon and Tiger. (*Ivory*).

The edict of the second Tokugawa shogun, Hidetada, in 1617, directed against the Christians, that made it compulsory for every house to contain the image of at least one Buddhist deity, had much to do with the many beautiful figure *netsuke* which came into being from that time on, but the universal use of tobacco, and the demand for pouches and pipe-cases, in the closing years of the 18th and the early years of the 19th century, provided the impetus for the more ornate *netsuke* that appeared at that time and afterwards.

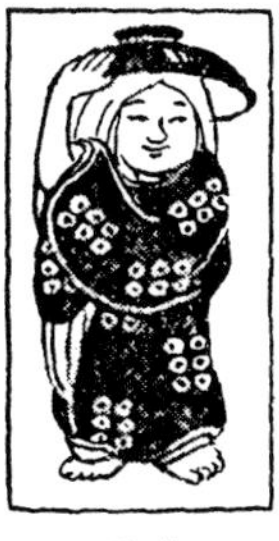

Shojo (Heavy drinker) (*Wood-colored*).

INRO (IN=SEAL, RO=CASE)

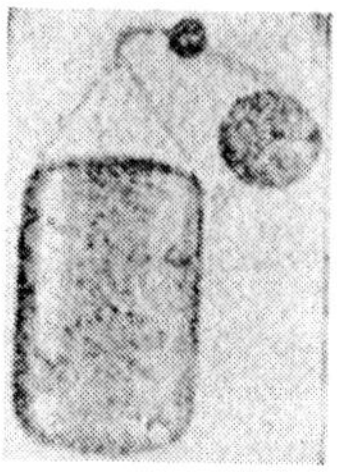

Gold ground 4 cases. Netsuke, carved-wood chrysanthemums. Early 19th century.

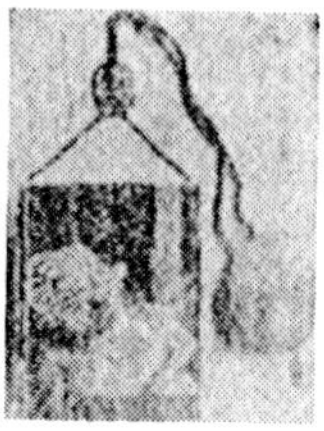

5 cases, black ground. Two Bugaku masks in gold and colors. Netsuke toggle-box for masks. Late 18th century.

Originally, an *inro* was probably a box with divisions for seal, ink pad, etc., and was not a necessary part of a gentleman's attire until later times when it was attached by a silk cord to a *netsuke* and hung through the wearer's sash. It was then used for medicines, either pills or aromatic conserves: of such ingredients as myrrh, dragon's blood, musk, cinnamon, ginseng, liquorice, etc.

An *inro* usually has four trays, sections or boxes, and a top lid, though there are *inro* of one, and up to seven boxes, each section fitting on to the other with marvelous mathematical precision, so much so that in a good specimen each piece is capable of transposition. *Inro* are made of metal, wood, ivory, crystal, etc., and lacquered wood, the last-named being preferred for medicines, as it keeps them in a moist condition.

As a nucleus for a collection of Japanese art work *inro* are desirable objects, especially if *netsuke* are attached to them. They are of surpassing value as specimens of the art of working in lacquer. In the small space available one often finds a treatment of a subject in miniature that would be inapplicable to a larger surface. On some *inro* there is such a wonderful harmony of color and composition, combined with minuteness of detail that one wonders what sort of eyes and hands the lacquerers possessed.

Inro frequently bear the name of the maker, but the omission of the signature is not a vital factor in the value of the piece, as many old artistic *inro* are without signature. The lacquer-work and *inro* of the most famous of all lacquerists, Korin (1661-1716), an artist also of great distinction with the brush, are much sought after by collectors, but fine examples of his work are now seldom put on the market. His best pieces are found in various museums. His masterpiece (generally so considered) a *tebako* (lit., small hand-box) is in the Imperial Museum, Tokyo.

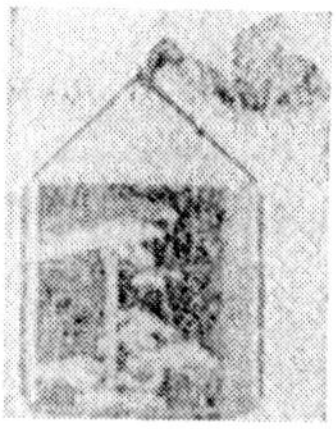

4 cases, black ground. Charm on cottage to exorcise demons, one of whom is flying away. Netsuke—(wood); a goat. Early 19th century.

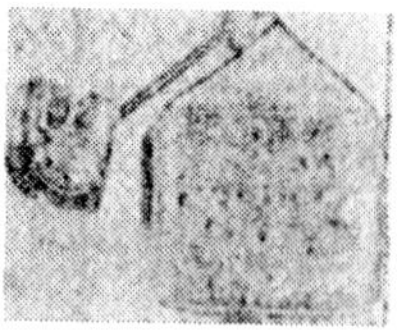

4 cases, black ground. Netsuke (wood)-carved; snail on leaf. Early 17th century.

Adapted, in part, from Huish's "Japan and Its Art." Engravings are from catalog of Victoria and Albert Museum.

BROCADES

"NISHIKI"—"BEAUTIFUL COMBINATIONS OF COLORS"

While Japanese brocades have been in existence for more than 1000 years, there are few authoritative documents on the subject of brocades. Old brocades, now highly valued, were most carefully selected for materials and treatment: silk threads, dyer, designs, hand-looms, weavers, etc., and in the olden days it took about 70 days for a weaver to produce one *tan* (12 yards)—and as to designs many were made by the famous artists, Eitoku Sotatsu, Korin, and Moronobu, among others. With the development of the *Cha-no-yu* ("Tea Ceremony") cult in the latter part of the 15th century, and with the institution of the *No* dance in the 17th century, a great impetus was given to the weaving of artistic brocades.

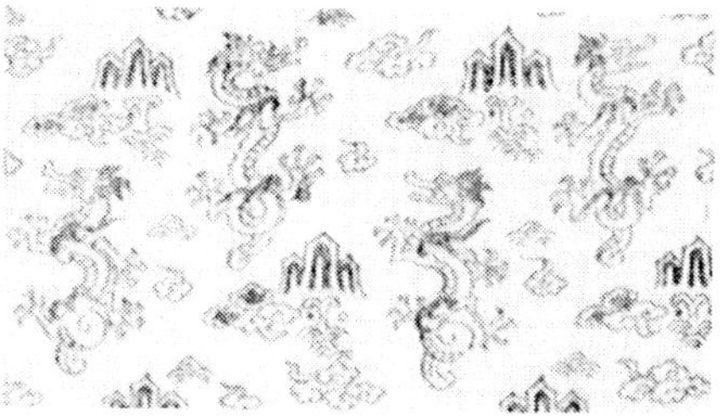

While brocades woven today for ladies' *obi* cost up to ¥5000 and more, they are not equal to the brocades made in the Momoyama or early Tokugawa periods (the former period about 400 years ago, the latter about 300), for the reason that the thread was then made by hand—much finer in its gloss and more durable than the machine-made thread of today, and the old vegetable dyes were greatly superior, and more suited to the silk than the chemical-dyes used in later days. In the Momoyama period a brocade called *karaori* or *yaeori* ("double weaving") was made with a background of raw silk with the raised design floss silk, sometimes an inch thick, sometimes extremely thin. These brocades are made today but are not so beautiful or artistic as the old brocades for the reason above stated, and also because the old-time artists and weavers were under the patronage of high-class *daimyo*—their living was secured, and they could give their time to designing and weaving, freed from care—a condition not possible in modern days.

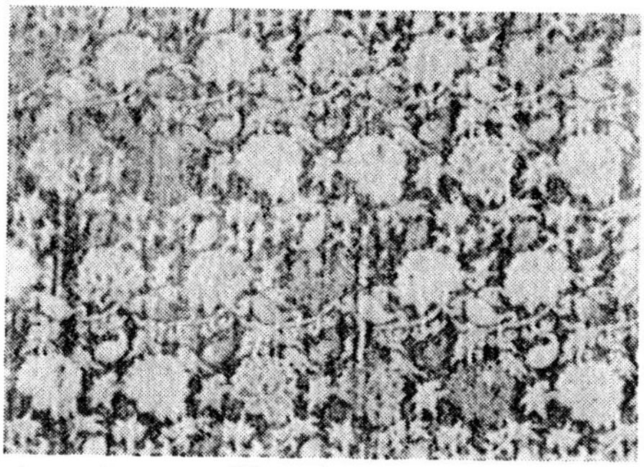

Today at curio and other shops selling brocades, priests' robes of 7 or 9 widths, and brocades used for the decoration of Buddhist altars, can be purchased. They are used by foreign visitors for bedspreads, table and cushion and sofa-covers, and as runners for tables and bureaus—also for wall decorations, and for other purposes.

LACQUER-WORK

The art of lacquering has been more highly developed in Japan than in any other country—but for carved lacquer, called *tsu-shi* in Japan, *tiao ch'i* in China, the palm still belongs to China. Though the Chinese originated the use of lacquer ware the Japanese quickly surpassed their Chinese teachers in its development, and they stand practically alone in its manufacture—an industry that was established in Japan before the Christian era. Japanese wares have won world-wide renown. So widespread is the fame of this varnish or lacquer that "japanned" or "to japan" (lacquer) long ago became current in the English language.

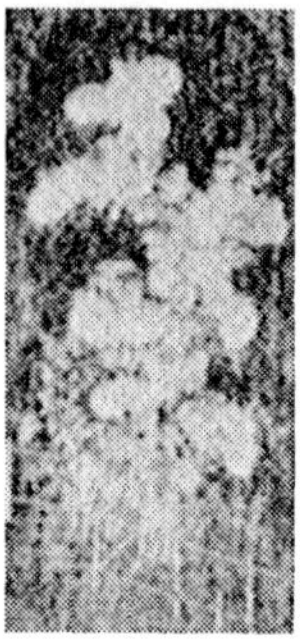

Lacquered Door. Inner Shrine of Toshogu, Nikko.

Lac is not a varnish in the usual acceptance of the word. It is the sap of *Rhus vernicifera* tree, and similar trees. These lacs dry not by heat but through dampness, so to speak. Lacquered objects have to be dried in a specially prepared air-tight cupboard called *muro*, made of rough wood kept damp by sponging with water, the temperature within the *muro* being maintained at from 68° to 80° F. In the best specimens many coats of lacquer are applied and this drying operation is many times repeated in the course of manufacture. The hardening thus produced is such that the various coats can be ground with whetstone to any required degree of fineness and given a wonderfully brilliant polish—superior even to that of enamel or pottery glaze—with fine burnt clay, charcoal, or similar substances, the final polish being given not by lacquer but with deer's horn ashes applied with the finger. Lacquer thus treated is extremely hard and will resist heat and acid. The S. S. Nile, returning the Japanese exhibits displayed at the Vienna Exhibition of 1873, was wrecked, but when the cargo was salvaged 17 months afterward, the wonderfully lacquered cabinets and stands were found to be uninjured by their immersion in sea-water.

Wood, seasoned and dried, of a soft and even grain, is generally the base of lacquered wares, and, in the smaller pieces, it is worked to an amazing thinness and evenness of texture; larger articles, such as cabinets, etc. of course have the necessary strength for use. These bases are strengthened with strong linen cloth. Space does not permit a description of the technique of manufacture as the process of lacquering is a long and delicate one, varying according to the quality of the object and its use, and involving months or years of work in perfect specimens, for which the Japanese pay liberally.

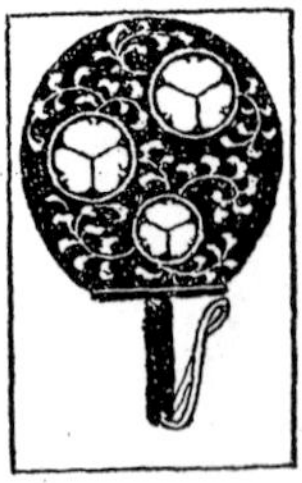

Lacquered Fan. "From Japan and Its Art."

Lacquered objects range from the commonest daily utensils to the most elaborate boxes, large and small, from chopsticks to saddles, from clogs to furniture, and they are finished in black and red lacquer, sometimes combined with other colors, in *hiramakiye* (flat-gold lacquer), *togidashi* (polished out)—where the pattern is the result of grinding and polishing, in *takamakiye* (raised-gold lacquer), or in *nashiji* (sprinkled gold dust producing the dotted appearance of pear skin). The common work made for export is usually just a plain wood article with a lacquered surface.

COLOR PRINTS

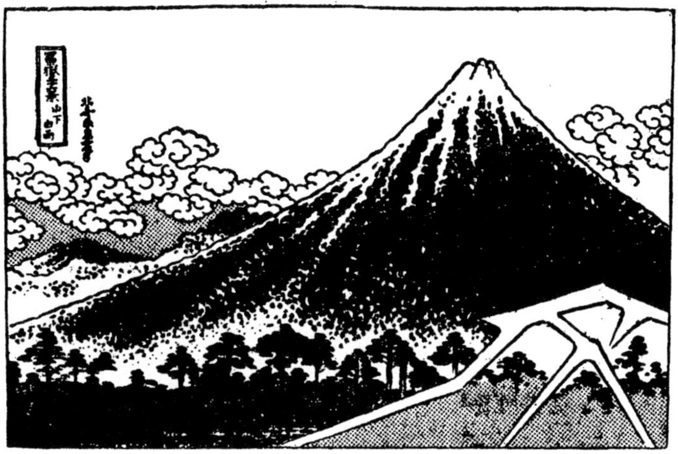

Color Prints (*Nishiki-ye*, "Brocade Pictures"), so called from their brilliant coloring, are products of *Ukiyo-ye* ("Passing world pictures") or genre painting school, depicting the everyday life and customs of ordinary folk, portraits of actors, courtesans, etc. They do not portray incidents of warfare, history, or the life of the Court, and were not highly regarded in aristocratic circles at the time they were printed and distributed in great quantities, selling for a fraction of a sen—even the best for very small sums. It was principally through the hundreds of prints taken to Holland by the Dutch who were allowed to trade at Nagasaki that European artists and collectors first became acquainted with the merits of these Japanese prints; but the real introduction of this art to Europe and America, it is said, dates from the 1850's when a few artists, often vistiting a Parisian shop called the Porte Chinoise, purchased for a few sous splendid specimens of these gaycolored sheets, and these artists became enthusiastic admirers of these prints.

Subsequently the monographs on Hokusai and Utamaro written by Edmond de Goncourt attracted public attention to Japanese color prints, and a demand was gradually developed—a demand which so keenly persists today that hundreds, and in some instances, thousands of dollars, or their equivalent in pounds, are paid for rare prints at the New York and London auctions, and wealthy Japanese are among the highest bidders for them. *(Continued)*

The picture portrays Mt. Fuji, with a thunder-storm at its base—one of the 36 color prints of Fuji, by the famous artist, Hokusai (1769—1849).

ARTISTIC, AESTHETIC, AND POETIC TASTES OF THE JAPANESE

COLOR PRINTS (**Ukiyoye**, "Passing World Pictures")

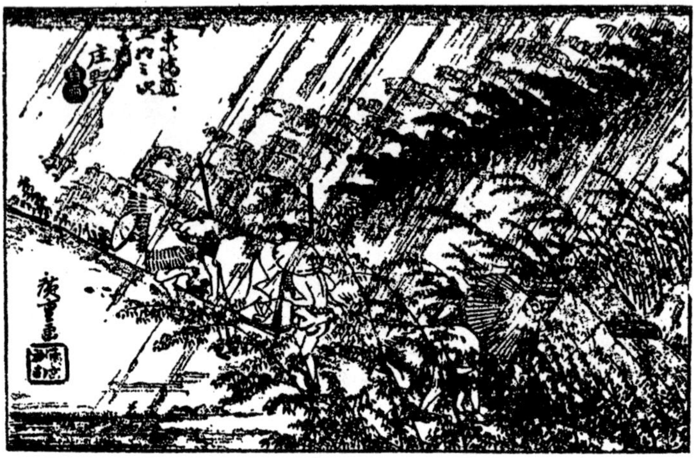

The chief stimulus to the vogue of the *ukiyoye*, beginning about 1785, came through the stage and its heroes—and to the popularity of the drama and of the actors is due the whole development of Japanese color prints. It was really the lower class of people in the social scale: laborers, peasants, tradesmen, and artisans who created this popularity, *samurai*, in accordance with an edict of the Shogun, being forbidden to attend theaters. Yet these stage heroes and "heroines,"* although basking in the adulation of the common people, ranked, socially, as one of the lowest grades—even the color-print artists who made portraits of them would not associate with them except in their unavoidable business association.

These prints reached their highest development in the latter part of the 18th century and the first half of the 19th, practically coincident with the Tokugawa regime, and modern prints have not shown improvement over them. They are, on the whole, free from vulgarity. The vegetable colors used by the old master-print artists were far superior to the mineral colors employed in modern times.

To quote Arthur Davison Fiske: "The color prints of Japan constitute almost the only pure Japanese art and the only graphic record of popular Japanese life. Therefore it may be regarded as the most definitely national of all the forms of expression used by the Japanese, an art which they alone in the history of the world have brought to perfection." Mr. Fiske, author, poet, art connoisseur, and collector, of Davenport, Iowa, and New York, is recognized as one of the outstanding authorities on Japanese prints, his *Chats on Japanese Prints* being one of the most widely read books on the subject.

The engraving depicts "Rainstorm at Shono Station"—near Ise, by Hiroshige (1797-1858), one of the master-artists of Ukiyoye—from his series "*53 Stations of the Tokaido.*"

* Female parts, as is almost universally the case up to the present day, were taken by men.

ARTISTIC, AESTHETIC, AND POETIC TASTES OF THE JAPANESE

COLOR PRINTS (Ukiyoye, "Passing World Pictures")

The production of a print is the joint work of the artist, a most skilful engraver, and the printer, the artist first making a black and white design with Indian ink (*sumi*), which has all the lines of the desired picture; this design is known as the Shita-ye, or foundation design. The technique is thus described by Wm. Anderson in "Japanese Wood Engravings":

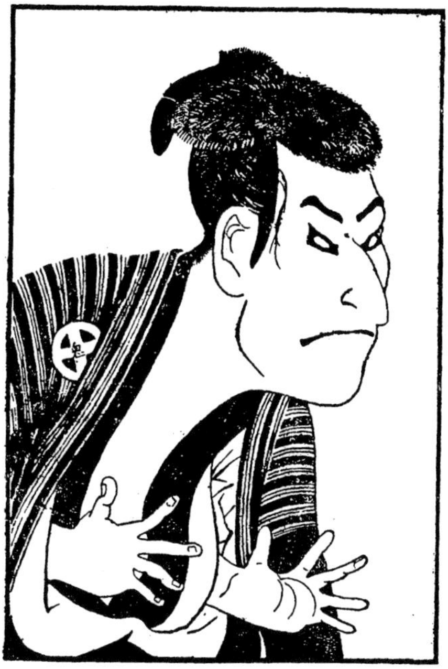

Otani Oniji (Actor). By Sharaku.

"The picture, drawn for the engraver upon thin translucent paper, is pasted face downwards upon a block of wood,* usually cherry—sawn in the direction of the grain, instead of across it, as in Europe—and the superfluous thickness of paper is removed by a process of scraping until the design is clearly visible; the borders of the outline are then incised with a knife, the interspaces between the lines of the drawing being excavated by means of tools of various shapes. The ink is applied with a brush, and the printing effected by hand pressure (assisted by a kind of pad), to which procedure may be attributed much of the beauty of the result. Gradations of tone and polychromatic effects may be produced from a single block by suitable application of ink or colour upon the wood; and a great deal of artistic feeling is exercised in the printing of the picture after the designer and engraver have finished their portion of the work.

"In ordinary colour prints, effects are obtained by the use of a number of additional blocks engraved in series from copies of the outline impression taken from the first or outline block. The correctness of register is secured by preserving two angles of the original block level with the surface of the lines of the engraving, and marking each of these with incisions in a certain direction. The angles are printed off upon the sheet bearing the first outline, and are repeated in facsimile in the cutting of all subsequent blocks, the corner marks left upon the paper after contact with block No. 1 thus being made to serve as an exact guide for the accurate apposition of the sheet upon each successive block. The printings are all effected by hand pressure"—not by a printing press.

Sharaku, whose few prints date from 1787 to 1795, made a specialty of actors' portraits in character. These are the most powerful and realistic of all Ukiyoye prints, and are very rare.

* Called Shita Han—In English, the "Key Block."

(*Continued*)

ARTISTIC, AESTHETIC, AND POETIC TASTES OF THE JAPANESE

(Concluded)

COLOR PRINTS (Ukiyoye, "Passing World Pictures")

Sometimes as many as 20 blocks are used for the necessary colors. The ordinary size of prints is 14 × 8 inches, blocks of larger size tending to warp.

In restricted space only a list can be given of the most noted color-print artists and the subjects they favored.

Actors in their favorite roles. Torii school artists: Shunsho, Sharaku, and Toyokuni.

Beautiful women (Bi-jin prints). Outstanding artists: Harunobu, Kiyonaga, Shunsho, Yeishi, Utamaro, and Toyokuni.

Landscapes (*Kei-shoku*). Hokusai and Hiroshige above all others. Foreign collectors are in constant quest of original prints of Hokusai's "36 color prints of Mt. Fuji," finally including 46 views in all, and of his Chinese Poets and their poems, a series of 10 long prints, where, in attractive manner, figures and landscapes are combined, and of Hiroshige's "Views of the Tokaido" and of Yedo, and particularly of his master-pieces, the "53 stations of the Tokaido," which, with the terminal stations, Kyoto and Yedo (Tokyo), make 55 in all—the stations whereat the great feudal processions of the *daimyo* stopped during their journeys to and from Yedo.

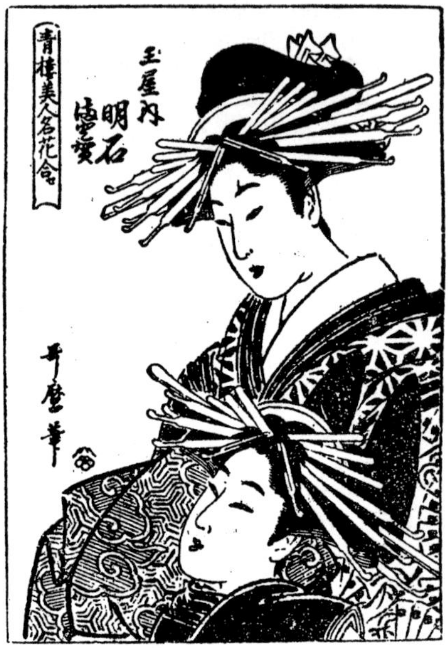

Courtesans by Utamaro (1754-1805).

Prints of birds and flowers (*Kwa-cho*), often with a few lines of what in English is known as "Free verse." Though a classical art of Chinese origin popularized by the Ukiyoye school, it was not confined to that school. Hiroshige's exquisite and delicate series of these prints are deservedly famous.

There are many cleverly executed imitations and fakes of Japanese prints, and the general rule of "let the buyer beware" applies in Japan, as in all countries. Before purchasing a high-priced print which is offered as an original an expert should be consulted. The prints handled by Mr. S. M. Shiba, and Yamatoya, Miyanoshita, experts on color prints, are guaranteed as to their genuineness. The Ukiyoye Society of Japan, 1127 Uyehara, Yokogi, Tokyo, will gladly furnish information relative to color prints. A book, "Process of Wood-cut Printing Explained," is on sale in the Fujiya Hotel Arcade, ¥2.

The best of Japanese prints may be found abroad in the United States at the Boston Museum, the Metropolitan Museum of Art in New York, and in the art galleries of Chicago and other Western cities; in London, at the British, and the Victoria and Albert Museums.

SATSUMA PORCELAIN

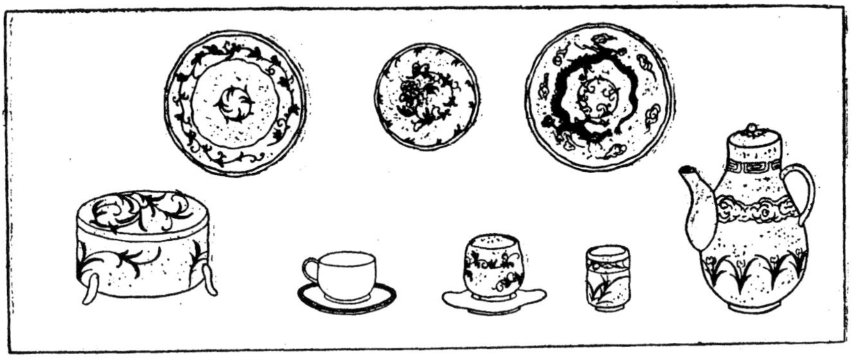

Satsuma-yaki, the beautifully decorated crackled porcelain, which has made the name Satsuma known to the whole artistic world, is produced at Kagoshima and Ijuin, in Kyushu. From the time that Kyoto took the lead in the production of this ware the Kyushu potters have not flourished as in the old days. The inhabitants of Ijuin are descendants of the potters who were brought over from Korea by Shimazu Yoshihisa, *daimyo* of Satsuma, one of Hideyoshi's generals, when in 1598 the army returned to Japan. These potters were given the rank of *samurai*, and, with their fellow countrymen in other parts of Kyushu, established the Japanese ceramic industry on an artistic basis. The earliest specimens of this ware are rarely seen. It is also called Awata-yaki, due to the similarity of the wares and the high reputation of the product of the Kinkozan Pottery, in the Awata District, Kyoto, which has been maintained since 1755.

The characteristic of Satsuma is its soft, warm, light-buff creamy ground of ivory-like lustrous glaze with a mazy crackled surface, adorned with a wealth of gold, red, green, and blue enamel —the whole exquisite in its rich mellowness. The maker's name is usually placed on the bottom of each piece of this ware.

Satsuma is generally regarded by collectors as the most representative national ceramic ware of Japan. "Satsuma" is an Ainu name, pronounced in that language "Satma"; it means "Dry Peninsula." The Ainu are the aborigines of Japan.

ARITA (—ALSO KNOWN AS IMARI—) PORCELAIN

Arita is situated in Saga Prefecture, N. W. Kyushu, 109 m. W. of Shimonoseki, Moji; 57 m. from Nagasaki. In olden days, Imari, 8 m. from Arita, was the seaport from which Arita porcelain was shipped, and its name became attached to these products (Imari-yaki), though it never was the seat of their manufacture.

The beginning of the ceramic art of Arita is traced to Shonzui Gorodayu, an Ise Province potter, early 16th century, the first in Japan to manufacture porcelain proper as distinguished from pottery; but the industry languished until it was given a new impulse with the return of Hideyoshi's army from Korea, in 1598, when one of his generals brought back several Korean potters, one of whom discovered near Arita the noted Izumiyama deposite, some of them almost pure kaolin, and all of incomparable quality,—which started the manufacture of real porcelain in Japan.

Arita porcelain became famous for its decoration with vitrifiable enamels: red oxid of iron and rich blues under glaze, and later with decorations over the glaze. The use of these enamels originated in the 17th century with two experts, Goroshichi and Kakiemon, who carried the art to a point of considerable excellence. From that time on Arita and other potteries turned out quantities of porcelain profusely decorated with blue under the glaze and colored enamels over it. Of the two experts, Kakiemon's early masterpieces are almost beyond price. Captain Brinkley warns collectors against being duped by specimens of Imari sold by unprincipled dealers as examples of the original Kakiemon's work. There were several generations of Kakiemons.

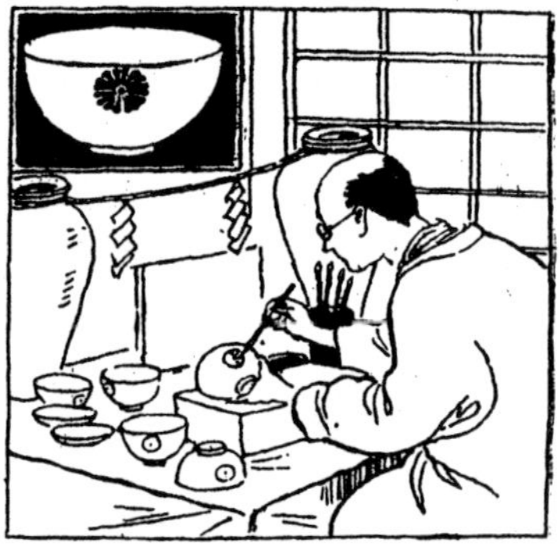

A senior artist decorating a set of rice bowls for the Imperial Household.

The earlier pieces were decorated with peonies and chrysanthemums, small landscapes, human figures in red and gold, sometimes with a little green. The blue, violet, yellow, and black muffle colors belong to a later period. Says Captain Brinkley: "Thus there came into existence the familar *Nishiki-de,* or "Brocade Pattern"—a brilliant ware, depending chiefly upon wealth of decoration and richness of coloring."

KUTANI ("NINE VALLEYS") PORCELAIN

The well-known Kutani ware is manufactured in Ishikawa Prefecture, N. W. Japan, but Yamashiro, with the workshops and kilns of the Kutani Pottery Co., and others, is regarded as the principal place of production of this ware.

This industry was developed about the middle of the 17th century principally through the efforts of Goto Saijiro, a Kyoto potter (under the patronage of Maeda Toshiharu, Daimyo of Daishoji), who discovered a good kaolin at the now moribund hamlet of Kutani (9 m. S-E. of Yamashiro), and who, at Arita, Kyushu, mastered the secrets of the potter's art so highly developed there. Upon his return in 1664, assisted by Hisazumi Morikage, a Kyoto painter, he helped the Kutani potters develop the production of "Old Kutani" wares, now so highly prized by connoisseurs. These ware were called *Ao-Kutani*, because *ao*, a deep-green transparent glaze, or enamel, brilliant and beautiful, was extensively used in their decoration. Together with yellow, purple, and soft Prussian blue, this glaze was applied in floral designs, scrolls and diapers. The main colors in other "Old Kutani" were green and red, to which were added purple, yellow, blue (enamel), silver, and gold. *Ao-Kutani* commands universal admiration, and probably is not equaled; it had few rivals in its fine harmony of colors and their massing, and the technical skill with which the enamels were applied. The best pieces, carefully, effectively and peculiarly decorated, are classed by ceramic experts among the most beautiful products of this art.

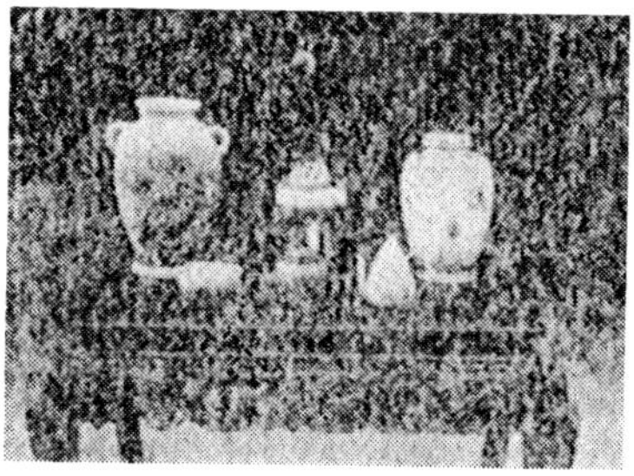

The industry suffered an extended decline, but in 1843 was revived, largely due to Iida-ya Hachiroemon, a porcelain painter, who originated a new style of design on a red ground, consisting of minute and elaborate tracings in gold of formal scrolls, diapers, and medallions enclosing conventional symbols, also copies of miniature landscapes, flowers blown by the breeze, birds among branches, and other aspects of nature in her simplest form. This "Red Painting" (*Aka-e*) quickly spread to other kilns of the district and has remained the distinguishing feature of Kutani pottery. The Kutani red, of soft opaque color, varies from rich Indian red to a russet brown.

Captain Brinkley says: "The amateur may be tolerably confident that specimens decorated with peacocks, masses of chrysanthemums and peonies, figures of wrinkled saints, brightly appareled ladies, cocks upon drums, etc. belong to the manufactures of modern times."

Kutani ware was further popularized by the introduction, about 1865, of a brocade pattern. This gold and red, or *kinrandei* (gold brocade) decoration is distinctively Chinese in character. During the past 50 years foreign orders have demanded flashy decoration of big vases, dinner and tea sets, etc., glittering with gilding, but wares, less gorgeous in coloring and more classical in design, are also produced to meet the taste of those who prefer a chaste and refined style.

The early pottery bears either the name Kutani, or the ideograph, 福, *fuku* ("Good Luck"). Since 1850 the pottery carries the name of its decorator (not of the potter).

THE LEGEND OF SILK

The Empress and the caterpillar

Once upon a time a dainty little Chinese Empress, while idling in her garden, had her attention drawn to a caterpillar which was building for itself a beautiful little house with threads spun from its own body. An idea came to the little Empress—could she—could she

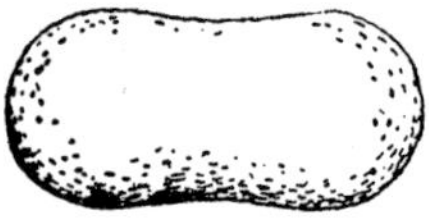
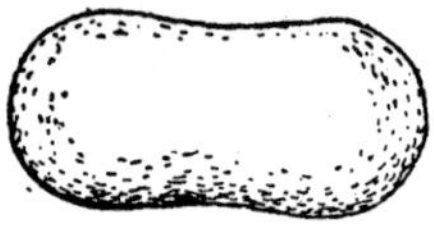
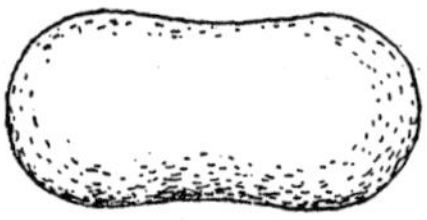

unravel the slender shiny thread which enveloped the tiny body and get one long thread—if so, what exquisite fabric it would make!

She asked the Emperor to give her a grove of choice mulberry trees, and there she worked, and cultivated the tiny worms which finally spun elaborate, beautiful threads with which they eneveloped their bodies. She took each cocoon, carefully unraveled the long threads, and one happy day she succeeded

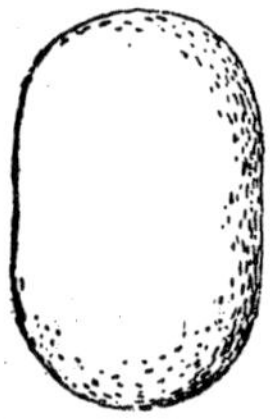
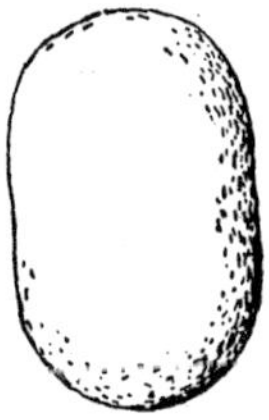

in twisting together the strands from several of the little silk balls into many long threads. Hundreds of yards she wound off, and from them she wove a shimmering fabric more wonderful than any that had ever been seen before—and ever since that eventful day the world has clothed itself in silk—and the world has honored the litttle Chinese Empress by calling the magic cloth she discovered by her name, which was Si Line-shi. In China her cloth is known as "si," in France as "soie" and in English-speaking lands as "silk."

The Empress died more than 4,500 years ago, and for more than 2,000 years after her death the manufacture of silk remained a secret with the Imperial family of China. Much silk was exported.

The penalty for exporting the silkworms or silk eggs from China was death, but legend says that the

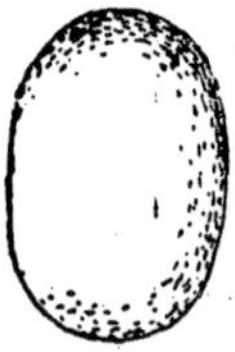
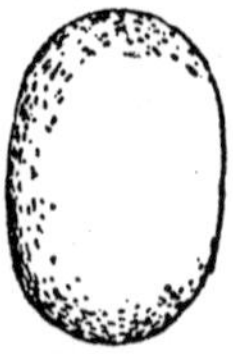

progressive Roman Emperor, Justinan, persuaded two Persian priests, who had lived in China for many years, to go and bring back some silk eggs with them. This they did, returning with the precious eggs concealed in a hollow in their pilgrim's staffs. It was from these eggs that the Western world was supplied with silk for twelve centuries, for the overland trade with China fell off, and Chinese silk became more and more rare.

THE MAGIC SILKWORM

According to the temperature, it takes from 3 to 7 days for the moth eggs, or "seed," to hatch the worm—which then commences a short span of life that scarcely ever exceeds 40 days. At first it is black in color, a short ⅛ in. in length, covered with long hair and with a shiny nose.

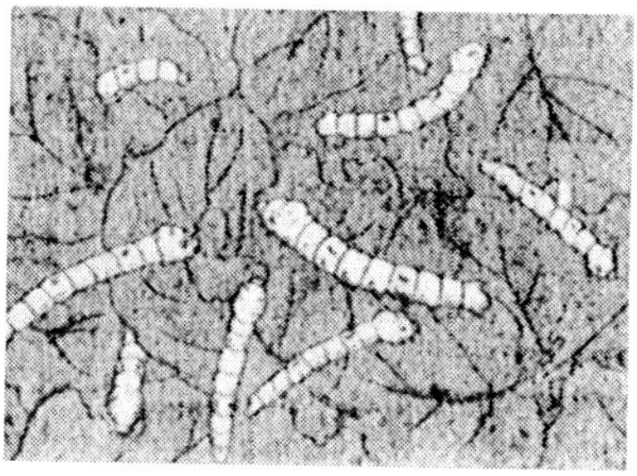

Silkworms eating mulberry leaves.

The worm has four molting periods or "sleeps," in each one shedding its old skin for a new one as the skin cannot keep pace with the worm's growth. The periods between these molts are called "ages," there being five, the first extending from the time of hatching to the end of the first molt, and the last from the end of the fourth molt to the transformation of the insect into a chrysalis. When the worm molts it ceases eating, grows slightly lighter in color, fastens itslf firmly to some object, and, holding up its head and the fore part of its body, remains in a torpid state for nearly two days. In molting, the old skin breaks at the nose, the head is pushed out, and the worm, by wriggling and twisting, gradually works the old skin back from segment to segment until it is entirely cast off.

By each successive molt the worm grows lighter in color, finally becoming slate or cream white; and the hair, long at first, gradually disappears. Weak and feeble after each molt, the worm gains strength by resting and then, freshened, supple and hungry, begins again to eat the mulberry leaves with such renewed vigor that several thousand of the worms eating make a noise like falling rain. They are fed with the tenderest leaves, assorted and chopped according to the age of the worms. In rainy weather each leaf is carefully wiped: dampness might be fatal. The worm lives for about 40 days as a worm, until it attains its full growth of about 3 in.—and in apppearance it is then one of the ugliest objects of animate nature—then the buzzing noise of the crunched leaves ceases and the worm, with the instinct of a perfect engineer, fastens its silken guy lines to a twig or bundle of straw so that the cocoon will be effectively secured in place.

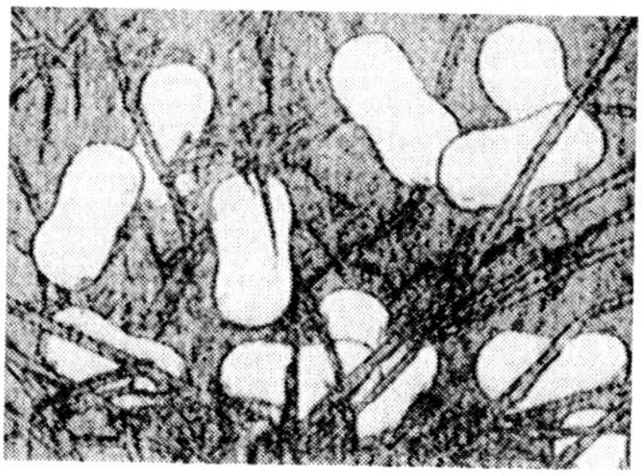

Cocoons on their straw beds.

Continued—

Concluding—

THE MAGIC SILKWORM

This worm now spins itself, in its precious white cocoon, into the sleep from which only the small minority reserved for breeding will ever awake. It is now only about 2 in. in length. The silk is elaborated in a semi-fluid condition in two long vessels inside the worm. Near the head of the worm these vessels grow more selender, finally uniting within the spinneret—the small orifice below the mouth, from which the silk issues in a glutinous state and apparently in a single thread. The worm works incessantly. The thin, gauze-like network which soon surrounds it gradually thickens until, in 24 hrs. after beginning to spin, the worm is nearly hidden from view.

The motion of the worm's head in starting the cocoon is very rapid and 9 to 10 in. (nearly a foot) of silk flows from the spinneret in a minute. Later, the average is about half this amount. The worm first makes the outline of the cocoon, after which it works from the inside, gradually enveloping itself. From 3 to 5 days are required to complete the cocoon, which then is about 1 in. in length and which, when unwound, gives from 800 to 1000 yards of firm, continuous thread. During the short life of the worm the temperature of the room must be maintained at about 72°F. Thus the worm provides a silk filament, derived from mulberry leaves, which has been transformed in its body by a magical process. The silk first spun by the worm in getting its bearings is loose and is known as "floss." This floss, or outside loose silk, is known as "waste silk." As there are more than 1000 breeds of silkworms, all cocoons are not of the same shape or color. Some are oval; some are like a peanut. In the domestic markets cocoons are the objects of lively transactions.

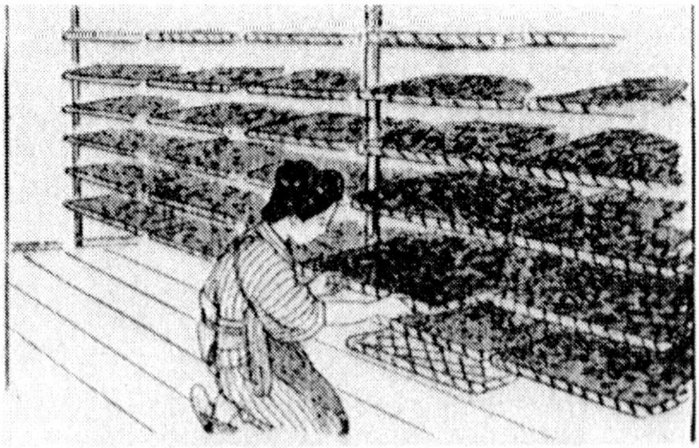

The farmer's wife rears the silkworms.

A cocoon may be unraveled by hand through several hours' patient labor. The unraveling is the work of the filatures, hand and steam, where the filaments of from 4 to 6 cocoons are united into a single thread—the raw silk of the commercial world gathered into skeins.

Some of the subject-matter of this silk series has been compiled from *Foundations of Japan* by Mr. J. W. Robertson Scott, and from a booklet on silk issued by Brainerd & Armstrong Co., for both of which acknowledgment is made.

THE PROGENITORS OF THE SILKWORM

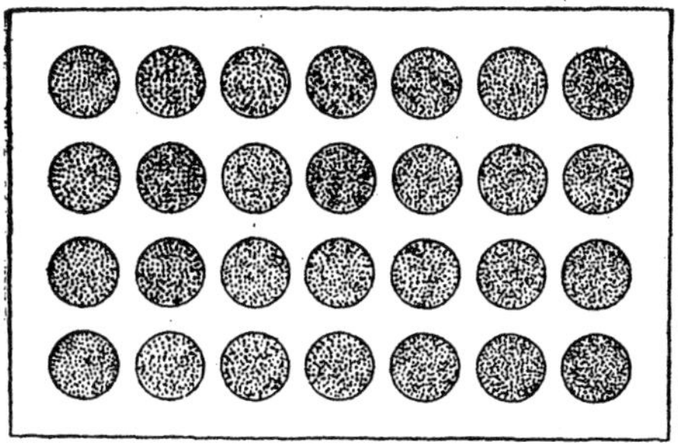

An egg card.

Introducing *Mr. and Mrs. Bombyx mori*—small moths half an inch long, wings of ashen white—the parents of the silkworm. In the whole world of stock raising there is nothing more remarkable than the birth of silk-worm moths. The cocoons on the racks in the farmer's home are covered by sheets of newspaper in which a number of round holes about ¾ in. in diameter have been cut. When the moths emerge from their cocoons* they seek these openings and creep through them towards the light. For newly-born creatures they evince astonishing ardor. On the newspaper the few males who have not found partners dance wildly, their wings whirring at a mad pace. From time to time they cease dancing and haunt the holes, through which the newly-born moths emerge.

When a female appears, a male instantly rushes towards her, or rather the two creatures rush toward each other and at once are locked in a fast embrace. Immediately their wings cease to flutter, the only commotion on the newspaper being made by the unmated males. In the hatching room these males on the stacks of trays are so numerous that the place is filled with the sound of their wings. From time to time the girls and women in charge of the silkworms lift down the trays and pick up and cast aside the superfluous male moths.

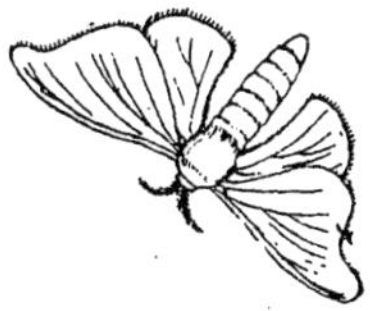

The female moths, when their partners have been removed, are each put within a half-inch-high tin ring 2 inches in diameter, placed on cards on which the eggs are laid, and each moth immediately begins to deposit eggs (usually from 600 to 800 of them), called "seed," in her ring. There are 28 of these tin rings on each card, which is about 10× 12 inches square. The bottom of each "compartment" becomes covered with eggs which, being sticky when laid, adhere to the card. The moth is destroyed. The egg is nearly round, slightly flattened, and closely resembles a turnip seed. It takes fully 30,000 eggs to make an ounce avoirdupois. Each egg has a small spot on one end, when hatched, the worm gnaws a hole through this spot.

The discovery that the hatching season can be controlled by regulating the temperature in which the eggs are kept made Spring, Summer, and Autumn rearing possible, thus increasing the cocoon production.

* Except with cocoons intended for seed, the moths are not allowd to emerge, as their escape would break so many threads that the cocoons would be ruined for reeling. To prevent this the chrysalis is stifled by steam or hot water.

SERICULTURE IN JAPAN

Raw silk is the principal and most important staple in the exports of Japan, constituting about 37% of the total amount of its foreign trade. By "raw silk" is meant the silk thread twisted into thick skeins of the natural color, the palest shade of buff, almost white. The product of the so-called wild silkworms is usually yellow, but, strictly speaking, there are no wild silks, all cocoons of commercial value are cultivated. The most important of this "wild silk", called "pongee", is produced by the tussar worm, which is an oak leaf feeder.

Japan supplies about 60%, as against about 30% from China, of the rest of the world's raw-silk needs, the United States taking from 85 to 90% of the quantity exported. The value of the raw silk exported increased from $3,040,500 in 1868 to $381,040,140 in the 1929 boom year, with a high rate of $2,200 a bale in 1919. In the memorable year 1929 when U.S. Steel sold for $260, raw silk touched $700 a bale. In August, 1932, when Steel was down to $26, raw silk was sold for the equivalent of $153 a bale on the Yokohama Silk Exchange. Nothing affects the Japanese silk market so quickly as the changes in American business conditions.

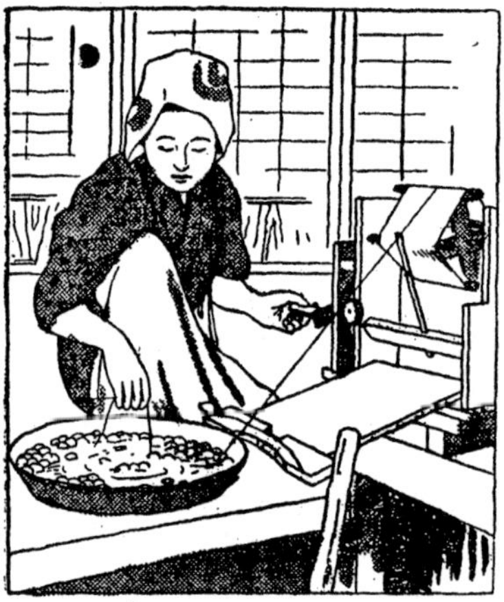

Farmer's wife unraveling cocoons.

Sericulture is next in importance to rice cultivation and raw silk is the foremost of Japanese exports. In 1931 the raw silk exported paid for all the cotton, coal, rubber, and automobiles Japan imported in that year. About 40% of the farmers of Japan, or more than 2,000,000 households, are engaged in sericulture, and about one-tenth of the arable land of the country is planted with mulberry trees, on the leaves of which the silkworm feeds.

Japan has become the world's chief source of raw silk because her large farming population, engaged in the intensive cultivation of very small farms, provides the mass of the virtually unpaid labor which is needed. Practically the entire cocoon output is produced as a subsidiary occupation for the farmer's wife and children whose painstaking care of the worms night and day at a time when they could not otherwise be gainfully employed adds nothing to the cost—which is mainly the cost of the egg-cards and the rent of the land on which the pollarded mulberry trees grow.

THE MULBERRY ("Kuwa")

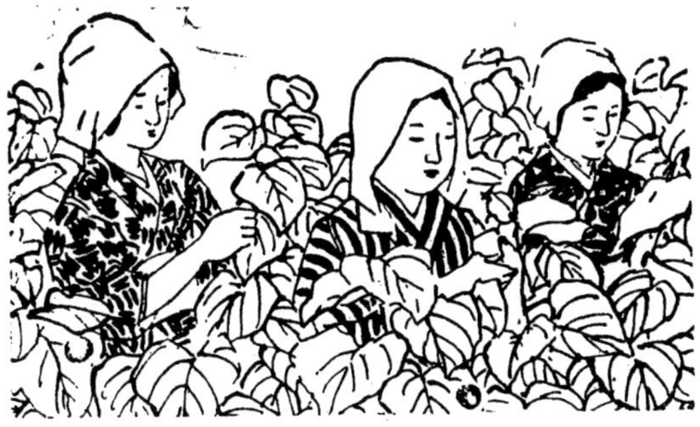

Inasmuch as in the description relative to silk-worms several references have been made to the tender leaves upon which the *Okaiko sama* ("Honorable Silkworms") feed—in fact, the only food they have—it is pertinent to write something about the Japanese mulberry, the leaves of which the silkworm by a marvelous process within its own body transforms into silk.

While there are large mulberry trees in Japan, the majority of them are small, seldom attaining a diameter larger than six or seven inches, and not often more than six or seven feet in height. The branches of these trees are cut off in spring to make way for new branches to grow. These branches grow rapidly, about as fast as grass. When traveling one sees patches of these dwarfed, pollarded trees—more like a shrub than a tree, with knobs around their trunks where the old branches have been cut off—near farmhouses whose occupants rear silkworms.

Besides its leaves the mulberry is valuable for other purposes. Its bark makes a very good grade of paper, and many kinds of Japanese paper are made from the pulp of the cut-off branches. Its wood, especially that of large trees, is highly valued in cabinet work and furniture. The mulberry bears a purplish-black berry somewhat like a blackberry, but longer, which has an agreeable taste, but the berries are not produced in any one locality in quantity that warrants sending them to market. They are gathered and relished by the farmers' children.

But this utilization of the mulberry is insignificant in comparison with the value of its leaves as food for silkworms. In the three seasons for rearing the worms, but especially in the spring season—the most important—the farmer's wife and children are busy from dawn to late at night picking leaves enough to satisfy the voracious appetites of the silkworms—with the added labor that should the leaves be damp from any cause each one must be wiped dry.

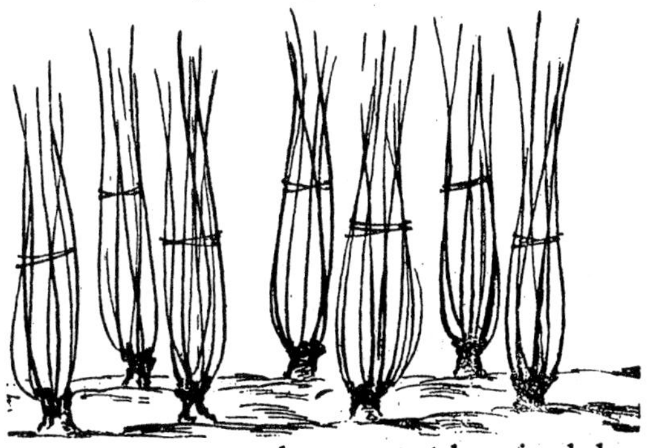

JAPANESE GREEN TEA

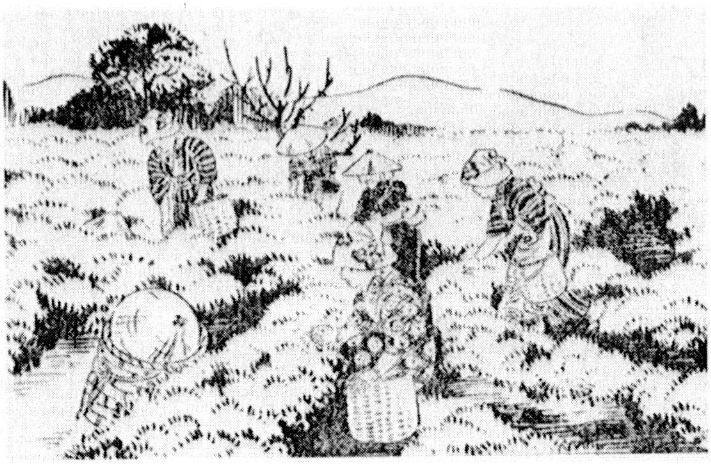

So far as known, the earliest reference to tea-drinking in Japan was recorded in the 8th century. It was first brought to Japan from China and was used more as a medicine than as a beverage. In the 12th century the tea-plant began to be cultivated in the Uji district, not far from Kyoto, the ancient capital of Japan, tea seeds having been brought there from China by a Japanese Buddhist priest, Yeisai. At the present time the tea plantations of Shizuoka prefecture are much more extensive than those of Uji and their product constitutes an important item in the foreign trade of Japan.

Japanese green tea is a mild and fragrant drink. It has a definite food value, according to chemical analysis, in that it contains the health-giving vitamins A and C in liberal portions. Recent researches disclose that all kinds of tea are highly alkaline, a property needed to counteract the undesirable effects of acids contained in fish and meat. Also that the mangan content of tea kills microbes, while its considerable iron content plays an important role in purifying the blood—thus present-day research endorses the ancient Chinese use of tea as a medicine.

One pound of Japanese green tea will make 200 to 250 cups of moderate strength. For making it, an earthen pot is best and should be scalded before using. A teaspoonful of tea for each cup should be put into the pot, and boiling water poured on it. With high grade tea, Japanese boil the water thoroughly and then allow it to become lukewarm before pouring it into the pot, then before drinking they eat something sweet, cake usually, claiming that only in this way can its subtle charm of taste and fragrance be realized.

The highest grade of Japanese green tea, named "Gyokuro," retails for ¥15 a pound—and from that price down to about 40 sen for the ordinary "Bancha."

The total tea area in Japan is about 106,000 acres, which produce about 90,000,000 lbs. of prepared tea annually.

BAMBOO ("TAKE")

"The most useful plant in the world"

The uses of bamboo are almost numberless, but 1400 ways of its use in Japan have been listed. It gives the Japanese chopsticks, umbrellas, building and fencing materials, fans, arrows, *fude* (writing brushes), baskets, pipes for conveying water, besides many other things of utility and value. It is also carved for ornamental purposes. Edison, when he first produced electric lamps, used bamboo filaments obtained from Yawata, a town situated between Kyoto and Osaka.

Bamboo is a grass; from a botanical point of view it is a tree grass. The biggest specimens come from Java and India, where the giant bamboo has been known to reach a height of 120 feet. There are about 490 known species of bamboo. The main plant runs underground, the canes as they grow up are only branches, therefore a grove of bamboos may be only one plant and anything that affects a part of it will affect the whole.

Take-no-ko (Baby Bamboo or Bamboo shoot) first comes up very slowly, generally in the spring and autumn and only occasionally in the summer. Its growth then gradually increases more rapidly until it reaches half its full height, after which the growth is less rapid. It has the most rapid rate of growth of any plant known. At maximum speed its growth is 49.5 to 50 centimeteres (19.5 to 20 in.) in 24 hours. Its greatest record growth is 91 centimetres (about 36 in.) in 24 hours. It has wonderful strength, elasticity and extreme hardness. It is so hard that some of its species, if struck by a piece of steel, will give off sparks. This is due to the amount of silicon it contains.

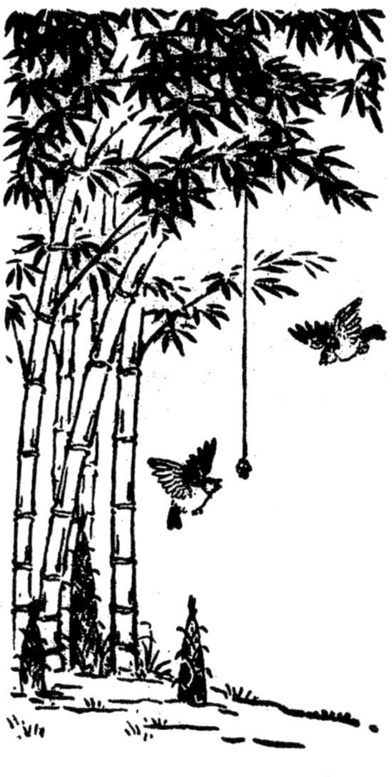

Take-no-ko supplies a delicate foodstuff which is sliced and cooked in various ways; cooked with rice it is called *Take-no-ko Meshi*. Some restaurants make a specialty of this dish.

Bamboo flowers, but only rarely. There is saying in the Far East that it only flowers in time of famine, and instances of this have been recorded.

A bamboo forest is worth much money and brings good return for the care and trouble given. At the time of a severe earthquake such forests are considered safe ground on account of the matted roots.

BAMBOO BASKETS

In Japan the best bamboo is found in the vicinity of Kyoto, and its use for artistic baskets constitutes the best known artcraft of ancient origin. At first bamboo baskets were imported from China, but about 1730, the mid-Tokugawa period, baskets far superior to the Chinese products were produced in Japan. At present the traditions of the profession of basket-weaving are maintained by Chikuryosai Yamamoto, of Osaka, an artistic workman.

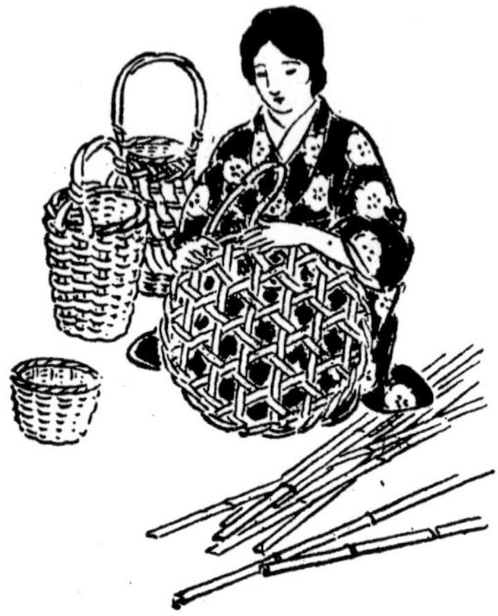

The basket material is selected from bamboos growing in the center of a grove for the reason that, not being exposed to strong winds, they grow straight. Bamboo is cut in early autumn, and is seasoned in the vicinity of the grove for about a year. Various climatic and weather conditions regulate bamboo cutting, which, when fulfilled, provide bamboo less likely to be worm-eaten.

Only the bark of the bamboo is used for baskets. This is cut by a sharp knife, then the skin is taken off. This process requires great skill, acquired only after years of experience. Forms of novel originality are produced by master-craftsmen, no especial pattern being followed, and recognized artists sign their names to their best productions.

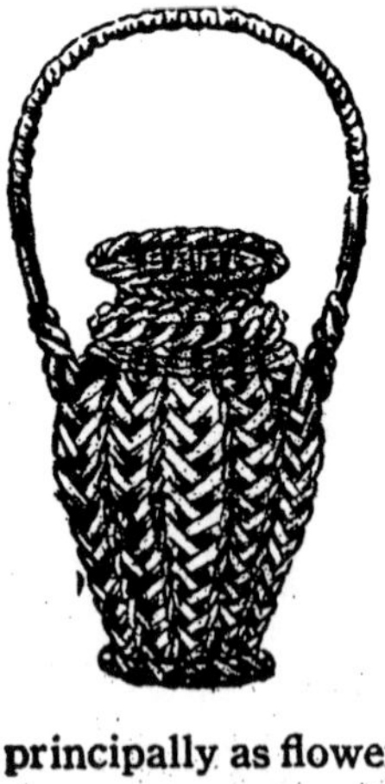

Roughly, bamboo baskets are of two forms: one symmetrical and elegant in appearance—for which only narrow materials are used—the other with an appearance of simplicity and coarseness, obtained through the use of wide materials. Sometimes old brown-colored bamboo is used. This is obtained from the ceilings of old farm-houses, which, because the houses have no chimneys, are colored through the years by smoke and soot from the family hearth. When woven into baskets such bamboos have a very soft, rich, silky appearance. Also, baskets made from new bamboo are painted brown or lemon color, and are used principally as flower-containers each holding a container for water. In the tea-ceremony bamboo-basket vases of the finest quality are used.

Varied forms of baskets are shown in the pictures.

STRAW-ROCK-BRICK-TILE-BERRIES

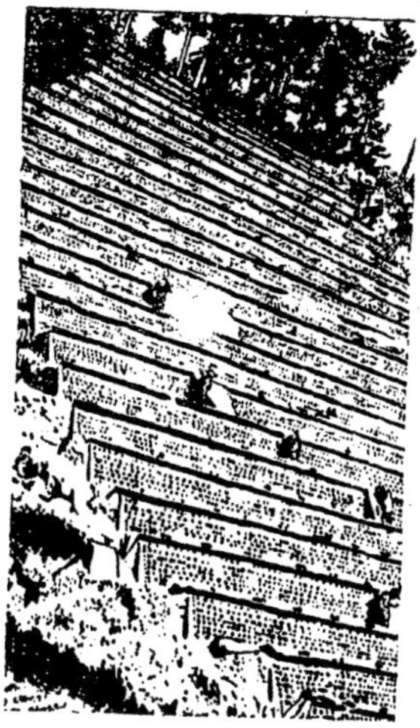

A novel method of strawberry cultivation has been developed in Shizuoka prefecture where steep slopes, useless as farm land, but exposed to the sun, have been cut into terraces, each terrace being faced with stone, brick, or by concrete tile, mortared together. The strawberry plants are placed in the junctures left for them—in tile in the V-shaped spaces, as shown. These tiles are about 18 in. long, 6 in. high, and 1½ in. thick. The various materials used retain the sun's heat and at night are covered with straw mats in order to conserve this heat. The plants are watered daily. Strawberries, large, and of superior flavor, are thus produced the year round.

The young shoots are placed in the fall, and are removed after they cease to bear. The tiles, or other materials, are then loosened and fertilizer (beancake and herring) is placed behind them. New shoots are taken from the discarded plants.

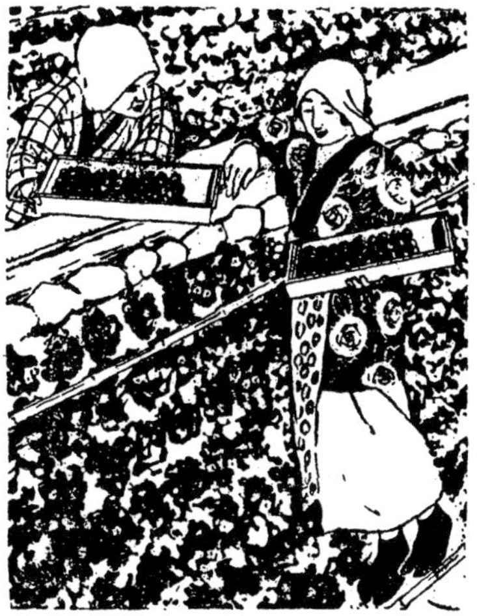

It is a profitable industry. Hebizuka, an ill-faring fishing hamlet before taking up the cultivation of strawberries, is said to produce about ¥400,000 worth of the fruit annually.

Pictures from the "Asahigraph" April, '33.

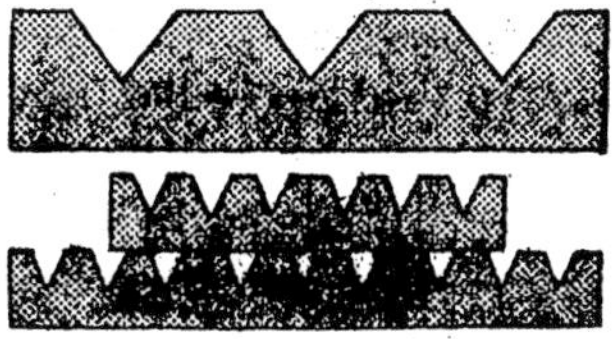

BICYCLES

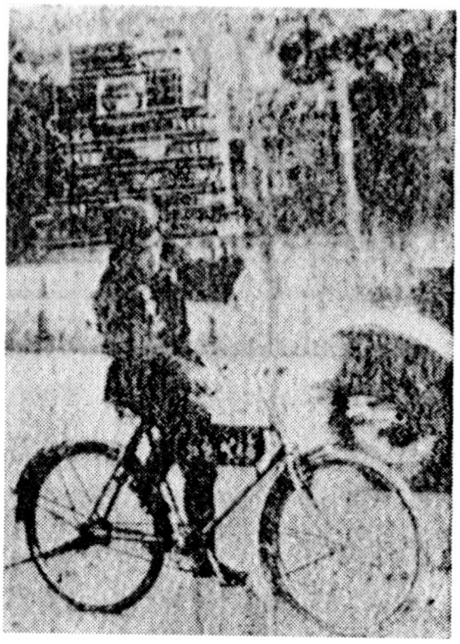

A soba (noodle) delivery boy. His balancing is almost acrobatic.

Foreign visitors, on their first trip to Japan, are amazed to find so many bicycles are used. The riders of these bicyles race with motorcars, trucks, and trams along congested city streets, narrow side streets and country roads. What the flivver is to America, the bicycle is to Japan. Schoolboys, messenger boys, bakery boys and restaurant delivery boys, glaziers' boys with a stock of glass on their backs, pedlers, and so on, all use bikes—and all are expert pedalers. They carry astonishing loads, making themselves and their vehicles anathema to motorists as well as to pedestrians, as they weave in and out at top speed through small lanes and chance openings in congested traffic.

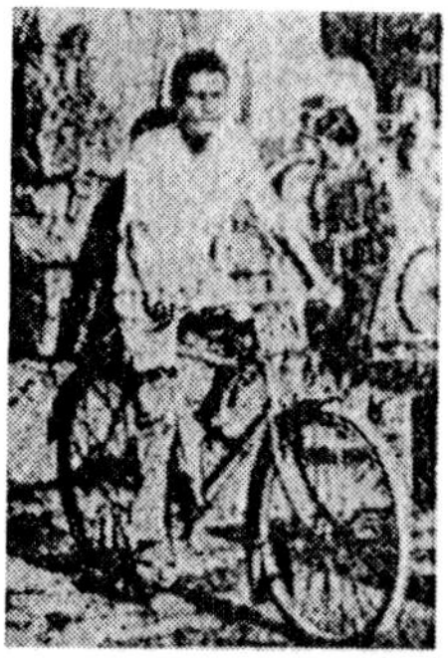

The lad with numerous trays, as pictured, is on his way to deliver *soba* (spaghetti) soup. The bowls contain warm *soba*, with fish; the boxes, cold *soba*. The young man pushing his load of boxes, tubs and cans, is a pedler of cooked food, etc., and pickles, on his daily rounds.

At the end of 1932 there were 6,356,157 bicycles in Japan proper, and, as the life of a bike is from 3 to 5 years, there is a steady demand for renewals—said to be about one million annually. In 1933 the export of Japanese bicycles and tires totaled nearly 12 million *yen*. This condition is the result of 30 years of strenuous effort in this industry. Large bicycle companies produce the bulk of the 2-wheelers, but small scale plants, producing bikes or accessories, constitute the majority of Japan's manufacturers of bicycles. At the end of 1933 there were approximately 770 bicycle factories, most of them making parts and accessories. Of these, 403 each employed more than five workers, but some of the factories do business on a huge scale. The manufacturing centers are Tokyo, Osaka, and Nagoya. China is the largest customer for Japanese bicycles, parts, and fittings, followed in the past by the Straits Settlements, and the Dutch East Indies. Recent tariff barriers have lessened bicycle exports to these countries.

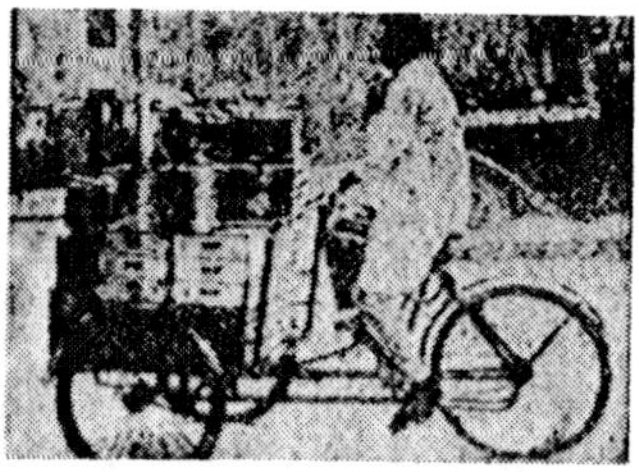

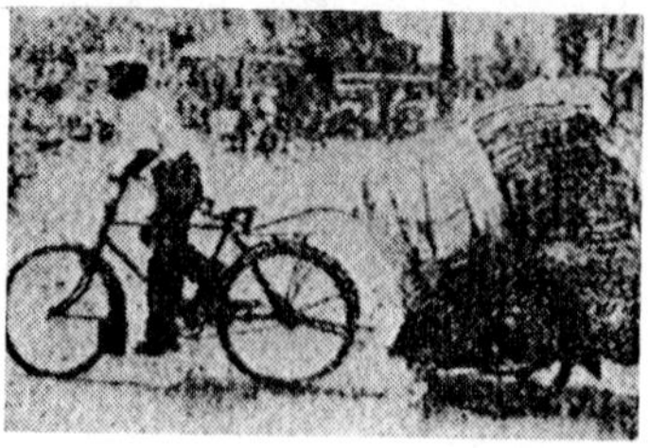

WILL ADAMS SHRINE

Kurofune-Fudo (*Kuro*=black, *fune*=ship). *Kurofune-Fudo* is the name of a shrine in Tokyo, dedicated in 1930 to *Fudo* (God of Achara), in which is enshrined the spirit of Will Adams, the English pilot of a Dutch fleet, whose vessel, "Charity," was the only one of the fleet to reach Japan (1600), at a small Kyushu Island port, after great hardships. Inscribed on the stone monument in front of the shrine is the following, in English:

IN MEMORY OF WILLIAM ADAMS KNOWN AS MIURA ANJIN THE FIRST ENGLISHMAN TO SETTLE IN JAPAN, COMING AS PILOT ON BOARD THE CHARITY IN 1600, WHO RESIDED IN A MANSION BUILT ON THIS SPOT, WHO INSTRUCTED IYEYASU THE FIRST TOKUGAWA SHOGUN ON GUNNERY, GEOGRAPHY, MATHEMATICS, ETC. AND CONSTRUCTED FOR HIM SEVERAL SHIPS ON THE EUROPEAN MODEL, WHILE RENDERING VALUABLE SERVICES IN FOREIGN AFFAIRS, AND WHO MARRIED A JAPANESE LADY, MISS MAGOME, AND DIED ON MAY 16, 1620 AT THE AGE OF FORTY-FIVE YEARS.

ERECTED BY THE PRINCIPAL RESIDENTS OF ANJIN-CHO, JULY 28, 1930.

Adams was known as *Miura Anjin* (*Miura*—the name of the county where he first lived, *Anjin*—Pilot), or "Miura Pilot."

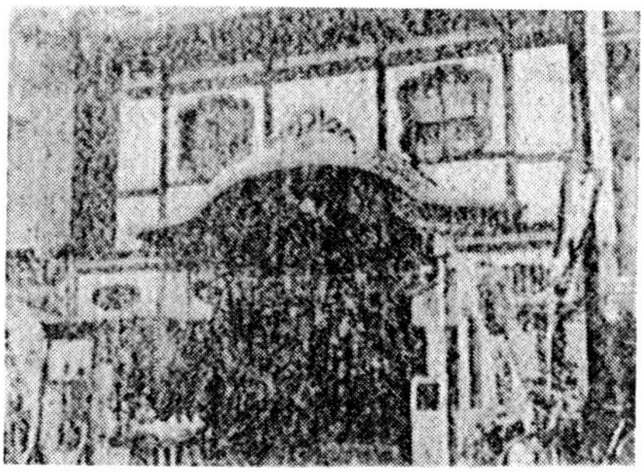

This shrine is near the Mitsukoshi department store, at Nihombashi.

Captain Quackernack, Will Adams, and Jan Joosten, a sailor, were among the 24 survivors of the original 110 composing the crew. They were taken to Sakai (near Osaka), and imprisoned. Later, the Captain left for Holland; Adams and Joosten were brought to Yedo (Tokyo), but as Adams rendered valuable service to Iyeyasu, the first Tokugawa Shogun, a plot of ground and a yearly revenue of rice was given him, as a recompense. The street on which his house stood was named *Anjin-cho* ("Pilot Street"), after him. In the reconstruction of Tokyo, after the 1923 earthquake, the street was obliterated, but the shrine, as stated, marks the site of his house.

Jan Joosten was given a plot of ground in Yedo, part of which is now occupied by the N.Y.K. building opposite the Imperial Palace. The street on which his house stood was called *Yaesu-cho* ("Eight-fold Sandbar Street"—which suggests the Imperial or Shogunate Palace). This, a Japanese rendering of Jan Joosten, was shortened to *Yaesu-cho*, as being less difficult to pronounce. Since the 1923 earthquake this street has been known as Marunouchi ("Inside the Circular Moat") street.

THE AINUS OF JAPAN

The Ainus (which in their own language means "man") are regarded as the aborigines of Japan, who, from meagre early records, it is surmised, came to Japan in some great wave of migration from Siberia, drove out their predecessors and took possession of the country. They say that their ancestors came from a land of ice and snow, a country devoid of forests and birds. Subsequently these semi-barbarians were gradually driven by the Japanese proper to the northern end of the main island, and, finally, they migrated to Yezo (Hokkaido) and to other islands farther north. For many years they were like a dying ember, their numbers gradually decreasing annually—but in recent years the Ainu population has remained stationary at around 17,500. Their present status with the Japaese Government more or less resembles that of the American Indians with the United States Government. In retreating, they left the country strewn with place-names belonging to their own language. For instance, *Fuji*, worshipped by them as the Goddess of Fire; *Noto*, the name of a promontory stretching out into the Japan Sea; the *Tonegawa*, or River Tone, near Tokyo, and hundreds of others. Likewise, it is stated, many geographical names in Siberia have been discovered to be of Ainu origin.

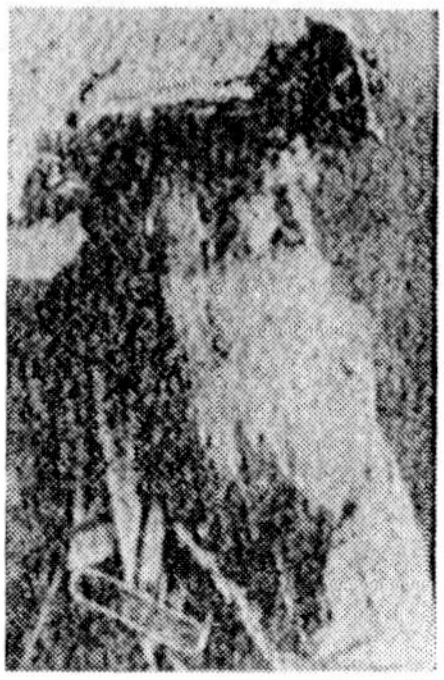

The Ainu are the hairiest race in the world. The most striking characteristic of the men is the abundance of their black hair and their luxuriant mustaches and beards, the latter sometimes a foot or more long. The women have mustaches tattooed on their upper lip and a small triangle just under the lower lip. These people are comparatively tall in stature, are of sturdy build, and possess pleasing and attractive faces. They have well-modeled features, brown eyes, black wavy hair, and cordial manners. They are distinguished by a flattening of certain bones of the arm and the leg (the *humerus* and, *tibia*), which has been observed nowhere else except in the remains of some of the cave-men of Europe.

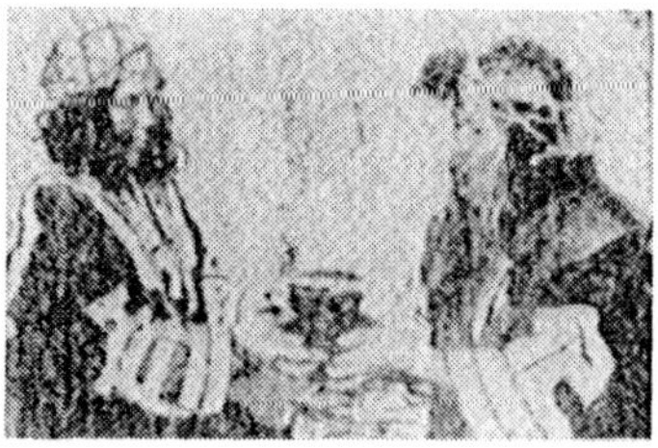

The Ainu nature has been radically changed by the struggles and calamities that have befallen the race, and which have gradually changed them from their savage state which early annals record, into a shiftless people of mild and amiable disposition, but with a pronounced addiction to drunkenness—their love of *sake* being partly accounted for in that *sake* drinking enters largely into their worship; the drunker an Ainu gets the more pleased are his gods supposed to be.

In dress, both men and women fancy gay colors. Their formal clothes are profusely decorated with striking designs, usually geometrical, and as each village has its own pattern—in this respect resembling the Scotch clans with their distinctive plaids—the native village of a traveling Ainu in native costume is quickly determined.

This description is continued—

THE AINUS OF JAPAN

The Ainu language is simple and devoid of gutterals. In great measure its structure resembles that of the Japanese, with a few fundamental divergencies. The vocabulary is quite distinct—but the younger generation, many of them intermarrying with Japanese, have discarded the native language altogether in favor of the Japanese.

In former years the Ainus lived on the produce of the chase and the sea-fisheries, but the former source of subsistence has diminished as Japanese settlements have grown. Fishing, at which they are expert, is their principal occupation. Their best craftsmanship is shown in their boats. Apart from this work their only production is that of a few rudely cut and carved wooden articles: spoons, coat-hangers, etc. A remarkable feature of the coat-hangers is the continuous links, whittled from a single piece of wood, and forming a chain from which the hanger depends. Corn and a few other vegetables are grown for their own use and that of their small stock of shaggy horses. They have never shown a liking for agriculture or any settled occupation, though in Kyushu especially, the Ainus have left evidences of their skill in moulding earth and clay pottery, profuse with varied and artistic designs, that are not excelled by any people of the contemporary Stone Age.

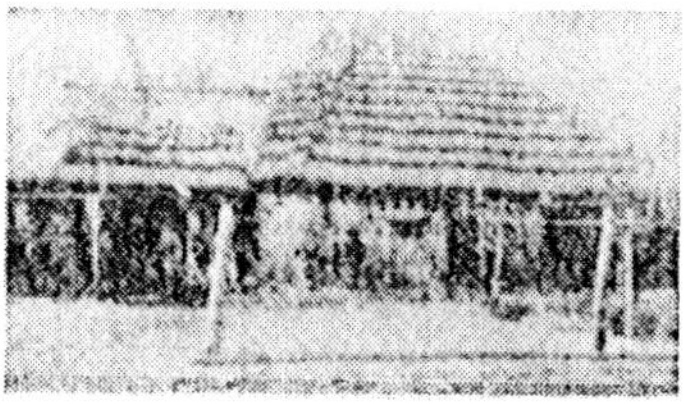

The type of house, or hut, of the Ainus is very similar to that used by many African tribes. These structures are one-story reed, or straw-thatched huts, with posts for the frame. The walls are double. The outside roof is neatly laid in ridges, in distinctive receding layers. At one end of the roof is a large triangular opening for the exit of smoke. A small windowless hut, called *shem*, forming a vestibule at the entrance, is where their millet, shelled peas, beans, etc. are pounded. It is a storehouse for firewood, for nets and other gear, and a shelter for their dogs.

Every house has two small, square windows, closed at night by wooden shutters with rope hinges. It is not considered polite to look into a hut through its windows, and it is a positive insult, both to gods and men, to look in at the east window, opposite the entrance. This, the *kamui-buyara*, or sacred "god-window," is where, towards the sunrise, they worship their gods, and they are watchful that this window is not desecrated in any way. A large fireplace at floor level is in the center of the house, the smoke from which gradually veneers the roof with an ebony polish. The floor is covered with coarse reed-mats, often polished to a rich glaze by the occupants walking and sliding over the soot that has dropped from the roof and been ground into the mats.

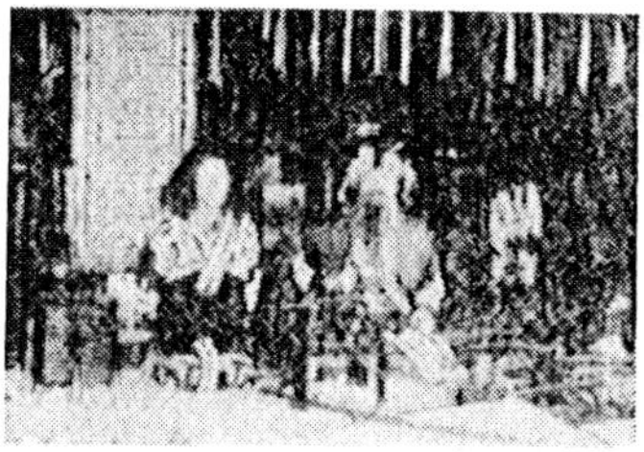

This description is continued—

THE AINUS OF JAPAN

The Ainu religion is a simple nature-worship. The sun, wind, ocean, bear, etc. are deified under the title Kamui "god," and sticks whittled into long shavings are set up in their honor.

The greatest events in Ainu life are the bear festivals. As stated, Ainus worship the bear and believe that after they have raised the cub, captured sometimes at the risk of life, and sacrificed him, they will find favor with his ancestors. The highest compliment they can pay a man is to compare him to a bear. With the killing of the bear, when two or three years old, by methods much resembling bull-baiting in Spanish countries, they pray that he will return to them for future sacrifice. These festivals are carried out with solemnities that form the most original and picturesque features of Ainu life.

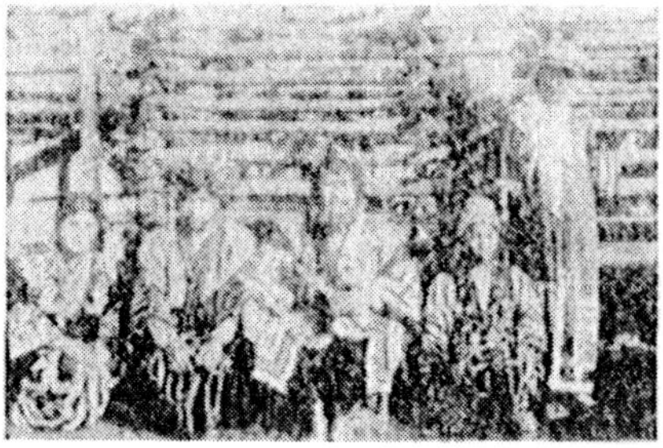

Grace is said before meat in a naive and touching form of words: "O thou Cereal Deity, we worship thee. Thou hast grown very well this year, and thy flavor will be sweet. Thou art good. The Goddess of Fire will be glad, and we shall rejoice greatly. O thou God! O thou divine Cereal! —do thou nourish the people. I now partake of thee. I worship thee and give thee thanks." The skulls are hung on a fence and preserved, in the belief that the spirits of the animals they worship dwell in the skulls. They also treasure up many charms or fetiches: feathers, snake skins, bird-skulls, etc., and their minds are saturated with a belief in various forms of magic and witchcraft. Their only literature are rude songs and quaint tales, many of them embodying an attempt to account for some natural phenomenon.

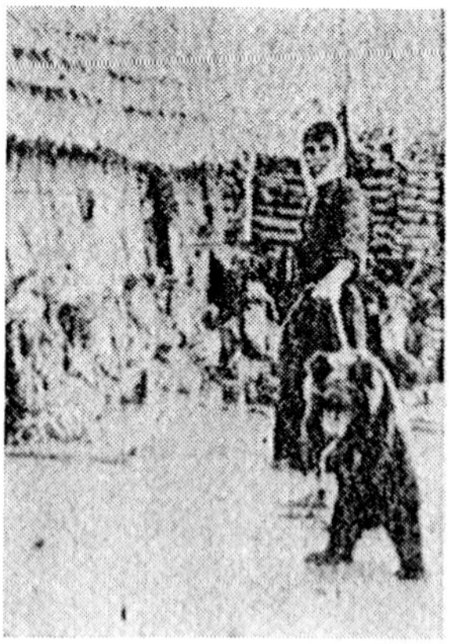

The largest and most typical Ainu village in Japan is that near Shiraoi, Hokkaido, 12 m. N. of Noboribetsu Hot Springs, easily accessible by railway.

Those who desire to know more about the Ainus are advised to procure the books and pamphlets written by the Venerable Archdeacon John Batchelor, D.D., of Sapporo, who has long resided among the Ainus, and is recognized as the highest authority on this subject. Among the Doctor's numerous and valuable books are: *The Ainu and Their Folk-Lore; Sea-girt Yezo; A Grammar of the Ainu Language; Ainu-English-Japanese Dictionary,* and *Ainu Place Names.*

MON or CRESTS

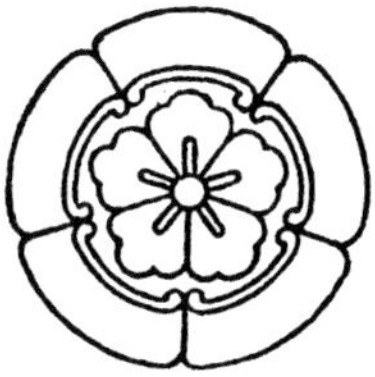

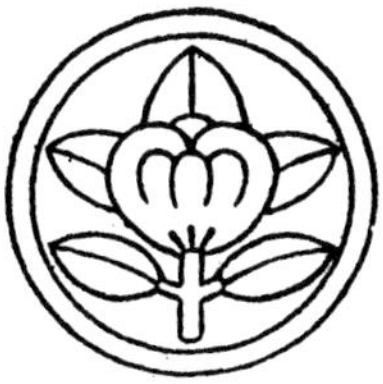

In Japan the use of crests is not a privilege confined to presons of quality—anyone may have one. Family crests are often used by private banks and business houses. The railways and municipalities use distinctive crests. In time of war, crests were conspicuous on the flags, and on the breast-plates and helmets of the warriors.

In time of peace the crest was worn as it still is, on the Japanese outer garment or kimono' in five places on the back of kimono, on each sleeve and each breast. Sometimes only in three places—on the back and sleeves. When the material for the kimono is dyed, a stencil of the crest is pasted on it and appears in white on the finished kimono. In olden days the family crest marked many of the family possessions, such as their lacquer-ware, their traveling cases, rickshas, etc.

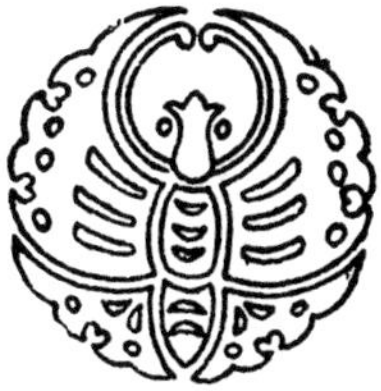

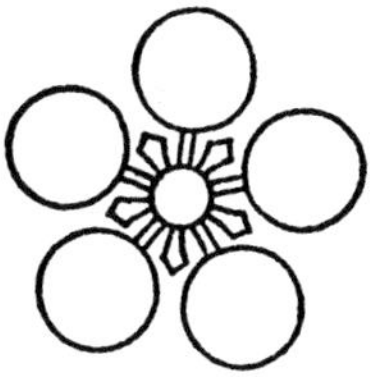

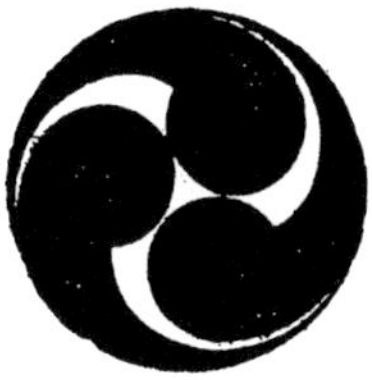

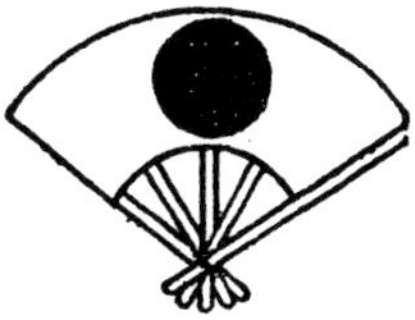

The Imperial Family has two crests, that of the Emperor, the 16-petaled chrysanthemum, and that of the Empress, the leaves and flowers of the paulownia. Japanese subjects are not permitted to use these crests in any way. The crest of the Tokugawa was three asarum leaves (hollyhock), with the points meeting in the center.

The cherry blossom, the bamboo, peony, and other flowers have furnished crests for noble families. Among other favorite designs are birds, butterflies, fans, Chinese characters, and geometrical figures. A daimyo named Aoki had for his crest the summit of Fuji with its peak issuing from the clouds. The great Shimazu family of Satsuma had a cross within a circle.

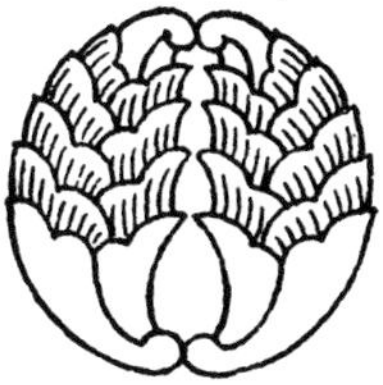

FUDE (FU—contraction of FUMI "WRITING," DE "HAND or INSTRUMENT")

THE JAPANESE WRITING BRUSH

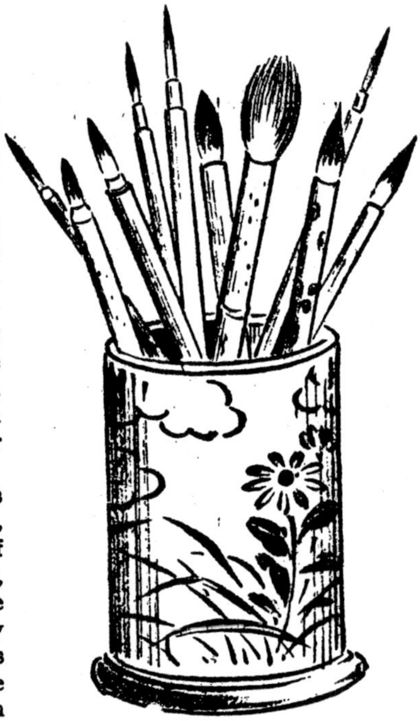

Although metal and fountain pens are widely used in Japan, there is perhaps not a single household in the land which is not in possession of a *fude* or two, and *fude* will continue to be used so long as the Chinese characters and the *kana* are employed as the written representatives of the Japanese language.

Handwriting, in both China and Japan, still ranks as one of the fine arts. It is an accomplishment necessary for all persons of culture, and invariably the *fude* is employed. Among the prized possessions of a family are *kakemono* and *gaku* (hanging tablets), written by some famous person, which conveys a lofty sentiment, maxim or precept.

A *fude* is a bunch of the hairs of a rabbit, badger, or other animal, bound together, or a combination of them, and inserted in a bamboo or, rarely, in a wooden handle. There are infinite varieties in size and quality and in the skill with which the *fude* is made. Concerning its size, there are brushes made of thousands of hairs which are thick enough to write a stroke two feet wide, then there are others made of only three whiskers of a rat that are used to write microscopic characters. The various schools of calligraphy have their special *fude*, some schools using brushes shaped like a Japanese awl, the brush tapering to a needle-like point; others prefer the acorn-shaped brush. Between these two there are many kinds and degrees of taperness, just as there are Spencerian, ball-pointed, stub and other pen nibs. The hairs are so bunched and tied that their ends taper to a fine point with not a single outstanding hair, and the stiff and soft hairs are bunched so that the stiff hairs surround the soft.

The large brushes are from 1 to 1½ in. in diameter at the place of their insertion in the handle. The non-brush end of such handles often has a disk attached on which the brush may be made to stand with the brush end upper-most—others sometimes have smaller brushes or a seal-stamp available in their hollow handles. Brushes of still larger sizes are made of rice-straw beards. They look like a round pointed whisk. The handle of such a brush is made so thick and long that it may rest on the shoulder while writing. Goat and horse hair, or the bark fibres of hemp-palm are also used for these brushes.

GEISHA (*Gei*-Art, *sha*-person; pron., Gay-shah)

Geisha are highly specialized types of Japanese women entertainers—mistresses of song and dance. A foreign writer describes them as "the perfect arrangement for the tired Japanese businessman." Fascinating and mysterious, geisha are like brilliant butterflies floating from flower to flower. Few ask what becomes of the joyous creatures when the winter winds blow. The geisha's glossy, jet-black hair, wonderfully arranged, her gay *kimono* and gorgeously-brocaded *obi*, her airs and graces, make her unlike any woman in the world. She forms a conspicuous feature of the life of Japan's chief cities. She sings, dances, and plays Japanese melodies on the *samisen*. When banquets or gatherings of merrymakers are held, she is hired to drive dull care away. She is a mistress of etiquette, and in her profession is usually an accomplished artist—and an expensive one. Also she is most trustworthy and loyal to her patrons. In the past, and even today, many important conferences of politicians and big businessmen are held in the *machiai*, or head geisha-houses—but whatever the geisha overhears seldom leaks out.

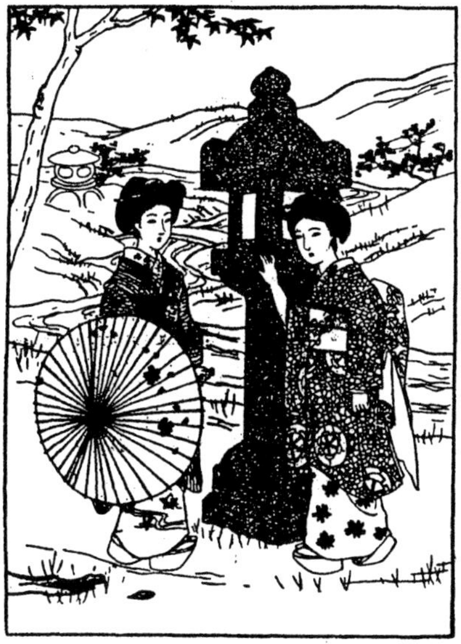

A budding geisha (called *han-gyoku* or *maiko*) embarks early on her career. From her 10th year to 16 or 18 years of age she is trained in singing, dancing, music, etiquette, deportment, writing, flower arrangement, the tea ceremony and other accomplishments. When proficient she takes on the duties of her profession in earnest. In her mature years she may become the mistress of a geisha establishment, or be fortunate enough to be chosen as a wife and preside over a house and family. Many are not so fortunate, and the butterfly wings are broken and soiled in the mire of a great city. Some of the geisha find wealthy patrons who buy them out of bondage. The majority are not so lucky, and the butterfly existence of the geisha does not always end happily.

A geisha is engaged for a period of from five to ten years, a certain sum of money being paid for her to parents or relatives, the highest prices being paid for the most beautiful. Her earnings go to her mistress, to whom she is always in debt for her training and resplendent clothing.

There are thousands of these professional women in Tokyo, Kyoto, and Osaka, while every provincial town has its quota, as well as all resorts.

The most noted geisha school in Japan is in Kyoto, in the Gion amusement quarter, reference to which is made in the *Odori* ("Dance") description. In Tokyo the geisha houses are grouped together in certain districts.

The vogue of Western dancing and entertainment means the eventual doom of the geisha, and to meet this competition many geisha are taking up the western style of dancing—but like other old-established customs in Japan the end of the geisha system is far in the future.

THE GOLDFISH OF JAPAN ("KINGYO")

Japan, where the culture of goldfish has been highly developed, is regarded as the home of goldfish. Because of their beauty of shape and color goldfish are bred by goldfish fanciers and commercial breeders, and are especially prized for their graceful appearance and for their brilliant coloring. While there are many varieties of this fish the most popular are:

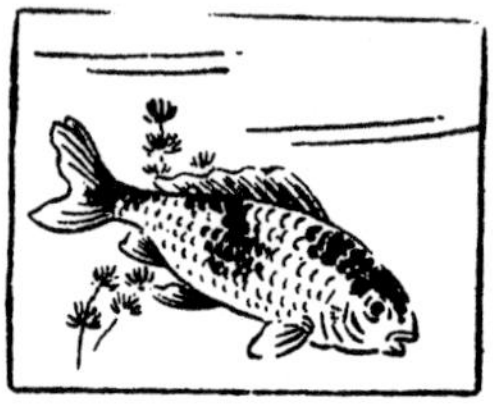

Wakin.

Wakin: Bright in color, with a longer body than other varieties. Short fins and tail. Average size when full grown 7 to 8 inches. *Wakin,* the most common goldfish, resembles a carp or gibel more than a real goldfish. They are cheap in price.

Ryukin: ("Loochoo goldfish"): Short, round body, with a long, swaying fantail. Including the tail it rarely grows longer than 8 to 10 inches. Somewhat higher in price than a *Wakin,* it is a sturdy fish, easy to keep.

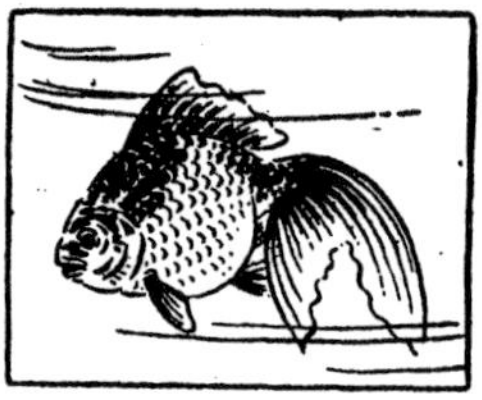

Ryukin.

Ranchu: Its special feature is that it has no dorsal fin and has a large head covered with small knobs. Its peculiar face makes one think of a bull-dog's face—in fact, it is called "bull-dog" by foreign fanciers of goldfish. It has an ovalshaped body, broad back which should curve gently from neck to tail. Its large abdomen must be symmetrical. A full grown *Ranchu* measures from 5 to 6 in. in length. Under proper feeding and water conditions this fish may live as long as 20 years, but it is easily affected by adverse conditions. In price, it ranges from ¥5 to several hundred yen apiece.

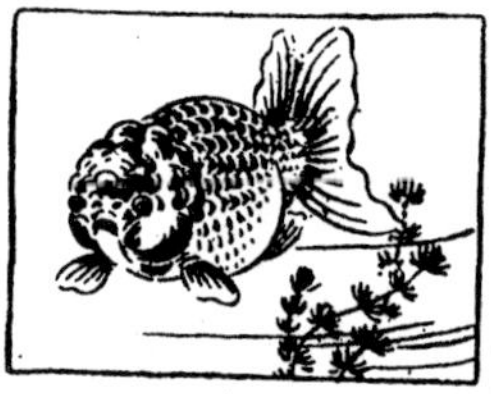

Ranchu.

Oranda-Shishi-Gashira: ("Lion-headed Hollander"): Oranda is the Japanese word for Holland. It really signifies something foreign. This fish is a half-breed, half *Ryukin* and half *Ranchu.* It has the head knobs of the *Ranchu* and may be described as a *Ranchu* with a dorsal fin. Full grown this fish sometimes measures about a foot in length.

Shina-kin or *Deme-kin:* ("Goggle-eyed goldfish"): The name *Shina-kin* means Chinese goldfish. In appearance these fish generally resemble the *Wakin*—apart from their characteristic eyes, of which there are two types: one having eyes that project sidewise, the other with protruding eyes that look forward. In color, this fish is either black, with white speckles or a yellowish red.

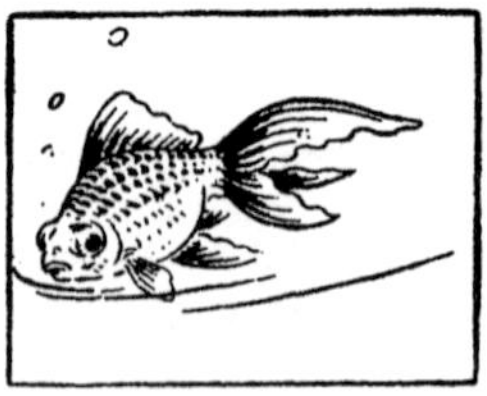

Shina-kin or Deme-kin.

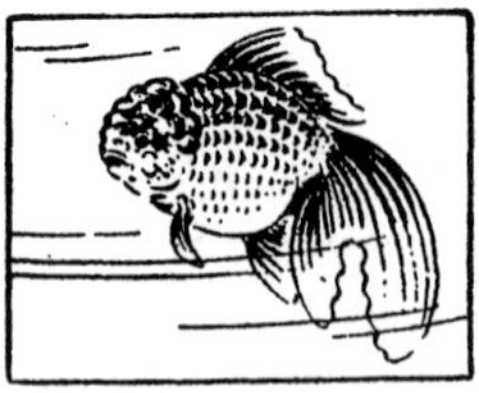

Oranda-Shishi-Gashira.

In 1932 there were exported to the United States 2,700,000 goldfish, worth about ¥405,000. The *Ryukin* type constitutes more than 50 per cent of the exports. The demand is steadily increasing.

The large fish seen in ponds are carp, often mistaken for goldfish.

THE CARE OF GOLDFISH

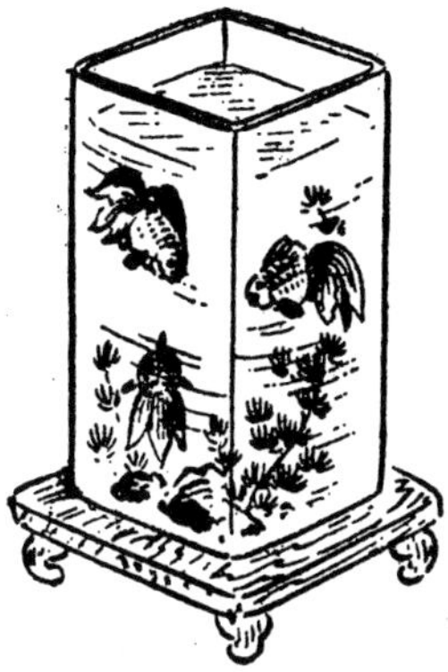

The treatment of goldfish in glass receptacles is considered here; space does not permit writing about goldfish kept in artificial ponds.

Water: Water at a temperature of 70°F is best. The fish thrive in standing water that has become somewhat cloudy, but as they require ample supplies of oxygen, fresh water, in quantity up to about one-third of the water content, should be poured in *gently* every 3 or 4 days, preferably between 10 and 11 a.m., after the old water has been siphoned off. The smaller the receptacle is the more often should the water be renewed.

When cleaning the vessel the minute deposits on its inner surfaces should not be entirely removed because the fish like to feed upon them. Goldfish need a sun bath daily, otherwise they lose color and die, but they are too delicate for long exposure during the hot season.

Food: Shrimp, dried and ground into powder, is good at any time. It also fattens the fish for winter. The larvae of mosquitoes is good—found on any stagnant water. Akamushi, or Red Worm, is much liked by goldfish. It is an infinitesimal, long, thread-like worm such as one sees in gutters. In Japan, dried, crushed silkworm cocoons are fed to goldfish. Boiled egg yolk is also good. The fish are given boiled barley, wheat gluten, noodles and macaroni (boiled first), and wheat bran; always in small pieces and quantities. Too much food should not be given—overfeeding will kill the fish. Should the morning supply of food not be consumed by 3 p.m. it should be taken out at once. Goldfish dealers usually have prepared food on sale. Place in the receptacle any fine weed that grows in water—watercress is suitable—place it in earth in a small pot, covering the earth with gravel.

Diseases: A sick goldfish does not swim about with the others; it stays at the bottom of the vessel, or moves slowly, as if exhausted. The most common disease is the water-lice disease, a white-like mold forming in bubbles on the body scales. The fish should be taken up and the bubbles squeezed out; it should then be placed in salt water that is strong enough so that the salt is evident to the taste. The fish will dart about as if pursued, but will soon calm down and should then be removed to fresh water.

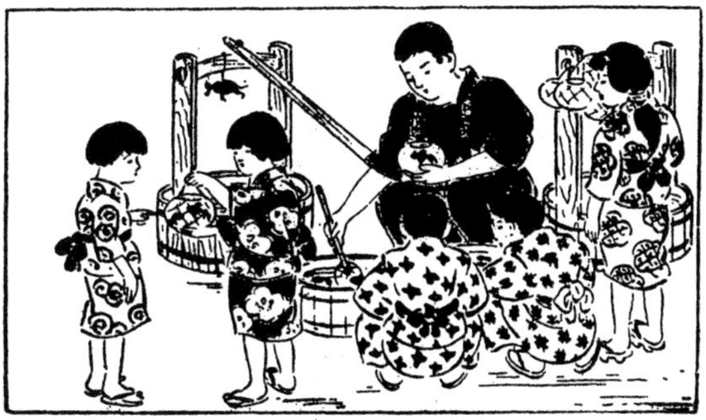

THE HEAD-HUNTERS OF FORMOSA (TAIWAN)

Continued—

The head-hunters make it their business and pleasure to lie in wait, slay, and decapitate the domesticated savages, the Japanese, and the Formosans who work near the GUARD-LINES (*Aiyu-sen*) which are established by cutting a path (*ai-ro*) along the side of the mountains, then clearing the jungle in front for sufficient distance for the guards to note the appproach of an enemy. The bamboo guard-houses are loopholed, supplied with firearms, grenades, telephones, etc. They are surrounded by barbed-wire fences, which in very risky districts are electrically charged, and sunken mines are laid for the savages. Five or more guard-houses, with 2 to 4 men in house, are placed at intervals in a mile. In localities where barter is permitted with the savages, a barter-house is erected near the superintendent's cabin, and interpreters are employed. There are over 100 of these trade stations, and the annual turnover is considerable. While one guard sleeps, the other watches, for the duty of the guard is not only to preserve his own life, but also to protect the villages and fields in his district. Formerly the savages attacked the men, who were in constant danger. Sometimes whole parties are ambushed and massacred. As the natives were subdued, or gave up their resistance, the guard-line was advanced, not always without disaster or hardship to the workers.

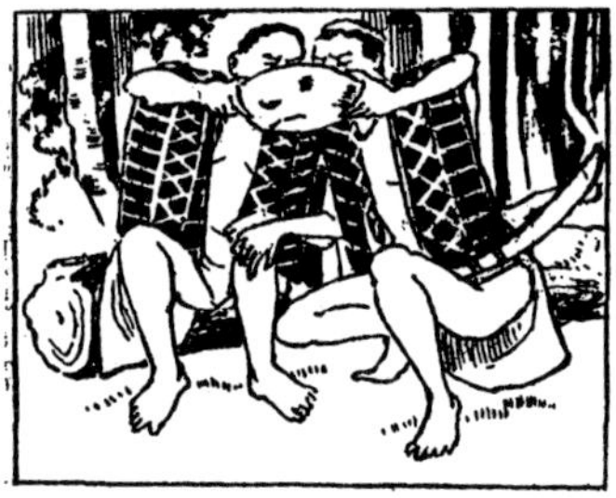

HEAD-HUNTERS on the war-path usually travel in squads. Equipping themselves with what firearms they have, with *krises*, poisoned arrows, and provisions, they approach as near as convenient to the guard-line and hide in the jungle near some frequented path. Here, whenever the opportunity comes, they shoot unsuspecting travelers, or, emerging from their lurking-places, they make a sudden and swift descent on some field or outlying house, murdering whomsoever they meet. The savage trails lie only through the dense forests, thick with underbrush, where hiding is easy. The decapitated heads are boiled, to separate the flesh from the bones; then the skull is adorned with various rude ornaments, and either hung up in the warrior's hut, or placed in a niche in the wall as a sort of curio. The bodies are left where they fall.

This description is continued—

THE HEAD-HUNTERS OF FORMOSA (TAIWAN)

Continued—

On the lakeshore of Jitsugetsu-tan ("Sun-Moon-Abyss," by foreigners called Dragon Lake), a beautiful lake (alt., 2,400 ft.) 10 m. in circumference—the largest in Formosa—dwell a small tribe of tame KABAN (*Ka*=become, *Ban*=savage), their ancestors having descended from Chinese who, after committing sundry major and minor crimes in the lowlands, have fled to this place from time to time and then degenerated into a semi-savage state. Mention of them is made especially for the purpose of describing their novel method of producing music. On a large flat stone, about 8×10 ft. in dimension, its surface about an inch above ground, they pound out their queer tunes and melancholy music by means of hard-wood instruments resembling giant pestles with a "pestle" at each end. These instruments range up to about 8 ft. in length. They sing while they "play" and the echo of their sorrowful music sweeps across the lake in a strain that is haunting. This village is reached by train from Taihoku to Nisui, changing cars there for Gaishatei, thence by push-car (8 m.) to the lake.

Musha, the principal village of the Musha aborigines, in a mountain district 4,000 ft. above sea level, is 33 m. N-E. of Gaishatei station, of which 27 m. is covered by light railway to Bikei, the rest of the way by push-car, called the "Savage Express."

The "Savage Express," also employed elsewhere in Formosa, is a unique means of conveyance. The "cars" are wicker canopy chairs, mounted on little springless factory-trucks, running on light rails 18 in. apart. The "locomotive" consists of two Chinese coolies who on each car push and perspire on the up-grades, but are recompensed on the down-grades when they swing on to the car, which, as it gains momentum, rushes along with terrific speed.

Kappan-san, another aboriginal village, is reached by train from Taihoku to Toen (35.7 m.), then by motor car to Taikei, thence by "Savage Express" up the mountain road. Along the way, here and there, are camphor distilleries where the process of manufacturing camphor can be inspected. Here, at this village, if you smile, you will be welcome, and perfectly safe. The villagers will show you their long knives (*kris*), their curious wooden hats, carved from a solid block of wood into the shape of a jockey cap and stained some vivid color, and you will note their barbaric ornaments.

From Taihoku, a 1-day trip can be made to the *Urai Aboriginal Community*, part of the journey being made by palanquin, or chair. Before visiting any aboriginal village it is advisable to consult the manager of the Taiwan Railway Hotel, or the Japan Tourist Bureau in that hotel.

This description is continued—

THE HEAD-HUNTERS OF FORMOSA (TAIWAN)

Continued—

Mention has been made of CAMPHOR-MAKING as an occupation for some of the aborigines, so a short description of the process may be pertinent.

Unfortunately, camphor cannot, like lacquer or maple-sugar, be extracted by tapping. The tree must be felled and cut into chips, which are steamed in a vat, the vapor being made to carry off the fumes into a cooling apparatus where condensation takes place and the camphor and camphor-oil are afterwards skimmed off and sent to a government refinery for further treatment, as camphor-refining is a government monopoly, and most of the camphor forests have been appropriated by the government. Cabinets made of camphor-wood are much esteemed, not only for the fine grain and silky sheen of wood, but for its efficacy against the attacks of insects.

The Camphor-laurel (*Kusuno-ki*) ranks among the stateliest of trees, frequently attaining an enormous height and girth—30, 40, and even 50 feet in circumference, and 130 ft. in height. Grand specimens may be seen in Japan at Atami, Ito, Atsuta, and at Dazaifu. Such giant trees are often worshipped by the simple country folk, who hang straw-ropes or paper round them in token of reverence.

The Formosa camphor-producing district, declared to be the largest in the world, covering an area of about 130 sq. m., chiefly in savage territory, is said to contain enough of the drug to supply the world's demand for 100 years—but synthetic camphor is a strong competitor. As the trees are felled, young trees are set out. At normal prices, a big tree will yield camphor worth ¥5,000 or more; comparatively small trees are worth from ¥150 to ¥300. A medium-sized tree about 12 ft. in circumference will yield about 50 piculs (about 6,666 lbs.—3⅓ tons of crystallized camphor, worth about ¥1,500. The bulk of the present output (about 8 million lbs., valued at 3 million *yen*) comes to Japan, though a considerable quantity of camphor, in a semi-refined state, is sent to Europe and America.

* * * *

A collection of weapons and wearing apparel of the head-hunting tribes and other aborigines of Formosa, may be seen at the Ueno Museum in Tokyo.

A JAPANESE BRIDE

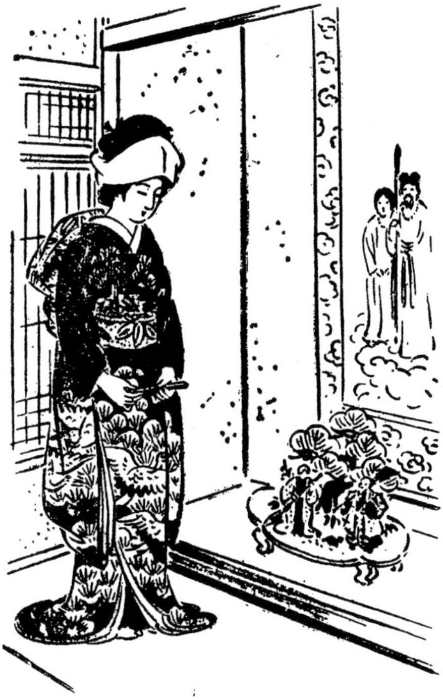

This picture shows the bridal attire of a young lady of the middle or upper class. In the very highest classes, a white costume is worn.

The young lady has her hair done in a style called "Bunkin Takashimada" and the strip of white gauze over pink silk on her head is popularly called a *tsuno-kakushi* (horn concealer). The hair is further adorned with amber or tortoise-shell bars and pins, their ends intricately carved in flower clusters.

There are three long-sleeved robes, each worn on top of the other, the outer one being of crepe silk designed in flowers and birds of auspicious wedding significance. The *obi* (sash) is of the finest product of the weaver's art and is tied in a special butterfly bow at the back. Large sums are spent on such sashes and outer robes.

The *hakoseko,* or mirror case, is tucked into the outer robe and a fan is carried in the hands.

In the room in which the ceremony is performed there is usually a scroll picture representing the gods, Izanagi and Izanami, the first married couple in Japanese history. Beneath it will be the *shimadai,* a tray on which are arranged pine, plum, and bamboo branches, signifying longevity and success, together with other felicitous symbols, including the ancient man and wife, Jo and Uba. At the left of the *shimadai* would be the long-handled *choshi* and at the right, the *hisago*—*sake* vessels used in the wedding ceremony.

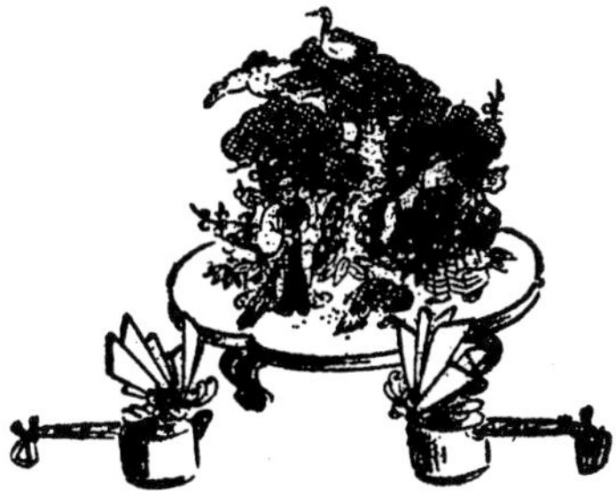

JAPANESE DRESS NOT CHEAP

The "cute little kimono," as tourists call them, that the Japanese lass wears are not as simple as they look. Many visitors think that the clothes of Japanese women are not very expensive and base this deduction on the presumption that the *kimono* is "quite a simple thing." If they faced a jury of long-suffering Japanese husbands they surely would be sentenced to pay for a few of these "simple things."

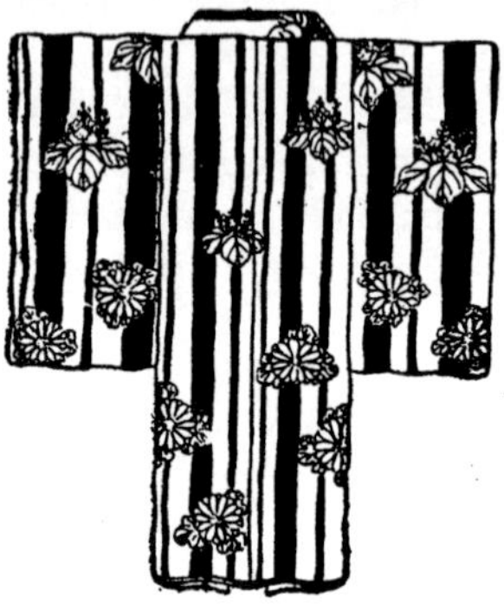

There are more parts to the Japanese *kimono* than appear on the surface. Leaving aside those undergarments next to the flesh that, it would seem, the lass of every country affects, the first requisite of Japanese dress is a garment very similar to the *kimono,* which is worn under the *kimono.* It reaches from shoulders to ankles. After it has been put on, a wide band of cloth is wound around it, while above its collar is arranged strip of silk. Her garment material thus far has cost from ¥30 up, inclusive of the undergarments.

The cost of silk material for the outer *kimono* of the average woman is from ¥20 up. The long sleeves and the lower part of the *kimono* have to be lined with bright-colored cloth, and the cost has now clicked up another ¥8 or ¥10.

The *kimono,* by the way, is five or more inches longer than is necessary. Consequently, the wearer draws it up carefully until its hem is just level with her heels, arranges a silken cord around her waist and over it smooths down what may be called the "slack" of the *kimono.* Then comes a very important part of the costume, called the *obi,* a long broad, stiff sash.

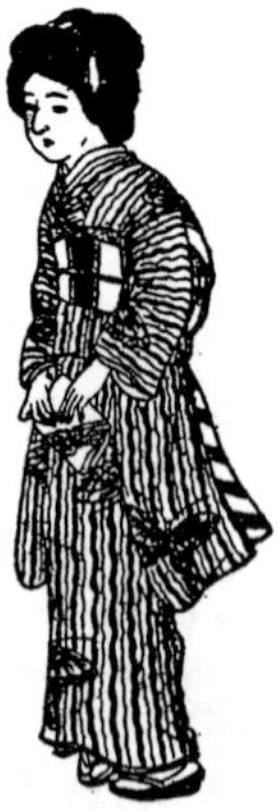

The *obi* generally is about 4½ yards long and its minimum width is twelve inches. It is very heavy, owing to the thick lining it must have to enable it to retain its stiffness, and, in summer, it is an actual torment .to the Japanese girl. The least cost of a decent *obi* is ¥20, but the cost of fine or *maruobi* may run into the thousands of yen because in place on a lining the *obi* material is doubled.

These are the most conspicuous parts of the Japanese woman's costume, but there are a number of minor details.

The *obi* must have two cords to hold it in place. One of these, which is worn at the top and drawn through the bow at the back of the *obi,* costs from ¥2 up. Then comes the jewelry of the *obi-dome,* the ornamental front buckle or clasp, which costs up to the thousands of yen.

Thus the *kimono* and its accessories are not as cheap as some think, nor is the *kimono* as simple as it looks.

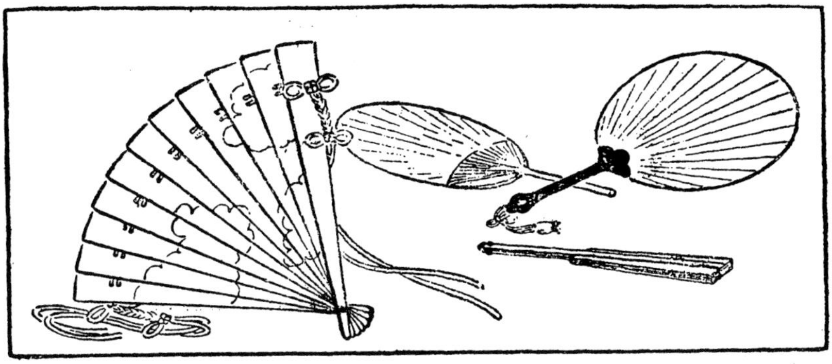

JAPANESE FANS

Incidental mention of fans occurs in the oldest official annals of Japan. The chief kinds of fans are the *uchiwa* or round fan, not capable of being shut, and the *ogi* or *sensu*, folding fan. A noble lady, widow of the youthful hero Atsumori, is credited with the invention of the folding fan. At the temple of Mieido in Kyoto, whither she had retired as a nun to hide her grief, she cured the abbot of a fever by fanning him with a folded piece of paper, over which she muttered incantations, and to the present day the priests of this temple are considered special adepts in the manufacture of fans, whence the name of "Mieido" adopted by many fan-shops in Japan.

Notable fans are the giant kind carried at the festival of the Sun-Goddess at Ise and by the firemen of Kyoto, and the war-fans formerly used by military commanders to direct their forces and give emphasis to their orders. Iron was the material usually employed for the war fans, the ornamentation consisting on one side of a red sun on a gold ground, on the other of a silver moon and stars on a black or dark blue ground.

Fans are used as bellows in winnowing rice, as trays on which to hand things, by umpires of wrestling matches to enforce their orders, and universally, by men as well as women, during the summer months. Their use to advertise business and wares is well nigh endless. The ordinary Japanese fans, made of paper over split bamboo, excel in cheapness as in beauty. Fan-makers adorn some of their wares with quaint and poetical conceits, and many of the small pictures on fans are often accompanied by a verse of poetry.

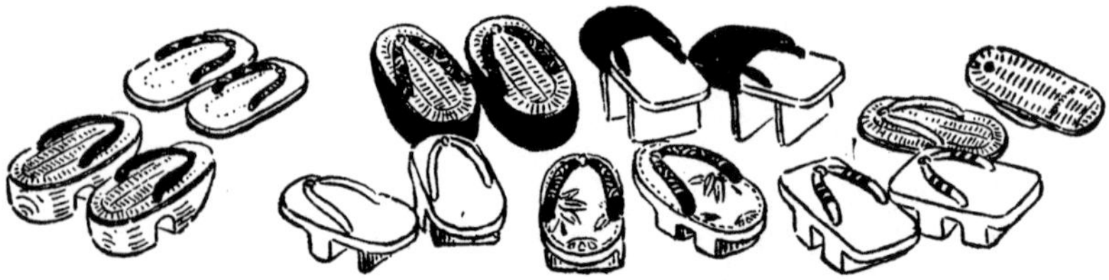

JAPANESE FOOTGEAR

Japanese footgear attracts the immediate attention of foreign visitors—as does the peculiar click-clack sound of *geta* on the pavement. The most distinctive feature of Japanese footwear is the Y-shaped cord or thong which passes between the big toe and the second toe—and it is a constant feature, since there is a great variety in Japanese footgear itself. However, all kinds may be roughly divided into two main classes, those for hard wear and those for easy wear. The former are known as *geta*, the latter as *zori*.

Geta may best be translated as "clog" or "patten." It is an oblong wooden piece raised on a crosswise support. A thong passes up through a hole in the forward end of the piece. This is attached to an ornamental cord whose ends are fastened down at either side of the wood. There are two main types of *geta*—one consisting of the oblong piece with two thin wooden cross-pieces under it, and one carved out of a solid block of wood. The former type is the most common. For rainy weather the cross-pieces are 2 or 3 or more inches high, lifting the foot well above muddy ground. Such geta have a toe cap of stiff oiled paper or leather. Well-nigh endless are the different styles of geta—some are lacquered, some have their tops covered with finely plaited rushes and the thongs are of velvet, silk brocade, cotton or velveteen, in many colors. *Geta* are only worn outdoors.

The *zori* is a sandal, not intended for such rough wear as the *geta*, though a coarse straw *zori*, selling for a few sen each, is made for mountain climbing and coolie wear. The ordinary *zori* is made of straw or reeds. There are many grades and styles for wear outside and inside the house, but even so the latter are never worn on the soft surface of the *tatami*, or thick straw mats which cover the floors of rooms—only bare or stocking-covered feet being allowed to touch the mats. The word stocking gives a wrong idea, for the Japanese do not wear stockings. They wear a sort of sock, known as *tabi*, which has a separate division for the big toe. It reaches just above the ankle and is fastend at the back by means of an overlap having metal hook tabs which engage with thread loops on the inner side. Above the *tabi* the legs are bare.

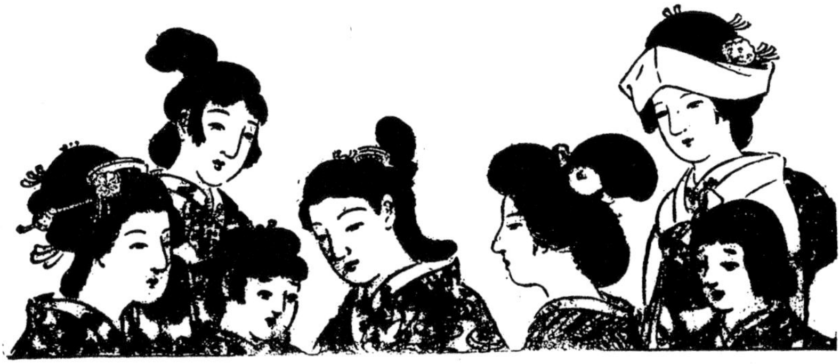

Different Styles of Coiffure

JAPANESE STYLES OF HAIR-DRESSING (MAGE)

Mage means "Style of Hair-dressing"

In Japan there are more than 35 styles of hair-dressing, the most common and most frequently seen being as follows:

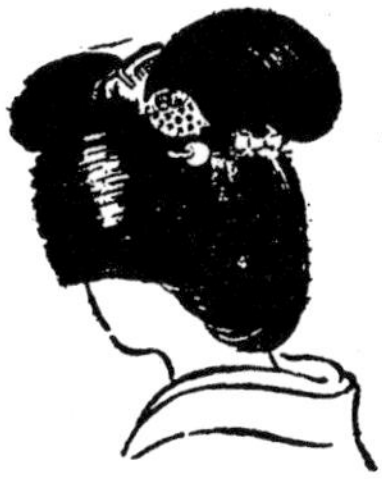

Maru mage. A common form of mage worn by married women of almost all classes.

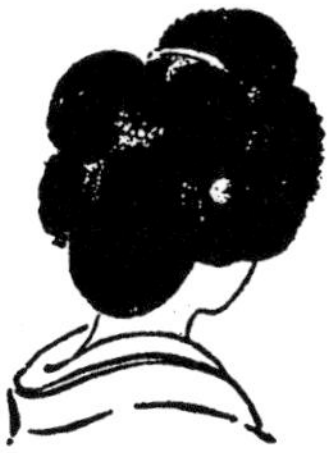

Icho-gaeshi. A Tokyo name for *chocho mage,* worn by young girls. It is so named because it resembles a *Chocho* or Butterfly.

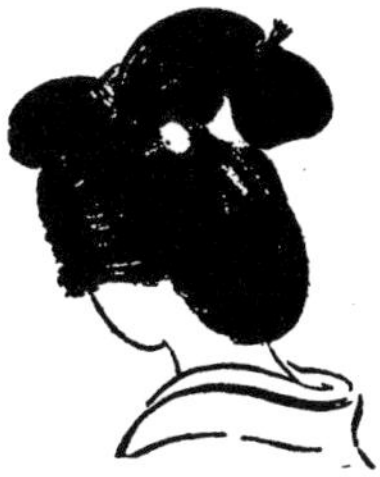

Shimada mage. A very common form of *mage* worn by girls of marriageable age of almost all classes.

The right-hand figure in the group above shows a bride's hair dressed for her wedding. The silk head-dress is called *tsuno-kakushi* or "to conceal the horns."

JAPANESE HOT SPRINGS

Regarding mineral springs, there are in Japan 951 hot springs and 155 cold springs of sufficient importance to be listed—and more than 250 of them possess radio-activity. The majority of the springs have valuable medicinal properties.

Because many of these springs are remote from beaten paths, and have poor hotel accommodations, they are unknown to the average tourist, but now a national enterprise proposes to erect modern hotels at some of the springs in order to attract visitors.

These springs are classified as simple cold, thermal, and carbon-dioxated springs, earthy carbon-dioxated and alkaline springs, common salt, bitter, iron carbonated, vitriol, and sulphur springs.

As to radio-activity our Masutomi cold spring ranks next to the famous water (909 ft. deep) in the Joachimsthal mine, Czechoslovakia (the ore from which produced the radium discovered by Madam Curie), and to that of Bramback, Germany.

Our Misasa hot spring ranks next to the Ischia, Italy, spring —the most radio-active hot spring in the world.

For further facts about Japanese hot springs, "The Hot Springs of Japan" (¥7), issued by the Japanese Government Railways, on sale at the Head Office of the Japan Tourist Bureau, Tokyo, is recommended.

LONG-TAILED COCKS OF MIYANOSHITA, HAKONE, JAPAN

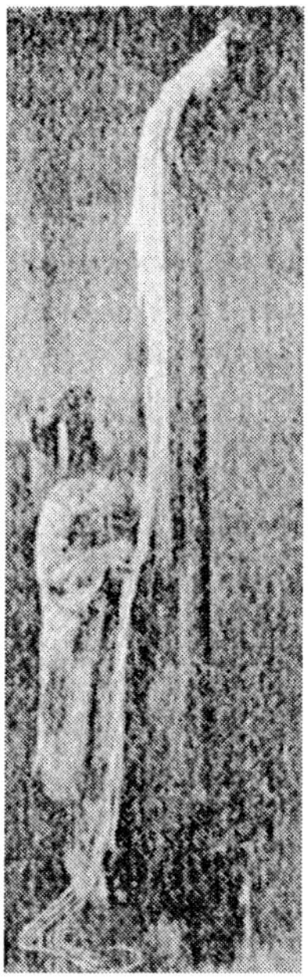

Three years old.
Tail, 12 ft. long.

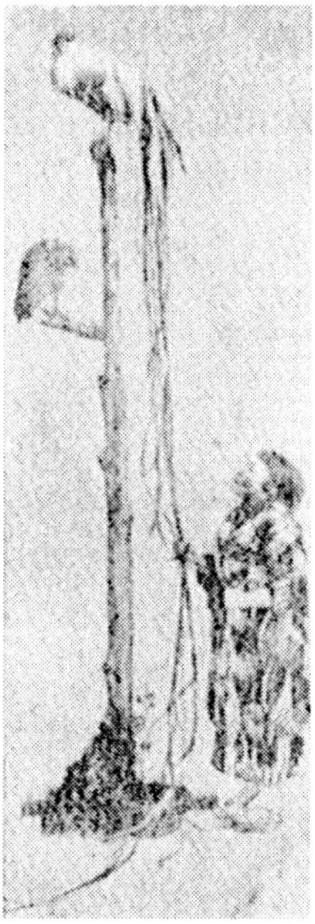

Five years old.
Tail, 15ft. long.

These rare, ornamental and beautiful birds—developed from common barnyard fowl after 150 years of careful selection and cross- and in-breeding with copper and green pheasants—are a specialty of Tosa, on Shikoku Island. They are black and white in color; sometimes of pure white (highly valued). The tail-feathers, 15 to 25 in number, are never moulted—ordinarily they grow from 8 to 11 ft. in length, occasionally to 25 ft. or more. They depend from five or more quills considerably larger and stronger than those of common fowl. Delicate in structure, these feathers may be coiled around the hand without breaking. In order to preserve them the tail-feathers must hang free, the bird sitting on a high perch. Every second day the fowl is taken out and allowed to walk about for an hour or so, someone holding up its tail to prevent it from getting torn or soiled.

Once or twice a month the tail is carefully washed with warm water and as carefully dried on some high place, the tail being held until quite dry.

The hen, although a handsome bird, cannot be compared with its splendid mate, the extreme length of its tail feathers being only about 8 inches. It lays in spring and autumn—about 30 eggs yearly—which are hatched by other hens. The birds are fed on unhulled rice, chopped greens, and small eel-like live fish, and are given plenty of water. They sometimes live to the age of nine years.

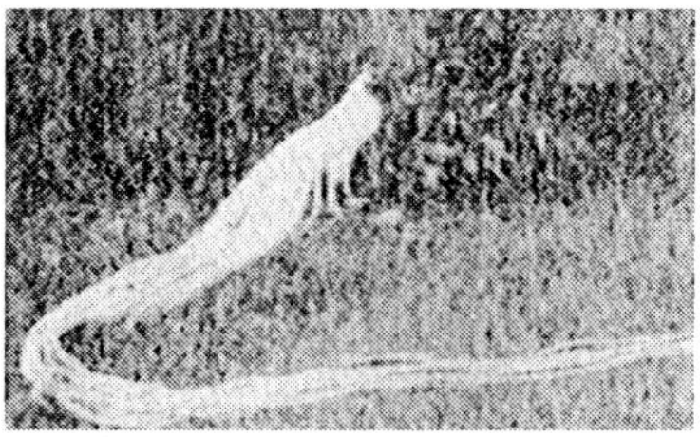

Three years old. Tail, 16ft long.

JAPANESE MUSICAL INSTRUMENTS

The koto, or Japanese horizontal harp, is somewhat like a zither. It has a wooden frame and curved sounding-board made of paulownia wood, with 13 strings of silk, mounted on ivory bridges. When played, the *koto* is laid flat and its strings are plucked by the thumb and the two first fingers of the right hand, to each of which is fastened a small ivory plectrum. In length the *koto* is slightly less than 8 feet.

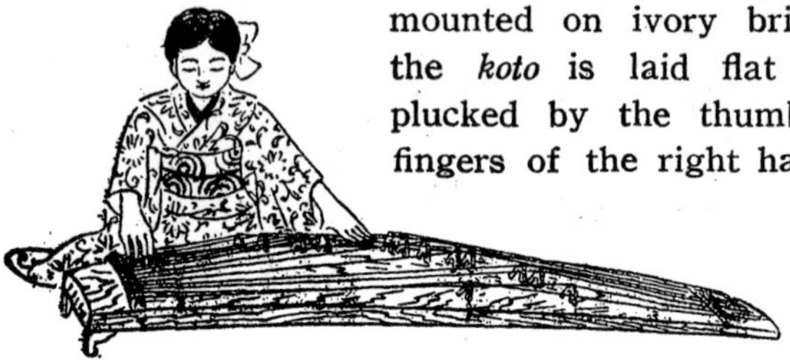

The samisen, 3-stringed, is the most popular of Japanese musical instruments. In skilful hands it is capable of rendering a great variety of tones. The frame of the body, almost square in shape, is made of quince or oak wood, and both faces are covered like a drum with cat's skin. Its neck and fingerboad, about 3 ft. long, is made of oak or red sandalwood. The bridge is made of buffalo-horn and the plectrum of ivory, buffalo-horn, or tortoise-shell. When playing, the performer holds the plectrum, quite large, in the right hand. The strings are graded in thickness. It may be called the Japanese banjo.

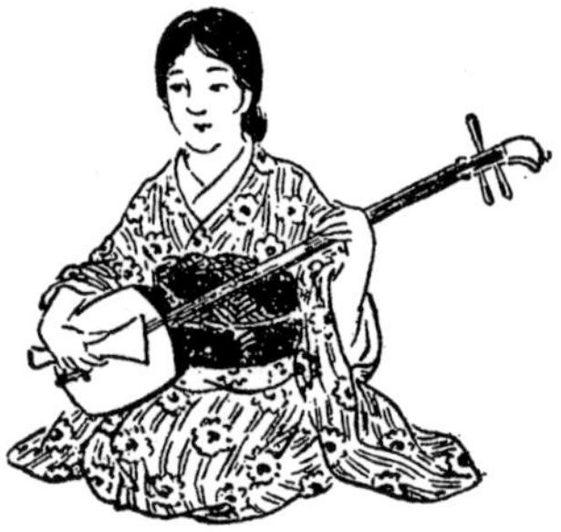

The biwa, a kind of lute, or mandolin, picked with the fingers, has a body semi-oval in shape, the extreme end of the neck being curved backward. It is a little over 4 ft. in length. Most biwa are 4-stringed. Biwa compositions are largely martial narratives, with a strong tinge of Buddhist fatalism.

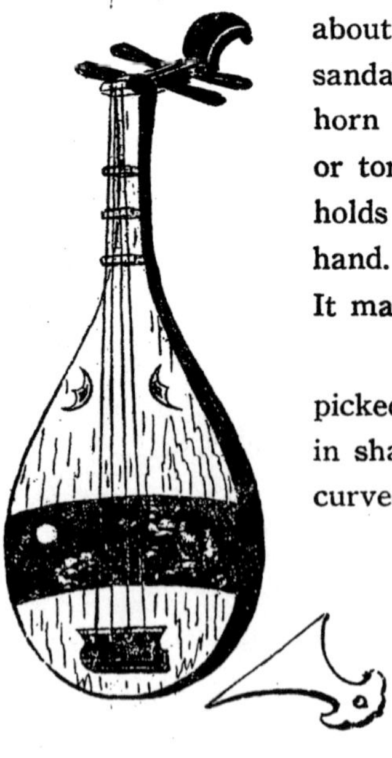

JAPANESE MUSICAL INSTRUMENTS

Drums. In the pictures A and B are drums, C is the *Tsuzumi* or "long snare-drum beaten with the hand." The drum-sticks of A are not held as are those of the West but are clinched at the top by the hands, turned downward at the wrists, and the drum is beaten as if the performer were trying to poke holes in its head. The drum-sticks of B are held more loosely in the hands and the strokes are made parallel to the drum-head.

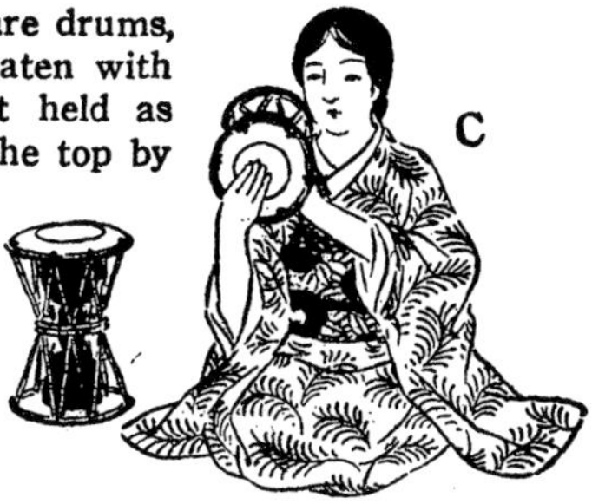

C

Shakuhachi (lit., 1 ft. 8 in.—the length of the flute) are bamboo flutes, played like a clarionet. In the streets, especially during the New Year holidays, *shakuhachi* players are sometimes seen, wearing a rush hat, like an inverted waste-basket, over their heads to conceal their faces while soliciting contributions. These players are known as *Komuso* (lit., *komo*, a coarse straw matting; *so*, a priest) for the reason that originally priests of a branch of the *Zen* sect played the *shakuhachi* while sitting on a coarse straw mat. This eventually evolved into the basket-shaped hat—which was used by spies disguised as *komuso* while endeavoring to discover military and political secrets, and by criminals as a means of concealment.

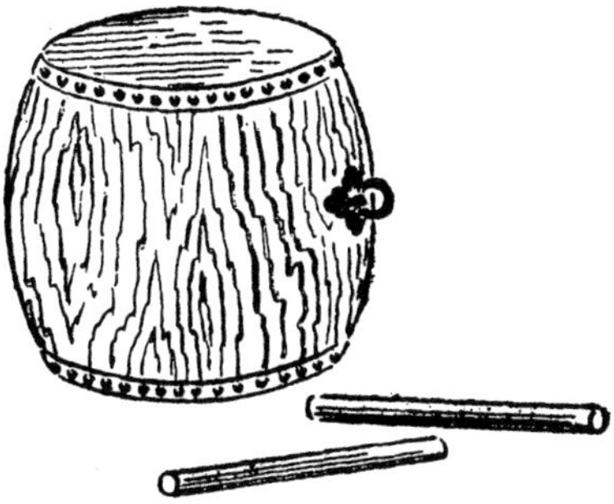

A

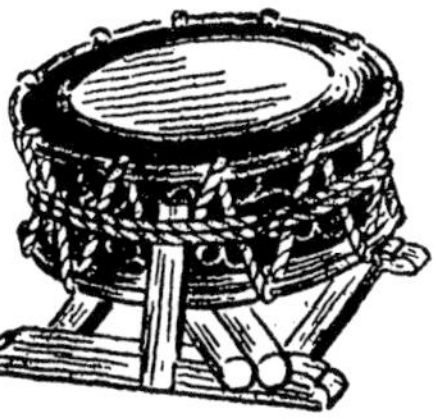

B

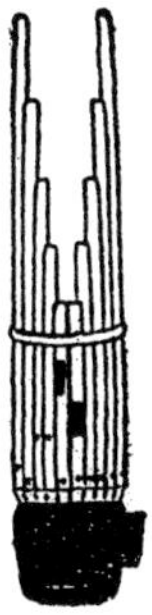

D

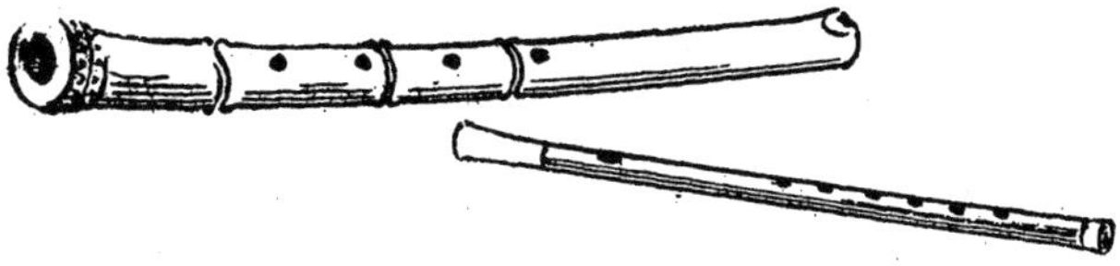

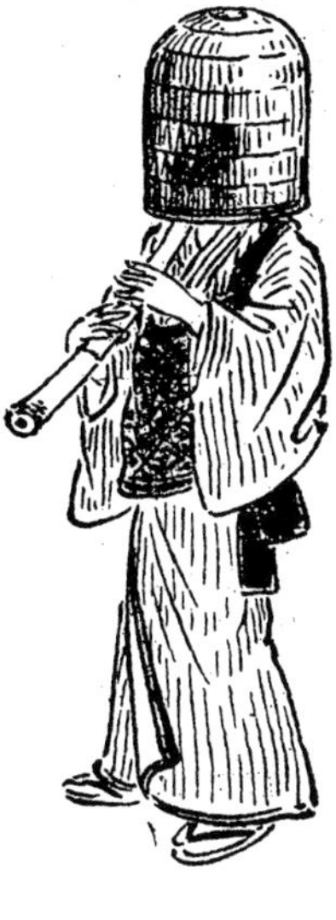

Sho. This instrument (D in the picture) consists of graduated bamboo reeds or pipes which are used in Shinto shrines while the address is being read, and at Shinto ceremonies. The player blows into the protruding mouth-piece shown, right, near the bottom. The sho is played in unison with other instruments, never alone. Its notes are soft and melodious.

THE JAPANESE UMBRELLA ("KASA")

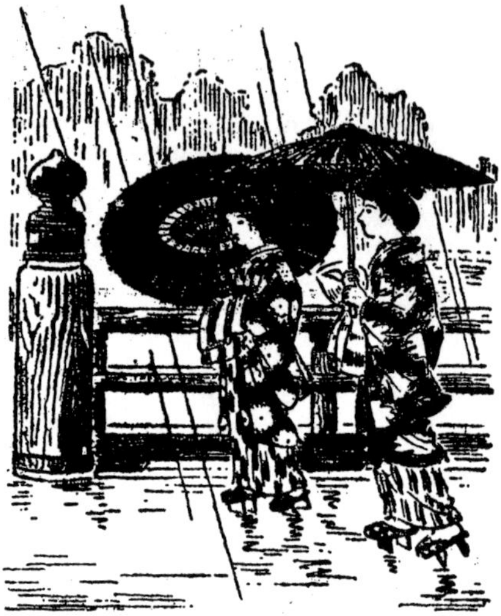

Japanese umbrellas are always of interest to foreign visitors, so different are they from their western cousins—which the Japanese call *komori-gasa* or "batlike umbrellas." *Kasa* are made of bamboo and oiled paper or silk and are decorated with painted designs, which vary. Many mercantile houses, inns, etc. provide kasa, called *bangasa,* for the convenience of their customers. These have the name of the house or their trade-mark painted on them. The picture shows the Fujiya Hotel *kasa.*

The ribs of *kasa* are made of split bamboo, and a circular piece of wood into which they are gathered at the top allows the *kasa* to be opened and shut freely. Waterproof paper or silk is stretched over the frame and a bamboo handle is attached. They are made usually in shops which also manufacture paper lanterns. *Kasa* include umbrellas for rain (*ama-gasa*) and those for protection against the heat of the sun (*higasa*) —parasol-like *kasa,* lighter than the *ama-gasa.*

Kasa are heavier than the western umbrellas and are not so handy to carry about—when closed they are carried handle down by means of a ring or loop at the top. Foreign-style umbrellas are being increasingly used in Japan on account of their convenience, whereas the exports of *kasa* to foreign countries are yearly on the increase, for beach use and other uses.

The standard size for men's use is about 20 in. in size with 40 to 50 ribs; for women, about 21 in., with 40 ribs.

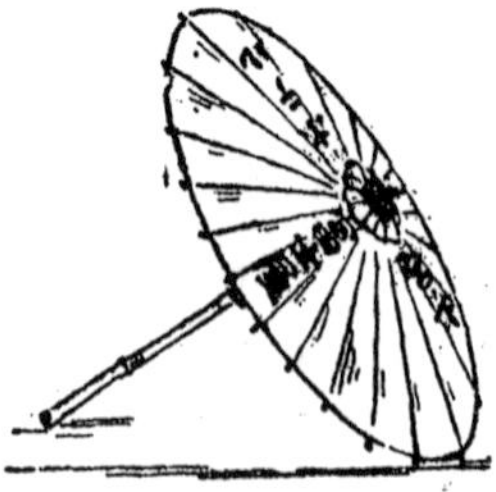

The oldest historical record of *kasa* is that during the reign of Emperor Kimmei, 539–71, when the King of Kudara, an ancient Korean province, sent, among other things, "several gorgeous *kasa*" to the Japanese Emperor as tribute. Prior to that time large rush hats were used in place of *kasa.*

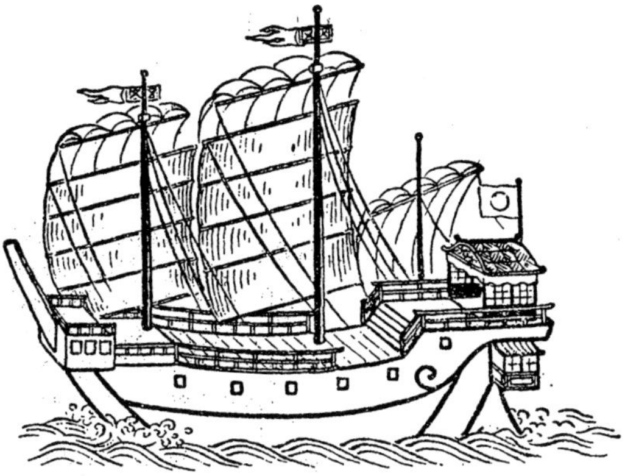

MARU

Maru (pron. mah-ru) has many meanings in Japan. The dictionary defines the word as meaning circle or ring when used as a noun, round or complete or something perfect when used as an adjective, and as a suffix for the name of a boy—and when applied in the last case it rather implies an affectionate meaning, as it did in olden days when used as a suffix to the name given to especially good sword blades. In feudal days it was applied to castles, and today the Emperor's main castle in Tokyo is known as *gohommaru*. Minor castles are called *hon-maru,* and certain buildings in castle compounds are described as various *maru.*

The Japanese national flag, a red ball on a white ground, representing the sun, bears the name *Hino Maru* (lit., "The Round of the Sun").

As a designation of Japanese ships, as in "Asama Maru," it is held that because a circles is complete so is a ship complete in its equipment, its independence, and its self-maintenance.

Maru is used only in the names of commercial vessels, never in those of war ships—where the suffix *Kan* takes the place of *maru.*

As an illustration of the use of maru in personal names, Mori Ran-maru and Ushiwaka-maru were names given to famous Japanese boys. Mori Ran-maru, a very intelligent youth, was the sword-bearer of the great general Nobunaga. He lost his life in defense of his master at the time when Nobunaga was killed by Akechi Mitsuhide, the latter also killing the boy. Ushiwaka-maru was the renowned Yoshitsune, brother of Yoritomo, founder of the Kamakura shogunate, which inaugurated the feudal system in Japan. These *maru* names are held until the lads attain man's estate, when other names are given them.

INTERNATIONAL MUSTACHE CLUB

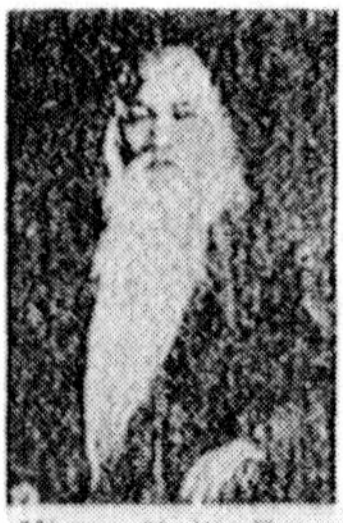

Hirota Fujii, Esq.

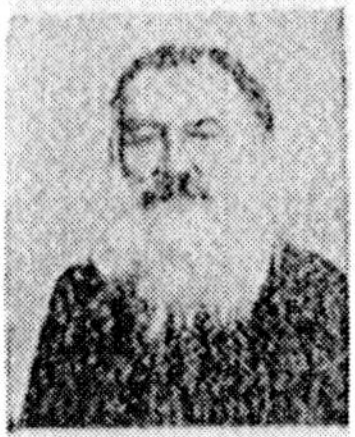

Herr Ernst Keller.

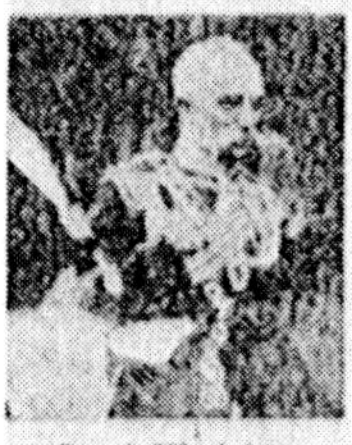

Lord Wyfold.

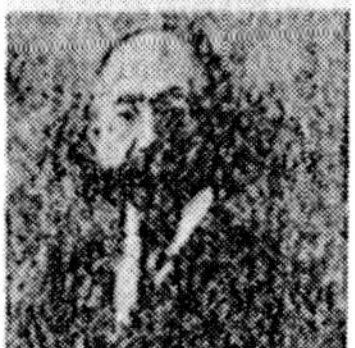

Professor Doctor Shiro Yamada.

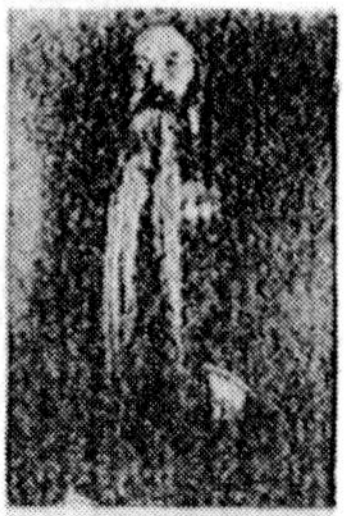

Naojiro Kato, Esq.

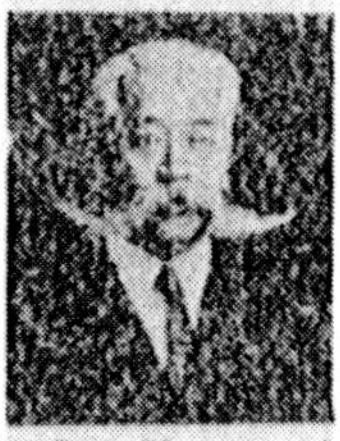

H.S.K. Yamaguchi, Esq.

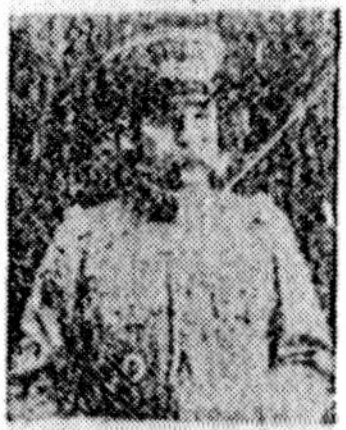

Lieut.-Gen. Hisashi Mori.

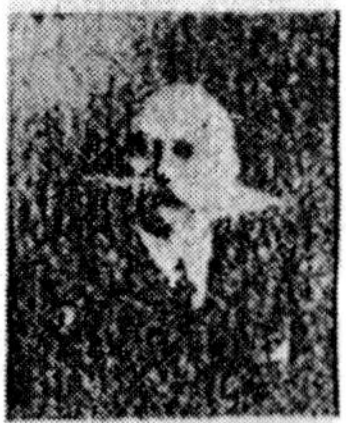

Herr W. Roloff.

The International Mustache Club was founded by Mr. H. S. K. Yamaguchi, managing director of the Fujiya Hotel, Miyanoshita, Hakone, Japan, who is the Honorable Secretary of the club. Its head office is at the hotel.

In Japanese, the name of the club is *Bankoku Hige Kurabu*—the word *hige* meaning a growth of hair on the face below the nose. As there is no corresponding word in English the club was named "The International Mustache Club," but men or women with beards or whiskers are welcome to become members, besides those with mustaches.

OBJECT: The object of the club is to do its bit in creating a feeling of good fellowship among its members, and to show that people of different nationalities are good fellows at heart, and that, after all, without distinction of race or creed or color, every one desires to live in peace and harmony with the rest of mankind.

MEMBERS: To become a member, all that is necessary is for the applicant to send his or her autographed photograph to the Honorable Secretary—which will automatically enroll the applicant as a member—and upon receipt of the application, with autographed photograph, an engraved Certificate of Membership will be forwarded to the applicant. A member must have *hige*, i.e., a mustache, whisker or beard that is at least two inches in length. Should this be shaved off the membership becomes void. Besides its Japanese members, the club has members in the United States, Great Britain, Germany, Czechoslovakia, India, Java, and Siam.

FEES: There are no fees or obligations of any kind.

GALLERY: The gallery for the display of photographs of members is in the Pagoda Tower of the Fujiya Hotel.

In a communication received from the Bald-headed Men's Club of Japan, which has many jovial members, the sympathy and get-together spirit of the International Mustache Club were solicited, and despite the apparently antagonistic requirements for membership in these clubs, the latter gladly extended its good fellowship to the bald-headed men, even though the hirsute adornments of its members could not be well transferred to the bald domes of the former's members as contributions for their lack of hair.

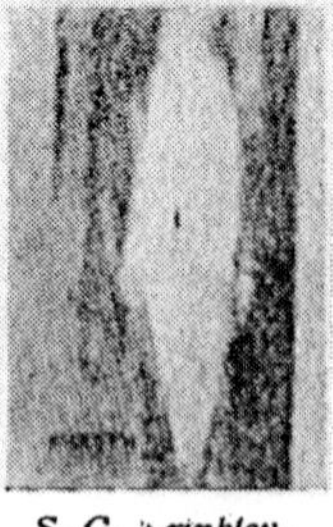

S. G. Brinkley, Esq.

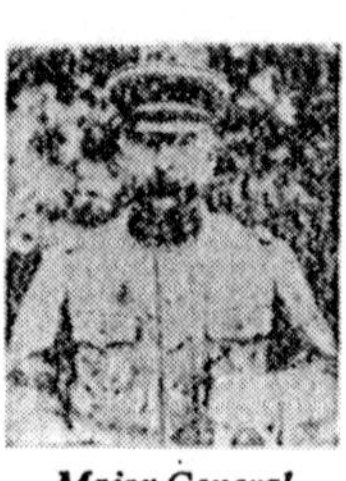

Major-General Kunizo Matsuda.

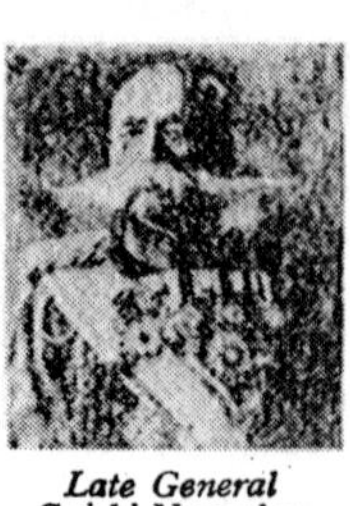

Late General Gaishi Nagaoka.

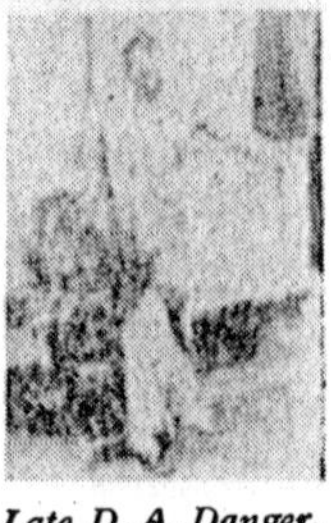

Late D. A. Danger, Esq.

MAZE-KOZE (MA-ZAY, KŌ-ZAY)

Here and There

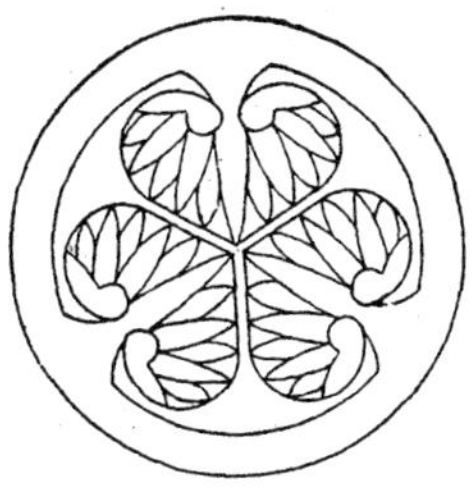

Mitsu-aoi, three leaves of *aoi* (hollyhock). Three of these leaves with their pointed tops in juxtaposition form the *mon* or crest of the great Tokugawa Family. It was adopted from the two-leaved *aoi* crest of the venerable Kamo Shrine, Kyoto, where, from ancient days, the ancestors of the Tokugawa worshipped. Almost every well-to-do family in Japan has its own *mon* (crest), shown principally in the *kimono* and *haori* (an outer garment) — worn by both sexes—that are used on ceremonial and other occasions. The *mon* is also shown on the lacquer-ware and other prized possessions of the family. See "Mon or Crest" description.

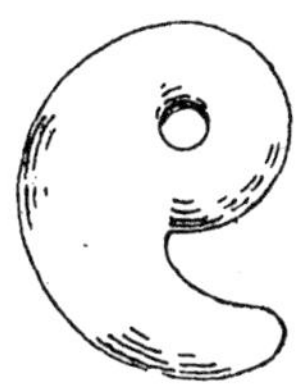

Maga-tama, comma-shaped ornaments made of stone, were anciently (say, prior to the 7th century) polished and strung together and used as necklaces and as ornaments that were worn by Japanese sovereigns and nobles. The necklace of the Imperial Japanese Regalia is made in *magatama* form. See "Imperial Regalia of Japan" engraving.

Walking Sticks at Court Functions: Permission is sometimes granted to aged men by the Imperial Household Office to use walking sticks at court functions as a reward for distinguished service. With this honor, a special stick is presented to the honored one by the Emperor. This is not an ordinary walking stick, it is a stick about five feet long, resembling more a staff of office. Its head is carved into the form of a pigeon.

There is a quaint symbolism in this use of the pigeon. It is believed that of all birds and beasts, the pigeon is the only one which cares for its aged parents. Thus the pigeon stands for the filial care and protection of the aged, and is a symbol singularly appropriate to adorn such a gift as this stick—which is called *Hato-no tsue* ("Pigeon-head cane"), sometimes *Kyuchujo* ("Imperial Palace Walking-stick").

Of course, the stick is highly prized and becomes one of the chief treasures of the family. The owner may, or may not, exercise his privilege of using it at court functions, but it may be assumed that he usually does, after such a distinction has been awarded him by the Emperor.

Pigeons are employed in many observances in Japan: at the launching of ships, at the time of a burial, and so on—and at principal temples and shrines one sees flocks of pigeons which pass their lives under the protection of the temple or shrine authorities, harbored presumably for the reason above stated, as an example to the young to care for the aged.

MAZE-KOZE (MA-ZAY, KO-ZAY)

Here and There

Mongolian Spot (English), ***Jihan*** (Japanese), ***Ji***=baby or child, ***han***=spot, Mongolenflecke (German): There are few Japanese babies without the "Mongolian Spot," which appears within a month after the birth of the child, and disappears when the baby is about two years old. In size, it is generally about that of the ball of a finger, but sometimes it is as large as the palm of an adult. Usually, there are one or two of these spots, occasionally three or four, but not more. They appear on the buttocks, waist, or base of the spinal column, sometimes (but rarely) on the limbs, breast, or stomach. Never on the palm or sole.

Chinese, Korean, Malayan, Hawaiian, and American Indian babies, besides Japanese, have this spot—and Ainu babies have numerous spots.

Histologically, the Mongolian spot is found on the skin, in the spindle-shaped pigment cell found in the corium, the innermost layer of the skin.

In the Occidental baby, this spot is not visible to the naked eye, but histologically it is found near the sacrum, the triangular lower bone of the vertebral column. *Adapted from Dr. Shigenobu Kuriyama's description in the "Modern Dictionary of Medicine"—30 volumes.*

There is a statement in this same dictionary that the name "Mongolian Spot" was given by the late Dr. E. Baelz, a noted savant, and for many years medical professor of the Tokyo Imperial University, who thought that this spot appeared only on Japanese (or Asiatic) children—a belief which now is found to be a mistaken one. Dr. Tokuji Ichikawa calls this mark, "Blue color Spot."

Lunar Calendar: Although the lunar calendar has been officially disestablished in Japan, it is still in use among ordinary folk; especially farmers —and many festivals and observances are held on lunar calendar dates, as of old. The lunar year is divided into 24 seasons of from 14 to 17 days in length. The lunar year begins anywhere from three to six weeks behind the solar year and never catches up. Every two or three years an extra month is intercalated into the lunar year.

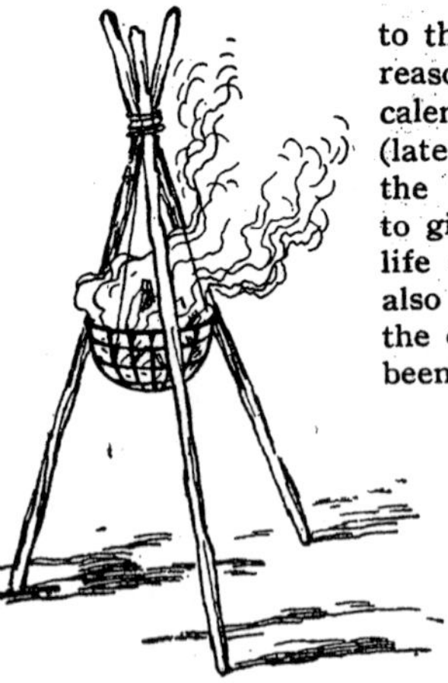

The farmer regulates his activities according to the lunar rather than the solar calendar, for the reason that experience has shown that the old lunar calendar has been fairly regular. The *Doyo* season (late July and early August), means a great deal to the farmer. He then drains his rice-fields in order to give them a sun-bath and to destroy the insect life that abounds in them. This is a merry time also for the farmer's children, who hunt through the drained fields in search of small fish that have been marooned in the puddles.

At night, in many localities, at this time, farmers foregather on the banks of a stream and, in the hope of ridding their fields from insect pests, burn pine knots in wire-baskets suspended from tripods, and repeat the formula:

"Okure, Okure, ine no mushi Okure."

"Go away, go away! Rice insects."

MAZE-KOZE (MA-ZAY, KO-ZAY)

Here and There

Conveyances in Old Japan: In medieval days the vehicles were those lumbering bullock-carts so often depicted in art and literature, particularly in the *Genji Monogatari.* For centuries these carts served the Japanese nobility in their ceremonial and pleasure parties round Kyoto, the old capital, and today upon the death of an Emperor, the body is conveyed to the tomb in a bullock-drawn cart, especially constructed. In old Japan horses were employed only to draw carts (*daihachi-guruma*) for conveying merchandise and as pack-horses.

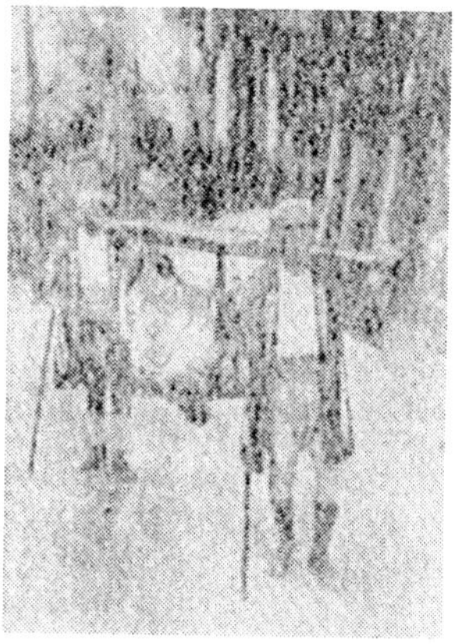

Kago, "basket" (the generic meaning) is the name now applied specifically to one particular kind made of split bamboo, being a seat of woven bamboo wicker-work which is hung from a long bamboo pole that rests on the shoulders of two men, one in front, one behind. Occasionally they are assisted by runners who, by means of a straw rope fastened to each end of the pole, help to draw the *kago* on up-grades and to hold it back on down-grades. The *kago* has a light roof and sometimes a strip of cotton stuff on one side to ward off the sun's rays. Japanese, with feet doubled under them, ride in a recumbent position in comfort, but foreigners find little comfort in such a cramped position and to obtain relief soon let their legs dangle from the sides. These *kago* are now employed only in mountainous districts where motorcars cannot penetrate.

A *Norimono* (vehicle; a palanquin) so often mentioned by travelers

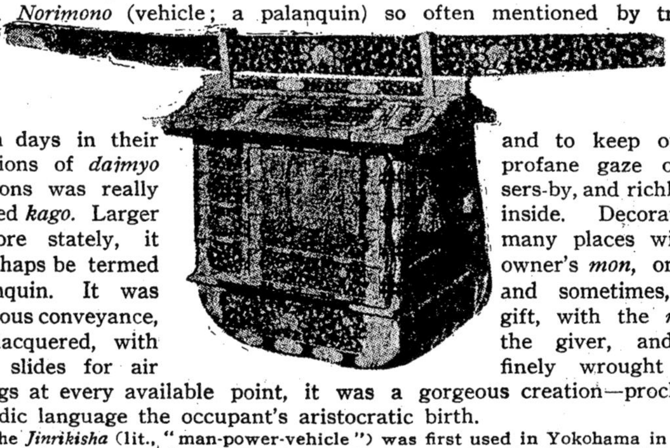

of olden days in their descriptions of *daimyo* processions was really a glorified *kago.* Larger and more stately, it may perhaps be termed a palanquin. It was a luxurious conveyance, highly lacquered, with latticed slides for air and to keep out the profane gaze of passers-by, and richly fitted inside. Decorated in many places with the owner's *mon,* or crest, and sometimes, if a gift, with the *mon* of the giver, and with finely wrought metal fastenings at every available point, it was a gorgeous creation—proclaiming in heraldic language the occupant's aristocratic birth.

The *Jinrikisha* (lit., "man-power-vehicle") was first used in Yokohama in the late sixties or early seventies of the 19th century. As its name implies it is a vehicle pulled by a man, or, as wittily suggested, a "pull-man-car." The word *jinrikisha* has had rather bad treatment at the hands of Japanese and foreigners alike. Japanese generally cut off its tail and call it *jinriki* or they translate the Chinese syllable *sha* into their own language, and call it *kuruma.* Foreigners cut off its head and maltreat the vowels, pronouncing it *rickshaw.*

Today from the thousands in use in the old days, these vehicles have dwindled to comparatively few in Japan. There are still a few at the port cities where the novelty of the ride appeals to foreign visitors. Motorcars and buses, taxis, and electric trams are taking the *rickshaw* and its picturesque puller out of the picture.

MAZE-KOZE (MA-ZAY, KO-ZAY)

Here and There

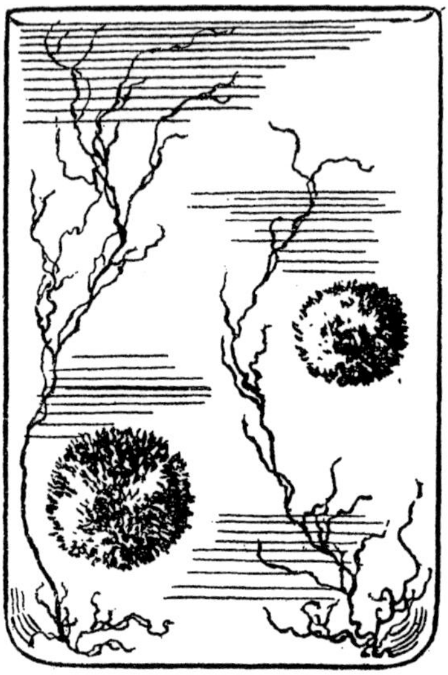

Mari-mo (*Mari*—ball, *mo*—weed). In Lake Akan, Hokkaidō, in the proposed National Park, best reached from Kushiro, is found a ball-like green weed of special interest to students of botany. Discovered in 1897, it was named *Mari-mo* by Professor Kingo Miyabe, of the Sapporo Agricultural College. Its botanical name is given by some authorities as *Aegagropila Sautari*, by others *Cladophora Sauteri*. This weed is also found in certain lakes of Saghalien (Karafuto), the Kurile Islands (Chishima), in some of the lakes of northern Europe, and in one of the Swiss lakes.

Marimo in form is a sponge-like dark-green ball which in diameter ranges from a half inch to nine inches. Its spores are much smaller than those of a sponge. In Lake Akan, triangularly shaped, there are mountain streams at each angle, and at the mouth of these streams the *marimo* are found, the smaller ones in shallow water, the larger at a depth of about 20 feet. Looking through a glass-bottom box or tube they appear as a mass of flabby balls. Sometimes they rise to the surface, sinking afterward, states Professor Makoto Nishimura, who has written a pamphlet on *Marimo*. The professor also states that *marimo* have remarkable vitality. He says that he took one of these weeds out of the water and placed it in a shady place, and after three months it was yet alive. The government authorities are preserving and propagating this rare species.

The illustration shows *marimo* owned by the Fujiya Hotel, Miyanoshita, Japan.

MAZE-KOZE (MA-ZAY, KO-ZAY)

Here and There

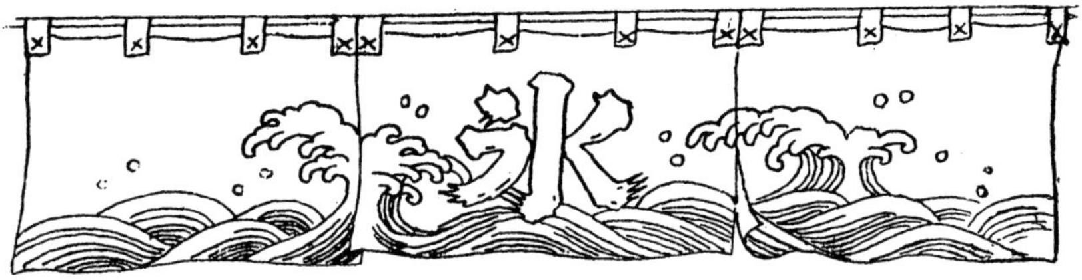

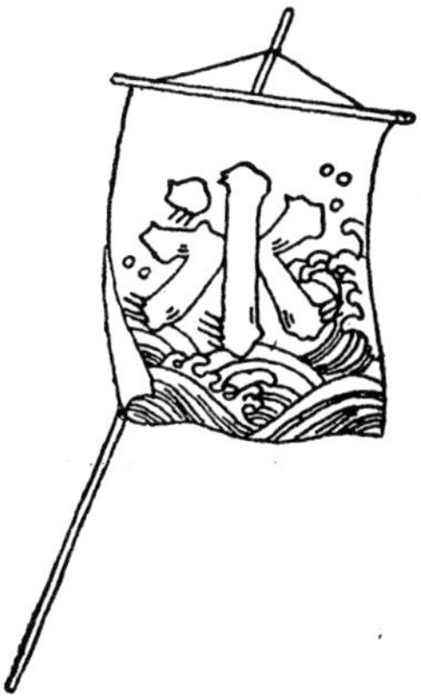

Kori-mizu (*Kori*—ice, *mizu*—water), shaved ice, is one of the most popular summer drinks of Japan. So far as known it is not served in other countries. On an upturned plane, somewhat similar to a carpenter's plane, or with machines made especially for the purpose, ice is shaved into very fine flakes from small blocks of ice, and various kinds of syrups are added for flavor: grape, strawberry, lemon, etc., or sugar. A glass of *kori-mizu* will cool one on the hottest of days.

In summer, little stalls, called *Kori-ya*, are opened in cities, towns, and villages, alongside traveled roads, near sea-beaches, at mountain passes, and on the approach to temples and shrines, and even in the shadow of metropolitan office buildings, and *kori-mizu* is served in many restaurants and ice-cream shops—and, invariably, wherever it is sold, a small flag or banner with the character for ice in the center, usually with a depiction of waves (representing water) is displayed outside that shop or stall. It is the sign of the *Kori-ya*. Many of these shops also have banners over the entrance, like that shown in the upper drawing.

A heaping glass of *kori-mizu* is sold for 5 to 10 sen, depending on the class of shop. It is a most refreshing drink on a hot day, and its cheapness creates a large demand.

ODDITIES—IN JAPAN

"Believe It or Not"

Memorial Services—

Color Prints: In Tokyo the members of the wood-print engravers' guild occasionally hold memorial services in honor of the spirits of countless cherry trees whose lives they and their fellow craftsmen have taken in making wood-print engravings. Up to 1911 all wood-print engravings made in Japan utilized cherry wood for the blocks; since that time about 20% of the blocks have been made of boxwood. Leaders of the guild, believing that Japanese culture owes much to wood-print engraving, hold such services as the only way they have of showing a sentimental regard for the tree which has contributed so much to the artistic life of Japan. The first service of this kind was held in Tokyo on April 1, 1923, at the Shinryoin Temple, at Sakuragicho, Shitaya, near Ueno Park.

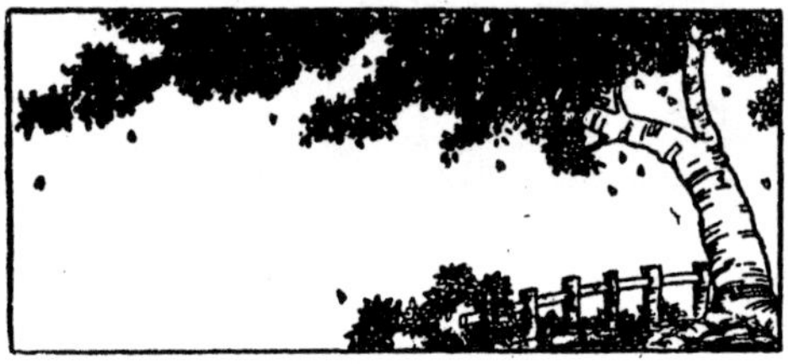

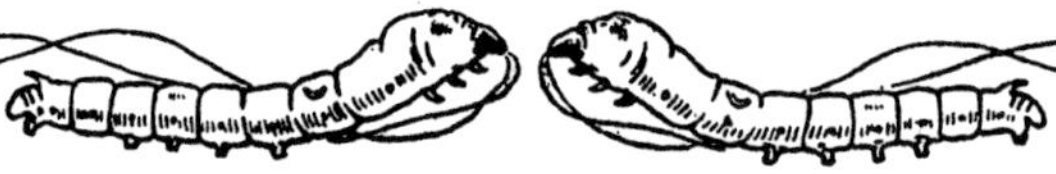

SILK-WORMS: On May 21, 1932, an elaborate Buddhist mass for all the silk-worms which have given their lives for the silk industry in Japan was said by 24 priests in the Asakusa Kwannon Temple, Tokyo. This memorial service was the idea of Mr. K. Kijima, the head of the 7th generation of a family of silk-thread dealers in Tokyo. It is expected to make this memorial service an annual event. At Uzumasa, near Kyoto, there is a small shrine called Kijima Jinja, dedicated originally to honor and to give thanks to silk-worms and weaving-machines for the production of silk thread, perhaps erected by an ancestor of the Mr. Kijima above mentioned.

Fish: On March 22, 1932, a Buddhist mass service for the purpose of comforting the spirits of fish that have been caught to feed the nation was held at the great Sodo sect temple, Sojiji, in Tsurumi, and at sect's Saijoji or Doryosan branch, near Odawara. The next day, the Tsurumi priests observed a "service on the sea" for fish that had died from natural causes. This took place on the waters of Tokyo Bay. These services were held under the auspices of organizations of marine-products dealers and local dealers throughout Japan, and the Government Department of Fishery, and were made possible through their monetary contributions. It is expected that this service will be observed annually.

Chrysanthemums: On November 6, 1932, a service was observed in Hibiya Park, Tokyo, in honor of the chrysanthemums which have beautified the November chrysanthemum exhibits in the park, held annually for many years.

ODDITIES—IN JAPAN

"Believe It or Not"

Memorial Services—

Broken Dolls: Annually, in early June, a Buddhist service is held at the Teikoku Primary School in Nishi-Sugamo, Tokyo, for dolls that have been broken beyond repair. The dolls are buried in the playground of the school, their grave being marked by a stone about 2 ft. high, inscribed "Grave of Dolls." Since the service was started in 1918 several hundred broken dolls have been buried there. The ceremony is always largely attended by school children and their mothers. Priests chant the sutra intended to compose the soul of the dead.

This service is an outgrowth of the Doll Hospital conducted by the school since 1913. An expert repairs all dolls turned in at the "hospital," and those broken beyond repair are saved for the annual ceremony—which never fails to delight and impress the children.

Dr. T. Nishiyama, the school principal, states: "The doll in Japan dates back to the days when clay images were buried in place of actual retainers of great men who previously had been sacrificed at the tombs of their masters. Since that time many a doll has been cast into river and sea under an old belief that misfortune and evil could be cast away by this ceremony. They have also been sacrificed in rites to obtain health and happiness of sons and daughters. Dolls have been the intimate friends and companions of children from time immemorial and they are regarded and treated by children as living beings and are factors in their education—which was our reason for establishing the hospital at this school. The dolls thus treated here have exceeded 10,000 in number."

At the Kosenji temple, near the Roppongi crossing, Tokyo, after entering the front gate, the first stone on the left is a gravestone for broken dolls and toys. It was placed there in 1931 through contributions of pupils of several girls' schools, each one giving a few sen. The names of the schools are on the back of the stone. The temple priest states that there are no set days for the burials but that broken dolls and toys are on occasion buried under the stone.

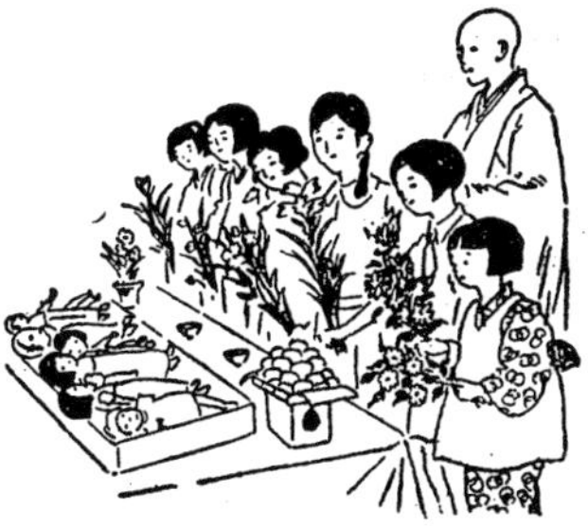

ODDITIES—IN JAPAN

"Believe It or Not"

Memorial Services—

Broken Needles Mass (*Hari-Kuyo*); Yearly, on December 8th, but more generally on February 8th, services for broken needles are held in many girls' schools, and in some private homes, to comfort the spirits of needles broken during the year—the needle being regarded as a living thing whose body has been sacrificed in service. An altar consisting of two or three steps is set up. In front of it is the Sacred Staff and Rope, *gohei* (cut-paper strips) being suspended from it. On the top step offerings of cake and fruit are placed. On the second step is a plate on which is a cube of *tofu* (bean-curd)—a jelly-like substance—into which the broken and crooked needles are thrust, the idea being to give the needles a soft rest after their hard work. Sewing accessories are displayed on the lowest step. In a Buddhist school a sutra is read to calm the spirit of the needles. In Tokyo, the *tofu,* with its needles, is offered to a Awashima shrine: at Asakusa, Shimo-Kitazawa, and elsewhere.

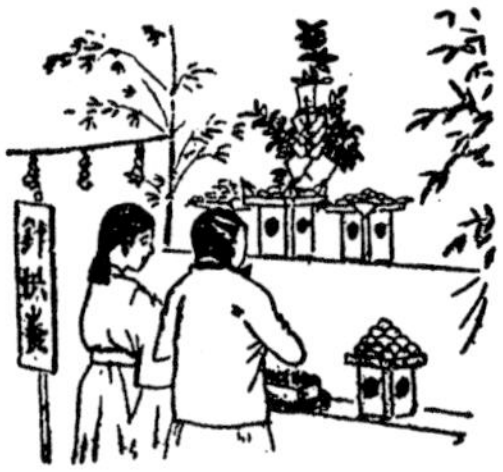

This ceremony, or ones nearly similar, is one of the traditional services observed by girls in Japan, which, with some lapses, can be traced back for about 1600 years to the time of Emperor Nintoku, and the Awashima shrines of the land are chosen for the offerings because it is said that the main Awashima Shrine, in the province of Kii (Wakayama) is dedicated to Emperor Nintoku.

ODDITIES—IN JAPAN

"Believe It or Not"

Memorial Services—

For the Samisen Inventor: Annually, on April 1 or 2, a Buddhist mass is held at the Taishin Temple, Mita, Shiba, Tokyo, to comfort the spirit of Omi Ishimura, who improved the old crude samisen, invented by an ancestor, to its present shape. The 300th anniversary of Ishimura's death was observed in 1929. The temple is known as the Samisen Temple because the graves of Ishimura and other celebrated samisen makers are located there. For picture of a samisen see *Japanese Musical Instruments* description.

* * * * *

Buried by the side of Ishimura's grave is a famous cat named Tama-chan, which died in October, 1925. Its elaborate Buddhist funeral service was held at the Zōjōji Temple, Shiba, and was conducted by the Lord Abbott of the temple, assisted by more than 70 priests, at a cost of ¥ 4000. More than 80 wreaths were offered to the spirit of the cat, which was buried by its owner, Mr. Tomijūro Kumazawa, proprietor of the Neko-ya, Yotsuya, Tokyo, to comfort the spirits of all cats whose skins had been used by samisen manufacturers. *Neko* means cat, and, after adopting Tama-chan, and naming his establishment "Neko-ya," Mr. Kumazawa's business prospered amazingly. He deposited money in the post-office savings department in the name of his cat, and when she died Tama-chan had about ¥ 1000 to her credit —which went toward the expense of her funeral and burial. Over ¥ 400 was offered to the spirit of Tama-chan by Mr. Kumazawa's friends and by lovers of cats, which, after the cat's burial, was given to various social welfare work organizations in the name of the cat. The spirit of Tama-chan now rests in a miniature family shrine at the Neko-ya and a bowl of rice is offered to it every morning.

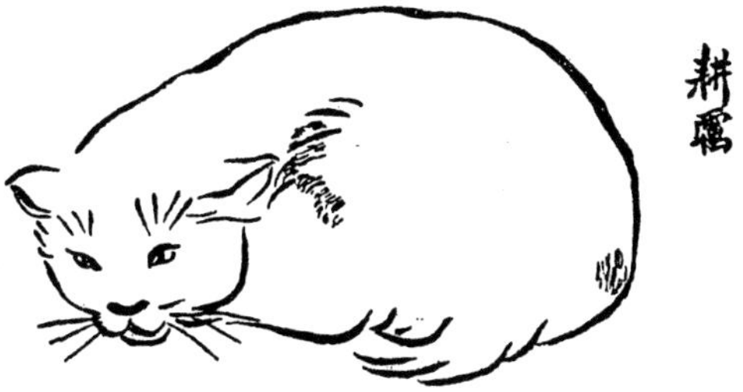

The Neko-ya has since adopted Tama-chan II. She is a beautiful cat, weighing about 12 pounds. Her usual sleeping place is in the window, where she serves as an advertisement for the establishment.

ODDITIES—IN JAPAN

Cats and Dogs: A bronze statue to console the spirits of dead cats and dogs stands on a lotus pedestal in the precinct of Kuonji, the Nichiren temple on Mt. Minobu, Yamanashi Prefecture. It is 7 ft. high and weighs 1,600 pounds. It was erected by Tokyo samisen makers and dealers to propitiate the revengeful spirits and for the repose of the souls of the hundreds of thousand cats and dogs which are killed annually to furnish samisen strings and drum coverings. The larger figure of the statue has the face of a dog and on its lap is a small figure with the face of a cat. Both figures are clothed in Buddhist robes, the cat in female robes. On top of the dog's head is a small statue of Buddha. The dog image is larger than that of the cat for the reason that many more dogs than cats have been killed for making the drum section of samisens. The samisen manufacturers and dealers felt that their business would be accused if the spirits of the sacrificed animals were not comforted, so the statue was erected for that purpose, and in gratitude to the cats and dogs that have contributed so much toward the livelihood of those in the business. See "Japanese Musical Instruments" descriptions.

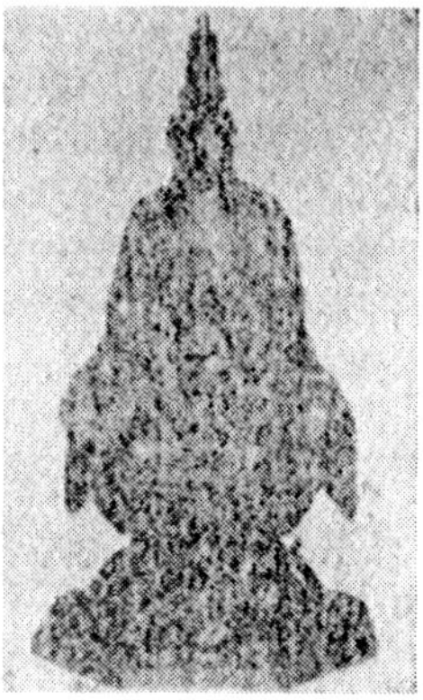

The average price of a tanned cat skin is about ¥4; that of a dog about ¥1.50—the latter is cheap because the raw skin costs the dealer very little. Two cat skins are required to cover one drum, one on each side; a dog's skin can cover several drums. About 20% of the samisens made in Japan are covered with cat skins.

To Tide over Unlucky Years: As stated elsewhere (see "Japanese Customs"), men at the age of 42 are believed in Japan to have reached the worst year of their life so far as fate and fortune are concerned—the 42nd year being considered the most unlucky year of a man's life. This is the reason that 27 men of Kinomoto, Shiga Prefecture, who were in this bad year, contributed to erect a large stone *torii* at the nearby Ifufura Shrine and dedicate it to its enshrined deity in the hope that they might pass through this critical year without serious mishap, through the protection of the shrine's guardian spirit. The formal dedication of the *torii* took place in April, 1932. Contributions, large and small, in money, trees, and in other ways, have for many years been offered to this shrine for the same purpose.

On the evening of February 3, when the *Setsubun* ceremony is observed, it is a custom of many Japanese who are in what are considered their unlucky years, i.e., men in their 25, 42, and 61 years; women, in their 19, 33, and 47 years, to wrap as many beans as correspond with their respective ages, in *hanshi* (Japanese paper), and drop the package at some quiet cross-roads, unseen by anyone. It is believed that this act will aid them in passing their unlucky year.

Snakes: At Yumoto, beyond Nikko and Chuzenji, on the lakeshore, is a monument to snakes, erected by a priest about 60 years ago. At that time snakes infested the mountains, to the terror of the people—who besought the aid of the priest, who prayed day and night for the departure or conversion of the snakes. His prayers prevailed, for since that time the snakes have been few and harmless, it is said.

ODDITIES—IN JAPAN

"Believe It or Not"

Monuments—

Elephants: In the precincts of Tennoji Temple, Osaka, is a bronze statue of a 6-tusked elephant standing on the back of a tortoise. On the elephant's back is an image of Fugen-Bosatsu, the Buddha of Wisdom. The six tusks of the elephant are accounted for by a belief that if elephants were allowed to live for their full span of life they would grow that number of tusks. The statue is about 36 ft. in height, and weighs close to 16 tons. It was dedicated on October 17th, 1929, in an elaborate Buddhist service, for the purpose of consoling the sprits of the elephants and tortoises whose lives have been sacrificed to furnish material for dealers, carvers, and workers of ivory and tortoise shell in the western part of Japan—and a memorial service is held yearly before the statue.

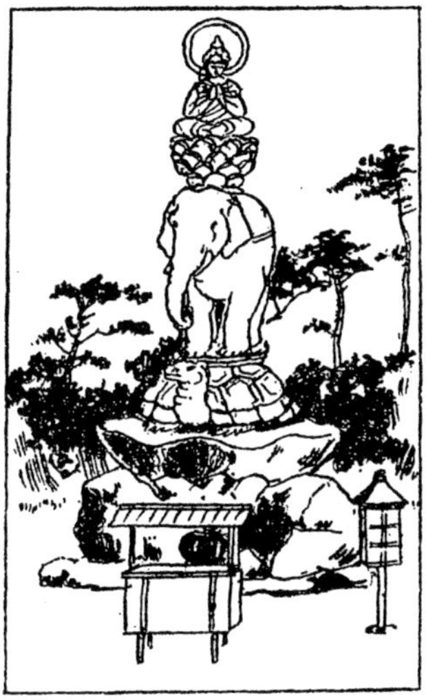

The statue was erected through the efforts of Mr. Fukumatsu Sunamoto, an Osaka ivory dealer who has been in the ivory business for over 40 years. Most of its considerable cost was paid for through the sale of two large informative volumes (¥30) about elephants, written in Japanese by Mr. Sunamoto's son. Each purchaser of these books was given a small ivory tablet with his name carved thereon—which was placed in the hollow interior of the Buddha. Contributions were also received from persons connected with the ivory and tortoise shell trades, and from the general public.

* * * * *

Under the auspices of the Tokyo Ivory Art Object Dealers' Association and the Association of Artists of Ivory Carving, a Buddhist mass for the spirits of elephants which have supplied ivory for ivory carving in Japan was celebrated by 21 priests, on April 15, 1926, at the Gokoku Temple in Otowa, Koishikawa, Tokyo. It was attended by more than 1000 persons. This was the first time that a mass to comfort the spirits of these elephants was ever held on such a large scale. It was celebrated by ivory dealers and carvers as an expression of their gratitude toward the elephants which have supplied them with material for their livelihood.

ODDITIES—IN JAPAN

"Believe It or Not"

Monuments—

Togyuboku-Kuyo-to, or The Butchered-Cow-Tree-Stupa, is a monument erected in the precinct of the Gyokusenji Temple, Shimoda, Izu, near the decaying stump of the citrus tree to which was tied the cow that was first butchered for meat in Japan. This was an unusual slaughter as the tenets of the Buddhist religion then strictly prohibited the use of meat for food. This historic event took place in 1856 so that Townsend Harris, the first U. S. consul-general to Japan, who was domiciled in the temple, could be supplied with beef as he requested—and incidentally it is revealed that when it became known that Mr. Harris was a beef-eater, the owners of cows throughout the neighborhood were so alarmed that they built high railings around their cow sheds in order to prevent their cows from being butchered for the consul. These cows were used for draft purposes. The stump of the cow tree is enclosed by a marble fence and is protected from the elements by a bronze lotus leaf. A new sapling has been planted back of the stump.

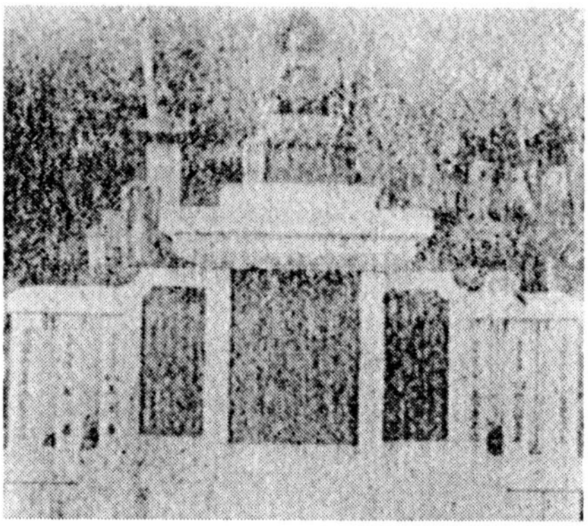

The monument, of marble and bronze, 10 ft. in height, topped with an image of Buddha, was unveiled on April 8, 1931—the birthday of Buddha. Its cost, ¥5,000, was met by contributions of dealers and users of beef in their various businesses in the eastern part of Japan, under the auspices of the Butchers' Guild of Shimoda, which promoted the project.

In shape and design the monument resembles the Tamamushi-Zushi or Tamamushi Sanctuary, a national treasure, now preserved in the Horyuji Temple, near Nara. This is the underlying story of the design: In a previous life the Buddha was a prince of high degree. In a wilderness he came across a tigress with seven hungry cubs. Taking pity on them, the Buddha gave himself to them. Because of this merciful and noble act he was in his next life born the Buddha. The Empress Suiko (592–628) had this story painted on the doors of the sanctuary above named. Because cows give their lives in order to feed mankind, Mr. Seigi Kobayashi, Tokyo, the designer of the monument, incorporated the idea of the story into the monument.

ODDITIES—IN JAPAN

"Believe It or Not"

A Memorial—

Monster Cat Bridge: In Tokyo, Koishikawa ward, between Otsuka and Kagomachi, is a bridge named Nekomata-Bashi or Monster Cat Bridge, spanning a small stream. Its story, by Bakin, a 19th century novelist, is thus given: During the Kanyei Era (1624–44) there lived in Kawagoye a silk merchant whose son died soon after his birth. While the merchant and his wife were mourning over the loss of their only son they heard a baby crying at their gate. Running out, they found a very young boy baby, with a sword alongside him. They adopted the baby as their own, naming him Monjiro ("Gate-second-boy"). Soon after this the merchant was killed by a ronin (a *samurai* without a master).

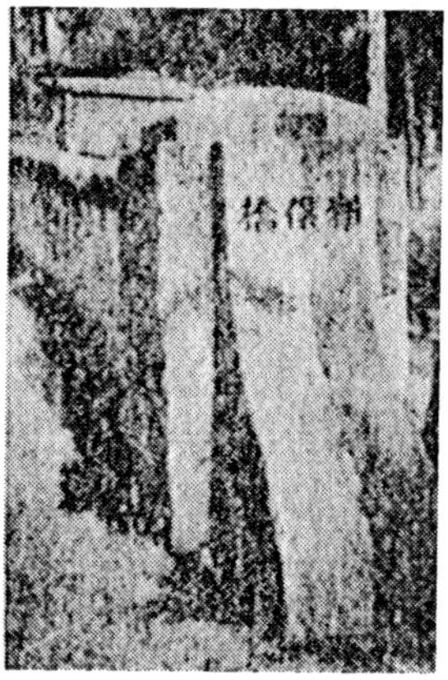

When Monjiro was 15 years old, he came to Yedo with his adoptive mother and an old cat which was a great pet of the family. They rented a house in Koishikawa, and the boy took fencing lessons so that he could qualify as a *samurai* in order to avenge his adoptive father's death. His mother became ill and was confined to her bed, and Monjiro had a very hard time to earn enough cash to purchase medicine and food for his sick mother. One night the old cat brought in something bright in her mouth. It was a gold piece, and for several consecutive nights she brought in similar pieces. Nearby was a pawnbroker's shop. Its owner soon noticed that a piece of gold was stolen every night. While pretending to be asleep, he kept watch. About midnight an old cat stole into his room and took a piece of gold out of his money-cabinet. The pawnbroker caught and killed the cat—and threw it into the stream.

When Monjiro heard that his cat had been killed by the pawnbroker, he went and asked him for the remains. At his first glance, the pawnbroker was startled by the resemblance of the boy to his dead wife, and a mole on Monjiro's face led them into conversation,—which revealed that they were father and son. "Soon after you were born," the pawnbroker told the boy, "your mother died of fever. Without a woman's hands to care for you, I could not bring you up, and, in spite of my love for you, I took you to Kawagoye, and deserted you leaving with you a sword as a keepsake."

Monjiro was taken back by his real father, and his adoptive mother was restored to health. Monjiro finally succeeded in tracing the murderer of his adoptive father and avenged his death. The pawnbroker made over all his property to his son.

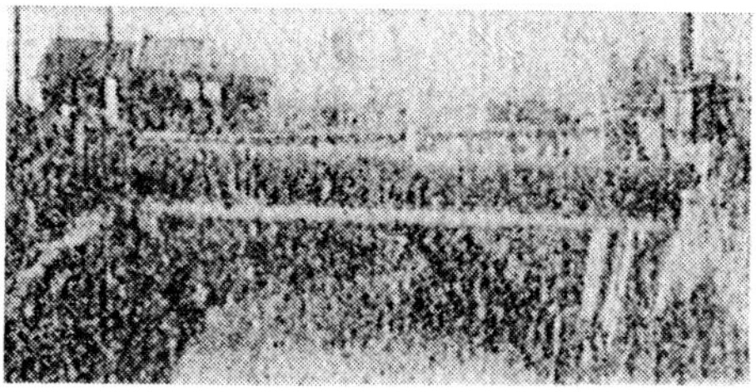

Monjiro attributed all his good fortune to the old cat and in commemoration of her faithful action he built a bridge over the place where her body had been thrown into the stream. This bridge is yet known as the Nekomata-Bashi, and its vicinity is known as Nekomata.

ODDITIES—IN JAPAN

Missing Child Stones. **So far as this writer is informed there are four of these stones in Tokyo. Probably there are more. When a lost child could not be identified, the finder of the child placed a description of it, and where the child could be found, in a recess cut in the stone. There was another recess in the stone in which the searcher for a lost child placed a description of the child, together with the address of its parents.**

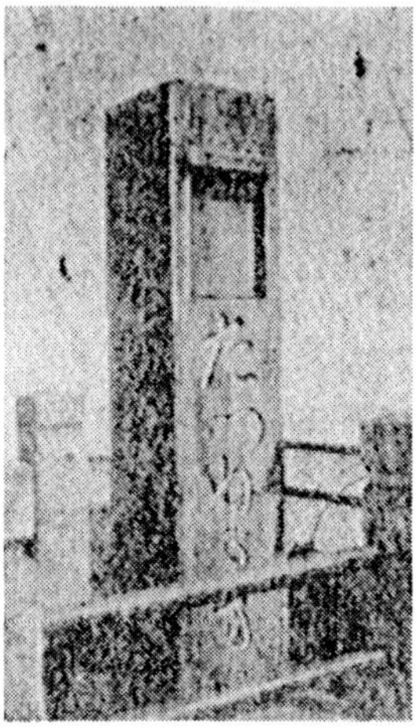

These stones are located: (1) Near the south end, left side, of Ikkokubashi Bridge, south of the Bank of Japan; (2) Near the Kaminari-mon (gate) of Senso-ji Temple; (3) In the precinct of the Yushima Tenjin Shrine; (4) In Tamachi, Akasaka (not far from Akasaka Mitsuke).

Salt for purification,, as well as to keep bad luck away, is an old superstition in Japan. Small pyramids of salt are often seen on the thresholds of restaurants, shops, houses of geisha, and sometimes at the gates of private residences in the belief that no evil will pass over them, and as a welcome to the guest or customer—and to attract customers. Should a customer, about to enter a restaurant, accidentally kick some of the salt towards it, this is considered a very lucky omen. A Japanese wrestler before grappling with his opponent will, in the frequent pauses in the ring preliminaries, scatter handfuls of salt here and there so that no evil spirits can enter the ring and prevent him from winning. According to the Japanese idea, salt purifies everything, and it is still the custom, in some Japanese families, inasmuch as meat was not eaten in olden days, that when meat is cooked, salt must be sprinkled on the fire —for the fire's purification. A story is told about Emperor Wu of the Chin Dynasty, who, after subduing his enemies in U, Wei, and Shu, lived such a luxurious life that he is said to have had an entourage of 3,000 beautiful women, each of them vying to monopolize the Emperor's attention. On one of his rounds through his city, his carriage being drawn by sheep, these animals suddenly stopped before the gate of one of his women—to the envy of all the other women—who did not know that this woman had been clever enough to place a liberal quantity of salt in front of her gate in order to attract the sheep. And it is said that the pyramids of salt are placed at the entrances of certain places as much to attract customers as to purify the premises.

Maigo-fuda ("Missing Child Tag"). In order to facilitate the recovery of lost children, parents were accustomed to attach to the *obi* of each of their children under 13 years of age an oblong brass tag on one side of which the child's name and address were engraved, thus enabling their finder to take them home. On the other side, the year of the child's birth was shown by its year symbol: rat, horse, sheep, cock, etc., as the fact might be, as a means of calculating and checking up further on the identity of the child. See "Year Names." The demand for these tags created a special business. This custom is still in vogue in the case of young children under school age.

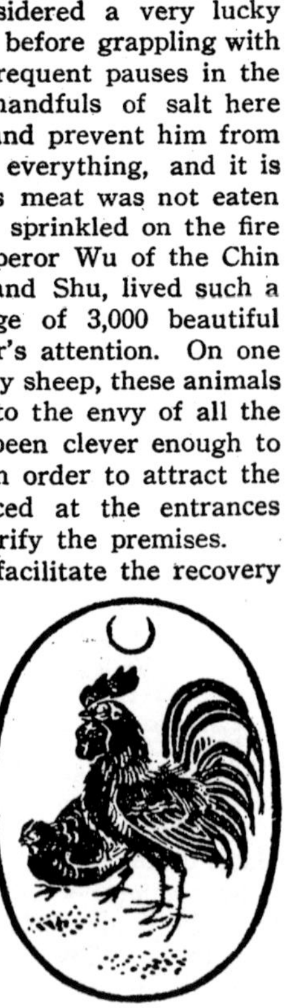

ODDITIES—IN JAPAN

"*Believe It or Not*"

Various—

Sticking Needles into Flesh ("*Harii*"): In Japan, the good old cure-all (acupuncture) is still in use, especially to relieve lumbago, sciatica, neuralgia, and toothache. The operation consists in perforating the skin and underlying tissues to a depth up to 2½ inches, depending on the part to be treated, with fine needles of gold, silver, or steel at the spot where the patient has pain. Needles of varying diameters and lengths, the latter from 1½ to 3 inches long, are employed, and in practice are worked up and down up to a dozen times, according to the strength and constitution of the patient. One to twenty needles may be used in one treatment. In the hands of a skilled practitioner the patient does not feel the needles, nor is blood drawn. This treatment is given by masseurs especially licensed by the government to practice acupuncture. There is a licensed masseur in Miyanoshita.

Komuso are men who play *shakuhachi* (a bamboo flute) from house to house, especially at New Year, soliciting contributions. They wear rush hats, like an inverted waste-basket, over their heads to conceal their faces.

In days past, the role of *komuso* was assumed by military spies as a means of obtaining desired information, or as a means of smelling out an enemy and securing the details of his dwelling in order to enter it easily and thus successfully carry out a planned revenge. The role of *komuso* was also taken by men who wished to make atonement for some sin, and by those who wished to make amends for an evil deed.

The term "Komuso" signifies adherents of the now extinct Fuke sect of Buddhism, a branch of the Zen sect. The former was started in 1249, in the Kamakura period. It became most prosperous in the early Tokugawa period, when *samurai*, wholly free from crime, and *ronin*, "wave men" or men without masters, were converted into the sect in ever-increasing numbers, finding shelter in its temples; but because of its abuses the Fuke sect became extinct in 1871 through an edict of the Meiji government.

The business center of the city of Sendai, *Basho-no-tsuji*, was so named by Date Masamune, the noted feudal lord, in memory of a faithful retainer, Basho, who in his wanderings as a strolling komuso player, served Date Masamune loyally, informing him about matters of interest, and the trend of people's talk. For pictures and further description of *komuso* and *shakuhachi* see *Japanese Musical Instruments* descriptions.

Chin-don-ya ("Men who make musical sounds") are men who go about the streets beating gongs and drums and cymbals for the purpose of advertising something. Their costumes, of various colors and make up, are fantastic and bizarre in order to attract attention. A banner describing the particular event or thing they are advertising is carried, also weird umbrellas. In Tokyo, the Chin-don-ya have a guild with 500 members.

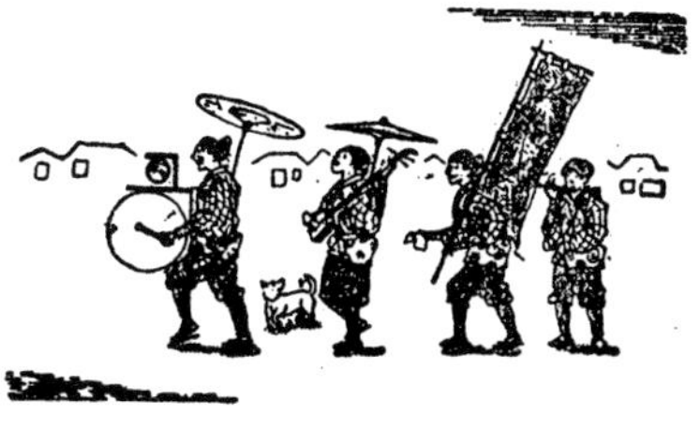

ODDITIES—IN JAPAN

"Believe It or Not"

Various—

University Caps: Marquis Okuma, one of the celebrated statesmen of Japan, the founder of Waseda University, Tokyo, desired that the university students should wear distinctive headgear.

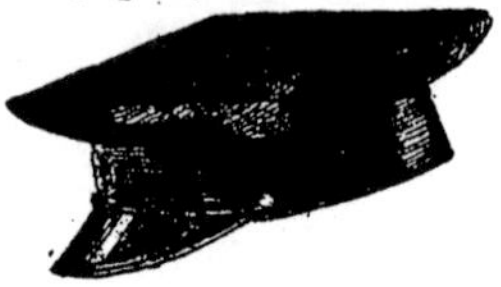

He therefore commissioned a cap manufacturer to design such a head piece. Several designs were evolved and submitted, but the one in use today was finally accepted. It consists of a cloth cap with a leather visor, its top being shaped like the conventional mortar-board worn by college and university graduates, but without the usual stiffening.

Heike Crabs: In April, 1185, a desperate battle was waged in Dan-no-ura bay, a section of the channel 3 m. east of Shimonoseki, between the Minamoto (*Genji*) and the Taira (*Heike*) clans to determine which of them should be supreme in Japan. The Heike fleet was annihilated. The battle is regarded as one of the three or four decisive battles in the history of Japan.

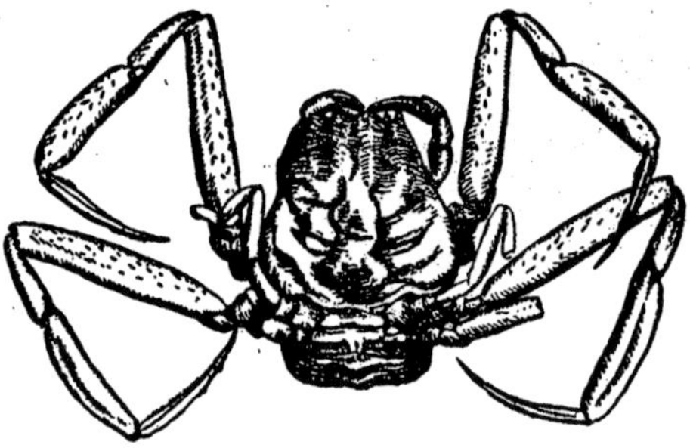

Since that time, tiny crabs, called *Heike-gani,* or Heike crabs, caught in Dan-no-ura have curious indentations in their shells, somewhat resembling a human face. Superstitious Japanese believe that these crabs are the wraiths of the Heike warriors that were drowned or killed at that place.

Trees in the middle of a Tokyo Street: In olden days, distances to various cities were reckoned from Nihombashi bridge, then regarded as the center of Tokyo. Ieyasu (b. 1542, d. 1616), founder of the Tokugawa regime, when Shogun, decided to mark every *ri* (2½ miles) along the principal highways leading to important places. The official in charge of this work asked the Shogun what marks he should use. "Well, you may plant er-er trees," said the Shogun, who, it is believed, may have faltered or mentioned some particular tree, but he was too dignified a personage for the official to dare ask again, so E-no-ki, or nettle trees (*celtis sinensis*) were planted.

There are two of these trees near the Komagome station of the Yamate line. The nearest stop to the trees of the tram line running past the station is Nishigahara. The place of the trees is called Ichirizuka ("One *ri* mound"). When the tram line was extended, the street-car officials were puzzled as to what to do with the "sacred" trees—sacred because the Shogun had planted them—they were too historic to be cut down to make way for a tram line. It was finally decided to run one track between the trees and move the houses on one side of the street far enough back to allow for the other track. This solution of the problem reveals a bit of the Japanese spirit and the reverence in which historic associations are held in Japan.

There is another marker tree of the same kind near the Denzuin temple, Koishikawa ward.

ODDITIES—IN JAPAN

"Believe It or Not"

Various—

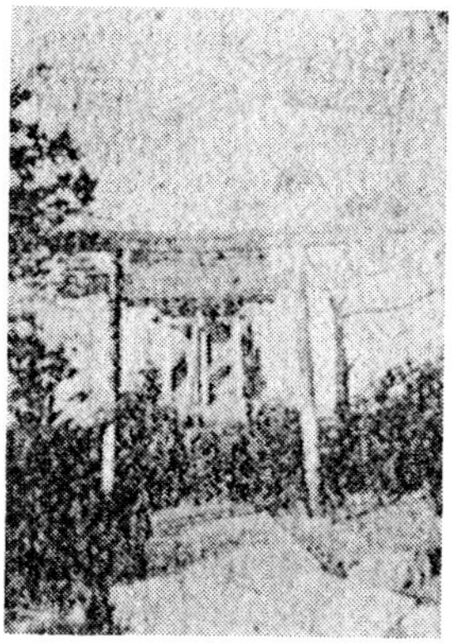

Shrines on the roofs of Tokyo Department Stores: At the Shirokiya, a department store established in 1662, there is a shrine in its roof-garden, and there is a well, with which the shrine is closely connected, in its basement. This is the story:

First, the well. When the store was started there was a lack of good drinking water in the city, and in 1712 a well was dug on the store's premises for the use of its patrons and neighbors. Water was found in abundance. Fed by a constantly flowing spring, the well yields 432,000 gallons of water daily. It was named Shiroki *Meisui* ("Clear Water").

While digging the well, one of the workmen unearthed a dirt-encrusted object that did not look like a stone. When cleansed, it was found to be a broze image, about 2 in. in height, of the goddess *Kwan-non.* The image was at once placed in a shrine, and was worshipped by the people until the Meiji Restoration (1868) when both the well and the shrine were accessible only on July 10 of each year, when a festival to the goddess was observed. In the earthquake-fire of 1923 the store was destroyed, but the image miraculously escaped destruction. When the store was rebuilt the consecrated image was placed in the shrine in the roof-garden. This image also came unscathed through the fire which wrecked the store on December 16th, 1932.

On the roof of the *Mitsukoshi* main department store is a Mimeguri Inari shrine. Its story is as follows:

During the Tokugawa Shogunate regime there was a great drought in Edo (Tokyo). On June 28, 1697, a ceremony to pray for rain was held in the precincts of the Mimeguri Shrine, near the Sumida River. On that day, Kikaku, a noted 17-syllable poet, went to the river for a row. Attracted by the large crowds he went to the shrine, and being recognized, he was asked to write a poem for the occasion. His poem, freely translated, reads:

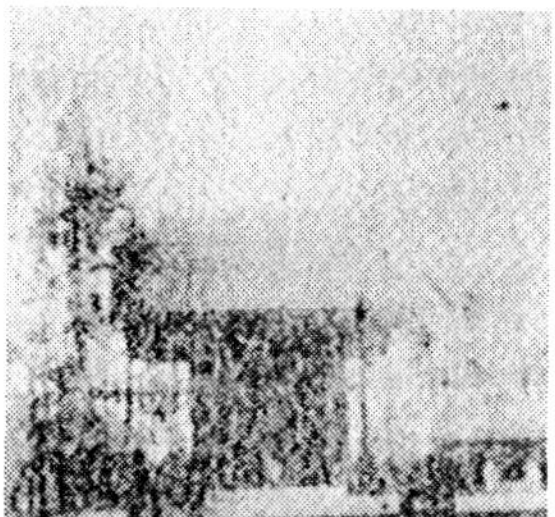

A shower, If thou, O God, carest
For the paddy fields
"Three times to go round."

Mi=three times: *meguri*=going round—also means honorable. Suggesting that the god go on his rounds for the protection of the fields.

Soon there appeared banks of clouds, from which a heavy shower fell.

One of the Mitsui ancestors was a devout worshipper at the Mimeguri Shrine. Hence the present shrine.

There are shrines on the roofs of many buildings throughout Japan, with interesting histories, but space here does not permit writing about them.

ODDITIES—IN JAPAN

"Believe It or Not"

Various—

Camellias, though noted for the singular beauty of their flowers, were never grown in the gardens of the *samurai,* for the reason that when their blossoms are in their full glory, they fall to the ground; they do not drop, petal by petal, like cherry blossoms. The profession of a *samurai* was to wage war, and consequently he was away from home much of the time in feudal and prior days, and if camellias were grown in the gardens of these warriors, their fallen blossoms would have too keenly suggested to the family that their distant fighter might lose his head in the same way—while in the full vigor of life.

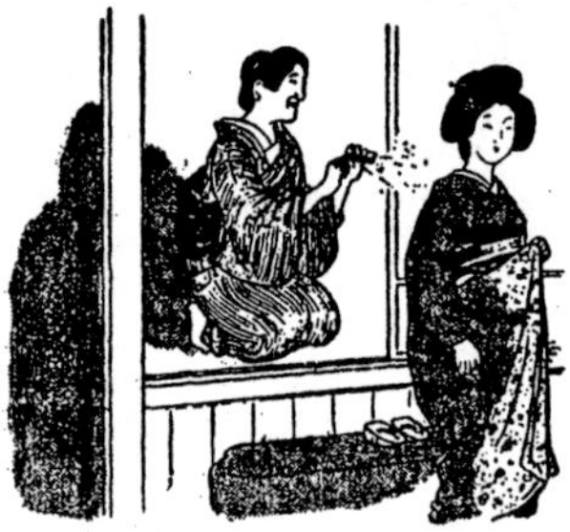

Striking Flints by keepers of geisha houses, so that the sparks will fly toward the *geisha* about to start on an assignment to a banqueting party, is an everyday practice. Such sparks are believed to drive away evil spirits, to purify the air surrounding the *geisha,* and to bring her good luck. This custom is also followed in many homes. After dusting and sweeping, and after lighted candles have been placed before the family altar, the master or mistress of the house goes from room to room and strikes a flint spark two or three times in each room—for purification, and to rout evil spirits.

Water Shrines, dedicated to the Water God, are often erected near the waterwheels seen all over Japan, as well as at many hydro-electric stations, so that those benefited by the water which constitutes to their livelihood may worship, and express their thanks to the god of the shrines; sailors on shore also pray before them.

Cat and Dog Cemetery: Paris, on the "Isle of Little Dogs," in the Seine, has, since 1899, maintained its Cimetière des Chiens, where over 25,000 friends of man are buried. Tokyo, too, since 1908, has required that pets shall be buried in the cat and dog cemetery of the Saishin Temple in Higashi-Nagasaki. More than 25,000 dogs, cats, birds, insects, and even fish have been buried there. Tombstones are erected over many of the graves and occasionally the owners of the dead pets burn incense before these stones. Every morning and evening a priest of the temple offers a Buddhist prayer for the spirits of the creatures buried in the cemetery—and on Sept. 21 (*Higan* or Equinoctial Day), a Buddhist animal mass, largely attended, is recited for their solace. The Tokyo Municipality assures a respectful burial. Burial costs are: ¥2 to ¥5 for a large dog, ¥1.50 for a medium sized one, ¥1 for a pup and 75 sen for a cat of any size. Special burials: from ¥1.50 to ¥10.

Coolie Raincoats, and raincoats worn by farmers and other laborers, are made of *minogusa,* a species of rush—and serve their purpose quite well. To foreign visitors it is an amusing sight to see a gang of workmen wearing these raincoats and umbrella-like hats of straw; they look like so many porcupines, especially when they squat to take a rest.

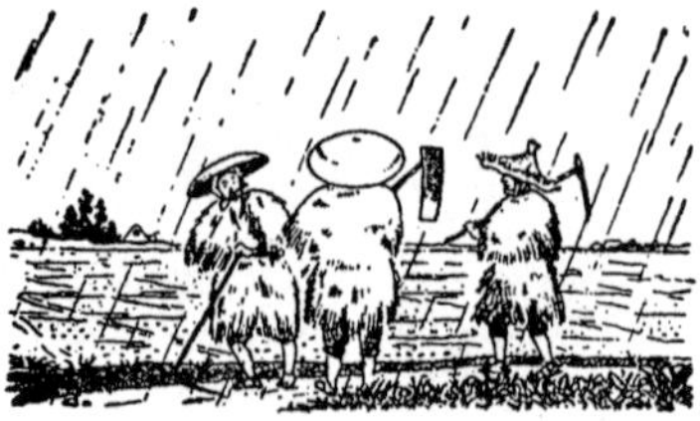

ODDITIES—IN JAPAN

"Believe It or Not"

Various—

Snakes as Medicine: While the medicinal value of snakes, taken in various preparations and eaten boiled, baked, and roasted, at the table, is unknown, yet it is estimated that every year fully 5,000,000 snakes, of all species find a place in the human systems of Japanese, and dealers state that the demand is increasing.

It is not only the persons discouraged because drugs and cures fail to restore them to health who resort to snake preparations, but many in good health do so in the belief that their mental energy and muscular strength will thereby be increased, and others eat snakes, they say, because dishes made from them are great delicacies, far superior to those made from frogs or turtles—and some folk relish the fresh blood of these reptiles. Many athletes, particularly *judo* wrestlers and marathon runners, have become snake devotees.

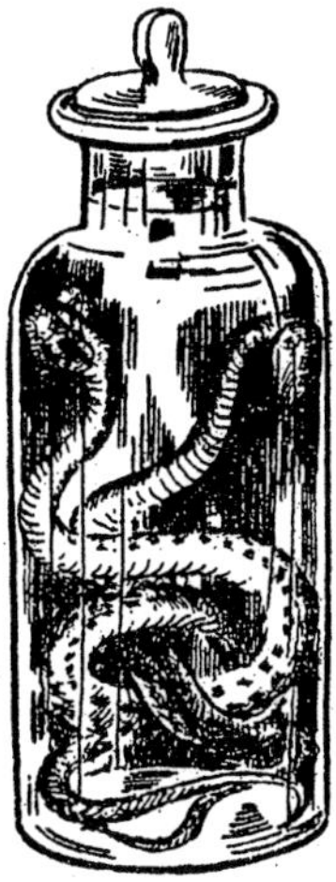

The superstitious belief that snakes increase muscular strength has its parallel in the belief that the use of angle-worm oil as a liniment is beneficial, that tigers' hearts are a courage-giving food, and that the flesh of deer make fast runners. Primitive peoples all over the world have had faith in these ideas from time immemorial—and such ideas are difficult to dislodge notwithstanding the advances made in civilization and education.

The latest report (1932) of the Tokyo Metropolitan Police shows that in Tokyo alone 2,000 snakes are purchased every week, at prices ranging from 90 sen to ¥2, the *shima-hebi*, or striped snake, being in greatest demand, for the reason that it is believed to have special medicinal value. Bottled snake's blood is sold for about ¥1 for the blood of one snake. About 80% of the snakes sold are charred and powdered, or dried and pulverized, and made into pills and capsules to be used as medicine, and about 20% go to the table boiled, baked, or roasted.

The 65 licensed snake dealers in Tokyo, constituting the Snake Dealers' Guild, maintain groups of professional snake catchers in several parts of the country. The best snake-hunting district is reported to be in Shimane Prefecture, notably around Lake Biwa, although there are numerous other noted snake regions throughout Japan.

ODDITIES—IN JAPAN

"Believe It or Not"

Various—

Sen-ka-ji Fuda **("1,000 Temple Cards") are cards or stickers that are pasted on every possible place on many temple and shrine buildings. Their origin is thus stated:**

When a person's relative or friend is seriously ill, that person will sometimes make a vow to the deity he worships declaring that if that deity will answer his prayers and restore the sick one to health he will visit a thousand temples and, after praying at each one, will stick his card on each temple as evidence of his vow and visit. Also when a person greatly desires to accomplish some particular thing, or in general wishes to be prosperous, he will make a similar vow that he will paste up one of these cards, on which his name will be printed, at 1,000 temples, in order to have his desires granted. Also this practice is followed when a man wishes to advertise his profession, office, or business and to be successful in it—and it is said that the higher the sticker is pasted the greater will be his prosperity. A pole, jointed like a fishpole, is carried for this purpose. Perhaps the inference to be drawn from this practice is that the practitioner, by visiting 1,000 temples, is bound to absorb some of their religious precepts—besides their atmosphere. In former days, instead of using a pole, the *fuda*, moistened side up, was laid on a bag of sand which was tossed or thrown to the desired spot—certainly a much more difficult method than with a pole. The picture shows the Fujiya Hotel *fuda*. It reads, from top to bottom: "Miyanoshita—Fujiya Hotel."

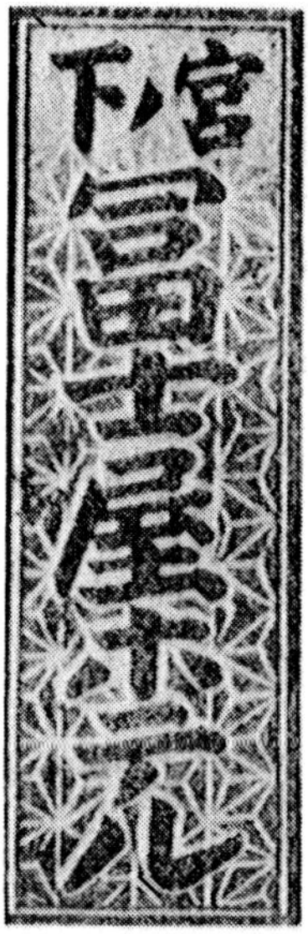

O-hyaku-do-mairi or 100-time visit. When a relative or friend is ill, or when a believer is in great trouble, or when a son or relative is in the army at the front, he, often accompanied by his wife, will visit the temple or shrine where he worships, one hundred times, one visit each night, when, in seclusion and quietness his devotions and prayers for the recovery of the sick person, for alleviation of his trouble, or for the safety of the soldier, will not be observed by outsiders. Some temples and shrines have certain designated places where believers walk back and forth one hundred times, praying and bowing each time before the image or the tablet of the enshrined deity, to attain the ends above named. This walk is repeated every night for a certain number of days: a week, a month or several months, depending upon the seriousness of the case or the trouble for the relief of which the prayer is made.

The *O-hyaku-do-fumi* or 100-time walk in a walk made by a devotee in his devotions. The Hon-do ("Main Hall") of temples has a wide porch on which he circles the building one hundred times. During the walk he keeps his record by counting one hundred beads on his rosary, or by means of white strings held in his hand. When the walk is finished, his sins are supposed to be forgiven.

ODDITIES—IN JAPAN

"Believe It or Not"

The Measles Stone: Near the entrance of the Yuten-ji Temple cemetery, Tokyo, there is a stone, called the *Measles Stone,* which is said to have a powerful influence in preventing attacks of measles, or at least of lessening the attacks. The stone is a couple of feet high, and it has a hole (about 15 in. in diameter) made in the stone block. Through this hole a mother puts her child three times, back and forth, murmuring, "I hope it will not be serious," in the belief that such action will ward off measles, or that the case will be a slight one. She will often murmur a prayer for the speedy recovery of the sick child, for an actual patient is often brought to the measles-stone and passed through the hole three times back and forth.

A temple authority stated that from February to May, when measles are more or less prevalent, long lines of parents, with their children, await their turn daily at the stone, and that yearly over a million charms against measles are sold at the temple. These are printed slips of paper, selling for three *sen* each.

The story is that Yuten, a learned priest of the Jodo sect, had a long argument about religion with the Devil—who was finally conquered, and with many sutras was placed in the hollow of one of the square blocks shown in the monument back of the stone—and the belief gradually spread that a priest so powerful as to subdue the Devil could also prevail against ailments of children. In former days, before vaccination was practised, Yuten's aid was also invoked against smallpox. At his death, the priest's residence was rebuilt by his disciples into the present temple. Yuten's tomb is a short distance back, and to the right, of the Measles Stone.

After the death of Priest Yuten a temple was dedicated to him and it was named the Yuten-ji Temple after him. The temple is reached by a 5 min. walk from the Yuten-ji station of the Tokyo-Yokohama Electric Line. One can reach the temple on foot in less than ten minutes from the American School in Meguro, Tokyo.

JAPANESE PROVERBS

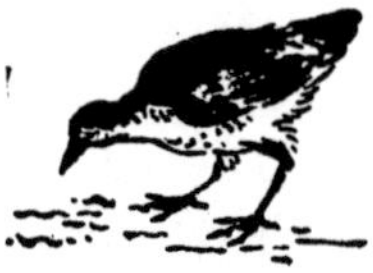

With the thought that some of the most popular Japanese proverbs will be of interest to guests of the Fujiya Hotel, a few are listed here translated as literally as possible, with their nearest English equivalents, liberally rendered:

惡事千里ヲ走ル
AKUJI SENRI O HASHIRU.
An evil act runs a thousand miles.
"Bad news has wings."

* * *

惡錢身ニ付カズ
AKU-SEN MI NI TSUKA-ZU.
One cannot keep ill-gotten money.
"Illy-got, illy-spent."

* * *

朝起ニ七ツノ
ASAOKI NI NANATSU NO
得アリ
TOKU ARI.
The early riser has seven gains.
"The early bird catches the worm."

* * *

明日ハ明日ノ
ASU WA ASU NO,
風ガ吹ク
KAZE GA FUKU.
To-morrow blows to-morrow's wind.
"To-morrow is another day."

* * *

塵積ッテ
CHIRI TSUMOTTE,
山トナル
YAMA TO NARU.
Dust amassed will make a mountain.
"Great oaks from little acorns grow."

* * *

出物腫物所
DEMONO HAREMONO, TOKORO
嫌ハズ
KIRAWAZU.
An ulcer or a boil comes out anywhere.
"Accidents will happen in the best-regulated families."

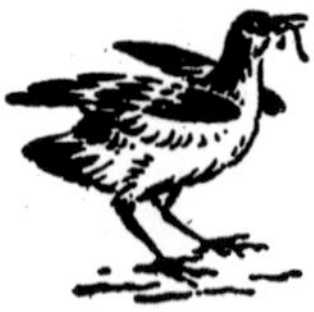

同病相憐ム
DOBYO AI AWAREMU.
People suffering from the same disease have mutual sympathy.
"Misery loves company."

* * *

覆水盆ニ返ラズ
FUKUSUI BON NI KAERAZU.
Spilt water never returns to the tray.
"It's no use crying over spilt milk."

* * *

郷ニ入ッテハ
GO NI ITTE WA,
郷ニ從ヘ
GO NI SHITAGAE.
Obey the customs of the place where you are.
"In Rome do as the Romans do."

* * *

畑カラ
HATAKE KARA,
蛤ハ取レヌ
HAMAGURI WA TORENU.
Clams are not obtainable from the field.
"One cannot get blood from a stone."

* * *

饑ジイ時ノ
HIMOJII TOKI NO,
不味モノナシ
MAZUI-MONO NASHI.
When hungry, all tastes delicious.
"Hunger is the best sauce."

* * *

火ノ無キ所ニ
HI NO NAKI TOKORO NI,
煙ハ立タヌ
KEMURI WA TATANU.
Where there is no fire, there is no smoke.
"Where there is smoke, there is fire."

JAPANESE PROVERBS

貧スレバ鈍スル
HIN SUREBA, DON SURU.

Poverty makes one stupid.

"Who goes a-borrowing, goes a-sorrowing."

* * *

人ノ噂モ
HITO NO UWASA MO,
七十五日
SHICHIJUGO-NICHI.

Rumor lasts but seventy-five days.

"A nine days' wonder."

* * *

人ハ見掛ケニ
HITO WA MIKAKE NI
ヨラヌモノ
YORANU MONO.

Man cannot be told by looks.

"Appearances are deceitful."

* * *

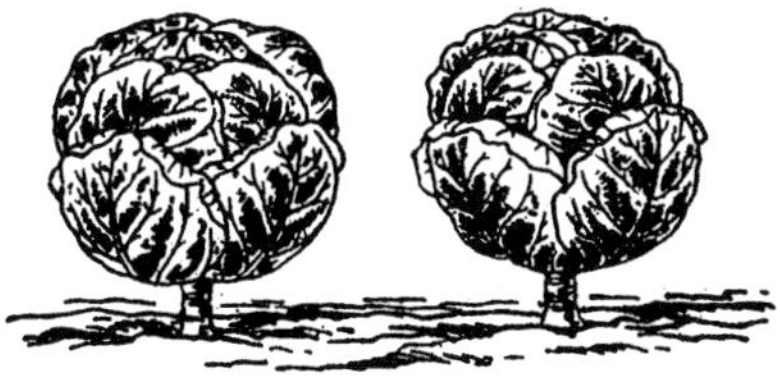

膝トモ談合
HIZA TOMO DANGO.

Consult any one, even if it be your own knees.

"Two heads are better than one."

* * *

惚レタ慾目
HORETA YOKUME.

Love's partial eyes.

"Love sees no faults."

* * *

細ク長ク
HOSOKU NAGAKU.

Narrow and long.

"Love me little, love me long."

* * *

佛ノ顔モ三度
HOTOKE-NO-KAO MO SANDO.

Even Buddha is provoked upon being importuned three times.

"Even a worm will turn."

* * *

百兩ノ抵當ニ
HYAKU-RYO NO KATA NI,
編笠一ツ
AMIGASA HITOTSU.

A wattle-hat for a debt of a hundred gold coins.

"Sue a beggar and catch a louse."

* * *

簞瓢鯰
HYOTAN NAMAZU.

You cannot catch a slippery fish with a gourd.

"Slippery as an eel."

* * *

一文惜ミノ
ICHIMO OSHIMI NO,
百損
HYAKU ZON.

One loses a hundred mon, by sparing one mon.

(One mon is a hundredth of a sen)

"Penny wise, pound foolish."

* * *

一ニ養生二ニ藥
ICHI NI YOJO, NI NI KUSURI.

Sanitation first, medicine next.

"An ounce of prevention is worth a pound of cure."

* * *

JAPANESE PROVERBS

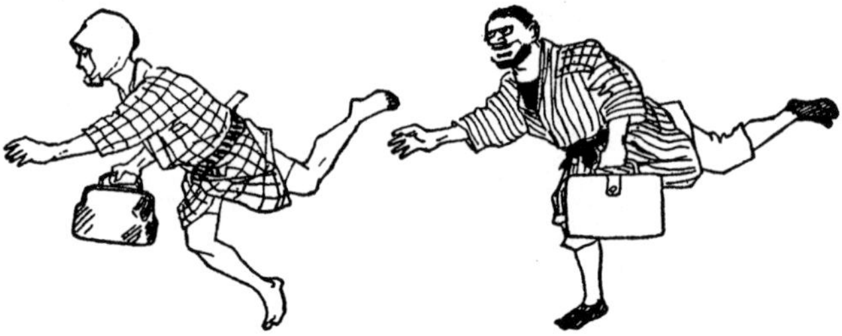

一擧兩得
IKKYO RYOTOKU.

Single effort, double gain.

"Kill two birds with one stone."

*　*　*

今ノ一針
IMA NO HITOHARI,
後ノ十針
NOCHI NO TOHARI.

One stitch now is worth ten stitches afterwards.

"A stitch in time saves nine."

*　*　*

今參リ廿日
IMA-MAIRI HATSUKA.

A new servant works hard but twenty days.

"A new broom sweeps clean."

*　*　*

急ガバ廻レ
ISOGABA MAWARE.

In haste, one goes in a circle.

"The more haste, the less speed."

*　*　*

頂クモノハ
ITADAKU MONO WA,
夏モ小袖
NATSU MO KOSODE.

As a gift, a wadded garment is acceptable even in summer.

"Never look a gift horse in the mouth."

言フハ易ク
IU WA YASUKU,
行フハ難シ
OKONAU WA KATASHI.

Easy to say, hard to do.

"Easier said than done."

*　*　*

言ハヌハ言フニ勝ル
IWANU WA, IU NI MASARU.

Not to say is better than to say.

"Silence is more eloquent than words."

*　*　*

ジヤ
蛇ノ道ハ蛇
JA NO MICHI WA HEBI.

Snakes follow the way of serpents.

"Set a theif to catch a theif.

*　*　*

地獄ノ沙汰モ
JIGOKU NO SATA MO,
金ノ次第
KANE SHIDAI.

Money controls even the order of Hell.

"Money is the key that opens all doors."

*　*　*

人生ハ
JINSEI WA,
風前ノ燈
FUZEN NO TOMOSHIBI.

Life is a candle-light before the wind.

"Our life is but a span."

JAPANESE PROVERBS

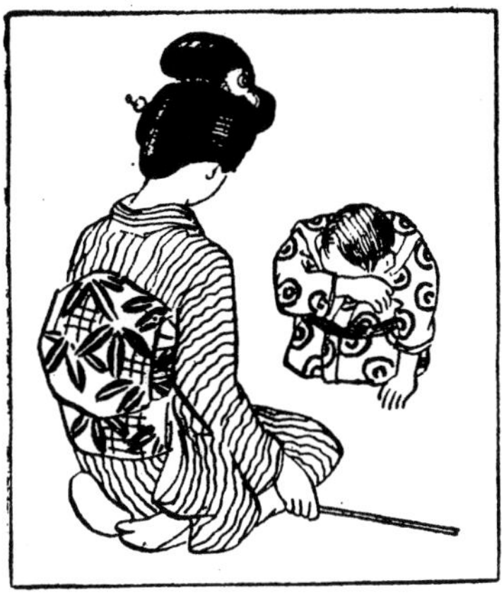

戯談 カラ
JODAN KARA,
誠 ガ 出ル
MAKOTO GA DERU.

Truth comes out of jest.
" Many an earnest word is spoken in jest."

* * *

上手 ノ 手 カラ
JOZU NO TE KARA,
水 ガ 漏ル
MIZU GA MORU.

An expert may sometimes miss.
" Even Homer sometimes nods."

* * *

十人 十色
JUNIN TOIRO.

Ten men, ten tastes.
" Many men, many minds."

* * *

壁 ニ 耳 アリ
KABE NI MIMI ARI,
障子 ニ 目 アリ
SHOJI NI ME ARI.

Walls have ears, *shoji* have eyes.
" Walls have ears."

* * *

蛙 ノ 面 ニ 水
KAERU-NO-TSURA NI MIZU.

Water on a fog's face.
" Like water off a duck's back."

* * *

金 アレバ
KANE AREBA,
馬鹿 モ 旦那
BAKA MO DANNA.

Wealth makes a fool a master.
" Money makes the man."

金 ノ 切レ目 ガ
KANE NO KIREME GA,
縁 ノ 切レ目
EN NO KIREME.

The parting of money is the parting of love.
" When proverty comes in at the door, love flies out of the window."

* * *

蟹 ハ 甲羅 ニ 似セテ
KANI WA KORA NI NISETE,
穴 ヲ 堀ル
ANA O HORU.

Crabs dig holes according to their size.
" Cut your coat according to your cloth."

* * *

可愛イ 子 ハ
KAWAII KO WA,
棒 デ 育テヨ
BO DE SODATEYO.

Bring up your beloved children with a stick.
" Spare the rod, spoil the child."

* * *

戀 ニ 上下 ノ
KOI NI JOGE NO
隔 ナシ
HEDATE NASHI.

Love makes no distinction between the high and the low.
" Love lives in a cottage as well as at Court."

* * *

戀 ハ 思安 ノ 外
KOI WA SHIAN NO HOKA

Love is beyond consideration.
" Love is blind."

* * *

光陰 矢 ノ 如シ
KOIN YA NO GOTOSHI.

Time flies like an arrow.
" Time and tide wait for no man."

* * *

心 ノ 鬼 ガ
KOKORO NO ONI GA,
身 ヲ 責メル
MI O SEMERU.

The devil in one's heart reproaches one's self.
" A guilty conscience needs no accuser."

* * *

紺屋 ノ 白 袴
KOYA NO SHIRO HAKAMA.

Dyers wear undeyed trousers.
" Shoemakers' children go barefoot."

* * *

轉バヌ 先 ノ 杖
KOROBANU SAKI NO TSUE.

Have a walking-stick before falling.
" Keep your powder dry."

JAPANESE PROVERBS

怖イモノ　見タシ
KOWAI-MONO MITASHI.

One is tempted to see a thing of fear.
" Forbidden fruit is the sweetest."

* * *

口　ハ
KUCHI WA
禍　ノ　門
WAZAWAI NO KADO.

The mouth is the entrance of calamity.
" The mouth is the gate of evil."

* * *

雲　ニ　梯
KUMO NI KAKEHASHI

Don't rest a ladder against a cloud.
" Hitch your wagon to a star."

* * *

臭イ者　身知ラズ
KUSAIMONO MI SHIRAZU.

An ill-smelling being does not know its own smell.
" One cannot see the beam in one's own eye."

* * *

馬子　ニモ　衣裳
MAGO NIMO ISHO.

A pack-horse driver looks fine in proper dress.
" Fine feathers make fine birds."

* * *

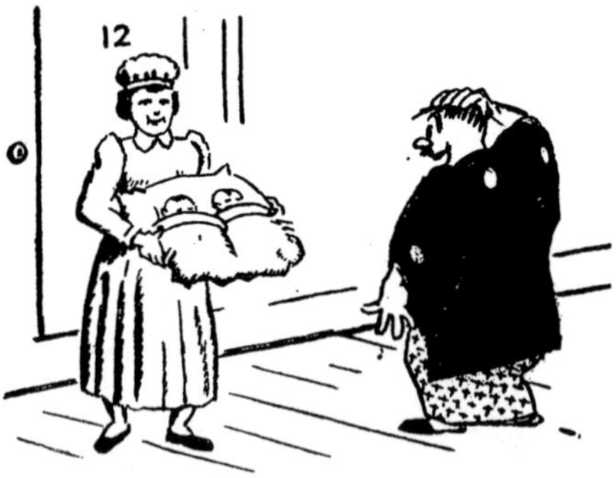

待テバ　甘露　ノ
MATEBA KANRO NO
日和　アリ
HIYORI ARI.

Waiting brings a happy day.
" Everything comes to him who waits-"

目　ノ　ヨル　所　ヘ
ME NO YORU TOKORO E
球　ガ　ヨル
TAMA GA YORU.

Where there are eyes there are eyeballs.
" Like begets like."

* * *

盲人　蛇　ニ　怯ヂズ
MEKURA HEBI NI OJIZU.

Blind men do not fear snakes.
" Fools rush in where angels fear to tread."

* * *

盲人　ノ　垣　覗キ
MEKURA NO KAKI NOZOKI.

A blind man peeps through a fence.
" Like looking for a needle in a haystack."

* * *

身　カラ　出タ　錆
MI KARA DETA SABI.

It is the effect of one's own fault.
" As you make your bed, so must you lie on it."

* * *

耳　ヲ　掩フテ　鈴　ヲ　盗ム
MIMI O OTE, SUZU O NUSUMU.

Covering one's ears, one steals a bell.
" The cat shuts its eyes while it steals the cream."

* * *

三ッ子　ノ　魂
MITSUGO NO TAMASHII,
百　マデ
HYAKU MADE.

A baby's soul remains a hundred years.
" The child is father to the man.

* * *

盈ツレバ　虧クル
MITSUREBA KAKURU,
世　ノ　習ヒ
YO NO NARAI.

The moon waxes and wanes; that is the way of the world.
" Every tide has its ebb."

JAPANESE PROVERBS

餅ハ餅屋
MOCHI WA MOCHIYA.

Rice cakes are best made by
the rice-cake maker.
"Every man to his trade."

* * *

貰ヒ物ニ苦情
MORAIMONO NI KUJO.

Don't complain about a gift.
"Beggars must not be choosers."

* * *

泣面ニ蜂
NAKI-TSURA NI HACHI.

A bee to a weeping face.
"Misfortunes never come singly."

* * *

二度アル事ハ
NI-DO ARU KOTO WA,
三度アル
SAN-DO ARU

What happens twice will happen thrice.
"Misfortunes never come singly."

* * *

生兵法ハ
NAMA-BYOHO WA,
大疵ノ基
OKIZU NO MOTO

Crude tactics are the source of a big wound.
"A little knowledge is a dangerous thing."

猫ニ鰹節
NEKO NI KATSUOBUSHI.

A dried bonito to a cat.
"Set a fox to watch the geese."

* * *

猫ニ小判
NEKO NI KOBAN.

Gold coins to a cat.
"Pearls cast before swine."

* * *

能アル鷹ハ
NO-ARU-TAKA WA,
爪ヲ匿ス
TSUME O KAKUSU.

An able hawk hides its claws.
"Still waters run deep."

* * *

能書筆ヲ擇バズ
NOSHO FUDE O ERABAZU

A skilful calligrapher never makes
a choice of his writing-brush.
"A bad workman quarrels with his tools."

* * *

濡レヌ先キノ傘
NURENU SAKI NO KASA

Have an umbrella ready before
you get wet.
"Make hay while the sun shines."

* * *

盗人ニ追銭
NUSUBITO NI OISEN.

Money spent on the pursuit of a thief.
"Throwing good money after bad."

* * *

JAPANESE PROVERBS

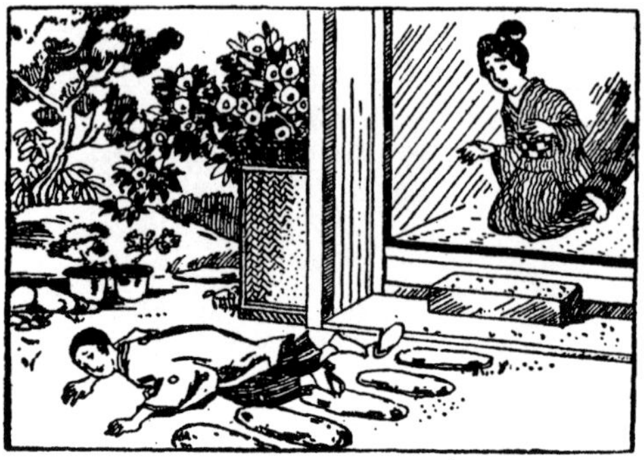

驕ル 者
OGORU MONO
久シ カラズ
HISASHI KARAZU.

A luxurious life never lasts long.
"Pride goes before a fall."

* * *

思ヒ 立ツタ ガ 吉 日
OMOI TATTA GA KICHI NICH.

The day on which a resolution is made is the best day to execute it.
"There is no time like the present."

* * *

鬼 ノ 目 ニモ 涙
ONI-NO-ME NIMO NAMIDA

Tears even in the devil's eyes.
"Crocodile tears."

* * *

親 ノ 慾 目
OYA NO YOKUME.

Parents' partial eyes.
"Everybody thinks his geese are swans."

* * *

親 ノ 因果 ガ
OYA NO INGA GA,
子 ニ 報ヒ
KO NI MUKUI.

The karma effect of parents visits their children with retribution.
"The sins of the father are visited on the children."

來年 ノ 事 ヲ
RAINEN NO KOTO O
言フト 鬼 ガ 笑フ
IUTO, ONI GA WARAU.

Don't talk of next year lest the devil should laugh at you.
"There is nothing sure under the sun."

* * *

樂 アレバ 苦 アリ
RAKU AREBA KU ARI.

Where there is comfort, there is suffering.
"There is no rose without a thorn."

* * *

論 ヨリ 證據
RON YORI SHOKO.

Proof is stronger than argument.
"The proof of the pudding is in the eating."

* * *

類 ヲ 以テ 集ル
RUI O MOTTE ATSUMARU.

The same kind gathers together.
"Birds of a feather flock together."

* * *

去ル モノ 日 ニ 疎シ
SARU-MONO HI NI UTOSHI.

One who has gone is forgotten day by day.
"Out of sight, out of mind."

* * *

觸ラヌ 神 ニ
SAWARANU KAMI NI,
祟 ナシ
TATARI NASHI.

One gets no curse from the god that has not been touched.
"Let sleeping dogs lie."

* * *

船頭 多ク シテ 船
SENDO OKU SHITE FUNE
山 ニ 登ル
YAMA NI NOBORU.

Too many boatmen bring a boat up the montain.
"Too many cooks spoil the broth."

JAPANESE PROVERBS

釋迦 ニ 説法
SHAKA NI SEPPO.

Preaching to Buddha.
"You can't teach your grandmother to such eggs."

* * *

辛抱 スル木 ニ
SHIMBO SURU-KI NI,
金 ガ ナル
KANE GA NARU.

Money grows upon a tree of perseverance.
"Perseverance brings success."
(As the ant said after swallowing the elephant.)

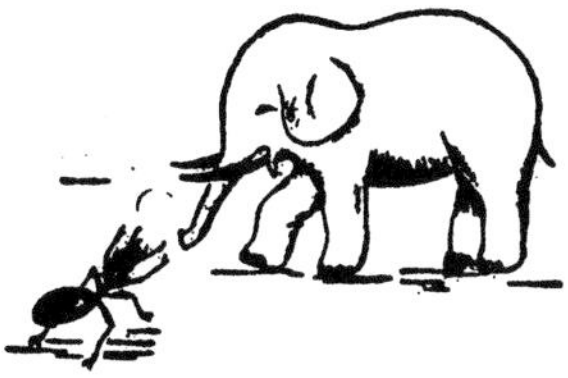

死人 ニ 口 ナシ
SHININ NI KUCHI NASHI.

The dead have no mouths.
"Dead men tell no tales."

* * *

知ラヌ ガ 佛
SHIRANU GA HOTOKE.

Ignorance is Buddha.
"Ignorance is bliss."

* * *

住メバ 都
SUMEBA MIYAKO.

It is the capital where you live.
"A man's house is his castle."

* * *

多藝 ハ 無藝
TAGEI WA MUGEI.

Too many accomplishments, no accomplishment after all.
"Jack of all trades, master of none."

* * *

高ミ ニ 土 盛リ
TAKAMI NI TSUCHI MORI.

Carrying earth on an eminence.
"Carrying coals to Newcastle."

玉 ニ 瑕
TAMA NI KIZU.

A flaw in the gem.
"The fly in the ointment."

* * *

他人 ヨリ 身内
TANIN YORI MIUCHI.

Relatives are better than strangers.
"Blood is thicker than water."

* * *

短氣 ハ 損氣
TANKI WA SONKI.

Short temper is liable to loss.
"Haste makes waste."

* * *

燈臺 下 暗シ
TODAI MOTO KURASHI.

It is dark at the foot of a lighthouse.
"Just below the candlestick is the darkest of all."

* * *

飛ンデ 火 ニ
TONDE HI NI
入ル 夏
IRU, NATSU
ノ 虫
NO MUSHI.

Summer insects jump into the fire.
"The fluttering moth about the candle flame at last gets burned."

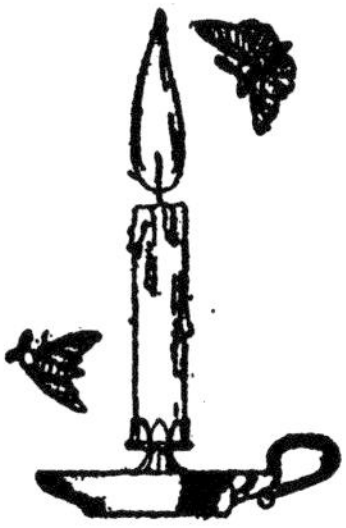

* * *

取ラヌ 狸 ノ
TORANU TANUKI NO,
皮 算用
KAWA ZANYO.

Don't count the badgers' skins before they are caught.
"Don't count your chickens before they are hatched."

JAPANESE PROVERBS

馬 ノ 耳 ニ 念 佛
UMA-NO-MIMI NI NEMBUTSU.

Saying prayers to a horse's ears.
"It is bad preaching to deaf ears."

* * *

運 ハ 天 ニ アリ
UN WA TEN NI ARI.
牡丹 餅 ハ 棚 ニ アリ
BOTAMOCHI WA TANA NI ARI.

Destiny is in Heaven; rice dumplings are on the shelf.
"Trust in Providence."

* * *

裏 ニ ハ 裏 ガ アル
URA NI WA, URA GA ARU.

The reverse side has its reverse side,
"The other side of the shield."

* * *

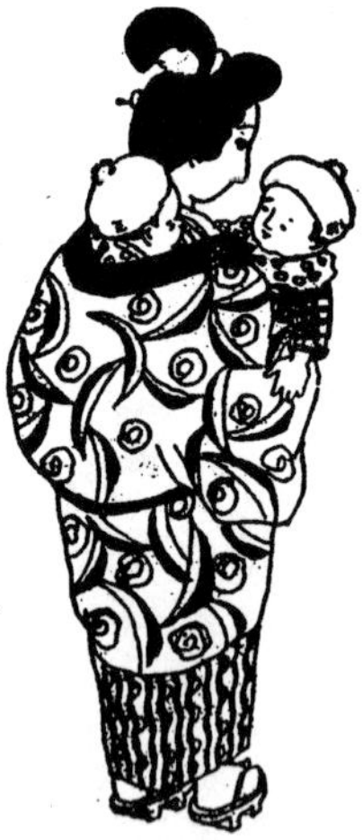

瓜 二ツ ニ 割ツタ 様
URI FUTATSU NI, WATTA YO.

As alike as a cucumber cut in half.
"As alike as two peas."

賣 物 ニ
URIMONO NI,
花 ヲ 飾レ
HANA O KAZARE.

Bedeck with flowers an article for sale
"No man belittles his wares."

* * *

瓜 ノ 蔓 ニ
URI-NO-TSURU NI,
茄子 ハ 生ラヌ
NASUBI WA NARANU

Egg-plants never grow on cucumber-vines.
"An onion will not produce a rose."

* * *

噓 カラ 出タ 誠
USO KARA DETA MAKOTO.

Truth coming out of falsehood.
"Many a true word is spoken in jest."

* * *

噓 ハ 泥 棒 ノ
USO WA DOROBO NO
始マリ
HAJIMARI.

To tell a lie is the beginning of a thief.
"Show me a liar and I'll show you a thief."

* * *

噂 ヲ スレバ
UWASA O SUREBA,
影 ガ サス
KAGE GA SASU.

Talk of a man, his shadow will turn up.
"Speak of angels and you hear the rustles of their wings."

* * *

我 身 ヲ 抓ツテ
WAGA-MI O TSUNETTE,
人 ノ 痛サ ヲ 知レ
HITO NO ITASA O SHIRE.

Judge of others' pain by pinching yourself.
"Do unto others as you would have them do unto you."
(But do them first)

JAPANESE PROVERBS

我田ヘ水ヲ引ク
WAGA-TA E, MIZU O HIKU.

One draws water into one's own field.
"Everyone draws the water to his own mill."

* * *

燒石ニ水
YAKE-ISHI NI MIZU.

It is like pouring water on a hot-stone.
"One can't carry water in a sieve.

* * *

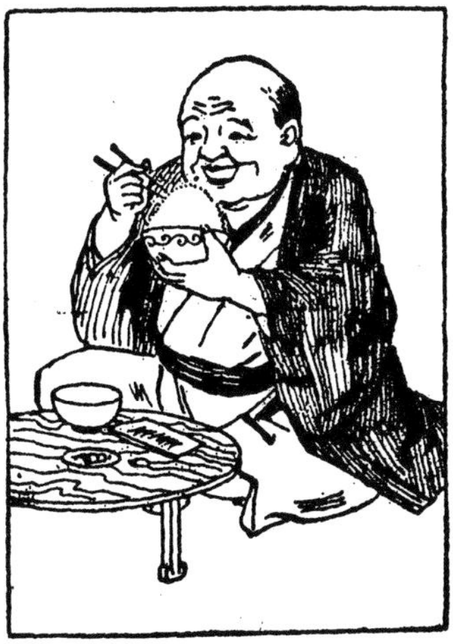

病ハ口カラ
YAMAI WA KUCHI KARA.

Illness starts from the mouth.
"Some men dig their graues with their teeth."

* * *

安物買ヒノ
YASUMONO-KAI NO
錢失ヒ
ZENI-USHINAI.

Money is lost in buying cheap articles.
"Cheap bargains are dear."

* * *

安受合ヒノ
YASU-UKEAI NO
早忘レ
HAYA-WASURE.

He who makes ready promises forgets them soon.
"A man apt to promise is apt to forget."

* * *

能ク泳グ者ハ
YOKU OYOGU-MONO WA,
能ク溺ル
YOKU OBORU.

Good swimmers are often drowned.
"The dog that kills wolves is killed by wolves."

* * *

嫁ト反物ハ
YOME TO TAMMONO WA,
晝間撰ベ
HIRUMA ERABE.

Choose a bride and piece-goods in the day-time.
"Choose neither a woman nor linen by candle-light."

* * *

油斷大敵
YUDAN TAITEKI.

Incautiousness is a great enemy.
"Danger comes soonest when it is despised."

* * *

善ハ急ゲ
ZEN WA ISOGE.

Do quickly what is good.
"Strike the iron while it is hot."

* * *

前車ノ覆ルハ
ZENSHA NO KUTSUGAERU WA,
後車ノ戒
KOSHA NO IMASHIME.

A front cart upset is a warning to a cart following.
"Learn wisdom from the follies of others."

* * *

We Japanese

BOOK II

Written by

ATSUHARU SAKAI

for

H. S. K. YAMAGUCHI,

Managing Director

THE NATIONAL HOLIDAYS OF JAPAN (1)

Shihohai or Four-direction-worship: This is one of the Four Great Holidays held by the Emperor at the time of the Tiger (4 o'clock) on the morning of January the first. He worships towards heaven and earth, the four directions, hills and mountains and the stars, so that peace may reign in the country, with good crops, in that year. This ceremony is of an unknown origin but it seems to have been held at court every year since 590, when its mention was made for the first time in history, though it was discontinued during the civil wars.

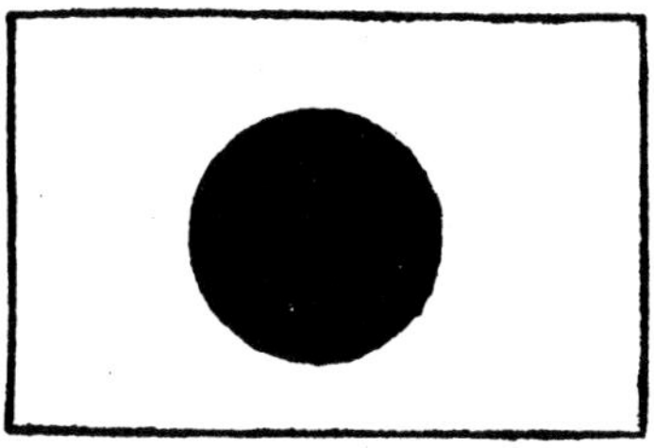

National flag of Japan.

Genshisai or First-beginning-ceremony: This ceremony is held at the Kashiko-dokoro, the Korei-den and the Shinden of the Imperial Palace, as well as at many local Shinto shrines, on the third of January each year. It was first held in the Imperial Palace on the third of the first month, 1870, when the "eight gods," viz. the celestial and territorial gods and the spirits of the Imperial ancestors, were worshipped. Early in the morning, offerings are made at the Sanctuaries mentioned above, and when the princes and princesses and high courtiers are seated at their respective seats, the Emperor makes his appearance to offer the Tamakushi (sacred offering) and reads the Imperial proclamation before the gods.

Kigensetsu or National-foundation-day: Kigensetsu (literally, "era-ceremony"), or National-foundation-day falls on the eleventh of February, which corresponds to the first day of the first month of the year in which Jimmu, the first Emperor of Japan, ascended the Throne 660 years before the Christian era. This day was specified in 1872 as one of the Four Great National Holidays.

The Vernal and Autumnal Equinoxes: Shunki-korei-sai (literally, "Spring-Imperial-spirit-festival") or the Vernal Equinox and Shuki-korei-sai (literally, "autumnal Imperial-spirit-festival") or Autumnal Equinox are celebrated on the days of the vernal and autumnal equinoxes, falling generally on March 23 and Sept. 23, respectively, when the Emperor pays respects to the spirits of his Imperial fathers. These festivals had their origin in the ceremony that the Emperor Jimmu held on the day of the Monkey in the 2nd month of the first year (660 B.C.) of his accession to the Imperial Throne to report to his ancestors on the conquest of the country.

The Anniversary of the Death of the Emperor Jimmu: The Emperor Jimmu, founder of the Japanese Empire, died at the time of the Dragon (8 o'clock) on the 11th day of the Horse in the third month, 585 B.C., at the age of 127 years, the day being fixed as the third of April at the time the solar calendar was adopted in 1873. (*Continued*)

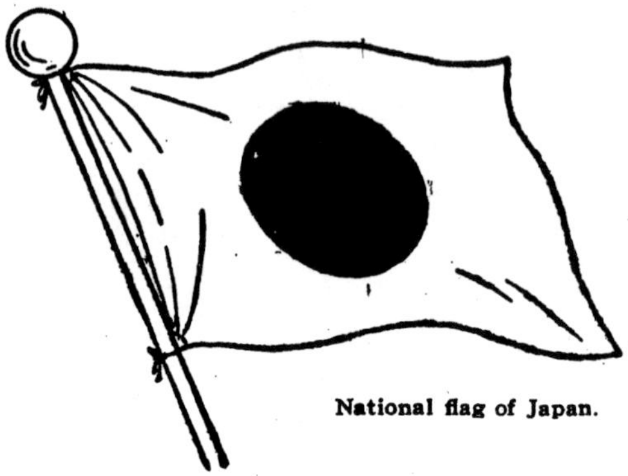

National flag of Japan.

The Birthdays of the Emperor and Empress: The birthdays of the Emperor and Empress are named Tencho-setsu (literally, "Heaven-long-festival") and Chikyu-setsu (literally, "Earth-eternal-festival"), respectively. The birth of the present Emperor and Empress is celebrated on Apr. 29 and Mar. 6, respectively, though the Empress's birthday is not a public holiday. Tencho-setsu is one of the Four National Holidays.

Kanname-sai or Thanksgiving-day: Kanname-sai (literally, "God-tasting festival") or Thanksgiving-day is celebrated on Oct. 17, when sake made of new grain, and boiled rice of a new crop, are offered to the Imperial ancestors. The ceremony is held both at the Imperial Court and at the Ise Shrines.

This ceremony originated in the historic fact that Princess Yamatohime offered a meal to the Sun Goddess by boiling with a sacred fire some rice she had obtained at Sashizu from a crane which had brought it.

Niiname-sai or Harvest Festival: Niiname-sai (literally, "New tasting Festival") or Harvest Festival is held on the 23 of November at the Imperial Palace, when the Emperor offers the first-fruits of the year to the Imperial ancestors. The Emperor himself also tastes of them, and in turn shares them with the courtiers.

This festival has its origin in the rice that the local gods are said to have offered to Prince Ninigi, the Imperial Grandson, as he is known in history, when he descended upon earth from the Celestial Abode of Takama-no-hara.

Meiji-setsu: The Emperor Meiji, who restored the Imperial administration in 1868, is regarded to be such a great emperor in the history of Japan that the anniversary of his birth is commemorated as a national holiday, and in fact as one of the Four Great Holidays. It falls on Nov. 3, as the Emperor was born on the 28th day of the ninth month (or Nov. 3, according to the solar calendar), in the year 1852.

Taisho-Tenno-sai: The anniversary of the death of the Emperor preceding the reigning monarch is one commemorated as a national holiday. The Emperor Taisho, august father of the present Emperor, died on Christmas Day, 1926, and the anniversary of his death is commemorated as a national holiday.

THF LONGEVITY OF THE JAPANESE

According to the census taken in 1935, the death rate of the Japanese under one year of age is 140 per thousand for males and 124 for females, i.e. an average of 1.3 babies die under one year of age, showing a decrease of 21.9 per thousand for males and 19.9 per thousand for females. The rate shows a gradual decrease after one year of age, and the lowest rate is seen for boys of 11 years, whose death rate is 2 per thousand, and for girls of 10 years, whose average death-rate is 3 per thousand. Therefore 11 years and 10 years are the safest ages for males and females, respectively. The rate rises again, till it reaches 9.8 for youths of 20 years and 10.6 for girls of the same age.

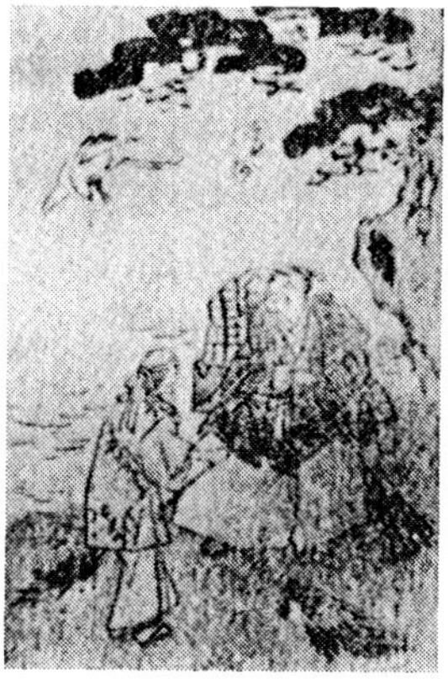

Symbols of longevity.

According to the 1935 census, the average longevity of the Japanese is 44.82 years for males and 46.54 years for females, showing an advance in the average age of 2.76 years for males and 3.34 years for females when compared with the results of the census taken in 1930.

THE DEATH-RATE OF THE JAPANESE

Age	Male Census 1930	Male Census 1935	Female Census 1930	Female Census 1935
Under 1 year	162.0	140.1	144.0	124.1
1 „	48.5	43.1	47.6	42.1
2 years	26.1	22.4	26.3	22.7
5 „	7.0	6.4	7.8	7.1
10 „	3.2	2.6	3.7	3.0
15 „	6.0	5.0	9.0	7.3
17 „	9.2	8.0	11.2	9.3
18 „	10.3	9.1	11.7	10.1
19 „	10.8	9.7	12.0	10.4
20 „	10.8	9.8	12.1	10.6
21 „	10.6	9.7	12.1	10.6
22 „	10.4	9.5	12.1	10.4
23 „	10.2	9.3	11.8	10.2
24 „	9.9	9.0	11.5	9.9
25 „	9.5	8.6	11.2	9.6
30 „	8.2	7.4	10.5	8.9
40 „	10.5	9.6	11.5	10.1
50 „	18.6	17.5	13.8	12.6
60 „	39.2	36.7	26.4	24.2
70 „	84.8	80.4	61.6	57.7
80 „	182.7	170.2	150.3	138.5
90 „	372.8	341.4	313.5	302.7
100 „	666.2	604.8	694.0	642.5

MINERAL SPAS IN JAPAN

Japan is situated in a zone of active volcanoes and is therefore dotted with mineral spas, numbering over two hundred, which attract people from all directions at all times of the year. A hot spring is traditionally considered in Japan to be the best and most efficacious resort for curing a protracted illness. We have a saying to the effect that a disease will prove fatal that is not healed by taking the baths at a hot spring, sometimes five or six times a day, for three cyclic periods of seven days in three consecutive years. The orthodox Japanese, particularly in the rural districts, seem to rely more upon the efficacy of a mineral spring than upon the effect of modern medicine for the cure of a disease, though as a general practice one does not stay at a hot spring more than three weeks at a time, or, as they say, three cyclic periods of seven days.

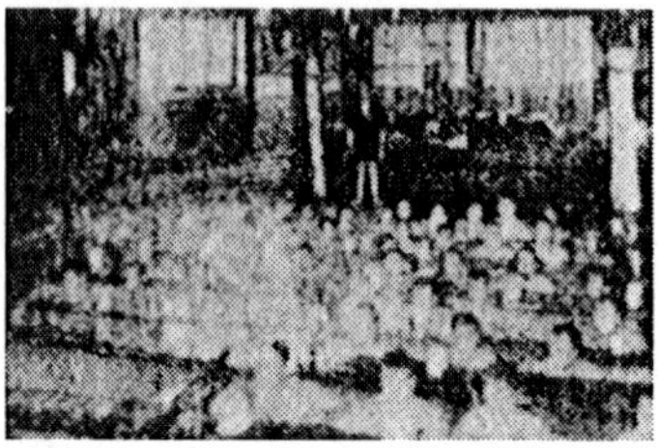

Public Bath at a Spa.

According to their components, the hot springs in Japan are classified under the following six kinds:

1. **Simple hot springs**
   Hakone, Kanagawa Prefecture
   Takeo, Saga Prefecture
   Iisaka, Fukushima Prefecture
   Nagaoka, Shizuoka Prefecture
   Ito, Shizuoka Prefecture
   Kamikochi, Nagano Prefecture
   Suwa, Nagano Prefecture
   Dogo, Ehime Prefecture
   Beppu, Oita Prefecture
   Nasu, Tochigi Prefecture
   Goshiki, Yamagata Prefecture
   Innai, Akita Prefecture, etc.
2. **Alkaline hot springs**
   Shiobara, Tochigi Prefecture
   Kasagi, Kyoto Prefecture
   Isobe, Gumma Prefecture
   Yumura, Hyogo Prefecture, etc.
3. **Carbonated hot springs**
   Beppu, Oita Prefecture
   Takaradzuka, Hyogo Prefecture
   Arima, Hyogo Prefecture
   Seto, Hyogo Prefecture
   Sawaguchi, Akita Prefecture
   Funakoya, Fukuoka Prefecture, etc.
4. **Saline hot springs**
   Miyanoshita, Kanagawa Prefecture
   Sokokura, Kanagawa Prefecture
   Yugawara, Kanagawa Prefecture
   Shiobara, Tochigi Prefecture
   Shima, Gumma Prefecture
   Arima, Hyogo Prefecture
   Wakura, Ishikawa Prefecture
   Atami, Shizuoka Prefecture
   Shuzenji, Shizuoka Prefecture
   Akayu, Yamagata Prefecture
   Yunohama, Yamagata Pref., etc.
5. **Sulphuric hot springs**
   Kusatsu, Gumma Prefecture
   Naruko, Miyagi Prefectute
   Awatsu, Ishikawa Prefecture
   Futami, Toyama Prefecture
   Akakura, Niigata Prefecture
   Yumoto, Tochigi Prefecture
   Nozawa, Nagano Prefecture
   Shionoye, Kagawa Prefecture
   Yumoto, Fukushima Pref., etc.
6. **Alum hot springs**
   Beppu, Oita Prefecture
   Aso, Kumamoto Prefecture
   Kirishima, Kagoshima Pref., etc.

A hot spring is always attributed to some divine agent so that a shrine is built for its god, especially as the appearance of a hot spring means prosperity and fortune to the owner of the land on which it appears.

BANKING IN JAPAN

It was in the year 1873, six years after the Restoration of the Imperial administration in 1868 that the first national bank was established in Japan, and it was followed in quick succession by many banks, till Japan had 153 national banks in 1878. Moreover,

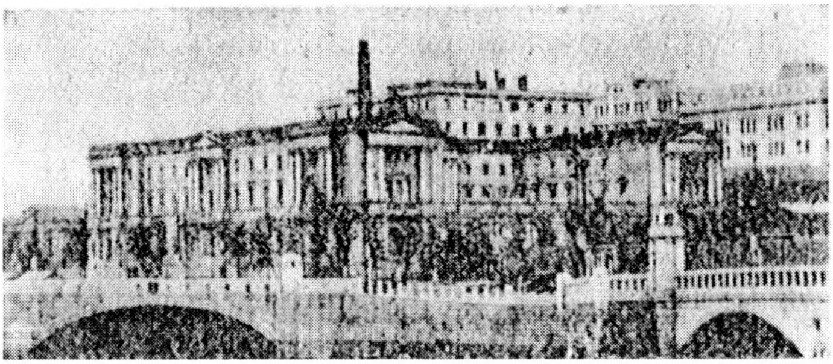

The Bank of Japan.

the National Bank Act was promulgated in November, 1872. The Yokohama Specie Bank was established in 1880, chiefly for conducting foreign exchange business, and it was followed in 1882 by the Bank of Japan, the central semi-government bank. In 1890, the Ordinary and Savings Bank Regulations were enacted for the control of banks, which by that time had grown considerably large in number, and the national banks were abolished in 1896-1899. The banks continued to increase so rapidly that at one time Japan had over 1,800 banks, though the number decreased to 652 in 1934, after the great economic depression, and to 554 in 1935, with the authorized capital of ¥2,395,266,000.

DEPOSITS IN THE BANKS OF JAPAN

(Unit: ¥1,000)

Year (Dec.)	Ordinary Banks	Savings Banks	Special Banks	Total
1921	6,327,436	1,900,131	779,171	9,006,738
1922	7,705,662	616,820	884,050	9,206,531
1923	7,651,510	623,983	828,017	9,103,510
1924	7,914,933	768,660	1,139,190	10,322,783
1925	8,702,065	890,108	1,451,520	11,043,693
1926	9,031,090	1,064,141	1,320,565	11,415,796
1927	8,906,473	1,083,098	1,475,266	11,464,837
1928	9,215,948	1,241,216	1,300,157	11,757,321
1929	9,213,171	1,421,138	1,342,530	11,976,785
1930	8,658,539	1,540,763	1,291,848	11,491,150
1931	8,174,255	1,636,255	1,155,238	10,965,767
1932	8,131,567	1,687,248	1,345,760	11,164,575
1933	8,727,313	1,825,258	1,331,112	11,883,683
1934	9,353,692	1,881,238	1,304,754	12,539,684
1935	9,873,685	2,004,578	1,391,611	13,309,874
1936	10,932,117	1,842,928	1,537,953	14,312,998

EARTHQUAKES IN JAPAN (1)

"Earthquakes, thunder, floods, fires and Dad" are proverbially said to be the five terrors in Japan. An earthquake is put at the head of the list possibly because Japan, situated on a zone of active volcanoes, has experienced disastrous tremors of the earth all through her history.

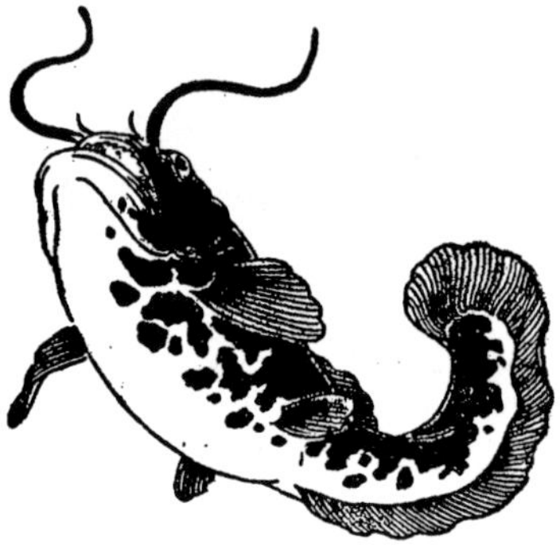

Cat-fish.

The first earthquake mentioned in the history of Japan took place in the 5th year (286 B.C.) of the reign of the Emperor Korei (the 7th). It is traditionally said that at this first earthquake Mt. Fuji and Lake Biwa made their sudden appearance simultaneously. The second large earthquake recorded in history occurred in the 5th year (416 A.D.) of the reign of the Emperor Inkyo (the 19th). The following quoted from a seismological chronology gives the years in which severe earthquakes took place in Japan:—

Year	Month	Day
286 B.C.	—	—
416 A.D.	July	24
559	April	27
676	Nov.	10
685	Oct.	4
707	June	5
744	Jan.	7
856	March	8
879	Sept.	29
887	July	1
939	April	2
976	June	18
1041	(summer)	—
1172	April	8
1179	Nov.	7
1185	July	9
1194	Aug.	27
1257	July	23
1293	April	23
1324	Nov.	15
1376	April	25
1402	Aug.	—
1406	Jan.	—
1407	Feb.	—
1410	June	21
1432	April	11
1432	Sept.	16
1448	—	—
1455	Dec.	30
1466	Dec.	29
1493	May	7
1495	Aug.	—
1510	Aug.	7
1533	Feb.	13
1544	—	—
1585	Nov.	29
1595	July	12
1621	Jan.	7
1648	April	22
1649	—	—
1662	May	1
1683	April	5
1697	—	—
1702	Nov.	23
1707	June	18
1707	Oct.	4
1707	Oct.	22
1732	Sept.	26
1751	Feb.	29
1751	April	25
1766	Jan.	28
1804	March	—
1822	June	12
1822	Nov.	12
1830	—	—
1835	—	—
1847	—	—
1855	Oct.	2
1892	Oct.	28
1894	June	20
1923	Sept.	1

EARTHQUAKES IN JAPAN (2)—*Concluded*

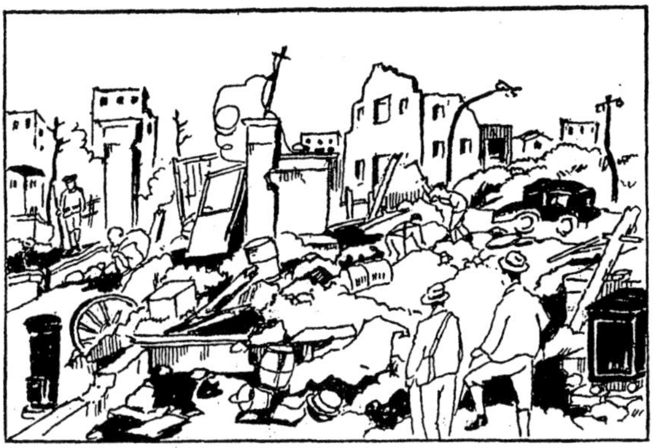

Debris of earthquake, 1923.

According to tradition in Japan, a huge cat-fish lies under the ground and every tremor of the earth is attributed to the movement of the fish. But this subterranean fish is controlled by the Kaname-ishi (literally, rivet-stone), which is situated in the precincts of the Kashima Shrine in Hitachi Province. Once a certain lord of the Mito clan tried to root the stone out, but in vain, and nobody knows how deep it goes down, for it is said to hold the seismic fish by the head. Experiments are now being made at the Tohoku Imperial University, Sendai, to discover whether or not the cat-fish has the power of foretelling an earthquake, and it has been scientifically proved that the fish can feel an earthquake much sooner than man can.

Then we have a saying that *glimmering* light is seen before an earthquake occurs. According to Col. James Churchward, authority on the lost continent of the Pacific Ocean, an earthquake is due to the escape from the earth of gas, and his theory seems to have been pretty well received by scientists.

Earthquake predicts: When an earthquake takes place, the Japanese are often seen to count time, generally with their fingers. They count it to see what it is, according to the old way of counting time, when the tremor has come, because an earthquake is generally believed in Japan to make a prediction of some kind as is seen from the following poem of 31 syllables:—

Ku wa Yamai; Go-shichi no Ame ni; Yotsu Hideri;
Mutsu-yatsu naraba; Kaze to shirubeshi.

Translation:

"Nine means sickness; five and seven show a rain; four is for sunshine; while from six and eight you must expect a wind."

This poem means: If an earthquake occurs at the time of nine (12 o'clock) sickness will prevail; if it comes up at five (8 o'clock) or seven (4 o'clock) a rain is coming; sunshine is predicted by an earthquake at the time of four (10 o'clock); but a wind is to be expected if an earthquake takes place at the time of six (6 o'clock) or eight (2 o'clock).

THE EARTHQUAKE MEMORIAL HALL (1)

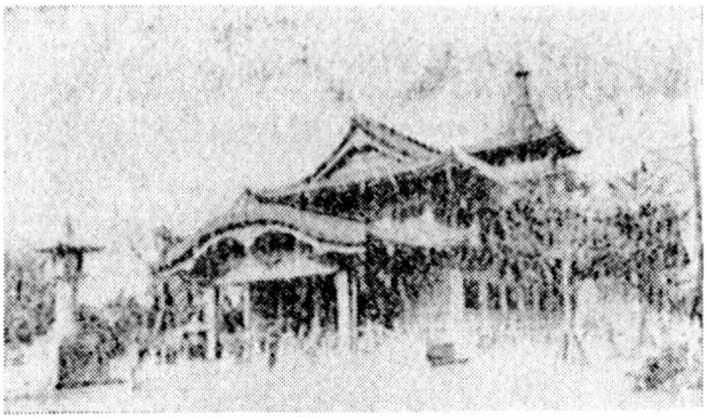

The Earthquake Memorial Hall.

Immediately after the Great Earthquake took place on Sept. 1, 1923, at 11.58 a.m., many fires broke out in Tokyo, reducing most of its buildings to ashes and burning many thousands of people to death, as shown below:—

Houses burned down and destroyed.........	366,262
Killed	59,065
Missing	1,055

At the old site of Hifuku-sho or Cloth Depot of the Army, which was an open space of over 16 acres, more than thirty thousand refugees, who took shelter from fire, were literally roasted to death by a whirlwind that swept over the place bringing fire in its wake, and their bones, after cremation, were piled up mountain-high. These bones were put in 260 barrels of 40 lit. each, and enshrined in a temple erected in the compound. The temple, which is called the Earthquake Memorial Hall, is a three-storeyed building and, besides the charred bones, preserves a record of twenty volumes, which contain the whole list of all the ill-fated people, not only of the old site of the Cloth Depot, but of the whole city of Tokyo, numbering altogether 58,885, excepting those whose bereft families desire to enshrine them in their own localities. On Sept. 1, every year, religious services are held at the Memorial Hall in honour of the ill-fated people, when tens of thousands of their bereft families and friends come to pay their respect to the memory of their unfortunate relatives.

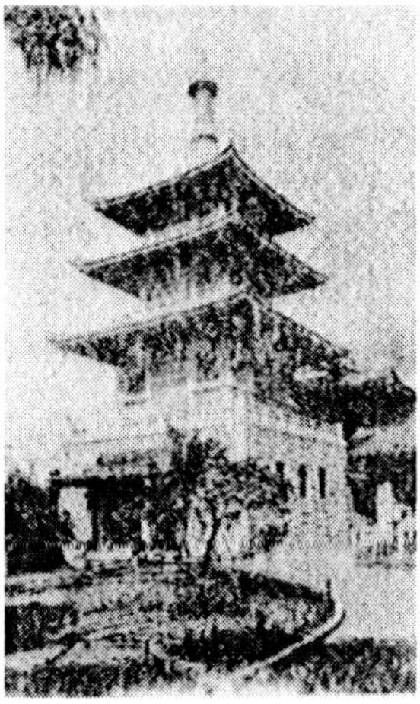

The Earthquake Memorial Tower.

Monument of the ill-fated school-children: Over 5,000 school-children were killed in the Great Earthquake and its subsequent fire, and a monument was erected to their memory in the same compound of the Memorial Hall. The fund contributed by 182,027 school teachers and children amounted to ¥14,066.47.

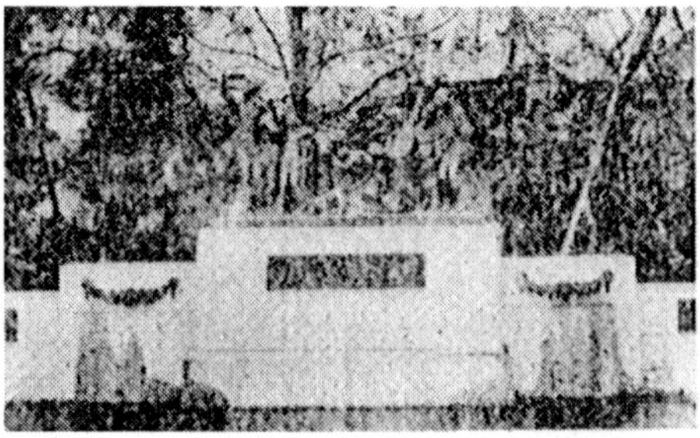

The Monument of the Ill-fated School-Children.

(Continued)

THE EARTHQUARE MEMORIAL HALL (2)

Buddhist statues of charred bones: Two Buddhist statues are made of the charred bones of the Cloth Depot. One of them is that of Amitabha, 3 ft. 3 inches high, and it is enshrined in the Jiko-in Temple near by the compound of the Earthquake Memorial Hall. The other statue called the Bankotsu-Kannon (or 10,000-bone-Kannon), of about the same size, is installed in the Bukkyo-Kaikan (Buddhist Hall), a few doors from the Jiko-in Temple. These two images, because of their being made of the bones, attract numerous visitors on September first every year.

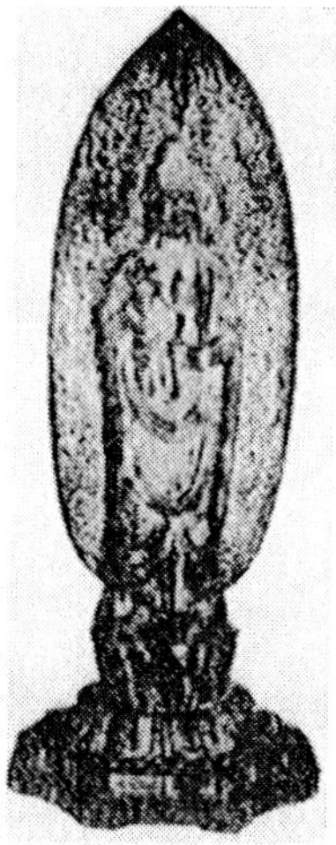

The 10,000-Bone Kannon.

A thousand images: The Bukkyo-Kaikan has a thousand small wooden images of Buddhism contributed by one Shingo Kurahashi with the prayer that the soul of his beloved son, Commander Shinji Kurahashi, who died at the age of forty-two, might have repose in the land of the dead.

The Eko-in Temple: The Eko-in Temple is situated near the eastern end of Ryogoku-bashi Bridge, Tokyo. It is a memorial temple built in commemoration of those burned dead at the big fire of Meireki. Umeno, 16-year-old daughter of Hikoye, a pawn-broker, fell in love with an apprentice-boy so deeply that when she saw that her love could not be realized, she contracted an illness, which proved fatal. Her funeral service was held at the Hommyo-ji Temple, Edo, on the 18th day of the first month (January), 1655. The Furisode, her favorite dress, which was used on her coffin at the funeral, was sold to an old-clothes dealer. On the anniversary of her funeral the next year, another was held at the same temple for another 16-year-old girl, Kino by name, a daughter of a paper-dealer. The same Furisode-dress was brought on her coffin, and again it was sold. On the 18th of the same month, 1657, the same Furisode-dress came to the temple for the third time when a funeral rite was observed for another 16-year-old girl, who was called Iku, daughter of Kiyemon, a koji (malt) maker. The horrified priest did not sell the dress this time, but he burned it up in his garden, when, the burning dress blown by a strong wind, the temple caught fire, resulting in one of the most destructive fires in Tokyo. The fire broke out at the Hommyo-ji Temple, Hongo, in Edo (Tokyo) at the zodiac time of the Dragon (8 a.m.) on the 18th day of the first month (January) in 1657 (the third year of Meireki era), and kept on burning for three days and nights before it was controlled, destroying two thirds of the Shogunate capital of Edo. It is said that no less than 107,000 were either burned dead or drowned in the River Sumida during the big fire. Priest Doyo, of the Zojo-ji Temple, built the Eko-in Temple to pray for the peaceful repose of those ill-fated people, and a mass service is still held at the temple on the seventh day of the seventh month (July 7), every year.

THE JAPANESE CASTLE (1)

The castle made its first appearance in Japanese history, according to the Nihon-shoki, when the Emperor Jimmu, the first of the Imperial line, built what may be literally translated a "castle-rice-field" on the camp during his expedition against Yasotakeru, a local chief. Prince Sahohiko, rising in revolt against the Emperor Suinin (the 11th) defended himself, for some time, in the Inaki or rice-straw-castle in the 5th year (25 B.C.) of his reign. Another straw-castle was built by Mononobe-no-Moriya, when Soga-no-Umako attacked him in 587 A.D. It was built of rice-straw piled up around a house. During the reign (640-644) the Soga father and son made a castle of their residence, beside which an arms store was built with a moat around it. The *Mizuki* or water-castle was built in Tsukushi in 670 by keeping water inside a large embankment. But it was during or after the reign (662-671) of the Emperor Tenji (the 38th) that a castle worthy of its name made its appearance in Japanese history, and castles were built in Tsukushi, Nagato, Iki, Yamato, Sanuki and Tsushima provinces for defence against the invasion of Shiragi, a kingdom in Korea. The castles of Akita, Taga and Izawa were among the largest built in the north, the last-mentioned occupying a plot of land which, according to the ruins recently brought to light, measured 5 cho (cho=60 ken) in the east, 38 ken (ken=6 Japanese feet) in the west, 5 cho 52 ken in the south and 5 cho 52 ken in the north. Castle-building made remarkable progress during the protracted hostility between the two military families of Minamoto and Taira in the 12th century, the castle of Ichinotani, which Yoshitsune Minamoto captured in 1184, being one of the best known in those days. Masashige Kusunoki, who is known as a typical tactician of great loyalty, built several castles in which he withstood the attacks of the Ashikaga forces.

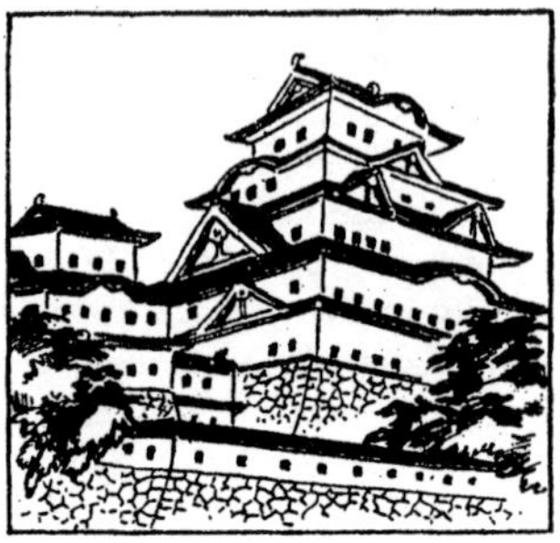
The Himeji Castle.

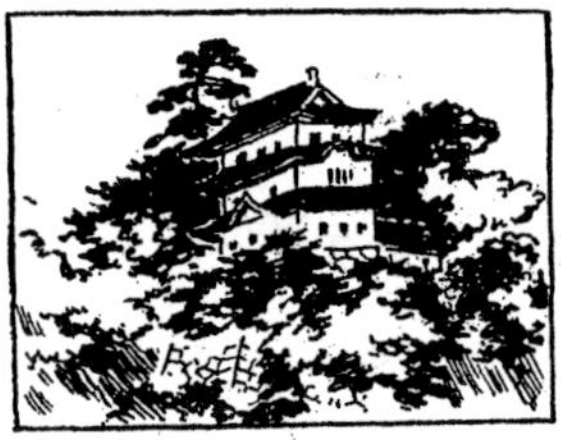
The Akashi Castle.

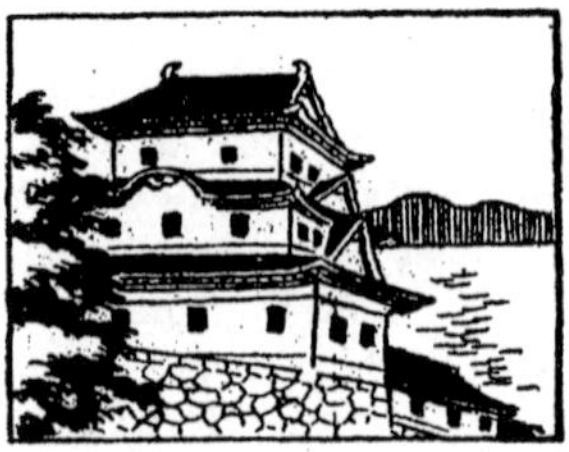
The Takamatsu Castle.

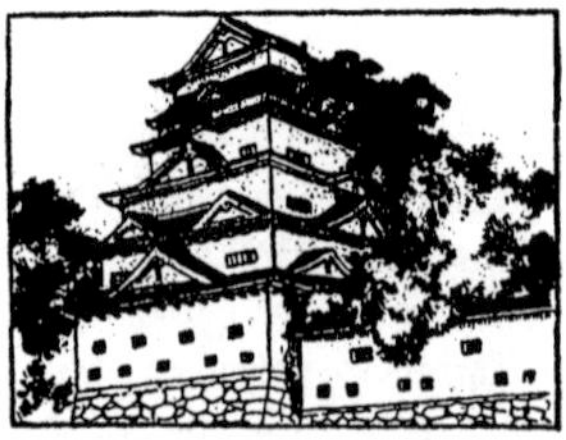
The Hiroshima Castle.

THE JAPANESE CASTLE (2)—*Concluded*

Then came the military dynasties of Ashikaga (1336-1574), Oda (1574-1583), Toyotomi (1583-1603) and Tokugawa (1603-1867), which were the most representative feudal days of Japan, and large numbers of castles were built in those days, since most local lords lived in castles or fortified residences. It is recorded that during a period of 446 years, 1183-1629, no fewer than 1,828 castles were destroyed. From this fact it is easy to imagine how thickly Japan was dotted with castles in her feudal days. In 1872, however, when prefectural governments were established in place of the abolished clans, most feudal castles were remorselessly pulled down, leaving less than a dozen standing.

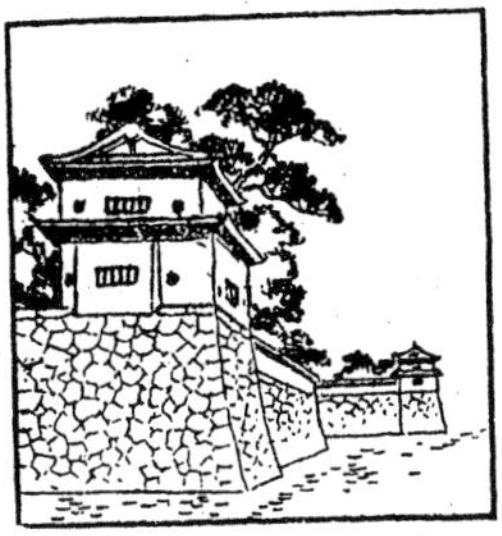

The Ohita Castle.

Castle-building: Of the ancient construction of a castle little is known, but the mediaeval and modern castles were constructed on the basis of Kuruwa or carved-circle, consisting of the outer and inner Kuruwa, with a moat between, which was, as a rule, about 15 ken (ken=6 Japanese feet) wide. The castle proper was called Hommaru or central citadel, and a castle usually had Ni-no-maru (2nd citadel). San-no-maru (3rd citadel), Higashi-maru (east-citadel), Nishi-maru (west-citadel) and Kita-maru (north-citadel), besides. The date of their appearance in the construction of a castle is not known, but these citadels are found in the Osaka castle, which was built by Hideyoshi Toyotomi in 1583. A castle had several entrances besides the front and back gates, which were called the Ohte and Karamete gates, respectively, and the Edo castle had thirty-six gates in all.

The Kumamoto Castle.

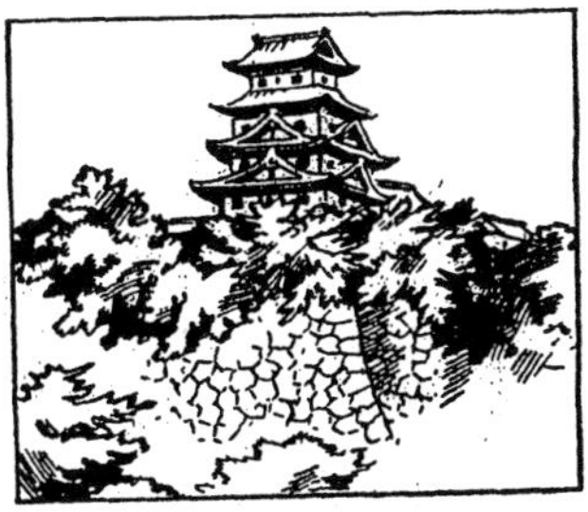

The Fukuyama Castle.

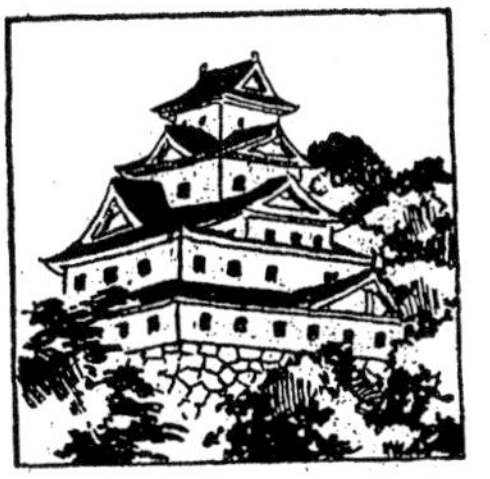

The Okayama Castle.

THE NAGOYA CASTLE

The Nagoya Castle, one of the few old-time ones still preserved in Japan was among the best and strongest of the kind in our feudal days. It was built in 1610, under the instruction of Iyeyasu, the founder of the Tokugawa regime, by such lords as Maeta, Mohri, Kuroda, Yamanouchi, Hachisuka, etc. The castle, which is 15.5 cho (cho=119 yards), east to west, and 17 cho, north to south, covers an area of 10 chobu (chobu=2.45 acres). It is built in such a situation that it commands extensive plains in all directions.

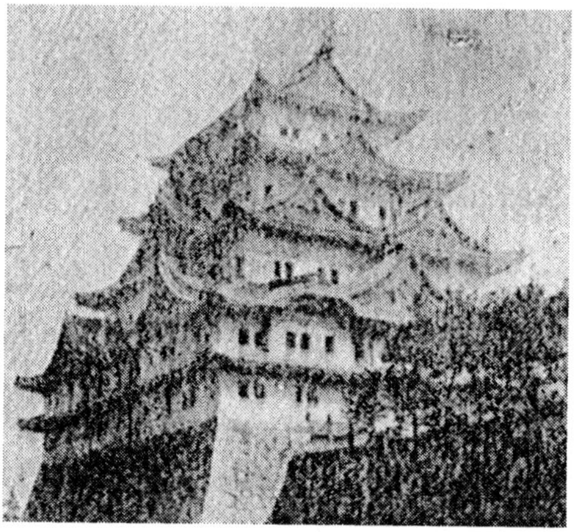

The Nagoya Castle.

Kiyomasa Kato, warlord of Kumamoto, who distinguished himself in the Japanese invasion of Korea in 1597, attended to the building of the Tenshukaku (castle-keep or donjon), which is of five storeys standing on strong basements built of huge stones by pouring melted lead between them. It is traditionally said in feudal days that no stone that touches the ground during its trip to its castle-site should be used in the building of a castle, and it is praiseworthy how Kato devised an ingenious way of transporting the tremendous stones from great distances in such a way that they did not touch the ground on their trip to Nagoya. In the castle-keep there is a well into which, it is said, Kato threw some gold pieces in order to keep its water pure and clean.

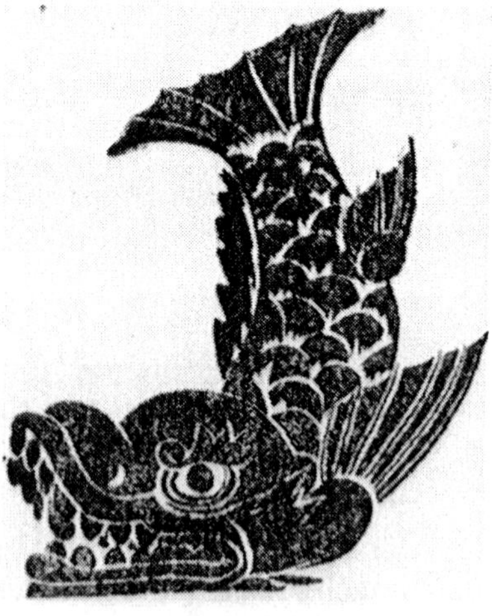

The Gold Dolphin.

The Nagoya Castle is famous for the two gold dolphins on its roof. The female dolphin is 2.51 metres high and 1.96 metres round, while the male one is 2.59 metres high and 2.07 metres round. The gold used in the two dolphins weighs 165,275 grams. The gold dolphins were once taken down during the Meiji era to be shown at an exposition held at Vienna, Austria. The Nagoya Castle is preserved as a national treasure but it is open to the public. It is the most typical castle of Old Japan.

THE SHIMENAWA OR SACRED ROPE

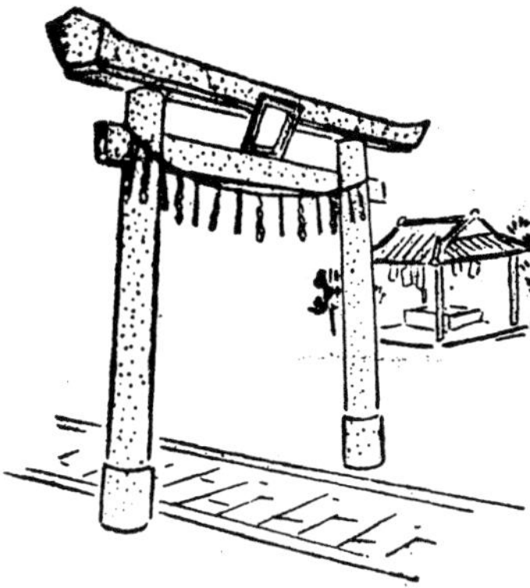

Shimenawa on a Torii.

The Shimenawa or sacred rope is hung before a Shinto shrine, over the entrance gate to a dwelling-house or else round a place which is considered sacred or has to be kept sacred. According to the Shinto belief, no evil can pass beyond the line of the Shimenawa.

The Shimenawa consists of two strands of rice-straw plaited together, in a left-handed or positive way, representing positivity and negativity, to which nature owes its existence. In the proper arrangement of the Shimenawa, its beginning or larger end should be on the left-hand side of the shrine or the god, though this rule seems to be little observed today. The rope has along it a few rice-stalks hanging at intervals. Formerly, as the original name of the rope indicates, the root-ends of the straws were plaited into the rope, with the head hung partly down. Though the straw is shorn of its ears and hung with the root-ends down, the ears were left on the stalks in former days, as they were the most significant part of the rope. Lastly, the Shimenawa has stripes of white paper or cloth, called "*nigite*" or "*nusa*," hanging between the clusters of the straws. According to a certain interpretation, these little pieces represent the hands of the Emperor reaching out for a good crop in the country.

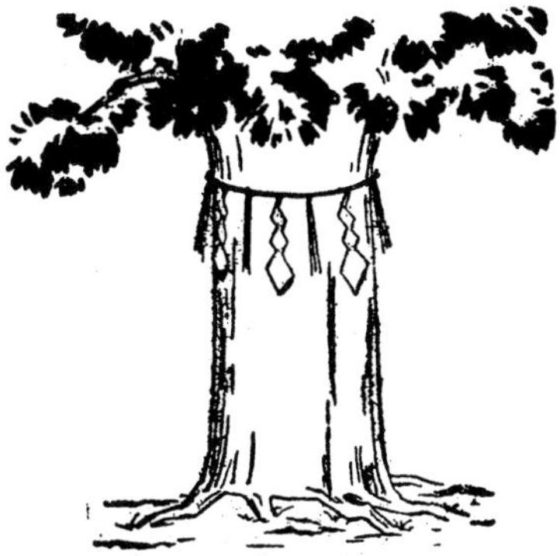

Shimenawa around a sacred tree.

When the Goddess Amaterasu, first ancestress of the Imperial family, was forced by Tajikarao or Prince Mighty-power, out of the Celestial Cave, in which she had hid herself because of the repeated offences of her brother, Prince Susanoo, a rope was put across the entrance of the cave by Prince Futodama to prevent the Sun Goddess from going back into the cave again. The rope was called "Shirikume-na-nawa" meaning "Don't-retreat-rope," which name was shortened to the present "shimenawa." Like the Torii, which cleanses the heart of the Shinto devotee, the Shimenawa sanctifies the place or thing around which it is put.

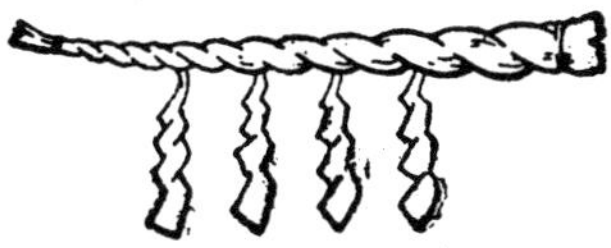

Shimenawa with Nigite hanging down.

THE WANAWA OR SACRED ROPE OF NEW YEAR (1)

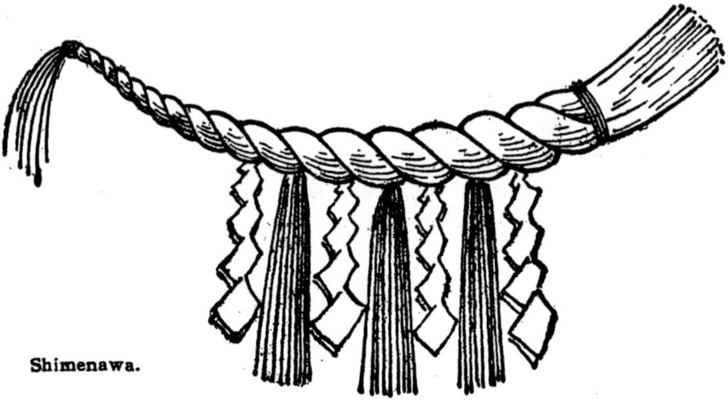

Shimenawa.

Every Japanese house is decorated, or, as the original Japanese means, "blessed" with what is called the Wanawa or circle-rope at New Year. It is a modern modification of the Shimenawa or sacred rope (which see). Decorated with the following articles for bringing luck, the rope is placed on the alcove (Toko-no-ma) or the sacred place of a Japanese home as well as at its front entrance:—

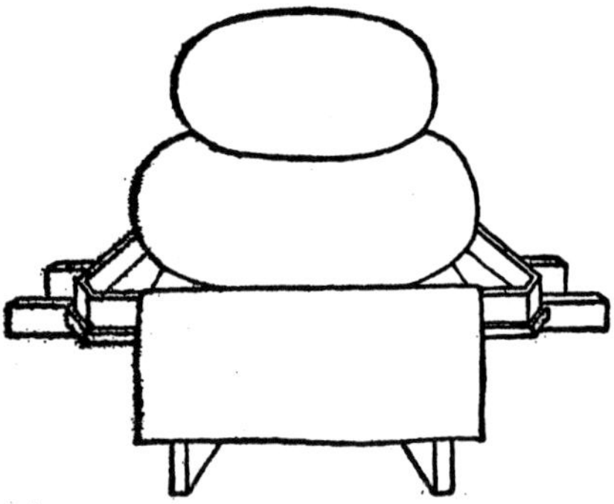

O-Sonae.

O-Sonae: O-Sonae (Honorable-offering) is also called "Kagami-mochi" (Mirror-rice-cake). It consists of two cakes of pounded rice, and represents the sacred mirror, one of the Imperial Regalia of Japan. The Sacred Rope is generally put on the O-Sonae.

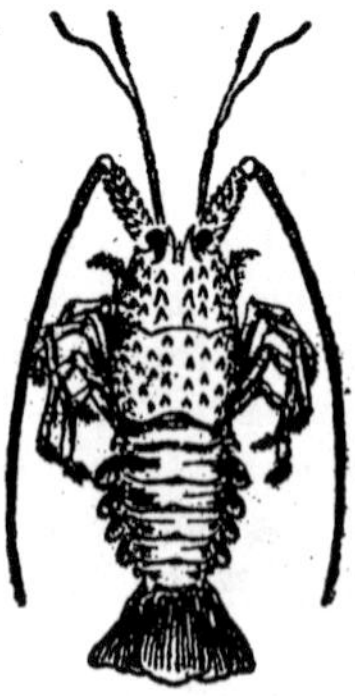

Lobster.

Lobster: A boiled lobster is indispensable to the New Year decoration. It is called "*ebi*" in the Japanese language, and expressed by two Chinese characters meaning "sea-old," because a lobster has a bent body like that of an old man. Hence in the New Year decoration, it signifies longevity.

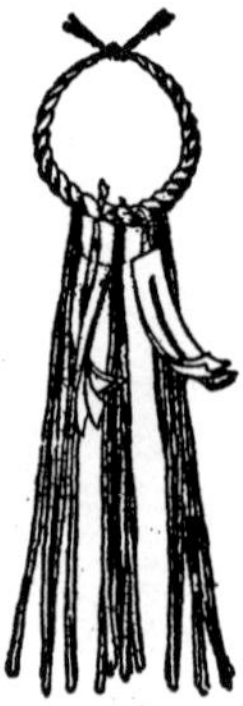

Wanawa.

(*Continued*)

THE WANAWA OR SACRED ROPE OF NEW YEAR (2)

(Concluded)

Kombu: The tangle is called in the Japanese language "kombu," which suggests "*yorokobu*" or "joy." Hence, it stands for joy or happiness in the Sacred Rope.

Daidai and Yuzuriha: *Daidai* (bigarade) and *Yuzuriha* (daphniphyllum macropodum) suggest homonymously "from generation to generation" (dai = generation) and "hereditary bequeathal." Hence, they are important in the Sacred Rope of Wanawa, because in our feudal days nothing was a greater disgrace to a samurai family than to be officially extinct since it had to continue in order to serve the lord for generations.

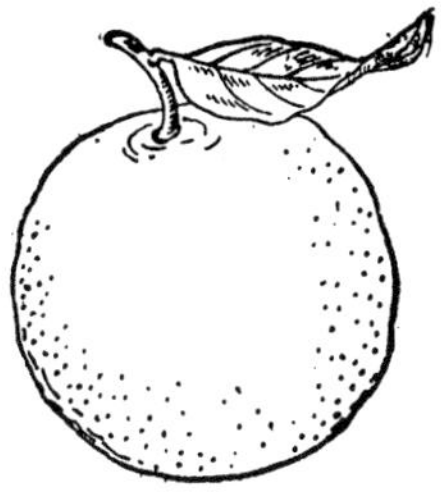

Daidai.

Hondawara: Hondawara (sargassum enerve) is a sea-weed, which bears numerous berry-like air-vessels. "Dawara" sounds like "tawara," which is the bale of rice. Now, rice was essential in the feudal days of Japan because the salary and allowance of the samurai were paid in it. Hence, hondawara signifies wealth in the New Year decoration.

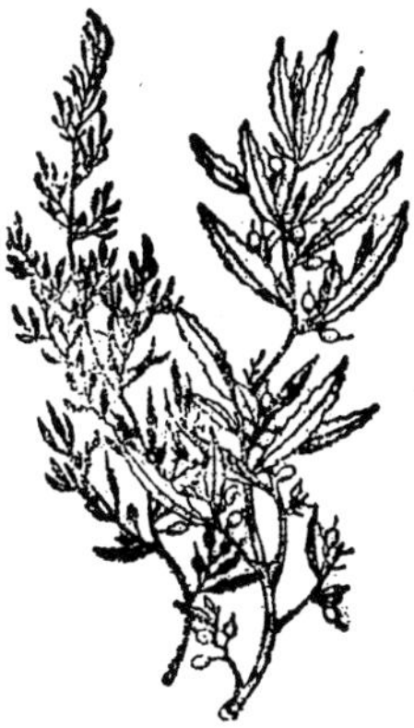

Hondawara.

Urashiro: Urashiro or gleicheniaceae is a kind of fern. Its leaves are white on one side from which comes its Japanese name (ura = back; shiro = white). It therefore stands for honesty and sincerity which the samurai of old so greatly prized.

Dried persimmon: Dried persimmons on skewers are also necessary in the New Year decoration, as they signify health and success in life.

Tokoro and sumi: Tokoro (polygonum multiflorum) and sumi (charcoal), homonymously meaning "place" and "dwell," respectively, are sometimes used in the Sacred Rope of the New Year, signifying "to live at a place." United with the bigarade (daidai = generations), these two objects, uninviting as they look, mean "to live at one place for generations," and this in turn implies loyalty to one lord.

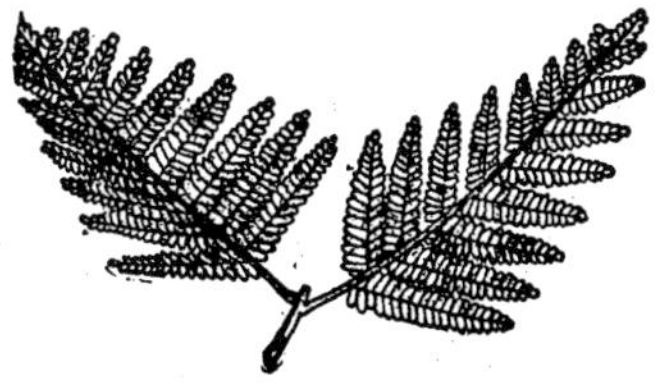

Urashiro.

THE TORII

The Torii is a simple gateway of rough logs erected on the approach to every Shinto shrine. The word "torii," which, as it stands, means a bird-perch, was derived from the Indian word "Torana," from which several European words, such as "tor," "door," etc. have come, though the Indian "Torana" has three cross-bars on the top while the Japanese torii has two.

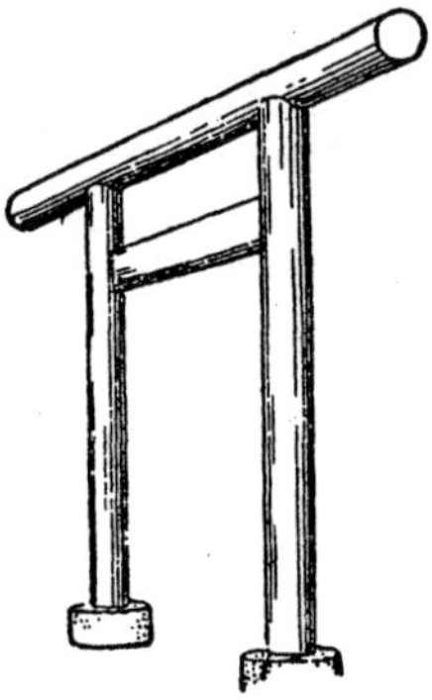

Torii.

The torii dates as far back in history as the pre-historic days of Japan. The Goddess Amaterasu, ancestress of the Imperial family, had a rude brother by the name of Prince Susanoo. According to the oldest record of the country, the prince laid waste his sister's gardens, defiled her new palace, threw a horse's hide over her loom, and proved himself unruly and wicked in many other ways. Disgusted by the repeated misconduct of her brother, the Sun Goddess hid herself behind the Ame-no-Iwato (or Celestial rock-door), and it is recorded that in consequence the world was thrown into utter darkness. The Eight-Million Gods sat in council at the Yasukawara (or Fields of Peace), and it was decided, among other things, that Tokoyo-Naganaki-dori (or Perpetual-daylight-long-singing-bird), as the long-crowing cock was called, should proclaim the break of day at the entrance to the cave. The torii is therefore an imitation of the gateway on which the mythological cock perched. The gods then made music and danced before the cave, so that the curious Goddess peeped out to see what all the noise was about. Tajikarao (or Prince Mighty-power) seized this opportunity to open the rock-door. The Goddess Amaterasu was now out of the cave and sunshine began to reign again over the country.

Now, the Japanese cock has been known, from time immemorial, to herald dawn. He is such a good time-keeper that he crows, or thrice announces the time regularly early in the morning, so that three torii before a Shinto shrine represent the three crowings or announcements of the cock. As the cock is an announcer of the passing of night and the coming of day, so do the three torii prepare the heart of a pious worshipper for his purified appearance before the god. His passing under the god-gate expels the darkness of his heart as darkness is lifted at dawn. The torii is therefore the purifier of an unclean body and soul. When the Japanese worships at a shrine, he claps his hands three times, (now generally twice) thereby making a rather loud sound. Then he reverently bends his head over them in adoration. This clapping of the hands is called "Kashiwade," meaning "clapping of clean palms," but phonetically the hands clapped are in imitation of a kashiwa-fowl (young cock), which flaps its wings when it crows or announces the time.

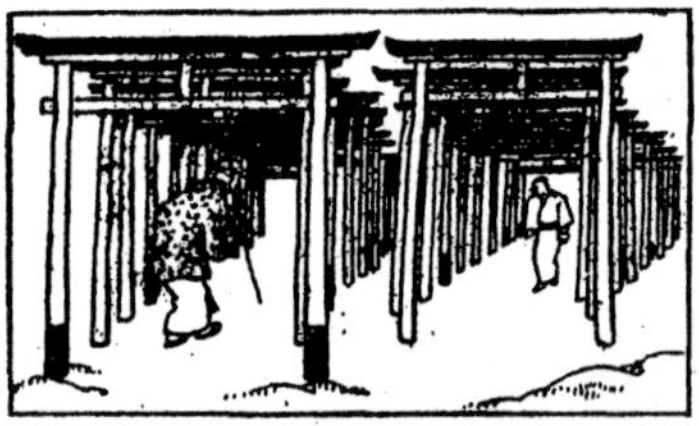

The Torii of Inari Shrine.

DIFFERENT KINDS OF TORII (1)

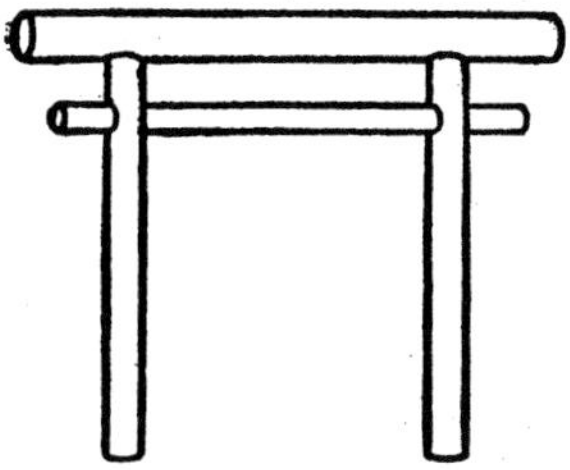

KUROKI TORII: Most primitive kind of Torii; made of round logs with their barks on; consists of two posts, Kasaki (top-bar) on top and Nuki (cross-bar).

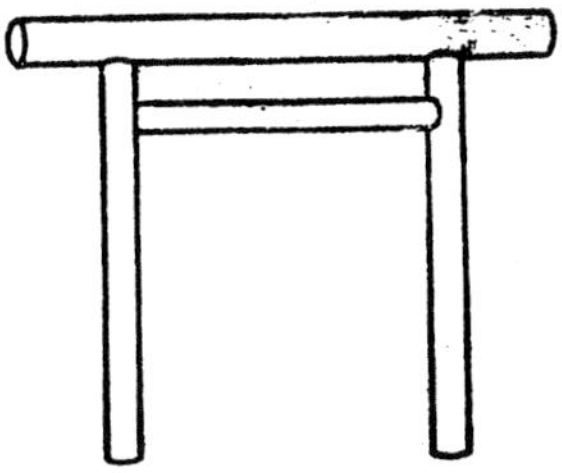

SHIMMEI TORII: The type of Torli standing in front of the Ise Shrines; simplest form of Torii; consists of two round posts, Kasaki (sometimes octagonal) and Nuki.

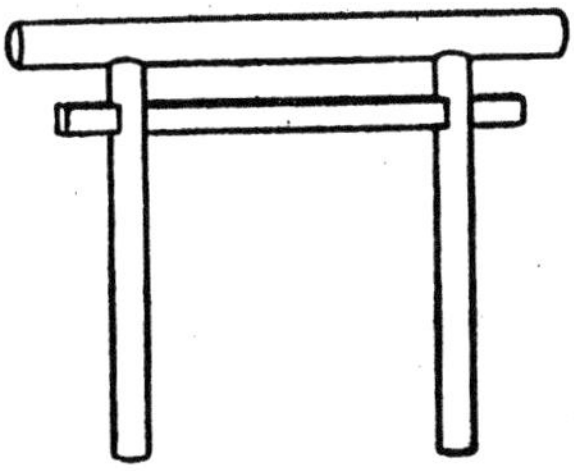

KASHIMA TORII: The type of Torii standing in front of the Kashima Shrine; both ends of Nuki (generally squre) run through the two posts.

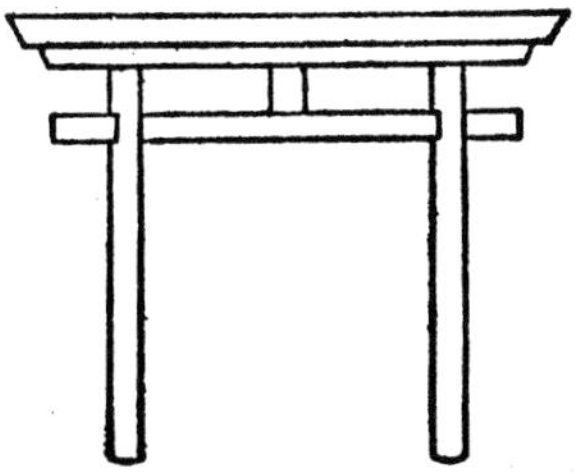

KASUGA TORII: This has Gakunuki (vertical bar between Kasaki and Nuki); Kasaki and Shimaki (below Kasaki) have both ends cut vertically straight; square Nuki running through round posts.

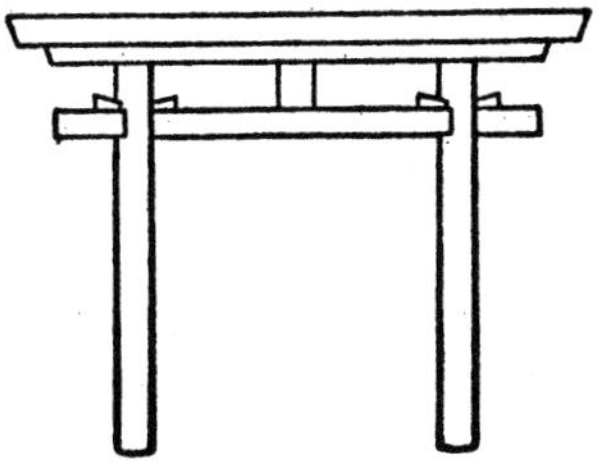

HACHIMAN TORII: Two posts are round and a little slant; Kasaki and Shimaki have both ends cut in a slantwise.

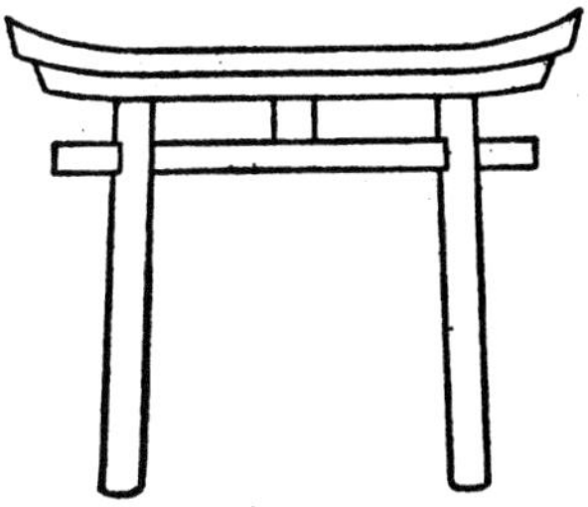

MYOJIN TORII: Most common type of Torii; Kasaki and Shimaki are a little inclined upwards at both ends.

(Continued)

DIFFERENT KINDS OF TORII (2)—*Concluded*

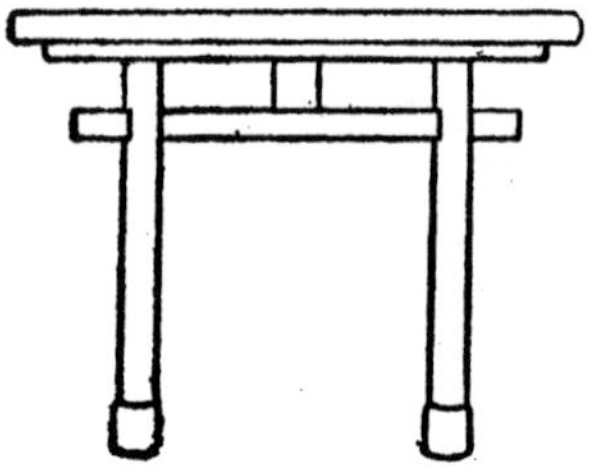

WARAZA TORII: Two posts have Netsutsumi (root-wrapper) to keep them from getting rotten; Kasaki has a metal protection.

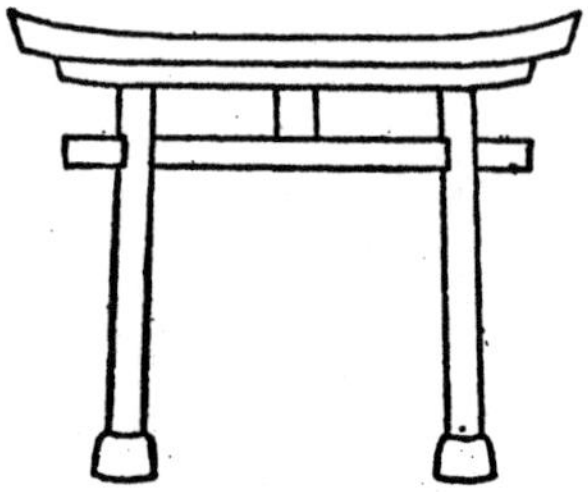

INARI TORII: The same type as that of the Myojin Torii; only it has Daiwa (stand-circle) between the posts and Shimaki.

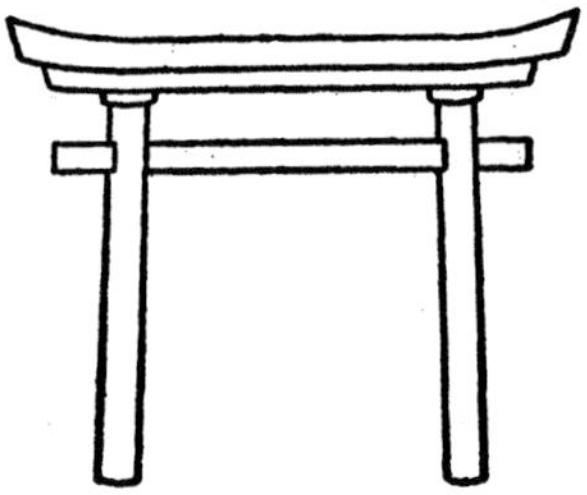

←
RYOBU TORII: Almost similar to Inari Torii; only it has Hikae-bashira (side-posts) to keep it from slanting.

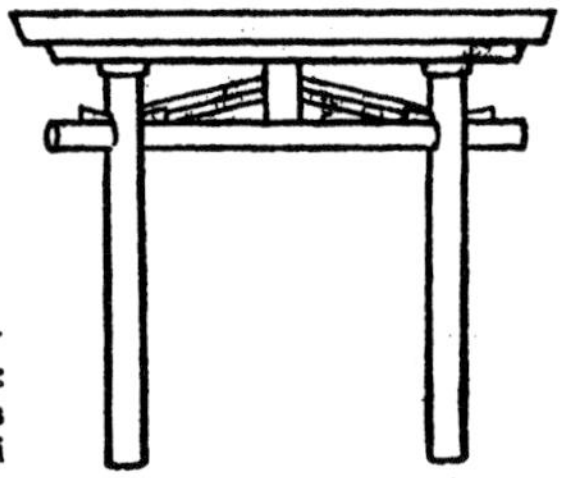

→
NUME TORII: This has gables between Shimaki and Nuki.

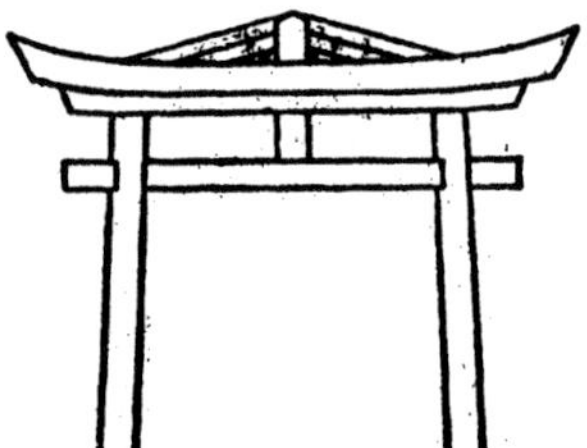

SANNO TORII: The same type as that of the Inari Torii with gables on the top of Kasaki.

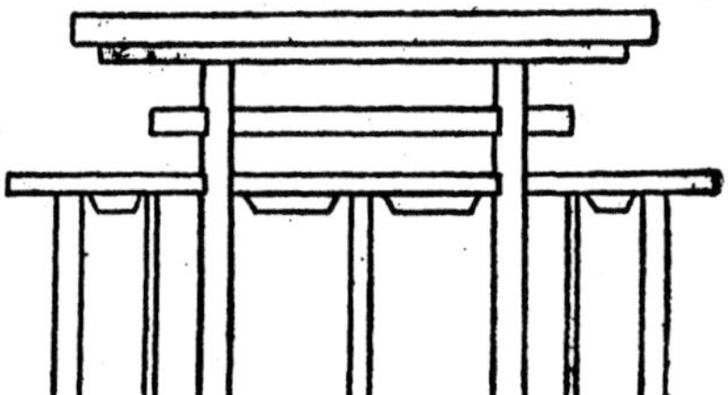

MIWA TORII: Special to the Miwa Shrine. It has two side-Torii beside the main one.

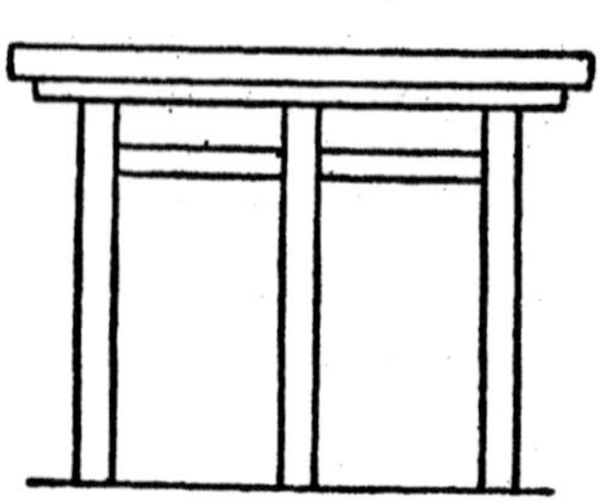

SUMIYOSHI TORII: Two posts are square.

THE DIET BUILDING OF JAPAN

The Diet Building stands majestic and imposing in Nagata-cho St., the White Hall St. of Tokyo, and its stepped white tower is seen from most parts of the city.

The Diet Building covers a site of 20,946 tsubo or 17.04 acres. It was completed in 1936 at the cost of ¥25,600,000, 27 years after the plan was first made and 19 years after the work got first under way. The building is in a modified Renaissance style, with its exterior finished with white granite. Its front entrance measures 681 ft. from end to end and it is 292 ft. wide, from the front to rear entrance, and 216 ft. high. There are 393 rooms in the structure and the auditoriums of the Upper and Lower Houses are provided with 635 seats each, while the gallery has 770 seats for the Upper and 922 seats for the Lower House.

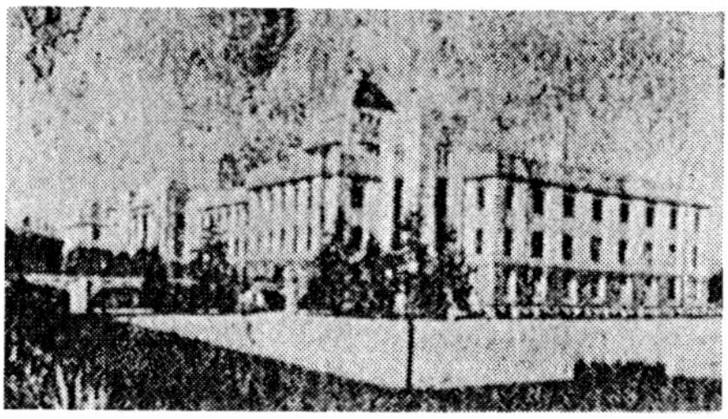

The Diet Building.

The basement of the building is occupied mainly by the heating plant, an electric transformer and a printing plant. The rooms of the first floor are chiefly for the clerks and other employees of the Diet. There are two audience halls, one for the House of Peers and the other for the House of Representatives, on the second floor, which is reached by a broad flight of steps leading up to the massive colonade. The assembly rooms for both Houses are two storeys in height with balconies that may be entered from the third floor, their seats being arranged in a semi-circular formation facing the long platform that runs across full length of the rooms.

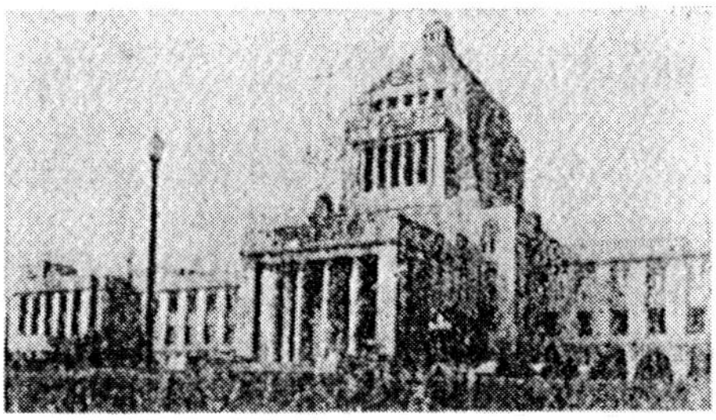

The Tower of the Diet Building.

The materials used in the building of the Diet are brought from different parts of the country; granite and marble from Hiroshima, Kyushu and Okayama Prefectures, and lumbers of keyaki (zelkova) and hinoki (Japanese cypress) from many different provinces. Most decorative motifs used in the wood carvings and mouldings represent ancient Japanese folklore and mythologies, the phoenix in bass relief being the Japanese symbol for eternity.

The new Diet Building was opened for assembly at the 70th session of the Diet in 1936.

THE INSIGNIA OF COMMAND (1)

Saihai: The Saihai is a baton of command. It has a bunch of narrow pieces of thick paper, which are either red, white, golden or silvery in colour and less than one inch wide and about a foot long. They number ninety-eight in representation of the ninety-eight thousand war-gods and are tied to one end of a lacquered handle of nuru-de-wood (rhus semialata), 1.2 to 1.8 ft. or sometimes 2.8 ft. long, with metal fittings at both ends. The nurude, for which we use two characters meaning "victory-tree," (捷木) is considered to be the best wood to be used for the handle of the saihai.

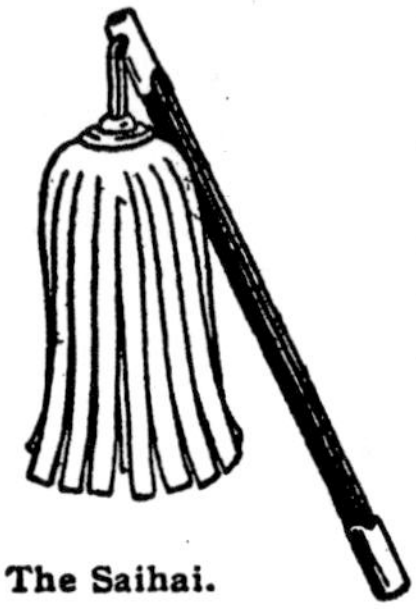
The Saihai.

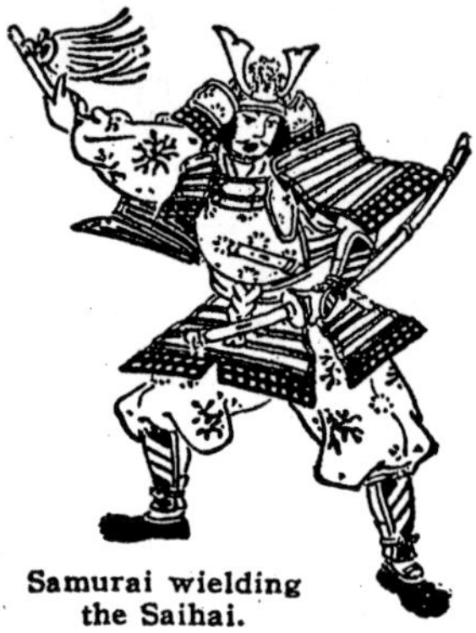
Samurai wielding the Saihai.

The word "Saihai" means "clearing the front" and the Saihai was considered to have a special power of leading soldiers to victory, for the Japanese baton seems to have been modelled after the Gohei or zigzag paper-offering used at the Shinto shrine. Yoriiye, a warlord of the Minamoto family, it is recorded, handed a red Saihai to Shinra-Saburo Yoshimitsu and this is the first time that the Saihai is mentioned in history. But generally the Saihai is believed to have been invented much later, and it was commonly used during the eras of Genki (1570–1572) and Tensho (1573–1591). The Japanese expression "Saihai wo furu" (to shake the Saihai) means "to take the lead" or "to assume the hegemony" (like "to wield the sceptre.")

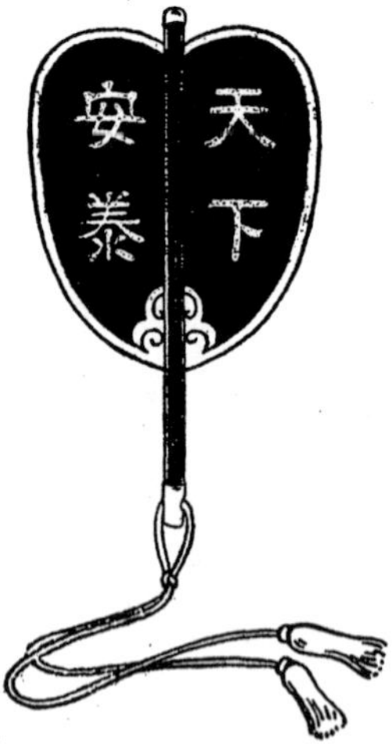

The Gumbai-Uchiwa.

Gumbai-uchiwa: The Gumbai-uchiwa is a war-fan. We quote a few lines from the Kokon-Yoran (Manual of Present and Past): "The war-fan clears dust, produces a wind and commands the soldiers. Hence it is for a general and not for a private soldier. Prince Jogu (or Shotoku) is said to have used one, which is preserved at the Koryu-ji Temple." Shingen Taketa defended himself with a war-fan, when attacked by Kenshin Uyesugi. Ujitsuna Hojo and Hideyoshi Toyotomi commanded their soldiers with the Gumbai-uchiwa on the battle-fields. In Sumo (Japanese wrestling) the Gyoji (umpire) wields a "Gumbai-uchiwa," which is lifted up for the winner.

(*Continued*)

THE INSIGNIA OF COMMAND (2)—*Concluded*

The Gumbai-uchiwa is made of iron leather with a lacquered handle of the nurude like the Saihai. The fan may be oval or round and sometimes it bears some mystic words.

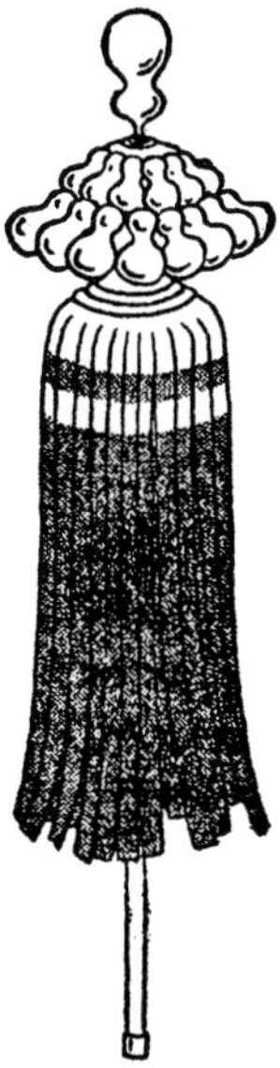

The Sennari-Hyotan.

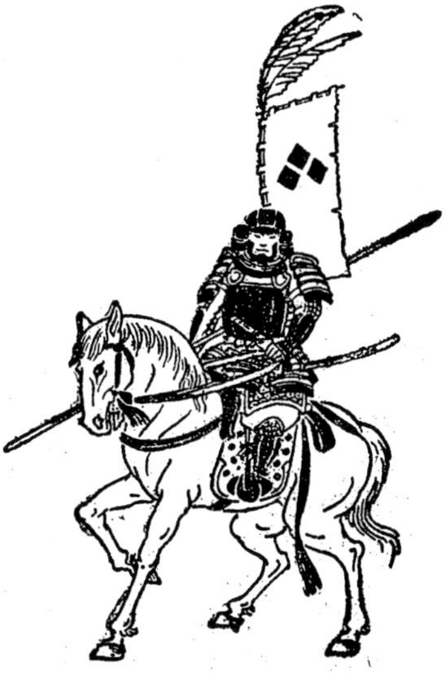

Samurai carrying a Matoi.

Umajirushi: The Umajirushi or horse-badge may not be properly called a sign of command, but it marks the place on the camp where the lord or general stands to stimulate the morale of the army. According to some record, the Umajirushi was first used by Ujiyasu Hojo in the 16th century, and it was quite popular during the latter periods of the same century.

Among the best known Umajirushi is that of Hideyoshi Toyotomi, who added one gourd to his Umajirushi every time he won a battle till his Umajirushi known as the Sennari-hyotan or 1,000-gourds was a scare to his enemy.

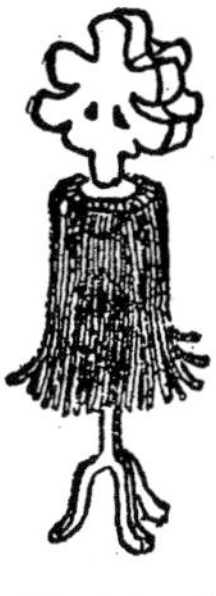

The Matoi

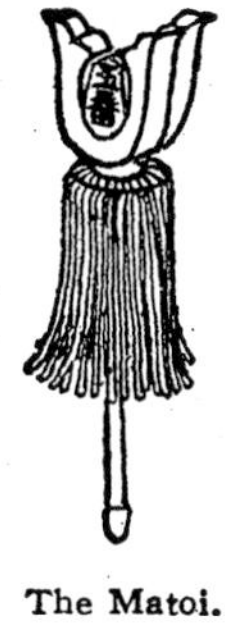

The Matoi.

The Matoi: No more sign of command than the Umajirushi is the Matoi, which also indicates the place where the leader stands. Or, it was often borne by him behind his helmet. The Matoi was of various shapes and sizes, but the commonest one consisted of a flag or ensign of the leader. It is said that the first Matoi in history was used by Daidoji, a samurai under Ujiyasu Hojo, who made a Matoi of the mark that he took from a warrior of the enemy. The Matoi is now commonly used by the fire-brigade.

COMMODORE PERRY MONUMENT (1)

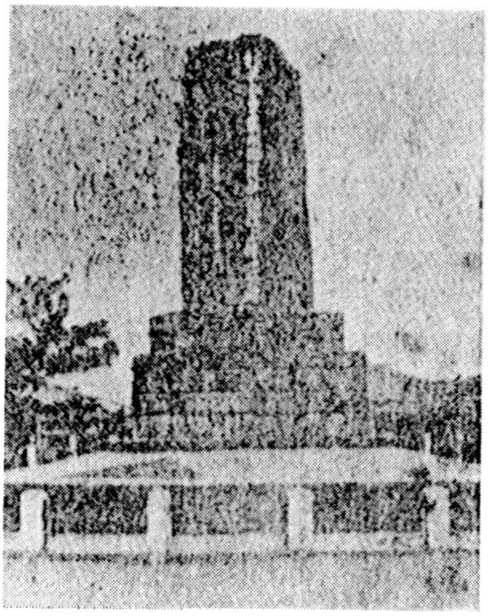

Monument at Landing-Place of Commodore Perry. (Erected July 14, 1901).

Rear-Admiral L. A. Beardslee was a naval cadet on board the U.S.N. "Plymouth" when Commodore Perry visited Japan as a messenger of peace in 1853.

In October, 1900, Rear-Admiral and Mrs. Beardslee came to Japan on a sight-seeing tour and the first place they visited on landing at Yokohama was Kurihama, where forty-seven years before Perry had landed. What was his disappointment to find that the landing place of the Commodore, whose coming to Japan in 1853 was epoch-making in her history, had been left quite unmarked.

Acting on the suggestion of Admiral Beardslee for marking the place, the America's Friends' Association, whose membership consisted of those Japanese who stayed in or visited the United States of America, appointed a committee for drawing up plans to raise the necessary funds for erecting a monument at Kurihama. The appeal made by the America's Friends' Association was quickly responded to, and the monument was completed on July 6, 1901. It is made of granite obtained in Miyagi prefecture, and it measures 15 ft. high, 8 ft. wide and 1.3 ft. thick, and weighs about ten tons. It stands on a foundation of stone taken from the Tone River, 18 ft. high, 11 ft. wide and 5 ft. thick, weighing nine tons, so that in all the monument stands 33 ft. high.

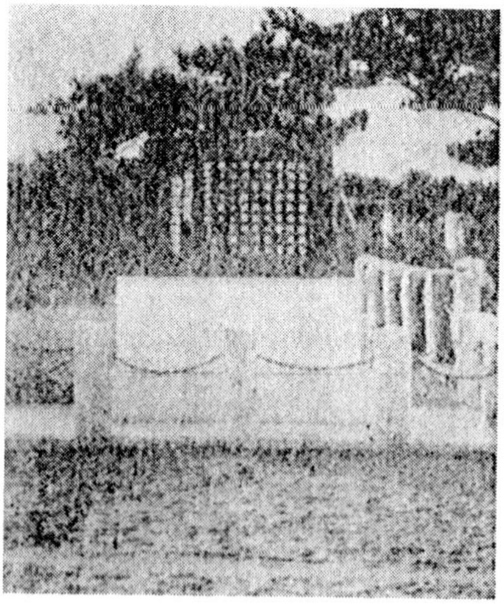

Monument of Commodore Perry Monument Preservation Society.

(*Continued*)

COMMODORE PERRY MONUMENT (2)—*Concluded*

The ceremony of unveiling the monument took place on July 14, 1901, or the 47th anniversary of the landing at Kurihama of Commdore Perry in 1853. The function proved very attractive and was attended by quite a large number of prominent people, both Japanese and foreign. The U. S. Government sent the three men-of-war, "New York," "Yorktown" and "New Orleans," commanded by Rear-Admiral F. Rogers, grandson of Commodore Perry. It was Rear-Admiral Rogers, who unveiled the monument.

The Japanese inscription on the front consists of sixteen Chinese ideograms meaning "Monument marking the landing place of Commodore Perry, U.S.A.", and on the back the Japanese reads "Landed June 9, 1853 (old calendar); erected July 14, 1901."

Kurihama, where the Commodore Perry Monument stands, is a fishing town, although it was a small village when Commodore Perry arrived in 1853. It is situated near Yokosuka at the southern end of the peninsula of Miura. Kurihama can be easily reached direct from Miyanoshita as well as from Tokyo and Yokohama. A government railway runs direct from Tokyo, via Yokohama and Kamakura. One can reach Kurihama in less than two hours from Tokyo. And there is a good motor road running from Tokyo and Yokohama to Kurihama.

One can motor from Miyanoshita to Kurihama. A government railway runs from Odawara, near Miyanoshita, to Kurihama, although one has to change trains at Ofuna, near Kamakura.

THIS MONUMENT
COMMEMORATES
The First Arrival
OF
COMMODORE PERRY
AMBASSADOR FROM THE
UNITED STATES OF AMERICA
WHO LANDED AT THIS PLACE
JULY 14, 1853
ERECTED JULY 14, 1901
BY
AMERICA'S FRIENDS' ASSOCIATION

TOWNSEND HARRIS MONUMENT

In memory of Townsend Harris, the first U.S. consular representative in Japan, a stone monument inlaid with a carved bronze plate of his head was erected by the America's Friends' Association in the compound of the Zempuku-ji (literally, Good-fortune), a Buddhist temple situated at the foot of the Sendaizaka Hill of Azabu, Tokyo. It was unveiled on Dec. 19, 1936.

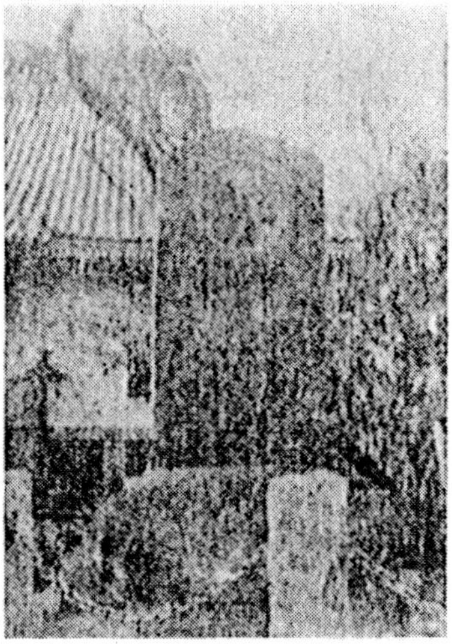
Townsend Harris Monument.

Townsend Harris was appointed Consul-general in Japan on Aug. 4, 1855, on the recommendation of Commodore Matthew Calbraith Perry and arrived at Shimoda, Izu Peninsula, on Aug. 21, 1856. In November, 1857, Harris came to Edo, the Shogunate capital (Tokyo), to conclude a treaty with Japan. This was signed at Kanagawa in June, 1858.

Harris was appointed U. S. Minister to Japan on Jan. 7, 1859, and he established at the Zempuku-ji Temple the American legation in Japan, the first diplomatic establishment of any foreign country in Tokyo. He remained until his retirement in 1862, and he died on Feb. 25, 1878. He lies buried in the Greenwood Cemetery, Brooklyn.

The American legation remained in the Zempuku-ji Temple until 1873, though the part of the temple where Harris stayed was destroyed by fire in 1863.

Harris used to say that he might tempt a patriotic Japanese to commit murder if he went out for a walk, of which he was very fond. In stead of going out of the temple, therefore, Harris took his exercise on the veranda of the temple till it was entirely worn out under his shoes. This veranda was lost when a fire destroyed a part of the temple several years ago, but most rooms of the temple where Harris lived are still preserved, and many articles that he used while there are exhibited in them. They are open to every tourist who visits the temple.

The Sakasa-icho: The gigantic gingko-tree of the temple is said to have grown up from a staff that Priest Shinran, the founder of the Jodo sect of Buddhism in Japan, put into the ground. It is called "Sakasa-icho" (inverted-gingko-tree).

The U.S. flag was hoisted on the top of an icho or gingko-tree that stood before his residence in the compound of the temple. The tree died some time ago, but a new gingko-tree has grown up at the same place where the old tree stood.

GENERAL GRANT'S TREES (1)

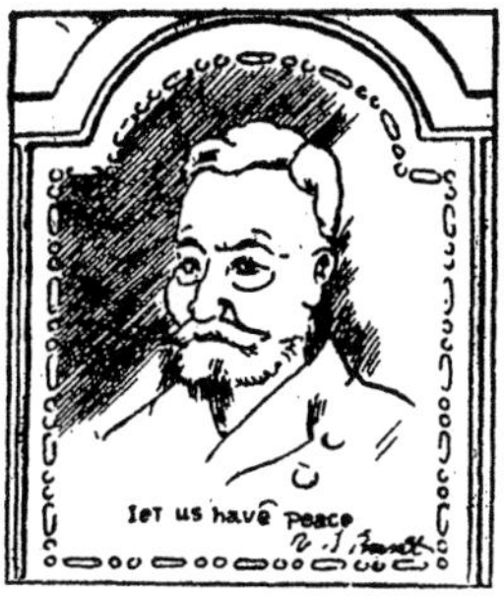

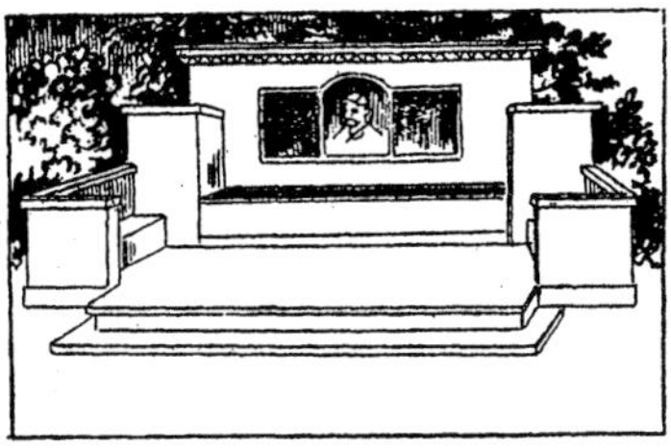

Ulysses Simpson Grant came to Japan on July 3, 1879, on a world tour he made after his second term as President of the U.S.A. was completed. During his stay in Tokyo, a reception was given at Uyeno Park in his honour by the Tokyo Municipality, where many classical games, which the Emperar Meiji honoured with his presence, such as shooting, fencing, and dog-racing, were shown for his entertainment. On Aug. 10, the Emperor Meiji proceeded to the Hama Detached Palace, where General Grant was received in audience at the Nakanoshima Tea Pavillion.

MEMORIAL TREES

planted by

General and Mrs. Ulysses S. Grant

General Ulysses Simpson Grant, ex-President of the United States of America, arrived at Nagasaki in 1879, whereupon Meiji Tenno despatched an Imperial envoy and a warship to greet him. On his arrival in Tokyo, July 3rd, the General was hailed with great enthusiasm by its leading citizens. Meiji Tenno welcomed him as the guest of the nation and placed the Hama Detached Palace at his disposal.

Imperial audiences, sight-seeing, and various kinds of entertainment were arranged for him. On August 25th, the final entertainment was held in honour of General and Mrs. Grant in Ueno Park, at which Meiji Tenno was graciously present.

In commemoration of this event, General Grant planted a hinoki (Cypressus lawsoniana), and Mrs. Grant a gyokuran (Magnolia grandiflora), both of which have grown thick and tall. But few people know the history of the trees. Therefore, we who had the privilege of participating in the welcome event fifty years ago, have erected this memorial tablet near them.

Viscount EIICHI SHIBUSAWA
Baron TAKASHI MASUDA

August 1929

(Continued)

GENERAL GRANT'S TREES (2)—*Concluded*

In commemoration of their visit to Tokyo, General and Mrs. Grant planted a hinoki (Cypressus lawsoniana) and a gyokuran (Magnolia grandiflora), respectively, in front of the Toshogu Shrine dedicated to Iyeyasu Tokugawa, in Uyeno Park. The General planted a pine-tree also in the precincts of the Zojo-ji Temple in Shiba Park. These trees, which were no more than a foot high when planted, are now gigantic trees, and tourists from the U.S.A. constantly visit them.

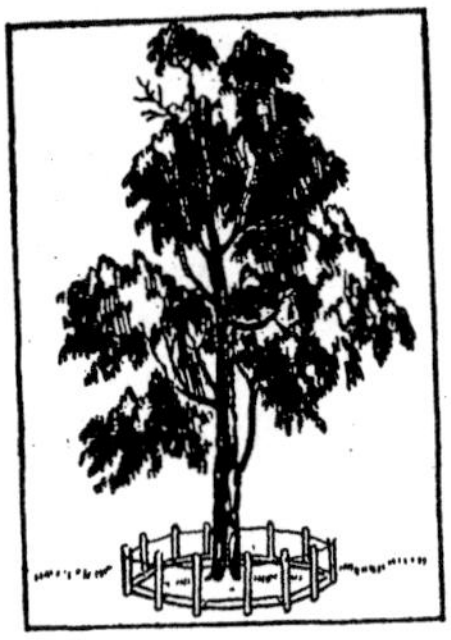

Grant Hinoki
Planted by Gen. U. S. Grant
August 25th 1879

Cypressus lawsoniana

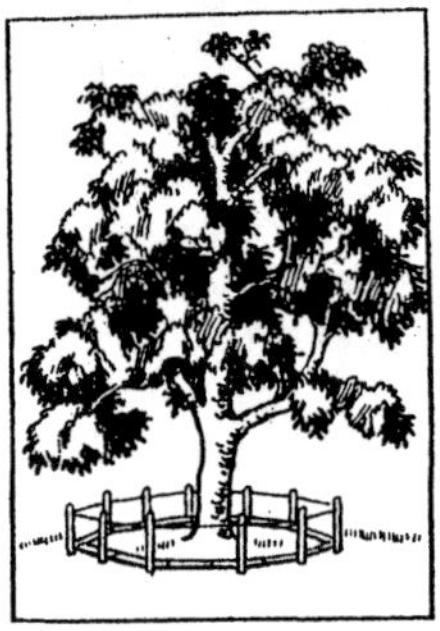

Grant Gyokuran
Planted by Mrs. Grant
August 25th 1879

Magnolia grandiflora

GRANT'S TREES AT UYENO PARK

GRANT PINE

Planted by General Ulysses S. Grant, 18th President of the United States of America, in July, 1879, when he visited Japan on his tour round the world with Mrs. Grant and their youngest son. During their stay in Japan they were guests of honour of the Emperor Meiji.

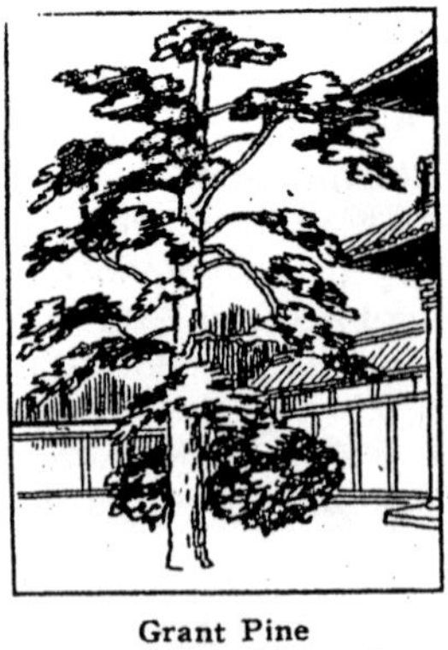

Grant Pine
at the Zojo-ji Temple

THE OLD TOKAIDO ROAD

Guests arriving from Odawara traverse a part of the old Tokaido ("East Sea Road"), between Odawara and the suspension bridge across the Hayakawa ("Rapid River"), below Yumoto. Guests who come or go by motor or bus between Yokohama-Miyanoshita (45 miles) journey for the greater part of the way over this road—which runs through regions famous in the history of Japan.

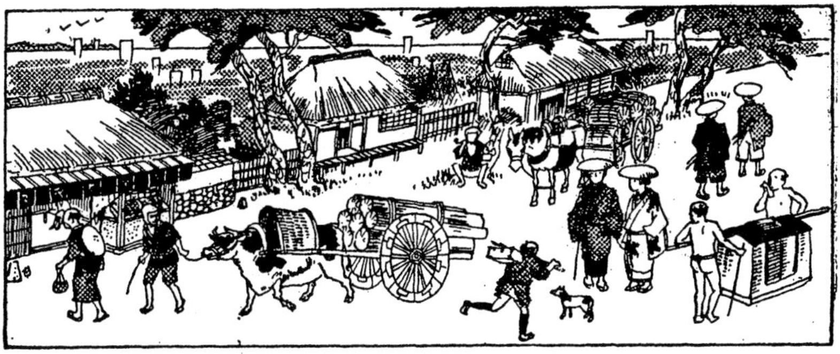

One of the Fifty-three Stages.

Along the Tokaido in feudal days passed gorgeous processions of the *daimyo*, or local lords, on their way to and from *Yedo* (Tokyo) and Kyoto. It was the main highway in the Eastern parts of Japan, and before the advent of railways it was crowded with a constant stream of traffic. Under an edict of the Shogun, *daimyo* and their wives were compelled to reside in Yedo for stipulated periods. This was done so that under the watchful eye of the Shogun there would be less tendency among powerful clans to rebel against the Shogunate government. Furthermore, the tremendous cost of these *daimyo* trains with their hundreds of retainers prevented the accumulation of funds necessary to equip and move armed forces. There were 53 post-stations where the *daimyo* stayed overnight. These have been immortalized in *Hiroshige's* color-print series: *The Fifty-three Stations of the Tokaido.*

The road is noted for its bordering pines which in places meet overhead, forming sylvan tunnels. In places age, the needs of an expanding populace, and the widening of the road for modern traffic have thinned out these trees, but there still remain enough of them for travelers to realize how beautiful the road must have been in feudal days and what interesting sights must have been presented by the vast number of people, mostly foot-travelers, along its entire route.

An interesting trip is to proceed by motor car or bus from the Fujiya Hotel to Lake Hakone, and there connect with the Tokaido bus line, rejoining the Miyanoshita road at the suspension bridge, which occupies the site of the old feudal bridge, thence journeying back to the hotel by bus, or on to Odawara, if desired. In many places along this route may still be seen the large stones which paved this winding road through the Hakone District. From it the views of mountains, sea and shore line are worthwhile.

THE FIFTY THREE STAGES OF THE TOKAIDO (1)

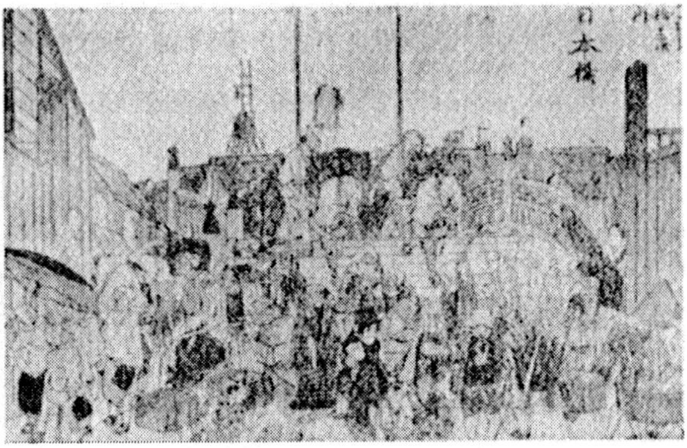

Old Nihombashi Bridge.

The Tokaido is one of the Eight Do's (literally, Roads) or Districts into which Japan was in feudal days and still is divided besides Kinai; namely, Tokaido (East-sea-road), Tosan-do (East-mountain-road), Hokuriku-do (North-land-road), San-yo-do (Mountain-sunshine-road), San-in-do (Mountain-shade-road), Nan-kai-do (South-sea-road), Sai-kai-do (West-sea-road) and Hokkai-do (North-sea-road), and the Tokaido consists of fifteen provinces, which are:

Iga	Ise	Shima	Owari	Mikawa
Totomi	Suruga	Kai	Izu	Sagami
Musashi	Awa	Kazusa	Shimosa	Hitachi

The first mention of the Tokaido was made in the Nihonshoki (720 A.D.) in connection with the appointment by the Emperor Sujin (the 10th) of Shido-Shogun (or Generals for Four Roads), of whom Takenunakawa was sent to the Tokaido, and this district has played an important role ever since in the history of Japan. Prince Yamatotake, for instance, came to Suruga, one of its provinces, on an expedition, during which he was attacked by the rebels who set fire to the grass around him. The prince defended himself by cutting the grass down with the Imperial sword, one of the Regalia, which from this incident was named Kusanagi-no-Tsurugi or Grass-cutting-sword. The two important shrines, the Kashima and Katori, are situated in the province of Shimosa. Then Yoritomo, of the Minamoto family, was the founder of Kamakura, where he established the Shogunate Government. Nobunaga, Hideyoshi and Iyeyasu, the founders of the Shogunate dynasties of Oda, Toyotomi and Tokugawa, respectively, hailed from this Do of Tokaido. During the Tokugawa regime, which lasted for a little over two centuries and a half, the Tokaido was perhaps the most important highway in Japan on account of the frequent communications made between the Imperial and Shogunate Governments at Kyoto and Edo (Tokyo), respectively.

(Continued)

THE FIFTY-THREE STAGES OF THE TOKAIDO (2)

Concluded

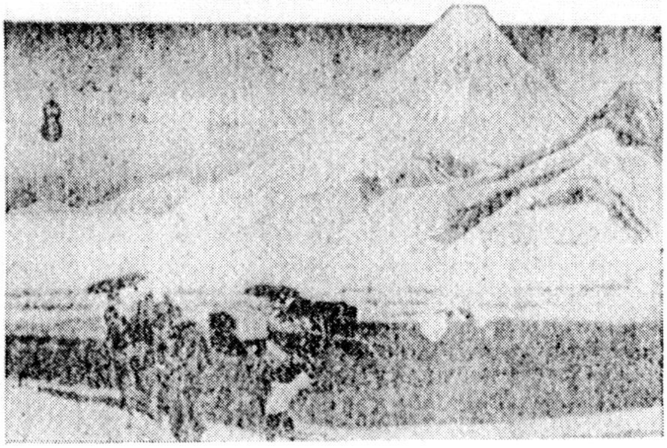

Mt. Fuji by Hiroshige.

The Tokaido is perpetuated by the immortal brush of Hiroshige, the Ukiyoye painter, who painted the "Fifty-three Stages of the Tokaido" between two capitals of the east and west. The Tokaido Railway is one of the main lines in Japan, and a quick train runs between Tokyo and Kyoto, 52[illegible].3 kilometers, in less than nine hours, but in feudal days it took an average pedestrian about two weeks, and an express messenger three or four days to cover the distance of 125 Japanese *ri* between the two capitals.

THE FIFTY-THREE STAGES OF THE TOKAIDO

Nihombashi	Fuchu	Fujikawa
Shinagawa	Maruko	Okazaki
Kawasaki	Okabe	Ikekoibuna
Kanagawa	Fujieda	Narumi
Hodogaya	Shimada	Miya
Totsuka	Kanaya	Kuwana
Fujisawa	Hisaka	Yokkaichi
Hiratsuka	Kakegawa	Ishiyakushi
Oiso	Fukuroi	Shono
Odawara	Mitsuke	Kameyama
Hakone	Hamamatsu	Seki
Mishima	Maisaka	Sakashita
Numazu	Arai	Tsuchiyama
Hara	Shirasuga	Mizuguchi
Yoshiwara	Futakawa	Ishibe
Kamahara	Yoshida	Kusatsu
Yui	Miabura	Otsu
Okitsu	Akasaka	Kyoto
Ejiri		

PRINCESS KONO-HANA-NO-SAKUYA-HIME

Name-sake of the Sakura or Cherry

When Prince Ninigi-no-Mikoto, popularly known as the Celestial Grandson because he was the grandson of the Goddess Amaterasu, ancestress of the Imperial family, was sent down to govern the earth, he alighted on Mt. Takachiho, at the foot of which the prince met a charming princess walking on the beach. "Who might you be?" the prince asked. The maid replied, "I am daughter of Oyamatsumi. My name is Kono-hana-no-Sakuya-Hime, and I have an elder sister, who is called Princess Iwanaga." When the prince asked her to marry him, she directed him to see her father, Prince Oyamatsumi, to ask for his permission. Oyamatsumi was so pleased to learn the wish of Prince Ninigi-no-Mikoto to marry one of his daughters that, by both daughters, he sent the prince a present of a hundred stands of food, so that by accepting them the prince might live as long as a rock, since the elder sister's name of Iwanaga suggested longevity (iwa = rock; naga = long-life). The younger sister's name stood for as great prosperity as that of flowers, her name meaning "Tree-flowers-blooming-princess." Prince Ninigi-no-Mikoto, however, accepted the younger sister, sending the elder sister back to her father. But when it was seen that Konohana-no-Sakuya-Hime was soon with child, the prince became suspicious and disowned the child. "I will go through fire," the suspected princess said to him, "and if I come out unhurt, the child is yours." The princess built an Uzumuro or doorless room, to which she set fire after secluding herself in it. But she was unhurt and the prince's doubts were dispelled. She is mother of Princes Ho-no-Teru-no-Mikoto, Ho-no-Suseri-no-Mikoto and Ho-no-Ori-no-Mikoto, the last-named being the grandfather of the Emperor Jimmu, the first of the Imperial line in Japan.

It is generally believed that "Sakuya" of Kono-hana-no-Sakuya-Hime has corrupted into "Sakura," which is the Japanese word for "cherry," and because the cherry-blossom is so well-known, the "tree-flowers" or "the flowers" was accepted to designate the cherry.

Few pines grow at Hakone. While Mt. Fuji and the Five-lake District abound in beautiful groves of pine-trees, Hakone and its vicinity are notorious for their lack of these trees, hardly any pines being found there excepting a few that were recently planted. According to tradition, Kono-hana-no-Sakuya-Hime once got one of her eyes hurt by a pine-needle. "No pine-trees shall ever grow in this part of the country," she said cursing the pine; hence few pines grow in Hakone and its vicinity, where the pious people will have no pine-decoration, but instead the sakaki-tree, before their gate at the New Year.

FAITHFUL UNTO DEATH

THE EMPRESS KEEPS HER PROMISE BY DEATH

"Which do you love better, your brother or your husband?" Prince Sahohiko asked his sister, Sahohime, in 26 B.C. She was the consort of the Emperor Suinin (the 11th) and had a baby-prince. She had little idea what her brother had in mind, and so innocently expressed her preference for her brother.

"Love is often replaced by love, sister," Prince Sahohiko went on. "You enjoy the exclusive love of the Emperor but he has many other ladies with him. You little know that some day you will entirely lose his love and affection. If therefore you will kill your husband on my behalf and help me to the Throne, you shall enjoy peace and happiness during the rest of your life."

When, soon after this, the Emperor visited the Empress at the Kume Palace, he took a nap with his head resting on her lap. This was a good chance for her, but she felt that sh could not commit regicide, yet neither could she disobey her brother. A tear trembled upon her eye-lids, and dropped upon the cheek of the sleeping Emperor.

"I had a queer dream" the Emperor said, waking up. "I had a small snake of brocade-colour about my neck and I was caught in a shower coming from the direction of Mt. Saho (after which Sahohiko and Sahohime were named.) I wonder what this dream portends."

"The small snake of brocade-colour, my lord, is the cord of the dagger I have, hidden here," the Empress replied, taking out the dagger her brother had handed her. "And the shower was my own tears." Then she went on to tell the Emperor all about the dark plot hatched by her brother, asking the Emperor to forgive him.

"You are innocent, so do not worry," the kind Emperor said to the Empress, but soon after he sent a punitive force against Sahohiko, who built a fort of rice-straw, which withstood the siege of the Imperial army for over a year.

"I shall be held responsible for the death of my brother," the Empress said to herself. "If my brother is killed, how can I avoid criticism and remain as Empress?"

Taking therefore her baby-prince, Sahohime ran into the straw-fort where her brother had entrenched himself, and no words of the Emperor could bring her out of it. At last the straw-fort was set on fire. Then the Empress, carrying the young prince in her arms, came out to the gate of the fort.

"I came into the fort" she said "in the hope that I might save my brother. But all is over now. I cannot outlive him, for I hold myself responsible for his death. The prince belongs to the Emperor, to whom he must be taken." "When I am gone," the Empress added after delivering the prince, "I should like the Emperor to marry one of the five daughters of the governor of Tamba Province, who are all reputed for fidelity and truthfulness."

The fort was burned down and Sahohime with her brother was burned to death. That was in the year of 24 B.C.

The Emperor Suinin, respecting the last wish of his faithful lamented wife, married Princess Hihasuhime, daughter of the governor of Tamba Province. She was the mother of the Emperor Keiko (the 12th).

SALT SUPPLIED TO INVETERATE FOE

THE MAGNANIMITY OF LORD UYESUGI

Terutora Uyesugi (also called Kenshin) and Harunobu Takeda (also called Shingen) were two great warlords and tacticians who fought each other at Kawanaka-jima in Shinano Province. They fought for over twelve years. The Kai clan, of which Taketa was lord, has no seas and it depended for the supply of salt upon its neighbouring clans. In 1567 Ujisato Imagawa and Ujiyasu Hojo, lords of his two neighbour-clans, made a secret agreement to supply the Kai clan with no salt. So Taketa was in great distress because of the shortage of salt.

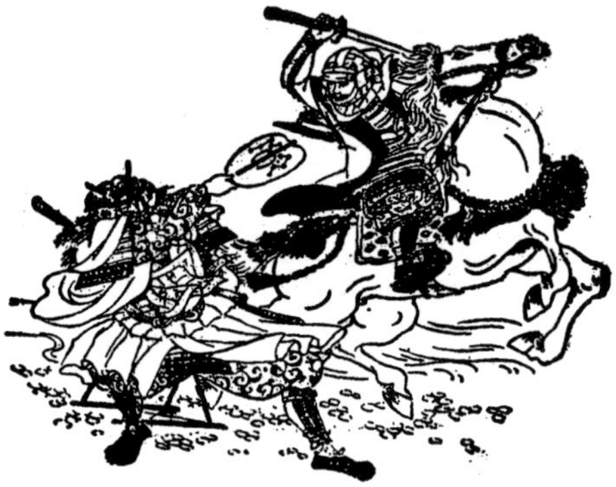

Uyesugi striking at Taketa at Kawanaka-jima.

Terutora Uyesugi, who heard of this inhuman act of stopping such an article of daily need, was indignant with Imagawa and Hojo, and he expressed his sympathy with his mortal enemy by offering salt to him.

" We have been fighting each other all these years," Uyesugi said to Taketa through a messenger, "but we mean nothing base, for we are meeting each other in fair play. It is mean of Imagawa and Hojo to cut off your supply of salt, which is an article of daily necessity. We have plenty of salt in my provinces. If you need salt, we can supply you with any quantity that you may require. I will see that it is supplied at a reasonable price."

Taketa and his clan were very grateful for this humane act of Uyesugi's.

Taketa died in 1573. When the news of his death reached the Kasuga castle, Uyesugi was taking his meal. He stopped his eating, spat out all food he had in his mouth, rinsed it in order to pay his respects to the deceased lord. And for three days, Uyesugi prohibited music in his clan in mourning for his inveterate foe.

Terutora Uyesugi died a little later in the same year, and before his death, he wrote a 31-syllable ode, which reads in effect:

" Whether Paradise or Hell,
My way is as right as a full moon
And my heart no less free of the clouds."

LADY KAZUTOYO YAMANOUCHI

One day in the autumn of 1578 there came to the Azuchi castle of Lord Nobunaga Oda, in the province of Ohmi, a horse-dealer from Sendai, a town famous for its fine horses in the northern part of Japan. He had with him a splendid stallion, which was too dear for any samurai of the clan to buy. Kazutoyo Yamanouchi, a low-rank samurai of promise, felt very sorry that he could not buy the horse and went home quite dejected.

"What is it that ails you?" his wife asked when he got home. "It is nothing that concerns a woman," was the cold reply, for in feudal days a samurai considered it a shame or something socially undignified to consult his wife on any matter relating to his duties. He appeared so disappointed, however, that his worried wife insisted upon knowing the nature of his trouble.

"There came a horse-dealer from Sendai," Yamanouchi said at last, "and he has a fine stallion, finer than any that we have here in the castle. But it is so dear that no samurai of the clan can afford to buy it, and I fear he may have to take the horse back. Its possession would mean immediate promotion for me. Nothing is harder indeed than poverty in this life."

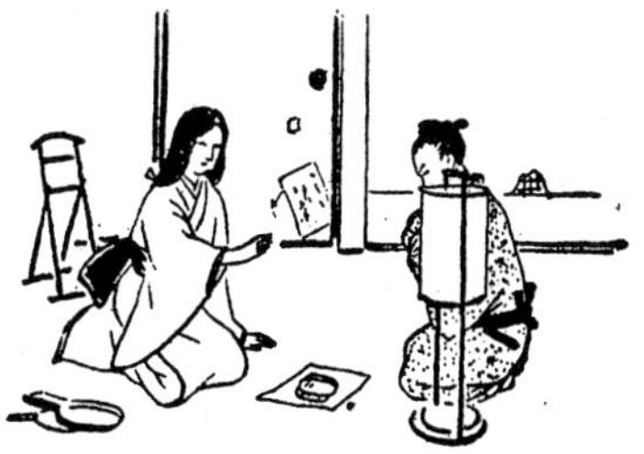

"How much is the horse?" his sympathetic wife asked, after listening to what her husband had to tell her. "Why, ten *ryo* of gold, and the dealer would take no less," Yamanouchi sighed crest-fallen. "Here is ten *ryo*" his wife said, offering her husband ten pieces of gold, which she took out of the drawer of her mirror-stand. "Take this and buy the horse." "Where on earth did you get this large sum of money?" demanded the surprised husband evidently in ecstacy.

"My mother gave it to me when I married," his wife said simply. "I have kept it in my mirror-stand all these years." "When my mother gave it to me," she went on to explain, "she told me never to spend it except on a thing of great consequence to my husband. When we were poverty-stricken, you being out of employment, for a long time, I never thought of using this money, but my mother's words always rang in my ears and I restrained myself. I am glad that I have not waited in vain. Take then the money immediately and buy the horse before it is too late."

There was a horse-display in the Azuchi castle a few days later, and Lord Oda took notice of the specially fine horse which Yamanouchi rode. The lord was very much pleased when it was explained how Yamanouchi, though of a low rank as samurai, had managed to buy the horse. "Double his allowance at once," Lord Oda said, "not because he owns that fine horse, but because he saved us from shame and dishonour. If the horse-dealer had gone back taking the horse, we should have been made a laughing-stock for having no samurai who could buy one horse."

Later on Yamanouchi was created a local daimyo or lord in the province of Tosa.

MADAM GALATIA, WIFE OF TADAOKI HOSOKAWA (1)

Lady Komano, wife of Lord Tadaoki Hosokawa, was daughter of Mitsuhide Akechi, a favorite lord of Shogun Nobunaga Oda. When Akechi assassinated Lord Oda in 1582 for personal grievances, Hosokawa, who was a daimyo on the side of the assassinated Shogun, divorced his wife, Lady Komano, because he did not wish to be called the husband of a woman whose father had committed regicide. Lady Komano returned no word of protest, but silently obeyed her husband, and taking leave of him lived a retired and solitary life in the mountains of Mitsuno in the province of Tamba.

Her mother was a pious lady, who always told her daughter to be true and faithful in all circumstances. Lady Komano therefore remained true to her mother's wise counsel. After the separation from her husband, Lady Komano was often sneered at as the daughter of a traitor, so that some of her friends even advised her to commit suicide.

"I know it is much harder to live in this way than to die," she said, "But it is cowardly to choose the easier way. Separated as I am from my husband, I am nevertheless still his wife. How can I commit suicide without his order? If my death is justified, my husband will send me word to that effect, and it will not be too late to die after I receive his instructions."

Hers was indeed a life of faith and devotion, for she was entirely given to praying for the repose of her departed father and mother. Her mother had died soon after her father had assassinated Oda. She also prayed fervently for the prosperity of her husband. News of her chastity and loyalty reached the ears of Hideyoshi Taiko. He therefore told Hosokawa to call back his divorced wife, so that Lady Komano was reunited to her husband in 1591, after a separation of some ten years.

It was after her reunion with Hosokawa that she learned of Christianity. One Takayama, a tea-master, who was very intimate with her father-in-law and a faithful believer in Christ, told her about his religion. Interested now in the teachings of Christ, Lady Komano, in disguise, made frequent visits to the Christian church, and when she could not attend it herself, she sent her lady attendant in her place. She was now determined to be baptized in spite of her difficult situation; and, she even told her Christian Father that she was willing to go to church in a coffin if necessary. This was of course a sin, and her confessor immediately told her so. He promised, moreover, to authorize her lady-in-waiting to give her baptism. Lady Komano was therefore baptized by her maid, and her baptismal name was Galatia, by which she was called among her Christian friends.

After her baptism, Madam Galatia studied Portuguese and Latin very diligently so that she might read the Scriptures and books of devotion.

Upon returning from Kyushu, where he had been sent on an expedition, Hosokawa found his wife almost a fanatic in her belief in Christianity, and no efforts whatever on his part could dissuade his wife from what he considered her folly. She would not on any account give up her faith even at the cost of her life.

(*Continued*)

MADAM GALATIA, WIFE OF TADAOKI HOSOKAWA (2)

Concluded

In May of 1600, Hosokawa was sent by Iyeyasu Tokugawa to lead an army against Kagekatsu Uyesugi in Aizu Province. Hosokawa knew that if he went east, Mitsunari Ishida, who was jealous of Tokugawa, would take Lady Komano as a hostage or prisoner. So Hosokawa left a 31-syllable poem with his wife, which read:

"*Nabiku-na yo, Waga Mase-gaki no Ominayeshi,*
Otokoyama yori Kaze wa fuku tomo."

Translated, the poem means in effect:

"Do not yield, Ominayeshi of my hedge,
Even though a wind should blow from Mt. Otoko."

Ominayeshi or patrinia scabiosaefolia, which is a tender plant, is often compared to the weaker sex, and Otoko means "man." Hence the poem implies that weak as Lady Komano was, like an ominayeshi-plant, she must not yield even when an adverse wind might blow from the mountain of man.

Sure enough, soon after the departure of her husband on the expedition, Lady Komano received a message from Mitsunari Ishida inviting her to come to the castle of Osaka. She at once replied that because her husband was away from home, she could not leave it. The message was repeated three times, and she replied in the same way. Then the indignant Mitsunari sent a few soldiers on the 16th of July, 1600, to take Lady Komano prisoner.

"Unreasonable as the enemy are," Lady Komano said to her people when she heard of the troops coming against her, "they belong to the Toyotomi family, to which we are too much indebted to raise our hands against the attacking troops." This she said because Mitsunari Ishida was one of the Shogunate ministers of Toyotomi.

Then she called to her side her two sons, one ten years old and the other nine, and explained the situation to them. She told them to be prepared for death as become sons of a samurai rather than be humiliated by the enemy. "We understand, mother," they said with one voice. "Say good-bye to your father and grandfather" she said, and they repeated it saying "Good-bye, father. Good-bye, grandfather," clasping their hands innocently in veneration, when their mother, steeling her heart, struck at them. Just at this moment, Shosai Ogasawara, a faithful retainer came in with a halberd.

"Shosai, help me," Lady Komano said to him, as she tried to lift her hair to receive the sword on her neck.

"That's not the way, Madam," Shosai explained. At this she bared her breast for him, saying: "Now then."

"But I cannot. Please move forth a little," he asked, since there was not enough room for him to cross the threshold of his mistress's chamber.

"With your permission," said Shosai, lifting his halberd. Then Galatia plunged forward and died upon the halberd.

Shosai also committed suicide on the verandah, and Galatia's ladies-in-waiting all followed their mistress's example, except one by the name of Shino, whom Komano ordered to survive her to tell her husband about the last moments of her mistress. Then Shino disguised herself as a maid-servant and escaped out of the castle to carry the message of Galatia's noble death to her Lord, Tadaoki Hosokawa.

KAGA-NO-CHIYO, GREATEST HOKKU-POETESS (1)

Every Japanese admits that Kaga-no-Chiyo is the greatest *Hokku*-poetess Japan has produced, *Hokku* being an ode of seventeen syllables. She has left many *Hokku* odes which are familiar to the Japanese.

When Chiyo married a man named Fukuoka at Kanazawa, she wrote an ode reading:

"*Shibu karo ka*
Shiranedo Kaki no
Hatsu-chigiri."

The ode as it stands means:

"Whether astringent or not,
I know not,
But this is my first picking of a persimmon."

But the play is upon the word "Hatsu-chigiri," which homonymously means "first picking" and "first engagement." In the ode Chiyo means to say that she will marry for the first time though she does not know whether her married life will be happy or not, like the picking of the first persimmon, of which one cannot tell whether it will be astringent or not.

But her married life was "astringent" and it did not last long, for she lost her husband when she was 27 years old. She wrote an ode on his death:

"*Oki-te mitsu*
Nete mitsu Kaya no
Hirosa kana."

Rough translated:

"I sit up and see;
I lie up and see;
O how wide the mosquito net is!"

When her only son died, who used to hunt dragon-flies, she expressed her grief in the following poem:

"*Tombo-tsuri*
Kyo wa dokomade
Itta yara."

"The dragon-fly catcher—
How far today,
Has he gone, I wonder!"

(*Continued*)

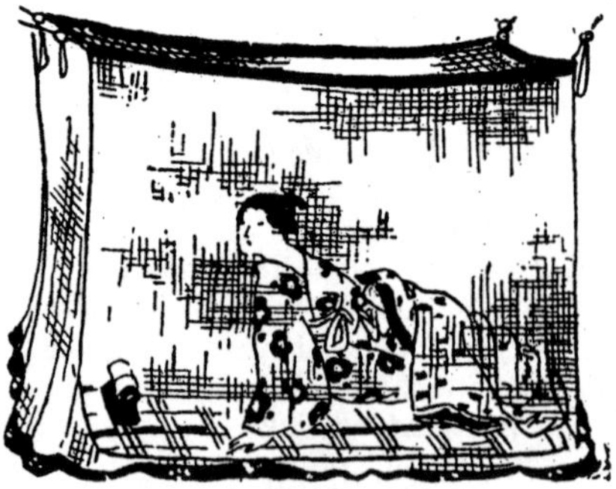

Chiyo in a mosquito-net.

KAGA-NO-CHIYO, GREATEST HOKKU-POETESS (2)

Concluded

In neither of these two odes, does Chiyo describe her sorrow direct, though it is fully implied in them, for implication is often more eloquent than expression.

A friend of hers sent her the following 17-syllable ode:

"*Hana sakanu*
Mi wa shizuka naru
Yanagi kana."

"One who bears no flowers
Leads as quiet a life
As does a willow-tree."

To this Chiyo replied in a *Hokku* also, reading:

"*Hana sakanu*
Mi wa kurui yoki
Yanagi kana."

"One who bears no flowers
Can act as freely
As can a willow-tree."

Her friend meant that one who has not the flowers of life leads as quiet a life as that of a willow-tree, which is not bothered by crowds of people who come to see its flowers. Chiyo, however, corrects it in her ode, which means that, as she has no flowers, her husband and son having died, she can act as freely as does a willow-tree, which having no flowers can toss about as the wind blows, without any fear of the flowers being shaken off.

Kaga-no-Chiyo died in 1795 at the age of 74 years. Her *Jisei* or death-bed ode reads:

"*Tsuki mo mite*
Ware wa Kono-Yo wo
Kashiku kana."

"Having viewed the moon even
I take leave of this life
With a blessing."

Her idea is: Of all things she has viewed, the moon is the most beautiful, and she has no wish to linger on in this life, which she leaves with her blessing.

THE SHOGITAI MILITARY UNIT

When, after the battle of Toba in January, 1868, Yoshinobu Tokugawa, the 15th Shogun, was determined to restore the administration to the Imperial Government, his dissatisfied loyal warriors held a secret meeting at the Entsu-ji Temple, Yotsuya, to discuss the question of supporting the Shogun. At their second meeting, which was held at the Hongan-ji Temple, Asakusa, they numbered over 500, and calling themselves the Shogitai, meaning "righteousness-upholding-party," pledged themselves to stand to the last by their master, the Shogun Yoshinobu Tokugawa, who had been put on his good behaviour at the Daiji-in Temple, Ueno. Meanwhile the castle of Edo was delivered to the Imperial Government on April 4, and soon after Edo was re-named Tokyo or "East-city" in contrast to Saikyo or "West-city," as Kyoto is sometimes called.

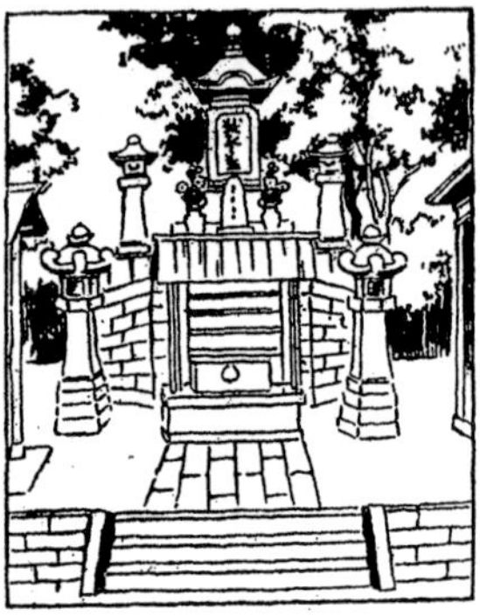
Graves of the Shogitai unit.

But the loyal warriors of the Shogun were disgruntled with the surrender of the castle, and the Kan-yei-ji Temple, the family temple of Tokugawa, gave every facility to the pro-Shogunate troops. When Yoshinobu Tokugawa left Tokyo for Mito, where he remained on his good behaviour, the Imperial army ordered the disbanding of the pro-Shogunate malcontents, including the Shogi-tai, Jinchu-tai, Byakko-tai, Garyu-tai, Manji-tai, Shimboku-tai, etc. who demanded that their ex-Shogun be appropriately appointed by the Emperor. They refused the order, so the Imperial army of some 15,000 strong, under the command of Masujiro Omura, whose statue now stands on Kudan Hill, made its general attack from three directions, on the pro-Shogunate troops. The Shogun's troops offered strong resistance, but brave as they were, they proved no match for the united forces of the six local clans, which, constituting the Imperial Expeditionary Army, soon occupied Ueno. The Kan-yei-ji Temple quickly caught fire and all its main buildings were reduced to ashes.

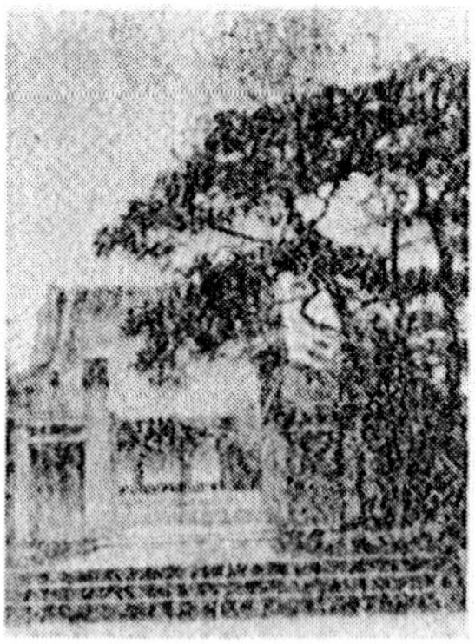
Kan-yei-ji Tempie.

After the bloody battle of Ueno, eighty-three slain pro-Shogunate warriors were left uncared for on the battle-field, because they were anti-Imperialists. Priest Bukki, of the Entsu-ji Temple, with government permission, therefore buried them after cremation, and he set up a grave-stone over them. In 1875 a monument was erected on the place of their cremation to the memory of the loyal pro-Shogunate warriors. It is 25.2 ft. high, and its simple Japanese inscription composed by Tetsutaro Yamaoka, a retainer of the Shogunate Government, reads: "The grave of the fallen in battle." A Buddhist service is held in their honour before their grave on May 5 every year.

THE LOYAL SUICIDE OF MUNEHARU SHIMIZU (1)

The Shogun Nobunaga Oda was desirous of taking possession of the western part of the San-yo or, as it is popularly known, Chugoku (Central Province) District, which belonged to Terumoto Mori, and Hideyoshi Toyotomi leading the van of 30,000 strong, arrived at Okayama, near the eastern frontier of the district, on the 15th of the 3rd month, 1582. Lord Mori had built seven castles on the frontier in his defence, and Muneharu Shimizu was appointed to take charge of the Takamatsu Castle, the strongest of them. It was garrisoned by only 5,000 troops and its fall or surrender would prove fatal to Lord Mori. So Hideyoshi was anxious to capture the castle.

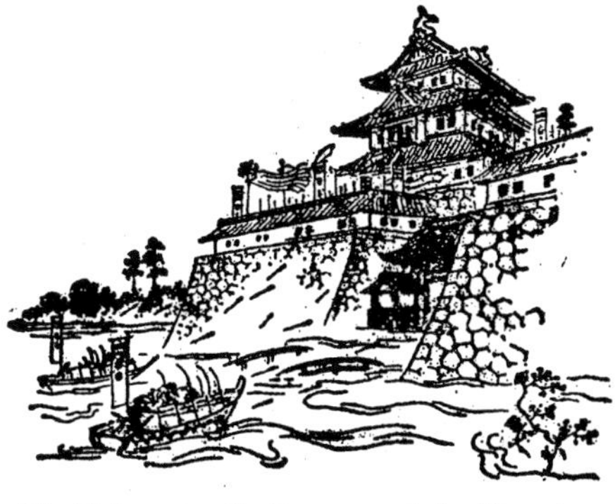
The Takamatsu Castle surrounded with water.

Lord Mori was no less aware of the importance of Takamatsu Castle so he offered to increase the feudal allowance made to Shimizu.

"No, my lord" Shimizu said, declining the promotion. "I am going to defend the castle at the risk of my own life against the odds of the enemy. Because Toyotomi invites many of our local chiefs with a lucrative offer, I may be suspected of betraying you. No, my lord, I have pledged my loyalty and I would not accept your offer at any cost."

Hideyoshi evidently made light of the small garrison, and thought he could capture the castle in no time. But every attack he made was repulsed by the brave garrison. One day Hideyoshi sent Lords Kuroda and Hachisuka as messengers of peace into the castle and offered Shimizu the whole province of Bitchu if he would surrender.

"No loyal samurai serves two lords," Shimizu replied resolutely. "I have been appointed keeper of this castle by Lord Mori, my master, who has full trust in me. It becomes the samurai of the Chugoku District to be tempted by no idea of gain or profit. We consider righteousness before life. You might offer me the whole land of Japan, but it would not move me in the least."

A short time later Kuroda visited Shimizu again by himself and said: "Lord Oda holds sway over the country. A wretched future awaits you, however persistent you may be. Ponder the matter carefully, and your future too, for you will enjoy a longer future if you come over to Lord Oda."

But Shimizu remained adamant, only repeating what he had said before. Finally he added: "I am determined to die in the cause of my master by sharing the same fate as this castle. It is my duty to the lord, who has been kind to me all these years. Say no more, but let us meet each other on the battle-field." *(Continued)*

THE LOYAL SUICIDE OF MUNEHARU SHIMIZU (2)

When every effort had proved abortive to capture the castle, Hideyoshi decided on what is known as Mizu-zeme (water-attack). By this the castle was to be surrounded with water from the River Ashimori. It is said that the dams built by the Toyotomi troops measured 28 *cho* (*cho*=360 Jap. ft.) 20 *ken* (*ken*=6 ft.) long, 4 *ken* high and 12 *ken* wide, costing 63,504 *koku* (*koku*=4 bushels) of rice and 635,040 *kan* (*kan*=10 sen in old currency) of coins, from the 7th to 19th of the 5th month. Then the Takamatsu Castle looked like a floating castle to the great glee of Hideyoshi, the leader of the besieging forces. The reinforcements of Lord Mori arrived on the 21st, but they could not approach the castle on account of the water, which was increasing every moment.

In the meantime Hideyoshi too asked for reinforcements, and the Shogun Oda leading an army of 35,000 strong was about to leave Kyoto for assistance, when Mitsuhide Akechi assassinated him on the eve of his departure. Mori then proposed peace by showing a samurai-like sympathy with Hideyoshi, who had lost his master. Hideyoshi accepted it on condition that Shimizu of the Takamatsu Castle should commit suicide, on account of his persistent resistance.

Shimizu was of course glad to die if his death could save his lord and troops of the besieged castle. Many of his brave warriors proposed to share death with him, but he permitted none of them to die. The sixth of the sixth month (June), 1582, was therefore appointed for his suicide.

On the day before, Shimizu put everything in order and wrote three 31-syllable poems for his son, who was taken as hostage by the enemy. When he had his face shaved, his attendant asked him what he had this cleansing himself before death for.

"My head will be taken to Lord Oda," Shimizu said in explanation. "If then my head and face were found to be unkempt with long hair, because of the siege which lasted for thirty-six days, the enemy would laugh at my having had hard times in the castle during the siege. This would be a shame to my lord's clan. I am not dying because I am defeated, but in order to save the lord and my men."

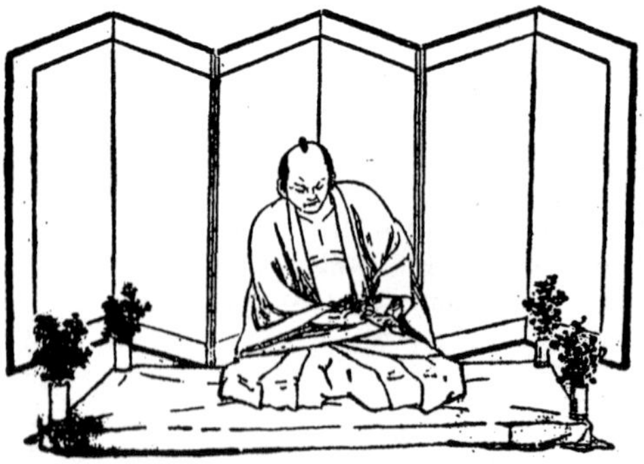

Hara-kiri.

THE LOYAL SUICIDE OF MUNEHARU SHIMIZU (3)

Concluded

On the evening before his suicide, Shimizu was called to the 2nd Citadel (Ni-no-maru) of the castle, where one Shirai, a special favorite of his, was garrisoned as keeper.

"You are to commit suicide tomorrow," Shirai said, after making an apology for calling his master to his keep. "I feared that it would prove disgraceful to you to behave yourself cowardly in the presence of the enemy's messenger tomorrow. I therefore have cut open my stomach in order to see whether or not suicide is hard. It is really easy, my lord, to commit suicide, so you need not feel worried about it."

So saying, Shirai uncovered his abdomen, which he had cut crosswise, and from which blood was gushing out.

"I thank you, Shirai," Shimizu said. "You have committed *hara-kiri* because you love me. You may therefore be sure that I will not be behaved cowardly or act disgracefully tomorrow. So be at ease." Shimizu then honoured his faithful retainer by "*kaishaku*," i.e., completed his suicide by cutting off his head.

On the sixth of the sixth month, at the time of the Snake (10 a.m.), Shimizu left the castle in a boat, in which a banquet was at once given with a sake and refreshments presented by Hideyoshi Toyotomi, his enemy. Shimizu acted calmly, evidently without minding death, which was so imminent. He drank and ate full and then suddenly stood up, sword in hand, to dance a piece of the *No* dance, after which he wrote his Jisei-poem (ode expressing farewell to the world):

"*Ukiyo oba*
Ima-koso watare
Mononofu no
Na wo Takamatsu no
Koke ni nokoshi te."

A free version:

I cross out of the Floating World,
leaving the name of a warrior on the
moss of Takamatsu (tall pine-tree)

He committed suicide in the presence of Mosuke Yokoo, the messenger from Hideyoshi Toyotomi. He was then 46 years old.

MISS UMEKO ISHIMOTO

THE HELEN KELLER OF JAPAN

Mark Twain, who said that Napoleon and Helen Keller were the two most interesting characters of the 19th century, (The Story of My life, p. 286) might have increased the number by one had he known Miss Umeko Ishimoto of Japan. She was born in Yokohama on July 7, 1874 and was just an average girl in looks. But Umeko San never knew the use of her limbs, which were paralysed at birth. She was therefore confined to bed all her life, and because her head was the only part of her body that she could move she was known by the nickname of the "Turtle-girl."

Now, Umeko San was an orphan, her parents having deserted her when she was a little child, so she was admitted to the orphanage run by Takejiro Yoshino. He took great pains to teach her how to read and write, so that after a time Umeko San could write as easily with her mouth as we do with our hand, and she always insisted on writing a letter of sympathy to anyone whom she heard to be afflicted with a lingering disease. Mr. Yoshino was a member of the Japan Methodist Church, Yokohama, so Miss Ishimoto embraced the Christian faith. She became such an optimistic Christian that she chose as her favorite text, "Godliness with contentment is great gain" (I Ti: VI, 6). And her favorite hymn was: "O Thou in whose presence my soul takes delight."

Mr. Yoshino trained her in the use of her mouth and she made truly marvellous development. Japanese children, for instance, fold pieces of paper into paper-boxes, paper-swallows, paper-storks, paper-flowers, etc., and Miss Ishimoto enjoyed herself by actually making such paper-toys with her mouth. She cut a piece of paper by handling a pair of scissors and a hair-pin with her mouth, just as easily as we do with our hands. Then she would fold the paper into a miniature paper-toy, which was so small that we could not do it even with the full use of our hands.

On the stand before her bed, there was a small doll, about three inches tall. It was beautifully dressed, and Umeko San would tell you that she had made the dress with her own mouth, and without anybody helping her at all. It was quite easy for her to thread a needle with her mouth. She put the point of the needle between leaves of a book and then threaded it with her tongue. Her step-father used to say: "Sewing was certainly a great and wonderful feat of Umeko's, who could work at it for days on end, if she was left with a needle, thread, a pair of scissors and a piece of cloth. But we were most surprised when we found that she could handle a razor. I lathered the head of each of my boys, and Umeko shaved it as closely and cleanly as I could. In fact, I used to leave the regular shaving of my boys to her 'mouth.'"

(Later, Miss Ishimoto was taken into the Municipal Orphanage of Yokohama, where she died in 1921.)

LIFE OF DEVOTION

KATSUGORO, THE CRIPPLE, AND HATSUHANA

A little farther up than To-no-Sawa, on your way to the Fujiya Hotel, Miyanoshita, from Odawara, you will notice a gigantic shii-tree (pasania), standing on the bank of the River Haya, under which tree, the bus-girl will explain, Katsugoro, the Cripple, and his devoted little wife, Hatsuhana (literally, First-flower) lived in a cottage. A small stone-monument marks the place.

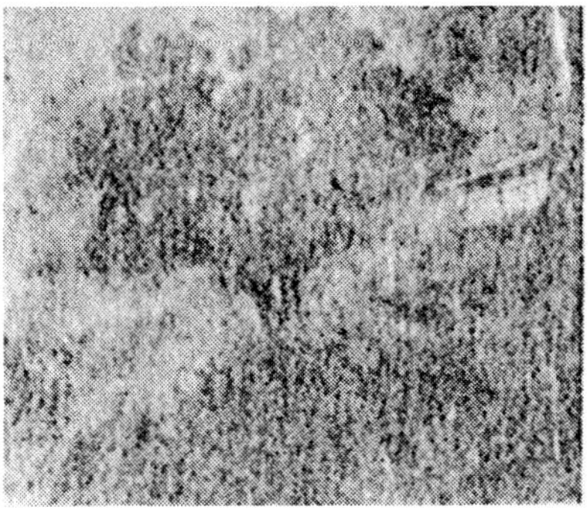

Pasania-tree.

Katsugoro, born in the province of Shimosa, came to Hakone in search of his enemy who had killed Katsugoro's father. He made a vow before a god that he would have nothing to do with any woman before he had avenged the death of his father. But at Hakone, he fell in love with Hatsuhana, daughter of one Shinzaemon Sukumo, with whom Katsugoro was staying, hoping that his enemy would go through Hakone, which was then known as one of the most difficult passes for anyone to go through. Soon, however, Katsugoro lost the use of his legs, probably, as it was thought, on account of his breach of the vow made before the god, and his young wife, instead of deserting her crippled husband, lived devotedly with him in a cottage that she built for him at the foot of the pasania-tree.

Night after night Hatsuhana repaired to the Kannon temple, which, the bus-girl will tell you, was situated on a hill across the river, and offered an earnest prayer for the recovery of her crippled husband. She also visited the Amida-ji (Amitabha-temple) on the old highway of Hakone for many a weary night to pray for him. When, however, she saw that no prayer offered to the gods restored the use of his legs, she was determined to undergo cold ablutions under a waterfall. And for a "circuit of seven days" she sat under the waterfall now known as the Hatsuhana Waterfall after her name, by offering her own life in order to restore Katsugoro to health again, and at the end of her long icy ablutions she died of shock and cold.

Strange to say, however, as the tradition goes, Katsugoro found the use of his crippled legs restored all of a sudden, and going to the waterfall he found Hatsuhana dead cold.

Katsugoro traced his enemy and succeeded in avenging his father's death at Isshiki, near Odawara. The remains of Katsugoro and Hatsuhana lie buried at the Saon-ji Temple on the old site of the residence of Shinzaemon, her father.

The Jomyo-in Temple, situated across the road from the pasania-tree, under which the lovers lived in a small cottage, has a monument erected to their memory over the top-knot hair of Katsugoro and a mirror that his wife used. The monument is called the Kagami-ishi or mirror-stone.

THE HITO-BASHIRA OR HUMAN-POST (1)

Every local province has some stories to tell of noble martyrs who offered themselves to be buried alive as *hito-bashira* or human-sacrifice for the sake of their fellow-creatures. When a great difficulty was met in the construction of a bridge, castle, embankment or anything else that was related to a river or sea, it was attributed to the anger or displeasure of the water-god, and a living person was offered to appease the angry deity. The victim was buried alive under the foundation of the construction as a *hito-bashira*.

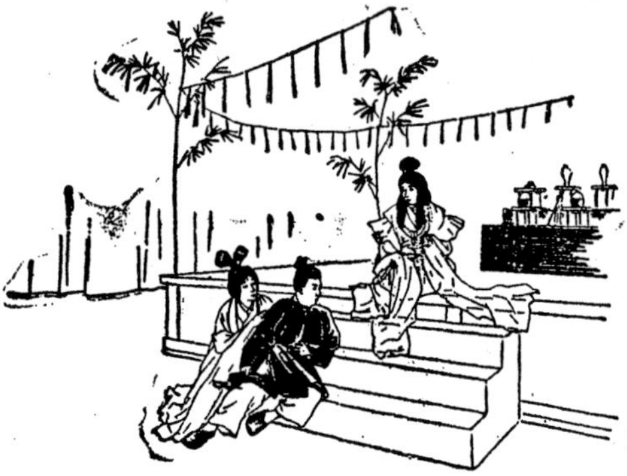

A scene from "Tarumizu" (Play).

The earliest "human-post" recorded in the history of Japan was offered to the river-deity of the River Yodo in 324 A.D. The banks of the River Yodo were destroyed by the rapid streams, and the Government failed repeatedly in its attempts to repair the broken embankments. One night the Emperor Nintoku was told in a dream that the torrent could not be checked unless two persons, Kawabuki of Musashi Province and Koromo-no-ko of Kawachi Province, were offered as *hito-bashira*. They were therefore buried alive at the broken parts of the river banks, and new embankments were built up over their bodies. Thereby the torrents were controlled.

The *hito-bashira* of the River Nagara, in the province of Settsu, is perhaps the best-known in Japan, and it is staged as a play. Upon the repeated failure to span a bridge over the River Nagara, Iwauji of Tarumizu Village told the authorities that the human-post was the only way to lay the foundation of the bridge, and so he was buried alive to serve as one. He was survived by a daughter, whom her mother told to pretend to be dumb when she married the son of a squire. Because he found her to be dumb, the squire took her to her mother's, when on their way to the village of Tarumizu he shot a pheasant which had cried out. "As with my father, who would have been spared had he kept silent, so the pheasant would not have been killed had it been silent," so the bride expressed her sorrow for the ill-fated bird in a poem. Her bridegroom was happy that after all she was not dumb and took her back to his own home where they lived happy till they grew old.

The most touching of all stories of *hito-bashira* is that of Seki-hachi Torazayemon, who offered his life as a human-post in order to save the people of thirty-six villages at Fujisaki in the province of Aomori. There is a shrine at Fujisaki by the name of Seki or "Dam Shrine," which is dedicated to the Dam-keeper Torazayemon, who died the death of a human-post. When a few years ago they repaired the Niju-Bashi, which is the front entrance to the Imperial Palace, Tokyo, they found some dozen human bodies buried there, some in a standing position and others lying. As this is not a cemetery at all, it was concluded that these bodies had been put there as *hito-bashira*.

THE HITO-BASHIRA OR HUMAN-POST (2)—*Concluded*

Tsukishima, Hyogo: After every attempt had failed to fill up a part of the sea off Hyogo, Kiyomori Taira asked Yasuuji Abe, the fortune-teller, to find out what would be the efficacious way of construction. According to an oracle, 30 human sacrifices were demanded by the angry god of the sea, but Abe made a false reply, telling Taira that the work would be successful if carried out on the lucky day, the 18th of the 3rd month, 1163. Fifty thousand coolies were raised from Yamato, Yamashiro, Ise, Iga, Harima, Settsu and Tamba Provinces, but the work met with no better success, until the fortune-teller told the truth to Kiyomori Taira. A barrier was at once built at Ikuno for taking thirty victims, who were to be buried alive as *hito-bashira.* But Matsuo, a young page of Taira's, offered his life in order to save the innocent people. He rode a horse into the sea and disappeared. The sea was easily filled up and Tsukishima (literally, artificial islet) was successfully constructed in 1173.

The River Yodo: In the eleventh year (324) of the reign of the Emperor Nintoku, the embankment of the River Yodo was repeatedly washed away by the rapids at Manda. The Emperor saw in a dream one night that the rapids could not be checked by anything but two human sacrifices, and Kawakubi of Musashi Province and Koromo-no-ko of Kawachi Province were named as victims in the Emperor's dream. They were therefore offered to the god of the river, and a strong embankment was successfully built to dam the rapids.

The River Fuji: The banks of the River Fuji frequently gave way, till the lord of the place decided to offer a human sacrifice to the god of the river. All his chief retainers offered themselves as victims to be buried alive for the benefit of his people, till they drew lots to decide who should have the honour of dying as a *hito-bashira.* Just at this moment a Buddhist pilgrim happened to come begging for alms, and he offered himself as a victim in their place.

"I will keep on beating the bell," the pilgrim added "and when its sound is heard no more, you must think that I am dead."

The pilgrim was buried alive and his bell was heard for over ten days, at the end of which he must have died. The dam was strongly built and the embankments of the River Fuji have not been destroyed by torrents for over three hundred years.

The Nijubashi Bridge: When the Nijubashi Bridge (Double Bridge) in front of the Imperial Palace, Tokyo, underwent repairs several years ago, some dozen bodies were brought to light under the foundation of the bridge, two or three of them being buried in a standing posture instead of lying. The bridge, being the front entrance of the Imperial Palace and originally of the Shogunate Palace in feudal days, is the last place for a dead body to be buried, so some orthodox Japanese were of the opinion that these bodies had been buried as human sacrifices.

KEIGYOKU (1)

BLIND MAN WHO SUPPORTED HIS AGED PARENTS

Atsumi is a sea-side spa in the prefecture of Yamagata, on the U-etsu Railway. Every visitor of the spa visits the Chotoku-ji Temple of the Sodo-shu Sect of Buddhism, a comparatively large temple for the small village, in veneration of Keigyoku, a blind man who most devotedly supported his aged father and mother. The temple has a stone monument erected in its precincts to the memory of the blind man, his wooden statue and ten framed pictures describing his life. Keigyoku is known as a typical man of filial devotion in the history of the Shonai Clan.

Keigyoku was born at Soda, a sea-side village near Nezugaseki in Yamagata Prefecture in 1712. Mosuke, his father, was in abject poverty, and Keigyoku, who could not go to school, had to help him by making straw sandals from childhood. He was very dutiful and obedient. One day when a little boy, he was sent on an errand. It was after a rain fall but the ground was almost dry. His mother said that he could go on a pair of sandals, while his father, who feared that it might rain again, told him to put on a pair of wooden clogs. The boy obeyed both of them by putting a straw sandal on one foot and a wooden clog on the other.

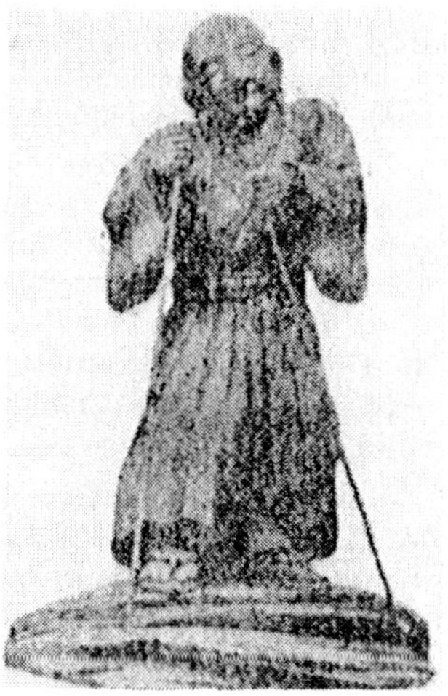

The wooden image of Keigyoku.

Now, Keigyoku had an eye-trouble when eighteen years old, but there was no eye-doctor at Soda, his native village, and so he lost his sight. But he kept on helping his father by making ropes and straw-sandals as before. Gradually his father failed in health, and the blind boy had to go out to collect fire-wood and buy materials for his work. Mosuke was very fond of sake, too, which the boy bought every day with the money he earned by selling the straw articles he made.

One day Mosuke, who was now sick in bed, desired to eat tai (sea-bream) before he died. It was a stormy day in winter and the fish could not be had at any of the neighbouring villages, till the blind boy walked for three and a half Japanese *ri* (about 8 miles) in a snow storm, before he found one. He had it wrapped in straw, and with his sticks he tapped his way homeward with ecstasy, the fish hanging from his side. But imagine his disappointment when on reaching home, he found the fish had disappeared, leaving the empty straw-wrapper at his side. The poor blind boy had therefore to retrace his steps, groping for it over a Japanese mile, before his canes, for he was always obliged to carry two canes, touched the fish. The blind boy could not refrain from lifting his sightless eyes to heaven to give thanks for the recovery of the fish.

It was when Keigyoku was 27 years old that his father, who had been sick for a long time, died at the age of 76, leaving his mother 62 years of age, who was also sick and bed-ridden. His devotion to his parents being known far and wide by this time, many gifts came pouring in, both in money and kind, and Keigyoku gave them all to his sick mother.

KEIGYOKU (2)—*Concluded*

BLIND MAN WHO SUPPORTED HIS AGED PARENTS

One cold winter's day, his mother expressed her desire to eat an ear-shell. Keigyoku searched for it at all the neighbouring villages, but in vain. He then remembered how, before he became blind, he caught ear-shells in the sea. So he stripped himself of his clothing and, blind as he was, jumped into the sea in search of an ear-shell. The fates were kind to him, for soon he found one, and he was just about to land when he was caught by a large octopus, which dragged him again into the sea with its long legs. He might easily have been drowned had it not been for a fisherman, who, seeing him at a distance, ran to his rescue. The octopus, which was caught, measured eight feet.

The lord of the Shonai clan, who was pleased with the filial devotion of the blind man, granted him 30 bales of rice in 1737. In the same year, Keigyoku, coming to Tsurugaoka, the capital of the clan, bought a bell, which he offered to the Chotoku-ji Temple, for it was his long-cherished desire to offer a bell to the temple so that the dead spirits of his parents might be at rest. Keigyoku carried the bell on his back for over eight Japanese *ri* from Tsurugaoka to Atsumi, the village where the temple was.

Keigyoku, who lived a bachelor, feared that the graves of his parents would be left uncared for after his death, and he yearned to leave a permanent fund with the temple so that his parents' graves might be attended to even after he was dead. He therefore presented the Chotoku-ji Temple with a few persimmon-trees and a rice-field. The trees bore fruit, which brought the temple some income for a long time, until they were rooted up by a storm. The temple used the wood of the trees to make cases in which to conserve the biography of Keigyoku. The rice-field, seven *tan* (0.171 acres) in size, we are told, is still owned by the temple, and yields a yearly crop of 6 *to* (12 gallons) of rice.

Judayu Sagara, a samurai of the Shonai clan, was an admirer of Keigyoku to whom he was always very kind. Once a fire broke out and destroyed his house. When Keigyoku heard that Sagara was distressed for want of money to build a new house, he walked to Tsurugaoka, where Sagara lived, and offered eighteen pieces of gold as a token of sympathy for the destruction of the house.

"These are not gold," Sagara said to Keigyoku, on opening the package, because all the pieces looked quite black. "Because you cannot see, you must have been deceived."

"No," Keigyoku said. "They are genuine gold pieces, which were given me by the Lord of the clan many years ago. As they are his gift, I have kept them next to my skin all these years; they are too precious for me to use."

Sagara polished the pieces, which proved to be true gold.

Keigyoku, the dutiful blind man, died at the age of 74 years on the 12th in the 11th month, 1785, and his remains were buried at the Dairyu-ji Temple in the province of Niigata, south of Yamagata. School children in the neighbourhood like to pay respects to the grave of the blind man, whose example of filial piety they venerate profoundly.

KINOKUNIYA-BUNZAEMON

Kinokuniya-Bunzaemon is generally regarded as one of the greatest parvenus that Japan has produced. He was born poor, lived rich and extravagant, and died ignored and obscure.

Bunzaemon was a son of a lumber merchant, who directed a firm named Ki-no-Kuni-ya (or Province-of-Ki Store) in the province of Kii. When he was eighteen years old, a crocodile made such havoc in Kuma-no-Ura (Creek of Kumano) and greatly molested the fishermen, because it scared the fish away. Young Bunzaemon therefore made a wooden doll, which after besmearing it with poison, he threw into the sea. The crocodile was thereby poisoned to the great relief of the people. When its stomach was cut open a leather bag was found containing a thousand pieces of gold. The lad took the bag to the local lord, who told him to keep it for himself. But the boy shared it with the people of his village, who began to look up at him with great admiration for his chivalrous conduct.

Now, the province of Kii was, and still is, noted for its oranges, which were exported to Edo in large quantities. One day, when a large ship laden with oranges was ready to sail for Edo, a great storm came on and the sailors would not dare to set sail. But the ship had to sail in spite of the foul weather, or the business would have been lost. So Bunzaemon recruited some young lads, who sailed at the risk of their lives. The ship crossed the rough seas of Enshunada Bay, and reached Edo just in time to keep the contract. On the return voyage the ship carried a large number of salted salmon back to Kii, and he made a fortune by repeating the voyage several times. It is said that he cleared in this way a fortune of 50,000 pieces of gold.

Later, a big fire broke out in Edo (Tokyo) reducing a large part of the city to ashes. Bunzaemon seized the opportunity to hasten to Kiso, where lumber of good quality is produced. He took large numbers of gold pieces, which he gave freely to children playing on the street, so that he could thus win the confidence of their parents, who agreed to sell a large amount of lumber, which he sent to Edo on credit. He thereby amassed a fabulous sum of money.

Bunzaemon built himself a huge mansion in the present ward of Nihombashi, where he lived an extravagant life, for he made it a rule to "earn much and spend much." At the time of Mame-maki (bean-throwing) one year, he called many licensed girls into his own mansion, where he threw basketfuls of gold pieces, instead of beans, crying "Devil in and Fortune out" instead of "Fortune in and devil out." Four times he closed all the gates of the Yoshiwara, the licensed quarters, and entertained all the girls himself, by spending an enormous sum of money on them and the licensed quarters. In this way he spent up all his fortune, leaving hardly anything with him when he died on the twenty-fourth day of the fourth month (April), 1734.

KOKICHI MIKIMOTO, THE PEARL-MAGNATE OF JAPAN (1)

The mere mention of a pearl brings up to the average Japanese mind the name of Kokichi Mikimoto, the Pearl-Magnate of Japan, of world renown, for he has thrown into the shade all other dealers in, and cultivators of, pearl-oysters in Japan. Mikimoto has devoted himself, whole-heartedly and exclusively for over seventy years to the cultured pearl industry, in which he made such remarkable progress that he may well be said to have made Japan one of the greatest pearl-cultivating countries of the world.

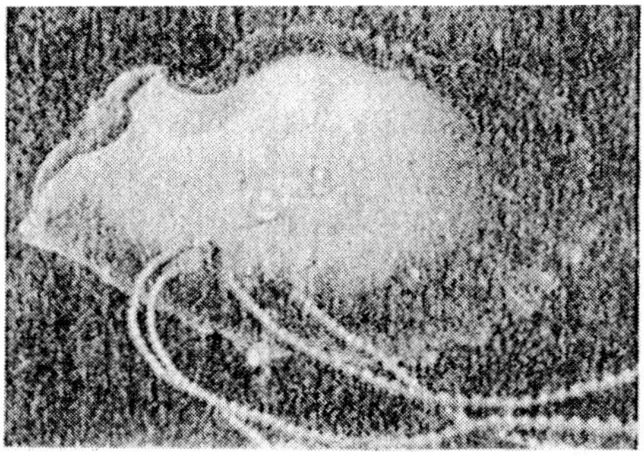

Cultured Pearls.

Kokichi Mikimoto was born at Toba in Ise Province in 1858. Ise, like Omura (near Nagasaki) and Owari, produces natural pearls that are somewhat inferior in lustre and colour to any produced abroad. Young Mikimoto took therefore a natural interest in pearl-oysters. It was in 1890, however, that Mikimoto first learned the possibility of cultivating pearls, and under the late Dr. Kakichi Mitsukuri he established a cultivating farm in the Bay of Ago, Miye Prefecture. After repeated failure, which made him the laughing-stock of his friends and neighbours, Mikimoto succeeded in 1894 in producing semi-spherical pearls, for which he was granted a patent two years later.

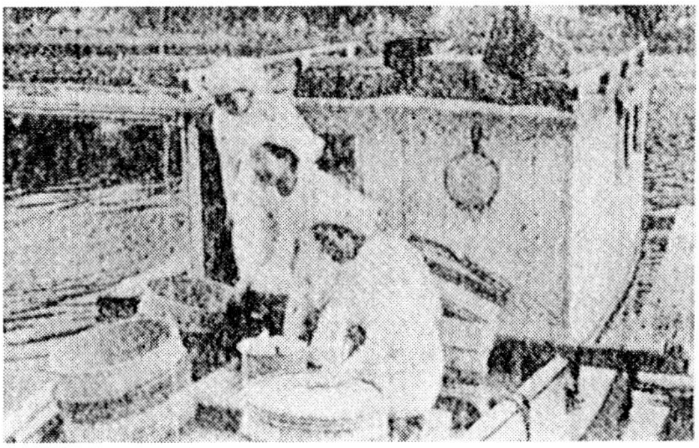

Pearl-culturing.

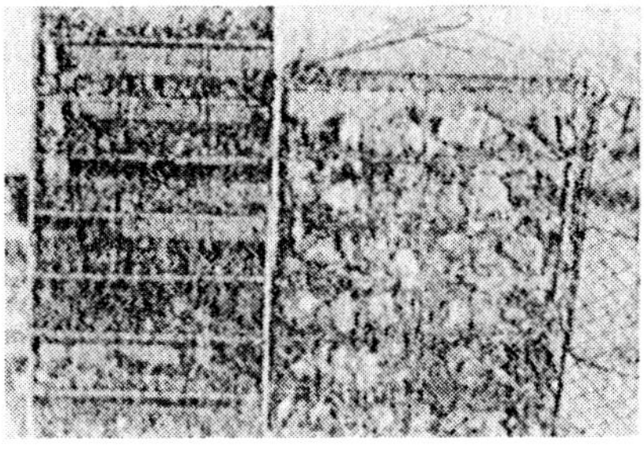

Pearl-oysters.

(*Continued*)

KOKICHI MIKIMOTO, THE PEARL-MAGNATE OF JAPAN (2)—*Concluded*

Mikimoto was not satisfied with this successful production of semi-spherical pearls, for he was ambitious to produce nothing short of a perfectly round pearl that would look as genuine as a natural one. He worked on vigorously and indefatigably against overwhelming odds and cynical enemies for over ten more years, till, thanks to his undaunted spirit, he produced in 1913 cultured pearls that looked equal in lustre and colour to the finest natural pearl ever produced anywhere in the world.

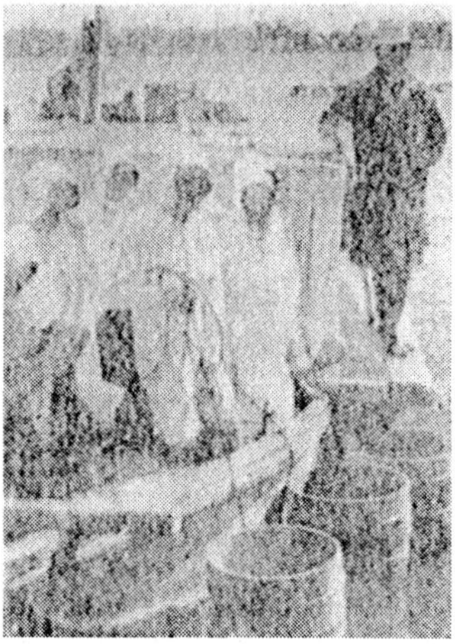

Pearl-oyster farm.

Mikimoto discovered that while a foreign substance had been considered necessary to the formation of a pearl, the essential element in the formation of a cultured pearl was the pearl sac formed from an epidermic, and not from any foreign substance. This was the most important discovery.

Mikimoto has also invented the "culturing cage" for holding about a hundred pearl-oysters, which will be saved from destruction when coloured brine called "akashio" appears. In the cage the pearl-oysters can be hauled up from the sea several times a year for the purpose of scraping sea-weed and barnacles off to help in their growth.

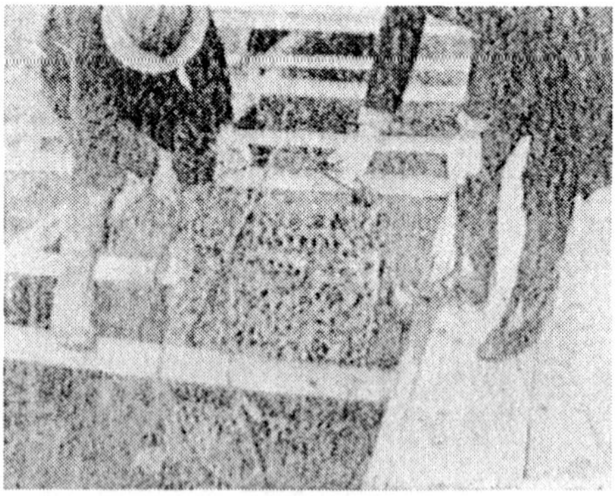

Culturing cage.

Mikimoto maintains a pearl-oyster farm at the following places in Japan: –

Gokasho Bay, Ago Bay, Hasama Bay, Hikimoto Bay, Kata Bay, Miye Prefecture; Omura Bay, Nagasaki Prefecture; Nanao Bay, Ishikawa Prefecture; Tanabe Bay, Wakayama Prefecture; Yayeyama Island, Okinawa Prefecture; Palao Islands, the Mandated South Sea Island.

The total area of the farms is 50,000,000 tsubo (40,830 acres), where over 10,000,000 pearl-oysters are cultivated and 3,000,000 more are bred every year.

PROF. SWEET POTATOES

KON-YO AOKI

"The Grave of Prof. Sweet Potatoes" is the inscription written on the tomb-stone erected over the remains of Kon-yo Aoki, who lies buried in the cemetery behind the Meguro Fudo (Acala), Tokyo.

Kon-yo Aoki was born son of a merchant in Edo (Tokyo) in 1700. He went to Kyoto, the then Imperial capital, where he studied Chinese classics, under Todai Ito, one of the greatest scholars of the day. Upon his return to Edo, he was employed as librarian of the Shogunate Government, and later he was elected the chief official in charge of the Government books.

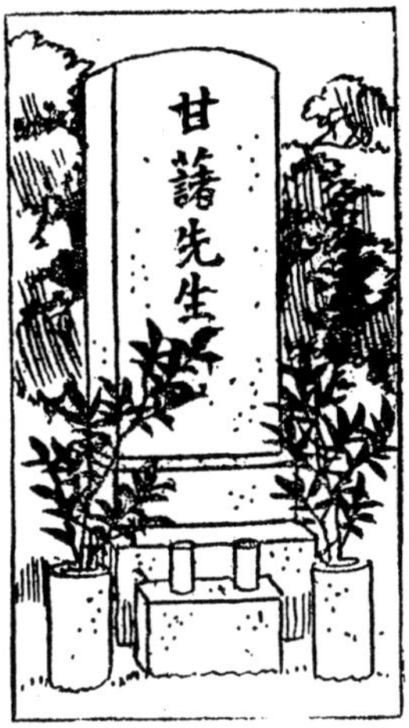

The Grave of Prof. Sweet Potatoes.

Kon-yo was grieved to see that many of the prisoners who were marooned in distant places were starved to death for lack of food because they were often exiled to barren lands. According to his idea, the marooned prisoners or exiles should be allowed to die a natural death, instead of being starved to death. Kon-yo therefore took seeds of sweet potatoes from Satsuma Province and planted them in many different provinces of the country. They grew abundantly and compensated for the shortage of rice and other grain when there was a crop failure. That Japan has sweet potatoes growing all over the country is attributed to the wise policy of Kon-yo Aoki.

Aoki also studied Dutch learning at Nagasaki and he was one of the first Japanese scholars of western learning.

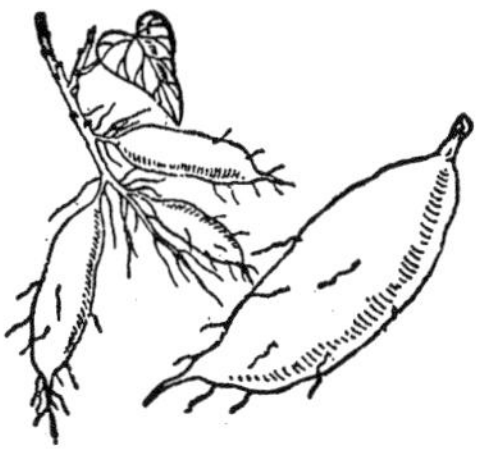

Sweet Potatoes.

Kon-yo Aoki died in 1771, and he was buried at Meguro, his tomb-stone bearing the inscription as cited at the beginning.

Sweet potatoes are called 'Satsuma-imo (potatoes of Satsuma Province) because they were introduced from that province to other parts of the country. In Satsuma Province they are called Ryukyu-imo (potatoes of the Loo-choo Islands) as they were introduced there through those islands. And in the Loo-choo Islands, they are known as Kara-imo (potatoes of Kara or China) because there the people say that the potatoes came from China. Some people of the Loo-choo Islands take sweet potatoes as daily food.

Roast sweet potatoes: The sweet potato, of which the Japanese are very fond, is cooked in most various ways, but Yaki-imo (or roast sweet potatoes) are perhaps most popular, specially in the cold season, and the Yaki-imo store is found in any street of a big city.

CHASTITY SAVED WITH LIFE

Lady Kesa-Gozen

"Kill me with this dagger," said Lady Kinugawa to Kesa-Gozen, her married daughter, on handing her a dagger. "Kill me with this dagger for I would rather die at your hands than anybody else's."

Lady Kesa-Gozen was wife of Wataru Minamoto, a court-warrior. She had a beautiful face, with which Morito Endo was charmed. Endo visited Lady Kinugawa, her mother, and forced her to promise, at the risk of her life, to give her married daughter as wife to him.

"It is my duty, mother," Lady Kesa-Gozen replied to her mother, "to save you. Leave the matter in my hands."

"I will obey you on condition that you do away with my husband," Lady Kesa said calmly to Endo, who came to demand her in marriage. She saw that nothing could dissuade him from his sinister deed should she refuse. "Come into our bedchamber and take the head that you will find has wet hair."

That evening Lady Kesa-Gozen gave a special dinner to her husband on the pretence that she wished to show her gratitude for the recovery from a protracted illness of her mother. Wataru was much more drunk than usual, and she helped him to bed Then she washed her own hair, and went to bed a little apart from her husband.

That night Morito stole in and cut off the head that he felt in the dark had wet hair. But looking at it he saw that it was his love's head and not Wataru's that he had taken. So he went to Wataru and confessed everything, asking him to avenge his wife's death by killing him on the spot.

"What good would it be were I to kill you" Wataru said, "when my wife is gone never to come back to life again?"

Then Wataru advised Morito to take the tonsure and become a Buddhist priest in order to devote himself to it and pray for the repose of the dead spirit of Lady Kesa-Gozen, whom he had murdered by mistake, and Morito, following the advice of his wronged friend, was converted to Buddhism under the priestly name of Mongaku.

Priest Mongaku was an adviser to Lord Yoritomo, the first Shogun, and he travelled round on pilgrimages in different provinces in which he caused many a ruined temple to be restored or repaired, though later he was sent an exile to the island of Sado, where he was starved to death by refusing to take anything to eat.

THE JAPANESE MIRROR

According to the Nihonshoki, the son of Kunitokotachi, a pre-historic prince, was named Prince Ame-no-Kagami or Celestial Mirror, and this is the first time that mention is made of a mirror in the history of Japan. When Prince Izanagi held a white-copper mirror in his left hand, Princess Ohirume-no-muchi or, as she is generally known in Japan, Amaterasu or Sun Goddess, was born, and when he held it in his right hand, Prince Tsukiyomi was born. When the Sun Goddess shut herself in the Celestial Cave at the repeated offences of Prince Susanoo, Princess Ishikoridome made the Yata-no-Kagami or Eight-foot-Mirror in imitation of the sun and put it on a branch of the sakaki-tree in order to attract the attention of the Sun Goddess.

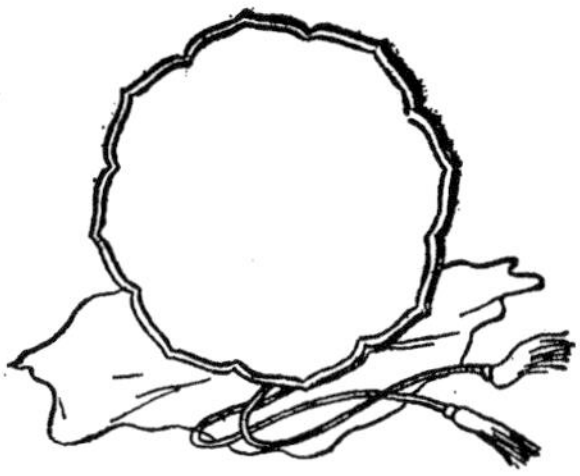

Ancient mirror.

When Prince Ninigi was about to leave the Celestial Abode of Takama-no-Hara to come to the land below, which he was to rule, the Sun Goddess handed him the Three Imperial Treasures, one of which was the Yata-no-Kagami. "You must look at this mirror as if you looked at me," said the goddess to the young prince. This mirror was removed into a shrine at Kasanui by the Emperor Sujin in 92 B.C. and enshrined at Ise by the Emperor Suinin in 5 B.C. It is on account of the Imperial command given by the Sun Goddess that a mirror is regarded not only as a practical and ornamental article, but as the esoteric representation of a spirit. Hence it is often enthroned in a Shinto shrine to represent the god or goddess to whom the shrine is dedicated.

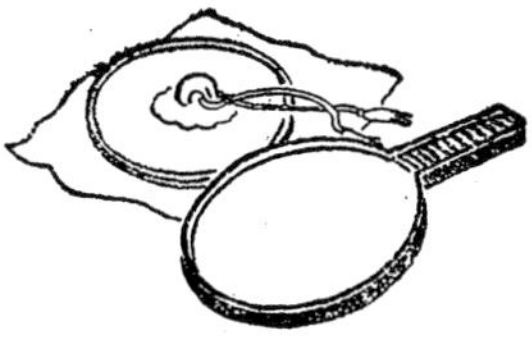

Mirrors.

It is also recorded that Prince Yamatotake had a mirror as the figurehead of his ship when he was sent fo subdue the rebellious local chiefs of the north. In 251, the King of Kudara, Korea, sent a messenger to Japan with a tribute which included a mirror, and in 272 the same king presented some swords and a large mirror to the Emperor Ojin. According to a Chinese story, the king of Wu gave a present of a hundred mirrors to the Japanese court in 238.

In those early days Japan received many mirrors from China and Korea, and made imitations of them in the country, judging from the mirrors that have been brought to light from some ancient graves, because these mirrors had somewhat similar figures on their back.

The ancient mirror was made of copper, silver or iron and rarely of enamel or stone. However, our pre-historic mirror was chiefly made of what is called white-copper, but the Chinese mirror was of bronze, though, it may be added, the oldest Japanese mirror seems to have been made of meteor. Silver and enamel mirrors were very rare. One mirror preserved in the Shosoin Museum measures 7 feet in diameter. During the Fujiwara days, a mirror sometimes had a handle, which became popular during the Tokugawa days. A mirror with bells is sometimes found in an ancient grave, and it seems to have been original in Japan. Glass mirrors were introduced comparatively late, as they came to Japan sometime during the Ashikaga days.

THE DWELLING-CAVES OF YOSHIMI (1)

A train-ride of a little over an hour from Ikebukuro, Tokyo, will take one to Matsuyama, Saitama Prefecture, which is known for its large number of ancient dwelling-caves.

Matsuyama was first the castle-town of Lord Uyesugi, and the castle changed hands several times before it was destroyed by fire in 1590, never to be rebuilt. The hill on which Matsuyama Castle stood has a cave known as the Cave of the Goddess Kannon, because it has several images of the goddess enshrined in it.

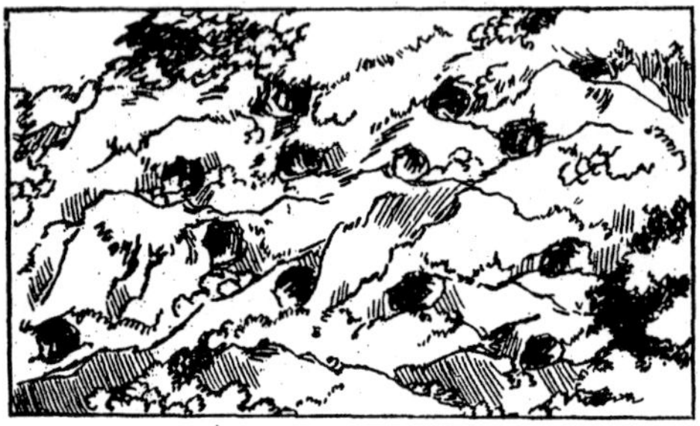

The 100-caves of Yoshimi.

Next to the castle hill, or at a distance of a few dozen yards from it, there stands another hill. This is honey-combed with ancient dwelling-caves on its southern side.

It was in 1870 that, after a great rainfall, a little landslide revealed a deep hole, 6 or 7 inches in diameter. This proved to be a horizontal cave. In the following year the owner of the land, Sankichi Takahashi, uncovered a few more caves by removing the shrubs which covered the hill.

Dr. Shogoro Tsuboi, then a student of the College of Anthropology, of the Tokyo Imperial University, uncovered over two hundred more caves while spending three months there in 1888. There are now altogether 237 caves, which are popularly called the "A Hundred Caves of Yoshimi," after the hill on which they are discovered. Scholars agree that these were dwelling caves in which lived ancient inhabitants of Japan. There is another group of some 200 caves 2 or 3 miles from Yoshimi. The following articles were brought to light by Dr. Tsuboi:—

Jewel: Magatama (comma-shaped beads) and Kudatama (pipe-beads).

Metal: Copper rings, iron rings, mirrors, swords and sword-guards.

Stone implements: Stone arrow-heads, stone axes, etc.

Bones: Human bones.

(*Continued*)

THE DWELLING-CAVES OF YOSHIMI (2)—*Concluded*

The old caves of Yoshimi are horizontal and they have each a square entrance, about 3'×4', without a door, though a stone slab about 2" thick seems to have been used in a few caves. The caves are 5' or 6' deep and a little less wide, and their arched ceilings are 4' or 5' high, though in some caves the ceiling is so high that one can easily stand up in them. The floor or ground on either side, or both in most caves, is 3" or 4" higher than the passage in the middle.

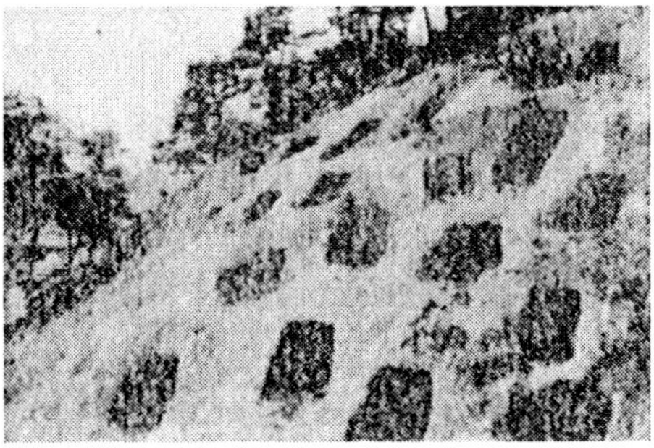

A part of caves.

On the walls of Cave No. 106, there are what one may take for ancient letters. There are many of them and some archaeologists conclude that they are ancient Korean characters. A kind of phosphorous moss (schisostega osmundacea) covers some of the caves and it is specially protected by the Government.

Near the caves there is a cave-hotel built by an old man, Minekichi Takahashi. He made up his mind to dig out a hotel in imitation of the caves, and worked at it for over twenty years, by the end of which he made several cave-rooms. Unfortunately, however, Takahashi died without completing his cave-hotel.

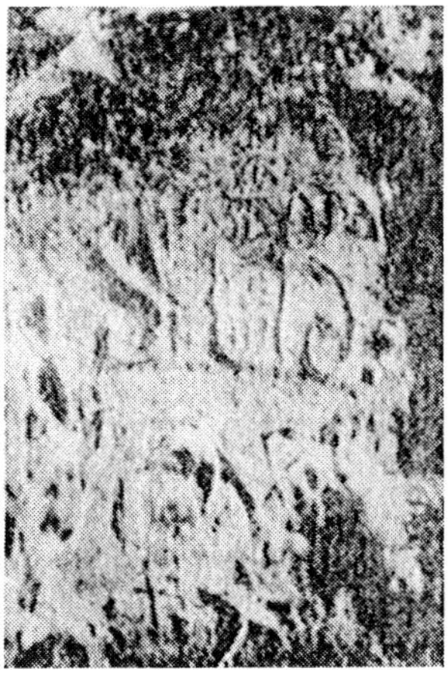

The Signature of Siebolt who visited the caves, 1873.

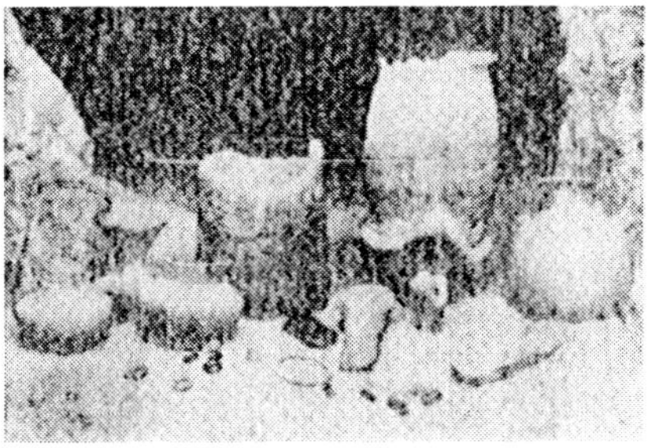

Some earthenware found in the caves.

THE BUDDHIST CAVE OF OFUNA

A 2.5-MILE-LONG CAVE NEAR KAMAKURA

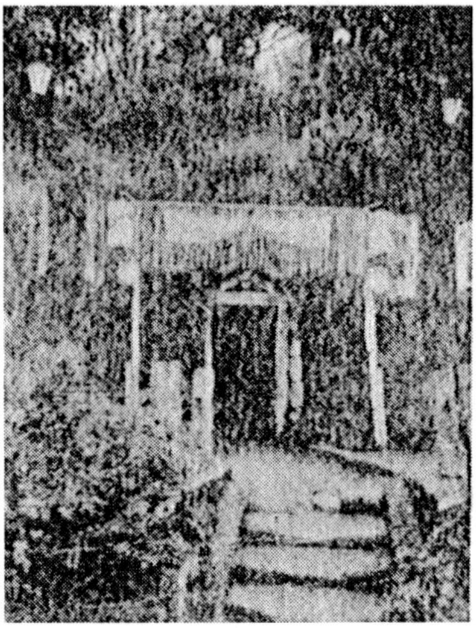

The entrance to the cave.

The Buddhist Cave of Ofuna is situated at 15 cho, or about one English mile, from Ofuna Station, near Kamakura. The cave was dug out by the founder of the Teisen-ji Temple a little over 200 years ago, during the last years of the Tokugawa Shogunate. It is five storeyed and measures 2.5 English miles. All along the dark passages there are numerous and varied carvings on both sides of the walls. There are altogether 531 Buddhist images, including 154 Kannon statues in representation of the famous sets of Chichibu, Bando and the Saikoku, and 16 Arhans, besides several legendary stories, such as Kintoki with his nurse Yama-uba and Ishidomaru with his mother. Mt. Koya is represented in a miniature way in the cave, with Priest Kobo enshrined in a niche in it. There are fifteen halls of meditation, in which several priests and feudal warriors sat in meditation, some of them fasting for forty-nine days in one of the halls. The cave can be reached by car in a few minutes from Ofuna Station.

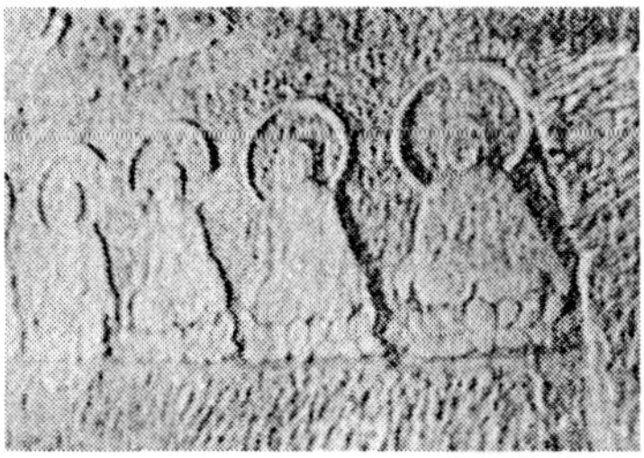

Buddhist images.

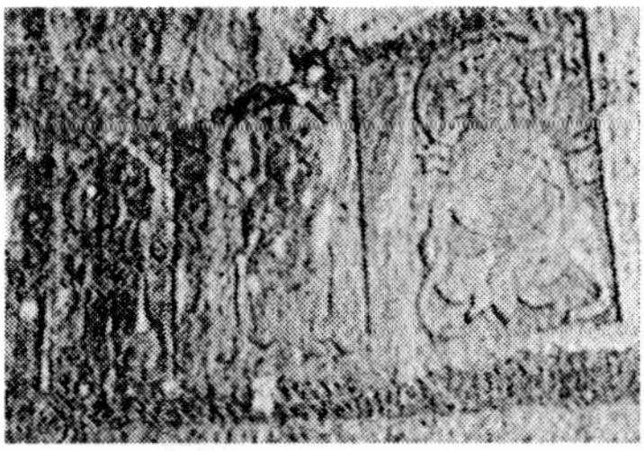

Buddhist images.

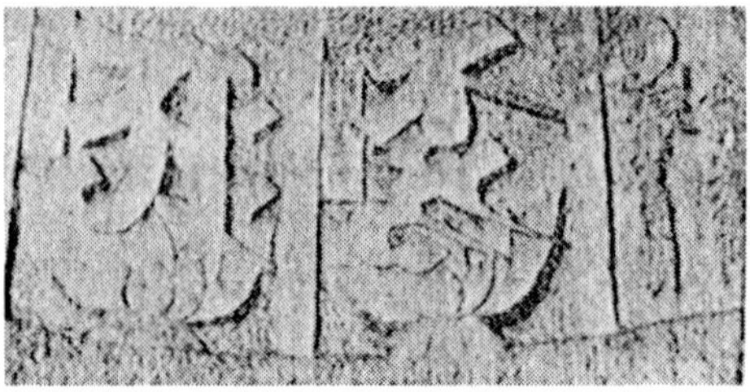

Buddhist characters.

NIHOMBASHI BRIDGE (1)

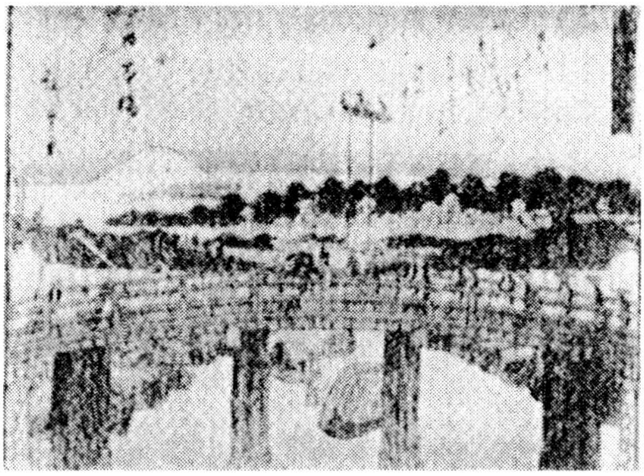

Old Nihombashi Bridge

Nihombashi Bridge was first built in 1603; it measured 226½ ft. long and 24½ ft. wide. It was so named because "the sun was seen rising from the eastern sea," though it is erroneously supposed by many to have been named so after "Japan" (Nippon). The bridge has been rebuilt thirteen times since it was first built. At the last disastrous earthquake of 1923 it was destroyed by fire like many other bridges in Tokyo, and the present bridge was completed in 1929 at the cost of ¥511,950. The bridge measures 49.091 metres long and 27,273 m. wide.

Nihombashi Bridge is considered to be the centre not only of the City of Tokyo, but of the whole Empire, for, when we say that a city or town is a certain number of miles away from Tokyo, the distance is measured from Nihombashi Bridge.

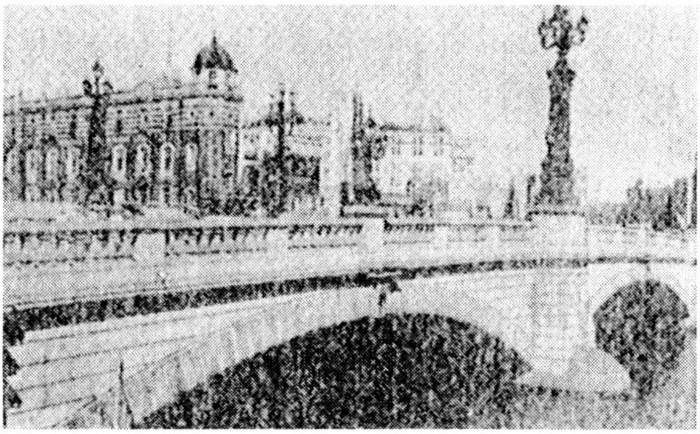

New Nihombashi Bridge

Nobunaga Oda who made a *ri* (Japanese mile) of 36 *cho* (*cho*=120 yds.) measured the distances of the local places in the Kinai District from Kyoto, the Imperial Capital, but Iyeyasu Tokugawa, the founder of the Tokugawa regime, measured all distances to the country from Nihombashi Bridge of Edo.

Mile-trees: We have many mile-trees. When Iyeyasu adopted the system of mileage, he ordered a mile-mound to be built up. When asked by his attendant-lord Okubo whether it was all right to plant a pine-tree on the mound, he told him to plant some other tree. Okubo failed to hear him distinctly, but he did not dare to ask Iyeyasu to repeat what he had once said. He therefore planted the E-no-ki (nettle-tree) on each mile-mound.

NIHOMBASHI BRIDGE (2)—*Concluded*

Public notices were often given at Nihombashi Bridge during the Tokugawa regime. The regular carriage rate, for instance, was kept posted up at Nihombashi Bridge for different places in the vicinity of Edo. The carriage of a load and the charge for a messenger are shown below:

To	*Carriage for a load*	*Charge for a messenger*
Shinagawa	94 mon	47 mon
Senju.....................	91 „	46 „
Kawaguchi	140 „	67 „
Itabashi	94 „	47 „
Kamitakaido	161 „	79 „
Shimotakaido	149 „	73 „

(mon=one tenth of a sen)

The weight of a load was fixed as follows:

40 kan for a horse
5 kan for a man
30 kan for Nagamochi (box)-carriers

(kan=3.75 kgs.)

There was a rush cottage near the bridge which served for gibbeting for three days the head of a Buddhist priest who had violated a woman, and that of a lover who had tried to commit *Shinju* or double suicide, which was as popular in those early days in Edo as today in modern Tokyo. The Shogun Yoshimune therefore declared double suicide a penal offence:—

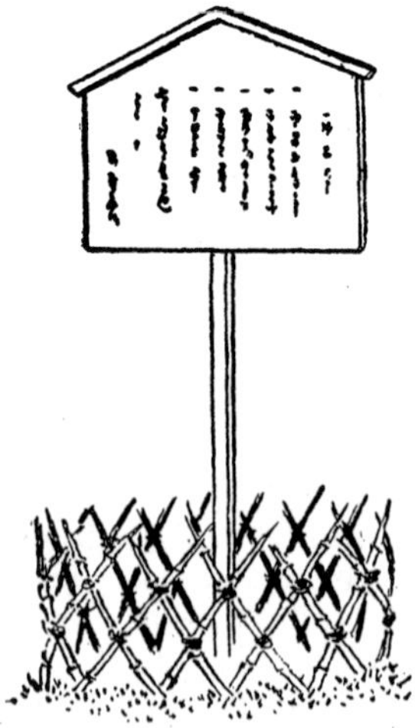

Notice-board at Nihombashi Bridge.

His edict said that,

1. When man and woman both die, their bodies shall be cast away;
2. When both are wounded but not mortally, they shall be social outcasts after being healed;
3. When the man survives the woman, he shall be put to death after being healed;
4. When the woman survives the man, penalty of death shall be commuted by one degree.

THE JAPANESE GRAVE (1)

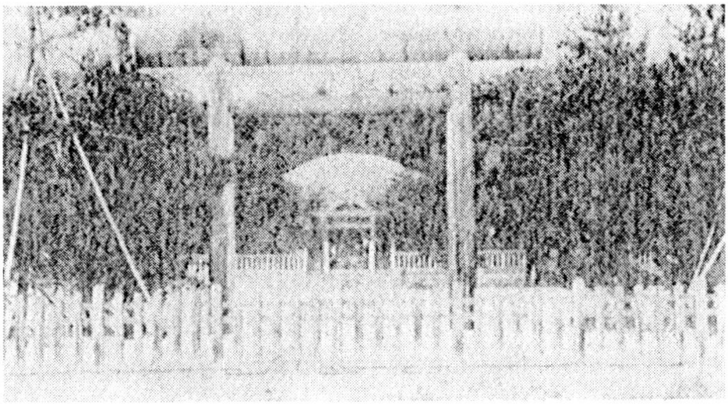

The Mausoleum of the Emperor Meiji at Momoyama, Kyoto.

In ancient times, the coffin, either stone, earth or wood, was put on the ground, instead of being buried in it as it is nowadays, covered over with earth to form a mound either in a single or double form. It was as much as 100 ft. or more in diameter and 20 ft. or more, high, although it was much smaller, on an average. As a rule, our mound-grave faces south, east, south-east or west, but never north.

Cremation introduced into Japan with Buddhism, was much in vogue because this faith became very popular in the Imperial court; many an Emperor and Empress as well as courtiers being great believers in it. A grave-stone was also introduced about the same time as Buddhism and it was erected not only over a dead body or its hair or some other part of it, but often over the personal effects of the deceased. A tomb is sometimes erected for a living person before he or she dies. When either of a couple dies, the would-be posthumous name of the survivor is inscribed in red on the grave-stone beside that of the deceased, indicating that the grave is to contain the remains of the two under it.

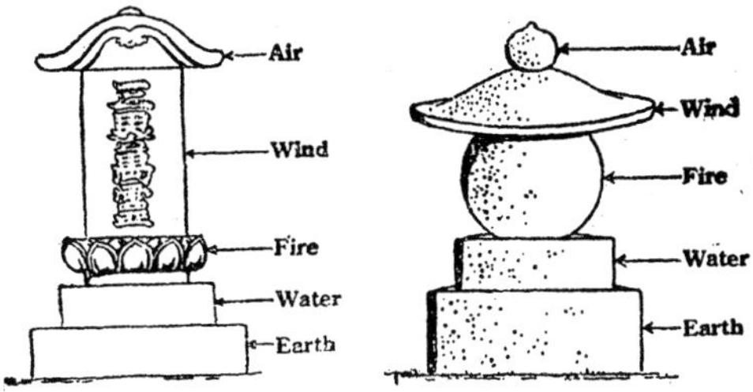

Form of a Japanese grave.

Properly speaking, the Japanese grave consists of five parts which represent the five elements: (1) earth, (2) water, (3) fire, (4) wind and (5) air, as we see in a regular grave of olden times, though this form is often departed from in modern graves. Our grave may be various in shape, but it is, as a rule, square and stands on two or three pedestals. It has the name, and very often the posthumous one, of the buried person, on its front side, and the date of his or her death and of its erection on its back or other side. There is an indented place for

(*Continued*)

water on a pedestal and a pair of bamboo or something else for flowers in front of the tomb-stone. An image of the Jizo (guardian deity of children) is often erected over the remains of a small baby.

SOME TYPICAL GRAVES

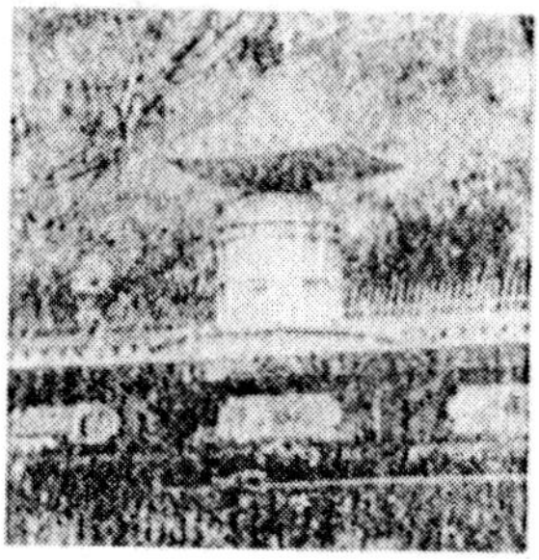
Iyeyasu Tokugawa, Nikko.

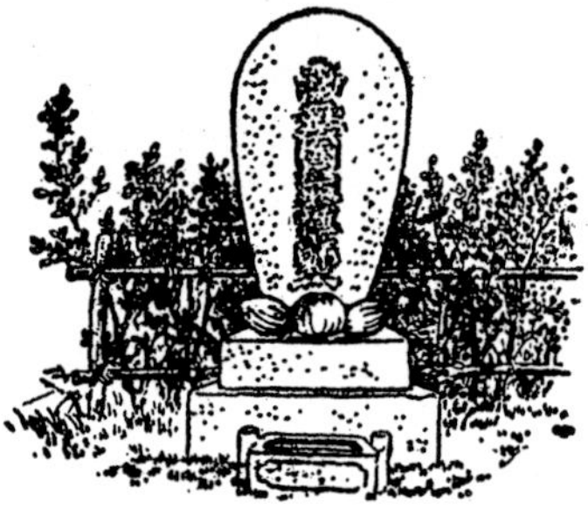
Priest's Tomb.

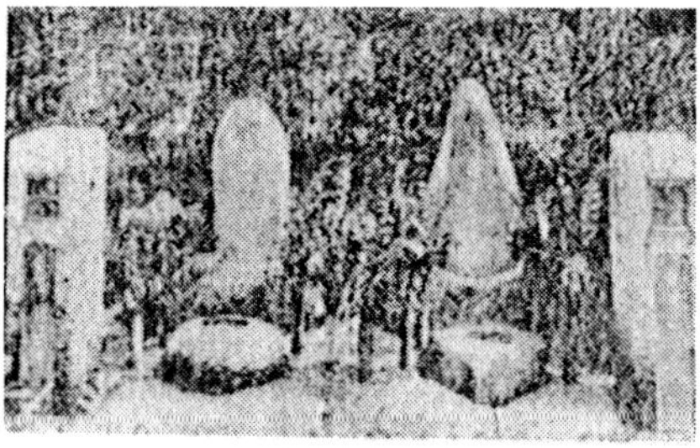
Gen. & Mrs. Maresuke Nogi.

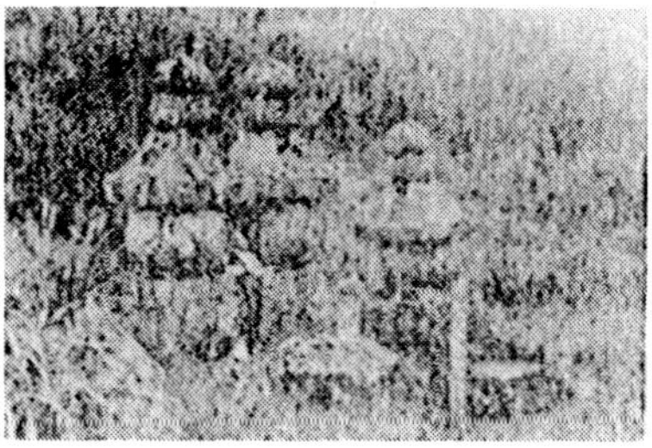
The Soga Brothers.

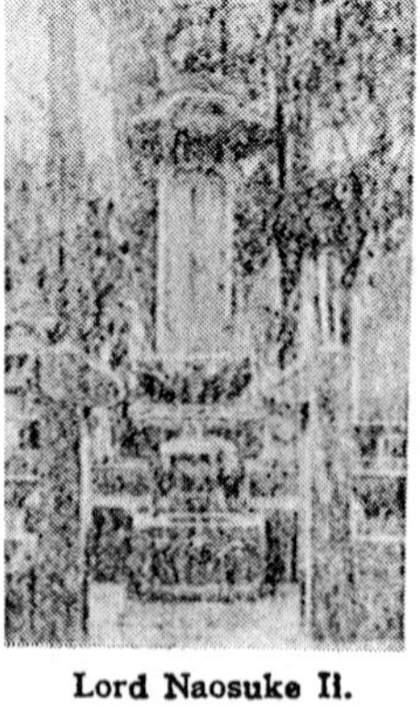
Lord Naosuke Ii.

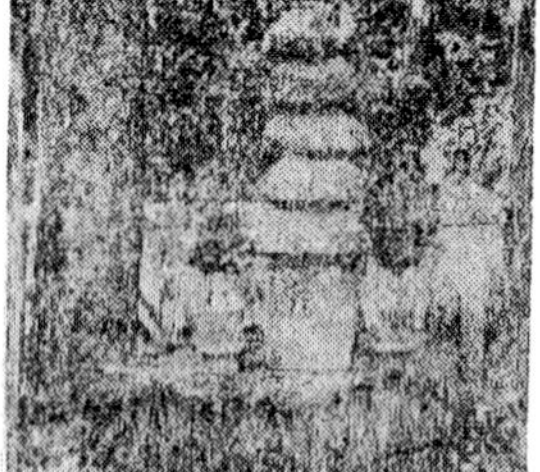
Yoritomo Minamoto.

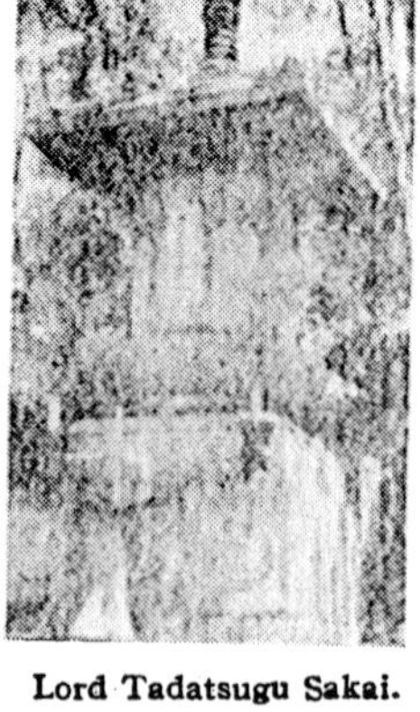
Lord Tadatsugu Sakai.

THE NOREN OR "GOODWILL"

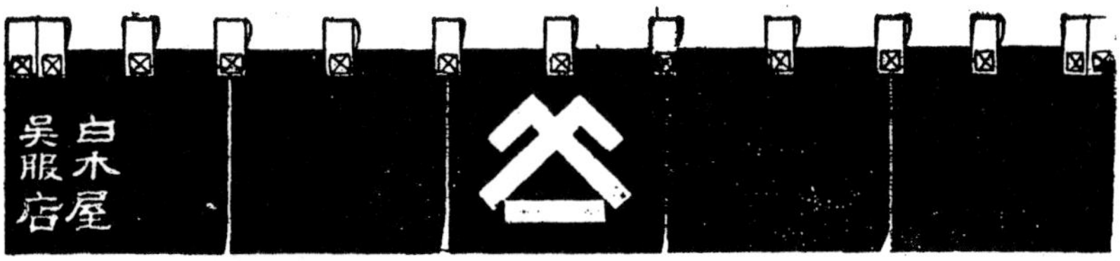

The Noren, which literally means a "warm blind or curtain," (暖簾) is found at the entrance of a commercial house. Originally means for keeping the wind, heat, cold and dust off, the Noren was made of cloth of some kind or often of matting, or even of rope, though blue cotton seems to have been popularly used. There is no fixed size for the curtain, but almost invariably it has the name, mark or brand of the firm dyed on it.

When the Noren was first used is little known, but it was in vogue about the middle of the Shogunate reign (1338-1573) of Ashikaga, and it was very extensively used by most of the leading merchants during the Tokugawa Shogunate (1603-1867), so that one could tell the business of a shop by just looking at the Noren.

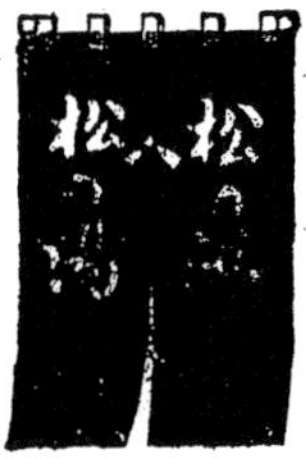

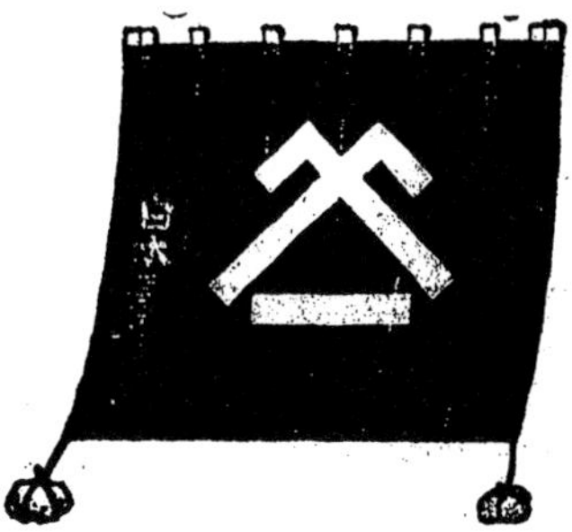

During the era of Genroku (1688-1703), a short Noren became so fashionable that a longer Noren was used at dry-goods stores, dryers' shops, public baths, barbers' shops, licensed houses, apothecaries, etc. In this way the Noren became almost as binding as the foreign "goodwill," and it sometimes changed hands. A clerk or apprentice who had served his term was privileged to "share the Noren" by establishing a branch of the firm where he had worked.

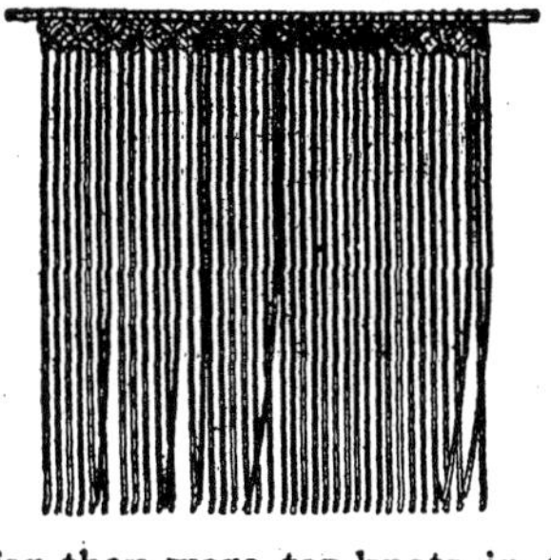

During the Tokugawa Shogunate, a restriction was placed on certain branches of business. The number of dealers in calendars, for instance, was limited to 81 in the era of Genroku (1688-1703); that of exchange brokers to 600 in the era of Kyoho (1716-1735); and the permits issued to hair-dressers in the era of Manji (1658-1660) numbered a little over 600, which increased in 1730 to 967 permits owned by 770 hair-dressers, some of whom operated several barber-shops. A hair-dresser, by the way, means one who dressed the hair of samurai or warriors, for they wore top-knots in the feudal days of Japan. So the Noren was a sort of patented permit, which was sellable and to own it cost several dozen or even hundred pieces of gold.

The Nawa-noren or rope-curtain, which is now seen in Tokyo, indicates a bar or cheap eating-house, so that "to go under the rope-curtain" means to get a cheap drink or meal.

THE JAPANESE NUMBERS AND NUMERALS

The Japanese have two ways of counting ten. They are:—

I.	Ichi (1)	ni (2)	san (3)	shi (4)	go (5)
	roku (6)	shichi (7)	hachi (8)	ku (9)	ju (10)
II.	Hitotsu (1)	Futatsu (2)	Mittsu (3)	Yottsu (4)	Itsutsu (5)
	Muttsu (6)	Nanatsu (7)	Yattsu (8)	Kokonotsu (9)	To (10)

While the first way of counting is said to be of foreign or Chinese origin, the second is a variation of the prehistoric way, which was:

Hi (1)	Fu (2)	Mi (3)	Yo (4)	Ii (5)
Mu (6)	Na (7)	Ya (8)	Kono (9)	To (10)

In counting on the fingers, the Occidentals begin with the small finger and end with the thumb, generally using the open fingers of one hand for one to five and those of the other hand for six to ten. In Japan, however, the open fingers are bent down for one to five, beginning with the thumb, and then the small finger, which is closed for five, is re-opened for six, to be followed by the other fingers till the thumb stands up again for ten.

According to Dr. Kurakichi Shiratori, our ancients counted ten on their fingers in the following way:—

The closed fingers are opened one after another, possibly beginning with the thumb, for one to five, which is the largest number for one hand. For six, three fingers of both hands are used, mi-mi (3.3) making mu (6). In the same way four fingers of both hands are used to show ya (8), which has come from yo-yo (4-4). But seven and nine cannot be expressed by the two same numbers such as six and eight. Dr. Shiratori holds that *nana* (7) is a corruption of na-nai, which means "no-pair" or "no equal" and seven was expressed by four fingers on one hand and three on the other. "Koko" (9), according to his explanation, has come from "kokona," meaning "no bending." This is because the number (9) is expressed by bending no fingers. And ten fingers were open to indicate the number ten.

Apropos, the Japanese names of the fingers are:

Thumb=Oya-yubi or parent-finger,
First finger=Hitosashi-yubi or man-pointing finger,
Middle finger=Naka-yubi or middle finger,
Ring finger=Kusuri-yubi or medicine finger,
Small finger=Ko-yubi or child-finger.

The Japanese use the Chinese numerals, which have the following derivations:—

一 (one) represents the horizon,
二 (two) stands for heaven and earth,
三 (three) means heaven and earth with a man between,
四 (four) consists of 囗 (earth) and the letter 八 (eight), indicating that the earth is divided into eight or many directions,
五 (five) means a hermaphroditic union of nature,
六 (six) is a number of divination indicating the positive and negative,
七 (seven) shows an affluvia coming up from Mother Earth.
八 (eight) means that two forces are opposed, for eight is easily divided:

$$\frac{8}{2}=4:\ \frac{4}{2}=2:\ \frac{2}{2}=1$$

九 (nine) stands for the ultimate number,
十 (ten) indicates the universe: "—" standing for east and west and "|" means south and north.

"WAITING ON THE 26TH NIGHT"

In the small hours of the 26th of the seventh month (July), according to the old and lunar calendar, which falls generally on a day in the early part of September, according to the new and solar calendar, high hills and eminences such as Kudan, Uyeno, Atago and Shinagawa in Tokyo, are crowded with pious people who gather there to worship, or rather to get a glance of, three Buddhist deitis, who are said to be visible only on that particular morning in the moon as it appears from behind a distant mountain. The three Buddhist deities are: Myojo (Bright-star) in the centre, Nittenshi (Sun-Emperor) on his right and Gettenshi (Moon-Emperor) on his left.

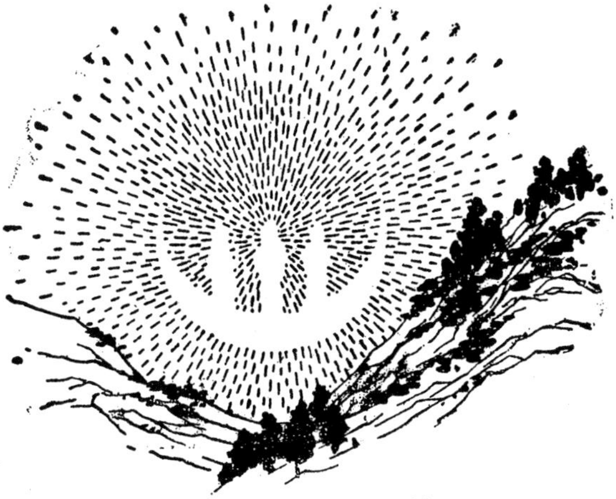

The Three Deities in the Moon.

They are seen standing in the moon just at the moment its two ends emerge like two lighted candles from the mountain in the distance.

This custom is commonly known as Nijurokuya-machi or "waiting on the 26th night," and it was very much in vogue during the latter period of the Tokugawa regime, though it is generally dying out in Japan.

THE NUMBER 108

108 booms of gongs: At midnight on New Year's eve every temple-gong in Japan tolls the passing year by booming 108 times in order thus to exorcise the evil of the old year and to ring the good of the new year in.

A year, according to the Chinese calendar, is divided into 12 months, 24 atmospheres (氣), and 72 climates (候), making the total of 108 in all. Hence the 108 booms of the gong.

A string of 108 beads: According to Buddhism, man has 108 worldly cares, which can be dispelled if one fingers a string of 108 beads by repeating or calling on the Three Ratnas. For this reason, the common rosary that a Buddhist devotee carries has 108 beads, which he always fingers while calling on the Three Ratnas or repeating the holy name of Nam-Amida-Butsu.

THE CITY-MARKS OR COATS OF ARMS (1)

In feudal days Japan had some three hundred local lords or daimyo, each with two or three hundred retainers or samurai under him. Each daimyo and samurai had a family crest or emblem of his own, and Japan was rich then in heraldic emblems. The significance of the crest has, however, considerably depreciated since the Restoration of the Imperial administration in 1868, though each Japanese still wears a crest sometimes. It is woven into the fabric of the "haori" or upper garment.

Each city now has its crest or city-mark, of which we give below the city-marks of the ten largest cities in Japan:—

Tokyo Population: 5,837,388 (1935).

Tokyo's coat of arms was adopted in 1899. It represents the character 東 for "east" of To-kyo (To=east; Kyo=city) combined with the characters for "kyo" (京) and "city" (市). It includes also the rising sun, which is on the Japanese flag.

Osaka Population: 2,989,866 (1935).

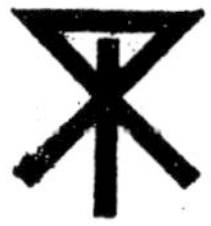

Osaka's coat of arms or city-mark was adopted in 1894. It represents a mooring-place on the beach, because Osaka was formerly called Naniwa (sea-beach).

Nagoya Population: 1,082,814 (1935).

The city-crest was adopted in 1907. It was the same crest that the Tokugawa family of Nagoya used in feudal days, the character 八 ("eight") standing for the eight districts, which the Nagoya clan embraced.

Kobe Population: 912,140 (1935).

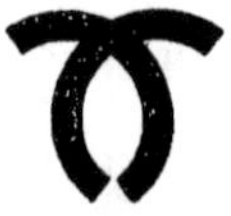

Kobe's coat of arms was adopted in 1907. It represents the paper of two folding fans, because Kobe was formerly called Ohgi-minato or "Fan-port."

(*Continued*)

Kyoto Population: 1,082,814 (1935).

Kyoto's city-mark represents the character 京 for "capital" skilfully stylized.

Yokohama Population: 704,290 (1935).

This was adopted in 1909 and represents the two Japanese kana ハ (ha) and マ (ma) of Yokohama.

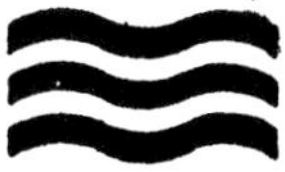

Hiroshima Population: 310,117 (1935).

Its crest was adopted in 1896. It represents a stream, which is the crest of Marquis Asano, the feudal lord of the clan of Hiroshima, also called "The City of Water."

Fukuoka Population: 291,157 (1935).

The city-mark was adopted in 1909. It consists of nine skilful reproductions of the Japanese Kana "フ" standing for the "Fu" of Fukuoka.

Nagasaki Population: 211,702 (1935).

Its city-mark represents the script style of the characters for "Naga" with five characters for "city" (市).

Hakodate Population: 207,488 (1935).

Its city-mark represents the Japanese character for "Tomoye" (巴) which corresponds to the swastika. The date of its adoption is not known.

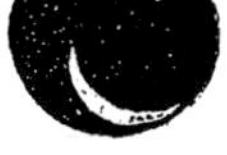

THE TSUBA OR SWORD-GUARD

The Tsuba or sword-guard seems to have been used since Japan's prehistoric days, because it is often brought to light from a shell-mound or an ancient grave. In those days, however, it was little better than a koiguchi or the mouth of a sheath. The Taiho decree (701 A.D.) specified the Tsuba as an accessory of the sword, but it was in the latter days of the Ashikaga era (1338-1573) that the manufacture of the Tsuba made any appreciable development, and it reached its zenith as a metallic art during the Tokugawa Shogunate. There are several schools of the sword-guard craft, but Myochin is generally regarded as the best Tsuba-maker. He lived in the 16th century and his school lasted for twenty generations.

TSUBA

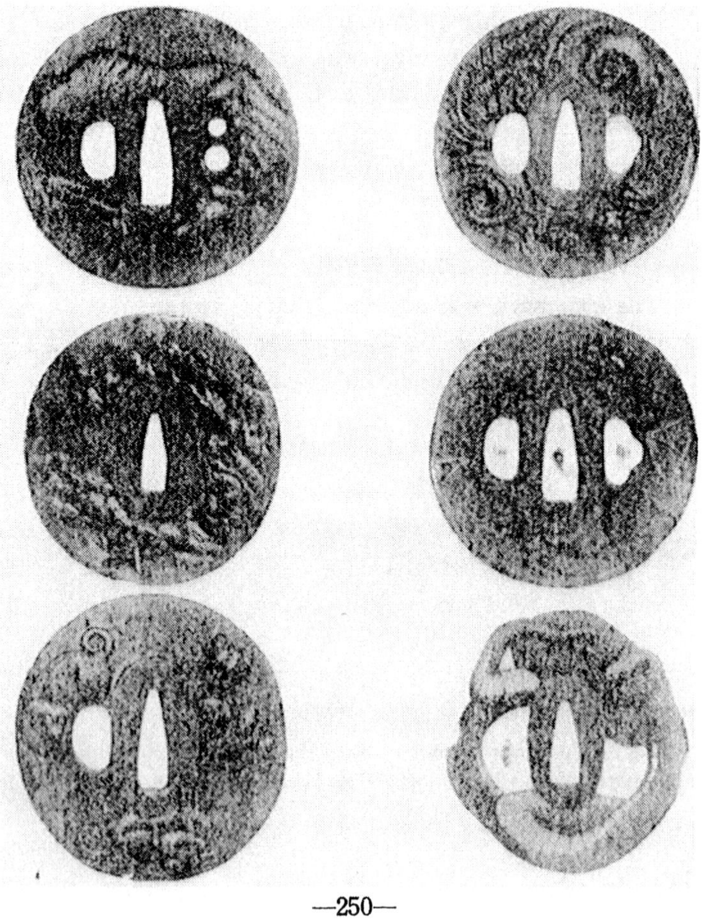

THE TEMPLE-BELL (1)

Most large temples in Japan have a temple-bell for tolling the time day and night. The bell has its origin in Buddhism. Ananda, a disciple of the Buddha, it is said, struck a bell to call the Bhikkus and Upavasathas to the services, while, according to a certain Buddhist sutra, the striking of the bell exorcises evil. In the old days of Edo, the capital of the Shogunate Government, the Zojo-ji Temple-bell boomed regularly at a certain time in the afternoon, so that its priests of the mendicant order might come back from their begging trip through the city.

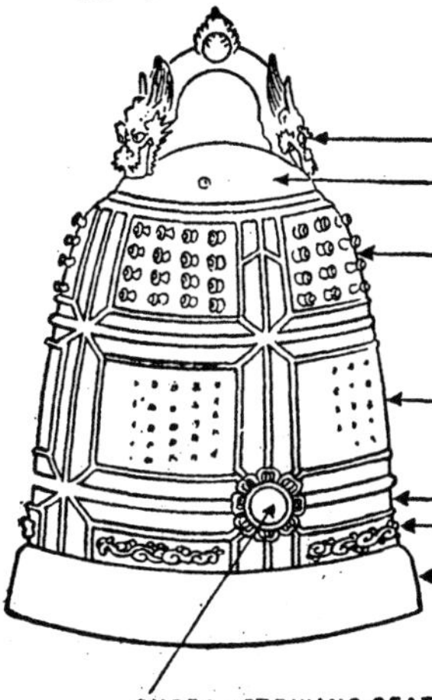

108 booms of the temple-bell: In former days each temple-bell boomed 108 times morning and evening in order to cast out evil. But now it only tolls the time day and night and booms 108 times on New Year's Eve and on certain special occasions. The number 108 represents 12 months, 24 atmospheres and 72 climates, though according to another interpretation the booming bell spells 108 worldly concerns (kuresas) of the old year. The Japanese temple-bell is cast in an alloy of copper and zinc.

Size of the Temple-bell: There is a fixed size for any temple-bell. Its height and weight are in proportion to its calibre, though this proportion is not always followed by every bell-caster. The measurement adopted by the bell-casters in the provinces of Shimotsuke and Ohmi is as follows:—

Height: Kasa 0.142 ft.; Chi-no-machi 0.355 ft.; Ike-no-machi 0.426 ft.; Kusa-no-machi 0.497 ft.; Total 1.42 ft. per 1 ft. of calibre.

Width: *Between* Kasa and Chi-no-machi 0.71 ft.; between Chi-no-machi and Ike-no-machi 0.931 ft.; between Ike-no-machi and Kusa-no-machi 0.994 ft.; Koma-no-tsume 0.1 ft. thick; Inside diameter 0.8 ft. thick.

Weight per calibre 1 ft. 5 kan (1 kan=3.7 kg.)

Weight of a temple-bell, proportionate to 2.2 or 2.3 ft. of calibre: Kusa-no-machi 50 kan; Ike-no-machi 25 kan; Chi-no-machi 13 kan 500 momme; Kasa 6 kan 250 momme; Ryuzu 6 kan 250 momme; Total 100 kan 1,000 momme.

(Continued)

THE TEMPLE-BELL (2)—*Concluded*

The Bell of the Dojo-ji Temple: In the 8th month (August) during the reign of the Emperor Daigo (the 60th), a pilgrim, Anchin by name, of Shirakawa, put up overnight at the house of Kiyotsugu Shoji in the village of Masago in the Kori (county) of Hidaka on his pilgrimage to Kumano in Kii Province. Shoji had a daughter, whose name was Kiyohime. She loved Anchin at first sight, and during night she stole into his room to make advances. Anchin refused on the ground that he could not defile himself before he had visited the god of Kumano, and promised that he would come back to Kiyohime on his way home. Kiyohime waited patiently for his return, until Anchin was overdue a few days, when she was told by a pilgrim that he had gone. Enraged at his treachery, Kiyohime turned into a dragon and started out to pursue Anchin. When Anchin saw the dragon running after him, he took refuge at the Dojo-ji Temple, when he was hidden under the large bell in the temple. The dragon arrived at the temple and coiled itself several times around the bell and then struck it with its tail, till sparks flew out.

The Bell of the Hoko-ji Temple: In 1614, a bell was cast by the Toyotomi family and its installation ceremony was held at the Hoko-ji Temple, Yamato. But the Tokugawa Government raised objection because it was at enmity with Toyotomi. The bell bore an inscription of four characters, namely 國家安康 (meaning "State tranquility"), and it was the original idea of Toyotomi's to pray for the peace of the country by offering the bell with these characters to the temple. But the Tokugawa family interpreted the inscription in a different way, though rather forcedly. The second (家) and fourth (康) letters, when put together, form the name of Iyeyasu (家康), the founder of Tokugawa. The Shogunate Government therefore accused Toyotomi of using his name in the inscription of the new bell in an insulting manner tantamount to exorcism of the Tokugawa Family. War was declared between the Tokugawa and Toyotomi families which resulted in the annihilation of the Toyotomi family. The bell is still preserved at the Hoko-ji Temple, Kyoto.

A Temple-bell and a Lake: Temple-bells and lakes are inseparably related in this country, since many a lake has a tragic tale of some bell which is sunk in it. Here is an example of one. The people of Kasumi-ga-ura often hear on a stormy day a faint voice coming from the depths of Lake Kasumi-ga-ura, saying "I wish to go back to Kokubun-ji." Now, this arises from the tradition that Benkei, a noted follower of Yoshitsune Minamoto, who carried a bell of the Kokubun-ji Temple, Fuchu, on his back, threw it into the lake. Again, no temple-bell is carried across the River Tone at Katori, Shimosa, since every temple-bell carried on a boat will drop into the water of its own accord unless well covered with a straw-mat. Then it is said that a booming sound is often heard coming from the pond of Rengedai near Hanadate in Akita Prefecture. Once a Buddhist temple there called the Kofuku-ji Temple, with its bell and all, was swallowed up by a great earthquake and the place is now marked by the present pond of Rengedai, which then appeared. The ringing of the bell is therefore always believed to be the herald of a brewing storm.

THE JINRIKISHA OR RICKSHAW

Few thought that the rickshaw or, as it is correctly pronounced in Japan, *jinrikisha*, would almost entirely disappear so suddenly from Japan. Until a few years ago the rickshaw and geisha-girl were two of the chief attractions for the foreign tourist, but the recent inroad of the motor-car has almost entirely driven the rickshaw from Japan.

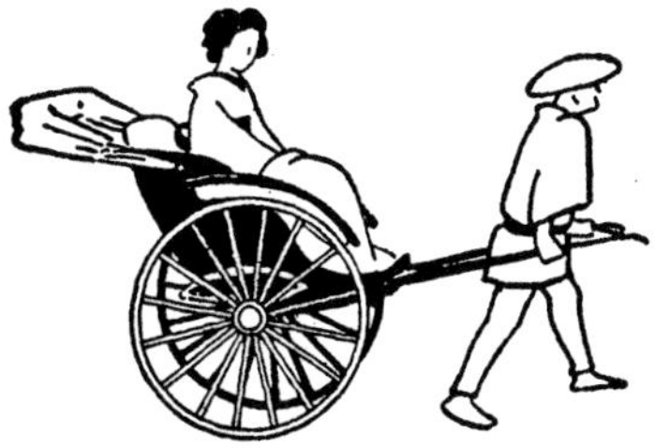

"Jinrikisha," as it stands, means "human-power-vehicle." It was invented by Yasuke Izumi and his two associates in 1869, and it was first used in the following year, 1870. Yasuke Izumi, who was born in the prefecture of Fukuoka, came in 1851 to Edo (Tokyo), where he was engaged in the manufacturing industry. When a carriage was introduced to Japan, Izumi at once saw the possibility of manufacturing a simpler kind of vehicle for use in Japan. Together with Kosuke Takayama and Tokichiro Suzuki, Izumi worked hard until they invented a simpler and lighter two-wheeled vehicle than the four-wheeled carriage. It was a marvel when compared with the slow *kago* or sedan-chair, which was soon replaced by the new rickshaw. Four poles were put on the four corners of the rickshaw for an awning and oil paper was used for protection on the rainy day, though the hood was invented in place of the awning, by Kanzayemon Uchida. The rickshaw was at first painted red. This was about 1872. Later, it was painted black as we see it now, a double-seater having been invented by this time.

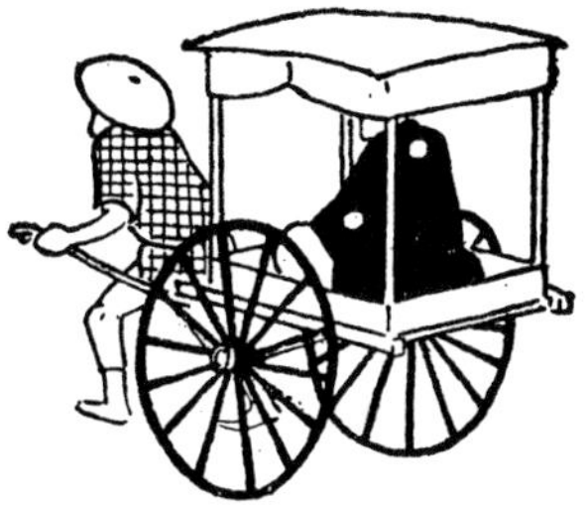

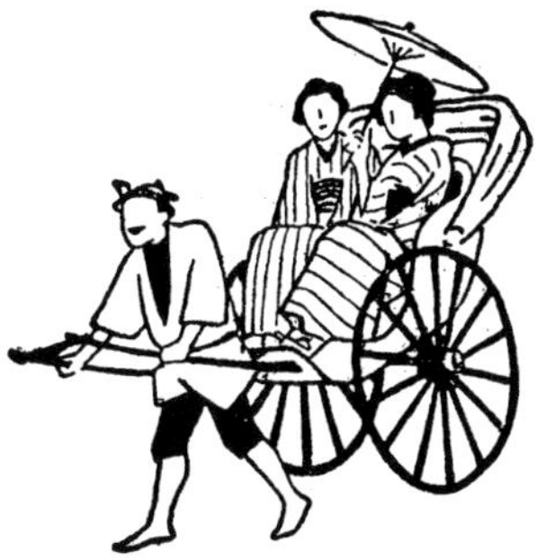

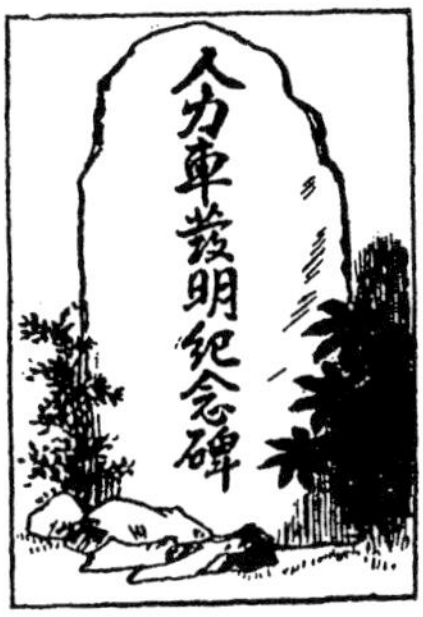

Izumi and his two associates received a reward of ¥200.00, a pretty big sum in those days, from the Imperial Government for their ingenious invention, and a monument was erected to their memory in the ground of the Zenko-ji Temple, which is a convent, at Aoyama, Tokyo.

The rickshaw is now seen more in the different ports of the Asiatic Continent than in Japan, the land of its invention, where it is practically a dead thing, except for tourists' amusement, conservative Japanese, and for those country districts where the road is so narrow that a motor-car cannot be driven over it.

THE FIRST FLYING MACHINE IN JAPAN

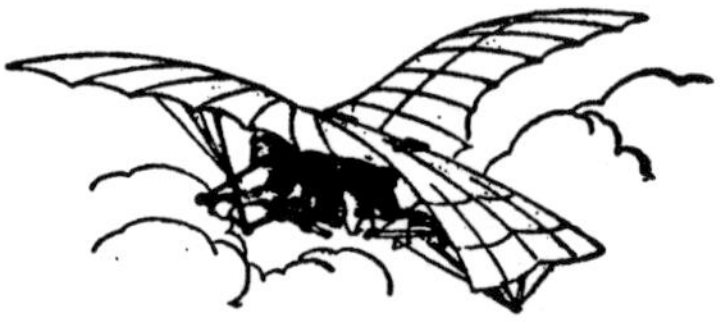

Kan Sazan (菅茶山) was a scholar of Chinese classics who lived in the province of Bingo in the 16th century. He operated a small school named the Renjiku (candid institute), where Rai-San-yo, one of the greatest historians Japan has produced, was once a pupil. In his little book titled "Fude-no-Susabi" (literary pursuits), Kan Sazan gives a detailed description of a flying machine invented a long time before him.

In the city of Okayama, Kan Sazan says, there lived a paper-mounter, Kokichi by name. He conceived the idea of flying up in the sky like a bird. He therefore caught a dove and made the measurement and weight of its body and wings, calculating their proportion. He then made two wings of paper large enough, according to his measurement, to carry up a man of his size and weight. With two strings which he tied to one end of each wing, he fanned the wings up and down. After several failures, Kokichi succeeded in flying up from the roof of his house; he was unable to fly up from the ground. In this way he flew about his house every day.

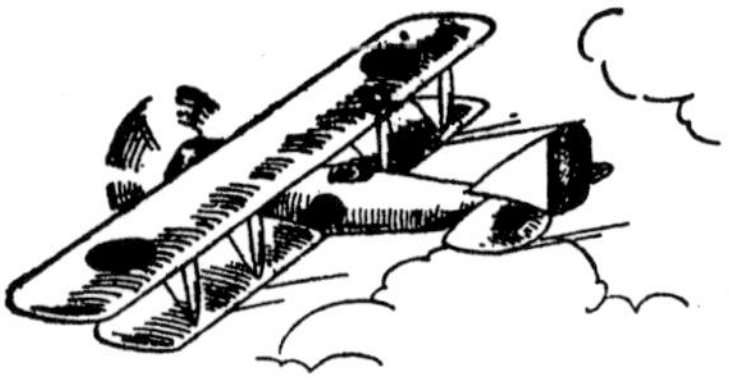

One day Kokichi ventured out farther than usual, flying over the fields, when he saw a picnic party at a distance. He flew on and thinking that he might find a friend in the party, he landed. The poor picnickers were scared off at the sight of the flying monster, so the flier had all their refreshments to himself. But, to his great dismay, Kokichi could not fly up from the ground, and he had therefore to walk back to his house, carrying his flying machine on his back.

The governor of the province summoned Kokichi to his office for his novel way of flying in the air, and deported him from the province and forfeited the machine, on the ground that it was a crime in the light of the law of the clan to scare the people, though it might be a pleasure to him to do what no other persons could.

ACUPUNCTURE IN JAPAN

Waichi Sugiyama, the inventor of acupuncture in Japan, lost his sight through an eye-disease when a baby, and he came to Edo, the Shogunate capital, when he was a little over ten years old, to study shampooing and massage under Ryomei Irie, the then best known in his profession. But the boy was so dull and slow of learning anything that his teacher, despaired of him, told him to go back to Kyoto, his native city. On his way back, Waichi stopped on the isle of Enoshima, near Kamakura, and underwent what is termed the "Seven-day confinement of devotion" in the little shrine of the Goddess Benten (Sarasvati). At the end of his devotional confinement, during which he prayed for help from on high, the young blind boy saw in a vision that his guardian goddess told him to go back to Edo once more and handed him a tube-needle to be used in acupuncture. Young Sugiyama therefore went back to Edo, where he studied acupuncture and invented a tube-needle, which is much used in needle-treatment in Japan today.

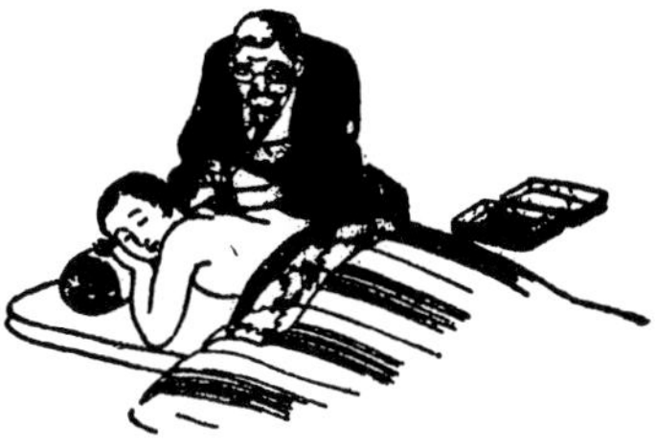

Needle-treatment.

Lord Tsunayoshi, the fifth Shogun of the Tokugawa regime, had a physical ailment of some kind, and Sugiyama was called to the Shogunate castle to give the Shogun a treatment, which cured him.

"I appreciate your treatment," the Shogun said to the blind needle-doctor. "Is there anything I can do for you in return, blind man? I will give you anything you may ask for. What then can I give you?"

"There is one thing, my lord, only one thing that I would like to have more than anything else."

"What is it? Tell me."

"I wish I could have an eye, my lord."

"Very well, blind man," Lord Tsunayoshi said calmly and kindly, "You shall have one."

The Shogun gave Waichi Sugiyama a lot of land in the street of Hitotsume or, as the ideograms go, "one-eye" (present Chitose St.) in Honjo, Edo, with an annual allowance of five hundred koku (koku=4.9 bushels) of rice.

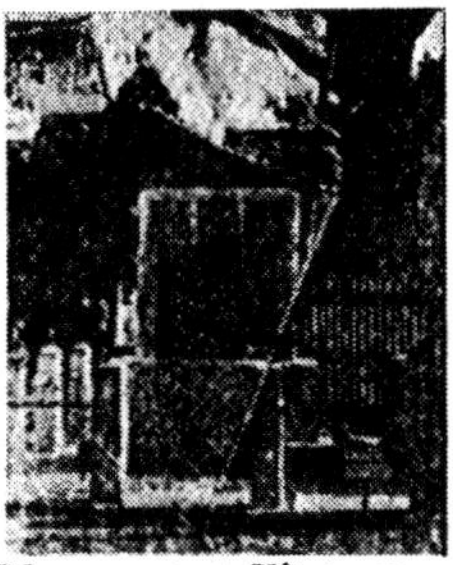

Monument at Hitotsume, Tokyo.

Sugiyama made a copy of the isle of Enoshima on his small lot of land, where he built a shrine dedicated to his guardian goddess. He also started a school for the blind, where he trained blind boys in the art of massage and needle-treatment. He was later appointed superintendent of the blind people, and he built schools for the blind at forty-five places throughout the country. They were the first schools for the blind in Japan.

Waichi Sugiyama died in 1694 at the age of 80, and his remains were buried on the isle of Enoshima.

Acupuncture is a recognized profession, and every acupuncturist has to obtain a government licence for its practice

HIBACHI OR THE BRAZIER (1)

Properly speaking, a genuine Japanese house has no glass-windows, though every modern-style house has them, and the shoji (paper sliding-door) is the only contrivance to keep out the cold, excepting the amado (literally, rain-door) or wooden sliding-door, which serves the same purpose as does the shutter of a foreign house. The shoji is a paper sliding-door with Japanese paper pasted on its frame-work. It keeps the room warmer than a foreigner may imagine that it does, for it preserves the heat of the room, and, at the same time, it helps its ventilation.

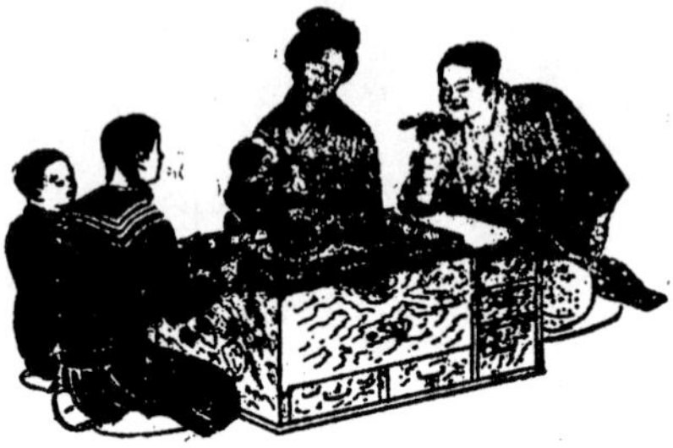

Family sitting around a Hibachi.

While the room of a foreign-style house is heated with a stove or fire-place, the Japanese seem to think little of warming their room. Strictly speaking, they have no heater for their room. The hibachi (literally, fire-basin) or fire-brazier is the only heater provided in a Japanese room, but it is used more for warming the hands than the room itself. The hibachi looks cozy and it is considered to be typically home-like in Japan to have all members of a home seated around a big hibachi and to talk while their hands are held out over the live charcoals in it.

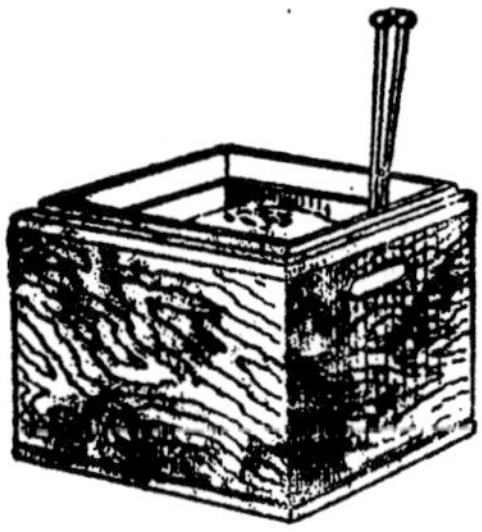

Hibachi.

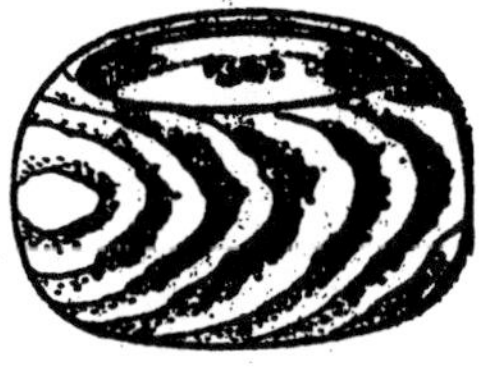

Hibachi.

The hibachi, possibly of Chinese origin, is of various shapes; square, round, oblong or fantastic, and of no less variety in size, being anywhere between about a foot and a foot and a half high and between about a foot and two feet long. Its materials may be wood, such as mulberry, paulownia, enju (pagoda-tree), persimmon-wood, etc., porcelain or bronze according to its owner's taste.

In a hibachi, we use charcoals, of which we have many kinds, those made of nara (quercus glandulifera), considered to be one of the best kinds in Japan. They are prepared in kilns of ever so many different kinds, as Japan has made special development in the preparation of charcoal, which has been used as the chief fuel for many generations. Many chemicals are obtained as by-products of charcoal.

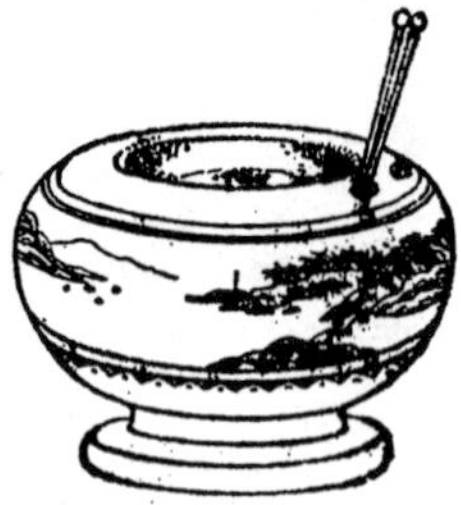

Hibachi.

HIBACHI OR THE BRAZIER (2)—*Concluded*

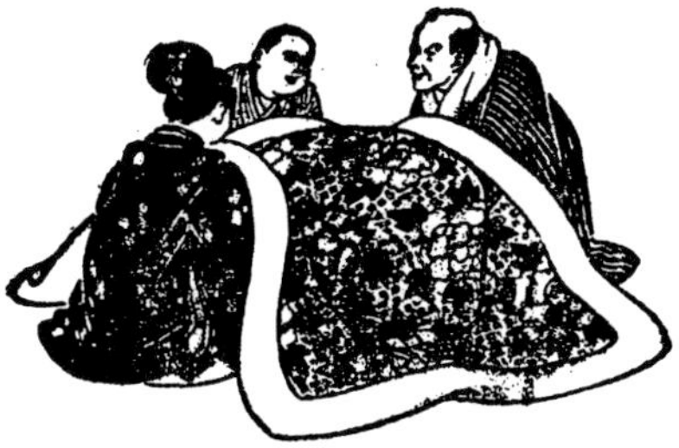

Kotatsu.

Kotatsu: The kotatsu is the popular footwarmer. A square container of charcoals is put into the tatami (mat-floor) with a wooden frame-work, over which a wadded cover is put to keep the kotatsu warm. The Japanese put their feet and sometimes their hands under the wadded cover to keep them warm. Children like to sit around a kotatsu and to listen to a nursery tale told by their father or mother. The kotatsu is a cozy warmer.

Irori: The irori (hearth) is no longer found in a modern-style house in Japan. It is a fire-place, which suggests the old-time home-life of Japan better than anything else does. Nothing is considered to be as entertaining as a chat around an old irori, black with soot, on a cold night after a hard day's work. The irori is the heater or stove of a room as well as a cooking place. It has what is called the jizai (literally, elasticity) made of bamboo, a contrivance for hanging a tea-kettle over the charcoal of the irori; so named because it can be "freely" stretched out or contracted.

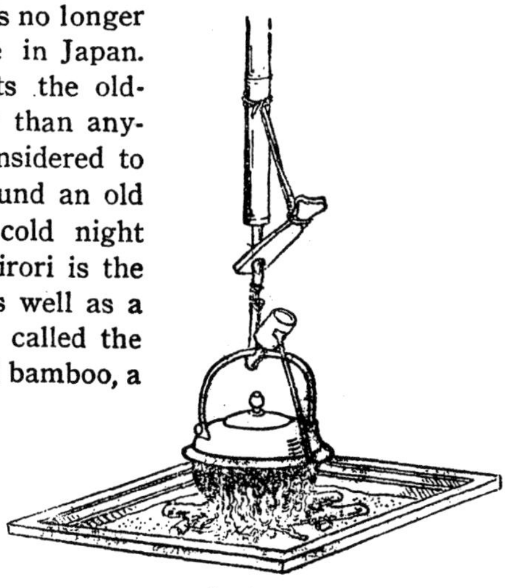

Irori.

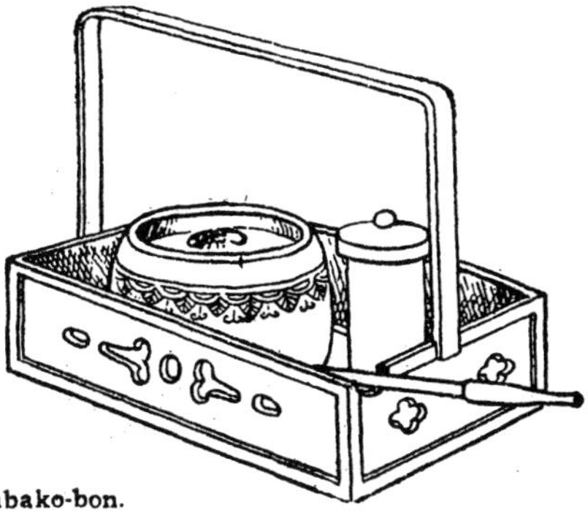

Tabako-bon.

Tabako-bon: The Tabako-bon (literally, tobacco-tray) is a portable box in which is carried live charcoal for lighting tobacco or a cigarette. It is most various and fantastic in shape.

THE CHOCHIN OR JAPANESE LANTERN (1)

The Chochin of Japan, or portable lantern as it means, is one of our most typical bamboo articles. Known the world over, the Japanese lantern is artistic in design but simple in construction, since it is made of bamboo-strips joined together with strings and covered with oiled paper. It is stretched out accordeon-fashion when in use, but collapsed when out of use. The use of a Japanese lantern is two-fold, practical and ornamental, as it is used to light the way in the night and also as an ornament. A lantern is necessary to the bride's escort at her wedding. Also, a funeral procession must have two or more plain and unpainted lanterns at the head, even when the funeral is held in the daytime, in order to lead the dead spirit, because, according to the Japanese belief, the land of the dead is dark and gloomy. This is why you see so many stone lanterns offered to a shrine. There are many kinds of lanterns in Japan; some of the chief are:

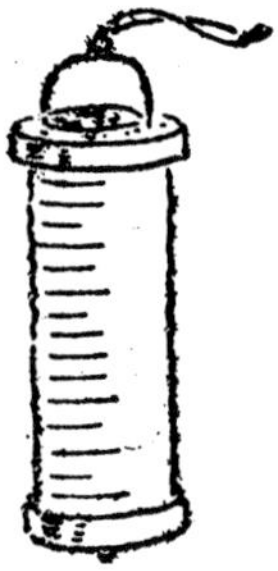

Odawara-chochin.

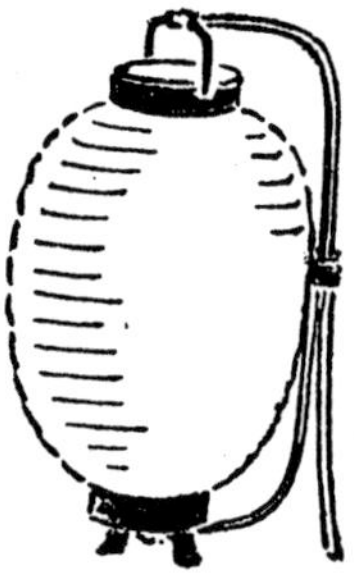

Yumihari-chochin.

Odawara-chochin: A cylindrical collapsible lantern, so named after the town of Odawara, where its inventor, Jinzaemon, lived in the 14th century. This lantern was commonly used by a rickshawman in the olden days.

Yumi-hari-chochin: A bow-supported lantern generally round and sometimes cylindrical. It is so named after its support which looks like a bow (yumi). Originally this lantern was used by the samurai on horseback; hence its other name of Uma-nori-chochin or horse-riding-lantern. In former days it had a long whale-bone handle. *Takahari-chochin:* This lantern is generally oval and is used at the time of festivals. It is not usually carried about like other lanterns, but it is put on the top of a tall pole or hung under the eaves of a house, though a lantern procession has this kind of lanterns as a guide or leader. *Hako-chochin:* This is a cylindrical lantern with a case at either end; hence the name meaning "case-lantern." The case, which is bell-shaped, may be made of a thin plate of wood or metal, and when the lantern is made to collapse, it is contained in the two cases. This lantern was invented in the 15th century.

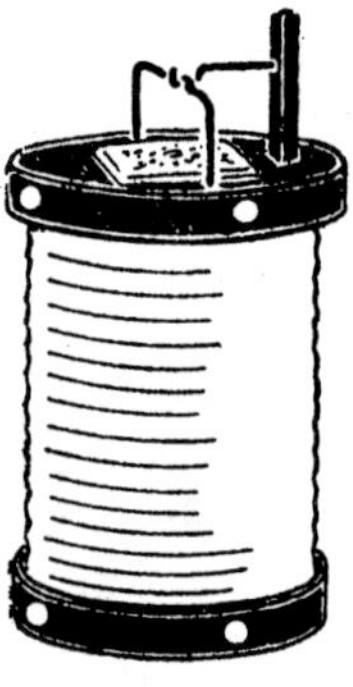

Hako-chochin.

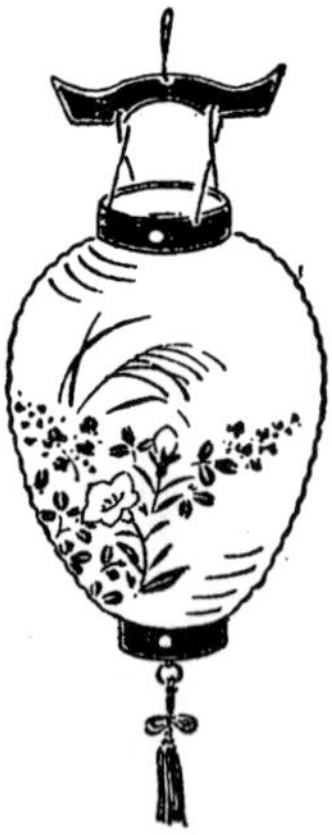

Gifu-chochin.

THE CHOCHIN OR JAPANESE LANTERN (2)

Concluded

Gifu-chochin: This lantern is so named because Gifu is the centre of its production. Oval, it is a kind of fancy lantern designed more for an ornamental use than practical, since, while most lanterns are made of oiled paper, the Gifu-chochin is made of silk with fantastic designs.

Hozuki-chochin: The Hozuki-chochin or "ground-cherry lantern" is round like a ground-cherry. Generally smaller in size than any other kind of lantern, it is either red or striped. It was originally designed as a toy, but it is now commonly used in lantern processions on happy occasions.

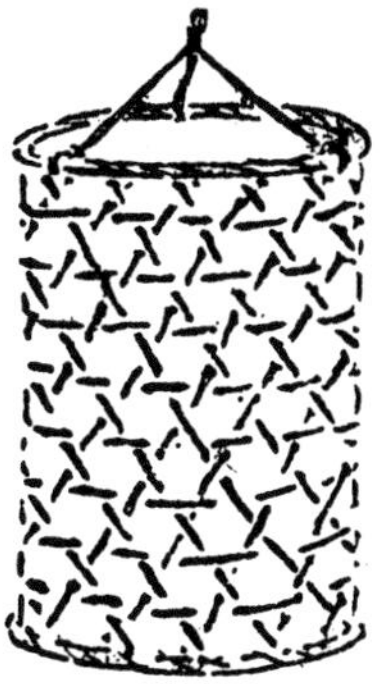

Kago-chochin.

Kago-chochin: - The Kago-chochin or "basket-lantern" is one designed like bamboo-basket and covered with oiled paper. It is still seen in the cold regions of North Japan.

Fugu-chochin: The Fugu-chochin or Globe-fish lantern is a novel kind made of the swollen globe-fish but it is intended more as an ornament than for practical use: Visitors to Kamakura and Enoshima are familiar with the Fugu-chochin as many globe-fish are caught in nearby waters. As it is a dangerous fish to eat, the fishermen prefer to convert it into a lantern.

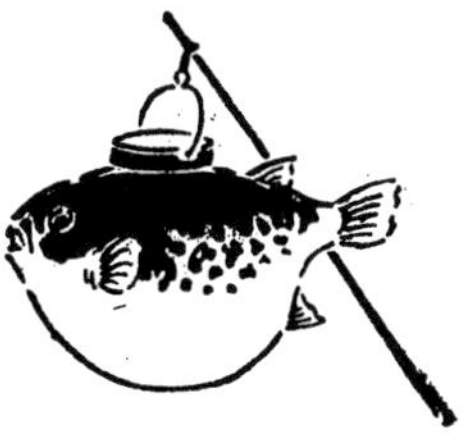

Fugu-chochin.

Some Japanese sayings about the lantern:

"Chochin-mochi" (The lantern-carrier), meaning a candle-holder or boaster.

"Chochin ni Tsurigane" (A lantern and a gong) often used as an instance of asymmetry, disproportion, ill-balance or ill-match.

"Chochin-mochi wa saki ni tatsu" (The lantern-carrier stands before). The candle that goes before gives the best light (German).

"Chochin-mochi Ashimoto kurai" (The lantern does not light the path before the feet of its carrier.) One must go abroad for news of home.

"Chochin wo karita On wa wasurenaku tomo, Tento no On wa wasureru." (One who does not forget the kindness of a friend who lends a lantern, forgets the sun.)

RICE-STRAW: HOW IT IS USED

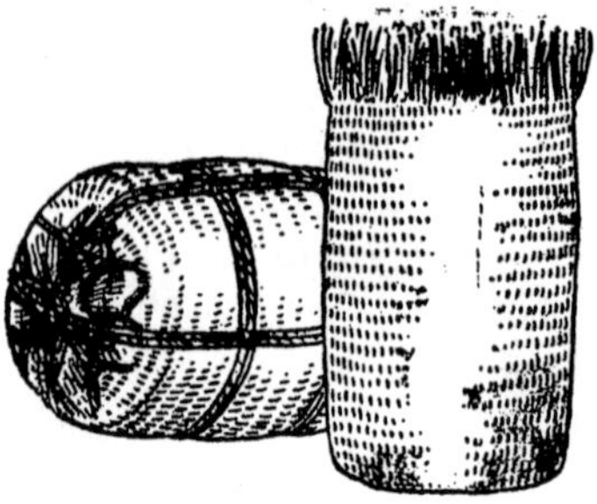

Bales.

Japan produces sixty million ***koku*** (***koku***=4.9 bushels) of rice a year on an average, and the disposal of rice-straw is a great problem to the Japanese. A large quantity of rice-straw is used in feeding cattle and horses, but at the same time rice-straw is put to many different uses, a few of the more important being as follows:—

Shimenawa or Sacred Rope: Because rice is the most important agricultural product in Japan, the Shimenawa, or Sacred Rope, placed before a Shinto shrine or around a place or article that has to be kept sacred, is made of rice-straw. Properly speaking, the Shimenawa should have the rice ears left on it.

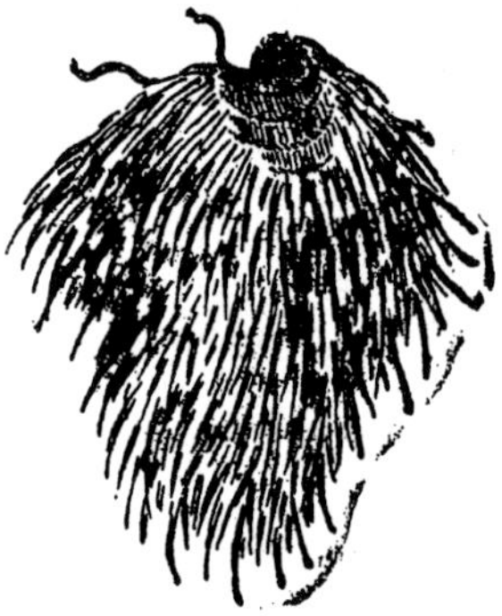

Rain-coat.

Rice-bale: The bale in which rice is put or preserved is made of rice-straw. A rice-bale generally contains 4 or 5 *to* (*to*=0.49 bushels) of rice.

Straw-bed: A bed made of rice-straw covered with cloth of some kind is cool in summer but warm in winter.

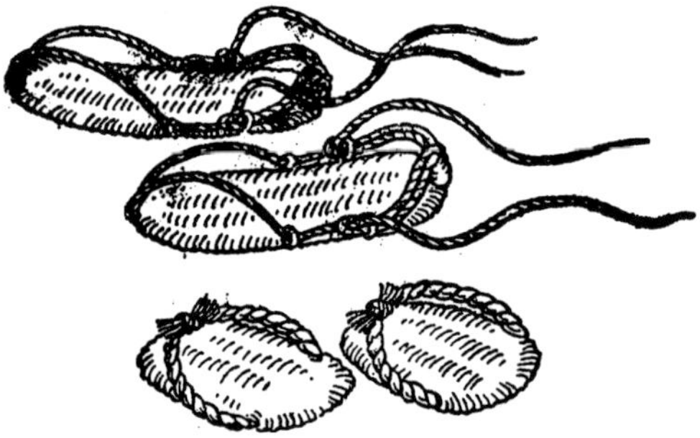

Foot-gears.

Straw-matting: Straw is made into a kind of matting, but it is generally used, in the tatami (matting), which is covered with a rush-mat.

Straw-rope: A straw-rope is not so strong as that of hemp or some other material, but it is both cheap and handy.

Straw rain-coat: Mino, or straw rain-coat, is very common and popular among our farmers and other out-door workers. It looks shabby, perhaps, but it is cool in summer and warm in winter, and also very cheap.

Straw-foot-gear: Zohri (footgear) is so cheap that a pair can be had for a copper or two.

Snow-boots and snow-shoes are made also of rice-straw, because they keep the feet warm in the snow.

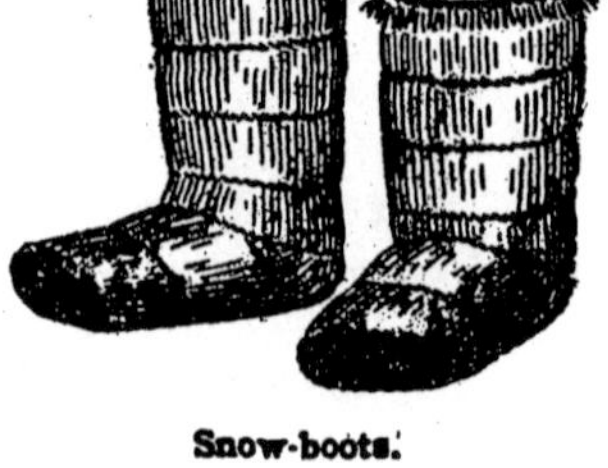

Snow-boots.

TAKAGARI—"HAWK-HUNTING" (1)

Takagari, or, as it is literally translated "hawk-hunting," by which is meant the catching of small birds by means of a trained hawk, was an amusement for emperors, courtiers and local lords in the feudal days of Japan. In the procession of a daimyo, for instance, a hawk was carried by its trainer or keeper, on whose fist it perched.

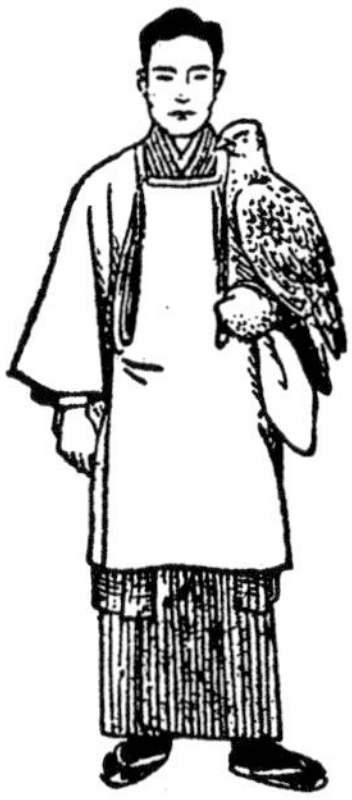

A trained-hawk.

In the forty-third year (355 A.D.) of the reign of the Emperor Nintoku (the 16th), a hawk was presented, for the first time in the history of Japan, to the Imperial court by Yosami-no-miyake Aniko, and the emperor told Sake-no-kimi to train it in the Korean manner. At one time the emperor went to catch birds by means of the hawk at Mozuno, when, it is recorded, dozens of pheasants were caught by the hawk. "Hawk-hunting" was in vogue after this, but the Empress Gemmyo (the 43rd), under the influence of Buddhism, prohibited the practice of catching birds with a trained hawk. The Emperors Kammu (the 50th), Saga (the 52nd), Uda (the 59th) and Daigo (the 60th) were so fond of "hawk-hunting" that they went out frequently to catch small birds on it and at one time, it is said, dozens of hawks were kept at the court. In 898, the Emperor Uda had a "hawking" contest by dividing his hawks into two parties. The left side caught ninety-four small birds, while the right side ninety-one small ones and a quail, which was counted as three small birds, and so the contest ended in a tie.

"Hawk-hunting" was much in fashion during the Shogunate dynasty of Tokugawa, and some of the Shogun were very fond of it. Every local lord, too, kept some trained hawks for the pleasure of catching birds, but it was generally prohibited for a private person to keep a hawk.

How to train a hawk: A wild hawk, when caught, is put in a dark room where it is kept for three to six days without anything to eat or drink, though a light is given for a few hours in the night. Then a little food, chiefly a pheasant, is given, and it is kept again without food or drink for two days, during which it is trained to perch on the fist of its trainer. The bird will recognize the voice and footsteps of its trainer, who gives it food, and becomes tame in two or three weeks. It is trained to pick up its food and come to its trainer for food. While in training, the hawk is fed on such birds as sparrows, buntings, thrushes, pigeons, herons, etc., though different birds are food to different kinds of hawks, and, as a rule, the hen-hawk is used to catch birds.

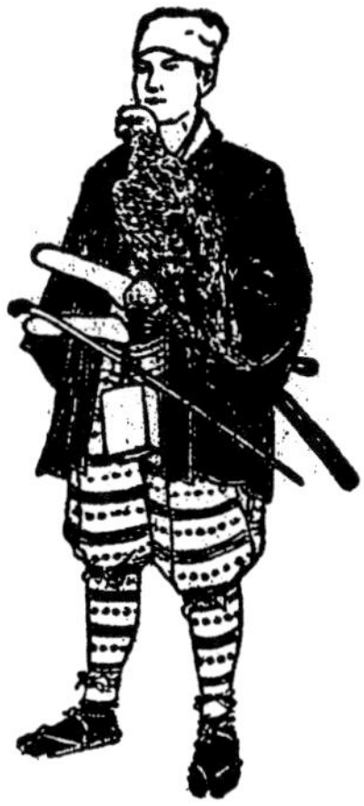

A hawk-keeper.

(*Continued*)

TAKAGARI—"HAWK-HUNTING" (2)—*Concluded*

Catching a crane: In feudal days there were many places in Japan where cranes came in flocks. When "hawk-hunting" is planned, a farmer is frequently sent to the place where the cranes gather thick, for a crane is said to be specially fearful of man. On the hunting day the keeper carries the hawk on his fist, and when he is near enough for the hawk to catch a crane a great noise is made to surprise the cranes. They start to fly. The hawk is set free and catches one of the cranes by the neck. The crane struggles to shake the hawk off, but it clings on to it. If the hawk appears too weak to bring the victim to the ground, another hawk is sent up to help the first, and the crane is brought to the ground.

Samurai learns a lesson from a crane: Ryoshun Imagawa, a samurai, was very fond of "hawk-hunting." Once on a "hawk-hunting," he sent his hawk up after a crane. It was too strong for his hawk, so another was sent up to assist the first. When the crane was brought down to the ground, his hawk-keeper came up to cut a bit of flesh from the crane as it was a custom to give every hawk a bit of flesh from each bird it caught. The crane, however, showed no sign of fear, but remained quiet as if it were resigned to the inevitable. Ryoshun, who watched it, was moved by the "samurai-like way" of the crane, as he termed it because he compared the calm attitude of the bird to that of a samurai who met death with defiance. Ryoshun gave up his "hawk-hunting" and he never caught a bird any more by means of a trained hawk.

Takajo-machi: Every large town or city, which was capital of its clan during feudal days, has a street called Takajo-machi (hawk-keepers' street). It was the street for the hawk trainers and keepers to live in.

Age of a hawk told by the colour of its talons: The age of a hawk can be told by the colour of its talons:

	Colour of talons	
Age	Upper side	Lower side
One to two years	black	red
Three "	black	blue
Four to five "	white	stripes
Six to seven "	black	red stripes
Eight to nine "	white	white
Ten to eleven "	yellow	black

CHIDORI-GARI OR PLOVER-CATCHING

The plover is called "chidori" meaning "thousand-birds" in the Japanese language. This is possibly because plovers are found in such large flocks. They are birds of passage and generally visit the Japanese shores in the autumn. Japan is rich in various kinds of the plover, of which the late Dr. S. Ogawa counted fifty-five with over two hundred varieties.

The plover was first mentioned in the Kojiki (712 A.D.), and Japanese literature is full of poems on plovers, which offered a favorite theme for verse. In former days the plover was found all over the country but it is gradually getting scare today.

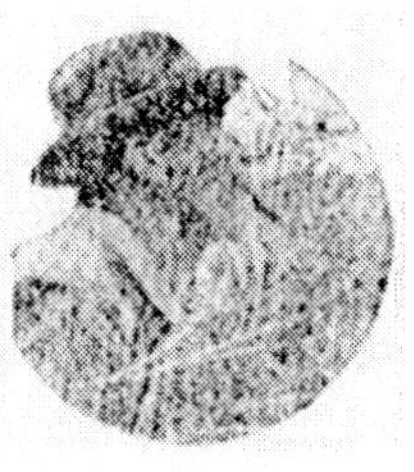

Mr. Kanzo Fukuda.

At Gyotoku, on the other side of Tokyo Bay, plovers flock together in large numbers, and an old man, Kanzo Fukuda by name, is a great expert in snaring plovers by a clever method.

At ebb tide, Fukuda builds up what he calls a Tsukiba (or mound) about 6 ken by 4 ken (ken=6 Jap. ft.), and high enough to remain above the water at flood tide.

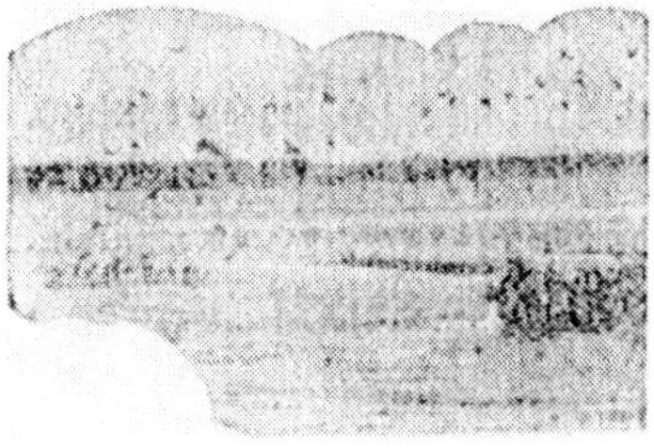

Flocks of plovers in the distance.

On the sand, near the mound, the old man sets 30 or 40 short bamboos, 2 or 3 feet long, each with a stuffed plover on it. These bamboos are hidden under the water at flood tide. A net, some 6 ken long and 7 ft. wide is provided on the mound, and Fukuda, with his assistants, hides himself in a small shed near the mound.

The old man is very clever at blowing a special whistle, which is an inch or two long. With it he can imitate the cries of different kinds of plovers. When he sees a flock of plovers in the distance, where they look no bigger than mere dots against the sky, he quickly recognizes them and imitates their cry, by blowing on his whistle. They are attracted by the whistle, and finding the call-birds, try to alight near them, only to find that the water is too deep for them. They then find their way to the mound, where the net is thrown over them to snare them at a cast.

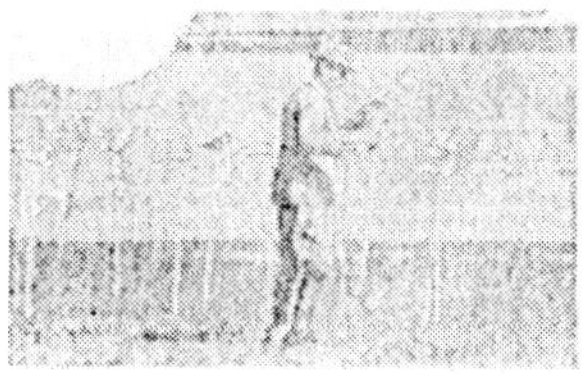

Call-plovers-on-bamboos.

This method of catching plovers is so effective that the Preserve Bureau of the Imperial Household is protecting the old man and his way of snaring plovers.

HOW "SUKIYAKI" IS SERVED (1)

The first thing to bear in mind is that all the cooking of Sukiyaki is done before the diner. He therefore has no fear of unseen dangers lurking in an unsanitary kitchen. This does not mean, however, that there is the least objectionable smell from the cooking. In fact, it is recognized by all who have eaten Sukiyaki that the cooking of it is not the least attraction. Its aroma is a great appetizer, for it seems to be a mixture of all those best kitchen smells which excite the salivary glands and thus make the mouth water.

Now, to create the Japanese atmosphere the first thing necessary at a Sukiyaki party is that the guests sit on cushions on the floor.

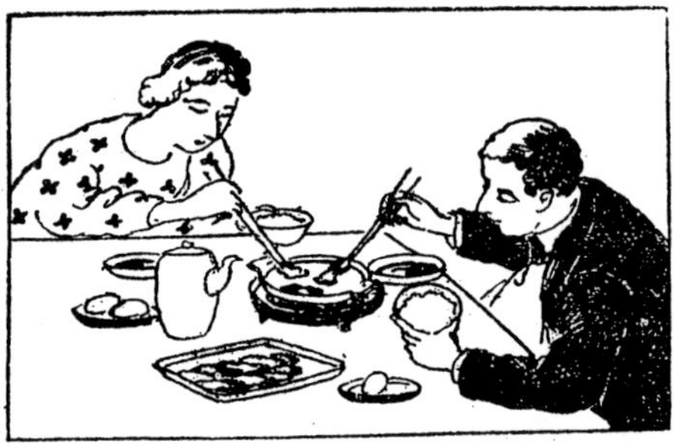

On this the guests squat in as near to the accustomed Japanese graceful style as their unaccustomed legs and spine will permit them. In the middle of each circular table providing for a party of four guests or more is a delightfully clean electric heater. Sometimes a charcoal brazier is used instead. On this is set the frying-pan or *nabe* as it is called in Japanese. It is from this word that this meal is often called *gyunabe.* Gyu means beef and *nabe,* pan. On plates, surrounding the *nabe* are the various constituents required for the meal. Most important of course is the beef. This must be tender and cut in small thin slices. Next in importance come the cut leeks, which are beautiful and white and contribute much to the delicious appeal which Sukiyaki makes. These, too, must be cut fine. Onions also are after mixed with the leeks. Now comes the highly-nutritious bean-curd known as *tofu* in Japan. This is very light and digestible, and of great value in Japanese soups and other dishes. A constituent known as *Konnyaku* is next used. This is a gelatine-like vegetable cut into thin strings so that it looks much like silvery spaghetti. Japanese doctors say that it has considerable medicinal value. As seasoning the Japanese usually put a little of what is called *Ajinomoto,* along with a little soup stock. This *Ajinomoto* is one of the most marvellous seasonings in the world, recognized even by the French as superior to their *sel de celeri,* in which French chefs have so much faith. It ought to be better known by housewives throughout the world. Housewives travelling make inquiries about it and buy quantities in Japan to take home. Now come two most important liquids. The first,

(*Continued*)

shoyu or *soy*, is indispensable. It is the Oriental sauce which is the basis of almost all sauces in the world, with the difference, however, that whereas so many Western sauces are strongly spiced and therefore too piquant, and consequently harmful to delicate stomachs, the Japanese *shoyu* is a natural soy bean-sauce, highly nutritious and an irresistible appetizer.

The second liquid is *sake* or Japanese rice-wine. This is optional in Sukiyaki. The teetotaller need not therefore fear breaking his pledge, unless he should chance to taste his neighbour's Sukiyaki, prepared with a little *sake* added, and find, as he is almost sure to do, that it is even more delicious than his own. Gourmets are unanimous in their opinion that, when a little *sake* is added to the *shoyu* or sauce, the Sukiyaki is better. It is of course the same with certain French dishes that would be much less appetizing, and in fact impossible, unless prepared in wine. Like Lamb's Bo-bo and his roast pork, therefore, the teetotaller who illicitly takes his Sukiyaki with a little *sake* may be absolved for committing moral sin by having acquired a gastronomical cardinal virtue.

Now, immediately the *nabe* or pan is heated through on the electric stove the hostess takes a piece of suet between her chop-sticks and rubs it around the hot pan to grease it, much as does the housewife who lards her baking-tin before putting the dough into it and then into the oven. For this greasing process there is now a pure animal fat prepared which is more convenient, and which melts quicker than suet. Next, the hostess (or the host, since Sukiyaki cooking is so simple that even a mere man can do it) puts in a little *shoyu* from the dainty Japanese pot resembling an invalid feeder. To this *shoyu* is added some sugar, which improves the taste when used to season Sukiyaki. Sometimes a small quantity of castor-sugar is spread over the vegetables instead. Here he adds a little *sake*, and then puts into the pan a fairly large proportion of leeks, onions, *konnyaku* and *tofu*. When these are getting brown, and smelling just right, the hostess begins to put in the meat. By this time the guest is feeling famished, and, usually too impatient to wait for the beef first, he begins to take the cooked vegetables from the pan with his chop-sticks, or *hashi* as they are called in Japanese. But of course the vegetables are too hot to transfer to the mouth direct. However, there is no need to blow them. The inventors of Sukiyaki have ordained that in the bowl provided to each guest there shall be beaten a raw egg. This, while being yet an additional sauce, serves also to cool the seething vegetables and hot meat. As for the meat, the hostess puts several pieces in the pan at a time. These she quickly turns over, and as soon as they are browned on both sides they should be taken by the guests. To leave the meat too long spoils it. It is best eaten before it has time to get browned all through. As piece after piece of meat goes into and comes out of the pan the sauce becomes richer, since it absorbs the blood from the succulent, sizzling, sirloin slices, so that the taste improves as the meal progresses. Thus, in eating Sukiyaki the appetite grows on what it feeds on.

(*Continued*)

HOW "SUKIYAKI" IS SERVED (3)—*Concluded*

Naturally the guests have other things served to them. On a small tray given to each guest is a lacquer bowl of delicious Japanese clear soup, and a porcelain bowl for rice. Then to drink he may choose first-class Japanese *sake* or beer, followed by green tea. It is another of Sukiyaki's virtues that it develops a wonderful thirst. This is due to the *shoyu*. As, however, there is always a sufficient variety of drinks at a Sukiyaki party to quench the most obstinate of thirsts there is no need to worry about that. Not the least joy therefore in taking Sukiyaki is in quenching the thirst it creates! All this means that at the conclusion of the meal the guest rises (if indeed he is capable) with a feeling of self-satisfaction that is rarely his after other meals.

Here it must be added that Sukiyaki may also be served with chicken instead of beef. Its correct name then is *torinabe*. In fact, almost any kind of meat may be used as the basic constituent of Sukiyaki, according to taste. For example, venison, wild-boar, rabbit, pork, mutton, pheasant and wild-duck. Even oysters and clams may serve, but when shellfish is used the dish is called *hamanabe*. There is also an endless variety of vegetables which may be used, according to the diner's tastes and the season of the year. The most popular, however, are celery, bamboo-shoots, mushrooms, spring and Bermuda onions, spinach, leeks, and a vegetable known in Japan as *shingiku* which belongs to the chrysanthemum family.

ORIGIN OF "SUKIYAKI"

In England and America the laborers insist that the most delicious bacon is that fried on the spade. This is natural, since they eat the bacon after that hard work which is the best appetizer, and after frying it on Nature's best and cleanest frying-pan, the spade, which has been cleansed and and polished in mother earth. Now, it is strange that, though many stories are told of the origin of Sukiyaki, what appears to be the most authentic is that Japanese farmers years ago found meat fried on the plow-share the most delicious. Especially did they find this so when, again like Bo-bo, they believed it a sin to eat meat in Buddhist Japan. To the succulent meat was added therefore the sauce of eating what was forbidden. The Japanese farmer consequently found the first Sukiyaki doubly delicious, since, added to its succulent taste was the even greater pleasure of eating this forbidden meat in mortal sin. The word literally means therefore "to fry on a plow." It is said that the Japanese "Bo-bos" of early times fried their prohibited meat on their plows. In support of this theory we have it from the old book "*Koji Ruien,*" published over a century ago, that "Sukiyaki is to grill chicken, seasoned in *soy*, on a plow-share over a fire." It was towards the end of the Tokugawa Era that Japanese progressives claimed the right to eat meat and thus advance with the times. It is happily no longer a sin to eat meat in Japan. In fact, it is becoming a patriotic duty, in these days of vitaminized victuals, in order to build up the nation's youth. Never was patriotic duty so delightful! It is not surprising therefore that the visitor to Japan may find on his arrival there large numbers of Sukiyaki restaurants.

Sukiyaki is universally admitted to be one of the most delicious meals in creation,

SEMBEI—WAFER OR CRACKER (1)

Sembei, literally meaning "baked rice-cake," looks like a wafer or rice-cracker, and it is one of the cheapest and most popular kinds of confectionery in Japan. It is made from rice or wheat flour, which is kneaded into dough and baked thin in a metal mould after being mixed with egg, sea-weed, sesame, Indian corn, spices or any other materials that the maker is pleased to put into it. According to its ingredients, Sembei has different names, such as:

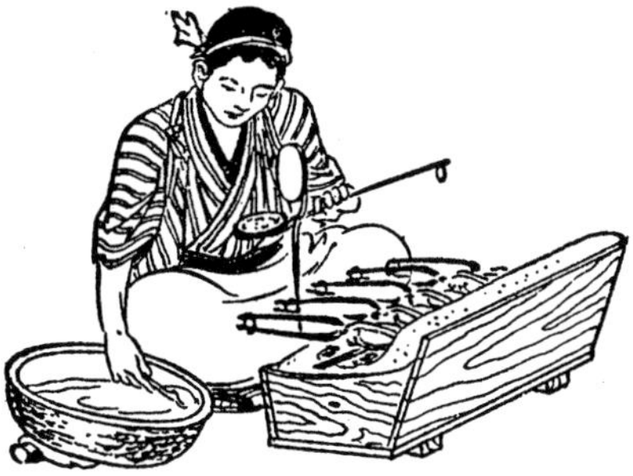
The baking of Sembei.

Tamago-sembei, with egg (tamago) mixed in,
Nori-sembei, with sea-weed (nori),
Morokoshi-sembei, with maize or Indian corn (morokoshi),
Goma-sembei, with sesame (goma),
Ebi-sembei, with shrimp (ebi).

Some kinds of Sembi are named after their shape, such as Kame-no-ko-sembei after a tortoise-shell (kame-no-ko) and Kawara-sembei after tiles (kawara). Kiraku-sembei, a famous Sembei in Yokohama, implies the happy idea of pleasure (raku) that will last as long as tortoise (ki indicating tortoise) lives which is proverbially said to live for a thousand years. Shio-sembei is perhaps one of the cheapest kinds of Sembei. It is a kind of rice-wafer, round or square or stick-shaped with Shoyu (Japanese soy) applied to make it salty. Tsujiura-sembei has a divining piece of paper or fortune-telling motto as the name indicates (tsuji = street; ura = divining), and it is very popular with orthodox and superstitious Japanese. Foreigners in Japan quickly learn to like Sembei, and foreign children are specially fond of the salty or Shio-Sembei, which is an ideal snack for almost any time of the day. A few more kinds of famous Sembei are:—

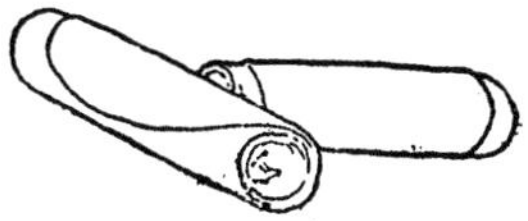
Rolled Sembei.

Chukei-sembei: So named after Ino Tadataka, commonly called Ino Chukei, a great geographer who made an accurate map of Japan after surveying the country thoroughly. His statue is erected at his birth-place, Sawara in Chiba Prefecture, and this Sembei bears his picture.

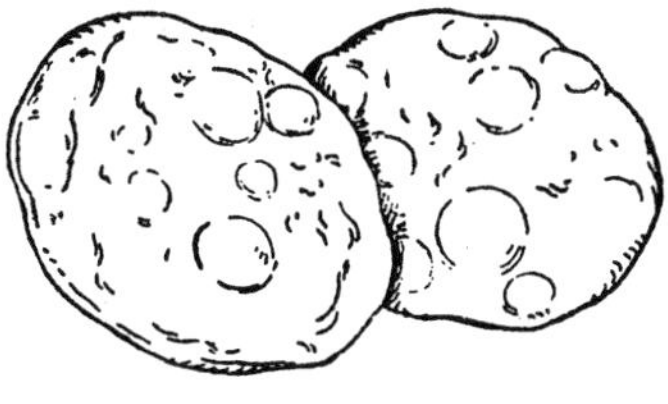
A kind of Sembei.

(Continued)

Imo-sembei: It has sweet potato (imo) in it. It is a famous product of Kawagoe, Saitama Prefecture, which produces a fine variety of sweet potato.

Taru-sembei: This kind of Sembei is made in imitation of a barrel (taru) of Shoyu or Japanese soy, of which a superior quality is manufactured at Choshi, Chiba Prefecture, where this Sembei is made.

Kawara-sembei: Kamakura, where this kind of Sembei is made, was the capital of the Minamoto Shogunate (1192–1204) and the Hojo Regency (1205–1333). This Sembei is so named because it represents different tiles (kawara) used at Kamakura in those early days.

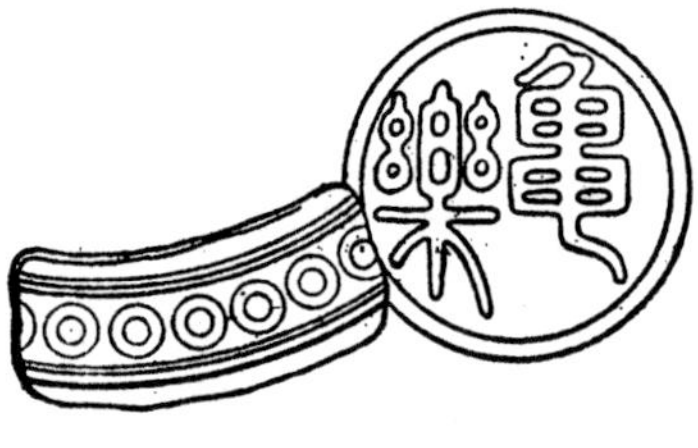

Kiraku-Sembei.

Kobe produces another kind of Kawara-sembei. As the city is always associated with, and noted for, the Minatogawa Shrine dedicated to Masashige Kusunoki, the royalist, who died at Minatogawa in the cause of the Emperor Godaigo in 1336, this Sembei has the picture of the pathetic separation between Masashige and his young son, Masatsura, who also died for the same emperor in 1349.

Kikusui-sembei: Kikusui, literally "chrysanthemum-water" represents the family crest of Masashige Kusunoki, one of the greatest royalists who died at Minatogawa in 1336. This is a famous product of Kobe, where stands the Minatogawa Shrine dedicated to the great royalist.

Heiji-sembei: This Sembei, which is baked in the shape of a straw-hat, has a touching story. Heiji was an ex-samurai, a descendant of the Taira family, and who was too poor to afford to buy fish for his sick old mother. He went to catch fish at Akogi-ga-ura, a fish-preserve, where the fish to be offered to the Ise Shrines were caught. One night he was detected by a government official, and he ran away leaving his straw-hat on the beach. The characters (平治) of his name written on the straw-hat he left there led to his arrest.

But Hirakawa Jirozo, who had been under great obligations to Heiji, appeared before the government official, and said: "I am told that Heiji is arrested because of the two characters written on the straw-hat that was found on the beach. I have come to establish his innocence, for the hat is mine. The two characters (平治) stand for my family and personal names, (平河治郎藏) because I have written their first characters.

Heiji was set free and Jirozo taken into custody in his place. The Heiji-Sembei is consequently made in the shape of the straw-hat that Heiji left when fleeing from the Akogi-ga-ura beach.

MISO OR BEAN-PASTE (1)

It is generally believed in Japan that miso or bean-paste is responsible in a great measure for the generally sound physical health of the Japanese. It is indispensable to Japanese cuisine, though miso is not used, as butter is used, at table. Meat or fish may be easily dispensed with, but bean-paste soup is de rigueur at the Japanese breakfast, which mainly consists of vegetables. What bread and butter is to a foreigner, boiled rice and bean-paste soup are to the Japanese. Bean-paste is also used in preserving foodstuffs, and vegetables pickled in good bean-paste will keep for years without going bad at all.

The word "miso" is of obscure derivation, but it is usually taken to mean "immature bean-soy." People often attribute it to the invention of Priest Kanshin, a Chinese Buddhist, who was naturalised in Japan during the Nara days (710–784). Priest Ingen (1591–1673), who introduced the Wobaku sect of Buddhism to Japan, and after whom the haricot beans are named "ingen," was such a great admirer of bean-paste that, it is said, he took its soup every day instead of a certain Chinese medicine that he had used many years.

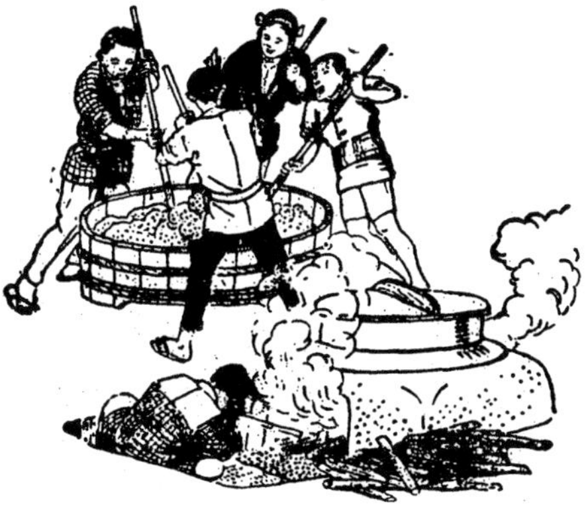

The preparation of Miso.

Bean paste is made from soya beans, which may be yellow, blue or white, according to the kind of paste to be made. The beans are soaked overnight in water and boiled so soft the following day that they are then pounded into paste which is in turn fully mixed with a certain quantity of salt and "*koji*" or malt prepared from wheat or rice. The mixture, after being stirred up several times, is kept in a tub for a long time or sometimes even several years until it matures by fermentation. One often finds in a local farmer's house bean paste that has been kept for several decades. The longer the paste is kept, it is believed, the better it tastes.

In the rural districts, every farmer makes bean-paste for his own use, but in the urban districts it is supplied by the maker, and according to a report issued by the Government, Japan manufactures hundreds of million kilograms, valued at tens of million yen every year.

(*Continued*)

MISO OR BEAN-PASTE (2)

There are several kinds of bean paste on the market, according to the different methods of preparation, and the following are some of the chief, most of which are named after the centres where they are made:—

Aka (red)-miso;
Inaka (local)-miso;
Sendai-miso;
Edo-miso;
Hatcho-miso;
Shiro (white)-miso.

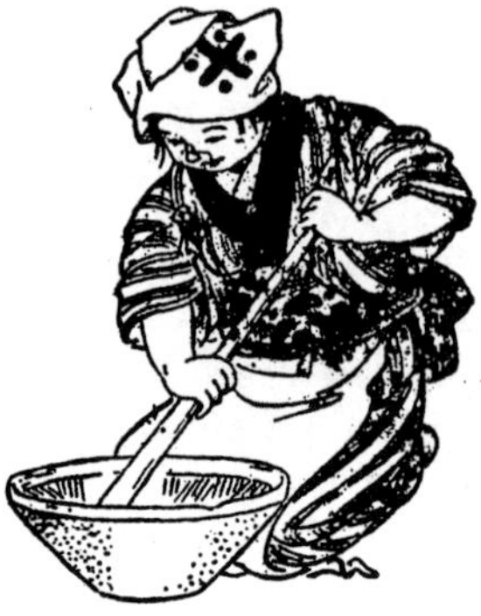
Maid preparing Miso-soup.

The analysis of Hatcho-miso, Sendai-miso and Inaka-miso is given below:—

	Hatcho-miso	Sendai-miso	Inaka-miso
	%	%	%
Water	46.873	50.923	51.410
Ash	13.794	12.816	12.213
Organic matter	59.333	36.262	36.377
Pure nitrogen	1.932	1.835	1.645
Soluble nitrogen	1.707	—	1.238
Albumen nitrogen	1.070	0.936	0.912
Soluble albumen nitrogen	0.916	—	0.892
Non-albumen nitrogen	0.949	—	0.734
Organic basic nitrogen	0.627	0.513	0.523
Ammonium nitrogen	0.024	—	0.022
Others (amino-acid) nitrogen	0.299	—	0.189
Fat	6.208	—	5.892
Chlorine	6.011	—	—
Salt	11.544	—	—
Alcohol	—	—	—

* * * * *

A few sayings about miso:

Miso wo tsukeru = to put miso on (to make a mess of it).

Temae miso = one's own miso (all geese are swans).

Miso no Miso kusaki wa jo-miso ni arazu = Miso savouring of miso is no good miso.

SHOYU OR JAPANESE SOY (1)

Shoyu or Japanese soy is more important in Japanese cooking than any other seasoning material or spice. In fact, the taste of Japanese food depends upon the quality and amount of soy used in it. Our soy is more necessary to Japanese cooking than foreign sauce is to foreign cuisine or indeed as useful as butter, sauce and gravy put together.

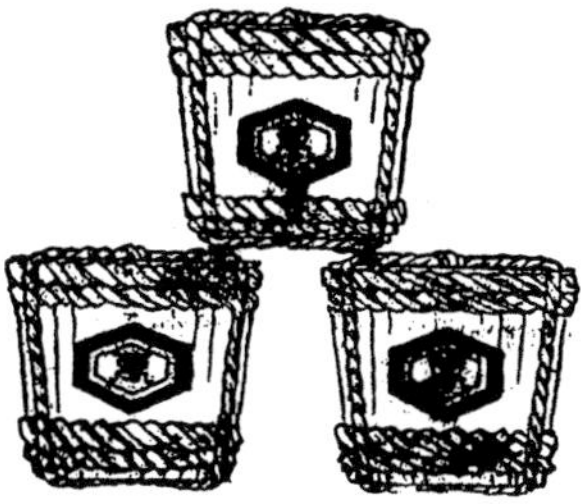

Kikko-man brand of Shoyu.

Neither the origin of shoyu nor the date of its invention is known for sure, but it is first mentioned in a record found in the Shoso-in, of the Totai-ji Temple, where the personal belongings of the Emperor Shomu (the 45th) and some other emperors are preserved. Also, it is mentioned in the Engi-shiki, a book of regulations of the Engi era (901–922). Chinese shoyu was imported during the early days of the Ashikaga regime (1338–1574), and it was in large quantities manufactured at Kyoto during the Shogunate of Yoshiharu Ashikaga (1521–1545). But it is certain that shoyu in those early days was not in liquid form, and it was not until the early period of the Tokugawa regime (1603–1867) that liquid shoyu was first made in Japan.

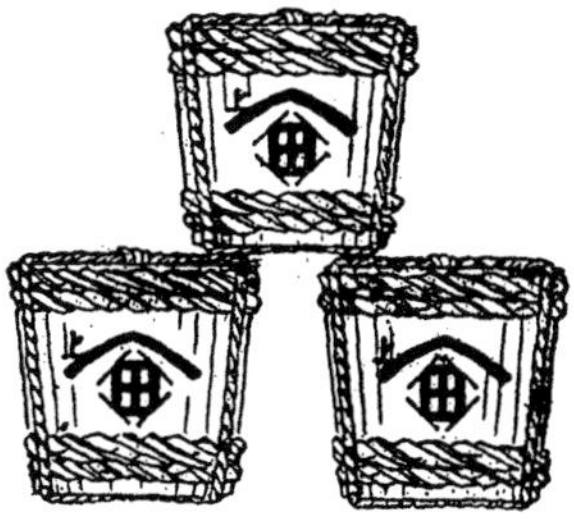

Higeta brand of Shoyu.

Tradition has it that in 1228 Gakushin, a Buddhist priest from China, taught the people of Wakayama the method of making shoyu, and the village of Yuasa in that province is known to be the oldest centre of shoyu manufacture. Shoyu was manufactured for the first time at Choshi, another centre, in Chiba prefecture, in 1616, and one shoyu-maker, Hamaguchi by name, came to Choshi from Wakayama in 1645 to coach others in shoyu manufacture. Noda in the same prefecture of Chiba began the manufacture of shoyu during the era of Genroku (1688–1703), and it is now one of the largest centres of shoyu manufacture in Japan. Shoyu was much used during the Tokugawa period (1603–1867) and greatly improved during the Meiji era (1868–1912). In 1933 Japan produced 512 million litres of shoyu valued at 57 million yen, of which the share of Chiba prefecture where Choshi and Noda are situated, amounted to 111 million litres valued at 17 million yen. These figures are not inclusive, as the farmer makes shoyu for his own use.

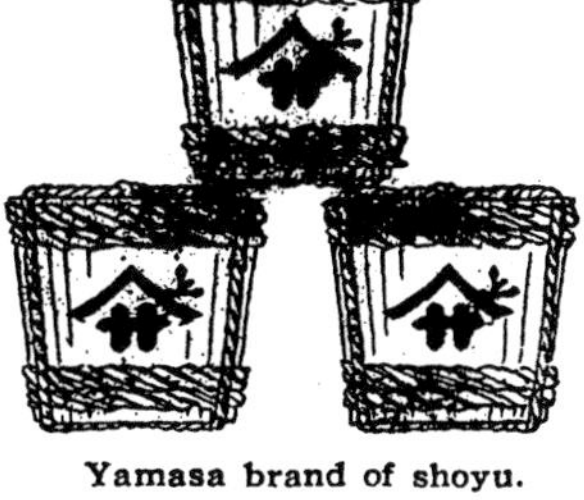

Yamasa brand of shoyu.

SHOYU OR JAPANESE SOY (2)

Prof. L. Lunge and A. Langgardt, who taught at the Tokyo Imperial University, in its early years (about 1877) took such a great interest in the manufacture of shoyu that they often visited the shoyu centres to study it in the making. Prof. A. Langgardt on his return home to Germany, made an imitation of Japanese soy and got it patented in Germany and "Moggi" now manufactured in Europe is a corruption of the name Mogi, who was a shoyu-maker of Noda.

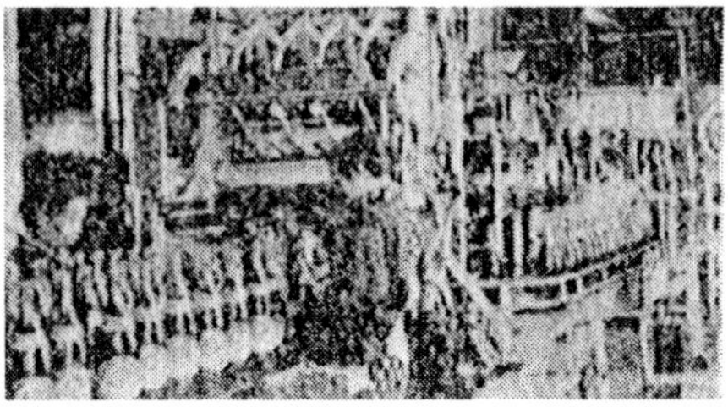

The bottling factory.

Shoyu is manufactured from wheat (sometimes barley), beans, salt and water. The wheat, upon the quality of which that of shoyu greatly depends, is grilled in a large iron-pan till by constant stirring it is burned brown. Then it is crushed. Beans are next boiled in a large couldron. A heavy weight is put on the lid of the kettle so that as little steam as possible may escape. After boiling for three or four hours, the fire is put out and the beans are kept overnight in the same kettle. They may be steamed instead for five or six hours. The grilled wheat and the boiled beans are now mixed and put into the malt-room where with some malt-seed added, they turn into malt in a few days. A certain amount of salt water or brine is put over the malt, which is kept for several days, by stirring it up every now and then, until it matures by fermentation. This combination is put in a press and thereby soy is obtained.

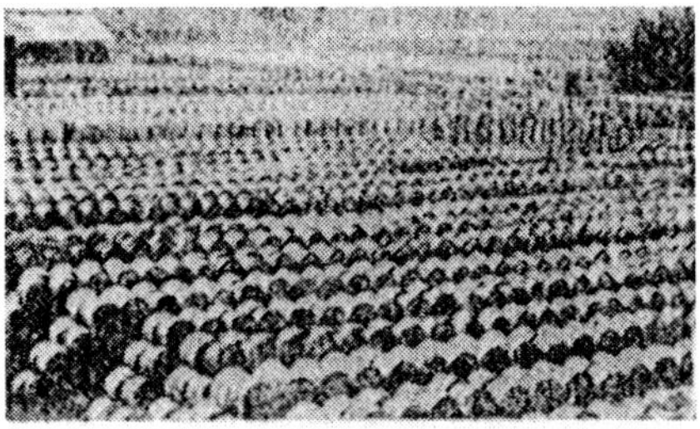

Wood for shoyu barrels.

There are several brands of Japanese soy, of which the following are the chief:—

Yama-sa (mountain ∧ and the letter "sa" サ)

Kikko-man (Tortoise-shell ⬡ and the ideogram for "10,000" 萬 (pronounced "man")

SHOYU OR JAPANESE SOY (3)—*Concluded*

Higeta (moustache ︿ and the ideogram for "field" 田)

Kagi-yamasa (key ┐ and yamasa ⌃サ)

Maru-kin (Circle ○ and the ideogram for "gold" 金)

The following is the average result obtained after analysing seventy-seven brands of Shoyu:—

Gravity (15°)	12.040
Solid matter	36.832
Albumen nitrogen	0.132
Non-albumen nitrogen	1.021
Sugar (as glocose)	3.381
Starch	0.483
Volatile acid	0.109
Non-volatile acid	0.880
Ash	21.543
Salt	19.734
Sulphuric acid	0.554
Epsom salts	1.117

(*Osaka Hygienic Laboratory*)

THE FIRE-BRIGADE OF TOKYO (1)

"A fire is necessary to Tokyo, for it makes an old street new," said the late Marquis Shigenobu Okuma, and a fire has been proverbially said to be the "Flower of Edo (Tokyo)." Tokyo is indeed a city of fires, which break out year in and year out. Roughly speaking, there are two thousand fires on an average in Tokyo in a year or three per day. The city was totally reduced to ashes in 1601, or 11 years after the castle of Edo was built by Iyeyasu Tokugawa. No less than 107 thousand lives were lost at what is known by the "big fire of Meireki" (1657), and 223 streets were entirely destroyed by fire in 1772. But by far the worst fire broke out after the Great Earthquake in 1923, when 366 thousand houses were burned down with 60 thousand people killed or missing. No wonder that the Shogunate capital adopted a very efficient fire-brigade system.

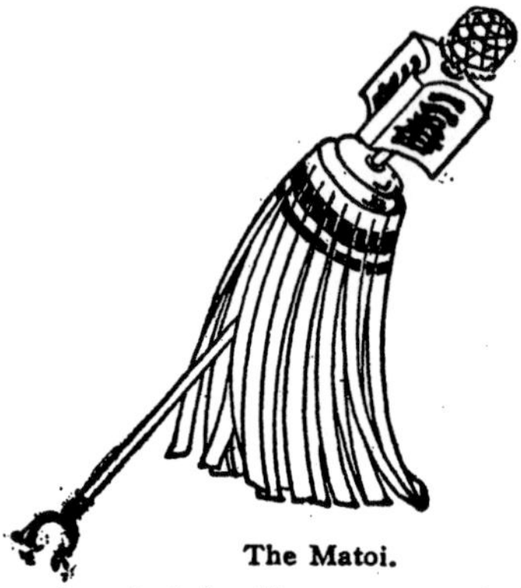

The Matoi.

It was soon after the Great Fire of 1601 that the Shogunate Government adopted the system of having a standing brigade of firemen always ready to act upon the outbreak of a fire in Edo. In 1629 some dozen Daimyo or lords were required to contribute to the fire brigade at the rate of 30 firemen for each 10,000 koku (koku=4.9 bushels) of rice that he received as an allowance, and these firemen took turns on duty each for a period of ten days. There were 15 units of firemen in Edo in 1648, though later on the responsibility for keeping a fire under control fell more upon the street-firemen than upon those appointed by the Government.

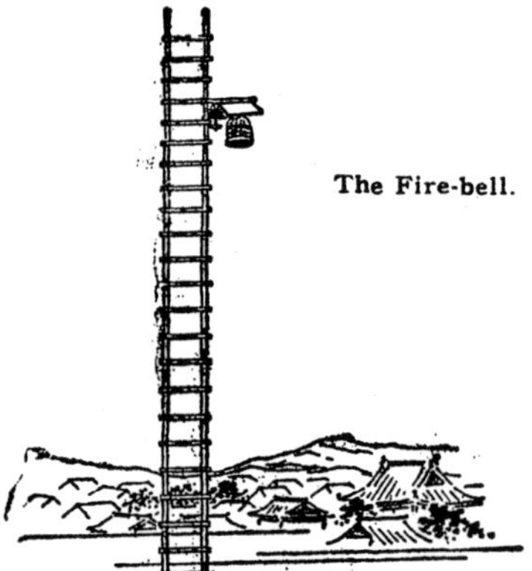

The Fire-bell.

Later on, the whole city of Edo was divided into 48 fire sections or units, each named after, or by, one or other letter of the Japanese alphabet assigned to it, though four letters homonymously considered ominous or unlucky were replaced by so many portentous characters. Each unit consisted of 70 firemen as follows:—

Head	1	Assistant	1
Ladder-carrier	6	Fireman	45
Sub-head	1	Standard-bearer	3
Horse-carrier	13	Total	70

(Continued)

THE FIRE-BRIGADE OF TOKYO (2)—*Concluded*

The "Matoi" or standard was no less important or even sacred than that of an army, for it was set up at a part where the fire was put out by the unit to which it belonged, and a quarrel often took place between units over a place where each claimed to have extinguished the fire. So each standard-bearer was held as responsible as is the ensign of an army.

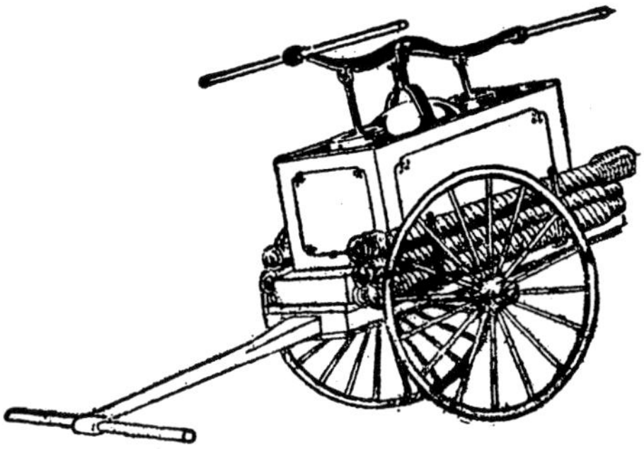

Old time Fire-engine.

There were 2,930 firemen in Tokyo at the time of the Restoration in 1868, and we have now over a thousand firemen all told in thirty-six wards in Tokyo.

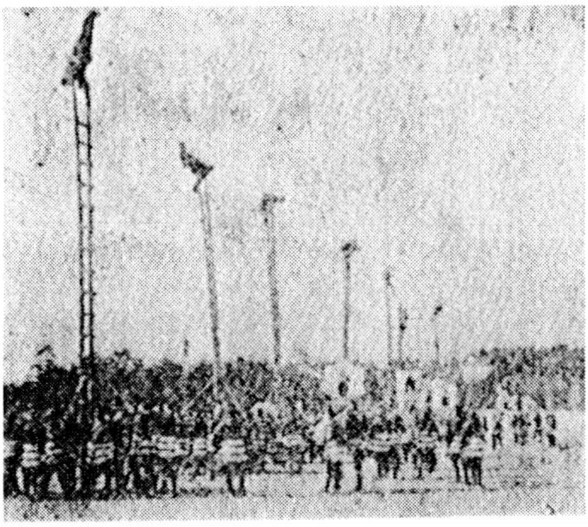

Climbing of ladders.

The Dezome-shiki: The Dezome-shiki or New Year's Parade of the fire-brigades is held on the 6th or thereabouts of January every year, when all the fire-brigades make a parade. The fire-men make all sorts of feats, of which the climbing of ladders and the shaking of the Matoi are the most attractive.

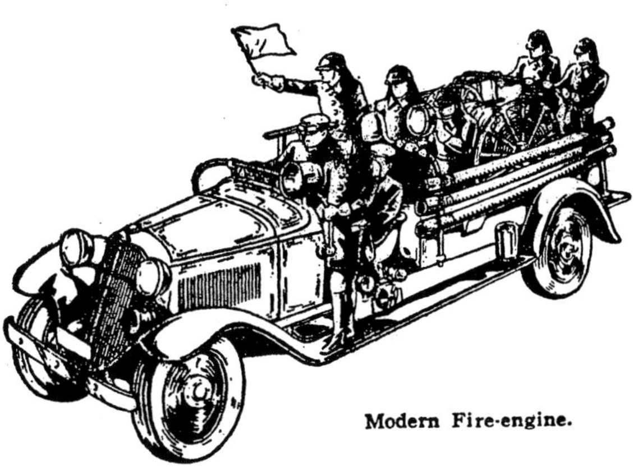

Modern Fire-engine.

THE NEW YEAR'S ODE PARTY AT IMPERIAL COURT

In the month of January every year, the New Year's Ode Party is held in the presence of T.I.M. the Emperor and Empress at court, when many Princes and Princesses of the Blood and court dignitaries attend the function. The theme of the ode is imposed by the Emperor towards the end of the preceding year, and any person of either sex can send in a short poem of thirty-one syllables that he or she may compose on the given subject. The judges are appointed by the Emperor in January, and the poems of their selection are announced at the meeting along with those of the Emperor and Empress and the Princes and Princesses of the Blood. The reading begins with the poems submitted by non-officials and courtiers of the lowest rank, followed by those of the higher courtiers so on up to the members of the Imperial family, until the poems of the Empress and Emperor are finally announced or sung out.

The annual court ceremony of the New Year's Ode Party is a very solemn one that a limited few can have the honour of attending it. But the management of the JOAK Broadcasting Station, Tokyo, has made it possible for the people to listen-in to the repetition by a radio broadcast of the grand function. The reading of the odes is done once for those written by the subjects, twice for those of the members of the Imperial families, three times for the one composed by Her Imperial Majesty the Empress and five times for the one by His Imperial Majesty the Emperor.

The ode party is of ancient origin, but only the courtiers of high rank were privileged to submit their compositions in former days. It was in the seventh year of the Meiji era (187[illegible]), that the privilege of submitting poems was granted to the people at large, and in the twelfth year (1879) that good poems composed by the general public were selected and announced at the party.

The theme for 1937 was "Snow on the Farm-House" and the New Year's Ode Party was held on Jan. 26th, this year in the Ho-o-no-ma (Phoenix Hall) of the Imperial Palace, which was used for a similar purpose for the first time in 1890. After the traditional historic ceremonies had been gone through, the poems were announced by the Reader in the presence of T.I.M. the Emperor and Empress and the Princes and Princesses of the Blood. It is reported that no less than 41,456 poems were submitted this year, but only forty-six poems were selected besides those of Their Imperial Majesties the Emperor and the Empress.

YABUSAME OR SHOOTING FROM A RUNNING HORSE

Yabusame, which means "shooting from a running horse," is of old origin, for it is generally believed to have had its origin in the shooting ceremony held by the ex-Emperor Shirakawa (the 72nd) in the fourth month of the year 1096, though according to a certain record, the practice was started during the reign of the Emperor Temmu (the 40th). The ceremony was adopted by Minamoto, one of the two military families of Feudal Japan, which seems to have held the ceremony of Yabusame generation after generation, until in 1266 it became an annual affair at the festival of the Hachiman Shrine at Kamakura, where Yoritomo, the first Shogun of Minamoto, established the Shogunate Government called the Bakufu or Camp Government, in 1186. The ceremony was often held at the Kasuga Shrine at Nara by Ashikaga, but it fell into disuse during the latter part of the Ashikaga Shogunate (1338-1573). When Iyeshige, the Shogunate heir, fell a victim to smallpox, the Shogun Yoshimune, his father, ordered Yabusame to be restored after the style given in old record, and the ceremonial shooting was performed as an offering before the Hachiman Shrine at Takada, Edo, on the 15th of the third month, 1728, with the prayer that the Shogunate heir might be restored to health. In 1875, seven years after the Restoration of 1868, Viscount Masanori Honda restored Yabusame, which had all but died, and Prince Tokugawa gave it at his private residence in 1887, when the Emperor Meiji was present at the performance.

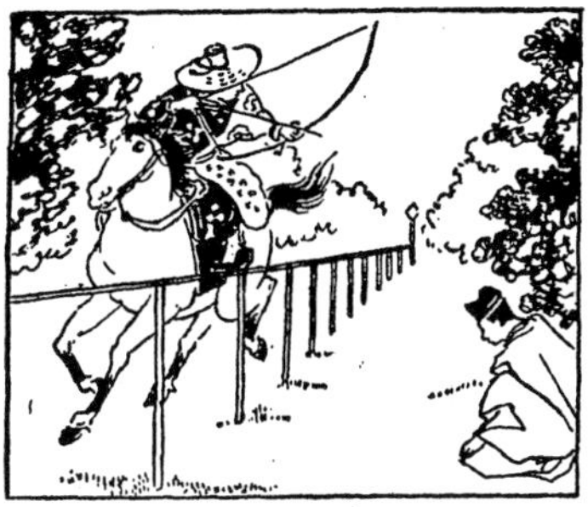

The classical ceremonial shooting of Yabusame had 16, 10, 7, or even 36 shooters in former days, but nowadays there are generally three shooters dressed in appropriate costume and mounted on horseback. While their horses gallop along a course of 2 cho (cho = about 119 yards), they shoot at three targets, 2 ft. sq. each put on a pole 3 or 4 ft. high, posted at some intervals.

Yabusame is now held on some felicitous occasions or at the festival of a local shrine. The Hachiman Shrine at Kamakura gives it as an annual ceremony on September 19. It is a ceremony of great interest, typical of ancient Japan, and many foreigners make a special visit to the shrine to see it.

THE CHRYSANTHEMUM-VIEWING PARTY (1)

In November every year, the Kangiku-no-Gyoen or Chrysanthemum-viewing Garden Party is held at the Shinjuku Imperial Garden. To it are invited government officials, military and naval officers, foreign diplomats in Japan, leading businessmen, educators, ministers of religion, social-workers and many other influential people of different ranks of society. A competitive show of chrysanthemum-flowers is also held about this time in almost every city of Japan, where the cultivation of the chrysanthemum has made a unique development, for chrysanthemum-viewing is an age-old practice in this country.

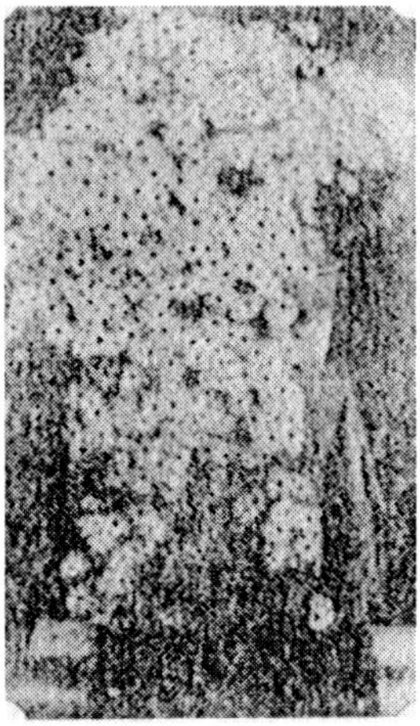

Cascade Chrysanthemum.

According to records, a chrysanthemum-viewing party was for the first time held by the Emperor Kao-tsu of the Han dynasty, China, on the ninth day of the ninth month, 200 B.C., in commemoration of his favorite Lady Ch'i. Because the sun (day) and the moon (month) meet together in the perfect number of nine, this festival was named the Choyo-no-Sekku or Seasonal festival of a double-positive figure, and the chrysanthemum-viewing was a great occasion in China. It was on the ninth day of the ninth month, 685 (or 686, according to the Nihon-Shoki) that the first chrysanthemum-viewing party was held in Japan. The Emperor Temmu (the 40th) attended the garden party, when a gift was given to every one there, from the Crown Prince down. The Emperor Heijo (the 51st) held also a chrysanthemum party in the Heian Imperial Garden in 807, and a certain authentic history gives this party as the first ever held in Japan for viewing the chrysanthemum.

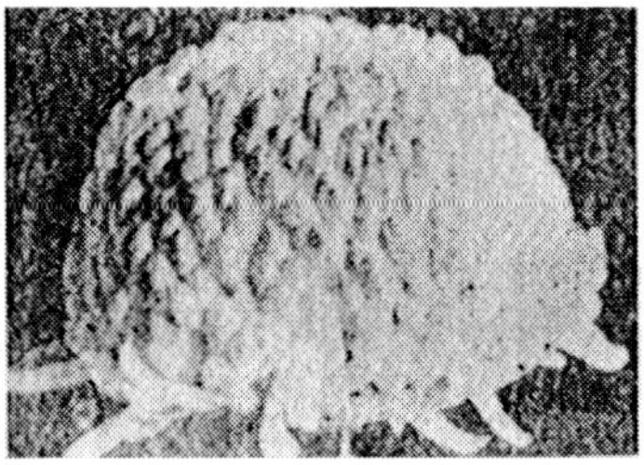

The Han people of China prized the chrysanthemum a great deal, probably because they were very fond of yellow. They lived in the valley of the Yellow River, where the soil looked yellow and this colour always suggested gold to them. So the Han people preferred the yellow chrysanthemum to that of any other colour.

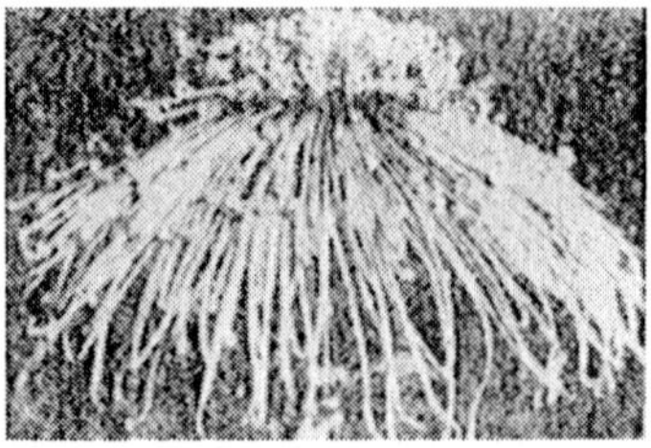

(Continued)

THE CHRYSANTHEMUM-VIEWING PARTY (2)

—Concluded

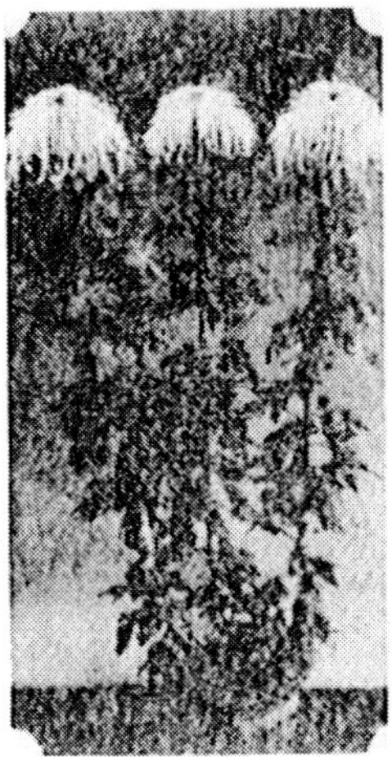

Kuan-ching was an inhabitant of Juan, China. He used to travel round with Jei-ch'ang-fang, a fortune-teller. One day, the fortune-teller said that on the ninth day of the ninth month a misfortune was to visit Kuan-ching's house where every living thing would be killed. "You should get therefore a bag of pepper made and go up a mountain, where you must drink chrysanthemum-wine, which will cast out the misfortune," the fortune-teller added. So Kuan-ching took his family up a mountain nearby, carrying the bag of pepper, and on coming down he found all his dogs, poultry, cows and sheep were dead. This is said to be the origin of the chrysanthemum-wine, which the Japanese still take on the occasion of a chrysanthemum party, and also of the Japanese pepper, which was used at a garden party in former days.

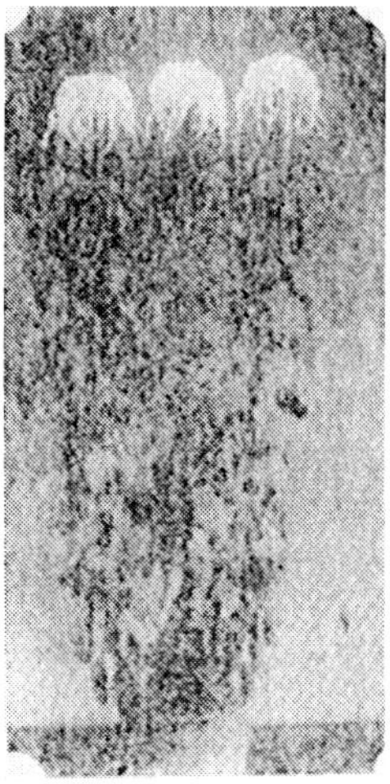

The Emperor Wen of the Wei dynasty was so weak that when he was seven years old, a fortune-teller said that he would not live to be older than fifteen years. But a hermit, P'eng-tsu by name, who had a great admiration for the personality of the young Emperor, gave him medicine made from the chrysanthemum, thanks to which, it is recorded, the Emperor lived till he was seventy years old. Hence in Japan, as well as in China, the chrysanthemum is called a "life-prolonging plant."

Japan had some varieties of wild chrysanthemums, but those which are now popularly cultivated were imported from China during the Nara days (710–784), though, according to a certain authentic history, the chrysanthemum was brought from Korea to Japan during the reign of the Emperor Nintoku (the 16th). ("Chrysanthemum of Japan," by Dr. T. Niwa.)

HIGAN OR PARAMITA (1)

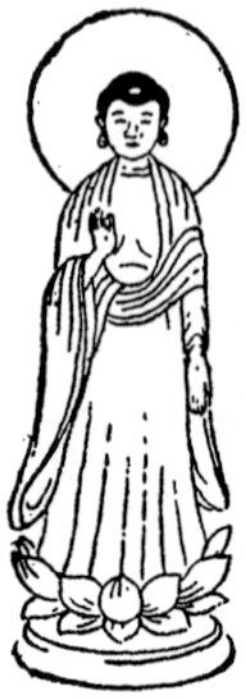
Amitabha.

"Higan," which comes twice a year, in March and September, i.e., at the spring and autumnal equinoxes, means "the other side," as the characters go; for, according to Buddhism, it is a translation of the Sanscrit "Paramita," (reaching the other side). Now our life and death are considered to be on "this side" Nirvana, which is on the "other side." This is because the worldly cares are compared to "the stream" that Bosatsu (Bodhisattva), the Saviour, crosses as "the ship" carrying the penitent and converted between the two sides. During the Higan period, which lasts for seven days, the Kongo-Hannya-Haramita or Vajracchedia-paramita sutra is therefore chanted at the temples of a certain Buddhist sect, and a prayer is offered for the salvation of the dead.

Higan seems to be of unknown origin, but it was widely observed in the eighth century. In February, 806, the Emperor Heizei (the 51st) issued an ordinance that Higan should be generally observed in the country.

The devout Buddhists of Tokyo would go on what is termed the Six-Amitabha Visit during the Higan period of seven days. During the reign of the Emperor Shomu (the 45th), it is recorded, a local chief by the name of Kiyomitsu, who lived at Toshima, near Edo (Tokyo) gave his daughter in marriage to another chief called Shosuke Adachi. Her mother-in-law was so ill-natured and cruel to her, that the daughter-in-law drowned herself in a stream called Numata, and her five (some say twelve) maids followed their beloved mistress in death. Kiyomitsu, her father, was so grieved over her death that he went on a pilgrimage through the country in order to pray at different temples and shrines for the repose of her departed spirit. At Kumano, in Kii Province, Kiyomitsu had a vision, in obedience to which he cut down a sacred tree and threw it into the sea. This tree drifted on the sea and came to the river in which his daughter had drowned herself. When Priest Gyoki came to the Kanto District, in which Kiyomitsu lived, he asked the priest to carve the Roku-Amida or Six Amitabha images of the sacred tree which made so mysterious a trip from Kii to the River Numata. Six statues of the Amitabha were carved and they were enshrined in the following temples near Edo (Tokyo):

(*Continued*)

1. The Saifuku-ji Temple, Ohji,
2. The Keimyo-ji Temple, Numata,
4. The Yoraku-ji Temple, Tabata,
3. The Muryo-ji Temple, Nishigahara,
6. The Joko-ji Temple, Kameido,
5. The Joraku-ji Temple, Uyeno,
7. The Shoo-ji Temple, Miyagi-mura

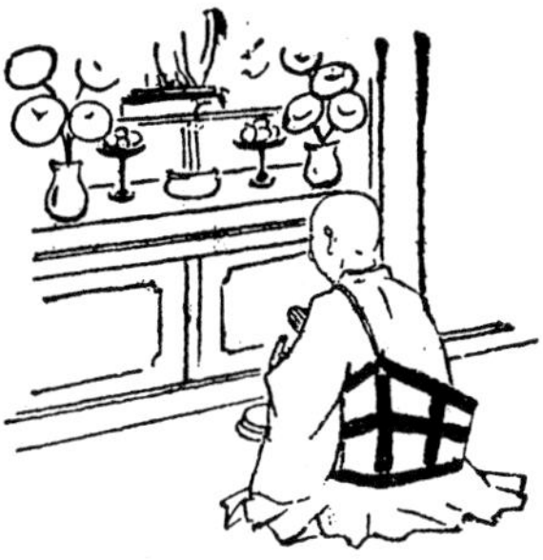
Buddhist Priest worshipping at an altar.

When Priest Gyoki had carved the Six Amitabha statues, he had some wood left over so he made another image. Hence the seventh image is enshrined at the Shoo-ji Temple as mentioned above, instead of six as is generally the case with Roku-Amida (Six Amitabha).

These six Amida-images, with the seventh, are enshrined at so many different Buddhist temples, which a devotee has to visit one after another in order to worship the Amida images. But there are several temples in different localities of Japan as well as in Tokyo, which have each a set of the Roku-Amida images standing side by side, as are found in the following temples:—

The Daiyo-ji Temple, Nishinokubo, Shibaku
The Zencho-ji Temple, Iikura, Azabuku
The Shunrin-ji Temple, Shikokumachi, Shibaku
The Shogaku-ji Temple, Takanawa, Shibaku
The Yuten-ji Temple, Meguro, Meguroku
The Kotoku-ji Temple, Aoyama, Akasakaku
The Sainen-ji Temple, Teramachi, Yotsuyaku
The Shimpo-in Temple, Jutchome, Kojimachiku
The Zenko-ji Temple, Aoyama, Akasakaku
The Baiso-in Temple, Aoyama, Akasakaku
The Shogen-ji Temple, Mita-daimachi, Shibaku

We have in Japan a saying that Higan is the limit of both heat and cold, i.e. the cold season will be over by the time of the spring equinox, and the hot season by the autumnal equinox.

NANAKUSA OR FESTIVAL OF THE SEVEN PLANTS

At the Nanakusa (nana=seven; kusa=plants) or the Seven Plants Festival, which is held on the morning of Jan. 7, every orthodox Japanese eats rice-broth that contains the Seven Plants; namely, shepherd's purse, chick-weed, seri (parsley), gogyo or hahakogusa (cotton-weed), suzushiro (radish), Hotoke-no-za, meaning "Buddha's seat" (lamium amylexicula), and aona (brasica chinensis), though the contents of the broth sometimes vary and turnip, trignotis pedunculare, etc. are used in some localities.

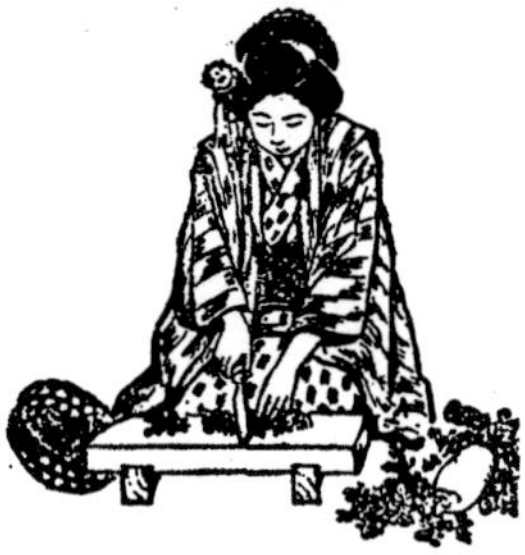

The preparation of the Nanakusa.

Formerly, the broth of the seven plants was served to the Emperor on the first zodiac day of the Rat, viz. in January, and the Emperor Saga, it is recorded, was very fond of this mixture. But during the era of Kampei (889–898 A.D.) the seven plants which are now used at the Seven Plants Festival were served to the Emperor Uda on the seventh of January, instead of the Rat day, and this custom of serving the Emperor with a broth of vegetables on Jan. 7 continued till the Tokugawa dynasty, during which the Seven Plants Festival began to be widely observed in the country. It was popularly believed, and is now scientifically proved, that these seven plants have a great medicinal value.

Tradition has it that on the western side of Mt. Sumeru there once lived a sacred bird called Hakuga, which took 8,000 years to attain maturity. This bird ate the seven plants on Jan. 7 every year and the Japanese imitated the manner of the traditional bird.

On the eve of the Seven Plants Festival, or on the evening of Jan. 6, the Japanese have the beating or mixing up of the seven plants on a kitchen-board (Manaita) of ligustrum japonicum (tara-tsubaki) wood with a willow-stick, singing the following song of the Seven Plants:—

"The seven plants; the shepherd's purse, etc.
Before the bird of China, or the bird of Japan,
Crosses the sea; the seven plants;
The shepherd's purse, etc."

While the seven plants are beaten or mixed up by using a willow-stick, the song is repeated 7×7 or forty-nine times, to represent so many constellations, into which, according to the astronomy of Old Japan, all the stars in heaven were divided.

In earlier days, however, these plants were beaten at different times on the Nanakusa eve, namely:

Parsley at the hour of the bird (6 p.m.); Shepherd's purse at the hour of the dog (8 p.m.); Cotton-weed at the hour of the wild-boar (10 p.m.); Trignotis pedunculare at the hour of the rat (midnight); Lamium amylexicula at the hour of the bull (2 a.m.); Turnip at the hour of the tiger (4 a.m.); Radish at the hour of the hare (6 a.m.).

"FIRE-WALKING"

Hiwatari ("Walking on Fire"), more properly *Chinkashiki* ("Ceremony of Fire-Control"), is a ceremony performed yearly on the afternoon of September 17 at the (Shinto) Shrine, Koma-Zawa, Greater Tokyo. The manner of its performance is as follows, as described in *Things Japanese:*

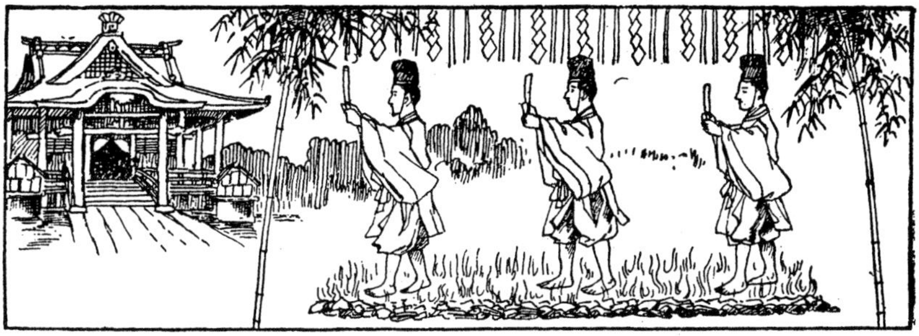

A bed of charcoal (about 10 bales), about one foot deep, is laid on a ground space 18 ft. long by 6 ft. wide, square to the points of the compass. Eight bamboos, with the fonds still on them, stuck into the ground on the sides and ends of the charcoal bed, are connected by a straw rope which is hung from fond to fond, about 5 ft. from the ground. From this hang 44 of the sacred *gohei* emblems—strips of white paper cut into angular form. A mat at either end of the bed of coals is spread with salt for those about to cross the fire to rub their feet on. Attendants busily fan the flames with open fans fastened to the ends of long poles, while others pound the coals flat with staves. Incantations (magic formulae) are made to the God of Water, who dwells in the moon, to descend and drive out the God of Fire. Prayers to conquer fire are offered up, and first one priest, then another begins slowly and solemnly to march around the charcoal bed, until all the priests join in the march. Round and round they go, gradually working themselves up into a state akin to ecstacy. When this is finished, each priest takes a handful of salt from a large bowl, and strews it upon the living coal. Then the high priest to drive away evil spirits makes four vertical and five horizontal strokes with a *chukei* (closed fan). He then salts his feet and steps on to the surface of the burning charcoal, over which he strides with dignified gait. The attendant priests follow his example, and when all have gone over, all go over again. The significance of the ceremony is to demonstrate that fire can be controlled and rendered harmless to believers.

The original shrine, situated at the foot of Kudan Hill, Tokyo, was destroyed in the earthquake-fire of 1923. It was rebuilt at its present place. When it was at Kudan, foreign visitors sometimes walked barefoot over the coals, without painful results, when their steps were lively. It is said there is no *hot* sensation at all. The priests declare that the protection of their head priest is a sufficient guard against accidents.

THE JAPANESE AS NOODLE-EATERS (1)

The Japanese are a noodle-eating people, for they take noodles of various kinds as a refreshment and at table, on a lucky as well as on an unlucky occasion, that is, at a festival, birth, wedding or even funeral. It is consequently deemed in some localities to be hospitality to force noodles upon a visitor.

Soba or buckwheat: Soba or buckwheat is one of the most popular noodles in Japan. It is made from the ears of soba (fagopyrum esculentum), which grows in temperate zones. It grew wild in Japan in olden days, and, according to the Zoku-Nippon-Koki, the cultivation of buckwheat was recommended and encouraged in the district of Kinai in the 7th month (July), 839, during the reign of the Emperor Nimmyo (the 54th). But the Shoku-Nippon-Shoki mentions an Imperial edict promulgated in the 7th month (July), 722, to the effect that because of a drought, the farmers should cultivate buckwheat, which grows both on barren and on rich soil. Buckwheat is now cultivated almost the country over, but Shinano and Kotsuke Provinces are best known for buckwheat, and it is now closely associated with Shinano Province.

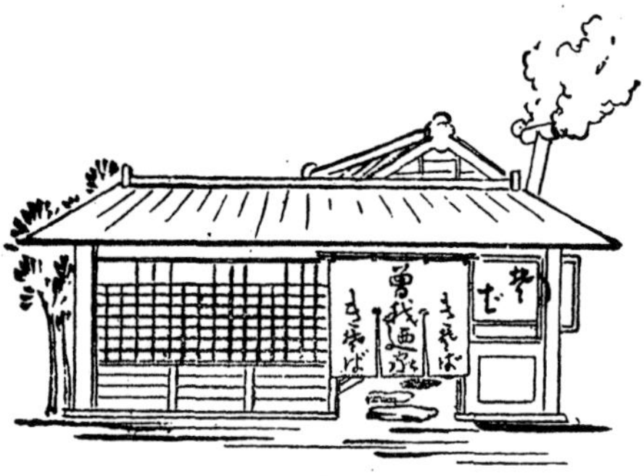

Soba-shop.

There are three chief varieties of soba: namely, *kisoba* (ordinary) *sarashina-soba* and *yabu-soba,* according to the ingredients that soba has in it. It is considered so nutritious that some Buddhist ascetics have lived on nothing but soba and fruits. Soba-dough is also a popular food in Japan. But it was about 1664 that soba in the form of noodles was first prepared in Japan. At that time Mt. Temmoku in the province of Kai had so many pious climbers that there was not an adequate stock of rice or wheat to feed them, so that a noodle made of soba-dough was served to them instead.

"Kake" and "Mori" may be said to be the most popular way in which soba is served. "Kake" (pour) is so called because soba is served in a bowl with its soup "poured" over it. By "Mori" is meant a kind of soba that is served on a "seiro" (steaming basket), on which soba is "piled up" (mori), with a bowl of soup accompanying it.

(*Continued*)

THE JAPANESE AS NOODLE-EATERS (2)—*Concluded*

There are many other ways in which soba is served: "O-kame," which contains mashed fish, mushrooms, *yuba* (fried bean-curd); "Gomoku-soba" (five-coloured soba), which has mashed fish, mushrooms, shrimps, egg, and arrow-head; "Kamo-namban," which has a few slices of duck meat.

It is a common custom in Tokyo that when a man removes from one place to another to live, he presents soba to his new neighbours, including, as we say, "three across the street and two on both sides," as a token of newly-made friendship. This custom seems to be of unknown origin, but it was adopted presumably because the word "soba" suggests a close-relation, "soba" homonymously meaning "beside or nearby."

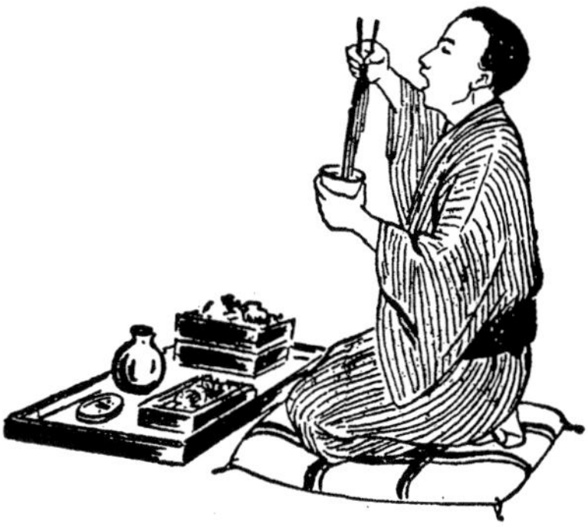

Eating Soba.

On New Year's Eve, most Japanese eat soba, which is accordingly called "toshikoshi-soba" or "year-crossing-soba." According to some authorities, goldsmiths and silversmiths of olden times used soba-dough in collecting scraps of gold and silver; hence it was associated with the earning of money. Thus soba came to be eaten on New Year's Eve as a lucky charm for the coming year.

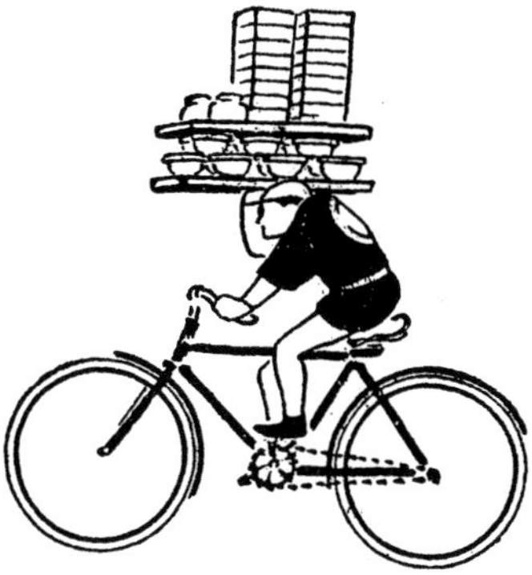

Employee carrying Seiro by bicycle.

The employee of a soba shop is trained to carry a pile of *seiro* or steaming bowls on his shoulder, while often riding a bicycle.

Other kinds of noodles: Somen and udon are two other kinds of noodles very common in Japan. They are made of wheat-flour.

While a foreigner tries to make no sound when eating a soup, the Japanese are taught to make a sipping noise when eating soba as a mark of their appreciation.

THE GOD OF POVERTY

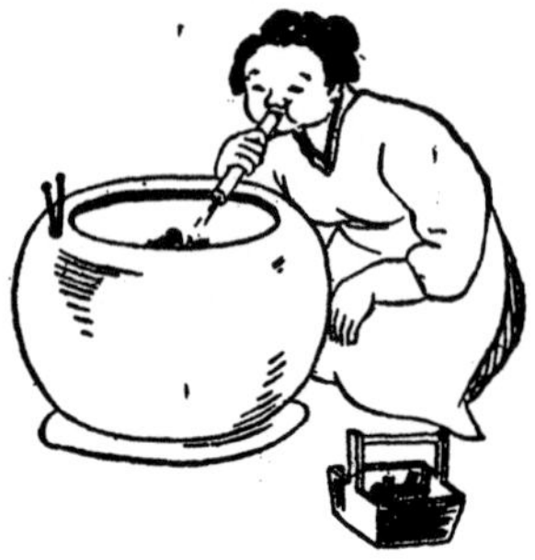

The hi-fuki-dake (fire-making-bamboo) is a primitive tool for making a fire. It is still used in most Japanese homes where a fire is made of charcoal in a hibachi (fire-brazier). It consists of a simple piece of bamboo, with one joint left at one end, and people blow at the fire through a small hole made in the joint.

Down in the old clan of Satsuma the southernmost end of Kyushu, it is a common practice for every piece of bamboo which has been used in making a fire through the year, to be thrown away on New Year's Eve. One end of the bamboo is stuffed with paper, and people believe that by thus throwing the bamboo away they get rid of the god of poverty. But the bamboo has to be thrown away without any one seeing it, else the exorcism would be of no avail.

At Nagasaki, however, the bamboo is generally thrown out of the dark at a pedestrian on the street, so that the god of poverty may be transferred to the innocent walker. Often the bamboo is thrown hard at the walker to make sure that the god of poverty is got rid of.

The festival for gods of poverty: On New Year's eve, some orthodox Japanese hold a festival for the gods of poverty. A miniature ship is prepared with willow-wood, and the gods of avarice, hunger and trouble, each written in Japanese on a small piece of paper, are "enshrined" in the ship, which, provided with a few grains of rice, a small bottle of sake and a lighted candle, is placed on the kitchen-range with a ceremony. They are all thrown into a river nearby and thus the gods of poverty are disposed of.

The Kama-jime or kettle-purification: Some down-town people of Tokyo have what is called the Kama-jime or kettle-purification when a Shinto priest purifies the kitchen at the end of each month or a year.

THE EMA OR VOTIVE OFFERING OF PICTURES (1)

In 1912 General Maresuke Nogi committed suicide (hara-kiri or seppuku) upon the firing of the signal-gun announcing the departure from the Imperial Palace of the cortege of the Emperor Meiji. Self-immolation, which means suicide, compulsory or voluntary, on the part of a retainer upon the death of his master, is as old in Japan as her history, which is full of pathetic stories of devoted retainers or samurai. In reality, this practice was prohibited by the Emperor Suinin (the 11th) in the 28th year (2 B.C.) of his reign, and some earthen dolls, representing men, horses, and others, were buried with the remains of the Empress Hihasu, his wife. In the 32nd year (2 A.D.) of his reign, later on, the earthen horse was replaced by a live one, which was offered to a shrine when a prayer was beard by the god, the idea being that the god would ride it. The horse thus offered is called "*Shimme*" or god's horse, and some shrines, such as the Imperial shrines at Ise and Atsuta and the Toshogu shrine at Nikko, still keep Shimme-horses.

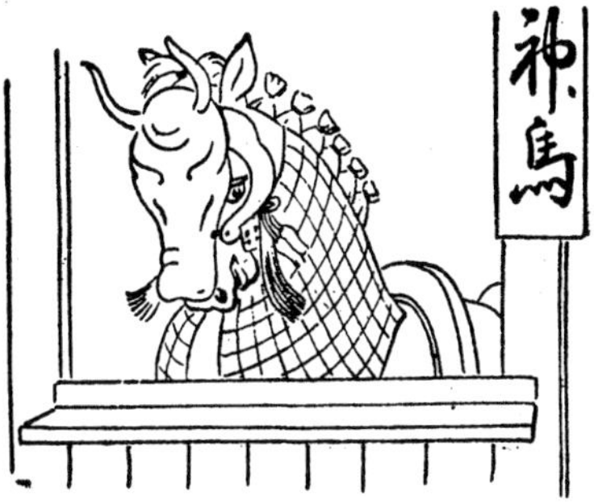

A Shimme.

But the shrine, on the one hand, was embarrassed by the many live horses offered to it, and, on the other, none but the rich could afford to offer a live horse every time a prayer was offered. So some 600 years ago, an artificial horse, either of wood, metal or paper, was introduced as a votive offering in the place of a live one, and it became fashionable in the country to offer a tablet of a painted horse as a votive offering to a shrine. Hence the name of "Ema," which means "picture-horse." Consequently, many of the larger shrines had to build the Ema-do or picture-horse-hall to keep the Ema in. But the original idea or significance of the votive offering is departed from and nowadays the Ema-tablets have all sorts of pictures, which can be roughly classified as follows:—

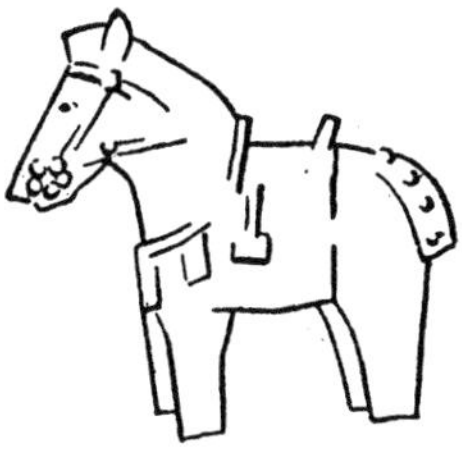

An earthen horse.

1. The picture of a horse offered with the original idea that the god would ride it.
2. The picture of a horse offered with a prayer that it will keep watch at the gate of the shrine.
3. The picture of the god to whom the prayer is offered: Fudo-image for Fudo; Jizo-image for Jizo, etc.
4. The picture of the god's messenger: the dove for Hachiman; the fox for Inari; the wolf for Sampozan; the snake for Benzaiten (Sarasvati), etc.

(*Continued*)

THE EMA OR VOTIVE OFFERING OF PICTURES (2)

(Concluded)

5. The picture of an article in which the god takes special interest: a sword for Fudo; a harp for Benzaiten (Sarasvati); forked radish for Daikoku; pomegranate for Kishimojin or Hariti, etc.
6. The picture of a zodiac sign assigned to the year in which the devotee was born: a rat for one born in the year of the Rat; a bull for one born in the year of the Bull; a tiger for one born in the year of the Tiger, etc.
7. The picture of anything that the devotee is specially fond of, and that he abstains from taking, so that his abstinence may so please the god as to cause him to accept the prayer: a bottle of sake; a cup of tea, etc.

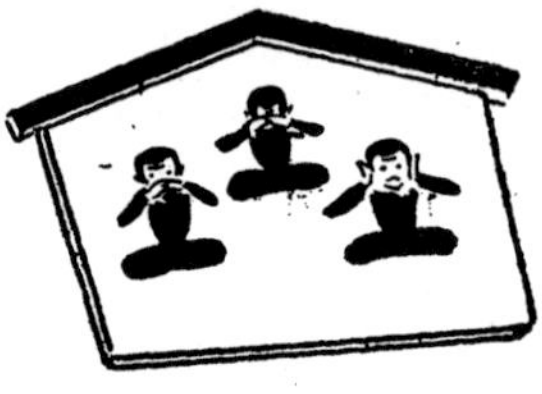

Ema of Three Monkeys.

8. The picture of anything suggestive of what the devotee is in need of: a wrestler for physical power or strength; a treasure-ship for a fortune, etc.
9. The picture of that part of the body which is cured of some sickness: an eye or the ideogram for it for an eye-disease; a child cured of illness, etc.
10. The picture of anything expressive of gratitude: an armour for one coming back from the front; a ship for one returning from abroad.

It should be added that, because the Ema is meant for a god, the painter does his very best in its painting. Consequently, Ema-painting has made great development as an art, so that we have fine Ema-pictures in Japan.

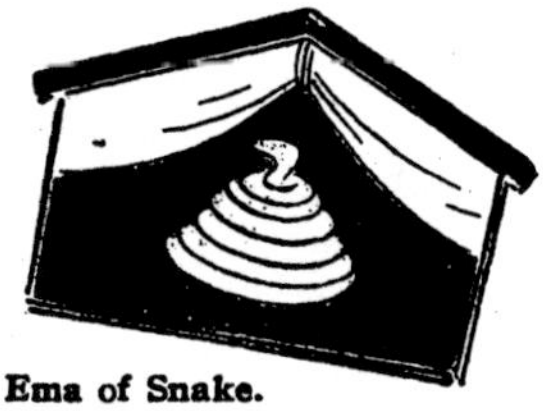

Ema of Snake.

At the village of Iogi, on the railway running from Takada-no-Baba, Tokyo, there is a shrine dedicated to the Kojin-sama or Rough-god. On the eve of Oct. 1, or on the night of Sept. 30, every year, on which a festival is held at the shrine, its visitors offer a set of seven horse-pictures to the shrine. The Kojin-sama are seven in number, and on Oct. 1 they go on a trip to Izumo, where a consultation is held of the eight million gods of the country to decide upon the marriages of young girls in Japan.

The Kannon-shrine at Asakusa, Tokyo, has a large Ema tablet representing a horse. It was painted by a certain master-painter of the Kano school. The villagers of the neighbourhood were much annoyed because night after night a horse came out to make havoc in the fields. Soon it was discovered that the horse of the large Ema-tablet had some greens around its mouth and mud on the hoofs. They concluded, therefore, that the Ema-horse made its nocturnal rounds and so they asked Hidari-Jingoro, the best sculptor of the day, to stop the horse from coming out. The sculptor put reins on the horse, which then ceased to come out.

THE MOKUGYO OR WOODEN BELL

The Mokugyo (moku = wood ; gyo = fish) is a most conventional object in Buddhist temples. It is generally made of camphor-wood, but sometimes of mulberry or rosewood, painted red or in a plainer colour. Somewhat round and hollow, it looks more like a wooden bell than a wooden fish, as the name literally indicates, though it has the scales of a fish, with its tail often bent up over its body. In a temple belonging to the Zen, the Jodo or some other Buddhist sect, the wooden bell is beaten to accompany the chanting of the Buddhist sutra. Sometimes, however, a mokugyo in the form of a fish is found in a temple, but it is not used in the Buddhist service.

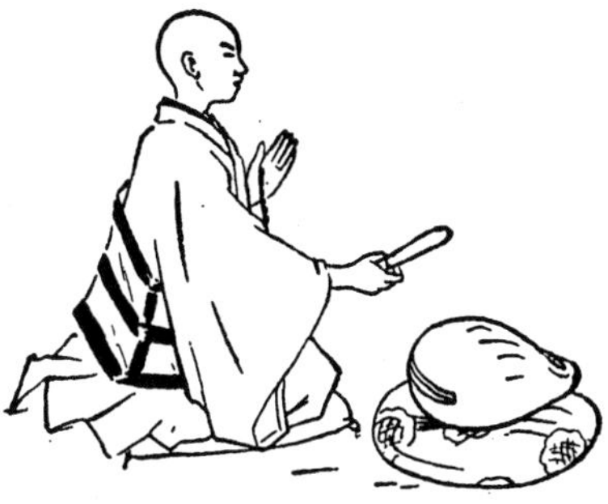

A priest and his Mokugyo.

The wooden bell is attributed to the invention of a Zen priest, Chih-ling by name, who lived during the Sui dynasty (581–617) in China. He made it after a fish mentioned in the Buddhist sutra, Subha Sastra.

Once upon a time, so the story goes, there lived a disobedient priest in India. Because of his misconduct he was born as a fish in the next life. A big tree grew on the back of the fish, which suffered terribly every time the tree was shaken or tossed by a big wave. The fish attributed its suffering to the insincere teaching of its master in its pre-existence, and it was looking for an opportunity of paying the old scores with him, when the master happened to cross the sea in a boat. "What did I do to deserve your resentment?" the master asked when he saw the retaliatory measures taken by the fish against him. "It is all due to your neglect in teaching that I suffer in this way." "No, I was not insincere, but you did not accept my teachings," the master admonished "for as one sows so one reaps." The fish was convinced of its folly and asked the master to make a Buddhist article of the tree growing on its back, so that its use in a service might help the fish to attain Nirvana. The master made a wooden fish or Mokugyo to be used in the Buddhist service, and it is said that its beating proved the fish's salvation.

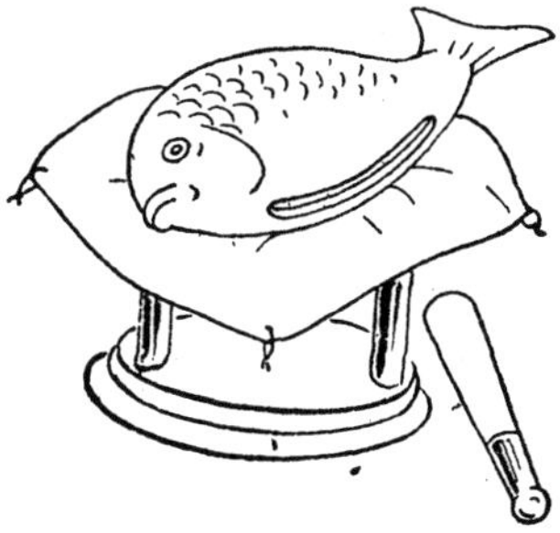

Mokugyo.

THE TORI-NO-ICHI OR RAKE FAIR (1)

On the zodiac day of the Cock (or Bird) in the month of November, of every year, a festival is held at the shrines dedicated to the pre-historic princes, Ame-no-Hihoko-no-Mikoto, Ame-no-Hiwashi-no-Mikoto and Ame-no-Torifune-no-Mikoto, and sometimes Prince Yamatotake. Like the dove, the fox and the monkey, which are messengers of the Hachiman, Inari and Sanno shrines, respectively, the eagle is the messenger of these pre-historic deities, whose shrines are popularly known as O-Tori-sama or Honorable-bird, the suffix "sama" being an honorific term for both sexes.

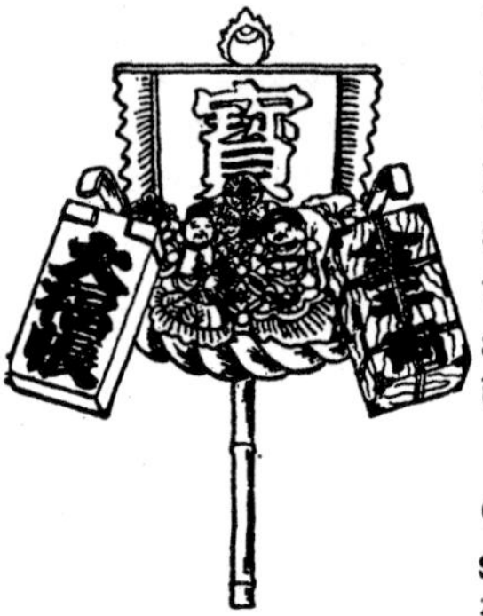

Decorated rake.

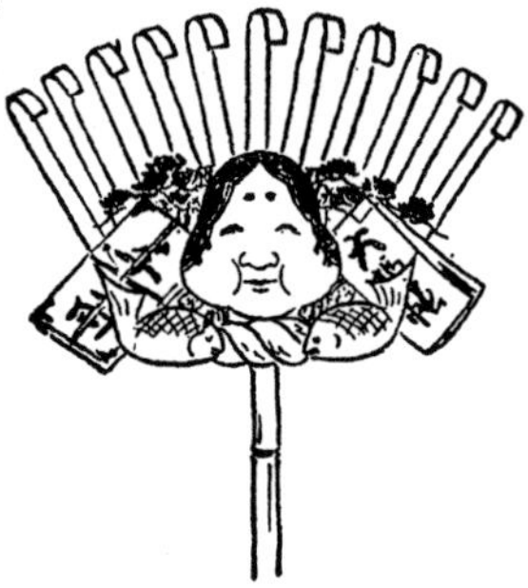

Decorated rake.

On the festival day of the eagle-shrine, a special fair known by the name of Tori-no-ichi or Bird-fair, is held at each shrine, and bamboo rakes of fancy decoration are almost exclusively sold at the stalls which line both sides of the approach to, as well as all the streets in the neighbourhood of, the eagle-shrine. These rakes, some no longer than a few inches, and others several feet long, are gorgeously decorated with lucky symbols representing bales of rice, a ledger-book, gold pieces, the bamboo, plum and pine, the crane and tortoise, the seven gods of fortune, the treasure-ship, the old couple of Elygium, the old man shouldering a rake to collect every good in and the old woman sweeping every evil out with a broom. As the mask of O-Kame is considered to be a lucky one, it is very commonly used on the rake.

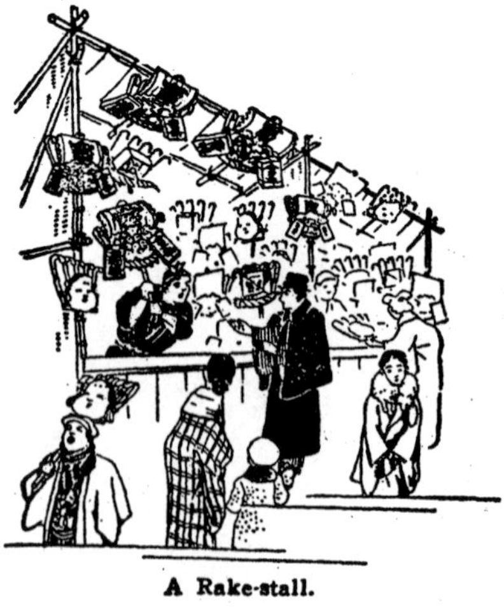

A Rake-stall.

The zodiac sign of the Cock ("tori" in the Japanese language) suggests the verb "to take," and so the rake is chiefly sold at this festival. Every orthodox Japanese

(*Continued*)

buys the rake, which will be kept as a luck-bringer or mascot at a conspicuous place in the house through the coming year.

Each eagle-shrine is so crowded on the fete-day, and particularly in the evening, that the street-cars run an hour or so longer than usual at night to carry the pious visitors to and from the shrines. It is generally said that the Rake Fair was first started at Yoshiwara, the licensed quarters of Tokyo.

One particular feature of the Bird or Rake Fair is that no decorated rake seems to have a fixed price. It is the only market in Japan where "One price only" is not applicable and the vendor will quote on his commodities whatever price his humour may dictate, in consideration of his prospective buyer who stands before his stall, expecting of course that price will be "jewed down." Every rake can be bought at half, or even at one third of the price asked for it, and much cheaper towards midnight as the vendor has to dispose of all the articles, which cannot be sold at any other time of the year. Every buyer is, moreover, expected to "jew" the price down, otherwise he would be "beaten" or fail in business during the coming year.

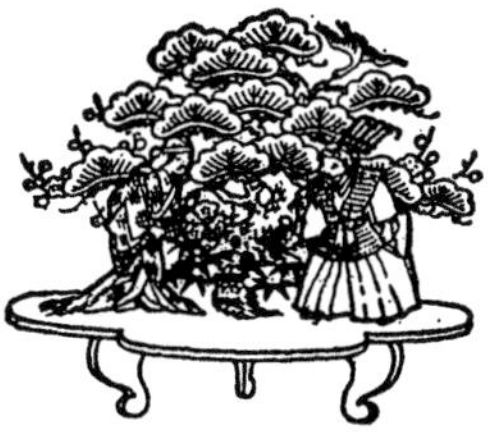

An old couple of Elygium.

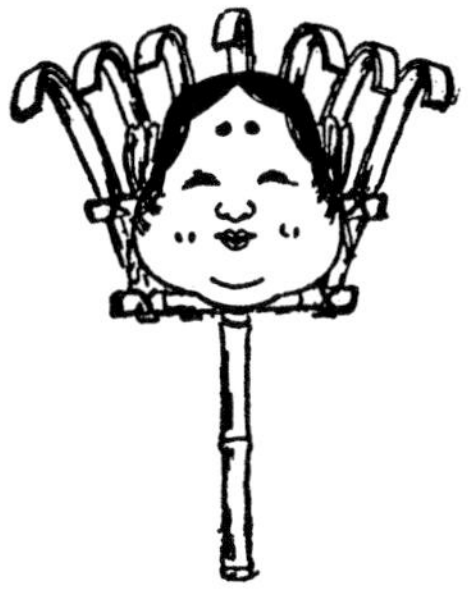

Rake decorated with O-Kame-mask.

Imo-kashira (a kind of taro-root) skewered on a vine or bamboo is also sold at the fair. The word "*kashira*" means "head" and its acquisition suggested a victory in battle in our feudal days, and the sale of skewered taro-roots is the survival of an old custom. The word "kashira" generally conveys the idea of "headway" or success.

A zodiac day is repeated every thirteenth day, as we have twelve signs, and if the day of the Cock comes three times or, in other words, the Rake Fair is held three times in November, it is superstitiously believed that more fires will break out in the coming winter than usual.

Some of the O-Tori-sama shrines, where the Rake Fair is held in and near Tokyo are:

The O-Washi	Shrine,	Shitaya
,, ,,	,,	Koishikawa
,, ,,	,,	Meguro
The Akiba	,,	Mukojima
The Suga	,,	Yotsuya
etc.		etc.

Sekihan and hot water: Sekihan is rice boiled with azuki or Indian beans. Few girls will eat Sekihan with hot water poured over it, though it is all right for them to eat white rice with hot water. This is because, if a girl should eat Sekihan with hot water, it is generally believed, she will have rain on her wedding day.

No nails trimmed after dark: Few Japanese will trim their nails after dark, for we say that if they do, they will not be in time to arrive at their parents' death-bed.

"*Reverse water*": By "reverse water" is meant hot water poured into cold water. When a dead person is finally washed before the remains are put into the coffin, water is poured into the tub in this way. "Reverse water" is considered unlucky and it is never used on an ordinary occasion.

Three slices of koko or pickles: While three is considered to be a lucky number, we never serve a person with three slices of koko or pickles, because "three slices" (*mikire* in the Japanese language) means homonymously "killing a person."

Tea kept overnight: The Japanese never take tea which has been kept overnight for the simple reason that a condemned criminal in olden times was served with such tea before his execution. However, most Japanese take tea every morning since they believe that they may meet with some accident if they leave home without taking tea in the morning.

The right side of clothing over the left: While foreign clothing has its right side over the left, the Japanese lady has the left side of her Japanese clothing folded over the right. The right side over the left is the way in which we fold the clothing of a dead person, for in Japan the dead are shrouded in a special kind of clothing for their trip for the land of the dead. Consequently Japanese clothing is never folded in the foreign way.

No funeral held on Tomobiki-day: According to the old or lunar calendar, there is a day called Tomobiki or friend-taking, which comes on in every sixth day. Few if any funerals are held on this particular day in Japan, for a funeral service observed on the Tomobiki-day will soon be followed by another funeral in the same family. If a funeral must be observed on this day, a doll is put with the dead body in the coffin, so that it will take the place of the one whom death would otherwise claim.

Nothing to be passed from chopsticks to chopsticks: At a crematory the relatives of the deceased will pass the cremated bones from chopsticks to chopsticks when the ashes are put in the urn. So the Japanese are told to pass nothing from chopsticks to chopsticks on an ordinary occasion.

Whistling at night: A Japanese boy is told not to whistle at night, for a whistle is the sign of burglary.

AMAGOI OR PRAYING FOR RAIN (1)

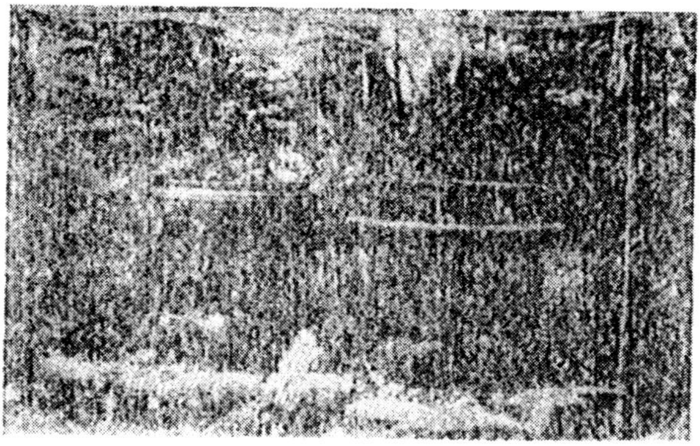

Amagoi-no-Kama.

On the roadside just before the 2nd or red Torii approaching the Hakone Shrine, on Lake Ashi, one will find two antiquated iron-kettles, which are about 700 years old. They are called the *Amagoi-no-Kama* or "Iron kettles used in praying for rain." At the time of drought, a farmer is seen to visit the iron-kettles with a bamboo tube. He offers a silent prayer to the kettles for rain, and takes home, from one of them, a little water in the bamboo, which he sprinkles over his rice-fields, that are cracked and parched for want of rain. Soon, it is believed, the clouds will burst to water the fields. The farmer will then have to take two bamboo-tubefuls back to the iron-kettles from which he took the sacramental water.

"On the day of the Horse in the fourth month (April) in the 2nd year (698) of the reign of the Emperor Mommu, a horse was offered to the god of Mizuwake-Peak, Yoshino, with a prayer for rain. On the first day of the fifth month (May) there was a drought in all the provinces, and a cloth-offering was made at different shrines. On the day of the Rat, a messenger was sent out to offer a prayer for rain to the gods of the famous mountains and long rivers in the vicinity of the Imperial capital of Kyoto." (The Shoku-Nihonshoki, Vol. I.)

This is the first mention ever made in Japanese history of a prayer offered for rain, though the book does not state whether any rain fell or not. A little further on, the same book says:—

"In the fifth month (May), the Emperor called the courtiers together, whom he instructed to send a messenger to the Ise Shrines and those of the seven Do (literally, Roads or Districts). Soon there was a great rainfall."

The same book mentions several instances of the prayer offered for rain. At Amagoi, the prayer was first offered at the two shrines of the River Nibu-kawa and Kibune. If it proved futile, offerings were made at the Hirose and Tatsuta Shrines, and prayer was continued until the appeal was made at no less than eighty-five shrines. At the ceremony of Amagoi, the prayer was read before the god, to whom several kinds of offerings were made, such as silk, cotton, hemp and vegetables. A black horse was offered in praying for rain, but a white one was used for stopping a long rain. But a private ceremony was held by the people on the top of a high mountain, where offerings were made of several edibles, such as rice, pease, fruit, vegetables, etc. and great noises were made by means of drums, gongs, and other musical instruments, or often kitchen utensils, and big fires were burned till a rain came down.

(Continued)

AMAGOI OR PRAYING FOR RAIN (2)—*Concluded*

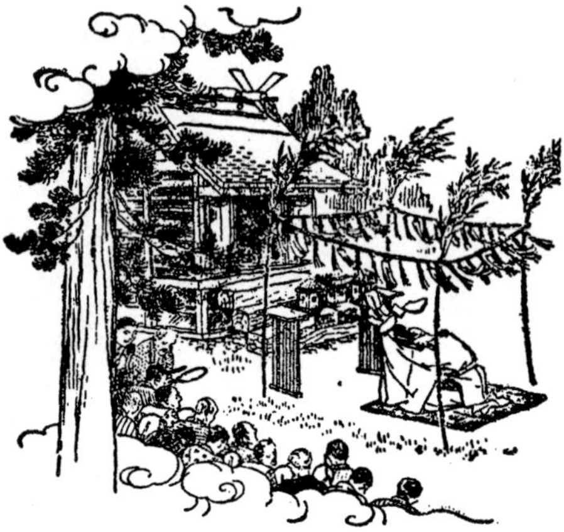

Praying for rain.

In the 7th year (788) of Enryaku era, no rain fell for five months. Then the Emperor Kammu took ablutions and offered a prayer for rain in the garden of the Palace. Soon black banks of clouds appeared over the mountains around the Imperial capital and a strong shower came, so that the courtiers lustily cheered the Emperor.

In the third year (1179) of Jisho era, a drought lasted for many a month. Moronaga Fujiwara, a courtier, in sympathy with the distressed people, made a pilgrimage to the Hiyei shrine, where he played on his favorite biwa (musical instrument) several times to palliate the god. The deity must have been pleased with his music, since, according to records, there followed a heavy rainfall.

When dry weather lasted for a long time in the 4th year (1174) of the Shoan era, the Emperor Takakura ordered prayers to be offered for rain. Priest Choken reasoned with the Blue Dragon, which is believed to have control over water, and soon a heavy rainfall came to the great relief of the people.

One year there was no rain for several months. A hundred Buddhist priests were therefore called from the Miidera, Tofuku-ji and Kofuku-ji Temples to read a sutra in prayer for rain in the Imperial Palace, but not a single drop of rain came. Then a hundred lovely girls were gathered together to perform a dance to appease the supposed anger of the God of Rain, but with no better success. Finally Lady Shizuka, who was known for her charming dance, was called in. No sooner had she begun her dance than dark clouds began to appear like a pall over the parched hills. The jealous Jupiter Pluveres was at last appeased, and he graciously permitted a rain for three days.

Priest Noin and Lady Ono-no-Komachi are widely known for their poems of 31 syllables that served as prayers to make it rain.

Priest Noin: "Ama-no-Gawa, Nawashiro-mizu ni, Sekikudase,
Amakudarimase, Kami naraba Kami."

(Open, O God, the Celestial River, none other than the Milky Way, to send water for the rice-nursery.)

Ono-no-Komachi: "Chihayafuru, Kami mo imasaba, Tachisawagi,
Ama-no-Togawa no, Higuchi ake tamae."

(If there be gods, then let them go about and open the Celestial Spring.)

Songs for calling rain down:

"Rain falling, the gods rejoice and the people prosper—the people prosper.

"How fruitful looks the rice crop of this year—rice-plants six feet high and ears two feet long."

THE OLD AND THE NEW IN JAPAN (1)

OLD

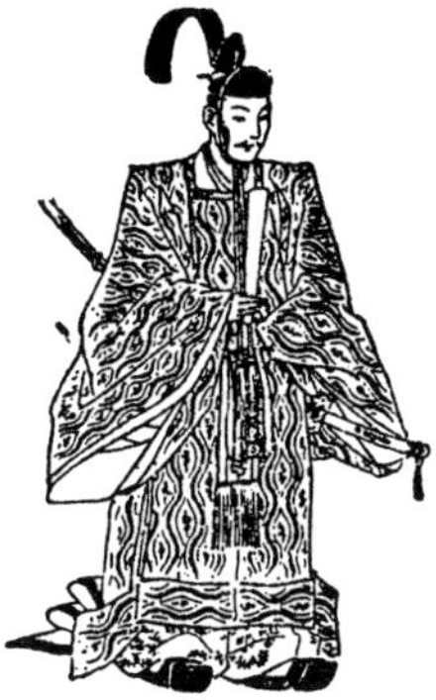

Courtier in Sokutai-dress.

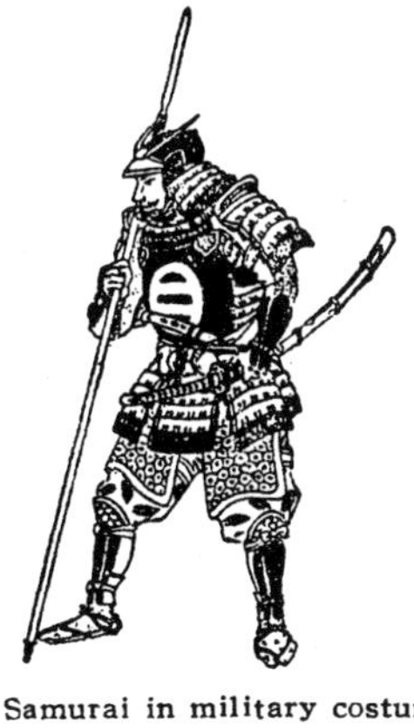

Old Samurai in military costume.

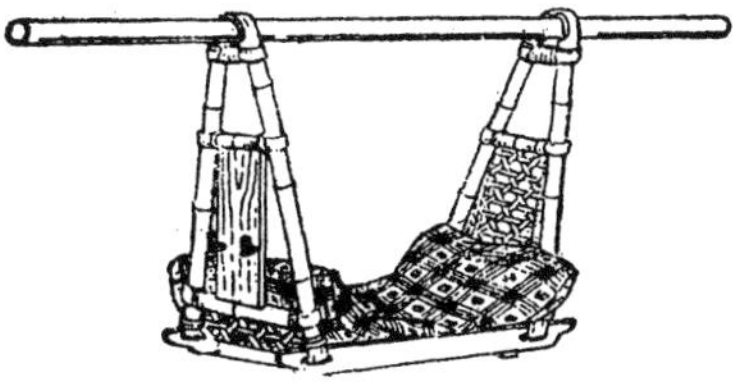

Kago or sedan chair.

NEW

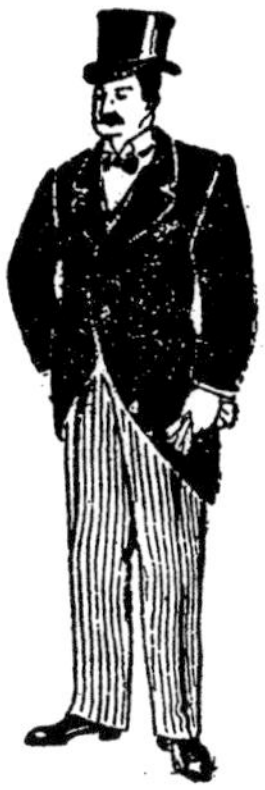

Modern Governmental Official in morning-coat.

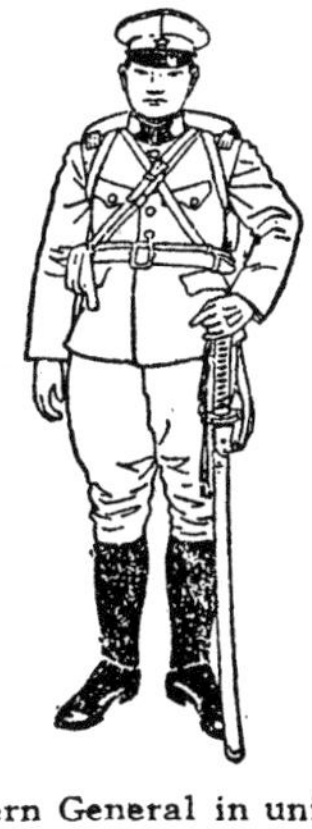

Modern General in uniform.

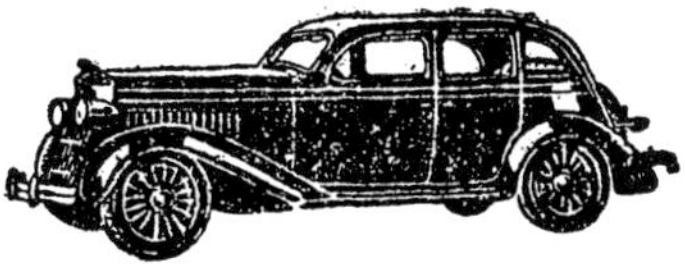

Motor-car.

(Continued)

THE OLD AND THE NEW IN JAPAN (2)

OLD	NEW

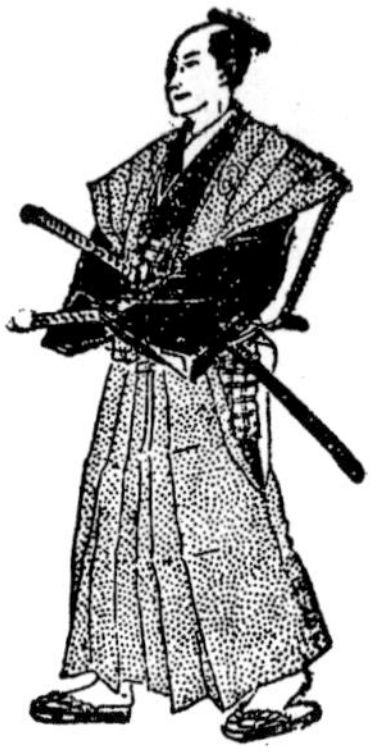

Samurai with top-knot.

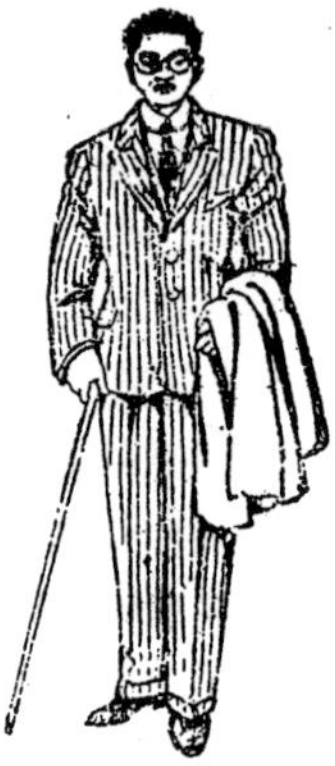

Gentleman with parted hair.

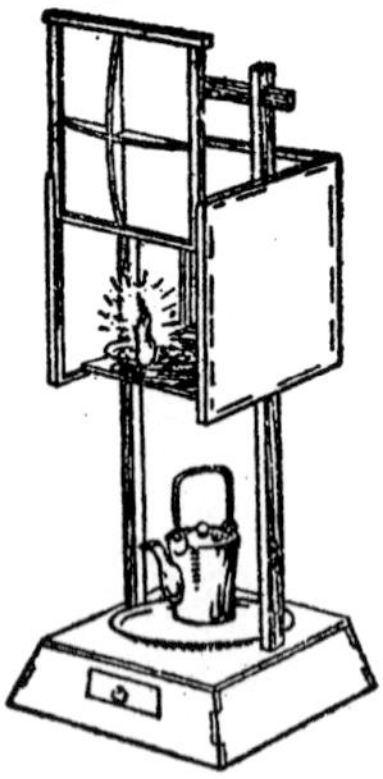

Andon or portable oil-lamp.

Electric lamp.

(Continued)

THE OLD AND THE NEW IN JAPAN (3)

(Concluded)

OLD

NEW

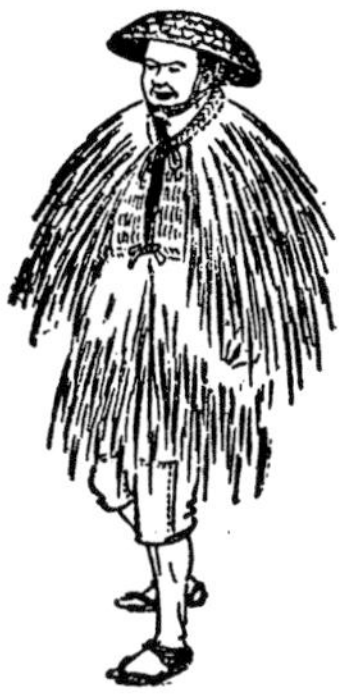

Mino or straw-raincoat.

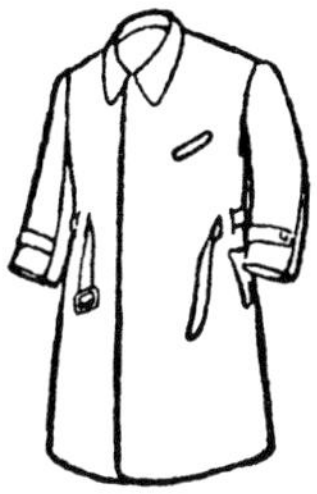

Modern raincoat.

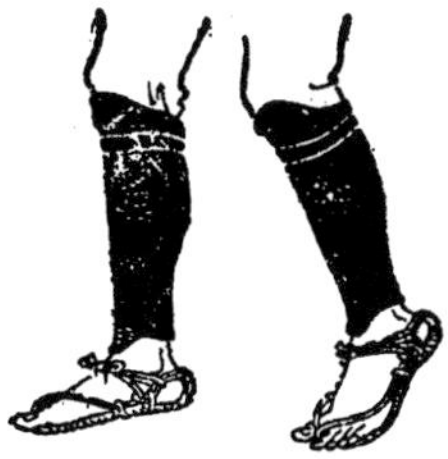

Waraji or straw-sandals.

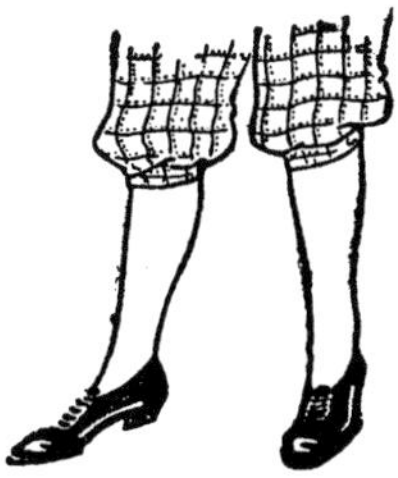

Shoes.

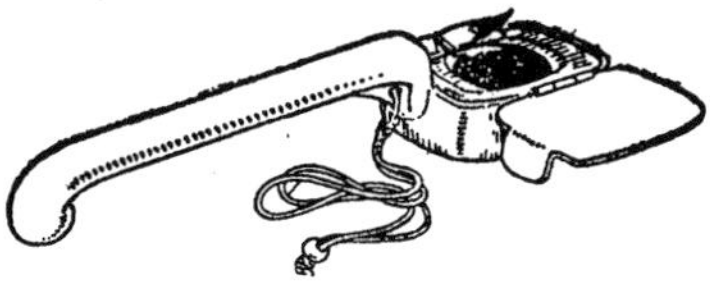

Yatate or case for Fude (brush-pen) with a pot in which is kept cotton soaked in Indian ink.

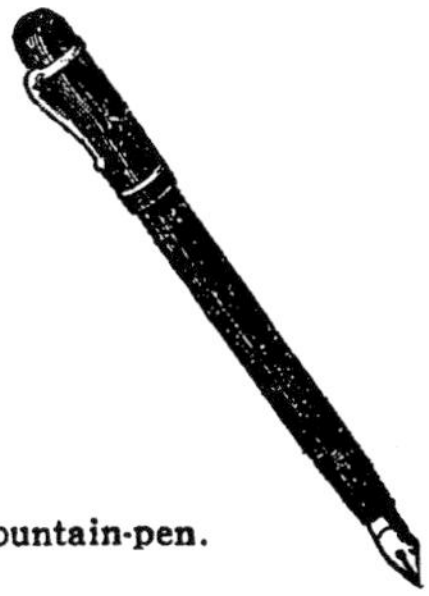

Fountain-pen.

THE HACHIMAN SHRINE

The Hachiman shrine, which was dedicated to the god of war, was one of the popular shrines in Japan's feudal days and it was found everywhere throughout the country. Its first mention in history was made in the Shoku-Nihongi. According to this book the Emperor Shomu (the 45th) sent an Imperial messenger to make an offering at the Sumiyoshi and Yawata shrines in the fourth month (April) of the year 737, the Hachiman Shrine at Usa in Tsukushi (Kyushu) being then the Yawata shrine.

In the ninth month, (September), 740, when Hirotsugu revolted against the Imperial court, the commander of the punitive forces prayed at the Hachiman Shrine for heavenly help.

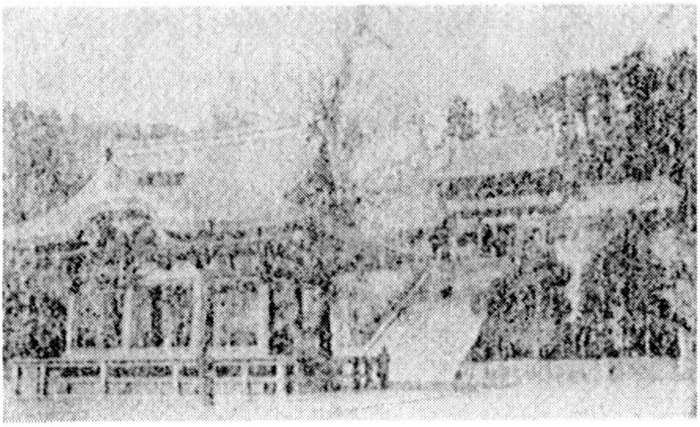

The Hachiman Shrine, Kamakura.

According to tradition, eight streamers, four red and four white ones, descended at Hakozaki, Tsukushi, and an oracle said "I am Honda-sumera-mikoto, the 16th." From this legendary story, a shrine was dedicated to Honda-sumera-mikoto (the Emperor Ohjin) and it was called the Hachiman shrine after the eight streamers though the Hachiman shrine at Usa is generally believed to be the oldest in Japan. Some scholars, however, hold that Prince Hikohohodemi was originally enshrined at the Hachiman shrine.

Yoriyoshi and Yoshiiye, two warlords of Minamoto, which was one of the two military families in Japan's feudal days, were such great devotees of Hachiman that they made him the tutelary deity of their family so that their retainers and descendants so fervently worshipped the god, till Hachiman became the Mars of Japan.

Buddhism seems, however, to offer a different explanation of "Hachiman." It claims that it means the "Eight Right Ways," namely, right seeing, right hearing, right thinking, right talking, right doing, right living, right walking and right enlightenment.

Some of the famous Hachiman shrines are Iwashimizu Hachiman, Kyoto; Tsurugaoka Hachiman, Kamakura; Hakodate Hachiman, Hakodate; Fujisaki Hachiman, Kumamoto; Yusuhara Hachiman, Oita-ken; Usa Hachiman, Oita-ken.

The Hachiman shrine being dedicated to the god of war, our samurai of old used to visit it before departing for the front in order to pray for victory, and the Japanese athletes of the last Olympic games prayed for success by visiting the Hachiman shrine, at Kamakura, before they left Japan for Germany.

THE INARI SHRINE (1)

Travel in any part of the country, and you will find no village or hamlet, however small, but has a shrine dedicated to the Inari. Because every shrine of the Inari has a pair of fox-images, a foreigner is often inclined to think that the Inari is dedicated to the fox or the Japanese worship it, while in reality the fox is a messenger of Princess Ugatama, the goddess of rice, enshrined in it.

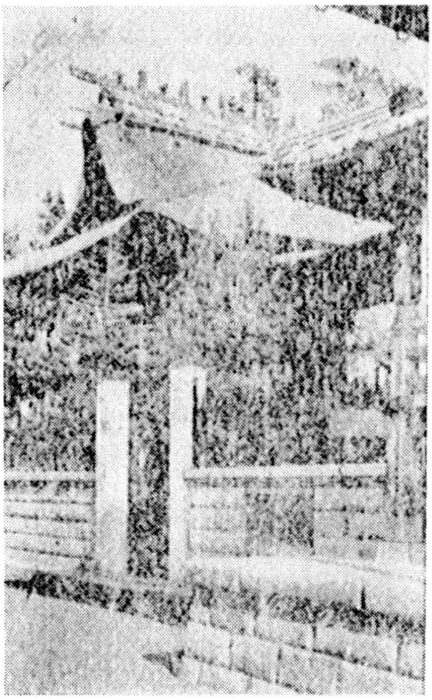

The Inari Shrine.

In 711 Iroko of the Hata family of Chinese descent, who had abundant "rice and paddies piled up," as the record goes, built a shrine at Fushimi, near Kyoto, in honor of Princess Ugatama (Barn-spirit). This is said to be the first built of all the innumerable Inari shrines in Japan.

It was on the first zodiac horse-day of the second month (February) in 711 that Iroko of the Hata family celebrated the dedication of the Inari shrine and hence the annual fete-day of the Inari falls on the first horse-day of February.

Priest Kobo, who lived in the 9th century, it is said, met at the gate of the Higashi-ji Temple, a white-haired old man who carried on his shoulders a rod with some rice-sheaves hanging from both ends and with a sickle in his right hand. When asked who he was, the old man answered that he was the deity of the Inari shrine at Fushimi, and immediately disappeared.

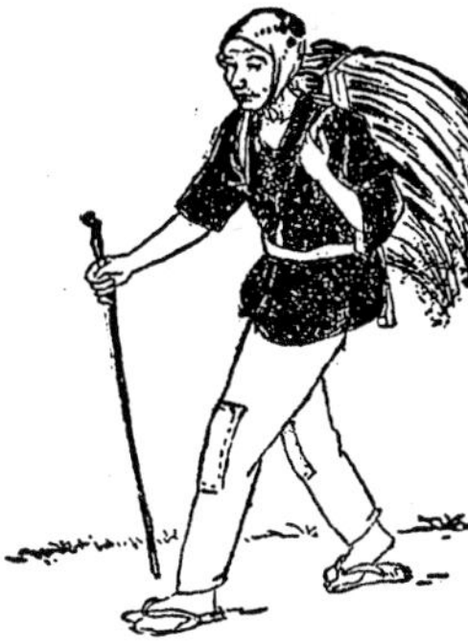

A farmer carrying
a sheaf of rice.

Some authorities attribute to this story the origin of the present ideograms for "Inari" meaning "rice-plant-bearer," though others find the origin of "Inari" in the name of Princess Ukemochi (or Foodholder), also called Ugatama, who was the goddess of the five cereals. It is said that rice grew within the stomach of this goddess, giving rise to "Ina-nari" (rice-growth), which has euphonically changed into the present name of "Inari."

According to some records, there lived in the 9th century two old foxes, a white male and a brown female, on Mt. Funaoka, near Kyoto. They made a den near the Inari shrine at Fushimi, till they were regarded as messengers of the Inari.

One fox-image of the Inari often carries a key in its mouth while the other has a ball under its forepaw. The key represents the barn of rice, while the ball stands for the spirit of Princess Ugatama. *(Continued)*

THE INARI SHRINE (2)—*Concluded*

(The Hatsu-uma Festival)

In the feudal days of Japan, the Inari Shrine, which is dedicated to Princess Ugatama, also called Princess Ukemochi, was founded in the castle of each clan, mainly for the following two reasons:

(1) Rice, a staple food in Japan, was so important, in the feudal days, that a hereditary salary and allowance were paid in rice, instead of money. The Inari Shrine was dedicated to the prehistoric princess, who is said to have told the Japanese how to raise rice.

(2) "Inari" has the homonymous meaning of "stay as you are" (i=to sit or stay; nari=as you are). The Inari Shrine was founded in the castle-grounds as a charm for keeping the feudal lord from being transferred to any other clan.

It was on the first zodiac day of the horse in the second month (February, old calendar) in 711 A.D. that the first Inari Shrine of Japan was founded at Fushimi. By the "first zodiac day of the horse" is meant the first one that may come after Kan, the coldest season, is over and the day comes usually on the second or third of February, new calendar. Thus was the first zodiac day of the horse selected for the festival of the Inari Shrine all over the country,

Each Inari Shrine in the country will observe its festival on the first zodiac day of the horse every year and it is called "Hatsu-uma" (lit. first horse). And the Hatsu-uma festival is one of the busiest festivals in Japan. Formerly the Hatsu-uma Festival was observed in the second month of the old or lunar calendar, but it is held in February, new calendar, which is about a month ahead of the lunar-calendar February.

At the festival of Hatsu-uma, the priest of the shrine will conduct a service, at which he will read an address to the Kami to whom the shrine is dedicated. All the approaches leading to the shrine will be lined with stalls of cheap articles, including food. In the former days, the fox-mask was one of the chief articles sold at the festival, for the fox is considered to be the messenger of the Inari Shrine. All the parishioners of the shrine will celebrate the occasion by preparing Sekihan, a special kind of boiled rice, and the children will be clad in their best dress.

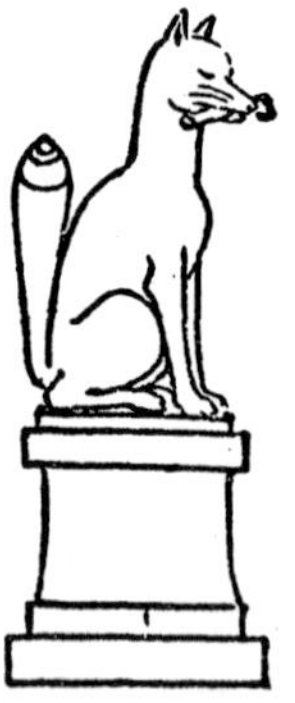

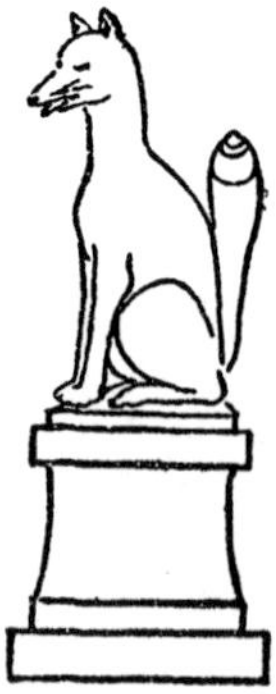

The Inari Shrine has a semi-annual festival: one in the spring to pray for a good crop and the other in the autumn to return thanks for the crop of the year.

The Inari Shrine is dedicated to Princess Ugatama, a prehistoric Kami and in this sense the Inari Shrine is Shintoistic. But it is, at the same time, Buddhistic, because the first Inari Shrine was founded by a Buddhist priest. The Inari Shrine is, therefore, Shinto-Buddhist. And its Torii is usually coloured red.

THE GOTOKU-JI TEMPLE AND ITS CAT-GRAVE

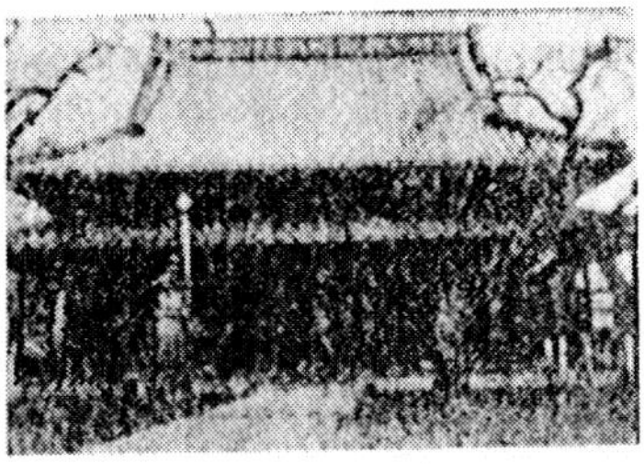

The Gotoku-ji Temple.

The Gotoku-ji Temple, which is situated at Setagaya in Tokyo, belongs to the Sodoshu sect of Buddhism. It is the family temple of Lord Ii, one of the Shogunate ministers. At a prominent place of his family grave-yard is seen an antiquated tomb under which the remains of a cat are buried. Incense is kept burning constantly before the tomb, and quite a large number of stupas are dedicated to the dead spirit of the cat.

The Gotoku-ji Temple was once, in the 17th century, so poor and humble that its resident priest made up his mind to look for another temple.

"Were you a human being," said the priest to his favorite cat one day, "you might earn money to help me out of my difficulties."

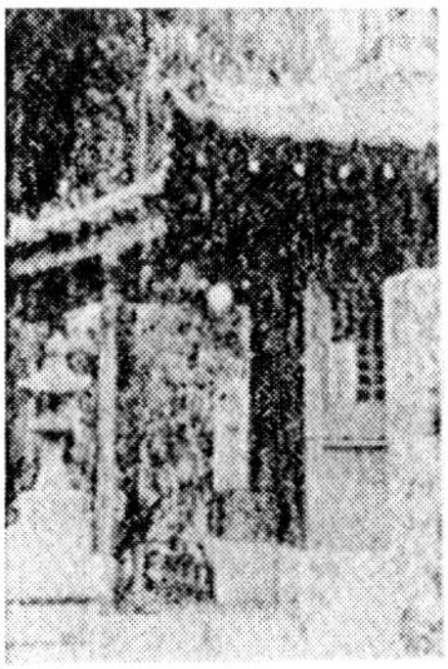

A shrine of the Gotoku-ji Temple.

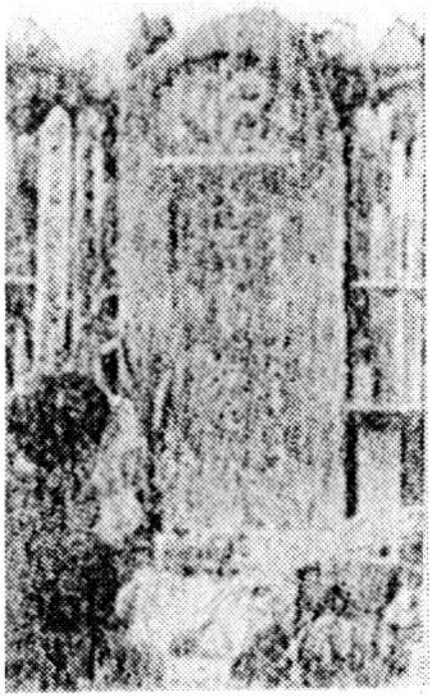

The Cat-grave.

A few days later, a noble-looking samurai on horseback came to the temple. He was Lord Naotaka Ii, ancestor of Naosuke Ii, who was assassinated at the Sakurada-mon Gate in 1860 for his pro-foreign sympathies. Taking a few retainers, Naotaka came to Setagaya, where he was caught in a shower. Looking for a shelter, he saw a cat beckoning to him under the gate of the temple. The curious samurai went to the temple, and he found the priest very learned. Lord Ii promised patronage, so the Gotoku-ji Temple has ever since been the family-temple of Lord Ii.

The cat-tomb enjoys a conspicuous place in the grave-yard of the Ii family, and it is a great source of income to the temple.

THE TALE OF THE SHUZEN-JI TEMPLE (1)

YASHAO, THE MASK-MAKER

"I have not come to hear the same old story," said Yoriiye, the ex-Shogun, in an angry voice to Yashao, the mask-maker. "You put off the obedience to my order every time I sent for the mask. I have now come myself to hear the reason of your delay."

Yoriie, son of Yoritomo, was appointed the second Shogun of the Minamoto family in 1202, only to the dethroned in 1204 and sent in exile to Izu Province, where he was confined in the Shuzen-ji Temple. He ordered a mask of his own face, but his mask-maker, who was considered to be one of the best mask-makers of the day, asked for time whenever the mask was sent for. Finally the impatient ex-Shogun came to urge the mask-maker, who only asked for another extension of time as before. It was on the 17th day of the seventh month (July), 1204.

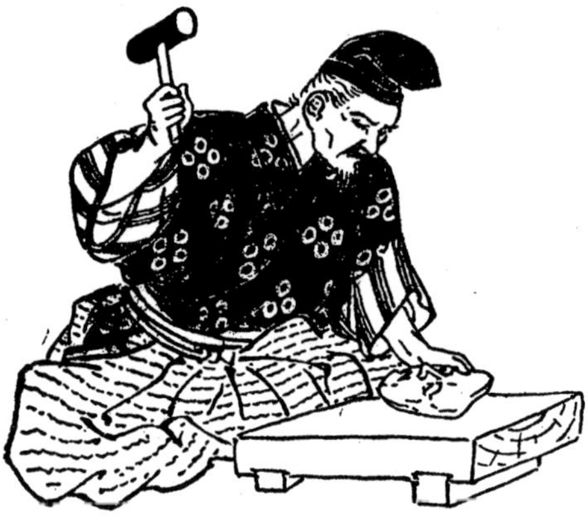

Yashao destroying his masks.

"I know you are angry" the mask-maker pleaded. "I know you are angry. It is of course a great honour to me to make your mask, and I would not neglect my work at all. And during the half-year, since I received your order, I have worked day and night to make a good mask, but none of the masks I have made is satisfactory to me. I must ask you, therefore, for another extension of time."

"I cannot tell you just when I shall be able to complete it," the mask-maker went on when the ex-Shogun demanded the time when he would execute the order. "You may think that a mask-maker can make a mask as easily with a chisel in one hand and a hammer in the other as a carpenter can build a house. A carpenter builds a dead house with dead lumber, but a mask-maker chisels out of a lifeless piece of wood the face of a man, woman, angel, devil, or any other good or bad living being. It is the inspiration which comes through his body that makes a good mask. It may come to me in half a month, in a month or it may not come for a year or two. I cannot tell you just when it will come to me." Yoriiye, who was at the end of his tether, drew his sword, which he lifted up to strike at the mask-maker, when his daughter, Kaede, stood between his father and the ex-Shogun. She asked the ex-Shogun to calm himself, for she would bring from her father's atelier a mask that he had finished the night before.

The mask was brought out. Yoriiye received it in his hands, and was lost in admiration of it. It was an exquisite piece of work.

(Continued)

THE TALE OF THE SHUZEN-JI TEMPLE (2)—*Concluded*

YASHAO, THE MASK-MAKER

"You are mistaken, my lord" Yashao, the mask-maker, said to the ex-Shogun, "to admire this mask. On the contrary, I consider it to be one of the worst masks I have made in my life, for it has a death feature. People say, and I myself think too, that most masks I make look alive; they have a spirit in them. But somehow every mask I have made of you looks dead. I do not know why. I meant to keep this mask hidden from every body."

But the ex-Shogun was so pleased with the fine workmanship of the mask that he went home proudly taking the mask and Kaede, the daughter of the mask-maker, as his maid.

"Mask after mask was made, but every one looked dead," Yashao said to himself after Yoriiye went away. "It will only bring disgrace upon myself and my family for generations to come, if that mask should be kept as a treasure of his family. I am undone. I will handle my chisel no more; I will make no more masks in my life."

So saying, Yashao took from his atelier all the masks there were in it and destroyed them one after another.

A few days later the pealing of the gong at the Shuzen-ji Temple told that something unusual was taking place, and soon Yashao heard of a night attack made on the residence of the ex-Shogun Yoriiye Minamoto by the Hojo troops. The mask-maker was worried about his daughter, Kaede, when, to his surprise, she came back, besmeared with blood. She had a halberd in one hand and the mask of the ex-Shogun Yoriiye in the other. According to her account, the ex-Shogun was taking a bath when the enemy attacked him. The quick-witted girl taking up his mask, put it on and shouted to the enemy that she was the ex-Shogun himself, so that Yoriiye ran away while the enemy chased her. Seeing him safely out of danger, Kaede made for her own home where, after telling the story, she fainted with fatigue. But while the mask-maker and his second daughter, Katsura, were nursing Kaede, there came the priest of the Shuzen-ji Temple. At his approach Kaede opened her eyes wide and asked in a faint voice what had become of the ex-Shogun. "He is killed, poor lord," the priest answered. At this Kaede let fall her head and breathed her last.

"You must be happy to die in defence of the lord, Kaede," the mask-maker said to his dead daughter. "So am I. I made many masks after his face, but to my great disappointment every one had a death feature. I see now that it was not my fault, but the ex-Shogun was destined to meet this sad fate. It must have been due to inspiration that the fate of a man which is known only to the gods was made manifest on a mask by my hand. After all, I am a master-artist as the people know and say that I am."

This mask, which Yashao made for Yoriiye Minamoto, is still preserved in the Shuzen-ji Temple, Izu, which can be reached within a few hours from the Fujiya Hotel.

THE MOKUBO JI TEMPLE

THE STORY OF UMEWAKA-MARO

A rickety old shrine and a dying willow-tree mark the place where young Umewaka-maro, a kidnapped boy, has slept in death for some thousand years.

Umewaka-maro was the son of Korefusa Yoshida, a Shosho (major-general) in the service of the Emperor Murakami (the 62nd). He lost his father when he was five years old, and he went up Mt. Hiyei, when he was seven years old, to pray for the peaceful repose of his dead father, and also to pursue his studies at the Getsurin-in Temple. He was so clever, it is said, that while he soon became a favorite among some of the priests, the others jealously made a sinister plot against his life so that he left the temple under cover of night when he was twelve years old. But he lost his way and came to Otsu, instead of the Imperial capital where his mother lived. There he was coaxed and cajoled by Toda, a slave-dealer, of Shi-nobu, a town in the northern part of Japan, and arrived at Azuma (a part of the later Edo) on the 15th day of the third month (March), 976. Through fatigue and sickness, Umewaka-maro could walk no farther, and so he was deserted by the heartless slave-dealer.

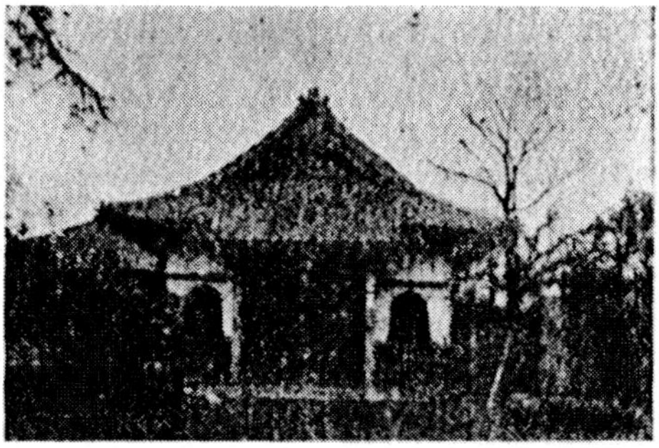

The Mokubo-ji Temple, Tokyo.

The people of Azuma, taking pity upon him, took good care of him. When asked who and how old he was, the boy said that he was the twelve-year-old son of Yoshida Shosho, Kyoto. Shortly after, he died, leaving a poem which, roughly translated, reads:

"Should one come and enquire after me, please reply,
O the birds-of-Miyako (plovers), that, like the dew on the dried
river-base of the Sumida, I have disappeared."

There happened to come a priest from Mt. Haguro of Dewa Province. His name was Chuen. He attended to the funeral service of the boy, over whose remains he planted a willow-tree.

On the anniversary of the death of the ill-fated boy, a year later, his mother happened to arrive at the Sumida River in search of her abducted son. When she asked her ferry-man why the people were gathering about the willow-tree on the banks of the river, he told her that a Buddhist service was being held for the peaceful repose of the soul of a boy who, having been kidnapped from the Imperial capital a year before, had died there. The poor mother then cried over the death of her son, for whom she was looking, and a small temple was dedicated to his dead spirit. It was named the Umewaka-ji Temple after him, but later it was re-named the Mokubo-ji Temple.

Though some thousand years elapsed since the kidnapped child died on the banks of the River Sumida, a Buddhist service is still held at the temple every year for the spirit of the young boy, Umewaka-maro.

THE SHINTOIST AND BUDDHIST FAMILY-ALTARS (1)

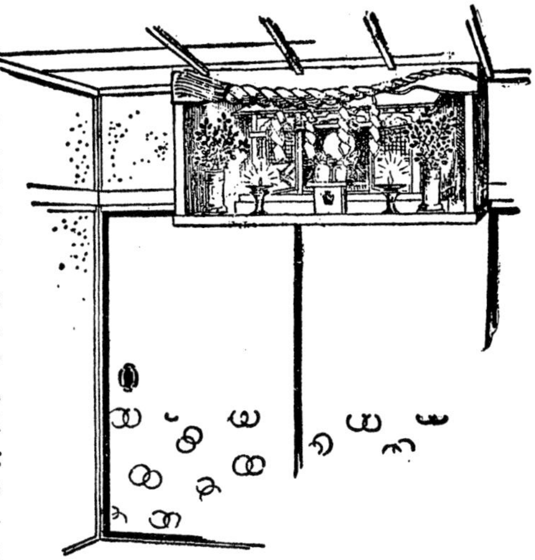
The Shinto Altar.

Practically every orthodox Japanese home is provided with a Shinto or Buddhist family-altar, or both. The Shinto family-altar, called "kami-dana" (or gods' shelf) seems to have had its origin in an altar in which was enshrined, according to the Kojiki, a string of beads that Prince Izanagi handed to the Goddess Amaterasu, her daughter. Generally speaking, the Shinto altar is provided for worshipping or venerating the Shinto deities, chiefly the Goddess Amaterasu, the ancestress of the Imperial Family of Japan, to represent whom an O-fuda (amulet or charm) is issued by the Daijingu Shrine, though Ebisu and Daikoku, two of the seven gods of fortune, as well as several other Shinto deities, are sometimes represented on the Shinto altar. The Shinto family-altar has no image or statue.

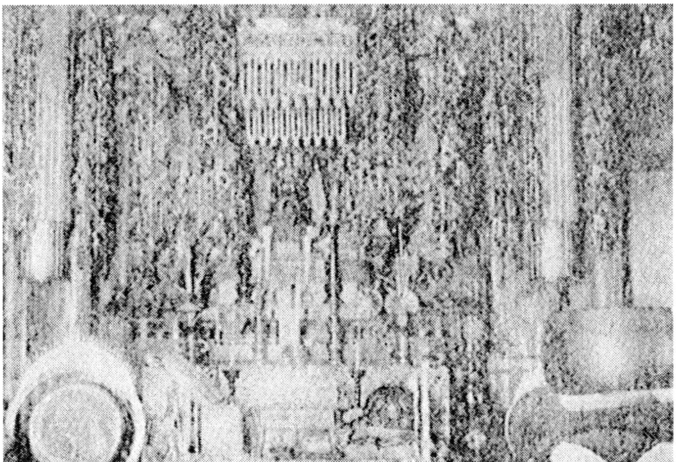
The Buddhist Altar.

(Continued)

THE SHINTOIST AND BUDDHIST FAMILY-ALTARS (2)

Concluded

The Butsudan, or Buddhist altar, became popular in Japan affer the Emperor Temmu issued in the third month (March), 686 A.D., a decree to the effect that every family in the Empire should be provided with a Buddhist family-altar and the sutra. The altar has in its sanctuary a statue of Buddha or of the founder of the Buddhist sect to which the family belongs, and sometimes the Ihai or Buddhist tablet with the posthumous name of the ancestor of the family written on it. The posthumous name means one that every Buddhist believer receives after his or her death. There are also in the altar Buddhist tablets of all the dead members of the family. The Buddhist family-altar is dedicated to the departed members of the family who are represented in the altar by their posthumous or Buddhist names written on these tablets.

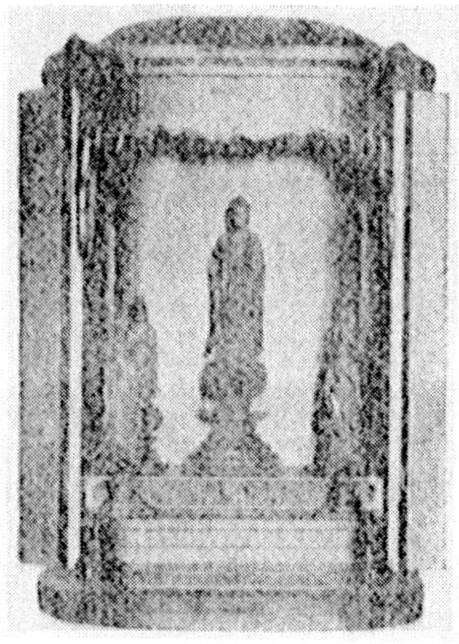

The Buddhist Niche.

Every morning, after all the rooms are cleaned, dusted and swept, a pair of candles are lighted on the family-altars, and each member of the family worships before them. We simply bow before the altars in order to show our respect to the Shinto deities and the departed members of our family, but we offer no prayer for anything. A bell is provided on the Buddhist altar, and it is rung every time we pay our respect to the departed. In lighting the candles, the fire ought really to be struck by a flint, and the light should not be blown out with the mouth, but waved out by the hand. If, for instance, good fortune of any kind visits the family, it has to be reported to the altars. Every gift received from a friend has to be first offered to the Buddhist altar before eating it, except when it consists of fish or meat, which is not offered to the Buddhist altar. This naturally means that the departed spirits are still considered among the members of the family, and they are invited to the family on the occasion of Obon or Feast of the Dead, which comes on the 13th of July.

One remarkable feature of Japanese religion is that though both the Shinto and Buddhist altars are found in the same family, there is no religious conflict between them in Japan, for there is a clear distinction between Shintoism and Buddhism in their sphere of influence or function. While Shintoism involves the pre-historic or historical deities of the country, Budhism venerates the Buddhist gods imported from India, as well as the departed spirits of the family. Each member of a family can worship at both altars without any compunction whatever.

MT. FUJI AND ITS "WONDERS"

Ascent: "It is as foolish not to climb Mt. Fuji as to climb it twice in life," is a common saying in Japan, and every Japanese of either sex makes it a life's cherished hope to ascend the "sacred mountain," as Mt. Fuji is regarded. It is considered to be a great honour to any climber to "worship the Goraiko" (literally, Honorable-coming-light) or the sun at its rising, from the top of the mountain.

There are several ways to climb up Mt. Fuji; the following five being the chief:—

1. via Gotemba (or eastern front side): This is perhaps the most convenient ascent as it runs through Gotemba, which can be reached by motor or bus from the Fujiya Hotel.
2. via Subashiri (or eastern side): by way of a route about six miles north-west of Gotemba;
3. via Yoshida: by way of Yamura by getting off the train at Otsuki Station, Central Railway line;
4. via Omiya (or front side): Omiya is about seven miles from Suzukawa Station; a new electric line runs from Fuji Station;
5. via Suyama: six miles from Sano Station; Mt. Fuji is best seen on the way.

Three lakes connected subterraneously: Lakes Seiko, Shoji and Motosu are situated over 900 metres above the sea-level and they are separated two or three miles one from another. But tradition has it, as geology proves, that they were one lake in ancient times and are still connected subterraneously. When, for instance, the water of Lake Seiko becomes low on account of a large quantity being used by an electric power house, that of Lake Shoji ebbs in proportion. When, on the other hand, a great rainfall increases the water of one lake, that of the two others will rise in a few hours, though they have no shower to swell it.

Ice Cave: The Ice Cave is situated at the northern foot of Mt. Omuro. It is dark inside and so a light of some kind is required when one enters it. The cave is several yards wide, a few feet high and over two hundred yards deep or long into the mountain. About a hundred yards inside, you come to a spacious room of ice, where large icicles hang from the ceiling and big ice-posts stand from the ground. You will see your light reflected in all directions by the ice which makes the room a fairy-like crystal palace. There are ever so many caves around Mt. Fuji.

Mt. Fuji inverted: Mt. Fuji is specially imposing when it is reflected upside down on the glassy surface of Lake Ashi. But by standing on the top of Mt. Fuji of an evening or morning, one may sometimes see the shadow of Mt. Fuji inverted above the mountain. It is only seen in fine weather and when there is much moisture in the air. The shadow will be dim and small at first, but it gradually grows clearer and larger until it appears perfectly clear.

MT. FUJI—ITS ROMANCES (1)

According to the Jodaiki (Imperial Administration Annals), land was submerged and Lake Biwa appeared in the province of Ohmi, in one night, in the 5th year (B.C. 286) of the reign of the Emperor Korei (the 7th). It is said that at the same time Mt. Fuji rose, though, according to another book, Mt. Fuji appeared in the 92nd year (B.C. 301) of the reign of the Emperor Koan (the 6th). The mountain was first opened to climbers by Priest En-no-Gyoja, who climbed it during the reign of the Emperor Mombu (the 42nd).

Ancestral God: Once upon a time the Mioya-no-kami, or Ancestral God, went paying visits to different gods in the country. During his journey, one afternoon, towards dark, he came to Mt. Fuji in the province of Suruga and asked the god of the mountain to let him stay there overnight.

"We are having the Good Crop Celebration," the god of Mt. Fuji said, "and so we cannot let you stay overnight as we are too busy."

"What has made you refuse your father" Mioya-no-Kami said indignantly. "Because of your want of filial piety, snow shall cover your top in summer as well as in winter. With cold thus reigning over the mountain, few will climb the mountain and offer food."

Mioya-no-kami then proceeded to Mt. Tsukuba, where he made the same request of its god, who, though busy with the same festival, hospitably received the visitor. A sumptuous feast was prepared for the ancestral god, whom the god of Tsukuba worshipped and served. The visiting god was so pleased with the hospitality accorded to him, that he blessed the god of Tsukuba, saying: "My son, how kind-hearted and noble you are! You will be blessed by the celestial and territorial gods, and loved by the people, who will come to pay respects to you all the year round."

Hence, Mt. Fuji is still covered with snow all the year round, while Mt. Tsukuba has innumerable climbers throughout the whole year.

Elixir of life: Lady Kaguyahime was an angel incarnate on earth. She had ever many suitors but she disappointed them all nor could the Emperor himself win her, for after living on earth many years Lady Kaguyahime went up to heaven on one full-moon night, the fifteenth of August, leaving all her wooers disappointed. At her departure, she left the elixir of life for the Emperor, who, however, was too grieved over her loss to care anything for the precious medicine. He therefore ordered the medicine to be burned up on the top of Mt. Fuji, the highest mountain in Japan, for it was the nearest place on earth to the moon, the abode of his love. Hence the mountain has still some smoke ascending to heaven. Also, the name "Fuji," which is often expressed by two Chinese characters, means "No-death."

Angels seen above Mt. Fuji: According to the "Record of Mt. Fuji" written by Miyako Yoshika (844–879), a great festival was held on the fifth day of November in the 17th year (875) of the era of Teikan, when about the time of the Horse (noon) two angels clad in the white were seen dancing on the top of Mt. Fuji. They appeared to be, as it were, a little above the top as the villagers saw them from the foot of the mountain.

Princess Konohana-no-Sakuya-hime: Prince Ninigi was once strolling about on the beach of Kosasa-saki, when he met a lovely maiden. She was Princess Konohana-no-Sakuya-Hime, daughter of Prince Ohyamatsumi. The young prince, charmed by her beauty, asked her to become his wife. But the princess told him to see her father, which he did. Prince Ohyamatsumi then sent his two daughters, Princesses Iwanaga-Hime and Konohana-no-Sakuya-Hime, with five hundred stands of foodstuff, so that the prince might select one of them. Prince Ninigi accepted the younger princess, Konohana-no-Sakuya-Hime, who became his wife. Princes Hoseri, Hikohohodemi and Hoakari were born of their union.

Konohana-no-Sakuya-Hime literally means "Tree-flower-blooming-princess," and it is said that the name of Sakura (cherry) was taken from her long name.

No pines at Hakone: It is traditionally said that Princess Konohana-no-Sakuya-Hime once had her eye hurt by a pine-needle. "No pines shall grow here," the Princess said. Hence, hardly any pine-trees are now found at Hakone and in its vicinity.

Hito-ana or Human-cave: The Hito-ana or Human-cave, situated at the vlllage of Hitoana at the western foot of Mt. Fuji is said to be connected with the famous cave of Enoshima, near Kamakura. The entrance is semi-circular in shape, 5 or 6 yards wide. When you enter the cave for some twenty yards, you come to the Pillar of Mt. Sumeru, the cave getting narrower and narrower, till you find a stand where, it is said, Priest Kakugyo sat in meditation for a thousand days. He died in 1646 at the age of 103.

CHARMS AND EXORCISM (1)

"Chinzei-Hachiro-Tametomo's Inn": Tradition has it that Chinzei-Hachiro-Tametomo, uncle of the Shogun Yoritomo Minamoto, had power over the god of a certain disease while an exile on the island of Hachijo-ga-Shima. Because of this legendary story, many "innocent" people in Tokyo and its vicinity will paste at the entrance to their houses a piece of red paper when small pox is prevalent. The paper has the Chinese characters reading "Chinzei-Hachiro-Tametomo's Inn."

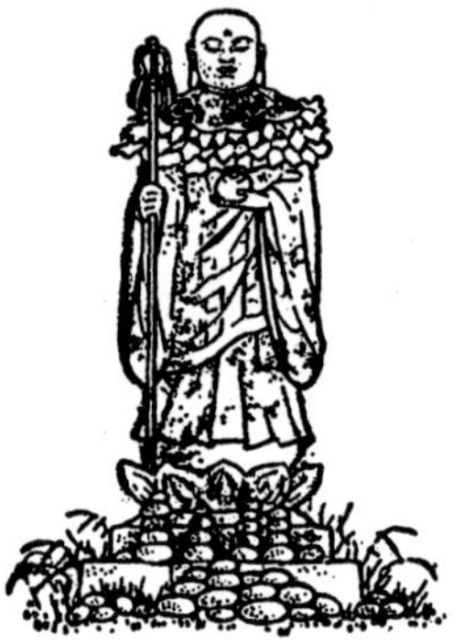

Jizo-image.

The Measles Stone: Pass your child three times through the hole of the Measles Stone in front of the grave of Priest Yuten in the Yuten-ji Temple, Meguro, and its measles will prove neither fatal nor even serious. This practice has its origin in the power that Priest Yuten is said to have had over some kind of sickness.

The Deaf Jizo: If a child is suffering from whooping-couph, or "One Hundred Days' Cough," as it is called in Japan, write your prayer on a piece of paper and mail it to the Tsunbo Jizo, or Deaf Ksitigarha, of Komagome, Hongo in Tokyo, and the child will be cured. However, you must promise to offer the deity a bottle of sake and spices, of which he is said to be very fond, and your promise must be kept if the child is cured. The Jizo being dead, no verbal prayer will be heard; hence it must be made in writing.

The Octopus-Stone: If you suffer from warts, the Tako-Yakushi or Octopus-Yakushi (Bhechadjaguru) at Meguro, Tokyo, will cure them. All you have to do is to get an "octopus-stone" for 30 sen and rub your warts with it until they disappear.

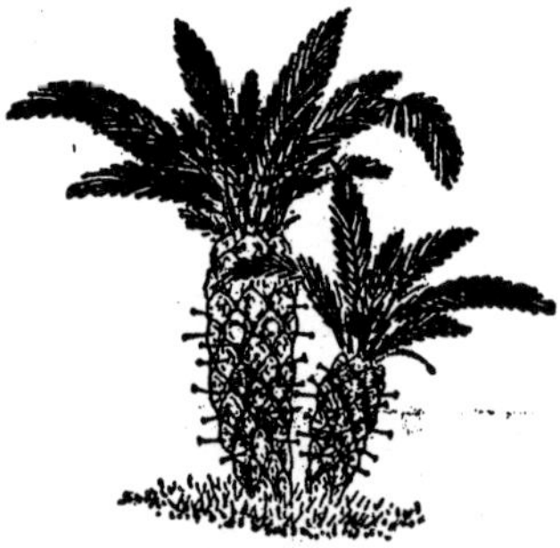

Sago-Palm with Needles.

Dipper with a broken bottom: Let a woman offer a dipper with its bottom broken to the god of birth at Fuchu, a suburb of Tokyo, and an easy delivery will be the result at childbirth.

Bibs: One sees countless bibs offered at different shrines. A bib is borrowed from a shrine for a weak baby to wear. When it gets stronger, two bibs are offered to the shrine as a token of thanks.

Needles on the Sago-palm: In some places in Japan the girl is taught to stick her broken needles on a sago-palm, which is traditionally said to be fond of iron; then she will not get hurt by a needle at her needle-work.

(Continaed)

CHARMS AND EXORCISM (2)—*Concluded*

Lost Needles: A lost needle will appear if you repeat the following poem of thirty-one syllables three times in Japanese:

"Kiyomizu no
Otowa-no-Taki wa
Tayuru tomo
Usetaru Hari no
Miyenu koto nashi."

(Free translation: Though the Otowa-waterfall of Kiyomizu might be dried up, there is no lost needle but will appear).

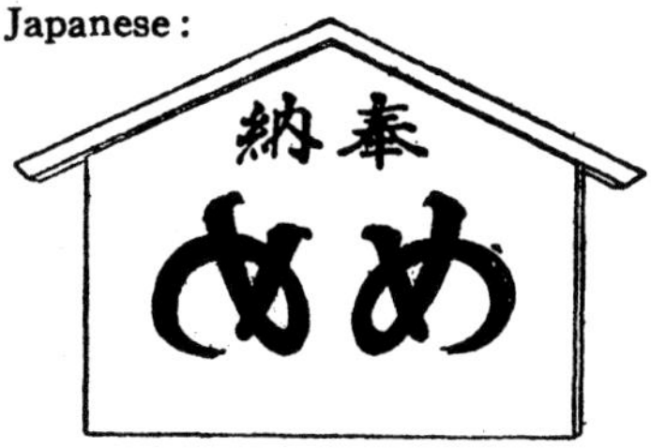

Ema Tablet.

Stones piled at the foot of the Jizo image: Every child has to cross the River Styx after death. A wicked woman will tell it to pile up stones on the river-bed and she will break down every pile that the child makes. If, however, a child piles stones at the foot of the Jizo-image in this life, the deity will help it in making a pile on the river-bed of Styx. Hence we see ever so many stones piled up at the foot of the Jizo all over the country.

Straw-sandals: When one is in poor health, one should offer a pair of straw-sandals to the Niwo or Deva-kings standing guardians at a temple-gate, and health will be restored.

The votive offering of Ema: The Ema, a votive offering of a picture on which is written the Japanese letter (め) for "eye" is presented to a shrine with a prayer for curing an eye-disease. It is generally believed that any eye-trouble can thus be cured.

Kitchen-brush: Suppose you have rheumatism. You should then visit the Tawashi (kitchen-brush) Jizo, of which we have many shrines in Tokyo, for insurance, at Shirogane, Shiba, Toriizaka, Sugamo, Toshima, Meguro, etc. Then you should wash, with one of the kitchen-brushes offered to the deity, the part of the sacred body corresponding to your affected part, and after that with the same brush, do as if you were rubbing the affected part. Visit the Jizo repeatedly till you are cured. When trouble is cured, you have then to offer two brushes to express your thanks to the Jizo. Of course you have to repeat the sacred name "Namu-Amida-Butsu" all the time by chanting while you undergo the mystic rite.

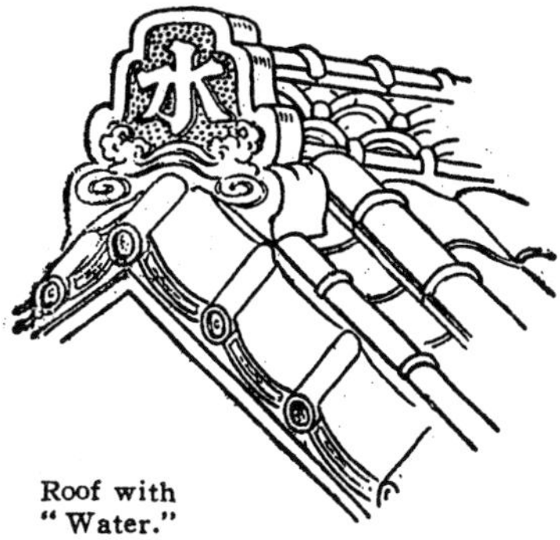

Roof with "Water."

Roof-tile with the character for "Water": One often sees the Chinese character (水) for "water" written on a roof-tile as a charm against fire. Most Japanese houses were thatched with straw or reeds in former days, and their roof could easily catch fire from the sparks flying from a burning house. So the character was used on a roof-tile as a preventive charm against fire.

SOME COMMON SIGN-BOARDS OF JAPAN (1)

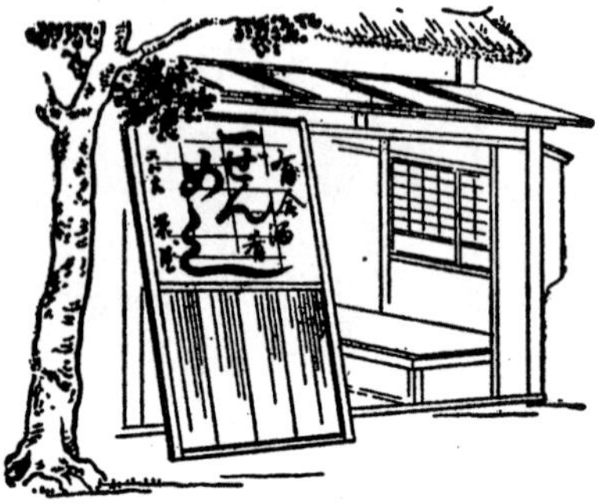

Cha-meshi (tea-rice) and Ichizen-meshi (one-bowl rice)—cheap restaurant where one can get a meal for a few coppers.

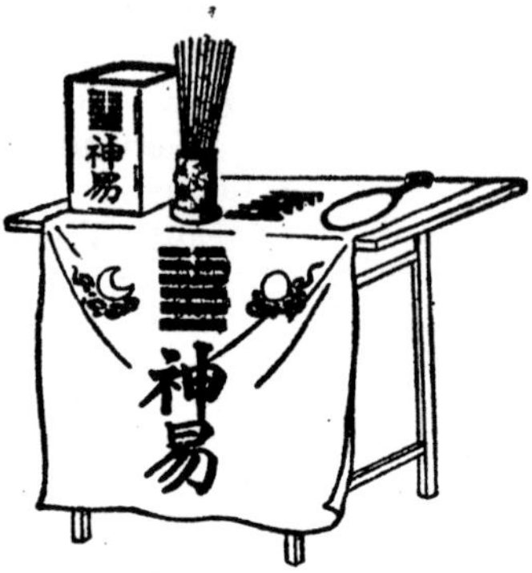

Tsuji-uranai or street fortune-teller and palmist, who charges 30 sen for each fortune-telling.

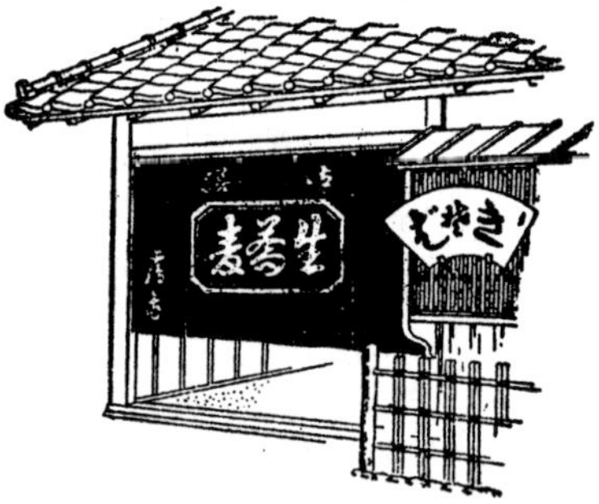

Soba-ya for sale of noodles, buckwheat or wheat.

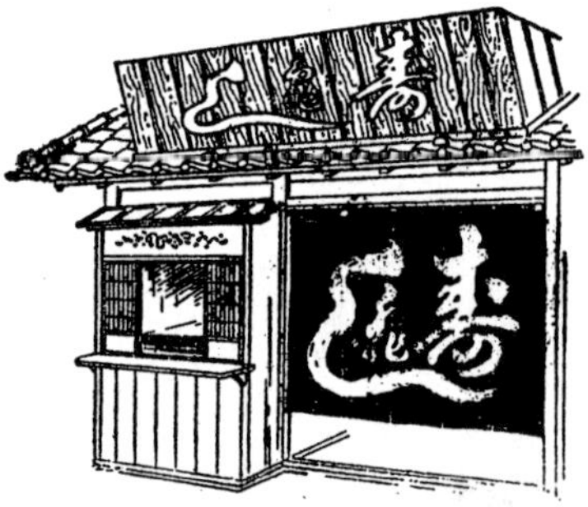

Sushi-stall, where Sushi is sold—boiled rice flavoured with vinegar, and either mounted or mixed with fish and some other food.

(Continued)

SOME COMMON SIGN-BOARDS OF JAPAN (2)

Concluded

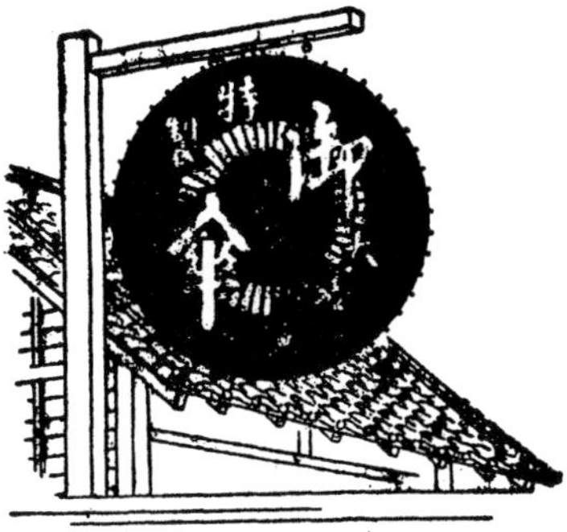

Kasa-ya for paper-umbrellas, also called Chinese umbrellas—cheap umbrellas of paper mounted on bamboo-frames.

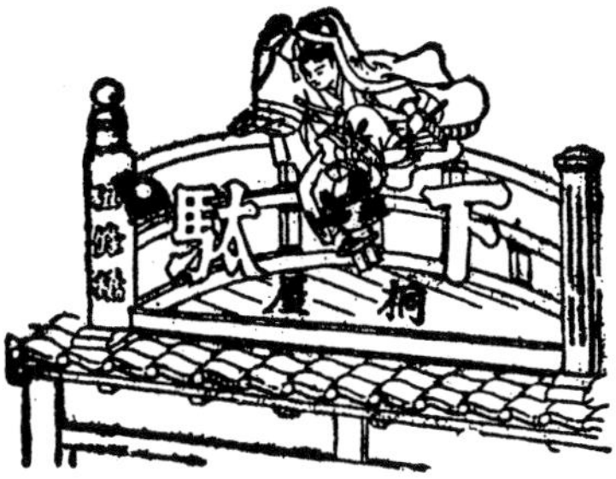

Geta-ya for Geta (wooden-clogs)—the sign-board representing a part of the railing of Gojo-Bashi Bridge, Kyoto.

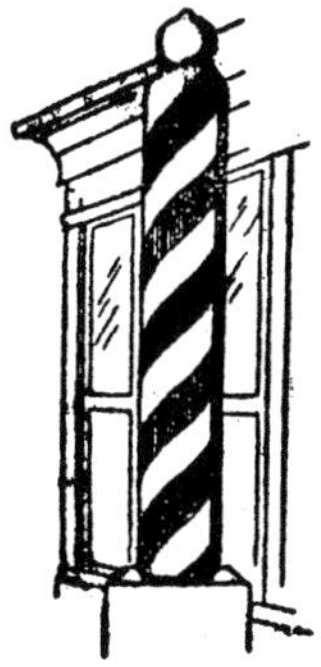

The three-coloured pole for a→ barber, introduced from the West to Japan during the Tokugawa regime.

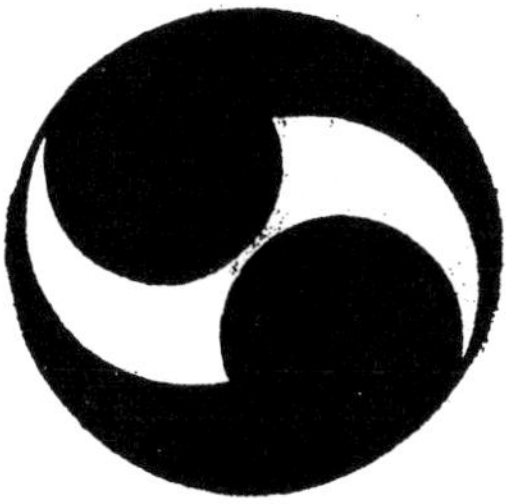

Imagawa-yaki—a cheap confectionery.

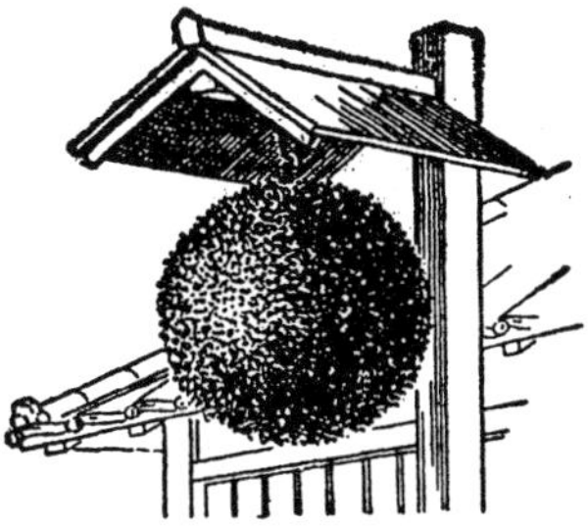

Sake-shop or bar—a ball of cryptomeria needles, found only in the country —the needles being said to keep sake unchanged.

YAKU-DOSHI OR UNLUCKY AGE

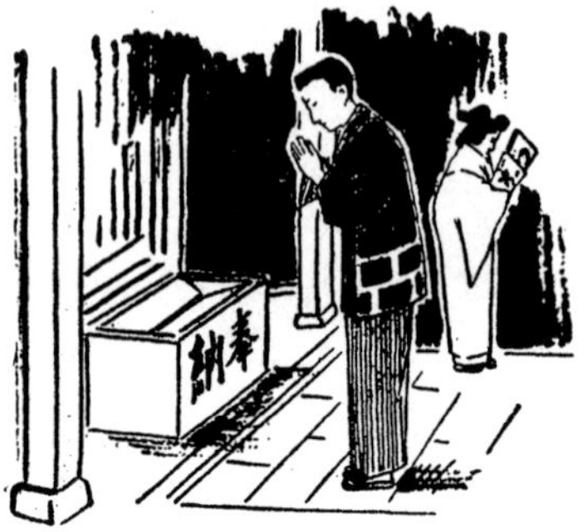

Praying for exorcism.

In Japan each year, each day and each hour has a zodiac sign allotted to it, and it is generally believed by the orthodox Japanese that his fate is determined by the zodiac sign of the year in which he was born. A man born in the year of the monkey, for instance, may be wise and clever, but he is often considered to be too independent, or dependent upon himself, to live in harmony with his friends. Then, according to some fortune-tellers, a person born in the year of the dog is generally wilful and headstrong. The Japanese are careful about what they do on the days of certain zodiac signs. A wedding ceremony, for example, is hardly held in Japan on the zodiac day of the tiger, for fear the bride may take leave as quickly as the tiger which is proverbially said to run a thousand miles in both ways on one day. There are zodiac days and hours when few Japanese start on a journey or begin business.

There are also unlucky years of age for men and women in this country. They are: seven years, sixteen (7+9) years, twenty-five (16+9) years and sixty-one (52+9) years. But, according to the present custom of Japan, the unlucky years are believed to be:—25, 42 and 61 years for men, and 19, 33 and 37 years for women.

The 42nd year and the 33rd year for men and women, respectively, are considered to be the years of greatest ill-luck so that a man of 42 and a woman of 33 years usually act more prudently and circumspectly in those years than in any other years of their life. *Yakuotoshi* (or *Yaku-harai*) or exorcist of evil: On New Year's Eve a street exorcist is heard crying along the streets: "Ill-luck shall be exorcised; evil shall be driven out!" At the entrance to the home which has a man or woman of an unlucky age, the exorcist will chant some words of exorcism, in which he calls upon the Seven Gods of Fortune and the tutelary deity of the locality to bless the home of the person who is of an evil age.

Ill-luck may also be exorcised by the person of ill-luck himself. He can expell his evil by throwing some coins away on New Year's Eve, or on the evening of the Setsubun or bean-throwing evening, which comes on the second or third of February, at the end of the Daikan or Great Cold. As many beans which were used at the Setsubun as the years of ill-luck are done up with some coins in a piece of paper, which the person concerned throws over his shoulder, without looking behind, at the cross-roads. Thereby the ill-luck will be dispelled.

In Kyushu there is a custom in which a piece of bamboo that has been used to make a fire through the year, is thrown away, without any one's knowledge, on New Year's Eve. Thereby it is believed that the god of poverty is done away with, though in some parts of the island the fire-making bamhoo is thrown at a passer-by in the street, in the dark, so that the god of poverty may be transferred to that unfortunate person.

THE SAMHARA, AMULET AGAINST ACCIDENT

It is widely known in Japan that during the Sino-Japanese War, which was fought in 1894-5, few soldiers who kept the amulet of the Samhara on their bodies were wounded by bullets. The Samhara, the origin and meaning of which are unknown, is a charm issued by some Shinto shrines. It has four characters or ideograms which are unintelligible to the ordinary Japanese as they are not found in any Japanese or Chinese dictionary, though according to some orthographers, the four characters are words of conjuration or incantation meaning that "The spiritual gods of heaven and earth protect against accident."

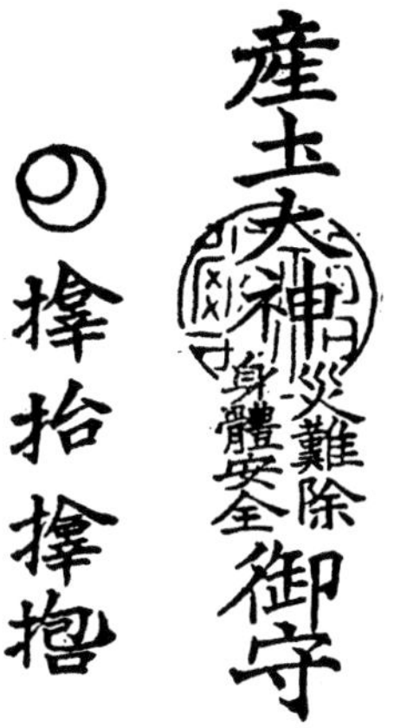

In 1625, Lord Iyemitsu of the Tokugawa Shogunate went "hawk-hunting," as the catching of small birds by means of a trained hawk was called. The hawk caught a wild goose and it was found to have the four words of conjuration on its breast. In 1668 a hunter by the name of Yagobei Yoshikawa, of Kii province, shot at a white pheasant, but every shot missed. On catching the bird in a trap, he found the four letters on its back. He thought that they might be the cause of his failure to hit the bird, so he wrote them on a board, which he found equally hard to hit at a distance. One samurai named Niimi rode on horseback down Kudan Hill, Edo (Tokyo). The hill was much steeper than it is now, and his horse losing its footing, Niimi was thrown several yards into the moat. He was quite uninjured, however, and he attributed his safety to the Samhara, which he then had on his body.

During the last Manchurian Incident, a certain Shinto shrine in Tokyo presented 5,000 Samhara charms to the Japanese soldiers in Manchuria, and it is reported that no less than three millions have been distributed in Japan by Mr. Tanaka of Okayama Prefecture, where the Samhara shrine was built in the spring of 1935. Many Japanese carry the Samhara on their bodies in order to be protected from an accident now that so many motor accidents take place, and the charm is also worn by many of the soldiers who go to the front.

"1000-persons one-needle vest": During the recent Sino-Japanese Incident, many women were seen standing at the entrance of the department stores or some other crowded places, and asking every woman they met to add a stitch each to the cotton cloth they carried with a threaded needle, for it is believed in this country that a vest or belly-band of cotton with a thousand stitches made by so many women will protect its bearer from a bullet in battle. It is called the "1000-persons-one-needle vest (or band)."

Charm of Narita Fudo: The charm issued by the Fudo shrine at Narita, Chiba Prefecture, is popularly known to be efficacious in preventing collision; hence it is used as an amulet against accident in most motor-cars running in Tokyo and its neighbourhood.

HOT-SPRING ROMANCES (1)

***Kusatsu, Gumma Prefecture*:** Tradition has it that Prince Yamatotake, son of the Emperor Keiko (the 12th), discovered the hot spring of Kusatsu in Gumma Prefecture during his eastern expedition in A.D. 110, but Priest Gyoki claims the discovery in 721.

According to the monument erected at Washi-no-yu (Eagle-spring), however, some villagers of Kusatsu claim to have seen one day a male eagle which cured its wounded leg by keeping it in a hot-spring. This is the origin of the Kusatsu spa. Shingen Taketa, a noted warlord of the 16th century, sent his wounded warriors to Kusatsu after a battle during the era of Eiroku (1558-1559).

***Shuzenji, Shizuoka Prefecture*:** The hot-spring of Shuzenji, Shizuoka Prefecture, is attributed to the discovery of Priest Kobo during the era of Daido (806-809). During his stay here, the priest put into the ground his cane of the judas-tree, which he had brought from China. The cane took root, and became what is now called the Katsura-tree (judas-tree) of the Shuzenji Temple, after which the River Katsura is named.

***Shika-no-yu at Nasu, Tochigi Prefecture*:** During the reign (629-641) of the Emperor Jomei (the 34th), Yukihiro Kano was appointed Governor of Nasu. There was a snow-white deer, large as a calf, making great havoc near the village of Myoga-sawa. One day Kano shot at the deer. He was sure that he had hit it, but it escaped. Going up a small stream of water, Kano met a white-haired old man, who said: "I am the god of hot-springs. Your deer is taking a bath a little farther up." Kano found the deer again, and killed it. He opened the spring, which was named the Shika-no-Yu (Deer-spring), and the founder was enshrined at the Onsen-jinja or Hot-spring-shrine.

***Dogo, Ehime Prefecture*:** Princes Ohnamuchi and Sukunahikona were two prehistoric local rulers. Prince Ohnamuchi ruled by militarism, and Prince Sukunahikona ruled humanely. One day they met together at Dogo, and talked about their administration. Ohnamuchi was so excited when he saw that his policy was less efficient than that of Sukunahikona, that he dropped senseless with shame. Sukunahikona, however, succeeded in restoring him to consciousness by pouring over his head some water that he fetched from a nearby hot spring. The Mitama-no-ishi (Spirit-stone), which one finds at Dogo, is said to be the identical stone on which Prince Ohnamuchi stood upon his recovery. The Dogo hot-spring has its origin in this legend.

***Yamashika, Kumamoto Prefecture*:** One samurai, Chikaharu Uno by name, went hunting on the 20th day in the 12th month, 1157, when he saw a deer standing in a hot-spring. Later, on the 16th of the first month, 1179, Shigemitsu Yamaga, another samurai, opened a bath-house for the first time. Hence the people of the Yamashika (literally, mountain-deer) hot-spring have the hot-bath festival on Dec. 20 and the bath-cleaning ceremony on Jan. 16th, every year.

***Kinosaki, Hyogo Prefecture*:** During the reign of the Emperor Jomei a crane came to Kinosaki and kept its wounded leg in hot water for some time. It repeated this for several days until the leg was entirely cured. The people opened a hot-spring, which they named the Ko-no-yu or Crane-spring.

During the era of Yoro (717-723), Priest Dochi kept reciting the Mandala sutra under a cryptomeria for three years, and the hot-spring which he opened at Kinosaki is named the Mandala-sutra spring. ***(Continued)***

HOT-SPRING ROMANCES (2)—*Concluded*

Takeo, Saga Prefecture: Yonemori, a villager of Takeo in the prefecture of Saga, once found a white heron standing still in the water. He tried to catch it but failed. Then, after the bird had gone, he found that the water was hot. A hot-spring was opened and a shrine was dedicated to the heron under the title of the Sagi-jinja or Heron Shrine.

When the Empress Jingo fell sick after her Korean invasion, she was cured by taking baths at Takeo. "It is a pity," the Empress said, "that there is no fresh water," and she struck the ground with the ferrule of her halberd, when lo! fresh water gushed out.

Yamanaka, Ishikawa Prefecture: Priest Gyoki discovered a hot-spring while on a pilgrimage in the prefecture of Ishikawa during the reign (724-748) of the Emperor Shomu (the 45th). He built the Iwoo-ji Temple (Medical-king Temple) by dedicating it to Yakushi, the god of medicine (Bhechadjaguru.)

While on "hawk-hunting" Nobuzure Hasebe, a warrior, saw a white heron sitting in a hot-spring. When it was caught, he found that it had a wounded leg. Hasebe opened a hot-spring at Yamanaka during the era of Kenkyu (1190-1198).

Yoshioka, Tottori Prefecture: A rich land-owner named Ashioka, who lived during the reign (947-967) of the Emperor Murakami (the 62nd), had an only daughter. The girl unfortunately had a boil, and the infection spread so badly that she had boils all over her body, till her physician gave her up. Her parents offered a prayer at the shrine of Yakushi (Bhechadjaguru) on Mt. Shobu (Iris) in whom they had great faith. One night they had a revelation in a dream that their daughter would be cured if she took baths in a hot-spring which they would find under a willow-tree in their compound. She did this and was cured, and this is the origin of the Yoshioka spa in Tottori.

Goshiki, Yamagata Prefecture: Priest En-no-gyoja, during a pilgrimage, stopped on the pass of Itaya. On the following morning he saw a five-coloured (goshiki) fog rising from the mountains. Following the fog, he discovered a hot-spring, which was later named Goshiki hot-spring, and there he took the baths for three cyclic periods of seven days, until he was thoroughly cured.

Onogawa, Yamagata Prefecture: Ono-no-Komachi was a lady of peerless beauty and in the service of the Emperor Nimmei (the 54th). Her father, a governor in the northern part of the country, was reported to have disappeared. Komachi, with the Imperial permission, left the court in search of her father, but when she came to Mikawa, she was taken ill. One night the God Yakushi (Bhechadjaguru) to whom she had offered a prayer for help, appeared to her in a dream to reveal to her a hot-spring about 100 Japanese miles farther north, where she would be cured and meet her father. She travelled on therefore and stopped at Onogawa, where her health was restored, and soon her father happened to come to the same village. The hot-spring was consequently called the Ono-Ama-yu or Nun-bath of Ono after this beautiful woman, who was also an example of filial piety.

THE NINGYO OR JAPAN'S MERMAID

Japan is rich in stories of mermaids or, as we call them, Ningyo (human-fish). The oldest record of the human-fish in Japan dates as far back as the 27th year (619) of the reign of the Empress Suiko (33rd). It reads as follows:—"A strange fish was caught on the coast of Horiye in the province of Settsu. It is of human shape, but it is neither a man nor a fish. It has a head like that of a woman, but it has scales like those of a fish, and the fins act like human hands."

When Tomomori of the Taira family drew a net at Beppo in the province of Ise, he caught a strange fish. It had a human head and a fish-like body. Its teeth looked like those of a fish, and it cried somewhat like a baby. Nobody knew then what it was.

The appearance of a mermaid was popularly taken for the foreboding of an unlucky occurrence. In the summer of 1189 the body of a dead mermaid was washed ashore on the beach of Soto-no-Hama. It was considered to be an ill omen because in the autumn of the same year Fujiwara Hidehira raised a war against the Emperor. In 1213, another dead mermaid was found near Akita in the northern part of Japan. When the report was received by the Hojo Government at Kamakura, a diviner regarded it as an unlucky sign, and soon Wada Yoshinori rose in revolt against the government. Another dead mermaid was found on the shore of Tsuruga in 1203, and the assassination of Sanetomo, the third Shogun of Minamoto, was generally considered to have been foretold by the appearance of the unlucky human-fish.

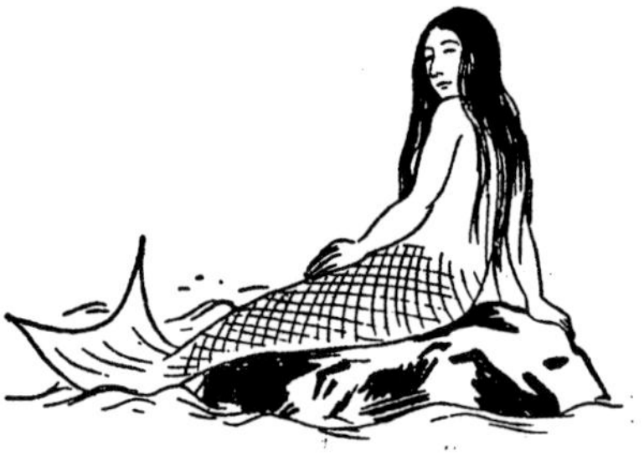

The report reached the Kamakura Government of a dead mermaid washed ashore at Tsuruga on March 11, 1247. A prayer was at once offered at the Hachiman shrine, Kamakura, against the occurrence of an unlucky event, but a war broke out between the Hojo regent and Miura Yasutoki on June 5 in the same year.

Otsuki Gentaku, a noted scholar, writes about a human-fish as follows:—

"In the beginning of the era of Enkyo (1744-1747), my uncle and aunt took a boat at Hirato (near Nagasaki). When their boat was running on the Genkai-nada, a human head came suddenly out of the water at a distance of about 3 yards from the boat. Every one on board was surprised as it was the last thing expected on the surface of the sea. It had a white face like that of a woman, with brown hair. It smiled at the people on board and soon went down again below the waves. But it came out a second time and then they saw its body, which resembled that of a fish. It was a Ningyo."

The appearance of a mermaid was considered to augur ill. Below are mentioned some more places where mermaids are said to have appeared:—

Yasuki-no-ura, Izumo Province, May 2, 756 A.D.; Susu-no-Misaki, Noto Province, April 3, 778 A.D.; Ietsu-no-Ura, Aki Province, August 14, 1189 A.D.; Seto-no-Hama, Autumn, 1248 A.D.; Tsugaru, Mutsu Province, September 10, 1248 A.D.; Futami-ga-Ura, Ise Province, April 3, 1357 A.D.; Ohama, Wakasa Province, April 11, 1310 A.D., etc.

THE SESSHOSEKI OR KILLING STONE OF NASU

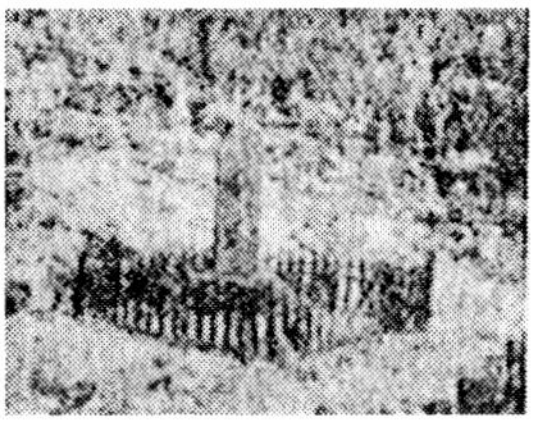

The killing stone at Nasu.

"Nothing flies above the stone but the clouds in the sky" is a free version of the noted 17-syllable poem written by Basho about the Sessho-seki or Killing Stone. Basho is by far the best poet in Japan of 17-syllable poems or *haiku*.

The stone is at the hot-spring spa of Nasu in the prefecture of Tochigi. Nasu is noted for a sulphur spring and the stone is on the dried river-base of the Yu-kawa (literally, Hot-water River), where sulphur gas evaporates in large quantities. There is a stone a few feet large in three dimensions, surrounded with a paling, and it is proverbially believed that, as Basho says, every bee, butterfly and any other insect drops dead when it flies over this stone on account of the gas generated from it.

During the reign of the Emperor Horikawa (the 73rd), Lady Tamamo-no-Maye of peerless beauty was taken into the Imperial service, and she became a great favorite with the Emperor. Soon he was taken ill, and when his court-physicians could not account for the cause of his disease, Abe-no-Yasunari, a fortune-teller, was called to see what the trouble was. Abe attributed the malady to the spell of Lady Tamamo-no-Maye, and he succeeded in counter-charming her. When she saw that her charm had been dispelled, she resumed her original shape of the fox, which had assumed human form. It ran from the Imperial palace and hid itself in the province of Tochigi, where it molested travellers as well as residents.

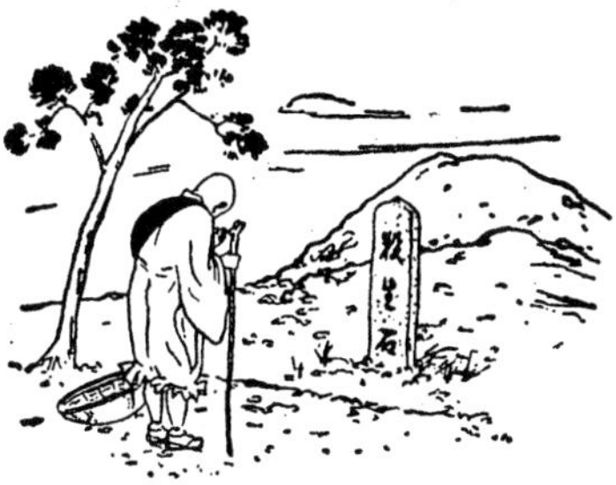

Poet Basho visiting the Sesshoseki.

At the command of the Emperor, Miura Yoshizumi and Kazusa Hirotsune, two warriors, led an army to Nasu, where the wizard fox had taken refuge and there they hunted for it. But it is recorded that the fox was so elusive that it took the shape of every living or dead thing in order to escape. It appeared sometimes as a small boy, then as a charming girl or a giant. At another time it wafted on the air like a feather, and yet again it appeared as a small bug on the tail of a horse.

The hunters were utterly bewildered, when one night a saintly hermit appeared to one of the leaders in a dream, in which he handed an arrow which would infallibly kill the fox. It did hit the fox, which at once turned into a stone, and generated a poisonous gas that killed every living thing coming near it, till the stone was covered with the dead bodies of the insects it had killed.

On the 13th of the eighth month, 1384, Priest Genno, of the Soji-ji Temple (now at Tsurumi, near Yokohama) of Noto Province, visited Nasu to calm the disturbed spirit of Lady Tamamo-no-Maye, who was now turned into the poisonous stone. The priest offered a prayer by reading the Buddhist sutra, and with a hammer, he then struck the stone, which split in two. Then there appeared before him a woman, who after thanking him for exorcising her power which had made it possible for her wicked spirit to attain Buddhahood, disappeared in the air. Therefore the stone lost its own power to kill.

DREAM DIVINATION

On the evening of January 2, the hawker is seen running along the streets crying "O-takara! O-takara! O-takara!" (Honorable treasure! etc.) By "treasure" is meant a picture of a treasure-ship, which is invariably a sailing one because a sail "swollen" before a fair wind is taken as a good augur in Japan. The treasure-ship has the Seven Gods of Fortune on board, and it is laden with various sorts of treasures, such as rice-bales, coral, gold and silver coins, Uchide-no-kozuchi ("Aladdin's" mallet), keys, etc. The picture has a 31-syllable poem written above the treasure-ship. The poem, which is said to have been composed by Prince Shotoku in order to save Hata-Kawakatsu from the evil effect of a bad dream, can be read similarly, with few phonetic changes, from both ends, thus:

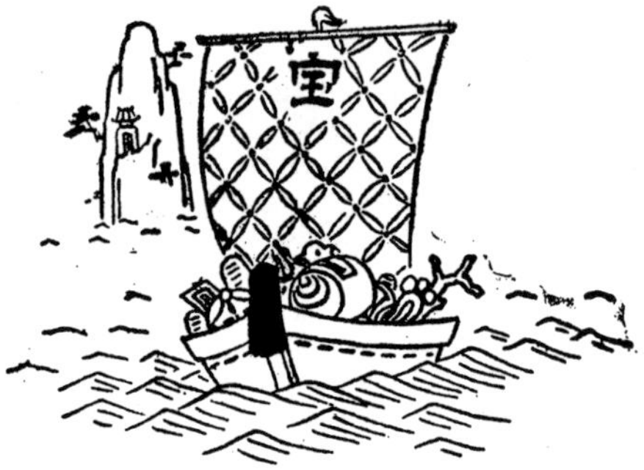

Treasure-ship.

"Na-ga-ki-yo no, To-o no ne-muri no, Mi-na me-sa-me, Na-mi nori-fu-ne no, O-to no yo-ki ka-na." (When we all wake up from a sound sleep of a long night, how sweet is the sound of the waves on which the ship is riding.)

You have to put the picture under your pillow when you go to bed on the eve of Jan. 3, and sleep on it. The dream that you may see on that particular night is regarded as the first one of the year, and it will predict what there will be in store for you during the year. The best dreams, according to tradition, are: "Mt. Fuji, the first best; the hawk, second, and the egg-plant, third." The dreams of a snake, the sun, and a fire destroying a house are among the good in Japan, but you have to be careful when you dream of a horse, a fish or a tooth coming out, for it portends something bad in this country.

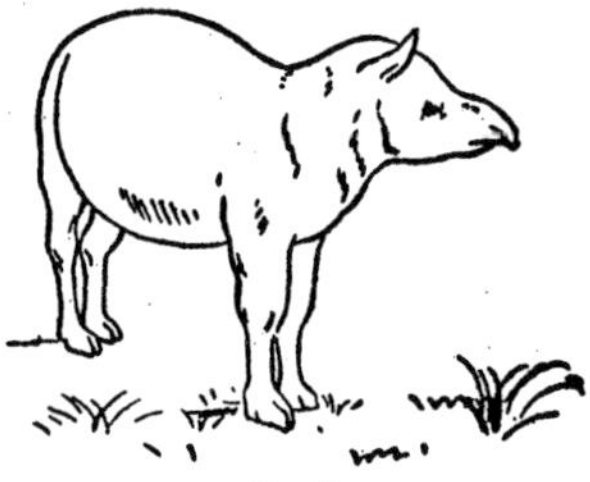
Tapir.

If you have a good dream, you must keep it secret from other people. But the picture of a bad dream has to be thrown into a river, otherwise the dream will have a bad effect upon you.

In former days the sail of the treasure-ship bore the Chinese character 貘 for "baku" (tapir), which according to tradition lives upon dreams.

***A few Japanese sayings about dreams*:**

A saint sees no dream.
Dream of your love, and your love will be lost.
Dream that you are cut with a blade, and money (metal) will come in.
The dream of a snake means promotion.
A dream is due to the debility of the five vital organs.
A red horse in a dream is the harbinger of a fire.
Pick up a chestnut in a dream and your father will die.
Throw to the baku (tapir) any bad dream that you may dream.
Dream of a bamboo sprout, and a friend will die.

"MOMOTARO," A NURSERY TALE (1)

The story of "Momotaro" is on the lips of every Japanese, for it is one of the first nursery tales that are told to every child in Japan. The story in a nutshell runs as follows:—

Once upon a time there lived an old man and his wife at a remote village in Japan. The old man used to go to the mountains to collect firewood and his wife to a river nearby to wash clothes in the water. One day a big peach came floating down the stream and the old woman took it home to share it with her husband. Soon after his return, the peach was divided into two by itself, and a baby walked out of it. Because he was born of a peach, he was named Momotaro (Peach-boy) and he became a great pet of the aged couple.

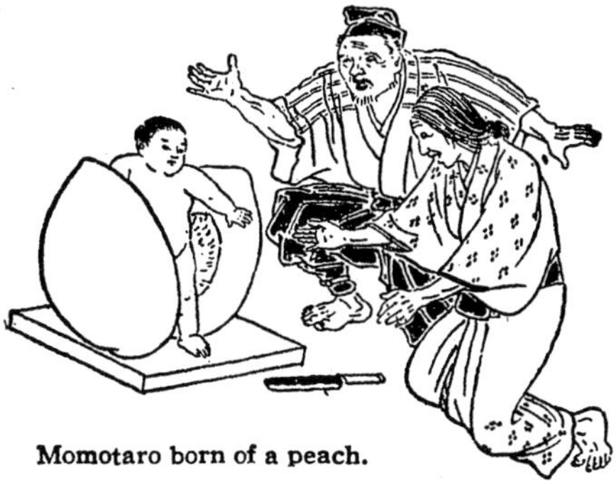

Momotaro born of a peach.

When he grew up, Momotaro wished to explore Oni-ga-Shima or the land of Oni (Ogres). Taking with him therefore some O-Nigiri (rice-balls) that his mother made for his luncheon, he started on his adventures. A pheasant, a dog and a monkey joined him on the way, and together they proceeded to the land of the Oni. The Oni, who are known to be cannibals

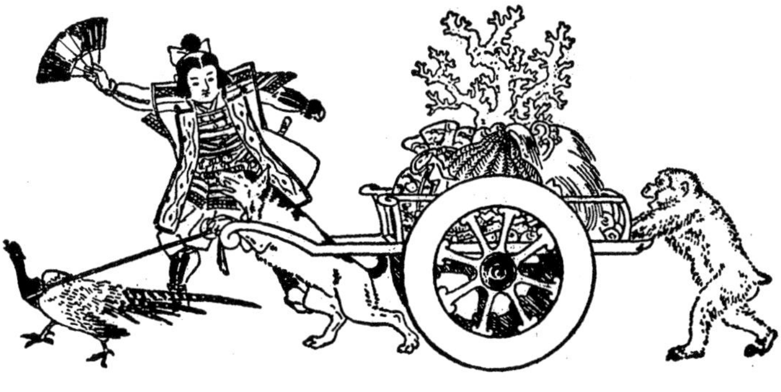

Momotaro returning in triumph.

scented the approach of Momotaro and his suite, whom they came out of their castle to attack and eat. But Momotaro proved the stronger, and they surrendered with little resistance. They offered all the treasures they had in the castle, consisting of "gold, silver, corals, damasks, brocades, etc." They were loaded on a cart, which the dog led, with the help of the pheasant that pulled it by means of a rope, and the monkey which pushed. Thus Momotaro returned home in triumph.

Scene of Story: Accoring to tradition, Momotaro, the hero of the story, personates Prince Kibitakehiko, grandson of the Emperor Keiko (the 12th) and nephew of Prince Yamatotake, and Oni-ga-Shima is located on an island off Takamatsu in the province of Sanuki, Shikoku, where one can still see the caves in which the Oni (a pirate) lived with his many followers. The prince was ordered by the Emperor to lead an expedition against the Oni. The story was first written by Michizane Sugawara (856-913), who was once the governor of the province.

But other scholars place the birthplace of Momotaro at Kiso in the province of Hida. There are several places, the names of which remind us of the story of Momotaro; such as the Momotaro shrine, Momotaro-Yashiki (Momotaro's residence), Saru-ga-Taki (Monkey-waterfall), Kiji-ga-Mine (Pheasant-peak), Inuyama (Mt. Dog), the Hoseki-ji Temple (Treasure-loading), etc., though no authentic record has been of course established to support the connection that these places may have with the story itself.

NURSERY SONG

MOMOTARO

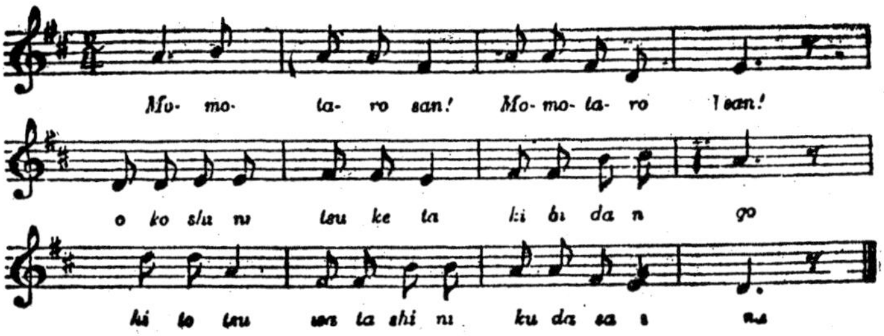

MOMOTARO

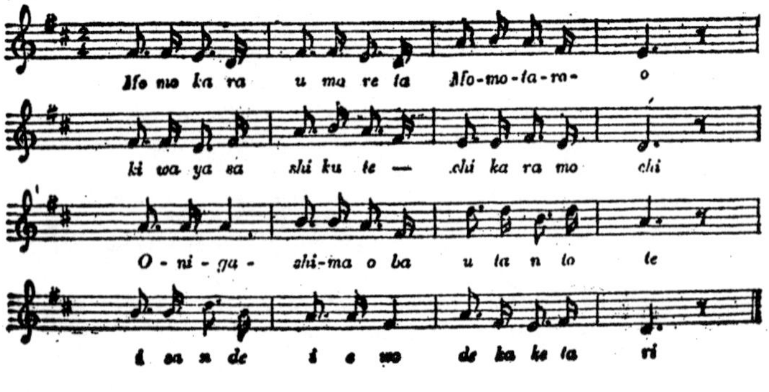

THE BUMBUKU TEA-KETTLE

The story of the Bumbuku-chagama or, as it literally means, the Fortune-distributing tea-kettle, which is kept at the Morin-ji (literally Luxuriant-forest) Temple at Tatebayashi in the prefecture of Gumma, is one of the most popular nursery tales in Japan. It has various versions, but briefly it runs as follows:—

Once upon a time a curio-dealer bought a tea-kettle. It was a fine iron-kettle, but, strange to tell, it disappeared night after night, though it was found in its place in the morning, so that the disgusted dealer sold it to the priest of the Morin-ji Temple. But when the priest put it over a fire, it turned into an old badger and scampered away.

But a more authentic record tells quite a different story about the mysterious tea-kettle. Priest Tenrin (literally, Celestial-forest), founder of the Morin-ji Temple once met at Ikaho, a hot-spring resort, an old man, by the name of Shukaku (literally, protecting-crane), whom he employed as a sexton for his temple during the era of Ohyei (1394-1427). He proved to be a devoted and faithful janitor and, so the story goes, he served with ten priests of the temple generation after generation.

In 1582 there was a great mass-meeting to be held at the Morin-ji Temple, when Priest Gingetsu (literally, peak-moon), the resident priest of the tenth generation, told Shukaku to prepare hot water for making tea for a thousand people whom the priest expected to attend the meeting. Shukaku brought an iron-kettle, which would contain about four gallons, and which he called the Bumbuku-chagama or Fortune-distributing tea-kettle, because, as he said, one who drank from it would never get thirsty again. And sure enough, all the congregation was fully served with tea from the tea-kettle, an actual fountain of hot-water.

Five years later, or on the 28th of February, 1587, the village of Tatebayashi had a great banquet and the sexton became so drunk that in his sleep he betrayed his transmogrification, for he was an old bager.

"Since my transmogrification is revealed," the old badger said to the surprised priests of the Morin-ji Temple, "I must take leave of you. I thank you all for having housed me in this temple for all these years. I was born in India, where I lived for 500 years, then I went to China, where I stayed for over 1,000 years, and then I came over to Japan, where I have lived for 1,800 years. It was my happy privilege to have met the saintly priest, founder of the Morin-ji Temple, who kindly engaged me as his sexton.

"But before I take leave of you, I will show you what magic power I have."

So saying, the badger-man conjured up before the priests of the temple the battle scene of Ichinotani, which was fought in 1184 and also the scene of a religious meeting held for the Lord Buddha in India. And the old badger took leave of them.

The Bumbuku Tea-kettle, with which Sexton Shukaku used to entertain the large congregation, is still kept at the Morin-ji Temple, where visitors may see it.

EMMA OR KING YAMA OF THE DEAD

"If you tell a lie, you will have your tongue pulled out by Emma-sama." Thus will a Japanese mother warn her child against telling a lie. Emma, or King Yama, presides over the land of the dead, and all souls that go down to the nether world will be judged by him according to their deeds in the upper world.

In feudal days, our shop-boys had only two days off in the whole year: the sixteenth of January and July. This custom of giving the shop-boys two holidays a year is still observed by most Japanese shops, and on these holidays most of the shop-boys will visit Emma or King Yama in their neighbourhood, though of course in these times many of them will go to a cinema theatre, or some other modern amusement as well.

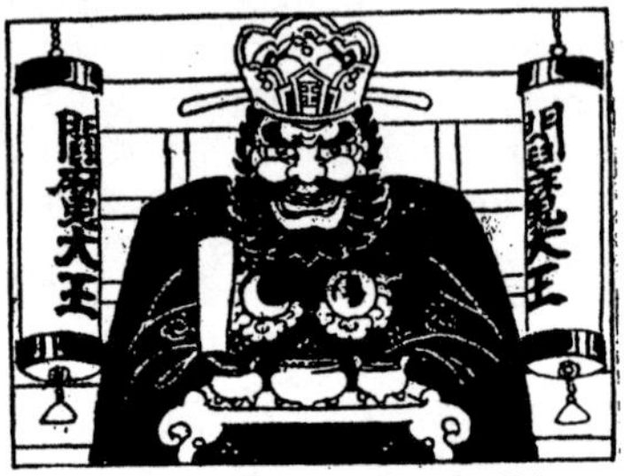

The largest Emma statue in Tokyo (Daiso-ji Temple, Shinjuku).

King Yama wears a Chinese crown, and has a dignified look, with a red face and angry eyes. He always holds a sceptre in his right hand and sometimes a banner of human heads in his left. The mirror of Harikyo and the scales of "go" (or deeds) are provided, for he judges all souls according to the reflections made in the mirror, which shows all deeds committed in this life.

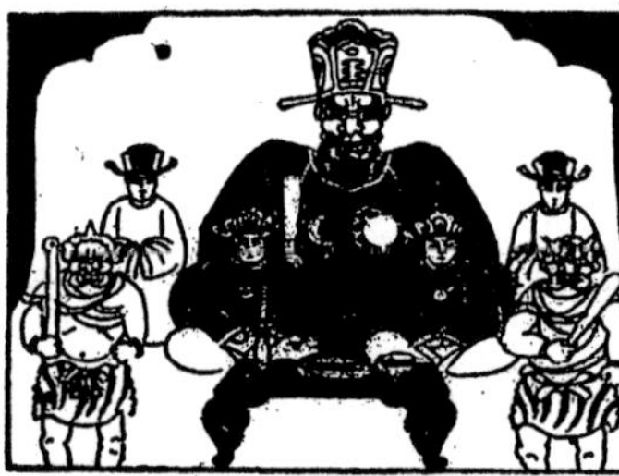

The Emma statue, Shinko-ji Temple, Toyama.

A wicked-looking woman often sits with King Yama. She is the keeper of the River Styx or the River of the Three Roads, after which she is named the old woman of the Three-Road-River. According to Buddhism, there are three ways of crossing the River Styx: those who did nothing but good in this life will cross the river by a bridge; those guilty of peccadilloes will wade its shallow parts, but the great sinners have to cross the river at deep places, only to be met, upon reaching the other side, by the vicious woman, who strips them of all their clothing.

There are two wicked Oni or ogres, one wearing a red loin-cloth and the other a blue one, of tiger's skin. They will drive the naked sinners up the mountains of needles and swords, and through the valleys of fire. Then he has three messengers. They are Old-age, Sickness and Death, who are constantly sent to the upper world in order to warn the people against committing sin. Those who heed the warning are allowed to cross the bridge of the River Styx to Paradise, but those who take no heed of it are tortured by the wicked keeper of the river and the two jailers of the dead.

THE 500 STONE-IMAGES OF THE RAKAN (ARHAN)

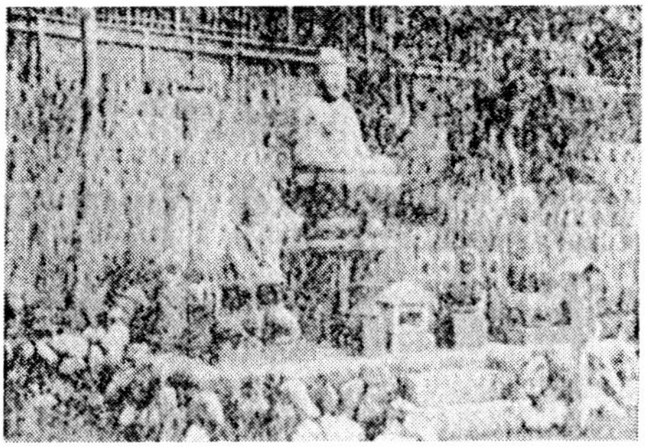

500 Arhan Images of the Daiyen-ji Temple, Tokyo.

On the hill behind the Daiyen-ji Temple situated at Meguro, Tokyo, there stand side by side 500 stone-images of the Arhan, who attained the enlightenment of Hinayama or the Lesser Vehicle. Each image is a little over a foot high. While, as a rule, the 500-Arhan images, of which we have many sets in the country, have so many different features and expressions, some happy and others gloomy, some fat and round, others thin and long, and so on, they are quite different from the 500 images of the Daiyen-ji Temple. There all the faces, without exception, look gloomy, and some even crying or weeping. But the wretchedness of their expressions is accounted for by the cause for which the images were erected. It is as follows:

Once there was a young priest by the name of Shinshu at the Daiyen-ji Temple. He had a personal grudge against the resident priest, and set fire to the temple at noon on the 29th day of the 2nd month, 1772. Fanned by a strong south-westerly wind the fire kept burning, and destroyed 157 streets of the Shogunate capital of Edo. Then the wind made a new turn, this time blowing northeast, till, according to records, no less than 223 streets were reduced to ashes, killing thousands upon thousands of people. The 500 Arhan images were set up therefore by the priest of the Daiyen-ji Temple in their memory, or for the peaceful repose of those ill-fated people who were burned to death in the great fire.

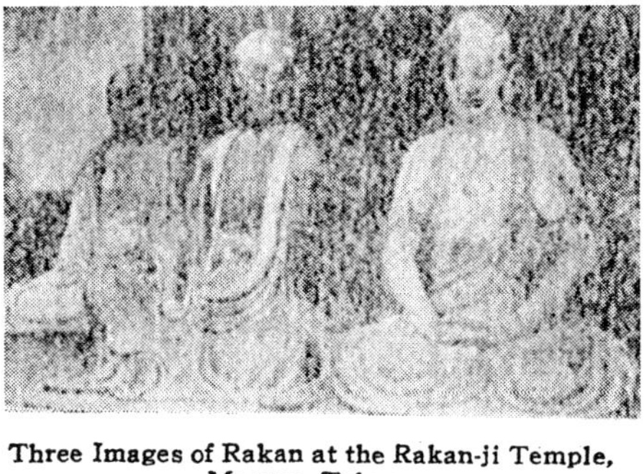

Three Images of Rakan at the Rakan-ji Temple, Meguro, Tokyo.

You will notice that one of the 500 Arhan of the Daiyen-ji Temple represents a hooded woman, carrying a baby in her arms. It is quite unusual to find a woman in a set of the 500 Arhan images, and the Christians claim that she represents the Virgin Mary. Indeed, it does look like the traditional image of the Virgin, but of course the priest of the temple will explain that this image stands for all the women who died in the great fire.

Mention may be made of another set of the 500 Arhan images, life-size and of wood, which Priest Shoun carved by spending some ten devoted years during the era of Genroku (1688–1704), and which he dedicated to the dead spirit of Lady Keisho-in, mother of the Shogun Tsunayoshi of the Tokugawa family. Over two hundred images of this set are preserved at the Rakan-ji or Arhan Temple, Meguro, Tokyo; all the others having been destroyed by the great earthquake of 1923.

THE DARUMA OR DHARMA (1)

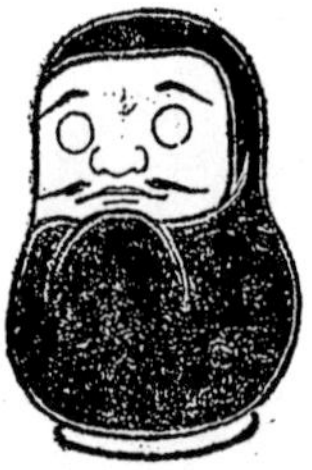

A Japanese Daruma-doll.

The Daruma is a doll representing a Buddhist priest generally wrapped up in a red cloth. It is on sale at every toy-shop in Japan. The doll has no legs, but it is made in such a way with a weight in it that it will immediately return to an upright position every time it is knocked down. Hence the doll is also called "okiagari-koboshi" meaning "a bonze who can easily get up." The doll is therefore used as a luck-bringer by orthodox Japanese, who consider it to be symbolical of an undaunted spirit against failure. They will keep, at a conspicuous place in the house, a Daruma-doll of papier-mache, which has two blank eyes, i.e. without the pupils, or which has its eyes covered with a piece of paper. When a prayer is answered or an object achieved, the paper is removed and the pupils are put with black Indian ink in the blank eyes.

The word "Daruma" is a perversion of the Indian word "Dharma," law, and our doll represents a Buddhist priest by the name of Bodhidharma. He was the third son of the king of Cochin in India. He studied Buddhism under Priest Prejnatara for forty years, and he went to China in 520, where he met King Wu of the Liang dynasty. When he saw that the King turned a deaf ear to his teachings, he took leave of the king to go to Wei, where he lived at the Shao-lin-ssu or Shorin-ji Temple. It is said that Dharma sat for nine years in meditation, without stirring, and all the time "facing the wall" until he lost the use of his legs. Hence, the Japanese doll of Daruma has no legs, his red cloth being accounted for by the fact the Indian monk always wore a red dhooty. In his nine years' meditation, the priest evolved the doctrine of Dhyana (or Zen, as it is called in Japan) or a method of training body and mind by sitting quiet in meditation, which makes his eyes see though looking at nothing. Hence our picture of Daruma has meditating eyes. Dharma died in 536, and his remains were buried on Mt. Yuji (literally, "bear's ears").

After an elaborate study, Dr. Junjiro Takakusu, a well-known authority on Buddhism, asserts that our Daruma does not represent Bodhidharma, but that it is modelled after Priest Dhyana-bhara, also called Sunyadsya or, as the name is pronounced in Japan, Priest

(*Continued*)

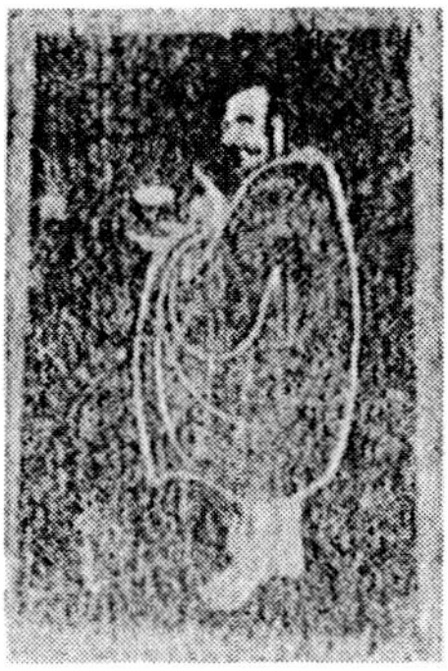

A mendicant dharma.

Shikuh (指空). He was a son of the king of Makada, India, and attended the University of Nalanda at the age of five. He went to Ceylon when nineteen years old, and later on to Tibet whence to China, and then to Koma, a kingdom in Korea, where he died on Nov. 20, 1363.

There is a temple on Mt. Kataoka, in Yamato Province, by the name of the Daruma-ji Temple, which is said to have been founded in commemoration of a Dharma, whom Prince Shotoku met while travelling in the province of Yamato on Dec. 1, 613. The Prince found the priest so learned and intelligent that on his death his body was buried on Mt. Kataoka, and the Daruma-ji Temple was dedicated to his dead spirit.

The Zen Sect: "The Dharma" says Chinese legendry, "came from the west; he knows no letters (meaning possibly that being an Indian he could read no Chinese characters), but he meditates all the time, so that if he wants to preach Buddhism by means of writing, he could use all the water of Lake Tung-tinghu up with brush-pens." To his meditation, which, as is said above, lasted for nine long years, is attributed the doctrine of the Zen sect of Buddhism in Japan. The word "Zen" is derived from the Sanscrit "Dhyana" (meditation). The believers of this sect have to sit in what is called Zasen (sitting-Zen) in which they meditate by sitting in a Buddha fashion for hours on end during which they concentrate their mind in order to attain supreme wisdom and spiritual enlightenments.

Nanakorobi-yaoki: This common phrase comes from Daruma. It means "seven falls and eight rises" indicating an undaunted spirit. One may fail seven times, but one will succeed at the eighth rise, so long as one has an undaunted spirit.

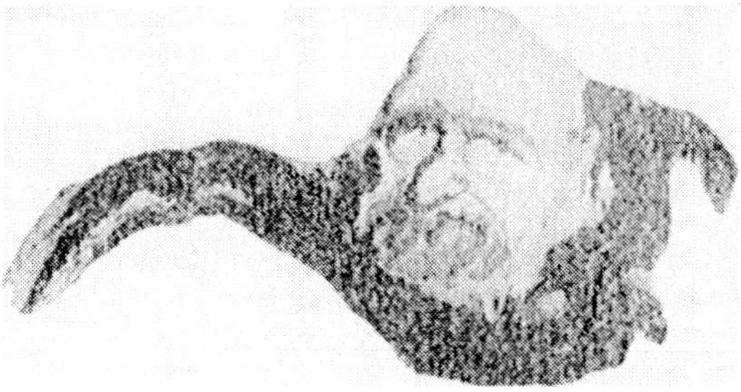

KURO-HONZON OR THE BLACK-IMAGE

Lord Iyeyasu, the founder of the Shogunate Dynasty of Tokugawa, had two images, the Shiro-Honzon and the Kuro-Honzon, in which he had great faith.

The Shiro-Honzon, or White-Image, was enshrined at the Daiju-ji Temple in Mikawa Province, and little is now known about it. The Kuro-Honzon, or Black-Image, was brought to Edo, when Iyeyasu entered the capital in 1590, and it was enshrined at the Zojo-ji Temple, the family temple of Tokugawa. Its origin is as follows:—

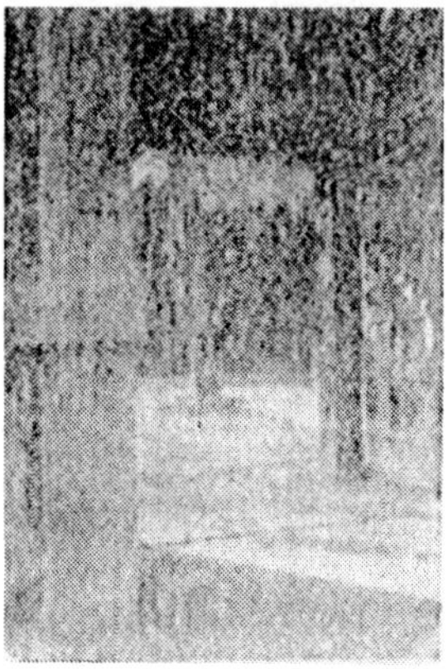

A Part of the Kuro-Honzon Temple.

Mitsunaka Minamoto, who lived in the 9th century, wished to make a priest of Bijomaru, his youngest son, who was rude and often cruel in his ways. He therefore sent him to the Nakayama-ji Temple in Settsu Province. But the boy preferred militarism to Buddhism and learning, or the practising of swordmanship to the study of Buddhism. Indignant at his disobedience, Mitsunaka called Bijomaru back and, after exchanging a few words with him, ordered Nakamitsu Fujiwara, his chief retainer, to put the boy to death. Nakamitsu, however, killed his own son, Kojumaru, instead and sent Bijomaru secretly to Yokowa on Mt. Eizan. This noble act of loyalty on the part of Nakamitsu touched Bijomaru to the heart, and he now turned over a new leaf, devoting himself to the study of Buddhism under Priest Genshin. Mitsunaka, his father, was so pleased that he gave him a wooden image of Amitabha or Amida Buddha, which was carved by Priest Eishin.

The Kuro-Honzon Altar.

This image was handed down from generation to generation in the family of Minamoto, till at last it fell into the hands of Iyeyasu Tokugawa, a descendant of Minamoto. It is said that the image became black on account of the incense burned thick by its devotees for many a century, until it is called by the name it now bears, Kuro-Honzon or Black-Image.

Iyeyasu was such a pious devotee of the sacred image that he took it with him on the battle-fields. During the many battles he fought against Taketa, Oda, Toyotomi and Sanada, Tokugawa had several narrow escapes, and was only saved miraculously, so that he attributed his escape to the gracious protection of the sacred image.

Upon the death of Iyeyasu in 1616, the Kuro-Honzon was enshrined at the Zojo-ji Temple, Edo, and it has since been a familiar object of worship in Edo, and incense is still kept burning before it by its devotees throughout the whole year.

THE KUHOMBUTSU OR NINE-RANK BUDDHAS (1)

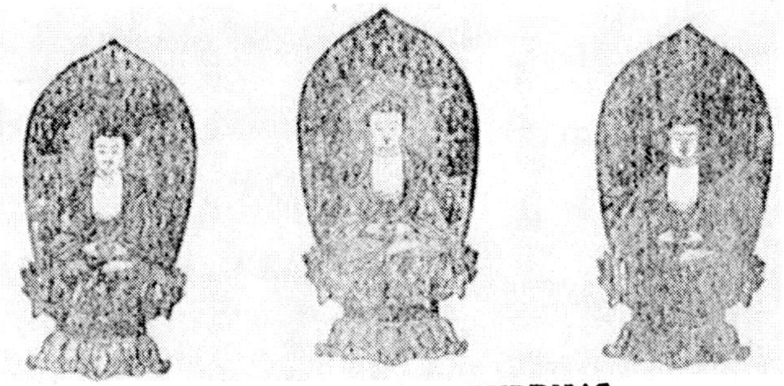

THE UPPER-RANK BUDDHAS

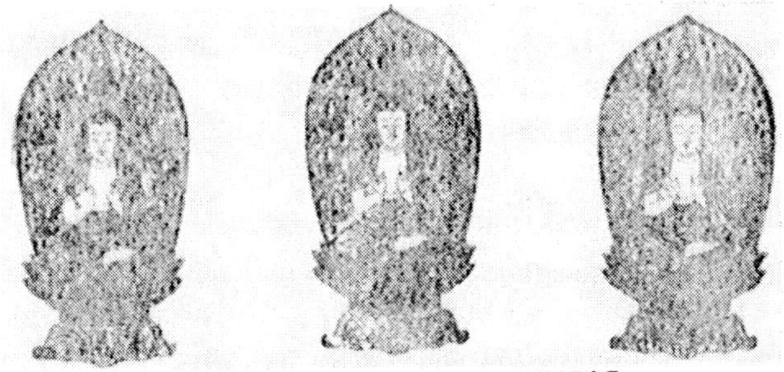

THE MIDDLE-RANK BUDDHAS

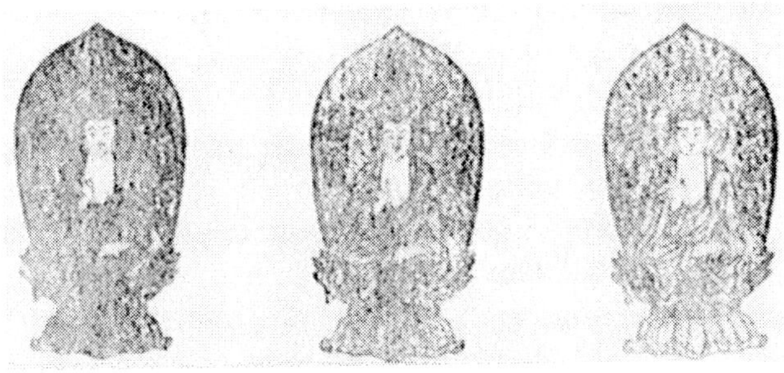

THE LOWER-RANK BUDDHAS

The Joshin-ji Temple, of the Jodo Sect, situated at Okuzawa, Tokyo, is known for nine wooden images of the Buddha, each 16 ft. high, illustrating the nine stages of Enthanasia or birth in Sudhavati (Paradise); namely, the upper, middle and lower ranks, each having the upper, middle and lower births, altogether nine ranks of birth. They were carved by Priest Kaseki.

THE KUHOMBUTSU OR NINE-RANK BUDDHAS (2)

Concluded

Priest Kaseki was born in Edo in 1618 and took the tonsure, under Priest Rengan, at the age of nine, by embracing the faith of Buddhism, when his father had committed suicide. The priest devoted his life to the carving of Buddhist images in order to pray for the peaceful repose of his father's spirit. By the time he was fifty years old, Priest Kaseki had carved ten thousand wooden images, which he enshrined at the Reigan-ji Temple, Fukagawa, in Edo (Tokyo).

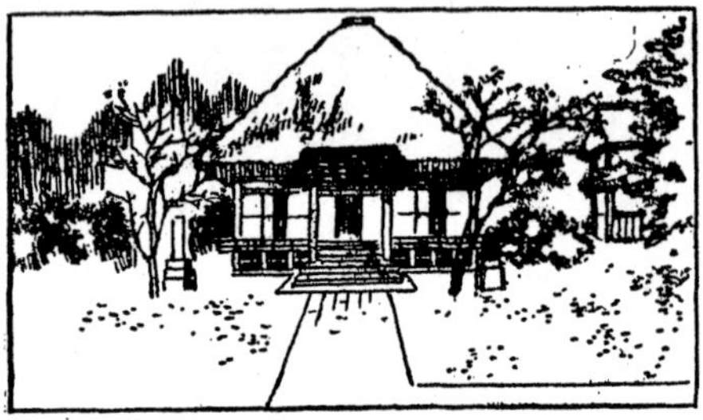

The Joshin-ji Temple.

In 1669, while Priest Kaseki was absent, staying with the resident priest of the Taiso-ji Temple, Echigo Province, a great tidal wave came up and washed all his images into the sea. "The Buddhas save the multitude by the Karma," the priest prayed when he heard of their being all washed away, "before they enter the life of Nirvana. O Buddhas, come back to the land of your Karma and help the people." And soon he received news that all the wooden images had been washed ashore again.

At the age of sixty-one, Priest Kaseki was called by the people of Okuzawa, a suburb village of Edo, and it was while he was the chief priest of the Joshin-ji Temple that he carved the Kuhombutsu, or Nine-rank Buddha, images, which are enshrined in the temple, each having a thousand smaller images on its halo. They are venerated in three Daibutsu-Hall, with three images in each.

Priest Kaseki was fond of the number 36,000, which is considered to be sacred in Buddhism. He carved 36,000 sacred images, it is said, during his life-time; he recited the Nembutsu-prayer of "Na-mu-Ami-da-Butsu" 36,000 times every day; his temple stood on a plot of 36,000 tsubo (tsubo=6 sq. ft.), and the main temple had 36 pillars.

The Joshin-ji Temple, of which Priest Kaseki was the chief priest, has a sacred image of Amitabha, which is said to have been carved by Priest Shotoku in order to keep evil away.

THE NIWO OR DEVA-KING OF MT. MINOBU

Eizen, the resident priest of the Shomyo-ji Temple at Kanazawa, near Yokohama, was a skilful player of Go or checkers. Every time he played he gambled and so amassed a large fortune which he won at the game, till his parishioners began to be disgusted with him so that his fellow-gamblers dropped him one after another.

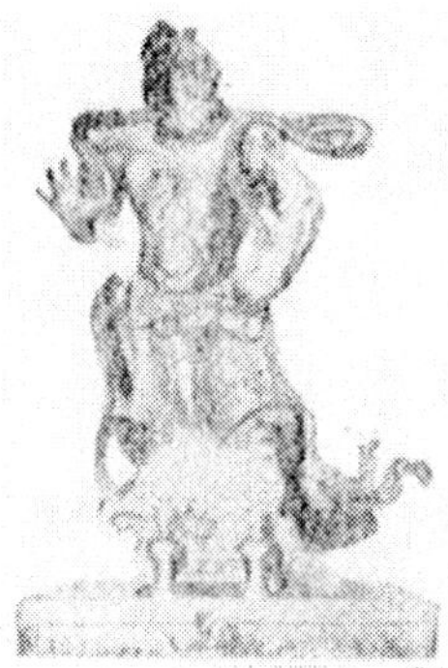

Niwo of Mt. Minobu.

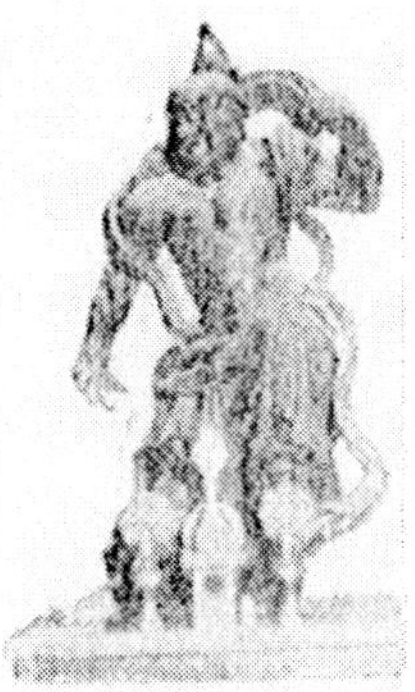

Niwo of Mt. Minobu.

While the priest was feeling lonely with no one to play with him, the squire of the village, Rokuro Rokuura by name, came to the temple to play with the priest. They played three times, betting ten, five and fifteen *ryo* respectively, which all fell into the hands of the priest, for he won again every time.

Dejected and disheartened, Rokuura took his leave of the priest. But when he came to the temple-gate, he stood and prayed to the Niwo, or Deva-king, enshrined there. Rokuura had longed for the image of the Niwo, on which he was willing to stake all his estate and property. On that particular day he had come to test the priest, only to find himself no match for him. He now prayed for help of the sacred image.

That night the gracious Deva-king appeared to Rokuura in a dream and told him to bet on the sacred image, as he would help the squire to win.

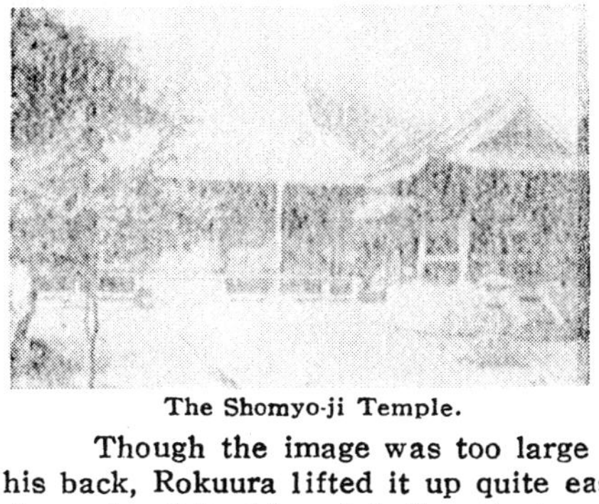

The Shomyo-ji Temple.

Early next morning Rokuura repaired to the temple and again challenged the priest, betting all his estate and property on the image of the Niwo, which the priest staked. Rokuura succeeded this time.

" If you take the holy image," the priest said to Rokuura when the image was about to be lifted up from the stand, " you must carry it by yourself without getting help from anyone else."

Though the image was too large for any ordinary person to carry on his back, Rokuura lifted it up quite easily and began to run down the hill. Amazed and dumbfounded, the priest rang the alarm-bell, to call the villagers, who, already disgusted with the priest, did nothing to recover the image. Rokuura ran on for two days and nights, till he came to Mt. Minobu, which is a sacred mountain for the devotees of the Nichiren sect, because Priest Nichiren secluded himself on the mountain for many years.

The Niwo image is still found enshrined on Mt. Minobu, which is a place of pilgrimage for Nichiren devotees.

THE GUARDIAN-IMAGES OF THE SHRINE AND THE TEMPLE (1)

The Niwo: Many Buddhist temples have the Niwo-mon Gate in front, in which the Niwo or Deva-kings are enshrined as guardian-deities. The Niwo represents Vajrayaksa, one of the five Buddhist Myowo or "Bright-kings." The one on the left (from the temple), with its mouth opened to pronounce the Sanscrit vowel sound "ah" is a positive image, which invites every good to come in, while the other, on the right, with its mouth closed to pronounce "um," is a negative image for shutting evil out. Many Deva-kings have lots of bibs, which are thanks-giving offerings. When, for instance, a child is sick with whooping cough or some other disease a bib is borrowed from the Niwo-image as a charm, and when the disease is cured, two bibs are offered as a token of gratitude.

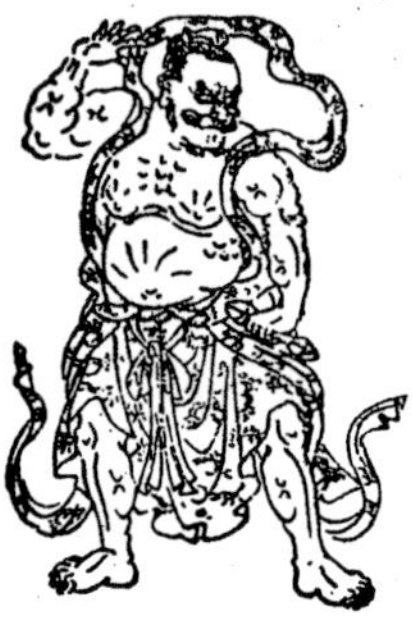

The Niwo.

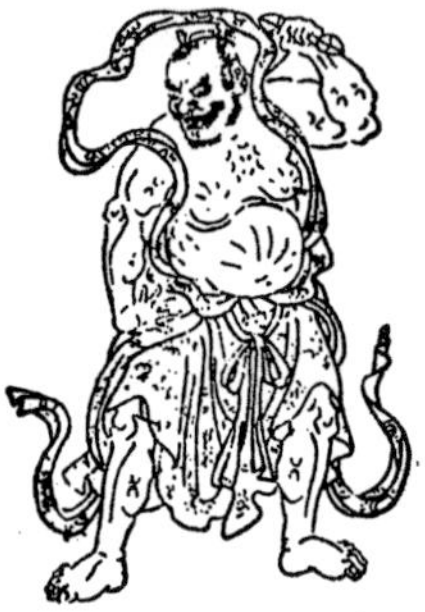

The Niwo.

The Kara-shishi and the Koma-inu: Most Shinto shrines have the Kara-shishi (Chinese-lion) on the left-hand side (from the shrine) and the Koma-inu (Korean-dog) on the right-hand side. They are of ancient and obscure origin. But some scholars say that Japanese adopted the Chinese practice of posting a stone-lion before a private residence, a shrine or a grave, while according to others the king of Korea is represented by the Koma-inu, because, when the Empress Jingo invaded the peninsula of Korea in 200 A.D., the Korean king pledged his fealty by promising to guard the Imperial palace of Japan for ever. Still others are of the opinion that the stone-images are placed as guardians before the Shinto shrine to represent Prince Hosori, who, through his admiration for the bravery of Prince Hikohohodemi, grandfather of the Emperor Jimmu, vowed allegiance by saying that his posterity would eternally guard the Imperial Palace. It must be added, however, that the original distinction of the two animals seems to have been forgotten, for the two guardian-animals look so alike that they are generally considered to represent one and the same animal. According to the old way of arrangement, the two stone-animals should stand face to face though nowadays they often face away from the shrine-precincts, instead of looking at each other.

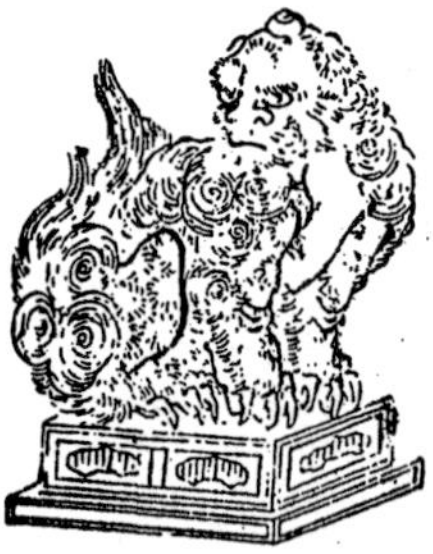

The Koma-inu.

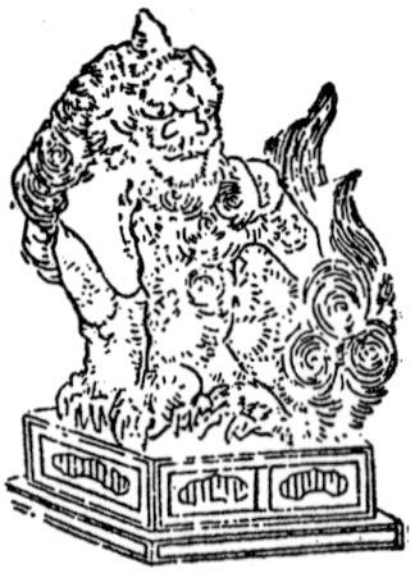

The Kara-shishi.

THE GUARDIAN-IMAGES OF THE SHRINE AND THE TEMPLE (2)—*Concluded*

The Korean-dog represents a fabulous unicorn called "ssu" in the Chinese language. According to tradition, it is a dark-brown animal as large as a bull, with so tough a skin on its head that it was used to make a military helmet. Sometimes the male and female animals are represented at a shrine, and then the one on the left-hand side (from the shrine) often has a baby under its paw. Also, we often find a stone-animal with a ball under its paw, because the lion represented by it, is fond of playing with a ball.

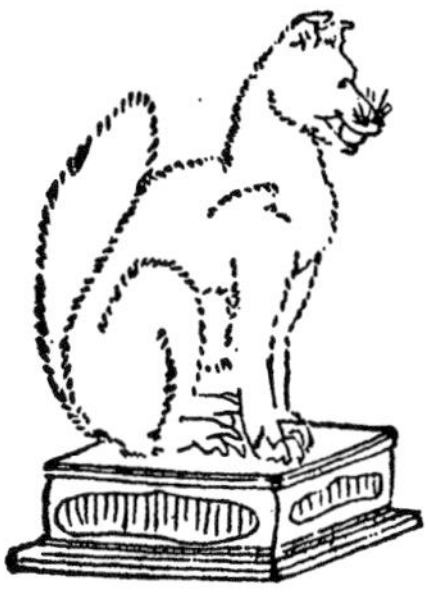

The Fox.

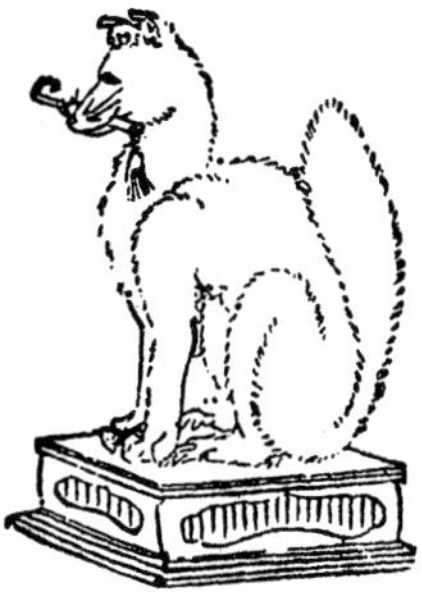

The Fox.

The Fox: A pair and some times many pairs of fox-images of either stone, wood or even porcelain stand before the Inari-shrine, which is dedicated to Princess Ugaji or Ugatama, the goddess of rice. Sometimes a key is found carried in the mouth of the fox-image, because it is supposed to keep the door of a barn in which rice is stored, and other images have the Hoshu-no-tama (treasure-ball) or "Aladdin's gem," so to speak, under its paw, signifying that the Inari, the deity of rice, is the source of all good.

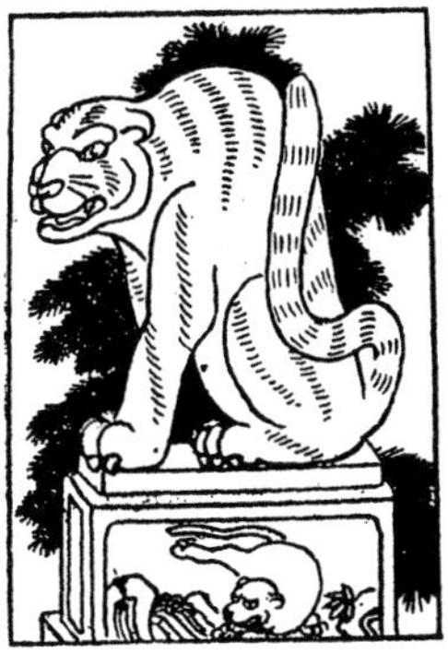

The Tiger.

The Sanno (literally, "mountain-king") shrine is dedicated to Prince Oyamakui, who is the god of hunting. He is always associated with mountains, and the monkey is the guardian-animal of his shrine, though the Sanno shrine of Tokyo, which had a part of Edo, the Shogunate capital, as its parish, has a pair of wooden images representing the court-ministers of the left and right.

The Bishamon shrine at Kagura-zaka (God-dance-hill) in Tokyo is dedicated to an Indian deity called Bishamon (Vaisravana), who being the guardian of the north, is armed with a sword in his left hand and a halberd in his right, and treading under his feet a devil called Ama-no-jaku (celestial-devil). Because this deity was brought over to Japan for the first time, according to tradition, on the zodiac day, month and year of the Tiger, during the reign of the Emperor Kimmei (the 34th), the Bishamon shrine has a pair of Stone-tigers standing as guardians before it.

THE ISHI-DORO OR STONE-LANTERN (1)

Every foreign tourist visiting Japan is surprised at the large number of Ishi-doro, or stone-lanterns, found in the precincts of a Buddhist temple or a Shinto shrine. It is said that there are over 1,700 stone-lanterns at the Kasuga Shrine, Nara, the earliest of which dates from the Choreki era (1037-1039), and the Toshogu Shrine at Ueno Park, Tokyo, dedicated to Iyeyasu, the founder of the Tokugawa regime, has 250 stone-lanterns and 50 bronze ones. All these lanterns were offered to the shrines by courtiers or daimyo of local provinces.

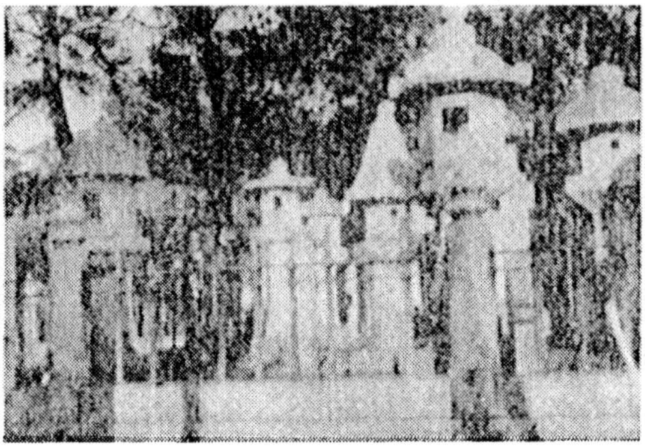

Stone-lanterns at the Gokoku-ji Temple, Tokyo.

A stone-lantern was originally put before a shrine, temple or grave for lighting purposes, although it is never lighted in modern times. Tradition has it that it was first made by the people of Yama-no-sato in Kawachi Province when the district was infested by highwaymen. Gradually the original object of the stone-lantern was forgotten and it was used as a mere ornament in a shrine, temple or Japanese garden. Today, however, the stone-lantern is quite indispensable to Japanese gardening. According to an old idea, a single stone-lantern was used, though today we generally find two, before a god.

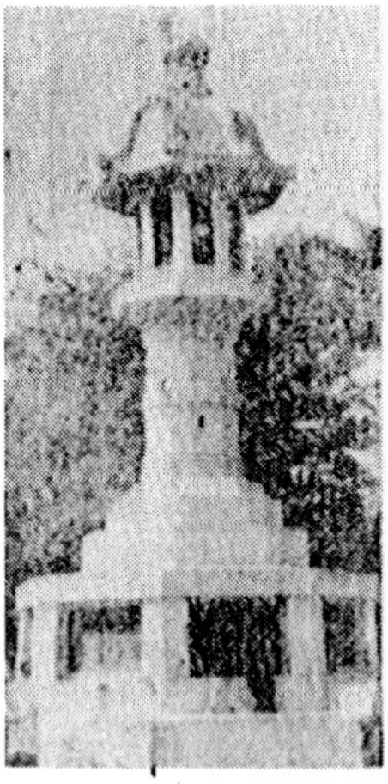

Stone-lantern of the Yasukuni Shrine, Tokyo.

The Tachibana-dera Temple, which was founded by Prince Shotoku, the father of Japanese Buddhism, has an old lantern, which is said to be the oldest in Japan, but the oldest on record is found at the Mimuroto-dera Temple in Kyoto, as it was erected in 1153, though the Todai-ji Temple, Nara, claims to have a bronze lantern made in 765. During the Tokugawa regime, the local lords vied with one another in erecting stone-lanterns or offering them to the shrines, as we can easily see by looking at those of the Zojo-ji Temple, Shiba Park, or of the Toshogu Shrine, Ueno, as well as of the famous Nikko Shrines.

(Continued)

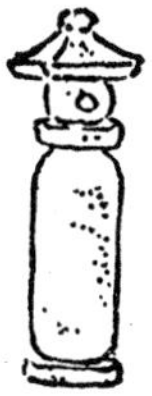

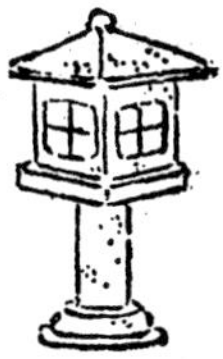

At the Gokoku-ji Temple, Tokyo, one may see replicas of the chief stone-lanterns in the Kansai districts.

While all the stone-lanterns are regularly arranged before the Toshogu Shrine, Ueno Park, we find one large one standing by itself. It is twice as large and high as the ordinary ones, and has a top-stone 12 ft. in diameter and the body about 3 times the width of the outstretched arms. This stone-lantern is said to be one of three carved by Katsuyuki Sakuma in 1631. Of the other two, one is at the Nanzen-ji Temple, Kyoto, and the other at Atsuta, Owari. It is treated with discrimination, being separate from the other stone lanterns, because Sakuma, who presented it, was no daimyo, but an ordinary samurai.

It is said that if a child hops on one leg round this stone-lantern, the one geta or wooden clog that is left behind will be carried off by an unseen power. Hence this stone-lantern is known as a "spook-lantern."

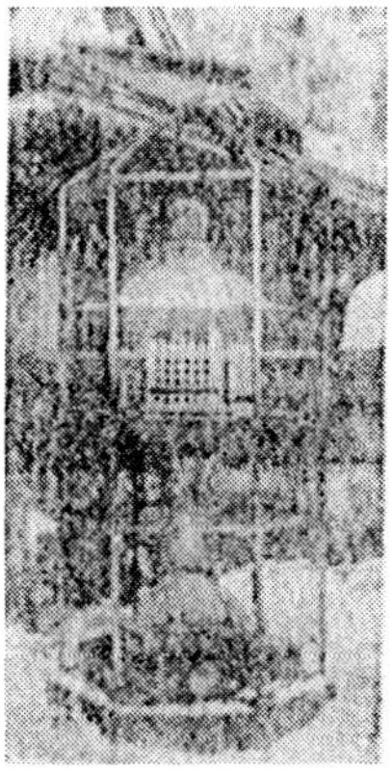

Spook-lantern at Nikko.

According to another explanation, however, the spook-lantern was so named because it is a copy of another spook-stone-lantern, which is found at the Futara Shrine, Nikko. One night, the story goes, a samurai, who passed by the shrine, met a spook. Instead of running away, the brave samurai struck at it with his sword until the spook disappeared. On the following morning the people of Nikko discovered that the stone-lantern of the Futara Shrine had several notches made with a sword. A wire-cage was therefore at once placed over the stone-lantern to prevent it from walking out any more to molest the people.

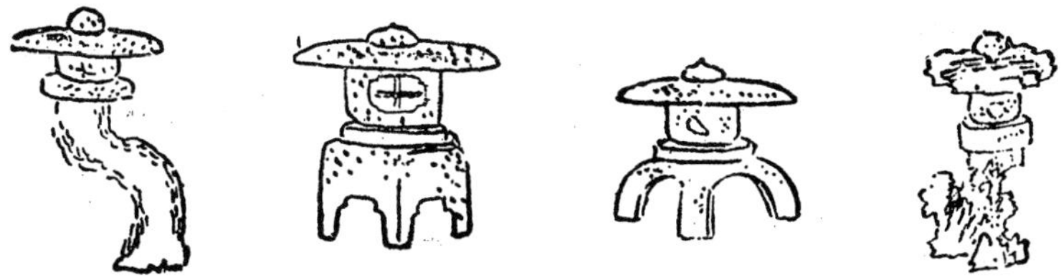

KISHIMOJIN OR HARITI

The Kishimojin or Kishibojin (literally, Devil-children-mother-deity), which is commonly found all over the country, is a shrine dedicated to Hariti (literally, great joy), an Indian goddess; those at Zoshigaya and Meguro being two famous Kishimojin shrines in Tokyo.

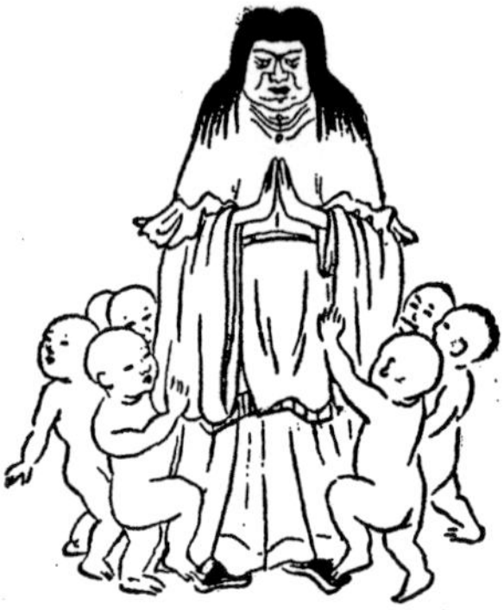

It is said that Hariti had five hundred children, whom she fed with the blood of the children she kllled by the dozen every day in the streets to the constant dread of mothers. These distracted mothers came therefore to the Lord Buddha and asked him to put a stop to her cruel ways. So one day the Lord Buddha went to see Hariti, but learning that she was away from home, he hid her youngest child under a basin. Hariti loved this child more than her other 499, and it was fed with the juice of pomegranates while the Lord Buddha kept it hidden. Hariti was almost mad with grief when, on coming home, she failed to find her favorite child. She looked everywhere for it, but all to no purpose. At last she went in despair to the Lord Buddha, whom she besought to restore her lost child.

" You miss your youngest child like that, when you have five hundred children," the Lord Buddha said to her quietly in admonition. "How much sadder do you suppose a mother will be when you kill her only child in order to feed your little ones with its blood? I will restore your child only on condition that you stop killing innocent children."

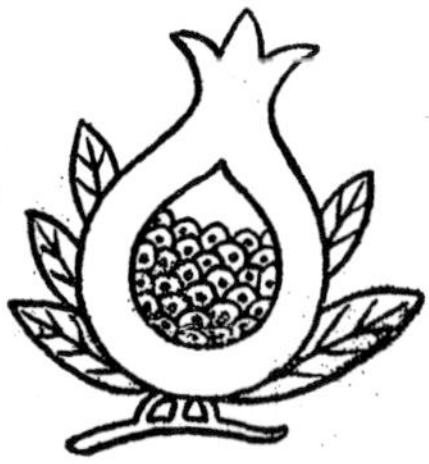

Hariti was at first too much enraged to accept what the Lord Buddha had to say to her, but at last she had to yield to his convincing argument. The Lord Buddha then restored the child to Hariti, to her great joy, and she devoted the rest of her life to protecting children. Hence her image or statue shows her surrounded by children, now her devotees but once her victims.

Hariti is believed to have a special power to cure children's diseases, so the Kishimojin shrine is visited by her devotees all the year round, and it has immense crowds at its festival, which falls on a day of November every year.

Because the youngest child of Hariti was fed with the juice of pomegranates, the Kishimojin shrine bears a crest representing a pomegranate. There is, moreover, a saying in Japan that the juice of the pomegranate has the taste of human flesh. This is possibly because of the tradition that the child was fed with its juice instead of the human blood on which Hariti used to feed her children, and also because the seeds of the pomegranate are blood-red.

THE BUGAKU DANCE (1)

The Bugaku Dance, a court-dance of ancient Continental origin, was first introduced to Japan from Shiragi, a kingdom in Korea, when the Empress Jingo sent an expedition against the peninsular kingdom in 200 A.D. The same kingdom sent a few more examples of Bugaku to Japan upon the death of the Emperor Inkyo (the 19th). The Emperor Keitai (26th) called some scholars and musicians from Kudara, another kingdom of Korea, in 513. Three more dancers came over from the kingdom of Kudara during the reign (540–571) of the Emperor Kimmei (the 29th). During the reign (593–629) of the Empress Suiko (the 33rd), Prince Umayado, more popularly called Prince Shotoku, who is regarded as the father of Japanese Buddhism, established a dancing institute at the Shitenno-ji Temple, Naniwa (Osaka), where Korean dancing was taught to the public so that it might be performed at the Buddhist services. The Emperor Kotoku (the 36th) and Tenji (the 38th), who adopted the Chinese system of administration, introduced Chinese dancing and music. In 736 a Buddhist priest, Buttetsu by name, came from Annam, and became a favorite with the Emperor Shomu (the 45th), who erected the Daibutsu or Great Buddha at Nara. The Rinyu Eight Pieces of Bugaku, which Priest Buttetsu brought from Annam, or, according to some Buddhist authority, from India (Rinyu being Lumbini, where the Buddha was born), are still highly prized in the Imperial court. In this way did Bugaku become popular in Japan till it was frequently performed during the Nara Period (710–784) and Heian Period (794–1185), for in those days foreign music was played at the Buddhist services, in which the Imperial family had great faith. (*Continued*)

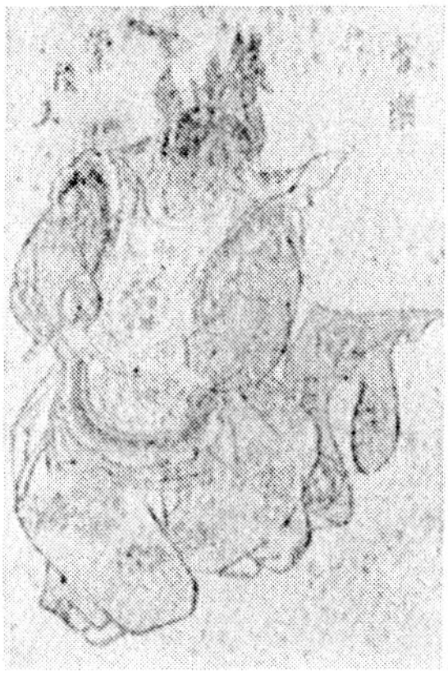

Bugaku Costume.

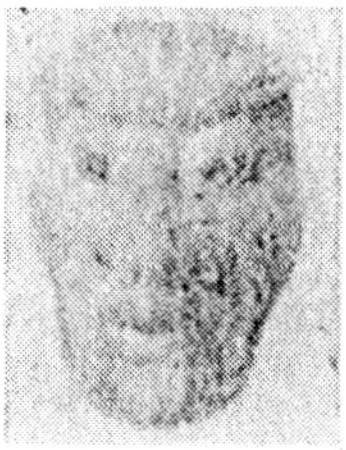

Bugaku Mask.

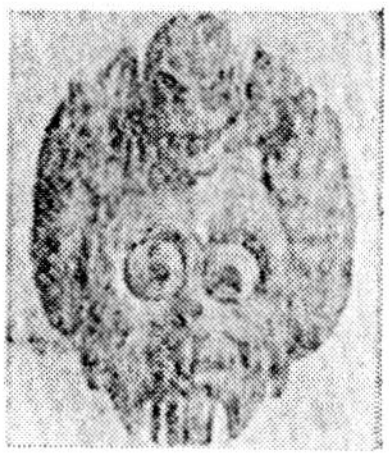

Bugaku Mask.

THE BUGAKU DANCE (2)—*Concluded*

During the Tokugawa regime (1603–1867), the Bugaku dances were performed at the Shishii-den Palace, Kyoto, every year, but it had begun to lose its popularity towards the end of the Tokugawa dynasty and gradually fell out of fashion. Upon the Restoration in 1868 of the Imperial administration, however, the court musicians were newly appointed and Bugaku has since been played at the New Year dinner-party held at court on Jan. 5th each year. It was given on a large scale when the Constitution was promulgated in 1889, and also at the time of the Silver Jubilee of the Emperor Meiji in 1892. Bugaku is now performed on felicitous occasions.

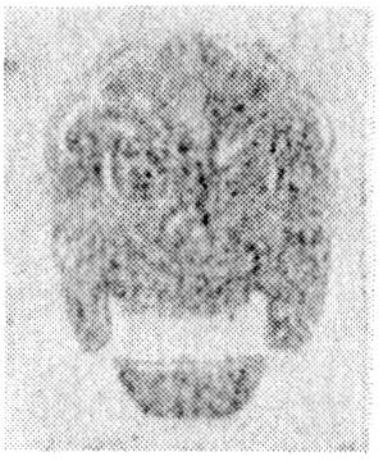

Bugaku Mask.

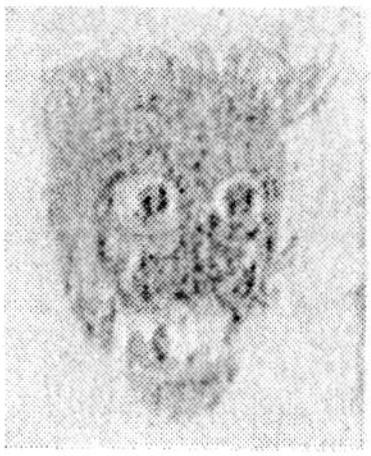

Bugaku Mask.

Bugaku includes dances from Tang (China), Rinyu (Annam or India), Tenjiku (India), Korea, Tibet, Pechili, Tartar, etc., representing battle-fields, court practices or the customs and manners of the countries where they were invented. The Tang dancing was most popular during the early period of the Heian days (794–1185). Later, Bugaku was divided into civil and military dances, but when the Emperor Ichijo (the 66th) changed the organization of the Bugaku dances to suit the Japanese taste, they were classified into the left and right dances; the Chinese and Indian dances belonging to the left, and the Korean and Pechili to the right.

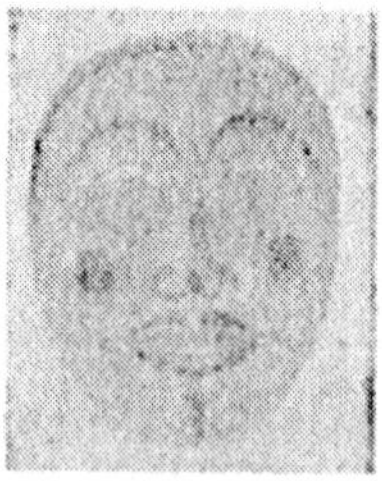

Bugaku Mask.

In 1888, the musicians of the Imperial court selected some fifty pieces of Bugaku, but the late Joden Otsuki, a recognized authority on Bugaku, gives 39 left and 26 right pieces of Bugaku in his little book called "The Illustrated Explanation of Bugaku," several other pieces being entirely lost.

The Bugaku masks are exquisite pieces of art, and many of of them are preserved as national treasures. It is remarkable how, while the ancient dances of Bugaku have disappeared in China, India, Korea and the other countries of their origin, they are well preserved and even improved upon in their adoptive country, Japan.

THE TAKETORI-MONOGATARI (1)

THE OLDEST NOVEL IN JAPAN

The Taketori-monogatari or, as the title indicates, "the tale of a bamboo-taker," which was written by an anonymous writer, is generally accredited to Shitago Minamoto, who died in 953 A.D. at the age of 73. Norinaga Motoori, one of the greatest scholars Japan has produced, dates the book in the era of Engi (901-923), but some other scholars put it further back in history. All agree, however, that the Taketori-monogatari is the oldest novel extant in the Japanese language.

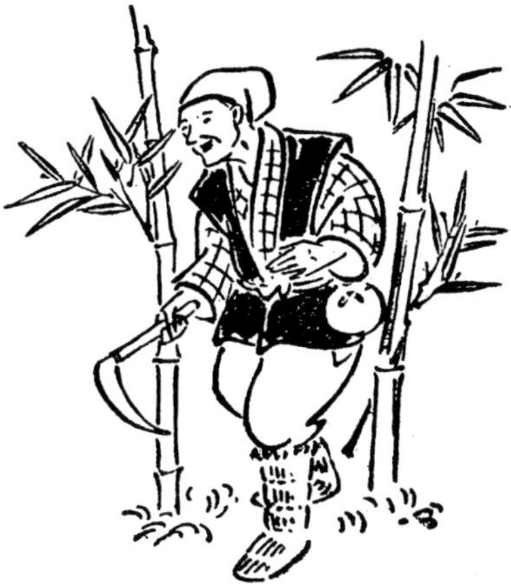

Taketori-no-Okina.

Synopsis

A long, long time ago there lived an old man and his wife at a remote village. He went out every day to get bamboo, so he was called Taketori-no-Okina, or "Bamboo-taking-old-man." One morning, as usual, he went bamboo-gathering, when he found a little baby-girl in a bamboo grôve. He took the baby to his wife as god-given because they had no child of their own, and they named her Kaguya-hime or "Shining Princess" as she appeared to shed light from her body. When she grew up, many young men came to seek her hand, but she always turned a deaf ear to them. There were five devoted lads who visited her day and night in order to win her. To each of them she gave a hard, or rather impossible, task to perform, telling that she would marry one who performed the allotted task. The first-comer, Prince Stone-mason, was told to get a stone-basin of the Buddha from Tenjiku, as India was then called. The second suitor, Prince Cart-owner, had to get a branch of white-gem flowers from a tree

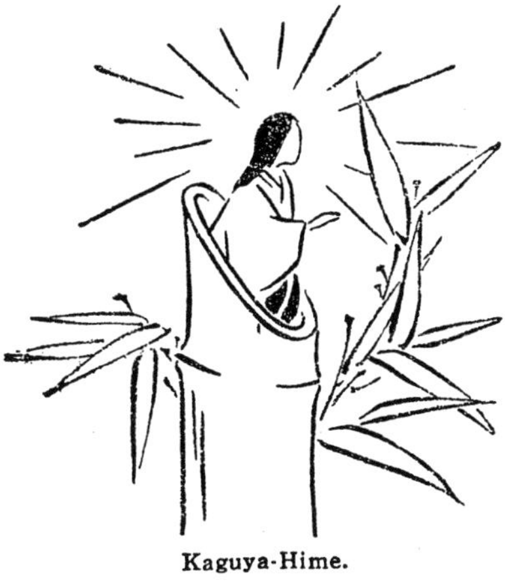

Kaguya-Hime.

(Continued)

THE TAKETORI-MONOGATARI (2)—*Concluded*

THE OLDEST NOVEL IN JAPAN

with a platinum root and gold trunk, on Horai or the islet of Elysium. The third, who was called the Minister of Abe, was asked for a fire-rat of China; the fourth, Otomo-no-Muraji, was to find a five-coloured gem in the neck of a dragon. The fifth, and last, Ishikamimaro by name, had to look for a cowrie brought by a swallow from the south. Every demand was of course seemingly beyond human power to satisfy, so one of the suitors indiscreetly brought a false gem, only to be undeceived by the Princess. Another lost his life in his adventurous attempt to acquire a gem she asked for, and the others gave up their search in despair. Soon, Kaguya-hime's beauty reached the ears of the Emperor, who sent for the Princess, but she would not even obey the Imperial command.

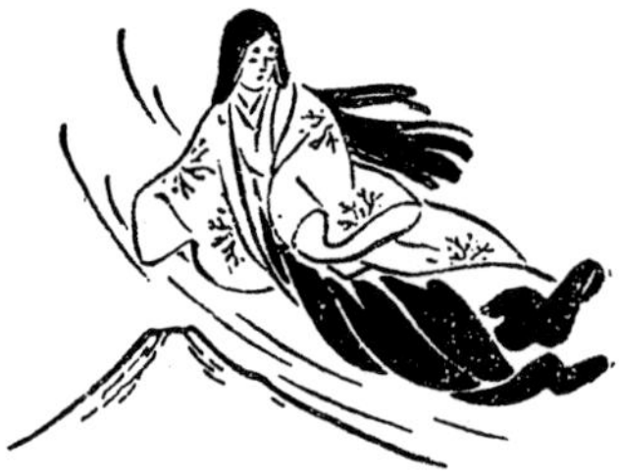

Twenty years had thus passed, when one spring she appeared gloomy every time she looked at the moon, and her melancholy increased as the year advanced till it was unbearable for her even to look at the moon. In reply to a question asked by her worried father and mother, she revealed that time was soon to come for her to return to the moon whence she had come. She was sorry that she had to take her leave of the old couple without repaying their kindness, for she belonged to the lunar world. The surprised old man went therefore to the Emperor and asked for a troop of two thousand strong to keep watch over the Princess. But on the fifteenth of the eighth month, when the moon was full, some celestial messengers came down to receive the Princess, and she ascended to the moon despite all that the troops did to retain her below.

Princess Kaguya-Hime left an elixir to give eternal life, but the Emperor, who hated anything that even reminded him of the Princess, burned it on a high mountain-top, near the heavens. Hence that mountain is called Fuji or "No-death," and smoke still keeps on rising from the burning elixir to heaven whose gates it might have opened to human-kind had not the Emperor burned the legacy of the Princess up.

Mt. Fuji, for which, according to the oldest novel of Japan, the characters (不死) meaning "no death" were used, is expressed now by 富士山 meaning "rich samurai-mountain," and sometimes by 不二山 (not-two or unique mountain). Smoke must therefore have been rising from its crater at the time this novel was written.

DIFFERENT KINDS OF SUMO OR JAPANESE WRESTLING

ORDINARY WRESTLING OR SUMO.

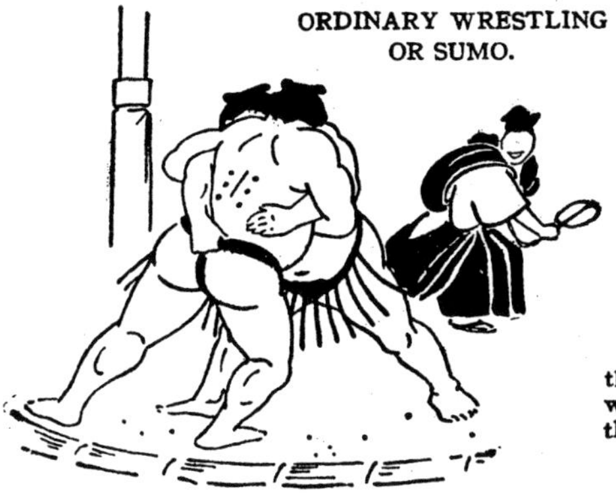

THUMB-WRESTLING.

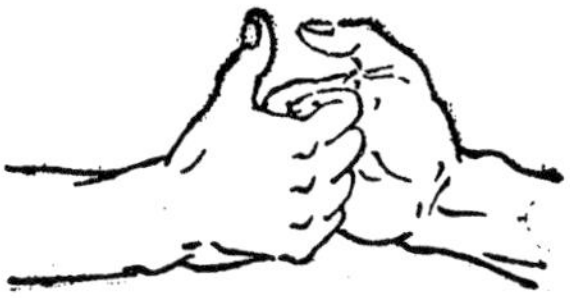

The two hands are clasped but with the thumbs free. The competitor who succeeds in holding down the thumb of the other wins.

PULLING-AT-NECK.

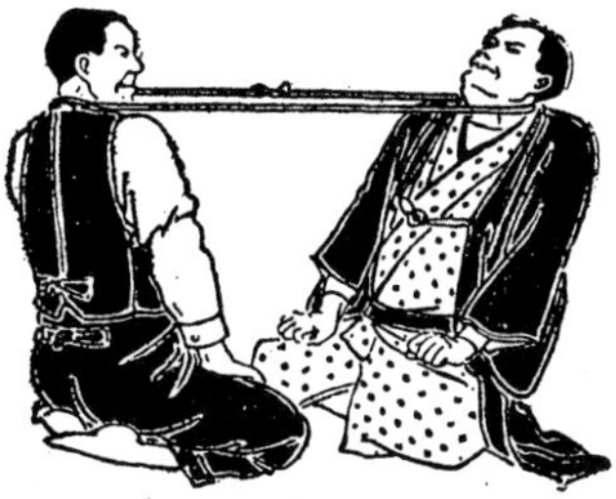

The player who is pulled forward is beaten.

ARM-WRESTLING.

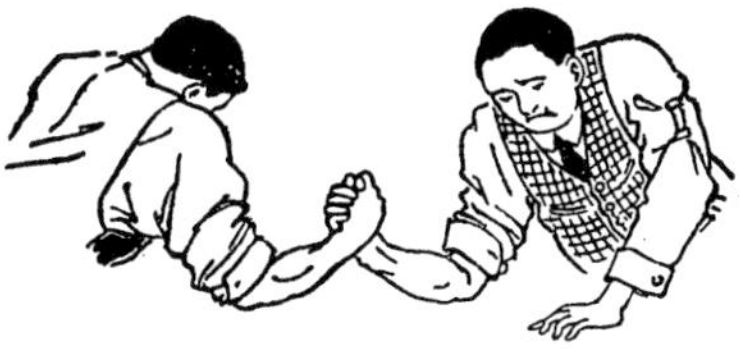

The two hands are clasped, and each competitor tries to push the other back. The one who succeeds in forcing the other's hand to touch the floor-mat wins. The elbow must be kept steady on the floor-mat.

PILLOW-PULLING.

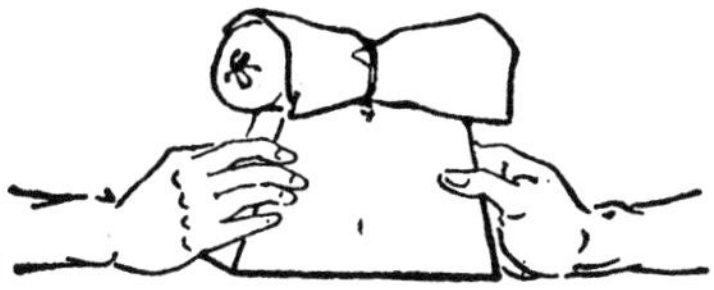

For this a Japanese wooden head-rest is used. But it must be pulled quite straight, turning neither to the left nor to the right. The one who lets it go is beaten.

LEG-WRESTLING.

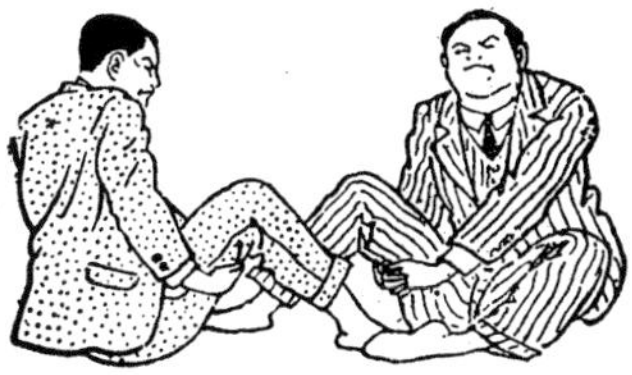

The one who succeeds in pushing the leg of the other to the floor-mat wins. The position of the feet must be kept steady.

KAKUBEI-JISHI

The Kakubei-jishi (Kakubei-lion) is a street acrobat or tumbler who goes from door to door on the street to earn a copper or two by doing an acrobatic turn to the playing of a drum and a flute. He is a little boy, hardly more than ten years old, dressed in a light uniform of black and red stripes, wearing a skirt and a tight pair of gaiters. He has a few feathers of a cock on his queer head-dress to symbolize the mane of a lion after which the name of Kakubei-lion is adopted.

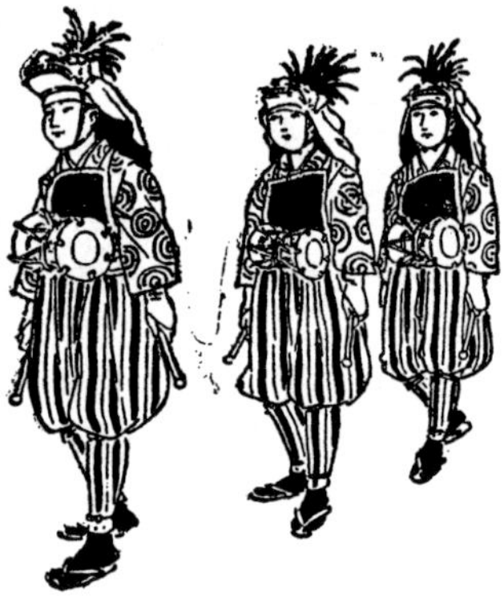

Kakubei was a farmer who was born at the modest village of Tsukigata in Echigo Province, early in the 14th century. In 1394 Kakubei invented a variety of acrobatic feats in which he trained the young children of his village. He took them out of his province to earn a livelihood so successfully that, it is said, Tsukigata sent out more than two hundred on professional trips all over the country till Echigo Province became associated with the acrobatic feats, which are known by the name of Kakubei-jishi or Echigo-jishi, or simply Kambara.

It is claimed, however, that Kakubei adopted his feats from some of ancient Indian plays or even that they had their origin in the pre-historic age of Japan.

Kakubei-jishi has some forty feats of which the following are among the most important: standing on the head or hands; walking on the hands; "dolphin" in which the player stands on his head and hands in imitation of the gold dolphin of the Nagoya castle; turning a somersault, sometimes more than once; "belly-turtle" in which the player stands backwards on all fours, often with his head between the legs; etc. The skill of the feat consists in the great flexibility of the "double-joined" body and so the player has to begin his training from his early childhood. It is traditionally said, though denied by the trainer of the feats, that vinegar is given to the player to give suppleness to his bones.

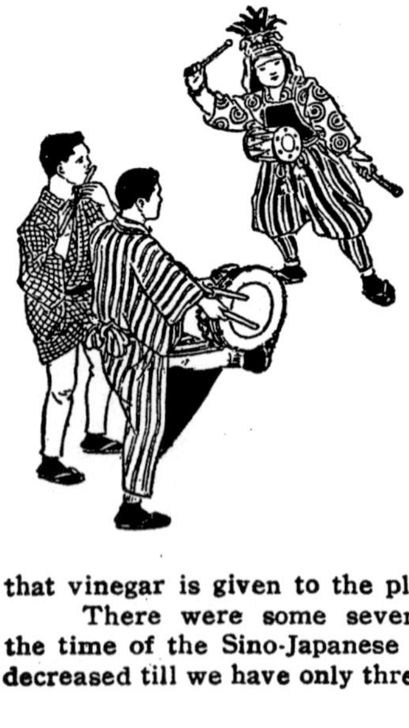

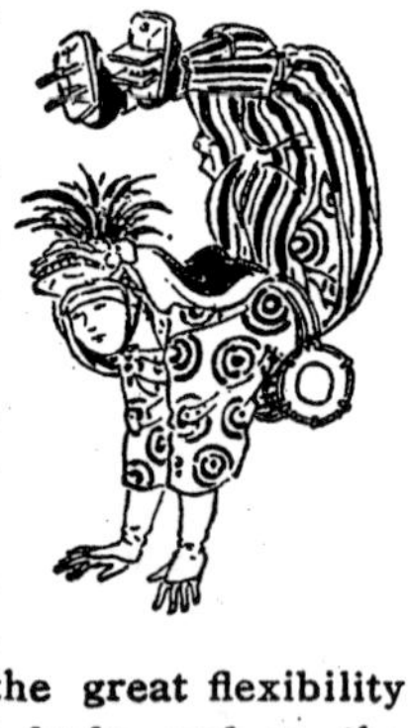

There were some seventy players of Kakubei-jishi in Tokyo about the time of the Sino-Japanese War (1894-95), but the number has gradually decreased till we have only three or four of these classical acrobats in Tokyo.

CHILDREN'S GAMES (1)

One feature common to many countries which travellers quickly discover is that children's games are universally similar. Here are a few Japanese children's games, which are common to the youngsters of many countries.

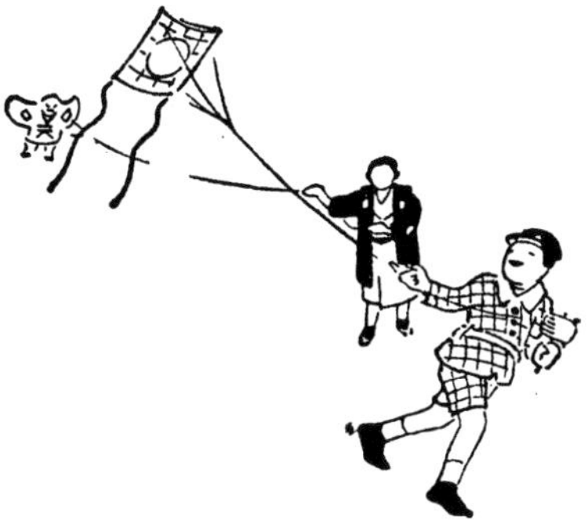

Kite-flying.

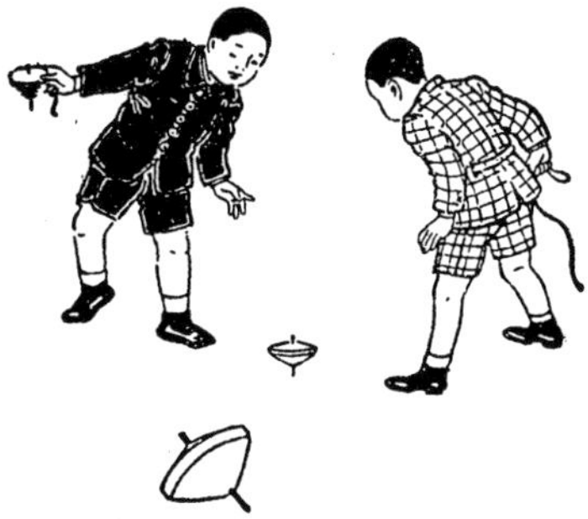

Top-spinning.

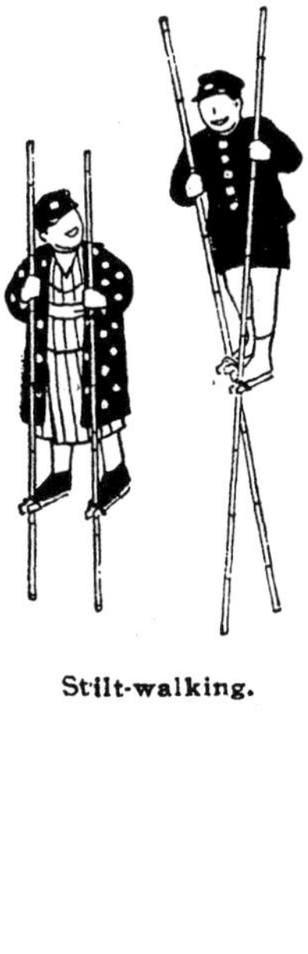

Stilt-walking.

(Continued)

CHILDREN'S GAMES (2)—*Concluded*

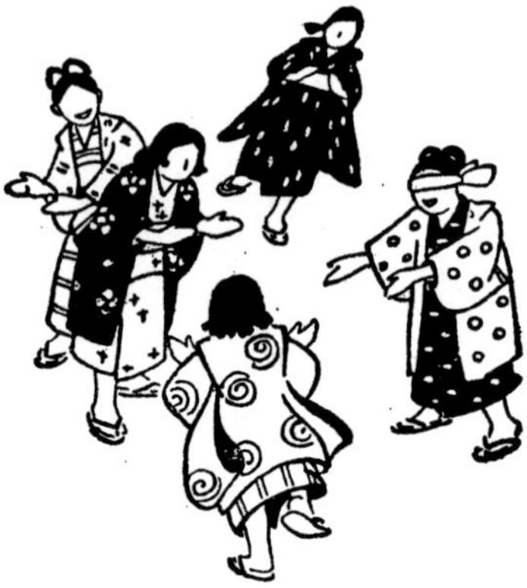

Blindman's buff.

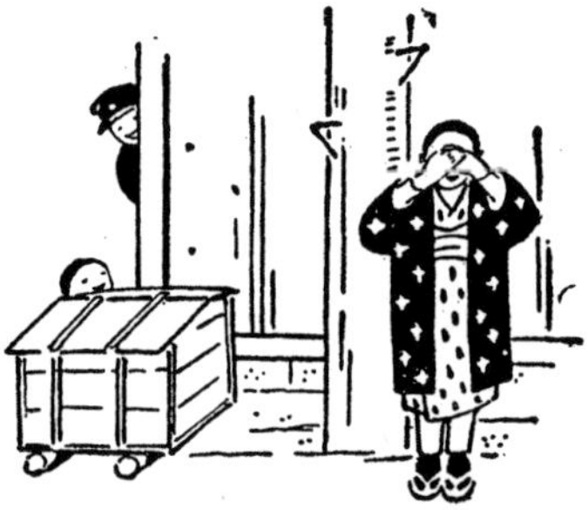

Hide-and-seek.

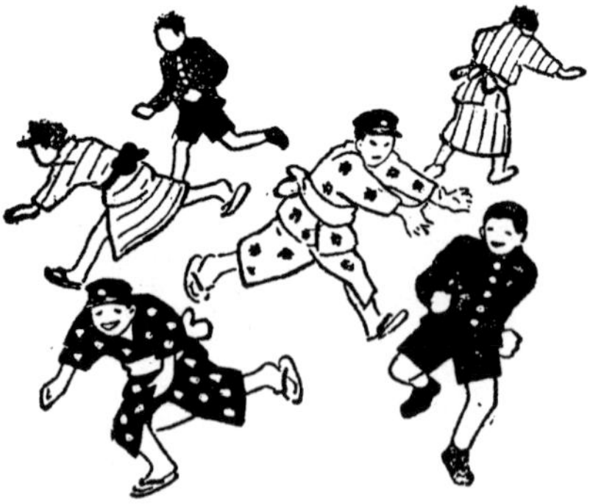

Tag.

KAMI-SHIBAI OR PAPER-PLAY

The popular street-dealer in cheap sweets visits small lanes where the lower-class people live. He beats his wooden clappers to call small children, who come to buy *sembei* (wafer), a bit of *ame* (jelly) or some other cheap sweets for one sen each. When the dealer gets a few children around him, he opens a box that he carries on his bicycle, and the curtain rises on the Kami-shibai or paper-play with the juvenile customers as a theatre party. The box contains a few sets of pictures, each about 1.5 ft.×1 ft. large, and each set is a theatrical play or drama. The young children who buy the cheap sweets for one sen can thereby enjoy the pictorial play, which the dealer explains in a most dramatic manner.

The Kami-shibai is very popular among the children of lower classes. The plays are of various kinds. Some are war-stories, others historical; some are real and others legendary; some tell of a social phase, others give the story of filial piety or patriotism, and so on. Every story is at once interesting and instructive, for otherwise it would not pass the necessary censorship of the local authorities. The children are so charmed that they are tempted to squeeze one sen each day from the limp purse of their mothers, so that they may enjoy all the stories since the shrewd proprietor of the paper-theatre always stops at a climax of each story. He then visits the same streets day after day and continues his stories, some of which will last for over a month. He is an ideal serial story teller.

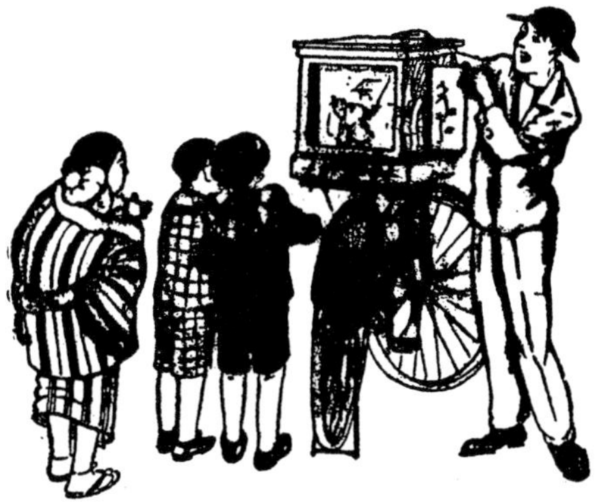

Children looking at the Kami-shibai.

The Kami-shibai is doing, however, a good social work among the children of the lower classes.

"SENDAI-HAGI" OR LADY MASAOKA

"Sendai-hagi" (bush-clover of Sendai) is one of the most popular classical dramatic plays in Japan. It is so named after Sendai, the clan-capital of Lord Date, because the scene of the drama is laid in Sendai, which is well known for hagi or bush-clovers (lespedeza). The heroine of the drama is Lady Masaoka.

Lady Masaoka was in charge of Prince Tsuruchiyo, the young scion of Lord Date, whom she had to protect from all sorts of sinister plots. She fought noble struggles against all the court ladies who had been won over by a treacherous retainer in an attempt to overthrow the clan. She gave the prince none of the food that was brought in for him lest it contain poison. Instead she herself cooked all his food without anyone knowing it. Often, therefore, the prince had to go so hungry while his noble nurse, Lady Masaoka, cooked his food that he even envied the freedom of the sparrow which can fly anywhere and eat when and what it likes.

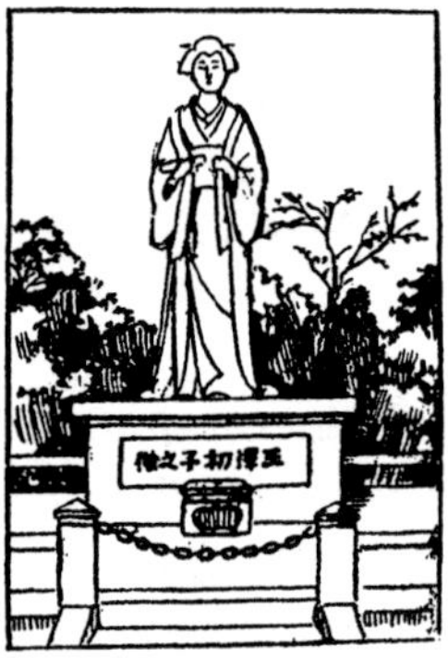

Stone statue of Masaoka, The Shogaku-ji Temple.

Lady Masaoka had a son of her own, Semmatsu by name, and he was the prince's playmate. She trained him to be loyal to his young lord and always ready to die for him. One day Lady Kajiwara, who was on the side of the false retainer, brought some sweets from the Shogun. They looked tempting, but Lady Masaoka warned the prince against eating them.

"This is a gift of the Honorable Shogun, Masaoka. What makes you suspect it and keep the Prince from eating it?" Lady Kajiwara demands this of Lady Masaoka, who looks too much troubled to know what to do, when Semmatsu, whom she had told to be always ready to run to the rescue of his young lord even at the risk of his own life, runs from an adjoining room, and snatches at the cake, and he swallows it almost at a gulp. This he does in obedience to his mother's teaching.

A maid, Lady Kajiwara, quick to grasp the occasion, stabs Semmatsu lest the poisoning plot be discovered. Semmatsu dies, but young Prince Tsuruchiyo is saved.

Left alone with her dead son, Lady Masaoka hugs his cold body to her breast and addresses him thus:—

"Semmatsu, it is a noble death that you have died. Your mother is happy that, true to her precepts, you swallowed the poisoned cake to save the young lord. You were born under an evil star to have a mother who, unlike all other mothers, teaches her son to die. But rest assured, my son, your death will unify the clan and cause it to stand on a firmer foundation."

Hatsuko Misawa, who is represented as Lady Masaoka on the stage, was born at Tottori in 1639. She married Lord Tsunamura Date and died at Shinagawa, Edo (Tokyo), in 1686. Her remains lie buried at the Shogaku-ji Temple, Meguro, in Tokyo, where a few years ago her admirers erected a stone statue to perpetuate her noble sacrifice as an example of fidelity to a lord.

THE CAT (1)

The cat-dance: If a towel is found missing in a Japanese family, suspicion is often thrown upon the cat, for people proverbially say in some localities in Japan that the cat dances the cat-dance of "Neko-ja! Neko-ja" ("We are cats, we are cats!"), with a towel tied around its head. There are also many stories told about cats that danced the cat-dance in the main hall of a temple or in a spacious barn.

In Japanese tradition, a cat is very often represented to transmogrify itself as a human being and talk like man. The cat of Saga, for example, is the most famous case of a transmogrified cats. The story is told of the family of Nabeshima, the lord of the Saga clan. One of his ancestors killed Ryuzoji, another local lord, whose pet-cat transmogrified itself as Lady Nabeshima, whom it had killed. Its feline followers murdered many court-ladies of Nabeshima and took their human forms. They wrought such mischief in the Nabeshima clan in order to pay off old scores with Nabeshima, who had killed their master, till one of the loyal subjects of Nabeshima discovered the cause of the trouble and exterminated the transmogrified cats.

The S/S "Tosa Maru" and her Cat: We have a saying that the cat and the rat will disappear before a fire or some other calamity destroys the house in which they live. In other words, they seem to have a premonition of a disaster.

The S/S "Tosa Maru" was a N.Y.K. liner berthed on the European line during the European war. She had a cat, which was a great pet of every seaman on board. Soon after the ship left Liverpool on Oct. 1, 1918, the pet-cat was found missing. It was to be found nowhere on board, and everybody wondered how and why the cat had disappeared, till the crew got nervous because the German submarines were then rampant on the high seas. Sure enough the ship was torpedoed by the Germans on Oct. 4 at 5.15 p.m. at 51° 12′ N and 7° 00′ W. The cat is still believed to have deserted the ship with the premonition that she was doomed.

The Cat-Graves: The cat is said to understand the human language, and we have many stories in which a cat helped its master to restore his ruined house, reciprocated its master's kindness or killed itself by cutting its own tongue with its teeth at the grave of its dead master. The Gotoku-ji Temple has a cat-grave that attracts more visitors than does that of Lord Ii, in whose grave-yard the cat lies buried; the Sairin-ji Temple at Omaezaki, in Totomi Province, has the grave of a cat that defended the temple at the cost of its own life against a big rat which stayed at the temple in the form of a mendicant priest. *(Continued)*

THE CAT (2)—*Concluded*

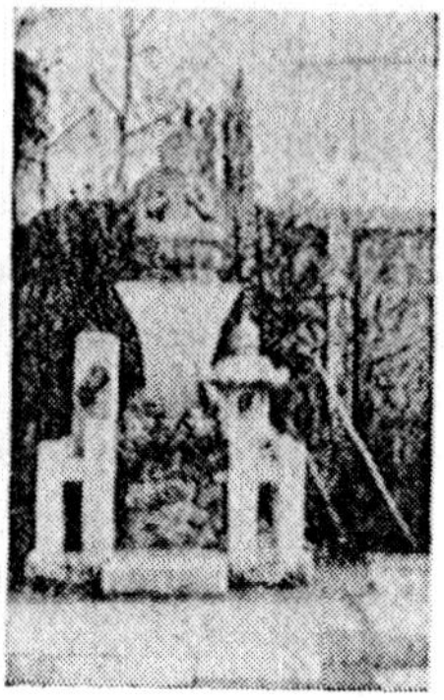

Monument at the Eko-in Temple.

In Koishikawa, Tokyo, a bridge marks a place where a faithful cat that stole gold-pieces to save its poor master, was killed, and in the cemetery of the Eko-in Temple at Ryogoku, Tokyo, there lies buried a cat that helped its sick benefactor by bringing him a gold-piece day after day. All these cats, according to tradition, acted on instructions given in the human language, which they understood.

Sword on a Coffin: It is a common custom in Japan to put a sword on the coffin of a dead body while it is kept at home before its burial, and no cat is allowed to enter the room where a coffin is kept, for, according to a common belief, a dead body would stir because of the electricity generated from its fur.

The Cat Temple: The Seizen-in Temple, situated at a short distance from Hitoyoshi, Kyushu, is widely known as the Cat-temple because there is a cat, called Tamadare, buried beside its mistress, at whose injunction the cat took revenge upon the death of its master, who was killed by Munemasu Yuyama in 1582. Now that over 3.5 centuries have elapsed, its grave is visited by its many admirers from one end of the year to the other.

No cat on the "Nirvana-stone": Before the Mausoleum of Hidetada, the second Shogun of the Tokugawa regime, Zojo-ji Temple in Tokyo, there stands a stone a few feet high, known as the "Nirvana-stone" or "Mandala-stone," because it has a most elaborate carving by Shigetsugu Yoshida, a famous sculptor, of the Nirvana or death of the Lord Buddha. All kinds of animals are represented in the carving as coming to mourn for his death, excepting the cat, which, according to tradition, was too busy chasing the rat to come to the death-bed of the Lord Buddha.

COMMON SAYINGS ABOUT THE CAT

The cat forgets in three days the kindness it has received for three years.

The tip of a cat's nose is cold all the year except on the day of the summer solstice.

Even three inches above the ground, a cat can turn a somersault.

If a cat "washes" its face while turning west, it will be fine on the following day; if it "washes" it while facing east, it will rain on the following day.

DOGS IN JAPAN (1)

The Japanese dog: Japan has indigenous dogs, such as Akita-inu, Tosa-inu, Kai-inu, Kishu-inu, Koshi-inu, Ainu-inu, etc. (inu = dog). As a rule, the Japanese dog is a good fighter, a good hunter, a good watch-dog and always faithful and devoted to his master. He is known to consider his life as nought should his master be in danger. But he is now fast disappearing from Japan under the pressure of the foreign dog, and a movement is now on foot to preserve the Japanese dog.

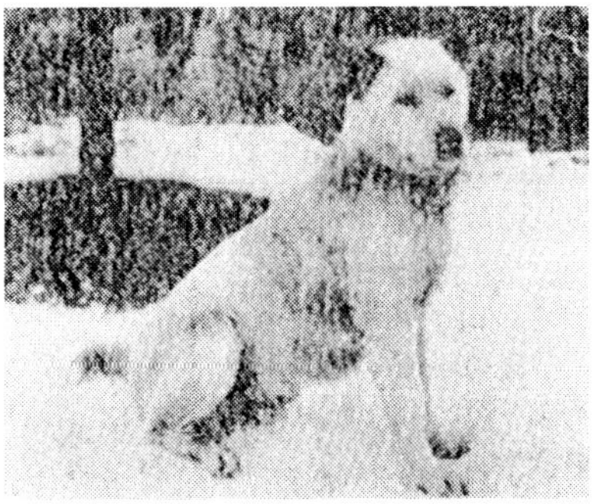

The Akita-inu.

Maternity belt on the dog-day: The zodiac day of the Dog comes on in every thirteenth day. On this day a woman with child will put on the maternity belt, because a dog is known for its easy delivery. A papier-mache dog is sometimes placed near a woman in labour for the same reason.

Temples for cats and dogs: There are three temples in Tokyo where dead cats and dogs are buried. The Kembyo-ji Temple (Dog-and-cat Temple), situated at Shimura in Itabashi Ward is built exclusively for their burial. But the Saishin-ji Temple, Koishikawa, is much older and larger, and it has some 40,000 stupas erected over the remains of cats and dogs, each bearing the posthumous name of the animal buried under it. A regular Buddhist service is held at the time of its burial, and we are told that some kind people hold memorial services for their departed pets, which are said to be entitled to the same Nirvana as their human masters.

Hakkenden: The Hakkenden, or Tales of Eight Dogs, was written by Sakichi Takizawa, generally known by his pen-name of Bakin (literally, horse-harp) (1768–1848), a great novelist who wrote no less than 250 novels until he became blind before he finished the Hakkenden of 180 chapters, which took him 27 years to write.

The story begins with the genealogy of Yoshizane Satomi (1417–1488), lord of Awa and Kazusa Provinces. His castle was besieged by Kagetsura Anzai, and when all hope had gone that the castle might stand the siege any longer, Satomi called his retainers and offered his daughter as wife to the one among them who took

(*Continued*)

the head of his enemy. She was called Fusehime or "Princess Dog-day," because she was born on the zodiac day of the Dog in the summer of the year 1442.

Now, Satomi had a favorite dog. He was named Yatsubusa (or Eight Tassels) because he had eight patches on his body. The dog disappeared that night, but on the following morning he came back carrying, in his mouth, a human head dripping with blood. It was the head of Kagetsura Anzai, and the siege of the castle was soon raised.

Fusehime remembered the promise her father made, and she offered herself to the dog on condition that he would not humiliate her. The dog therefore carried the princess on his back deep into mountains, where they lived together. The dog collected berries and fruits for her, and she, on her part, talked Buddhism to the dog so that he would be reborn as a human being at his second birth. The princess had a string of eight crystal beads, each engraved with one of the eight Chinese monograms, namely, humanity, righteousness, propriety, wisdom, loyalty, faith, filial piety, and fraternal love.

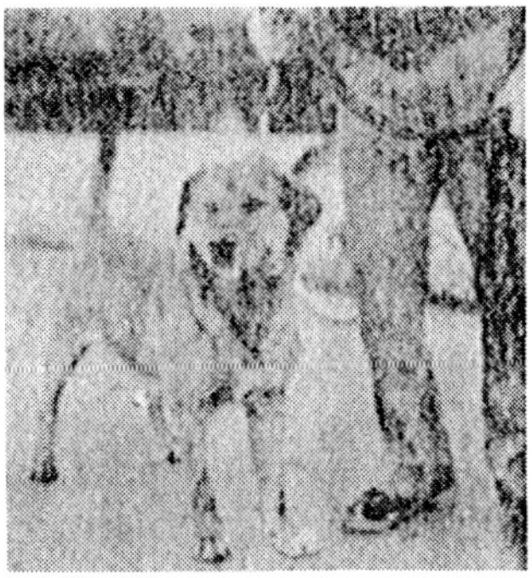
The Tosa-inu.

A year went by, when one day a retainer of Satomi fired at the dog from a distance in an attempt to save Fusehime by killing him. The bullet struck the dog and then glancing off killed the princess too, but the crystal beads disappeared mysteriously.

The story gives a full description of how the mysterious beads were finally located. They were found in the hands of eight babies whose family-names had "inu" (dog) in them; namely:

Inukai (dog-keeper)	Inuyama (dog-mountain)	Inutsuka (dog-mound)
Inuta (dog-fields)	Inumura (dog-village)	Inusaka (dog-hill)
Inuye (dog-creek)	Inukawa (dog-river)	

They grew up to be brave warriors, and each lived up to the principle indicated by the monogram of the bead he owned. Then, after undergoing all sorts of adventures the warriors realized that they were brothers bound by the mysterious beads, so they finally made their way to Lord Satomi, whose loyal retainers they became.

(*Continued*)

DOGS IN JAPAN (3)

Maru: In 1860 Heiyemon Ishiwara, a samurai of the Shonai clan, received a few foreign rabbits from his lord and he took such good care of them as a samurai should do of any royal gift. One morning one of them was found missing, and this unfortunate event took place three mornings in succession, no less than seven rabbits being stolen by nobody knew whom. Now, it was considered a sign of disloyalty or faithlessness on the part of a samurai to lose any royal gift, but it would have been none the less humiliating for Ishiwara to discover the thief of the rabbits among his own retainers. So, finally, Ishiwara pinned the fault upon Maru, his favorite dog, which he drove out as the criminal who had stolen his precious rabbits. It was in the depth of winter and the snow lay several feet deep on the ground.

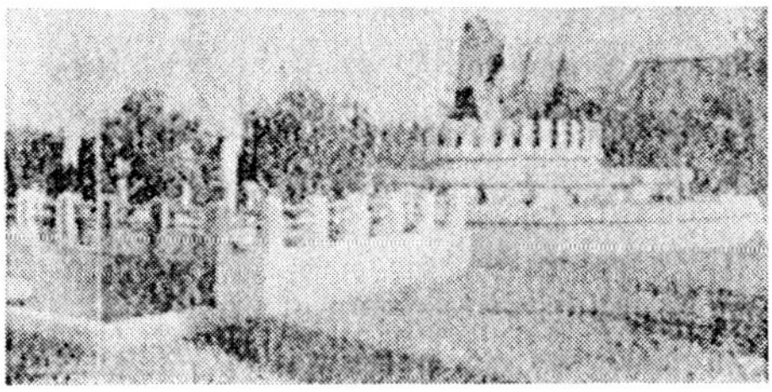

The dog-crypt of the Saishin-ji Temple.

In the small hours on the fifth night after the scape-goat-dog had been forced out, Ishiwara heard the noise of a violent struggle out in his garden. Taking a lighted candle in his hand, he went out to see what the noise was about. What was his surprise to see three dead wolves on the snow, and Maru, the scapegoat, biting at the throat of a fourth. He was almost dead with the wound that he had received in the struggle. Ishiwara realized that it was these wolves that had stolen his rabbits.

"O Maru, forgive me. I was wrong, Maru," Ishiwara said with tears in his eyes, when the faithful dog breathed his last. "Do forgive me, for I did not know that the rabbits had been killed by the wolves."

Maru was buried very politely in the garden of Heiyemon Isbiwara, and a stone still marks the burial place of this faithful dog.

White-dog Monument: The wife of the daimyo of Sanuki Province, Shikoku, died at Edo (Tokyo) and her remains were carried to his clan, when her pet, a white dog, followed the funeral procession all the way to Sanuki for hundreds of miles. When her body was buried at the Bussho-ji Temple, the faithful dog would not leave her burial-place. It was taken by force to the residence of the daimyo, but it soon returned to the burial-place of its dead mistress. The dog was taken back again, this time on a boat, but it jumped into the water on the way and was drowned in an attempt to return to the grave-yard. A monument was therefore erected to the memory of the faithful dog in the temple precincts and it is called the White-dog Monument. *(Continued)*

DOGS IN JAPAN (4)—*Concluded*

Dog kills python: A certain samurai went out hunting and took his favorite dog with him. In the woods, he sat on a stone, and he was just about to doze off when his dog barked loudly. He saw nothing strange about him and began to doze off again. The dog barked again. Every time he tried to sleep, the dog awoke him to make his sleep impossible, till the samurai suspected that the dog had resumed its wild nature. So he drew his sword and killed the dog, when its head, so the story runs, flew up as it was cut off. There was a thud heard behind him, and on turning back, he saw a large python, 30 ft. long that fell from the branches of a big overhanging tree. The dog's head was still clinging to the throat of the python.

Priest Kobo and "dog charm": Priest Kobo went on a pilgrimage to Matsuyama in Shikoku. He stopped overnight at a farmer's and he was so pleased with the devoted services of the farmer that he would comply with any request that the farmer made.

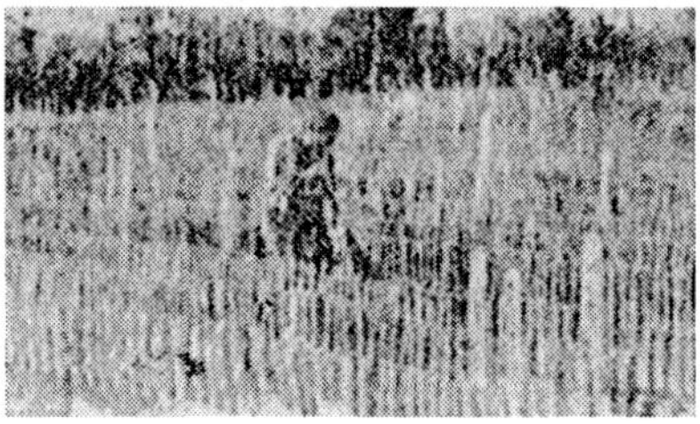

The dog-graves of the Saishin-ji Temple.

"We are troubled with wild boars here," the farmer said. "They make such a havoc in our gardens. Please give us a charm against them.

The priest took up a brush-pen and painted something on a piece of paper, which he handed the farmer after he sealed it, telling him to hang it in his gardens. Sure enough the wild boars ceased to come out any more after the charm was put over the gardens. But when the priest went away the curious farmer opened the charm, when a dog that the priest had painted on the paper flew away from it. This is, the people would tell you, the origin of the Inu-kami (dog-god) in Japan.

Dog-fight: Dog-fight was much in vogue during the Kamakura days. It is said that Takatoki Hojo, the Shogunate Regent, was so fond of it, that there were no less than four or five thousand dogs kept in the Government at one time for the purpose of dog-fighting which was practised till the middle of the Tokugawa regime. This practice has almost died out, though it may be still seen in some localities. The Tosa dog, which is stout and strong, is known as the strongest dog for dog-fighting.

Dog-chase: Dog-chase is another amusement that was much practised at one time at the Shogunate court. This amusement began also during the Kamakura days, and lasted till the end of the Tokugawa Shogunate. It was at one time carried on very extensively. Sometimes, over a hundred dogs were chased and shot at by thirty-six horsemen, who were divided into three groups, and in the presence of the Shogun and many lords. But it is now no longer practised.

THE HERON (1)

(Japanese "Sagi")

The Emperor Daigo (the 60th) was holding a party in the Shinsen-en Garden, when he saw a heron (sagi) in one corner of the garden. A courtier of the fourth court-rank was ordered to catch the bird. But the heron started to fly away when he approached it. "It is the august command of His Majesty and you must not fly off," the courtier said. And so, says the legend, the bird remained still on the same spot. The heron was caught and brought before the Emperor, who was so pleased with the beautiful bird that he "appointed" the bird to the "fifth court-rank." Hence the bird was named "Goi-sagi" (goi = fifth rank). This story is staged under the title of "Sagi," a popular Noh play.

There are several species of the heron in Japan, which have the word "goi" in their names, such as Sanka-no-goi, miso-goi, mino-goi, etc.

The heron (ardeidae) is called "sagi" in the Japanese language, which, according to some authorities, means "purity" because the bird is of pure white. It is a common bird in Japan, though some species are only of passage, coming to Japan in summer. Japan has the following thirteen species of the heron:

1. Ao-sagi or common or grey heron (Ardia cinerea),
2. Shojo-sagi or eastern buff-backed heron (A. coromanda),
3. Oh-sagi or great white egret (Herodias timoriansis),
4. Komomo-jiro (A. alba modesta),
5. Shira-sagi or little egret (A. garzetta),
6. Chusagi or plumed egret (A. intermedia),
7. Yoshi-goi or Oriental little bittern (Ardetta sinensis),
8. Oh-yoshi-goi or Schrenck's little bittern (Nannocnus eurythmus),
9. Sanka-no-goi or bittern (Bolaurus stellaris,
10. Miso-goi or Japanese night-heron (Gorsachius goisagi),
11. Mino-goi or green heron (Nyclicorax javanicus stagnatilis),
12. Akagashira-sagi or Chinese squacco heron (N. prasionsceles),
13. Goi-sagi or grey night-heron (N. nyclicorax).

(Continued)

THE HERON (2)—*Concluded*

(Japanese "Sagi")

The Toki: The Toki or Japanese crested ibis (ibis nippon) is an almost extinct kind of bird resembling the heron. It is rarely found in Korea and China, but it now thrives on the isle of Sado, in the Sea of Japan. It lives wild on the isle, but at one time it was not seen there for over ten years. In February, 1932, however, the bird was again found on the isle, and after a careful investigation, the authorities have discovered that the ibis lives in deep forests of the villages of Kamo, Kawasaki, Niiho, Miho, Iwakubi, Kaifu and Takachi of the island. The bird has a long bill, somewhat curving downwards. It is greyish white, with a flesh tint on its wings and a part of the tail-feathers, which number twelve, so that the bird on the wing looks pink or, in the Japanese language, *toki*: hence its Japanese name. It lays two to three or four eggs in May in a nest made of dead sticks. The *toki* was put under special protection by the Imperial Government in December, 1934.

The Heron Roosts: About 2 or 3 Japanese miles south-west of Omiya, in the prefecture of Saitama, near Tokyo, there is a heron-preserve, about 70 acres wide, in the village of Noda, which is better known as the "heron mountain" (Sagi-no-Yama). Herons of various kinds, including such as the Goi-sagi, Oh-sagi, Chu-sagi, Ko-sagi, Shojo-sagi, etc., come in May or June, tens of thousands in number, and it is a marvellous sight to see these herons perching on the branches of trees as far as the eye can reach till the trees look as if they "bore herons." They make such a noise that talking under their trees is impossible. They nest and bring up their young to leave again in August or September.

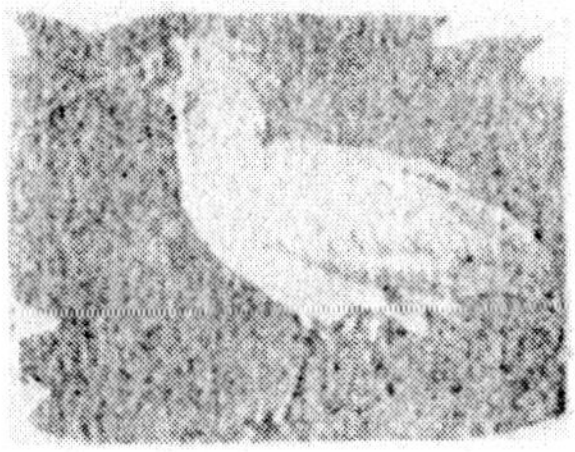

The Japanese crested ibis.

According to records, the herons and cormorants began to come to the village of Noda during the era of Kyoho (1716–1735), and they increased year after year, so that every Shogun of the Tokugawa regime who visited the Shogunate shrines at Nikko, used to stop at Noda to look at them. In 1921, a plot of land, 28 cho (cho = 2.45 acres), was specified as a preserve, in accordance with the game law, to provide a breeding place for the herons.

THE FLOATING ISLETS OF LAKE OHNUMA

Lake Ohnuma, which is situated in the province of Uzen (Yamagata Prefecture) in the northern part of Japan, is an object of great interest to the limnologist of Japan on account of the islets floating on its surface.

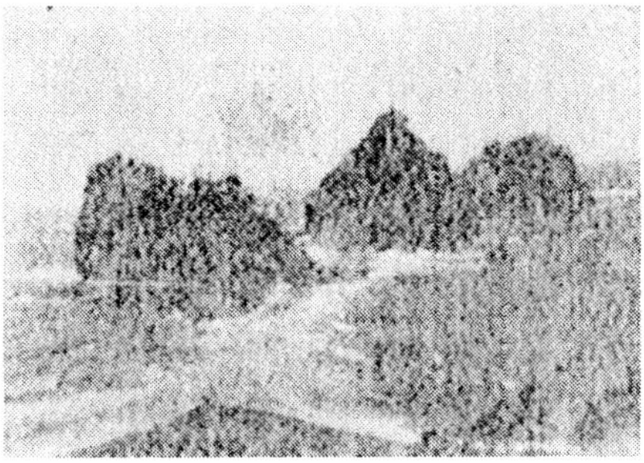

Floating islets of Lake Ohnuma.

In the ninth year (681) of the era of Hakuho (White phoenix) during the reign of the Emperor Temmu (the 40th), it is said, Priest En-no-Shokaku first discovered the floating islets of Lake Ohnuma. In the year 739 Priest Gyoki counted 66 islets on the lake and named them after so many provinces into which Jápan was divided. Ohye Hiromoto, lord of Sagaye, in the province of Uzen, built the Ukishima or Floating-Islet shrine in 1193, and the present Shinto priest of the shrine is said to be the 55th descendant of the first to hold the post.

During the Tokugawa regime, the islets were considered as means of divination, for the fortune of a province was divined by the floating movements of a particular islet which was named after the province. It is still said that no islet will move about if anyone who is wicked at heart is looking at it, and the one is considered to be lucky who sees the islets move about.

Lake Ohnuma is 600 meters long, and from 150 to 350 meters wide, its greatest depth being 3 meters. The largest islet, which was named Ohshu after the northern provinces of Japan Proper, is about 10 meters by 2 meters with some luxuriant shrubs growing on it. However, a meter or two is the average size of the islets.

The islets consist chiefly of sod or rotten leaves of plants which rose to the surface on account of gas generated from them. Each islet has a luxuriant growth of reeds or some other plants on it.

The islets move round on the surface of the lake, usually in the morning or towards evening, on a bright sunny day, but remain still during the rest of the day. The lake is about 200 feet above the sea level, and high banks stand all around it. In other words, the lake is, so to speak, at the bottom of a basin. It has several small bays, which are covered with thick growth. The lake has, therefore, no uniform temperature, and the difference in temperature of the water in various parts of the lake sets the water in motion, which drives the islets from one part of the lake to another.

Lake Kobuta: Lake Kobuta, two Japanese miles northwest of Kusatsu in the prefecture of Gumma, has two floating islets which consist chiefly of lava from Mt. Shirane. Then also on the island of Sado on the Sea of Japan there is a lake which has a few floating islets.

THE CHERRY AS THE NATIONAL FLOWER OF JAPAN (1)

The cherry is called in the Japanese language "sakura," which is generally believed to be a corruption of the word "sakuya" (blooming) from the name of Princess Kono-hana-no-sakuya-Hime, who is enshrined on the top of Mt. Fuji. This long name literally means "tree-flowers-blooming-princess," for the cherry was so well-known in those early days in Japan that the flower meant the cherry. This princess was so named because, it is said, she dropped from heaven upon a cherry tree. Hence, the cherry-blossoms are considered to be the national flowers of Japan.

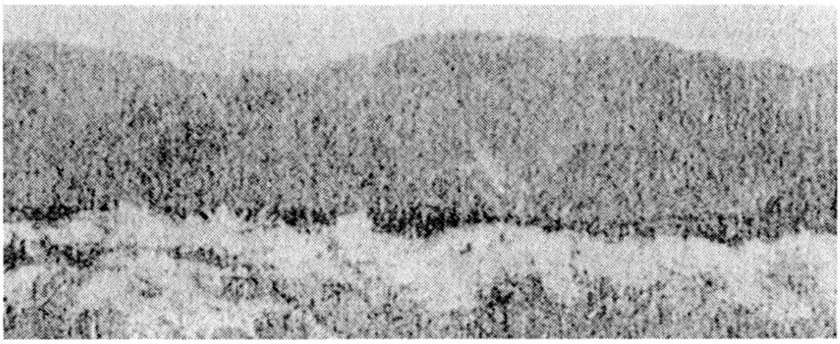

The Cherry-blossoms of Kowakidani, Hakone.

The cherry is extensively cultivated in Japan, though it grows wild on plains and in deep mountains in the country. When forty or fifty years old, it is some twenty or thirty feet high, with a trunk three, four, or even six or eight feet in circumference. Its flowers open in April or May, though the *Higan-zakura*, viz., the equinoctial or paramita cherry, often blooms in October, and, when seen at a distance, its blossoms look like a white mist, to which they are often compared. The tree bears small edible cherries.

The first mention of the cherry is made in the Kojiki in connection with the Goddess Amaterasu, who hid herself in the Celestial Cave because of the repeated offences of Prince Susanoo, her brother. A branch of *hahaka* is used for divination, and it is said to be a branch of the cherry. But the term "sakura" appears in Japanese literature under the name of the Waka-sakura Palace, which the Empress Jingo built at Iware in the province of Yamato. A little later on the Emperor Inkyo (the 19th) wrote a Japanese poem about the cherry at the Fujiwara Palace.

The cherry symbolizes the national character of the Japanese. This is because the life of a samurai of feudal times was proverbially compared to the short-lived cherry-blossoms, which last "no more than three days," for our samurai was always fully prepared to sacrifice his life at any time in the cause of his master. Another saying is that what "the cherry is among flowers is the samurai among men." Norinaga Motoori, a great scholar, wrote a 31-syllable poem on the Yamato-kokoro or the spirit of the Yamato-race, as the Japanese call themselves.

(Continued)

THE CHERRY AS THE NATIONAL FLOWER OF JAPAN (3)

This poem, freely translated, reads as follows :—

"The spirit of Yamato's isles
If, chance, a stranger should inquire,
Go, show the morning sun that smiles
Upon the mountain-cherry fair."

—Prof. H. Saito.

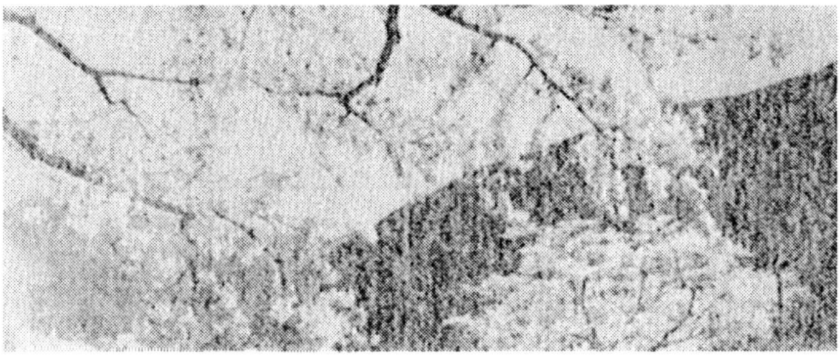

The Cherry-blossoms at Ashi-no-yu, Hakone.

Cherry-blossom-viewing was no less in vogue in old Japan than it is today, for Japanese literature is full of poems composed by the Emperors, the Empresses, the courtiers and court-ladies on the occasion of viewing the cherry-blossoms. The party which Lord Taigo took to Yoshino for flower-viewing on the twenty-fourth of the second month (February, old calendar), 1594, consisted of about 5,000 people. The cherry season is perhaps the most lively in the calendar in Japan, because the whole country is decorated with flowers, as spring turns its back on winter.

There are many old cherry-trees, which are historically famous, such as the Sakon-no-sakura of the Shishiiden Palace, Priest Saigyo's cherry at Saga, Kyoto, the cherry planted by Prince Shotoku in Shiga Prefecture, the White-Flag-cherry, which is said to have been planted by Yoshiiye Minamoto in 1084, etc. Of all places known for cherry-trees, none perhaps is more familiar than Yoshino in Yamato Province, on which a poem reads in effect: "As far as the eye can reach, nothing is visible but the cherry blossoms though what are hidden behind are invisible." Arashiyama is another popular place for cherry-blossoms. Tokyo falls behind no other places in the number of places known for cherry-blossoms; such as Koganei, Asukayama, the Sumida, Sanritsuka, Uyeno and Shiba Park.

(*Continued*)

THE CHERRY AS THE NATIONAL FLOWER OF JAPAN (4)—*Concluded*

Kowakidani situated about three miles from the Fujiya Hotel at the heart of the Fuji-Hakone National Park is said to have thirty thousand cherries under the eye. It commands one of the best scenic beauties in the neighbourhood of Tokyo and Yokohama.

In 1681, Motokatsu Mizuno counted forty different kinds of the cherry in his little book on flowers and the number increased to fifty-four in the Sansaizue published in 1713. Later, a hundred and fifty different species were given by a certain horticulturist who lived in the 19th century, but at present Japan has over four hundred varieties of the cherry. Here are some of the principal ones:—

1. Yama-zakura (prunus pseudo-cerasus, var. spontanea) or mountain-cherry.
2. Yoshino-zakura (p. yedonensis), called also Somei-yoshino.
3. Ito-zakura (p. ito-sakura: p. pendula), called also Shidare-sakura or weeping-cherry.
4. Higan-zakura (p. subhirtella), or equinoctial or paramita cherry.
5. Takane-zakura (p. miquelianna), called also Minezakura or peak-cherry.
6. Kan-zakura (p. campanulata), called also Ganjitsu-zakura or New Year-cherry.
7. Shiro-zakura (p. marimowiczii), called also Miyama-zakura or Deep-mountain-cherry.
8. Mejiro-zakura (p. ceraseidos), called also Kome-zakura or rice-cherry.
9. Mame-zakura (p. ineisa).
10. Hime-zakura (p. pogostyla).
11. Takasago-zakura (p. formosana).
12. Musha-zakura (p. taiwaniana).
13. Karakuni-zakura (p. glandulifolia).
14. Niwa-ume (p. japonica).
15. Yusura-ume (p. tomentosa).
16. Shima-sumomo (p. Kawakamii).

SOME NOTED SAKURA-TREES IN JAPAN

1. Usuzumi-zakura or light-black cherry: at the village of Neo, Gifu Prefecture. It is 26 ft. in girth.
2. Jindai-zakura or God-days-cherry: at the Jisso-ji Temple in Yamanashi prefecture. It is the largest yet found, being 35 ft. in girth.
3. Shidare-zakura or weeping-cherry: at the village of Nakazato in Fukushima prefecture. Also called Taki-zakura or waterfall-cherry. It is 31 ft. in girth.
4. Yaye-zakura: at Nara. Noted for its double flowers. (Note: We generally prefer the single to the double flowers).
5. Kiku-zakura or chrysanthemum-cherry: at Kenroku Park, Kanazawa. It has many small petals; hence its name.
6. Ishiwari-zakura or stone-breaking cherry: at Morioka, Iwate prefecture. It grows through a crevice in a large rock.

THE BAMBOO (1)

The bamboo, which is a plant belonging to the tropics and subtropics, grows wild throughout Japan, over mountains, valleys and plains. No other country has so large a variety of bamboos as Japan is boast of. Being an evergreen, and therefore a symbol of constancy and devotion, the bamboo is interwoven with the daily life of the Japanese, and with the plum and the pine, it is always thought of as a lucky plant. We have many sayings and proverbs concerning the bamboo; such as "grafting a bamboo on a tree" meaning an unbecoming match; "Dream of a bamboo and a friend dies"; "A bad year when a bamboo blooms," for a bamboo dies when it bears flowers; "Like a splitting bamboo" meaning frankness.

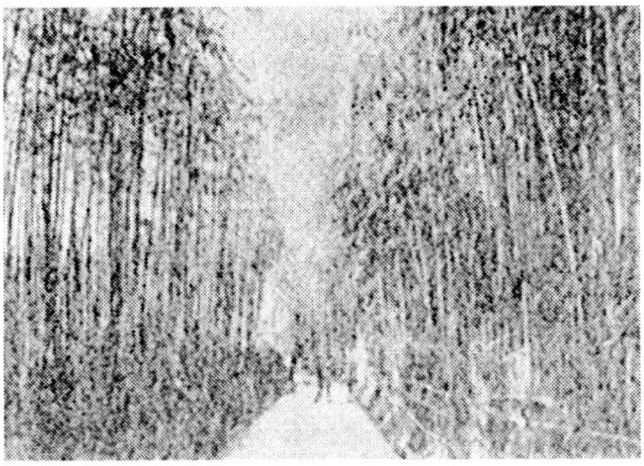

Bamboo-thicket.

According to the Kojiki and the Nihonshoki, Izanagi, a prehistoric prince, threw away a fine-toothed comb, from which a bamboo-shoot sprang up, and an ugly-looking woman pulled it out and ate it. Prince Hikohohodemi had his umbilical cord cut off with a bamboo-knife. From a comb, which Shiotsuchi-no-Okina threw away, a grove of 500 bamboos sprang up and they were used to make baskets.

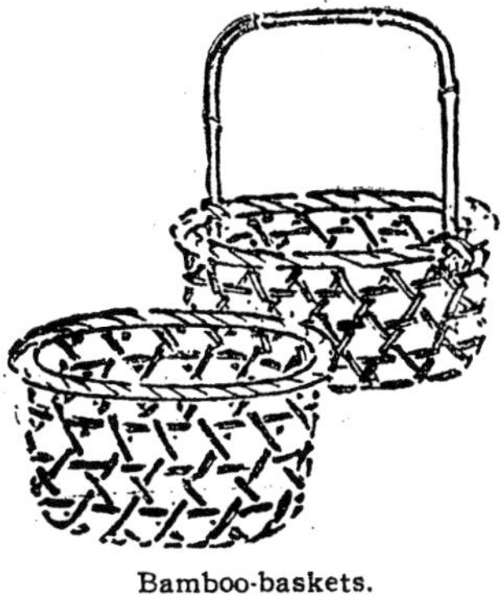

Bamboo-baskets.

In Japan the bamboo is used in many varied ways, and indeed it is one of the daily necessaries in our domestic life. The bamboo is first of all used as a New Year decoration from one end of the country to the other. It adds to natural scenery in Japanese gardening and a potted bamboo is a gem. It also plays an important role in Japanese architecture, for it is often used as an imposing pillar before the alcove, the sacred place in a Japanese house Then it is used for the baths in the plastered walls, and forms an elegant hedge around the home. Furniture of all sorts is made of bamboo. Among the many articles are a table, chair, tea-tray, blind, basket, lantern, umbrella-handle, umbrella, bookshelf and ever so many other utensils and vessels for domestic use. Several musical instruments, such as a flute and *shakuhachi* are made of bamboo.

(*Continued*)

THE BAMBOO (2)

The Japanese are known as good archers, and their bows and arrows are of bamboo. Then the bamboo furnishes good material as pulp for making high-class paper and a fine filament for the electric bulb is made from bamboo-fibre. A bamboo sprout is a delicacy, of which the Japanese are very fond, and it is pickled for domestic use and canned for exportation. Bamboo toys are exported all over the world in large quantities. According to the statistical report of the Japanese Government, our production of bamboo-baskets in 1935 amounted to 1.5 million yen, which figure, it has to be added, excludes those manufactured in domestic industry, and our exports of bamboo articles totalled 95 thousand yen. Indeed, no part of the bamboo is wasted, for its root makes a good walking-cane and its leaves and sheath are used for wrapping purposes.

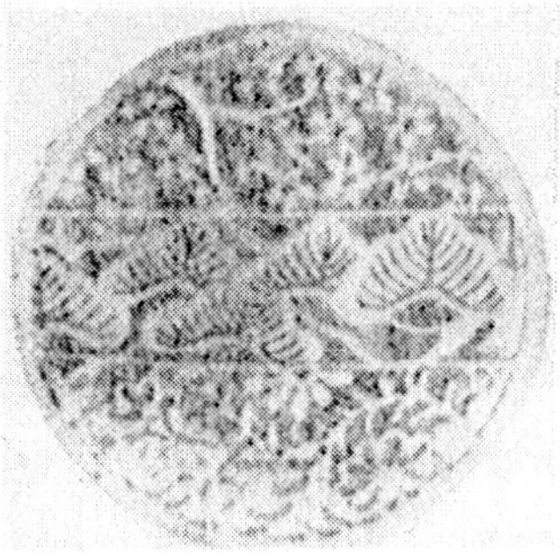

Bamboo-button.

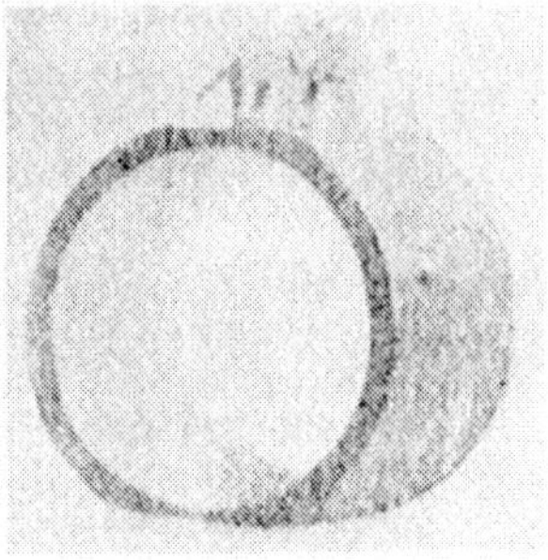

Bamboo napkin-ring.

Out of more than 200 varieties of the bamboo, Japan has over 100, ranging in size from 50 or 60 feet high to a few inches. The largest bamboo measures 2 or 3 feet in circumference. While the bamboo is as a rule, hollow, *madake* (phyllostachys bambusiodes), which is found on the isle of Take (bamboo) at Matsushima, and on Mt. Ichiu in Awa province, is long-joined like the wangee cane. Shiho-chiku or square bamboo (p. quadrangulais), which is found in a part of Kyushu, is so called because it is square, while *kurotake* (p. nigra), which is black as its name indicates, is found only in the province of Satsuma, the southern end of Kyushu. The chief varieties of bamboo in Japan are as follows:—

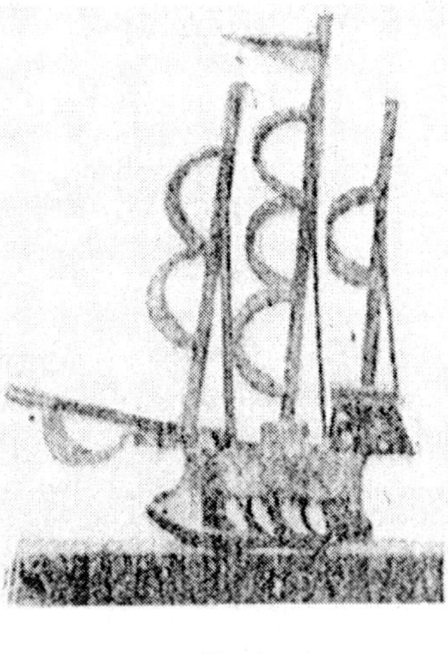

Bamboo-toy.

(Continued)

I. *Medake* (Arundinaria)
1. Medake (A. simond)
2. Hakone-dake (A. chino)
3. Chigo-zasa (A. variegata)
4. Taimin-chiku (A. graminia)
5. Kanzan-chiku (A. Hindsii)
6. Ryukyu-chiku (A. linearis)
7. Narihira-dake (A. fastuosa)
8. Tochiku (A. tootsik)
9. Kan-chiku (A. marmorea)

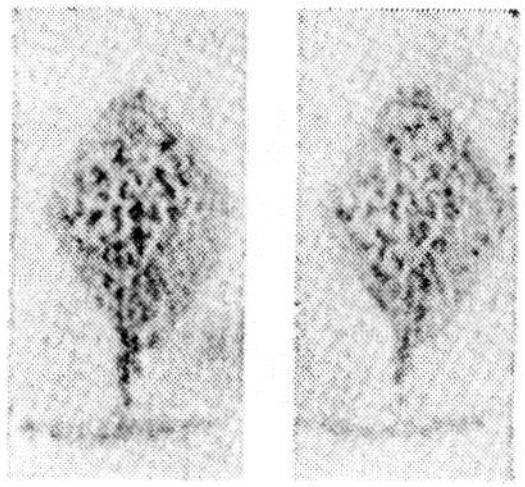

Cuff-buttons.

II. *Madake* (Phyllostachys)
1. Madake (P. bambusoides)
2. Hachiku (P. nigra var. Henonis)
3. Kurochiku (P. nigra)
4. Moso-chiku (P. edulis)
5. Bungo-zasa (P. kumasasa)
6. Shiho-chiku (P. quadrangularis)

III. *Kuma-zasa* (Sasa)
1. Susu-dake (S. spielosu)
2. Miyama-suzu (S. nana)
3. Nemagari-dake (S. paniculata)
4. Kumazasa (S. albo-marginata)
5. Miyako-zasa (S. nipponica)
6. Adzuma-zasa (S. ramosa)
7. Yadake (S. japonica)
8. Chishima-zasa (S. kurilensis)
9. Ohkuma-zasa (S. chartacea)
10. Yakushima-zasa (S. owatarii)
11. Tsuboi-zasa (S. tsuboiana)

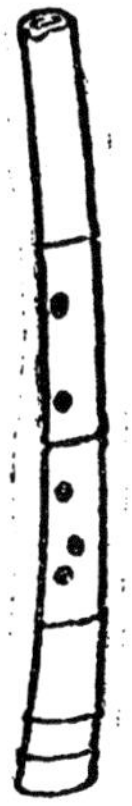

Shakuhachi.

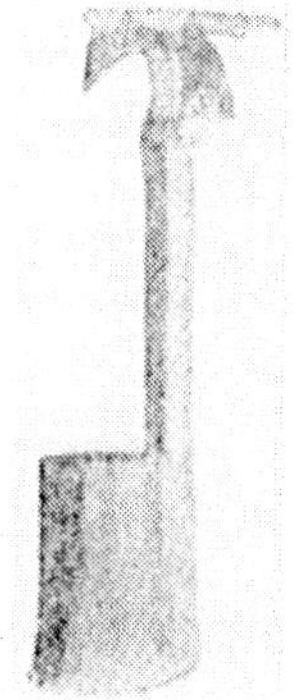

A Bamboo-toy.

IV. *Hoo-chiku* (Eubambuseoe)
1. Hoo-chiku (Bambusanana)
2. Taizan-chiku (Bambusavulgaris var. striata)
3. Shichiku (B. stenostachya)
4. Kakudake (B. angulata)
5. Kobana-dake (B. breviflora)
6. Hori-dake (B. fauriei)

V. *Machiku* (Dendrocalamus)

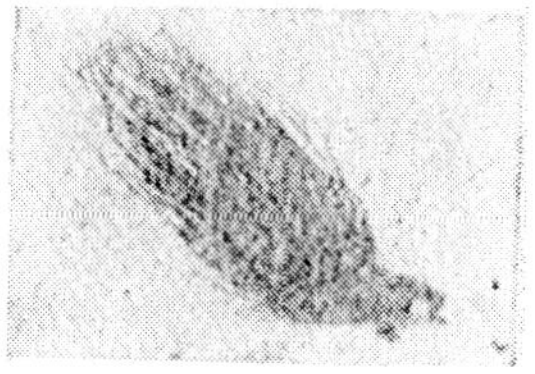

Bamboo-tortoise.

THE HOUSE OF SPARROWS

(SUZUME-NO-YADO)

For 230 years the "House of Sparrows" has been well known in Kyoto and its vicinity. The present owner of the House is Mr. Yoshio Kagimoto, of the 7th generation of this family. This is the story of the House:

The first Kagimoto, while walking one day in his garden, noticed that a pair of sparrows were flying back and forth from his nearby trees to his garden. They appeared to be hungry; so Mr. Kagimoto gave them food, which they ate voraciously and flew away chirping. After that, the sparrows came to the garden every day to be fed—and evidently sensing the kindly motives of Mr. Kagimoto, and becoming familiar with the premises, they flew in and out of his house and eventually made a nest on the back of a picture-frame on the wall of his sitting-room. Here the eggs were laid and their young were hatched. When these youngsters grew up they also made nests in the house and reared their families, and this process was repeated again and again, the number of sparrows increasing year by year, despite the ravages made on them by rats.

Noticing that many of them were killed by those rats and taking pity on his feathered friends, Mr. Kagimoto finally procured a number of gourds, made holes in them and hung them in one of his rooms, thus providing safe havens for the birds. Also, he hung lanterns and gourds under the eaves of his house and on the branches of his trees—all of which provided protection from the rats. In course of time the hundreds of sparrows flying about the house and garden and in and out of their room, chirping happily, afforded a remarkable sight.

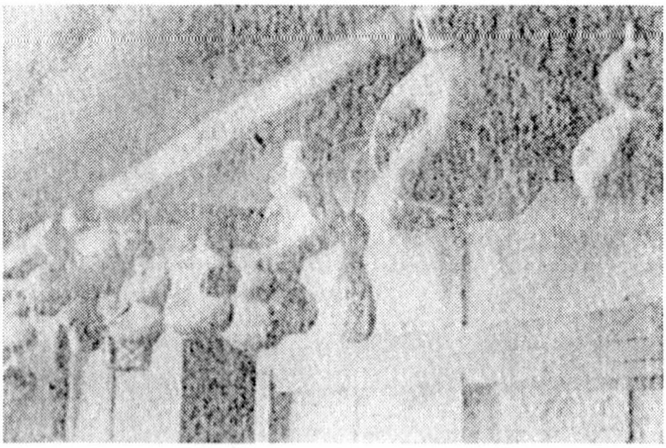

After the death of this benevolent man, and up to the present time—a full 230 years—both the name of Mr. Kagimoto and the House of Sparrows have become famous. Many gourds and lanterns have been contributed by bird-lovers. These, on which are inscribed the names of the donors, have been hung about the premises.

Compared with times past, the number of sparrows has decreased, due to the sound of the guns of the nearby army division, but, when in Kyoto, a visit to the "House of Sparrows" is worth while.

ICHO OR GINNAN—GINGKO-TREE (1)

Icho or Ginnan (gingko biloba) is a deciduous forest-tree of the last botanical period, and it is found in only China and Japan. It grows over 30 to 40 feet tall, with a girth of 10 yards or more at the base. The gingko, which is anemophilous is of both sexes, and its unisexual flowers coming out in spring send out their pollen over ten miles. The leaves are fan-shaped with parallel veins and look like the web-foot of a wild duck; hence the Japanese name of "icho," which is a perversion of the Chinese pronunciation of the two characters 鴨脚 meaning "duck-foot." They turn yellowish in the fall and make an excellent fertilizer. Also, the Japanese school-children keep them in their books to scare the worms away. The gingko-fruit, which is called "ginnan" or silver-prune, is used in high-class cooking in Japan. You will also notice that an old gingko-tree always bends northwards in Tokyo and its vicinity.

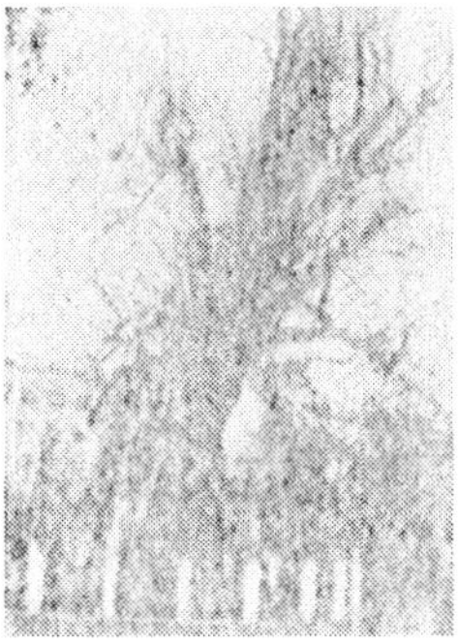

The gingko-tree in Hongo, Tokyo.

In Japan most of the oldest gingko-trees are found in the precincts of a shrine or temple, and many of them are specified as natural monuments in Japan. Here are some of the most famous gingko-trees:—

Icho at Kamakura. The gingko-tree of the Hachiman shrine, Kamakura, is perhaps the most famous gingko-tree in Japan, for when Sanetomo, son of Yoritomo Minamoto, visited the Hachiman Shrine, Kamakura, in 1219, Kugyo, his nephew, running out from behind the tree, assassinated his uncle.

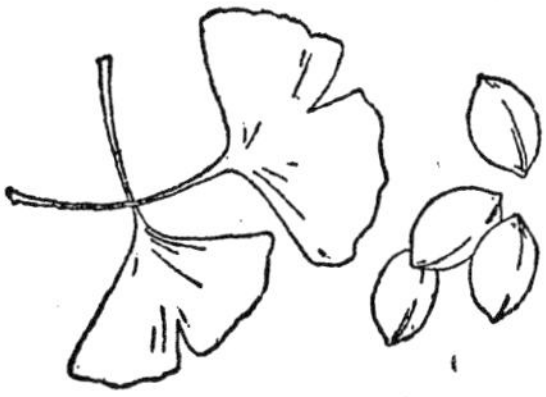

Sakasa-icho. Sakasa-icho or inverted-gingko-tree of the Zempuku-ji Temple, Tokyo, is said to have sprung up from a cane that Priest Shinran, founder of the temple, had left stuck in the ground. It is over 30 feet. in girth at 5 ft. above the ground. There is another gingko-tree in the compound of the Zempuku-ji Temple. It is a young tree much smaller than the inverted-gingko. The priest of the temple will tell you that Townsend Harris, the first U.S. Minister to Japan, hoisted his flag on the top of the gingko-tree that then stood on the place where the young one now stands. *(Continued)*

ICHO OR GINNAN—GINGKO-TREE (2)—*Concluded*

Weeping-Gingko: At the third anniversary of the death of Priest Nichiren, founder of the Nichiren Sect of Buddhism, which was held at the Hokekyo-ji Temple, in Chiba Prefecture, on the 13th of October, 1284, Priest Nitcho, one of his greatest favorites, came too late for the memorial service and Priest Nichijo, his father who was in charge of the temple, was very angry with his disrespectful son, who was not allowed to burn incense by way of paying his respects to the invited spirit of the founder of their sect. As repentance, it is said, Priest Nitcho kept reciting the Buddhist sutra for seven consecutive days and nights by walking round a big gingko-tree of the temple. Hence its name of Naki-icho or weeping-gingko; and it still stands in the compound of the Hokekyo-ji Temple.

Gingko-tree of Horyo, Okuzawa Village in Aomori Prefecture:
40 ft. in girth at 5 ft. above the ground.

Old gingko-tree of Nigatake, Miyagi Prefecture:
26 ft. in girth at 5 ft. above the ground.

Gingko-tree of the Jonichi-ji Temple, Toyama Prefecture:
36 ft. in girth at 5 ft. above the ground.

Gingko-tree of Arita, Saga Prefecture:
50 ft. in girth at foot.

Gingko-tree of the Chiba-ji Temple, Chiba Prefecture:
27 ft. in girth at foot.

Gingko-tree of the Kosho-ji Temple, Chiba Prefecture:
This tree is not tall for a gingko-tree, but it has many "milks," for which it is noted.

Fossilized gingko-tree: The following kinds of fossilized gingko-trees are found in Japan, namely:

1. Gingko digitata.
2. Gingko sibirica.
3. Gingko nathorsli.
4. Czekanowskia rigida.

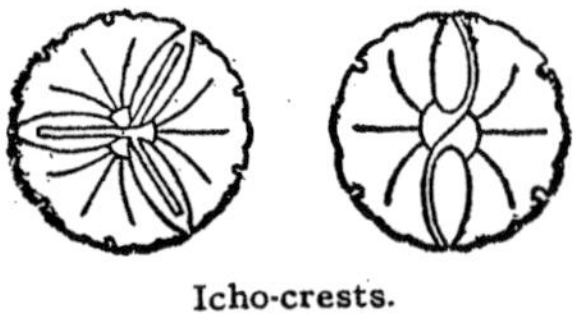

Icho-crests.

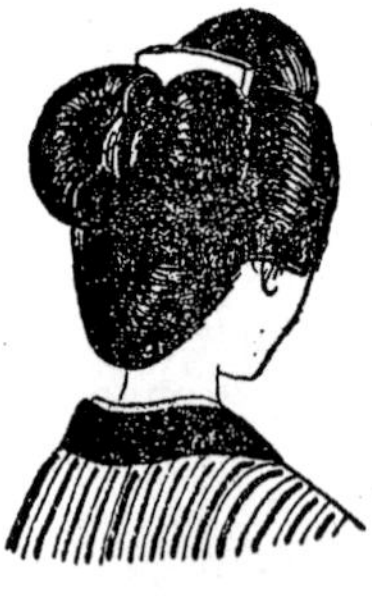

Icho-mage.

Icho-mage: Icho-mage is a kind of coiffure for a young girl in Japan. It is named after the leaf of the icho-tree.

Crests of icho-leaves: We have several kinds of crests which are modelled after the icho-leaves, such as:

Icho-hishi	Icho-tsuru	Janome-icho
Yotsuwari-icho	Tsurugi-icho	Suji-chigai-icho.

SUGI—THE JAPANESE CEDAR OR CRYPTOMERIA (1)

Sugi—the Japanese cedar or cryptomeria—which is found all over the country, is so named because the tree grows up straight (sugu=straight), sometimes attaining the enormous height of 200 to 300 feet, with a girth of 20 to 30 feet or more. It is known for its old age as well as for its straightness, and we have many sugi-trees that are more than a thousand years old.

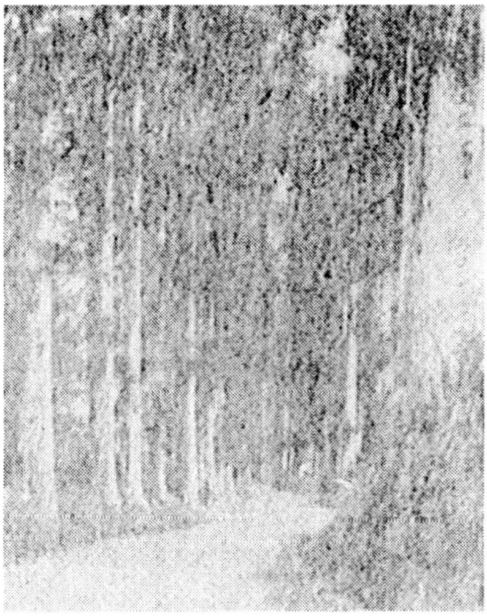

The Sugi-avenue of Nikko.

Because it is straight, sugi makes a good post or pillar for a big building or a lofty telegraph pole, and it furnishes fine building material. Our bridges in olden times were built of sugi, and one often finds still a log-bridge of a single sugi-tree across a stream. It is said that sake keeps longer when a few sugi-needles are soaked in it, and it improves its flavour. Hence our sake-casks are made of sugi-wood. One can find a sake shop in many local places by looking for a shop-sign made of sugi-needles in the form of a round sake-barrel. In the northern and western parts of Japan, the sugi-bark is widely used as a roofing material, and sugi-needles furnish materials for incense "Senko."

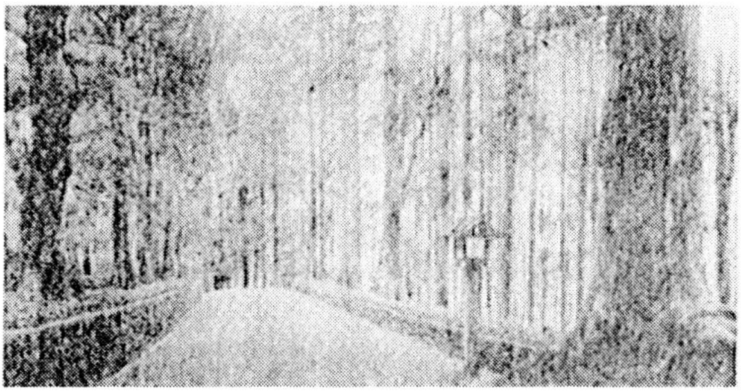

The Sugi-avenue of the Hakone Gongen Shrine.

According to the Nihonshoki, Prince Susanoo cut and cast his hair away and from it several trees sprang up: sugi from his beard, hinoki (Japanese cypress) from his waist-hair, the camphor-tree from his eye-brow and kaya (torreya nucifera) from his whisker; sugi- and the camphor being for the building of the "floating-treasure" (ship) and *hinoki* for the palace.

Jindai-sugi: By jindai-sugi, which, as the name goes, indicates the god-day-sugi or mythological cryptomeria, is meant fossil-wood, which was obtained chiefly at Hakone, or according to a certain book, from the bottom of Lake Hakone, Hakone being well-known for the Hakone work made of

(Continued)

SUGI—THE JAPANESE CEDAR OR CRYPTOMERIA (2)

Concluded

the Jindai-sugi; though fossil-wood is found on the sea-shore of Tamba and Wakasa provinces and taken from the beds of the River Hirose and Natori in Sendai.

The oldest sugi-tree in Japan: The oldest sugi-tree in Japan is found in the village of Ohsugi (big-sugi), Kochi prefecture. It is estimated to be more than 2,000 years old. The lowest part of the trunks measures 30 metres in girth, and it forks off into two trunks about a foot from the ground. They are called the Me-oto-sugi or "man-and-wife-sugi." The "female" or southern trunk, which is the larger, is 18.91 metres in girth, and stands 64.21 metres high, while the "male" or northern tree measures 16.1 metres in girth, and 53.64 meters high. Probably because of its name, the tree attracts many believers from far and wide, who offer prayers for issue. If a girl keeps a bit of a bark from the "female" trunk on her left breast, she believes that a daughter will be born to her, and the bark from the "male" trunk on her right breast will mean the birth of a son.

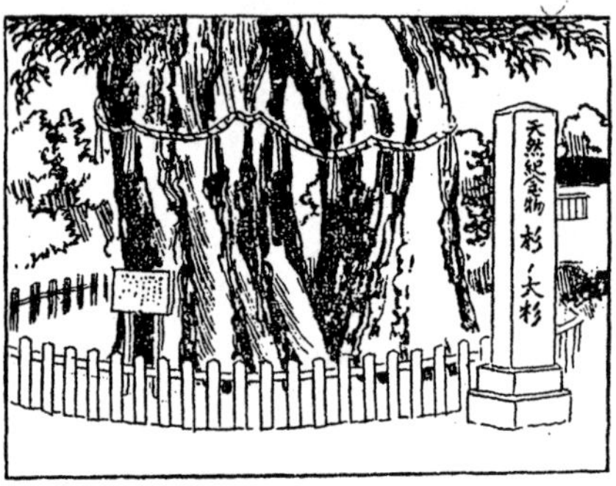

The Me-oto-Sugi of Kochi Prefecture.

Sugi-avenue at Nikko: The approach to Nikko has a beautiful avenue of gigantic trees standing along the highway for a distance of 24 miles (18,404 trees). Upon the building of the Toshogu shrine dedicated to Iye-yasu, the first Shogun of Tokugawa, the local daimyo, or lords, made offerings of various kinds, such as *torii* and lanterns. But Masatsuna Matsudaira, lord of Kawagoe, was too poor to offer anything expensive, so he made a humble offering of many sprouts of sugi, which he planted along the highway leading to the town of Nikko. Insignificant as they may have been at the time of their planting, these sugi-trees present an unforgetable sight now that some 300 years have elapsed and the tourists who visit Nikko usually exhaust their superlatives in expressing their admiration of them.

Sugi-avenue at Annaka: No less imposing than the sugi-avenue of Nikko is that of Annaka, a little town in Gumma prefecture on the old Nakasendo Highway. This avenue, which was placed under special protection by the Education Department in 1933, extends for half a mile with 321 gigantic sugi-trees standing on both sides of the highway. The date of their planting is not exactly known, but some authorities consider that it was somewhere about the ninth year (1604) of Keicho era, and that they are older than the sugi-trees of Nikko.

THE SAGO-PALM OF THE MYOKOKU-JI TEMPLE (1)

The Myokoku-ji Temple at Sakai, near Osaka, which belongs to the Nichiren sect of Buddhism, is known far and wide for its enormous sago-palm of 127 stems, each 15 or 16 ft. high, and 56 ft. in girth. It is oldest and largest sago-palm in Japan, which is said to have been brought from Korea some 800 years ago.

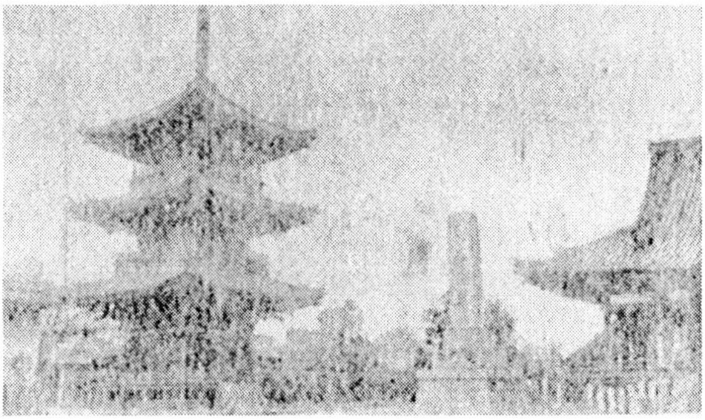

The Myokoku-ji Temple.

At one time the palm-tree lost its verdure, apparently dying, in spite of all that the priests of the temple did to restore it to health, till, as the last resort, some priests were called from another temple of the same sect in Kyoto to chant a sutra for the recovery of the plant. They recited a thousand volumes of the Hokke sutra, which contains one of the most important tenets of the Nichiren sect. Strange to tell, the dying tree was soon restored to life. The Myokoku-ji Temple was overcrowded with people, old and young, of both sexes, who came to see the mysterious tree, which seemed to believe in Buddhism.

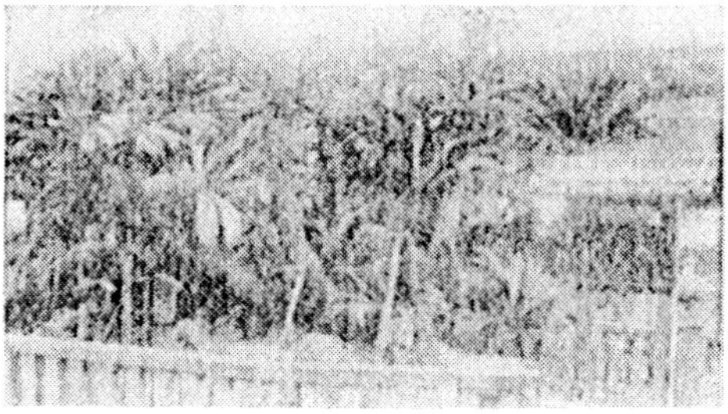

The Sago-palm of the Myokoku-ji Temple.

The Shogun Nobunaga Oda was provoked to anger by the fuss that the people made over a mere plant, and he ordered Hyosuke Inoko, a retainer, to transplant the sago-palm into the castle of Azuchi, where Oda was then residing. When a few days later Lord Oda woke up in the small hours, he heard a faint voice saying, "Let me go back to the Myokoku-ji Temple; let me go back to the Myokoku-ji Temple." Rammaru Mori, his page, was called from an adjoining room in which he was sleeping, and told to find out who was speaking. The page stole into the garden from which the voice seemed to come, and he was surprised to hear that it came from the sago-palm that had been brought from the Myokoku-ji Temple.

(Continued)

THE SAGO-PALM OF THE MYOKOKU-JI TEMPLE (2)

Concluded

"I thought it strange that the tree should have revived at the reading of the sutra," Lord Oda said after listening to what Mori had to say in his report. " No wonder that the tree hundreds of years old should be haunted and have an evil spirit: I will cut it down in the morning."

On the following morning Lord Oda got up earlier than usual, and ordered the tree to be cut down by Kyuyemon Sugaya, who led an army of 300 coolies into the garden of the castle. Lord Oda sat on a camp-stool, attended by many retainers and pages. The coolies stood around the tree, and at the command of Sugaya one of them stepped out to strike the tree down, when suddenly he fell with a thud on the ground and died on the spot, vomitting blood.

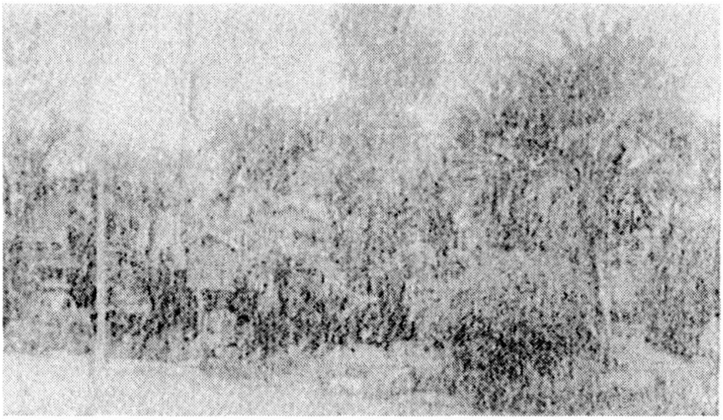

The Myokoku-ji Temple.

" We are told that Ts'ao-ts'ao of the Wei dynasty died when he tried to cut an old pear-tree down," Lord Oda said, clearly awe-stricken." This old palm-tree may have an invulnerable spirit in it. Better leave it untouched and restore it to its former place in the Myokoku-ji Temple."

The sago-palm was then carried back to the temple, where it stands as a mystery to many visitors. On the 2nd of the 6th month (June), 1582, just three years after transplanting the tree, Nobunaga Oda was assassinated by Mitsuhide Akechi at the Honno-ji Temple.

When later on the Emperor Reigen (112th) was seriously ill, no medicine proving of any avail, a prayer was offered for his recovery at the shrine dedicated to the spirit of the mysterious tree, and he was soon cured. He offered a gate to the shrine, now known as the Imperial Messenger Gate.

Broken needles: Women in the vicinity of Sakai " offer " their broken needles to the sago-palm of the Myokoku-ji Temple, in the superstitious belief that they will not then be hurt by a needle; possibly because of the scientific fact that iron is good for the growth of the sago-palm. There are huge numbers of broken needles at the root of the sago-palm in the Myokoku-ji Temple.

AYU (plecoglossus altivelis) (1)

Of all fresh-water fish in Japan ayu (plecoglossus altivelis) is perhaps the most prized in season on account of its special flavour, though the eel may be said to be among the most popular. "Ayu," according to some scholars, means "small-white-fish," but others are of opinion that the word "ayu" is derived from the verb "ayuru" meaning "coming down," the fish being so called because it comes down the river. Its name is written by two ideograms meaning "year-fish," because, according to the Wamyosho, "ayu is born in spring, grows up in summer, weakens in autumn and dies in winter."

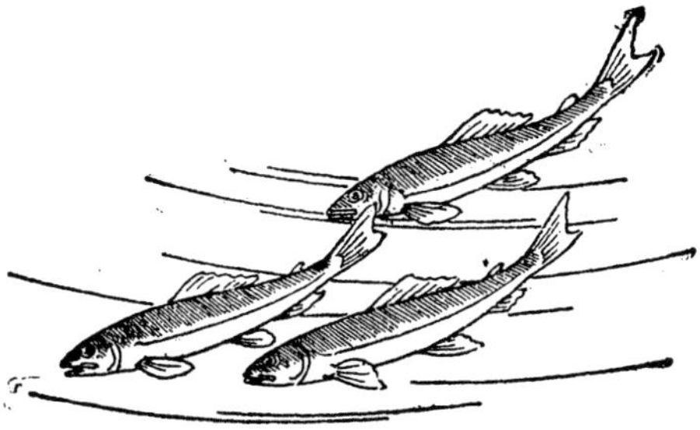

Ayu.

It is traditionally said that in the fourth month of the year 200 A.D., while the Empress Jingo was staying at the village of Tamashima, Kyushu, on her expedition to Shiragi, a kingdom in Korea, she caught some "fine-scaled fish" by using as bait boiled rice tied to the end of a thread taken from her dress. This fish, it is now known, was ayu. Because of this the place was named *Mezura* ("unusual"), which later on changed into *Matsuura*, as the place is now known. The Nihonshoki mentions this custom of fishing ayu with boiled rice.

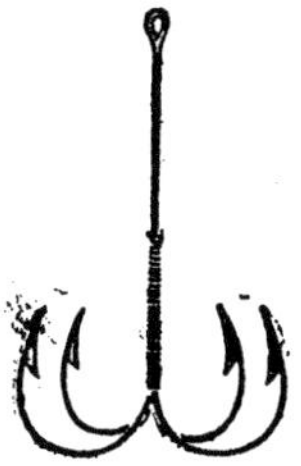

Fishing-hook.

Ayu has fine scales and a wide mouth with rows of fine teeth. When grown up, it is black-backed, yellowish white on the belly, and reddish about its head. It is born in the river and goes down to the sea, to return up the river, in April or May. When young, it lives on animal food in the river, till it is 3 or 4 inches long and after that it eats only moss. It measures over a foot when fully grown, though a special kind found in Lake Biwa does not grow larger than 2 or 3 inches, and it does not go down into the sea. The fish lays its eggs in October, when many of them die through fatigue from their long swim. Some ayu, however, survive the winter in a deep river. The close season for the fishing of ayu, is from the first of October, when its spawning season begins, till the end of May.

Ayu is found nearly all over the country, but the following rivers are specially known for ayu and ayu-fishing in Japan: namely the River Nagara, Mino province; the River Tama, Musashi province; the River Chikuma, Kyushu; the River Gokase, Hiuga province; the River Niyodo, Tosa province, the River Iwakuni, Suwo province, the River Ohta, Aki province; etc.

(Continued)

AYU (plecoglossus altivelis) (2)—*Concluded*

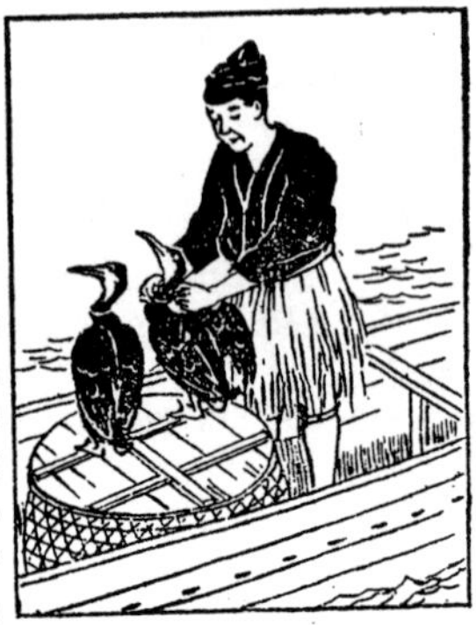

Cormorant-Handler.

There are four principal ways of fishing ayu: They are (1) with rod and line; (2) with what is called the "cormorant-rope" and a net; (3) by means of a trained cormorant, (4) by what is called Tomozuri (literally, catching by means of a friend). In catching ayu with rod and line, we generally use false hooks because it is hard to catch it with bait. In the second way of catching ayu, the "Unawa" or "cormorant-rope" with black feathers put at intervals on it, is used to chase the fish. Ayu takes this rope for cormorants, and few dare swim out of the range of the rope. When they are encircled by the rope, a net is thrown over them for a catch at a single cast. In Tomozuri we use an ayu as a decoy. It is tied fast with a few hooks about it and other ayu are caught of their own accord. The fishing of ayu by means of trained cormorants is a most clever and ingenious method. The cormorant is employed usually at night, after the moon has set, for it does not work well on a moonlight night. The boat, lighted with torches, has a cormorant handler, an assistant and two rowers. The chief handler generally manipulates twelve cormorants i.e. six by each hand, while his assistant handles four or five. Each cormorant is tethered, and a hook is put round its neck in order to prevent it from swallowing the ayu it catches. Great skill is required to manipulate the cormorants, which, swimming in zig-zag fashion, and in great disorder, in their wild chase after ayu in the water, would cause an endless entanglement of the cords in less skillful hands. Then from time to time the fisherman pulls the cormorants one after another to the prow of the boat to take out of their mouth all the fish they catch. Ayu-fishing by means of trained cormorants shows the typically clever and ingenious way of the Japanese cormorant fishers.

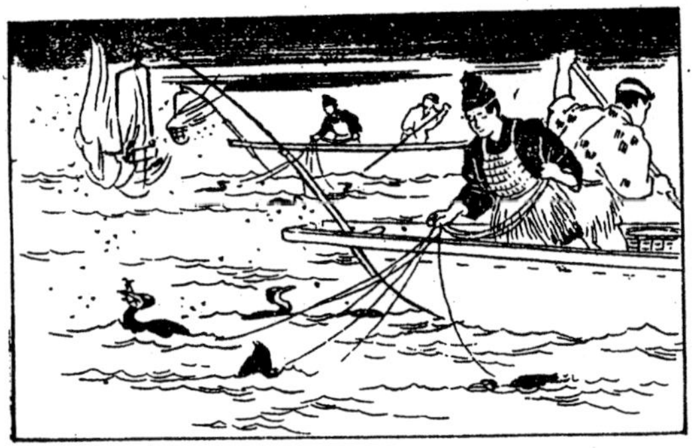

Ayu-fishing.

HANZAKI OR SANSHOUO—GIANT SALAMANDER (1)

The giant salamander (Megalobatrachus japonicus), which is a tailed amphibian resembling a water lizard, is called in the Japanese language "hanzaki" or, as it is more popularly known, "sanshouo." The name "hanzaki" was given to the amphibian because it is alive even when it is cut in two (han=half; zaki or saki=torn), and sanshouo means "sansho-fish" because it has the smell of a Japanese pepper called "sansho" (xanylum piperitum). This fish or amphibian, sometimes measuring five feet, is known for its grotesque looks and limited geographical distribution. In fact, it is scarcely found in any other countries of the world than China and Japan, but Japan is the recognized home of the giant salamander.

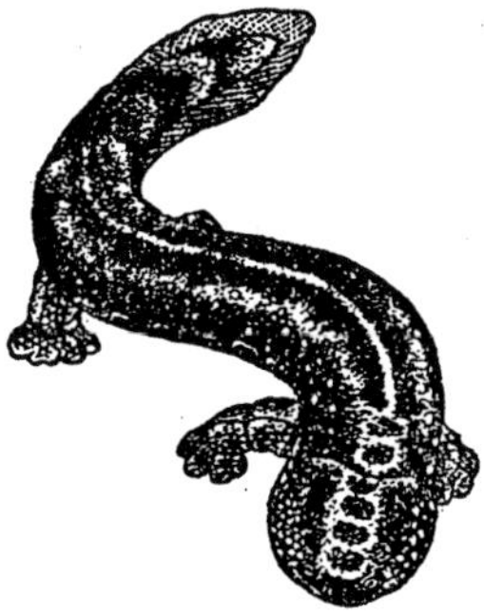
Giant salamander.

In Japan the geographical distribution of the giant salamander lies between Oita and Fukuoka in Kyushu, in the south, and Gifu in the main island of Japan Proper, in the north, or between 33° and 36° N and 131° and 137° E, the fish being found chiefly in the following rivers:—R. Yakkan, Oita; R. Ota, Hiroshima; R. Takahashi and R. Asahi, Okayama; R. Haruyama, Hyogo; R. Go, Shimane; R. Tenjin, Tottori; R. Katsura, Kyoto; R. Yodo, Osaka; R. Kiso and R. Nagara, Gifu. Generally speaking, the giant salamander is found in a river, which empties itself not into the Pacific Ocean, but into the Inland or Japan Sea or the Bay of Ise. It lives at an altitude of 200 to 1,000 meters above the sea-level, though it lays its eggs generally at 400 to 500 meters above the sea.

The giant salamader is negative to the sun, which it avoids, hiding itself under a stone or rock in the daytime, though it is quite active during the night, when it travels out of its nest for two or three hundred yards in search of food.

When small, it keeps on going upstream till it reaches the altitude of about 1,000 meters, where it is generally found. It is very fond of crab-meat and usually lives upon frogs, small fish or any molluscs found in the water. It swallows fish head foremost.

The breeding season of the giant salamander is from the middle of August to the latter part of September, and it lays more eggs between Aug. 25 to Sept. 5 than at any other time. Those eggs, which are laid in the early part of September, are hatched in the latter part of the same month, if they are kept at a temperature of 23° to 25° C. The eggs are hatched generally in four weeks, though some eggs may remain unhatched till about the 10th of October.

(*Continued*)

HANZAKI OR SANSHOUO—GIANT SALAMANDER (2)

(Concluded)

The egg of the giant salamander is about 3 c.m. large, and it looks transparent like gelatine, but with a yolk at the center like that of a hen's egg. A medium-sized salamander, about 2.5 ft. large, lays a mass of 150 to 300 eggs, but a large one of over 3 ft. will lay about 600 eggs at one time, and all the eggs are bound together with a transparent cord. They are laid either on sand or soft earth, near stone or rock walls, or in a hole which is some three or four feet square. Some salamanders lay their eggs in a quick stream; others in a slow stream, and still others in quiet or stagnant water. The mother-salamander takes tender care of her eggs, which she keeps on moving gently with her flat tail, though according to some foreign scholar only the male salamander takes care of the eggs. If any one touches the eggs with a stick, the mother will angrily bite at it.

A young salamander, when hatched from an egg, looks black, but when it is a year old, it turns brown, and three pairs of gills may be seen. It grows 7 or 8 inches in three years, 1.5 ft. in four years, and weighs over 2 or 3 lbs. P. F. von Siebolt tells of a giant salamander, which was kept for 50 years, and which measured 4.5 ft.

The flesh of the giant salamander is edible, but because the soup in which its flesh is cooked turns red, we have a saying in some localities that the salamander should be eaten in the evening. Young salamanders are considered to be a good cure for dysentery. Japan exports quite a large number of giant salamanders and their eggs every year.

Hakone salamander: Hakone-sanshouo or Hakone salamander (onychodactylus japonicus), so named because it was first found at Hakone, lives in mountainous localities, such as Hakone, Amaki (Izu province), and Nikko. It is about 5 inches long, reddish brown in colour, striped in yellow, with brown spots. It is also negative to the sun, which it avoids. The people of these localities will catch this salamander in the spring and keep it dry as medicine.

Salamander swallowed alive: A small kind of salamander, an inch or two large, is found in different localities of Japan. Our children will swallow this small fish alive because they are told that it is a cure of nervous weakness or some kind of illness, though possibly more for curiosity's sake, as the fish is felt moving about in the stomach for a short time after it is swallowed down.

THE SACRED FISH OF KOYA-SAN

Ame-no-uo (" *Rain Fish* ")

Numerous miracles are attributed to *Kobo Daishi* (A.D. 774–834), the great Buddhist saint who founded the monastery of the Shingon sect on Koya-san (" Plateau Mountain "), near Nara, in A.D. 816. Among them is the legend that one day, on his way to the monastery, he noticed that a pilgrim on the roadside was about to eat a fish which he had roasted, as part of his lunch. The saint stopped and asked the man if he would sell him the fish. The man was willing. Thereupon, after paying for it, Kobo Daishi threw the fish into a nearby stream—when, lo!—the fish came to life and swam away.

At another time, according to another legend, on one of the mountain trails he saw that a man was about to cook a fish which he had impaled on a skewer. Moved with pity, and wishing to save the life of the fish, he gave the man a little money and placed the fish in brook, where it revived and swam down stream in the current.

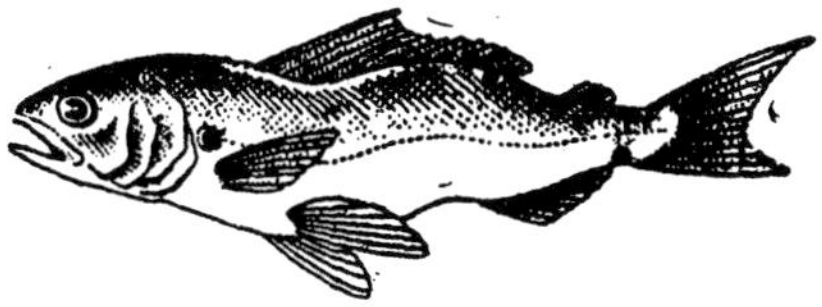

In a small stream of the inner Sacred Hall, Koya-san, there swim fish with marks on them as if made by a skewer.

These fish are named " rain fish " because in the streams of the district similar fish are caught in quantity during a rain. This species, with a black mark on the back, is abundant in the streams of the province of Omi, in which Lake Biwa is located. Some of the Omi fish grow to about two feet in length.

A FROG COMES TO LIFE AFTER ELEVEN DAYS' ANABIOSIS

In November, 1935, the experiment was made of freezing alive some reptiles, namely, a bull-frog, a green frog, a tree-frog, a tadpole, a snake and a snail, by Prof. Senzo Wada, Aomori Normal School, at the ice storage of the Aomori Ice Manufacturing Co., Aomori Prefecture. This he did in order to see what possibility there was of keeping them in a state of anabiosis.

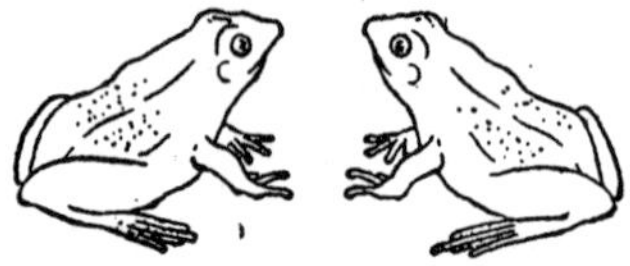

The reptiles were taken into the ice storage at the temperature of 0.3° C at 5 p.m. on November 6, and there thoroughly frozen. The room was examined every two hours to see that the temperature of 0.3° C was maintained. Five days after, namely on Nov. 11, and at noon, the door of the storage was opened and the frozen reptiles were taken into the laboratory of Prof. Wada in the service of the company. The room was gradually heated by an electric stove and the temperature went up to 1°C at 4 p.m. The thawing process was conducted slowly, since a sudden rise in temperature would destroy the cellulous structure of the frozen reptiles. The experiment was then stopped for the day.

The temperature was raised to 7°C on the 12th, and to 13°C on the 13th. The experiment of bringing the frozen reptiles back to life was made at noon on the 14th Nov., i.e., 8 days after they had been transformed into a state of anabiosis. When no sign of life was observed, the impatient professor took up his lancet and began to dissect the bull-frog.

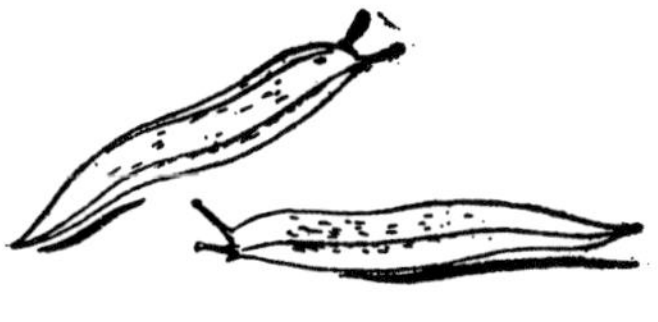

"Pshaw! it was alive!" the professor cried with great disappointment, as soon as he had opened the unlucky reptile. No change in the blood of the frog was observed. The professor had been too hasty!

"I will bring the other animals to life, without fail," he said to himself, but with apparent confidence on his face.

On the 16th the tree-frog and the snail were taken out again. They were put into water, 7° C and kept in it for 20 minutes. The ice thawed, but the bodies of the reptiles remained as hard as stone. Nor did their eyes move at all. The professor then took them before the stove, where the temperature was 15° C. He and his witnesses watched them carefully. Five minutes passed, ten minutes, a quarter of an hour, and yet no sign of recovery was seen. In twenty minutes, Prof. Wada shouted "There!" with great ecstacy. Sure enough, the tree-frog had moved its legs a fraction. Then its eyes opened but soon closed again, and the frog stood as still as if it were no more alive than before. For another twenty minutes the frog remained still. The witnesses were about to give it up for dead, when suddenly to every one's amazement it opened its eyes again. It had indeed come to life again! Then it jumped off the professor's hand, and in forty minutes it actually ate a fly.

Thus the tree-frog came to life again after it had been kept in a state of anabiosis for eleven days.

THE DAIKON OR RADISH

The radish (raphanus sativus) or, as it is called in Japan, Daikon, (dai=large; kon=root), and which contains a high percentage of diastase is such a good digestive of starch that it is considered to be one of the necessary greens for a rice-eating people such as the Japanese, who are very fond of it. We have a saying to the effect that however much one may overeat with boiled rice, or with *mochi*, which is a kind of rice cake, a bit of raw radish will digest all in no time. The radish is therefore a wholesome and popular vegetable in Japan.

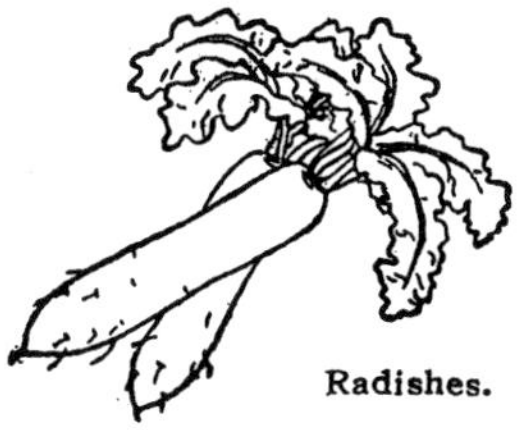

Radishes.

The radish is used in various ways in Japanese cooking. Raw radish, first of all, is considered to be a sure cure for dyspepsia, and grated raw radish, taken with *shoyu* or bean-soy, is a good appetiser. It is commonly used in *miso-shiru* or bean-paste soup, which is an indispensable drink at breakfast, and it is also cooked with fish or meat. The radish preserved in rice-bran is perhaps the most popular pickle eaten by all classes throughout the year. It is called Takuan-zuke (Takuan-pickle), so named after Priest Takuan (1573-1645), who invented this method of preserving the radish. According to his method, the radish is dried in the sun and preserved in rice-bran and salt, by pressing it with a heavy stone. Some might say this pickle was named Takuan-zuke because the weighty stone used on it resembles the grave-stone of Priest Takuan's tomb in the Tokai-ji Temple, at Shinagawa, Tokyo. Boiled rice and Takuan-zuke make the simplest meal that the Japanese can take. Asa-zuke is another pickle of the radish preserved in salt and malt.

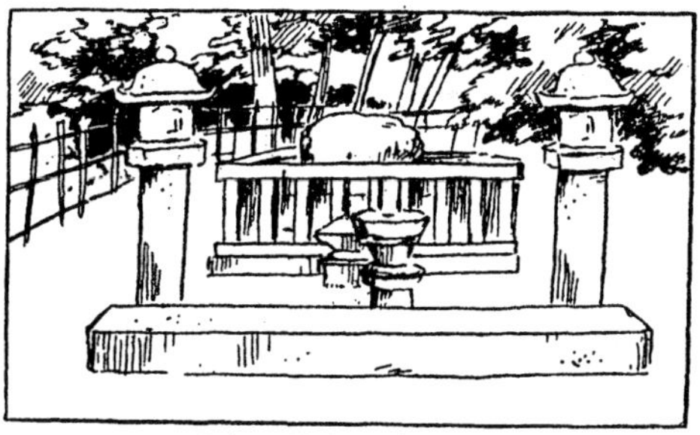

Priest Takuan's grave.

The radish, which is an annual and biannual plant, grows about a foot long and an inch or two in diameter, but there are several different kinds, of which some of the chief are given below:—

1. Nerima-daikon: about 2 ft. long and 3 or 4 inches in diameter, grown particularly at Nerima, Tokyo.
2. Sakurajima-daikon: more like a turnip than a radish; often 1.5 to 2 ft. in diameter and less high, weighing sometimes 10 to 15 kilogrammes. Cultivated only on the isle of Sakurajima, in Satsuma Province.
3. Kameido-daikon: over a foot long and a little over an inch in diameter. Cultivated at Kameido, Tokyo.
4. Moriguchi-daikon: 4 to 5 ft. long and less than an inch in diameter. Cultivated at Moriguchi in Kawachi Province.

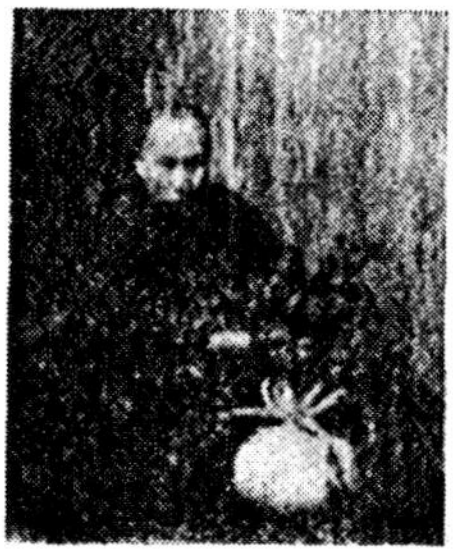

Sakurajima radish.

We Japanese

BOOK III

Written by

ATSUHARU SAKAI

for

K. M. YAMAGUCHI,

President

THE DIFFERENT NAMES OF JAPAN

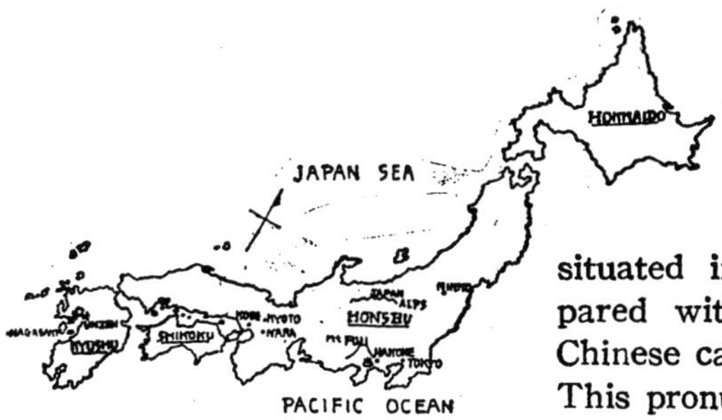

Japan: The Japanese call their country by the name of Nihon or Nippon (日本), which means the "origin of the sun" as Japan is situated in the east when compared with China. The ancient Chinese called the country Zippon. This pronunciation was expressed by Marco Polo with the spelling of "Zipangu," from which "Japan" (English), "Japon" (French), "Japan" (German), "Giappone" (Italian), etc. have been derived.

Toyoashihara-no-Chiaki-Nagaioaki-no-Mitsuho-no-Kuni: This long name was used in the Imperial command that the Goddess Amaterasu gave to Prince Ame-no-Oshihomimi, when he was about to leave the Celestial Abode for the land below.

Akitsushima: Two sets of characters are used for this name: one meaning "autumn-creek-land" (秋津洲) while the other indicates the Dragon-fly-land, the latter name being given to the island of Japan because, according to scholars, the country looks like two dragon-flies on the wing.

Yamato: The characters now used for this name mean "great peace" (大和), but little is known about the origin of this name, Yamato. Some scholars hold that Japan was so named after the central and most influential province of Yamato, while others attribute the name to the mountainous conditions of the country. (Yama = "mountain"; to = "place").

Fusokoku: No more is known about the origin of this name than that "Fusokoku" means a country of mulberry-trees. According to an old Chinese record, there was a land of that name, 20,000 Chinese miles east of China, where sacred mulberry-trees grew in abundance. Japan was evidently regarded as an Elygium, as the name of Fuso was taken to mean by the Chinese.

O-Yashima: Because, according to the Kojiki, Prince Izanagi and Princess Izanami "gave birth" to the "eight islands", Japan was named O-Yashima or Great-Eight-Lands.

There are more than ten other names, which are found in ancient records and annals as indicative of Japan.

THE NATIONAL EMBLEM

The first ancestress of the Imperial Family of Japan is called Amaterasu (Ama = heaven; terasu = shining) or the Sun Goddess. Hence the Japanese Emperor is in the Japanese language "Hi-no-Mitsugi" or the "heir to the sun", while the Japanese "Hime" for "princess" means "sun-daughter" (Hi = sun; me = woman), in contrast to "Hiko" (Hi = sun; ko = child) for "prince." In a letter addressed to the Emperor Yang of the Sui dynasty, China, in 607 A.D., the Empress Suiko (the 33rd) said: "The Sovereign of the Land of the Rising Sun greets the Sovereign of the Land of the Setting Sun." No wonder, therefore, that the Japanese are a heliolatory people as one still sees many Japanese worshipping the sun early in the morning, and their national flag represents or symbolizes the rising sun.

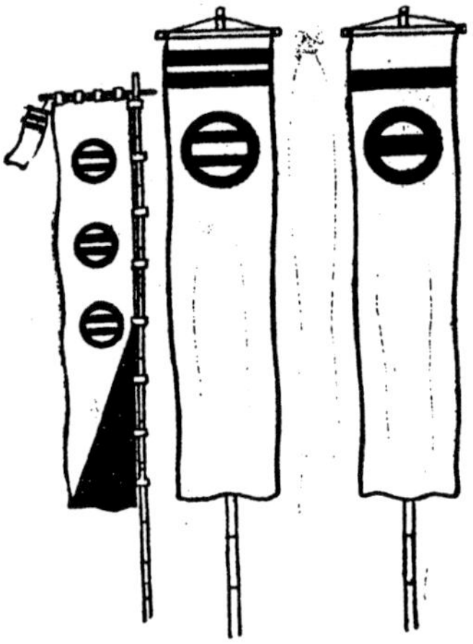

Crests of the Nitta and Ashikaga families. the origin of Hinomaru

The Emperor Goreizei (the 70th) conferred upon Yoriyoshi Minamoto two brocade flags, one with the sun and the other with the moon, embroidered in gold and silver, respectively, in recognition of the meritorious services rendered by the Minamoto family for several generations. These flags were handed down to Yoshikuni Minamoto after the civil wars known by the names of the Former Nine Years' and the Latter Three Years' wars that the Minamoto family fought against the northern rebels in the 11th century. Yoshikuni made two new flags of the sun and the moon in imitation of the Imperial gifts and gave them to his two sons. The one bearing the sun hierographically symbolized by a circle with a horizontal line across it, was given to Yoshishige Minamoto, who became the first ancestor of the later Nitta family, while the other embodying the moon in a hierographical circle with two lines across it, was handed to Yoshiyasu Minamoto, whose descendants are the family of the Ashikaga Shogun (1338–1573). These symbols became their respective family-crests.

From Yoshishige Minamoto, the ancestor of the Nitta family, came the two families of Tokugawa and Sakai, which latter adopted a new crest or ensign, representing the sun in a red disk on white cloth, like the present national flag of the country some time during the fifteenth century. This was the first appearance in the heraldic history of Japan of the rising sun as a feudal flag.

In 1854, the Shogunate Government issued a decree by which the Rising Sun was made a maritime flag for all Japanese ships, and subsequently, upon the abolition of the clans in 1869, the Rising Sun was declared to be the national flag of Japan in 1870.

Shintoism: Its Gods and Their Representation

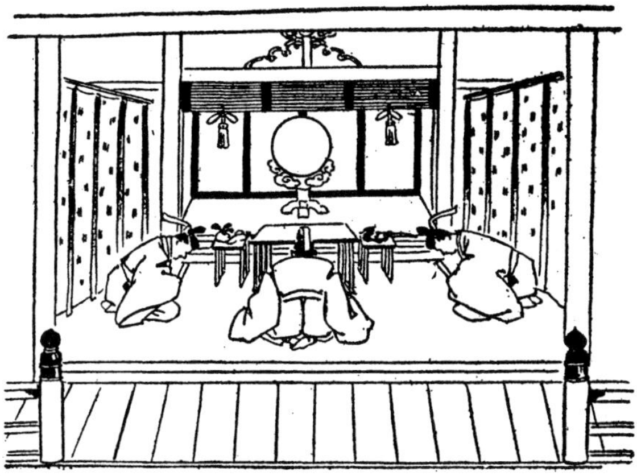

Shinto priests worshipping Kami of their shrine; a mirror symbolizing Kami

Shintoism, which literally means the "way" of Kami or "gods", is the worship of Kami (gods), who are of two kinds in Shintoism, mythological or prehistoric and historic, though most of its gods belong to the former category; such as the Goddess Amaterasu, of the Imperial shrines at Ise, Prince Izanagi and Princess Izanami, Prince Susanoo, Prince Oyamakui, etc. being among the most widely venerated all over the country. Among the Kami of the latter category are found the Emperors Jimmu, Chuai, Ojin, Kammu, Godaigo, Meiji and several other Emperors and Empresses, besides some historic figures of great distinction, such as Masashige Kusunoki, Iyeyasu Tokugawa, Kiyomaro Wake, General Nogi, Admiral Togo, etc.

A Shinto shrine is called in the Japanese language "Yashiro" and "Omiya", which etymologically mean "house-substitute" and "honorable house", respectively, and it is, according to our idea, a temporary residence on earth for a Kami (god), who lives in heaven. It is generally built of Hi-no-ki (lit. tree of fire) or Japanese cypress, but because purity is one of the most important requisites in Shintoism, it is of plain wood with little, if any, decoration, as one sees in the Meiji Shrine, Tokyo, and the Shinto shrines, Ise.

Nor is there any image, or idol, enshrined in a Shinto shrine. A Shinto god is represented in its shrine by what is called Mi-tama-shiro or spirit-substitute. Some of the common Mi-tama-shiro are: mirror, bead, stone, sword, arrow, halberd, Gohei (paper-offering), bell, sceptor, or any other article preserved in representation, or commemoration, of Kami enshrined in the shrine. Sometimes, however, a hoary old tree, a giganic rock and a mountain are venerated as objects of worship.

Before a shrine was built, it seems, the Shinto Kami was worshipped at Iwakura, which literally means "rock-throne". It was a huge rock, a place of worship for the prehistoric people of Japan, who worshipped their Kami on the top of a high mountain. The late Masao Toyama, a Shinto priest, discovered over sixty rock-thrones in the Kinai district and its vicinity.

THE KASHIMA AND KATORI SHRINES

When, according to Kojiki and Nihongi, two oldest annals of Japan, it was decided to send Prince Ninigi from the Celestial Above of Takama-no-Hara to the land below, Goddess Amaterasu ordered Futsunushi to come down in advance to prepare the way for the advent of the prince. Takemikazuchi also offered to come down to help Futsunushi in subjugating the disobedient local chieftains. Together they came down and after their unification of the country they received Prince Ninigi, who founded the country of Japan.

Takemikazuchi and Futsunushi are enshrined at the Kashima Shrine, Hitachi Province, and the Katori Shrine, Shimosa Province, respectively, situated about one hour's drive by taxi from each other; the former established in B. C. 600 and the latter in B. C. 643. The shrines are now rebuilt in every twenty years, but they are very old in the style of architecture. The Oku-no-In (inner sanctuary) of the Kashima Shrine, built by Iyeyasu of the Tokugawa regime, is over 300 years old and specified as a national treasure.

Kashima and Katori have some interesting festivals, such as the White-horse Festival, Jan. 7, and the Military Festival, Sept. 1, held at Kashima.

The sword "Futsu-no-Mitama": The Emperor Jimmu during his eastern expedition was caught in a poisonous fog, and many of his troops fell sick. One night Takakuraji saw in a dream that he received a sword from the Sun Goddess and on waking up Takakuraji found the sword, near his pillow. This sword is still preserved as a treasure in the Kashima Shrine.

The Rivet Stone. In Japan every earthquake is attributed to the of a subterranean catfish. This mysterious fish, encircling around the earth, its head and tail meet each other at Kashima, where the Kami of the shrine placed a "rivet," as the stone in the Kashima precincts is called, to keep them under control. The stone is about a foot in diameter, but nobody knows how deeply rooted it is. It is also said that Takemikazuchi sat on the stone when he came down from Takama-no-Hara.

The Grape-mirror: One of three ancient mirrors manufactured during the T'ang dynasty of China is preserved in the Katori Shrine and specified as a national treasure. It has many grapes carved on its back; hence its name.

Mitarashi-no-Mizu. It is a small mysterious pool, which furnishes the Kashima Shrine with its purifying water. Nobody knows how deep the pool is, but it is believed that the water will not go higher than the breast of any one who enters it, irrespective of his stature.

Kashima and Katori are situated at a place, which is rich in prehistoric relics. The former has a large number of prehistoric earthen vases brought to light in its precincts, and some of them are very valuable.

The precincts of the two shrines are little less sacred and awe-inspiring than the Ise Shrines, with gigantic hoary trees, some of which are dozens of feet in girth. They are situated within the reach of a few hours' ride by steam-train or taxi, from Tokyo.

THE MEIJI SHRINE

The Meiji Shrine is dedicated to the Emperor Meiji and his consort, the Empress Dowager Shoken. The Emperor Meiji was and is much adored because he effected the Restoration of 1868, by which it is meant that he restored to the Imperial Government the administrative power of the country which had been in the hands of the Shogun; the Emperors having been little better than nominal rulers. The shrine was bombed out during the war, but the Japanese take every opportunity to pay homage to the Emperor and Empress at the shrine, at all times of the year and especially on its festival days; i. e., April 11, July 30 and Nov. 3, besides the New Year's days. They enjoy the honour of being in the solemn presence of the spirits of the illustrious ruler and his Imperial consort.

The original Meiji Shrine built in 1920 was a majestic shrine and awe-inspiring to the Japanese. All the wood used in its building was brought over from the Kiso mountains and Taiwan, and the three Torii standing on its approach are just grand. Hinoki (Japanese cypress) shingles used in thatching the roofs of the shrine, it is reported, weighed no less than 118,000 kan (kan=3.75 kg). All the trees in the shrine precincts, numbering hundreds of thousands, are contributed by the local prefectures all over the country.

The Gardens: There are beautiful Japanese gardens on the compound of the shrine. They are opened to the general public once or twice a year, and almost regularly during the season of the iris flowers, for which the gardens are specially known. Clear water bubbles from a fountain at the root of a majestic cryptomeria-tree. The fountain is known as "Kato Kiyomasa's well", for this warlord resided at this place over three hundred years ago.

Yoyogi: One notices a dead old tree kept sacred with the sacred rope of Shimenawa by the roadside between the first and second Torii of the shrine. It is called "Yoyogi" (lit. generation-generation-tree), after which the place where the Meiji Shrine now stands is named Yoyogi.

The Meiji Art Gallery: The Meiji Art Gallery is situated in the outer gardens of the shrine. It is a magnificient edifice standing on the very spot where the cortege of the Emperor Meiji took the train when it left Tokyo for burial in Kyoto on Sept. 13, 1912. The Gallery contains eighty pictures, or forty Japanese and forty oil paintings, all painted by first-class master-painters of Japan, depicting so many chief events that took place during the illustrious reign of the Emperor Meiji.

NENGO OR YEAR-NAME (ERA)

No other country has a more complicated calendar than Japan has. First we have the solar calendar of the West, which is generally adopted all over the Empire. But many of the local customs are still observed in accordance with the old lunar calendar, which is about a month behind the solar one; a full moon coming always on the night of the fifteenth each month. Then we are in the 2,609th year (1949) of the Imperial reign, for according to the *Kojiki* (712 A.D.) and the *Nihonshoki* (720 A.D.), Jimmu, the first Emperor was enthroned 660 years before the Christian era. Then again we are now in the 24th (1949) year of Showa era (lit. radiant-peace) in the reign of the present Emperor, who ascended the Throne in 1926. It was the Emperor Kotoku (the 36th) who adopted the Nengo (year-name) or era by calling the first year (645 A.D.) of his reign the era of Taika (lit. great innovation), for in that year he effected a thorough reorganization of the political system of the country. A white pheasant was presented to the Imperial court in 650, A.D., and the year-name of Hakuchi (white-pheasant) was adopted for that year. It lasted for five years and after some interval the era of Hakuho (white phoenix) and Shucho (red-bird) were adopted in 673 and 686 A.D. respectively. After these a new year-name was inaugurated on every lucky or unlucky occasion; even the death of an Emperor often requiring the adoption of a new year-name. The Emperor Meiji stipulated in 1868 that every Emperor should have a new year-name at his enthronement. Japan had 250 different Nengo (year-names) or eras in her history, inclusive of eighteen year-names that the Northern Court adopted during the duarchal period (1331–1392).

YEAR-NAMES

Taika	645–649	Shingo-keiun	767–769
Hakuchi	650–654	Hoki	770–780
Shucho	687–696	Ten-o	781
Taiho	701–703	Enryaku	782–805
Keiun	704–707	Daido	806–809
Wado	708–714	Konin	810–823
Reiki	715–716	Tencho	824–833
Yoro	717–723	Showa	834–847
Shinki	724–728	Kasho	848–850
Tempei	729–748	Ninju	851–853
Tempyo-shoho	749–756	Seiko	854–856
Tempyo-hoji	757–764	Ten-an	857–858
Tempyo-shingo	765–766	Teikan	859–876

Continued

Genkei	877–884
Ninna	885–888
Kampei	889–897
Shotai	898–900
Engi	901–922
Encho	923–930
Shohei	931–937
Tenkei	938–946
Tenryaku	947–956
Tentoku	957–960
Owa	961–963
Koho	964–967
Anwa	968–969
Tenroku	970–972
Tenen	973–975
Teigen	976–977
Tengen	978–982
Eikan	983–984
Kanwa	985–986
Eien	987–988
Eiso	989
Shoryaku	990–994
Chotoku	995–998
Choho	999–1003
Kanko	1004–1011
Chowa	1012–1016
Kanjin	1017–1020
Jian	1021–1023
Manju	1024–1027
Chogen	1028–1036
Choreki	1037–1039
Chokyu	1040–1043
Kantoku	1044–1045
Eisho	1046–1052
Tenki	1053–1057
Kohei	1058–1064
Chiryaku	1065–1068
Enkyu	1069–1073
Shoho	1074–1076
Shoreki	1077–1080
Eiho	1081–1083
Otoku	1084–1086
Kanji	1087–1093
Kaho	1094–1095
Eicho	1096
Shotoku	1097–1098
Kowa	1099–1103
Choji	1104–1105
Kasho	1106–1107
Tennin	1108–1109
Ten-ei	1110–1112
Eikyu	1113–1117
Gen-ei	1118–1119
Hoan	1120–1123
Tenji	1124–1125
Daiji	1126–1130
Tensho	1131
Chosho	1132–1134
Hoan	1135–1140
Eiji	1141
Koji	1142–1143
Tenyo	1144
Kyuan	1145–1150
Nimpei	1151–1153
Kyuji	1154–1155
Hogen	1156–1158
Heiji	1159
Eiryaku	1160
Oho	1161–1162
Chokan	1163–1164
Eiman	1165
Nin-an	1166–1168
Kao	1169–1170
Shoan	1171–1174
Angen	1175–1176
Chisho	1177–1180
Yowa	1181
Juei	1182–1183
Genryaku	1184
Bunji	1185–1189
Kenkyu	1190–1198
Shoji	1199–1200
Kennin	1201–1203
Genkyu	1204–1205
Ken-ei	1206
Shogen	1207–1210

Continued

Kenryaku	1211–1212
Kempo	1213–1218
Shokyu	1219–1221
Teio	1222–1223
Gennin	1224
Karoku	1225–1226
Antei	1227–1228
Kanki	1229–1231
Teiei	1232
Tempuku	1233
Bunreki	1234
Katei	1235–1237
Rekinin	1238
En-o	1239
Jinji	1240–1242
Kangen	1243–1246
Hoji	1247–1248
Kencho	1249–1255
Kogen	1256
Shoka	1257–1258
Shogen	1259
Bun-o	1260
Kocho	1261–1263
Bun-ei	1264–1274
Kenji	1275–1277
Koan	1278–1287
Shoo	1288–1292
Einin	1293–1298
Shoan	1299–1301
Kangen	1302
Kagen	1303–1305
Tokuji	1306–1307
Enkei	1308–1310
Ocho	1311
Showa	1312–1316
Bumpo	1317–1318
Gen-o	1319–1320
Genkyo	1321–1323
Shochu	1324–1325
Kareki	1326–1328
Gentoku	1329–1330
Genko	1331–1333
Kemmu	1334–1335
Engen	1336–1339
Kokoku	1340–1345
Teiwashohei	1346–1369
Kentoku	1370–1371
Bunchu	1372–1374
Tenju	1375–1380
Kowa	1381–1383
Genchu	1384–1392
Meitoku	1393
Oei	1394–1427

Northern court

Shokei	1332–1333
Rekio	1338–1341
Koei	1342–1344
Teiwa	1345–1349
Kan-o	1350–1351
Bunna	1352–1355
Embun	1356–1360
Koan	1361
Teiji	1362–1367
Oan	1368–1374
Eiwa	1375–1378
Koreki	1379–1380
Eitoku	1381–1383
Shitoku	1384–1386

Continued

Kakei	1387–1388
Ko-o	1389
Meitoku	1390–1392

Shocho	1428
Eikyo	1429–1440
Kakichi	1441–1443
Bun-an	1444–1448
Hotoku	1449–1451
Kyotoku	1452–1454
Kosho	1455–1456
Choroku	1457–1459
Kansei	1460–1465
Bunsho	1466
Onin	1467–1468
Bummei	1469–1486
Chokyo	1487–1488
Entoku	1489–1491
Meio	1492–1500
Bunki	1501–1503
Eisho	1504–1520
Taiei	1521–1527
Kyoroku	1528–1531
Tembun	1532–1554
Koji	1555–1557
Eiroku	1558–1569
Genki	1570–1572
Tensho	1573–1591
Bunroku	1592–1595
Keicho	1596–1614
Genna	1615–1623
Kan-ei	1624–1643
Shoho	1644–1647
Keian	1648–1651
Shoo	1652–1654
Meireki	1655–1657
Manji	1658–1660
Kambun	1661–1672
Empo	1673–1680
Tenwa	1681–1683
Teikyo	1684–1687
Genroku	1688–1703
Hoei	1704–1710
Shotoku	1711–1715
Kyoho	1716–1735
Gembun	1736–1740
Kampo	1741–1743
Enkyo	1744–1747
Kan-en	1748–1750
Horeki	1751–1763
Meiwa	1764–1771
An-ei	1772–1780
Temmei	1781–1788
Kansei	1789–1800
Kyowa	1801–1803
Bunka	1804–1817
Bunsei	1818–1829
Tempo	1830–1843
Koka	1844–1847
Kaei	1848–1853
Ansei	1854–1859
Man-en	1860
Bunkyu	1861–1863
Genji	1864
Keio	1865–1867
Meiji	1868–1911
Taisho	1912–1925
Showa	1926–

SCHOOLS IN FEUDAL JAPAN

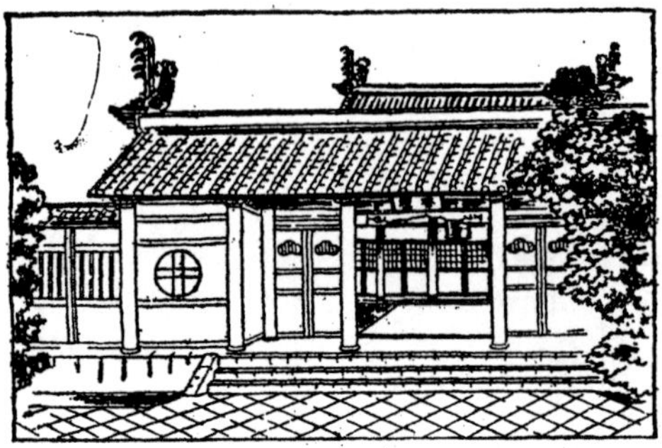

Seido (Sacred Hall)

The first school in Japan made its appearance in 663 A.D., the first law of education enacted in 701, A.D. when Daigaku (lit. great learning) was founded at the Imperial Capital for educating the sons of the courtiers above the fifth court-rank, while Kokugaku (lit. local learning) was established for the benefit of the children of the local chiefs and governors. The central school had a capacity for admitting 400 students, but the local ones accommodated no more than twenty to fifty; the school-age for both the institutes being thirteen to sixteen years of age. Classics, history, law and mathematics were the subjects taught at Daigaku, which had rice-fields attached to it for raising necessary provisions for its expenses. Soon several private schools made their appearance, such as Kobun-in, Kangaku-in, Junna-in, Shogaku-in, etc.

During the Kamakura days (1186–1333), when the military art was considered to be more important than civil learning in general, schools were in the state of being much neglected. But learning was resuscitated a great deal during the Ashikaga regime (1338–1573), when the Ashikaga School played an important role in the education of the warriors and courtiers. Yoshimitsu Ashikaga was the President of the Junna-in and Shogaku-in schools.

Iyeyasu, founder of the Tokugawa Shogunate, promoted learning among all the clans of the country, and a Government school was established at Fushimi, near Kyoto, and another at Shinobu-ga-Oka, Edo, which was his Shogunate Capital (now Tokyo). The latter, which was later removed to Yushima, was called the Seido (lit. Sacred Hall), where Chinese classics and Confucianism were exclusively taught. It was a Confucian school during our feudal days, and it still stands at Yushima, Bunkyo-ku in Tokyo, though it is now nothing but a memorial hall for Confucius and Confucianism.

Continued

During the Tokugawa dynasty (1603-1867), every local clan had a school for instructing its samurai-children at the expenses of the clan government. Besides, there was a small class of learning, known by the popular name of Terakoya (temple-school), where the sons of the people in general received lessons in the 3 R's.

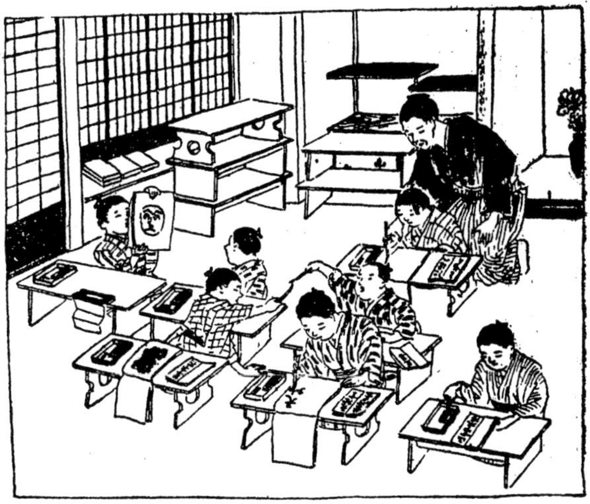

Terakoya or temple-school

Generally speaking, the samurai, priests and physicians belonged to the intelligentsia classes of people in our feudal days, and the first-mentioned, in particular, considered it to be a great shame to be illiterate, so that most of our samurai of old were scholars.

On March 14th, 1868, the Emperor Meiji proclaimed the Imperial oath of five articles, one of which reads in part: "Seek knowledge far and wide in the world," thus laying the fundamental principles for modern education in Japan. In 1871 the Department of Education was founded in the Imperial Government and in the following year the national system of education was reorganized. But the national policy of education was laid by the Imperial Rescript on Education, which was proclaimed by the Emperor Meiji on Oct. 30, 1890. This Rescript was read in every school in the Empire at all important national festivals, in the prewar days, although it is now nullified under the New Constitution adopted in the postwar days.

KANA, THE JAPANESE ALPHABET

While the ideograms of Chinese invention are used in China, Japan and Korea, the Japanese language employs Kana or the syllabic alphabet of Japanese origin as particles to express the inflection, declension and other grammatical changes of the parts of speech.

"Kana", which, according to some scholars, is a perversion of the Sanscrit "Karana" (letter), is expressed in the Japanese language by two Chinese characters (假名), meaning "temporary name (or letter)" and it is so called in contrast to Mana (眞名), which, meaning "true name (or letter)", designates the complicate and elaborate Chinese characters that constitute the main part of the written Japanese language.

Kana has two kinds; namely, Kata-kana and Hira-kana. The former, written in a stiff or square form has fifty (or fifty-one inclusive of "n") syllabic letters, and hence it is also called the "Goju-on" (or fifty-sounds). It is said that Kibi-no-Mabi, who lived in the 8th century, invented this alphabet after his return from China, where he stayed for study for several years. "Kata" means "side" and each of the Kata-kana letters was invented by adopting one side, or part, of a Chinese character. The first letter (ア) pronounced "a", for instance, is adopted from the left-hand side of the Chinese character 阿, also pronounced "a"; the second letter (イ) is taken from the Chinese ideogram (伊) pronounced "i"; ウ, the third letter, is taken from the top of the Chinese (宇) pronounced "u"; and so on. In this way every letter of the Kata-kana letters is taken from a Chinese character. They are arranged in the order of "a, i, u, e and o", with the consonant sounds of k(g), s(z), t(d), n, h(b and p), m, y, r and w combined with the vowels.

Hira-kana or plain-kana is written in a script or running style. It is considered to be a simplified form of Chinese characters. This alphabet, also syllabic, consists of forty-seven (or forty-eight inclusive of "n") letters and is attributed to the invention of Priest Kobo, who arranged the letters in the present order. Translated, this alphabet has the following Buddhist idea:

Hira-Gana	Meaning
I-ro-ha-ni-ho-he-to	Fragrant though bright flowers are,
chi-ri-nu-ru-wo	Nethertheless they scatter;
wa-ka-yo-ta-re-so	Who in this world
tsu-ne-na-ra-mu	Remains unchanged?
u-i-no-o-ku-ya-ma	The deep mountains of viscistudes ever
ke-fu-ko-e-te	changing, which we crossing to-day
a-sa-ki-yu-me-mi-shi	Evanescent dreams will be seen no more,
e-hi-mo-se-su	Nor shall we drink too deep.

Continued

Kata-kana Letters

ア	イ	ウ	エ	オ	ハ	ヒ	フ	ヘ	ホ
(a)	(i)	(u)	(e)	(o)	(ha)	(hi)	(fu)	(he)	(ho)
カ	キ	ク	ケ	コ	マ	ミ	ム	メ	モ
(ka)	(ki)	(ku)	(ke)	(ko)	(ma)	(mi)	(mu)	(me)	(mo)
サ	シ	ス	セ	ソ	ヤ	ヰ	ユ	エ	ヨ
(sa)	(shi)	(su)	(se)	(so)	(ya)	(i)	(yu)	(ye)	(yo)
タ	チ	ツ	テ	ト	ラ	リ	ル	レ	ロ
(ta)	(chi)	(tsu)	(te)	(to)	(ra)	(ri)	(ru)	(re)	(ro)
ナ	ニ	ヌ	ネ	ノ	ワ	ヰ	ウ	ヱ	ヲ
(na)	(ni)	(nu)	(ne)	(no)	(wa)	(wi)	(u)	(e)	(wo)
					ン				
					(n)				

Read "a" to "o", "ka" to "ko", "sa" to "so" and so on to end with "n"

Flat Sounds

ガ	ギ	グ	ゲ	ゴ	バ	ビ	ブ	ベ	ボ
(ga)	(gi)	(gu)	(ge)	(go)	(ba)	(bi)	(bu)	(be)	(bo)
ザ	ジ	ズ	ゼ	ゾ					
(za)	(ji)	(dzu)	(ze)	(zo)					
ダ	ヂ		デ	ド	パ	ピ	プ	ペ	ポ
(da)	(ji)	(dzu)	(de)	(do)	(pa)	(pi)	(pu)	(pe)	(po)

Read "ga" to "go", "za" to "zo and so on to end with "po"

Hira-kana Letters

い	ろ	は	に	ほ	へ	と	ち	り	ぬ
(i)	(ro)	(ha)	(ni)	(ho)	(he)	(to)	(chi)	(ri)	(nu)
る	を	わ	か	よ	た	れ	そ	つ	ね
(ru)	(wo)	(wa)	(ka)	(yo)	(ta)	(re)	(so)	(tsu)	(ne)
な	ら	む	う	ゐ	の	お	く	や	ま
(na)	(ra)	(mu)	(u)	(wi)	(no)	(o)	(ku)	(ya)	(ma)
け	ふ	こ	え	て	あ	さ	き	ゆ	め
(ke)	(fu)	(ko)	(e)	(te)	(a)	(sa)	(ki)	(yu)	(me)
み	し	ゑ	ひ	も	せ	す	ん		
(mi)	(shi)	(we)	(hi)	(mo)	(se)	(su)	(n)		

ば	ぱ	ぼ	ぽ	べ	ぺ	ど	ぢ	が
(ba)	(pa)	(bo)	(po)	(be)	(pe)	(do)	(ji)	(ga)
だ	ぞ	づ	ぐ	げ	ぶ	ぷ	ご	で
(da)	(zo)	(dzu)	(gu)	(ge)	(bu)	(pu)	(go)	(de)
ざ	ぎ	じ	び	ぴ	ぜ	ず		
(za)	(gi)	(ji)	(bi)	(pi)	(ze)	(dzu)		

(1) The flat sounds are expressed by putting two dots on the right-hand upper corner of the letters.

(2) Read "i" to "nu", "ru" to "ne" and so on to end with "n"

The Chinese Ideographs in the Japanese Language

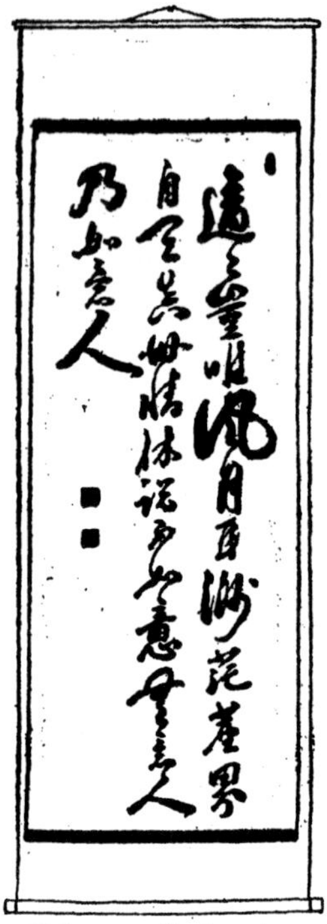

Kakemono (lit. hanging scroll) of calligraphic writings

The history of Japan began with the enthronement in 660 B. C. of Jimmu, the first Emperor of the Imperial line, but the *Kojiki*, the *Nihon-shoki* and the *Kogo-shui*, the oldest annals of the country, go back much earlier by hundreds or even thousands of years. And yet Japan is not found in the state of savagism or barbarism, but, on the contrary, she was a much civilized country if we judge by what is brought to light from under the ground or ancient graves. It is very possible and even probable, therefore, that Japan had some letters of her own invention, and some scholars hold that she had a kind of syllabic letters called the Jindai-moji (lit. god-days letters) as we still see in the charms issued by the Shinto shrines, though they seem to have little authenticity for their prehistoric existence.

In default of letters or characters of her own originality, Japan borrowed the ideographs of Chinese origin to express her own language. They are called "Kan-ji" (lit. letters of the Kan or Han dynasty) and are universally used in Japan together with Kana, or syllabic letters, of her later invention. These Chinese characters are used by the Chinese, Japanese and Koreans, but, strange to say, these peoples pronounce or read each Chinese ideograph in different ways, with the same meaning.

The Chinese ideographs were introduced to Japan for the first time in 284 A. D., and after that they were brought over to Japan through various geographical and chronological channels, till they were inseparably intermingled with the Japanese language. Consequently, every ideograph, now in use in Japan, has two or more different pronunciations, making it terribly hard for a foreigner to master Japanese, which is usually expressed in Chinese ideographs. Many linguists say that the Japanese language is the hardest to master in the world and this is why, while many foreigners speak Japanese as fluently and correctly as does a native, few have as yet mastered the written language of the Japanese in reading and much less in writing it.

According to the *Gyokuhen* (a dictionary), the Chinese ideographs number 22,726, while the *Koki-jiten*, (another dictionary) has 42,174 ideographs and the *Kaibe* 55,425. There are a few ideographs of Japanese invention expressing some things indigenous to Japan.

JINDAI-MOJI OR PREHISTORIC LETTERS

"Did Japan have no letters of her originality before the Chinese characters, now in use, were introduced?" Such is a question often asked by a foreign tourist, and it is a reasonable one in view of the civilization that Japan seems to have had during her prehistoric or ancient days; the Emperor Jimmu, founder of the Imperial dynasty, having been enthroned, (as no monarch of Japan was crowned), 660 years before the Christian era, though Japanese history is of much older origin if the Jindai (literally, gods' days) is included. It is, therefore, more probable than otherwise that Japan had letters of some kind that she invented before the introduction of the Chinese ideographs.

As a matter of fact, Japan had and still has letters, which are known as the Jindai-moji (lit. gods' day letters) or prehistoric letters. So entirely different from the ordinary letters found in Japan, that they are all but unintelligible to most Japanese. They are found chiefly on the O-Fuda (lit. honourable-card), (erroneously translated "amulet" or "charm"), issued by the Shinto shrine. Scholars assert that the use of the Jindai-moji was restricted to the Imperial family during the prehistoric days, and that, as they now are, they were employed to designate the name of the deity venerated in the shrine which issues the O-Fuda. These letters, however, seem to have become obsolete with the introduction of the Chinese characters during the reign of the Emperor Ohjin (the 15th), although they are still extensively used by the Shinto shrines on their O-Fuda. The pious Japanese, however, it may be added, never try to open any O-Fuda, much less to try to read the letters written on it.

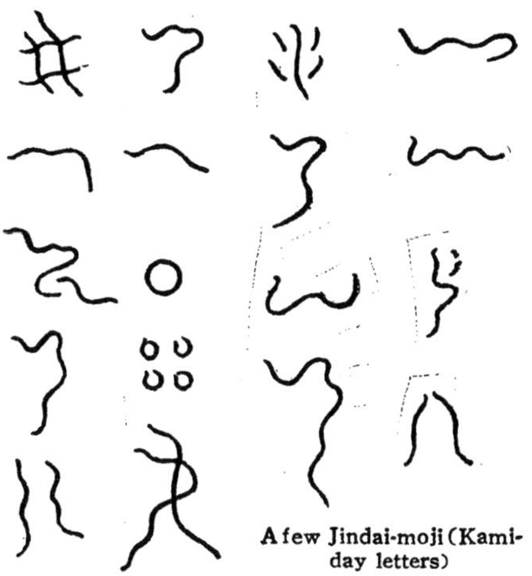

A few Jindai-moji (Kami-day letters)

Kana: Japan has two sets of Kana or syllabic alphabets. Each set consists of simplified letters, as they are now believed, taken from characters of Chinese origin, but nevertheless they are called Kana (假名) meaning "temporary name" instead of Kaji (假字) or temporary letters, as they should be called with more propriety if they are of temporary use. Some Shinto priests, however, explain this paradoism in this way that the present Kana (or temporary name) was used "temporarily" in place of the Jindai-moji, which were employed to designate the names of the deities in the prehistoric days. According to these Shinto scholars, Kana is not "temporary or simplified letters," but they have been perverted to their present form from some of the Jindai-moji letters.

The Japanese Names of the Twelve Months

Some months of the year are in the English language named after deities, like January from Janus, March from Mars, May from Maie and June from Juno, although the other months are erroneously numbered, like October indicating the tenth month, instead of the eighth, and December for the twelfth month, instead of the tenth month. But all the twelve months of the year are numbered in the Japanese language, as follows:

English	Japanese	Literal meaning
January	Ichi-gatsu	one-month (first)
February	Ni-gatsu	two-month (second)
March	San-gatsu	three-month (third)
April	Shi-gatsu	four-month (fourth)
May	Go-gatsu	five-month (fifth)
June	Roku-gatsu	six-month (sixth)
July	Shichi-gatsu	seven-month (seventh)
August	Hachi-gatsu	eight-month (eighth)
September	Ku-gatsu	nine-month (ninth)
October	Ju-gatsu	ten-month (tenth)
November	Juichi-gatsu	eleven-month (eleventh)
December	Juni-gatsu	twelve-month (twelfth)

But in literary writings or specially poetry, the following names are often used for the twelve months of the year:—

English	Japanese	Meaning
January	Mu-tsuki	social-month
February	Kisaragi	put-more-dress-on
March	Yayoi	more-growth (because plants grow and grow in this month)
April	U-tsuki	month of U-flowers (deutzia scabia)
May	Sa-tsuki	month of early rice-ears
June	Mina-tsuki	no-water month, (but possibly corrupted from "full-water month")
July	Fu-tsuki	literary month, or month for reading
August	Ha-tsuki	month of leaves, (possibly month for leaves to fall off)
September	Naga-tsuki	long-month (possibly long-night-month)

Continued

October	Kamina-tsuki	no-god month, as the gods are said to meet at the Izumo shrine to discuss the marriage of all young ones in Japan
November	Shimo-tsuki	frost month
December	Shiwasu	all-ending (month)

Floral Calendar

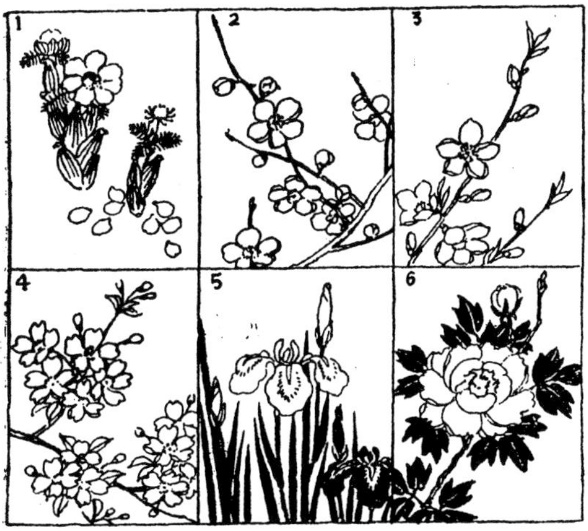

(1) January: adnis
(2) February: plum
(3) March: peach
(4) April: cherry
(5) May: iris
(6) June: peony

(7) July: morning-glory
(8) August: lespedeza
(9) September: chrysanthemum
(10) October: hibiscus
(11) November: camellia
(12) December: narcissus

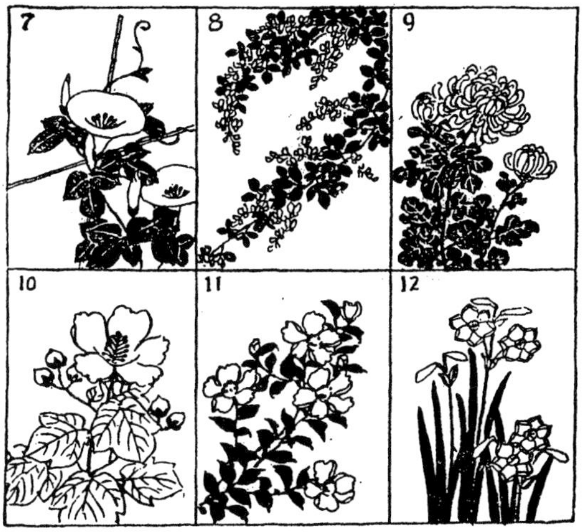

Typical flowers of twelve months

THE THIRTEEN NATIONAL PARKS OF JAPAN

The selection of national parks, which was startcd by the Home Department in 1934, was completed in February, 1936, by specifying twelve national parks in Japan with one later addition. They scatter from the Hokkaido in the north to Kyushu in the south. Here is a brief description of the thirteen national parks:

Fuji-Hakone National Park

Area: about 71,751 hectares

Situation: Shizuoka, Yamanashi and Kanagawa Prefectures, with Mt. Fuji and the Hakone Hot Spa District as its center.

Approaches: Otsuki station of the Chuosen Railway; Kofu Station, the same line, Fuji Station of the Tokaido Railway Line and Gotemba of the Gotemba Railway Line.

Akan National Park

Area: about 87,498 hectares

Situation: Kushiro and Kitami Provinces, Hokkaido, with Lake Akan as its beauty center.

Approaches: Abashiri Railway Line, Kushiro-Honsen Railway Line, Kitami Aioi Railway Line, etc.

Daisetsuzan National Park

Area: about 231,929 hectares

Situation: Ishikari, Sorachi and Tokatsu Provinces, Hokkaido

Approaches: Asahikawa City, Kamifurano and Obihiro.

Towada National Park

Area: 82,862 hectares

Situation: Aomori and Akita Prefectures, with Lake Towada as its scenic center.

Approaches: Aomori City, Komagi Station, Tohoku-Honsen Railway Line, Sannohe and Gonohe Stations the same railway Line

Nikko National Park

Area: about 56,923 hectares

Situation: Niigata, Gumma, Tochigi and Fukushima Prefectures, with Nikko as its scenic center.

Approaches: Nikko City, Numata, Wakamatsu and Aizu of the Joetsu Railway Line.

Continued

Central Mountains National Park

Area: 169,768 hectares

Situation: Niigata, Nagano, Toyama and Gifu Prefectures

Approaches: Matsumoto Station of the Chuosen Railway Line, Toyama Station of the Hokuriku Honsen Railway Line and Takayama Station of the Takayama Railway Line

Yoshino-Kumano National Park

Area: about 55,086 hectares

Situation: Nara, Miye and Wakayama Prefectures.

Approaches: Osaka City, by rail or by sea.

Setouchi or Inland Sea National Park

Area: 184,600 hectares inclusive of land and sea

Situation: Okayama, Hiroshima and Kagawa Prefectures.

Approaches: Being the only sea-park in Japan, can be reached by rail or ship.

Aso National Park

Area: about 67,827 hectares

Situation: Kumamoto and Oita Prefectures.

Approaches: Oita, Beppu, Nakatsu, Kurume and Kumamoto.

Unzen National Park

Area: about 13,029 hectares

Situation: Nagasaki Prefecture.

Approaches: Can be reached from many different directions especially from Shimabara, in the east, Chichiishi in the west and Obama hot spa.

Kirishima National Park

Area: about 21,560 hectares

Situation: Miyazaki and Kagoshima Prefectures, with Mt. Takachiho as its scenic center.

Approaches: Miyazaki City and Kagoshima City.

Daisen National Park

Area: about 12,403 hectares

Situation: Tottori Prefecture; the only national park on the Japan Sea side.

Approaches: Daisenguchi Station of the San-in Honsen Railway Line and Daisen Station of the Hakubi Railway Line

Ise-Shima National Park

Area 52,036 hectares

Situation: Ise Province, where the Ise Shinto shrines are situated.

Approaches: Sangu Line.

PRAYING FOR THE ENEMY

Foes cared for as well as friends

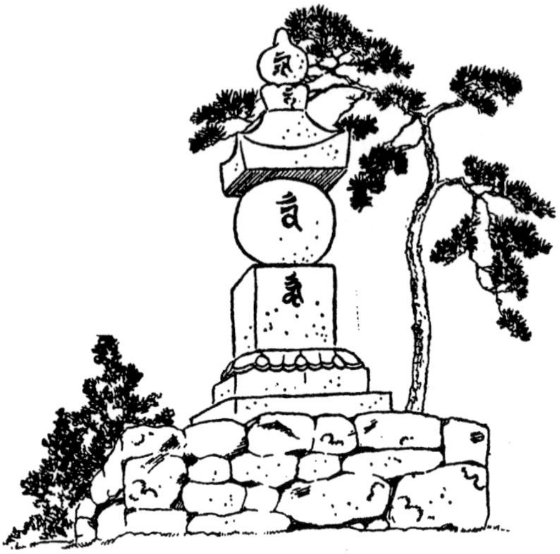

Stone-monument dedicated to friends and foes

The Ear-Shrine: In 1056 Yoriyoshi Minamoto, a court-warrior, was despatched by the Emperor Goreizei to tranquilize a rebellion that was raised by Yoritoki Abe, and his two sons, Sadato and Muneto, in the northern part of Japan. On his triumphal return in 1064, Yoriyoshi brought two skin-baskets containing many dried ears that were taken one each from those who fell on the enemy's side during the war, instead of their heads as was the custom in our feudal days. These ears were buried with Buddhist rites in the Seido-in Temple at Rokujo, Kyoto, and Yoriyoshi enshrined a life-size image of Buddha in a small shrine dedicated to the ears buried under it.

The Ear-Mound: Early in the Japanese invasion of Korea, 1592–1598, the heads of all the Koreans killed in battle were brought over to Japan for inspection, for it was a common practice for every samurai in our feudal days to present, for inspection of his master or lord, all the heads that he took in battle. Later on, in the war, however, the Japanese troops in Korea sent home the noses of Koreans they killed. In 1597 Hideyoshi Toyotomi buried these noses in the Hoko-ji Temple, Kyoto, and great Buddhist services were held to offer a prayer for the peaceful repose of these ill-fated Koreans The monument erected over the buried noses is now known, by mistake, as the Ear-Mound, and it is one of the chief attractions for tourists in Kyoto.

The foes-and-friends-equally-fed monument: In the compounds of the Yugyo-ji Temple at Fujisawa in Kanagawa Prefecture, there stands an antiquated monument a few feet high. It is called the Onshu-Byodo-Kuyo-Hi or Foes-and-friends-equally-fed Monument and it was erected to offer a prayer for the repose of those fallen on both sides in a battle in 1416. Priest Son-ei, or Yugyo-Shonin XV, who, being a religionist, stood neutral like the Red Cross people and erected the monument so that the battle-dead might have a peaceful repose. The monument is specified as a national sovenir by the Government of Kanagawa Prefecture.

THE JAPANESE AS A RELIGIOUS PEOPLE

The Japanese are considered to be extremely religious, and no wonder they are so considered, judging from the way they live. They believe in "Ten" (Heaven), both cosmic and spiritual, and every inevitable occurrence is piously and resignedly attributed to the power of Heaven, though, it may be added, their conception of Heaven is anything but vague. When you see a small grove of trees along a railway line, you are sure to find Torii, for there is a shrine in it. Japan has over a hundred thousand Shinto shrines and a little fewer Buddhist temples, which the pious people visit regularly once or twice a month. It is a remarkable fact, however, that the Japanese visit the shrines and temples more to pay their respects to the deities venerated there than to offer a prayer for anything.

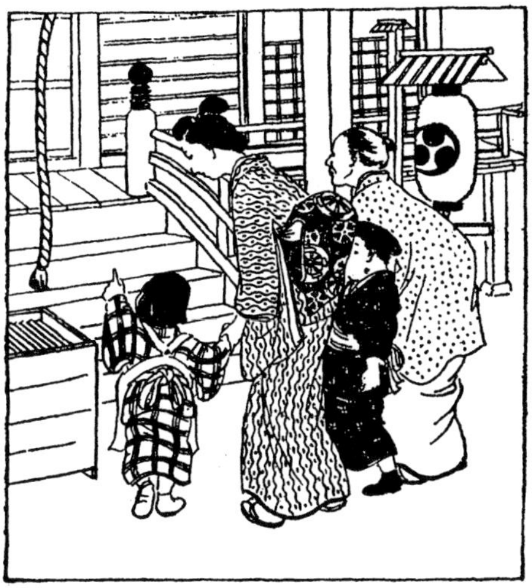

Visit to Shinto shrine

Family altar: Almost every orthodox Japanese family has a family-altar, either Shintoitic or Buddhist, and very often both altars, in one house and each member pays his respects to them every morning, the first thing to be done after the teeth are brushed and the face is washed in the morning.

Charm: Many a child has an O-Mamori (lit. honorable protection) or charm on its body, for it is believed to protect its bearer in representation of the deity of the shrine or temple which issues it. Almost all motor-cars in Japan have a charm against a crush.

Miyamairi: When a baby is 31 or 32 days old, it is taken to its tutelary shrine and committed to the protection and patronage of its deity. In November every year, a boy and girl, who are three, five or seven years old, are taken to their respective tutelary shrines. These visits of shrines are called Miyamairi (shrine-visit).

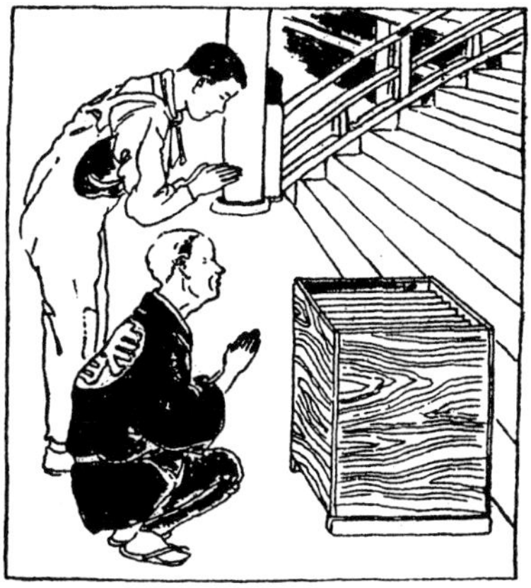

Worshipping before shrine

Continued

Shinto Palanquin: At the festival of each shrine of Shintoism, its palanquin or portable shrine makes its rounds along the streets of its parish, so that the parishioners may be blessed by the deity who is symbolically represented by a Nigite (paper offering) or some other Shinto article in the palanquin. The procession of the palanquin is a great occasion at each festival.

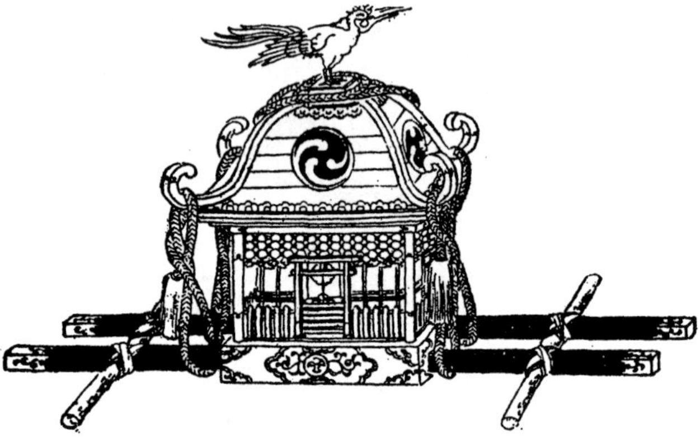

Palanquin, a portable shrine

Direction-stone: One will notice a stone standing at every important fork of a local highway in Japan. The stone is a pointer or direction-stone indicating the way to a village to the left and to the right. But on the front side the stone has the name of a deity, either Shintoist or Buddhist, for the wayfaring pedestrian is thus piously committed to the kind care of the deity represented by the stone. The names of Priest Kobo, Kannon (Goddess of Mercy), etc. are very commonly engraven on the stones.

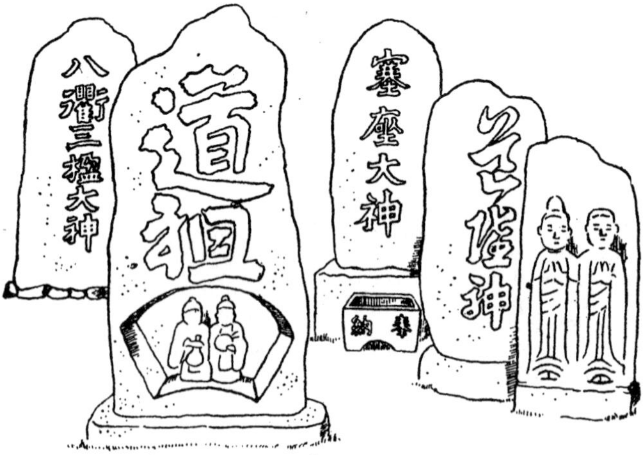

Roadside direction-stones

SECRET OF JAPAN'S PROGRESS

"What is the secret of the great progress that Japan has made in such a short space of time, since Commodore Perry visited Japan in 1853 ?" is a question that is asked by ever so many foreign tourists who are surprised at the prodigious progress that Japan has since made in civilization.

In the first place, it is a mistake to think that Japan's civilization has been effected in so short a space of time. It is based upon the preparation that she made during the Tokugawa regime, during which she was apparently in a state of dormancy, by closing her doors against foreign intercourses. During that period, when Japan was in peace and tranquility, the local clans vied with one another in every line of culture. In no other periods of her history did Japan make a greater progress in art, literature and industry, than she did in the feudal days of Tokugawa, excepting of course the Meiji and its subsequent eras. In this sense feudalism did real blessings on Japan, for her present culture had its foundation laid during our feudal days.

In the second place, Japan has a longer history to support her civilization than is generally supposed by foreigners. It seems that Japan was much advanced in civilization and culture in her pre-historic days, and she has not attained her present civilization in a short time, but it is based on, and backed by, a long history of some two thousand years.

This much said, we come to the secret of Japan's great progress. It is usually attributed to the typical characteristics of the Japanese people; such as loyalty, patriotism, devotion, energy, efficiency, etc. These characteristics will well apply to the Japanese for the stupendous stride that Japan has made, for certainly the Japanese are loyal, patriotic, devoted, energetic and efficient, and the great progress of Japan is well attributed to these typical attributes of the Japanese nation.

In the feudal days of Japan, it was the ambition of every samurai or warrior to serve his lord better than did any of his fellow-samurai, and every local lord made efforts to stand higher in the favour of the Shogun and the Emperor than did any other lords in the country. Now that she has entered the world-arena, it is her greatest ambition to be better than the best in the world in any line of culture. In the prewar days the world charged Japan with exporting commodities cheaper than their manufactures would cost in other countries. She was not dumping them at all, but, on the contrary, she endeavoured to supply the world with cheaper articles than were supplied by any other countries in the world. In art, science, literature, trade, industry and what-not does every single Japanese aspire to stand higher in his own profession and occupation than anybody else, and in her effort to be better than the best lies indeed the secret of the great progress that Japan has made and will make to rise up from her defeated ruins.

JISEI OR DEATH-BED ODE

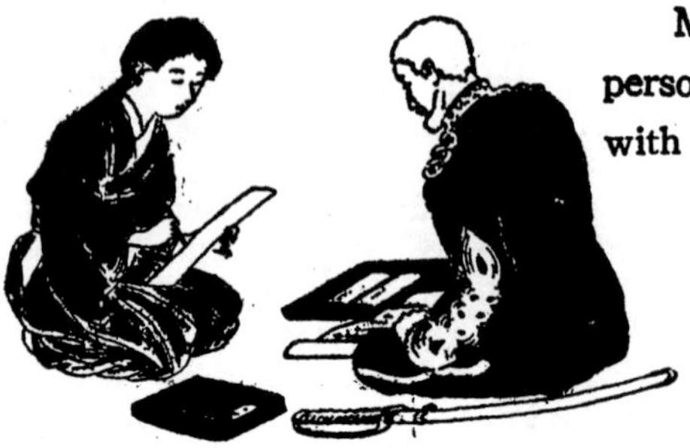

Nogi and his wife writing their Jisei

Maresuke Nogi, a man of great personality, served most loyally with the Emperor Meiji, whose favorite he was, and he thought that his work was over with the death of the Emperor, which took place on July 30, 1912. On Sept. 13, on which the Imperial cortege was to depart from the Imperial Palace, Tokyo, for Kyoto, where his funeral services were to be observed, when a signal was fired at 8 p.m. to announce its departure from the Palace, Nogi and his wife killed themselves at their private residence; he committing harakiri with a sword after the classical manner of an old samurai, while his wife died by cutting her throat with a dagger in the same way that our feudal lady of old did when she committed suicide. Nogi and his wife left a Jisei (death-bed ode) each, which runs as follows:—

"Utsushi-yo wo
Kami-sari mashishi
Oh-kimi no
Ato wo shitaite
Ware wa yuku-nari"—Nogi

(Free translation: Following the foot-steps of the Great Lord, who has departed from the transient world to join the gods, I go.)

"Ide mashite
Kaeri-masu Hi no
Nashi to kiku
Kyo no Miyuki ni
Au zo kanashiki"—Mrs. Nogi

(Free translation: It is sad to see the Emperor proceed today on a trip from which I am told he will on no day return.)

"Jisei", which literally means "taking leave of the world", is an

Continued

ode of 31 or 17 syllables that a dying man or woman improvises at the last moment. Life is compared in this country to the short-lived cherry-blossoms that fall off in three days, and the Japanese are trained to stare death in the face with perfect calm. So they consider it a shame to be flurried in their last hours, but try to be calm enough to compose a Jisei in the face of death. Our history is full of such Jisei-odes written by dying men. To give one or two more:

Ujisato Gamo, lord of Aizu, was falsely accused by Mitsunari Ishida, who was jealous of his growing influence, and Gamo was served with poisoned tea by Hideyoshi Toyotomi, his master. He was aware of the dark attempt on his life, but he swallowed the tea with perfect calm, leaving a Jisei:—

"Kagiri areba
Fukanedo Hanawa
Chirumono wo
Kokoro mijikaki
Haru no Yama-kaze."

(Because the flowers are short-lived, they fall off without the wind blowing: how hasty and impatient the mountain-breeze of the spring is.)

Ujisato compared his life to the cherry-blossoms, and his short-tempered Hideyoshi to a mountain wind. He scorned at the short-temper of the latter.

Kaga-no-Chiyo, a famous poetess said in her Jisei: "Having viewed the moon, of all things, I say God-be-with-ye to the world."

Chiyo means that, as she has seen all beautiful things on earth and even the moon in the sky, she sees no need of staying in this world any longer, so she says good-bye to it.

Sokan, a poet, wrote a Jisei of 31 syllables, which reads in effect:

"Should any one enquire
Where Sokan has gone,
Tell that a small business
Has taken him to the life beyond."

REIGI OR ETIQUETTE

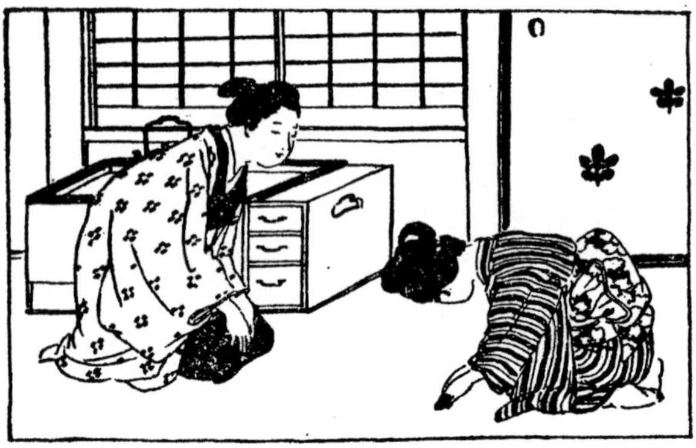

A girl bowing "Good morning," to her mother

Japan calls herself a land of etiquette, but in her case it is a sort of negative formalities. Instead of being told to do this or that, as the Golden Rule demands, the Japanese are trained not to act in such and such a way, " dont's " playing so much importance in Japanese etiquette. From their childhood the Japanese are told to control themselves in the expression of their " pleasure, anger, love and joy." At table the Japanese children are told to talk little, because talking at table is against good manners, though a meal-time is considered to be a most enjoyable time in a foreign home. It is ill-behaved, according to good manners, for a girl to give free vent to her opinion in the public, and especially in the presence of a superior has she to sit still and look as wise as an owl, without moving her eyes, not to say her head or hands. A Japanese girl will often return a smile, instead of an answer, when asked a question by a foreigner. She speaks with her lips half closed, for loud speaking is a sign of rude manners. If you give a seat to a Japanese visitor, for instance, you will be surprised at the number of times he has to be asked before

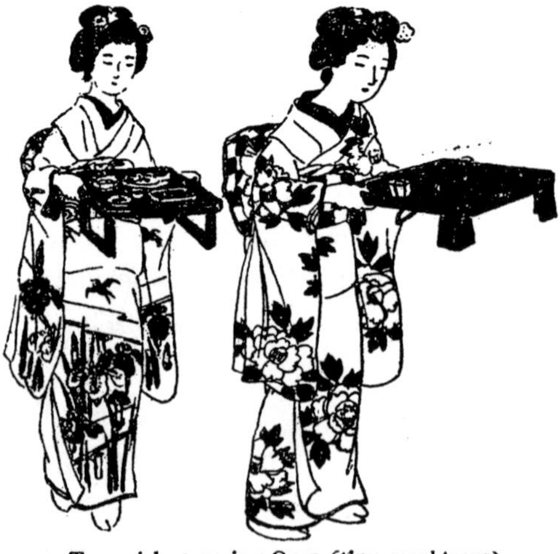

Two girls carrying Ozen (tiny meal-trays)

Continued

he gets seated, and he says it is in conformity with etiquette to decline several times. The Japanese are a polite people, and very hospitable, too. But politeness with them means much formality, which restricts the free actions of the people. According to good manners, there is no movement either of a hand or foot that is not governed by etiquette, for there is a form for sitting down or standing up, for opening or closing a door, (no girl will open a sliding-door standing, but she kneels down), for carrying a tray with something on, for handling chopsticks at table, for holding a bowl of rice or sipping tea when on a visit, for putting hands together on the floor-mat in bowing, so on and so forth.

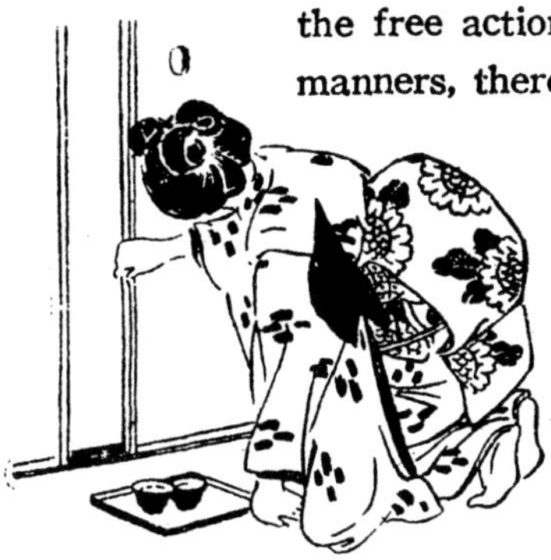

A girl opening a sliding-door on bent knees

But the present formality of etiquette is but an issue of our time-honoured discipline. From time immemorial the Japanese have been trained to maintain order in everything and trained themselves to keep in good order. Discipline often means discrimination with the Japanese, for it demands self-denial, obedience and reverence. "Should the father fail to act as such," our samurai of old was told, "the son must act as such; should the elder brother fail to act as such, the younger brother must act as such." This is absolute obedience to a senior and superior. Japan is strong as a fighting nation chiefly because her children are well disciplined and obedient, and etiquette or formality accounts a great deal for devotion the Japanese are known for. Their devotion will account more for their bravery in fighting than does anything else, although it is oftener blind than otherwise.

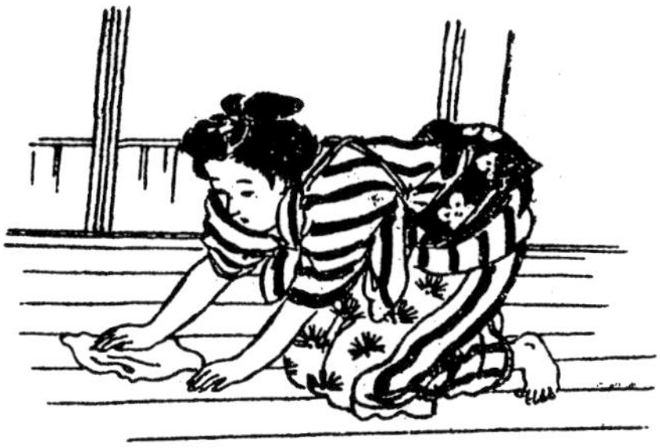

A maid wiping the floor

O-JIGI OR HONORABLE BOW

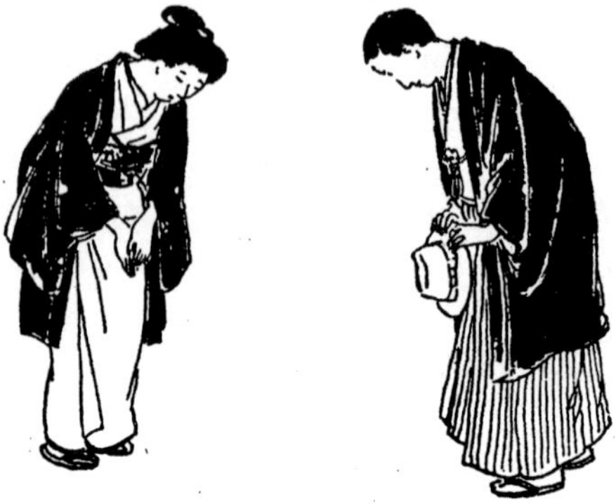

A full-dressed gentleman and lady bowing to each other

"How many times has one to bow in Japan?" is a question often asked by a foreign tourist. This is a matter of small wonder because our O-jigi (honorable bow), as a bow is called in the Japanese language, must look queer or funny to him, for, on meeting on the street, for instance, two Japanese, specially women, bend double for what appears to a foreigner to be a dozen times in greeting each other.

"How do you do, Miss Suzuki?" Mrs. Sato asks, and she bows, when the addressee bows low, too, saying "How do you do, Mrs. Sato?" or "I am well, thank you." "I missed the meeting you the other day", one says with an apologetic bow, and the other responds with "And we also missed you," also accompanied with a bow. "How is your baby? Is she all right now?" "She is all right, thank you." And both bow to each other. In this way do they bow for five or six times and even more for anything and everything they may have to thank or make an apology for.

The Japanese do not shake hands with each other for meeting or separation, no matter how long they have been separated or they are going to be separated, from each other. They are trained to suppress their emotions of joy or sorrow, which they express by a simple smile.

In a formal bow, in a house, the Japanese sit squarely in a Japanese style on the mat, with the tips of their forefingers and thumbs almost touching each other, while their faces bend over them. On the street, they bow by bending very low with their hands resting on the lap or knees.

Dogeza: In feudal days the Japanese commoners had to sit squarely on the ground when they met a local lord or other high dignitary on Daimyo-gyoretsu or feudal procession. This way of bowing on the ground was called Dogeza. In our bowing, either modern or feudal, the Japanese do not look each other in the face because their heads are bent low, while in the foreign manners they have to cast their eyes at each other.

MAN AND WIFE IN JAPAN

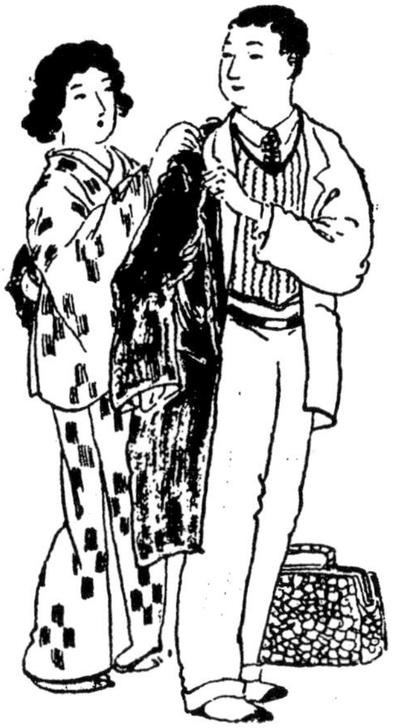

A wife helping her husband with his coat

"Man initiates and woman follows" is the principle that governs a Japanese home as well as the Japanese Empire. The husband rules, the wife obeying, and hen-pecking, or a curtain lecture, is considered, according to the precepts for women in this country, to be no more out of order than "the earth covering the Heaven." To a wife, her husband is "the heaven and lord". She addresses him "Anata" (lit. yonder-side) and speaks of him as "Taku" (lit. house) and "Shuji" (lit. master), while he calls her "Omae" (lit. honorable presence), a term usually used in addressing an inferior and mentions her, in talking or writing, as "Kanai" (lit. house-interior) or "Sai" (lit. wife). A Japanese wife refers to her husband as "Ryojin" (lit. good-man) in a letter or some other writings; he mentions her as "Gusai" (lit. stupid wife) on a similar occasion, simply on account of usage, though he does not mean it at all.

While in the West a wife walks in front, or side by side, or arm in arm, with her husband, standing on the principle of equality of man and wife, a Japanese wife does not usually walk before her husband, on principle, but she always lags behind, walking a step or two after him, simply

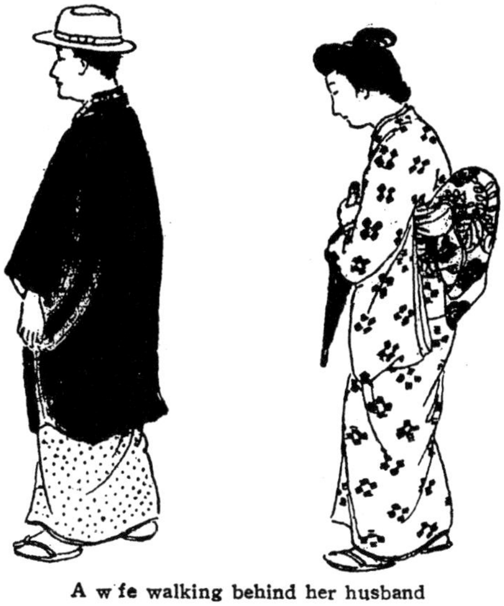

A wfe walking behind her husband

Continued

because she is trained from her childhood to be modest before the other sex and, in particular, her husband. Nor is our lady helped with her overcoat by her husband, who, on the contrary, is helped by her in putting on his coat or Haori. When you visit a Japanese home, it is always the mistress of the family that will help you with your overcoat, whether you be a man or woman.

We have a saying to the effect that "A sagacious woman causes her country to ruin" (Onna sagashiu-shite Kuni horobu), and the Japanese womanhood is governed by this saying. This is one reason why woman suffrage was not so popular in Japan before.

Formerly the bridegroom sat at the left-hand side of the bride at their wedding, for in this country the left, the positive, is regarded to be more important than the right. But nowadays he sits at the right-hand side of his bride, possibly under the influence of the West.

If a husband and a wife have two different hobbies or specialties, the former taking interest in science and the latter in music, for instance, chances are very often that the wife will give up her hobby to chime with his. She will often ignore her own interest before his. A Japanese wife is modest and most self-sacrificing and she makes nothing of herself in helping her husband.

In Japan marriage is usually attributed to En (or karma) or "cause and effect" and the Japanese have a faint belief in the preordination of marriage. Most Japanese do not get married through their own choice or selection, but they are contented with marriage arranged by their parents or friends. Love appears after marriage in Japan. Should a marriage prove unhappy, it will be put up with, becaue the couple believe that they are joined by some unseen power. Separation is usually quite foreign to married people in Japan, which has a low rate of divorces. We have a common saying to the effect that it is as much a shame for a girl to marry a second time as it is for samurai to serve two masters.

KOKO OR FILIAL PIETY

Filial piety is of no less prime importance in Japan than are loyalty and patriotism, for which the Japanese are reputed the world over. The *Kokyo* (lit. book of filial piety), which was one of the classical books that a samurai of old had to master, ranks filial duty as the first of all human virtues. The character 孝 for this virtue consists of 老 for "old age" and 子 for "child", the lower part of the former eclipsed or hidden, for the reason that an old man is supported by, or carried on the back of, his son. While in the West a young couple lives, as a rule, separated from its parents, a Japanese young man will live, after he gets married, with his parents, so that he may take care of them in their old age. So this virtue of filial duty was strongly emphasized by the lord of every locality in our feudal days.

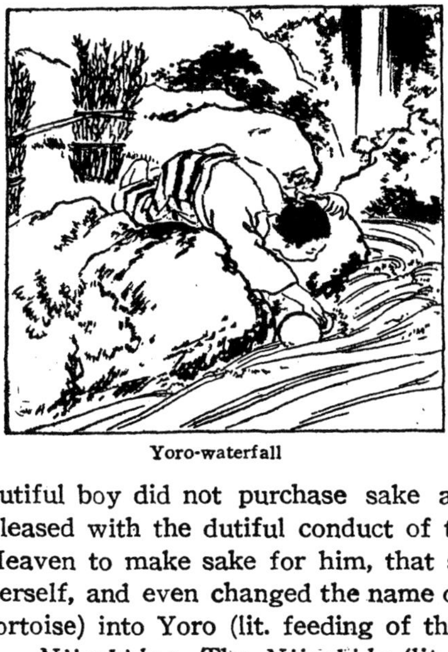
Yoro-waterfall

Yoro-no-Taki: During the reign of the Empress Genshō (44th) there lived a poor old farmer in the province of Mino. He was so fond of sake that, poor as he was, he could not live a single day without it, so that his young son bought it for him every day with what little money he earned by working for his neighbours. One day he, stumbling down, fell into a spring, the water of which tasted like sake, which he put into a container. The dutiful boy did not purchase sake any more. The Empress was so pleased with the dutiful conduct of the boy, who must have moved Heaven to make sake for him, that she visited the spring of water herself, and even changed the name of her era from Reiki (lit. sacred tortoise) into Yoro (lit. feeding of the old) in 717.

Nijushi-ko: The *Nijushi-ko* (lit. 24 dutiful sons) is a little book written by Kakukyogyo (Japanese pronunciation), a Chinese scholar of the Yuan dynasty, but its stories are so influentially inculcated upon the mind of the Japanese that the book may as well be called a Japanese. Here are a few of the more interesting stories of it.

Binson (Jap. pronunciation): Binson was a pupil of Confucius. His step-mother loved her two sons much better than him, but he made no complaints, always serving her very obediently. His father found

Continued

him shivering with cold in the winter because he was thinly clothed while his half-brothers were warmly clad, and he was going to divorce her for her discrimination in treating the three sons; when Binson said to his father: "Please do not send her away. I am all right so long as my brothers are warmly clad." The step-mother was moved and she mended her ways.

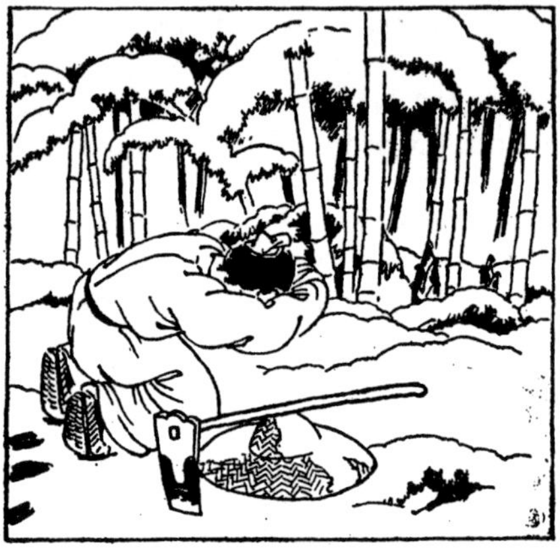

Moso praying for bamboos in winter

Moso: Moso had a sick old mother. She had lost her sense of taste, but always demanded nice food. He made no complaints, but he always tried to satisfy her wishes. One winter's day, his mother asked for a bamboo-shoot. Moso went out on the snow and prayed Heaven for a bamboo-shoot, when lo! a large one shot through deep snow before him. In Japan a large bamboo is called "Moso" after his name.

Oho: Oho had his father killed by the Emperor Wen of the Sa-kuo dynasty for giving a bit of advice. Oho never sat with his face turned towards the palace of the Emperor in resentment during his life-time. After the death of his father, he visited his grave every day and wept so hard that a tree growing near it was killed by his tears. After the death of his mother, who was afraid of a thunder, Oho visited her grave every time when a thunder pealed and shouted into it: "Mother, do not get afraid; for your son is beside you."

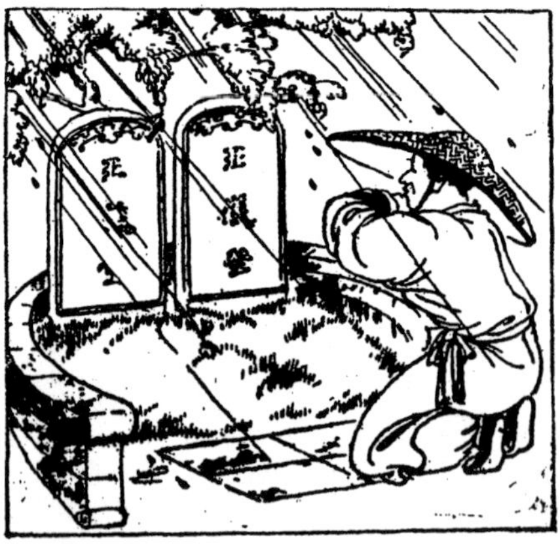

Oho visiting his parents' graves in a storm

Continued

Gomo: Gomo was such a dutiful child that, when his father was too poor to buy a mosquito-net in summer, Gomo, eight years old, stripped himself naked and slept beside his father, so that mosquitoes might stop on his naked body instead of his father's, which he covered with his own clothing.

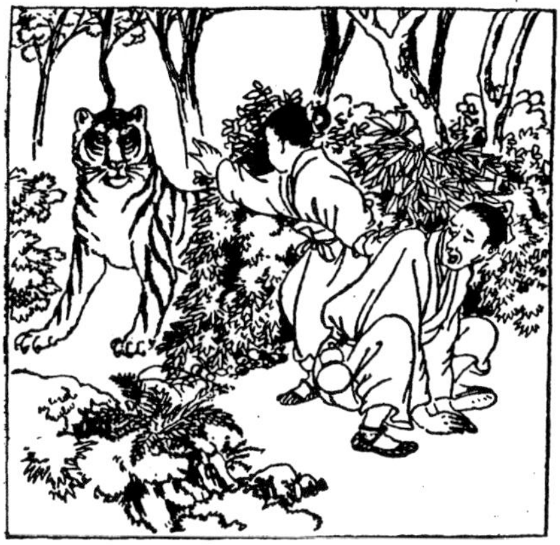

Osho: Osho served his step-mother most faithfully. One winter's day, when she was sick, she wanted to have a carp. He went to a river; it was frozen over with ice. He sat on it till the ice, thawing under him, made a large hole, through which a large carp jumped out, for, as it was believed, Heaven was moved by the dutiful behaviors of Osho.

Roraishi: Roraishi, 70 years old, wanted to have his aged parents forget that they were old. So he dressed himself like a small baby, and ran about in the room with some toys, even by falling down on the ground to please them. He was invited by the king of Ch'u, but he declined the invitation and lived an obscure life, though he wrote several books.

Kakukyo: Kakukyo was so poor that he could not afford to give enough food to his mother, who always shared her food with his little child. "We can have another child, but no more mother," he said to his wife, and he was going to bury his child alive, when a gold kettle was brought to light. The child was saved because the dug-out kettle brought much money.

Emperor Shun (2255-2205 B.C.): Shun had a step-mother who was hard upon him, being partial to his half-brother, her own son. Shun, however, served her faithfully and devotedly. When he was sent to fields, a large elephant appeared to help his cultivation. Even birds came out to help him in his hard work. His filial devotion reached the ears of Emperor Yao, who made Shun his successor. Emperors Yao and Shun are among the wisest rulers in the history of China.

VICARIOUS SELF-SACRIFICE

The Japanese have been trained from time out of memory to make nothing of life at duty's call, and they gladly give up their lives in the cause of patriotism. They are above dying an ignoble death, which they term "Inu-jini" (lit. dog-death), but they are always prepared to lay down their lives in the cause of justice. It is remarkable, however, how they brave death without any religious consideration for future life. Our history is beautifully dotted with noble deeds of self-sacrifice, of which Migawari (lit. body-substitute) or vicarious self-sacrifice stands conspicuous. Indeed has every locallity many beautiful stories of devotion in which a Japanese died in defence of justice. A few cases of self-sacrifice follow:—

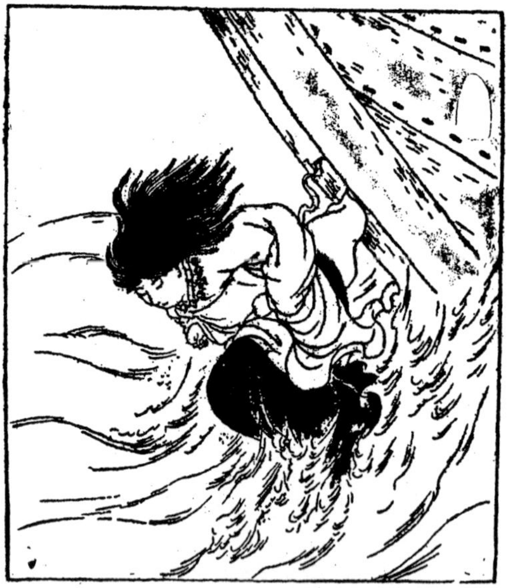
Princess Ototachibana drowing herself to save her husband

Princess Ototachibana: Prince Yamatotake was sent by his father, the Emperor Keiko (12th), to subjugate the rebels of the north in 110 A. D. He came to Musashino Province, in which Tokyo is now situated, and was crossing the present Bay of Tokyo, when, a heavy storm raging, his ship was rolled and tossed as if it were going to be capsized. "I fear the god of the sea is offended," Princess Ototachibana, his wife, said. "I will go into the sea and pacify his anger on behalf of the Prince." So saying the princess jumped into the angry waves which

Continued

soon subsiding, Prince Yamatotake landed safely on the other side of the bay.

The Sato brothers: Tsuginobu and Tadanobu were two brothers of the Sato family in the service of Yoshitsune Minamoto. During the battle of Yashima fought in 1186, Noritsune Taira, a good archer of the enemy, shot an arrow at Yoshitsune, when Tsuginobu, stepping forth, received the mortal arrow on his own body. "I am glad I am dying in your defence," the dying man said. "But I am sorry that I shall not live to see you get victory." It was on the 19th of the second month (February), 1186, that Tsuginobu Sato died.

In the 11th month (November) of the same year, a band of Buddhist priests attacked Yoshitsune at Yoshino, where he was taking shelter. Tadanobu younger brother of Sato borrowed his coat-of-mail, in which he impersonated his master. He, too, died in defence of his master in the same year.

Yoshiteru Murakami: Prince Morinaga, son of the Emperor Godaigo (96th), garrisoned the castle of Yoshino in the province of Yamato. Takauji Ashikaga sent some troops to lay siege to the castle. When it could stand the siege little longer, Yoshiteru Murakami donned the dress of the prince and, standing on the castle-walls, he shouted: "I am Prince Morinaga. You look at me and see what a true warrior should do." So saying Murakami disemboweled himself under the very eye of the enemy, who rushed into the castle. In the meantime, Prince Morinaga escaped out of the castle at the back-gate.

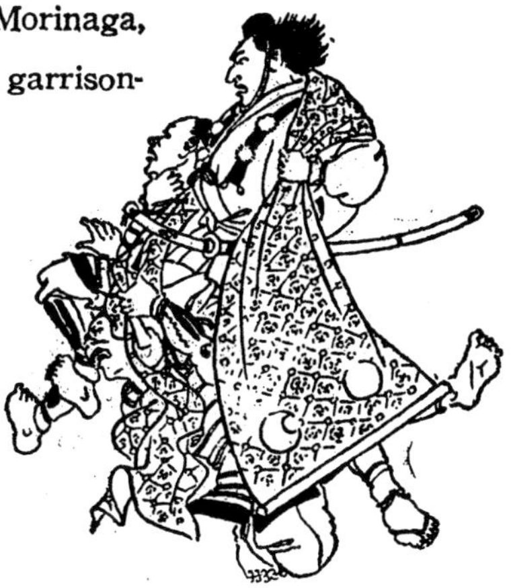

Yoshiteru Murakami recovering the Imperial banner from enemy

KODO OR CEREMONIAL INCENSE-BURNING

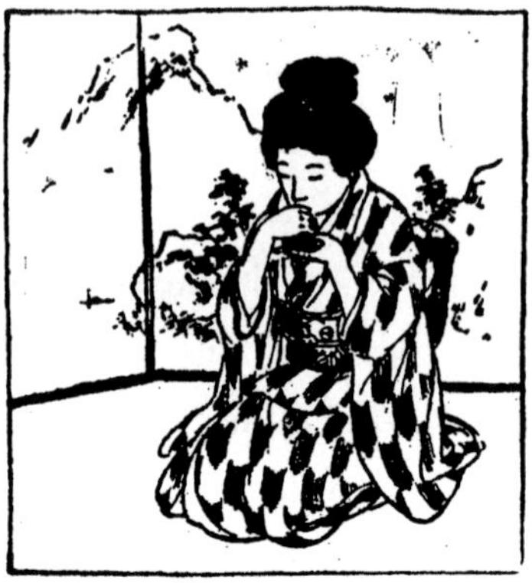

A maiden smelling incense, which is screened with her right hand

According to the *Shotoku-Taishi Den* (Life of Prince Shotoku), the people of Awaji, an island off Kobe, were found using as a fuel some aromatic wood, which Prince Shotoku (574–621), ordering to be sent to the court, found it to be aloe-wood, possibly, as the book says, coming adrift from the southern part of Asia. The prince was pleased to receive a large piece, 18 ft. And he is generally believed to be the founder of Kodo, ceremonial incense-burning, in Japan.

Japan has hardly any kind of aromatic wood and her incense is mostly imported from the South Seas, India and some other southern countries of Asia. But the Japanese, as a nation, use a great deal of incense, not only at religious services, but also at home to keep the rooms perfumed. Incense-burning or its appreciation is an art in this country, called Kodo (lit. way of incense), a refined and artistic way of appreciating incense. There were at one time 61 kinds of composite incense, says the *Kindai-Sejidan* (Modern-times news), made of 186 different kinds of aromatic wood. But the most important part of Kodo consists in what is termed, in the Japanese language, "the hearing of incense." In this art, by the way, the Japanese use the word "hear" (kiku) instead of "smell' (kagu), for some reasons, to express the smelling of incense.

But ceremonial incense-burning is a sort of contest or a pastime for telling the kinds of incense, which are burned at a gathering. It requires some power of sense, memory and judgment, for a very minute difference has to be told by smelling different composites of incense. There are several ways of this contest, but the Genji-ko (incense of Genji) is perhaps the most popular. It is so named after the famous novel *Genji-Monogatari* written by Lady Murasaki-Shikibu.

Continued

At the Genji-Ko contest, five different kinds of incense are used, and a party, usually ten in number, makes a guess at their composites. At the beginning, the five kinds are separately burned, and all present "hear" (smell) their smell. Five dozes of each kind are made, making twenty-five dozes altogether, of which a set of five dozes is taken by the choise of the leader and burned one after another. Taken at random by the leader, the set may be of one kind of incense or all different kinds, or else it may have two or three kinds. Each member of the party notes down, on a piece of paper provided

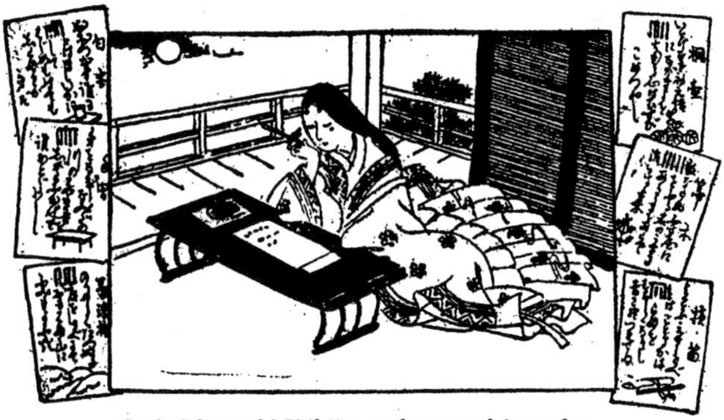

Lady Murasaki-Shikibu and some of her odes

for the occasion, the name and diagram of the set or composite incense. The second set of another five dozes is taken at random, and the same process is repeated five times till all the dozes are thus tested and smelled. At the end of "the hearing" of all incense, the leader gives marks for the guesses of each member. Five kinds of incense make fifty-two composite kinds of incense possible, and they are named after so many chapters of the *Genji-Monogatari* as diagramed below:

The diagram should be read:

 called Hahaki (sweeping-tree) means that all dozes are different from one another.

 called Tenarai (penmanship) means that all dozes are of one kind.

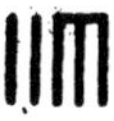 called Hanano-en (flower-banquet) means that dozes 1 & 3 are of the same kind, the rest being different.

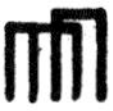 called Nio-miya (fragrant shrine) means that dozes 1 & 3 are of the same kind, while dozes 2, 4 & 5 are also of the same kind.

 called Yokobuye (horizontal flute) means that dozes 1, 2 & 5 are of the same kind, the rest being different,

and so on and so forth. It has to be added that the names of the diagrams have little to do with the game because they are names simply adopted, as said above, after so many chapters of the *Genji-Monogatari*.

GIANTS IN JAPAN

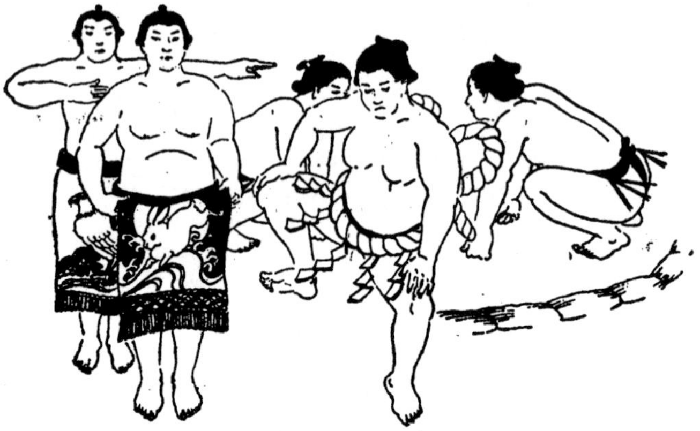

Professional wrestlers

Prince Yamatotake, son of the Emperor Keiko (12th), says the *Kojiki,* stood 10 Jap. ft. (9.94 ft.) high, strong enough to "lift a tripod up." Otoneri-Shishifuto-Umamaro, who lived during the reign of the Emperor Junna (53rd), according to an ancient annal of Japan, stood 9 ft. and odds high. In the fifth month (May), 866 A.D., an Imperial decree was issued, says the *Sandai-Jitsuroku,* to the effect that all "long men" standing above 6.3 ft. (190.89 cm.) should be reported to the Imperial court, though little is known about the results of this Imperial order. A giantess standing 7 ft. (212.1 cm.) was reported from the province of Tamba in the fourth month (April), 1026 A.D.

Here is a list of some giants and giantesses of modern times in Japan:—

	Jap. ft.	cm.	Weight
Osora Buzayemon	7.6	230.30	429 lbs.
Iketsuki Keitazayemon	7.5	227.27	396 „
Ishikiri Unzo	7.5	227.27	
Shakagatake Kumoyemon	7.5	227.27	
Kumonryu Seikichi	7.3	221.21	
Onikachi Shonosuke	7.3	221.21	248 „
Giantesses (woman-wrestlers)			
Yone	7.3	221.21	
Taki	7.3	221.21	
Matsu	6.2	187.87	248 „

Japanese Weights, Measures, and Moneys with Foreign Equivalents

Japanese system	Metric system	British system	U.S.A. system
Length			
Measure:			
Shaku (尺) = 10 sun (寸)	3.030 decimeter	11.93 inch	11.93 inch
Ken (間) = 6 shaku	1.818 meter	1.988 yd.	1.988 yd.
Cho (町) = 60 ken	1.090 hectometer	119.30 yd.	119.30 yd.
Ri (里) = 36 cho	3.926 kilometer	2.440 mile	2.440 mile
Cloth Measure:			
Shaku = 10 sun	3.787 decimeter	14.9128 inch	14.9128 inch
Jo = 10 shaku	3.787 meter	4.1424 yd.	4.1424 yd.
Surface			
Tsubo (坪) (6 Shaku sq.)	3.3058 sq. m	3.954 sq. yd.	3.954 sq. yd.
Se (畝) = 30 tsubo (or bu)	99.174 sq. m	118.61 sq. yd.	118.61 sq. yd.
Tan (反) = 10 se	9.917 acre	0.245 acres	0.245 acres
Cho (町) = 10 tan	0.9917 hectare	2.4507 acres	2.4507 acres
Sq. Ri (方里)	15.423 sq. km	5.955 sq. mile	5.955 sq. mile
Capacity (Dry and liquid)			
Sho (升) = 10 go	1.8039 litre	0.397 gallons	0.4765 gallons (liq.)
To (斗) = 10 sho	1.80 decalitre	3.970 gallons	4.7654 gallons (do.)
Koku (石) = 10 to	1.80 hectolitre	39.703 gallons 4.963 bushels	47.654 gallons (do. 5.119 bushels(dry)
Weigths			
Momme (匁)	3.75 gramme	57.8703 grs.(av.)	57.8703 grs. (avoir.)
Kin (斤) = 160 momme	0.60 kg.	1.323 lbs. (do.)	1.323 lbs. (do.)
Kwan (貫) = 1000 momme	3.75 kg.	8.2672 lbs. (do.)	8.2672 lbs. (do.)

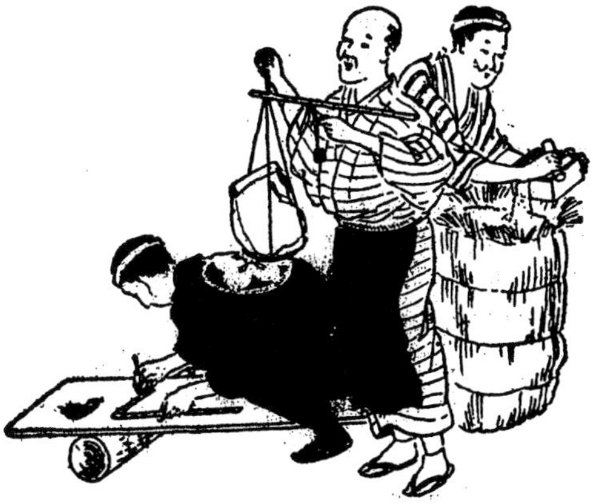

Carpenter (left); merchant (middle) and farmer (right)

JAPANESE PAPER

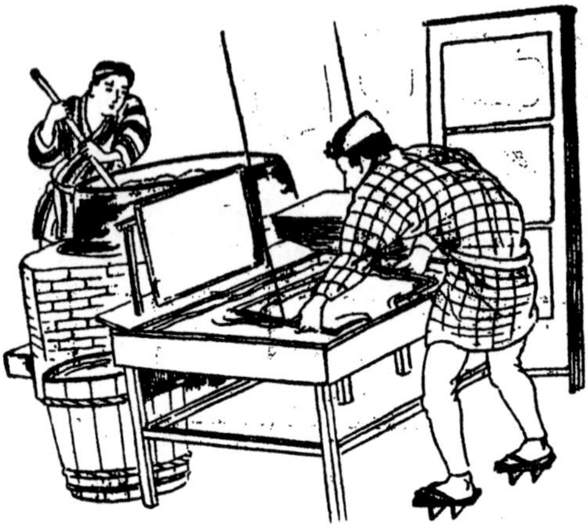

Japanese paper-manufacture

Generally speaking, Priest Doncho, who came from Koguryu of the Korean Peninsula, is said to be the first introducer of paper in Japan, for he made it in the seventh year (610 A. D.) of the reign of the Empress Suiko (the 33rd), though Japan seems to have had paper of some kind in her prehistoric days. Prince Shotoku invented a method of making paper by boiling the barks of Kozo (paper-mulberry) and his method was employed extensively in Japan for over ten centuries. The paper manufacture made great progress in Japan during the Muromachi (1338–1573) and Tokugawa (1603–1867) periods.

Japanese paper is considered to be very good in quality, for it is at once strong and tenacious. It is made chiefly from two kinds of barks: Kozo or paper-mulberry and Mitsumata (edgeworthia papyrifera).

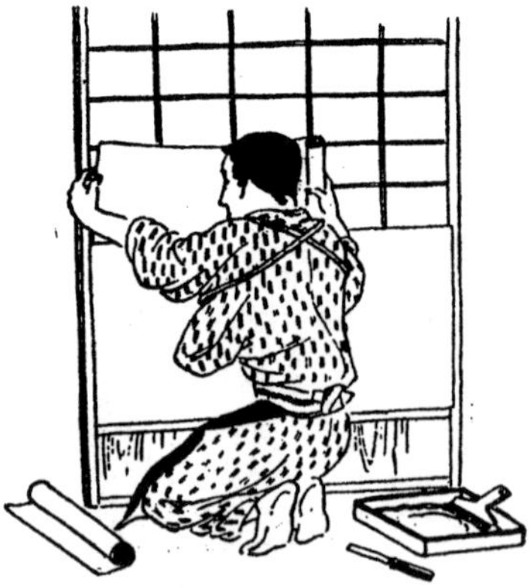

Paper pasted on sliding-door

There are several species of Kozo, such as Kojiki, Tsunkyo, Akaso, Kuroso, etc., while Mitsumata is divided into two: Aoki and Akaki with some varieties.

Continued

Gampi paper is quite typical of Japan. It is made of the barks of Gampi (lychnis coronata), including Kogampi, Tosa-gampi, Miyama-gampi, etc., which grow wild in the province of Kii.

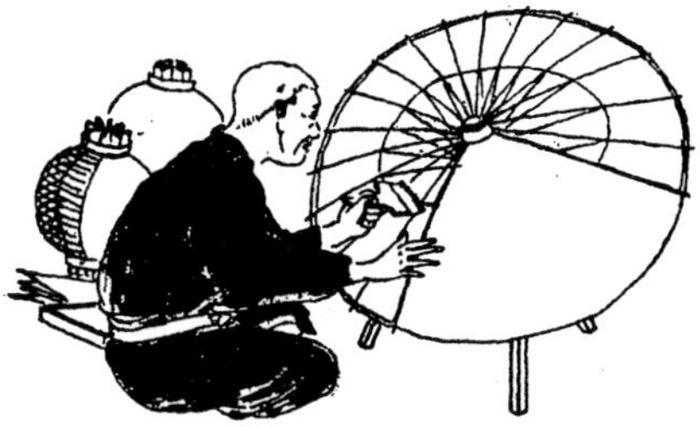

Umbrella and lanterns made of paper

Mitsukuni Tokugawa and paper: Mitsukuni Tokugawa, lord of the Mito clan, is known for his wise administration. He was very careful about the use of paper, which he never wasted, and he used to tell his maid-attendants to be as careful in their use of paper. When he saw, however, that they paid little attention to his admonition, he took them one day to see how paper was made. He chose a cold day when it snowed hard and showed them how hard on such a stormy day the workers had to work with their chappy hands. The ladies stopped wasting paper.

Kamitsubute (paper-pellets): We often see a high bronze statue, for instance, dotted with small pieces of paper called "Kami-tsubute" or paper-pellets (Tsubute=stones thrown). One will put a piece of paper in one's mouth and spits it up on the statue. The higher one throws it up with the mouth, the greater luck will be in store for one. Children are often seen competing with one another in reaching a high mark on a statue with a stone-pellet.

Chief kinds of Japanese paper: Hanshi. Hosho, Torinoko, Mino-gami, Tosagami, Awa-kami, Gampi, etc.

Hanshi is paper of daily or ordinary use; Hosho is used on a ceremonial occasion, and Mino-gami (lit. Mino-province paper) is used in writing official papers,

COINAGE IN JAPAN

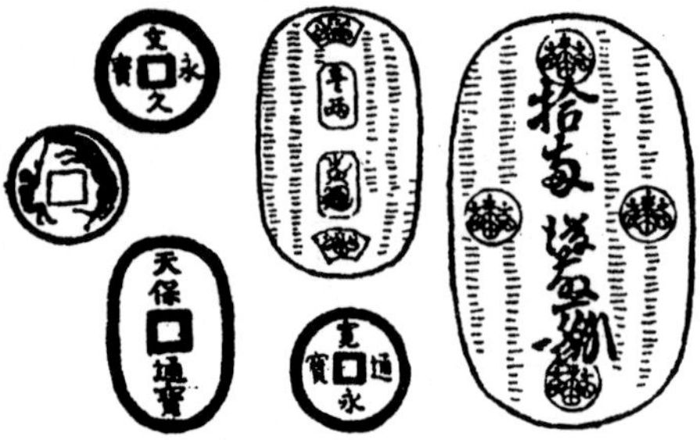

Old-time coins

The Wado-kaichin, which was minted with copper dug out in the province of Musashi during the era of Wado (708–714), was, so far as records go, the first currency ever circulated in Japan though bartering must have been practised before. It was after Japan exchanged envoys with China that the former established a monetary system of any kind. After the Wado-kaichin eleven different kinds of currency were circulated, reign after reign, till according to some authorities, the Emperor Murakami stopped coining money, because copper production in the country much decreased.

From the Fujiwara premiership in the 9th century down to the Ashikaga Shogunate in the 14th century, Japan imported Chinese coins, such as the Eiraku-Tsuho, which was circulated as a national currency. These coins were minted also in Japan, and they are still in existence, though not in circulation, in the country. During the Toyotomi Shogunate, (1585–1602), when some of the currency systems of the country were restored, the Ohban (lit. large-stamp) pieces of gold, were circulated and the currency system of Japan began to manifest itself. But the Toyotomi dynasty was of short duration, and it was under the Tokugawa Government that the currency system of the country began to take shape.

During the Tokugawa Shogunate, there were two kinds of gold pieces: Ohban (larger-stamp) and Koban (smaller-stamp). The former, which was oval in shape, was not freely circulated, but the Shogun bestowed it upon his local lords on felicitous occasions. It

Continued

was minted in Kyoto, and had the Japanese words for "ten Ryo" written on it. The letters, when effaced, were written again on paying the necessary charges. The latter, or the Koban, which was also oval in shape, was circulated on the market, and it was a unit of currency during the Tokugawa Shogunate. Then there were two subsidiary pieces of silver: Shu and Bu.

The Teigin were grains of silver, which were counted by weight in comparison with gold pieces, as the former had no fixed value in themselves. It was about the middle of the Tokugawa Shogunate that the Government issued silver pieces that had any fixed value like the present coins: namely, five-momme pieces, one-bu pieces, three-shu pieces and one-shu pieces.

In 1882 the Bank of Japan was founded and in 1884 the Government issued convertible Yen pieces of silver, which made Japan a silver-standard country, so far as the circulation of currency was concerned, till a new monetary law was enacted in 1897. Japan adopted the gold standard as a result of her war with China or Japan paid dear for her gold standard, which she thus adopted after great bloodshed and 20-yen and 10-yen gold pieces were ciculated in Japan. The adoption of the gold standard abolished the circulation of the Yen silver coin, and 50-sen coins became the largest subsidiary coins in Japan. The Government reminted the 50-sen coin, gradually deminishing the standard and weight of the coin, but the world-war raised the price of silver so much that Japan saw a great outflow of her silver coins, till their debasement was found necessary and the 50-sen silver pieces were minted.

The 10-sen and 5-sen nickel coins were other subsidiary coins, which were circulatcd first in 1888. They had each a hole in imitation of a foreign coin, so that it might be easily distinguished from any other coins, while the hole makes it difficult to counterfeit the coin. Besides, we had 1-sen bronze pieces, which were first minted in 1897. On account of the shortage of copper, in this country, they replaced copper coins previously circulated.

But the world war effected a thorough change in the Japanese currency, and Japan has chiefly paper-notes, most coins making their disappeance.

SEA-FORTUNE AND MOUNTAIN-FORTUNE

Prince Hoseri and Prince Hoori, who is generally called Prince Hikohohodemi, were brothers. Prince Hoseri, the elder, was fond of fishing, and the younger Prince Hikohohodemi was much given to hunting on mountains. One day they exchanged occupations, the younger going to the sea to fish while the elder went hunting. Neither caught anything on that particular day. Moreover, Prince Hoori lost his brother's fishing-book. Prince Hoseri, angry at the loss of his favorite hook, sent his brother down to the bottom of the sea in search for it. Aided by an old fisherman, Prince Hoori soon reached the Ryugu, or Dragon Palace, at the bottom of the sea. He found great favours with the Dragon-King, and fell in love with Princess Toyotama-Hime, the royal daughter, who helped him in recovering the lost hook. When, after staying in the Dragon Kingdom for three years, Prince Hoori expressed his desire to go back to the land. Princess Toyotama, who was with child, said that she would soon follow him. And when she came to the land soon after the prince, she wanted to be confined for delivery, telling her husband never to look into the delivery-room, Unable to overcome his curiosity, however, Prince Hoori looked in. Lo! what should he see in the room but a huge crocodile (Japanese *Wani*)? "Now that I am discovered, I must go back to my own home" Princess Toyotama said, and leaving her baby, Princess Toyotama left the Imperial Palace. The baby is Ugaya-Fukiaezu, father of Emperor Jimmu, the first Emperor of Japan.

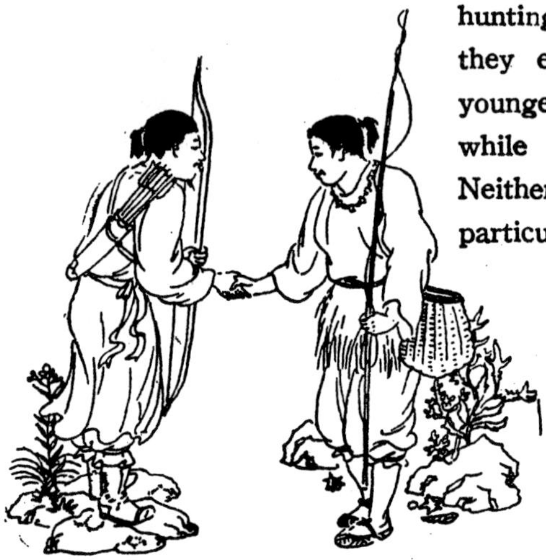

MAMA-NO-TEKONA

The Guho-ji Temple is an old temple situated at Mama of Ichikawa, in the prefecture of Chiba. It was founded by Priest Nitcho, a disciple of Priest Nichiren, who founded the Nichiren sect of Buddhism. Priest Nitcho left his temple never to be heard of again, in 1299, when Priest Jonin, his adoptive father died. The main image of the temple was wrought by Priest Jonin, while the statues of Vajra in the temple-gate were carved by Unkei, by far the greatest sculptor that Japan has produced. Besides these, the temple owns several valuable treasures.

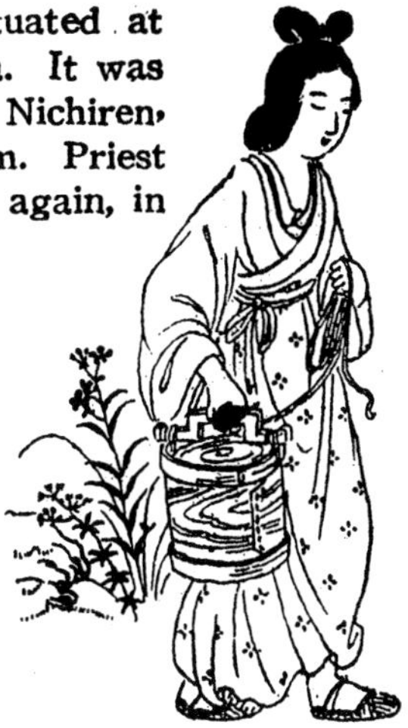

Mama-no-Tekona carrying water from a well

Near the stone-steps that lead to the temple there is a small shrine dedicated to Mama-no-Tekona (lit. Maiden Tekona of Mama Village). The shrine was erected by Priest Nikko of the Guho-ji Temple in 1501 near the grave of the ill-starred girl, Tekona, of the village of Mama.

Tekona of Mama, according to the Manyoshu, an anthology of ancient Japanese poems, was a girl of exceeding beauty, who lived during the reign (540–571) of the Emperor Kimmei (29th). She used to come to draw water from the well of the village, when, it is said:

> "She was clad in rough hemp, bare-foot, her hair unkempt, but she was a thousand times as beautiful as a nobleman's daughter, for her face looked as round as a full moon and as charming as flowers in their prime. When she drew water from the well, the people of the village were attracted to see her like insects that are drawn by the fire in summer or like a ships that are pulled into a harbour. The young lads vied with one another in seeking her hands, but all were disappointed."

Tekona was sad to see so many young men were mortified or ruined on her account, and in order to save them any more mortification she plunged herself into a river, which runs by Mama. Mushimaro Takahashi, Akahito Yamabe, and many other poets wrote odes in admiration for her chastity, which made her still revered now that little less than fifteen centuries have elapsed since she drowned herself in the river; for the people visit her little shrine constantly from one end of the year to the other.

But somehow the deity of the Tekona shrine has been made a protector of children, and the people come from great distances to offer a prayer for the patronage and protection of their children.

Prince Shotoku, Father of Japanese Buddhism

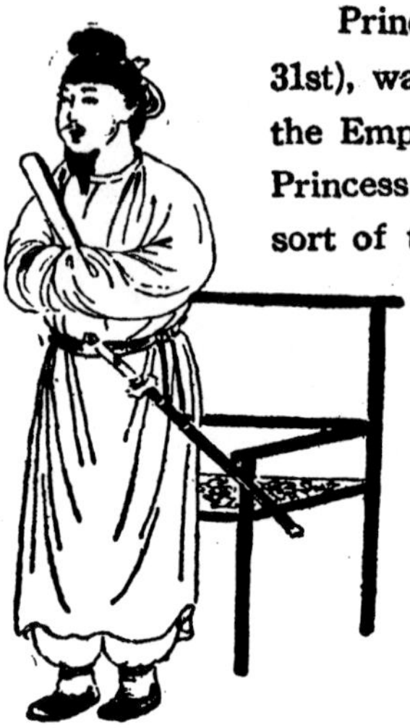

Prince Shotoku

Prince Shotoku, son of the Emperor Yomei (the 31st), was born in the 3rd year (574) of the reign of the Emperor Bitatsu (the 30th). When his mother, Princess Anahobe-hashihito (later the Imperial Consort of the Emperor Yomei), came before a court stable, while walking in the Imperial Palace, she suddenly gave birth to the prince without having any labour-pains, when, according to the Nihon-shoki, "he talked". Hence his name of Prince Umayado or Barn-door. He is also called Prince Toyotomimi (lit. quick-eared) because, it is said, he could listen to ten suits at the same time without making any mistake in his judgment. The name of Shotoku, or Sacred-virtue, was given him by his admirers in later generations.

It was in 587 when Prince Shotoku was thirteen years old that his father, the Emperor Yomei, became critically ill. The prince, who had studied Buddhism under Eiji, a Korean priest, prayed to the Three Ratnas for the recovery of his father. He began carving a statue of Yakushi-nyorai (Physian Buddha) or Bhechajaguru to offer a prayer to, though the Emperor died before the completion of the image. This image is still preserved at the Horyu-ji Temple.

When Mononobe-no-Moriya, an anti-Buddhist minister, broke out with Soga-no-Umako, a Buddhist, the prince took the side of the latter and sent an army in his support. The prince again carved the images of the Shitenno or Four Deva-kings promising to them that he would build a temple for them in case he should succeed over Mononobe. The Shitenno-ji Temple in the province of Settsu was built by him in return of his thanks for the help which he believed was given him by the images during his battle with Mononobe.

The Emperor Sushun, successor to the Emperor Yomei, was assassinated by Yamato-no-Aya-no-Ataigoma of Korean descent,

Continued

under the instigation of Soga-no-Umako, who, however, condemned him to death for regicide.

"Your execution of the actual assassin" said Prince Shotoku to Umako, "will not save you the disgrace of being slandered as a regicide by posterity."

Upon the enthronement of the Empress Suiko in 593, Prince Shotoku, a lad of 19 years, was appointed Regent to her, and he achieved great administrative renovations during his regency.

Prince Shotoku was a great student and admirer of the Continental culture and he adopted many Chinese and Korean systems of administration. In 603, he adopted the system of coronets and ranks for the courtiers. There were twelve ranks; namely, major and minor virtue, major and minor humanity, major and minor etiquette, major and minor faith, major and minor justice and major and minor wisdom, which were distinguished from one another by the colour of the coronet each courtier wore, as, for instance, purple for the major and minor virtue and red for the major and minor humanity. This system indicates, at the same time, what great importance he attached to morals and personal characters.

In the following year, Prince Shotoku issued the Seventeen-article Constitution, which is a great literature. Its spirits may be condensed in three main points written in the first three articles; namely, peace among men, the worship of the Three Ratnas, and the importance of the Imperial line.

Prince Shotoku exchanged envoys with the Chinese court to introduce the Continental civilization, but great discretion seems to have been exercised by the prince to maintain the disgnity of an independent country in his correspondence, in which the Japanese sovereign was called the "Emperor of the sun-rising country", while the Chinese ruler was the "Emperor of the sun-setting country."

Prince Shotoku built several large Buddhist temples, among which are such as the Shitenno-ji, Chugu-ji, Hoko-ji, etc. At the time of his death there were 46 Buddhist temples, 816 monasteries and 569 nunneries in Japan. Prince Shotoku is generally regarded as the father of Japanese Buddhism.

His mother died in 621 and Prince Shotoku, who was grieved over her death, fell ill on the 22nd of the first month in the following year. His wife also took to sick bed and died on the 21st of the second month, and Prince Shotoku followed her on the following day.

OOKA ECHIZEN-NO-KAMI TADASUKE

The Daniel of Old Japan

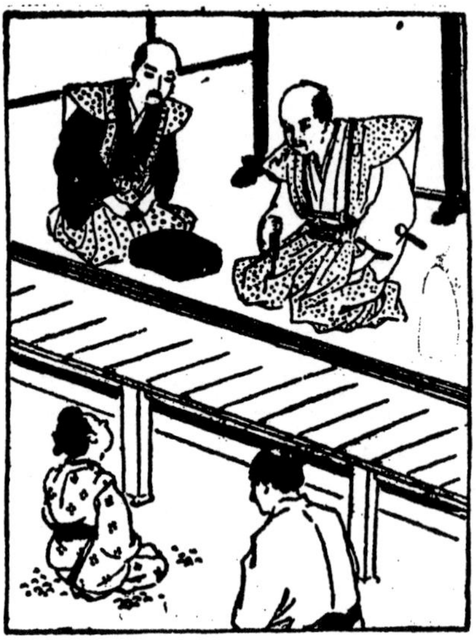

Judge Ooka in the bench

Ooka Echizen-no-Kami Tadasuke was the governor of Yamada, which belonged to a branch-family of Tokugawa. Once there was a dispute between Kii and Ise Provinces concerning their boundaries, when the people of Kii, which was under the direct control of Tokugawa, tried to overpower Ise in borrowed plumes, but Ooka did not hesitate to give a just judgment and declared the Kii people to be in the wrong. Yoshimune, lord of Kii Province, was so pleased with the judgment of Ooka that, when he was appointed the Shogun, he made Ooka the Mayor of Edo, the Shogunate capital. He was known for the good judgments that he gave. He died in the year 1751 at the age of 77 years.

Genrokuro fishing in the fish preserve: Genrokuro was the third son of Mitsusada Tokugawa, lord of Kii Province, and he was an obstinate and wilful prince, it is said, who wanted to have his own way in everything he did. He often went to Akogi-ga-Ura, a fish preserve, where he could catch more fish than anywhere else.

"I am my father's son" the haughty prince would say if any of his attendants protested or objected to his fishing at Akogi-ga-Ura. "Who dare object to my catching fish at any place that belongs to my father?".

Tadasuke Ooka, the governor of Yamada, who heard of the violation of the fishing law, wanted to put an end to it whether the violator be a prince or not, and one day he told his men to bring the prince to court.

"Who could you be?" the governor demanded in an angry voice when the prince, bound hand and foot, was brought before him, "to violate the law of the province? Fishing is prohibited at Akogi-ga-Ura, as you must know."

"I am the third son of Lord Tokugawa of Kii Province and

Continued

Genrokuro is my name" the proud prince said in great exitement. "I am perfectly at liberty to catch fish anywhere in my father's territory."

"You don't say—you are a liar" the governor said with dignity. "A prince should know better than fishing in the fish preserve."

The prince pointed to the crest of Tokugawa that was on his coat, but Ooka said that it must be a false crest because a true prince could not violate any law that his father made for the benefit of his people.

"You must be a liar or else mad," Ooka went on. "I could send you to prison for violating the law, but, because I see you are under age, I will forgive you this once, if you observe the law hereafter."

Genrokuro was of course glad to go home, and he never went to Akogi-ga-Ura for fishing. He was rechristened Yoshimune when he came of age, and it was he that, upon his appointment as the Shogun in 1716, made Tadasuke Ooka the Mayor of Edo, the Shogunate capital.

Hachirobei and his fifty pieces of gold: Hachirobei was a dealer in old metal who lived near Otama-ga-Ike Pond in Kanda, Edo. He lived a single life and alone. By dint of great frugality, he saved fifty pieces of gold, which, for fear a thief might steal, he kept in a jar of a rice-bran paste in which pickles were preserved. Every time he came home from business, he took his gold out of the jar and chuckled to himself over it, as he thought, without anyone seeing him.

One day, after a tiresome day's work, Hachirobei repaired to his jar and put his hand in the jar with the happy thought of enjoying the gold, as usual. What was his surprise when his hand failed to touch it? The gold was stolen. So he reported his case to Mayor Tadasuke Ooka.

"Hachirobei has lost his fifty pieces of gold" Mayor Ooka said when he called all the tenants of the tenement-house in which Hachirobei lived. "He kept it in a jar of pickles. If any of you has borrowed it without his permission, it must be returned; or else he shall be dealt hard".

"I know that the gold cannot have gone out of its own accord" the Mayor went on when none stepped forth to confess to his theft. "It must have been stolen by one who saw Hachirobei put it in the jar. A rice-bran paste has a strong smell that will remain long on the hand which is once put in it. I will smell every hand now. Every one of you must step out to let me smell his hand."

Just at this moment one of the tenants put his hand to his nose. The Mayor caught sight of it.

"That fellow over there" Mayor Ooka said instantly. "You come forth; none other needs come forth."

The thief was caught and, in accordance with the law, he was driven out of town, after the money was returned to its owner.

LADY SEIKAN-IN

Shoguness Iyemochi Tokugawa

Lady Seikan-in, whose childhood name was Princess Kadzu (lit. peace), was the eighth daughter of the Emperor Ninko (the 120th). She was born on the tenth day of the eighth month (July 3rd, according to the lunar calendar), in 1846, the year in which her Emperor-father died.

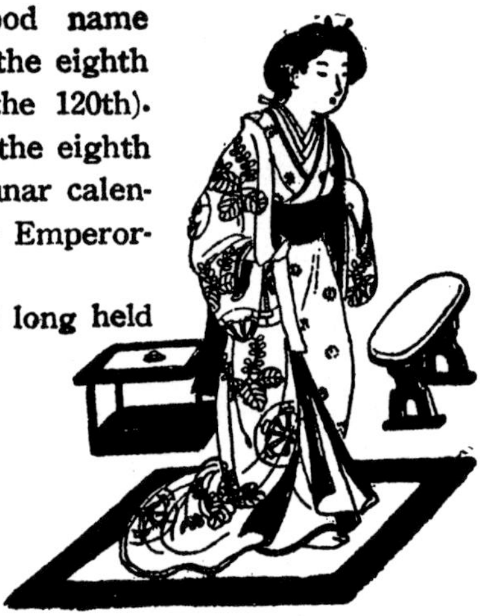

Lady Seikan-in

The Shogunate court, which had long held the real suzerainty of the country, appeared to get alienated from the Imperial court, because the nation was awakened to the importance of the Imperial administration, instead of the Shogunate, and Japan had never been in greater need of co-operation between the two courts, Imperial and Shogunal, in her history than at that time. Consequently, the engagement was concluded, as a political expediency, between the Shogun Iyemochi Tokugawa and Princess Kadzu, and their wedding took place on the 19th of the fourth month in 1861. The princess expressed her feelings in a 31-syllable poem, which runs as follows:—

> "Oshimaji na
> Kimi to Tami tono
> Tame naraba
> Mi wa Musashino no
> Tsuyu to kiyutomo"

(Free translation: What do I care if, for the sake of the Lord and the people, my body should disappear like a dew on the fields of Musashino?)

Princess Kadzu came from Kyoto to Musashino, where Edo was situated.

She had been engaged to Prince Arisugawa, but their engagement was cancelled so that she might get married to the Shogun. It must have been hard on her to break the engagement with the prince, but she was willing to sacrifice herself for the sake of the Emperor and the people and to die in Musashino, where Edo (Tokyo) was situated.

Continued

In 1865, after four years of their married life, the Shogun was appointed the leader of the Imperial punitive army against the clan of Nagato, but he died of beriberi at Osaka on the 11th of the eighth month, 1866. The princess, now a widow, took the tonsure, assuming the Buddhist name of Lady Seikan-in (lit. quiet and peaceful) in order to devote the rest of her life to Buddhism.

At his departure on the expedition, the Shogun Iyemochi Tokugawa promised that he would purchase for his wife a piece of Nishijin, (a kind of silk brocade), one of the chief products of Kyoto. When his remains were brought to Edo, she also received the brocade that her husband had purchased for her. She wrote another famous poem of thirty-one syllables:—

"Utsu-semi no
Kara-ori-koromo
Nani ka sen
Aya mo Nishiki mo
Kimi arite koso."

(Free translation: What need is there for Kara-orikoromo, or China-woven fabric, which is as worthless as the cast-off skin of a cicada, for damask and brocade are prized only when the Lord is alive?)

The princess was now a devout Buddhist leading a pious religious life in order to pray for the repose of the spirit of her husband. She also made great contributions towards the Imperial restoration of administration by helping the Emperor Komei, her brother, and the Emperor Meiji, her nephew. When the royal army marched against the Shogunate capital of Edo (Tokyo), in 1867, she endeavoured to plead for the innocence of the Shogunate court of Tokugawa, into which she married.

Lady Seikan-in died at To-no-sawa, Hakone, on Sept. 2,1877, at the age of 30 years, and her remains were buried, in accordance with her will, beside her husband, at the Zojo-ji Temple, Tokyo.

She is looked up to as a typical Japanese woman, and a great memorial service is held every year to her memory at the Zojo-ji Temple, when girl-students of Tokyo, numbering tens of thousands, attend the religious function in admiration for her personal characters.

LADY KASUGA

Lady Kasuga was born in 1579. She was the daughter of one Rizo Saito and her maiden name was O-Fuku. She was married to Inaba Masanari, who was daimyo under Lord Taiko, or Hideyoshi Toyotomi, as he is better known. When Lord Iyemitsu, the third Shogun of the Tokugawa family, was born in 1604, Lady Kasuga offered her services as wet-nurse for the young prince, whose childhood name was Takechiyo. Her honest devotion to her charge soon won her such great favour in the eyes of the Shogun, his father, that a high position was offered to her husband, Masanari Inaba, who for a certain reason was leading a retired life.

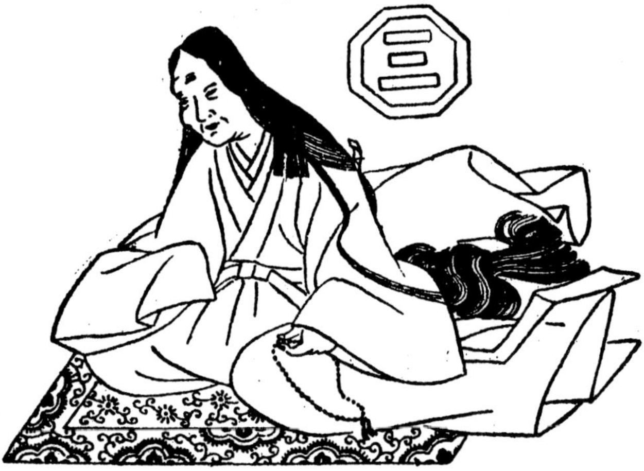

Lady Kasuga

Inaba, however, like an orthodox samurai, declined the Shogunate invitation on the ground that, humble as he was, he was above availing himself of his wife's influence in acquiring a position. Lady Kasuga bore three sons for Masanari Inaba.

Lady Kasuga was as brave and strong as any samurai, and she was skilled in the handling of a naginata-halberd, which was the chief weapon for a feudal lady.

While living with her husband, a band of three burglars broke into her residence. Lady Kasuga fought againstt hem and killed two; the other making good his escape in the darkness.

The wife of Lord Hidetada, the Shogun, showed greater affection for her second son, Prince Kunichiyo, than for her eldest son and

Continued

heir to Hidetada, Prince Takechiyo, of whom Lady Kasuga was in charge, and on that account all of the Shogun's court-ladies, as well as the courtiers, sought to ingratiate themselves with Lady Tokugawa, the Shoguness.

In the Shogunate court, Lady Kasuga was hissed at and abuses showered upon her because she was in favour with Prince Takechiyo. Nothing daunted, she was determined to stand true to her trust and to support her charge against all difficulties, for she knew that Prince was the legitimate heir of the Shogun.

Her appeal made through a court-lady to Lord Iyeyasu, father of the Shogun, was fruitless as it was coolly received by the ex-Shogun, who attributed everything to the jealousy of Lady Kasuga. Things went from bad to worse at the Shogun's court, and Prince Kunichiyo was on the point of being nominated as heir to the Shogun. No time was to be lost now, and Lady Kasuga saw no way open for her but to see the ex-Shogun himself, and explain to him the real conditions of the Shogunate court at Edo.

Under the false pretence, therefore, that she was going on a pilgrimage to the Imperial shrines at Ise, Lady Kasuga obtained from the Shogun permission for leave of absence. She hastened to Shizuoka, where Lord Iyeyasu, ex-Shogun, was then residing and watched for an opportunity to see him. Fate was certainly kind to her, for, in a few days, the ex-Shogun went "hawk-hunting" in which small birds were caught by a trained hawk. Lady Kasuga waited for him by the roadside. Lord Iyeyasu recognized her at once though she was dressed in travelling attire. She told him why she had travelled so far from the Shogunate castle down to Shizuoka and in what precarious situation Prince Takechiyo stood in the Shogunate court at Yedo. The surprised ex-Shogun promised shortly to visit the Shogunate court and to see to it that things were straightened out.

The unexpected advent at Edo of the ex-Shogun, father of the Shogun, was a great occasion at the Shogunate court. All the Shogun's princes were received in audience by their grandfather. The ex-Shogun, who was specially pleased with the growth of Prince Takechiyo, the eldest son of the Shogun, invited him to sit with him on the High-Seat of Honour. The spoiled Prince Kunichiyo followed his brother, wishing to share the privilege. "No," said the ex-Shogun in an angry voice, "you have no right to come up here." The Lord then handed some cakes to Prince Takechiyo, but he threw some others to Prince Kunichiyo. "Even cakes are given in that way!" escaped from the lips of the Shoguness, who betrayed her displeasure at this

Continued

discriminative treament of her favorite son. Lord Iyeyasu seized the opportunity to give her a lecture on the distinction between the eldest and other princes. "It is against order and discipline," said the ex-Shogun, "to give preference to a younger prince in anything. The eldest son should be the heir, and the other sons his subjects." These words uttered by the father of the Shogun brought the Shogunate court to its senses, and the dispute concerning the Shogunate heir was at once settled.

In 1623 Lord Hidetada retired in favour of his son, Prince Takechiyo, who was rechristened Iyemitsu Tokugawa, the third Shogun. Lady Kasuga was assigned to more important duties. In recognation of her devotion to the Shogunate family, the Emperor Gomidzunoo gave her the second court rank in 1629, granting her the honorific title of Lady Kasuga, by which name she is generally known in the history of Japan.

When Lord Iyemitsu was seriously ill, with pernicious smallpocks in 1628, Lady Kasuga repaired to the mausoleum of Lord Iyeyasu and offered her life as a substitute for that of the Shogun, praying for his quick recovery. She swore that, if his life was spared, she would take no medicine in case she should be taken ill. Lord Iyemitsu recovered.

When Lady Kasuga herself was taken ill in 1643, she remembered her promise made before the shrine of Lord Iyeyasu and refused to take any medicine. Lord Iyemitsu was worried over her illness and came often to see her. When she became seriously ill, the Shogun offered medicine, with his own hands. Lady Kasuga did not refuse it this time, but she put it into her mouth, only to spit it out at once. It was only to show her respect and obedience to the Shogun that she accepted the medicine. When the Shogun asked if there was anything she desired to have done after her death, she only expressed her gratification at seeing the Shogun well and sound and thanked him for all the goodness she had received at his hands during her life.

The devoted life of Lady Kasuga came to an end on the fourteenth of the ninth month (September), 1643, and her remains were buried at Karatachi (lit. citrus) Temple, Bunkyo-ku, Tokyo. People still visit the temple to express their admiration for the devoted life of Lady Kasuga, who is one of the greatest women Japan has produced, and incense is kept burning from one end of the year to the other at her antiquated tomb.

HOKIICHI HANAWA

Japan's Greatest Blind Scholar

"Bancho de, Meaki Mekura ni, Michi wo kiki!" (freely rendered: In the street of Bancho, the eye-open were taught the Way by the eye-closed).

This is a well-known satirical poem of 17 syllables written by, or about, Hokiichi Hanawa, one of the greatest blind men of letters that Japan has produced. Though blind, Hanawa had many open-eyed pupils who studied classics under him. In this ode, the "Way" suggests the road as well as learning, Bancho (lit. watch-street) being the street where the blind scholar ran a private school.

Hokiichi Hanawa, son of Uhei Ogiwara, was born in 1747 at Hokino in the province of Musashi. He lost his sight at the age of seven years, and, his mother dying when he was ten years old, young Hokiichi was sent to Edo to study poetry. But he could not write verse. Nor did accupuncture, which he studied for four years, any more suit his taste. He found literature best to his liking.

In the meantime Hokiichi was told that Tenjin was the guardian deity of letters, and he offered a prayer for help at every Tenjin shrine he came across. He also started what was called a 1,000-day prayer, during which he recited the sutra of Prajna of 100 volumes each morning. At the end of the prayer he was granted the official title of Shibu on Aug. 26, 1763. At the end of another 1,000-day prayer, during which he recited a certain sutra of 10 volumes, another and higher official title of Koto was granted on him.

It was in 1778 that his attention was attracted to the fact that many of the classical books written during the era of Hogen (1156–1158 A.D.) were lost, and the blind scholar made up his mind to make classified quotations of all classical books of Japan. He often repaired to the Tenjin shrine to offer a prayer for help, and he even abstained from tasting salt or anything salty, in conformity with the old custom of Japan, in order that his prayers might be heard by Tenjin. Soon Hokiichi was appointed Kenko, the highest office for blind men, and he was employed in the service of the lord of Mito to revise the Dai-Nihon-shi (History of Great Japan).

In 1819, full 39 years after Hanawa began his undying work of classifying the classical books, he completed the publication of 1,530 books.

One summer's evening, it is said, the blind teacher was giving a lecture on Chinese classics, when a breeze coming in put out the light. The blind lecturer went on reading the book by heart.

"Mr. Teacher," said one of the pupils. "The light has gone out. Please stop your lecture till we get a light."

"Can't you see when the light is gone?" the blind teacher asked nonchalantly, because darkness did not affect him. "My! my! how inconvenient it is to be open-eyed."

Hokiichi Hanawa died in 1822, and his remains lie buried at the Aizen-in Temple, Yotsuya in Tokyo.

SONTOKU NINOMIYA

A great financier of Old Japan

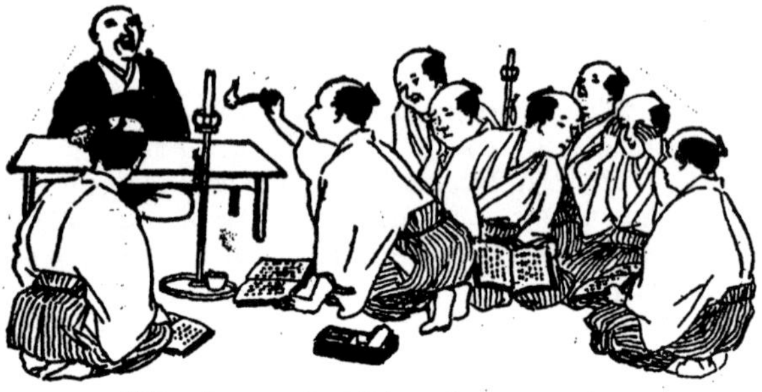

"How inconvenient it is to be open-eyed!"
(See P. 55)

Sontoku Ninomiya was one of the greatest financiers that Old Japan produced, and his soul is venerated at the Ninomiya Shrine dedicated to him at Odawara, situated at the foot of the national park of Hakone.

He was born at the village of Kayama, near Odawara, in 1787. His childhood name was Kinjiro. When he was only twelve years old, the River Sakawa overflowed its banks and all the land owned by Farmer Riyemon, his father, was laid waste. It was at this time that young Ninomiya was determined to be a social worker to restore his father's estates and help the people of his village. He lost his father at the age of fourteen years, and he, now the main stay of his family, had to work day and night to help his mother. Unable to attend school, young Ninomiya taught himself reading while carrying firewood for neighbours of his village. When he was sixteen years old, his mother died, and young Kinjiro, was taken into the family of his uncle on his father's side, Mampei by name, while his two younger brothers were sent to their grandfather on their mother's side. Mampei, however, was a great miser and he did not allow his nephew to use oil for his light in the evening. Ninomiya sowed some rape-seeds on a spare lot that belonged to nobody, and got some oil-seeds. He obtained some oil in exchange for the seeds, and he studied hard, after the members of the family went to bed, by using the oil he thus obtained. Ninomiya planted rice on a small land and harvested a bale in the autumn. In the following year he got a crop of four bales, which increased to twenty bales two years later. In the meantime Ninomiya saved

Continued

what little money he could out of his earnings, small as they were, and he purchased some three acres of rice-fields by the time when he was twenty-six years old. So he left his uncle's to live an independent life with one brother (the other brother died soon after he was taken by his grandfather).

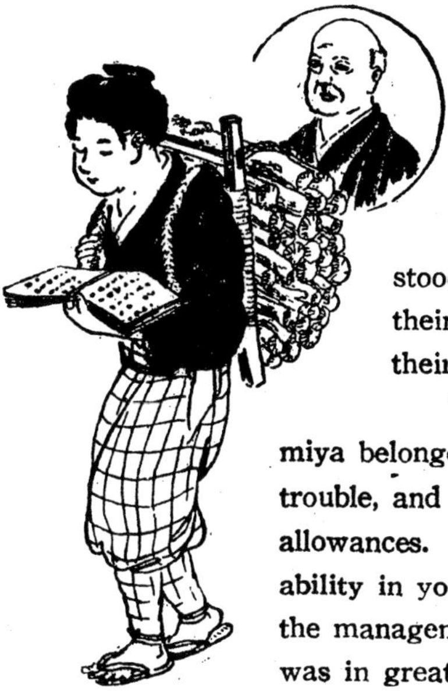
Sontoku Ninomiya reading a book while carrying faggots for neighbours to earn money

It was when Ninomiya was twenty-six years old that he was employed by Hattori Jurobei, the clan-minister, as the care-taker of his three sons. Ninomiya accompanied them to school, where he stood outside the class-room listening to their lessons, so that he could answer their questions at home.

The Odawara clan, to which Ninomiya belonged, was at that time in a financial trouble, and its samurai had a great cut in their allowances. Hattori, who noticed a financing ability in young Ninomiya, asked him to readjust the management of his house, because he himself was in great debts. After repeatedly declining, Ninomiya accepted the duty of financing the household of Hattori, provided that Hattori should agree to the proposal that Ninomiya made; namely:

1. To have rice and soup only at each meal
2. To wear nothing but cotton
3. To do nothing uneconomical

This was his first public appearance as a financier, and upon its successful discharge, much of his future career depended. In five years, however, Ninomiya paid all the debts of Hattori, and he had three hundred ryo (ryo was a unit corresponding to the Yen) in cash. Hattori gave Ninomiya one hundred ryo, which he distributed among

Continued

the servants of Hattori to whose sympathetic cooperation Ninomiya attributed his success.

His success in readjusting the household management of Ha tori recommended Ninomiya to Lord Okubo, of the Odawara clan, who told him to attend to the readjustment of two ruined villages of his clan. Ninomiya was no less successful in the resuscitation of the villages, and he was then told to go to the village of Sakura-mura in the province of Shimotsuke. Ninomiya modestly declined the commission, and his kind lord waited patiently for three long years for him to accept the task. He found the village entirely devastated and ruined, and its population decreased from 450 families to 140 or 150. Ninomiya removed, with his wife and child, to the village of Sakura-machi, and lived with the people, whom he found extremely ill-behaved. He visited every family and showed his kindness to every person in the village. He reproved the bad and admired the good, and in a few years' time he succeeded in restoring the whole village to its former prosperity.

Sontoku Ninomiya, whose financing ability became known far and wide, was invited by several local lords to attend to their finances, such as the lords of Yatabe in Hitachi Province, of Karasu-yama in Shimotsuke Province and of Shimotate in Hitachi Province, and he discharged all duties very successfully.

It was when Sontoku Ninomiya was fifty-six years old that he was called by the Tokugawa Government to do some engineering work on Lake Imba and the River Tone. Then Ninomiya was appointed by the Government to be in charge of the engineering work of Nikko.

Sontoku Ninomiya died at Nikko at the age of 70 years in 1856. He is now an object of great admiration for our school-children, many of whom have on their desks a replica of his image representing him reading a book while he carried faggots on his back for his neighbours.

PRIEST IKKYU

Priest Ikkyu is one of the wittiest and most humorous priests that Japan has produced. Born the second son of the Emperor Gokomatsu (the 100th), he was sent to the Daitoku-ji Temple to study Buddhism under Priest Yoso. He called himself Ikkyu (lit. one-rest), because in his belief our life is but a short stay or rest between the two other lives, past and future. He died on the 21st of the eleventh month in 1481, after having had his own portrait painted by a painter two days before his death. Many comical stories are told about him. One or two follow:—

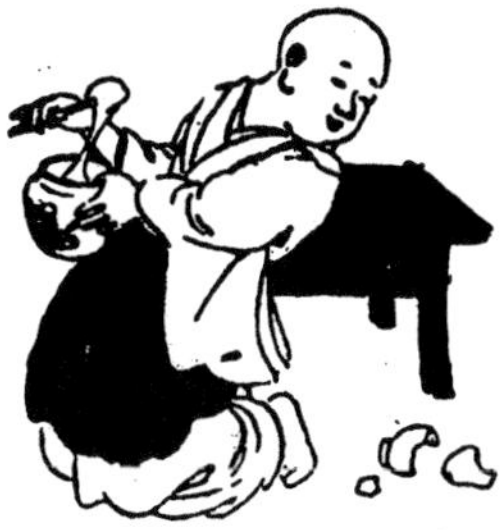

Ikkyu tasting Ame with a broken cup behind him

A precious cup broken for excuse: Priest Yoso, of the Daitoku-ji Temple, was so fond of Ame, a kind of jelly, that he always kept a jar of it in his sitting-room. He never gave a taste of it to young Ikkyu or any other acolytes of the temple. "Ikkyu, my dear," said Priest Yoso when he was going out one day. "This jar contains something good for a grown-up person, but it is nstant death to a youngster to taste it. It is dangerous. You must not touch it." "No, I will keep my hands off" responded the apparently obedient young priest. As soon as Priest Yoso went out, however, Ikkyu repaired to the sitting-room of his master-priest and shared the precious Ame with his fellow-priests. When the Ame was all gone, Ikkyu broke into pieces, a cup that Priest Yoso prized very much. And when Priest Yoso came home, Ikkyu, in tears, said: "I ask your forgiveness, Reverend Priest, but I broke your precious cup. I was dusting the room when my duster catching your precious cup broke it. I tasted your Ame at once to die in apology for my mistake, because you told me that it would be instant death to a youngster to taste it. I did not die. I tasted it again, but I was as sound as before. I took it all, but here I am, still unable to die. I do not know how to excuse myself."

How to catch a painted tiger: "Is it possible to catch a tiger?" the Shogun Yoshimochi of the Ashikaga regime, who had heard much of Ikkyu's witty ways, asked him by way of putting him to a test. "Yes, it is, my lord." "Can you catch that tiger?" the Shogun asked again, pointing to a tiger that was painted on a screen before him. "O yes, my lord" replied the young priest calmly, "nothing is easier." "Give me a rope and I will show you how to catch it." When a rope was brought in, Ikkyu stood before the screen, with the rope in his outstretched hands, ready to catch the tiger, and said: "Please drive the tiger out. I am ready to catch him."

PRIEST HAKUIN

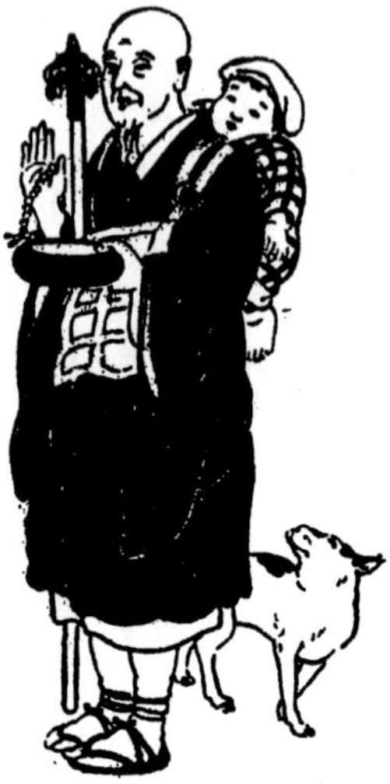

Priest Hakuin on a mendicant trip carrying a baby

Priest Hakuin was born at Hara in Suruga Province in 1685. He entered into Buddhism at the age of ten years. He served at several temples, such as the Shoin-ji Temple of Hara, Daisho-ji Temple of Numadzu, Zuiun-ji Temple of Mino, Shoso-ji Temple of Iyo, Joko-ji Temple of Wakasa, Eigan-ji Temple of Takada, etc., and finally he came back to the Shoin-ji Temple again, where he died in 1768 at the age of 82 years.

Many stories are told about the generosity of Priest Hakuin, who was famous for his religious enlightenment. We give here one or two of the best-known stories regarding his generosity or broad-mindedness.

One day a dealer in Tofu (bean curd) brought a baby born of his daughter, and said to the priest: "People call you a saint, but you are a recreant priest after all. Here is a result of your sin." The dealer went back by leaving the baby.

Priest Hakuin did not retort to the abuses and insults that the indignant Tofu-dealer showered upon him, but gently accepted the new-born baby. Having no maid with him in the temple, Priest Hakuin had to do everything for his new charge. He even washed the swaddling-clothes himself, he went round in the village to ask for milk to give to the baby, and he carried it with him on every pilgrimage and a mendicant trip. He made no complaints about the baby or the insults that the Tofu-dealer made, but he gave the best care he could silently to the baby.

A couple of years went by. One cold morning, the mother of the baby saw Priest Hakuin, who was going on a pilgrimage with her baby on his back. Her conscience smote her. On returning home, she confessed that the baby was not Priest Hakuin's, but that Carpenter Kyusan was its father. The surprised Tofu-dealer went to Priest Hakuin and explained the matter to him with thousand apologies. "All right. You may take the baby to her" was all that Priest Hakuin said in reply, but he showed no sign of offense or indignation and went on discharging his religious duties as if nothing had happened to him. The priest fed the baby for three years without making any complaints.

EMPEROR JIMMU

The Emperor Jimmu, founder of the Imperial line, was the 4th son of Prince Ugaya-Fukiaezu, and his real name was Prince Kamu-Yamato-Iware-Hiko, Jimmu being his posthumous name. He lived in the province of Hiuga in Kyushu, but when he heard of rebels rampant in the eastern, or central, part of Japan, he was determined to lead an army against them. With Prince Itsuse, his brother, Prince Iware-Hiko started on an eastern expedition, and taking Uzuhiko, a hunter, as a guide and pilot, they sailed on the Inland Sea and arrived at Naniwa (Osaka), where they landed to proceed to Yamato Province by way of Mt. Ikoma. Nagasunehiko, a local chieftain, offered them resistance, and a severe battle ensued when Prince Itsuse was mortally wounded by an arrow.

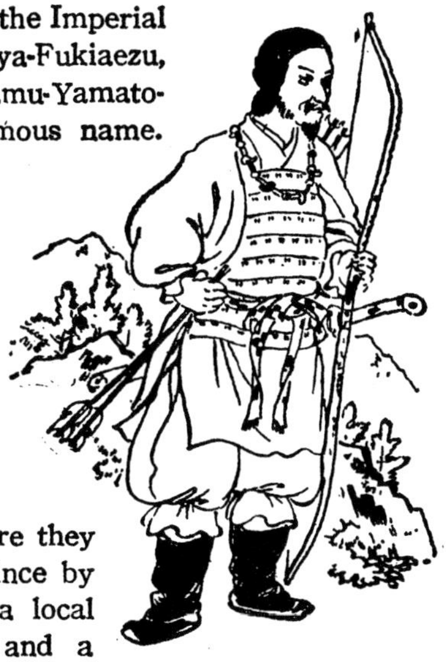

Emperor Jimmu

"I am a descendant of the sun" Prince Iware-Hiko said, for he was offspring of the Sun Goddess, Prince Amaterasu, "and it is not meet that I should fight facing the sun. I will fight with the sun on our side."

So saying Prince Iware-Hiko made a round-about way in order to attack the enemy from his back. He lost his way in the mountains of Kumano. A kite came flying and led the Imperial army, till the prince succeeded in defeating the enemy. This kite, by the way, is the origin of the Golden Kite, a decoration for the army and navy during the prewar days.

All rebels surrendering, Prince Iware-Hiko made his capital at Kashiwara, southeast of Mt. Unebi, where he organized a government by appointing courtiers and officials, and he was enthroned as the first Emperor of Japan on the day in 660 B. C., which is said to correspond to Feb. 11, the day of our prewar national-foundation day or Kigensetsu.

Prince Iware-Hiko died, according to Kojiki, the oldest annals of Japan, at the age of 127 years in 585 B. C. on the day now corresponding to Apr. 3, a prewar national holiday, and he was posthumously named the Emperor Jimmu (lit. divine-bravery). He lies buried on Mt. Unebi in the province of Yamato.

EMPEROR NINTOKU

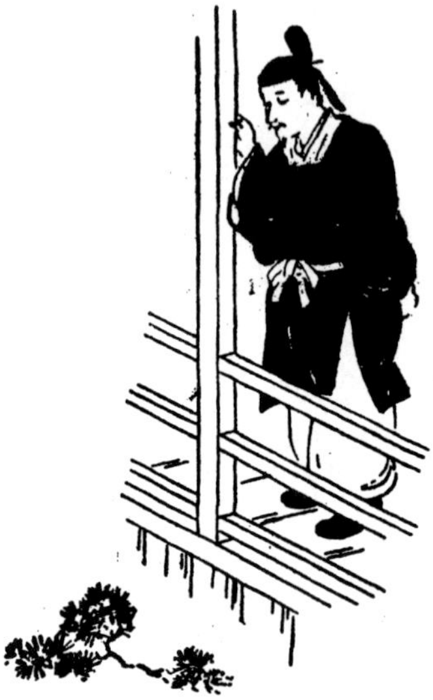
Emperor Nintoku on a tower

The Emperor Ohjin (15th) had two princes, Osasagi and Wakairatsuko, the latter of whom he loved so much that he appointed him crown prince, with the concent of the former, who was his heir by birth.

The Emperor Ohjin died in 310 A. D. But Wakairatsuko would not ascend the throne by ignoring his elder brother, who in turn dared not act against the wishes of their deceased father; each devolving his rights upon the other for three years, during which no tribute was accepted by the court. One fisherwoman, it is said, presented a tribute of fish, which she had to carry between the two princes till it became bad because each told her to take it to the other.

When Prince Wakairatsu saw that nothing could induce his brother to ascend the throne, he committed suicide in 312 A. D. in order to transfer the Imperial prerogative to his brother. Prince Osasagi was enthroned in 313 A. D., and he is the Emperor Nintoku (lit. humane-virtue).

In 316 A. D., the Emperor Nintoku saw from a tower of his palace at Naniwa (Osaka) that few smokes rose up from the neighbouring villages. He concluded that the people must be in insufficiency, and exempted them of taxes for three years.

"We are rich now" the Emperor Nintoku said to his Consort when, at the end of three years, he looked down again upon the neighbouring villages, where he saw many more smokes rising than before.

"How can you say we are rich, Sire" the Consort objected "when our palace is in a ruined condition with rotten roofs and falling walls?" The palace had been left unrepaired during the three years.

"The people's happiness is ours" the Emperor replied. "The smokes rising up from the villages indicate that they are now in plenty. We can now take taxes."

The people were in plenty, and they brought the taxes and tributes of their own accord, and repaired the palace with their own hands. The Emperor Nintoku encouraged agriculture and it is said that there were no criminals in the country during his reign.

The Emperor Nintoku died in 399 A. D. after governing the country for eighty-six years.

SHOGUN OR MILITARY EMPEROR

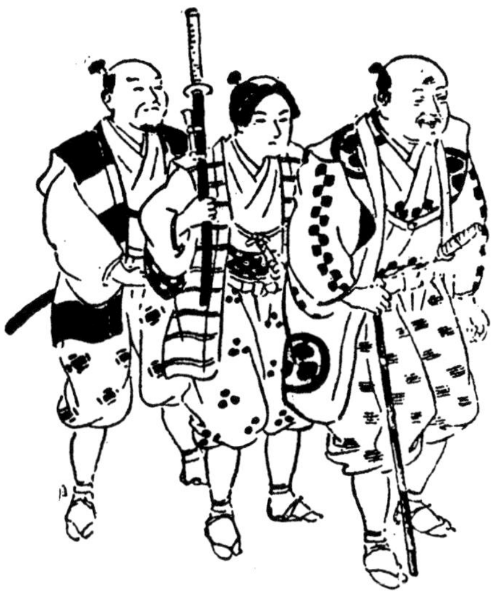

Shogun on a trip in cognito

By the Restoration of 1868 is meant that the state administration of Japan, which had been in the hands of the civil Daijin (minister) or the military Shogun (general) for many a century, was restored to the Imperial court by the Emperor Meiji in that year. The term "Shogun", which is commonly translated "general", like Nogi-Shogun or General Nogi, means the commander-in-chief of the army, but, properly speaking, it is abbreviated from "Seii-Taishogun" or "great general for subjugating the barbarian rebels." Its first mention was made in history when the Emperor Suijin appointed the Shido-Shogun or the Governor-generals for the Four Do or Districts, in 88 B. C. There were several Shogun appointed after them, but they were thrown into the shade by the civil courtiers, chiefly of the Fujiwara family, which wielded the actual power of administration after 859 A. D.

It was Yoritomo Minamoto, founder of the Minamoto Shogunate, that, as the Shogun, held the sway over the country in place of the Emperor. He was appointed "Seii-Taishogun" by the Emperor Gotoba in 1185, but with his death, which took place in 1190, the Hojo family from which his wife, Lady Masako, came, held the actual administrative power of the country, the Shogun holding the sinecure no better than did the Emperor himself. The Hojo regency lasted from 1199 to 1333.

Then came the Ashikaga regime, which lasted from 1338 to 1574. It was followed by Oda and Toyotomi, whose dynasties lasted no more than for a generation or two. Lastly, we had the Tokugawa

Continued

dynasty, which, founded in 1603 after Toyotomi, lasted till 1867, and the feudalism of Japan was abolished by the Emperor Meiji in 1868. Prince Iyesato Tokugawa, who was for many years the President of the House of Peers before the war, would have been the Shogun the XVI had not feudalism been abolished.

THE SHOGUN

Minamoto dynasty
- Yoritomo (1192—1199)
  - Regent Tokimasa Hojo
- Yoriiye (1202—1203)
- Sanetomo (1203)
  - Regent Yoshitoki Hojo

Yoritsune Fujiwara (1220—1244)
- Regent Yasutoki Hojo
- Regent Tsunetoki Hojo

Yoritsugu Fujiwara (1244—1251)
- Regent Tokiyori Hojo

Prince Munetaka (1252—1265)
- Regent Tokimune Hojo

Prince Koreyasu (1266—1289)
- Regent Sadatoki Hojo

Prince Hisaakira (1289—1307)
- Regent Morotoki Hojo

Prince Morikuni (1308—1333)
- Regent Takatoki Hojo

Prince Morinaga (1333—1335)

Prince Shigenaga (1335)

Ashikaga dynasty
- Takauji (1338—1358)
- Yoshiaki (1358—1368)
- Yoshimitsu (1368—1394)
- Yoshimochi (1394—1423)
- Yoshikazu (1423—1425)
- Yoshinori (1429—1441)
- Yoshikatsu (1441—1449)
- Yoshimasa (1449—1473)
- Yoshihisa (1473—1489)
- Yoshitane (1490-1493) (1508-1522)
- Yoshizumi (1493—1508)
- Yoshiharu (1522—1545)
- Yoshiteru (1546—1565)
- Yoshihide (1566—1567)
- Yoshiaki (1568—1573)

Nobunaga Oda (1574—1582)

Toyotomi dynasty
- Hideyoshi (1580—1591)
- Hidetsugu (1591—1595)
- Hideyori (1598—1603)

Tokugawa dynasty
- Iyeyasu (1603—1605)
- Hidetada (1605—1623)
- Iyemitsu (1623—1651)
- Iyetsuna (1651—1681)
- Tsunayoshi (1681—1709)
- Iyenobu (1709—1712)
- Iyetsugu (1713—1716)
- Yoshimune (1716—1745)
- Iyeshige (1745—1761)
- Iyeharu (1761—1786)
- Iyenari (1786—1837)
- Iyeyoshi (1837—1853)
- Iyesada (1853—1858)
- Iyeshige (1858—1866)
- Yoshinobu (1866—1867)

PRINCE YAMATOTAKE

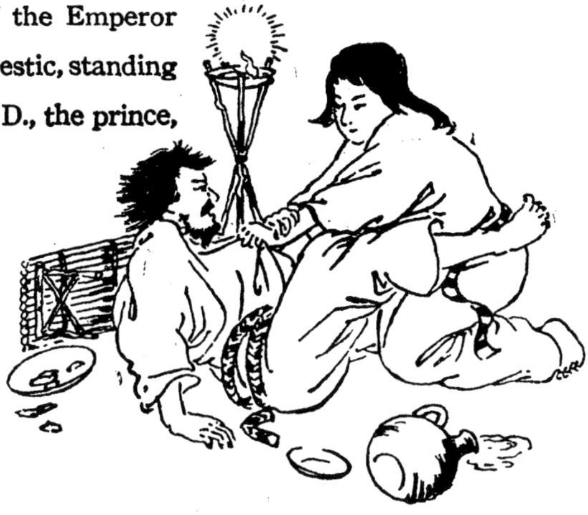

Prince Ousu killing Takeru

Prince Ousu, son of the Emperor Keiko (12th), looked majestic, standing ten feet high. In 97 A. D., the prince, then sixteen years old, was sent to subdue Kawakami-takeru, a rebellious local chief of Kumaso in Kyushu. Disguised as a girl, he mingled among the waitresses who entertained the Takeru (chief) at a banquet, and stabbed him to death with a sword after the prince woke him up. "Hold! Who could you be?" the dying chieftain querried, and when he was told who the assassin was, he went on: "You are the bravest I have ever seen. May I offer you the name of Yamatotake (lit. brave hero of Japan)?" Prince Ousu is, therefore, more generally known by that name, Prince Yamatotake.

In 110 A. D., the eastern rebels rose against the Imperial court, and Prince Yamatotake was again sent on an expedition to subjugate them. He stopped at Ise on the way, where Princess Yamato-hime loaned him the sacred sword of the Ise shrines. When the prince came to the province of Sugura, the rebels took him under the false pretense of hunting deer and they set fire to the fields with the prince to the leawards. The prince saved himself by cutting the grass with the sword. The place is still known as Yaizu (lit. burned-ford) and the sword with which he defended himself is thenceforth called the Kusanagi-no-Tsurugi (lit. grass-cutting sword). The sword is still enshrined in the Shinto shrine at Atsuta, near Nagoya.

Continued

The prince took a boat to cross the present Bay of Sagami. A heavy storm came on, and his ship was tossed in danger. "This must be due to the anger of the sea-god" Princess Oto-tachibana, his consort, said. "I will go to the bottom to appease him." She jumped into the angry sea and the storm soon subsided. Kisarazu, which, according to tradition, is a corruption of Kimi-sarazu (lit. lord-not-leaving), is the place where the prince landing the prince fell into deep thought of his wife.

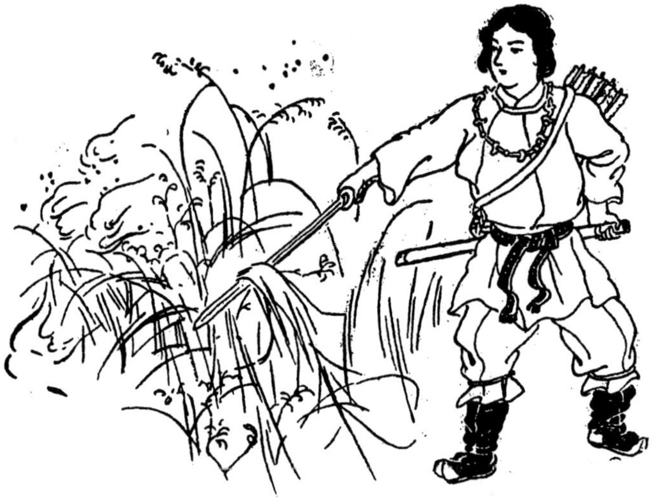

Prince Yamatotake cutting grass down

The prince went on to the pass of Usui, where, looking back towards the Bay of Tokyo, he signed "Azuma-haya!" (Ah my wife), after which the locality in the neighbourhood of Tokyo is called Azuma. Usui, by the way, was for a long time believed to be a pass situated near Karuizawa, but recent studies reveal that it is situated at Miyagino, near Miyanoshita, in Hakone.

All the rebels subjugating, Prince Yamatotake started in triumph for the Imperial capital, but he was taken ill on his way home, and he died at the age of thirty years in the province of Owari. He lies buried at Nobonu in Ise Province.

EMPERORS KENSO AND NINKEN

Prince Ichinobe-no-Oiwa, grandson of the Emperor Richu (17th), had two sons of the same name, Princes Oke (of different Chinese characters). When their father was killed by the Emperor Yuryaku (21st), the two princes took refuge at Yosa in Harima Province, under false names. In the 11th month, 481 A. D., the Governor of the province, on his rounds, stopped at the residence of Hosome, for whom the princes were working as servants.

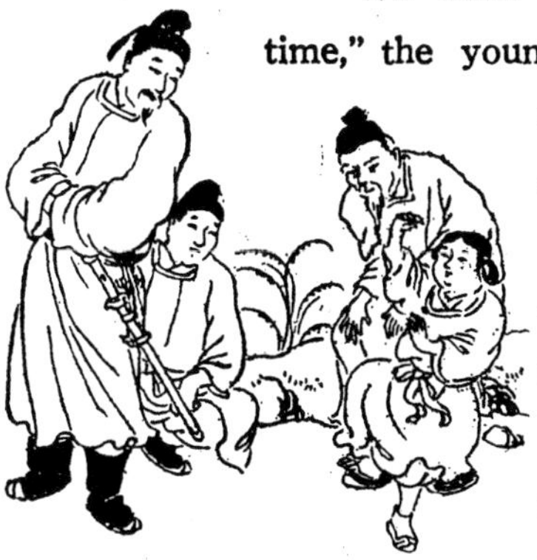
Prince dancing a dance at a banquet

"We have been in disguise for quite a long time," the younger prince said to his elder. "We might seize this opportunity to reveal ourselves to the Governor."

"But which do you prefer," the elder prince asked, "we stay on safely in disguise or get known and killed?"

"We are descendants of the Emperor Iwahowake (Richu) and tired of this life of servitude" the younger Oke said, and they hugged each other in crying over their obscure and miserable life.

At a banquet, Hosome, their master, told the princes to hold the candles and, when dancing began, the Governor asked them to join. The elder prince was too shy to dance, but the younger brother stood up and danced, singing a song which hinted that they were of Imperial descent. The Governor, in great surprise, made a report on them, and the Emperor Seinei (22nd), who had no issue, was so pleased at the good news that the two princes were at once called to the court. The elder prince was soon appointed the successor to the throne.

Continued

When the Emperor Seinei died in 484 A. D., the elder prince refused to ascend the throne, asking his brother to be enthroned in his place.

"The late Emperor made me his heir because I am your elder brother" the elder prince said. "But since we were brought back to the court on your account, you must be first enthroned."

Neither accepting the throne, Princess Iitoyo-no-Ao, their aunt, attended to the administration, but she died within a year of the death of the Emperor Seinei. After a long talk with his brother, therefore, the younger prince ascended the throne, and he is the Emperor Kenso, (23rd).

"When our father was killed by the Emperor Yuryaku," the new Emperor said to his brother when the grave of their father was discovered after a long search. "I was too young to do anything by way of revenge. We must now take revenge upon the death of our father by opening the grave of our enemy."

"Nothing would be a greater disgrace to the dead than to have their graves opened" Prince Oke, the elder, denied." "Our father was a mere prince, but his enemy was an Emperor, who is higher than anybody else. Why should we open the grave to put him to disgrace? And we are taken back to the court through the goodness of the late Emperor, son of our enemy. We should do nothing so outrageous as to open the grave of an Emperor."

The Emperor Kenso obeyed and abandoned his desire of opening the grave of the Emperor Yuryaku.

When the Emperor Kenso died in 487 A. D., the elder prince was enthroned, and he is the Emperor Ninken (24th).

Yoshiiye Minamoto, Warlord of Great Popularity

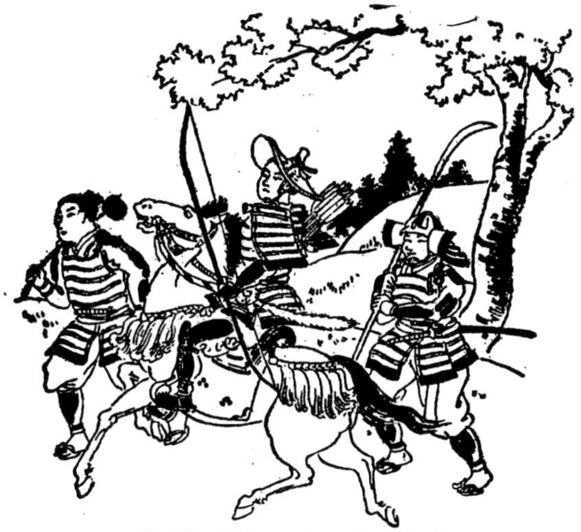

Yoshiiye Minamoto on horseback

Minamoto-no-Yoshiiye is perhaps one of the most popular warlords of Feudal Japan. He was a great tactician, known for his humane acts and well versed in literature.

After the fall in 1091 of the fort of Koromo-gawa (lit. dress-river) of the north, Yoshiiye pursued Sadato, son of a local chief, in hot chase, and, while chasing him, he addressed his enemy in verse:

"Koromo-no-Tate wa
Hokorobi ni keri"

This 14-syllable verse means, as it stands, that the warp of Koromo (dress) is broken, but enigmatically the verse implies that the fort of Koromo is fallen.

Uta, the Japanese poem, by the way, consists of two parts; the first part of seventeen syllables and the second part of fourteen, and it was a common practice in our feudal days that, if a warrior was addressed either in the first or in the second verse, by his enemy in battle, he had to improvise the other part in reply. Yoshiiye's verse being the second part of fourteen syllables, Sadato at once replied in a verse of seventeen, reading:—

"Toshi wo heshi
Ito no Midare no
Kurushisa ni."

Continued

(The lapse of years having told hard upon the worn dress.)

The two verses mean literally that the warp of the dress is broken because of its old age, and, at the same time, they refer to the fall of Koromo, Sadato's fortress. The literary warlord gave up his chase, suffering his literary enemy to escape, though later on they became fast friends.

Yoshiiye led an army against Takehira Kiyowara and his brother in the north. When he approached their fort, he saw a confused flight of wild geese.

"It is recorded in a book of tactics" said our tactician lord, "that a disordered flight of wild geese betrays an ambuscade."

A search was at once instituted, and a number of soldiers were found in ambuscade.

Yoshiiye is perhaps best known for a poem that he improvised at a barrier called Nakoso (lit. don't-come) in the province of Iwaki. It runs:

"Fuku-kaze mo
Nakoso-no-Seki to
Omoishi ni
Michi mo Seni chiru
Yama-zakura-bana."

(Even to the blowing wind, I thought, this was the Don't-come Barrier, but lo! how the roads are the running rapids of the fallen mountain-cherry-blossoms!)

At one time Yoshiiye shot at a fox that he saw in the distance. It was hit, and rolled down. Sadato running forth, said "It's dead." "No," said the good archer. "No, it has only fainted because I shot through its ears." Sure enough, when Sadato pulled the arrow off, the fox, coming to its senses, scampered off.

Yoshiiye Minamoto died in 1108.

GENZAMMI YORIMASA AND "NUE"

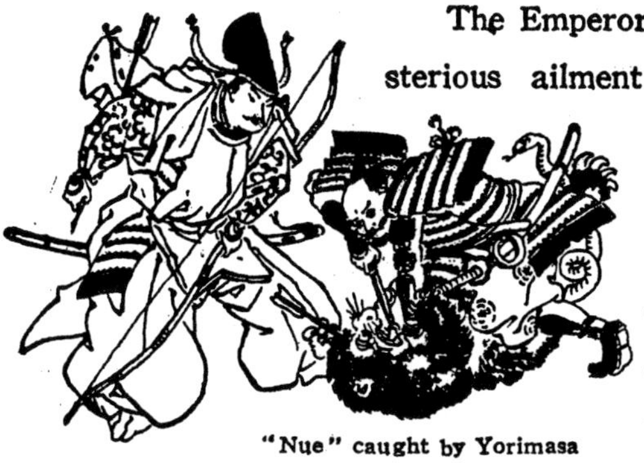

"Nue" caught by Yorimasa

The Emperor Nijo (78th) had a mysterious ailment in the fourth month (April) in the year 1160. Every night, after midnight, or, to be more exact, at the zodiac time of the Bull, the Emperor was seized with agony, which no medicine, offered by the court-physician, could alleviate nor was a prayer, offered at the shrines and temples, of any more avail. It was discovered that every time when the Emperor suffered, some dark banks of clouds were seen appearing in the direction of Sanjo in Kyoto, the Imperial capital, which, moving on, settled over the Nanden-Palace and a strange voice, sounding "nue," was heard from the clouds. At last it was decided at court to call Genzammi Yorimasa of the Minamoto family, one of the best archers of the day, and tell him to shoot at the mysterious animal in the clouds. On the appointed night Yorimasa, clad in an archer's attire, went to the Imperial Palace and waited for the mysterious clouds to appear. In the zodiac time of the Bull (2 a. m.) there appeared, as usual, dark banks of clouds over the forest of Sanjo, and when they settled over the Imperial Palace, the Emperor began to suffer. Yorimasa put an arrow on his bow, offered an inward prayer to Hachiman, the guardian god of his Minamoto family, and shot it into the clouds. He felt that it told. Another arrow was shot immediately after it and again it must have hit something in the clouds. Sure enough, something dropped dead from the clouds upon the roof of the Palace—a strange

Continued

animal, which had the head of a monkey, the back of a tiger, the tail of a fox and the legs of a badger. Nobody knew what it was, but it was named "Nue" because it made a sound like "nue".

The strange animal was soon buried in the grounds of the Kiyomizu Temple and the Emperor conferred upon Genzammi Yorimasa a sword and a suit of dress as a token of his appreciation.

Yorimasa and Lady Ayame: Lady Ayame (lit. iris) was a favorite court-lady with the ex-Emperor Toba (74th). Yorimasa, who was a court-warrior, was charmed with her beauty and he loved her. One day Yorimasa was called to the court by the Emperor, who asked him if he loved Lady Ayame. Yorimasa, abashed, could make no reply, when the Emperor called three ladies so similarly dressed that they could not be told one from another.

"I know that you love Lady Ayame" the Emperor said to Yorimasa. "One of these girls is she. You find her and she shall be yours."

Yorimasa was too much embarrassed to know what to do, but he improvised an ode of 31 syllables. It read:

"Samidare ni
Numa no Ishigaki
Mizu koete
Izure ka Ayame
Hikizo hatsuro."

Free translation: "The water overflowing the stone-walls of the pond due to an early summer-rain, it is impossible to know which is Ayame (iris)."

The Emperor was so pleased with the improvization that, stepping forth, with tears of joy in his eyes, he took Lady Ayame by the hand and handed her to Yorimasa, saying "You shall have Ayame."

Yorimasa and Lady Ayame were married and they lived a happy life in the peninsula of Izu, not far from Hakone.

DOKAN OHTA

FOUNDER OF EDO CASTLE

So long as the Imperial Palace of Tokyo exists, the name of Dokan Ohta will be gratefully remembered, for it was he who, in 1456, built the Chiyoda castle of Edo, the forerunner of the present Imperial Palace of Tokyo. Little must Ohta have imagined that his capital should grow up to be the second largest city in the world, with a population of no less than eight millions, as Tokyo was before the war.

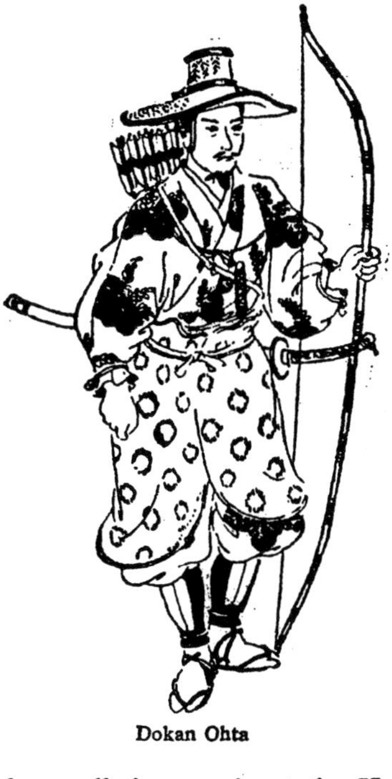

Dokan Ohta

Ohta was born in 1432, and his childhood name was Tsuruchiyo, which was changed into Mochisuke when he came of age, though he is better known by the name of Dokan, which he assumed upon his conversion to Buddhism.

He was a clever boy and could write as well at eleven years of age as any grown-up people. When he was fifteen years old, his father, who felt a little uneasy with his over-sagacity for his age, told him, by way of precepts, that a board-fence would fall down when crooked, but stand safe when straight. Young Ohta brought out Byobu (Japanese folding-screen) to show his father that it would fall down when straight whereas it stands when bent.

Ohta was one of the most active and powerful lords in the Kanto districts in which Edo, as Tokyo was then called, was situated. He lived at the Chiyoda or Edo castle, into which Iyeyasu, the founder of the Tokugawa regime later removed, but after the Restoration of the Imperial administration in 1868 it was made the site of the Imperial Palace.

Ohta was once out hunting and was caught in a shower. He called at a cottage close by and asked for a rain-coat. A girl of sixteen came out. She held out to him an open fan with a small branch of *Yamabuki*, or yellow rose, on. Ohta could make nothing

Continued

of it, but on returning home he was told by a retainer that the girl must have meant to quote an old poem of 31 syllables about the yellow rose, reading:

"Nanae-yae
Hana wa sakedomo
Yamabuki no
Mino hitotsu dani
Nakizo kanashiki"

The poem means, as it stands, that it is a pity that the yellow rose, with its double flowers, bears no fruit. But "Mino" here has a double meaning: "of fruit" and "rain-coat". So the girl evidently meant that she had no rain-coat.

Ohta, being a warrior, made light of learning, to say little of poetry, for he thought that militarism was the only art necessary to a warrior of his position. But this little incident put him to shame and also to thinking, and he became a poet. Once he was received in audience by the Emperor Go-tsuchimikado, who asked him how extensive the plain of Musashino, where Edo was situated, was. Ohta replied in poetry, saying in effect that the plain was so vast that there are some places where dew falling from the wide sky cannot cover. "My house", Ohta again said in poetry when the Emperor asked a question about his residence, "is connected with the sea by pine-avenues and Mt. Fuji is viewed from under my eaves."

In 1486 Sadamasa Uyesugi, who was jealous of the growing influence of Ohta, invited him to a banquet, and, while Ohta was taking a bath, several warriors assailed him with spears from behind the walls of the bath-room. Ohta caught a few spears in his hands and improvised his *Jisei* (farewell-to-the-world poem) or death-bed poem of 31 syallables, reading:

"Kino made
Mama-moshu wo
Ire-okishi
Hennashi Bukuro
Ima yabure ken".

The poem means in effect that the seamless or worthless bag, meaning his body, which contained delusions until yesterday, is now broken, namely, dead.

He was fifty-five years old when he was assassinated, and he lies buried at Isehara in Kanagawa Prefecture.

PRIEST TEIA, THE TATTOOED

A drama written on fact by Shigemaru Sugiyama

It was in spring that two pilgrims, evidently brother and sister, in their teens were dragging their weary steps up the steep path of Mt. Kenji in the Shikoku Provinces. They had been travelling from place to place, apparently on a pilgrimage, but really in search of their enemy, for over ten long years. Disappointed at their fruitless trips to trace him, they were now climbing Mt. Kenji, which was founded by Priest Kobo, and known for miracles wrought by Zo-o Gongen, who is enshrined on the mountain.

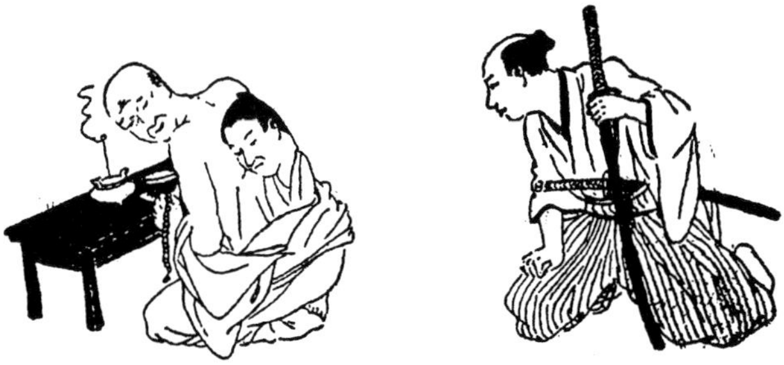

Son finds his father's picture tattooed on the back of enemy

On the way they met an old man, Jihei by name, over 70 years of age, carrying a stone-image of Jizo on his back. He spoke highly of the virtues of Priest Teia, a saintly resident-priest of Mt. Kenji, who had initiated the erection, on the mountain, of eighty-eight stone-images of Jizo, which the old man had to carry up on his back like the one that he had. When he told the pilgrims that the priest hailed from a northern province, the sister betrayed a start. He may be their enemy! So she urged her brother to hasten on in order to meet the holy priest.

They found Priest Teia undergoing his regular asceticism under a large waterfall of 80 feet long, as he was wont to have it twice a day. He was chanting the sutra loudly all the time.

Continued

"We are Kiyoharu and Matae, two children of Kiyonari Magara of the Ishikawa clan, whom you murdered ten years ago" the two young pilgrims shouted the moment they cast their eyes on the priest. They recognized their enemy at once in him, for whom they had been searching all these years. "You are no doubt Tosai Ishikawa, though you disguise yourself as a dog of a priest."

They challenged the priest to come out at once and have a fight with them. Nothing daunted, Priest Teia went on with his cold ablutions as hard as ever, and when his austerities were over, he slowly walked out of the waterfall and stood before them.

Tosai Ishikawa, for that was the worldly name of Priest Teia, and Kiyonari Magara, father of the young pilgrims, were cousins in the clan of Ishikawa. When there was a civil trouble in the clan, Ishikawa killed Magara by mistake, and he disappeared from the clan. He first went to Mt. Hiyei, where he was converted into Buddhism under Priest Gakunen, and then he came to Mt. Kenji in Shikoku Provinces.

"I am willing to receive your blow," Priest Teia went on after he explained his situation. "I am willing to receive your blow, but I fear that your sword will be powerless, sharp as it may be—too weak to kill me."

So saying, Priest Teia stripped himself naked, and he had the picture of their father beautifully tattooed on his back. He always carried on his back the picture of his wronged cousin, and himself underwent the ascetic ablutions with a prayer that his cousin might have a peaceful rest. He had renounced the world for the sake of Magara, his cousin.

The young pilgrims were too much touched with the noble deed of their supposed enemy to attack him, and they both, converted into Buddhism, took the tonsure under Priest Teia in order to join him in praying for the peaceful rest of their father.

KIKEN MURAKAMI

There are forty-eight tombs, instead of forty-seven, in the little burial-place of the 47-Ronin at the Senagku-ji Temple, Tokyo, because one is erected over the remains of Kiken Murakami, who was given the privilege of sleeping buried in the same cemetery as the 47 Ronin, though he was not one of the party.

Kiken Murakami was a warrior of the Satsuma clan at the southern end of Kyushu. When Naganori Asano, lord of the Ako clan, was condemned to suicide by the Shogun for his unsuccessful attempt at the life of Yashinaka Kira in the Shogunate castle, Murakami was indignant at the indifferent attitude of the ex-warriors, or Ronin (lit. men on the waves) of the clan, which was abolished on account of the ignoble death of their lord. According to Murakami's samurai-idea, the ex-warriors of the clan should take revenge upon the death of their lord, but Yoshio Oishi, the Karo or clan-minister, took to a life of dissipation, and frequented ill-famed houses where he stayed for days and nights on end, apparently forgetting his important duty of avenging the humiliation of Lord Asano. One day Murakami caught Oishi in making merry in a bevy of girls in a house of ill repute. He called names at the shameless ex-Karo of the Ako clan, kicked at him and spat upon him. He abused Oishi with all sorts of insults conceivable and yet the ex-Karo might have been wood or stone, for he simply smiled a blank smile at Kiken Muraki, his

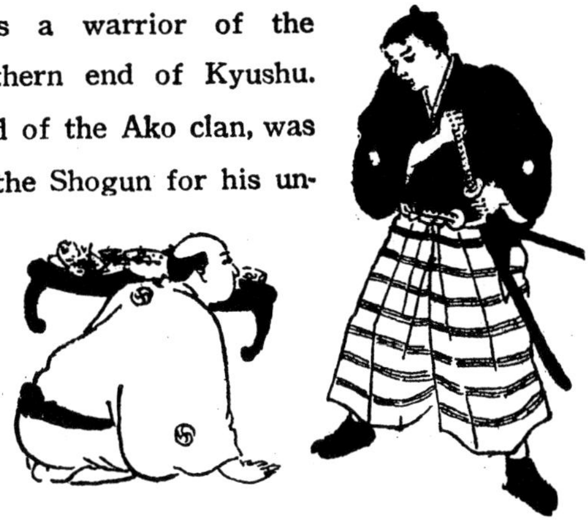

Kiken Murakami abusing Yoshio Oishi

Continued

abuser, who, utterly disgusted with Yoshio Oishi, went home to his clan of Satsuma.

But what was his surprise when, on arriving at Satsuma, his native clan, Murakami heard that Yoshio Oishi, whom he had abused and humiliated in every way possible, succeeded in avenging the death of their lord, with forty-six other Ronin, in the Shogunate Capital of Edo on the 14th of the twelfth month (December), 1702.

Murakami was so mortified with his misplaced, though well-meant, insults that he started again for the Shogunate capital of Edo (Tokyo) with no loss of time. But he arrived there too late, for the 47 Ronin, having surrendering themselves to the Government authorities, after offering the head of Kira, to the grave of Lord Asano, had committed suicide at the Sengaku-ji Temple, where their disgraced lord lay buried.

"I never thought" the penitent Murakami said, when he sat before the grave of Yoshio Oishi, leader of the party, whom he had insulted. "I never thought that you were making secret preparations for taking revenge by beguiling the public with apparent debauchery. I only feared that you had forgot your duties with your dead lord in leading a reckless life. I will follow you to the other world and make an apology in person."

Kiken Murakami committed *harakiri* before the grave of Yoshio Oishi and the admirers of Murakami's spirit buried his remains in the cemetery as those of the 47 Ronins. You will find his tomb at the left-hand end of the row when you enter the little burial-place where the 47 Ronin lay buried. His grave is No. 48th in the graveyard of 47 Ronins.

Murder was not the object of the 47 Ronin in taking revenge, but they offered the head of the enemy to the grave of their lord, whose departed spirit it was their only object in view to comfort and they killed themselves.

MENCIUS'S MOTHER AND THREE REMOVALS

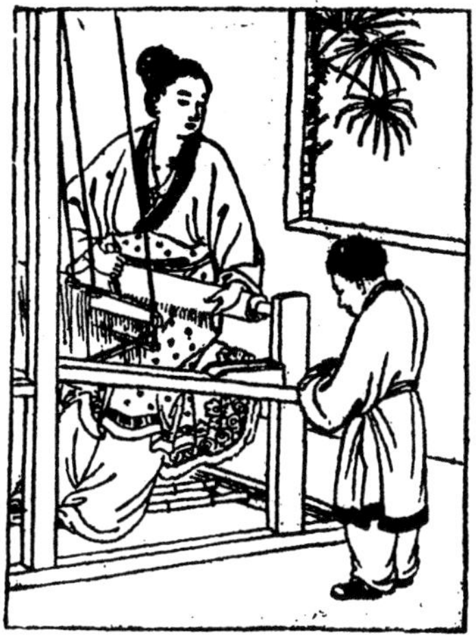

Mencius's mother snaps the thread of her loom

Mencius is a Chinese savant whose doctrine and philosophy were as extensively followed by our samusai of old as were those of Confucius, and his mother is generally regarded among the most influential in moulding the personality of Japan's womanhood.

When a boy, Mencius was not a diligent pupil, but he often played truant, coming home without the permission of the teacher. One day, when he came home, as usual, before school was over, his mother, who was working at a weaving-loom, snapped all the thread off with a pair of scissors, and said: "My son, learning done by halves is no more of use than is cloth that is cut off while being woven."

Mencius's mother is well known in Japan for three removals that she made in order to give her son the better bringing-up. First she lived near a graveyard. Our innocent boy imitated the priest and played at the burial of the dead or some other religious matter. "This is no place for the boy" his mother said to herself and she shifted off.

She then lived in the business quarters of her town. Young Mencius imitated hawkers and other dealers, with whose children he was associated, playing at selling things, till his mother removed off again, for a merchant, who makes a profit at the cost of other people, is not held in esteem in the Orient

At the third time Mencius's mother selected a place near a school for living. Her son played with the school-children, after whose manners he studied learning. This time his mother was satisfied, and she was settled there permanently.

Mencius's mother is regarded as an ideal woman in Japan, and her "three removals" is a proverbial saying in Japan as showing an ideal method of bringing up a child.

KOJIKI, THE OLDEST HISTORY OF JAPAN

The *Kojiki* (lit. old-annals) is the oldest record of Japan. It was compiled by Futo-no-Yasumaro. According to its preface, the Emperor Temmu (40th), who wanted to have an authentic history of Japan and the Imperial family, ordered Hiyeda-no-Are, then a lad (possibly a girl) of twenty-eight years, to study old records and write a history. Hiyeda-no-Are studied many records, but did not write a history. The Empress Gemmyo (43rd) then ordered Futo-no-Yasumaro, on the 18th of the ninth month (September), 711 A. D., to write a history, and he wrote down what was verbally told by Hiyeda-no-Are, then about sixty years old, out of his (her) memory. The book was completed on the 28th of the first month (January), 712 A. D.

The *Kojiki* consists of three books or 48 volumes; the first treating of the Jindai (lit. Gods' dynasty) or pre-historic days, from Ame-no-Minakanushi-no-Kami (lit. Heaven's Central-master-god) down to Prince Ugaya-Fuki-Aezu (lit. maternity-roof-not-yet-thatched-Prince), father of the Emperor Jimmu, so named, according to tradition, because he was born before his maternity-room was fully prepared; the second book recording the reigns from the first Emperor who was enthroned in 660 B. C. down to the Emperor Ojin (15th); and the third book from the Emperor Nintoku (16th) to the Empress Suiko (33rd). The *Kojiki*, therefore, is a history of Japan from the mythological days up to the Empress Suiko.

Scholars do not agree as to the sex of Hiyeda-no-Are, who dictated the book, for Norinaga Motoori, who wrote the *Kojiki-den*, a commentary on the *Kojiki*, thinks that Hiyeda-no-Are was a man, while Atsutane Hirata, one of the greatest authorities on Shintoism, is of opinion that Hiyeda-no-Are was a woman.

The oldest copy of the *Kojiki* extant, written by Priest Ken-yu in 1371, is preserved at the Shinfuku-ji Temple in the province of Saitama.

Manyoshu or an Anthology of 10,000 Poems

The Manyoshu, which literally means a "collection of ten thousand leaves", is the oldest anthology of poetry in Japan. It consists of twenty volumes containing 4,496 poems written during a period of 440 years between the reigns of the Emperor Nintoku (the 16th) and the Emperor Junnin (the 47th).

The Manyoshu is generally believed to have been compiled by Tachibana-no-Moroe, the Minister of the Left, at the command of the Empress Koken (the 46th), but the latest poem contained in the book dates A. D. 759, while Tachibana-no-Moroe died in 757, two years before the book was completed. It seems that the selection was suspended on account of the death in 756 of the Emperor Shomu. It is more authentically proved that larger contributions are made to the selection by Ohtomo-no-Yakamochi, in whose family the Manyoshu was found preserved. The Manyoshu was made public in 808 during the reign of the Emperor Heijo (the 52nd). The original copy of the Manyoshu has been lost, though we have several very old hand-written copies of it.

The Manyoshu has 4,173 Tanka (or short poems), 262 Choka (or long poems) and 61 Sedoka (or poems 7 syllables longer than Tanka), totalling 4,496, which are also classified into the following four kinds; viz., 1. miscellaneous poems, 2. love poems, 3. elegies and 4. symbolics. This anthology contains poems written by Emperors, Empresses, courtiers, court-ladies, ordinary citizens and villagers, practically representing all scales of society, so that the Manyoshu may well be said to be the voice of the whole nation during the periods of time that the book covers, though a majority of the poems belong to a period of 130 years, from the Emperor Jomei (the 34th) to the Emperor Junnin.

Here are a few poems of the Manyoshu translated into English:—(Translator Tetsuzo Okada)

With a Basket

Emperor Yuryaku

"With a basket, a fine basket,

Continued

With a digge , a fine digger,
Thou maiden who gatherest the herbs
On this hillside,
Where is thy house ?
What is thy name ?
Knowest thou that all Yamato's land
Is mine, over it all I reign ?
Call me thy lord and tell me ;
Where is thy house ?
What is thy name ? "

MOON NIGHT

Otomo-no-Yotsuna

" Fine is the moon-light night,
Clear is the river sound.
They who on a journey go,
They who at home remain,
Let both enjoy the night."

ON HIS WIFE'S DEATH

Kakinomoto-no-Hitomaro

" My love wanders her way
Lost among the red leaves
Of autumn's forest deep.
Yet not knowing the paths
Of hills, for her I weep."

AN ADMONITION

Otomo-no-Yakamochi

" Know that scarlet will soon fade.
It compares ill with the dress
Dyed with common chestnut juice."

INCONSTANT LIFE

Anon

" Life that inconstant is
E'en when at home we' stay—
Now drifting o'er sea waves,
Where it ends who can say ? "

ONNA-DAIGAKU OR ANALECTS FOR WOMEN

In the feudal days of Japan the daughter of a samurai included in her trousseau a book titled the *Onna-daigaku* (lit. women's great learning), the word "Daigaku" being now translated "university". What the *Rongo,* the *Analects* of Confucius, which every samurai had to master, was to a young man of old, the *Onna-daigaku* was to a young woman, who had to have the whole book on the tips of her fingers, so to speak, before she reached marriageable age, because this was the only book of morals for young womanhood in our feudal days.

The *Great learning of women* was written by Ekiken Kaibara, a great scholar of Chinese classics, who lived in the 17th century, although some scholars attribute it pretty authentically to the pen of his wife. It has eighteen items which every woman should bear in mind. Greatest emphasis is first laid on the importance of obedience, on the part of a bride, especially to her husband and parents-in-law. Kaibara then places personality above good looking, and warns against luxury. A young man and woman, he says, should not sit together without the permission of their parents, nor should their clothing put together lest some mistake should ensue between them. To a woman, he goes on, her husband is her all-in-all, her only master on earth. Kaibara then warns against jealousy, rude word, ill-behavior, cruelty to maids, drinking, extravagant living and several other misconducts on the part of a woman.

"Many do not mind, it is said, spending 1,000,000 coins in order to give their daughter in marriage", Ekiken Kaibara says in the conclusion of his book, "but they grudge spending 100,000 coins on the education of their children. It would be of greater importance and effect to have a girl get all these items by heart one by one than wed her with a trousseau of fine dresses."

Kaibara bases his precepts on the theory of woman's inferiority to man, and he places a wife under her husband. This book has been entirely forgotten as being quite out of date in modern Japan.

ROMANCE OF O-SHICHI AND KICHIZA

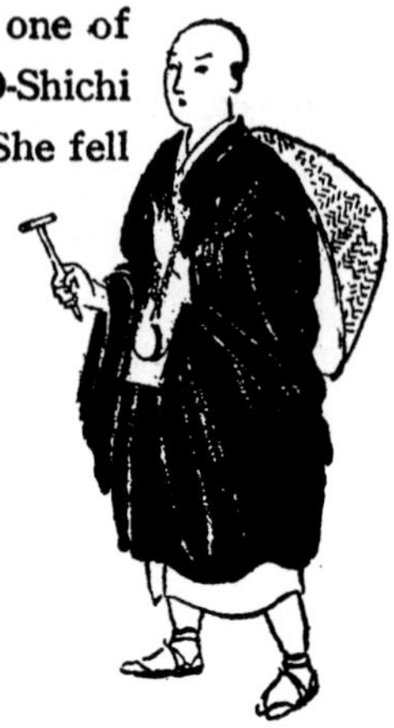

Priest on a pilgimage

The love affair of O-Shichi and Kichiza is one of the most romantic stories staged in Japan. O-Shichi was born daughter of a green-grocer in 1668. She fell in love with Kichiza, sexton of the Enrin-ji Temple, in Bunkyo Ward, Edo (Tokyo.) Because they could not see each other so often as they wished, the foolish girl set fire to her own house on the 28th of the 12th month (December), 1682, in the hopes that her father might take shelter in the Enrin-ji Temple, where she could see her lover as often as she wished. But, contrary to her expectation, O-Shichi was taken, not to the temple she desired, but to the execution-grounds, where she was put to death for incendiarism at the age of sixteen years, on the 29th of the third month (March), 1683.

Kichiza, now left to himself, became a priest assuming the Buddhist name of Saiun (lit. western-fate) and lived at the Fudo shrine, Meguro. He was determined to pray for the peaceful rest of his love's departed spirit by living a life of pilgrimage for her, and he walked every other day, for ten thousand days, over ten miles, back and forth between Meguro and the Kannon shrine at Asakusa, always repeating the Buddhist formula of "Namu-Amida-Butsu."

Priest Saiun died on the 4th of the tenth month (October), 1740, and he was buried in the cemetery of the Daien-ji Temple, Meguro, which many lovers still visit in order to pay their sympathetic respects to the disappointed lovers. O-Shichi lies buried at the Enjo-ji Temple, Koishikawa.

The Daien-ji Temple, Meguro, has a wooden image of Jichiza attired like a pilgrim, and a deep-indented metal-bell that the love-lorn priest kept beating during his tertian trips to Asakusa shows how devoted and faithful he was to his love.

WAKA OR JAPANESE POEMS

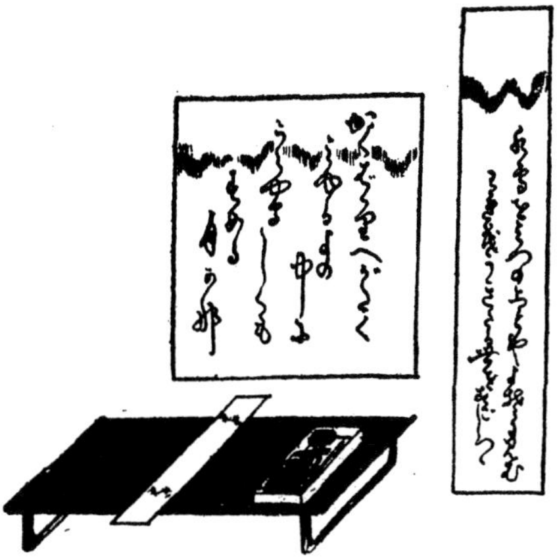

Two Waka written on paper and a Japanese desk

Every Japanese has a poetic nature and is, so to speak, a poet by nature, possibly because, born in a country of scenic and artistic beauty, he is naturally charmed to express himself in verse, by which in our case is generally meant an ode called Waka (lit. Japanese poem) of thirty-one syllables. Waka, short as it is, is not at all easy to compose, but, on the contrary, it is, to some extent, harder than is a prose or a longer poem, because a complete thought has to be expressed in so few syllables. Our ode is, therefore, concise and suggestive, and nevertheless expressive, and one often has to read between the lines to get or appreciate its real meaning.

There are many anthologies of Waka in Japan, of which the Manyoshu (lit. 10,000-leaf collection), the Kokinshu (lit. ancient and modern collection), and the Shin-Kokinshu (lit. new Kokinshu) are among the most noted. The Emperor Meiji wrote over sixty thousand Waka-poems during his life-time.

A Waka-ode is composed of thirty-one syllables, which are divided into the Kami-ku (lit. upper clause) of 5, 7 and 5 meters and the Shimo-ku (lit. lower clause) of 7 and 7 meters, as is illustrated by the following verse of the "spirit of the Japanese":—

Kami-ku	5	Shikishima no
	7	Yamato kokoro wo
	5	Hito towaba
Shimo-ku	7	Asahi ni niou
	7	Yama-zakura bana

"The spirit of Yamato's isles
If, chance, a stranger shall inquire,

Continued

Go show the morning sun that smiles
Upon the mountain-cherry fair!"

(Translated by Prof. H. Saito)

Here are a few more Waka and their free translations:

"Yomo no Umi
Mina Harakara to
Omou yo ni
Nado Namikaze no
Tachi-sawagu ran"

— the Emperor Meiji

Translation;
"All seas of the Four Sides
As brothers and sisters are considered:
Why should in life
The wind and the waves turbulent be?"

"Koto tareba
Taru ni makasete
Koto tarazu
Tarade Koto-taru
Miko koso yasukere"

—Michizane Sugawara

Translation:
"Sufficiency becomes insufficiency because of its own sufficiency; happy is one who can make sufficiency out of insufficiency."

"Morotomo ni
Aware to omoe
Yamazakura
Hana yori hoka ni
Shiru Hito mo nashi"

— Priest Gyoson

"With thee, O mountain Sakura-tree!
A lonely fate I moan
The blossom alone cheers me—
The only friend I own."

(Translated by F. V. Dickins)

RENGA OR POETIC CAPPING

In 1062 A. D. Yoshiiye, a warlord of the military family of Minamoto, attacked Sadato Abe at the fort of Koromo-gawa (lit. dress-river), at the fall of which, when Abe escaped, Yoshiiye, pursuing, addressed him in an ode of 14 syllables, reading:—

"Koromo-no-Tate wa
Hokorobi ni keri."

Literally translated, the verse means that the warp (tate) of his dress (koromo) was torn, but enignatically it implies that the fort (tate) of *Koromo*-gawa was defeated. The escaping enemy also improvised a reply in verse, reading:

"Toshi wo heshi
Ito no Midare no
Kurushisa ni,"

which may be freely rendered: "The old shabby yarn being unable to stand it."

Uta or Japanese ode consists of 31 syllables, which are divided into Kami-ku (upper section) of 5, 7 and 5 syllables and Shimo-ku (lower section) of 7 and 7 syllables.

In Renga or poetic capping, one person writes one section, either Kami-ku or Shimo-ku, and another person caps it with the other. In the case cited above, Yoshiiye improvised a lower section, which Abe capped with an upper section.

When Prince Izanagi, father of the Goddess Amaterasu, said a certain thing in verse to Princess Izanami, she replied in verse, and Prince Yamatotake, who asked a question in verse during his eastern expedition in 112 A. D., was answered in verse also. And these are considered to be the two oldest cases of Renga, verse capping, in Japan.

Renga, which is witty improvization of verse, was much in vogue among court-nobles and warriors during the feudal times of Japan. A Renga contest was an annual affair held at the Shogunate court of Edo (Tokyo) on the 11th of the first month (January), when the Shogun himself participated in the contest.

Continued

Once a Renga contest was held somewhere by many Renga poets, when a shabbily clad priest, who happened to come along the way, stopped and sat much interested on the veranda of the room where the contest was held. One of the party, getting a hint from the mendicant, wrote:

"Kukuri mo tokazu
Ashi mo nurasazu."

meaning: "One need not untie one's skirt-cord or get one's feet wet." Nobody present could cap this Shimo-ku (latter) verse, when the onlooking priest, with permission, put in, to the joy of all present; thus:

"Nanishi ou
Hana-no-Shirakawa
Wataru niwa."

Freely translated: "When one wades across the flowery white-river of great renown." The two sections combined mean: "One need not take off one's skirt or get one's feet wet when one crosses reputed rapids scattered over with white flowers."

A famous astronomer had a wife who had an illicit relation with a priest, whose name was Asahi-no-Ajari (lit. rising-sun acharya or priest), who used to visit her in his absence One day the astronomer came home at an unexpected time, and the priest, whose retreat was cut off, ran out at the western entrance of the house, when the pursuing astronomer improvised:

"Ayashikute
Nishi ni Asahi ga
Izuru kana."

"Suspiciously in the west Asahi (morning-sun) comes out" and the suspected priest replied in verse:

"Temmon-hakase
Ikaga miru-ran."

"How does the astronomer-professor account for it, I wonder?"

Both burst out laughing, and the priest was forgiven, they becoming fast friends.

Shigenari Kimura, A Typical Samurai of Old

Shigenari Kimura served with the Toyotomi dynasty (1585–1603) in its declining days. He died at the unripe age of 21 years, but he may be said to have lived longer than the average span of human life if his life could be measured by its usefulness, for he was one of the most important samurai during the last years of the Toyotomi family. He was a typical samurai of old and died as such.

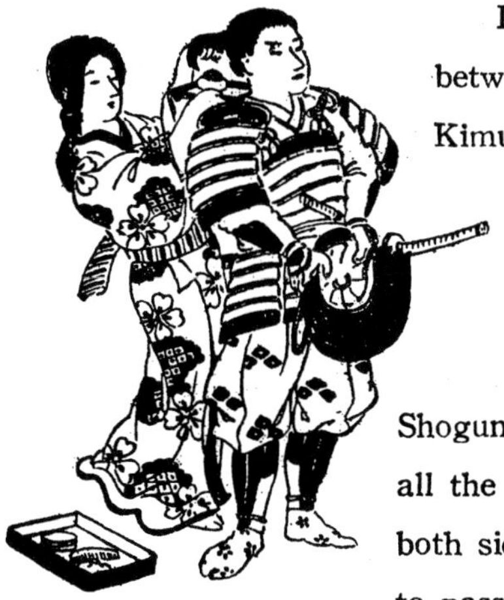

Shigenari Kimura starting for the front

In 1614, when peace was concluded between Toyotomi and Tokugawa, Kimura, just out of his teens, was sent on an important mission of getting the peace agreement signed by Iyeyasu, the ex-Shogun of Tokugawa. On his arrival at the Shogunate Palace, young Kimura saw all the Shogunate dignitaries sitting on both sides of a long passage-way he had to pass along, but he walked straight on with dignity, but no sign of fear, without even returning the greetings of the Shogunate lords, until he came into the presence of the ex-Shogun, whose signature he received. When he retired from the ex-Shogunate presence, Kimura bowed politely at every Shogunate lord and said: "Last time when I passed along this hall, I carried an important mission in representation of my lord, Toyotomi, and so I did not return your greetings. I ask your forgiveness."

Peace was soon broken between the two Shogunate families, and Kimura was aware that he was not going to return alive from the

Continued

battle they were to fight against each other, and he ate much less than usual at meals.

"I want to save myself the disgrace" Kimura answered when his worried young wife asked him why he ate so little, "of having undigested rice in my throat when my head is cut off by the enemy. Early in history, I am told, a certain warrior was shot dead with an arrow, which hit him on the throat, when rice that he ate at breakfast ran out."

That night his young wife, 19 years old, retired into her chamber. She wrote a testment. "Man has a time for everything," she said among other things, "and it will be a disgrace to survive the time of death". And she committed suicide.

On the morning of the battle, which totally ruined the Toyotomi family in 1615, Kimura took a bath, washed his hair cleaner and dressed it neater than usual, and showed such presence of mind that he sang a favorite "No" drama before his retainers. Then he held his helmet over burning incense to give it its fragrance before his departure for the front.

Shigenari Kimura was killed in a battle against Naotaka Ii, a lord on the Tokugawa side. When his head was brought for inspection, Iyeyasu admired his samurai-like death and bade his attendant lords smell the helmet, which he said Kimura made scented because his head would soon smell bad in hot summer, in which the battle was fought. Naotaka Ii, who killed Kimura, was so much touched with his samurai-like death. He buried Kimura's head in his clan, and built a head-mound over it offering a prayer for the repose of his departed soul. Kimura is indeed looked up to as a true samurai.

KAIZUKA OR SHELL-MOUND

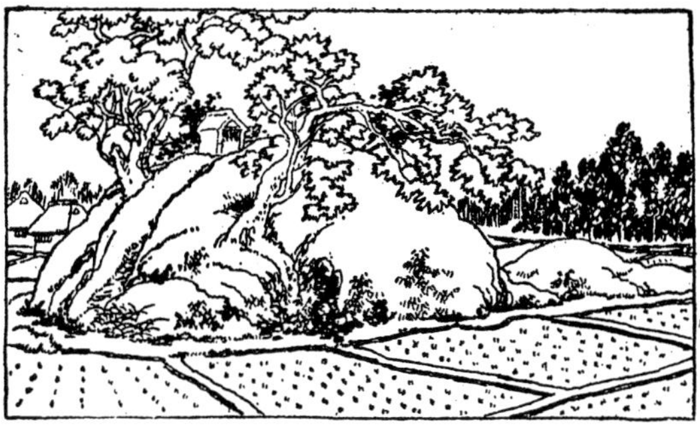

Shell-mound

The first mention in Japan of Kaizuka or the shell-mound is made in the *Hitachi-Fudo-Ki* (Records of land and customs of Hitachi) written in 713 A. D. at the orders of the Empress Gemmyo (43rd). There was a mound, says the book, by the name of Okushi at the distance of 12 ri (ri=4 kilos), west of Hiratsu, in the province of Hitachi, the mound consisting of the refuse of shell-fish and other kinds of food upon which the "giant" dwellers of the province lived.

We have several villages called Kaizuka (lit. shell-mound) in the country, but they seem to have attracted little attention on the part of the Japanese anthropologists, till in 1878 the attention of Prof. Edward S. Morris, of the Imperial University, Tokyo, was attracted to some white shells lying loose near Omori Station (now in Tokyo) on the then Tokyo-Yokohama Railway line, on his very first trip to Tokyo after landing at Yokohama. A further study of the place led Prof. Morris to the first discovery of shell-mounds in Japan. Over 600 shell-mounds have since been discovered in the vicinity of Tokyo and its neighbouring provinces, and indeed is Japan dotted abundantly with shell-mounds, which made valuable contributions to the study of our prehistoric dwellers, for the shell-mound is generally believed to be their refuse-heaps.

Besides fresh-water and sea shells of various kinds, some human skulls and other bones, 16 in total, were found in the shell-mound of Omori. Scholars do not agree as to whether these human bones represent the Japanese or Ainu or some other prehistoric dwellers. Certain it is, however, that monkeys and deer, which are represented by the bones brought to light at Omori and some other shell-mounds of Japan, are much larger than are those now existent in Japan.

WATER WORKS OF OLD TOKYO

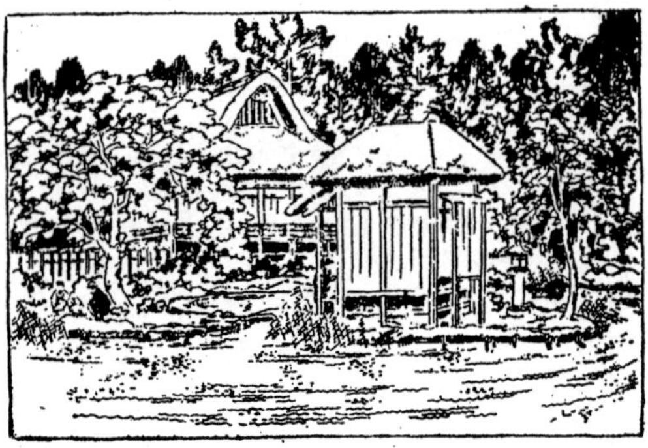

Inokashira Park, feudal fountain of water-works for Edo (Tokyo)

Tokyo, with its population almost reaching the 7-million level (prewar days) as one of the largest cities in the world, requires some 40 million cubic meters of water a year, which is supplied chiefly by three large reservoirs at Murayama and Yamaguchi. In view of the growing population of the city, the metropolis is now planning to make the fourth reservoir, which, when completed, will be six or seven times as large as the three, now in existence, put together, and the largest in the world, except the Hoover Dam.

It was early in the 17th century that water was for the first time conducted to Edo, the castle-city of Tokugawa, by means of water-works. In the tenth year (1605) A. D. of Keicho era, Iyeyasu, founder of the Tokugawa dynasty, visited the village of Mure, known for its beautiful pond of Nana-no-i-Ike (lit. seven-well-pond). He was so pleased with its clear water that he had his tea made with it. Japanese tea, by the way, is never made nice but with pure and clean water. It was Hidetada, his son, who ordered this water to be conducted to Edo, (Tokyo) for a distance of some twenty kilometers, for the benefit of the people of his capital-city. This is the origin of the Kanda-josui (drinking water of Kanda), so well-known during the Edo days. When Iyemitsu, son of Hidetada, who is known in the history of Japan for the seclusion policy that shut the country against foreign intercourse, visited this pond in 1629, A. D., he called it I-no-Kashira (lit. fountain-head), which he wrote in two Chinese ideographs on a standing tree with a Kotsuka (a small knife attached to a sword).

Inokashira, now a public park in Tokyo, still attracts large crowds of people with its picturesque scenery in all seasons. It can be reached from Tokyo by the Government railways running from Shinjuku or by a private line called the Inokashira line from Shibuya, Tokyo.

THE EDO CASTLE

The old castle of Edo stood where the Imperial Palace of Tokyo now stands. It was first built by Dokan Ohta, a retainer of Sadamasa Uyesugi, in 1457, and it changed hands several times. When Iyeyasu Tokugawa got possession of the Eight Provinces of the Kanto District, he made Edo his capital city, and the castle was rebuilt.

The Edo castle was mainly divided into two parts: the inner and outer castles. The former consisted of Hommaru (main citadel), Nishi-maru (west citadel), Nishi-no-marushita, Fukiage, Kita-no-maru (north citadel) and San-no-maru (3rd citadel), while the present Marunouchi and its vicinity were within the outer castle. It was during the era of Kan-ei (1624–1643) that the outer moats, which extended to Akasaka, Kojimachi, Ichigaya, Ushigome, Koishikawa and Kanda were completed. The Hommaru (main citadel) was situated on the north-eastern side of the inner castle, but all were destroyed by fire after they were delivered to the Imperial Government by Tokugawa in 1868.

There were altogether thirty-six gates around the old castle, but we have only a few still existent; such as the Front Gate, Sakurada-mon Gate, Sakashita-mon Gate, Inui-mon Gate, Hanzo-mon Gate, etc.

Population of Edo: According to the census taken in 1723, the population of Edo was as follows:—1,676 streets; 128,505 families; 565,482 persons.

Dokan Ohta and Yamabuki flowers: Dokan Ohta, the founder of the Edo castle, was out hunting. He was caught in a rain and took shelter at a small cottage. When he asked for a raincoat, a girl of sixteen held an open Japanese fan to him. It had a few flowers of the Yamabuki (kerria japonica) with a poem on it. Ohta could make nothing of the flower. Her poem runs as follows!

"Nanaye yaye
Hana wa sake domo
Yamabuki no
Mi no Hitotsu dani
Nakizo kanashiki."

(Seven petaled or eight petaled flowers Yamabuki has, but I am sorry that they have no fruits.)

The poem has a hidden meaning. Pun is laid upon "Mi-no-Hitotsu dani", which, as they stand, mean that "no fruits even", but, written "Mino-Hitotsu dani", they would mean "no rain-coat even." So the maid meant that she had no rain-coat.

Ohta was ashamed of his ignorance, and he took to learning till he became a great man of learning.

THE OSAKA CASTLE

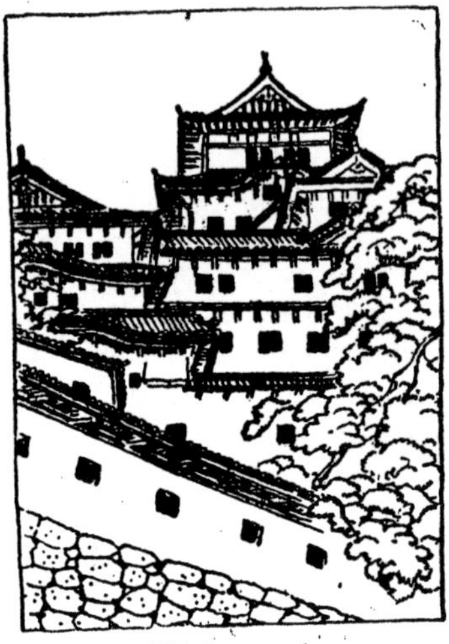

Old-time castle

The Osaka castle is situated in the north-eastern part of Osaka city. It is surrounded by water on three sides; namely the River Yodo on the north and moats on the east and west; the castle facing south. Situated, as it did in olden times, in a natural defence, the castle stood majestic and imposing, visible from all directions around it. It is 3 ri (ri=3.927 kilos) large in circumference.

Priest Rennyo, of the Hongan-ji Temple, built a detached temple at Osaka in 1496. Priest Kenjo, of the same temple, rose in revolt against Shogun Nobunaga Oda in 1574. Oda sent troops against the priest, who offered such strong resistance that the Emperor Ogimachi (106th) acted between them, and peace was restored in 1580. In the same year, however, the temple was destroyed by fire.

Hideyoshi Toyotomi noticed the military importance of Osaka and he built the Osaka castle, which consisted of the Hommaru (main citadel), Ni-no-Maru (2nd citadel) and San-no-Maru (3rd citadel), with Tenshukaku (donjon) in the center. The construction was started in 1582 and completed in 1585, taking 3 years and ten months.

Soon after the death in 1598 of Hideyoshi Toyotomi, a war broke out between Hideyori, his son, and Iyeyasu Tokugawa, who laid siege to the castle, leading an enormous army of 1,380,000 strong, it is said, against the Toyotomi of 135,000 strong. The castle fell in 1615, when Hideyori and his mother, Lady Yodo, committed suicide within the castle.

ICHIYA-JO OR CASTLE BUILT IN ONE-NIGHT

"The hill that you see over there, on the other side of the River Haya-kawa (literally, Quick-river) is Mt. Ishigaki (literally, Hedge)" the bus girl will explain by pointing to a hill covered over with citrus-trees, to your left, soon after your bus leaves Odawara on your way to Miyanoshita. "It is noted in the history of Japan for a castle that Hideyoshi Toyotomi built in one night in 1590."

When Ujisato Hojo, lord of the Odawara castle, proved disobedient, Hideyoshi Toyotomi, or, as he is more popularly known, Taiko, the Great, led an army against Hojo in 1590. He came by way of Hakone, and pitched a camp behind Mt. Ishigaki. On the following morning, the beseiged people of the Odawara castle could not believe their own eyes when towering over their own castle, they saw a new castle, which they had not seen the day before. The castle was built during a short time of one night. Hojo was no match for Toyotomi, and he soon surrendered. The castle that Toyotomi erected in one night was built of paper, and it is known in history as the Ichiya-jo or One-night Castle of Toyotomi.

Hideyoshi built another one-night castle at Su-no-Mata in Mino Province, when he was sent by Nobunaga Oda, his master, to attack Tatsuoki Saito in 1560.

When Nobuna Oda led his troops to attack another castle, he stopped at a Shinto shrine. "I am going to offer a prayer for victory. If we are going to get victorious, all the coins I throw in will show their head up."

So saying, Nobunaga threw in some coins with a prayer for victory. Sure enough all the coins he threw in showed their head-side up and the troops marched in high spirits. And they captured the castle they attacked.

It was found that all the coins were in pairs, all joined with the head-side out.

Letter to Davy Jones: It was said that no ships that sailed off the cape of Omae-saki in Ohmi Province could carry any horses or trappings nor could one say " horse " on board, for else some mishap was sure to befall the ship. So when his troops were to sail of the cape, on their way to Odawara, Hideyoshi handed an autographic letter to the leader of his troops. It was addressed to the King of Ryugu or Dragon-land (or Davy Jones) whom he asked in it to allow his troops to pass off the ill-omened cape without any trouble. The ships sailed in safety and Hojo soon surrendered.

THE SHOSO-IN REPOSITORY

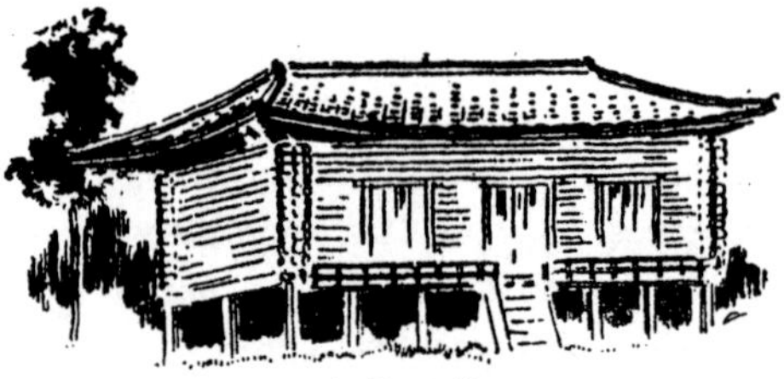
Shoso-in Repository

In the Shoso-in Repository, at Nara, which is one of the oldest buildings in Japan, are preserved thousands of precious articles that were used in the Imperial court during the reigns (724–823) between the Emperors Shomu (the 45th) and Saga (the 52nd).

The Shoso-in, all built of prism-shaped lumbers, consisted at first of two premises, the South Hall and the North Hall, which were later connected by the Middle Hall. They are altogether 18 ken (ken=6 Jap. ft.) 8 inches wide, 5 ken 12 inches deep and 5 ken high, the floor being 9 ft. above the ground. The Shoso-in was so named according to the Shoku-Todai-ji Yoran (Supplementary Todai-ji Temple Manuel), during the Kamakura days (1186–1333). It was damaged by thunderbolt which hit it on a southern part on the 17th of the sixth month (June), 1243, but otherwise it has been preserved intact for over twelve centuries.

The Shoso-in Repository was built originally to contain the treasures of the Todai-ji Temple, which was built by the Emperor Shomu, a great Buddhist believer, who erected the Daibutsu (Great Buddha) at Nara. But, according to a certain scholar, the Shosoin Repository was built when the Empress Komyo (literally, bright-light), who was so named because light emanated from her body on account of her faith in Buddhism, presented to the Great Buddha on the 21st of the sixth month (June), 756, all the precious articles that her deceased husband, the Emperor Shomu, had used. Indeed the Shoso-in Repository contains all sorts of ancient articles, all over 1,000 years old, such as ancient records, mirrors, weapons, musical instruments, Gigaku masks, incense burners, trappings, gold and silver-ware, porcelain-ware, lacquer-ware, glass-ware, brush pens, paper, screens, paintings, sculptures, etc. counting several thousands in number.

In China, which knows no period free from a civil war in her history, little is left of the culture or art of the Sui or Tang dunasty, to say nothing of a previous regime. Nor can we find anything so old in Korea. But the Shoso-in Repository contains many rare implements and utensils that show the ancient culture not only of the Nara days (710–784) A. D. in Japanese history, but of the early periods of Chinese and Korean civilizations. And in this sense the Shoso-in Repository constributes valuable data to the history of the East.

THE HAKONE SHRINE

The Hakone Shrine is situated on the banks of Lake Ashi or Hakone. The shrine, according to Shintoism, was founded by Take-no-uchi-no-Sukune during the reign of the Empress Jingo (3rd century), and it was dedicated to Prince Ninigi-no-Mikoto, Princess Konohana-no-Sakuya-Hime and Prince Hikohohodemi-no-Mikoto. Prince Ninigi, generally known as the Imperial Grandson, descended from the Celestial Abode of the Gods to govern the land of reeds, as Japan was called in the ancient times. Princess Konohana-no-Sakuya-Hime, his spouse, who was apotheosized on Mt. Fuji, is the name-sake of Sakura (cherry), the national flower of Japan; and Prince Hikohoho-demi, the son of Prince Ninigi, is the grandfather of the Emperor Jimmu, first of the Imperial line.

Buddhism, however, claims that Sensei-Shonin first founded the Hakone Shrine during the reign of the Emperor Kosho (the 5th), before the official introduction of Buddhism to Japan. Kiko-Shonin came to Hakone during the reign of the Emperor Sujin (the 10th) and Priest Genri during the reign of the Empress Kokyoku (the 36th). These are known as the three founders of the Hakone Shrine, which is dedicated, according to Buddhism, to its three deities: Miroku (Maitreya), Kanzeon (Avalokitesvara) and Monju (Manjusri).

But Priest Mangan is generally regarded as the founder of Hakone. Mangan (lit. 10,000-volumes) was so called because, it is said, he studied so many volumes of the Buddhist sutras. He was born in Kyoto during the era of Yoro (717–724 A. D.) and came to Hakone during the era of Tempyo-Hoji (757–764 A. D.). It is said that Priest Mangan saw in a dream three Buddhist deities, whom he enshrined at Hakone; hence the three Buddhist deities at the Hakone Shrine. Priest Mangan died in 816 A. D. at the age of 97 years, and

Continued

his remains are buried on the mountain behind the shrine.

The Hakone Shrine had devout adherents in several Shogun. Yoritomo Minamoto, the first of all Shogun, came to worship at the shrine before he raised his standard against the Taira family, which he finally succeeded in annihilating. Hideyoshi Toyotomi placed the Hakone Shrine under his special protection, and Iyeyasu Tokugawa offered 200 Koku (koku=4.9 bushels) of rice annually in the province of Izu and made an annual tribute to the shrine. Iyetsuna Tokugawa, another devotee, rebuilt the shrine in 1667.

Hakone is known for its Sekisho or barrier, which was one of the most famous in feudal days. It is said to have been established in 1618, though, according to some authorities, there was a barrier as early as 1222.

Dragon Festival: During the era of Tempyo-Hoji (757–764 B. D.), the people on the western side of Lake Hakone were much molested by a nine-headed dragon. Priest Mangan read the Buddhist sutra to placate its spirit by tying it to a large tree on the banks till it was released on condition that it would be the guardian deity of the lake. A festival has since been held in honour of the dragon, when 3.333 To (To=0.49 bushels) of Sekihan or rice steamed with red beans, is offered to it. Two Shinto priests of the shrine row a boat with the steamed rice on board, and when the middle of the lake is reached, the rice is thrown overboard into the lake. They must not look behind when they row back to the banks. If the rice sinks to the bottom, they say, the dragon-deity accepts it; but if it floats on the wake of the boat, the god is out of humours. The villagers have a great cermony of offering lighted lanterns to the dragon-deity on the occasion. The festival is held usually on the evening of July 31 every year.

THE KOMPIRA SHRINE

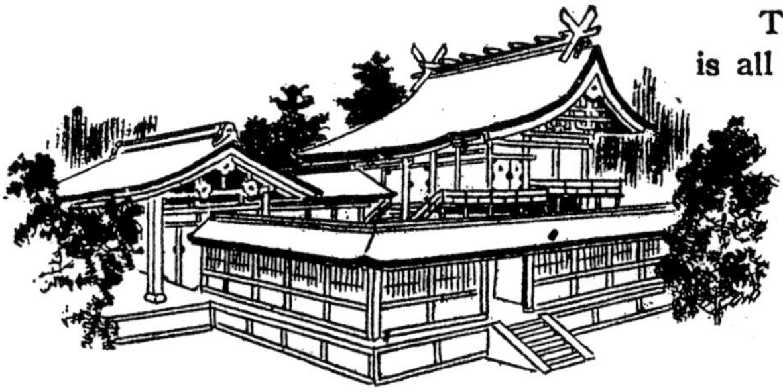

Kompira Shrine

The Kompira shrine is all but ubiquitous all over the country, found practically in every town and village of any locality. Though it is now generally believed to be dedicated to Prince Onamuchi, a prehistoric figure of Japan, there was originally venerated in the shrine an Indian and Buddhist deity called Kumohira, of which Kompira is undoubtedly a perversion. This Indian word means a crocodile, or a fish, with a snake body. Kompira is the guardian deity of sailors or a sea-faring people, and this is why we have a Kompira shrine at every sea-side village or hamlet in Japan.

The Kompira shrine in the province of Sanuki is the largest of the kind in Japan. The Emperor Sutoku (75th), who was sent an exile to Sanuki after the battle of Hogen in 1156, is also enshrined in the Kompira shrine of Sanuki. In the feudal days of Japan this shrine claimed the largest number of devotees visiting it, of all shrines in Japan, (the Imperial shrines at Ise excepted), and it was a cherished hope of every pious Japanese to have the opportunity of making a trip to Sanuki during his life-time.

Many an interesting story is told about miraculous deeds done by Kompira. A pious sailor distressed in a storm at sea, it is said, will be led by a mysterious light if he calls in a prayer upon the deity of Kompira. Once a young man was thrown overboard into the sea by his employees, but he was saved because, it was believed, his father was a faithful believer of Kompira, and his faithless employees were soon arrested. You will see that all local boats and ships of Japan, without exception, have a charm issued by the Kompira shrine of their respective localities. Every fisherman carries a small amulet of the Kompira on his body, next to the skin.

The festival of the Kompira shrine is observed on Oct. 10th every year, and the Sanuki shrine is widely known for the most fantastic and classical perfromances given on this fete-day. While the Emperor Sutoku stayed as an exile in Sanuki, the people, who were not allowed to see him openly, visited him in disguise. This custom still remaining, many visitors of the shrine are clad in quaintest ways when they come to the shrine. According to tradition, Kompira claimed a human victim on the 10th day, every month, till the people observed a fete-day in honour of the Kompira deity.

THE DOG-SHRINE AND THE CAT-SHRINE

The Dog-shrine and the Cat-shrine stand opposite each other, across a street in the town of Takahata in Higashi-Okitama-gun, Yamagata Prefecture. They have the following legendary stories related about them:—

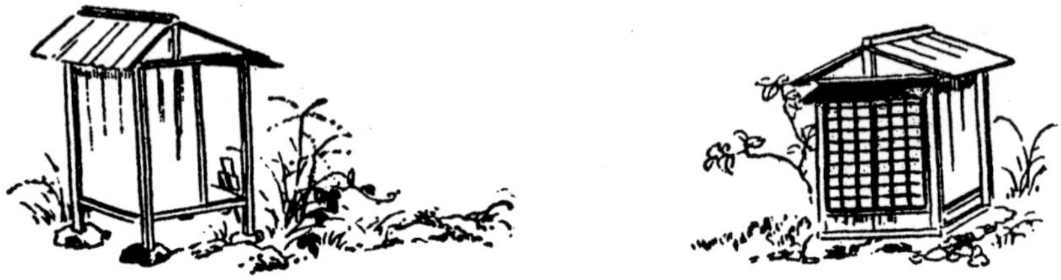

The cat and dog shrines

The Dog-shrine: Once a blindman lost his way in the neighbourhood of Takahata and went astray in a wood, where he made up his mind to stay overnight. Late in the night he heard a strange noise coming from somewhere in the woods. Probably there was a party of some sort going on, and he could clearly hear the following song repeated over and over again:

"The three-coloured and the four-coloured dogs of Kai Province should not know that we are here."

On the following morning when the blindman went back to his village, he told all about the noises to the squire of the town, who attributed it to the working of some badgers. He sent for the three-coloured and the four-coloured dogs of the Kai Province, which were sent out into the woods, and a short time later a huge badger was found killed by the dogs, which, however, died from fatigue caused by the fight they had with the badger. The Dog-shrine is dedicated to the ill-fated dogs which lost their lives in killing the badger.

The Cat-shrine: The Cat-shrine stands opposite the Dog-shrine across a street. It is dedicated to a cat which saved her master with her own life. She was a meek cat and a great pet of her master, but one day she turned almost mad, and she forgot evidently every word of her master's, to whom she had been very obedient.

"They say" her master said, "that a cat forgets in three days the kindness that she received for three years, though a dog remembers for three years the kindness that he received during three days. This cat must have turned mad."

So the master killed the cat by cutting her head off with a sword, when lo! it jumped up only to bring something down with a thud. It was a large snake, with the head of the cat still clinging on its neck! The cat saw the imminent danger that her master was in, and warned him of it, but her master, unable to understand her conducts, killed her without taking her warning. He built the Cat-shrine, which he dedicated to his faithful pet-cat.

THE HORYU-JI TEMPLE

Oldest art-treasure of Japan

The Horyu-ji Temple, situated near Nara, is the oldest wooden building of Japan, and the Japanese may well be proud of it because the temple, wooden as it is, has stood almost intact for over 1,300 years.

When the Emperor Yomei (31st) was seriously ill, he made up his mind to erect a Buddhist temple upon his recovery, but he died without seeing his wish realized. The Empress Suiko (33rd), his consort, and Prince Shotoku, who were great believers of Buddhism,

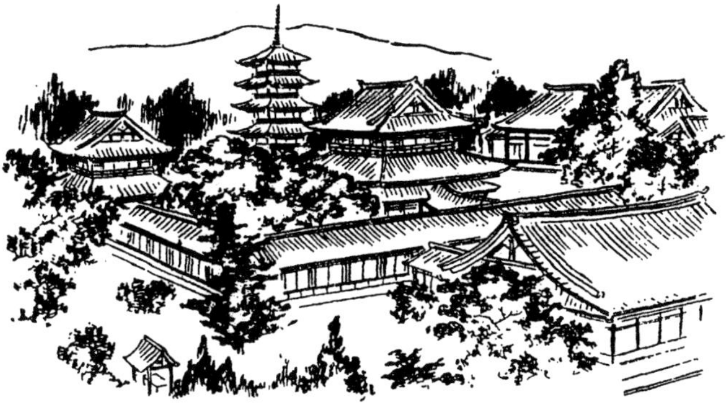

Horyu-ji Temple, Nara

built the Horyu-ji Temple in dedication to the Emperor Yomei. It was one of the temples that Prince Shotoku, known as Father of Japan's Buddhism, built during his life-time.

The Horyu-ji Temple was started in 593 A. D., and completed in 607 A. D. A fire destroyed a part of the temple during the reign of the Emperor Tenji (38th), but most of the buildings, with their Buddhist images as well as other pieces of art, have been preserved as they were when first enshrined there. Most scholars, however, agree that the temple was not all destroyed by fire, and the part that

Continued

survived the fire is said to be the oldest wooden building in the world. Out of 1,243 pieces of art therein preserved, buildings included, 768 pieces have been so far declared as national treasures, and it is believed that the rest, which include many ancient mirrors, masks, swords, etc. will also be specified among the national treasures.

The principal buildings of the Horyu-ji Temple are: Kondo (Golden Hall), Goju-no-To (5-storeyed pagoda), Kodo (Main Hall), Seireido (Sacred spirit Hall), Yume-domo (Dream-Hall), Sharido (Ashes-Hall), Eden (Picture-Hall), Shoro (Bell-tower), etc. The Dream-Hall, an octagonal building, stands on the former site of a palace where Prince Shotoku died, in 621 A. D. Therein enshrined is the Buddhist statue, Kyusei-Kannon (lit. Salvation-Kannon), which is said to have been carved by the prince himself.

Tamamushi-no-Zushi: The Tamamushi-no-Zushi (lit. Beetle-Niche) is perhaps among the most-widely reputed pieces of Buddhist art in Japan, so called because the niche is decorated, or covered over, with the wings of Tamamushi (chrysomeridae), a kind of beetle, and its inside walls are all painted with mardasang-oil. It is 7–8 Japanese feet high, and three Buddhist statues, in which the Empress Suiko was a great believer, are enshrined in it.

Wall Paintings: The Kondo (lit. golden hall) is an excellent example of the Asuka-period architecture. It had twelve wall paintings, four larger and eight smaller. They were excellent master-pieces depicting Buddhist portraits and scenes, and they have been preserved intact over 13 centuries. A fire broke out in the Hall of Kondo in 1949, and all the 13-century-old Buddhist wall-paintings were reduced to ashes, excepting one portrait.

WORSHIP AT A SHRINE AND A TEMPLE

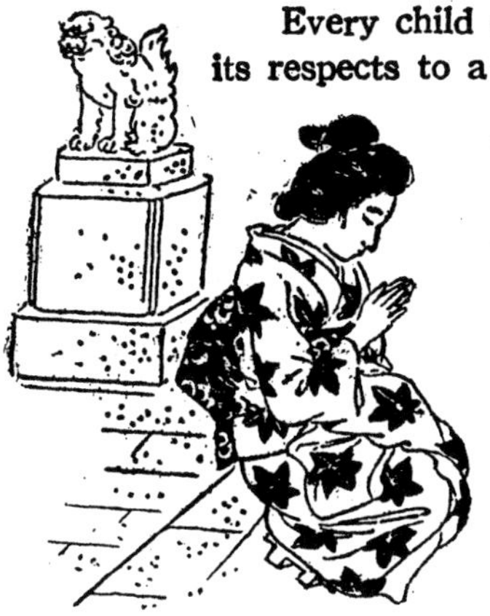

Girl in prayer

Every child of Japan is taught and trained to pay its respects to a Shinto shrine, and, therefore, it will bow squarely to every shrine it may pass by. We pay a visit to a shrine and a temple regularly or otherwise and worship the deity therein venerated, generally speaking, not so much to offer a prayer for anything, except on a special occasion, as because we do homage to the god.

Temple: At a Buddhist temple, which is dedicated to a Buddhist or chiefly Indian deity, we generally join our hands together and bow our head over them in worshipping the image. Oftentimes there is a metal gong called "Wani-guchi" (lit. crocodile-mouth) at the entrance to the main front of a temple, with a rope hanging from it. A visitor will strike the gong with the rope before bowing his head. Incense is sometimes burned at a Buddhist temple by a visitor before he worships its image.

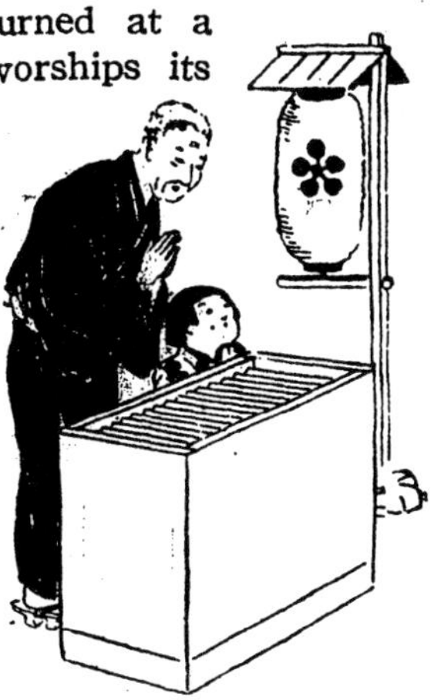

Old man in prayer

Shrine: A Shinto shrine has what is called "Mitarashi" (lit. honorable-hand-washer), which is a basin or tub of stone or some other material containing water for every visitor to wash his mouth and hands before bowing his head to the deity enshrined in the shrine. Many Shinto shrines have bells, like the Buddhist "Waniguchi", with cotton-stripes of five colours hanging from them. The visitor will shake the stripes to ring the bells, and then he claps his hands, generally twice, over which he bows his head in worship. A Shinto shrine will sometimes have Sakaki-branches (eurya ochnacea), sacred to Shinto gods, which a devotee will offer before worshipping, with his hands, the stem-end of a branch turned to the deity venerated in the shrine.

You will notice that many a visitor of a shrine and a temple throws a copper or two in when he worships the deity, more as a mere custom than for anything else.

O-SAISEN OR OFFERTORY

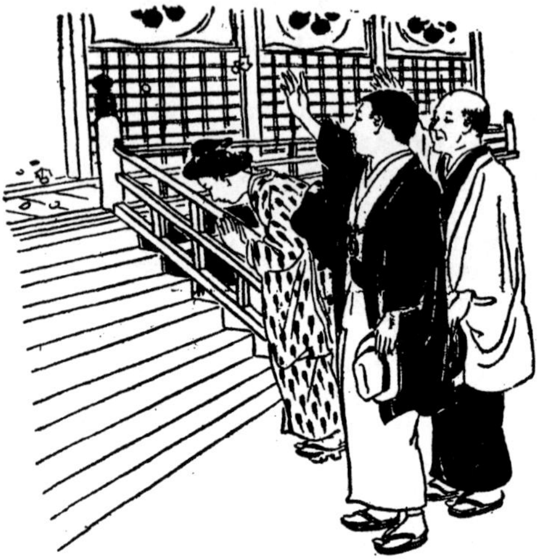

Visitors throwing coins of offertory

When a Japanese visits a shrine or temple to worship its deity, he throws a few coins in it or into its offertory-box (Saisen-bako) provided for the purpose, and he claps his hands two (or three) times before a Shinto god or joins them in case of a Buddhist deity, then bending his head over them. The money thus offered is called Osaisen (honorable offertory) or also Saisen (lit. scattered-money) because the worshipper scatters it in disorder in the hall of a shrine or temple.

Saisen, as its characters now stand, means "return-money" or money offered in return either in a crop or kind, for a blessing bestowed by the god venerated in the shrine or temple or in the realization of a prayer offered. In former days an offertory was called Hatsuho (lit. first ears of rice) and also Hayaho (lit. early ears of rice) and it was offered in kind, instead of coins, by way of returning thanks for the protection of the rice-fields. It was a real offering of thanks given for a crop.

But the original idea of Osaisen has been forgotten or entirely departed from, and an offertory now consists of a few coppers, of which there is no fixed amount. It is offered, not for a blessing already received, but, on the contrary, for one for which a prayer is offered. Or we may go a little further and say that our offertory has no more significance in it than that it is a simple token of

Continued

respects paid to the god. Look at a visitor or worshipper of a shrine or temple. He offers a few coppers, claps or joins his hands and bends his head over them for a few seconds of time, too short for saying any prayer. In other words, the Japanese visit a shrine or temple not so much because they have any special prayer to offer, as to pay their respects to the deity therein enshrined.

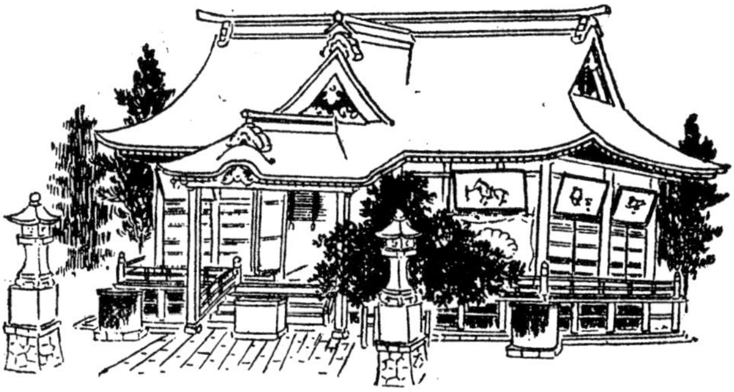

Shinto shrine with an offertory-box in front

We have the saying "Jigoku no Sata mo Kane shidai", which, freely translated, will mean that the judgment of Hell depends upon the amount of the money. According to Buddhism, every soul has to be judged by the King Yama, Judge of the Dead, who condemns bad ones to Hell, and this saying ironically implies that an avaricious Buddhist priest is often influenced, in his religious services, by the amount of money offered by his laiety.

Shintoism, which was maintained by the Government in the former days, had no definite parishioners, although it will be supported by the Government no longer under the new Constitution. Buddhism, which has a graveyard attached to its temple, has parishioners who are represented by those who are buried in the cementery. These parishioners will pay optional offerings to support their temple.

RASHO-MON GATE

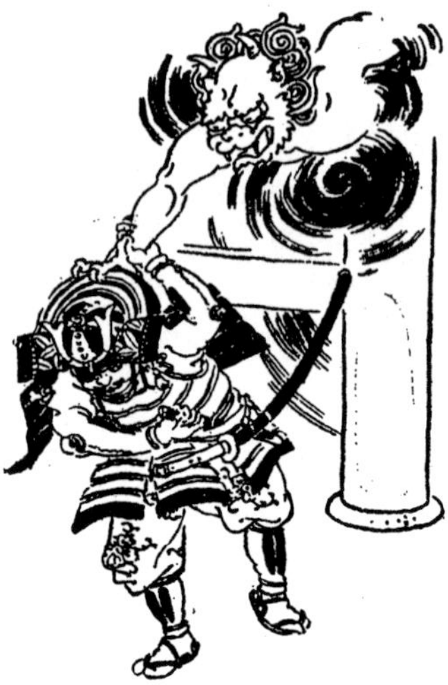
Tsuna Watanabe caught by Oni

Once there appeared night after night on the Rasho-mon, the southern gate of Kyoto, an Oni (ogre or bogy) to the great distress of the people. Tsuna Watanabe, one of the Shitenno or four Deva-retainers of Yorimitsu Minamoto, a court-warlord, who distinguished himself by killing Shutendoji, a cave-dwelling bandit, of Mt. Ohyeyama, did not believe in the existence of any ogre, and he offered to find out what it was like and to kill it if it really existed. Armed and attired like a regular samurai of old, Watanabe proceeded by himself to the Rasho-mon Gate one night. He saw no spectre or bogy, and, nothing strange happening, he climbed up the gate and was about to set up, as a mark of his visit, a tablet that he had taken with him, when he felt a strong grip on the crown of his helmet. He even felt that he was slowly lifted up into the air. He caught the arm that held his helmet and cut it off with a sword. It was a hairy arm which resembled no human one.

Watanabe was ordered by the Emperor to shut himself at home for a cycle of seven days because he was defiled by touching the body of a bogy. On the last day of his confinement, he received a visit from an elderly woman, who introduced herself as his aunt that lived far away in the country and whom he had never seen before. Watanabe could not see her or any other visitor during his time of confinement, but, coming all the distance from the province of Ise, as she told him, she must see him by all means. Watanabe yielded and saw her. When among other things he told her of his recent adventures, she insisted upon seeing the mysterious arm. Watanabe refused, but she even pleaded that it was harsh of him to refuse anything to his own aunt. He again gave in. But the moment when she caught sight of the arm, which Watanabe brought out, she snatched at it, and, saying "This is my own arm", she turned into a terrific ogre and flew out at the garble of the roof. This story is often represented on the stage in both No and Kabuki plays.

RYU OR DRAGON

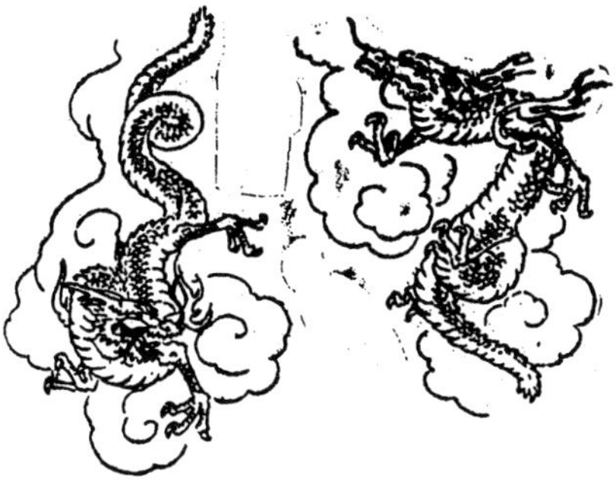

Ascending dragon and descending dragon

Ryu (dragon), Kirin (Oriental Pegasus), Ho-o (Phoenix) and Kame (toroise) are said to be the four signs of wise royal administration, which appear only when there is a saintly sovereign in the country. But Ryu (also Ryo) or dragon is a fabulous kind of a phython, which calls forth wind and live in clouds. Ryu affords a popular theme for painters and sculptors, many of whom specialize in Ryu, and indeed Japan is specially rich in pieces of art representing this fabulous animal. At Nikko, for instance, the Naki-ryu, or crying dragon, which vibrates at the slightest clapping of hands under its head, is painted on the ceiling of a temple close by the famous Yomei-mon Gate; the Tosho-gu Shrine has the Nobori-ryu (ascending dragon) and Kudari-ryu (descending dragon) carved on its gate and a hundred phases of a dragon painted on the composite ceiling of its main shrine. Because Ryu is said to live in the water in autumn and goes back to heaven in spring, almost every lake and pond in the country has some story told about a dragon that lived, or even is said to live still in it. There are several kinds of Ryu: Ko-ryu with scales, O-ryu with wings, Kyu-ryu with horns and Han-ryu which has not yet been to heaven. It is said in China that a viper, 500 years old, is Mizute; a Mizute, 1,000 years old, is Ryu, a Ryu, 500 years old, gets horns and another 1,000 years will give it wings. As for a dragon's colour, Ryu is yellow, red, blue, white or black. An emperor is often compared to a Ryu: his face is metaphorically called Ryu-gan (lit. dragon-face); his virtue Ryu-toku (lit. dragon-virtue); his car Ryu-ga (lit. dragon-palanquin), etc.

Continued

Ryugu: Ryugu (lit. Dragon-palace) is among the most popular stories of the dragon in Japan. Urashima-taro, a fisherman, who saved a turtle, was taken on its back to the land of Ryugu or dragons, where he stayed for three days and nights. On coming home, however, he found that he had stayed away from home for so many hundred years. He is narrated in Nihonshoki (720 A. D.) one of the oldest annals of Japan, and he is Japan's Rip Van Winkle.

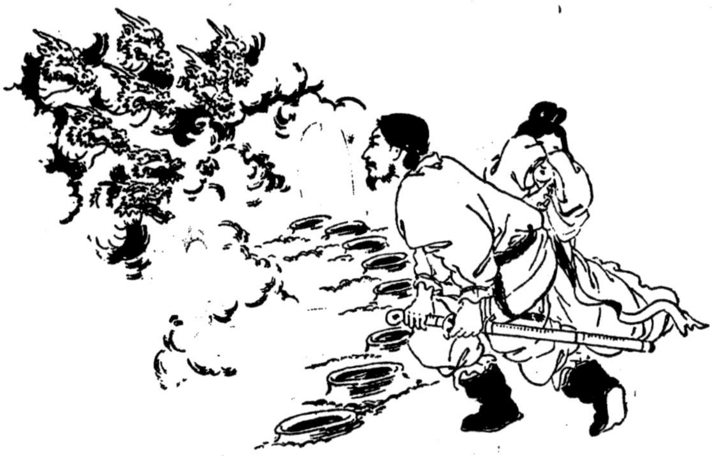

Prince Susanoo killing a 8-headed dragon to save a princess

Lake Hakone and the nine-headed dragon: It was during the reign of the Empress Koken (46th) that a nine-headed dragon, which lived in a western part of Lake Hakone, (properly Lake Ashi), wrought havoc by ravaging the land in the vicinity of Hakone. It demanded a live child every year, and Priest Mangan, who happened to come to Hakone, tied the mischievous dragon to a huge tree till, when the priest offered to give it a certain amount of boiled rice annually, it promised to take no more live child.

On the 31 of July every year, the people of Hakone offers Sekihan (lit. red steamed rice) or rice coloured red by steaming with Indian beans, to the legendary dragon. The rice is carried aboard a boat by two Shinto priests and thrown into the lake at its center, the priests then rowing to the banks without turning their heads back till they reach the land.

KIMON OR "DEVIL-GATE" DIRECTION

According to Chinese mythology there sit in state four guardian-deities at the cardinal points of the universe; namely.

(1) The Blue Dragon on the stream of the east

(2) The White Tiger on the large highway of the west

(3) The Red Sparrow on the swamp of the south

(4) The Black Militant on the high mountain of the north

And the universe is guarded by these guardian-deities at the following four gates:

(1) Temmon (lit. heaven-gate), north-west

(2) Kimon (lit. Devil-gate), north-east

(3) Chimon (lit. earth-gate), south-east

(4) Jimmon (lit. man-gate), south-west

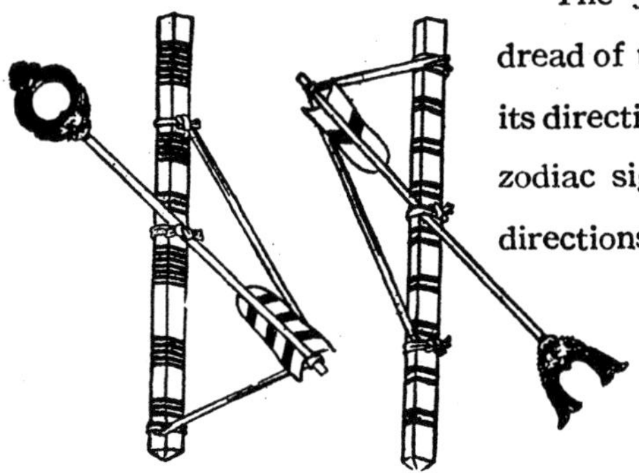

Evil-driving arrows set up against Devil-Gate Direction

The Japanese have a traditional dread of the Kimon, or Devil-gate, and its direction of north-east. The twelve zodiac signs are assigned to so many directions (see "We Japanese," Vol. I, p. 100), and every direction is lucky or unlucky, according to the year which has a zodiac sign assigned to it in the lunar calendar; with the only exception of the Kimon, which is closed at all times. In building a house, for instance, the Japanese will avoid making a kitchen or a toilet in its devil-gate direction. They will not remove into a house which is situated in the evil direction of the one they are living in. If an orthodox Japanese has to remove into a house which is situated in the unlucky direction of Kimon, he will first take a

Continued

house in another direction, and then after staying there for a little while he will go intò the "unlucky" house, so that ill-luck may thus be avoided or exorcised. Thus he will avoid going direct into the unlucky direction.

On the eastern sea, tradition says, there was a mountain called Mt. Dosaku. It had a large peach-tree, whose luxuriant branches extended for 300 miles. The north-eastern direction of the peach-tree was guarded by devils. In imi ation of this enormous peach-tree, the Emperor Puang-fi of China planted a peach as a charm against evil. Nobody knows where Mt. Dosaku or the big peach-tree was, though, according to some authorities, this story was first told in India and that Mt. Dosaku was in Cochin-China, where there is a place which is expressed by three characters meaning the Devil-gate-pass.

When the Emperor Kammu (45th) removed the Imperial capital from Nara to Heian (lit. peace) or Kyoto in 794, he told Priest Saicho to found a temple on Mt. Hiyei, which is situated in the Devil-gate direction from Kyoto, the Imperial capital. The "100 seat prayer" has since been offered annually at the temple for the protection of the Imperial family at Kyoto. The Kan-ey-ji Temple, situated at Uyeno, Tokyo, was founded to close up the evil direction of Kimon when Iyeyasu, founder of the Tokugawa regime, built the castle of Edo (Tokyo) in 1606, because Ueno Hill stands in the Devil-gate direction of Edo (now Tokyo).

Every Buddhist temple has a central altar called Sumeru, a Buddhist world, which is guarded by the following Buddhist guardians:

East:	Jikokuten	(Dhritarastra)
South:	Zochoten	(Virudhaka)
North:	Tamonten	(Dhanada)
West:	Komokuten	(Virupaksa)

KAPPA OR RIVER-BOY

The accidental drowning of a boy in a stream was often, and still sometimes is, attributed to a mischievous prank of Kappa (lit. river-boy), an amphibious biped, 2 or 3 ft. high, which is very fond of a human liver. We have ever so many stories, mostly incredible, told about this "fabulous" biped, which seems to understand the human language, and one is often inclined to believe in its existence in the past from the strange fact that many an authentic writer makes mention of this amphibian in his books. Kyushu, the insular provinces of the south, seems to have been much more abundant in Kappa than anywhere else in the country. In some cases Kappa tried to pull into its river a horse that was tethered near its banks, only to be pulled out of the water by the horse and caught by the people; in other cases, Kappa had one of its arms cut off for a prank it did, and recovered it by showing the people that it could rejoin the broken arm with a medicine, which it taught them how to prepare. Such a medicine, known by the name of "Kappa-medicine," is found in several localities of Japan. When spared from death, Kappa gave a written oath in which it promised to molest the people no more, as we see in a tablet still preserved in some local temples and shrines. Kappa is so fond of a cucumber that a boy who throws one into the river where he is going to have a swim, will not be bothered by it. It is also known for its acts of reciprocation and retaliation.

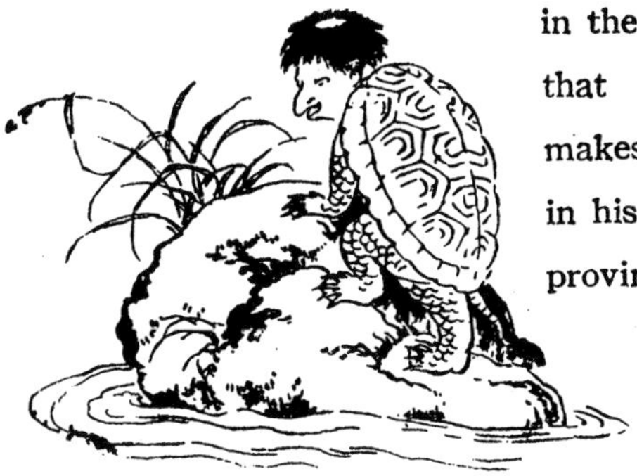

Kappa or River-boy

Continued

Kappa-no-Myoyaku (Kappa's mysterious medicine): A certain widow was sitting one night by a window when a strange hairy hand was put in to take hold of her. She struck at it, and being a brave woman, she looked out of the window, but she saw no trace of anything. The same hand came again on the next evening. On the third night she had a knife ready with her and when the same hand came the third time she cut it off. On the following morning her maid traced the blood to a river behind her house. On the fourth evening, the widow had a visit from an old stranger. He had no right arm. He wanted to see the curious arm that he had heard the widow had got, and after an exchange of a few words it was found that he was its real owner, who came to restore it.

"But I am afraid that it will be of no use to you now that it is cut off", she said, when the visitor, who revealed herself to be a Kappa that had lived in the river behind her house for a long time, showed a medicine which it said would join the arm back.

The arm was handed back, and the Kappa put it on its body so perfectly that it looked as if it had never been cut off.

Kappa told the widow how to prepare the medicine, which is now known as Kappa-no-Myoyaku (Kappa's mysterious medicine), and it is still on sale in the Kumagaye in Saitama Prefecture.

Kappa has bobbed hair, with a bowl on its crown. So long as Kappa has water in its bowl, it is very powerful, and it can pull a horse into a river. When, however, its bowl is dry, it is utterly powerless. A Japanese child of old had bobbed hair, with its crown shaved. Bobbed hair is called O-Kappa (lit. honorable Kappa) in Japan after the head of Kappa, which it imitates.

CAT-TOMB

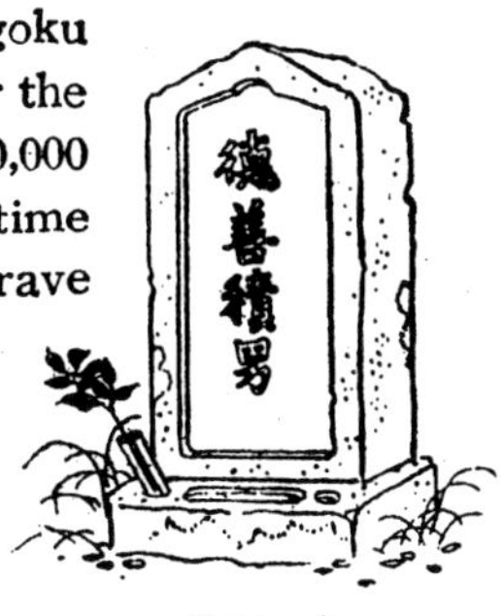
Cat-tomb

In the precincts of the Eko-in Temple, Ryogoku in Tokyo, which was erected with a prayer for the peaceful repose of the ill-fated people over 100,000 in number who were burned to death at the time of a great fire in 1657, there is a regular grave erected over the remains of a male cat on Mar. 11,1816 The grave has the following story.

A certain fish-monger used to visit a money-changer, Kisaburo Tokita by name, to do business with him. Every time when the fish-dealer visited Tokita, he gave a piece of fish to a male cat, which Tokita kept.

One day the fish-dealer fell sick, and he was confined to bed for several days, too sick to go out to sell his fish.

One morning the fish-monger found two gold-coins by his bed-side, but he did not know who had brought them to him.

On recovery, the fish-dealer visited the money-changer again. The cat was not to be seen and he asked the money-changer what had become of it. "I killed him," was a quick reply and then he went on to say:

"One morning I missed two gold-coins. They must have been stolen from my drawer, but I could not find the thief. On the following morning I saw the cat going out with a gold-coin in his mouth. I recovered it. On the third morning the cat stole another gold-coin, which I took back. So I made up my mind to kill the thief-cat."

Then it was the fish-monger's turn to tell his story. The money-changer, who listened with great interest to what the fish-monger had to tell, was so moved with the acts of the male cat, which must have stolen the gold-coins to repay the fish-dealer for his kindnesses. Tokita then handed to the fish-dealer two more gold-coins, which the cat evidently intended to give the fish-monger.

A tomb was erected over the place where the cat was buried and its inscription reads: "Virtue and good-accumulating male-animal."

FOX OF SHINODA FOREST

Several stories are told in Japan about foxes, which, escaping death through the kindness of men, assumed the human shape and married them by way of reciprocating their benefaction. The most typical of this kind of stories is the "Fox of Shinoda," which never fails to draw a full house when represented on the stage.

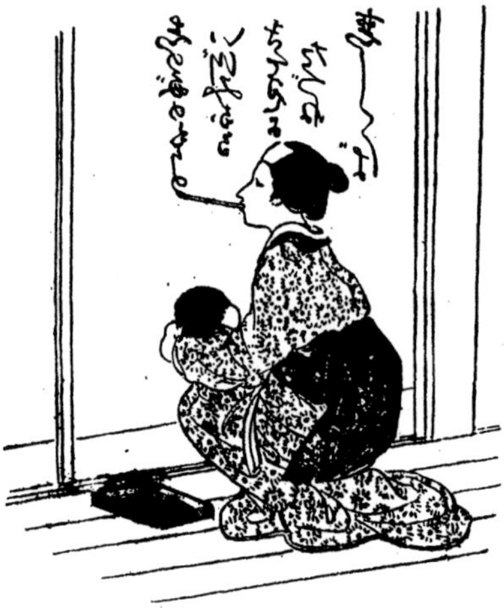

Transmogrified fox-mother writing her 31-syllable ode on Shoji sliding-door before she leaves the house

Yasuna Abe, son of Governor Yasuaki Abe, who lived at Tennoji (now in Osaka) during the reign of the Emperor Murakami (62nd), was a pious and devoted warrior and he often visited the Shinoda shrine in the province of Izumi Province. Once when he took a rest by pitching a tent near the main shrine, there came a female fox running in a scare, and hid itself under the tent. Tsuneharu Ishikawa, widely reputed for his wicked and cruel deeds, came in chase of the fox, which he demanded of Abe. Ishikawa had a sick wife, whose only remedy, according to her physician, was to eat the liver of a live fox, and Ishikawa came to Shinoda, which was known for a large number of foxes. He found three foxes, two of which scampered off, while the third came to the tent of Abe. Abe, however, pleaded that he had no knowledge of it, and he protested when the retainers of Ishikawa began searching for the fox. A heavy affray ensued, and Abe, overnumbered, was taken prisoner by the troops of Ishikawa, the fox running away in the meantime.

Continued

Ishikawa was about to kill Abe, when there suddenly came Priest Raihan, for whom Ishikawa had such admiration that, when the priest asked for Abe, Ishikawa delivered him with great reluctance, at the pursuasion of the priest, who, however, as it was later revealed, was none other than the fox transmogrified in order to save its benefactor.

Yasuna, thus unexpectedly spared, went down to a small stream to quench his thirst. He was just in time to save a handsome-looking girl, who, dropping into the stream by mistake, was almost drowned. Tired as he was with the wounds he received at the fight, Yasuna escorted the girl to her home, which was in a wood close by, where he stayed for some time under the kind care of the girl he saved, till they fell in love with each other and eventually they got married.

In the meantime Yasuaki, father of Yasuna, was killed in a fight with Ishikawa, who, however, was killed by Yasuna, with the help of Zenji Mita, his retainer. His father dead, Yasuna stayed on at his wife's, till their son was seven years old. One autumn's day, his wife looked out into their gardens to enjoy the chrysanthemums, and, charmed by their beauty, she betrayed her real shape of a fox, unawares because the girl that Yasuna found drowing in the river was the selfsame fox that Yasuna had saved from the cruel hands of Tsuneharu Ishikawa. Her transmogrification discovered, she suddenly disappeared, leaving the following 31-syllable poem on Shoji, (paper-sliding door) for her son:

"Koishikuba
Tazune kite miyo
Izumi ,naru
Shinoda-no-Mori no
Urami-Kuzu-no-Ha."

(If you miss mother, come and see her at Shinoda Forest in the province of Izumi, whither moth r goes with sorrow.)

MAJINAI OR EXORCISM

Every sort of misfortune and illness is popularly attributed to the working of some evil spirit in Japan, and the Japanese have invented strange ways of Majinai or spelling evil out. Here are a few of them, which are still practised more or less:

Lover expected: When a Geisha-girl misses her lover, she will make a paper-frog and stick a needle into it. It is taken out when he comes. The Japanese for "frog" is "kaeru", which homonymously means "coming back". Hence this charm. The Chinese character (馬) for a horse, when written in a reverse way, has the same effect in bringing a lover.

Charm against pestilence: When smallpox is prevalent, one often sees a small piece of red paper pasted at the entrance of a house in an affected locality. The paper has a few characters meaning the lodging place of a certain person who is said to have controlled evil, such as "Chinzei-Hachiro-Tametomo," "Shinagawa Matsuemon," "Somin Shorai," etc., the idea being that the names of such warriors will scare the epidemic-evil away.

Charm against an eye-disease: A person suffering from an eye-disease will get a few mud-snails from an irrigated rice-field and set them free in a river. In many local places mud snails are eaten, but they must be caught in the irrigated rice-field; none that live in a river being eaten.

Charm against thunderbolt: Our children are told never to keep their front naked because *Kaminari*, or the god of thunder, is fond of a navel. When it thunders hard, incense is burned to keep lightning off and one often gets in a mosquito-net. But if you cry "Kuwabara! kuwabara! (mulberry-fields, mulberry-fields), it was said, you will not be struck by lightning, because it is popularly believed that the mulberry-tree is non-conductive.

Charm against falling down: A Geisha-girl has sometimes a small gourd-shaped ornament on her Obi (sash) in order that she may not fall down. A dried gourd, which is very buoyant, is believed to make the body of its bearer very light.

Continued

Charm for a lost needle: When a needle is lost, a pair of scissors are tied up with a cord in such a way that they cannot be used to cut a thing. They are untied when the needle is found out. Or the following 31-syllable was repeated three times in olden days:

"Kiyomizu no
Otowa no Taki wa
Tayuru-tomo
Use-taru Hari no
Miyenu koto nashi"

(The Otowa waterfall of Kiyomizu may sometimes cease to fall, but there is no lost needle but is found out.)

Charm for one who starts on a long trip: In some localities, a pair of Geta (wooden clogs) of one who starts on a long trip are arranged on the door-step, when one leaves the home, with one turned forth and the other turned back, so that the traveller will go and come back.

Charm against a barking dog: When you are barked at by a dog, you turn your palm to the dog after imitating to write the Chinese character for a tiger on it with a finger of the other hand, and the dog will stop barking at you.

Charm for second dentition: A tooth from the upper jaw has to be thrown under the floor by saying " Let a tooth take its place"; a tooth from the lower jaw has to be thrown on the roof by saying "Let an Oni's (devil's) tooth take its place". Good teeth will come out for the second dentition.

Charm against a visitor: When you are bothered by a visitor who stays unduly for a long time, put a broom against the wall with its handle down and, they say, he will leave you soon.

Charm for easy delivery: A papier-machie dog is placed beside the pillow of a labouring woman as a charm for an easy delivery because a dog is known for an easy delivery.

Charm against the crying of a baby: When a baby cries hard, its mother is often heard to say "Mo! Mo!" in a loud voice. "Mo" means "Mongolians" and it seems to have its origin in the Mongolian invasion of 1281. The mother means to warn the baby against crying, because "the Mongolians will come if it keeps on crying." The Mongolian invasion must have struck such a terror into the heart of every Japanese.

SALT AS CHARM

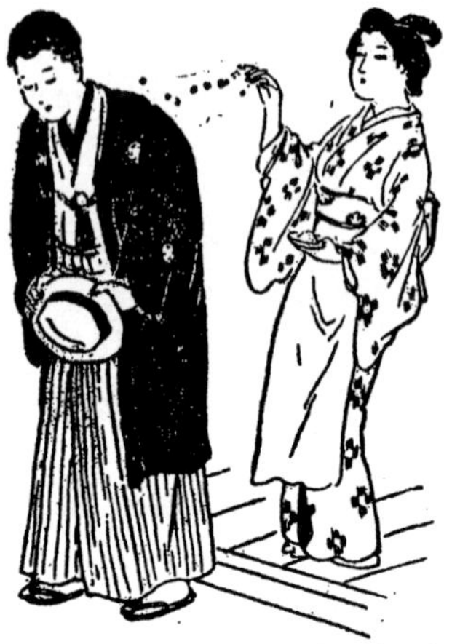

Wife purifying husband with salt

"Salt! Salt!" an orthodox Japanese, on coming home from a visit, demands at the front entrance of his house, without getting in.

His wife or maid comes out taking a pinch of salt, which she sprinkles piously over his body. He is now free to enter the house. This means that he has been to a funeral and the salt, thrown over his body, purifies him, so that he may get rid of uncleanliness generally supposed to come to him on account of his attending a funeral, for death is considered in this country to be dark and unclean or filthy, while life is bright and clean.

When a dead body is taken to a crematory for cremation those who accompany the remains, will step on some salt at the entrance for purification on coming back. One still sees in a remote locality that a bit of salt is thrown into fire after beef, pork or any other meat is cooked over it, for flesh of any kind is still supposed to be unclean in many localities or at least not pleasing to the god of fire, who is purity itself.

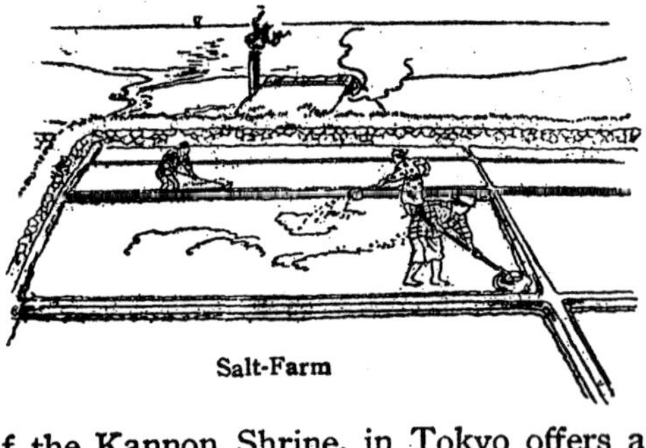

Salt-Farm

Three small stacks of salt are always seen at an entrance to a Japanese restaurant, a Geisha-house, a Yose (vaudeville), etc. This practice is of Chinese origin and salt is put there as a luck-bringer to invite customers and guests, as well as a purifying charm. (See We Japanese Vol. I. P. 177).

Every devotee of the Salt-tasting Jizo enshrined close by the Kaminari-mon Gate of the Kannon Shrine, in Tokyo offers a small dishful of salt to the deity, so that his or her sin may be cleansed. You will also see a sacred statue covered thick with salt offered by its pious believers at the Daiso-in Temple, Shinjuku in Tokyo.

This custom of using salt originated in the prehistoric days when Prince Izanagi purified himself with salt-water after coming back from the land of Tokoyo-no-Kuni (lit. perpetual night) or the dead.

Shiotsuchi-no-Okina: A prehistoric prince to whose invention salt is attributed in this country is said to have taken salt by boiling sea-water. He is enshrined at the Shio-gama (lit. salt-kettle) shrine at Shiogama in Miyagi Prefecture, where he taught the people how to get salt from brine. The very kettle with which he made salt is said to be preserved as a shrine-treasure.

HUMAN PREORDINATION

Japan has twelve signs of the Zodiac; namely, Rat, Bull, Tiger, Hare, Dragon, Snake, Horse, Sheep, Monkey, Cock, Dog and Wild Boar. Each year and each day has had a zodiac sign assigned to it from time out of memory. The year 1947, for instance, was that of the Wild Boar, 1948 is that of the Rat, 1949 is that of the Bull, and so on; while the first of January, 1948, was the day

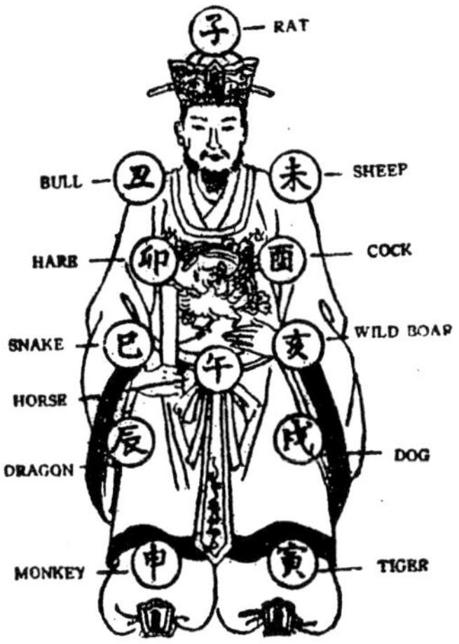

Emperor in Summer

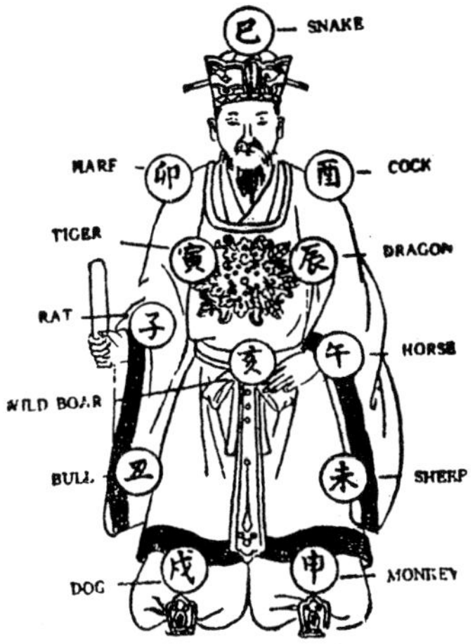

Emperor in Winter

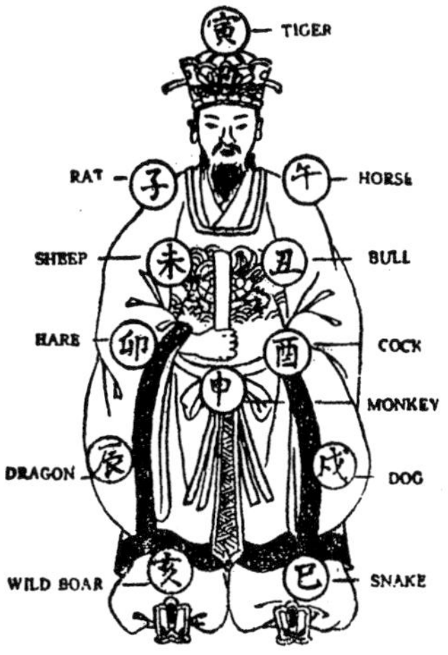

Emperor in Autumn

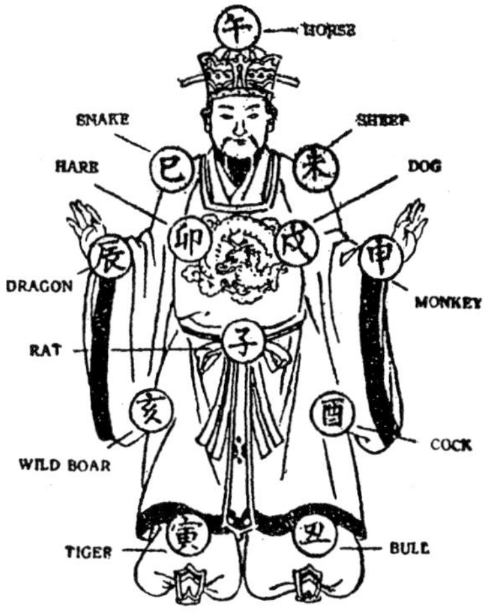

Emperor in Spring

Kotei (Emperor) for the four seasons Ideagraphs in circles show zodiac signs

Continued

of the Horse, the second was that of the Sheep, the third of the Monkey and so forth till the last day of the year 1948 will be that of the Wild Boar to be followed by that of the Rat again in 1949. So each man and each woman has the same zodiac sign assigned as that of the year of his or her birth, and it is believed in Japan that our destiny in life is determined according to the position that the zodiac sign of the year of birth has on the body of Kotei (Emperor) or the Heavenly Father :—

The fortune-teller will say concerning the preördination of men as follows:

The head of the Emperor: One whose zodiac sign falls on the head of the Emperor is rich and noble in character; promoted fast in life; much respected and admired; and will live a long and affluent life.

The shoulders of the Emperor: One whose zodiac sign falls on the shoulders of the Emperor is quiet and peaceful; will live rich and affluent; will be well-to-do when old, though many harships will take place while young; will have many horses and cattle; will have good connections in relatives and kinsmen.

The hands of the Emperor: One whose zodiac sign falls on the hands of the Emperor is clever and dexterous; wise and sagacious; but difficult in love matters; will live happy until an old age.

The front of the Emperor: One whose zodiac sign falls on the front side of the Emperor will be versed in civil and military arts; good at literary work, such as poetry, singing, etc.; but will have trouble of different kinds through life; should worship the stars.

The thighs of the Emperor: One whose zodiac sign falls on the thighs of the Emperor will live rich and honoured; but is fickle and whimscal; will marry a rich wife or husband; will have many children, who will rise in life; should be careful not to fall gloomy.

The knees of the Emperor: One whose zodiac sign falls on the knees of the Emperor is always fickle and changeable; cannot live at one place for a long time; will be always troubled in some way or other; will have more failure than success; is not dutiful to parents; should be behaved well.

The feet of the Emperor: One whose zodiac sign falls upon the feet of the Emperor cannot live long in parents' home; will fail in business; will not have a good conjugal relations; will be always distressed in one way or other.

PORTENTS OR SIGNS

Udonge-no-Hana, eggs of a lacewing: Nothing is more dreaded as a bad sign in this country than are the eggs of a lacewing laid on the ceiling, walls, lamp-shade or anything else within a house. They are named Udonge-no-Hana after Udombara, which is said to come out once in 3,000 years. If a lacewing lays its eggs within the house, a death or else a serious disease is generally expected in the household.

Spider coming down from the ceiling: "A spider in the evening must be killed even though it might be taken for a parent" says a proverb, "but a spider appearing in the morning must be spared even though it might be taken for an enemy." A spider in the evening is a sign of a burglar, but one coming down from the ceiling in the morning is a good sign.

A tea-stem floating vertically in a tea-cup: "Good news is waiting for me" one would say if a tea-stem is found floating vertically in a tea-cup served at a friend's. A tea-stem in a tea-cup is always a good sign.

A comb dropped in the street: One will rather be glad than sorry to drop a comb (Kushi) unawares in the street, for with it homonymously trouble (ku) and death (shi) are done away with. No Japanese will pick up a comb that he may find on the street.

Itchy ears: If one feels itchy in the right ear, good news will come; but itch in the left ear is a bad sign.

Weasel crossing the road in front: If a weasel crosses the street in front of you, the friend whom you are going to see will be found absent.

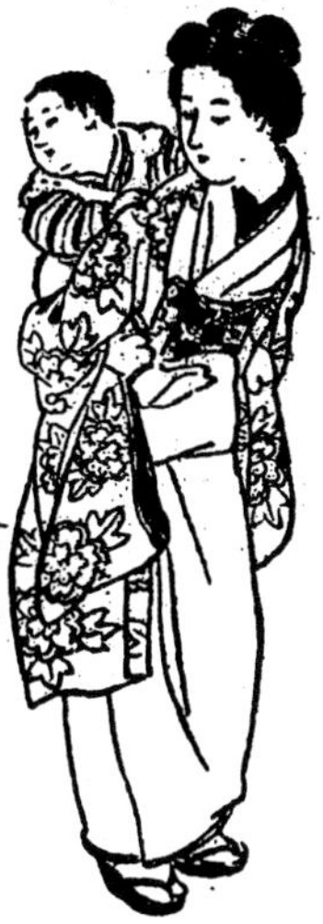

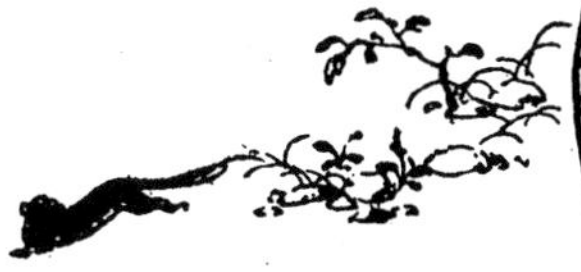

A weasel crossing the road

TENGU STORIES

Every festive procession of a Shinto shrine is led by a man wearing a red mask with an enormously long nose. He is said to represent a Tengu (see "We Japanese", Vol. I, P. 18), an aerial and fabulous being which haunted or lived in deep mountains, though every Shinto priest will tell you that the long-nosed leader represents Prince Saruda-Hiko, who, according to the Nihon-Shoki, led the Imperial party of Prince Ninigi-no-Mikoto when he came down from Heaven to rule the country below. There is no locality in Japan but has some stories told about the Tengu.

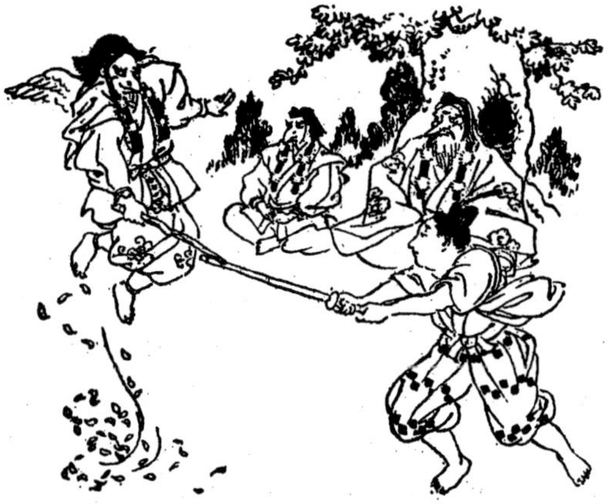
Young Ushiwaka-maru practising swordsmanship under Tengu on Mt. Kurama

Ushiwaka-maru on Mt. Kurama: Of all Tengu stories, that of Ushiwaka-maru is perhaps the most famous. Ushiwaka-maru, better known by his later name of Yoshitsune, was brother to Yoritomo Minamoto, the first Shogun of the Minamoto Dynasty. When their father, Yoshitomo, was killed by Kiyomori Taira, in 1159, young Ushiwaka-maru was sent up Mt. Kurama for the study of Buddhism, but the ambitious young man practised swordsmanship night after night, it is said, under the instructions of Tengu, till he became one of the best swordsmen in the history of Japan, and he helped his brother, Yoritomo, in destroying the Taira family in 1185.

Continued

Tengu's letter of apology: The Butsugen-ji Temple at Ito, Izu Peninsula, keeps a "letter of apology" written by a Tengu. Several hundred years ago or, to be more exact, in 1659, so the Priest of the temple says, every traveller walking on the beach of Ito was troubled by the mischiefs of some unseen being which lived in the woods. Priest Nichian of the Butsugen-ji Temple recited the Buddhist sutra asking the superhuman being to quit its mischief. At the end of the sutra-reading, a scroll came down from the forest, and no traveller was molested any longer. The scroll, about 2 ft. by 9 ft., contains some three thousand letters or characters, which are beyond decipherment for any human being, and it is concluded that it was written by a Tengu by way of apology for molesting the people.

The Kaya-ji Temple and the Kaya-tree: The Kaya-ji was a famous temple in Asakusa, Edo. At one time it had a resident priest, Gen-ei by name, who was very fond of the play of Go (checkers). One day there came a Yamabushi (mountain-monk), who offered to play at checkers with the priest, provided that the latter would bet a large Kaya-tree (torreya nucefera), of which the priest was very proud. They played and the priest was beaten. "All the fruits of this tree shall be mine" the mountain-monk said, and he mysteriously disappeared after telling the priest that he was a Tengu from Mt. Akiba, which is known as a dwelling-place of the Tengu. The tree kept growing on, but it ceased to bear any fruits afterwards.

Tengu borrowed use of hands: Shotei was the chief priest of the Seiko-ji Temple, near Utsunomiya. He was noted for his skill in calligraphy. One evening there came to his temple a Tengu, who asked for the skill of his hands, saying "May 1 borrow your hands for a while?" The priest replied that he could not lend them because he could not cut them off, when the Tengu said: "I need not take them with me. All you have to do is just to say that you will let me have them."

Continued

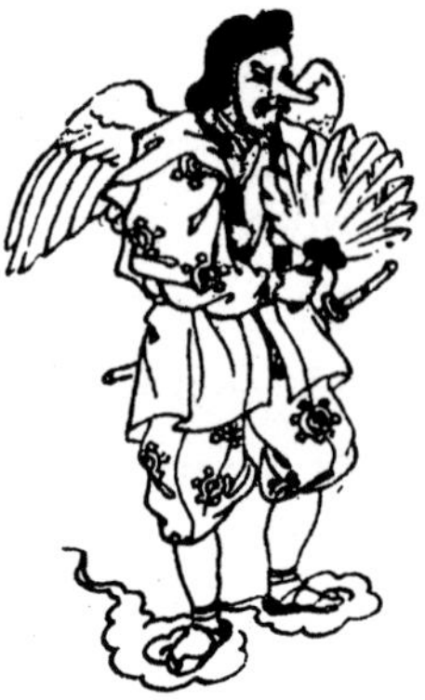

Tengu, fabulous aerial being

"You are welcome then," said Priest Shotei, and the Tengu went away after thanking the priest.

That night Priest Shotei lost the use of his hands, which were suddenly paralyzed and maimed. About a month went by, when the Tengu again visited him, saying: "I have come to return your hands. As a taken of my appreciation for your kindness, I have brought a talisman for averting a fire."

Priest Shotei recovered the use of his hands that moment, and ever since his temple has sold a famous charm against a fire.

A lad carried from Kyoto to Edo by Tengu: On the 20th of the seventh month (July), 1810, a young man, about 25 years old, fell suddenly from the sky on the street of Umamichi, Asakusa, in Edo (Tokyo). He was stark-naked and he fainted from the fall.

"Where am I?" the young man asked, when, on coming to himself, he opened his eyes to see large crowds of people gathered around him. And when he was told that he was in a street of Edo, he went on: "I am son of Ito Naizen, a retainer of Lord Yasui in the Imperial capital of Kyoto. My name is Yajiro."

Early on the 18th, the same month, according to his story, young Yajiro, taking a servant with him, went up Mt. Atago, famous for the dwelling of many Tengu, where a stranger offered to show him fine views. He followed him, but he could recollect no more.

Yajiro was taken back to Kyoto, and it was commonly believed that it was a prank of Tengu that carried him mysteriously from Kyoto to Edo.

In Japan, the mysterious disappearance of a boy is always attributed to a prank of Tengu, of which Japan has many mysterious stories.

Yonaki-Ishi or Night-Crying Stone, of Sayo-no-Nakayama

Sayo-no-Nakayama on the Tokaido Road is proverbially known for the Yonaki-ishi stone that "cries at night." The stone is reported to have been the cause of a law suit once instituted at Shizuoka regarding the rights of its possession.

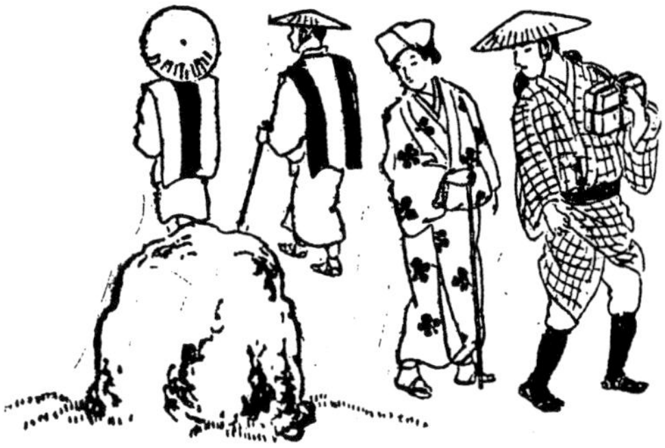

Yonaki-Ishi of Sayo-no-Nakayama

During the era of Eikyo (1429–1440 A. D.), a young girl, by the name of Sayohime, the name-sake of the legendary stone, who was then with child, was travelling by herself through Nakayama in the prefecture of Shizuoka. A highwayman, appearing, attacked and killed her for her money, for Nakayama was famous for highwaymen.

Sayohime was a great believer of Kannon, Goddess of Mercy, who, assuming the human form of a Buddhist priest, took her baby, a boy, through the wound that proved fatal to her, and brought it up. This boy grew up to be a brave warrior and took revenge upon the wronged murder of his mother by tracing the highwayman who had killed her.

According to local tradition, however, there was once a pine-tree growing where the stone now stands. It is said that a child stopped crying at night if a few needles of this pine were burned in its house. Consequently the pine-tree was called the Yonaki-Matsu or "pine-tree that cries at night." When the pine-tree was struck by lightning, the villagers of Nakayama discovered a stone in the place where the pine-tree had stood. Hence the name of the stone, Yonaki-ishi (lit. night-crying stone). The stone, which weighs 350 *kan* (kan=3.75 kilos), is kept in the compound of the Kyuen-ji Temple at Nakayama.

Ghost brings baby up: O-Shino, wife of Farmer Sagenji, of the village of Ishizaki at the foot of Mt. Tsukuba, Ibaragi Prefecture, was going from her bridegroom's house back to her native home, as was usual with every young wife of that locality, to be delivered of child. But she was killed by a highwayman on the way. Her poor husband went on a pilgrimage, for four years, in order to pray for the rest of her departed spirit. On his way home Farmer Sagenji stopped at a neighbouring village where he was told by an old woman who dealt in Dango (or dumpling), of a young woman who came to buy a few dumplings every day by paying two coppers. When asked who she was, the old dealer told him, the young one said that she was O-Shino of Ishizaki Village.

It was discovered that O-Shino, wife of Farmer Sagenji, was delivered of a baby after her murder, and that she brought it up by coming out of the grave every night to buy a few dumplings for the baby. The boy was taken to the Toko-ji Temple, in the cemetery of which she lay buried, and then to his own father, Farmer Sagenji, who brought him up.

SHICHIFUKUJIN OR SEVEN GODS OF FORTUNE

(Where to get their images)

The seven gods of fortune are: Ebisu, Daikoku, Bishamon, Benzaiten, Fukurokuju, Jurojin and Hotei, (see We Japanese Vol. I). They are very popular with the Japanese all over the country; the first two, in particular, being venerated in almost every Japanese home. There are three sets of shrines and temples dedicated to the seven gods of fortune in Tokyo; namely, the Mukojima, Yamate (Bluff) and Meguro sets, of which the first-mentioned is the best-known, and the pious people of Tokyo make regular visits to the shrines and temples specially during the New Year's time, when the images are available at their respective shrines and temples. The Mukojima set of the seven gods is available at the following shrines and temples:—

Ebisu	Mimeguri shrine,	Mukojima
Daikoku	" "	"
Bishamon	Tamon-ji Temple,	"
Benzaiten	Chomei-ji Temple,	"
Fukurokuju	Hyakka-en Garden,	"
Jurojin	Shirahige Shrine,	"
Hotei	Kofukuji Temple,	"

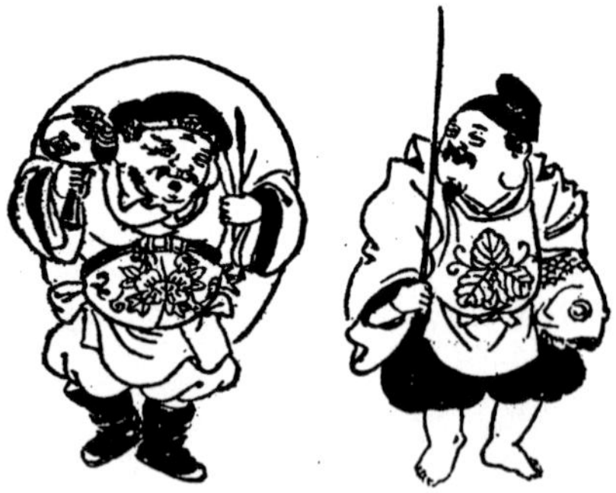

Ebisu (right) and Daikoku (left)

Ebisu: said to be the third child of Prince Izanagi and Princess Izanami, and brother of the ancestress of the Imperial family of Japan. He was first enshrined at Nishinomiya between Osaka and Kobe, but his real identity is quite obscure. He always carries a Tai (sea-bream) under his left arm and a fishing-rod in his right hand.

Daikoku: A combination of the Indian deity, Mahakala (lit. great black) and the Japanese prehistoric prince, Okuninushi (Okuni 大國

Continued

pronounced also "Daikoku"), who is enshrined at the Izumo shrine. The rat is his messenger.

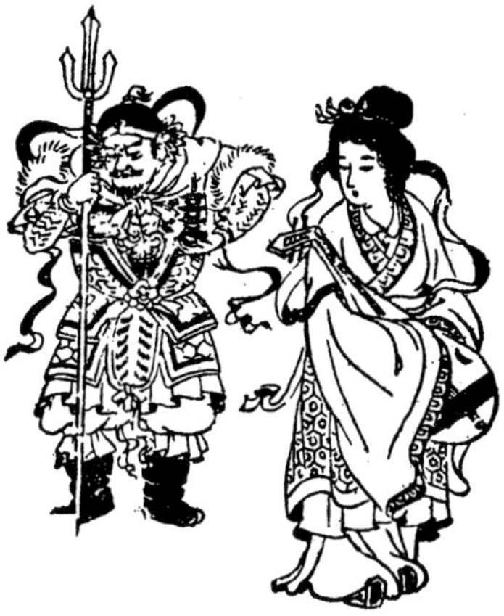

Benten (right) and Bishamon (left)

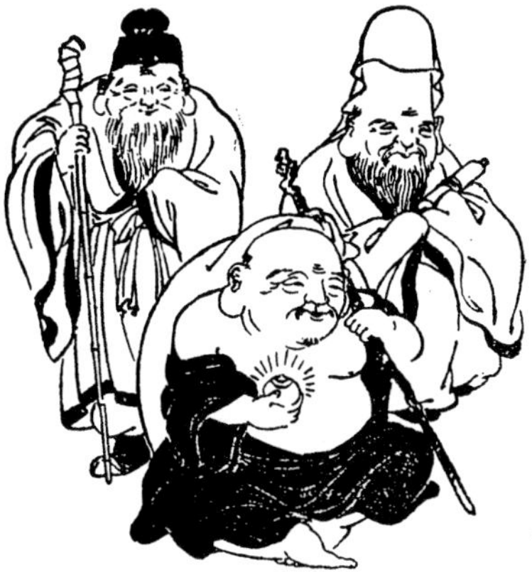

Jurojin (left), Fukurokuju (right) and Hotei (front)

Bishamon: The Indian deity, Vaisravana, who is a protector of Buddhism; always clad in an armour and armed with a halberd. The centiped is his messenger.

Benzaiten, also called Benten for short; Sarasvati, an Indian angel, always carrying the Biwa-lute and often with a white snake. She is considered to be a goddess of music and art.

Fukurokuju (lit. fortune-fief-longevity): A Chinese hermit, also said to be the god of the south polar star. The stork is his messenger.

Jurojin (lit. longevity-old-man): said to be identical also with Fukurokuju and added only to make the lucky number of seven. The deer is his messenger, according to some scholars.

Hotei: A mendicant priest called Keishi (Japanese pronunciation of 契此), who lived in China during the Tang dynasty. He owned hardly anything but the personal effects contained in a large bag that he is represented always to carry on his back, living entirely upon alms. He died on the third of the third month (March), 917 A. D. The name Hotei means "cloth-bag."

DAIKOKU, GOD OF FORTUNE

Daikoku, a god of fortune, is one of the most popular household deities in Japan. He is so important that the main pillar of a dwelling or warehouse is called Daikoku-bashira (pillar) after him in this country. Originally Daikoku is an Indian deity called Mahakala (lit. great-black) as the two ideographs (大黒), possibly its translation, now used for "Daikoku" in Japan, mean. Mahakala is always put near a kitchen in India, and so is Daikoku enshrined on a shelf above a hearth in a Japanese home so that his sacred image is always kept black with soot. Daikoku seems to have been imported to Japan during the Heian era (794–1185 A. D.).

But in Shintoism Daikoku is considered to be identical with Okuninushi, a prehistoric prince, to whom the Izumo shrine is dedicated, and indeed, so far as the costume and paraphernalia of Daikoku are concerned, both seem to be quite confused in Japan; the confusion being accounted for by the ideographs (大國主) used for the name of the prehistoric prince, which can be pronounced "Daikoku" as well. Daikoku is clad in the *kariginu*-dress, at all resembling none of Indian clothing. He sits, or often stands, on two bales of rice, the most important staple food in Japan, where all salaries and allowances of Daimyo (lord) and samurai (warrior) were paid in rice in her feudal days. He carries on his back a large bag, which the Indian deity never does, while, according to history, Prince Okuninushi carried a large bag on his back for his brothers when they went on a trip in the province of Inaba. Daikoku has in his right hand a hammer called "Uchide-no-Kotsuchi, (lit. little hammer that brings everything by beating), a sort of an "Aladdin's" hammer, at the beating of which anything and everything will come out. And the rat is the messenger of Daikoku, and it was a rat that saved Prince Okuninushi from the danger of being burned to death by a wicked brother in the grass. The festival of Daikoku is held always on the zodiac day of the Rat.

KANNON, GODDESS OF MERCY

The Kanzeon or, more popularly, Kannon is the Indian deity, Avalokitesvara (avalokite = see; isvara = free existence), for which we have three Chinese characters meaning "Observation of life-sounds" or the worldly worries. The deity is regarded in Japan as the Goddess of Mercy and very popularly worshipped the country over. She was first introduced to Japan during the reign of the Empress Suito (33rd), whose Crown Prince, Prince Umayado (lit. barn-door) or, as he is generally called, Prince Shotoku (lit. sacred-virtue) was a great devotee of the Goddess, who is believed to have a miraculous power. We have several phases of Kannon, of which the most popular are:

Byakui-Kannon (white-dress Kannon)
Medzu-Kannon (Horse-head-Kannon)
Yoryu-Kannon (Willow-Kannon)
Gyoran-Kannon (Fish-basket-Kannon)
Juichi-men-Kannon (11-faced Kannon)
Senju-Kannon (Thousand-hand-Kannon)

Asakusa Kannon: The Asakusa Kannon of the Senso-ji Temple, Tokyo, attracts thousands upon thousands of devotees every day all through the year. It is said that, during the reign of the Empress Suiko (33rd), Hashi Nakatomo, with his two retainers, Hamanari and Takenari of the Hinokuma family, went fishing on the River Sumida. They threw their net repeatedly for a long time, but, strange to say, no fish were caught on that day and they were about to return home in disappointment when a gold image of the Kannon, 1.8 inches high, was caught in the net. The Goddess was at once enshrined at Asakusa, which has since been the Mecca of the Kannon believers for over 13 centuries. But the statue is known as Hibutsu or Secret-Buddha, and nobody has ever seen it. Another statue, 18 inches high, which was carved by Priest Jigaku (794–864 A. D.) stands before a niche in which the secret image is installed.

Vice-Admiral Viscount Ogasawara and his Kannon Image: Vice-Admiral Viscount Ogasawara was a midshipman on board N. M. S. Takachiho during the Russo-Japanese war, 1904–5. At the time of his departure for the front, his pious mother gave him a Kannon image, telling him to offer the Goddess a cup of water every morning. The young officer kept the sacred image in his cabin and did as his mother had told him to do, not so much on account of his own belief in the goddess, as because the image reminded him of his mother at home.

One night early in August, 1904, the Viscount saw a great

Continued

naval operation in a dream. In the battle, he lost his right arm and he awoke. On the following morning he wrote a letter to his mother giving a description of the naval campaign that he saw in the dream, though he made no mention of the cannon ball that hit him on the right arm.

A little over ten days later, the battle of the Yellow Sea took place. Strange to tell, the array of the ships was exactly the same as he had seen in the dream. It was a sanguine battle, and his ship, which received a few balls, was a scene of veritable carnage after the battle. A cannon visited his own cabin, destroying anything and everything in it. One of his overcoats, which was hanging on a rack, had thirteen holes. His Kannon niche, however, stood as it had been. He opened the door with a kind of reverence and what was his surprise to see that the Kannon had lost one of her right arms, for the image was Senju-Kannon (lit. many-armed Kannon). Viscount Ogasawara clasped his hands together without intending, to worship the holy image out of pure reverence for the first time in his life, and "O mother!" escaped his lips unconsciously.

Scapegoat Kannon: We have many stories in which a holy image of Jizo or Kannon is wounded as a scapegoat for its devout believers.

A farmer was a devout believer of the Kannon of the Senso-ji Temple, Asakusa, whose printed image he always carried next to the skin. One day, after midnight, the farmer met a drunken man, on the embankments of Yoshiwara. He was struck with a sword, and feeling that he was wounded on the shoulder he fell senseless on the ground, apparently dead. When he was brought to himself again, however, it was discovered that he was not wounded at all, but the sacred picture of Kannon, which he had in his pocket was torn to pieces. It was concluded that, because of his faith in Kannon, the Goddess received the blow of the sword in his stead.

The Nunobiki Kannon: There was a stingy old woman near Mt. Nunobiki in the province of Shinano. She kept herself too busy in earning money to pay a monthly visit to the Kannon image of the Zenko-ji Temple, by making endless excuses for staying at home when her neighbours paid their regular visits to the Goddess. One day when the old woman was putting a piece of white cotton to dry on a bamboo pole, a strange bull made its sudden appearance and caught her cotton on its horns. The old woman ran after the bull to recover the cotton till at length she came into the precincts of the Zenko-ji Temple, where the bull made a mysterious disappearance, leaving the old woman in great bewilderment. Reluctantly she paid a visit to Kannon, and she was converted into Buddhism. It is said that her white cotton is still visible on Mt. Nunobiki (lit. cotton-pulling), which has a white stratum horizontally across it.

SHIROKI KANNON

One summer, early in the Tokugawa regime, there was a great scarcity of rain in Edo (Tokyo), and the ancestor of the present Shiroki Department Store decided to drill a well in his compounds, in order to help out those suffering from the drought. An 1.8-inch gold image of Kannon appeared when the ground was dug out a few feet deep. Encouraged by the blissful find, the workers dug further down, when clear water gushed out, to the great joy and relief of the people of Edo.

When, it is said, the lord of the Fukui clan, then staying in Edo, was taken very ill, a drink of water from this well cured him, and the well became so famous in the city of Edo that the residences of many lords were furnished with water from it every morning at the time of "four" (10 a. m.), during the Shogunate regime of Tokugawa.

The water is still bubbling out at the basement of the Shiroki Building and the sacred image of Kannon, which happily surrived the big earthquake of 1923 and the war, is enshrined in a little shrine on the roof of the building. A great ceremony of *Kaicho* (lit. curtain-opening) is held on the roof every year on what is termed in Buddhism "46,000 days" (April 10), on which day, it is popularly believed, a visit to Kannon will have as much effect on the visitor as if he made a daily visit for 46,000 days.

Hikotaro Omura, ancestor of Shiroki: Hikotaro Omura, the first ancestor and founder of the Shiroki Department Store, was a son of a lumber merchant in the province of Ohmi. He was an ambitious lad. One day he met his cousin, Shissai Miwa, at the Temman Shrine of Kitano, Kyoto, where they made a promise that they would vie with each other in leading a successful life. They made an appointment to meet again on Nihombashi Bridge, the center of Edo, in three years thence. Both came to Edo, where Hikotaro started a small dry-goods store, while Shissai began the study of Chinese classics. On the appointed day, three years after, they met each other on Nihombashi Bridge, when Omura brought an apprentice-boy with him, while Miwa had a servant with him showing that both started a successful life. At the end of the second three years, Omura had over a dozen clerks in his service and Miwa was running a private school where he taught Chinese classics to many young boys. The end of another three years saw Omura operating one of the largest dry-goods stores in Edo, which was the forerunner of the present Shiroki Department Store, while Miwa had been appointed tutor to Lord Mayeta of the Kaga clan, one of the largest in Japan.

Omura named his dry-goods store Shiroki-ya (lit. white-wood-store) because his family had dealt in cedar and cryptomeria, which were commonly called "shiroki" (white-wood) in his province.

PRAYING FOR THE DEAD IN JAPAN

The Japanese pay great respects to the dead by holding a religious meeting once in a while in commemoration of, or rather to pray for the peaceful repose of, the dead members of their families, for it is considered to be disgraceful for any Japanese to disregard or neglect them. The Japanese are religiously trained to take good care of the graves of their forefathers and other dead family-members, which they visit every now and then.

The first tenth day is observed by Shintoism and the first seventh day by Buddhism, after death, when, after a Buddhist sutra or a Shinto prayer is read by a priest, all the mourners who are the relatives and intimate friends of the deceased, are invited usually to dinner given in honor of the dead. Few Christians, needless to say, observe such a function for their dead. A similar meeting is held, on a smaller scale, on every tenth day by Shintoism and on every seventh day by Buddhism. On the 35th day (5×7 days) or 49th day (7×7 days) for Buddhism and on the 50th or 100th day for Shintoism, a gift is returned to those who showed their sympathy or condolence by making an offering in kind or money to the bereft family. According to a popular belief of Buddhism, a dead soul will linger about its earthly abode for 49 (7×7) days, by which time the remains have to be buried. A Buddhist service is held for the repose of their dead (either of a family or the nation) on the following anniversaries of death :—

1st year, 3rd year, 7th year, 13th year, 17th year, 23rd year, 27th year, 33rd year, 37th year. 47th year, 50th year and so on.

A Japanese school-child or student can absent himself from school, without affecting his days of attendance, for a period of seven days when death takes place in the family. Nor will a Japanese who is in mourning for a kinsman send out greetings in the following New Year or attend a public meeting during the period of mourning. No pine-decorations are used to decorate a house in mourning in the New Year. In conformity with Confucian teachings, the Japanese of old observed the following periods of mourning, though this custom has long been dead :—

Kinsman	Time of mourning	Kinsman	Time of mourning
For father and mother...	13 months	For adoptive parent.........	150 days
„ Husband	30 days	„ Wife	30 „
„ Eldest child	90 „	„ Other child	30 „
„ Parent-in-law	150 „	„ Grand parents	150 „
„ Great grandparents.	90 „	„ Uncle and aunt.........	90 „
„ Brother and sister .	90 „	„ Half-brother and sister.	20 „
„ Grandchild............	7 „	„ Great grandchild	7 „
„ Cousin..................	7 „	„ Nephew and niece ...	7 „

Our mourning is based on an idea that, death being impurity, a person who has lost a kinsman is in the state of contamination and hence he or she avoids public appearance during the period of mourning. And all persons in mourning were clad in plain white, instead of black, in former days.

THE RICE-PLANTING JIZO

Japan is rich in stories of a sacred image that helped its devotees by working on their behalf. Jizo (Ksitigarbha), guardian deity of children and caretaker of departed souls, in particular, is believed to have the attribute or power of taking the human form, and many are indeed stories in which this merciful deity worked in the rice-fields when its pious owner was too sick in bed to work. Hence the name of Taue-Jizo (Rice-planting Ksitigarbha).

The special features of Rice-planting Jizo are that the sacred image has muddy feet because it works in the paddy fields which are muddy with irrigation. Here are a story or two of Jizo.

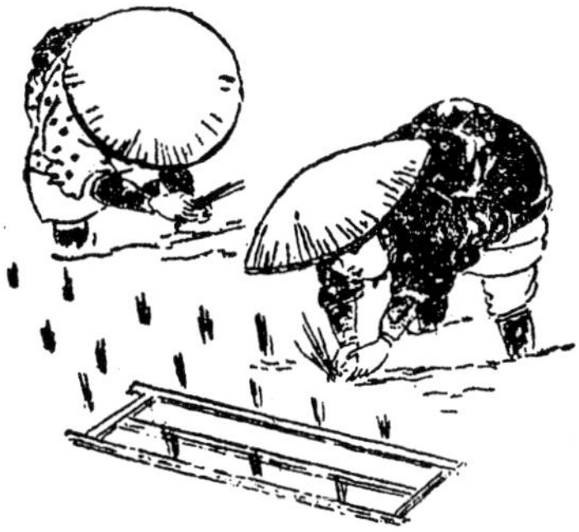

Rice-planting

Taue-Jizo of Nanzen-in Temple: The Nanzen-in Temple, situated at Daigo, near Kyoto, is dedicated to Jizo, now known as Taue-Jizo or Rice-planting Ksitigarbha. When a certain farmer, a great devotee of Jizo, was once laid up with illness, some one worked on his fields and finished the planting of rice while he was still in bed. It was soon discovered that Jizo of the Nanzen-in Temple had much mud on its feet, so it was concluded that the sacred image worked on the rice-fields on behalf of the sick farmer. Jizo was subsequently called Taue-Jizo.

Honzon-Jizo of the Emmei-ji Temple: The Emmei-ji Temple stands at the village of Muko-ga-Oka in Kanagawa Prefecture. It has another Taue-Jizo venerated in it. This Jizo is said to have taken the appearance of a young apprentice-boy, on whose behalf the sacred image ploughed the fields by leading the horse of his master by the bits. Jizo is also known by the name of Hanatori (lit. Nose-holding) Jizo, meaning that the horse is led by its reins.

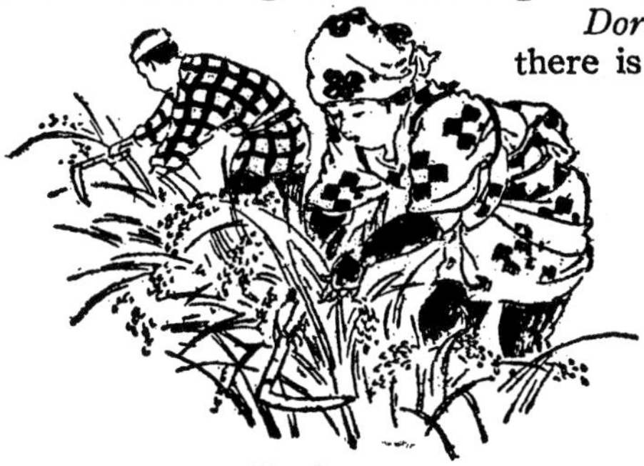

Rice harvest

Doro-nuri Jizo: In some localities there is a custom in which, after rice planting is over in the spring, the villagers throw a handful of mud to one another or put a handful of mud on the image of Jizo, so that Jizo may protect the rice-fields. Doro-nuri Jizo (lit. mud-daubing-Jizo) at the village of Abe in Nara Prefecture is known for the miraculous power of healing a skin disease. All you will have to do is to put a bit of mud on a part of the sacred image corresponding to the affected part of your body, and you will soon be cured.

O-ESHIKI-FESTIVAL

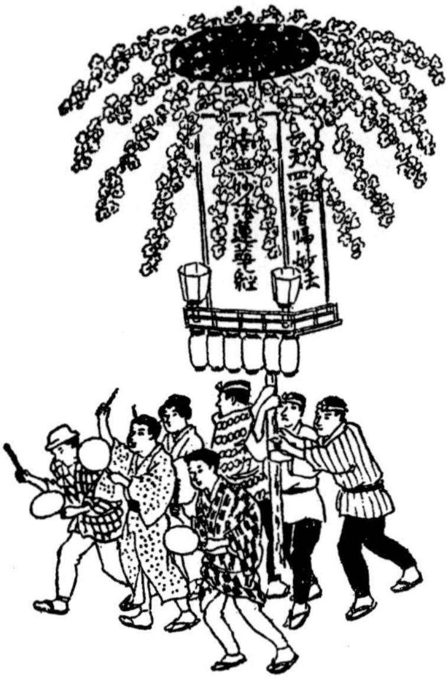

Mando (lit. 10,000-lanterns) at Oeshiki

O-Eshiki (lit. honorable-meeting-ceremony) is a festival observed at every Buddhist temple of the Nichiren sect on the 13th of October each year in commemoration of the death of Priest Nichiren, its founder, who died on the 13th day of the tenth month (October) in the year 1283. The Nichiren sect is justly called by some the Salvation Army of Buddhism, because it is no less lively and persuasive than is its sister organization of the West, and its pious believers march in great processions, on this particular fete-day of O-Eshiki, to the Nichiren temple of their respective localities to do homage to Saint Nichiren, founder of their sect. Many of them come from such long distances that they have to walk all day and night.

The Hommon-ji Temple at Ikegami, Tokyo, in particular, where Priest Nichiren died in 1283 is a great center of pilgrimage for these pious visitors, numbering literally hundreds of thousands, for the accommodation of whom all railways, which led to the temple, the Government railways not excepted, used to run in all-night services on the night of Oct. 12, the day before the anniversary of the death of Nichiren.

Uchiwa-daiko: Uchiwa-daiko (lit. fan-drum), which is a round disk of leather with a handle, is a typical instrument of this sect of Buddhism. The pilgrims of O-Eshiki will keep on beating the fan-drums, as hard as their hands permit, chanting the Nichiren formula "Na-mu-Myo-Ho-Ren-Ge-Kyo" (Nam-Lotus-Sutra) on their way to and from the temple they visit. Thus they will beat sin and evil away.

Mando: Mando (lit. 10,000-lanterns) consists of a simple frame of wood with long splinters of bamboo decorated with red or white pieces of paper in representation of as many lights as are indicated by its name. A symbolic lantern marches usually at the head of each pilgrimage procession, as a sign for cleansing evil by driving darkness with its imaginary light.

Hojoe or Ceremony of Setting Animals Free

In a funeral procession, one often sees a big bamboo-cage of birds carried immediately after the coffin. These birds are set free after the burial of the dead body at the cemetery, so that the philantholopic act of setting the birds free may contribute towards the post-mortem salvation of the departed souls which may be doomed to Buddhist Hell on account of sins committed in this life.

This practice of setting birds free at a Buddhist funeral was adopted from the custom of Hojoe (the ceremony of setting living things free), such as birds, fish, etc., after giving them the commandment of Sanki-kai or returning to the Three Ratnas.

Hojoe was of Chinese origin, and it was adopted in Japan during the reign of the Emperor Bitatsu in the sixth century, when he prohibited killing of any kind on the six Posadha-days, namely, the 8th, 14th, 15th, 23rd, 29th and 30th days of each month.

The Emperor Temmu commanded that the Prohibition Day should be observed when the birds, fish and any other animals that were kept should be set free. In 717, A. D. the two provinces of Osumi and Hiuga revolted against the Imperial court, when a prayer was offered for peace at the shrine of Usa-Hachiman and its priest led the Imperial troops against the rebels. Upon his triumphal return, the priest received an oracle from the deity of his shrine to the effect that the ceremony of Hojoe should be observed by setting living animals free in atonement for the many lives which were lost during the war. It was observed on the fifteenth day of the eighth month (August) in the same year. This was the first ceremony of Hojoe ever held officially in Japan. Another Hojoe was observed for the freedom of animals at the shrine of Iwashimizu-Hachiman on the 14th day of the eighth month in 1220 A. D.

The ceremony of Hojoe was celebrated both officially and privately once in a while chiefly on a Buddhist occasion, but its official observation was discontinued after the Restoration of 1868, though at a Buddhist funeral one still sees the custom of setting birds free. In 1948 this ceremony was observed before memorial trees of Gen. & Mrs. U. S. Grant with a prayer for their peaceful repose

SPEAR FESTIVAL OF OHJI

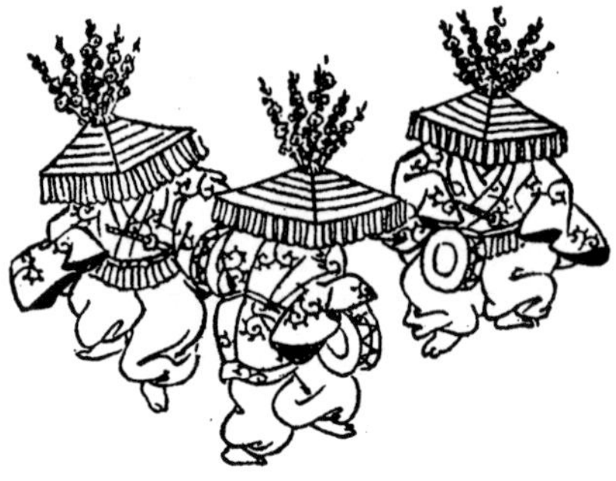

Festival of Ohji Shrine

The Ohji shrine of Ohji, Tokyo, was founded during the era of Genko (1321-1323 A. D.) in dedication to Prince Izanagi and Princess Izanami. The village (now a ward of Tokyo) of Ohji, which means "royal child" was so named after the prehistoric prince enshrined there. During the Tokugawa Shogunate, the shrine was much venerated by the Shogun, some of whom offered annual tributes to the shrine, and samurai used to offer a prayer for victory and promotion in life.

A classical festival is held at the Ohji shrine on the 13th of August (properly the seventh month in the lunar calendar), when a military dance is performed by a party of dancers. Two of them, clad like samurai of old, wear seven swords, 4 ft. long, three on the right-hand side and four on the left. One of them has a Gohei (Shinto offering) on his helmet while the other carries a bunch of bulrushes on his, and each is armed with a halberd. Eight other dancers come after the warriors. Two wear the Eboshi-headdress of paper and six others have flower-headdresses covered with five-coloured pieces of paper, and each has a small Tsuzumi drum in front. All the dancers appear in the main hall of the shrine, and dance a dance to the music played by the band of the shrine. Towards the end of the dance the fancy flower-dresses are thrown into the crowds which look at the dance in the court-yard, and they scramble and struggle for the flowers, which are torn into pieces until nothing is left but smashed and destroyed pieces of paper. But happy is one who can carry small pieces of the flower-headdresses home as a luck-bringer to be kept during the rest of the year.

This festival, however, is known by the name of Yari-matsuri (lit. spear-festival) and miniature-spears are special articles sold on the occasion of the festival. You will find quite big numbers of stalls dealing in miniature spears all along the approaches to the shrine. The visitors of the shrine buy them and offer them to the shrine. According to tradition, Lady Kasuga, nurse and governess of Iyemitsu, the third Shogun of the Tokugawa dynasty, was a great believer in the Ohji shrine, and she offered a spear to the shrine every time when a prayer she offered was answered. Hence the custom of offering miniature-spears to the shrine on the occasion of its festival.

MANZAI OR STREET EXORCIST

In the New Year two men are seen visiting door after door on the street in order to spell evil out for the New Year, by singing a prayer for exorcism or blessing. They represent Ebisu and Daikoku, two gods of good luck, and they are street-exorcists called Manzai (lit. 10,000 years); the one in front, called Tayu, who carries a fan, sings the prayer, just for a handful of rice or a copper or two, to the sound of a Tsuzumi-drum beaten by Saizo, the other. The exorcising song is full of lucky expressions.

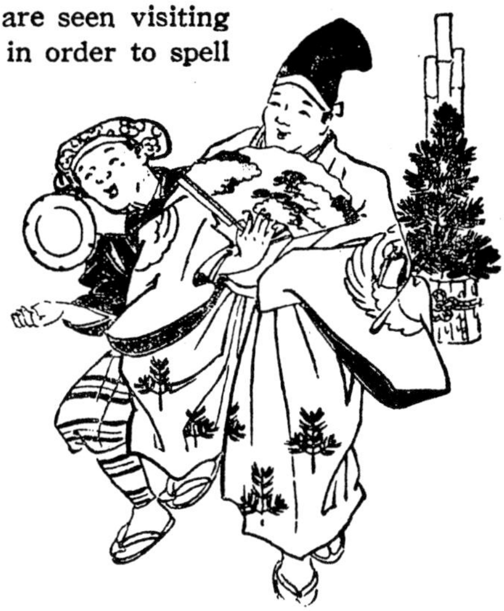

Manzai, street-exorcists of New Year

In former days Manzai had a fixed costume of Suho-dress, green in colour, with wide sleeves and large crests on and they wore a special kind of headgear called Ori-eboshi, like that of Ebisu, while the other wore Daikoku-hood. But they do not wear such a costume of a classical style no longer.

According to some authorities, this exorcising practice was performed after a dance danced at Kashiwabara during the reign of the Emperor Jimmu, the first of the Imperial line, while other scholars think that it was introduced from China during the reign of the Empress Jito (41st). It became very popular at Kamakura, the Shogunate capital (118S–1333 A. D.). It was performed regularly on the seventh of the first month (January) every year in the courtyard of the Ashikaga Government, but later on the fifth of the same month during the Tokugawa regime. It was performed at the Imperial court by the Manzai-singer of the Yamato school, and at the Shogunate court of Edo by those of the Mikawa school, with which the province of Mikawa was, and still is, always associated.

Manzai is no more performed in the Imperial court and its performance is not limited to the fifth or seventh of January, but the Manzai singers go on their rounds all through the seven days of "Matsu-no-Uchi" (lit. within the pines), which are our New Year's days.

SAN-EN OR THREE MONKEYS

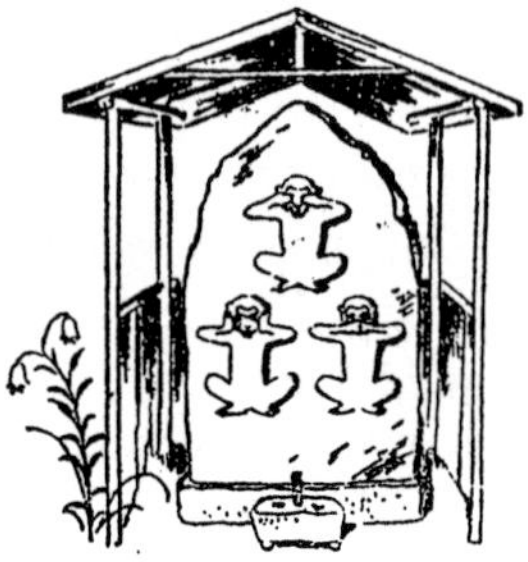
Three-monkeys on crossroads

San-en (Three Monkeys) are among the most popular products that many tourists both Japanese and foreign, of Nikko, take home as a keepsake. They usually represent a set of three joined monkeys, one covering its eyes, another its month and the third its ears, with its forepaws. They are very popular in Japan, so that they are often painted on a kakemono (hanging scroll) and carved as an ornament. You will find the Three Monkeys carved in many Buddhist temples and on a stone-sign that stands on the crossroads pointing the way. The Three Monkeys are said to have their origin in the Hanuman, an Indian deity, but they are attributed in Japan to the invention of Priest Dengyo, founder of the Tendai sect, who lived in the ninth century.

In the Japanese language "saru" or euphonically, "zaru", means both "don't" and "monkey". "Iwa-zaru", for instance, which really means "don't speak" makes a homonymous suggestion of "monkey" to the Japanese ear. In a similar way is a monkey suggested by "Mi-zaru" (don't see) and "Kika-zaru" (don't hear); "evil" of course being understood in the three cases of "don'ts": The three monkeys are:

Mi-zaru = Don't-see-evil Monkey

Iwa-zaru = Don't-say-evil Monkey

Kika-zaru = Don't-hear-evil Monkey

Kakizome or First Calligraphic Writing of the Year

Military art was certainly outstandingly important in the feudal days of Japan, but no more was learning neglected by our samurai of old who regarded it a shame to be ignorant, if not illiterate. Great importance was, therefore, attached by them to calligraphic practice not so much for its literary value from a viewpoint of learning, as because they regarded it a means of self-culture. With calligraphical practice the Japanese of old fostered their presence of mind as well as their personality, for one easily forgets oneself and all the worldly cares during its practice,

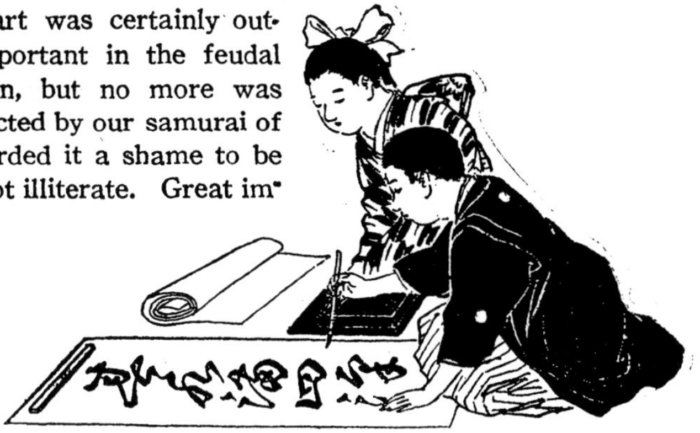

A school-boy, in full dress, writing New Year calligraphy

Kakizome (kaki = writing; zome or some = beginning) is the ceremony of writing for the first time in the New Year. It is held on Jan. 2, because, according to our idea, New Year's day should be kept little short of sacred and the Japanese did hardly anything on that day, excepting exchanges of calls and respects by way of expressing thanks for the past favours.

The children and oftentimes grownup people of most Japanese families sit squarely upright at their writing desks and write some good proverbs, Chinese or Japanese poems, common sayings, etc. most carefully, always suggestive of loyalty, patriotism, good morals, or anything else that may sound good or lucky, on Japanese paper with Fude or brush-pen. Here are Just two or three expressions that a elementary-school child writes at Kakizome :

"Kimi-ga-yo" (the Lord's reign) (君ヶ代)
"Hatsu-Hinode" (The first sun-rise) (初日の出)
"Hi-no-Maru no Hata" (The flag of the rising sun) (旭の旗)
"Chuko" (Loyalty and filial piety) (忠孝)

These writings are put up high on the wall or under the lintel of a room, where they may be kept for a few days or sometimes during the whole year, so that the writer may "go up" or make progress in hand-writing. In this way do the school-children vie with one another in calligraphic writings.

Sometimes the first writings of the year are taken to the shrine of Tenjin dedicated to Michizane Sugahara (845-903 A. D.) who is regarded as the deity of calligraphy and literature in this country.

Ga-no-Iwai or the Celebration of Longevity

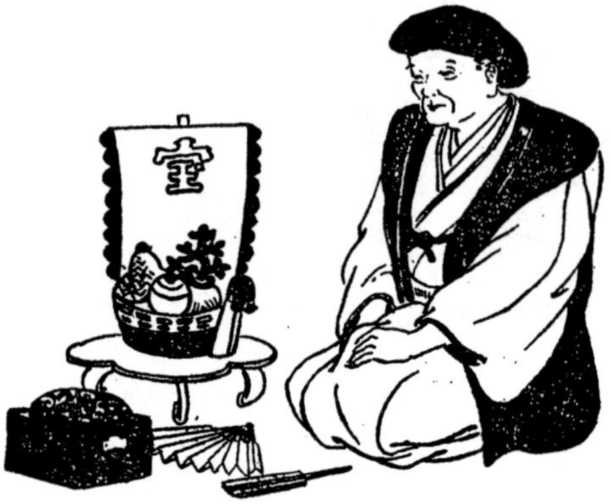

An old man at the celebration of calendar-returning

The celebration of a long life was initiated in Japan during the Nara days (710–784 A. D.) when a celebration was held in honour of one who reached the age of 40, 50, 60, 70, 80, 90 and 100 years and so on. But during the last years of the Ashikaga days (1338–1578 A. D.) the 42nd, 61st, 77th and 88th years of age were added to the list of years for celebration.

One congratulated oneself upon one's arrival at 40 years of age because, according to Confucius, one attains discretion at that age. The figure forty-two suggests death in the Japanese language and an orthodox Japanese will have a great celebration on his arrival at that age so that evil may be exorcised. As regards the other years of the list, a celebration is held for the happiness of reaching them. Some years of age have special names as shown below:—

Kanreki or Calendar-returning: We have the twelve branch-signs and the ten trunk-signs (of the zodiac) and a year has one sign of each set assigned to it. Because they are repeated in every sixty years (L. C. M. of 12 and 10), one who is 61 years old is said in Japan to have reached the age of Kanreki (calendar-returning) or a second birth; hence a great celebration is held for him.

Continued

Koki or Rare-old age: Confucius says that the age of three score and ten is rare and far between. Hence one who is 70 years old has a great celebration of Koki or Rare-old age.

Kiju or Pleasure-longevity: The age of 77 years is named "Kiju" (pleasure-longevity) because the character for "pleasure", when written in a running style, resembles our figures for seventy-seven.

Beiju or Rice-longevity: The Chinese character for rice resembles the figures for eighty-eight. Hence one who is 88 years old will have the celebration of Beiju (lit. rice-longevity), so named after the resemblance between the two characters.

Needless to say, a great celebration is held in honour of an octogenarian, nonagenarian, centenarian, and so on. On the occasion of such a celebration, a dinner party is held by inviting the relatives and intimate friends of one whose longevity is celebrated. Two indispensable dishes on such an occasion are Sekihan (or rice steamed with Indian beans) and Tai (sea-bream), which are always suggestive of good luck. A veteran old man or woman will sometimes be clad in red, with a red hood and red dress because of his or her second childhood.

Common saying of a happy life:

"Omae hyaku made
Washa kuju-ku made
Tomo ni shiraga no haeru made."
(You till 100 years
I till 99 years,
Both having white hair)

TANJO OR CHILD-BIRTH

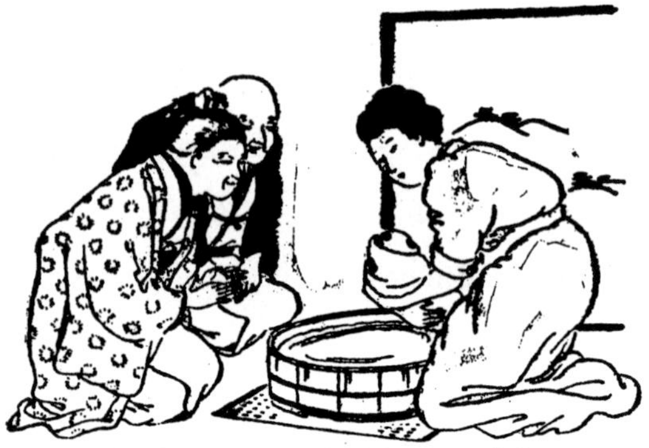
A midwife giving a birth-bath to a baby

Chakutai: When a woman has been with child for five months, a day of luck is selected for observing the ceremony of Chakutai (lit. wearing a maternity band). Her native family makes a present of red and white pieces, eight feet each, of silk (nowadays of cotton), which is tied up with the Noshi and Mizuhiki, signs of a gift, and accompanied with Sake (rice-wine) and fish, with the double meaning of congratulation and blessing. Her midwife puts the band on her. A zodiac day of the Dog is generally selected for this ceremony because of an idea that a dog is known for an easy delivery.

Ubuyu: Ubuyu means birth-bath. It is given to a baby at its birth. The midwife comes every day, usually for a week, to give it to the baby. After that the bath is given by some one else of the family.

First seventh-evening: On the seventh evening after birth a celebration is held when the relatives and intimate friends of the family are invited to a dinner. Sekihan (lit. red steamed-rice), which is rice steamed with red or Indian beans, is indispensably served on the occasion. The native family of the woman in childbed presents the baby with a dress. The baby is christened on this day, and its name is reported to a town or village office, where it is registered.

Miyamairi: The baby is taken to the tutelary deity on the 32nd day in case of a boy and on the 33rd day in case of a girl, to offer a prayer for the safe growth of the baby. Relatives and friends are invited to a dinner given at home. It is a custom still preserved in some localities that those invited give a dog made of papier-machie as a gift.

Kuisome: The celebration of Kuisome (lit. first eating) is held on the 120th day after birth. A good dinner of many dishes, which are set on an O-zen (meal-tray), is served before the baby, who is carried on the lap of its father in case of a boy and of its mother in case of a girl and helped to the imitation of eating the food. The baby is of course too small to eat anything. Sekihan is again prepared, instead of ordinary white rice, for the occasion.

HANAMATSURI OR FLOWER FESTIVAL

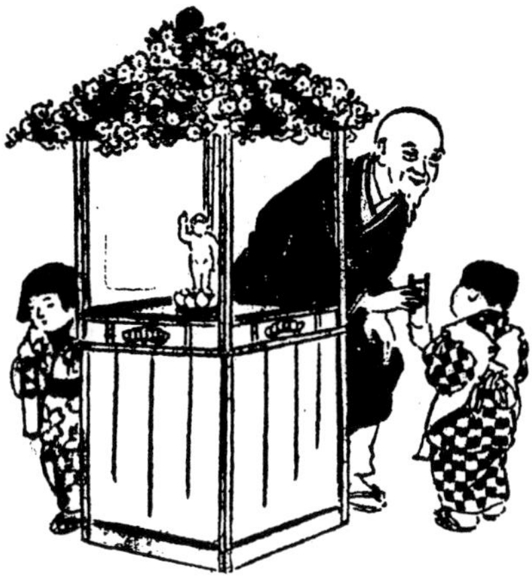

Priest handing a tube of Amacha (sweet-tea) to children

Annually, on April 8th, the birthday of Sakyamun (or Shaka in Japanese), as the founder of Buddhism was called, is celebrated throughout the country. The celebration is called the Busshoe (Buddha's birthday celebration), or, as it is more popularly called, Hanamatsuri or Flower Festival, because Japan is decorated by cherries, the national flower of Japan, in full bloom in this month. On that day every Buddhist temple observes the ceremony of Kambutsue (Baptism of the Lord Buddha), in imitation of the annointment of a king in ancient India.

A miniature-temple called Hanamido, or Flower Temple, is temporarily built over a statue of the Infant Buddha, namely 12 to 16 inches tall, beautifully decorated with various flowers. The Infant Buddha is generally represented standing in a floral basin, because the moment when he was born of the right side of his mother, Queen Maya, it is said, he stood up and, walking seven steps without help, pointed to heaven with his right hand and to the earth with his left, saying "I am the only lord in heaven and under heaven." All pious Buddhists visit the temples to which they belong, and over the sacred image they pour, with a small ladle, Amacha (lit. sweet-tea) or Indian amrita, which is a decoction of the juice of "amacha", a kind of the hydrangea. Each devotee will carry a little Amacha home in a small tube of bamboo, for it is generally believed to have a medicinal value. One often sees some pious visitors rub their eyes with amrita juice on their palms, a symbol of making a spiritual eye clear.

Hana-matsuri (Flower Festival) is now quite in vogue and every Buddhist temple of note observes it very extensively. In large cities, the celebration of the festival is getting increasingly popular. In Tokyo, for instance, thousands of young Buddhists, in gala attire, each carrying some flowers, assembles in large temples or some other public places, where the Hana-Mido (Flower Temple) is temporarily installed. They then hold exercises and dances in honour of the Lord Buddha, founder of their religion.

O-BON OR ALL-SOULS FESTIVAL

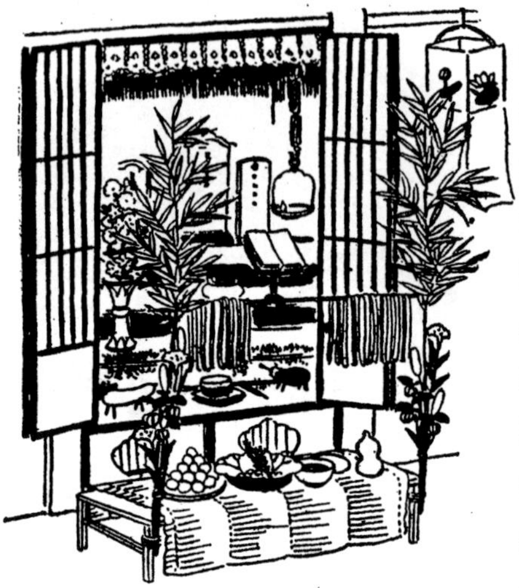
Obon-altar, with various offerings

According to a popular belief, a dead soul hovers about its earthly abode for seven circuits of seven days, namely, forty-nine days, after its death, and hence its remains, if necessary, may be kept so long, but no more, at home without interment. After their burial, the spirit will make an annual visit to its former house on the 13th of July (old calendar) to stay for a space of three days. On that evening, every orthodox Japanese family, which has a dead member, will make what is called O-Mukae-bi (welcome-fire) in front of the house by burning a few dried stems of hemp on a clay-plate in order to welcome its home-coming spirit or light its way home. This invitation of a dead family-member is called O-Shoro (spirit-invitation).

While the fire is burned, some of the members are seen to rub their bodies with their hands warmed by the fire, for it is believed that any physical ailment will be cured by thus rubbing the affected part of the body. If a woman step over the flickering flame of the fire, she will not suffer from a woman's complaint.

At home a service is conducted by a Buddhist priest who reads the sutra before an altar prepared for the occasion. On the altar you will find wooden tablets with the posthumous, or Buddhist names, of the departed members written on them, and before them

Continued

all sorts of edible things are offered; such as vegetables, fruits, melons, egg-plants, cucumbers, grapes, beans, Indian corns, etc., but no fish, meat or bird is offered to the spirits. Some egg-plants cut in small cubes are offered on a lotus-leaf, and water is sprinkled from a basin over the offerings by using loosestrife leaves. While no fish or meat is offered, a bull and a horse made of an egg-plant and a Shiro-uri (white-melon), respectively, with dried stems of the hemp for their legs, are quite indispensable to the occasion. All these offerings are placed on a mat made of dried stalks of water-rice.

The spiritual visitors are supposed to stay in their earthly abode for three days, at the end of which they will ride the egg-plant bull and the white-melon horse to their celestial abode and then all the offerings are thrown into a river nearby.

This practice of feeding the departed members is called O-Bon, shortened from Ullambana (Ullam=head down; bana=stand), an Indian practice. Priest Maudgalya (Mokuren in Japanese), a disciple of the Lord Buddha, as a dutiful son, with his power of seeing the dead, saw that his mother, who had been dead for many years, was suffering in the inferno of starvation, where everything she tried to eat became a flame. Priest Mokuren consulted the Lord Buddha, who told him to offer food on the fifteenth of the seventh month (July), in order to save his mother from the inferno of starvation. This is the origin of O-Bon or all-souls festival.

This practice of feeding the dead came to Japan during the reign of the Empress Saimei, and it was observed for the first time in 658 A. D. to be practised ever since. During the O-Bon days, the farmers take an off-day when many an interesting thing takes place; Bon-Odori (Bon-dance) and Toro-nagashi (lantern-festival) being among them.

CHUGEN OR MID-YEAR GIFT

According to Chinese practice, the fifteenth days of January, July and October are celebrated as the San-Gen or three "Gen", namely, the Upper Gen, the Middle Gen and the Lower Gen, respectively; the word "Gen" being of an obscure meaning, although it gives an idea of beginning (元).

On Jan. 15th, at the zodiac time of the wild boar (10 p. m.), the Japanese take a kind of gruel made of rice and *Azuki* (red or Indian beans), which is traditionally believed to keep evil and bad disease off during the year. The shop-boys have on this day, or the following, what is called Yabuiri (etym. going to one's father) and visit their own homes, though they were sure to visit the shrine of the Emma, or King of the dead, in former days. The Japanese children are told that the King Yama will pull their tongue out if they tell a single lie. This custom of eating gruel is now much more widely observed than before by orthodox Japanese, who will take it on the first and fifteenth days of each month, besides Jan. 15th.

July 15th, the second of the set, is known by the common name of Chugen or Middle Gen, and it is much more widely observed all through the country. On this day the Japanese exchange mid-year gifts with their relatives and friends just as they do year-end's and New Year's gifts, which correspond to the Christmas presents of the West. Consequently, the streets of a large town or city are decorated for bargain sales on or about this day, as they are towards the end of the year. This day has thrown the other two days into the shade, because O-Bon or Ullambana on which the dead are invited for feasting, is also observed on the same occasion, so that most people have come to think that Chugen, on which the mid-year gifts are exchanged, is a part of O-Bon. And in former days, a gift offered on the day of Chugen, was tied with a black-and-white cord, instead of a red-and-white one with which an ordinary gift has to be tied up. A mid-year gift was in former days to have a Buddhist significance.

The third of the San Gen (three Gen) comes on the fifteenth day of October, on which the Chinese had a whole-night celebration for the North Polar-Star. Japan has not adopted this practice nor is any celebration held on this day of October. In short, the Japanese have almost forgotten the words Jogen (Upper-Gen) and Kagen (Lower-Gen), but Chugen (Middle-Gen) seems to gain in popularity because of the proganda made by the merchants, who have a bargain-sales day for the mid-year gifts on July 15th, one of the O-bon days or all-souls festival.

"UKAI" OR FISHING WITH CORMORANTS

Ayu, or plecoglossus altivelis, is a fresh-water fish that is much prized by the Japanese for its relishable flavour. It lives in almost any rivers of the country, from Kyushu in the south to the northern part of Honshu or Main Land. It is 5 or 6 inches large, though in the southern part of Japan the fish grows as large as 6 or 7 inches. It feeds upon animal matter when young, but chiefly on water-moss when grown up.

Its close season is from November to May in the following year. It is caught with rod and line with a false bait, or hooked without a bait. The Unawa (lit. cormorant-rope) is often used to catch the fish in a large number. The rope has black feathers, or something similar, hanging from it at intervals of one foot or so in imitation of a cormorant-feather to scare the fish. It is drawn under the water and a net is cast over a place where the fish are thick.

But by far the most interesting method of catching Ayu is "Ukai" (lit. cormorant-keeping) in which a trained cormorant is used to catch Ayu.

The cormorant is a black water-bird, a little larger than a crow. It lives near a river or the sea and lives upon the fish it catches in the water. A wild cormorant is caught and trained to catch the Ayu. Japan has four species of the cormorant; namely, phalacrocorax carbo, p. capillatus, p. pelagicus and p. bicristatus.

The cormorant is used in catching the Ayu in different localities in Japan, but the River Nagara in Gifu Prefecture is the outstandingly best known for Ukai, and many a tourist is attracted to see this novel way of fishing. There are now a dozen families which have been engaged in Ukai fishing generation after generation hereditarily for centuries.

Continued

Ukai-fishing is held generally in the dark night, before the moon is up or after it has set. The bird has a ring around its neck for keeping it from swallowing the fish it may catch, and it is tethered to the hand of a fisherman with a rope made of the cypress bark. A fishing party consists of half a dozen or more boats, each manned by four fishermen clad in a classical way; namely, the chief cormorant-handler, who manipulates twelve cormorants at the bow, an assistant handler who has six birds, and two rowers of the boat. The boats first go upstream to a certain part of the stream and then slide down catching the fish by means of the trained cormorants. The birds swim in the water with great agility in all directions in pursuit of the fish, but a skilful fisherman keeps all the ropes, in good order in his hands, from getting tangled up. The cormorants are taken out of the water one after another at intervals, and it puts all the fish out of its mouth, almost of its own accord.

According to tradition, Prince Onamuchi invited Prince Takemikatsuchi in Izumo Province, in the prehistoric days, when Prince Kushiyatama turned into a cormorant. But the mention of a cormorant is made in the Kojiki in connection with a cormorant-keeper appointed by the Emperor Jimmu, and so the fish was evidently caught in ancient times in Japan by using a cormorant. During the era of Engi (901–922 A. D.) the Imperial court gave seven cormorant-keeping families a fief each to cover the expenses of torches to be used in catching Ayu for the Imperial family. During the Shogunate regimes, most cormorant-keeping families received special allowances from the Shogunate Government. Ukai is one of the chief attractions for foreign tourists who visit Japan.

JAPANESE INNS

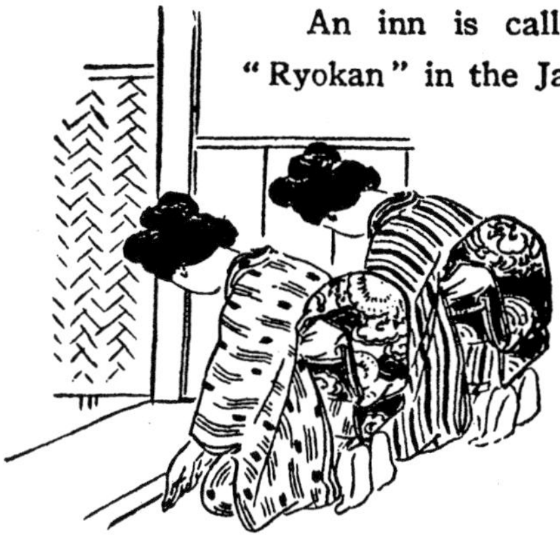

Two inn-girls bowing low at the entrance

An inn is called "Yadoya", "Hatagoya" or "Ryokan" in the Japanese language.

You will be greeted, at the porch of a Japanese inn, by a number of maids, who, sitting in the Japanese way, on the floor, either of matting or of wood, bow so politely with their hands nicely put side by side on the floor. Your shoes have to be taken off, for the Japanese wear no shoes inside a dwelling-house, and a pair of slippers will be given you instead.

A maid will take you into a nice Japanese room, almost devoid of furniture, in the foreign sense of the term; no table, no chair, no bed-stead, no wash-stand; there being in the room a low Japanese desk and a Hibachi (fire-brazier), which is the only heater in the room, containing a fire made of charcoals and an iron-kettle on it for boiling water for tea. The room is simple but artistically decorated in the Japanese way with a few pieces of art. A Japanese kimono is soon brought in, because a Japanese feels more comfortable and at home in it than in foreign clothing.

The proprietor of the hotel or a chief clerk comes in with a register-book, in which you have to write your name, address, age, where from and where-to, etc.

Japanese tea is served by a maid in a small tea-cup, with no sugar or milk in it because the Japanese take their tea plain. There being no fixed time for tea in Japan, you will be served with a cup of tea no matter at what time of the day you visit a Japanese inn.

No guest-room, in a Japanese inn, for so it is called in Japan, has a bath-tub attached to it, but all its guests take a bath in a common bath-room one after another, or sometimes several persons together in the same bath-tub, instead of throwing the water every

Continued

time when one takes a bath. Hence the bath-tub of an inn is large enough to accommodate several persons at one time. Soap is never used in a bath-tub, but you must soap yourself outside the bath-tub, which you enter after rinsing all soap off your body. Nor is a towel properly used in it.

Every Japanese inn is operated on the Japanese plan, and two meals, evening and morning, are included in the hotel rate. But while a foreign hotel has a menu, leaving the choice of food to its guest, a Japanese inn serves its guest with food of its selection, and he has to eat whatever is served him for the hotel rate he has accepted. And instead of being served with food dish after dish in a course, as in a foreign hotel, all food is brought in all at once, in a Japanese inn, on what is called "Ozen" (lit. honorable meal-tray), which will be placed before the cushion on which you sit. Unless you order for bread, you will have to eat Gohan (boiled-rice), which is served in a bowl on the same meal-tray. Nor is a knife or fork brought in, but instead you will have to manipulate a pair of chopsticks, 5 inches or so long. A maid will sit before you while you eat, so that she may serve you with more bowlfuls of rice, if you require, and you can have as many bowlfuls of rice as you please, though usually we do not ask for a second help of any other food. And it is considered to be ill-behaved in Japan to leave any grains of rice in a rice-bowl; though any other kinds of food may be left over with little impropriety. When you finish eating, the maid will give you a cup of what is called Bancha (inferior tea) to wash your throat down.

You will see no bedding in your room when you get in, for it is kept in a closet, usually attached to your guest-room, and it will be spread out when you go to bed. Our bedding consists generally of two wadded beds with two or three wadded covers, which an average foreigner finds rather too heavy. Bedding is folded up and put into a closet again when you get up on the following morning.

In the morning you go to the same wash-place as do the other guests. A maid will make tea for you before she brings breakfast, also on a meal-tray, consisting generally of rice and a vegetable soup, with two or three other light kinds of food.

THE OPENING OF KITCHEN BOARD

The Ho-on-ji Temple, Asakusa, in Tokyo, has the ceremony of opening the kitchen board on Jan. 12th every year, when two carp are cut into pieces on a kitchen board while a Buddhist sutra is being chanted by the resident priests of the temple. This ceremony has its origin in the following story.

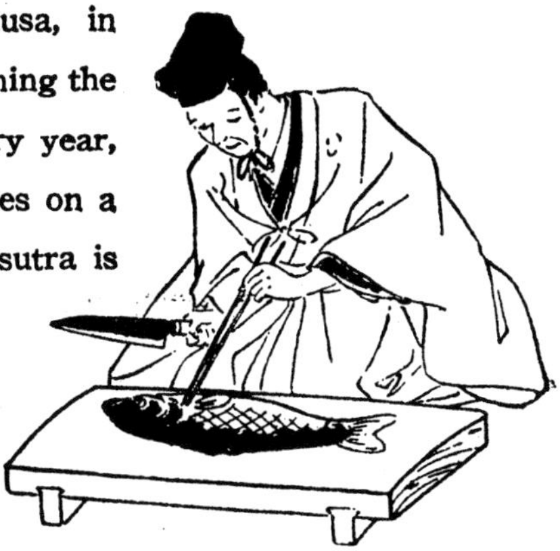

Kitchen-Board opening (a carp cut to pieces)

Priest Seishin was a favorite with Priest Shinran (1173-1162 A. D.), founder of the Shinshu sect of Buddhism. He lived at a small temple that he built at Iinuma in the province of Shimosa, taking charge of preaching Buddhism in the Kanto districts. Among his admirers, Priest Seishin had an old Buddhist adherent, whom he christened Seikai after his own name.

One day Priest Seikai said to his master: "I will present you with two carp regularly every year in reciprocation of your kindness shown to me all these years" and so saying he disappeared all of a sudden, to be heard from, no more.

A little while later a Shinto priest of the Temman-gu shrine, at the same village of Iinuma, saw his deity Tenjin in a dream. "I was christened Priest Seikai" the god said "by Priest Seishin, for whom I have great admiration. I have promised to present him with two carp every year. So you must take them annually to his temple."

The Shinto priest, waking up, found two carp in the holy hand-

Continued

washing cistern of the shrine, and took them immediately to Priest Seishin.

The temple of which Priest Seishin was the résident priest, was named the Ho-on-ji Temple (lit. Requital-temple) possibly on account of the above story. It is now situated in the street of Kita-Kiyoshima, Asakusa in Tokyo. The Temmangu shrine of Iinuma still keeps the practice of presenting two large carp, over a foot in size, regularly in New Year, to the Buddhist temple, where the ceremony of "Opening the Kitchen Board" is observed on Jan. 12th every year. The fish are put on a kitchen board in the center of the temple-hall and a priest, dressed in a special costume for the occasion, cuts them into slices while the other priests keep chanting a Buddhist sutra in chorus. The priest in charge of cutting the fish makes on the board two Chinese characters (長 and 久, both meaning "long life") with the fins and bones of the fish, of which every participant of the ceremony receives two slices.

Two slices of carp, dried up, are sent on a bamboo hurdle to the Hongan-ji Temple, Kyoto, the head temple of the Shinshu sect, to which the Ho-on-ji Temple belongs, and the former will send to the latter Kagami-mochi or two mirror-shaped cakes of pounded rice in return. This practice of opening the kitchen board is remarkable no less because of all things two live carp are killed and cut into pieces in a Buddhist temple in spite of a strong Buddhist teaching against killing any animals than that the ceremony has been observed ever since the time of Priest Shinran in the twelfth century.

A carp, by the way, which keeps still when it is put on a kitchen-board, is a symbol of resignation and our samurai of old were trained to be resigned to their environments.

KOHAKU OR RED-AND-WHITE

While purple is considered to be the royal colour, the double colour of Kohaku, as red-and-white is called, is no less prized in Japan. According to a certain scholar, white represents the Imperial court of Prince Ninigi, who made his advent in Japan, to found the Imperial dynasty of Japan in the province of Yamato, while red was the court colour of the Izumo tribe, which surrendered to the Prince to offer Izumo to him. So the double-territory colour stands for the union of the two prehistoric courts of Izumo and Yamato provinces.

O-Sonae: O-Sonae, which literally means "honorable offering" consists of two disks of pounded rice, a red one on top of a white. The Japanese make this double rice-cake in New Year' time or on any other felicitous occasion.

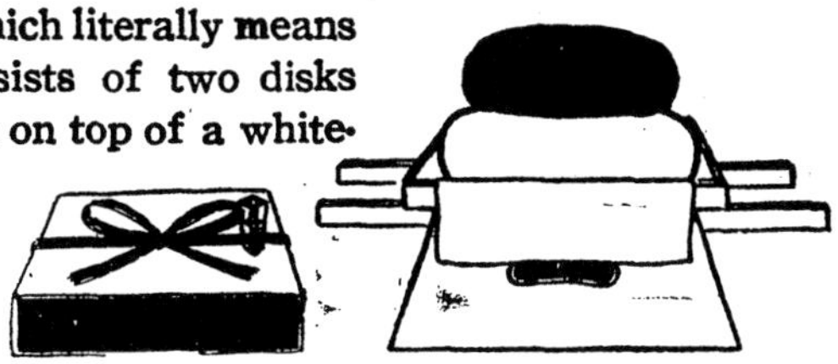

Kohaku (lit. red and white): (right) rice-cakes and (left) a gift tied with a Mizuhiki-cord

The War of the White and Red Flags: The two military families of Minamoto and Taira, which fought each other in the 12th century used the white and red flags, respectively.

It is said that the white flag now universally used as a sigh of surrender has its origin in the white flag of the Minamoto family. The white flag of surrender was first used in Europe by those who surrendered to Genghis Khan, who swept over Europe with his Mongolian hordes in the beginning of the 13th century, and Genghis Khan is said by some Japanese scholars to be a descendant of the Minamoto family.

Mizuhiki: Noshi (lit. stretched) and Mizuhiki are two signs of a Japanese gift. Mizuhiki literally means "water-drawing" (mizu = water; hiki = to draw), and it consists of five (or three) red-and-white cords made of paper. The idea of red and white has a prehistoric origin as explained above, while five, for which we use a Chinese ideograph in representation of the hermaphroditic union of nature, stands for the origin of everything in the universe. The cord, as its name indicates, represents a stream of purifying water. Every gift has to be tied up with this cord of purification, excepting a gift which is given on the occasion of a funeral or some unfortunate occasion.

In India a present is often accompanied with a cup of water with a few tulsi-leaves floating on it. It is called Krishna arpan (offering to Krishna) and no gift so accompanied must be refused. The Japanese Mizuhiki may have been influenced by this Indian custom of Krishna arpan.

SIGNS OF VICTORY

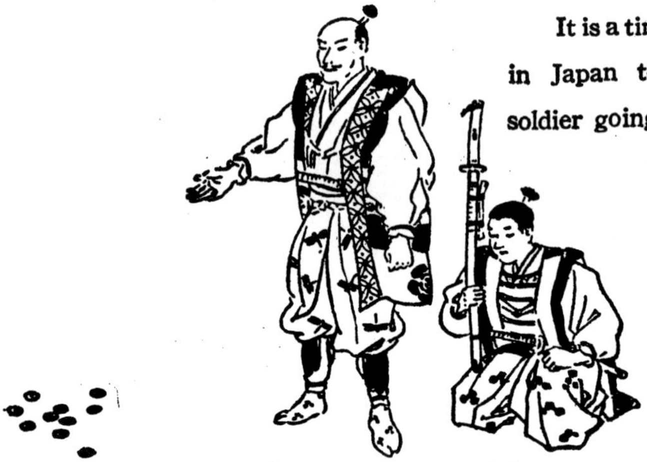
Lord Oda-Nobunaga throwing coins into a shrine

It is a time-old custom in Japan to present a soldier going to the front with a gift consisting of Katsubushi (dried bonito), because its Japanese name homonymously suggests a victorious warrior (homonymously katsu=victorious; bushi=warrior); hence as a luck-bringer or mascot. Dried chestnuts (katsuguri) were also presented to a Samurai in former days because of their suggestive triumph (katsu=victorious: guri or kuri=return).

One-chopstick: On the eve of marching to the front Nobunaga Oda, a warlord, was served with a meal, possibly by mistake, with one chopstick, instead of two. He was very angry, because serving with a chopstick was considered to be a sign of ill-luck. But Hideyoshi Toyotomi, one of his favorite retainers, explained the matter in a different light, saying: "It must be a good sign, sire, because it suggests our occupation of the enemy's territory from one side on." Nobunaga was pleased and he won the battle he fought next.

Coins in "head": Nobunaga was on his march to Okehazama to have a decisive fight with Yoshimoto Imagawa, when he stopped at Atsuta to offer a prayer for help from Kami at the Imperial shrine there.

Continued

"If we are to win this battle", Nobunaga said, after offering some coins to the deity of the Atsuta shrine, "All the coins I throw in will show their head up."

Sure enough, all the coins that he threw in showed their head side and Nobunaga defeated his inveterate enemy. But, as it was later found, the coins were joined in pairs all with their head side out.

Big persimmon: When Iyeyasu Tokugawa was on the eve of marching to Sekigahara, where a pitched battle was to be fought against Toyotomi, in 1600 A. D., he received a large persimmon. "I am glad" Iyeyasu said in ecstacy. "I am glad that I have got this large persimmon. This surely means that the enemy, who is at Ogaki (lit. big-persimmon) will fall into my hands." Iyeyasu was to march to a place called Ogaki or "large persimmon".

Iyeyasu was victorious, and consequently he founded a Shogunate dynasty that lasted for over two hundred and fifty years till Emperor Meiji restored the Imperial administration in 1868.

Shigemori Taira and "Peace": Shigemori Taira was appointed the Mayor of Heian (Kyoto), the Imperial capital. He accepted the appointment, saying:

> "I am unworthy of this important post. But we are in the era of Heiji (lit. peaceful-reign), the capital is called Heian (lit. peace and transquility), and my family is Heishi (another way of reading his family name, Taira, which means "peace"). In view of these good signs, I am glad to accept this post."

And Shigemori was one of the best mayors that Kyoto had for many years.

STREET FORTUNE-TELLER

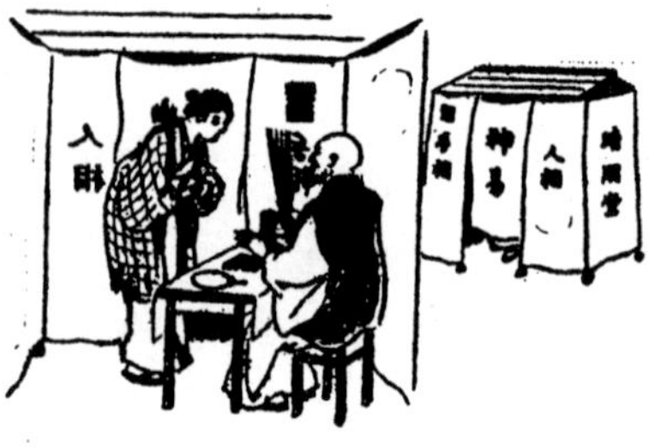

Street-fortune-teller running a road-side office

By the side of a dark and out-of-the-way street in the city of Tokyo, you will often find, of a quiet evening, a solitary man, often moustached and clad in a rather faded black *Haori*-coat, standing at a table, with or without a filthy whitish cloth and lighted with a dim lantern that wears the mark, the sign, of fortune-telling in Japan. He is a street fortune-teller and the table constitutes his open-air office, with hardly any more tools of fortune-telling than a batch of fine bamboo-pieces called "Zei-chiku" and a set of wooden sticks called "Sangi".

When a client comes to consult him, various questions are asked concerning the cause and condition of his or her trouble, age, family relations and any other information that may be required in telling his or her fortune. Then the fortune-teller takes out the *Zei*-pieces of bamboo most respectfully; concentrates his mind in a praying attitude; he grasps a handful of them; he counts the number of the pieces he grasps; and then he moves and removes the *Sangi*-pieces accordingly in order that he may tell the fortune or bad luck of his client.

The street fortune-teller is very popular in Japan, for the orthodox Japanese consult him on various occasions. If, for instance, an orthodox Japanese has to move away from one dwelling place to another, he will see a fortune-teller concerning the lucky direction for him, for in this country a direction is lucky or unlucky according to the circumstances of each person of either sex. If a person is laid up with a protracted or serious disease, a fortune-teller is consulted to see under what evil star the patient was born and whether or not his attendant physician is good for him. When a young man or girl is going to get married, his or her mother or father will see a fortune-teller to ask whether or not the match proposed will be a good one. In this way is a fortune-teller consulted on every good or bad occasion, and his advice has a strong bearing upon the daily-life of the orthodox Japanese, who seem to believe in fortune-telling or divination.

YOMAWARI OR NIGHT-WATCHMAN

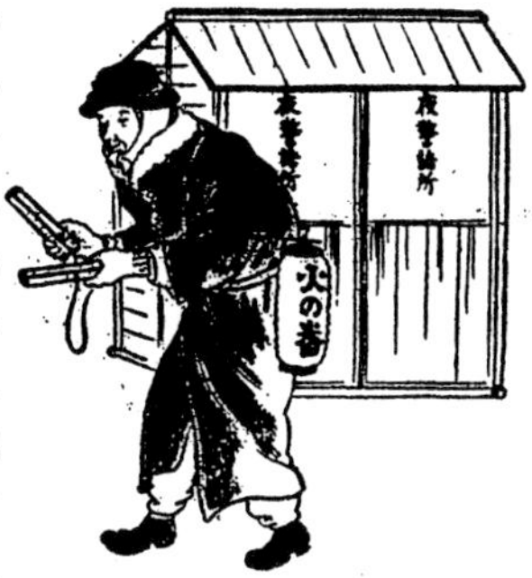

Yomawari or night-watchman

The late Marquis Shigenobu Okuma, one of the elder statesmen of the Meiji era and a maker of Modern Japan, said sarcastically that fires which take place so often in Edo (Tokyo) that they are said to be "the flowers of Edo" (Edo-no-Hana), are necessary to Tokyo because they make an old street a new one with new houses built in place of the old ones. Indeed no other country has so many fires breaking out in a year than Japan, and Tokyo is notoriously famous for the large number of fires breaking in one year. According to an official report, Japan has over 20,000 cases of fire destroying houses valued indeed enormously, while Tokyo alone has cases destroying houses valued at millions of yen annually. This is due partly to the Japanese dwelling-houses being built of wood which makes it easy for a house to catch fire and partly to their being heated with charcoals by means of an open Hibachi or fire-brazier, which exposes a house to the danger of being burned down.

Every city, town and village is divided into several sections or units with the chief object of maintaining the welfare and order of the people and the prevention of a fire is one of the chief works of each unit. During the winter season, say from October or November to March or April, when a fire breaks out most frequently in the year, every unit keeps a night-watchman or two, called Yomawari (lit. night-going-rounds), who goes on his rounds during the night, from late in the evening till dawn on the following morning. Warmly clad, a night-watchman goes on his rounds, carrying a Japanese lantern and beating wooden clappers. "Click! click! click-click!" they go, resounding far and wide in the quietude of a dark night, and it is quite classical to listen to their sounds. Sometimes, however, the night-watchman will carry a stick with jingling bells, which go clanking along as he patrols along the streets and lanes in the night.

"STAMP-COLLECTION"

A new hobby peculiar to the Japanese

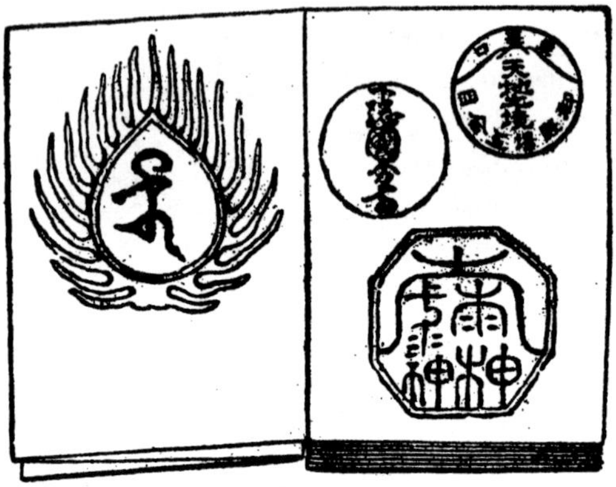

By "Stamp-Collection" is not meant the collection of postage stamps so very prevalent all over the world. Many Japanese of course collect postage stamps and match-box paper like foreign collectionists. But our "stamp-collection" means something entirely different in nature and it is peculiar to the Japanese.

"Stamp-collection" is done not only by young school-children and boys, but by grown-ups as well, and it is very much in vogue in Japan. The collectionists, young or old, of either sex, make trips by carrying folded albums and collect on them the marks of stamps used by the Shinto shrines and Buddhist temples that they visit. And we have over a hundred thousand shrines and seventy thousand temples, all possessing wooden stamps which the curious collectionists get pressed on their albums. Every large post-office and railway station also has such a stamp engraven with a scenic picture of its neighbourhood, to say little of a tea-house at each beauty spot in the country.

"The stamp-collection" is an interesting hobby peculiar and even new to the Japanese. A stamp may be pressed on an album free of charge, or it may be charged.

KAMMURI, CROWN AND CORONET

The word "Kammuri" derived from the Japanese "kamuru" for "putting on" a headwear of any kind, now means a crown for the Emperor and a coronet for a courtier. Kammuri seems to be of ancient origin in Japan, for the *Kojiki*, the oldest annals of Japan, mentions the name in connection with Izanagi, a prehistoric prince.

It was the Empress Suiko (33rd), however, who adopted the system of coronets of different colours for twelve different court-ranks in 603 A. D. after the manner of the Chinese court, while the Emperor Kotoku (36th) changed the system into that of seven colours and thirteen, and later nineteen, court-ranks, though the Emperor Tenji (38th) adopted twenty-six ranks. After many such reforms and changes of the system of coronets for the courtiers, the Japanese court still retains the system of classical coronets worn by courtiers on the occasion of great ceremonies at court; the chief headgears, of the court being: the Ben-kan for the Emperor, Hokan (lit. treasure crown), Kin-kan (lit. brocade-coronet), Rai-kan (lit. etiquette-coronet), Burai-kan (lit. military-etiquette-coronet), etc.

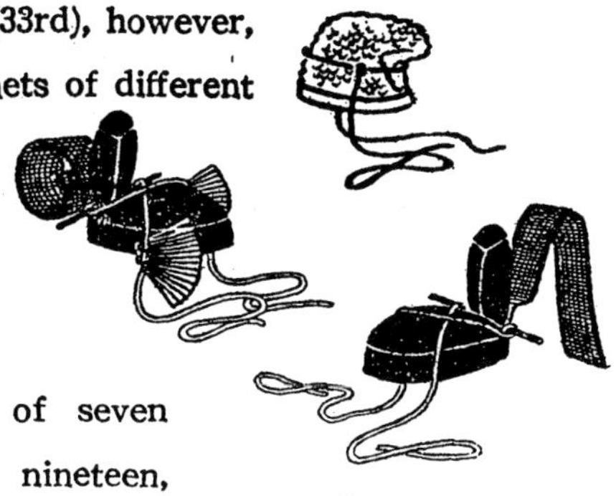

Coronets

There are different kinds of Ei (lit. pendant) also called Embi (lit. swallow-tail) used on the court-headgear. The Ritsu-ei (lit. standing-pendant) is used only on the crown for the Emperor, some of the other kinds being: Sui-ei (lit. hanging-pendant), Ken-ei (lit. wound-pendant), Hoso-ei (lit. fine or slender pendant) and Nawa-ei (lit. rope-pendant).

FURO OR BATH

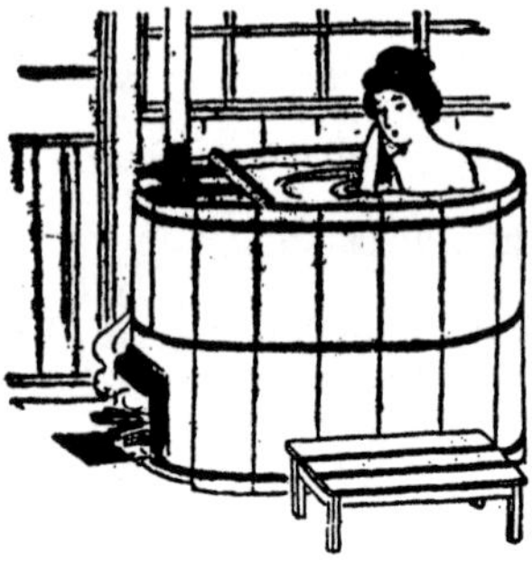

Bath-tub

The Japanese are extremely fond of a hot-water bath, which they take irregularly or regularly, once a day, or once, twice or three times a week, and so on, sometimes in the morning, but generally in the evening after a day's work is done. The cold ablutions are taken for a religious purpose, and a cold-water bath seems to be of early introduction. When we take a bath, we first wash our face, and then get into the bath-tub after pouring a pailful or two of hot water over our body. Our bath-tub, which is made, as a rule, of zelkova or some other hard wood, may be round, oval or square in shape, and it is full of hot water, which is deep enough to cover your shoulders when you bend down in the tub. While a foreigner can hardly stand the heat of 25° C, the Japanese will get in water 45° to 50° C hot. After we stay in the hot water for a few minutes to get warm, we get out and wash and soap ourselves on the sink. Soap is never used in a bath-tub, but everybody washes or soaps his body clean outside the tub and rinses soap off before he gets again into the tub because all the members of a family take a bath in the same water one after another, instead of throwing the water away every time one has taken a bath. Nor is it proper to use a towel in the water. This process we re-

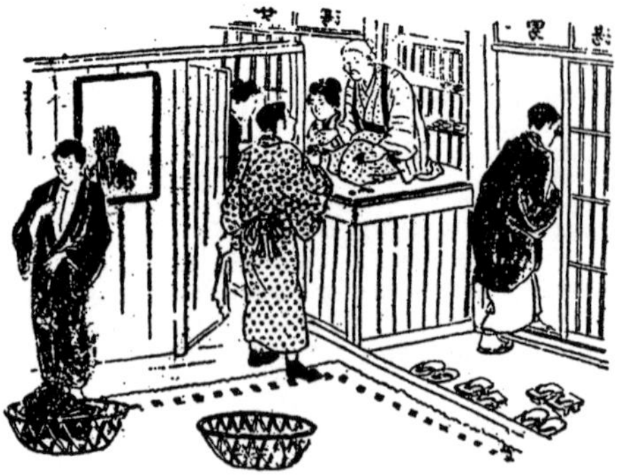

Entrance to a public bath-house

Continue

peat two or three times by getting in and out of the tub and washing ourselves on the sink, and then we wipe the water off with the same wet towel that we use in washing the body, instead of a dry one, as most foreigners do. Our towel, by the way, is much smaller in size than a foreign one, being about 7 or 8″×2.5′ and it is commonly used for various other purposes.

Public bath-house: For those who cannot afford to have a bath tub at home, we have a public bath-house, where the charge for a bath is very cheap. While in feudal days, mixed bathing was allowed or overlooked of both sexes, each public bath-house has a bath-tub in a separate compartment for either sex. Each compartment has a large bath-tub that will accommodate a dozen or more people at one time in it while others will wash their bodies on the sink.

You will notice that a public bath-house is a sort of an information office, where one can have the first-hand news, and all the customers of a public bath will talk with one another either in the tub or on the sink. At rural places they are served with a cup of tea, after they have taken a bath, and they have chats before they go home. A public bath-house is open from early morning till late in the evening.

Shobuyu (lit. iris-bath): On May 5th, when the Boys' Festival is observed in Japan, many orthodox Japanese will take Shobuyu or iris-bath. A few blades of the iris are put into a bath-tub when they take a bath.

Daidai-yu (lit. citrus-bath): On the day of the winter solistice, Daidai-yu or citrus-bath is prepared in many orthodox Japanese families. A few pieces of citrus-skins are put into a bath-tub when they take a bath. Even a public bath-house will put some citrus-pieces into its bath-tub. They seem to believe that this kind of a bath has a medicinal value.

SMOKING IN JAPAN

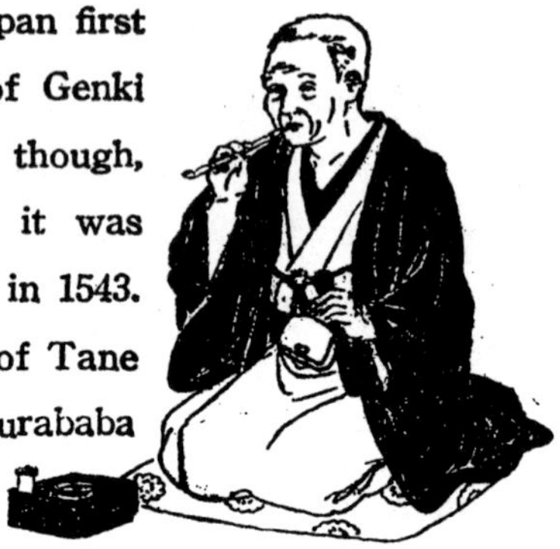

Old man smoking

Tobacco was introduced into Japan first by the Portuguese during the era of Genki (1570—1572) or Tensho (1573—1591), though, according to a certain authority, it was brought to Japan for the first time in 1543. Tobacco was planted on the island of Tane in Osumi Province, and then at Sakurababa near Nagasaki, to be cultivated later on in several other provinces. In 1609 and 1616 the Shogunate Government prohibited smoking, and all the pipes in Edo that were confiscated by the Government were destroyed near Nihombashi Bridge. But the people kept on smoking, ignoring the law, which gradually died of itself. In Japan the best tobacco is produced in the prefectures of Kanagawa, Kagoshima, Nagasaki, Mito, etc., although we import large quantities of tobacco.

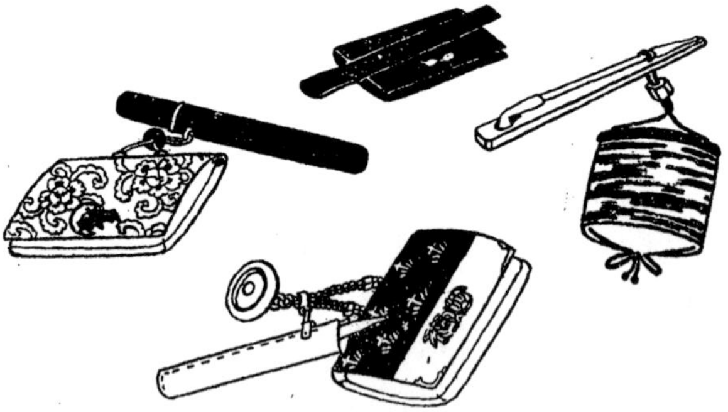

Tobacco-pouches

Almost every Japanese smoker will tell you that tobacco tastes better when smoked through *Kiseru*, a tiny tobacco-pipe, than in any other way. So he prefers cut tobacco to a cigar or cigarette.

Continued

Because our tobacco pipe has a small bowl, its pinch of tobacco lasts only for a puff or two, and the smoker has to refill it very often. Its ashes are blown out and very often kept on the palm of a hand, while the bowl is refilled with a pinch of tobacco with the other hand.

Kiseru: The *Kiseru* (a corruption of some Spanish word) is a tobacco-pipe, about 5 or 6 inches long, which is used in smoking cut tobacco. It consists of three parts:—

1. *Gankubi* (lit. "wild goose's head") or metal bowl
2. *Rao*, made of bamboo or some other tubular plant, so named because a special kind of bamboo, of which a pipe is made, grows in *Lao*, a province in South Asia, from which the word is corrupted
3. *Suikuchi* or mouth-piece

Tobacco-pouch: At first tobacco was carried by its smoker in paper, but a cloth bag was later invented. A tobacco-pouch is now made chiefly of leather as it keeps tobacco in a better condition than does a container of any other material. It is hung from the sash of a smoker by means of *Netsuke*, which is a toggle fixed to a cord.

Tobacco-bon: Nothing is considered in Japan to be more typical of a care-free life than an old man who, retired from an active life, is smoking his *Kiseru*-pipe leisurely with a *tobacco-bon* beside him. It is a portable case or container of a small fire-brazier in which a live charcoal or two are kept. The smoker lights his *Kiseru* from the fire, curls the smoke leisurely, and then empties the pipe ashes by striking the *Kiseru* lightly at the bamboo-spittoon that *tobacco-bon* contains besides the fire-brazier. The sound of the pipe striking the spittoon is to the Japanese most suggestive of an easy life.

TABI OR JAPANESE SOCKS

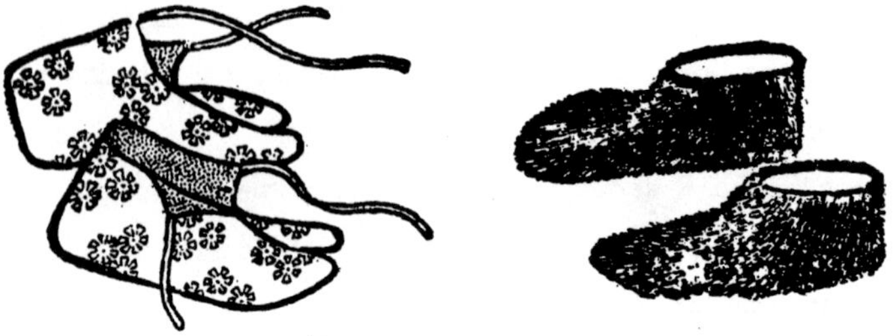

Tabi

While it is against good taste to go barefoot even in summer, stocking feet were considered in feudal days no less ill-mannered than a covered head is in the presence of a superior, as we still see in South Asia, where every visitor of some shrines has to take his shoes off and go barefoot. Of this we are humorously reminded in "Around the World in Eighty Days." It was in the Shogunate period that a warrior over fifty years of age, as well as in weak health under that age, was allowed by the Emperor to wear the *tabi* or Japanese socks at court.

Tabi seems to have been in use during the reign of the Emperor Yenyu (64th) in the tenth century, but it was in the Kamakura days (1186—1333) that *tabi* in the present shape was invented. *Tabi*, as its characters now go, means "foot-bag" (足袋), but in early days it meant "single-leather" (單皮) or "stepping-leather" (踏皮) for it was first made of deer-hide. It may have been a simplified form of the fur-shoes that a *samurai* of a high rank wore in early days of feudalism in Japan. It was after the era of Meireki (1555—1657) when leather became rather of scarce that cotton was used to make *tabi*.

There are several kinds of cloth of which *tabi* is manufactured; cotton, silk, woolen cloth, hosiery, velvet, serge, etc., but cotton and silk are used most in making the *tabi*. *Tabi* is in various colours, such as white, black, blue, red, purple, etc., but white and black are most in vogue, white being chiefly for women and black for men, though man also wears white for formal dress.

Tabi is not measured by the inch or foot, but by the number of *mon*, which is one tenth in value of a *sen*. A mon-coin was an iron one with a hole through it. We say that a certain *tabi* is 8 *mon* or 9.3 *mon* large, for instance, when by these figures we mean that so many iron-coins can be placed along the *tabi* measured.

OGI OR FOLDING-FAN

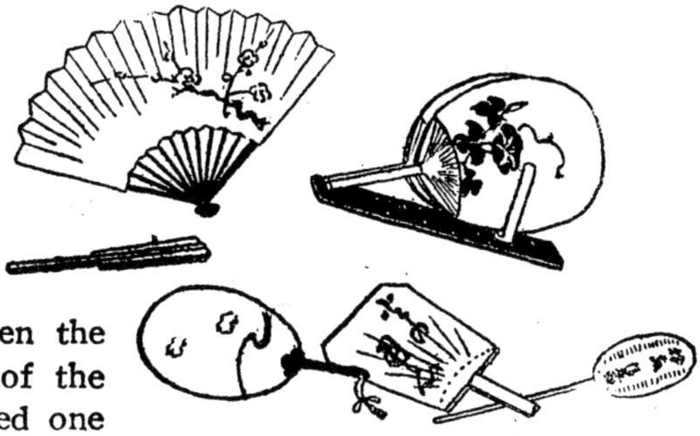

Differont fans, round and folding

Ogi or the folding-fan is of Japanese origin, and it is said to have been made in its present shape after the wing of a bat. Its first mention appears in Japanese history when the Empress Jingo, mother of the Emperor Ojin (15th), used one during her Korean expedition.

Formerly a folding-fan was used by a court-lady more for hiding her face than for any other purpose. Later it was much used by warriors in the feudal days of Japan. While Uchiwa, or a round fan, was introduced from China to Japan, the folding-fan took a reverse course, for, according to the Ryozan-Bokudan (兩山墨談), a folding-fan was for the first time taken to China during the reign of the Emperor Shoko (101st), namely, the Ming dydasty in China.

When a fan has a good picture painted by a master-painter or a calligraphy written by a noted calligrapher, it is taken off its ribs and put into a frame for decoration.

In former days a folding-fan had 5 bambo-ribs, which later increased to 7, 8, or 10 and even 18 and 20 ribs or more. They have a piece of paper or silk either painted or otherwise.

Tokyo, Kyoto and Nagoya are three largest centers for manufacturing folding-fans in Japan.

Suyehiro: A folding-fan is also called Suyehiro, which literally means "future prosperity" and, therefore, it is regarded as a luck-bringer. The fan is worn by a Japanese on a lucky occasion, such as a wedding, festival and a celebration of some kind. An actor, dancer or public singer, who is on a formal call, usually wears a fan under his Obi or sash as a sign of etiquette.

Hi-no-Maru-no-Ogi: Hi-no-Maru-no-Ogi or sun-fan, about 1.2 ft. long, is one that has the sun painted on it, or, to be more exact, a red circle for the sun on a golden ground, on one side, and a golden circle for the moon on a red ground, on the reverse side. This fan usually had iron ribs and a warrior of old always carried one when he went to the front. He challenged his enemy by waving it.

Fan-crest: There are several crests which are modelled after a fan; such as Mitsu-Ogi (three-fans), Chigai Ogi (crossed-fans), Ogi-kuruma (fan-wheel), etc.

O-ZEN OR MEAL-TRAY

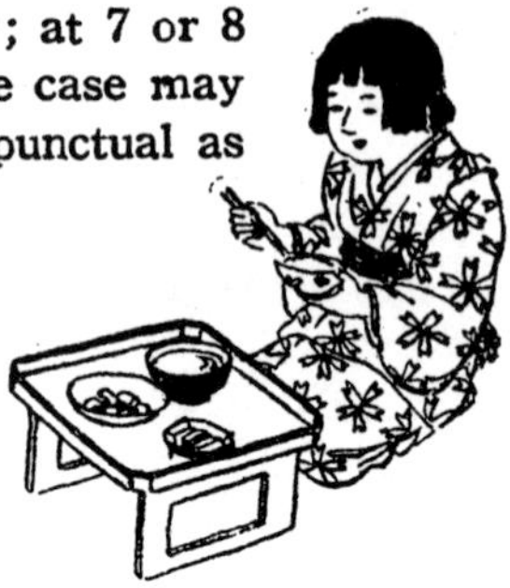
A girl at Ozen

The Japanese take three meals a day; at 7 or 8 a. m., at noon and at 6 or 7 p. m., as the case may be, though they are not so particular or punctual as most foreigners are, about the time of eating. Most urban people use a small table around which a whole family sit at meal, after the manner of the Western people. But, properly speaking, as one still sees in the country or at a regular Japanese restaurant, a meal is served on an O-zen (meal-tray), about a foot square (formerly a stand 2 or 3 inches high), on which all food is served in small bowls or dishes at once at the beginning of the meal, instead of being brought in dish after dish in a course.

Boiled-rice is main food for the Japanese. It is served in a porcelain bowl, placed in the nearer corner on the left-hand side of O-zen, side by side with a wooden bowl, on the right, in which a vegetable soup is served. One may take three bowlfuls or a third help of boiled-rice without violating good manners, or, on the contrary, a polite Japanese will ask for a second help at least. But it is a sign of ill-behavior to leave a single grain of boiled-rice over in a bowl. If you leave any grains over in it, you must eat them when you drink tea or hot water at the end of the meal. We never had cold water at meal, though modern people seem to prefer cold water to hot. All dishes are served at once, artistically arranged on O-zen.

Japanese food consists more of vegetables than of meat, of which beef, pork and chicken, milk included, are of recent introduction. The Togyu-boku or the first-butchered-cow-tree (see We Japanese Vol. 1, P. 175) marks the place where the first cow was butchered with the object of meeting the desire of Townsend Harris, the first U. S. Minister to Japan. But the Japanese are great eaters of fish, perhaps the greatest in the world, because Japan, surrounded by clean seas on all sides, has many good fishing-places where fish can be caught all the year round.

The Japanese do not use a knife, or a fork or a spoon at table, but they use a pair of chopsticks, 5 or 6 inches long, of wood, bamboo, metal, glass, or ivory, either painted, lacquered or plain. It is against good manners to touch any food with fingers, and the Japanese are very clever at the manipulation of chopsticks, which are as useful to them as a knife, a fork and a spoon combined, or even more.

NOSHI AND MIZUHIKI

A Japanese wraps up his gift usually in a piece of paper when he presents it. It is then tied up with 3 or 5 cords, called Mizuhiki, and accompanied with a folded piece of paper known by the common name of Noshi or, more properly, Noshi-awabi (lit. stretched-abalone).

Noshi-awabi: Noshi-awabi, commonly called Noshi for short, is a small piece of sea-ear, cut, dried and stretched or ironed, and put in a folded piece of paper. It is always put on a gift excepting when it consists of fish, bird or meet (namely, animal-food) and when it is presented as a token of condolence for death.

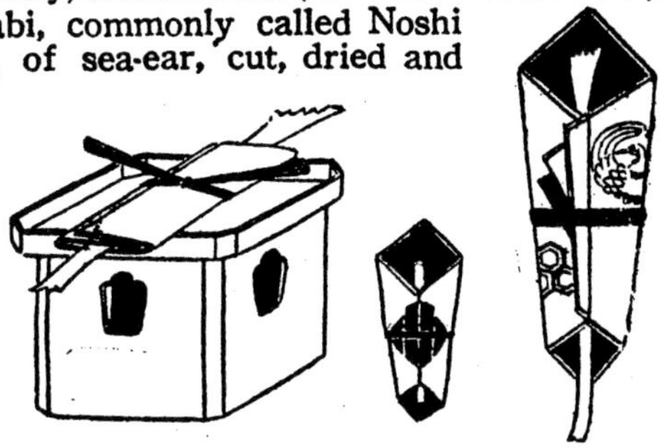

Noshi

The Emperor Shih Hwang, founder of the Tsin dysnasty, China, who was known as a great tyrant and despot, wished to get an elixir of life, which he sent Jofuku (Hsu-fu) to secure in the land of Horai (P'eng-lai) or eternal youth. Jofuku came to Japan and landed in the present province of Kii in the 72nd year (219 B. C.) of the reign of the Emperor Korei (7th). Failing, however, to find the medicine he was sent for, Jofuku stayed and died in Japan, without going back to China. He lies buried in the province of Kii.

It is believed that the elixir of life that Jofuku came to obtain in Japan was nothing but sea-ear, or abalone, which was considered in Japan to be very wholesome and healthful. Hence the Japanese still use Noshi, made of sea-ear, as a sort of luck-bringer on the New Year's day; "noshi" signifying "prosperity" in Japan.

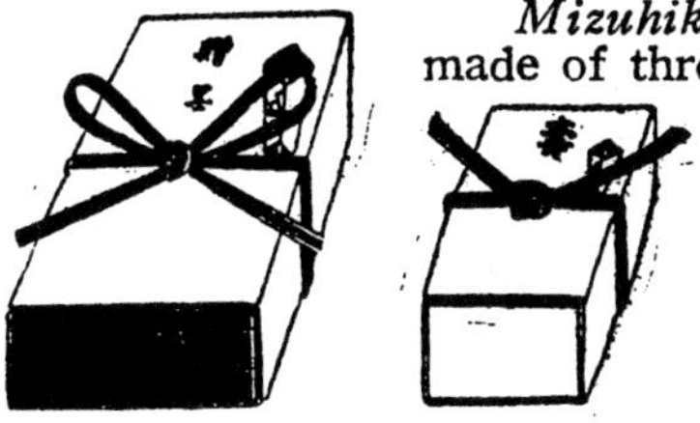

Gifts decorated with Mizuhiki and Noshi

Mizuhiki: Mizuhiki (lit. water-drawing) is made of three paper-strings stiffened with paste. It is used in tying a piece of paper in which a gift is done up in Japan. Mizuhiki is of various lengths; anywhere between a foot and eight feet. It is dyed, a half in white and the other half in red or black, although it may be golden or silver in colour. Red and white, which, according to some authorities, represent the two courts of Izumo and Yamato which Japan had in her prehistoric days, as well as golden and silver cords, are used on an ordinary gift or on a lucky occasion, but black and white cords, representing condolence, are used only at the time of a funeral.

In tying Mizuhiki, its white or silver part comes on your left-hand side and the red or golden part, is on your right while a gift for condolence has black on your right-hand side when it is tied on a gift.

In some locality of India, a tulsi leaf is put in an earthen cup of water accompanying a gift. It is called the Krishna arpan, meaning that the gift is presented in the name of the god Krishna, and the donee must accept it. The Japanese custom of using the Mizuhiki or water-drawer, as name signifies, is believed by some people to have come from India.

CHA OR TEA

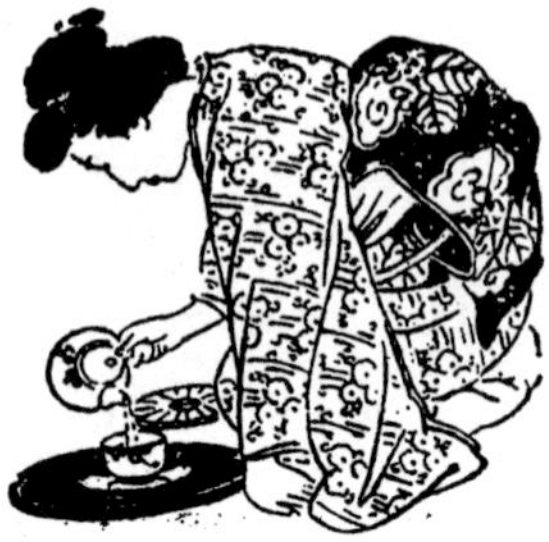

Woman pouring tea

The Japanese are great tea-drinkers. But they drink usually green, and not black, tea, which is called in Japan, Kocha (lit. red tea), and they take it plain without any sugar or milk in it. Nor are they particular about the time of drinking tea, but they take it almost at any time of the day. A Japanese drinks tea early in the morning because, it is said, early tea keeps him calm and steady all day; before he starts on a trip because tea will keep him strong; when he comes home from work or a trip because tea gives him a good rest, and so on. When you visit a Japanese friend in his home or at his office, tea is always served, no matter at what time of the day you call on him.

Tea-making looks very simple. You put a bit of dry tea-leaves in a small tea-pot (ours is very small), pour hot water in, keep it just two or three minutes and then pour it out into a tea-cup, which is also much smaller than a foreign one. But with us tea-making is considered to be very difficult: you must have a good iron-kettle and real good charcoals; water has to be pure and must be properly heated and then cooled properly just "enough" to make good tea and the water is kept in the tea-pot just for a necessary space of time, for else tea is spoiled, being too light or thick or bitter. Japanese tea tastes sweet without any sugar in it when it is properly prepared, and it is said that it is more costly to treat one to proper ceremonial tea than to a regular dinner.

Cha, as tea is called in Japan, was first introduced to Japan when Priest Kobo came back from China, where he went for studies, and he presented it to the Emperor Saga (52nd), while Priest Eisai is said to have planted tea in Japan in 1202. Among the tea producing centers in Japan are Uji of Yamashiro Province, (near Kyoto) Abe of Suruga Province and Sayama of Musashi Province, in which Tokyo is situated.

There are several grades of Japanese tea but Gyokuro (lit. gem-dew) is considered to be far better than any other grades while Bancha, cheap and of inferior quality of tea, is very popular and it is used almost in every Japanese home. Habu-cha (cassia occidentalis) and Kombu-cha (sea-weed-tea) are two popular beverages used like tea in Japan.

Cha-bashira: Cha-bashira (lit. tea-pillar) is a tea-stem found floating vertically in a tea-cup. It is traditionally believed to be a sign of good luck.

Tea kept overnight: We never drink tea which has been kept overnight. Such tea was given in feudal days to a condemned prisoner before his execution.

AKABO OR STATION-PORTER

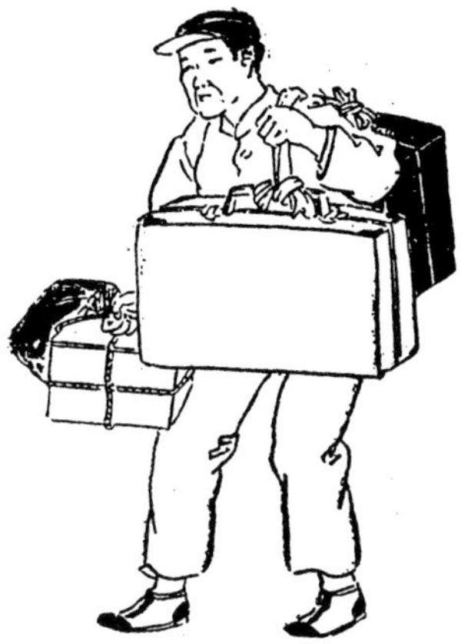

Station-porter

The Akabo (lit. red-cap) is a station-porter, whom you will find at every large railway station in Japan. He wears a black uniform and a red regulation cap (hence his popular name), well fitted up for quick activity with a pair of gaiters. Honest, polite and energetic, he is always ready to render help to a passenger at a call. When you board a train, the porter carries your luggage into your compartment and helps you in securing a comfortable seat, and when you alight from the cars your personal effects will be carried to the entrance of the station. He is regarded to be a typical Japanese, in whom, it is said, a foreign tourist finds a real Japan when he alights from a railway at a station.

Although the red-cap asks for an optional pay per pieoe of luggage he may carry for you, there is a fixed amount of charge. Because no receipt or check is handed by a red-cap for a parcel or luggage that he receives for his care, a foreign tourist sometimes feels worried about it. But he is perfectly honest and always true to his trust so he is sure to hand all luggage back when you board the train or leave the station. Our red-cap always remembers and never fails his client. If, however, you should feel concerned, all that you will then have to do is to remember the number your red-cap bears on his breast, as a foreign face is often hard to remember.

The red-cap is not an employee of the Government Railways or of a railway or station where he works, but he is engaged usually by a private concern which makes a special contract with the station concerned for keeping "Akabo" in it.

Every foreign tourist who has the experience of having engaged a red-cap at a railway station in Japan attests to the fact that our station-porter is 100% honest and trustworthy; for he never cheats or hides anything from his client.

THE LOTUS-THREAD MANDALA

The Tayuma-ji Temple, built by Prince Moroko, fourth son of the Emperor Yomei (31st) at the foot of Mt. Futakami, Nara, has among its temple-treasures a mandala woven of lotus-thread, a most unique piece of art in Japan.

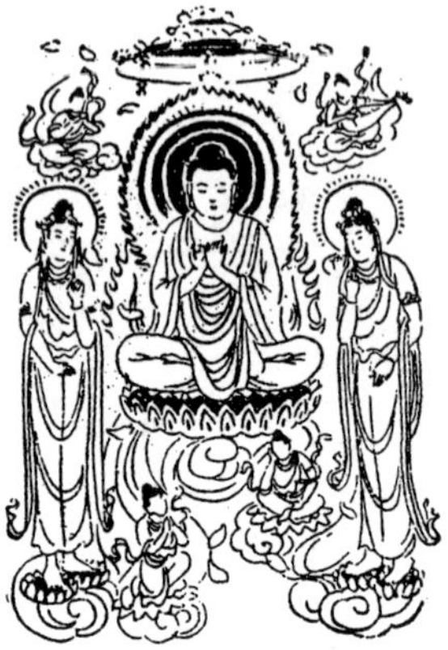

Mandala

Chujohime, to whose invention the Lotus-thread Mandala is attributed, was daughter of a court-minister. Pious and devoted to Buddhism, she left her parents in 763 A. D. at the age of sixteen years, and took the tonsure, by assuming the Buddhist name of Nun Nyoho, under the virtuous priest Jitsuin at the Zenrin-ji Temple, more commonly called by the name of the Tayuma-ji Temple.

Nun Nyoho dedicated to the Mida Buddha a complete hand-written copy of a certain Buddhist sutra of a thousand volumes, which she completed in the course of three years by copying three volumes each day. The hand-written sutra is still preserved in the Tayuma-ji Temple.

Once Nun Nyoho shut herself up in meditation and prayer with a strong determination that she would not leave the Hall before she saw the Mida Buddha face to face. A few days later a young nun appeared to her in a vision and said that, her prayer answered, Nun Nyoho would see the Mida Buddha because of her devotion. The nun in the vision told her to collect a hundred horse-loads of the lotus for weaving a mandala. So saying the nun in the vision disappeared. With the help of her father, therefore, Nun Nyoho obtained so much lotus in two days, and took or extracted all the webs she could from the stems and roots, of the lotus. The mysterious nun made her second appearance, and wove in one night, from the zodiac time of the Rat (midnight) to that of the Tiger (4 a. m.), an exquisite mandala, 15 ft. long, under a light made of three sheaves of rice-straws and two *sho* (*sho*=1.5 gallons) of oil. The nun disappeared as mysteriously as she had come. When the mandala was washed in the water of a well drilled in the north-eastern corner of the temple-grounds, it became a five-coloured beautiful mandala, as is now preserved in the Tayuma-ji Temple.

When the mandala was completed, there appeared to Nun Nyoho another elderly nun who said that she was the Mida Buddha, the mysterious young nun being one of her attendant-deities.

THE "MASK"

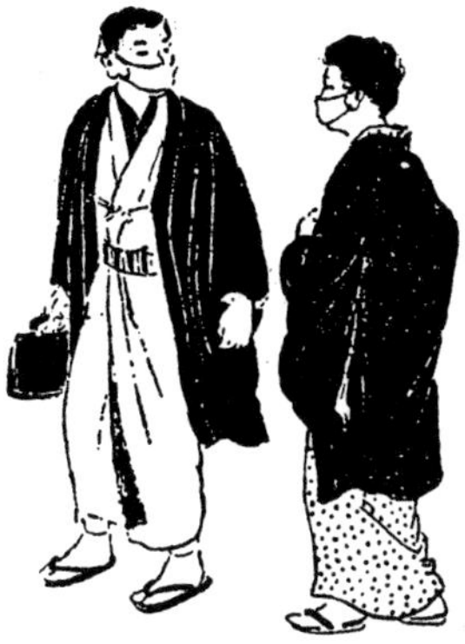
Two persons in "Mask"

"What is that?" is a question that is invariably asked by a new visitor of Japan when he sees a Japanese with what we call "Masuku" over his nose. It must be something most strongly queer to a foreign tourist and indeed it is even remarked by some foreigners that the "mask" spoils the handsome looks of a Japanese girl.

The "mask" is used all through the year by some people, such as a hospital nurse or some other medical people, but it is used most during the winter-time. It came to vogue some thirty years ago when Japan was visited by the Spanish flu. It is used for a double purpose: namely, for the benefit of the wearer as well as of those in contact with him.

The "mask" is a simple affair, made of double clothing; with a small metal frame in. A piece of cotton gauze, usually three or four fold, is put in it, and some people put a little bit of menthol crystal. Some foreigners object that the "mask" will keep the carbon dioxide that comes from the mouth of the wearer. It may be so, but, at the same time, as you will experience by wearing it, it keeps its wearer very warm and surely it keeps cold off, as is medically and statistically proved in Japan. One thing is quite certain, however, that the "mask" is very efficient in keeping dust off in the dusty street-car of Tokyo and many other cities of Japan, as clearly seen from the fact that the cotton gauze has to be renewed every day or at least in two days because it gets soiled with dust.

A careful Japanese will hide his mouth with a palm while talking. He will put his hand just an inch or so before his mouth, in order to keep his breath from a person he is speaking to. In putting a lighted candle of a family-altar, the Japanese will fan it out with his hand, instead of browing it off.

In a theatre or some other public places, the polite Japanese will hide their eating with their palm while eating a lunch with the other. It is not their food, but their mouths that are hidden because the Japanese consider it ill-mannered to eat in public. It is a custom of recent introduction to Japan for the Japanese to dine with friends. In olden times, a visitor was served with a meal, which he ate by himself, his host eating in another room, and it was an honour for the host to sit at the same table as his superior.

NO PLAY

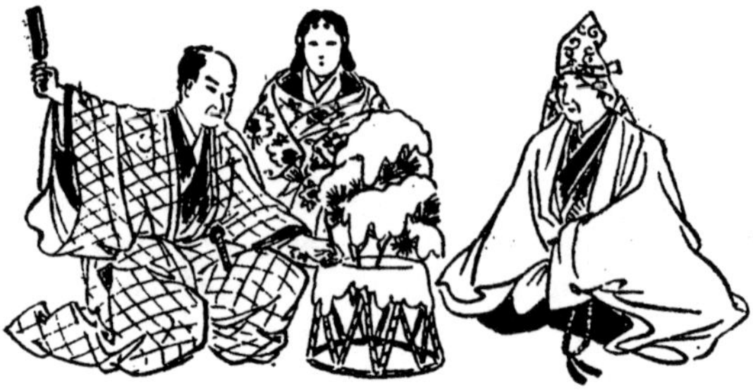

No Play

It is said with some truth that no study of Japan would be complete without that of the No play, a classical and historical drama, which played such an important part in the promotion of patriotism and devotion in samurai of old. The No play was the only theatrical performance that a samurai could visit, for he was not allowed to see the Kabuki or ordinary play, which had much love-scene in it. The No play was so popular among the samurai class that it was often performed on the point of their departure for the front, for the reason that the play, being slow of motion, cultivated presence of mind among the warriors.

The word "No" (能), as it stands, means "performance" or "accomplishment" and Rev. Eikai Kawaguchi, an authority on Tibetan culture, asserts that it is a Tibetan word. But this play seems to be of unknown origin in Japan; some holding that it originated in Japan, others that it was imported from Tibet or some other parts of the Asiatic Continent and still others that it is Buddhistic in its origin. Certain it is, however, that Sarugaku (lit. monkey-dance), corrupted from the Tibetan word "Sanro", as Rev. Kawaguchi holds, was the forerunner of this classical play of Japan.

The No play made great development under the patronage of the Ashikaga regime (1338–1573), of which Yoshimitsu Ashikaga, the third Shogun, was very fond of this play. Its pieces underwent great improvement in word and performance, till the No drama became real literature in Japan. Great emphasis is laid on patriotism and devotion, the central spirit of samurai of old.

The No play consists of three parts: players, minstrels and an orchestra. The players play to the singing of the minstrels, who sing the story, and to the music of the orchestra which plays three kinds of drums and a flute. No woman takes part in the No play, but a man plays a female role. Every important actor wears a mask, the manufacture of which is a great art in Japan. We have many No masks preserved as national treasures, some of them being over a thousand years old. The No player wears a peculiar costume, which is quite gorgeous in appearance; it must have been adopted from that of an old courtier.

Buddhism exercises a great influence on the No play, and every piece is associated with it. And no matter how tragic a piece may be at its beginning, it invariably ends with a Mai, or dance, in a most optimistic way. Certainly is the No play a religious and spiritual performance.

JAPANESE DOLL

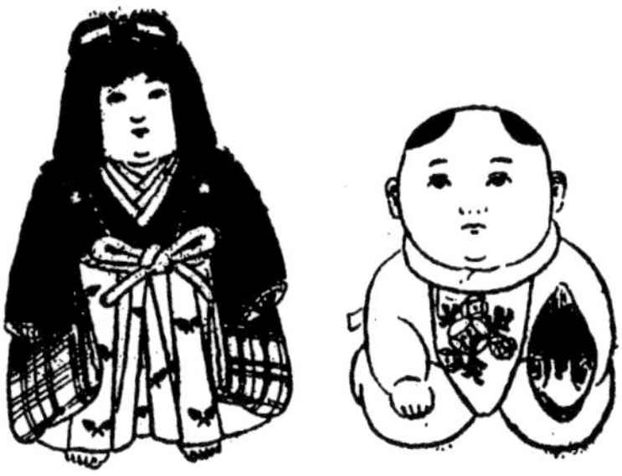

Dolls

The Japanese doll was originally of twofold significance: one as a scapegoat and the other for decoration. According to the *Shoku-Nihongi*, Susanoo, a prehistoric prince, cut his nails to make them a sort of substitution to atone for a crime he had committed, and the Japanese doll called Ningyo (Nin = man; gyo = shape) is said to indicate something that stands for, or serves as, a scapegoat to atone for a human sin or crime. In many localities in Japan, a doll, made of paper in human form, is still offered to a shrine or thrown into a river as an exorcism of evil or a cleanser of impurity or filth on behalf of a person afflicted with illness, which in this country is often attributed to the mischievous prank of an evil spirit. *Amakatsu*, for instance, possibly meaning "heaven's punishment", is a substitute for an afflicted person. It consists of two pieces of bamboo in the shape of the letter T with the picture of a human face. When a baby is born, this doll is often placed as a charm at its bedside. *Hoko*, (lit. creeping baby) is another charm against evil. It is a doll made of silk, with black thread for hair.

Haniwa, which is often brought to light from an ancient grave, is a kind of earthen doll that was buried with the remains of a nobleman or a local chief. When Prince Yamatohiko died in 659 A. D. many of his favorite retainers were buried alive to follow their master to the land of the dead. The Emperor Suinin (the 11th), who was moved by their cruel death ordered that a substitute of some kind should be buried instead of a live person. Nomi-no-

Continued

Sukune, therefore, invented ***Haniwa***, an earthen doll, to be buried for this purpose.

Dolls made gradual but steady progress, and their manufacture became an art during the Kamakura and Ashikaga days, when many different kinds of dolls for decorative purposes made their appearance. *Hina-ningyo* (lit. fledgeling-doll) or baby-doll is perhaps the most typical of this category. It was a small doll, and at first used as a sort of scapegoat, as we still see practised in such provinces as Tottori, Kii and Awa, where it is thrown into a river as a charm against evil. Little is known, however, as to when *Hina-ningyo* began to be celebrated on the first Snake-day (generally the 3rd) in the third month (March), though it is generally believed that it was started during the era of Tensho (1573–1591 A. D.) The doll celebration was in vogue during the Tokugawa dynasty, when the doll manufacture made remarkable progress.

Straw-Ningyo: A straw-ningyo is used as a means of cursing. It is said, and to some extent believed, that, if you strike an iron nail into a straw-doll, at the dead of night with a prayer to curse anyone you may have a grudge against, he (or she) will suffer. And we have many a story of a black magic curse thus perpetrated by means of a straw-doll.

To a Japanese girl, a doll is not a mere toy, but a play-mate. She will take care of it as if it were alive, like a baby. She will carry it on her back in the same way that she is carried on her mother's back. When she plays at house-keeping, a doll will be her visitor or guest and it will be treated as such.

When a doll is broken, our girl will often bury it in a corner of her garden. A stone is put over it as a tomb, and she is seen clapping her small hands in the way of worship. Flowers are often offered to the doll-grave as we do to a human grave.

I-RO-HA KARUTA OR A JUVENILE CARD-PLAY

I-ro-ha Karuta (*karuta* corrupted from "card") is a juvenile card-play very popular among young children, especially in New Year's time. It is so named after the Japanese syllabic alphabet of forty-eight letters beginning with "I-ro-ha" (or a-b-c). This game has two sets of so many cards each, one for "reading" and the other for "taking".

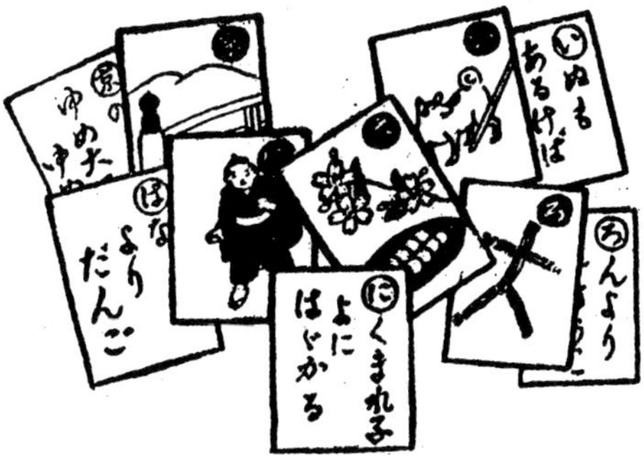

Playing-cards

Each letter of the Japanese alphabet has a popular proverb beginning with it. The first letter "i" (い), for instance, has "*I*nu mo arukeba Bo ni ataru" (lit. Even a dog, walking out, catches a cudgel), interpreted generally to have the same meaning as "A flying crow gets something;" for the second letter "ro" (ろ) we have "*Ro*n yori Shoko" meaning "Proof speaks more eloquently than argument"; the third letter "ha" (は) often suggests "*Ha*na yori Dango" (lit. Dumpling is better than a flower), meaning that food is better than a flower, and so on. Each syllabic letter standing at the beginning of a proverb it represents, these forty-eight proverbs, commonly called "I-ro-ha Tatoye" (lit. a-b-c proverbs) are written in simple letters, one each, on so many cards of the "reading" set.

Continued

Each card of the other set, that is, for "taking", also forty-eight letters in number, has one of the alphabet in a conspicuous type and also a picture depicting the proverb it represents: "a dog with a cudgel" for the first letter "i", "a child with some sweets standing under a tree in full bloom," for the third letter "ha", and so on. These cards are illustrated in a simplest way so that any small children may understand the pictures.

This game can be played by many children. The illustrated cards are scattered quite in disorder on the mat-floor on which the players are seated in a circle, or, as is often the case in these days, on a table, with the players sitting around it. The leader, or, in this case, the reader, reads loudly the "reading" cards of proverbs one after another, after shuffling them well, and the players vie with one another in picking up the illustrated cards corresponding to those which the reader reads out. The larger number of cards one picks up, the greater winner one is.

The game can be played in partners. In this case the players are divided into two parties, or sides, sitting face to face with each other, and the illustrated cards, divided equally between the two sides, are displayed side by side, in good order before each party. The reader reads the proverbs one after another, in the same way, and the players pick up the corresponding ones from either side. If a child takes a card from the rival's side, it hands one from its side over to the other, in order to make the cards of its side the less, because in this method of play the side that gets rid of its cards sooner is the winner.

This is an exiciting game, and it fosters retentive memory and quickness of action on the part of the juvenile players. It can be played by such young children, under school-age, as can remember the cards by looking at the pictures.

WATERFALLS IN JAPAN

Kegon Waterfall: Nikko is said to have forty-eight waterfalls, of which Kegon Waterfall is the largest and it is perhaps the most famous in the whole country of Japan. It has its origin in Lake Chuzenji and it is the origin of the River Ohya, which runs through the streets of Nikko city. Kegon Waterfall, 750 ft. long, top to bottom, which is a grand sight to look at, is named after a Buddhist sutra and attracts many local and foreign tourists all through the year. This waterfall is also notoriously known the country over because many a pessimist throws himself into the waterfall to commit suicide, so that the authorities made a railing around the top of the waterfall to keep the pessimistic people from getting near the cascade. The waterfall can be seen in full by getting down by an elevator.

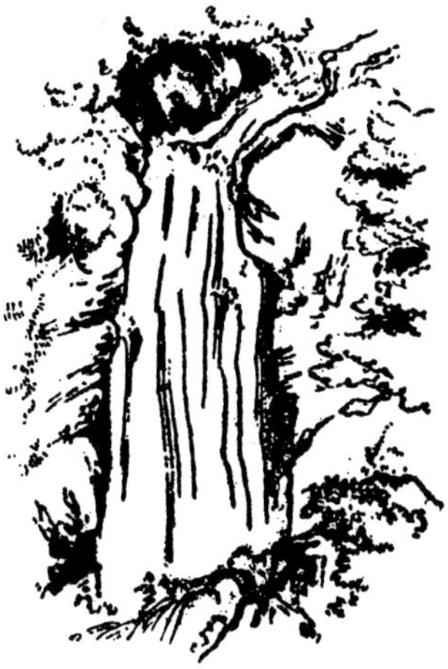

Waterfall

Nachi Waterfalls: Nachi Waterfalls, which also are forty-eight in number, are situated in the province of Kii; the largest one being 840 ft. long and about 100 ft. wide. It is said to have been exploitered by Priest Kobo and it has since been a place of religious asceticism, so that many prominent priests, such as En-no-Gyoja, Priest Denkyo, Priest Chisho, etc. practised asceticism under these waterfalls. Priest Mongaku, in particular, who killed Lady Kesa by mistake, sat for several days in meditation and asceticism under the waterfalls.

The ex-Emperor Kazan visited the Nachi Waterfalls, where he stayed for three years, during which a dragon appeared to him and handed him two gems and a sea-shell. The gems were enshrined in Buddhist temples nearby, and the shell was thrown into the waterfalls.

Yoro-no-Taki: Yoro-no-Taki, (lit. waterfall for feeding the old), is located midway on Mt. Yoro in the province of Mino. "Yoro" means "feeding the old", the waterfall so named after a dutiful son whose story in brief runs as follows:—

During the reign of the Empress Gensho (44th), there lived a dutiful farmer near Mt. Yoro in the province of Mino. He worked hard day and night to purchase sake or rice-wine for his aged father, who was very fond of it. One day he found a spring from which sake bubbled up, because, it was believed, the gods who were moved by his filial devotion, turned the water of the spring into sake. He took a bottleful of the sake every day to his father, till the story of devotion reaching the ears of the Empress, she visited the spring of sake, and she adopted the name of Yoro for her era (717–723) in appreciation of his dutifulness, and waterfall has ever since known as Yoro-no-Taki. The waterfall can be reached in one day from Nagoya.

Setsubun or Bean-Throwing Ceremony

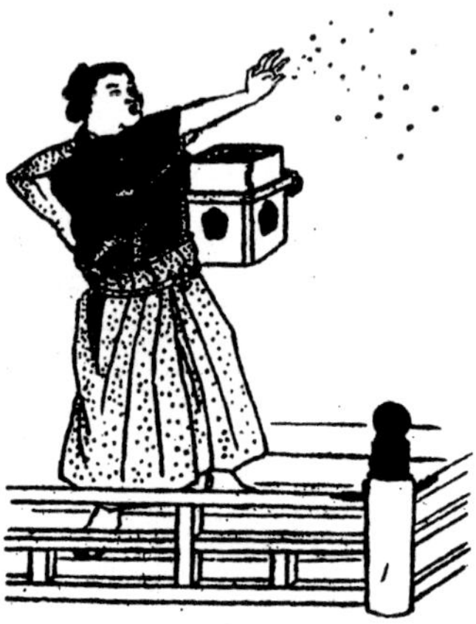

Bean-Throwing

"Fuku wa uchi! (Fortune in)
Fuku wa uchi! (Fortune in)
Oni wa soto! (Devil out)"

This is a cry heard from almost every orthodox Japanese home on the evening of the Setsubun (lit. season-change), which comes on at the end of Kan or coldest season. The Kan season, which lasts for thirty days, inclusive of Daikan (major-cold) and Shokan (minor-cold), ends usually on the 2nd or 3rd of February, when the ceremony of Mame-maki (bean-throwing) or Tsunan (devil-driving) is held in most Japanese houses.

On the day of Setsubun, a small branch of *Hiiragi-tree* (osmanthus aquifolium), which resembles the holly, and the head of a dried sardine are put at the entrance of each house (though in former days a nayoshi, or magil aphalotus, was used instead of a sardine). In the evening, the ceremony of Mame-maki, or bean-throwing, is held to "bring fortune in and drive evil out." The bean-thrower, who is the master or scion of a family (never a woman in olden days), is dressed in Kamishimo-dress and he throws a handful of parched beans from a dry-measure, which he carries on a Sambon-tray, crying as quoted above. He throws a handful twice in the lucky direction of the year where resides the Year-virtue God, and once in the direction opposite to him. He repeats the same cries in every room and closet that there may be in the house, one of its doors being open while he throws the beans, possibly, as an exit

Continued

for the Devil. Thus is the fortune invited and evil driven out for the year.

Some of the beans that are thrown in the room are kept on account of a common belief that, if you eat three of these beans at the time when the first thunder peals in the year, you will escape a thunder bolt during the year. A man or woman in his or her "unlucky years of age," i. e. 25 and 42 years for men and 19 and 33 years for women, will wrap in a piece of white paper as many of beans used at Setsubun as his or her years of age, together with some coins, which are thrown away at crossroads so that evil may be done away with for the year.

Recently the ceremony of bean-throwing is held at every large Shinto shrine and Buddhist temple, when some champion wrestlers or noted actors act as what are called "Toshi-otoko" (lit. year-man) as the bean-thrower is commonly called. Happy are those indeed who succeed in catching a few beans that are thrown by these year-men, for great are crowds who assemble to catch a few of the beans. These beans, which the luckier people of the crowds catch, are kept at home as a luck-bringer for the year.

Tradition has it that during the reign of the Emperor Uda (59th) a devil of some kind lived in a cave near Lake Misoro in Kumano. It came out in the night to make havoc in the neighbourhood, till, by following the oracle of Vaiscavana, seven wise men were ordered by the Emperor to kill the evil spirit. They threw parched beans into the cave by closing its entrance with the leaves of the Hiiragi-tree and heads of sardines. This is said to be the origin of the practice of throwing parched beans in the evil direction with a few Hiiragi-leaves and the head of a dried sardine outside a door which is open at the time when the beans are thrown out.

HORSE STORIES

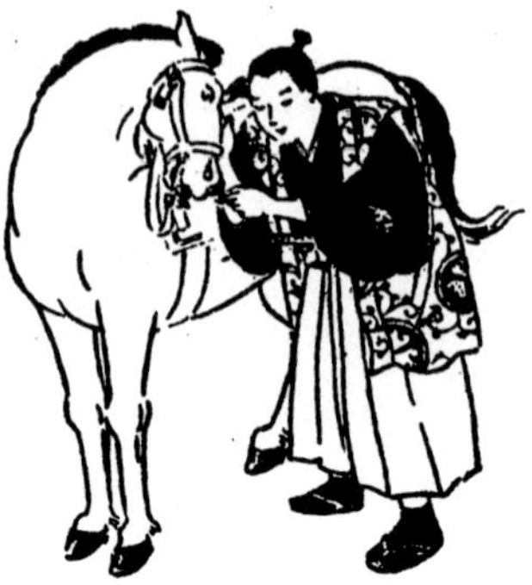
A lord with his horse

Mitsuhisa Matsudaira and Oikaze: Oikaze (lit. fair-wind) was a favorite horse that Mitsuhisa Matsudaira, lord of Osumi, kept for twenty years. When Matsudaira was about to leave Edo (Tokyo) for his local clan, he thought that the horse was now too old to accompany him.

"You tell Oikaze" Matsudaira said to his horse-keeper, "that he is to stay here this time without accompanying me."

The horse must have understood what was told him, for crestfallen, after that, he refused to eat anything offered him.

"It is not because I do not like you," said Matsudaira to his horse, patting him on the head when he heard of its disappointment, "but through my sympathy with you for your old age that I have decided to leave you here. If you wish to go, of course you shall."

The horse understood him, and became as cheerful and active as before. Matsudaira took his horse to his local clan, where it soon died.

Grave of Gotogo: Masamune Date, lord of the Sendai clan, had an old horse, Gotogo by name, which he had ridden for 30 years. Date was over 70 years, too old to use the horse. So when he was called to Edo (Tokyo) by the Shogun Iyemitsu Tokugawa, Date took his favorite horse out of the stable and said to him:

"Gotogo, I appreciate your faithful services in which you carried me all these years. I am now called to Edo and I do not know when I shall come back. You stay at Sendai and take a rest."

That night Gotogo broke through the stable, kicked to death the stable-keeper, who was known for his cruel treatment of the horse, and threw itself down the steep castle-walls to die.

Date mourned over his death and buried him with religious rites, erecting a stone monument in appreciation for the faithful service of Gotogo. His grave, which is in the city of Sendai, is still visited by many admirers.

Takatsuna Sasaki and Ikezuki: Yoritomo Minamoto had two favorite horses, Ikezuki and Surusumi. On the eve of the battle of the River Uji, fought in 1184, Kagesuye Kajiwara had a private interview with Yoritomo and asked for Ikezuki, on which, he said, he would distinguish himself in the battle. But Yoritomo gave

Continued

him Surusumi instead, keeping the other horse for his own use. Soon after Takatsuna Sasaki, another warrior, came and asked for Ikezuki, promising that he would be the first to land on the enemy's side of the river if he could have the horse. Yoritomo gave him Ikezuki. When Kajiwara saw that his rival had the horse he could not get, he was jealous of Sasaki, and he was almost determined to kill him and then himself, so that his master would lose two of his important retainers. But when Kajiwara asked how Sasaki had got Ikezuki, he only said: "I knew that the Lord would not give me the horse, which he refused you. So I stole it on the eve of my departure from Kamakura." Kajiwara laughed and wished he had done the same.

When the Minamoto army came to the River Uji, which was overflowed with water running from Lake Biwa, all the bridges had been destroyed by the enemy. Soon Kajiwara and Sasaki rode into the rapids, the former leading.

"Kajiwara," Sasaki said to his rival in a diplomatic way, "the band of your horse looks loose."

Kajiwara thanked Sasaki and pulled up to put the band to rights. In the meantime, Sasaki shot forth, and he was the first to land on the other side of the river. Minamoto won, and Yoshinaka Kiso, his enemy, was ruined.

The Nambu horse: Nambu of Aomori Prefecture is known for good horses raised there. The origin of the Nambu horse is briefly described as follows:—

Masamune Date, lord of the Sendai clan, sent Rokuyemon Hasekura as an envoy to Europe in 1613. Hasekura crossed the Pacific Ocean and went on to Europe via Mexico and the Atlantic Ocean. He visited the Spanish and Vatican courts and came back to Japan in 1620. He brought with him some stallions from Europe, but by that time Japan had closed her doors to foreign intercourse, so he could not keep the horses, which were brought from abroad. So he drove all of them out of his clan, and the Nambu clan, with or without an understanding, caught them and kept them as stray horses. This is why Nambu now produces the best horses in Japan.

Lord Sakai *and his horse:* Lord Sakai of the Shonai clan had an old horse which he rode for some twenty years. Once when he was going back to his clan from Edo, he told his horse, through a retainer that it would be left behind. The horse then dropped its head and refused to eat anything after that. Lord Sakai who heard of his favorite horse being in a dejected mode, said to it, stroking its head "I do not mean to desert you, but I thought you were too old to stand the long trip. You may go with me, if you do not like to be left behind." The horse seemed to understand its master's words, and ate as before. It was taken to Shonai with its master, and died a little while later.

KARASU OR CROW

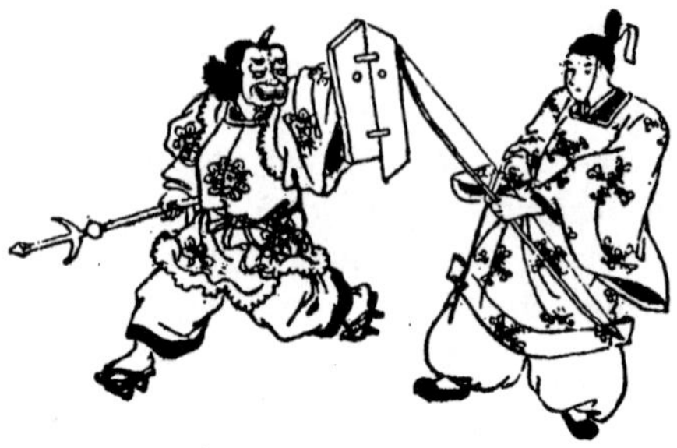

Evil-driving

The crow includes most birds of the genus corvus and of the family corvidoe. There are five species of the crow in Japan; namely :—

1. Corvus corone
2. „ macrorrhynchus
3. „ corax
4. „ dauricus
5. „ neglictus

"The pigeon has the etiquette of three branches and the crow has the filial sense of feeding back."

By this common saying is meant that the pigeon perches itself modestly three branches lower than its parents sit, while the crow reciprocates the love of its parents by feeding them after it is grown up. People say that a young crow will feed its parents for sixty days.

"Crow! crow!
Your house is on fire.
Hurry home to pour cold water over it.
If there is no cold water, pour hot water.
If there is no hot water, pour tea."

The crow is often associated with a fire, because it is said to be the only bird that can fly towards the sun without minding its rays. We say that the crow roosts in the west, and it flies towards the rising sun in the morning and towards the setting sun in the evening. The crow never feels the heat of the sun because, they say, it is already scorched black in the sun.

Continued

Once upon a time the owl was running a dyeing shop, which many birds visited to have their feathers dved in various colours. The crow had as yet no colour, but nevertheless he was much of a dandy. One day he asked the owl to dye his feather as stylish as there was no equal in the world. The dyer-bird put the crow head and all into a pot of indigo. When the crow was taken out, he was glossy black. The angry crow made a protest, but the owl simply replied that the crow was dyed in a colour of which there was no like. Thus the two birds became inveterate enemies and this accounts for the owl avoiding daytime lest the crow should catch it.

During the reign of the Empress Suiko (the 33rd), Kuramoto Saeki crossed to Itsukushima to look for a place where Princess Ichikushi could be venerated. When he was strolling along on the beach, two crows, male and female, came flying from he did not know where, and guided Saeki to the place where the Itsukushima Shrine now stands.

The two crows, it is said, served the Princess Ichikushi for a long time and then disappeared after bringing up two young ones, male and female. Generation after generation two birds raised only two successors and then disappeared.

The ceremony of Otokui, or bird-feeding, is held on Oct. 28 every year at dawn, in front of the Yabusaki (father-feeding-cape) Shrine, when it is said two parent-birds take leave of their young ones. A priest rows out a boat for a mile and a half, and throws some dumplings of boiled rice into the sea after observing some rituals. The birds come flying from a forest nearby and eat all the dumplings up to fly away never to come back.

It is traditionally believed that the crows would fail to make their appearance if on board the boat there were any one who is defiled or filthy.

GAMBLING - TREE

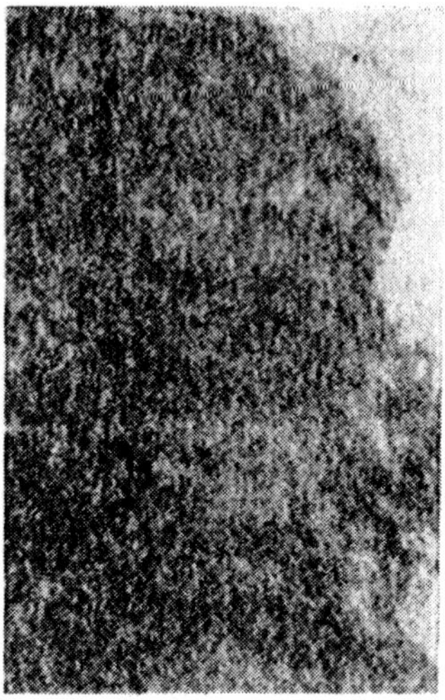

Biranji-tree

"Where is the famous Biranji?" Tadamasa Okubo, lord of Odawara, asked on his way from Kyoto to Edo of a chief retainer who came to meet him at Mishima. "There is no temple of that name" was the innocent reply, because while the lord meant a tree of that name (Biranji), his retainer took the name for a temple, as "ji" homonymously means "temple" in Japanese.

Biranji is the Japanese name for *bakuti* or *prunus macrophylla*, a tropical tree, which is scarcely discovered in Japan, excepting Kyushu and Shikoku. But a big bakuti-tree is found on Mt. Ishigaki a mile south of Odawara. This mountain was made famous by Hideyoshi Toyotomi, who, during his attack of the Odawara castle in 1590, built there in one night a huge paper-castle, which, looking down upon the enemy's castle, so scared him that he soon surrendered. No scientist seems to be able to account for the existence of this tropical tree so far north in Japan, though some scholars try to explain it by saying that the seed of the tree came drifting from the south hundreds of years ago when this part was on the beach.

On the sunny side of Mt. Ishigaki (lit. stone-wall), which is now covered with orange-trees there stands the gigantic bakuti-tree, old and hoary, with five large trunks growing luxuriant from one root. It is an evergreen tree and bears flowers like those of a laurel in October. Because of its extraordinary size and exceptional position, this tree was put in 1924 under special protection of the Japanese Government. An extract taken from its leaves is used as cough medicine called aqua prunus macrophylla.

During the reign of the Tokugawa family, this tree offered a sort of a gamble-house, for gambling went on night after night under the protection of its wide-speading branches. Hence, it is said, the tree is called Bakuchi-no-ki (bakuti) or gambling-tree, though, according to some scholars, the tree was so named because its barks peel off so easily as an unsparing gambler bets on his clothing.

FUKUJUSO OR ADONIS AMURENSIS

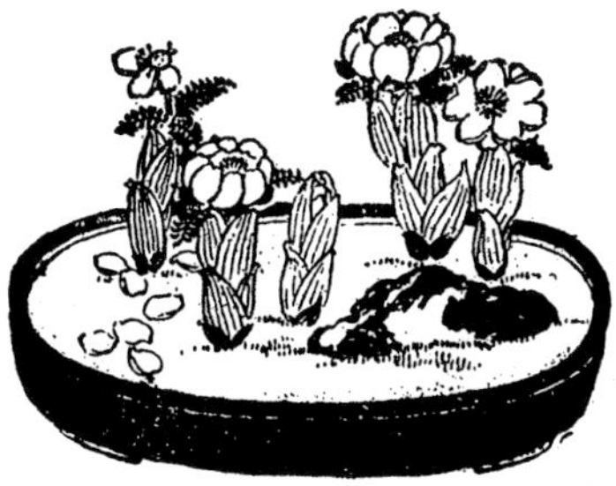
Adonis in a pot

Fukujuso (福壽草) means, as the characters stand, "fortune-longevity-plant", and moreover it is suggestive of gold with its yellow flowers. It is a symbol of wealth in Japan, and therefore it is much used at the time of New Year. Many Japanese families will have potted Fukujuso-flowers in the alcove in the New Year because of their suggestion of gold.

Fukujuso (adonis amurensis) belongs to Ranunculacae. It is a perennial plant, 3 or 4 inches to 10 inches high, and its leaves are pennate like those of the carrot. Its golden flowers, of 12 to 20 petals, come out early in the year. Fukujuso grows wild in Japan, especially in the northern part.

Once upon a time, so the tradition of the Ainu says, there was a very beautiful maid. Kuno was her name. Her god-father selected the mole, the deity under the ground, for her bridegroom, and, disappointed as she was with his selection, she obeyed him, like a dutiful daughter in the Ainu race. The wedding ceremony was observed on a lucky day in the palace of the subterranean deity, but when the ceremony was at its best, the bride made her sudden disappearance. The enraged mole-bridegroom searched for his faithless bride everywhere around his palace till he found her hidden in the grass.

"You have disobeyed your father and deserted your husband whom he selected for you" the mole said in anger. "You shall not return to my palace any more, but turn into earth on the spot."

Forthwith the princess turned into a beautiful flower, which the Ainu call Kuno after her maiden name, meaning "Fukujuso." It is said among the Ainu that this plant, small as it is, looks beautiful because it was a charming princess in its former existence.

INTRODUCTION OF RAW COTTON

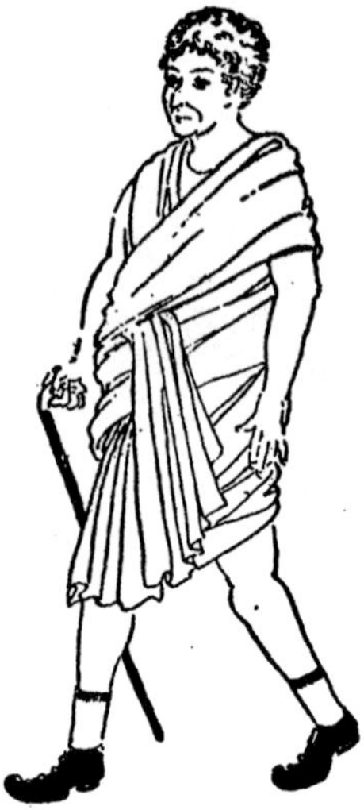

In the seventh month (July) of the year 799, during the reign of the Emperor Kammu (the 50th), a small boat went aground at the mouth of the River Yahazu in the province of Mikawa, and a queer-looking young man stepped out of the boat. He was a young man of 20, standing 5 ft. 5 in (Japanese measure) with curly hair. He was not clad at all in our sense of clothing, for he had only a piece of blue cloth hanging from his left shoulder, as the record goes, in the fashion of a surplice generally worn by a Buddhist priest in Japan. His language was quite unintelligible to the Japanese; nor did he understand a single Japanese word. He carried with him a one-stringed musical instrument. Nobody knew what nationality he belonged to nor what country he had come from. According to a Chinese priest living in the neighbourhood, the stranger had come from the Konglong Mountains of China. But when the castaway had learned the Japanese language enough to make himself understood, it was found that he was an Indian.

Among the personal effects he had saved from his wreck, was some seed of raw cotton, from which the first cotton ever produced in Japan was obtained. Then cotton was soon introduced to such provinces as Kii, Awaji, Awa, Sanuki, Iyo and Tosa, and some provinces in Kyushu. The Indian lived first in the Kawara-ji Temple

Continued

near the beach, where he got stranded, but later he was removed to the Kokubun-ji Temple in the province of Ohmi, and then to a temple of the same name in Kawachi province. The village where this Indian landed with the cotton seed was called Tenjiku-mura (天竺) (Indian village). This name, however, sounded rather queer to the ears of the average Japanese, so that later on the two characters (天竹), meaning (celestial bamboo), were used in place of the former ones. There is now a shrine dedicated to the first Indian who brought raw cotton to Japan. It was first called the Tenjiku-jinja or Indian shrine, but it is popularly known as the Shibata shrine, meaning "the new Hata shrine".

During the reign of the Emperor Ohjin (the 15th), Japan had several hundred immigrants, who, so far as the record goes, came from Korea, though, judging from the name, Rev. Eikai Kawaguchi, a great authority on Tibetology, holds they were Tibetans coming thorough the peninsular kingdom of Korea. Their manager or leader was called Hata. He was a weaver, and the Emperor Ohjin made him an official in charge of weaving in the country. The Japanese words "hata" for "loom" and "hata-ori" for "weaver" are derived from the name of the Hata family. The Indian who brought the seed of raw cotton, was also connected with weaving, and his visit was another epoch-making in the history of Japan's weaving. Hence the Indian was called, or regarded as, "a new Hata" (Shin-Hata), which has corrupted into Shibata, as his name-sake shrine is now called.

LIFE-SIZE STATUES OF ARHAN

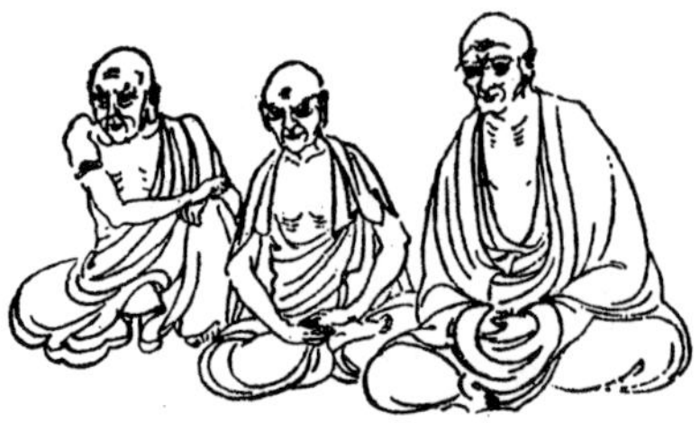

Arhan statues

Not far from Meguro Fudo (lit. Eye-black) or Acala at Meguro in the ward of Meguro, Tokyo, there is a small Buddhist temple called Rakan-ji or Arhan Temple, in which some two hundred life-size statues of Arhan (Buddha's disciples) are enshrined. Arhan, which literally means "enlightenment" in Hinayana (lit. small vehicle) represents some of the disciples of Buddha, and these Arhan images were carved by Priest Shoun.

Priest Shoun was a Buddhist sculptor in the 17th century. When he visited the 500 statues of Arhan at the Rakan-ji Temple in Bungo Province, Kyushu, he conceived the idea of carving so many images himself. He came to Edo (now Tokyo) during the era of Teikyo (1684–1687) and confined himself in a small cottage belonging to the Senso-ji Temple, Asakusa, so that he might devote himself to the carving of the sacred images. He had little fund to fall back upon nor did any supporter finance him. So he went about as a mendicant priest begging in the day-time for alms on which he lived while he betook himself to the sculpture work at night with a dim light until he became a laughing stock of the people in his neighborhood. When he had made some fifty statues, however, Lady Keishoin, mother of the Shogun Tsunayoshi, herself a devout Buddhist, heard of his pious undertaking and donated a sum of money in his encouragement. Her example was followed by a number of people who contributed to his fund. Free from financial care, Priest Shoun could now give all his time to the attainment of his religious object. He completed his work in 1695 when he had made no less than five hundred life-size, or even larger, statues of the Buddha and Arhan.

Priest Shoun built a temple which he called Rakan-ji Temple at Honjo, Edo, for the veneration of his statues, and he dedicated it to Lady Keishoin, who supported him financially as well as morally. Priest Shoun died in 1710 at the age of 63 years.

The Rakan-ji Temple, in which the Arhan set was enshrined, was removed to the present site of Meguro in 1897, but there are only a little over two hundred images, the rest being either lost or destroyed.

Mokugyo: Mokugyo, or, as it literally means, a wooden-fish, is something most conventionalized with its tail and scales merely symbolized; for it is more in the form of a wooden bell as it is generally called in English than anything else. But the Rakan-ji Temple has a Mokugyo in the form of a fish, a rare case of a musical instrument used in a temple.

500 stone-Rakan: Not far from the Rakan-ji Temple there is another Buddhist temple famous for a set of 500 Rakan statues standing on a hill behind the temple. They were erected with a prayer for the peaceful repose of the ill-fated people who were burned to death in a big fire which destroyed a large part of Edo in 1772.

ISSUN-HOSHI

TOM THUMB OF JAPAN

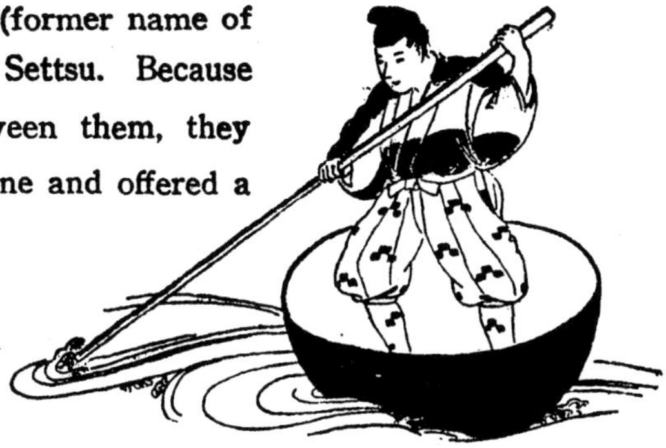

Once upon a time there lived a man and his wife at Naniwa (former name of Osaka) in the province of Settsu. Because they had no child between them, they visited the Sumiyoshi shrine and offered a prayer for a baby, "any baby," they said in their prayer, "even as small as a thumb." Their prayer was heard, and in course of time a boy-baby was born to them. But it was no more than an inch large. Some eight or ten years elapsed, but the baby grew little bigger, till the people called him Issun-hoshi (lit. inch-bonze) and his parents recalled the prayer they offered at Sumiyoshi.

One day Issun-hoshi asked permission of his father and mother for going to Kyoto, the Imperial capital, where he would work his way up to make something of himself. The permission given, the boy asked for a wooden bowl and a pair of chopsticks, which he asked them to carry for him when they came to see him off at Yodo whence he was to row his bowl-boat on his way to Kyoto. Issun-hoshi got into the bowl and rowed it with the chopsticks up the River Yodo, through great difficulties, till he came to Toba, where he landed to go to Kyoto on foot.

Upon his arrival at the Imperial capital, our brave inch-boy called at one of the largest mansions in the city, with self-introduction. It was the private residence of the Premier, where Issun-hoshi offered his services. The Premier employed him through curiosity,

Continued

and the boy worked his best till he became a favorite with everybody in the family, and particularly with the Princess, daughter of the Premier.

One day the Princess visited Kiyomizu, taking Issun-hoshi with her, to worship Kannon, Goddess of Mercy. It was no fete-day and there were few visitors. On her way home the Princess was attacked by two Oni (ogres), and our brave inch-boy struck at the Oni with his needle-sword to defend the Princess. "None of your sauce!" one of the Oni said, and he swallowed the boy up. But Issun-hoshi pricked all about in the stomach of the Oni, who vomitted him out with great pains. Nothing daunted, the boy kept his brave resistance to save his young mistress, but he was again swallowed up, this time by the other Oni. But he managed to jump from throat into the nose, instead of going down into the stomach, and then he managed to enter one of his eyes When the Oni lifted his hand to rub the eye, Issun-hoshi jumped down. Annoyed thus by the small boy, the Oni took to their heels without molesting the Princess any more.

When the two Oni were gone, the Princess found on the road a hammer, which is called Uchide-no-Kozuchi (lit. hammer that strikes anything out), which the Oni must have left behind. Like the Aladdin's lamp, this hammer brings anything that its bearer may desire to have.

"This hammer will give you anything you want," the Princess said. "What would you like to have?"

"I want to be an ordinary man" the little man said, and at her shaking of the hammer, Issun-hoshi became an ordinary man all of a sudden.

The Premier was so pleased with the adventures in which Issun-hoshi saved his daughter, that he recommended him to the Emperor, who appointed him high in the Imperial court, and our ex-inch-boy was adopted by the Premier as his son-in-law.

NURSERY TALE

Kachi-kachi-yama

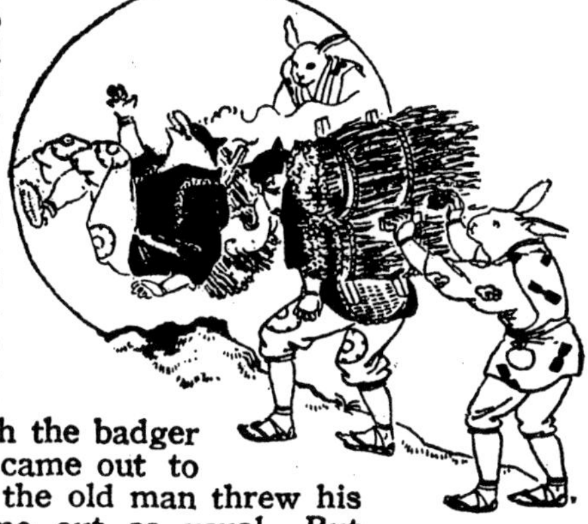

Once upon a time there was an old farmer who used to shout: "The seeds that the old man sows shall each become a thousand", every time he scattered a handful of seeds on the field.

"The seeds that the old man sows shall each be one and no more" shouted a badger that came running from the wood nearby every time when the old man threw his handful of seeds.

The old man put some bird's lime on a stone on which the badger used to sit everytime when it came out to undo the old man's cry. When the old man threw his seeds, as usual, the badger came out as usual. But this time the badger was captured with the bird's lime and the old man took it home, its limbs bound with a straw-rope.

"You make a soup of badger this evening when I come home," he said to his old wife when he went out again. His wife began the preparation of the soup, when the badger asked her to loosen a little the rope with which it was tied up painfully tight. When through pity she tried to help it, the badger got off and at once killed her. It assumed her shape, and prepared a soup of her flesh.

"Is the soup ready?" the old man asked the moment when he came home.

"O yes, it is made delicious" the human-shape badger replied. The old man unloaded himself and sat at his Ozen (meal-tray) to eat the soup, when the badger, running out, shouted loudly: "You are eating the soup of your own wife, instead of the badger. Look under the floor."

The old man curiously looked in, and sure enough there he found the mutilated remains of his wife. He burst out into tears over her death, when there came a hare to ask why he was crying. After it listened to the tale that the old man told, the hare offered to help take revenge upon the death of the old woman.

Once the hare took the badger out into mountains to collect faggots. On their way home, the badger walking before, the hare struck a flint to set fire to the faggots the badger had on its back. The flint went click! click!

"What is it I hear clicking?" the badger asked.

"Why, it is a sound coming from Kachi-kachi-yama (Mt. Click-click", the hare explained. But the faggots catching fire, the badger got burned on the back. The hare, the quack, gave it a medicine prepared from pepper, which gave the badger nothing but pain.

When the badger got well, the hare took it on a row on a river. The hare had a wooden boat for itself, but it gave the badger an earthen one. Soon after they rowed out, water got into the earthen boat, which sinking the badger was drowned.

NURSERY TALE

Trio: Monkey, Hare and Bull-frog

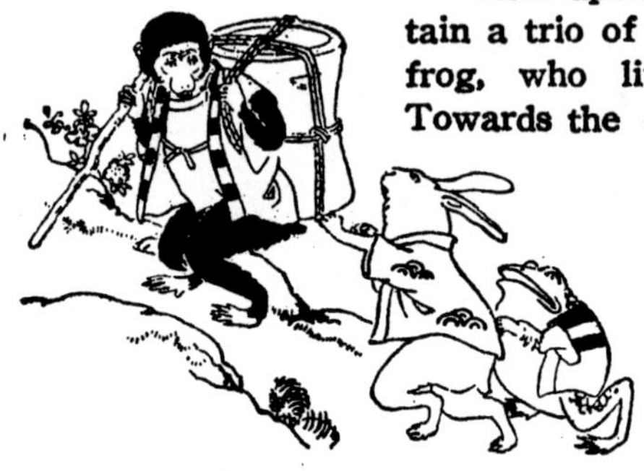

Once upon a time there was on a mountain a trio of a monkey, a hare and a bull-frog, who lived together most friendly. Towards the end of the year, when every Japanese home prepares Mochi or rice-cake, which is indispensably necessary for the New Year in Japan, the trio wished to have some for themselves and so they went down the mountain to look for some Mochi at the nearest village. Soon they found a mortar of Mochi, and the monkey, the strongest of the trio, carried it on his back up the mountain back to their dwelling. The greedy monkey, however, wanted to have all the Mochi to himself, instead of sharing it with the other two. So he said: "I have a good idea. We will throw the mortar down the mountain and any of us who may get to it first shall have all the Mochi to himself." The monkey was sure that he would get it because he thought he was the quickest of the three in running, but the hare, being no less a good runner, agreed to the proposal made by the monkey. The bull-frog, however, who was slow of walking, made a protest, but he was overpowered by his quicker-footed friends

"One! two! three! go!" shouted the monkey, and he threw the mortar down the mountain. It rolled down and down. The monkey and the hare ran quickly after it; the bull-frog slowly following them. The monkey was the first in running, but when he came to a steep part of the mountain, he stumbled down, falling on his haunches. This is why the monkey has two red scratches on his haunches.

The hare was the first to reach the foot of the mountain. He saw the mortar rolling down. "There it comes" he thought. "I can have it all to myself." He held his arms out to receive the heavy mortar, which, however, was so heavy that the poor hare had its fore-paws broken by the heavy mortar. This explains why the hare has short fore-paws. Nor did he get the Mochi, the mortar being empty because the Mochi had rolled out of it on the way.

The bull-frog, despaired of any hope in his competition with two quick-footed rivals, toddled slowly down the mountain, when, quite unexpectedly, he discovered the Mochi, still steaming hot, caught in bushes. He made a hearty meal of the rice-cake, all to himself, and this accounts for the potbelly that the bull-frog has.

KAMINARI OR THUNDER

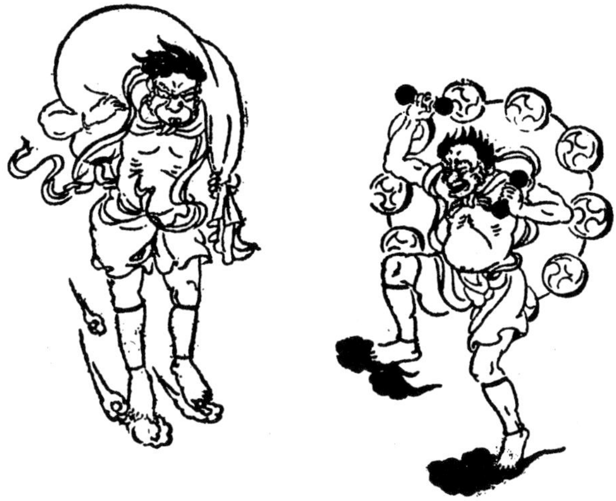

Princess Izanami, says the *Nihonshoki*, gave birth to eight gods of thunder; namely, the great thunder, fire-thunder, earth-thunder, bursting-thunder, black-thunder, mountain-thunder, field-thunder and pealing thunder.

According to a popular belief, the god of thunder has a number of drums over his shoulders, with a drum-stick in each hand, and their beating makes the peals of thunder; hence the Japanese name "Kami-nari" (lit. god-pealing) for "thunder." You can see a wooden image of thunder preserved as a national treasure in the San-Butsu-den (lit. three-Buddha-Hall) at Nikko.

Japanese child warned against uncovered front: A Japanese child is told never to leave its front uncovered, because if it does, Kaminari, the god of thunder, will come down, to get its navel, which has, therefore, to be always protected with a belly-band.

Charm against thunderbolt: Some Shinto shrines, such as is dedicated to Princess Oichi-hime in Kii Province, issue a charm which will protect its bearer from a thunderbolt. Thunder is also

Continued

kept off if you shout "Kuwambara! Kuwambara!" (lit. mulberry) when it peals; because it is popularly believed that the mulberry-tree being non-conductive, no thunderbolt strikes it.

According to a legend, however, Kaminari once fell into a well by the name of Kuwabara-ido (ido = well) in Izumi Province. The villagers closed the well with a cover, till the god of Kaminari promised never to molest them any more, when he was released. Hence, "Kuwambara! Kuwambara!"

Most Japanese families preserve some beans, which are used at the bean-throwing ceremony held at the end of Kan, the coldest season, which falls usually on Feb. 2 or 3 each year, and the Japanese swallow a few of them at the first pealing of thunder, for, it is popularly believed, they will not then be struck by lightning during the year.

Obo visited mother's grave at every pealing: Obo is one of the Nijushiko (lit. 24 dutiful sons) who are selected as typically dutiful. His mother was so afraid of thunder, while alive, that, after her death, Obo used to visit her grave every time when thunder pealed, and shouted in a loud voice, "Mother, don't be afraid, for I am here with you!"

Tokihira Fujiwara killed by lightning: Tokihira Fujiwara, a court Minister, accused Michizane Sugawara, a fellow-courtier, falsely to the Emperor, who sent Sugawara to a place of exilement, where he died. Soon after his death, Fujiwara was killed by lightning, which the people attributed to the vindictive spirit of Michizane Sugawara, who was deified as Tenjin (lit. celestial deity.)

"HACHI-NO-KI" OR POTTED TREES

"Hachi-no-Ki" (lit. potted trees) is an outstandingly famous piece of the No play. It is a dramatized story of one ronin (ex-samurai), Sano Genzaemon Tsuneyo by name, who did not forget loyalty even though he was reduced to penury.

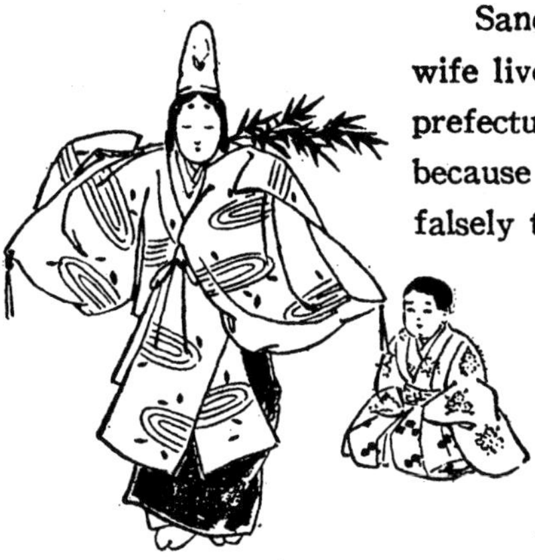
No Play

Sano Genzaemon Tsuneyo and his wife lived at Sano, a remote village in the prefecture of Gumma, after his retirement, because his relatives had slandered him falsely to his lord, and he was deprived of all his possessions. One cold winter's day, toward dusk, an old Buddhist priest called at his house and asked for night's lodgings. He was out, and his wife, having hardly any food to offer, asked the priest to go a little farther on to the next village where he would find a better place to stay overnight. Disappointed and forlorn, the priest went on in the snow and that towards dusk. Sano coming home, remorse took him for having heartlessly refused a holy man, who is privileged to have hospitality at any home. The priest was called back, but he was served with nothing better than boiled millet, instead of boiled rice. It was a snowy night, but Sano had no firewood to make a fire with for him. So he burned his favorite potted trees, a plum, a pine and a bamboo to warm the stranger.

"I used to have better days," Sano said to the priest, "when I collected quite a number of potted trees, of which I have all disposed, excepting these three, which I will break up to make a fire for you."

The priest objected, intimidating that Sano might come again into power, when he replied saying: "That would no more be possible for me than fossilized wood can bloom."

The priest now noticed that Sano was no ordinary warrior and

Continued

asked what made him live such a reduced life. Sano told him how his wicked relatives had falsely deprived him of all his possessions.

"The fates are against me", Sano explained when asked why he had not brought his case before the attention of the Shogun. "Lord Saimyoji (the Buddhist name of Regent Tokiyori Hojo) is now on his religious tour. But poor as I am, I am always ready to respond to a summons that may come from Kamakura at any time. Should the need for my services arise at Kamakura, I will put on this coat-of-mail, worn out as it looks, take this sword, rusty as it appears, and hasten to the court to prove my loyalty, old and reduced as I am. And if I am allowed to fight, I will dash into the thickest part of the enemy's ranks, and, fighting to the last of my strength, I will die a glorious death."

The scene changes. The daimyo or local lords are all summoned to hasten to the Shogunate court at Kamakura. Sano Genzaemon Tsuneyo, clad in a worn and shabby armour, rides on a jade. Though his horse and accoutrements are poor, still he looked no less brave than any other daimyo, for his heart was brave and his honour untarnished.

Regent Tokiyori Hojo sat on the Regent's dais, and told his attendant to bring before him "an aged warrior clad in a threadbare coat-of-mail and with an unusually long sword, riding a poor thin horse." Sano was brought before the Shogunate regent.

"Do you remember one cold night last year when you gave shelter to an itinerant priest, who asked lodgings for the night. You had no firewood in your house and, to warm the priest, you cut up three potted trees, your most valued possessions? You also said that pennilessly poor though you were, you were still a loyal retainer of the Shogun. I was that poor priest, and your action in burning your favorite trees for me will never be forgotten."

The regent then restored to Sano his possessions which had been taken falsely from him, and, in addition, three local fiefs named after the plum, the pine and the bamboo were conferred upon Sano.

USHI OR COW

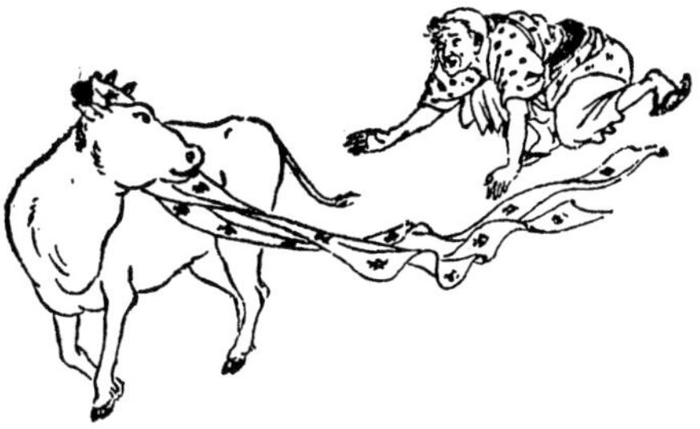

Ushi (bull or cow) was no less sacred in this country than is in India, and some people still worship a stone-image of a bull often found in the precincts of the Tenjin (lit. celestial god) shrine, which is dedicated to Michizane Sugawara, who is, therefore, often associated with a bull because he was carried on a bull when he was sent exile to Kyushu. But, at the same time, the Japanese paradoxially regarded the cow as a "quadruped too unclean to eat", nor did they drink a cow's milk, until Japan came in contact with the Westerners a little over three quarters of a century ago. One would look like a beast, it was believed by Japanese of old, if one ate its meat and a Westerner is more hairy because he eats beef and other kinds of meat.

Cow leads woman to temple: Once there lived an old woman of seventy in the province of Shinano. She was so selfish and avaricious that she kept herself too busy to visit the Zenko-ji Temple even on a fete-day. On one anniversary of the birth of the Buddha, namely, on the eighth of the fourth month (April), when she was starching clothing as usual, a cow coming along caught a piece of cloth on its horns. The old woman ran after it till it vanished mysteriously with the cloth, within the sacred grounds of the Zenko-ji Temple. She worshipped the Kannon image of the temple and thenceforth she turned to be a pious woman. On looking up, she found that a mountain before her marked, as it had been marked, with a white band around it. That mountain is now called Mt. Nunobiki (lit. cloth-pulling).

Curse at Bull-time: Ushimitsu-mairi (lit. worship at the zodiac time of the Bull) is a visit or worship made in olden days by a jealous woman to a shrine situated in a lonely and desolate place, at the zodiac time of Ushimitsu (lit. Bull-three) or about 2.30 a.m., for the purpose of imprecating a curse on her rival. She wears her hair hanging unkempt and dishevelled on her back and carries on her head a triped with three lighted candles on its legs. At the dead of night she repairs to a lonely part of shrine precincts, where she nails on a giantic tree a straw-doll in representation of her vival. She must repeat this, without anyone knowing it, for a circuit of 3×7 or 21 days, at the end of which, it was believed, her rival will die in agony. If, however, she should be spied on her way to or from the shrine, her prayer will be lost.

WANI OR CROCODILE

Japan, situated as it is out of the tropical zone, has few crocodiles living in its waters, and little is mentioned, therefore about it in Japanese literature. Nor has Japan any geographical places which have the crocodile as their name-sake, excepting one or two, such as Waniura (lit. crocodile-creek) in Nagasaki prefecture and Wanibuchi (lit. crocodile-abyss) in Shimane prefecture, so named possibly because once a crocodile made its appearance at those places. Inaba-no-Usagi (lit. hare of Inaba Province), which is found in *Kojiki*, one of the oldest records of Japan, is perhaps the best-known story in which mention is made of crocodiles.

Hare of Inaba Province: There was once a great flood in the province of Inaba, and a hare was washed down, on a floating piece of wood, far into the sea till it reached the isle of Oki in the Japan Sea.

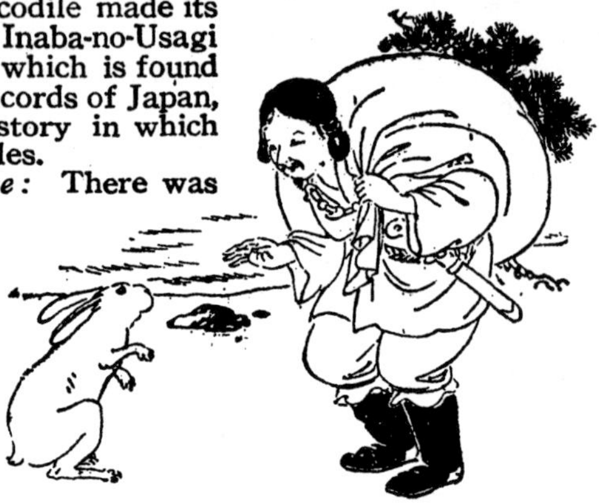

Prince Okuninushi and hare

One day the hare stood on the beach longing to get back to Inaba, when he saw a crocodile.

"Mr. Crocodile," the hare said after a few words of greetings. "Mr. Crocodile, I wonder which has a greater number of fellows, you or I."

"Of course my host is greater than yours," said the crocodile.

At the suggestion of the hare, which proposed to count the crocodiles if they line up in the sea, the crocodile called all its tribe and had them line up landwards from Oki, so that the hare might count them. The hare jumped on their backs one after another by counting them.

"I only wanted to come back to Inaba, foolish crocodiles," the hare said when, stepping on the back of the last crocodile, it was about to step on the land, but it was caught by the tail by the last crocodile. The angry crocodiles skinned it all up. When the hare lay suffering from cold and pain, there came Prince Okuninushi, the kind and merciful lord of the province, and he cured the hare.

Sobei and his crocodile: Sobei was a wrestler in the province of Suruga. Once he shot at a deer, which escaped him by jumping into the sea. Sobei swam after it, and killed it. When he was swimming back, carrying the deer, a crocodile came after him. He gave it a leg from his deer, and swam on as hard as possible while the crocodile ate it. It came again; he threw another leg. The crocodile came a third time, and Sobei gave it another leg, but he was now near the beach, he boldly caught the crocodile, and turned it back up. The crocodile was caguht; it measured over ten feet. (*Konjaku-monogatari* or Tales of the Present and Past)

DOG STORIES

White dog monument: The wife of daimyo in Shikoku Province died in Edo (Tokyo). When her remains were carried to his clan, her white pet-dog followed the funeral procession all the way to Sanuki Province of Shikoku, for hundreds of miles. It is even recorded that, like men who abstain from eating fish while in mourning, the white dog ate no fish or bones which were given it during the long journey. When the remains were buried in the daimyo's family-cemetery in the Bus-sho-zan Temple, the dog would not leave the burial place. The people took it away by force, but it soon went back to the grave of its dead mistress. The dog was again taken back, this time on a boat when it jumped into the water in an attempt to go back to the grave-yard, only to get drowned. A stone-monument was erected over the remains of the faithful dog. It is called "white dog monument."

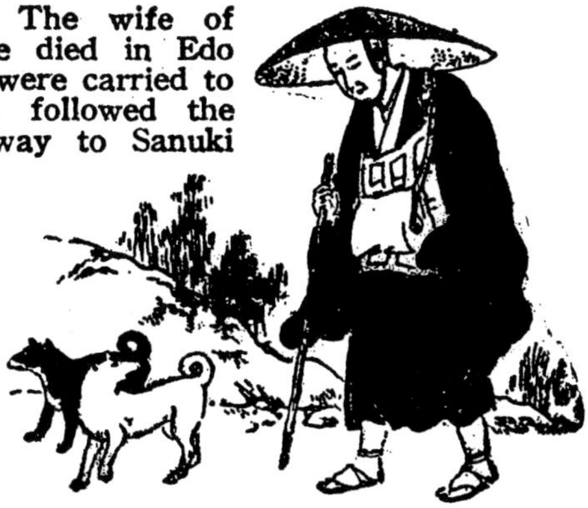

Priest Kobo and two dogs

Dog receiving a court-rank: Lord Sakai of Himeji had a spaniel, which he used to take with him everywhere he went. When once he was sent from Edo (Tokyo) to Kyoto, the Imperial Capital, as a Shogunal messenger, in 1781, Lord Sakai was determined to leave the spaniel in Edo, as it was considered improper to take a beast on such an important mission. The spaniel, however, considered the matter in a different way, for it insisted upon going with his master. No angry words or threat could keep away the dog which had always been very obedient. Lord Sakai took the dog with him in the procession intending to send it back from Shinagawa. The spaniel was no less disobedient at Shinagawa, and it bit at those who tried to force it back, till the lord permitted the dog to go on in the procession. And the dog trotted along the lord all the way from Edo (Tokyo) to Kyoto. When Emperor Kokoku heard of the fidelity of the spaniel, he gave the dog the 5th court-rank.

Python killed by dog: A samurai went out hunting, taking a pet-dog with him. In the woods, he sat on a stone and he was about to doze off to sleep when his dog barked loudly. The samurai saw nothing strange about him and again he fell into a little doze. The dog again barked loudly. Every time he began to nod, the dog barked to wake him up and sleep was impossible. Tame as the dog had been, it acted in such a strange way that the samurai, disgusted with the mad and stubborn way of the dog, killed it on the spot by cutting its head off with his sword, when lo! the head jumping up bit at a large snake, which dropped down with the head of the dog still clinging to the neck of the snake.

INDEX

The numbers refer to the pages